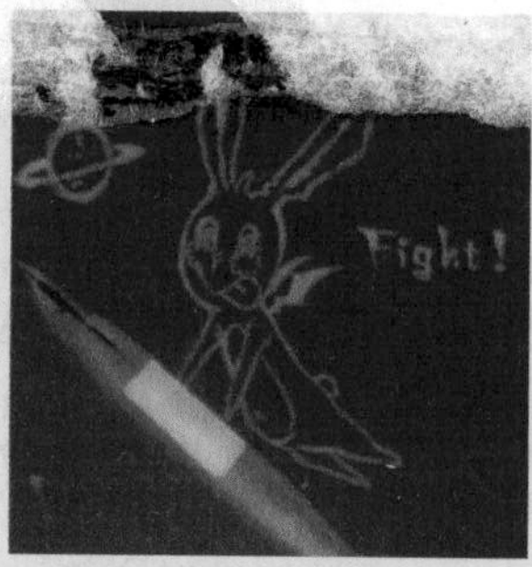
Fight!

It was my dream to become an astronaut, but it seems like it wasn't meant to be. Instead, I'm thinking about traveling to space inside my head. If you're not busy, please join me.

—Katsura Hoshino

Shiga Prefecture native Katsura Hoshino's hit manga series *D.Gray-man* has been serialized in Weekly Shonen Jump since 2004. Katsura's first series "Continue" first appeared in Weekly Shonen Jump in 2003.

Katsura adores cats.

D.GRAY-MAN
3-in-1 Edition
Volume 1

SHONEN JUMP Manga Omnibus Edition
A compilation of the graphic novel volumes 1–3

STORY AND ART BY
KATSURA HOSHINO

English Adaptation/Mayumi Kobayashi, Lance Caselman
Translation/Mayumi Kobayashi, Toshifumi Yoshida
Touch-up Art & Lettering/Elizabeth Watasin
Design/Yukiko Whitley (Graphic Novel and 3-in-1 Editions)
Editors/Michelle Pangilinan, Urian Brown (Graphic Novel Edition)
Editor/Nancy Thistlethwaite (3-in-1 Edition)

Printed in the U.S.A.

Published by VIZ Media, LLC
P.O. Box 77010
San Francisco, CA 94107

10 9 8 7 6 5 4 3 2
3-in-1 edition first printing, July 2013
Second printing, June 2015

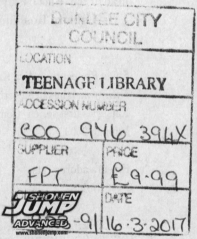

www.viz.com

www.shonenjump.com

SHONEN JUMP ADVANCED MANGA EDITION

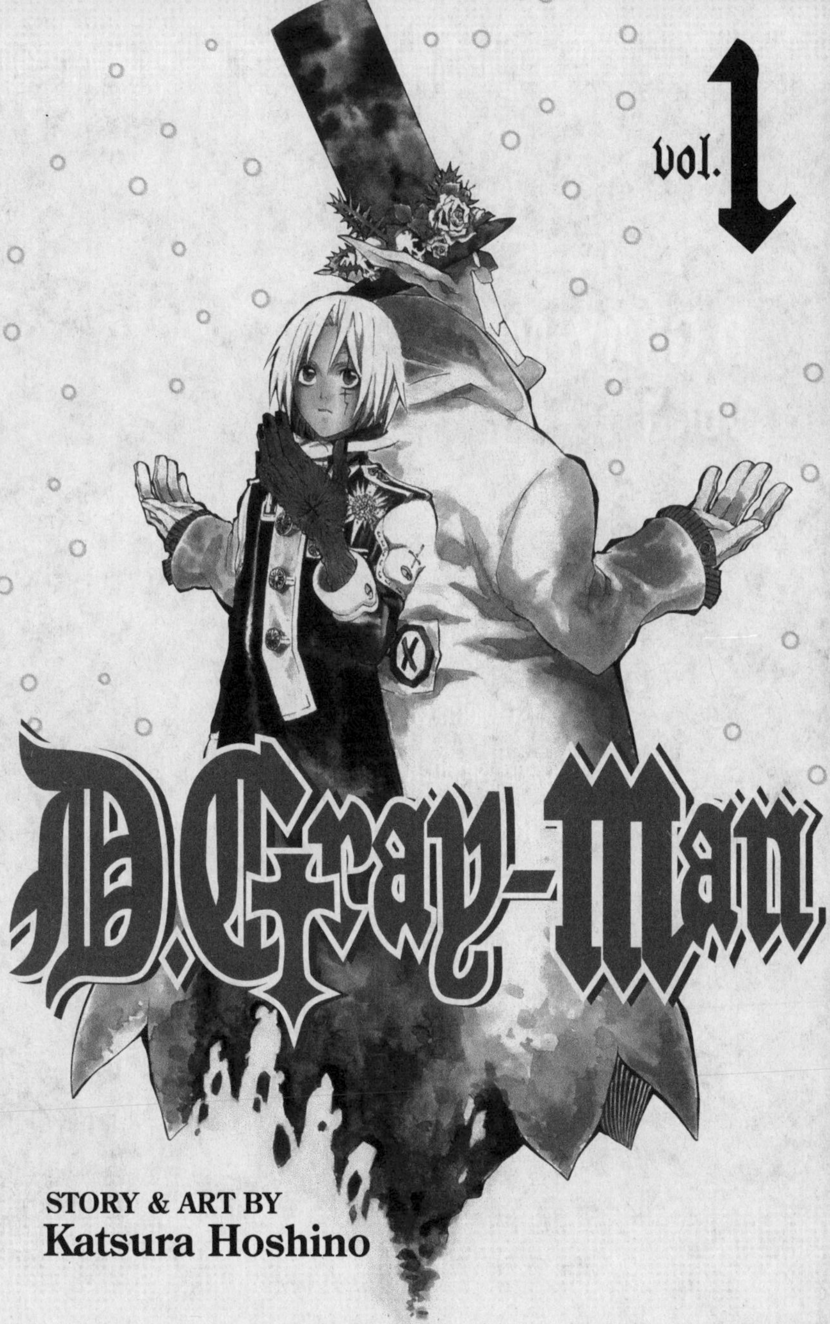

D.Gray-man

vol. 1

STORY & ART BY
Katsura Hoshino

D.GRAY-MAN
Vol. 1

CONTENTS

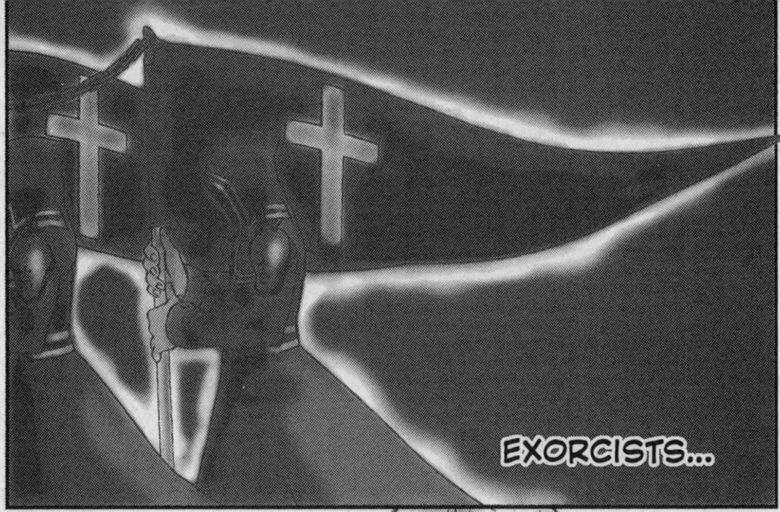
EXORCISTS...

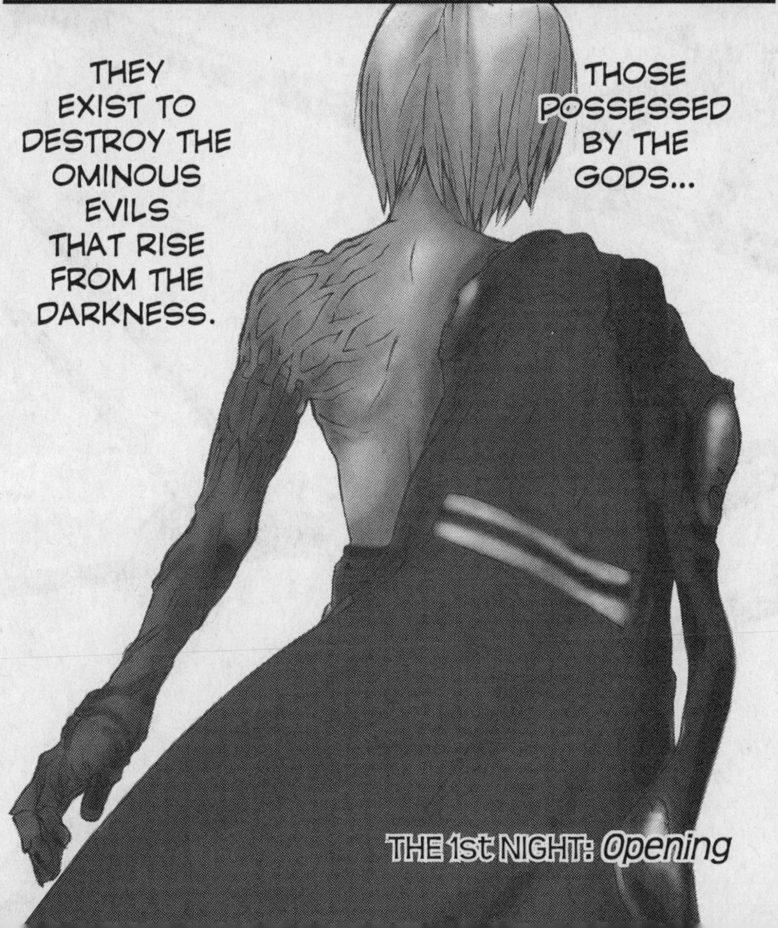
THOSE POSSESSED BY THE GODS...
THEY EXIST TO DESTROY THE OMINOUS EVILS THAT RISE FROM THE DARKNESS.
THE 1st NIGHT: Opening

THE 1st NIGHT: *Opening*

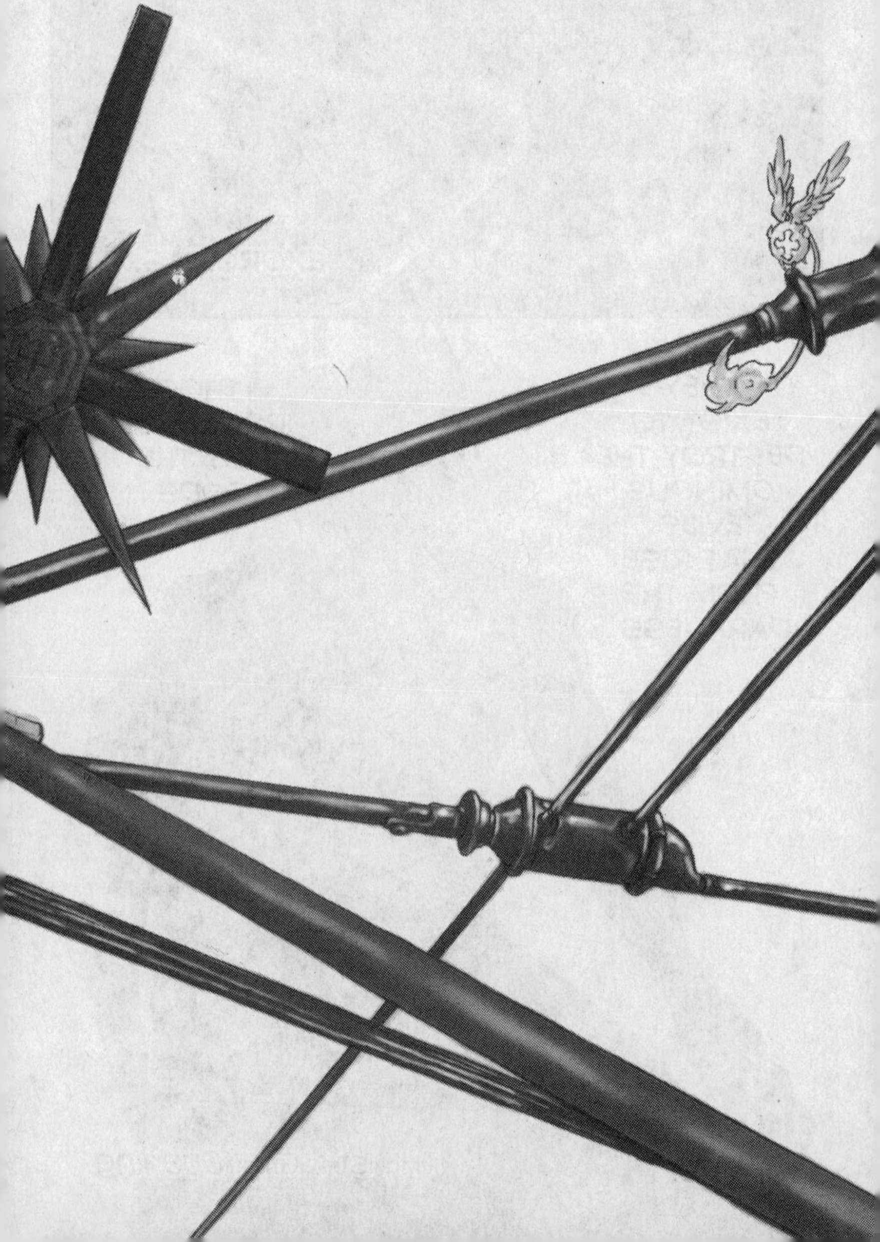

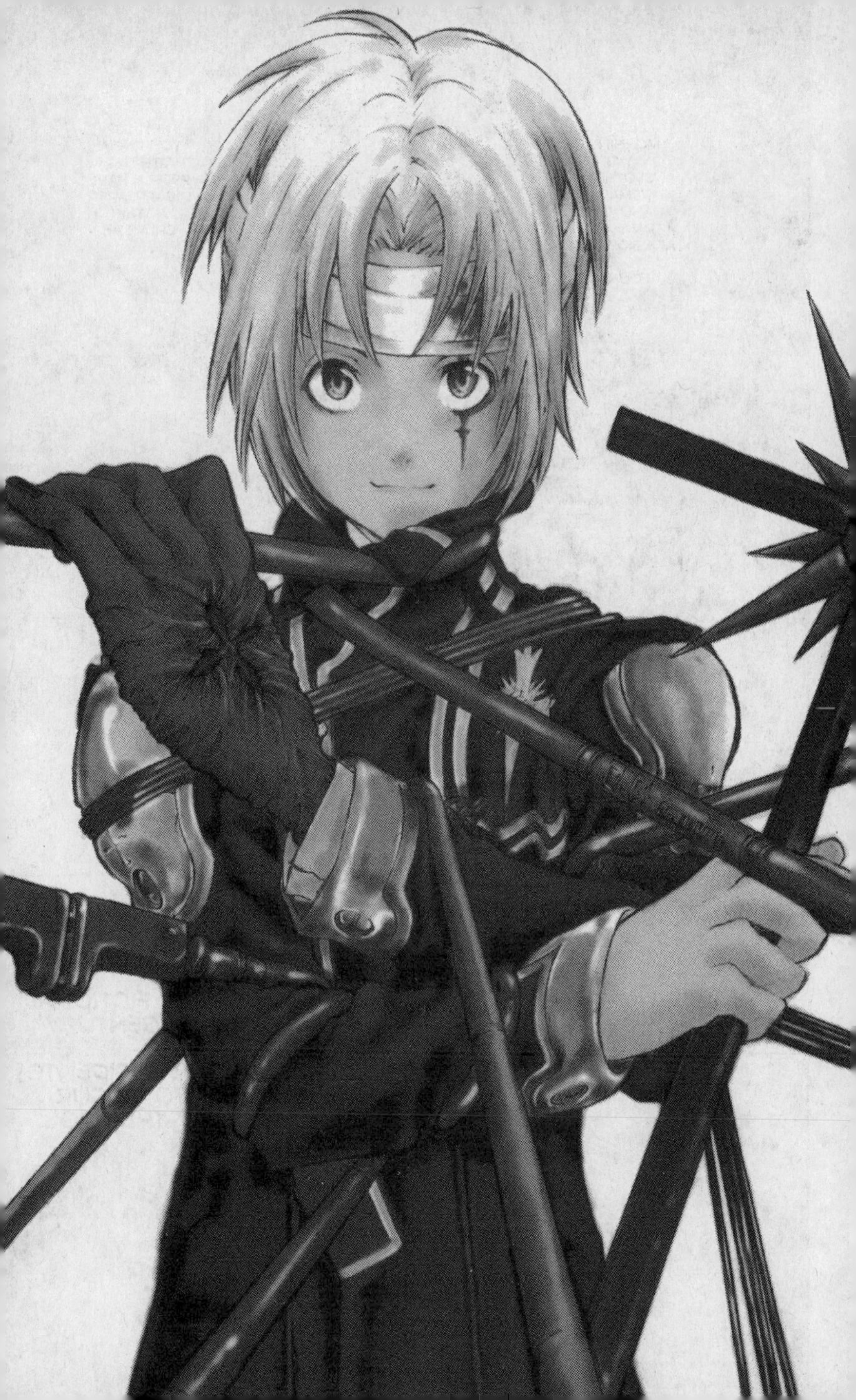

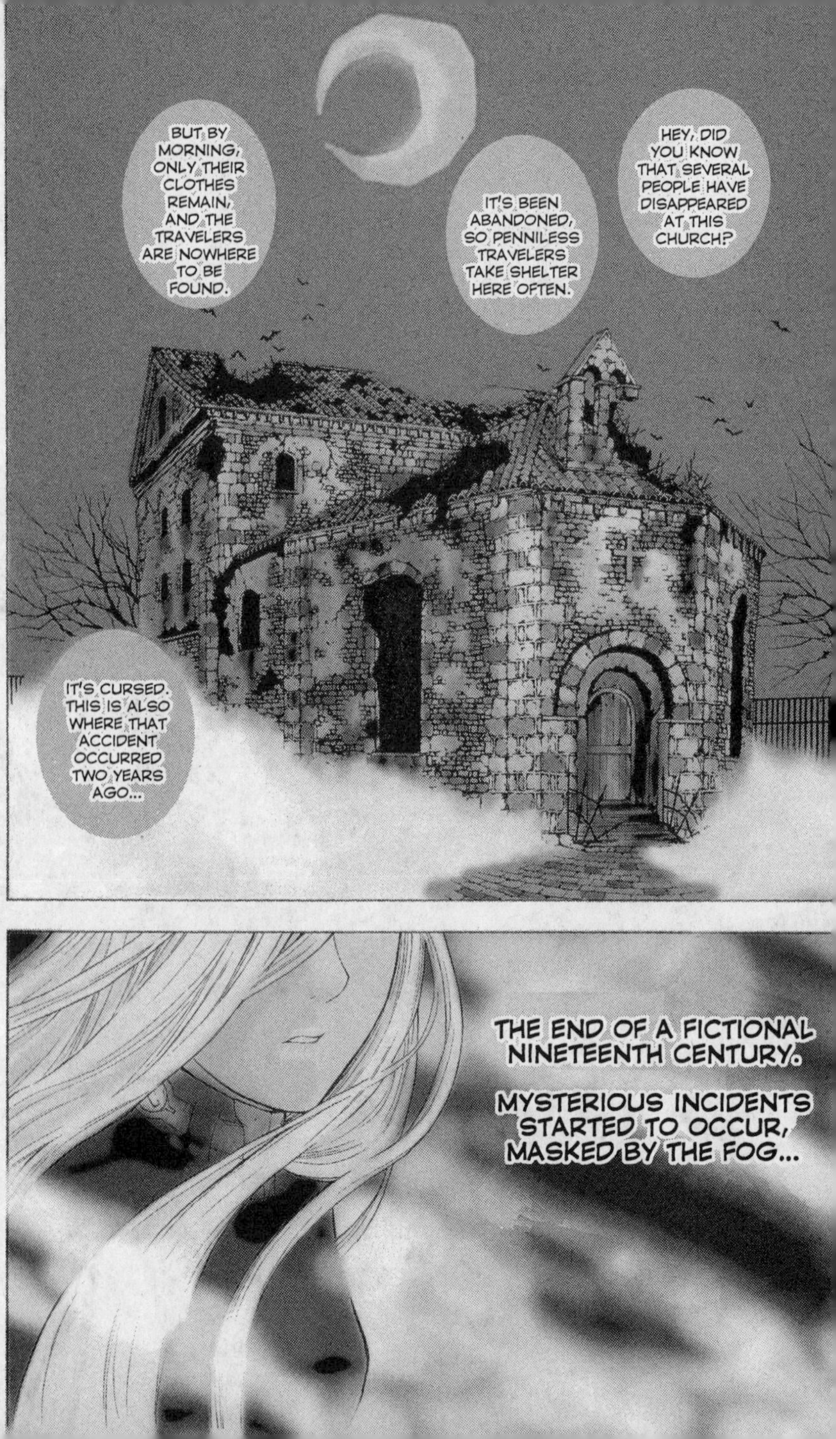
HEY, DID YOU KNOW THAT SEVERAL PEOPLE HAVE DISAPPEARED AT THIS CHURCH?
IT'S BEEN ABANDONED, SO PENNILESS TRAVELERS TAKE SHELTER HERE OFTEN.
BUT BY MORNING, ONLY THEIR CLOTHES REMAIN, AND THE TRAVELERS ARE NOWHERE TO BE FOUND.
IT'S CURSED. THIS IS ALSO WHERE THAT ACCIDENT OCCURRED TWO YEARS AGO...
THE END OF A FICTIONAL NINETEENTH CENTURY.
MYSTERIOUS INCIDENTS STARTED TO OCCUR, MASKED BY THE FOG...

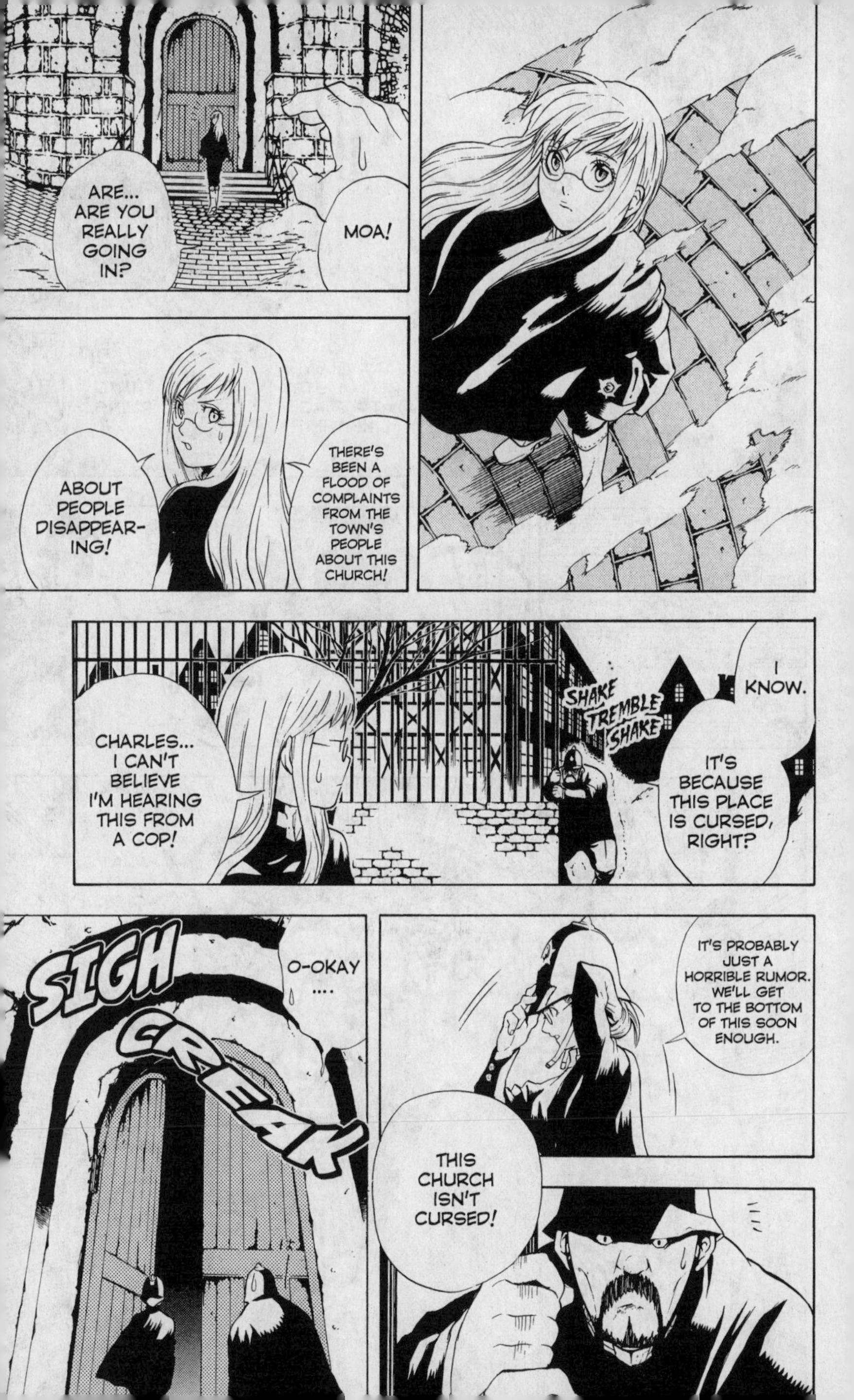
MOA!
ARE... ARE YOU REALLY GOING IN?
THERE'S BEEN A FLOOD OF COMPLAINTS FROM THE TOWN'S PEOPLE ABOUT THIS CHURCH!
ABOUT PEOPLE DISAPPEAR-ING!
I KNOW.
IT'S BECAUSE THIS PLACE IS CURSED, RIGHT?
SHAKE TREMBLE SHAKE
CHARLES... I CAN'T BELIEVE I'M HEARING THIS FROM A COP!
IT'S PROBABLY JUST A HORRIBLE RUMOR. WE'LL GET TO THE BOTTOM OF THIS SOON ENOUGH.
THIS CHURCH ISN'T CURSED!
O-OKAY ....
SIGH
CREAK

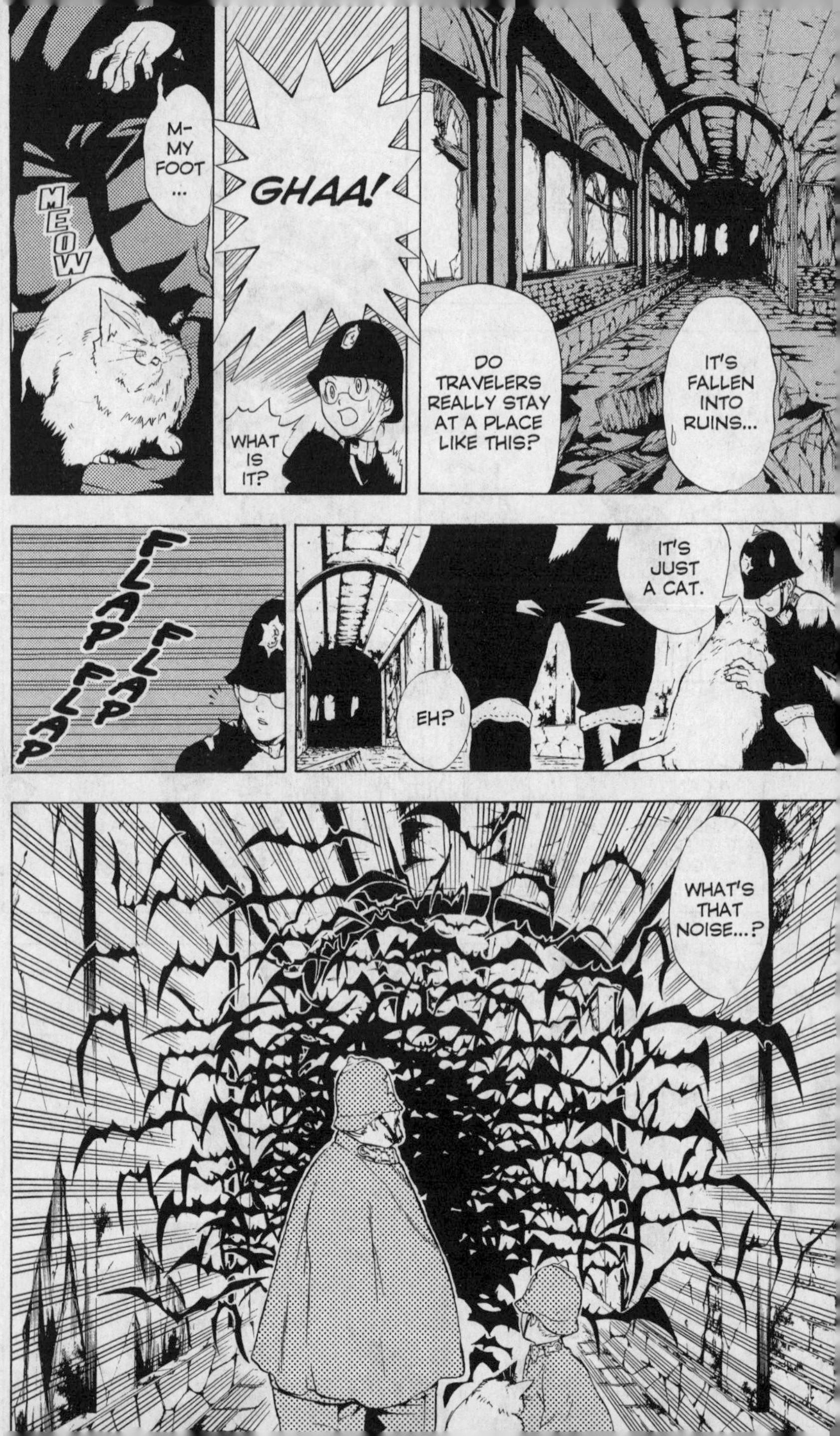
IT'S FALLEN INTO RUINS...
DO TRAVELERS REALLY STAY AT A PLACE LIKE THIS?
GHAA!
WHAT IS IT?
M-MY FOOT...
MEOW
IT'S JUST A CAT.
EH?
FLAP FLAP
FLAP FLAP
WHAT'S THAT NOISE...?

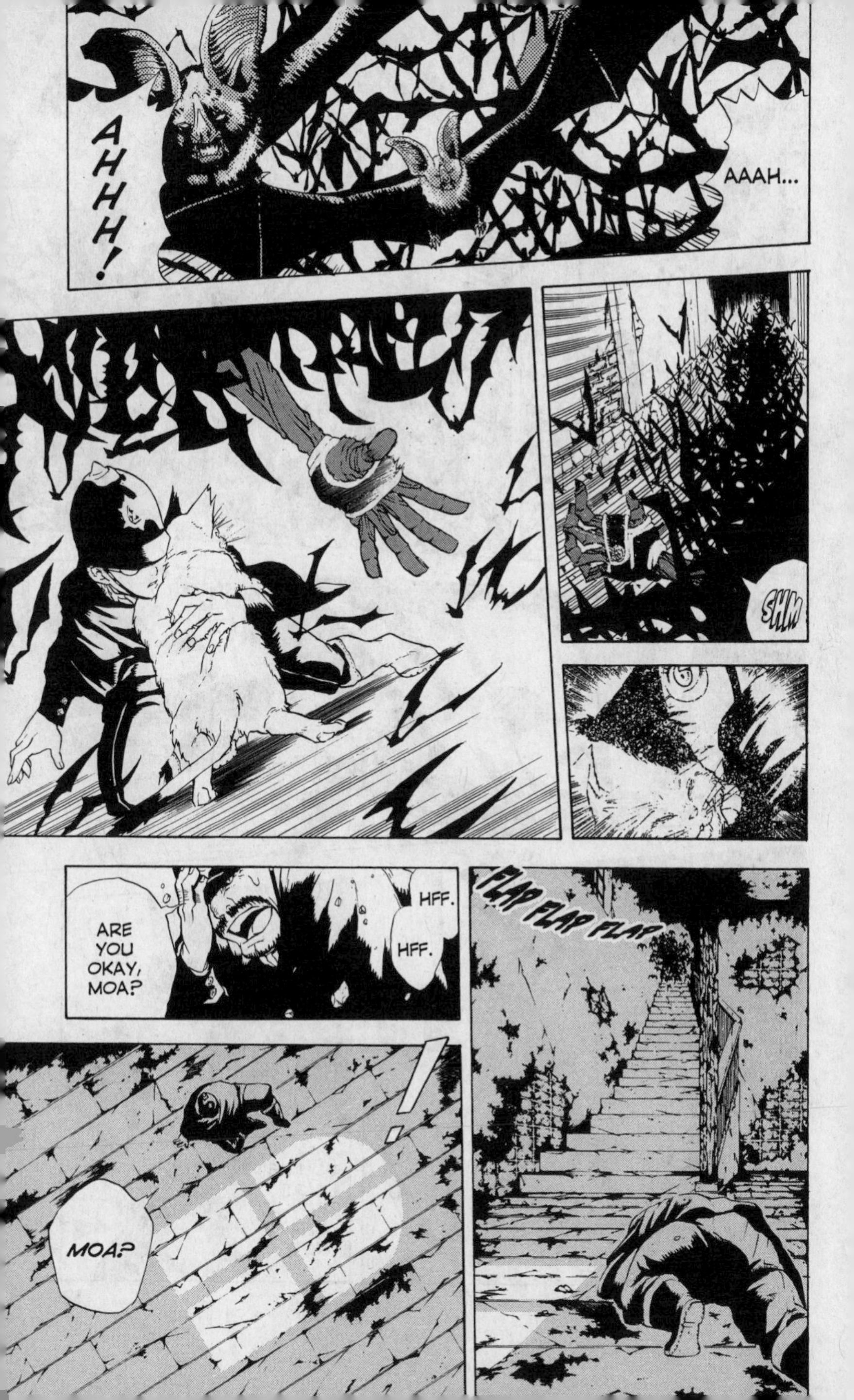
AAAH...
AHHHH!
SHM
FLAP FLAP FLAP
HFF.
HFF.
ARE YOU OKAY, MOA?
!
MOA?

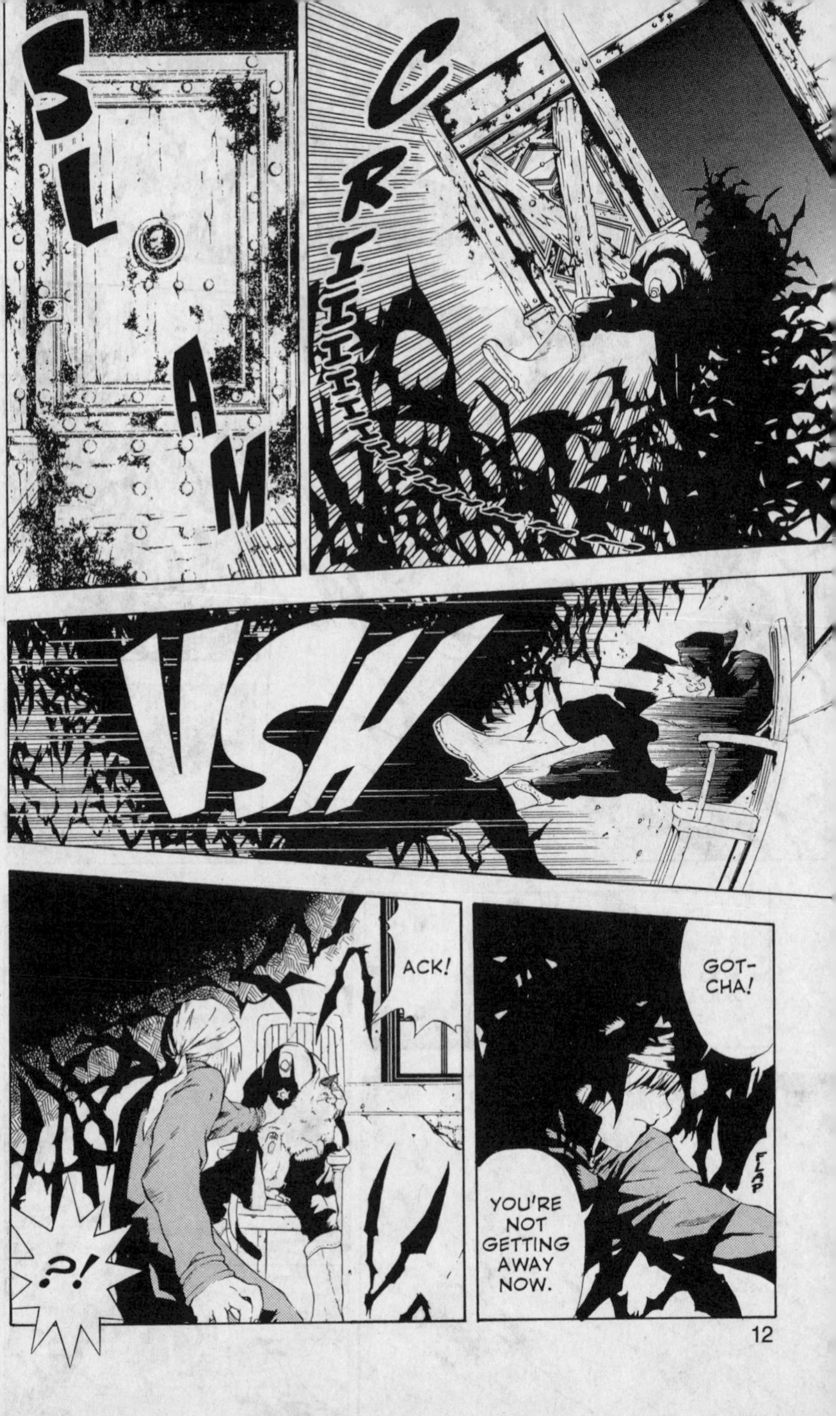
CRIIIIIIIIIIII
SLAM
VSH
GOT-CHA!
FLAP
YOU'RE NOT GETTING AWAY NOW.
ACK!
?!

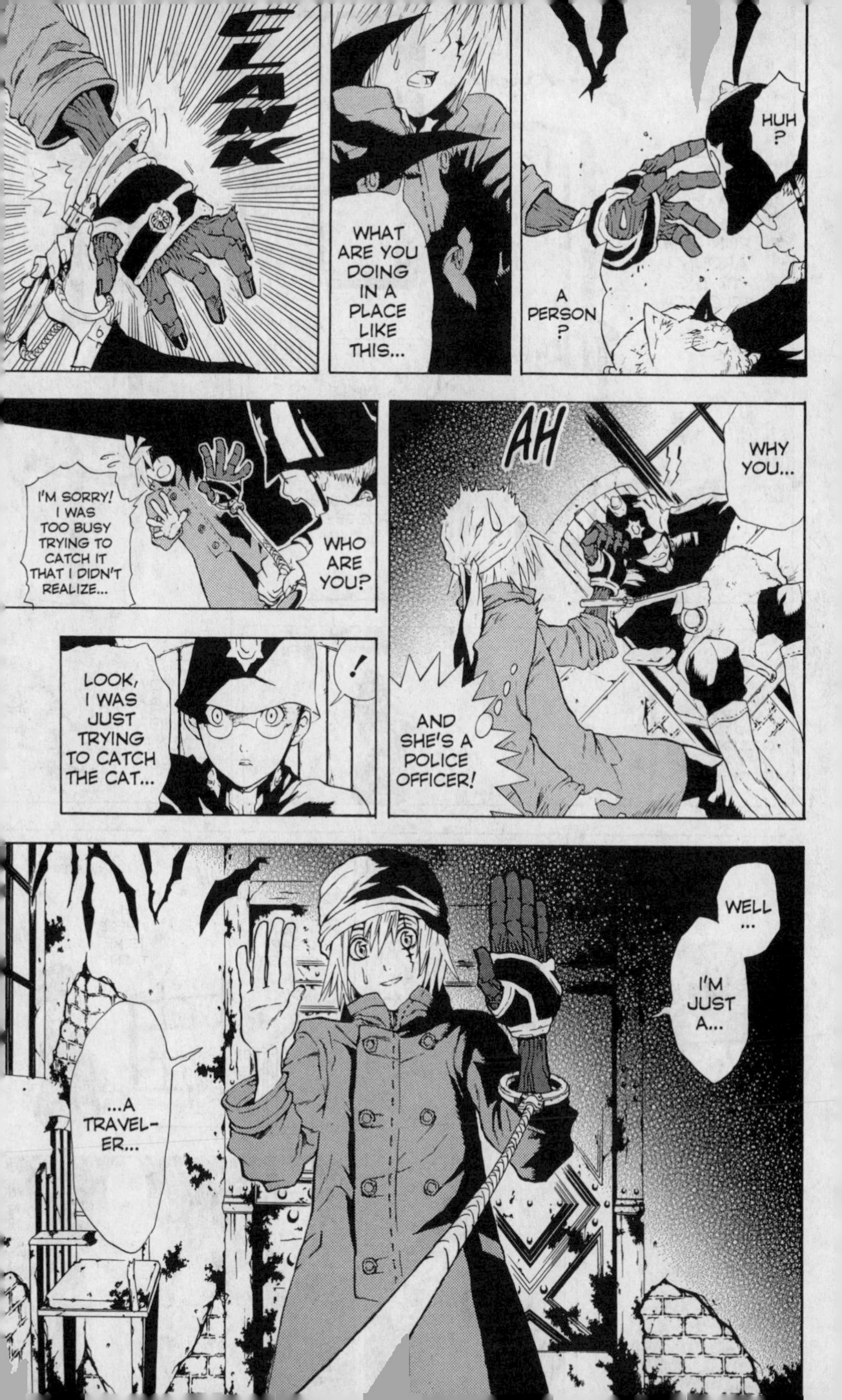
HUH?
A PERSON?
WHAT ARE YOU DOING IN A PLACE LIKE THIS...
CLANK
WHY YOU...
AH
AND SHE'S A POLICE OFFICER!
WHO ARE YOU?
I'M SORRY! I WAS TOO BUSY TRYING TO CATCH IT THAT I DIDN'T REALIZE...
!
LOOK, I WAS JUST TRYING TO CATCH THE CAT...
WELL...
I'M JUST A...
...A TRAVEL-ER...

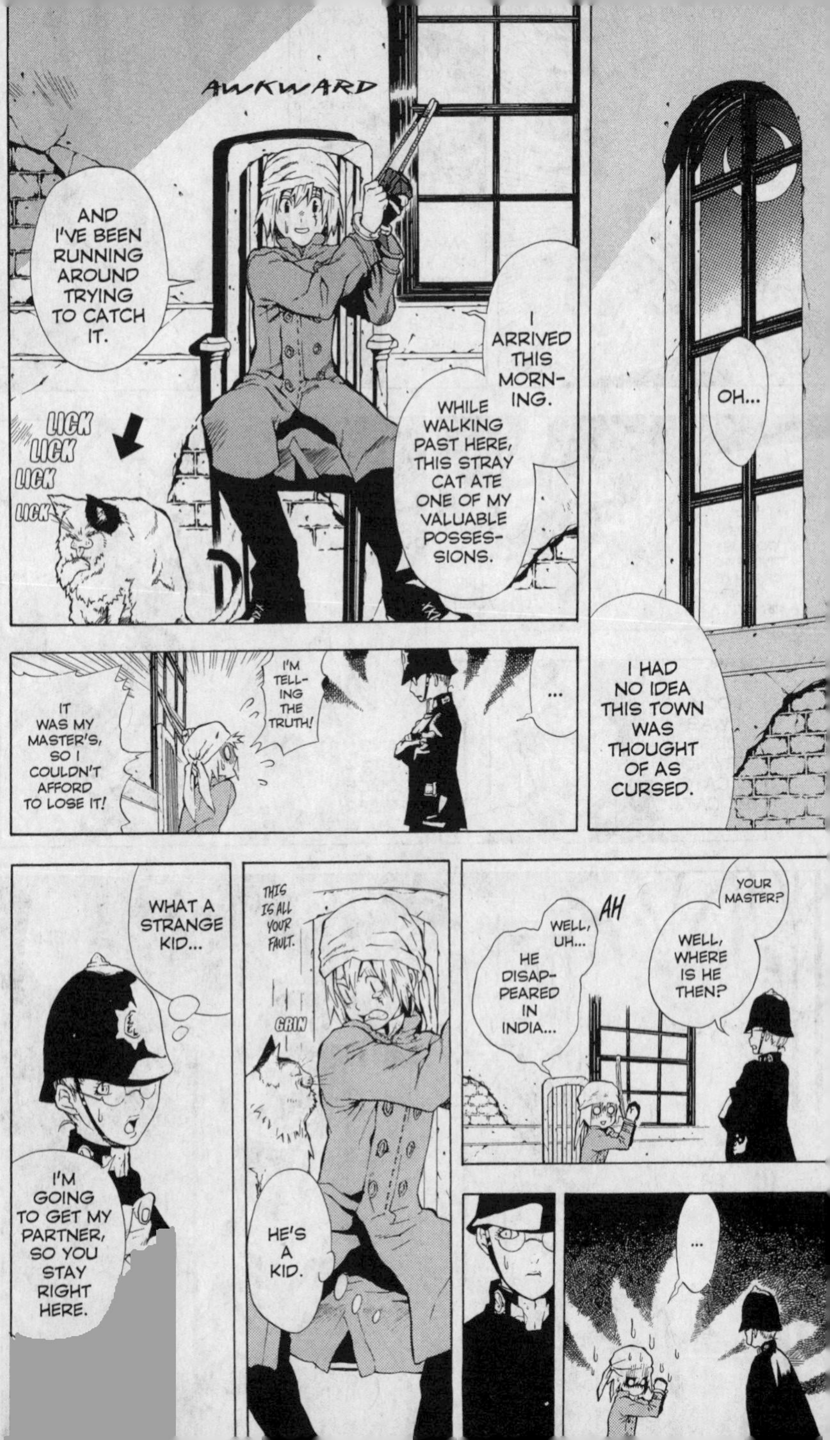
OH...
I HAD NO IDEA THIS TOWN WAS THOUGHT OF AS CURSED.
AWKWARD
I ARRIVED THIS MORN-ING.
WHILE WALKING PAST HERE, THIS STRAY CAT ATE ONE OF MY VALUABLE POSSES-SIONS.
AND I'VE BEEN RUNNING AROUND TRYING TO CATCH IT.
LICK LICK LICK LICK
...
I'M TELL-ING THE TRUTH!
IT WAS MY MASTER'S, SO I COULDN'T AFFORD TO LOSE IT!
YOUR MASTER?
WELL, WHERE IS HE THEN?
AH
WELL, UH...
HE DISAP-PEARED IN INDIA...
...
THIS IS ALL YOUR FAULT.
GRIN
HE'S A KID.
WHAT A STRANGE KID...
I'M GOING TO GET MY PARTNER, SO YOU STAY RIGHT HERE.

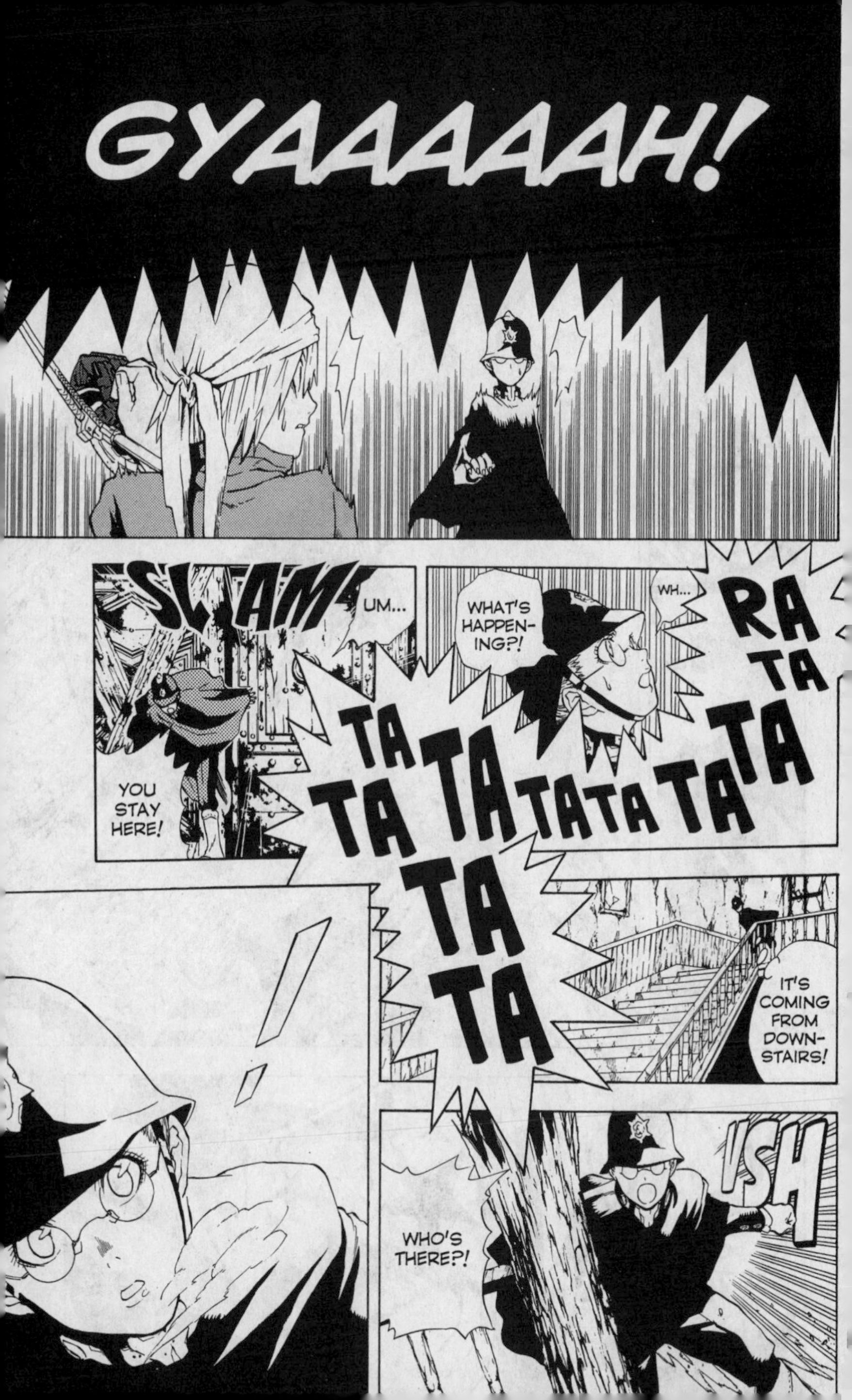
GYAAAAAH!
RA TA
WH...
WHAT'S HAPPEN-ING?!
TA TA TA TA TATA TA TA TA TA TA
SLAM
UM...
YOU STAY HERE!
IT'S COMING FROM DOWN-STAIRS!
!
VSH
WHO'S THERE?!

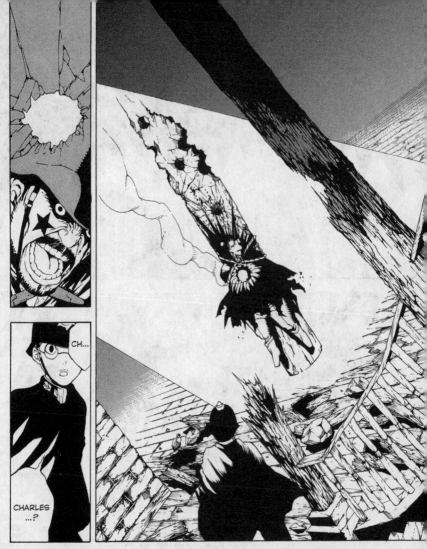

CH...

CHARLES ...?

WSSH

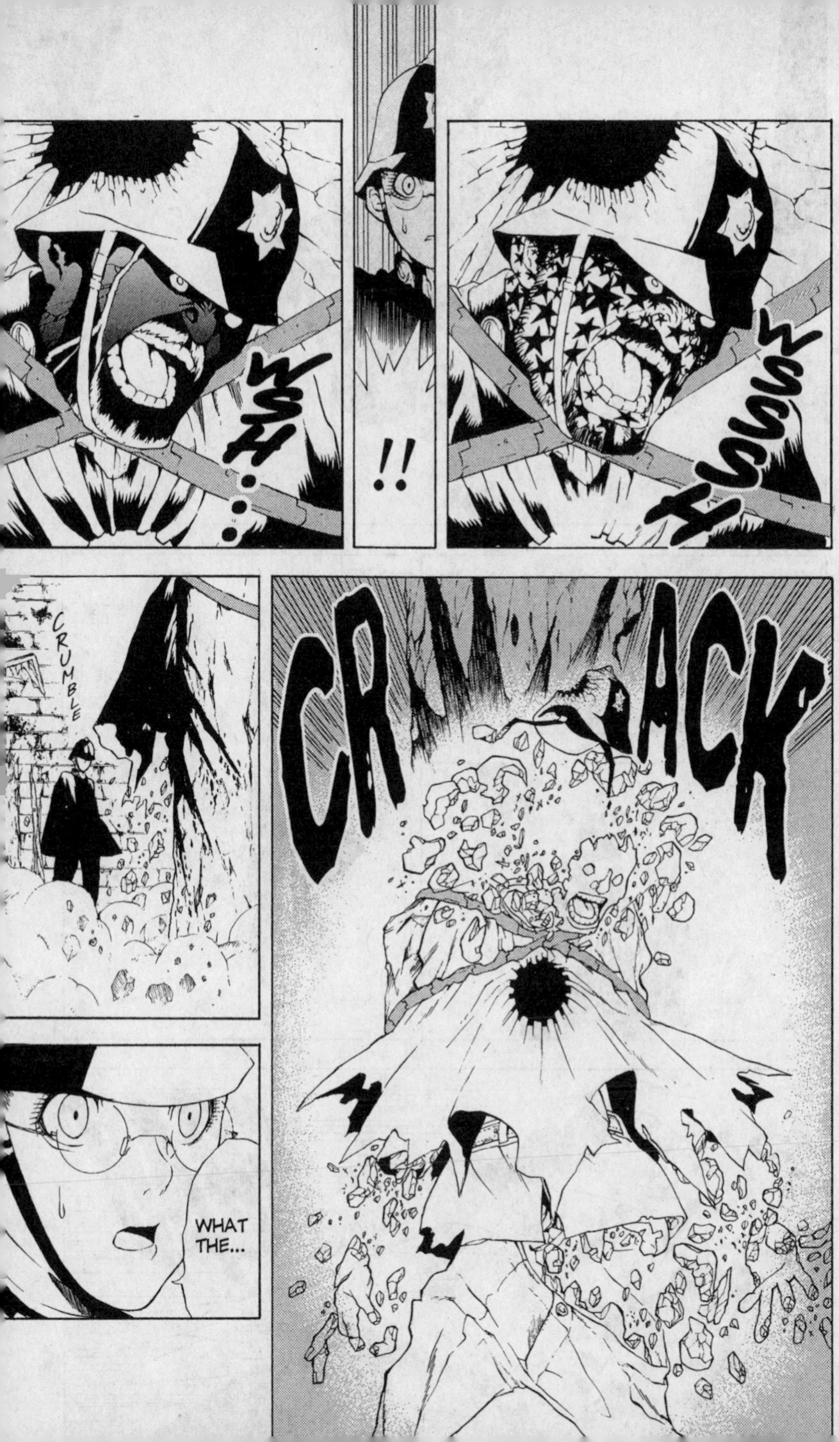
WSSSH
!!
WSH...
CRACK
CRUMBLE
WHAT THE...

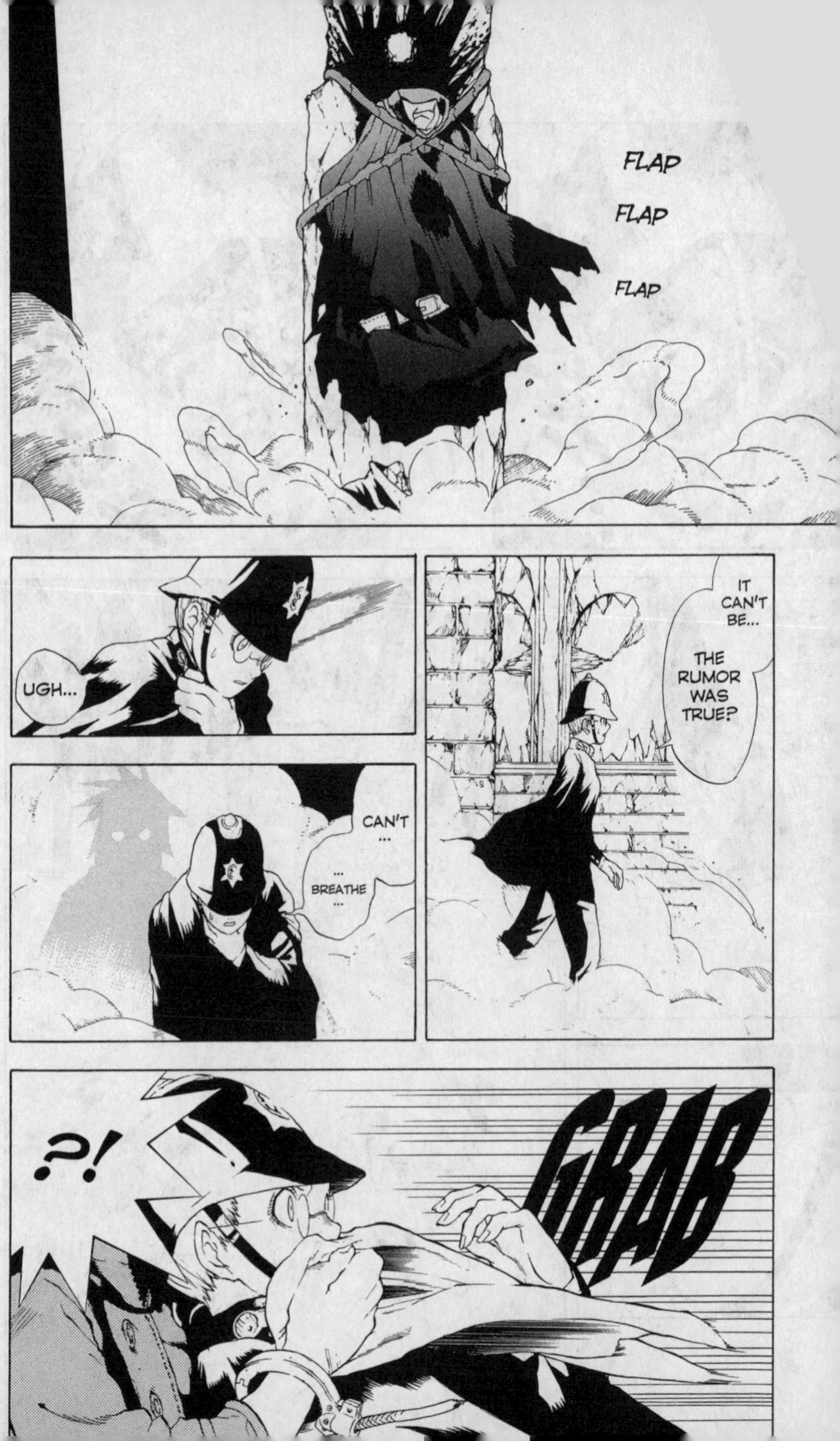
FLAP
FLAP
FLAP
IT CAN'T BE...
THE RUMOR WAS TRUE?
UGH...
CAN'T ...
... BREATHE ...
GRAB
?!

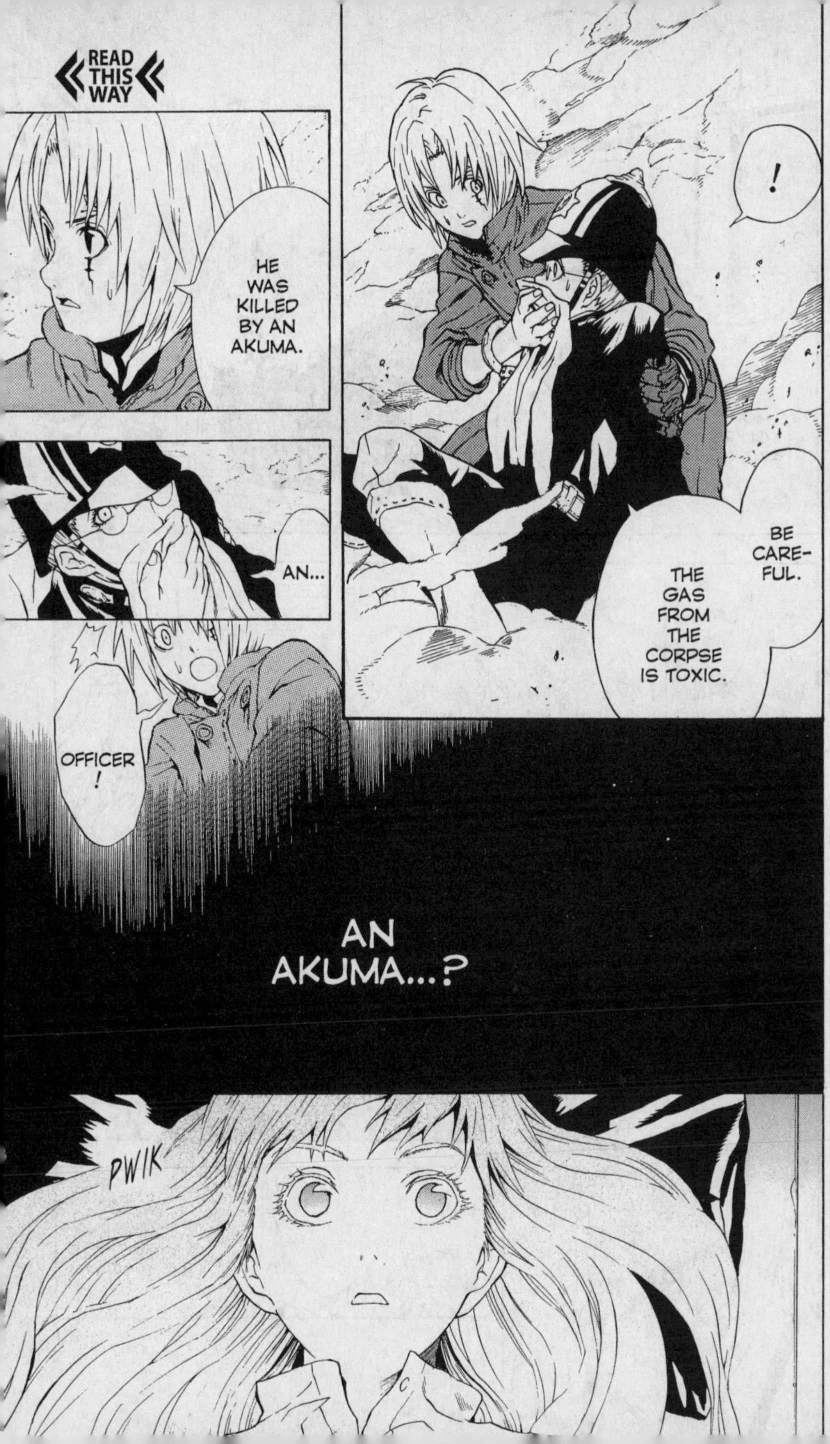
READ THIS WAY
!
BE CAREFUL.
THE GAS FROM THE CORPSE IS TOXIC.
HE WAS KILLED BY AN AKUMA.
AN...
OFFICER!
AN AKUMA...?
PWIK

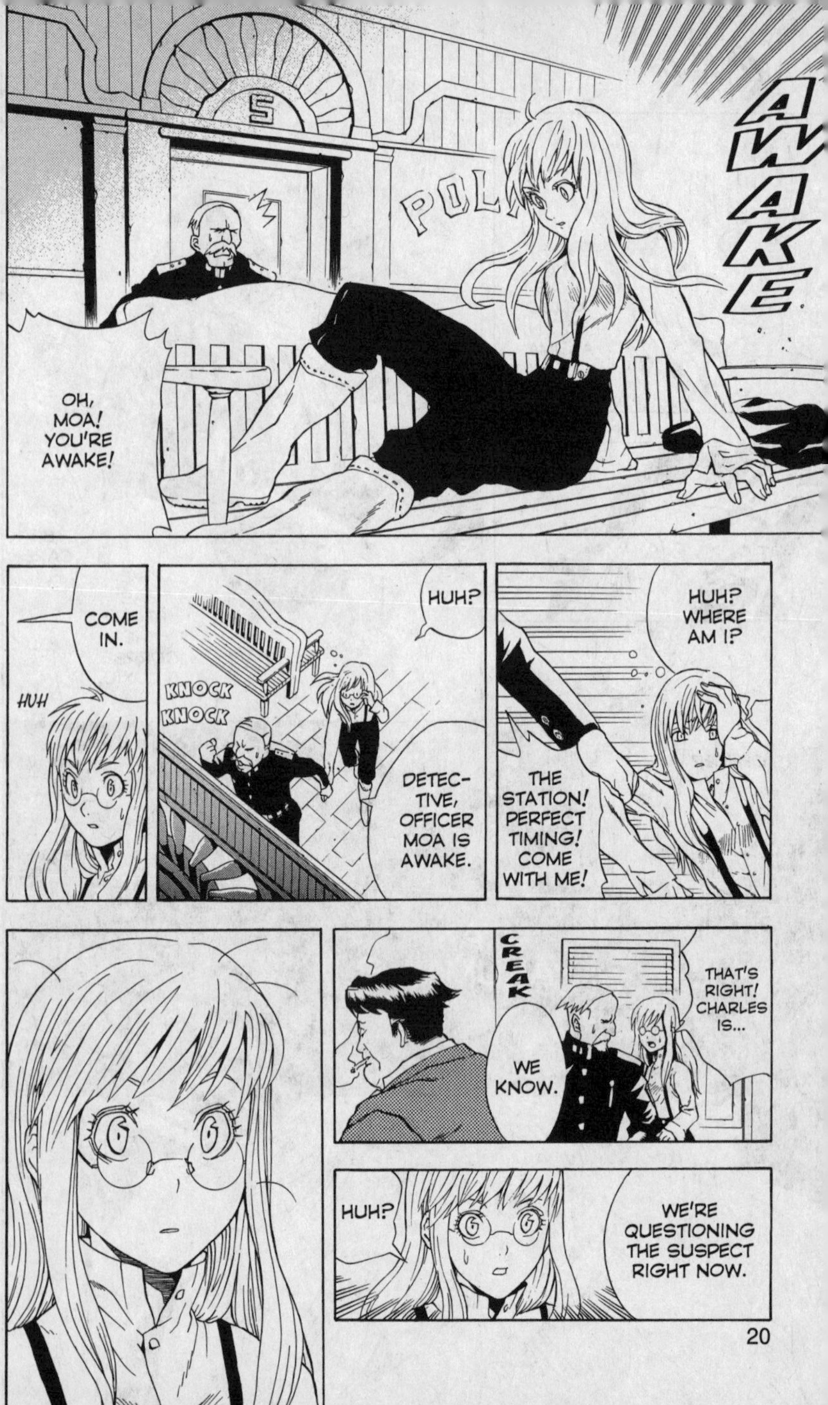
AWAKE
POL
OH, MOA! YOU'RE AWAKE!
HUH? WHERE AM I?
THE STATION! PERFECT TIMING! COME WITH ME!
HUH?
KNOCK KNOCK
DETEC-TIVE, OFFICER MOA IS AWAKE.
COME IN.
HUH
THAT'S RIGHT! CHARLES IS...
CREAK
WE KNOW.
WE'RE QUESTIONING THE SUSPECT RIGHT NOW.
HUH?

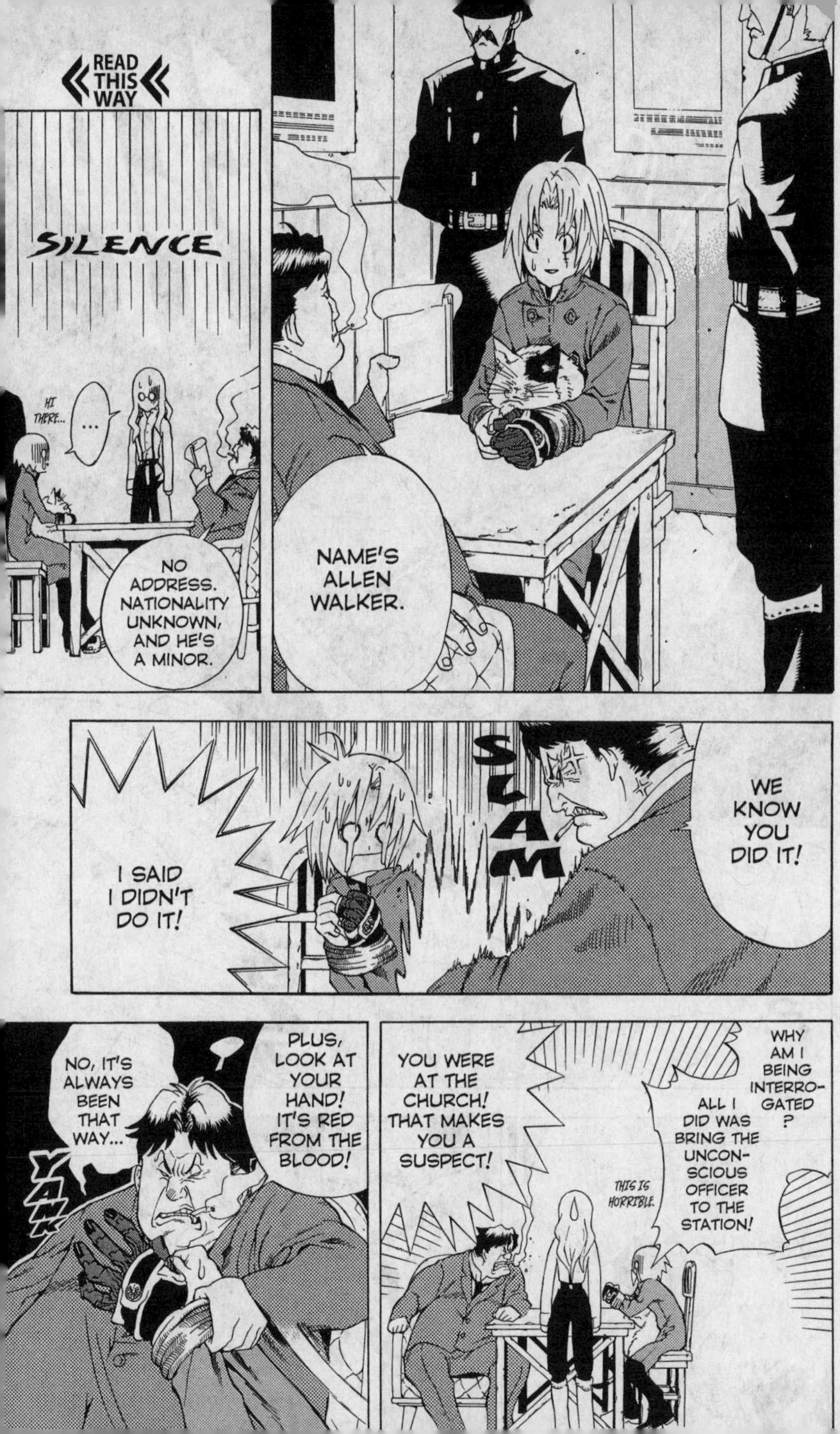
READ THIS WAY
NAME'S ALLEN WALKER.
SILENCE
HI THERE...
...
NO ADDRESS. NATIONALITY UNKNOWN, AND HE'S A MINOR.
WE KNOW YOU DID IT!
SLAM
I SAID I DIDN'T DO IT!
WHY AM I BEING INTERROGATED?
ALL I DID WAS BRING THE UNCONSCIOUS OFFICER TO THE STATION!
THIS IS HORRIBLE.
YOU WERE AT THE CHURCH! THAT MAKES YOU A SUSPECT!
PLUS, LOOK AT YOUR HAND! IT'S RED FROM THE BLOOD!
NO, IT'S ALWAYS BEEN THAT WAY...
YANK

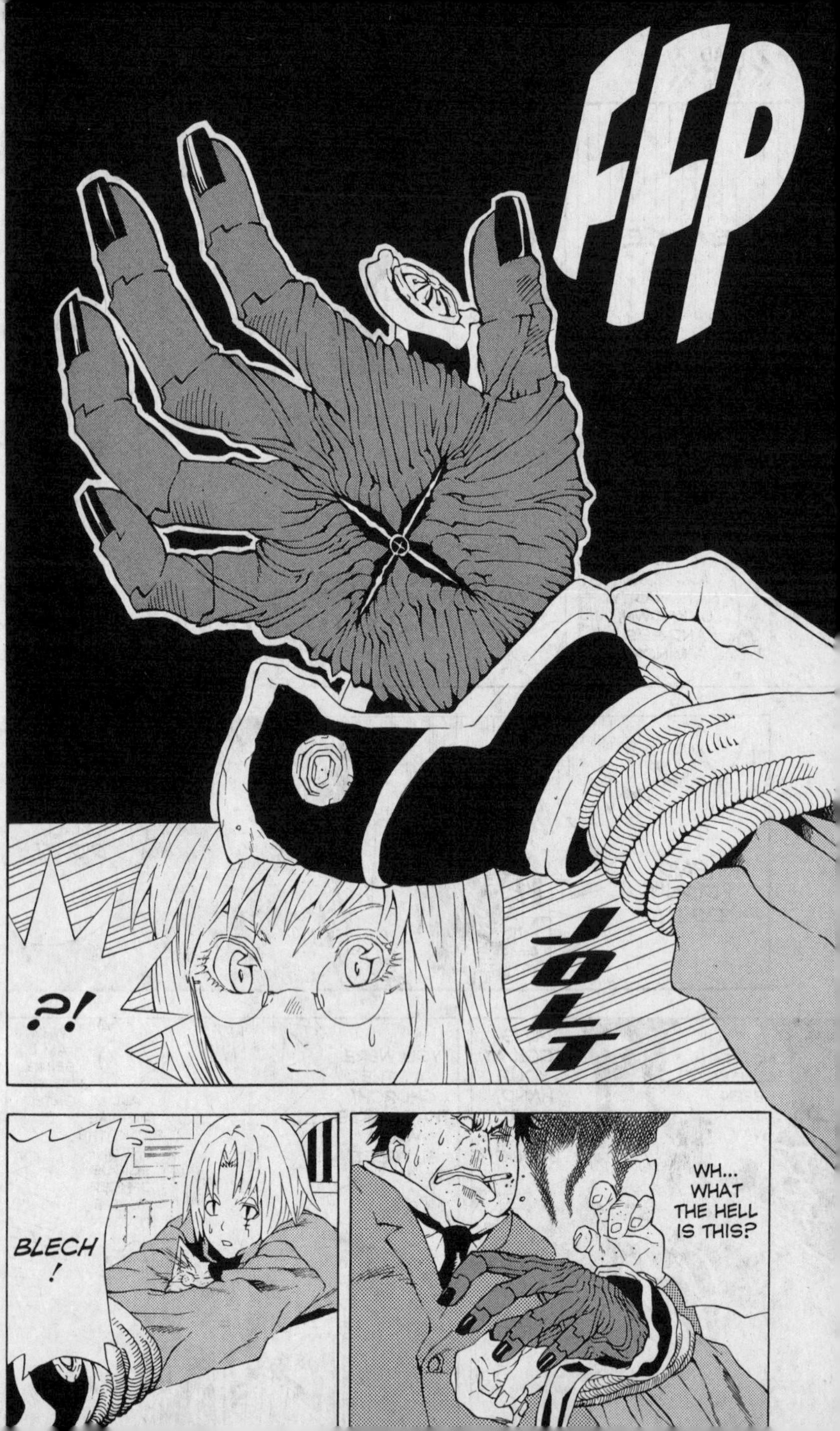
FFP
JOLT
?!
WH... WHAT THE HELL IS THIS?
BLECH!

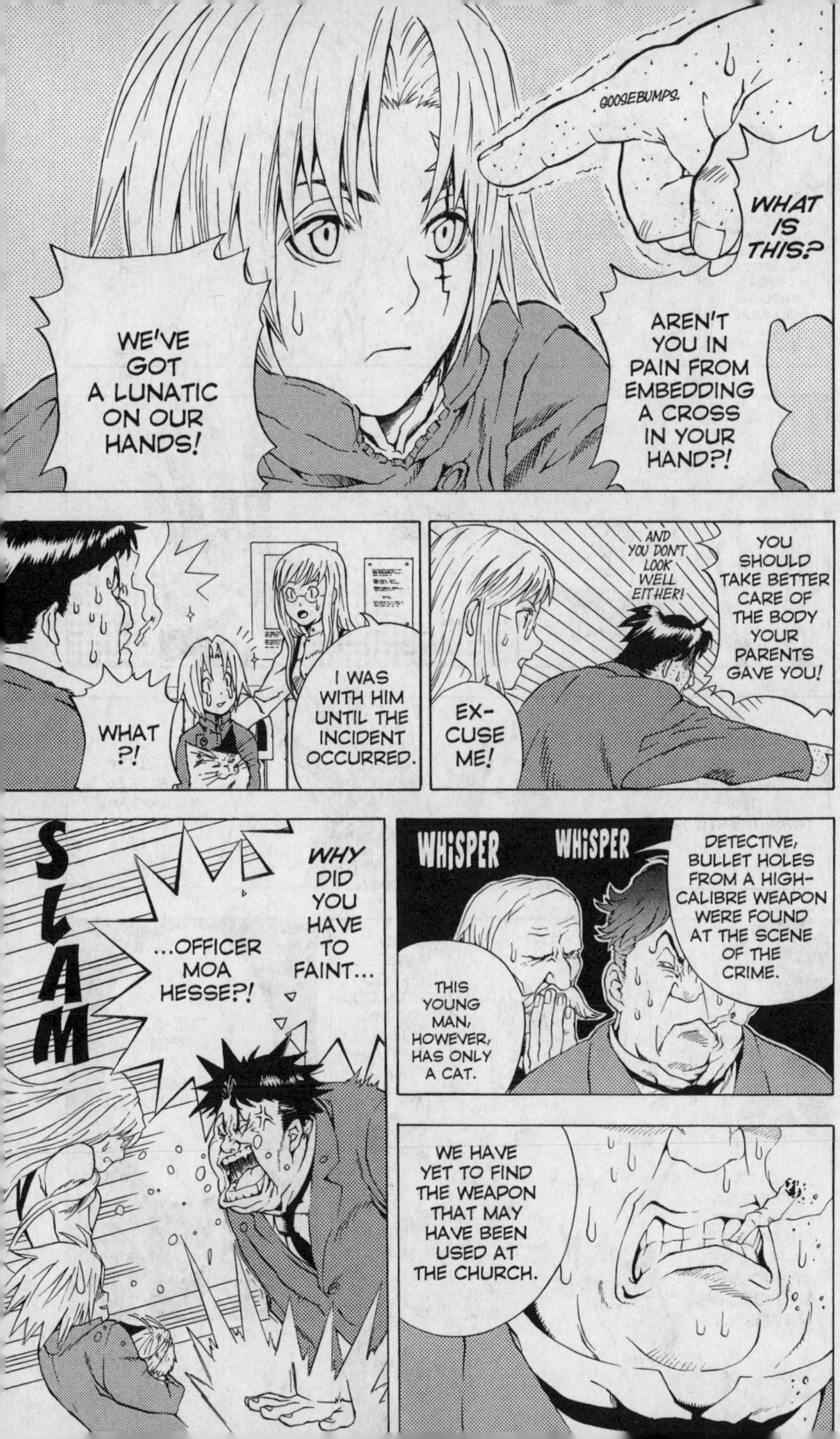
GOOSEBUMPS.
WHAT IS THIS?
AREN'T YOU IN PAIN FROM EMBEDDING A CROSS IN YOUR HAND?!
WE'VE GOT A LUNATIC ON OUR HANDS!
YOU SHOULD TAKE BETTER CARE OF THE BODY YOUR PARENTS GAVE YOU!
AND YOU DON'T LOOK WELL EITHER!
EX-CUSE ME!
I WAS WITH HIM UNTIL THE INCIDENT OCCURRED.
WHAT?!
WHISPER
WHISPER
DETECTIVE, BULLET HOLES FROM A HIGH-CALIBRE WEAPON WERE FOUND AT THE SCENE OF THE CRIME.
THIS YOUNG MAN, HOWEVER, HAS ONLY A CAT.
WE HAVE YET TO FIND THE WEAPON THAT MAY HAVE BEEN USED AT THE CHURCH.
SLAM
WHY DID YOU HAVE TO FAINT...
...OFFICER MOA HESSE?!

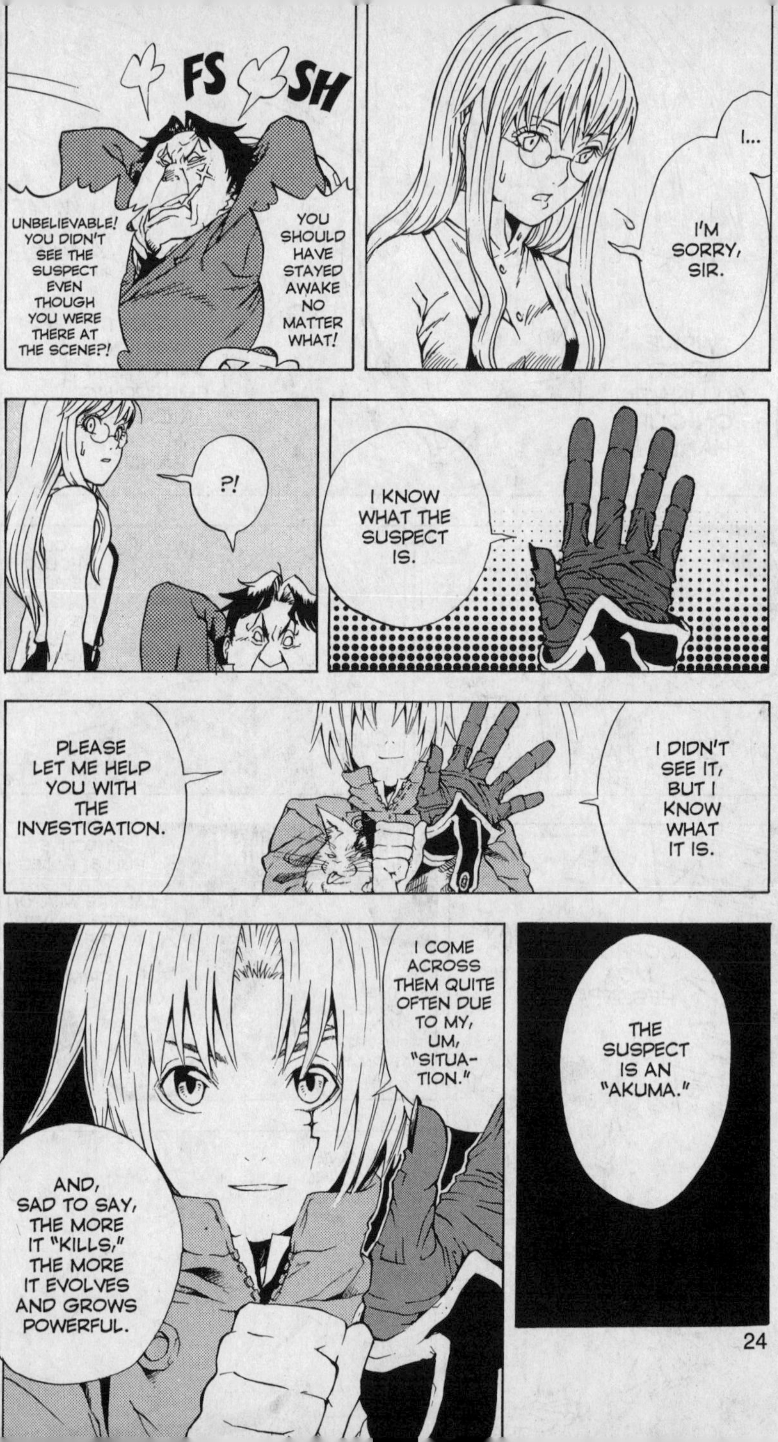
I...
I'M SORRY, SIR.
FS SH
YOU SHOULD HAVE STAYED AWAKE NO MATTER WHAT!
UNBELIEVABLE! YOU DIDN'T SEE THE SUSPECT EVEN THOUGH YOU WERE THERE AT THE SCENE?!
I KNOW WHAT THE SUSPECT IS.
?!
I DIDN'T SEE IT, BUT I KNOW WHAT IT IS.
PLEASE LET ME HELP YOU WITH THE INVESTIGATION.
THE SUSPECT IS AN "AKUMA."
I COME ACROSS THEM QUITE OFTEN DUE TO MY, UM, "SITUA-TION."
AND, SAD TO SAY, THE MORE IT "KILLS," THE MORE IT EVOLVES AND GROWS POWERFUL.

READ THIS WAY

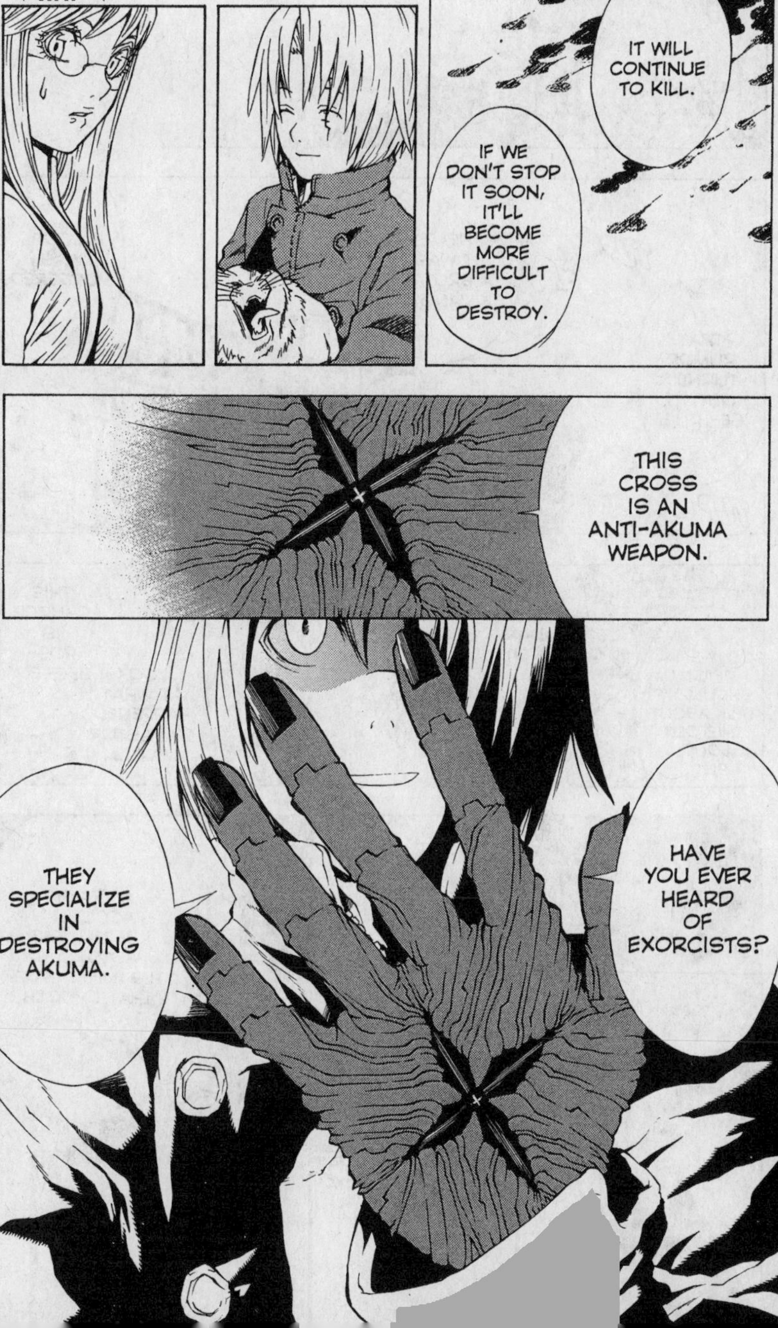
IT WILL CONTINUE TO KILL.
IF WE DON'T STOP IT SOON, IT'LL BECOME MORE DIFFICULT TO DESTROY.
THIS CROSS IS AN ANTI-AKUMA WEAPON.
HAVE YOU EVER HEARD OF EXORCISTS?
THEY SPECIALIZE IN DESTROYING AKUMA.

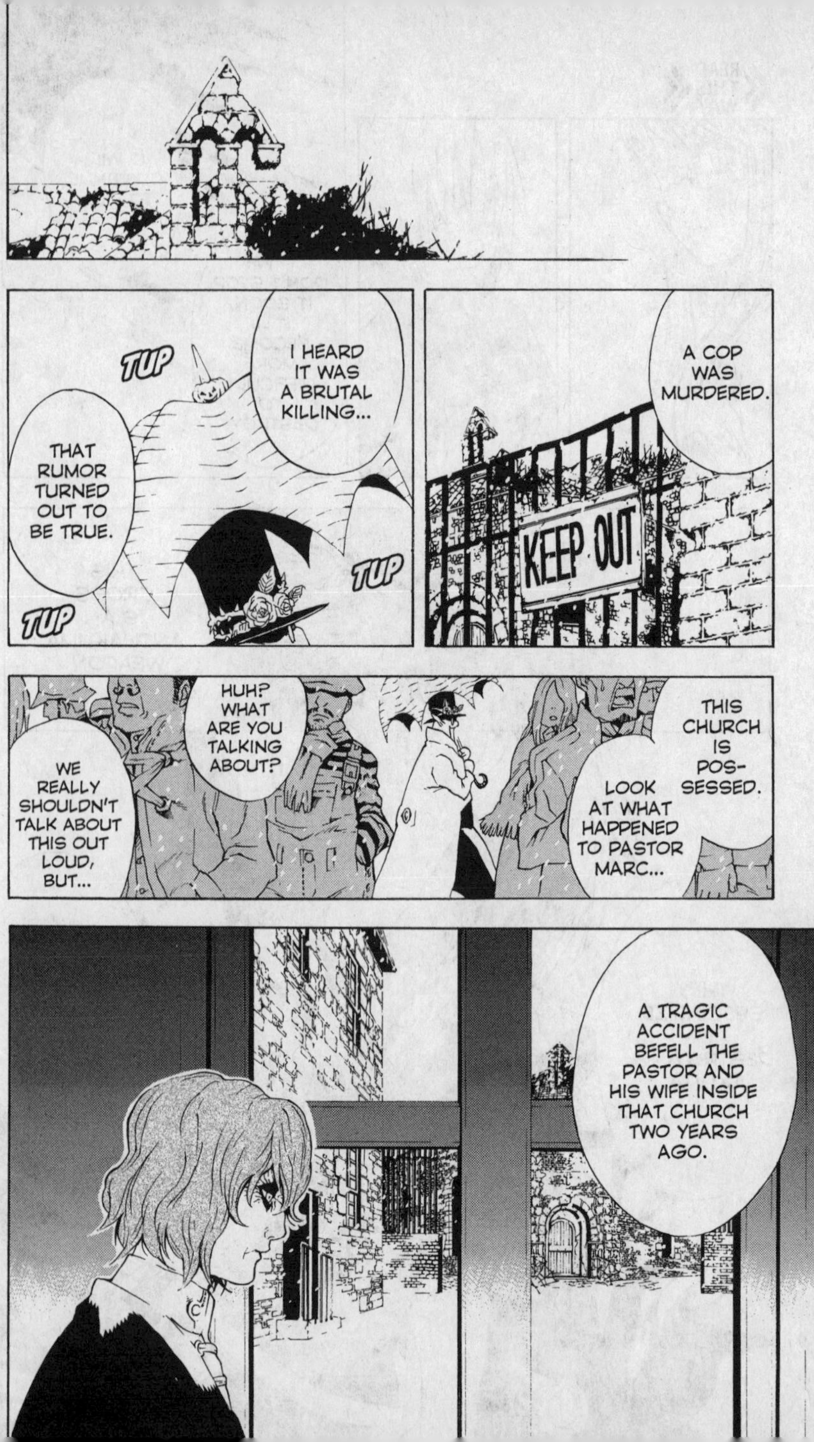
A COP WAS MURDERED.
I HEARD IT WAS A BRUTAL KILLING...
TUP
THAT RUMOR TURNED OUT TO BE TRUE.
TUP
TUP
THIS CHURCH IS POS-SESSED.
LOOK AT WHAT HAPPENED TO PASTOR MARC...
HUH? WHAT ARE YOU TALKING ABOUT?
WE REALLY SHOULDN'T TALK ABOUT THIS OUT LOUD, BUT...
A TRAGIC ACCIDENT BEFELL THE PASTOR AND HIS WIFE INSIDE THAT CHURCH TWO YEARS AGO.

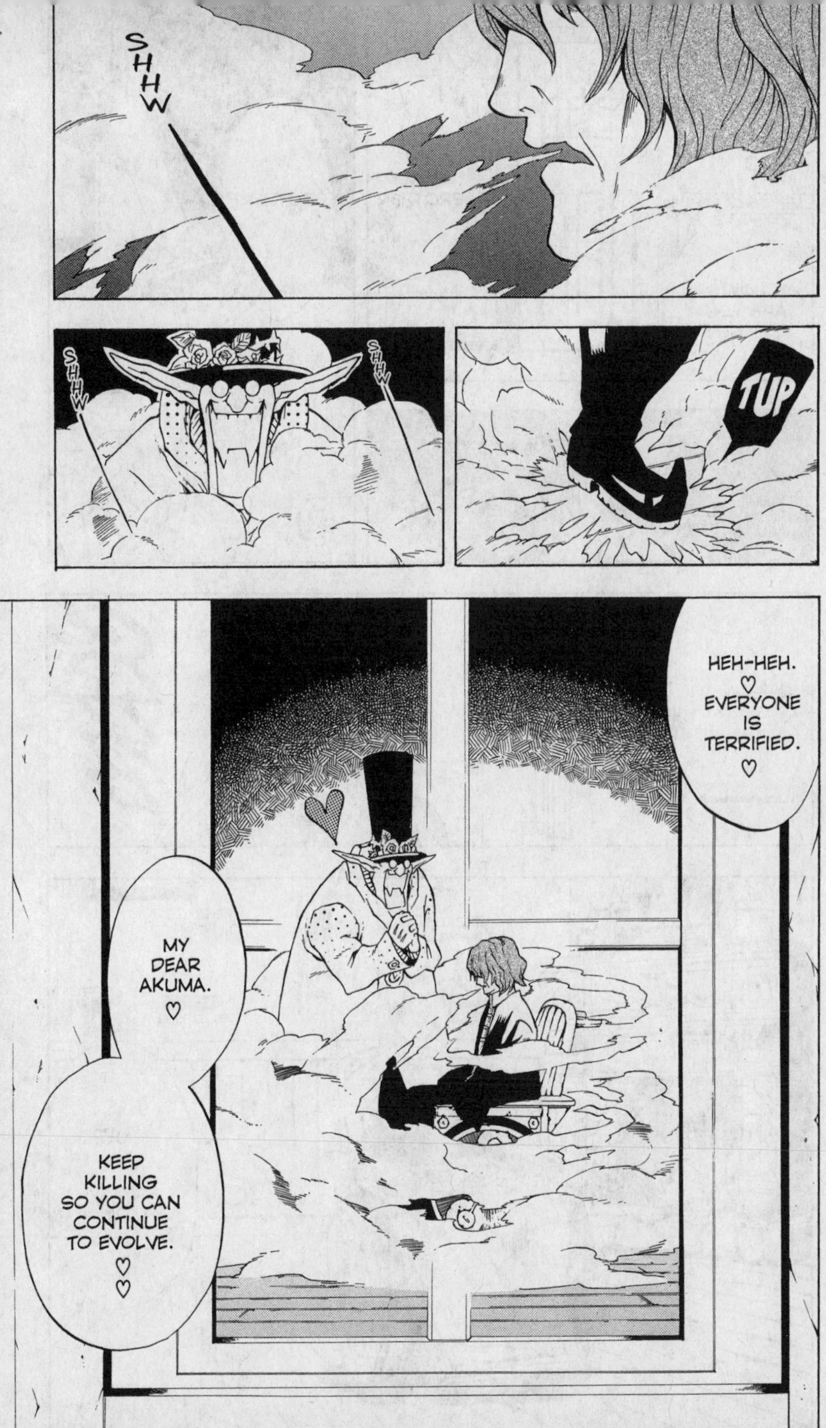

SHHW
TUP
SHHW
SHHW
HEH-HEH. ♡ EVERYONE IS TERRIFIED. ♡
MY DEAR AKUMA. ♡
KEEP KILLING SO YOU CAN CONTINUE TO EVOLVE. ♡ ♡

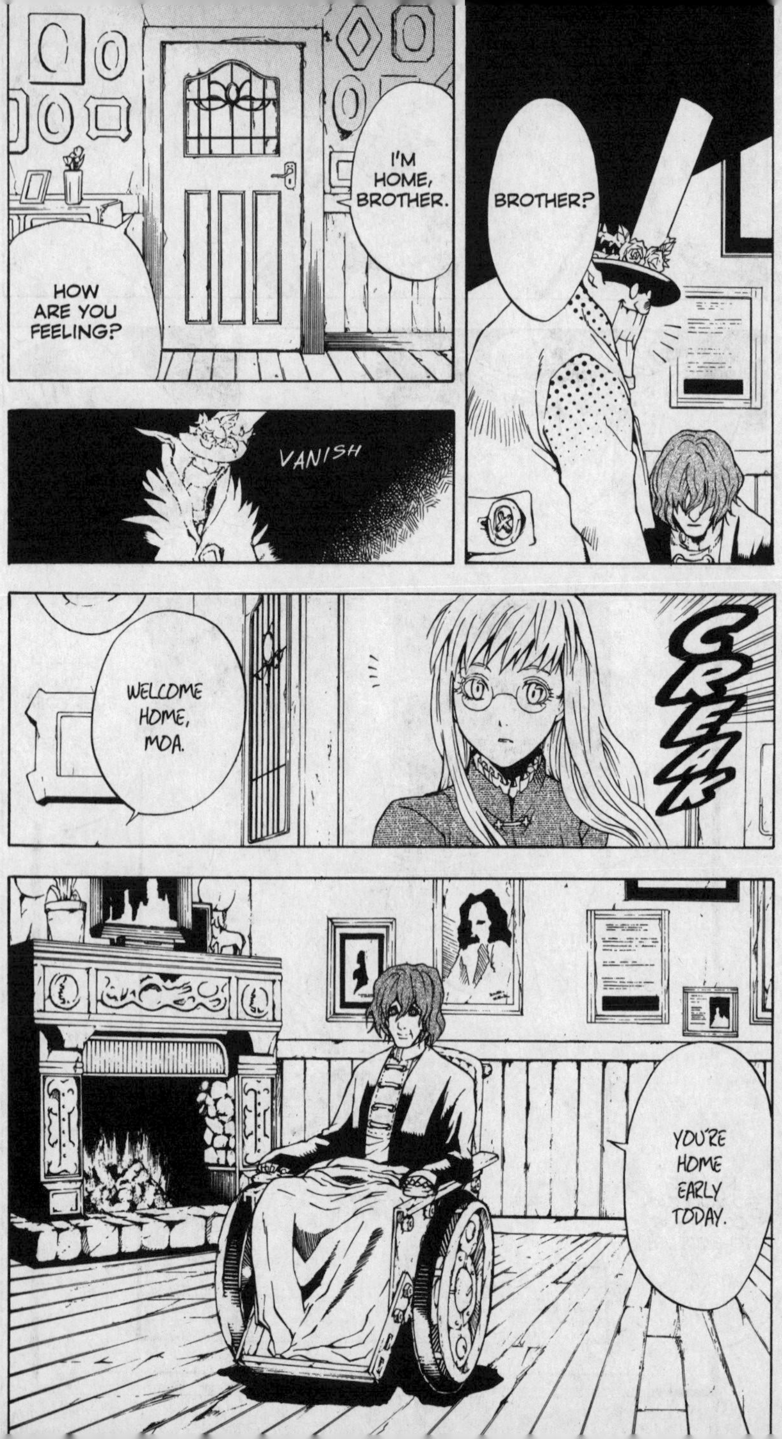
BROTHER?
I'M HOME, BROTHER.
HOW ARE YOU FEELING?
VANISH
CREAK
WELCOME HOME, MOA.
YOU'RE HOME EARLY TODAY.

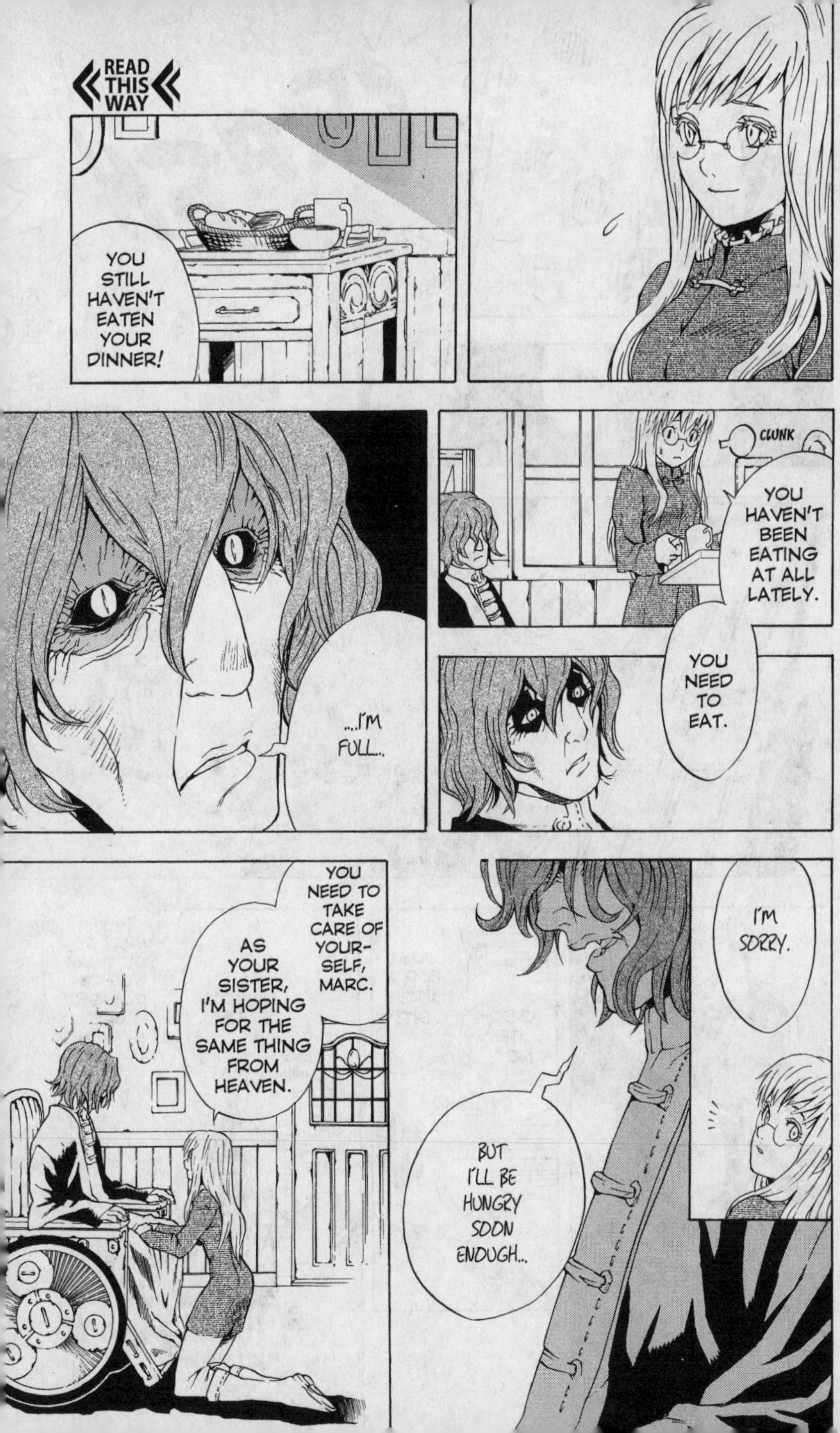
READ THIS WAY
YOU STILL HAVEN'T EATEN YOUR DINNER!
CLUNK
YOU HAVEN'T BEEN EATING AT ALL LATELY.
YOU NEED TO EAT.
...I'M FULL...
I'M SORRY.
BUT I'LL BE HUNGRY SOON ENOUGH...
YOU NEED TO TAKE CARE OF YOUR-SELF, MARC.
AS YOUR SISTER, I'M HOPING FOR THE SAME THING FROM HEAVEN.

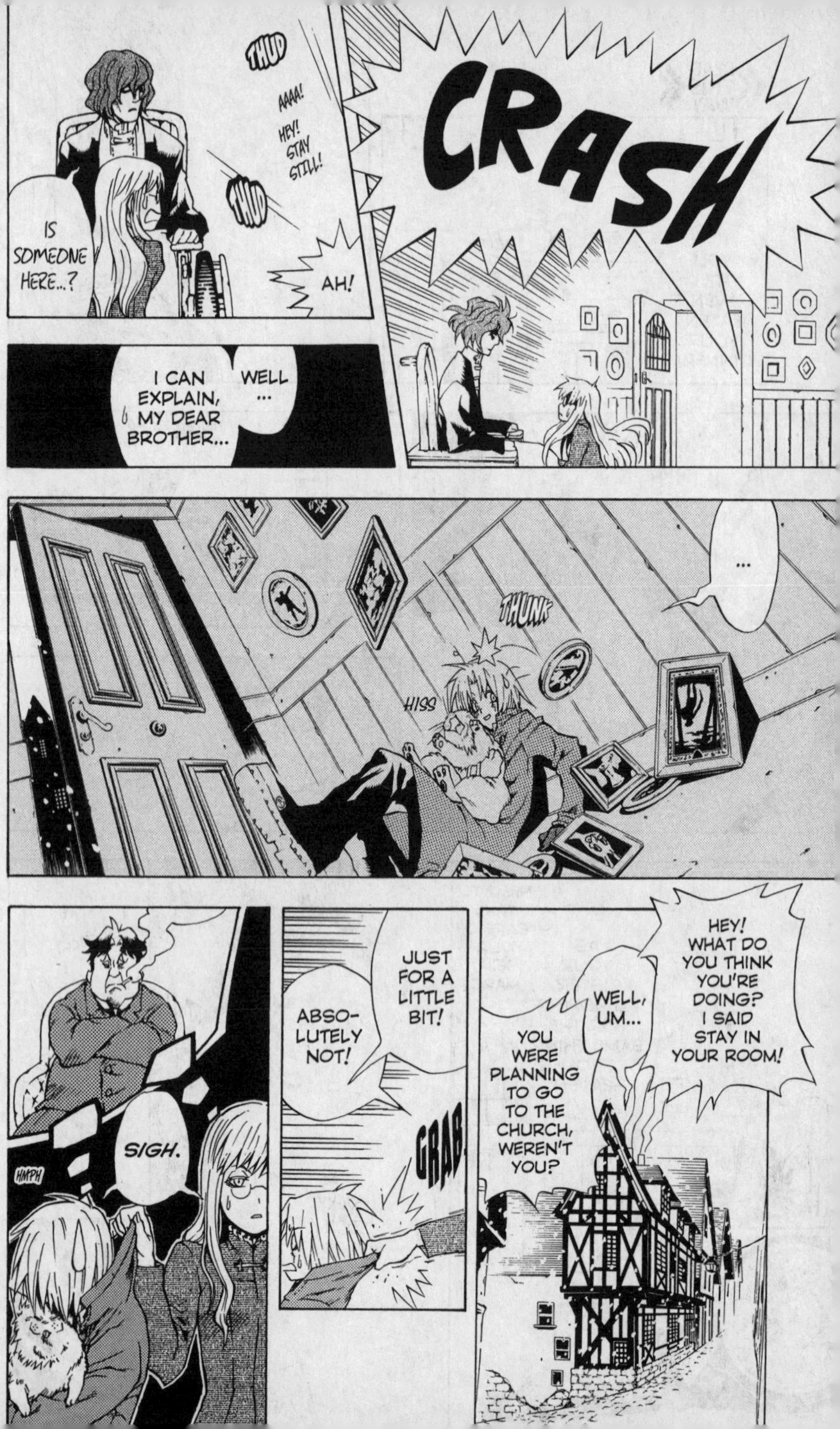
CRASH
THUD
AAAA!
HEY! STAY STILL!
THUD
AH!
IS SOMEONE HERE...?
WELL ...
I CAN EXPLAIN, MY DEAR BROTHER...
...
THUNK
HISS
HEY! WHAT DO YOU THINK YOU'RE DOING? I SAID STAY IN YOUR ROOM!
WELL, UM...
YOU WERE PLANNING TO GO TO THE CHURCH, WEREN'T YOU?
JUST FOR A LITTLE BIT!
ABSO-LUTELY NOT!
GRAB
SIGH.
HMPH

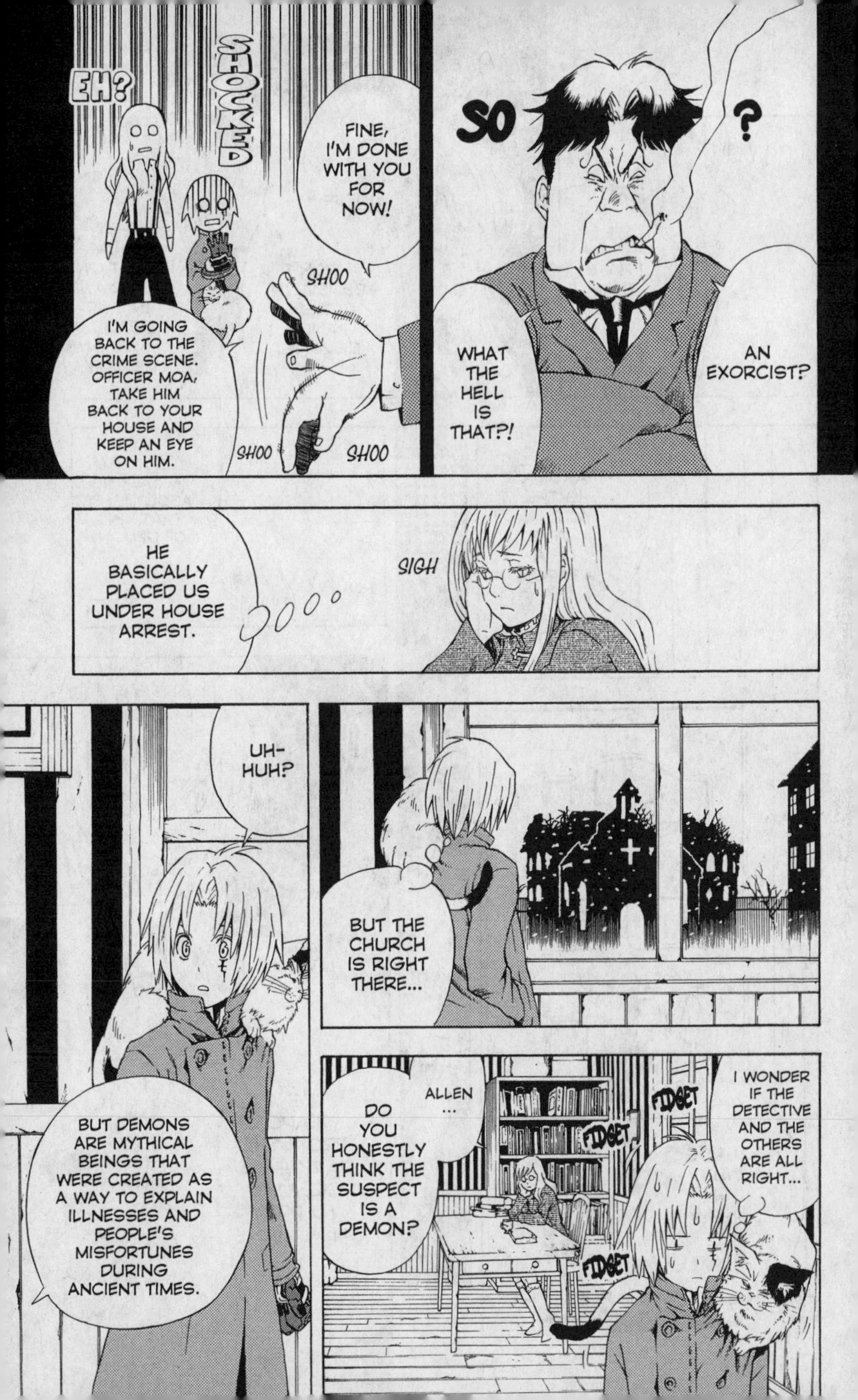
SO
?
AN EXORCIST?
WHAT THE HELL IS THAT?!
FINE, I'M DONE WITH YOU FOR NOW!
SHOO
SHOO
SHOO
SHOCKED
EH?
I'M GOING BACK TO THE CRIME SCENE. OFFICER MOA, TAKE HIM BACK TO YOUR HOUSE AND KEEP AN EYE ON HIM.
SIGH
HE BASICALLY PLACED US UNDER HOUSE ARREST.
BUT THE CHURCH IS RIGHT THERE...
I WONDER IF THE DETECTIVE AND THE OTHERS ARE ALL RIGHT...
FIDGET
FIDGET
FIDGET
ALLEN ...
DO YOU HONESTLY THINK THE SUSPECT IS A DEMON?
UH-HUH?
BUT DEMONS ARE MYTHICAL BEINGS THAT WERE CREATED AS A WAY TO EXPLAIN ILLNESSES AND PEOPLE'S MISFORTUNES DURING ANCIENT TIMES.

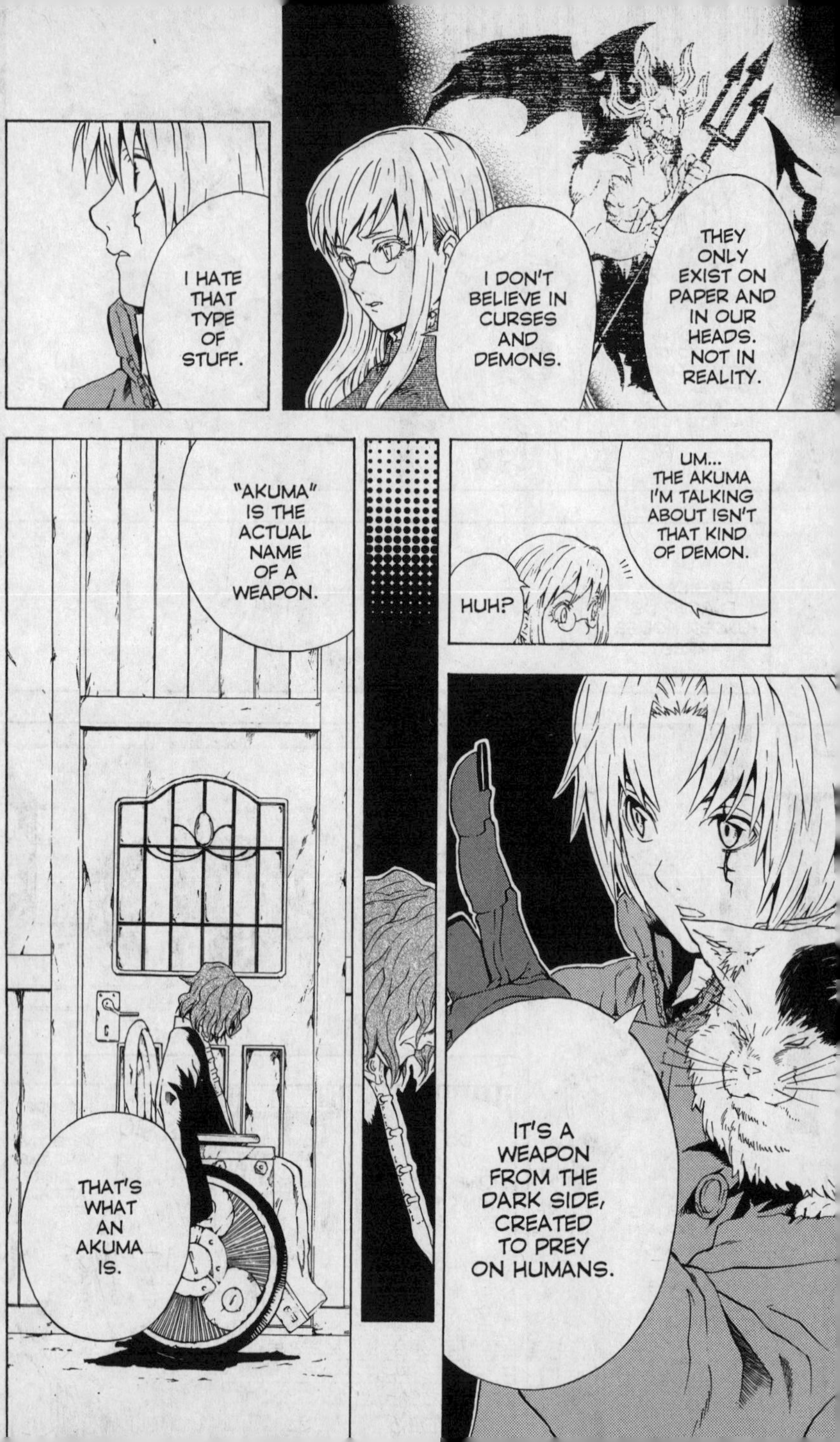
THEY ONLY EXIST ON PAPER AND IN OUR HEADS. NOT IN REALITY.
I DON'T BELIEVE IN CURSES AND DEMONS.
I HATE THAT TYPE OF STUFF.
UM... THE AKUMA I'M TALKING ABOUT ISN'T THAT KIND OF DEMON.
HUH?
IT'S A WEAPON FROM THE DARK SIDE, CREATED TO PREY ON HUMANS.
"AKUMA" IS THE ACTUAL NAME OF A WEAPON.
THAT'S WHAT AN AKUMA IS.

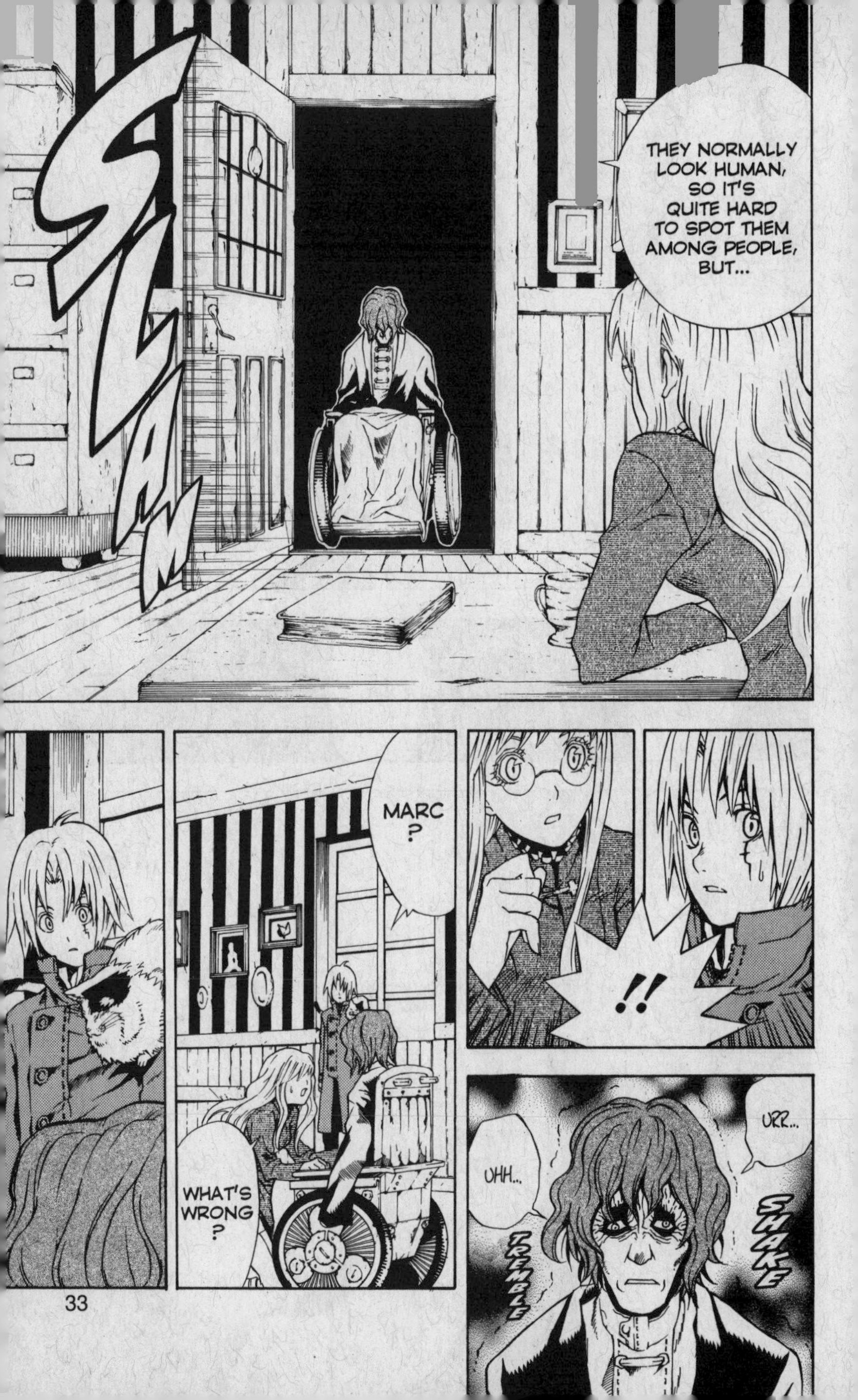
THEY NORMALLY LOOK HUMAN, SO IT'S QUITE HARD TO SPOT THEM AMONG PEOPLE, BUT...
SLAM
!!
URR...
UHH...
SHAKE
TREMBLE
MARC?
WHAT'S WRONG?

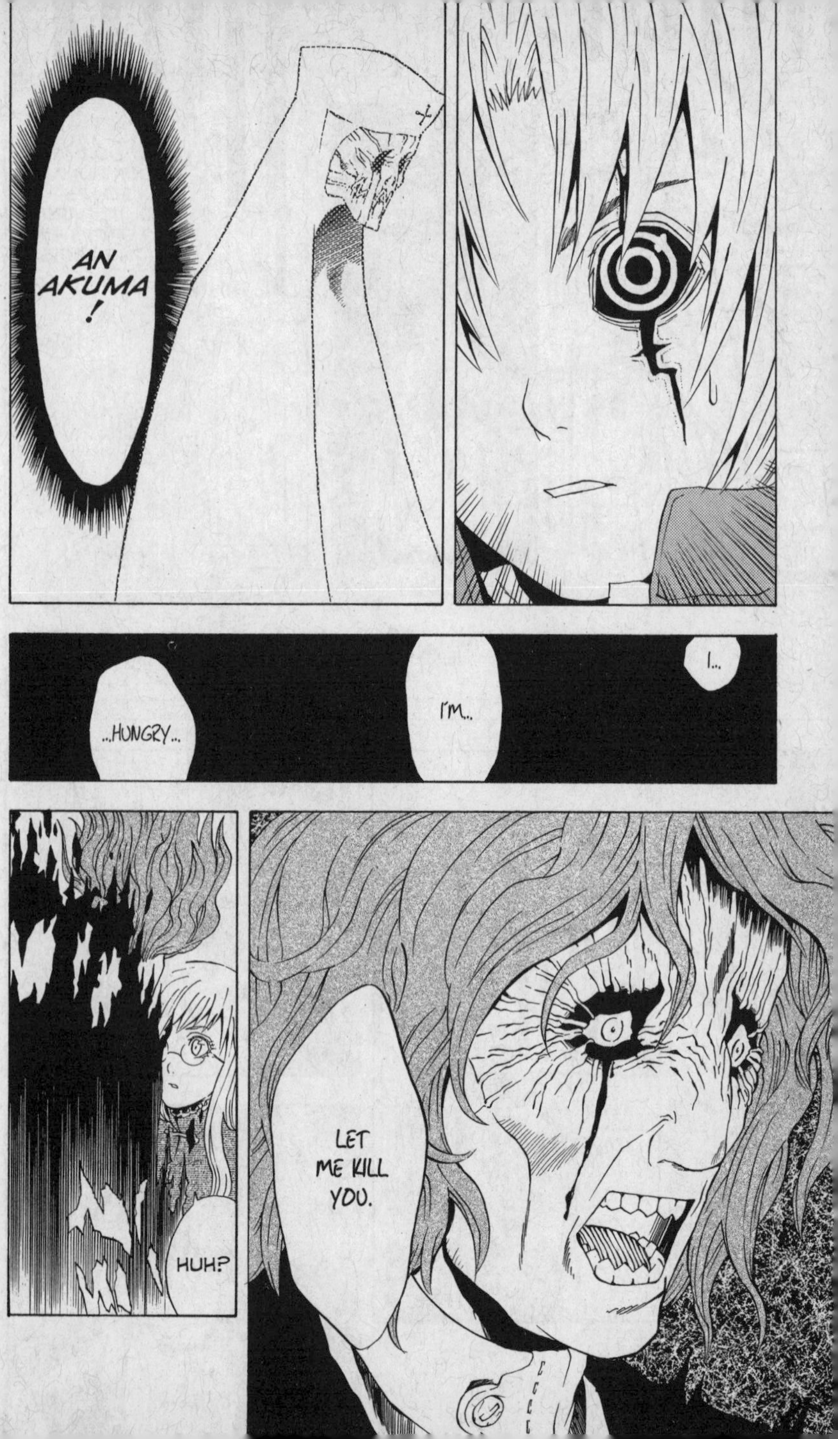
AN AKUMA!
I..
I'M..
...HUNGRY...
LET ME KILL YOU.
HUH?

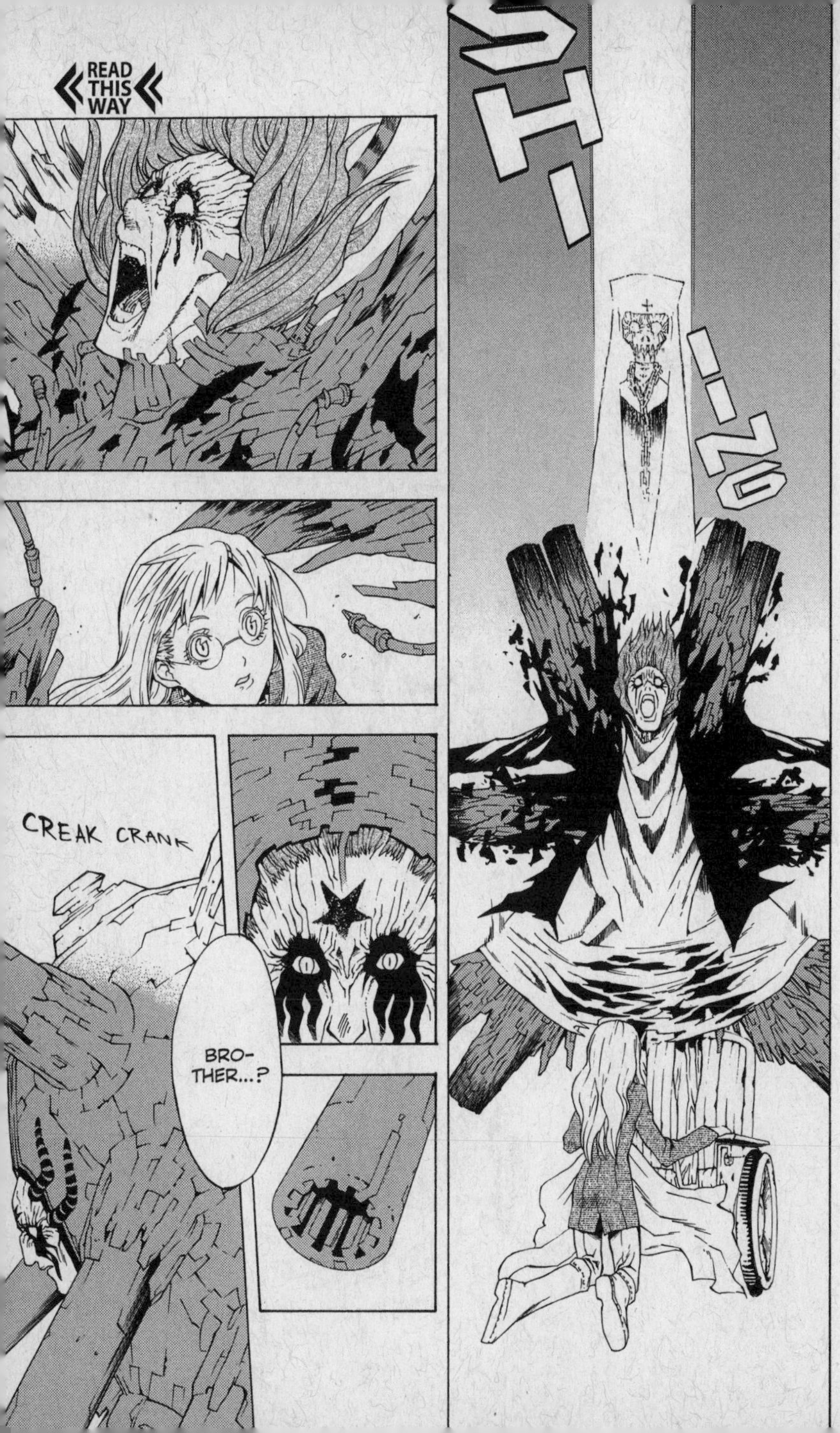
READ THIS WAY
SHIIIING
BRO-THER...?
CREAK CRANK

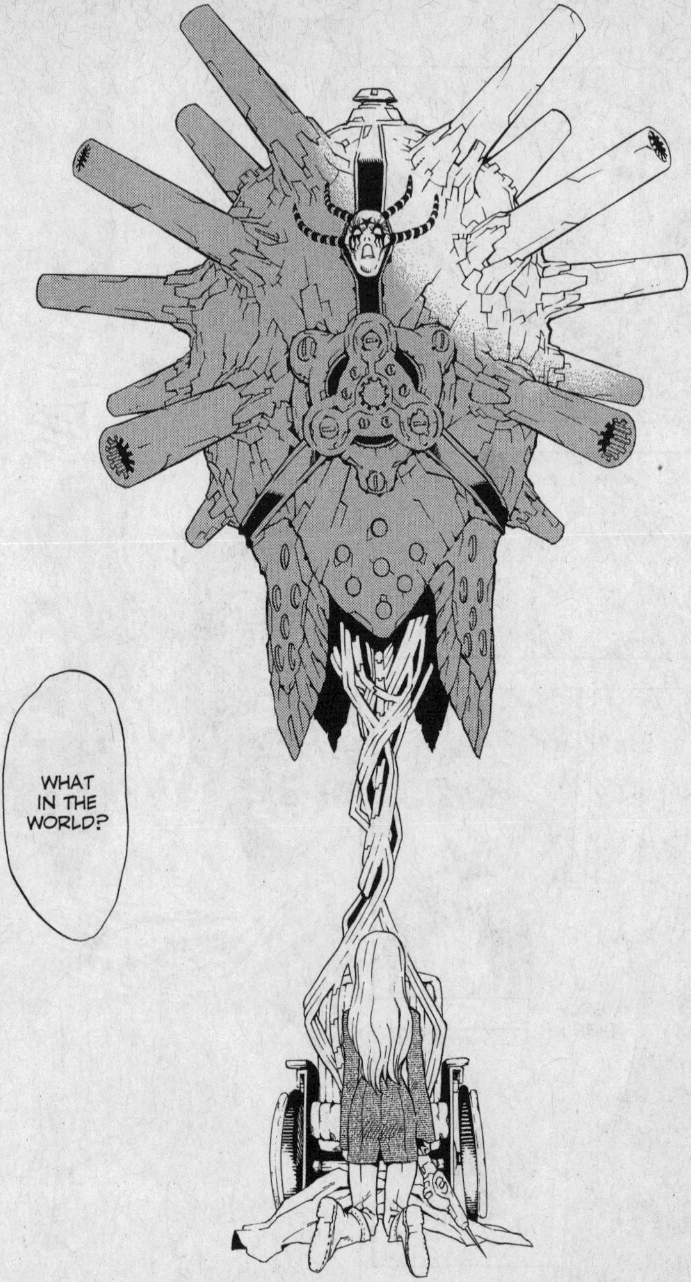
WHAT IN THE WORLD?

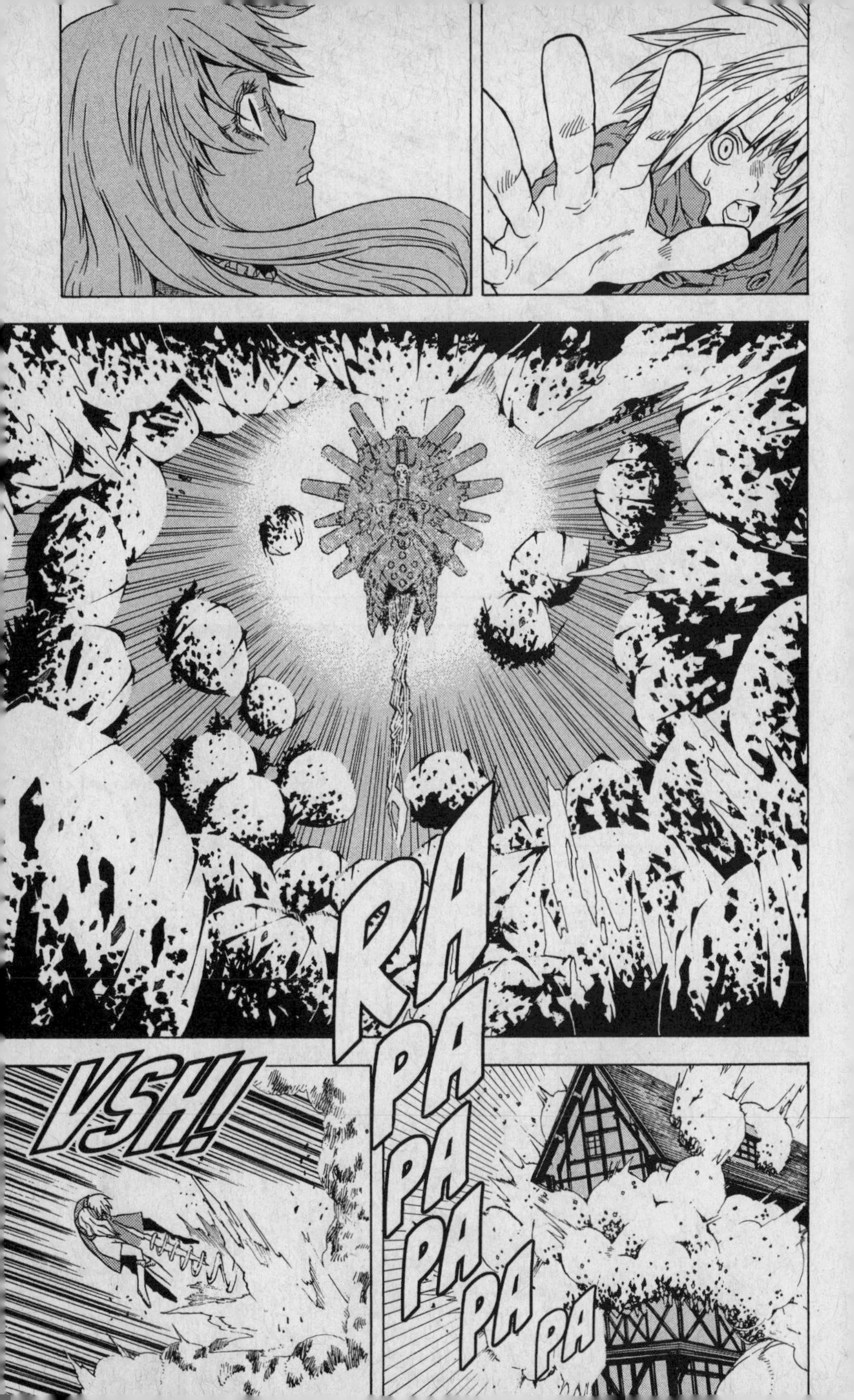
RA PA PA PA PA PA PA
VSH!

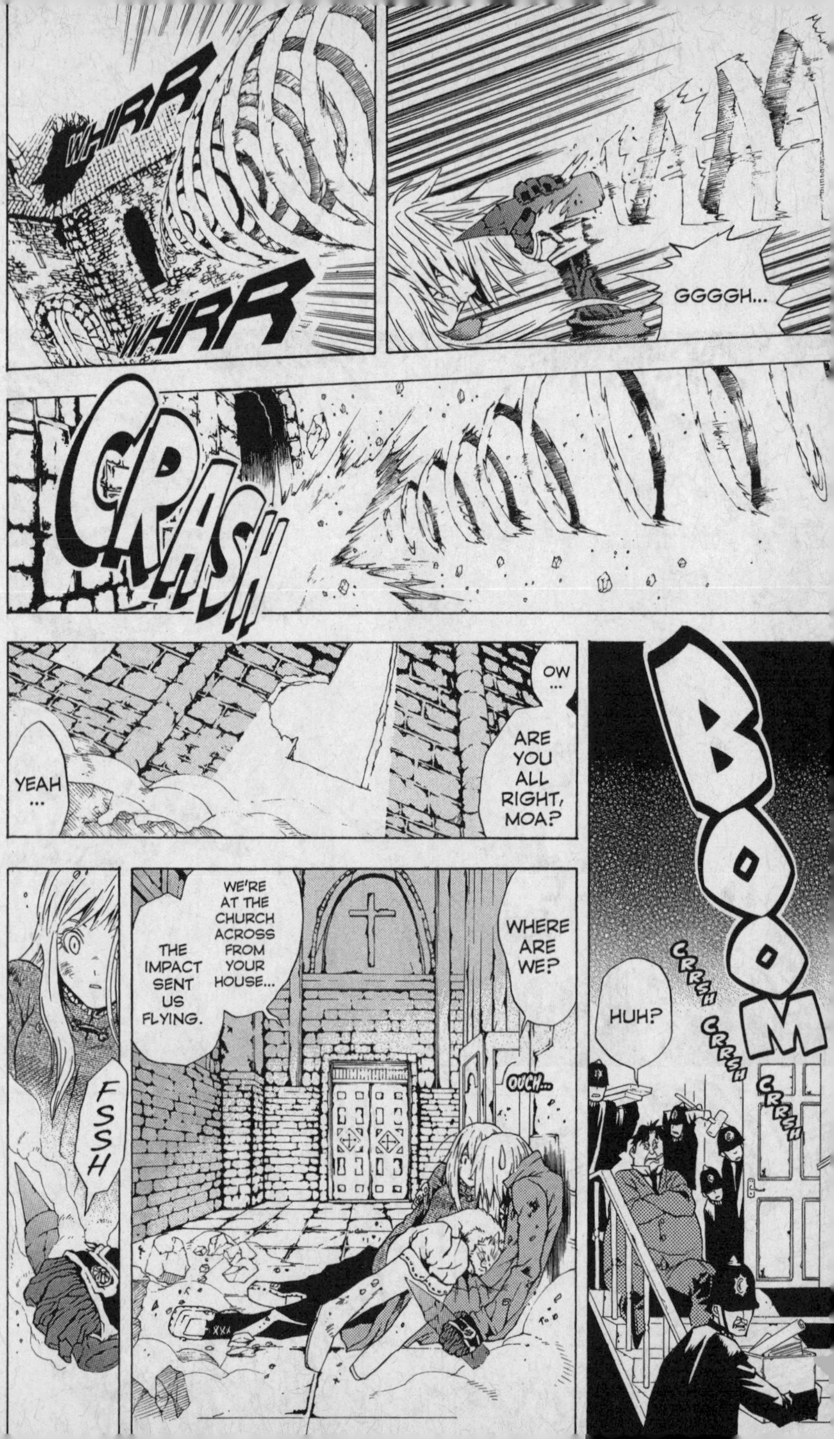
GGGGH...
WHRR
WHRR
CRASH
BOOOM
CRRSH CRRSH CRRSH
HUH?
OW...
ARE YOU ALL RIGHT, MOA?
YEAH...
WHERE ARE WE?
WE'RE AT THE CHURCH ACROSS FROM YOUR HOUSE...
THE IMPACT SENT US FLYING.
OUCH...
FSSH

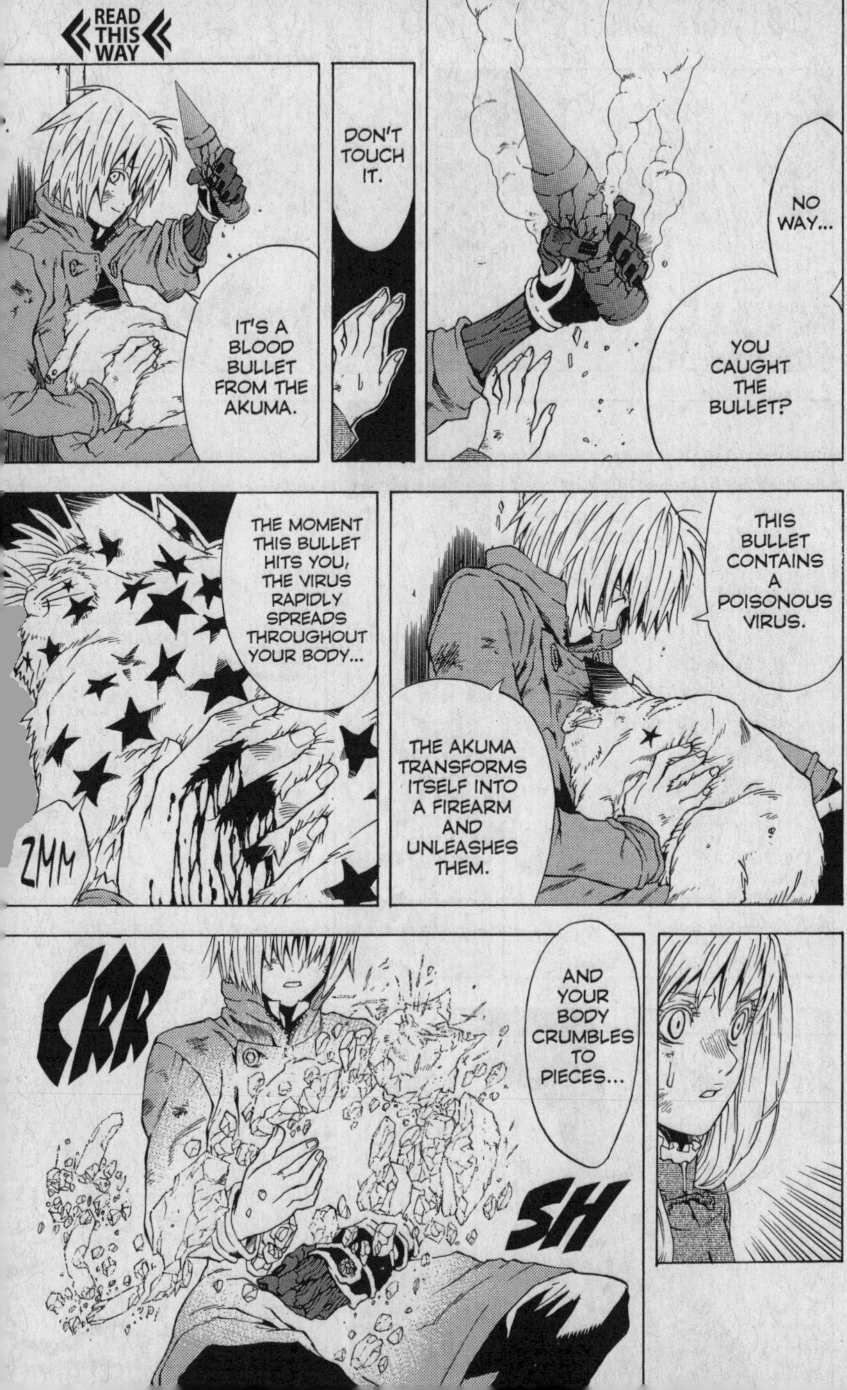
READ THIS WAY
NO WAY...
YOU CAUGHT THE BULLET?
DON'T TOUCH IT.
IT'S A BLOOD BULLET FROM THE AKUMA.
THIS BULLET CONTAINS A POISONOUS VIRUS.
THE AKUMA TRANSFORMS ITSELF INTO A FIREARM AND UNLEASHES THEM.
THE MOMENT THIS BULLET HITS YOU, THE VIRUS RAPIDLY SPREADS THROUGHOUT YOUR BODY...
ZMM
AND YOUR BODY CRUMBLES TO PIECES...
CRR
SH

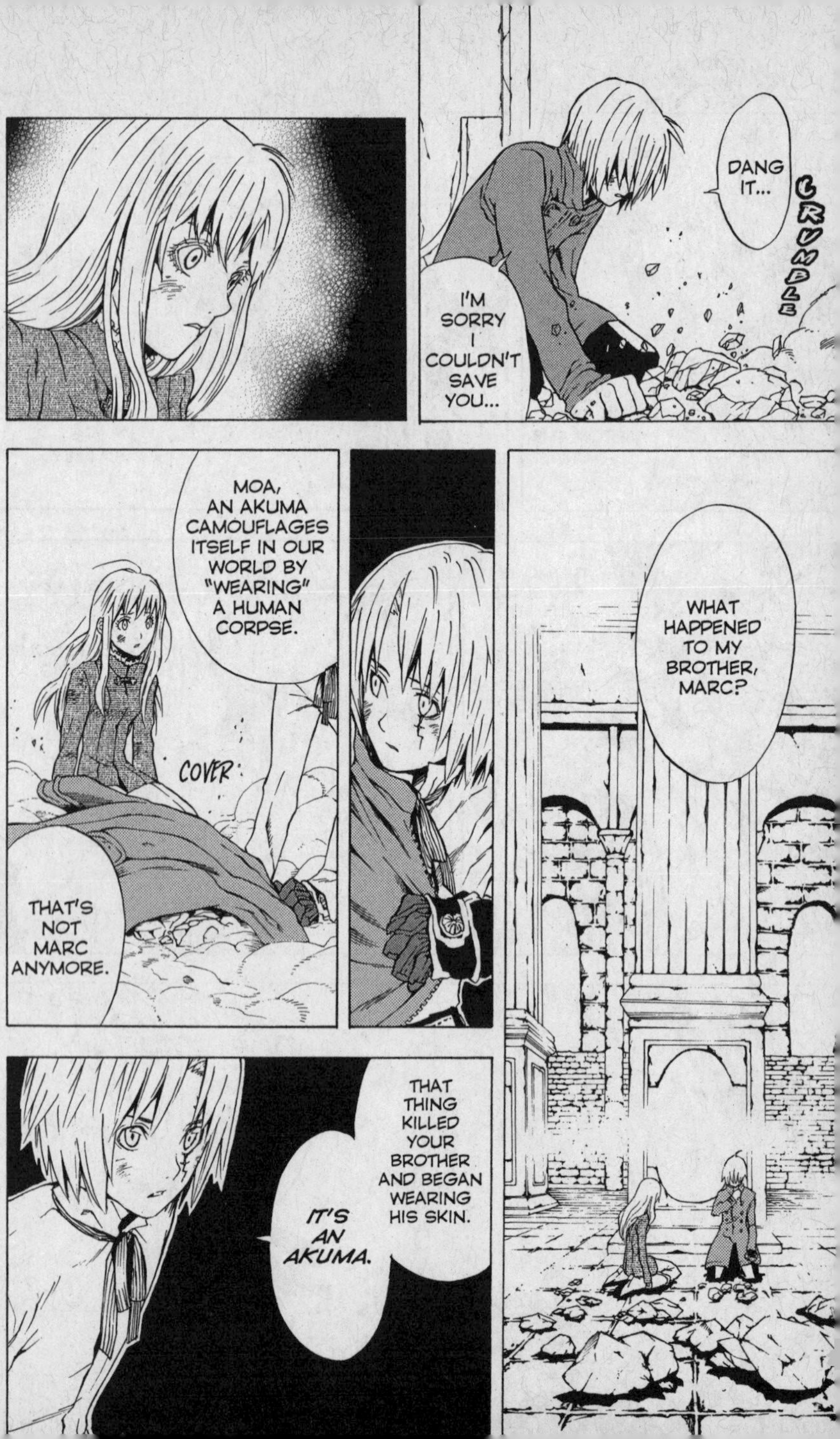
DANG IT...
CRUMBLE
I'M SORRY I COULDN'T SAVE YOU...
WHAT HAPPENED TO MY BROTHER, MARC?
MOA, AN AKUMA CAMOUFLAGES ITSELF IN OUR WORLD BY "WEARING" A HUMAN CORPSE.
COVER
THAT'S NOT MARC ANYMORE.
THAT THING KILLED YOUR BROTHER AND BEGAN WEARING HIS SKIN.
IT'S AN AKUMA.

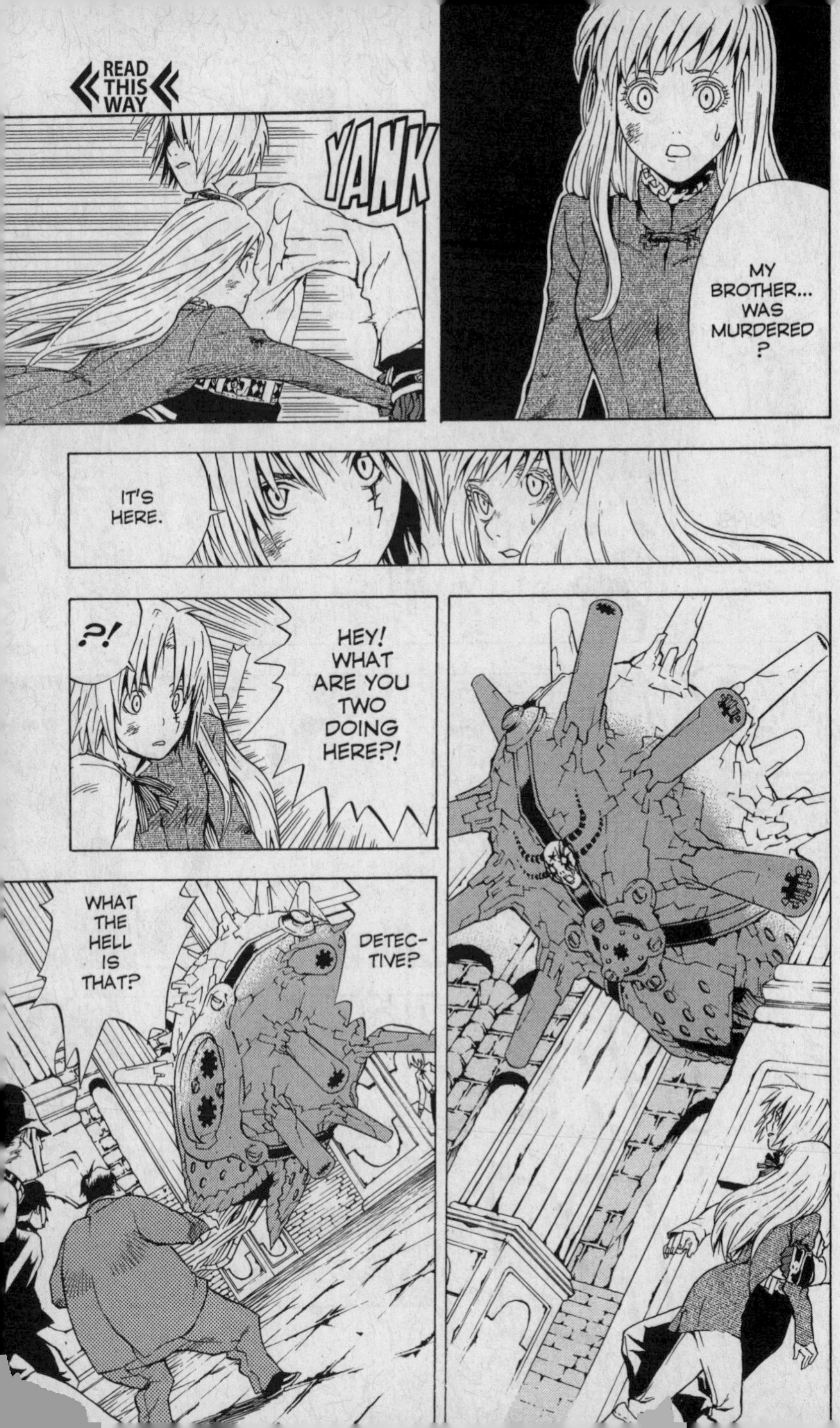
READ THIS WAY
MY BROTHER... WAS MURDERED?
YANK
IT'S HERE.
?!
HEY! WHAT ARE YOU TWO DOING HERE?!
DETECTIVE?
WHAT THE HELL IS THAT?

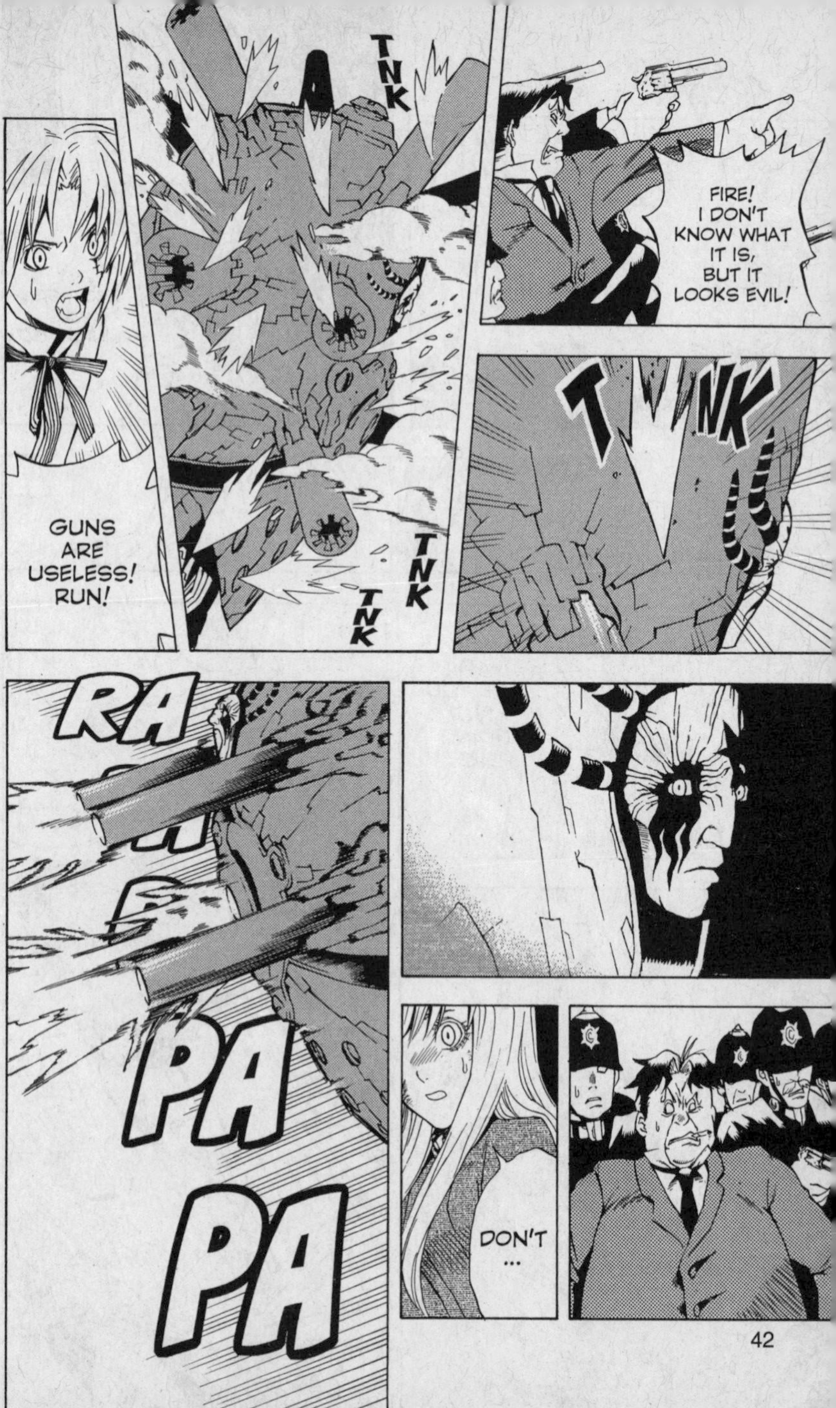
FIRE! I DON'T KNOW WHAT IT IS, BUT IT LOOKS EVIL!
TNK
TNK
TNK
TNK
GUNS ARE USELESS! RUN!
DON'T ...
RA
PA
PA

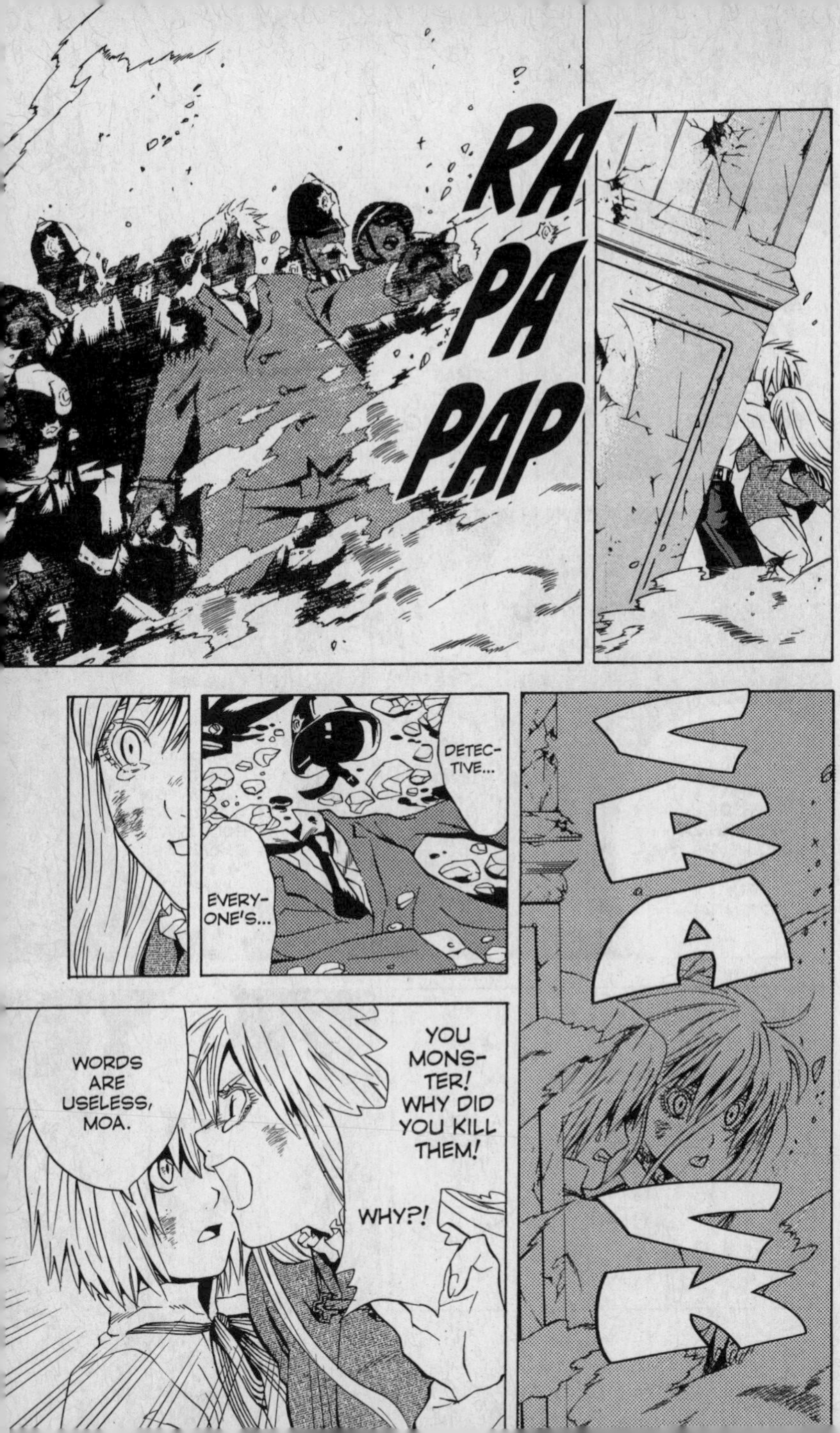
RA PA PAP
VRAK
DETECTIVE...
EVERYONE'S...
YOU MONSTER! WHY DID YOU KILL THEM!
WHY?!
WORDS ARE USELESS, MOA.

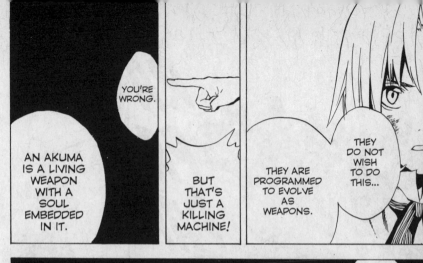

THEY DO NOT WISH TO DO THIS...
THEY ARE PROGRAMMED TO EVOLVE AS WEAPONS.
BUT THAT'S JUST A KILLING MACHINE!
YOU'RE WRONG.
AN AKUMA IS A LIVING WEAPON WITH A SOUL EMBEDDED IN IT.
THE SOUL IS RULED BY THE "MAKER." THESE LOST SOULS ARE THOSE THAT ARE TORMENTED BY THEIR SINS. THEY HATE THIS WORLD.
AND IT IS ALL THE PAIN AND FRUSTRATION OF A TORMENTED SOUL THAT SERVES AS THE ENERGY SOURCE...
THAT FEEDS THE AKUMA AND HELPS IT REACH ITS FULL POTENTIAL.
EVEN THAT AKUMA... ONCE HAD A SOUL EMBEDDED IN IT.

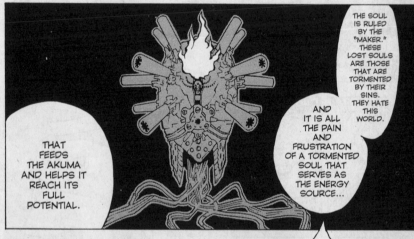

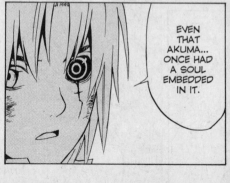

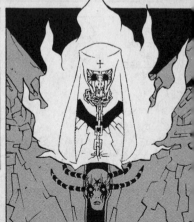

READ THIS WAY

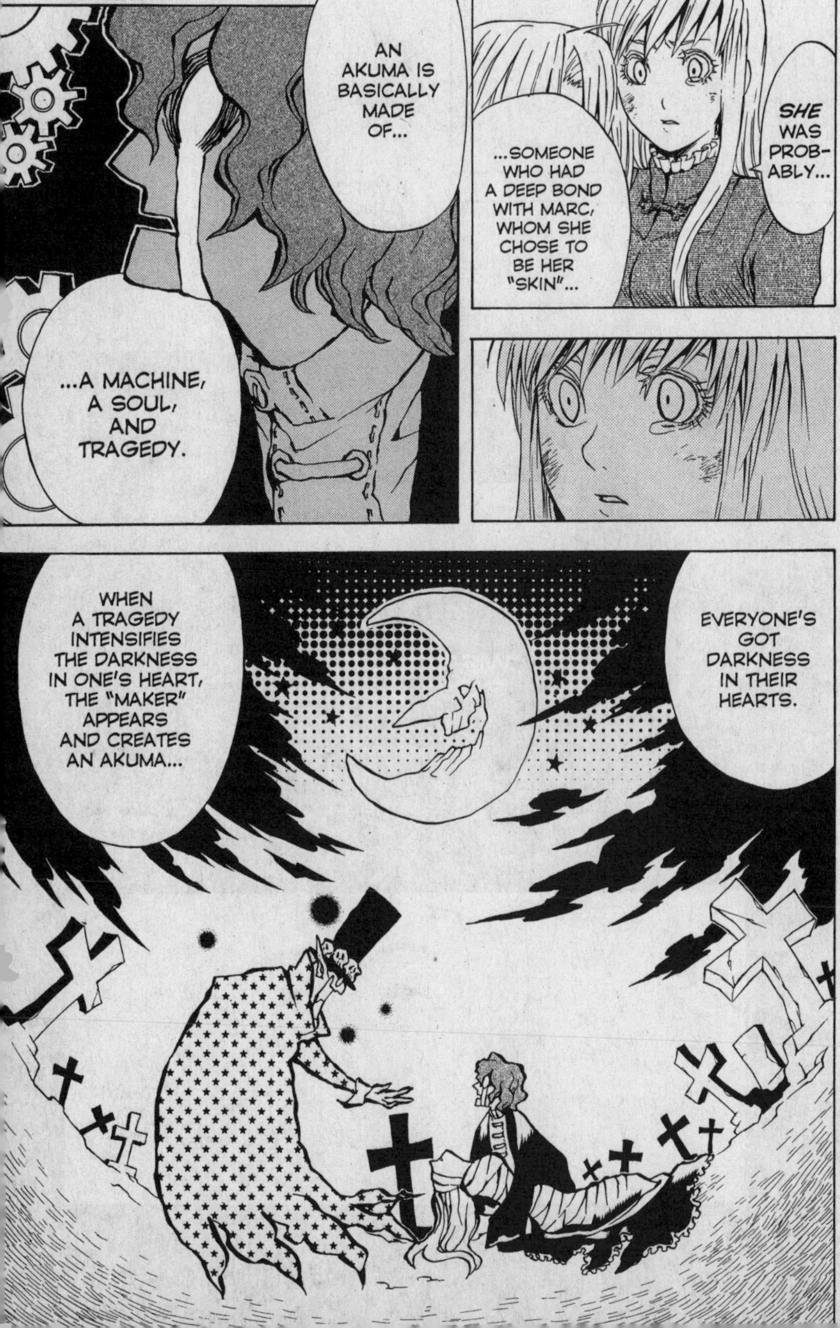
SHE WAS PROBABLY...
...SOMEONE WHO HAD A DEEP BOND WITH MARC, WHOM SHE CHOSE TO BE HER "SKIN"...
AN AKUMA IS BASICALLY MADE OF...
...A MACHINE, A SOUL, AND TRAGEDY.
EVERYONE'S GOT DARKNESS IN THEIR HEARTS.
WHEN A TRAGEDY INTENSIFIES THE DARKNESS IN ONE'S HEART, THE "MAKER" APPEARS AND CREATES AN AKUMA...

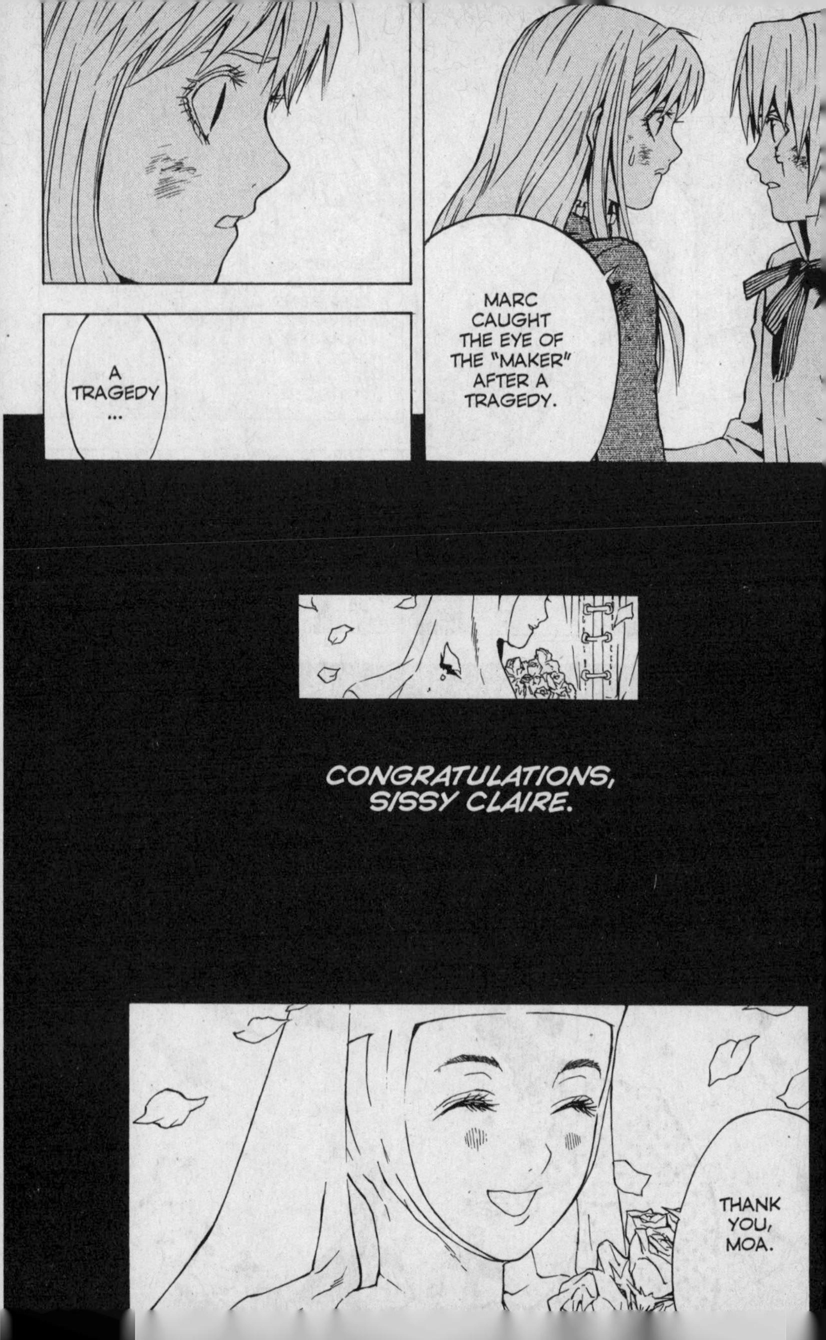
MARC CAUGHT THE EYE OF THE "MAKER" AFTER A TRAGEDY.
A TRAGEDY ...
CONGRATULATIONS, SISSY CLAIRE.
THANK YOU, MOA.

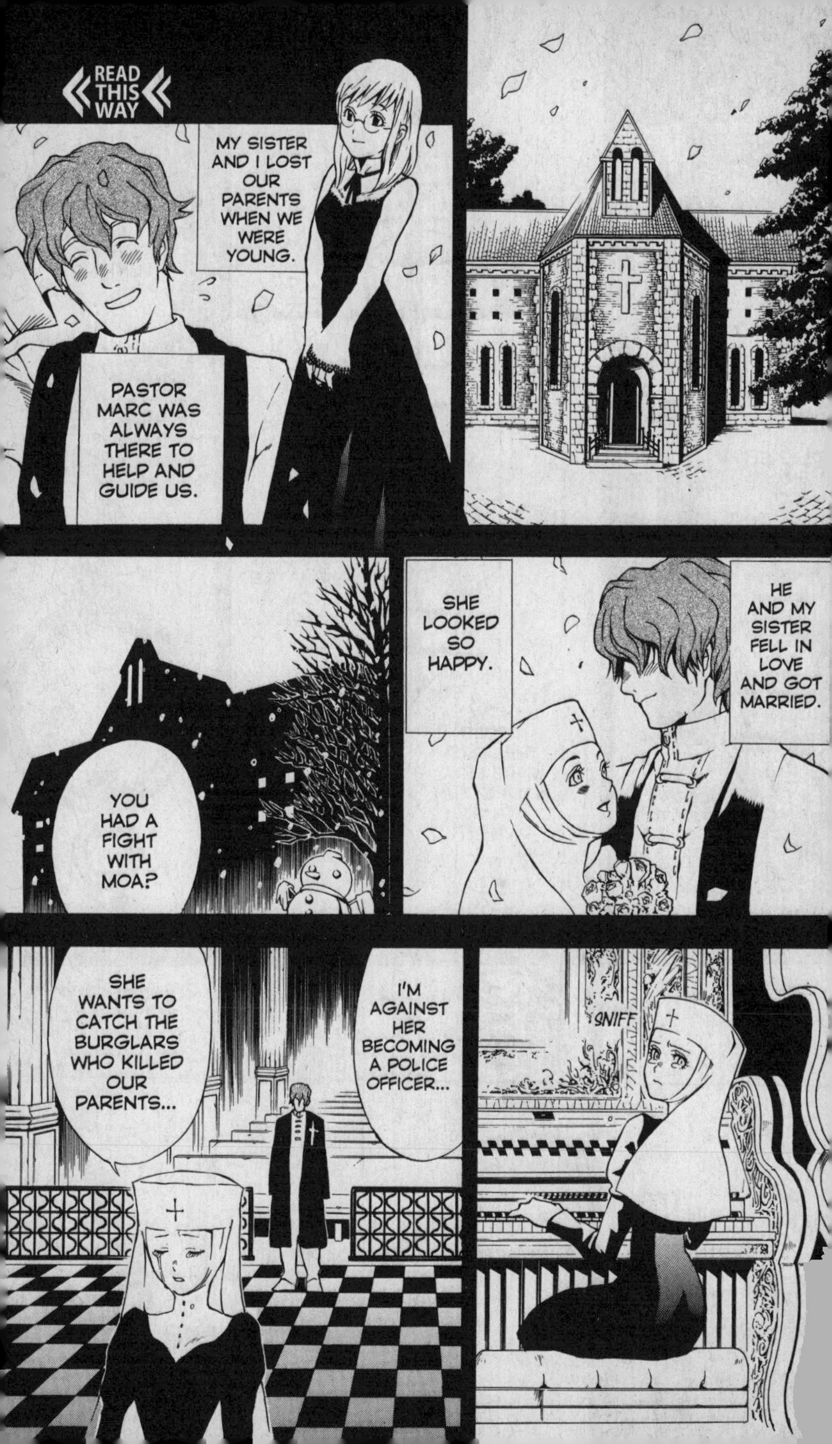
READ THIS WAY
MY SISTER AND I LOST OUR PARENTS WHEN WE WERE YOUNG.
PASTOR MARC WAS ALWAYS THERE TO HELP AND GUIDE US.
HE AND MY SISTER FELL IN LOVE AND GOT MARRIED.
SHE LOOKED SO HAPPY.
YOU HAD A FIGHT WITH MOA?
SNIFF
I'M AGAINST HER BECOMING A POLICE OFFICER...
SHE WANTS TO CATCH THE BURGLARS WHO KILLED OUR PARENTS...

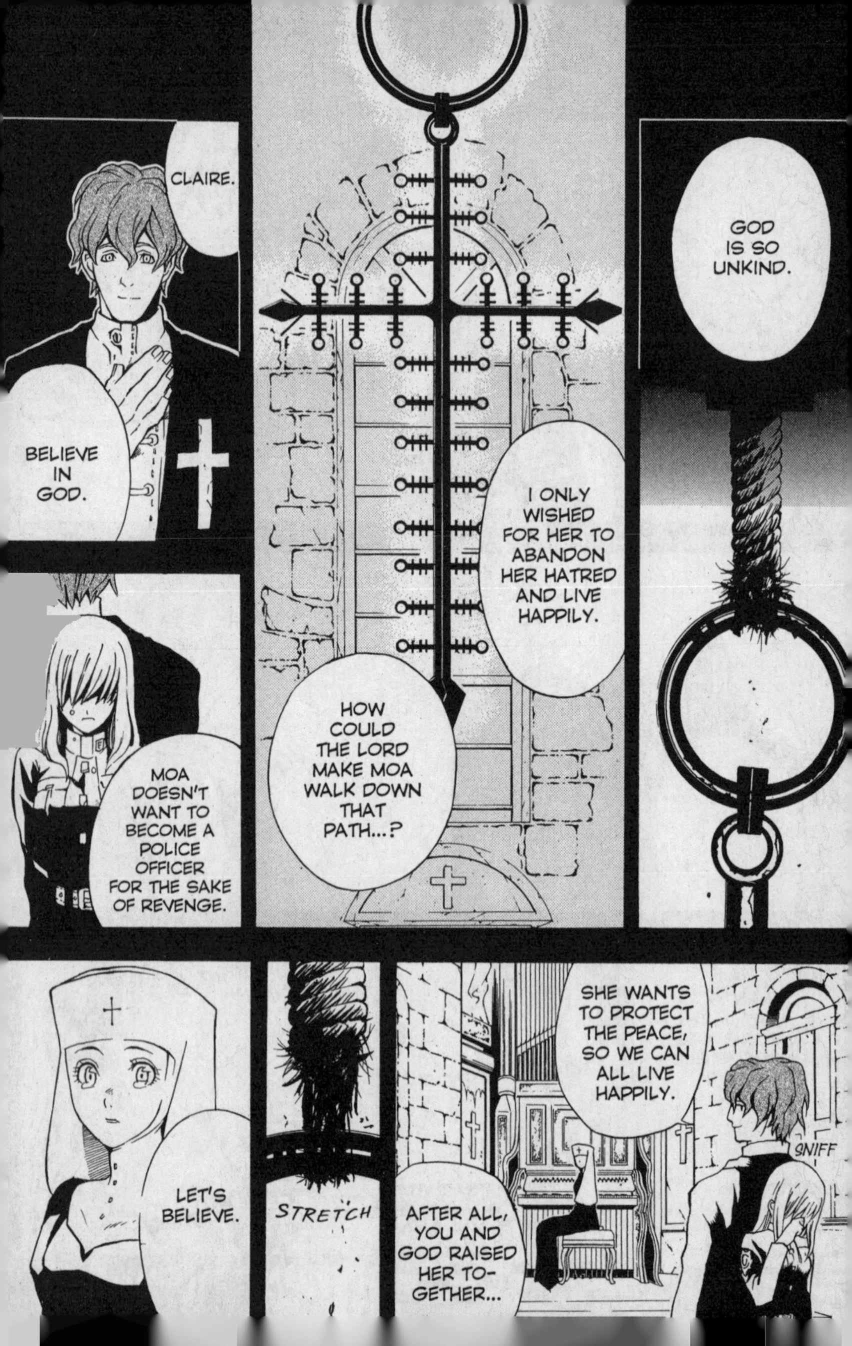
GOD IS SO UNKIND.
I ONLY WISHED FOR HER TO ABANDON HER HATRED AND LIVE HAPPILY.
HOW COULD THE LORD MAKE MOA WALK DOWN THAT PATH...?
CLAIRE.
BELIEVE IN GOD.
MOA DOESN'T WANT TO BECOME A POLICE OFFICER FOR THE SAKE OF REVENGE.
SHE WANTS TO PROTECT THE PEACE, SO WE CAN ALL LIVE HAPPILY.
SNIFF
AFTER ALL, YOU AND GOD RAISED HER TO-GETHER...
STRETCH
LET'S BELIEVE.

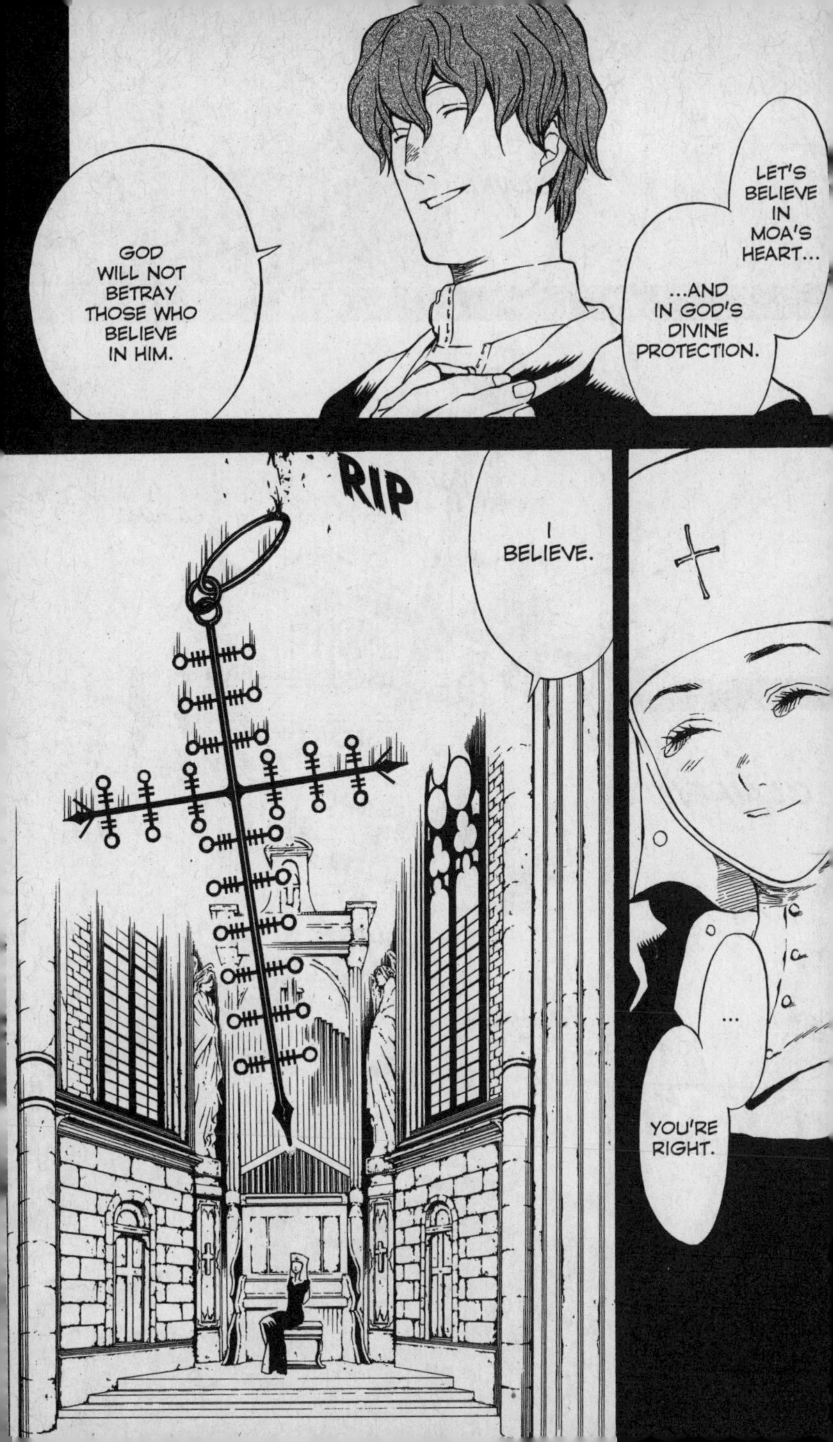
LET'S BELIEVE IN MOA'S HEART...
...AND IN GOD'S DIVINE PROTECTION.
GOD WILL NOT BETRAY THOSE WHO BELIEVE IN HIM.
...
YOU'RE RIGHT.
I BELIEVE.
RIP

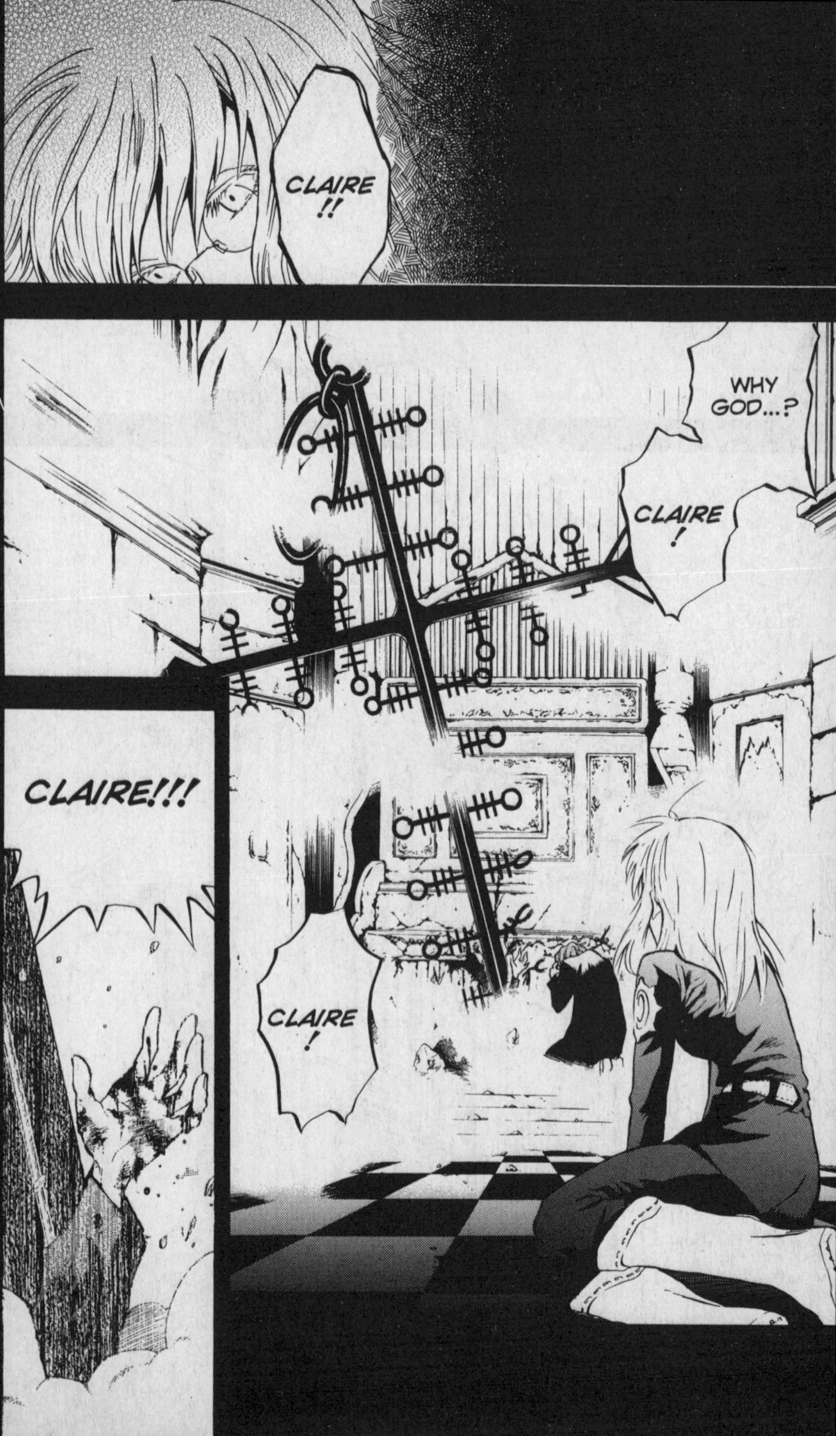
CLAIRE !!
WHY GOD...?
CLAIRE !
CLAIRE !
CLAIRE!!!

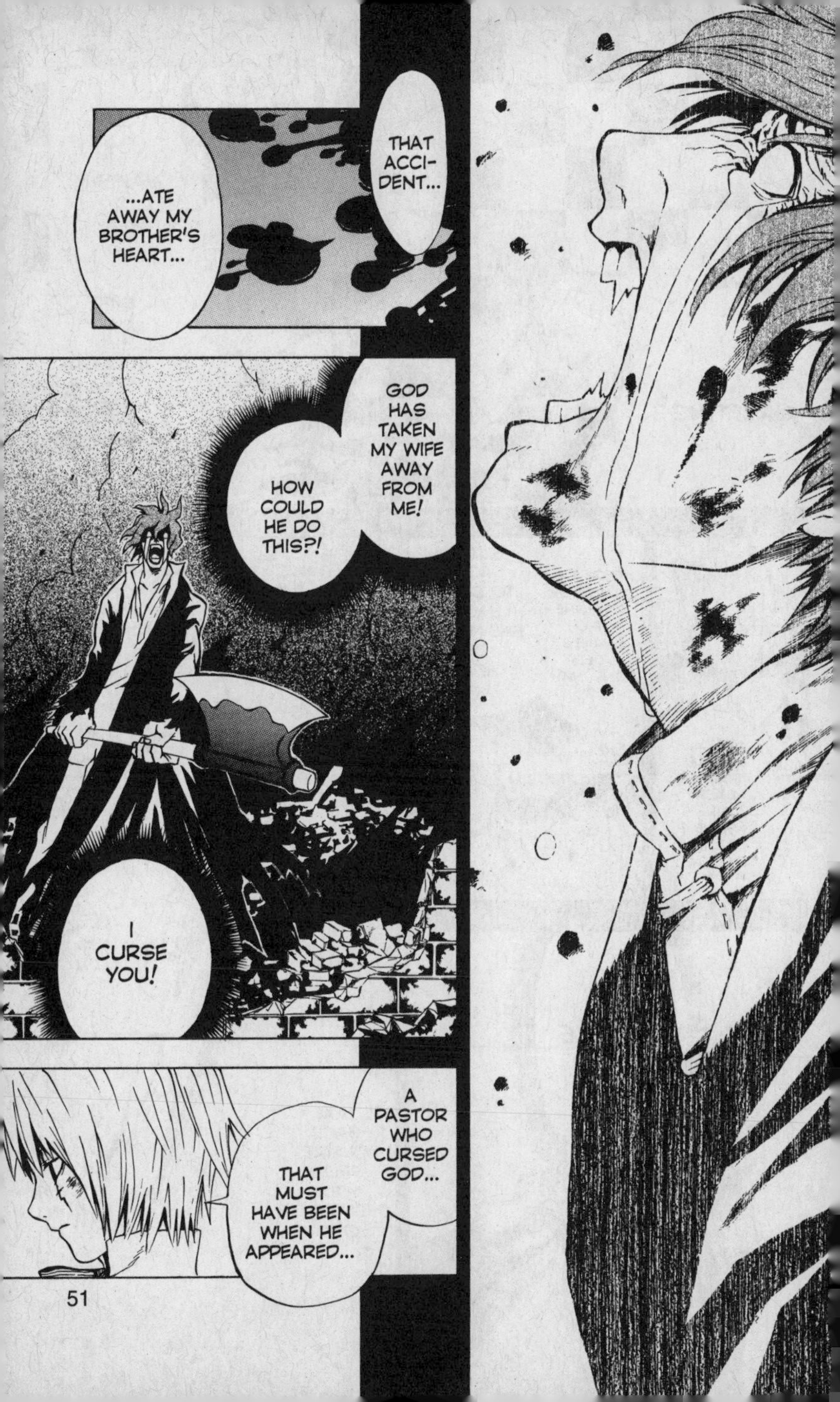
THAT ACCI-DENT...
...ATE AWAY MY BROTHER'S HEART...
GOD HAS TAKEN MY WIFE AWAY FROM ME!
HOW COULD HE DO THIS?!
I CURSE YOU!
A PASTOR WHO CURSED GOD...
THAT MUST HAVE BEEN WHEN HE APPEARED...

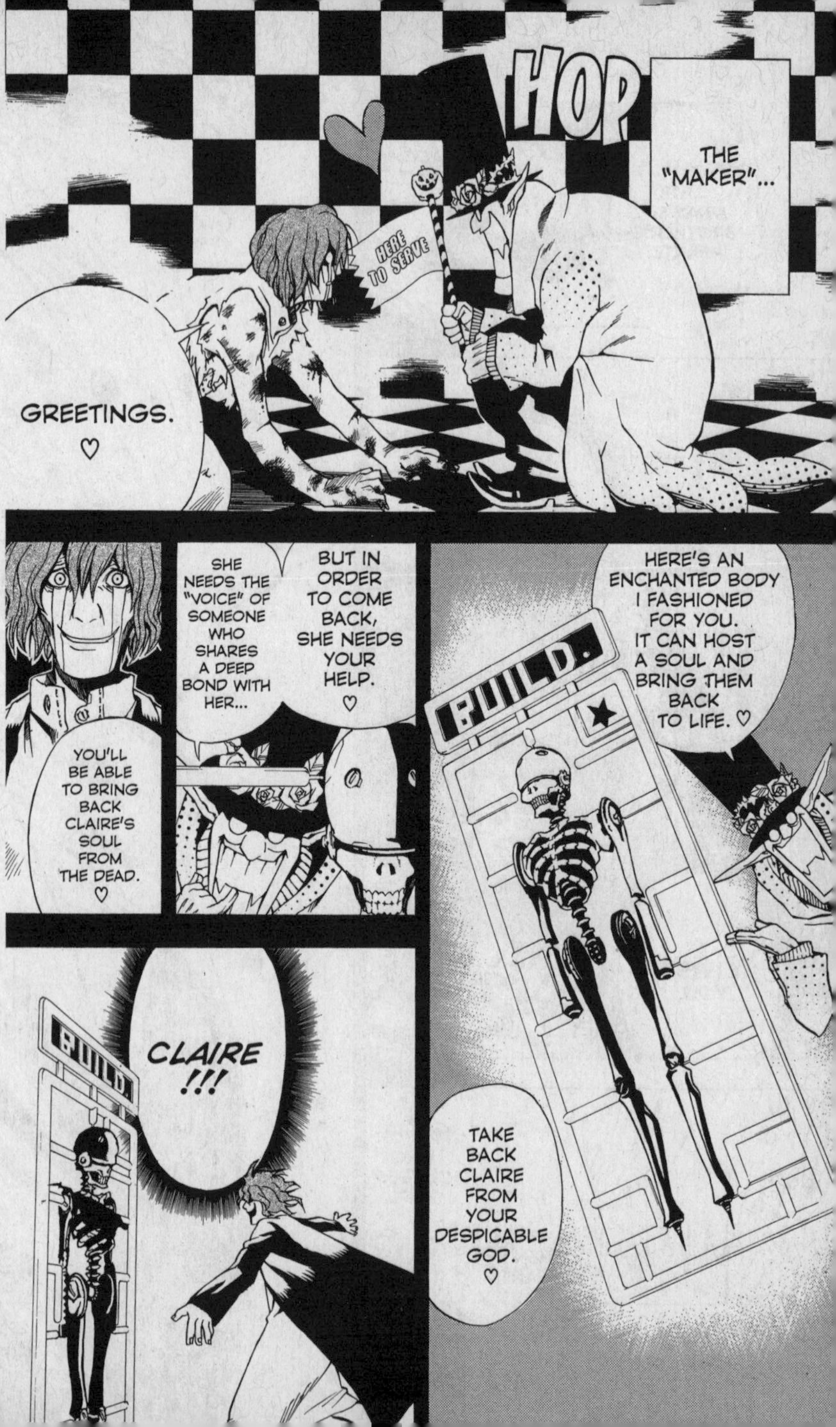
THE "MAKER"...
HOP
HERE TO SERVE
GREETINGS. ♡
HERE'S AN ENCHANTED BODY I FASHIONED FOR YOU. IT CAN HOST A SOUL AND BRING THEM BACK TO LIFE. ♡
BUILD.
TAKE BACK CLAIRE FROM YOUR DESPICABLE GOD. ♡
BUT IN ORDER TO COME BACK, SHE NEEDS YOUR HELP. ♡
SHE NEEDS THE "VOICE" OF SOMEONE WHO SHARES A DEEP BOND WITH HER...
YOU'LL BE ABLE TO BRING BACK CLAIRE'S SOUL FROM THE DEAD. ♡
BUILD.
CLAIRE !!!

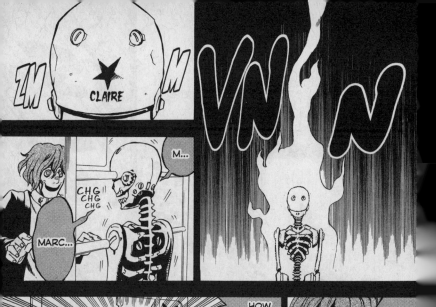

ZM
M
CLAIRE
VN N

M...

MARC...

CHG
CHG
CHG

HOW DARE YOU TURN ME INTO AN AKUMA!

I'M TRAPPED! THERE'S NO ESCAPE!

HOW COULD YOU...?

HUH?

UGG-GH...

GRAB

TEE-HEE. ♡ AND YOU'RE ALL MINE NOW, CLAIRE. ♡

THIS IS AN ORDER. KILL THIS MAN AND PUT ON HIS SKIN. ♡

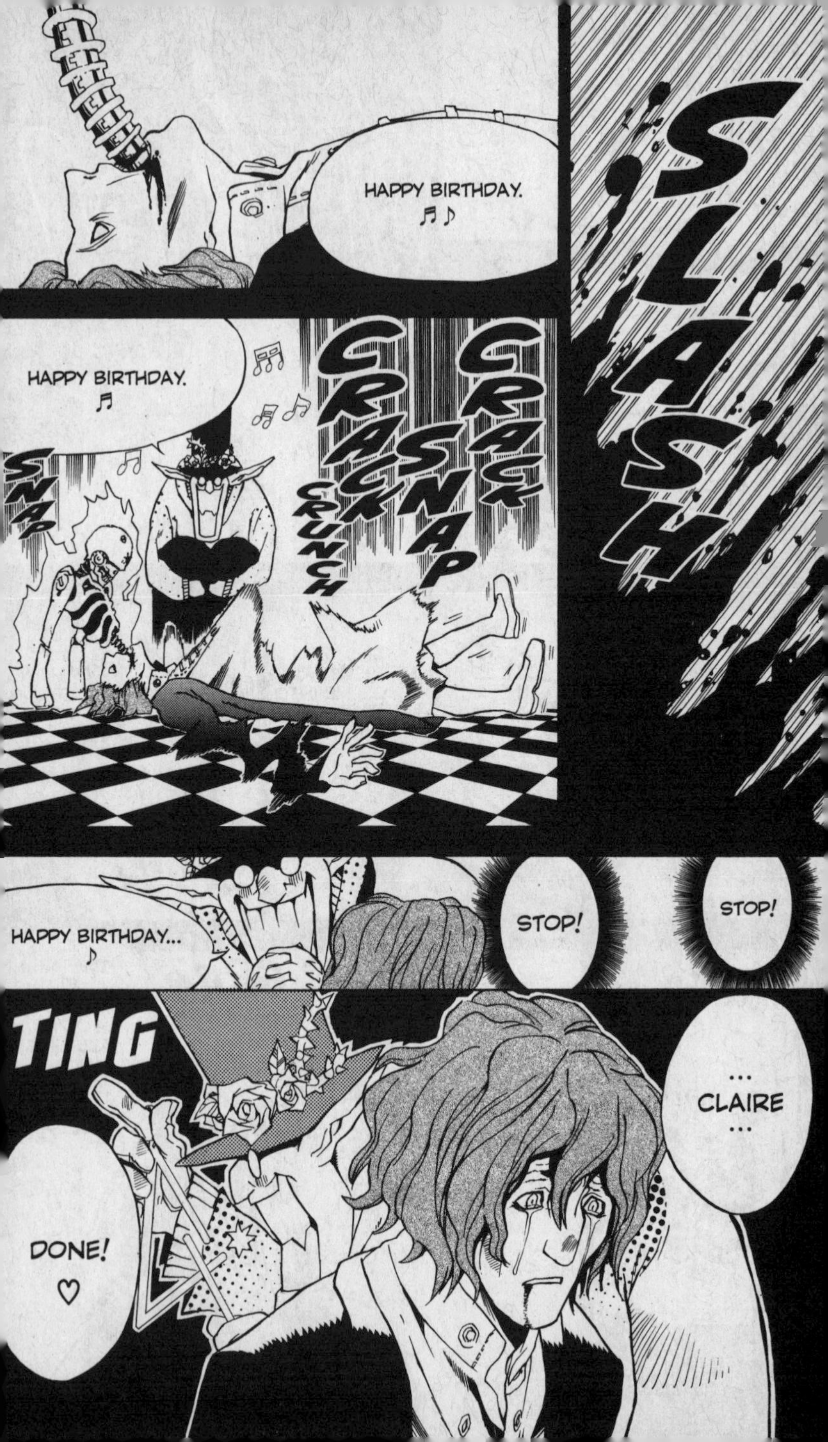
SLASH
HAPPY BIRTHDAY. ♬♪
CRACK SNAP SNAP
CRACK CRACK CRUNCH
HAPPY BIRTHDAY. ♬
SNAP
STOP!
STOP!
HAPPY BIRTHDAY... ♪
... CLAIRE ...
TING
DONE! ♡

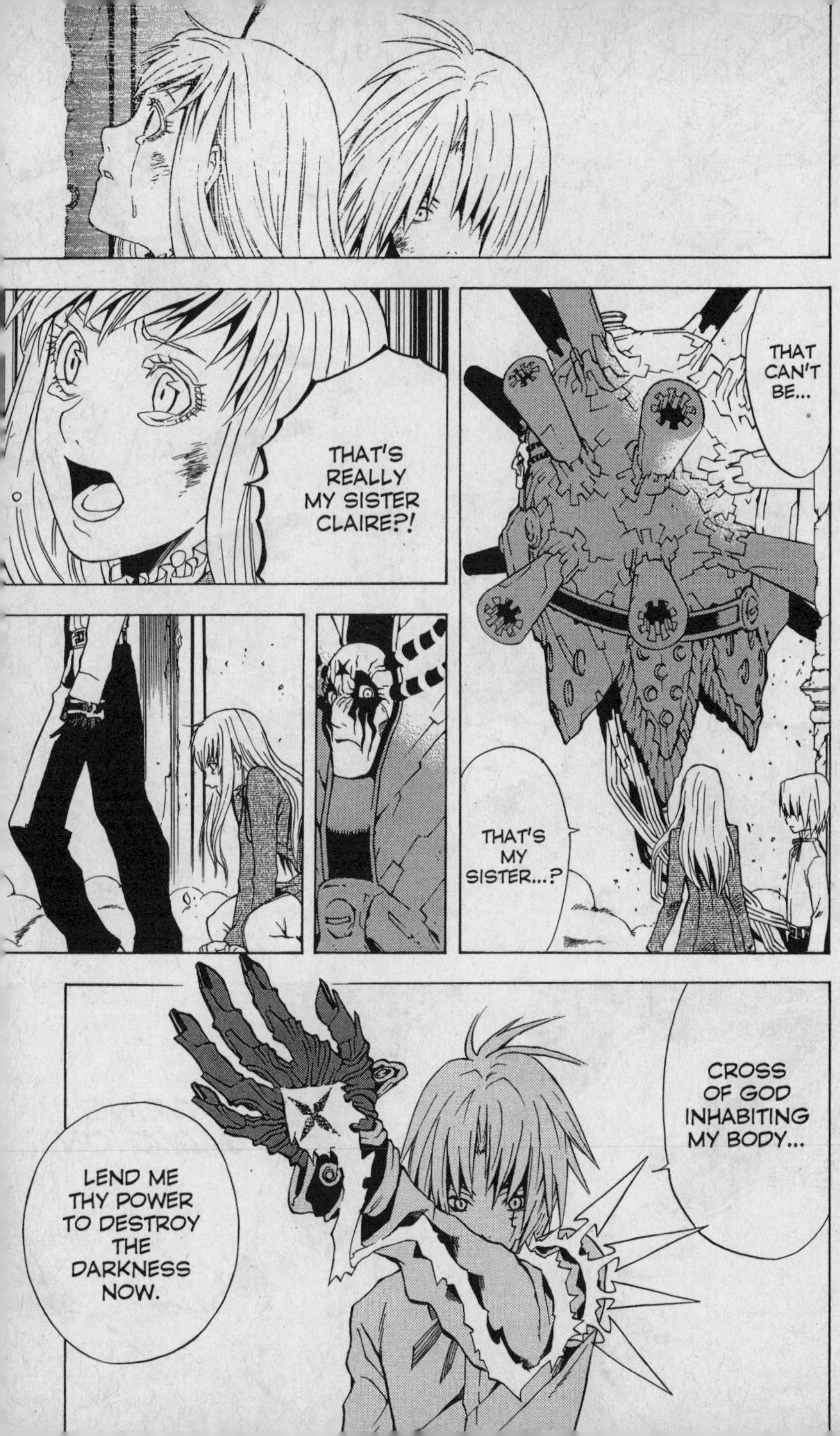
THAT CAN'T BE...
THAT'S MY SISTER...?
THAT'S REALLY MY SISTER CLAIRE?!
CROSS OF GOD INHABITING MY BODY...
LEND ME THY POWER TO DESTROY THE DARKNESS NOW.

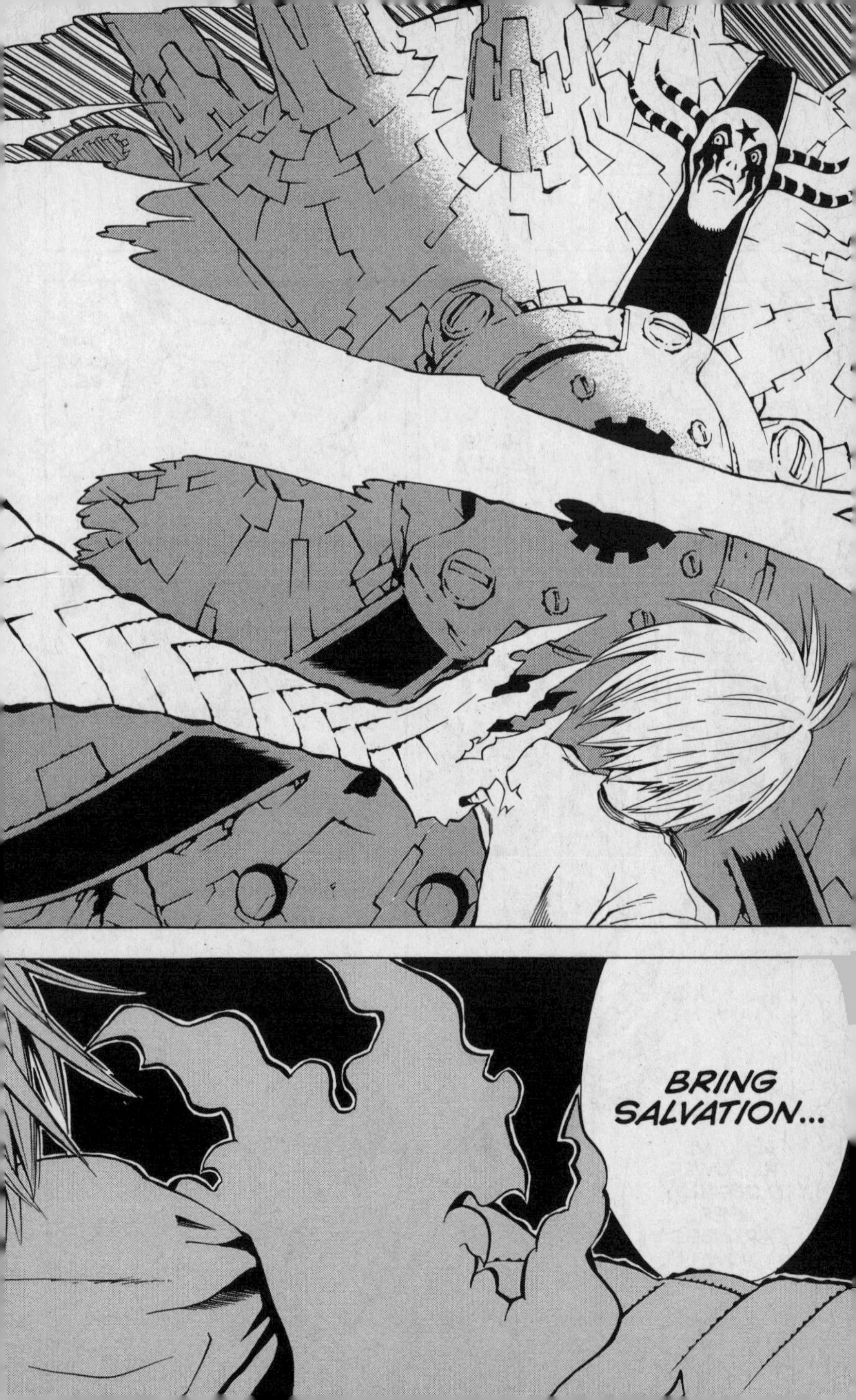
BRING SALVATION...

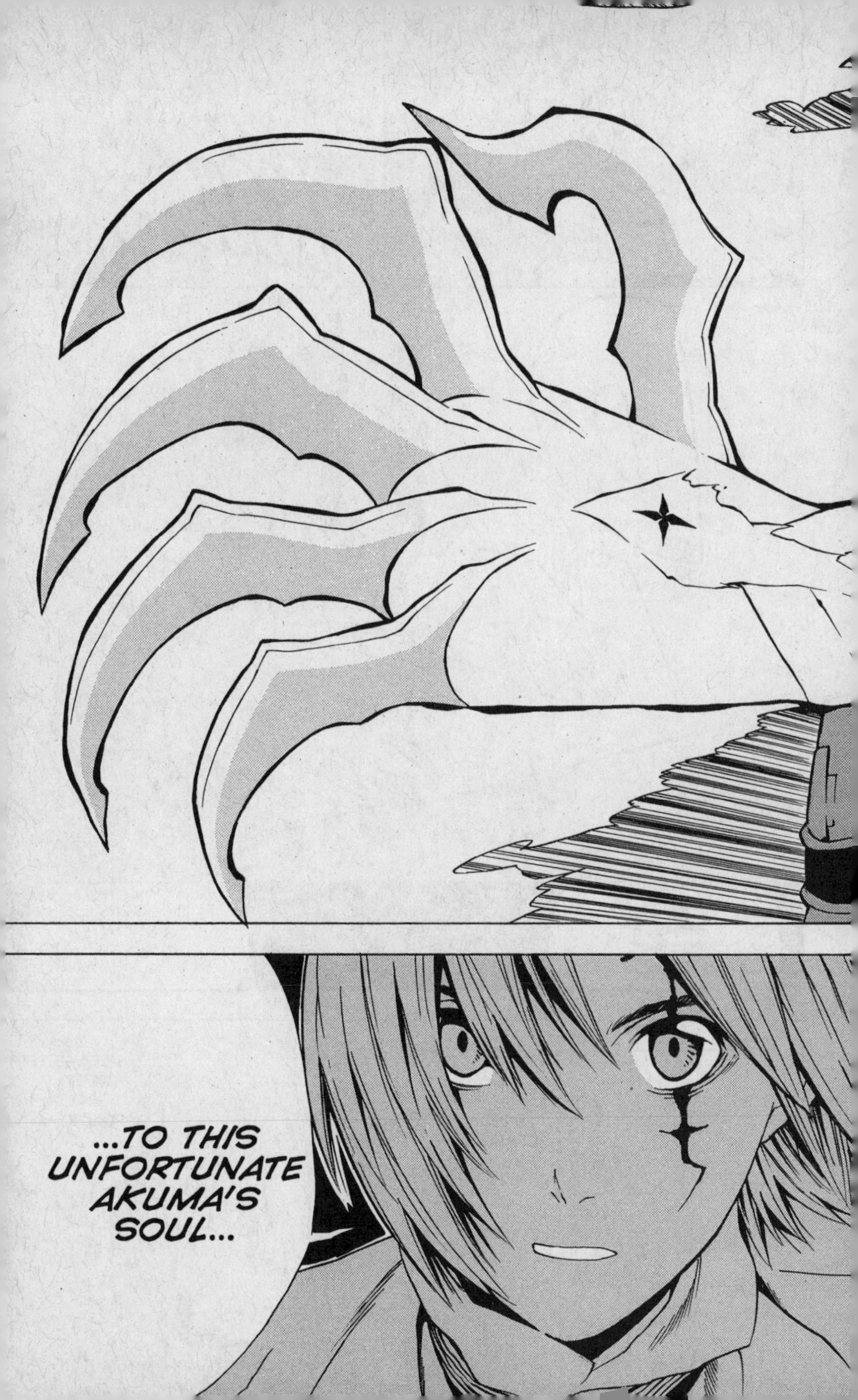
...TO THIS UNFORTUNATE AKUMA'S SOUL...

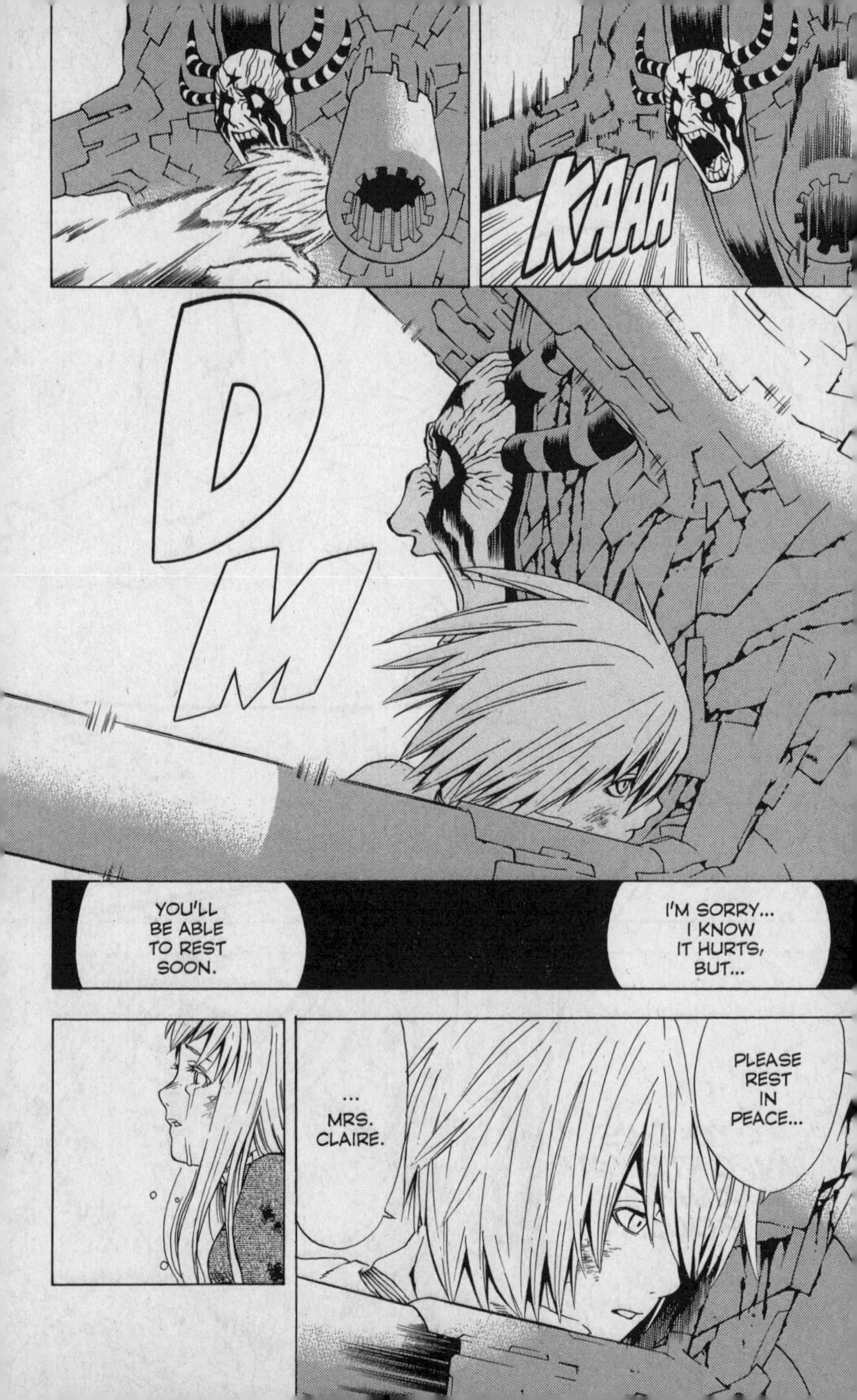
KAAA
DM
I'M SORRY... I KNOW IT HURTS, BUT...
YOU'LL BE ABLE TO REST SOON.
PLEASE REST IN PEACE...
... MRS. CLAIRE.

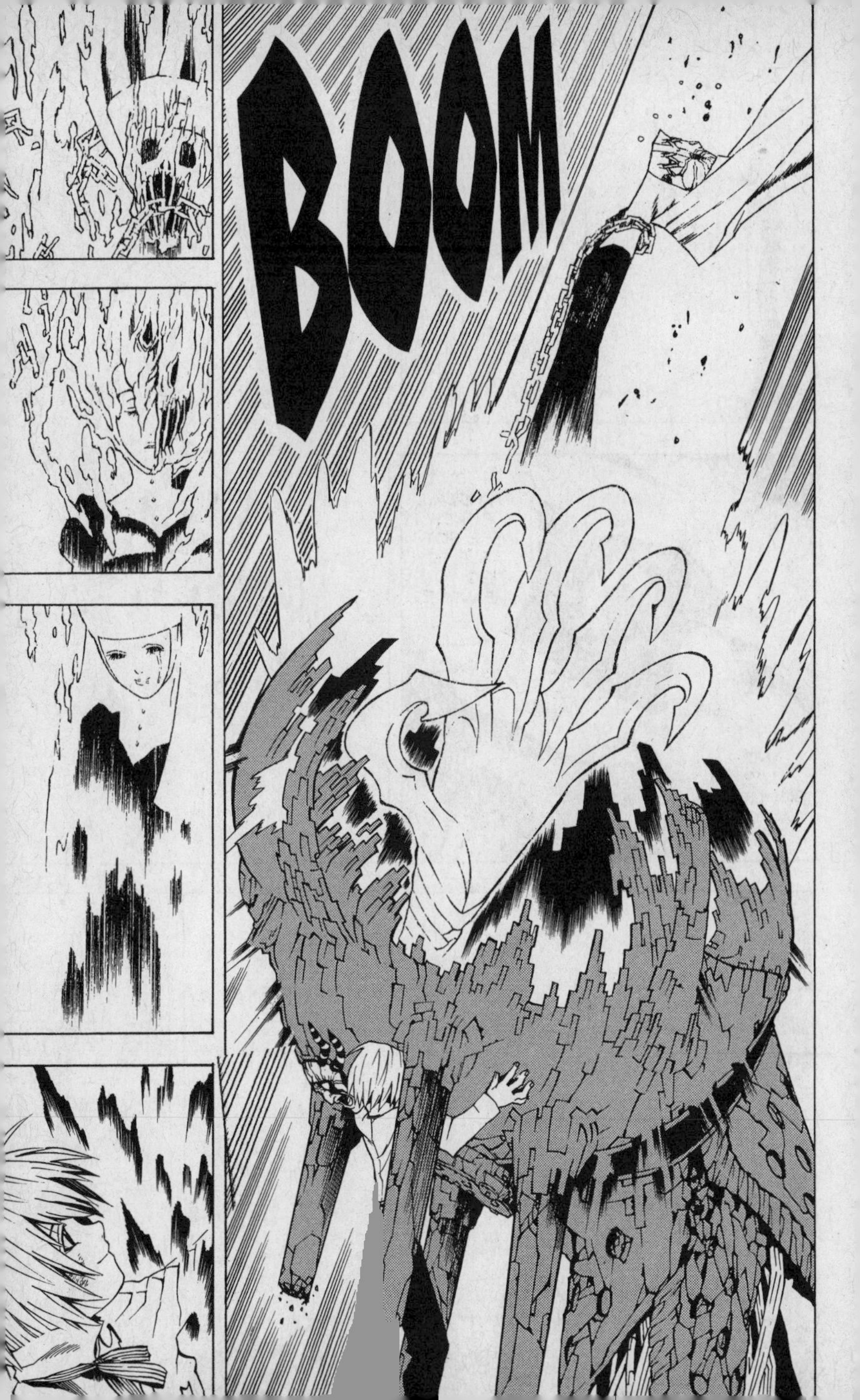
BOOM

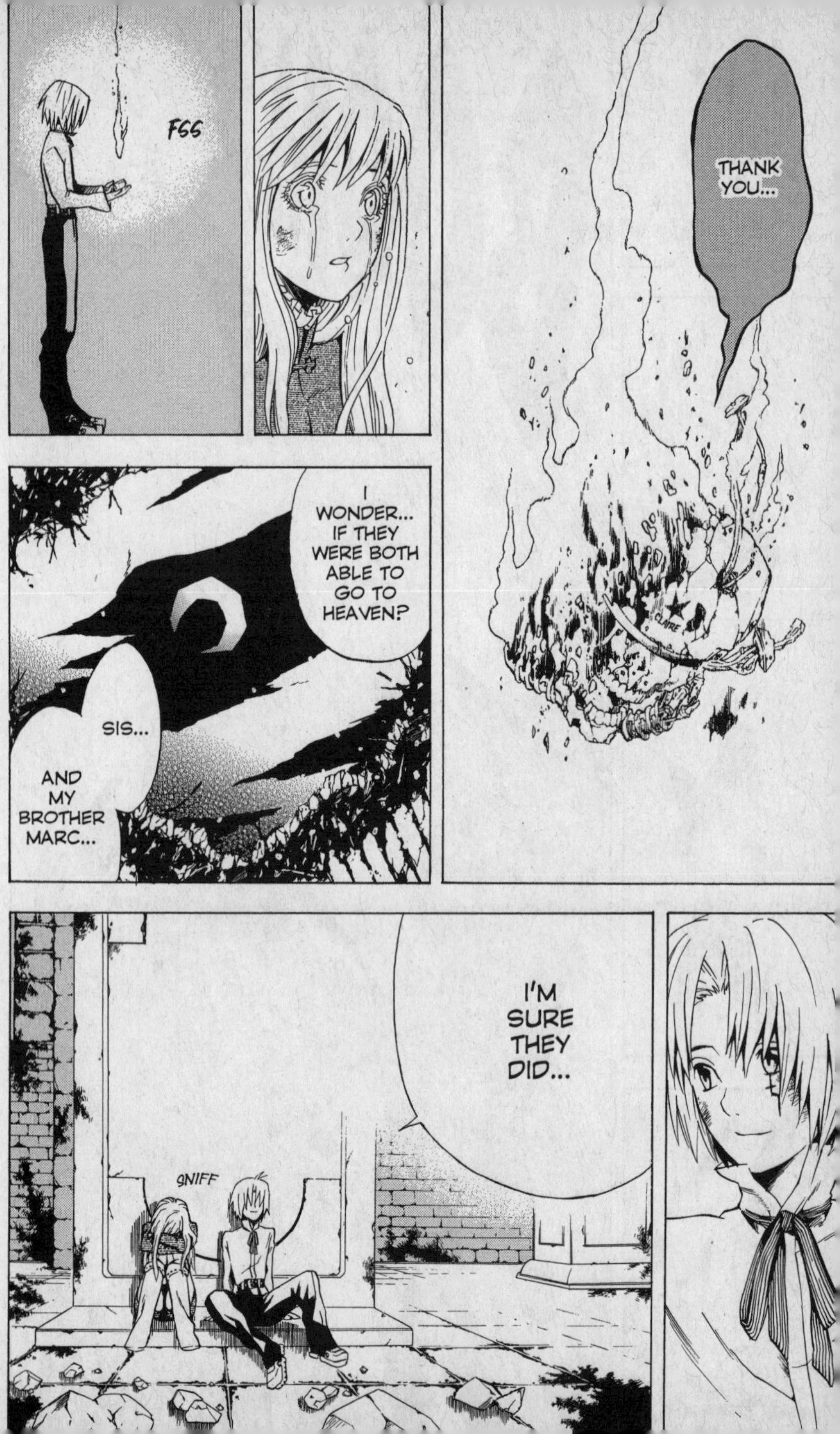
THANK YOU...
FSS
I WONDER... IF THEY WERE BOTH ABLE TO GO TO HEAVEN?
SIS... AND MY BROTHER MARC...
I'M SURE THEY DID...
SNIFF

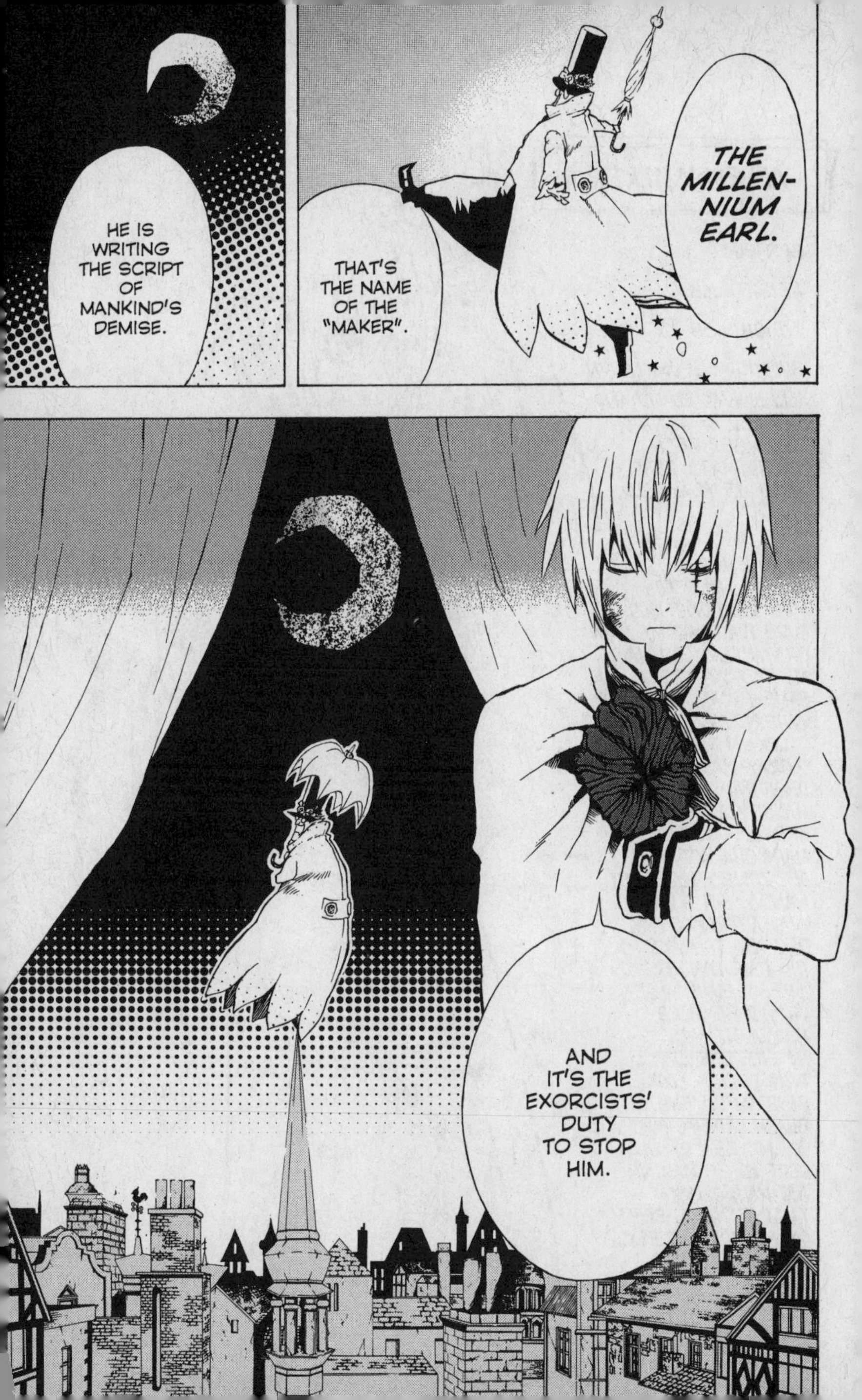
THE MILLEN-NIUM EARL.
THAT'S THE NAME OF THE "MAKER".
HE IS WRITING THE SCRIPT OF MANKIND'S DEMISE.
AND IT'S THE EXORCISTS' DUTY TO STOP HIM.

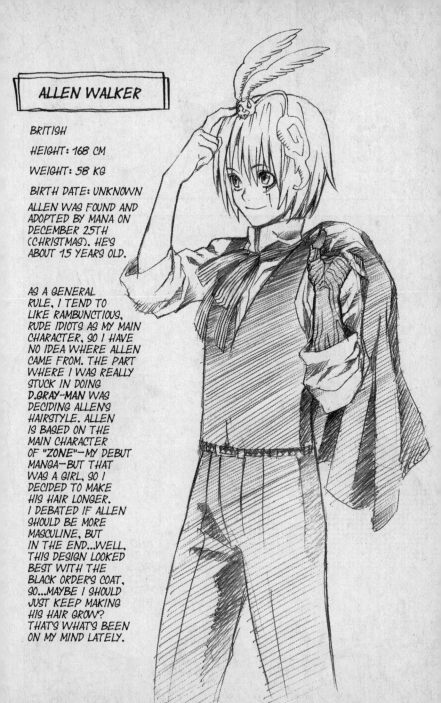

ALLEN WALKER

BRITISH

HEIGHT: 168 CM

WEIGHT: 58 KG

BIRTH DATE: UNKNOWN

ALLEN WAS FOUND AND ADOPTED BY MANA ON DECEMBER 25TH (CHRISTMAS). HE'S ABOUT 15 YEARS OLD.

AS A GENERAL RULE, I TEND TO LIKE RAMBUNCTIOUS, RUDE IDIOTS AS MY MAIN CHARACTER, SO I HAVE NO IDEA WHERE ALLEN CAME FROM. THE PART WHERE I WAS REALLY STUCK IN DOING D.GRAY-MAN WAS DECIDING ALLEN'S HAIRSTYLE. ALLEN IS BASED ON THE MAIN CHARACTER OF "ZONE"—MY DEBUT MANGA—BUT THAT WAS A GIRL, SO I DECIDED TO MAKE HIS HAIR LONGER. I DEBATED IF ALLEN SHOULD BE MORE MASCULINE, BUT IN THE END...WELL, THIS DESIGN LOOKED BEST WITH THE BLACK ORDER'S COAT. SO...MAYBE I SHOULD JUST KEEP MAKING HIS HAIR GROW? THAT'S WHAT'S BEEN ON MY MIND LATELY.

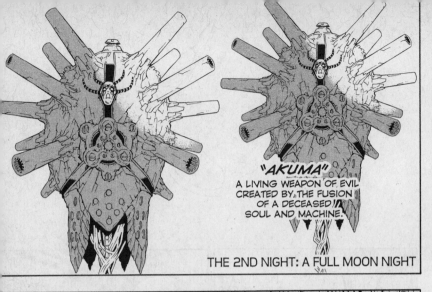

"AKUMA"
A LIVING WEAPON OF EVIL CREATED BY THE FUSION OF A DECEASED SOUL AND MACHINE.
THE 2ND NIGHT: A FULL MOON NIGHT
"EXORCIST"
A MEMBER OF THE BLACK ORDER WHO DESTROYS AKUMA.
THE END OF A FICTIONAL NINE-TEENTH CENTURY.
A MYSTERIOUS EVENT WAS TAKING PLACE NIGHT AFTER NIGHT.

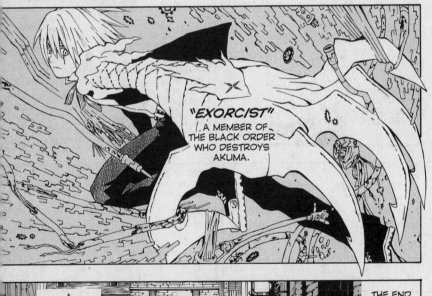

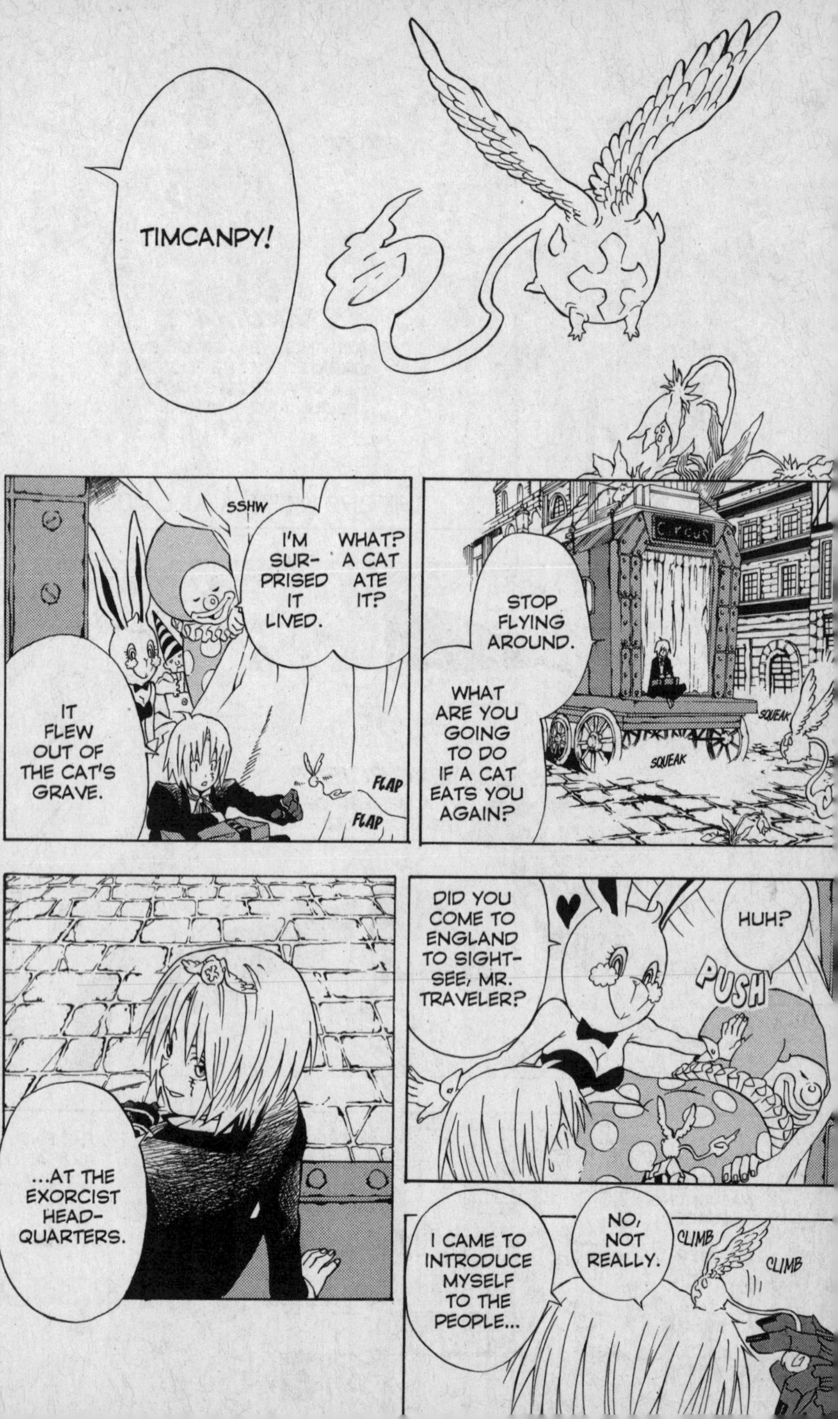
TIMCANPY!
STOP FLYING AROUND.
WHAT ARE YOU GOING TO DO IF A CAT EATS YOU AGAIN?
SQUEAK
SQUEAK
SSHW
WHAT? A CAT ATE IT?
I'M SURPRISED IT LIVED.
IT FLEW OUT OF THE CAT'S GRAVE.
FLAP
FLAP
HUH?
PUSH
DID YOU COME TO ENGLAND TO SIGHT-SEE, MR. TRAVELER?
CLIMB
CLIMB
NO, NOT REALLY.
I CAME TO INTRODUCE MYSELF TO THE PEOPLE...
...AT THE EXORCIST HEAD-QUARTERS.

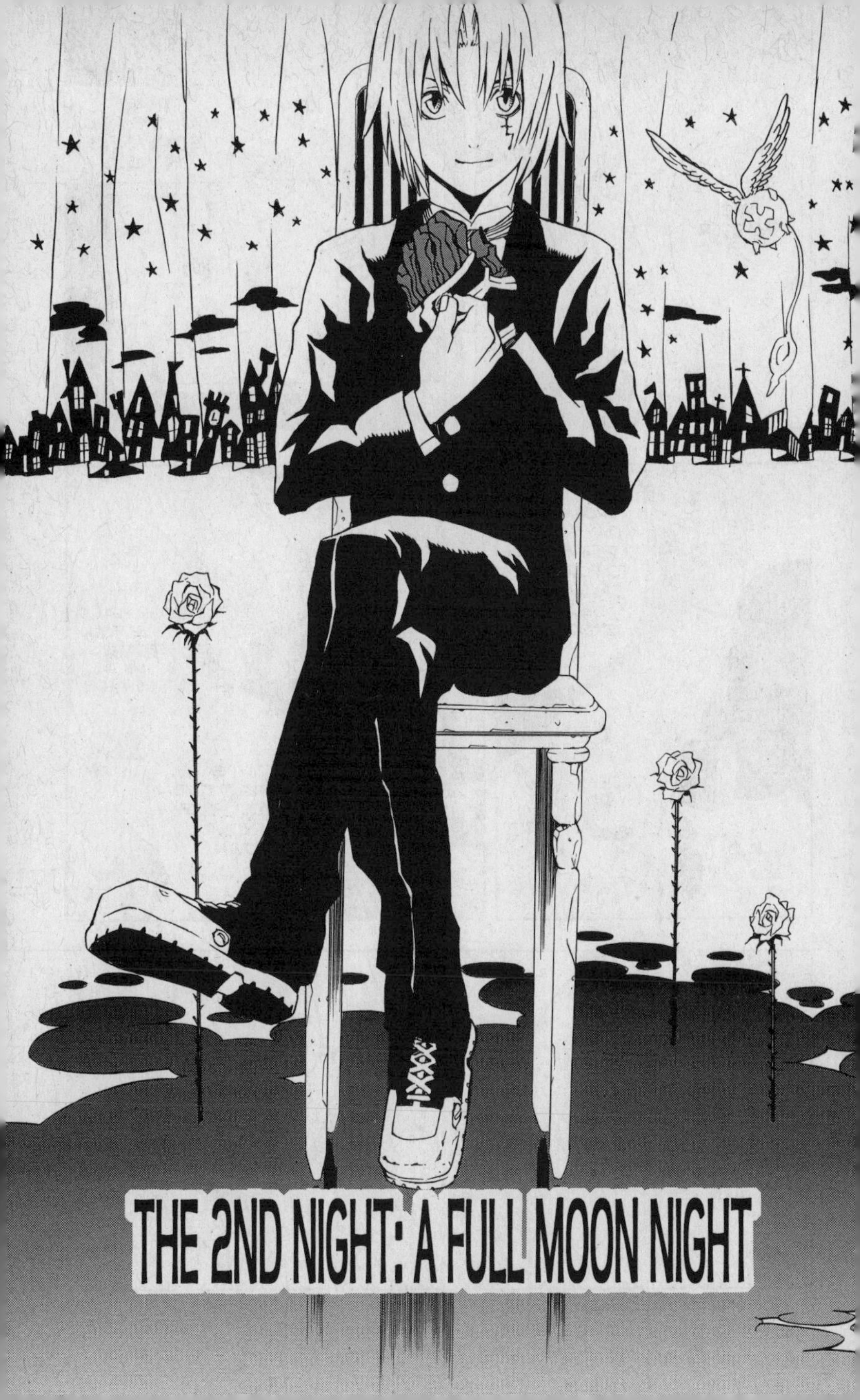
THE 2ND NIGHT: A FULL MOON NIGHT

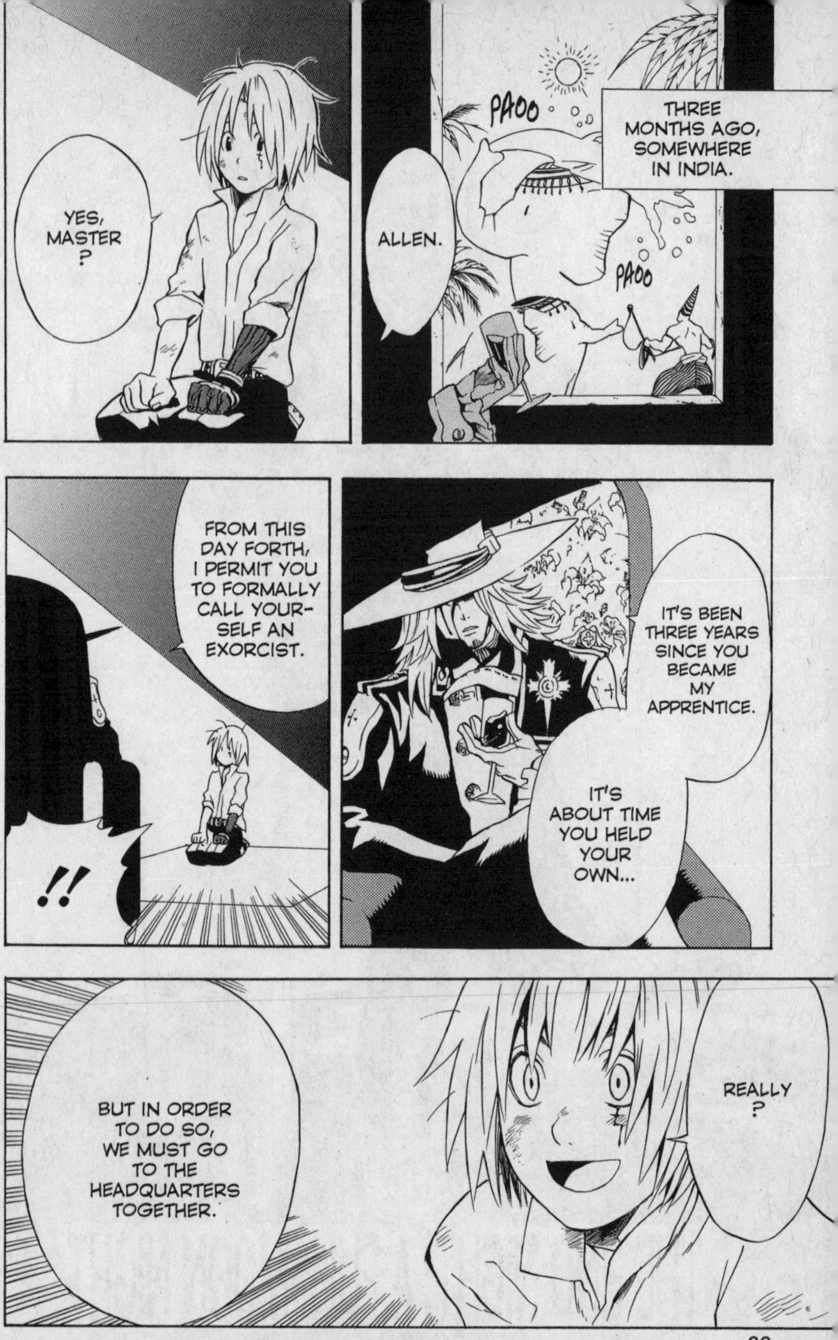

THREE MONTHS AGO, SOMEWHERE IN INDIA.
PAOO
PAOO
ALLEN.
YES, MASTER?
IT'S BEEN THREE YEARS SINCE YOU BECAME MY APPRENTICE.
IT'S ABOUT TIME YOU HELD YOUR OWN...
FROM THIS DAY FORTH, I PERMIT YOU TO FORMALLY CALL YOUR-SELF AN EXORCIST.
!!
REALLY?
BUT IN ORDER TO DO SO, WE MUST GO TO THE HEADQUARTERS TOGETHER.

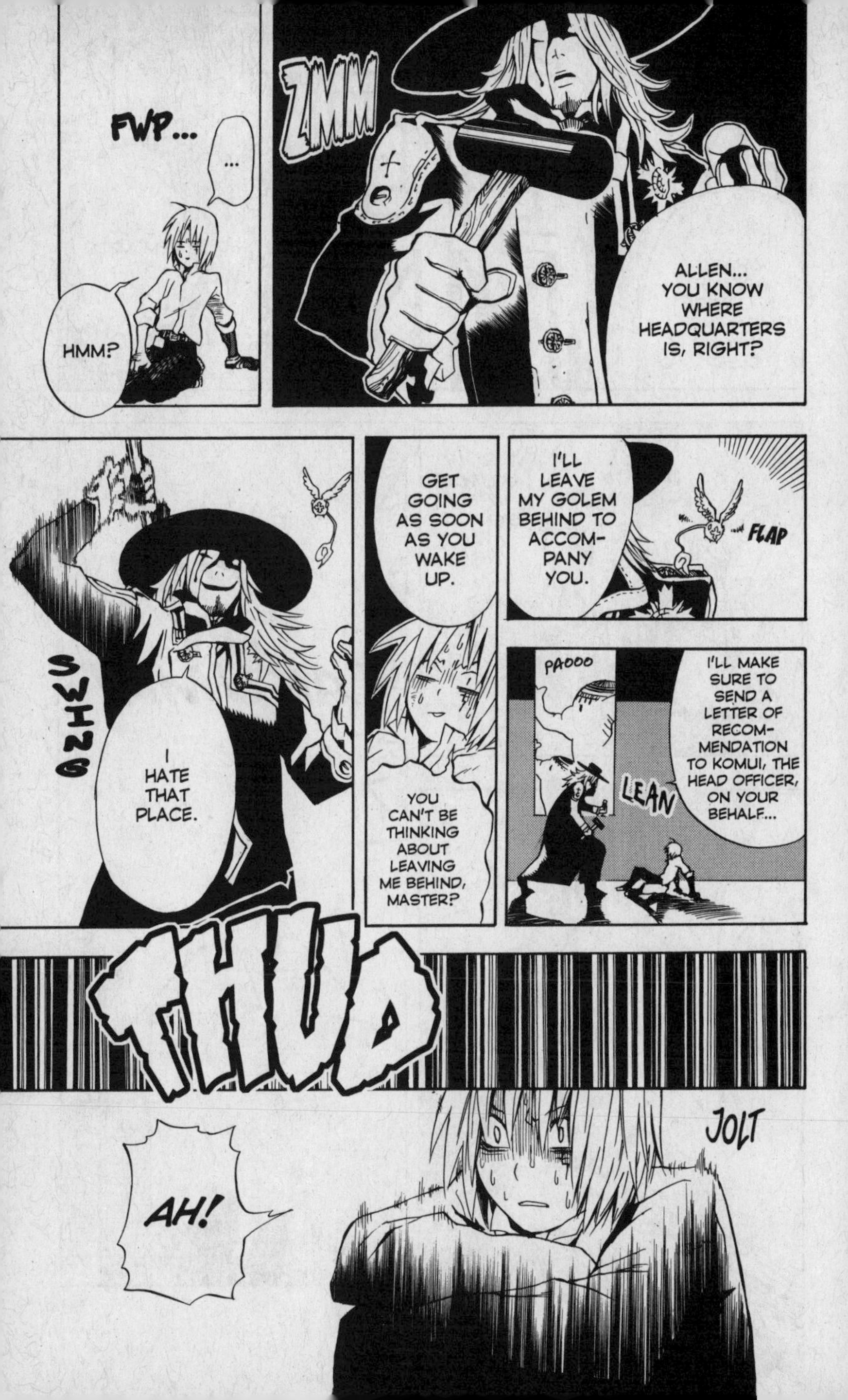
ZMM
ALLEN... YOU KNOW WHERE HEADQUARTERS IS, RIGHT?
FWP...
...
HMM?
I'LL LEAVE MY GOLEM BEHIND TO ACCOMPANY YOU.
FLAP
PAOOO
I'LL MAKE SURE TO SEND A LETTER OF RECOMMENDATION TO KOMUI, THE HEAD OFFICER, ON YOUR BEHALF...
LEAN
GET GOING AS SOON AS YOU WAKE UP.
YOU CAN'T BE THINKING ABOUT LEAVING ME BEHIND, MASTER?
SWING
I HATE THAT PLACE.
THUD
JOLT
AH!

PEAK

IT... IT WAS JUST A DREAM...

I STILL REMEMBER IT...

WHAT'S WRONG? YOU WERE MOANING IN YOUR SLEEP.

HFF

HFF

HFF

!!

IT'S AN AKUMA! IT'S GONNA KILL US!

W... WHAT?

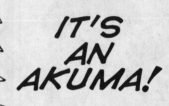

IT'S AN AKUMA!

JUMP

THANKS FOR THE RIDE!

OH MY!

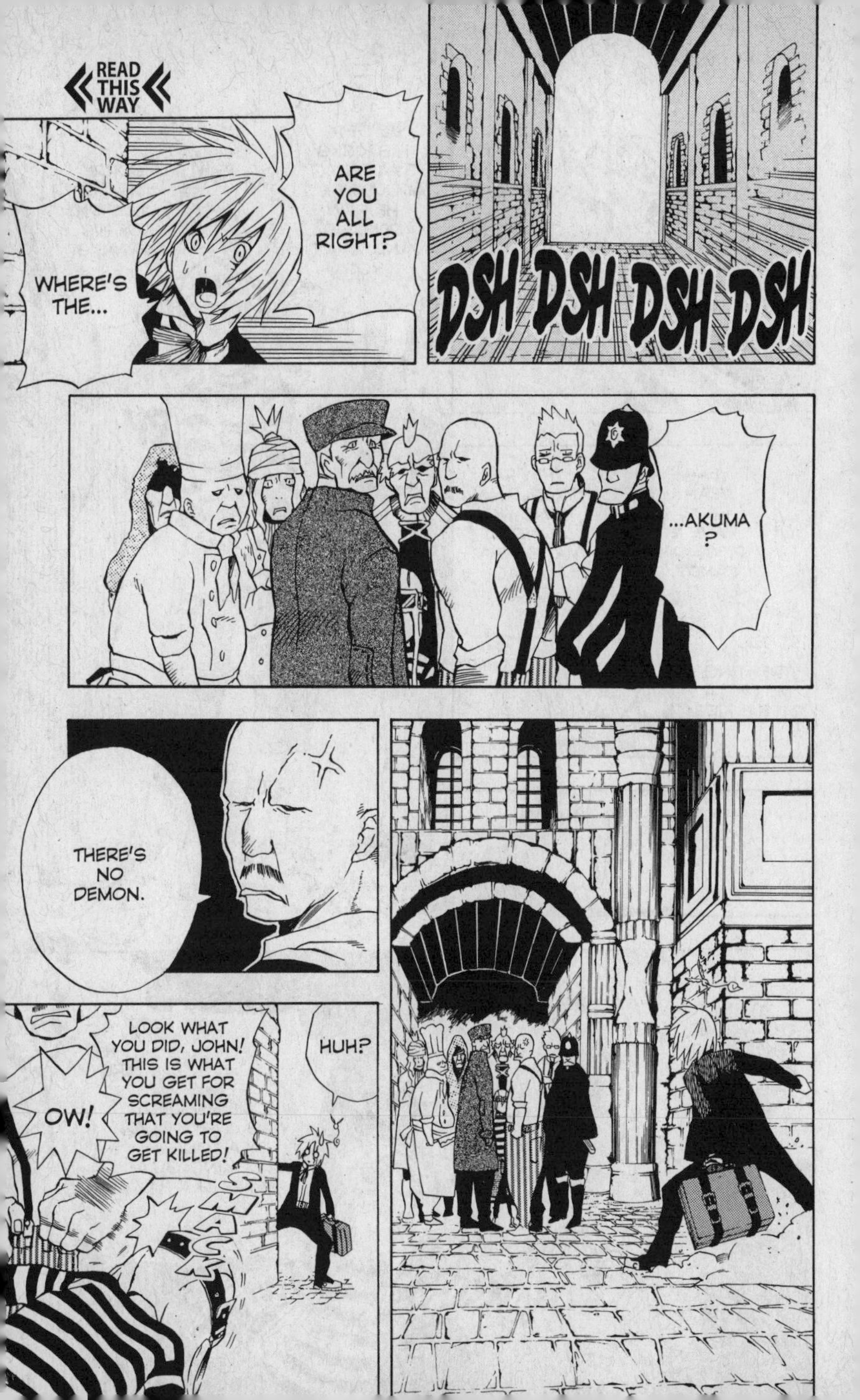

READ THIS WAY
DSH DSH DSH DSH
ARE YOU ALL RIGHT?
WHERE'S THE...
...AKUMA?
THERE'S NO DEMON.
HUH?
LOOK WHAT YOU DID, JOHN! THIS IS WHAT YOU GET FOR SCREAMING THAT YOU'RE GOING TO GET KILLED!
OW!
SMACK

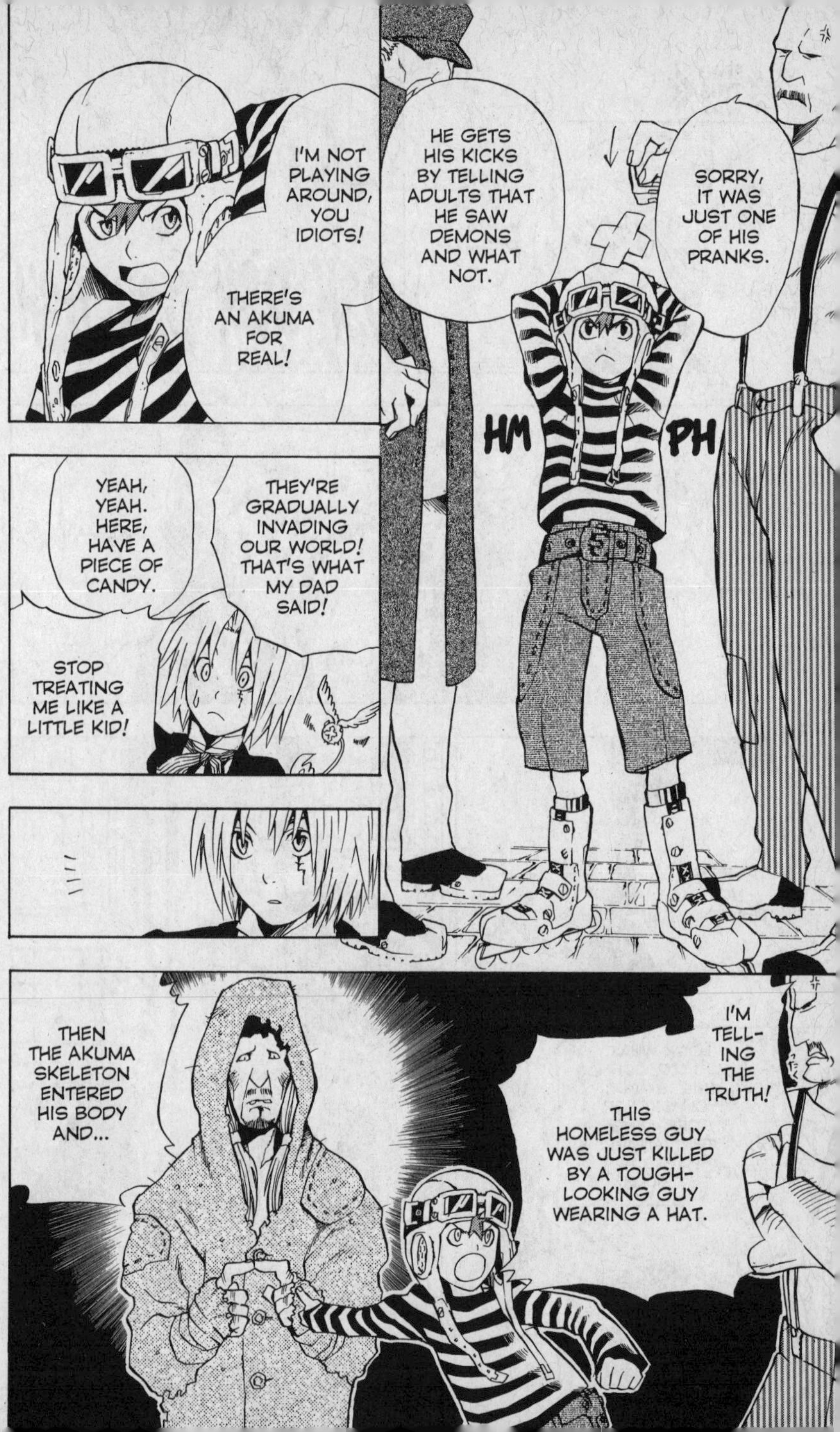
SORRY, IT WAS JUST ONE OF HIS PRANKS.
HE GETS HIS KICKS BY TELLING ADULTS THAT HE SAW DEMONS AND WHAT NOT.
HMPH
I'M NOT PLAYING AROUND, YOU IDIOTS!
THERE'S AN AKUMA FOR REAL!
THEY'RE GRADUALLY INVADING OUR WORLD! THAT'S WHAT MY DAD SAID!
YEAH, YEAH. HERE, HAVE A PIECE OF CANDY.
STOP TREATING ME LIKE A LITTLE KID!
I'M TELL-ING THE TRUTH!
THIS HOMELESS GUY WAS JUST KILLED BY A TOUGH-LOOKING GUY WEARING A HAT.
THEN THE AKUMA SKELETON ENTERED HIS BODY AND...

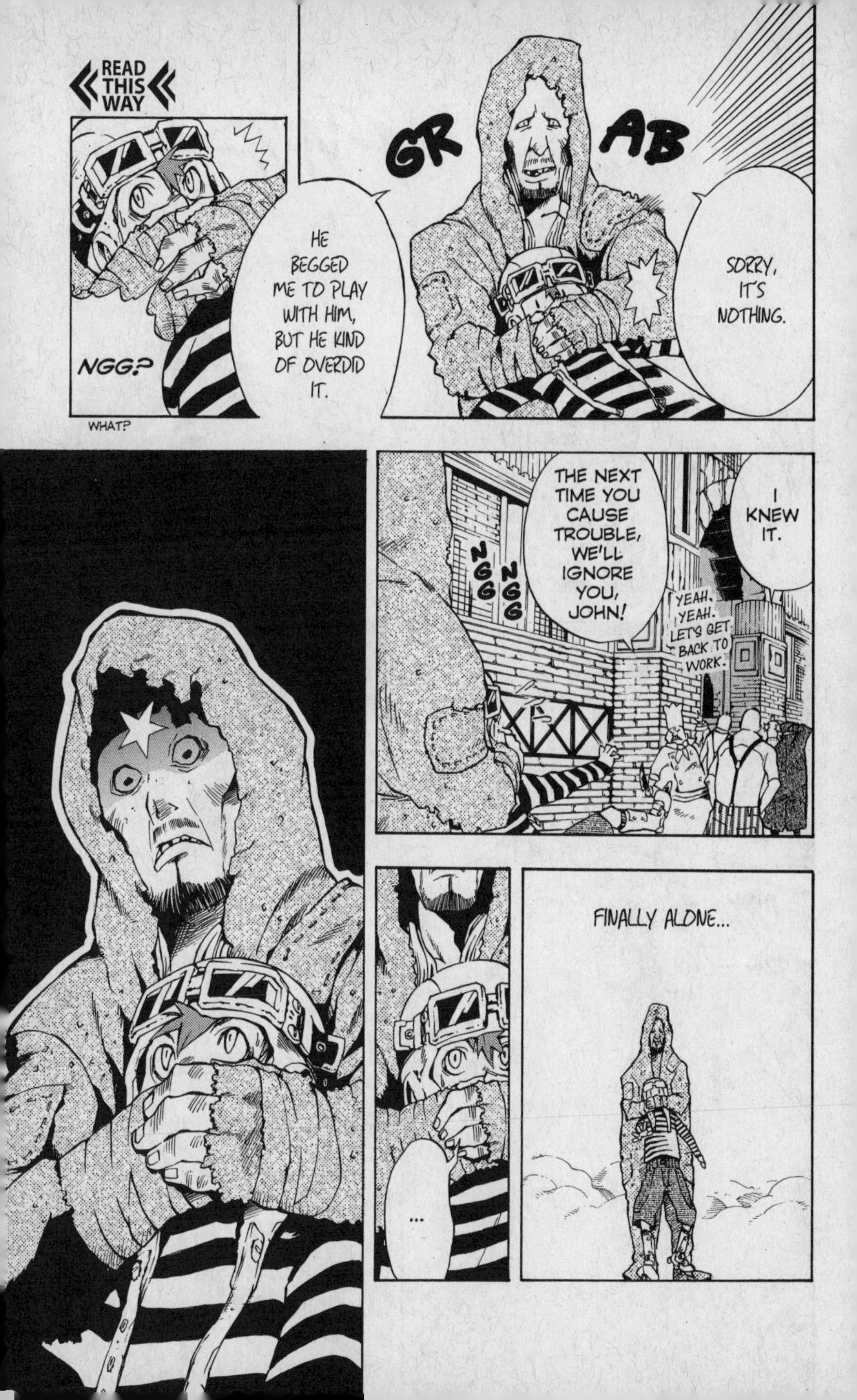

READ THIS WAY
SORRY, IT'S NOTHING.
GRAB
HE BEGGED ME TO PLAY WITH HIM, BUT HE KIND OF OVERDID IT.
NGG?
WHAT?
I KNEW IT.
THE NEXT TIME YOU CAUSE TROUBLE, WE'LL IGNORE YOU, JOHN!
YEAH, YEAH. LET'S GET BACK TO WORK.
NGG NGG
FINALLY ALONE...
...

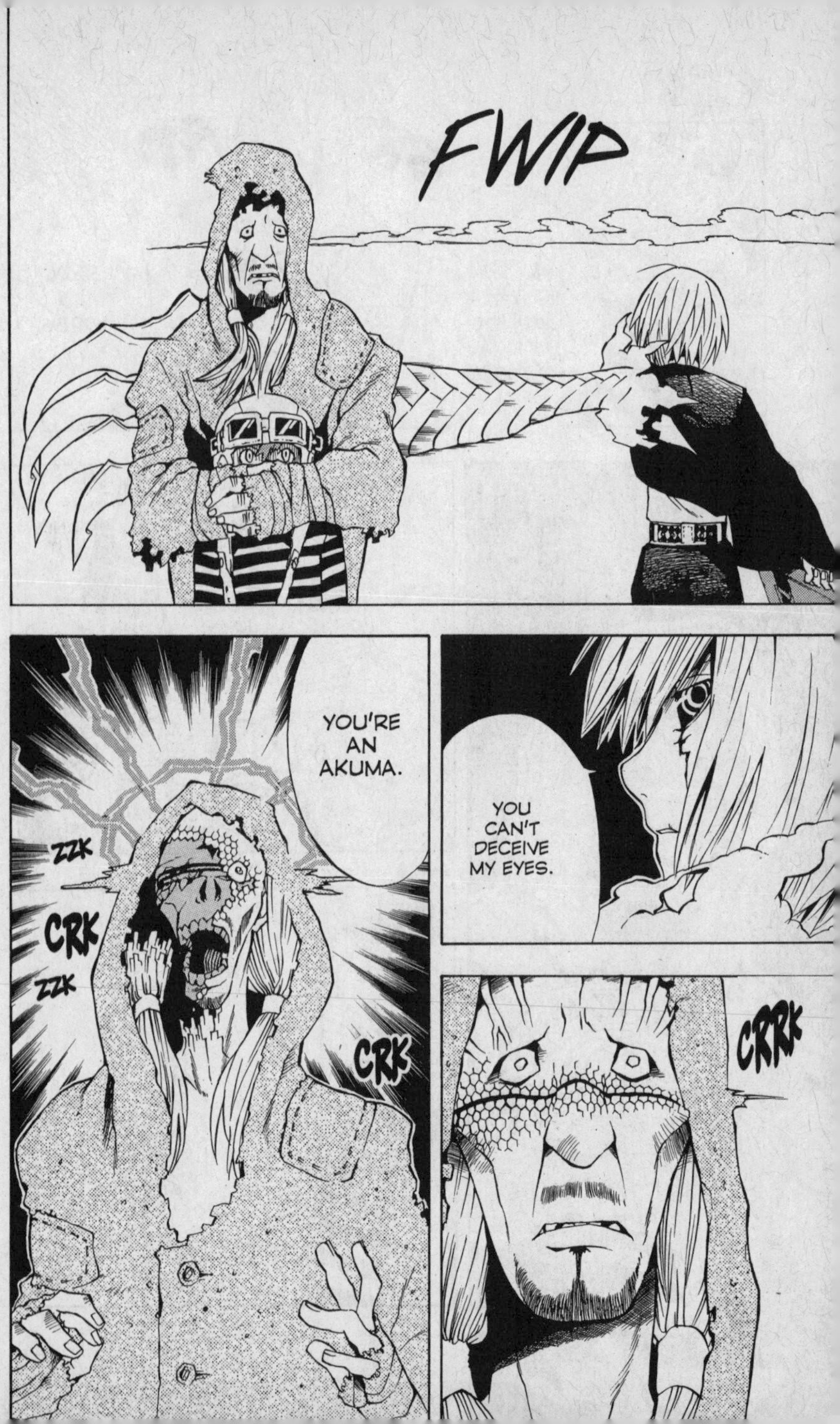
FWIP
YOU CAN'T DECEIVE MY EYES.
CRRK
YOU'RE AN AKUMA.
ZZK
CRK
ZZK
CRK

READ THIS WAY

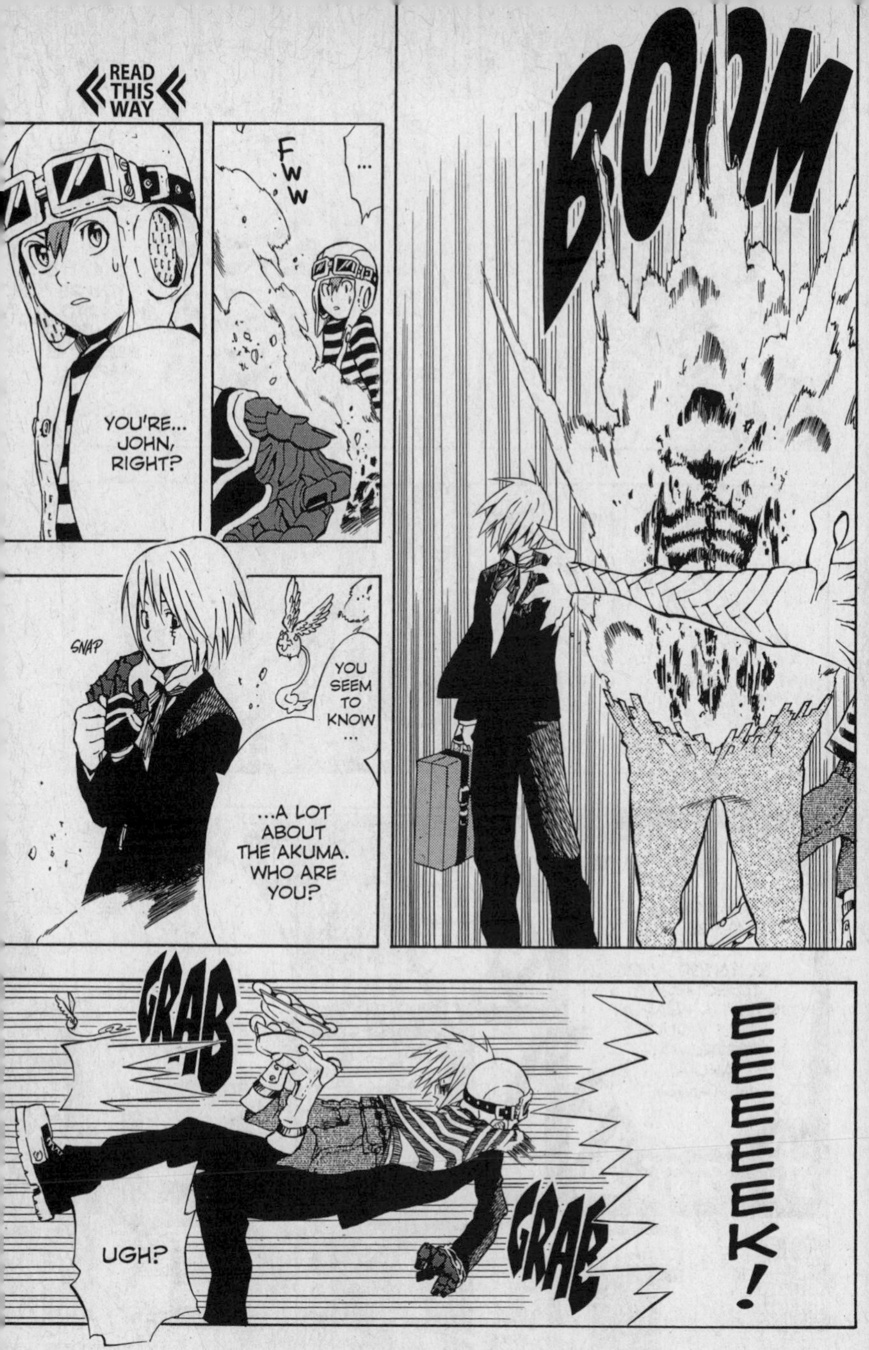
BOOM
FWW
...
YOU'RE... JOHN, RIGHT?
SNAP
YOU SEEM TO KNOW...
...A LOT ABOUT THE AKUMA. WHO ARE YOU?
EEEEEEK!
GRAB
GRAB
UGH?

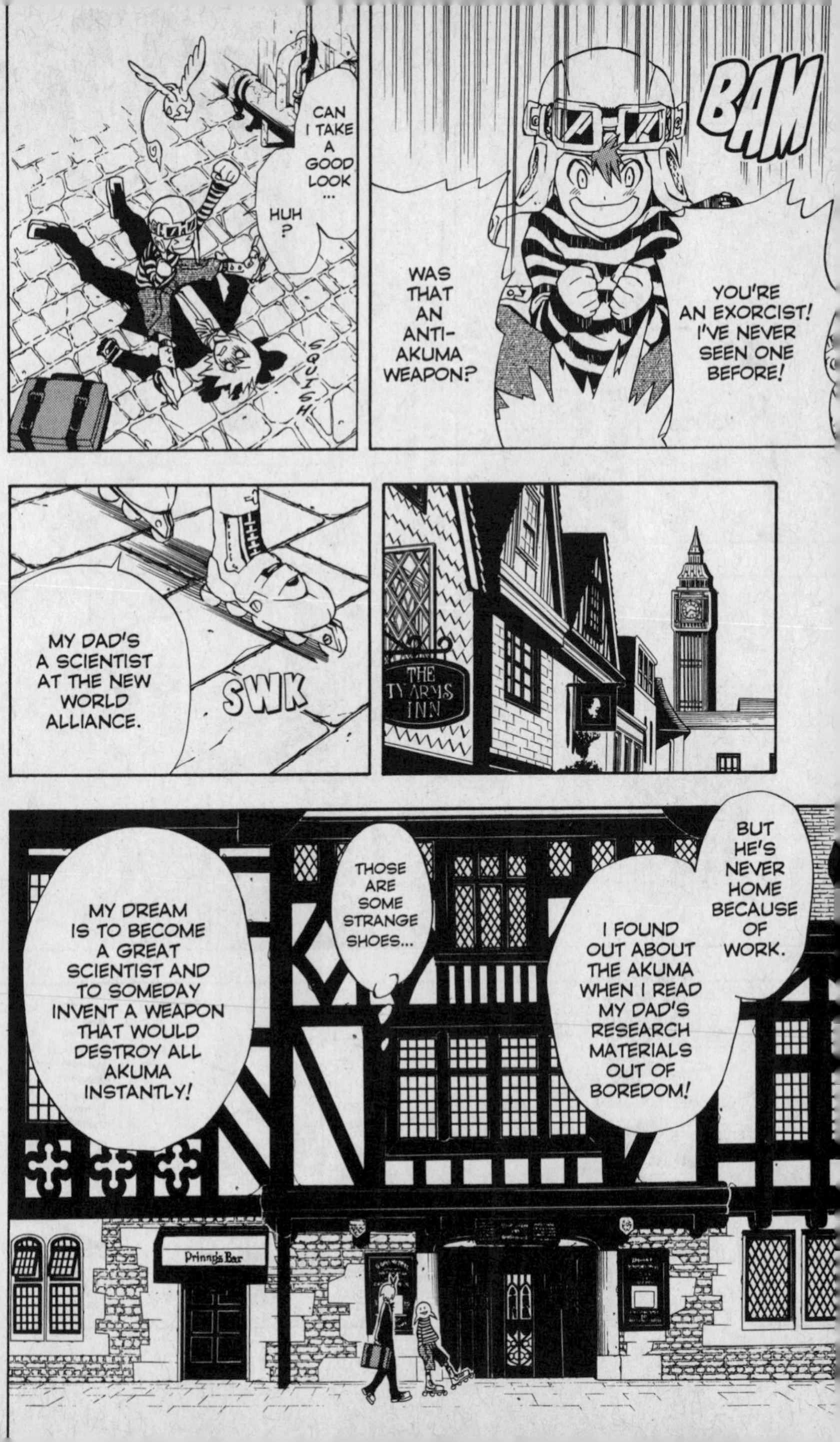
BAM
YOU'RE AN EXORCIST! I'VE NEVER SEEN ONE BEFORE!
WAS THAT AN ANTI-AKUMA WEAPON?
CAN I TAKE A GOOD LOOK ...
HUH ?
SQUISH
MY DAD'S A SCIENTIST AT THE NEW WORLD ALLIANCE.
SWK
BUT HE'S NEVER HOME BECAUSE OF WORK.
I FOUND OUT ABOUT THE AKUMA WHEN I READ MY DAD'S RESEARCH MATERIALS OUT OF BOREDOM!
THOSE ARE SOME STRANGE SHOES...
MY DREAM IS TO BECOME A GREAT SCIENTIST AND TO SOMEDAY INVENT A WEAPON THAT WOULD DESTROY ALL AKUMA INSTANTLY!

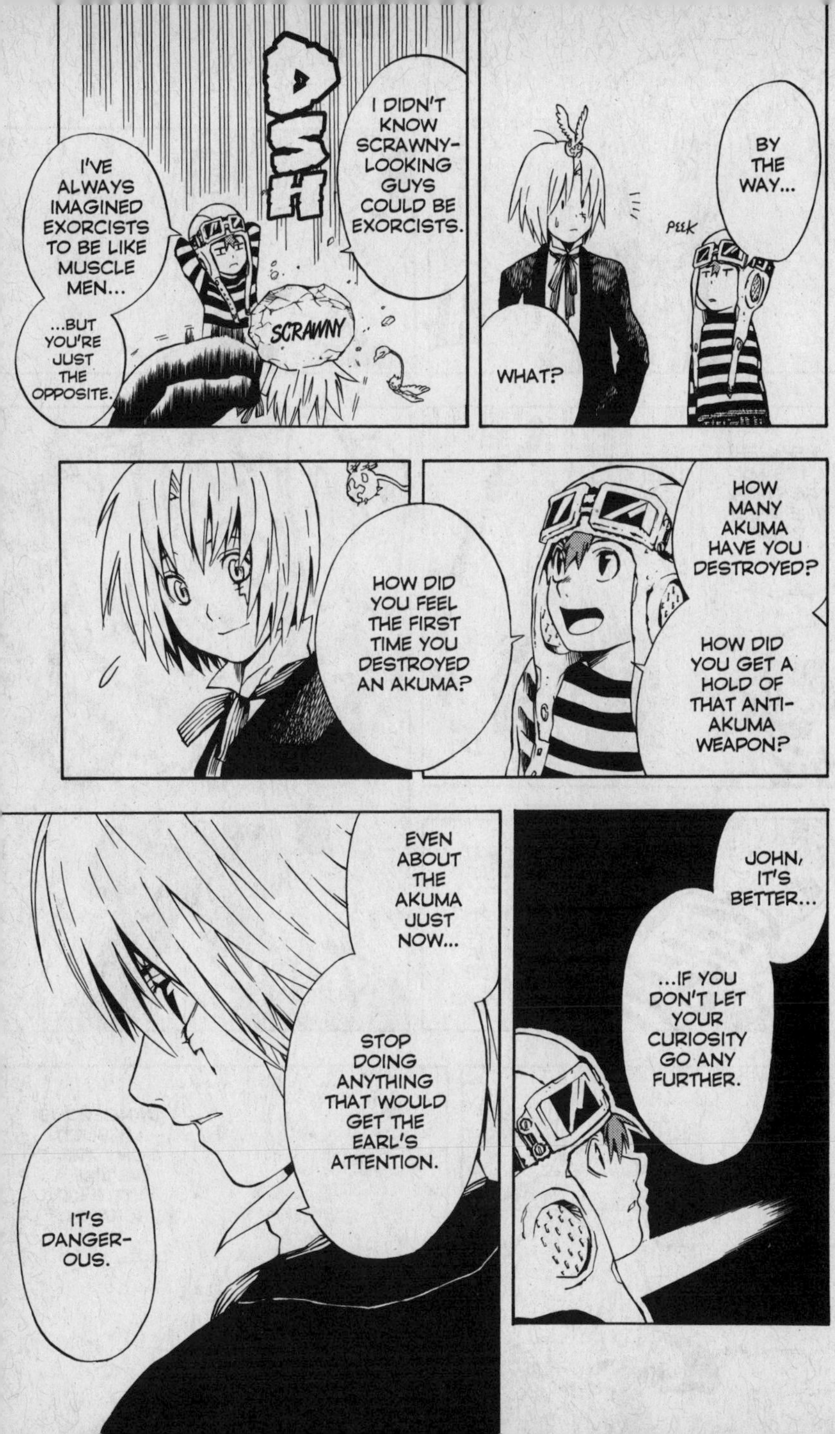
BY THE WAY...
PEEK
WHAT?
I DIDN'T KNOW SCRAWNY-LOOKING GUYS COULD BE EXORCISTS.
DSH
SCRAWNY
I'VE ALWAYS IMAGINED EXORCISTS TO BE LIKE MUSCLE MEN...
...BUT YOU'RE JUST THE OPPOSITE.
HOW MANY AKUMA HAVE YOU DESTROYED?
HOW DID YOU GET A HOLD OF THAT ANTI-AKUMA WEAPON?
HOW DID YOU FEEL THE FIRST TIME YOU DESTROYED AN AKUMA?
JOHN, IT'S BETTER...
...IF YOU DON'T LET YOUR CURIOSITY GO ANY FURTHER.
EVEN ABOUT THE AKUMA JUST NOW...
STOP DOING ANYTHING THAT WOULD GET THE EARL'S ATTENTION.
IT'S DANGER-OUS.

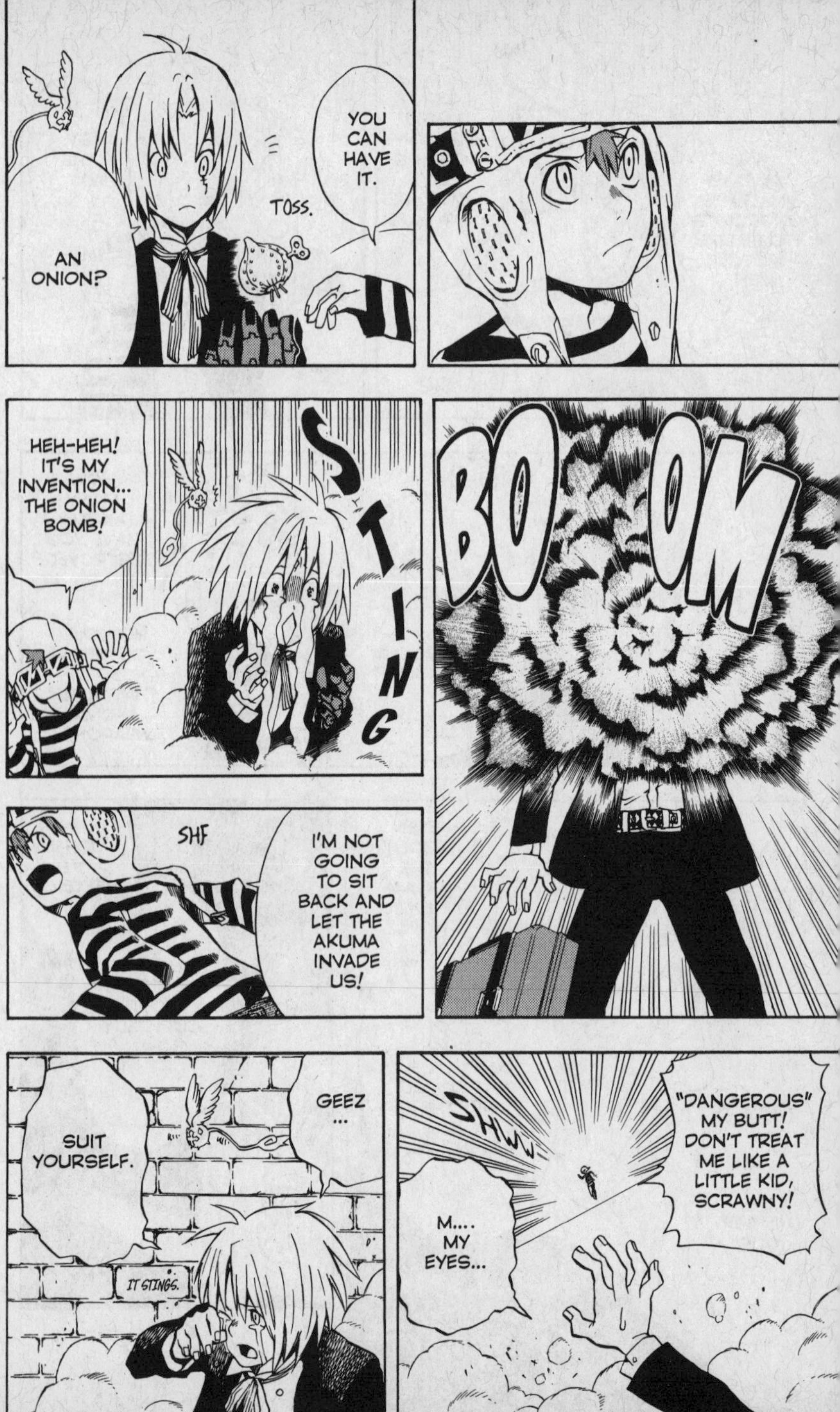
YOU CAN HAVE IT.
TOSS.
AN ONION?
BOOM
STING
HEH-HEH! IT'S MY INVENTION... THE ONION BOMB!
I'M NOT GOING TO SIT BACK AND LET THE AKUMA INVADE US!
SHF
"DANGEROUS" MY BUTT! DON'T TREAT ME LIKE A LITTLE KID, SCRAWNY!
SHWW
M.... MY EYES...
GEEZ ...
SUIT YOURSELF.
IT STINGS.

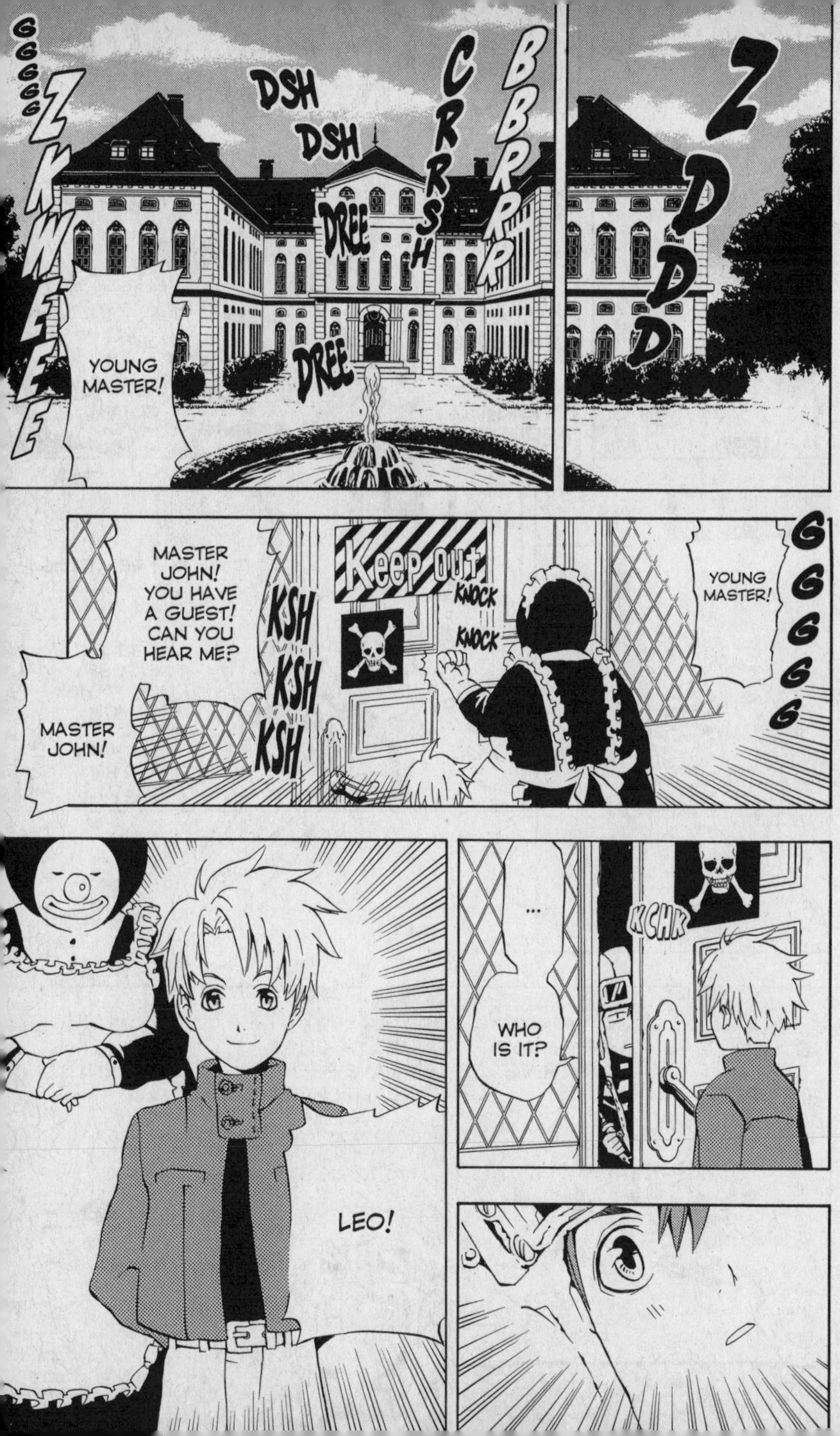
ZDDDD
BBRRRR
CRRRSH
DSH DSH
DREE DREE
GGGG
ZKWEEEEE
YOUNG MASTER!
GGGGG
YOUNG MASTER!
KNOCK KNOCK
Keep out
KSH KSH KSH
MASTER JOHN! YOU HAVE A GUEST! CAN YOU HEAR ME?
MASTER JOHN!
KCHK
...
WHO IS IT?
LEO!

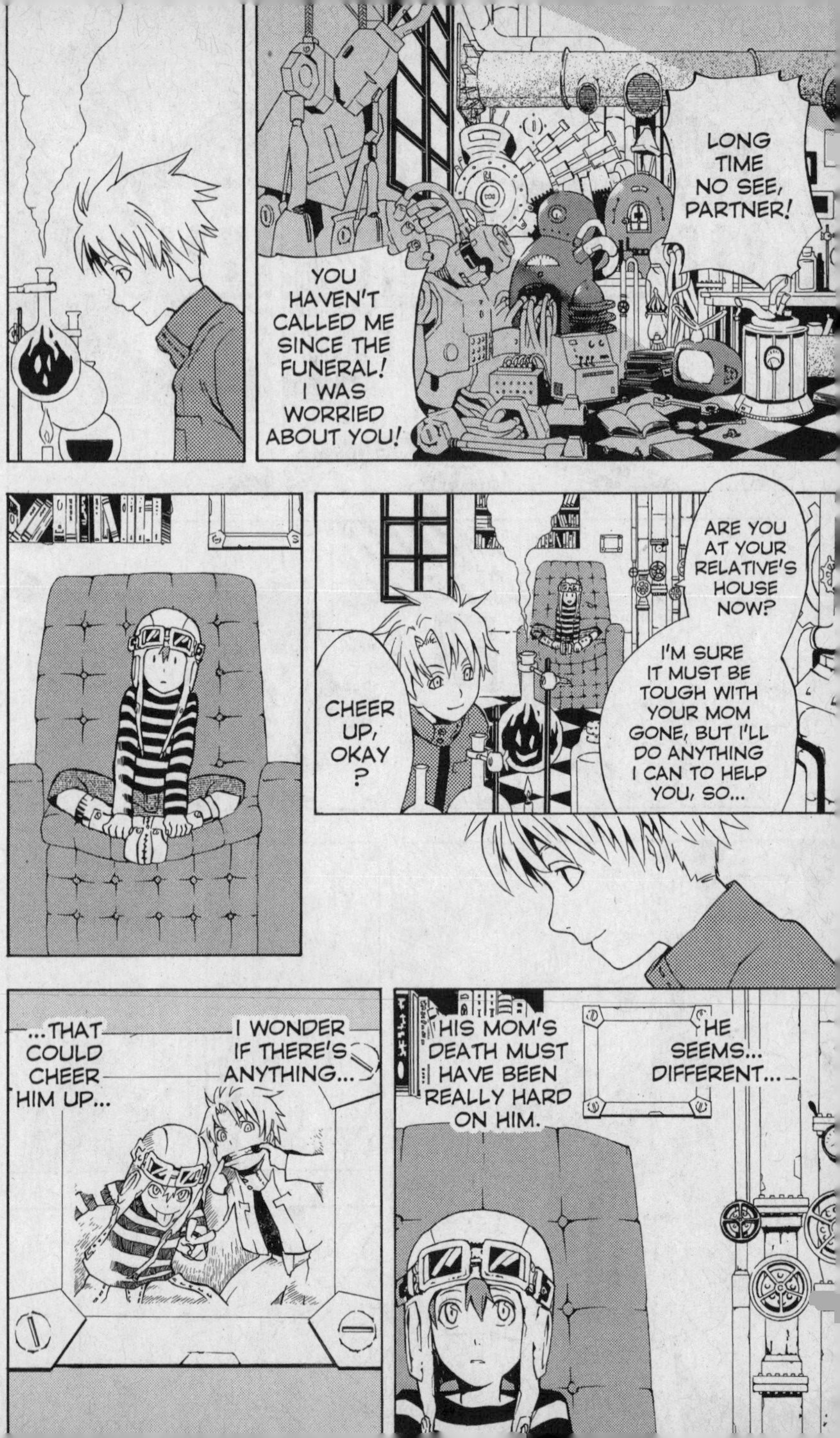
LONG TIME NO SEE, PARTNER!
YOU HAVEN'T CALLED ME SINCE THE FUNERAL! I WAS WORRIED ABOUT YOU!
ARE YOU AT YOUR RELATIVE'S HOUSE NOW?
I'M SURE IT MUST BE TOUGH WITH YOUR MOM GONE, BUT I'LL DO ANYTHING I CAN TO HELP YOU, SO...
CHEER UP, OKAY?
HE SEEMS... DIFFERENT...
HIS MOM'S DEATH MUST HAVE BEEN REALLY HARD ON HIM.
I WONDER IF THERE'S ANYTHING...
...THAT COULD CHEER HIM UP...

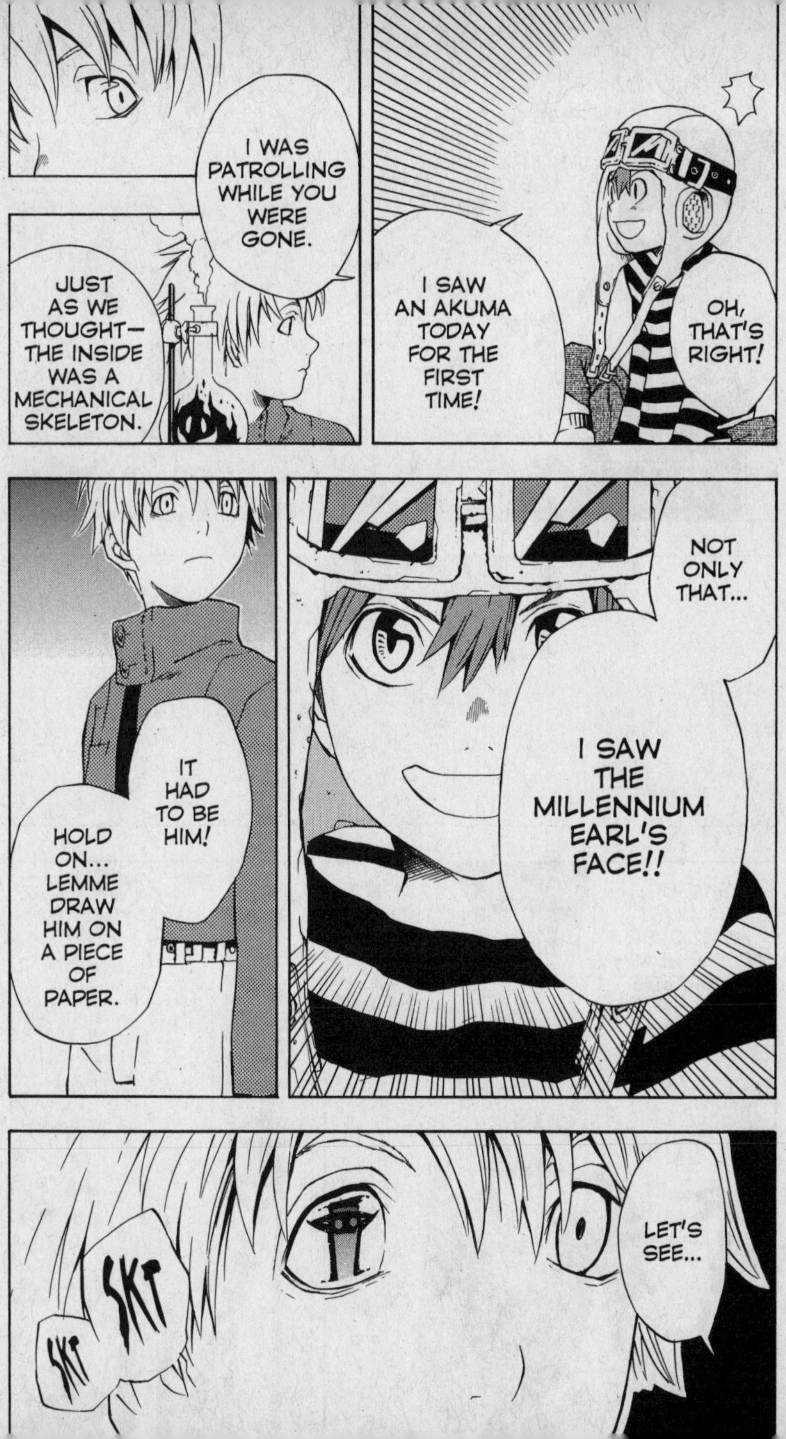
OH, THAT'S RIGHT!
I SAW AN AKUMA TODAY FOR THE FIRST TIME!
I WAS PATROLLING WHILE YOU WERE GONE.
JUST AS WE THOUGHT—THE INSIDE WAS A MECHANICAL SKELETON.
NOT ONLY THAT...
I SAW THE MILLENNIUM EARL'S FACE!!
IT HAD TO BE HIM!
HOLD ON... LEMME DRAW HIM ON A PIECE OF PAPER.
LET'S SEE...
SKT
SKT

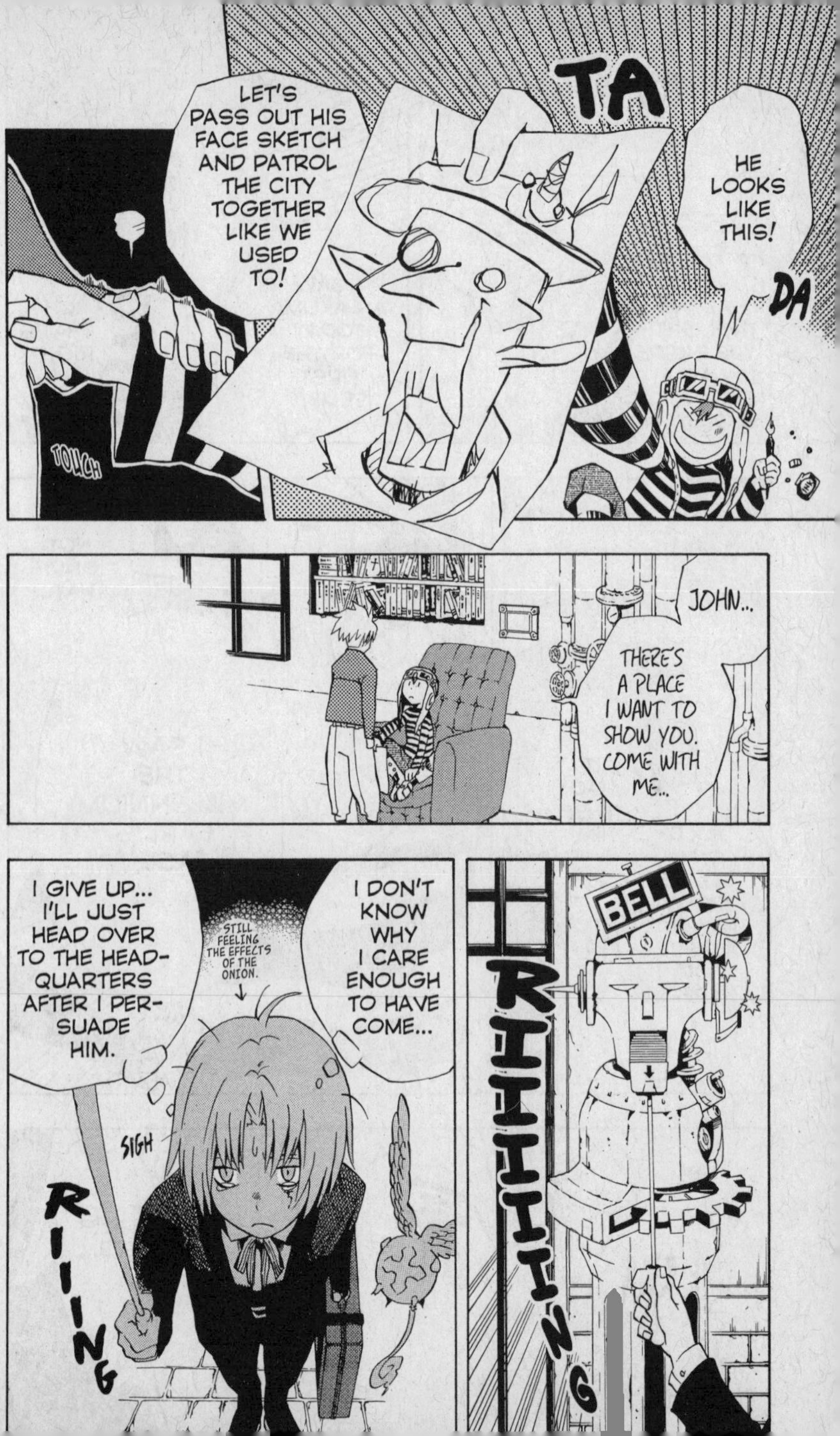
TA
HE LOOKS LIKE THIS!
DA
LET'S PASS OUT HIS FACE SKETCH AND PATROL THE CITY TOGETHER LIKE WE USED TO!
TOUCH
JOHN...
THERE'S A PLACE I WANT TO SHOW YOU. COME WITH ME...
BELL
RIIIIIIING
I DON'T KNOW WHY I CARE ENOUGH TO HAVE COME...
I GIVE UP... I'LL JUST HEAD OVER TO THE HEAD-QUARTERS AFTER I PER-SUADE HIM.
STILL FEELING THE EFFECTS OF THE ONION.
SIGH
RIIING

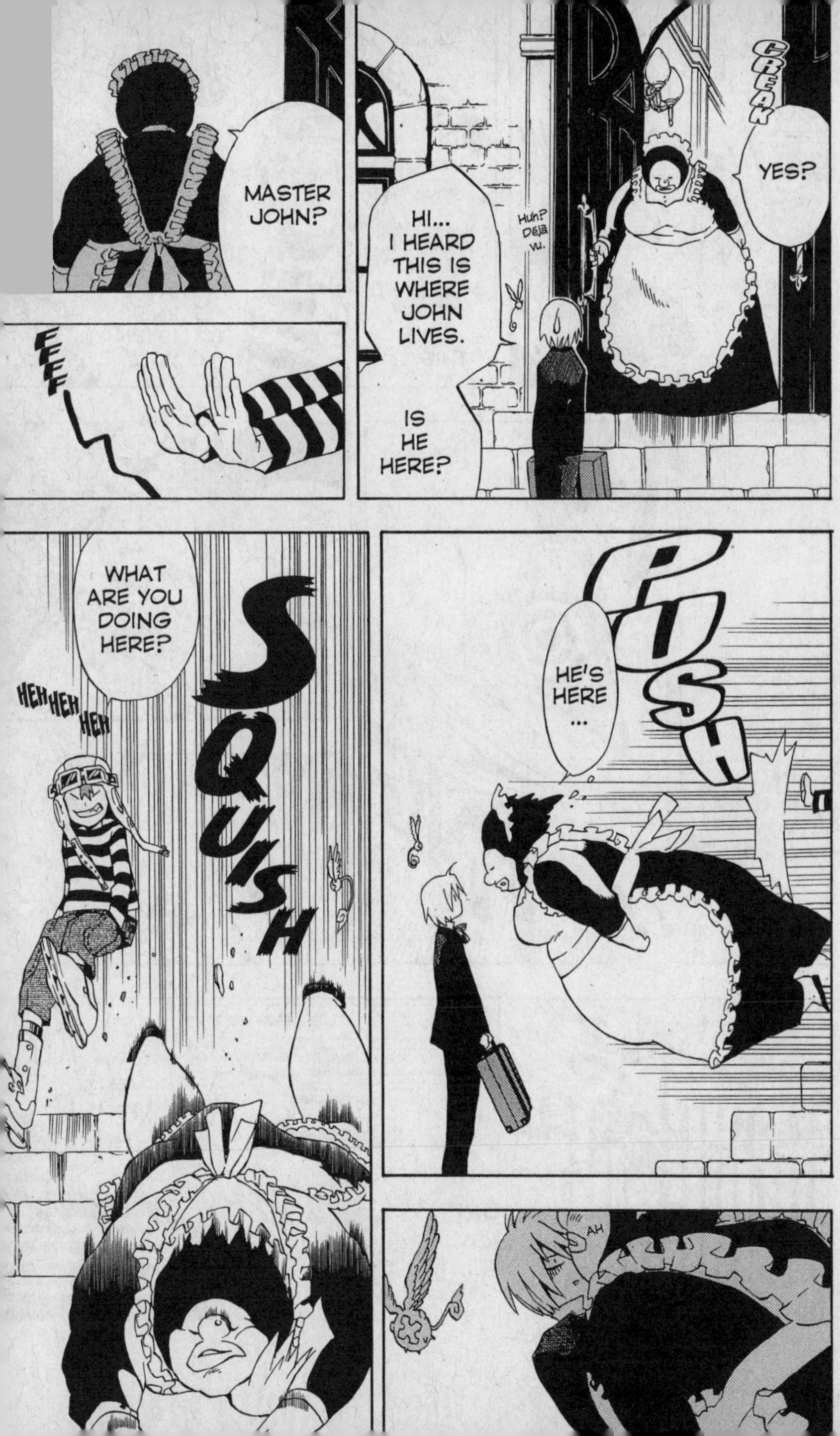
CREAK
YES?
Huh? Déjà vu.
HI... I HEARD THIS IS WHERE JOHN LIVES.
IS HE HERE?
MASTER JOHN?
FFFF
PUSH
HE'S HERE ...
AH
WHAT ARE YOU DOING HERE?
HEH HEH HEH
SQUISH

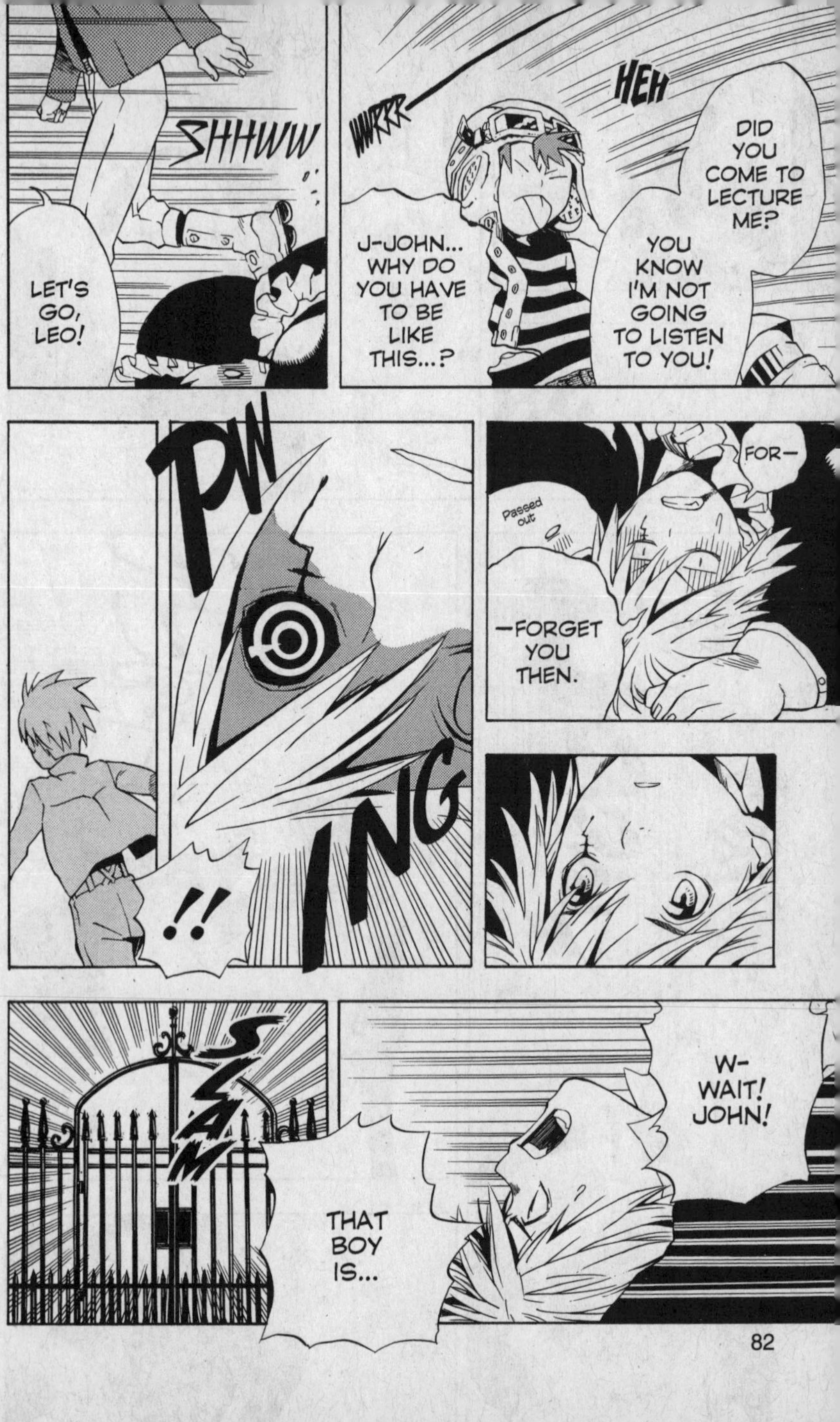
HEH
DID YOU COME TO LECTURE ME?
YOU KNOW I'M NOT GOING TO LISTEN TO YOU!
WWRRR
J-JOHN... WHY DO YOU HAVE TO BE LIKE THIS...?
SHHWW
LET'S GO, LEO!
FOR—
Passed out
—FORGET YOU THEN.
PWING
!!
W-WAIT! JOHN!
THAT BOY IS...
SLAM

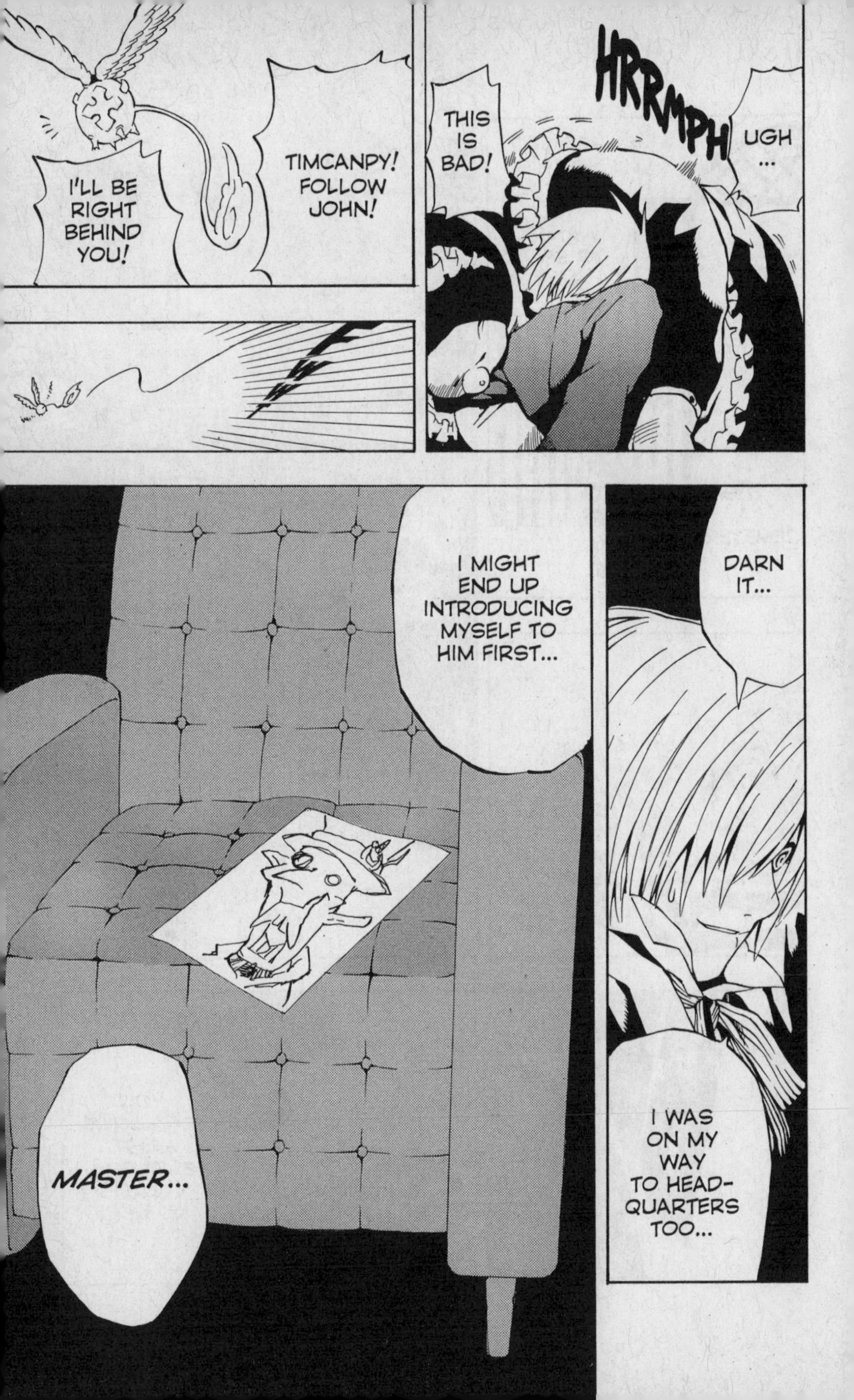

HRRMPH
UGH ...
THIS IS BAD!
TIMCANPY! FOLLOW JOHN!
I'LL BE RIGHT BEHIND YOU!
DARN IT...
I WAS ON MY WAY TO HEAD-QUARTERS TOO...
I MIGHT END UP INTRODUCING MYSELF TO HIM FIRST...
MASTER...

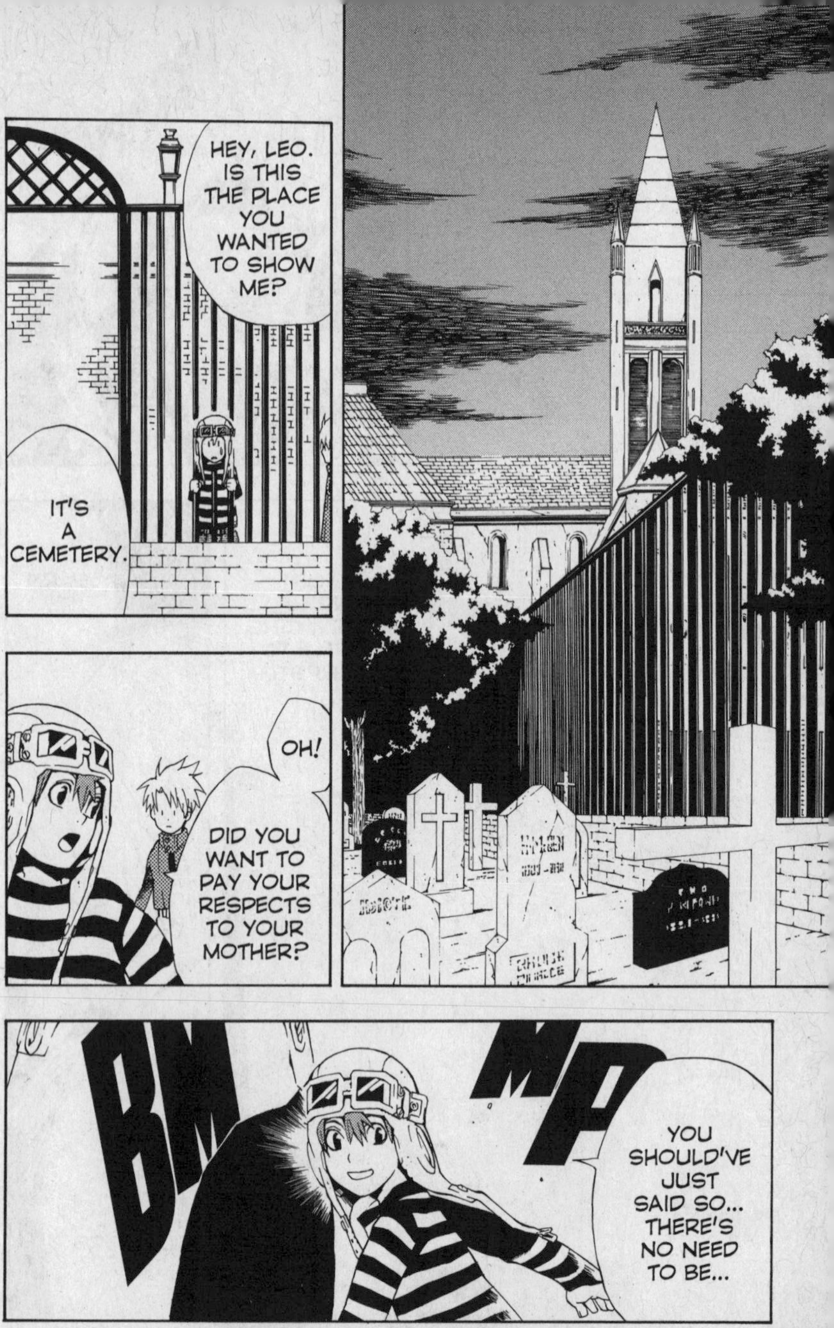
HEY, LEO. IS THIS THE PLACE YOU WANTED TO SHOW ME?
IT'S A CEMETERY.
OH!
DID YOU WANT TO PAY YOUR RESPECTS TO YOUR MOTHER?
BMMP
YOU SHOULD'VE JUST SAID SO... THERE'S NO NEED TO BE...

PAT

GOOD EVEN-ING. ♡

NICE TO MEET YOU, JOHN. ♡

VSSH

...!

THE M...

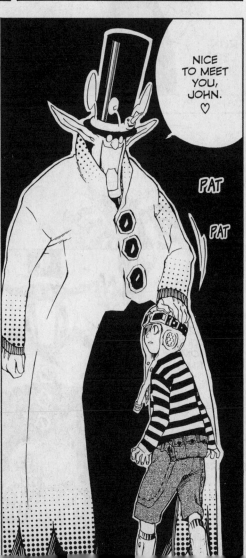

PAT

PAT

...MILLEN-NIUM EARL?

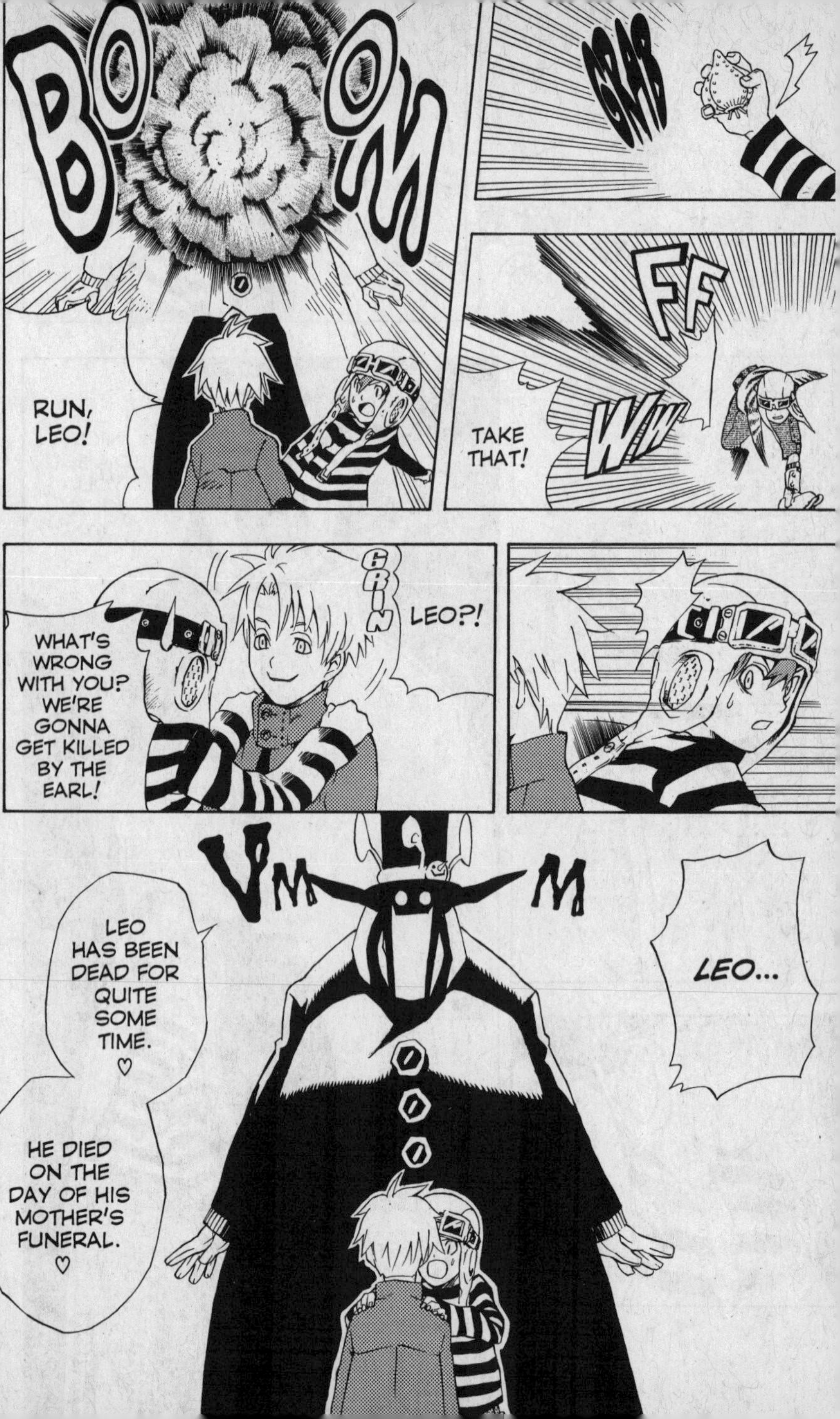

GRAB
FFWW
TAKE THAT!
BOOM
RUN, LEO!
GRIN
LEO?!
WHAT'S WRONG WITH YOU? WE'RE GONNA GET KILLED BY THE EARL!
VMM
LEO...
LEO HAS BEEN DEAD FOR QUITE SOME TIME. ♡
HE DIED ON THE DAY OF HIS MOTHER'S FUNERAL. ♡

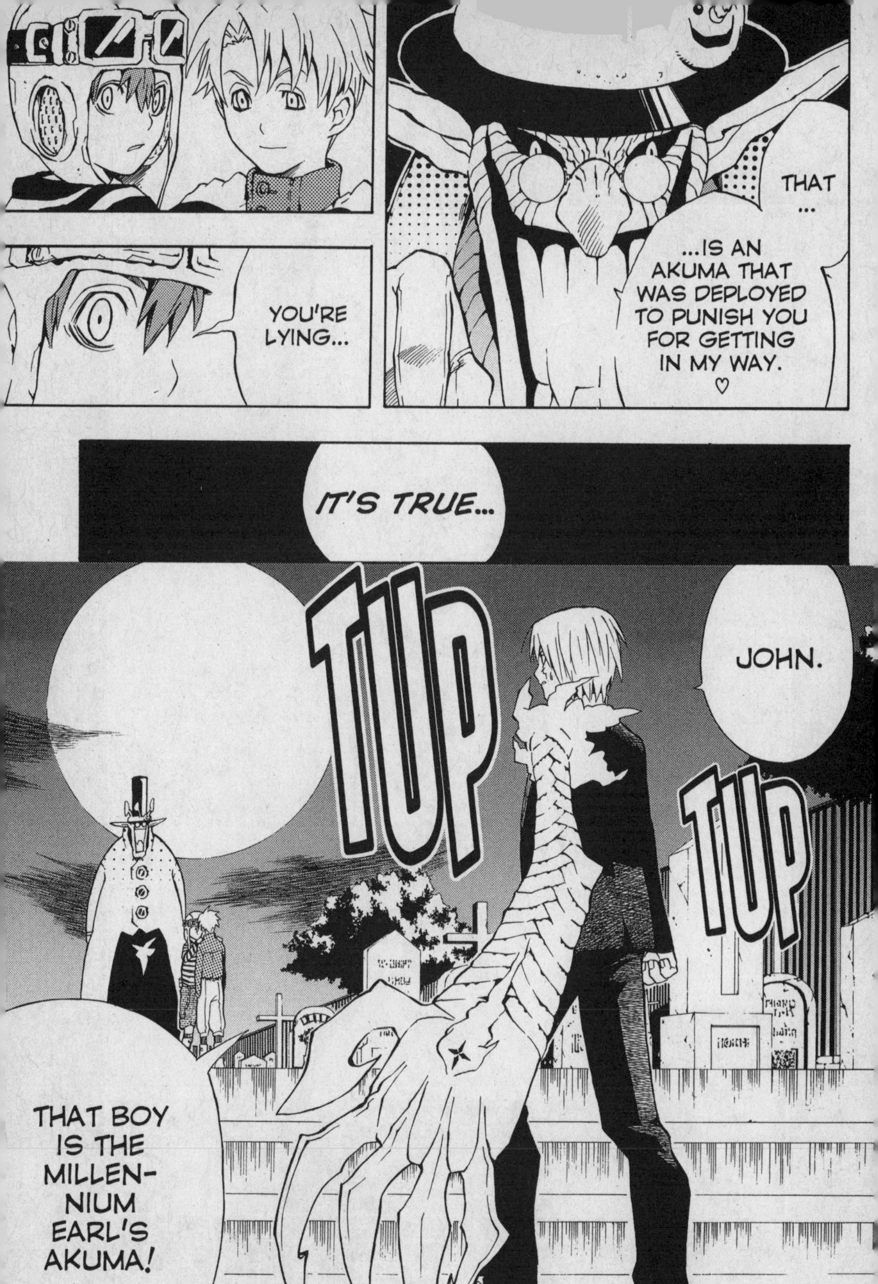
THAT ...
...IS AN AKUMA THAT WAS DEPLOYED TO PUNISH YOU FOR GETTING IN MY WAY. ♡
YOU'RE LYING...
IT'S TRUE...
JOHN.
TUP
TUP
THAT BOY IS THE MILLEN-NIUM EARL'S AKUMA!

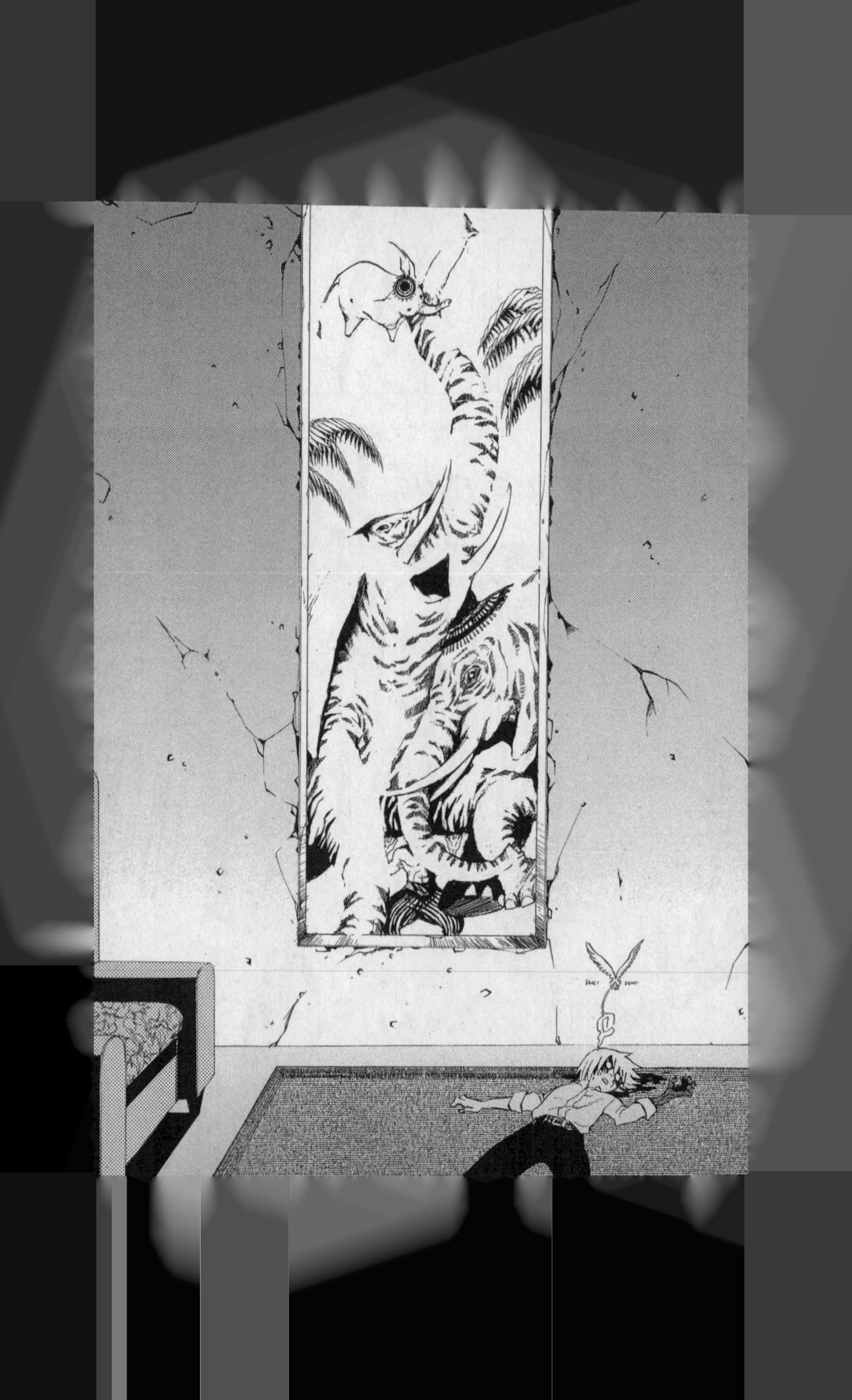

THE 3RD NIGHT: THE PENTACLE

DESTROY...

RUN...

DESTROY...

RUN, MANA!

DESTROY...

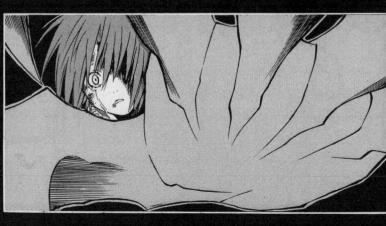

DESTROY ME!

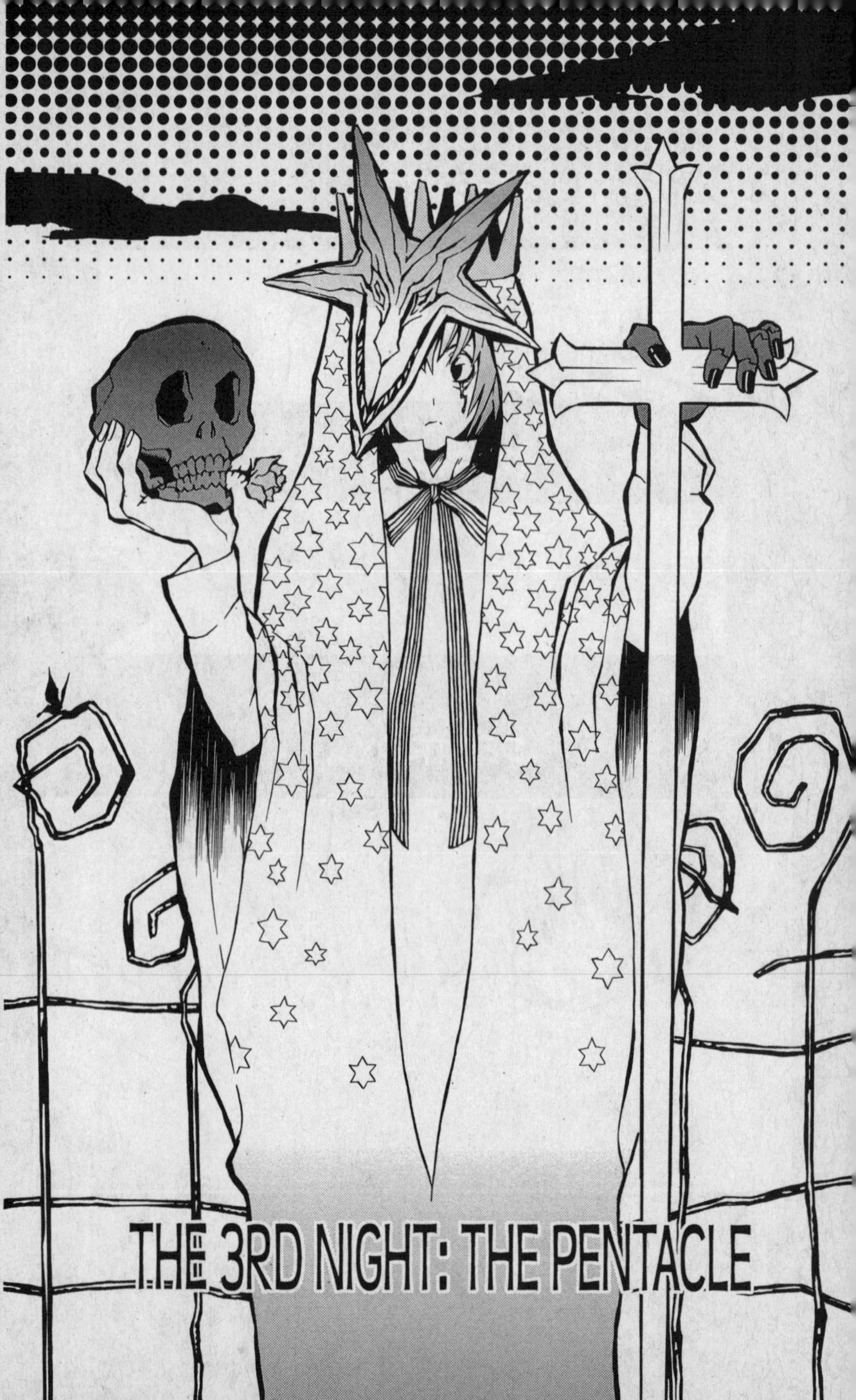
THE 3RD NIGHT: THE PENTACLE

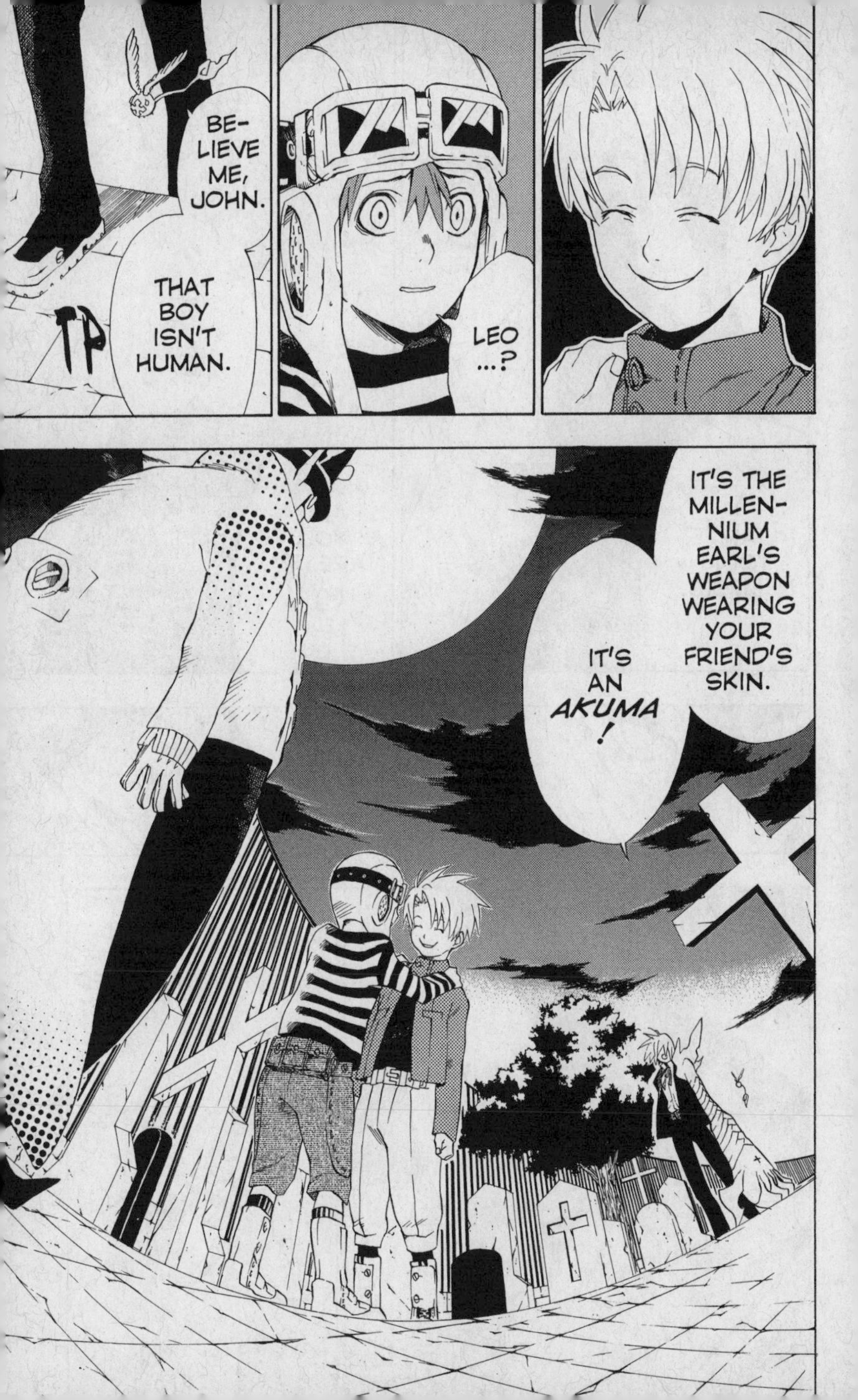
LEO ...?
BE-LIEVE ME, JOHN.
THAT BOY ISN'T HUMAN.
TP
IT'S THE MILLEN-NIUM EARL'S WEAPON WEARING YOUR FRIEND'S SKIN.
IT'S AN *AKUMA*!

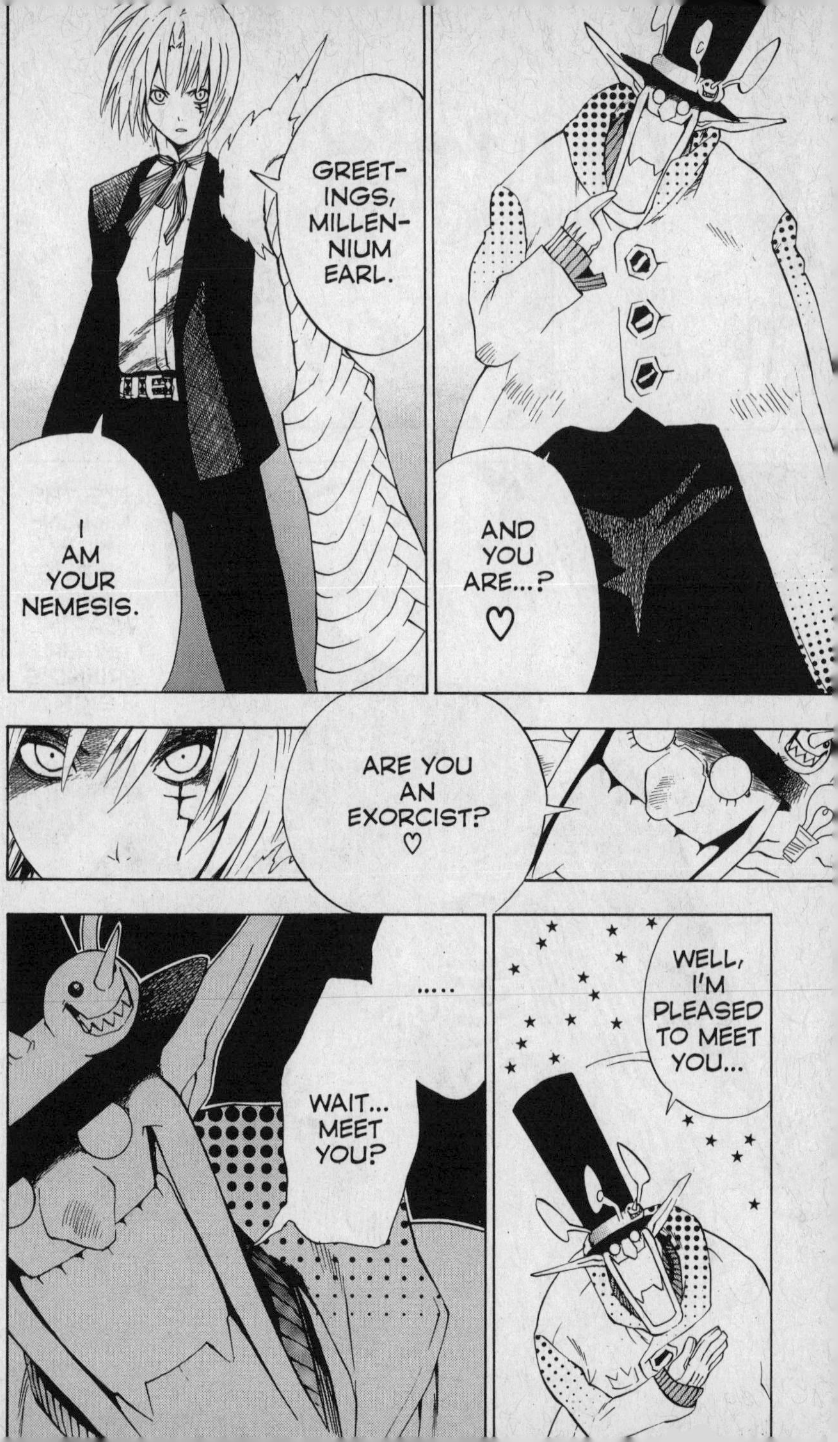
AND YOU ARE...? ♡
GREET-INGS, MILLEN-NIUM EARL.
I AM YOUR NEMESIS.
ARE YOU AN EXORCIST? ♡
WELL, I'M PLEASED TO MEET YOU...
.....
WAIT... MEET YOU?

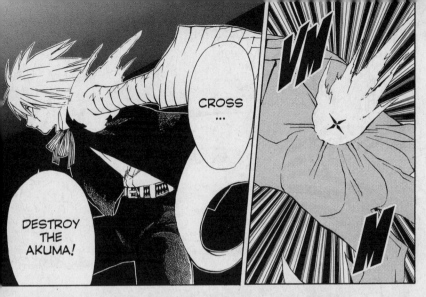

CROSS...

DESTROY THE AKUMA!

VM

M

BRING SALVATION...

...TO HIS SOUL!

ZAZ ZAZAZA

OOH

HUSSSH

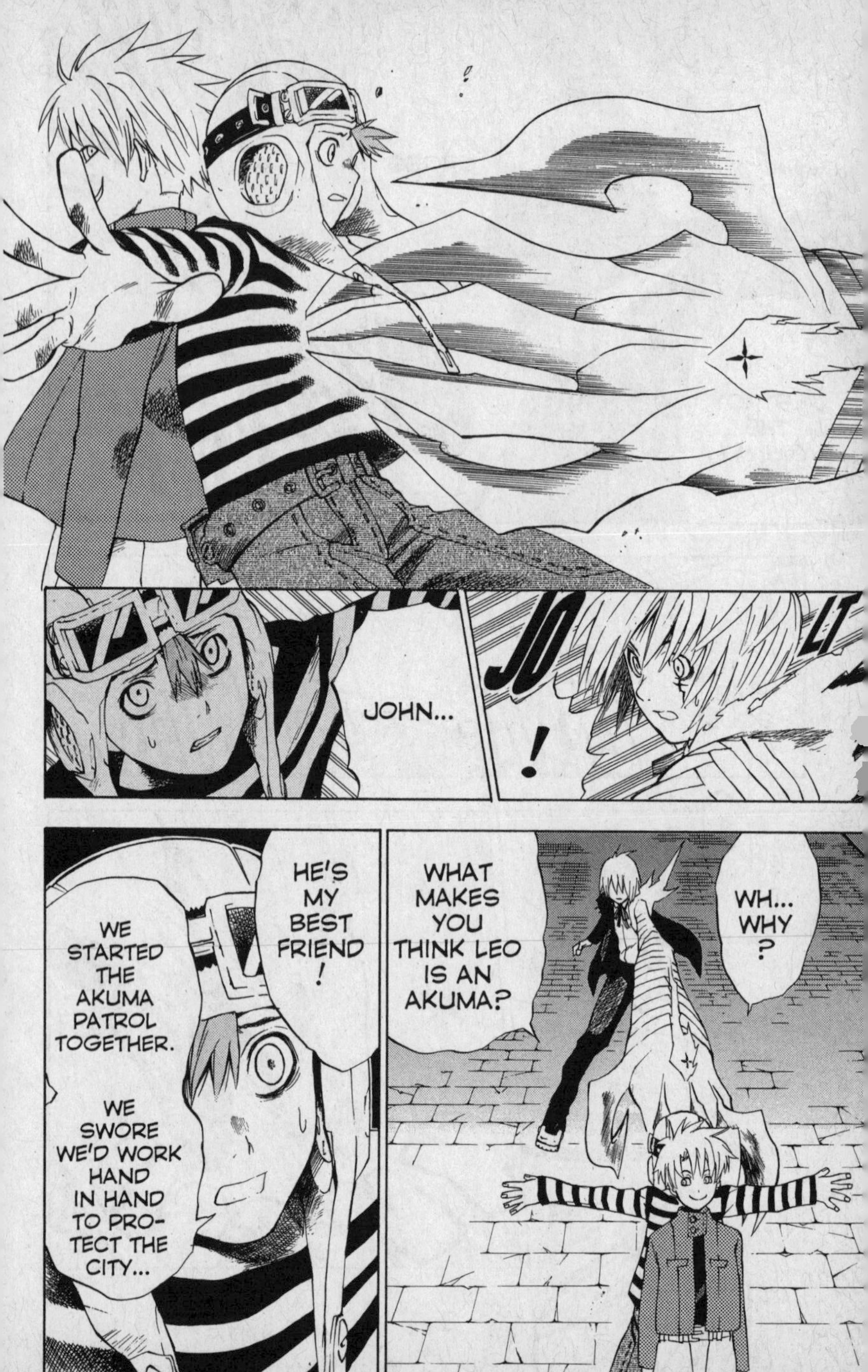
JOLT
!
JOHN...
WH... WHY?
WHAT MAKES YOU THINK LEO IS AN AKUMA?
HE'S MY BEST FRIEND!
WE STARTED THE AKUMA PATROL TOGETHER.
WE SWORE WE'D WORK HAND IN HAND TO PROTECT THE CITY...

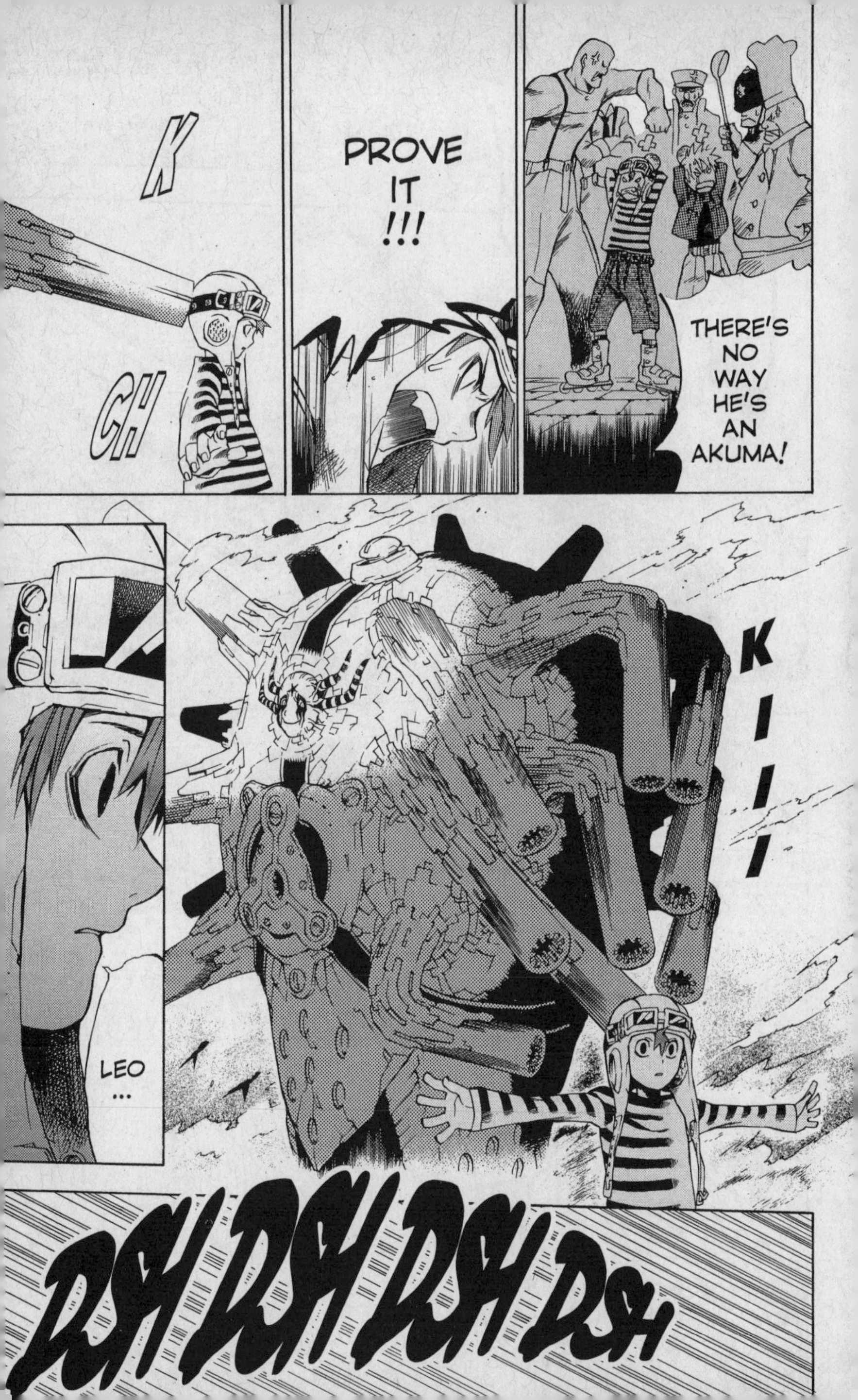
THERE'S NO WAY HE'S AN AKUMA!
PROVE IT!!!
K
CH
KIII
LEO ...
DSH DSH DSH DSH

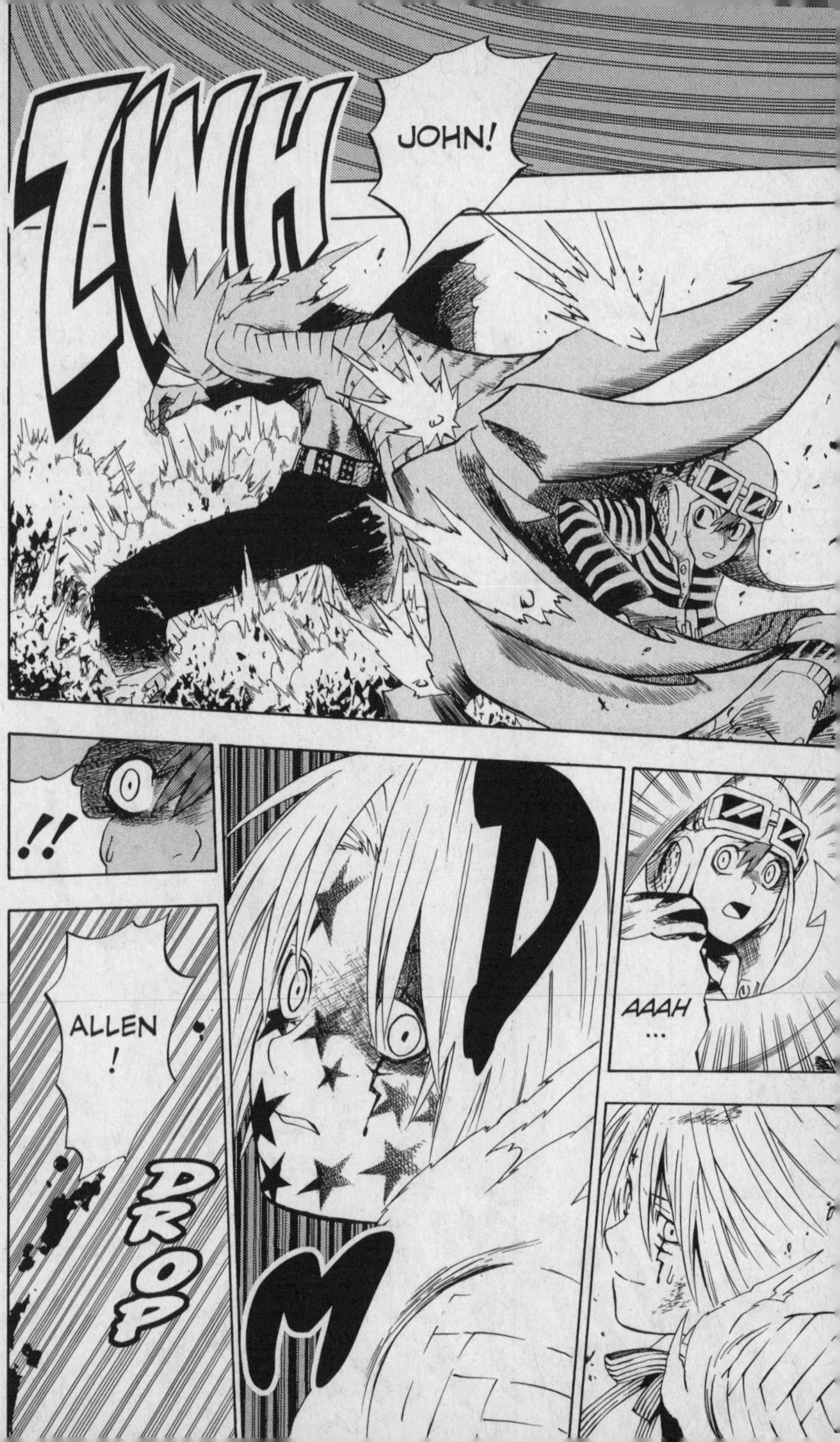
JOHN!
ZWH
AAAH ...
DM
!!
ALLEN!
DROP

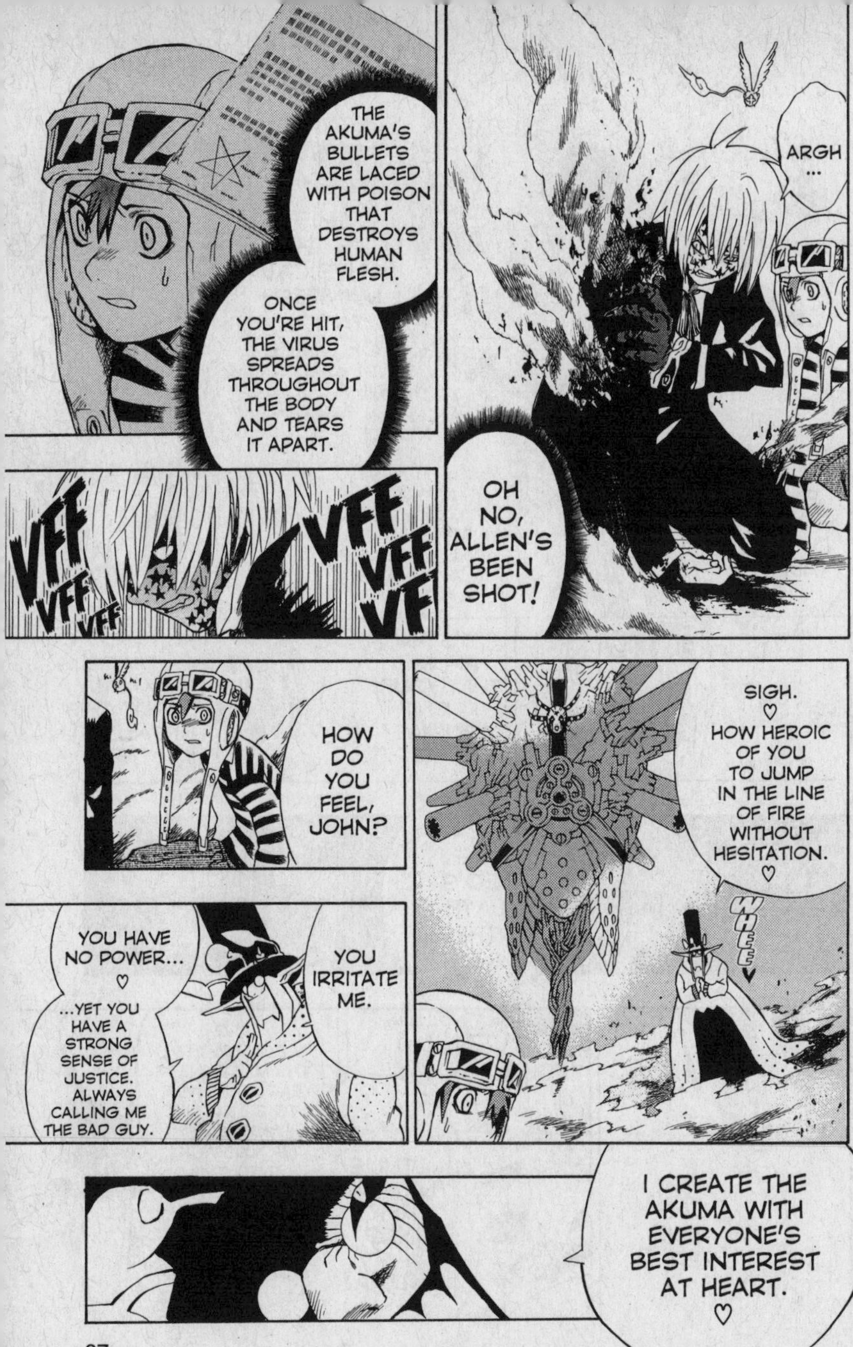
ARGH ...
OH NO, ALLEN'S BEEN SHOT!
THE AKUMA'S BULLETS ARE LACED WITH POISON THAT DESTROYS HUMAN FLESH.
ONCE YOU'RE HIT, THE VIRUS SPREADS THROUGHOUT THE BODY AND TEARS IT APART.
VFF VFF VFF VF
VFF VFF VFF
SIGH. ♡ HOW HEROIC OF YOU TO JUMP IN THE LINE OF FIRE WITHOUT HESITATION. ♡
WHEE
HOW DO YOU FEEL, JOHN?
YOU IRRITATE ME.
YOU HAVE NO POWER... ♡
...YET YOU HAVE A STRONG SENSE OF JUSTICE. ALWAYS CALLING ME THE BAD GUY.
I CREATE THE AKUMA WITH EVERYONE'S BEST INTEREST AT HEART. ♡

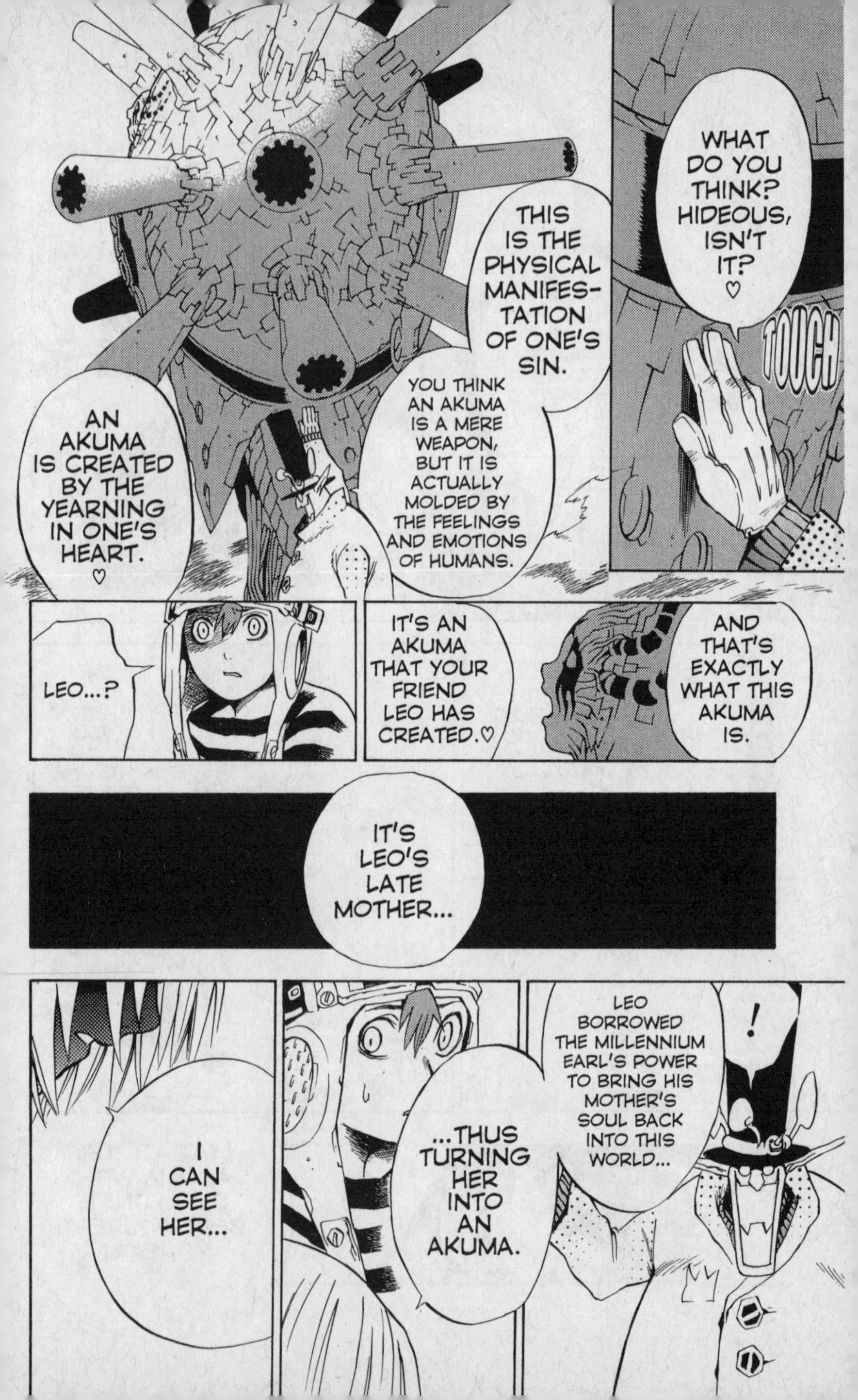
WHAT DO YOU THINK? HIDEOUS, ISN'T IT? ♡
TOUCH
THIS IS THE PHYSICAL MANIFES-TATION OF ONE'S SIN.
YOU THINK AN AKUMA IS A MERE WEAPON, BUT IT IS ACTUALLY MOLDED BY THE FEELINGS AND EMOTIONS OF HUMANS.
AN AKUMA IS CREATED BY THE YEARNING IN ONE'S HEART. ♡
AND THAT'S EXACTLY WHAT THIS AKUMA IS.
IT'S AN AKUMA THAT YOUR FRIEND LEO HAS CREATED.♡
LEO...?
IT'S LEO'S LATE MOTHER...
!
LEO BORROWED THE MILLENNIUM EARL'S POWER TO BRING HIS MOTHER'S SOUL BACK INTO THIS WORLD...
...THUS TURNING HER INTO AN AKUMA.
I CAN SEE HER...

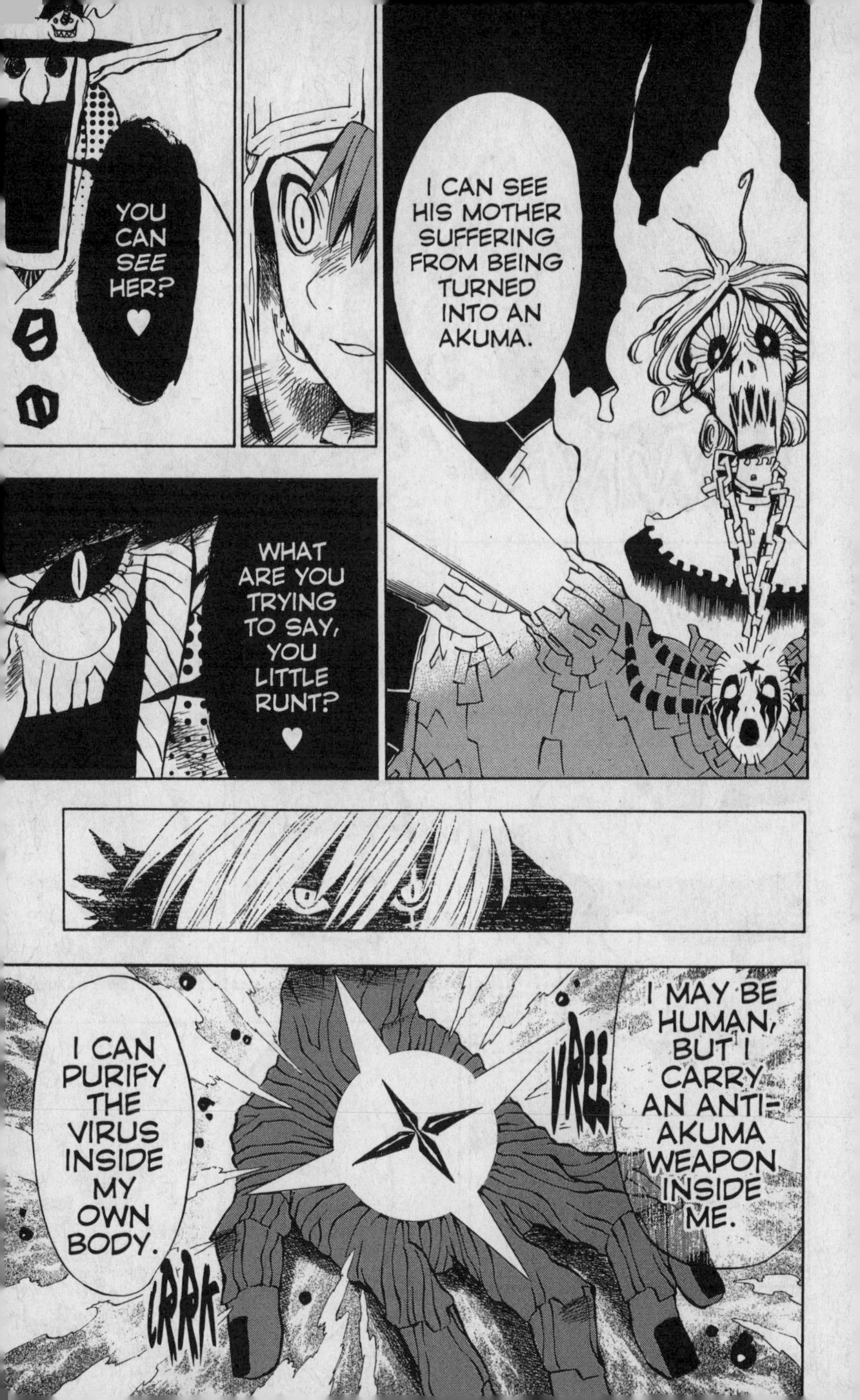
I CAN SEE HIS MOTHER SUFFERING FROM BEING TURNED INTO AN AKUMA.
YOU CAN SEE HER? ♥
WHAT ARE YOU TRYING TO SAY, YOU LITTLE RUNT? ♥
I MAY BE HUMAN, BUT I CARRY AN ANTI-AKUMA WEAPON INSIDE ME.
VREE
I CAN PURIFY THE VIRUS INSIDE MY OWN BODY.
CRRK

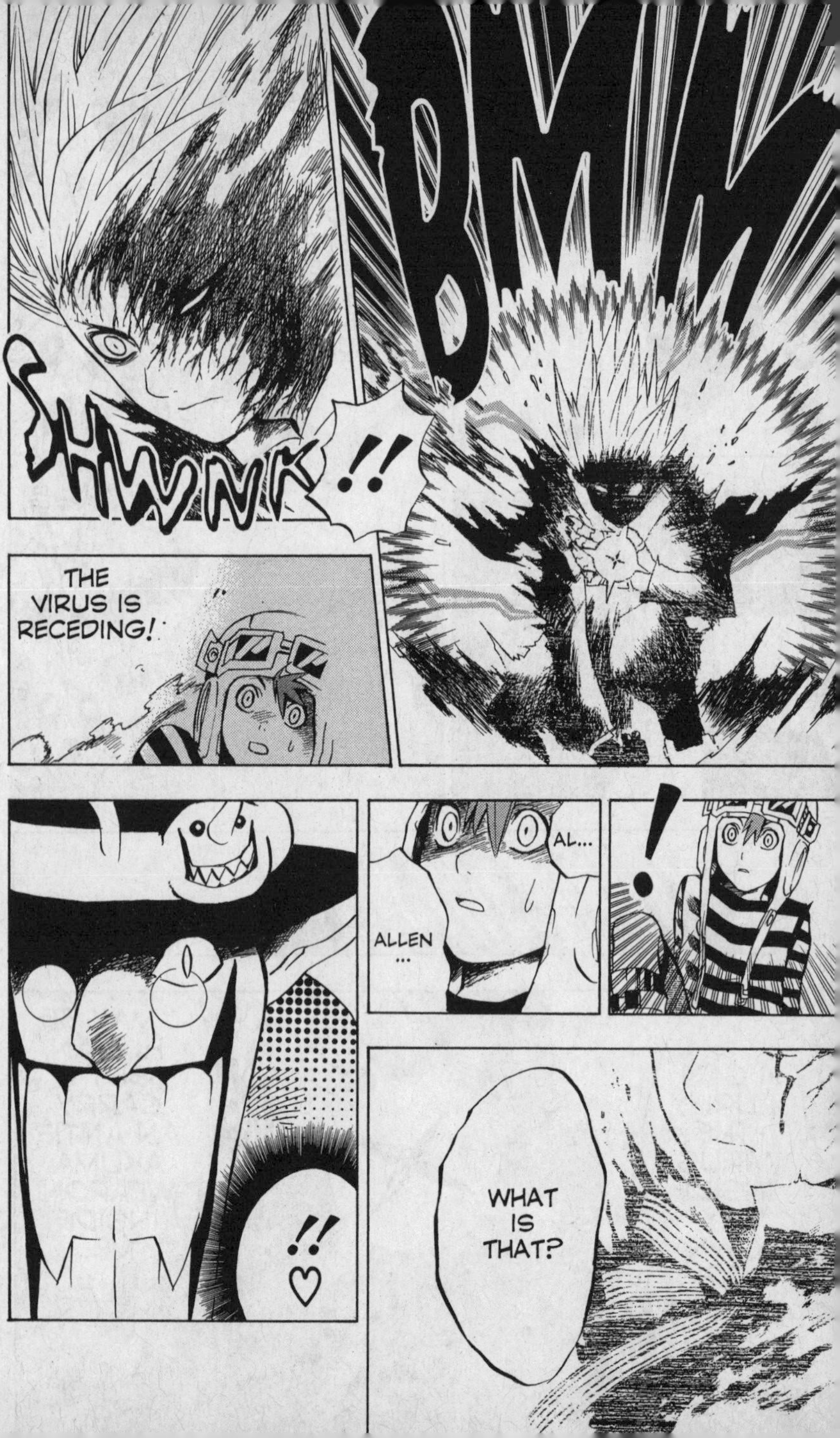

SHWNK!!
THE VIRUS IS RECEDING!
!
AL...
ALLEN ...
WHAT IS THAT?
!!
♥

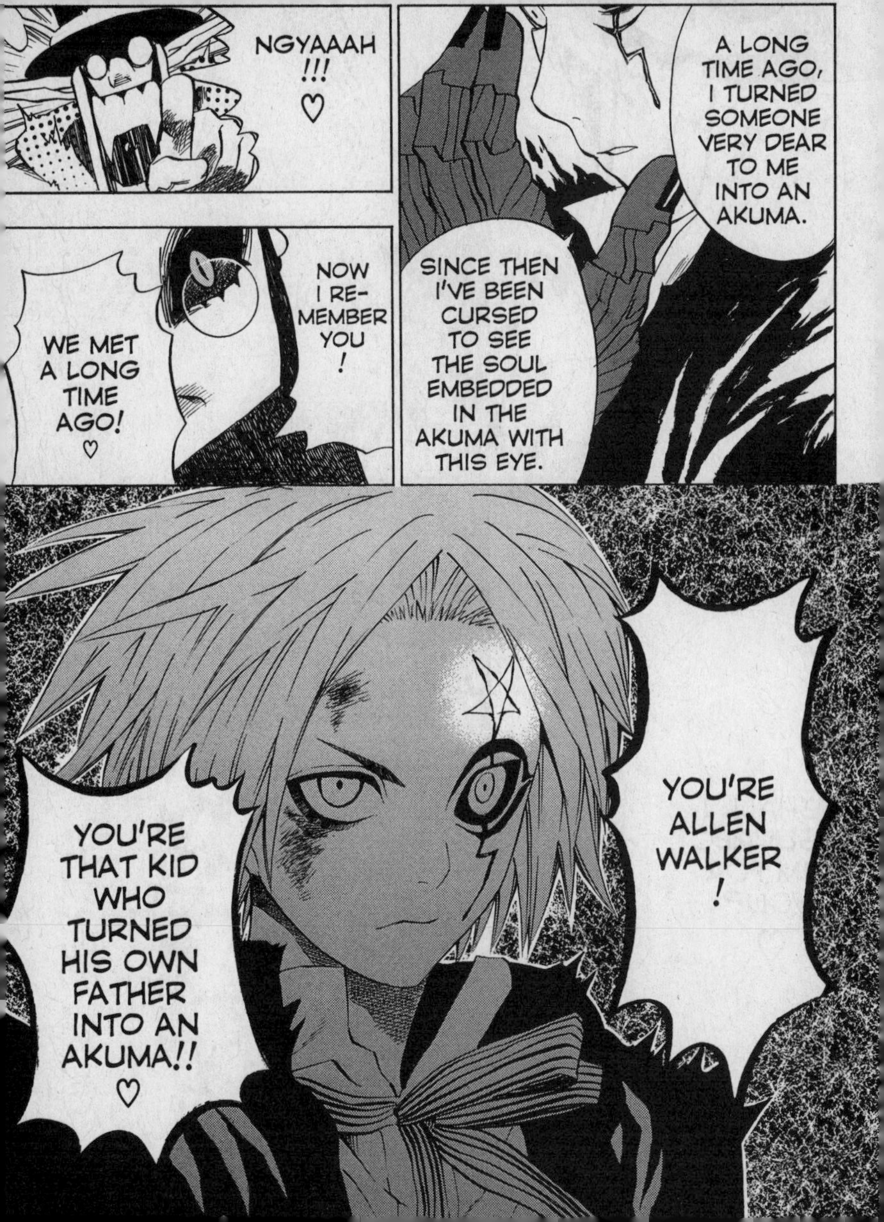
A LONG TIME AGO, I TURNED SOMEONE VERY DEAR TO ME INTO AN AKUMA.
SINCE THEN I'VE BEEN CURSED TO SEE THE SOUL EMBEDDED IN THE AKUMA WITH THIS EYE.
NGYAAAH!!! ♡
NOW I RE-MEMBER YOU!
WE MET A LONG TIME AGO! ♡
YOU'RE ALLEN WALKER!
YOU'RE THAT KID WHO TURNED HIS OWN FATHER INTO AN AKUMA!! ♡

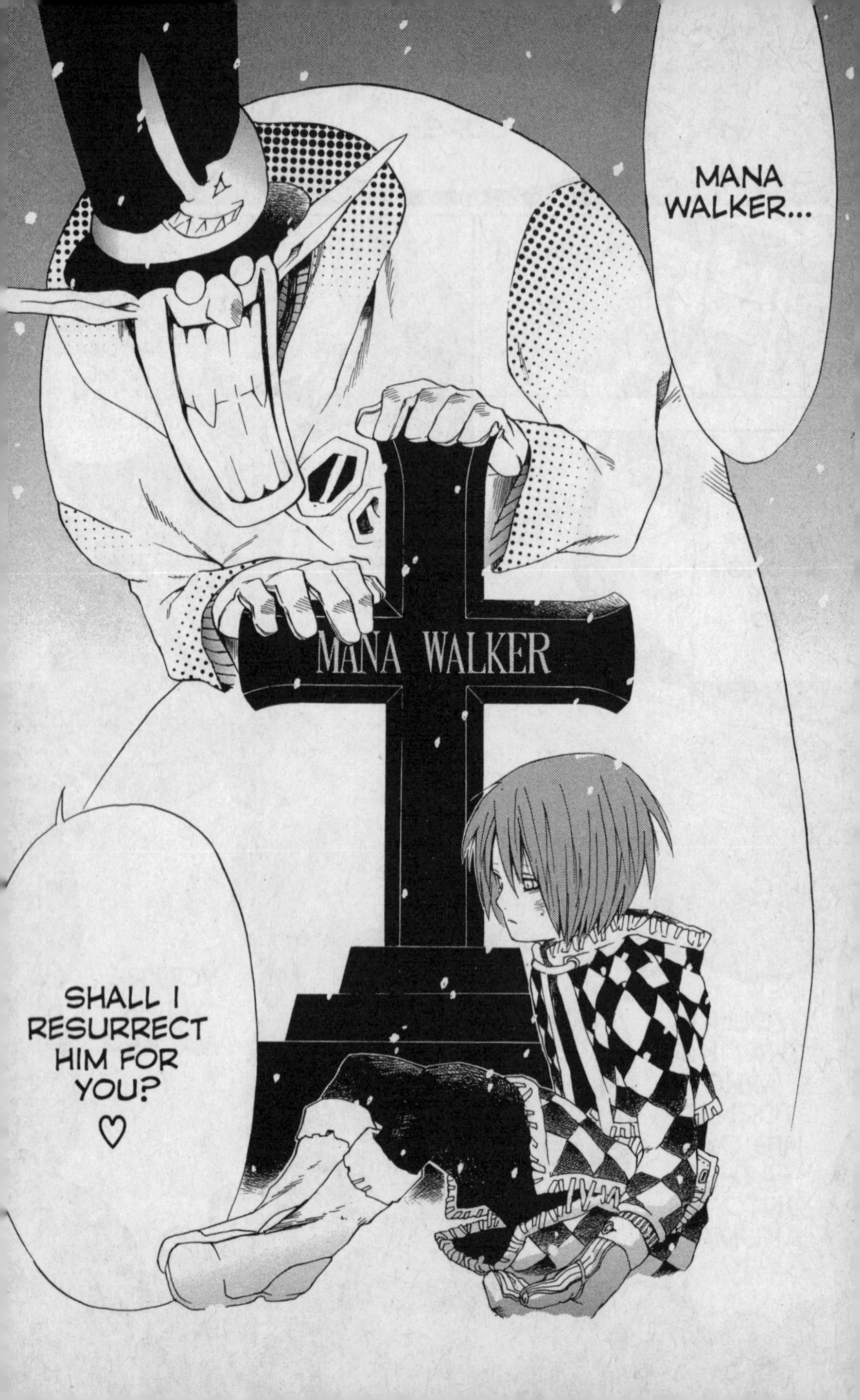
MANA WALKER...
MANA WALKER
SHALL I RESURRECT HIM FOR YOU? ♡

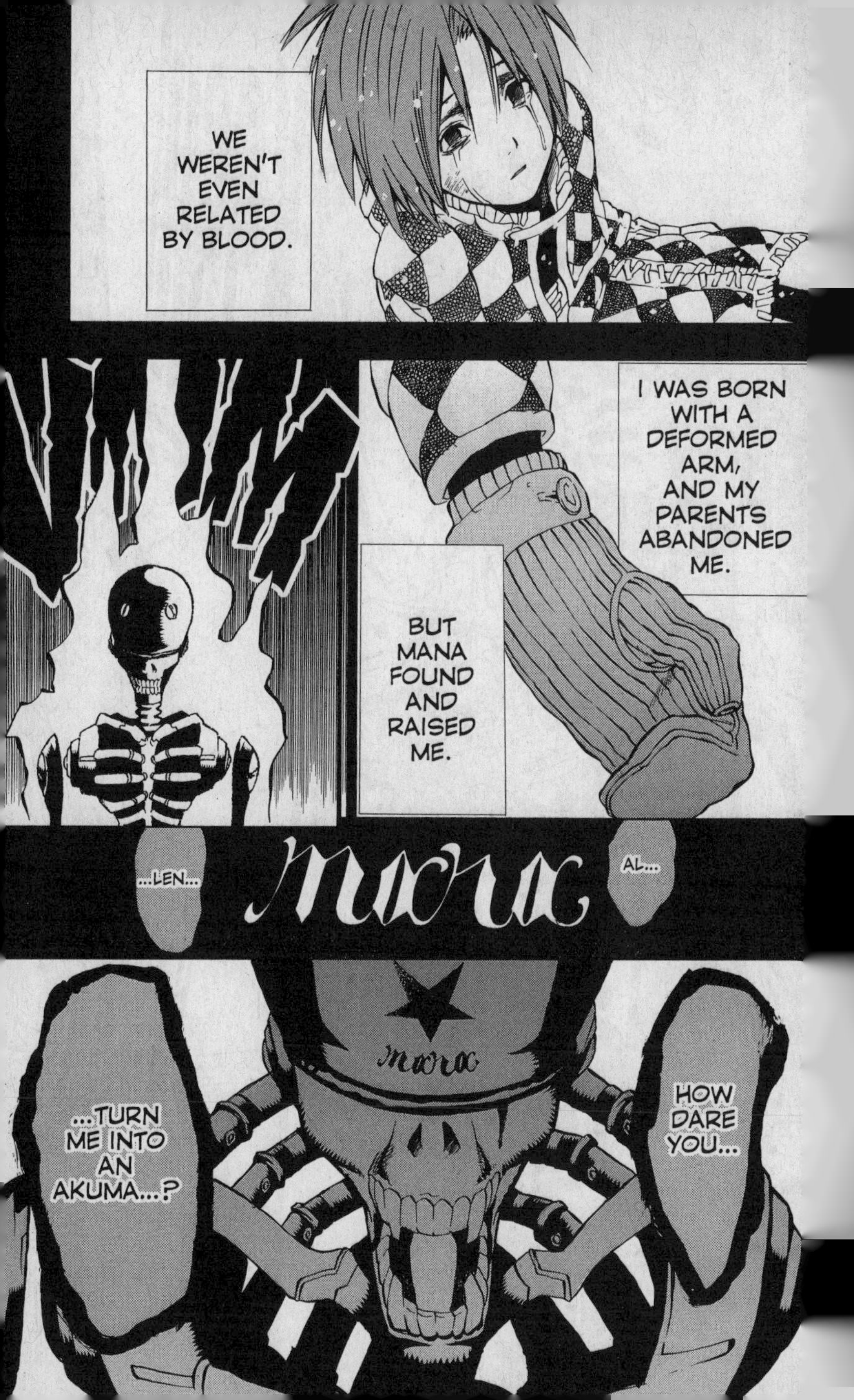
WE WEREN'T EVEN RELATED BY BLOOD.
I WAS BORN WITH A DEFORMED ARM, AND MY PARENTS ABANDONED ME.
BUT MANA FOUND AND RAISED ME.
AL...
...LEN...
HOW DARE YOU...
...TURN ME INTO AN AKUMA...?

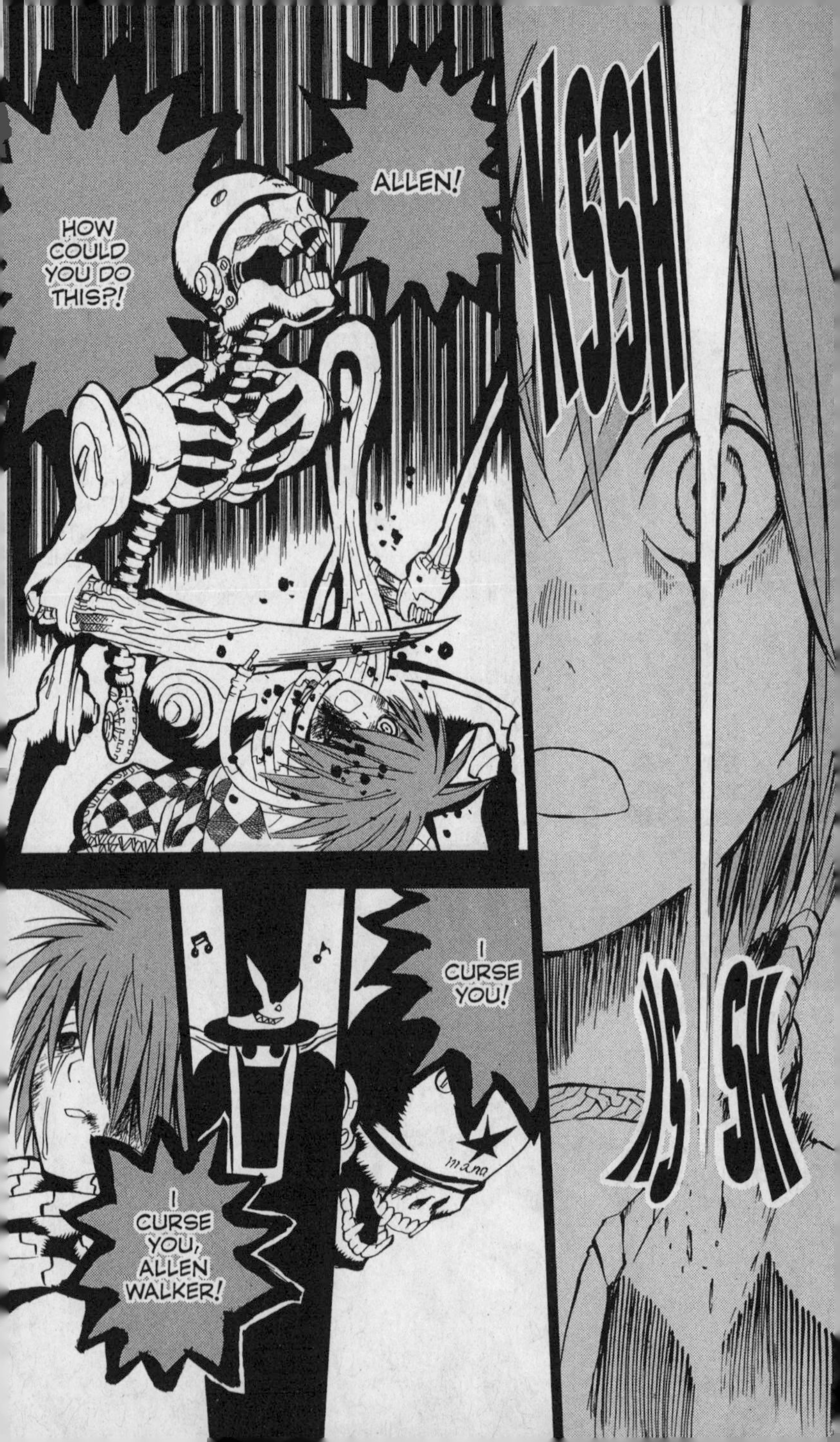
KSSH
SK
ALLEN!
HOW COULD YOU DO THIS?!
I CURSE YOU!
I CURSE YOU, ALLEN WALKER!

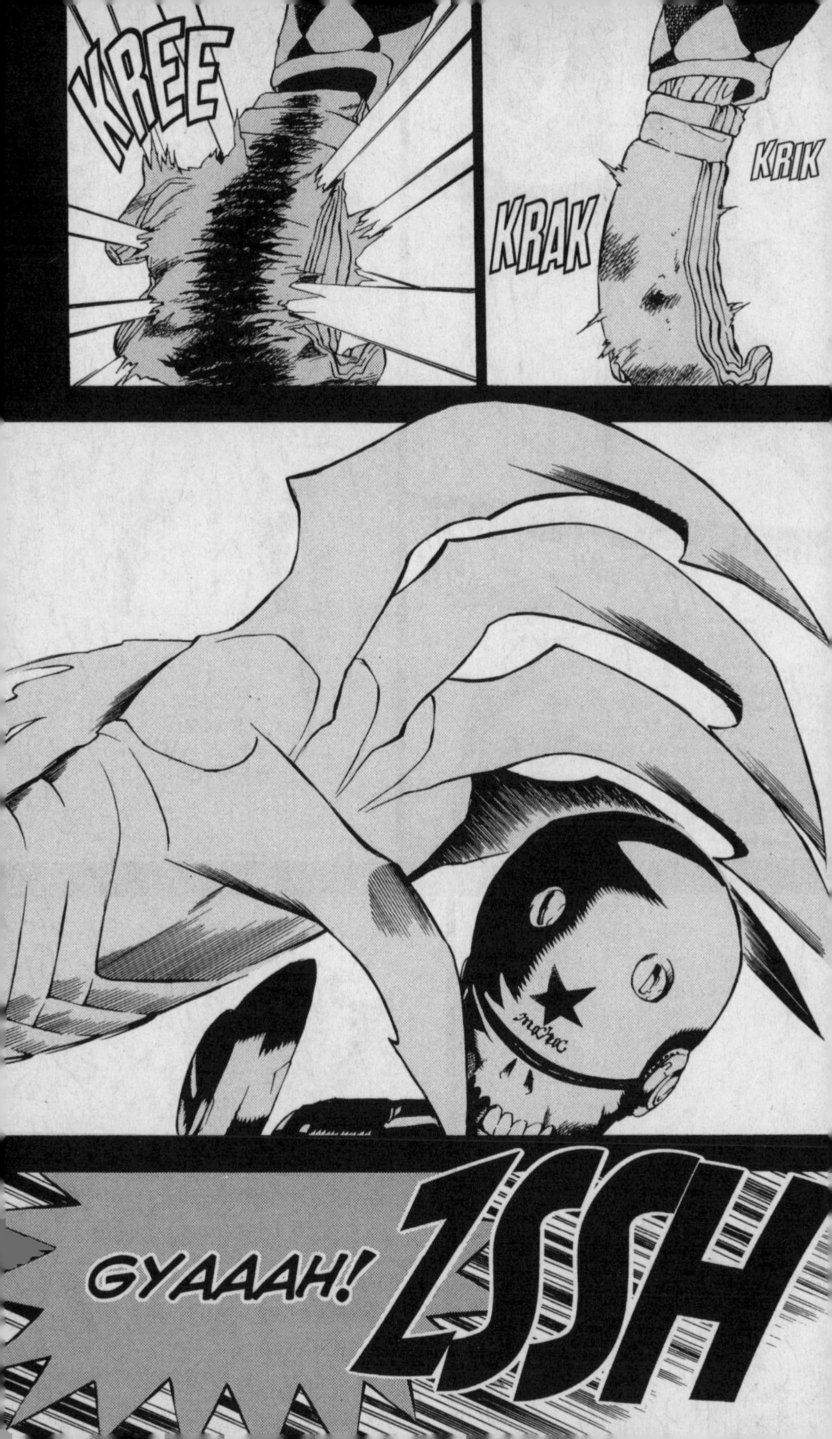
KRIK
KRAK
KREE
ZSSH
GYAAAH!

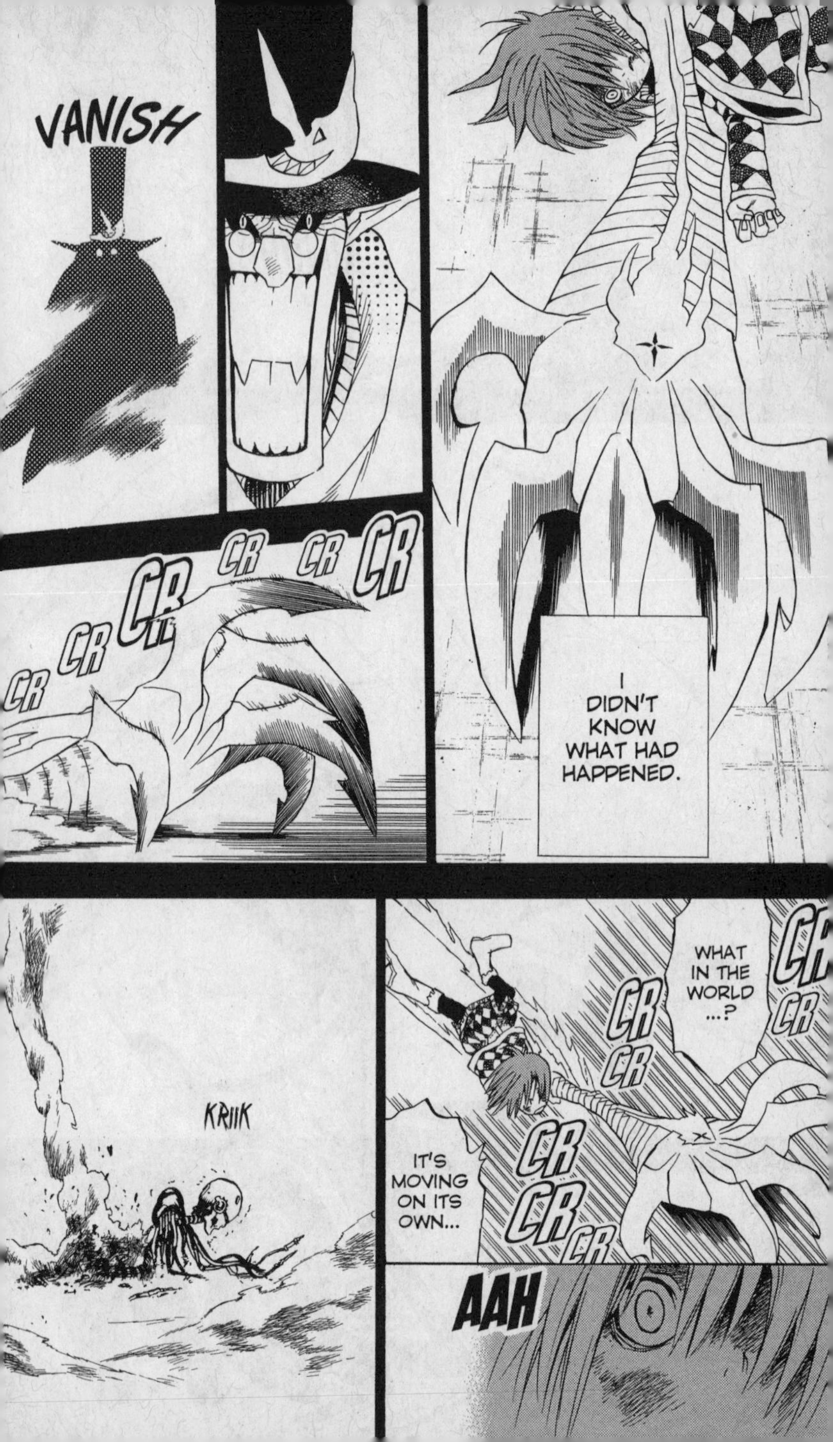
I DIDN'T KNOW WHAT HAD HAPPENED.
VANISH
CR CR CR
CR CR CR
WHAT IN THE WORLD ...?
CR CR
CR CR
IT'S MOVING ON ITS OWN...
CR CR CR
AAH
KRIIK

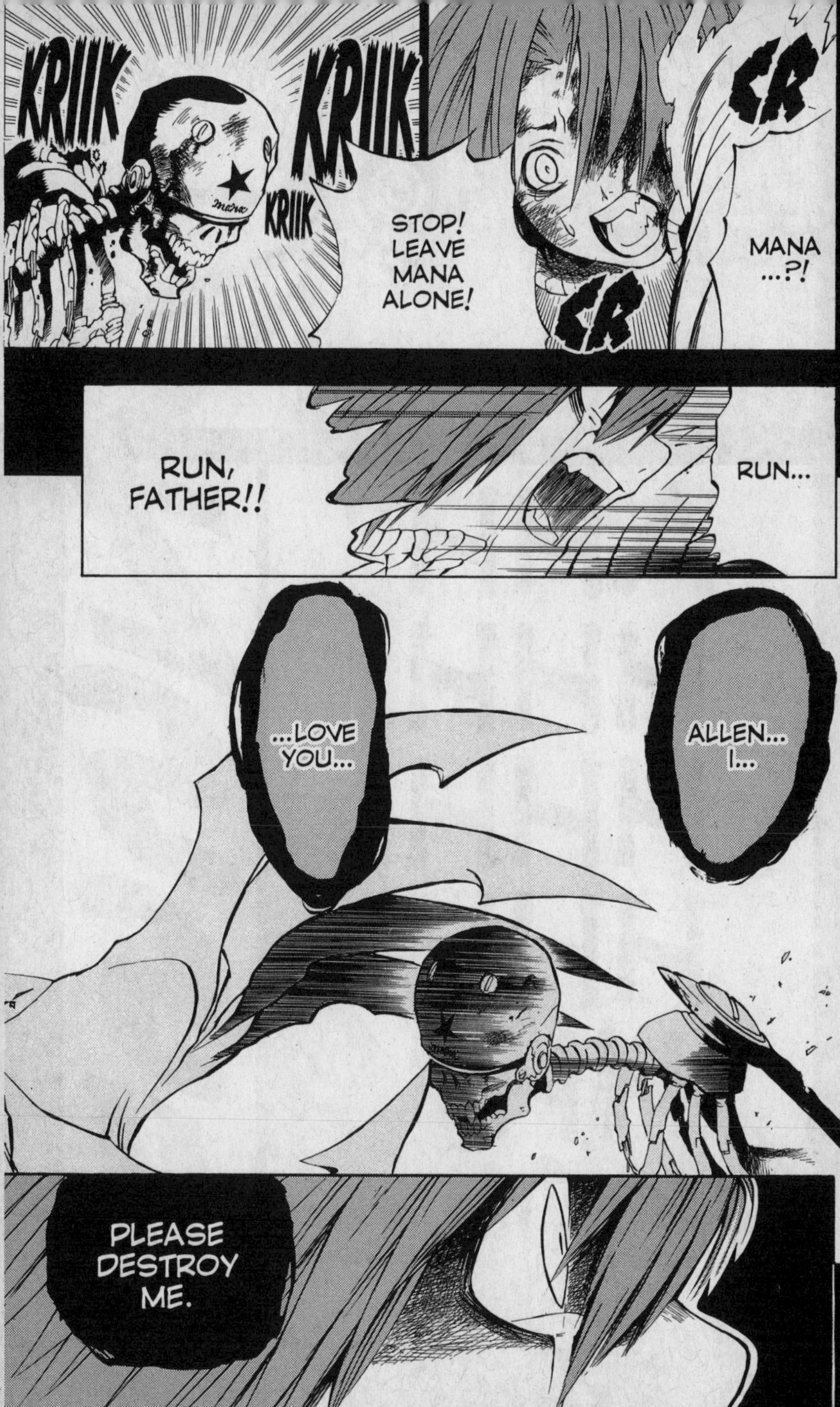

CR
MANA ...?!
CR
STOP! LEAVE MANA ALONE!
KRIIK
KRIIK
KRIIK
RUN...
RUN, FATHER!!
ALLEN... I...
...LOVE YOU...
PLEASE DESTROY ME.

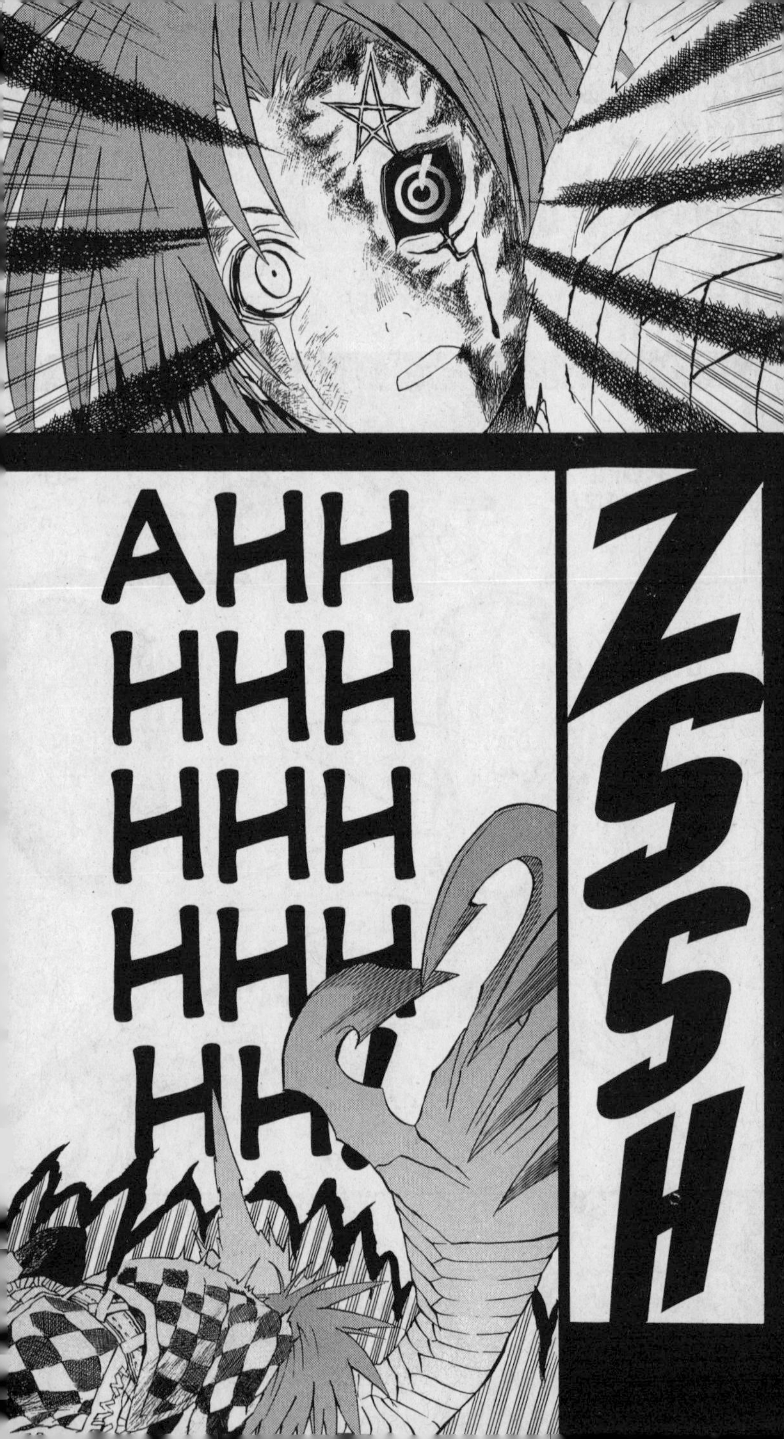
ZSSH
AHHHHHHHHHHHHH...

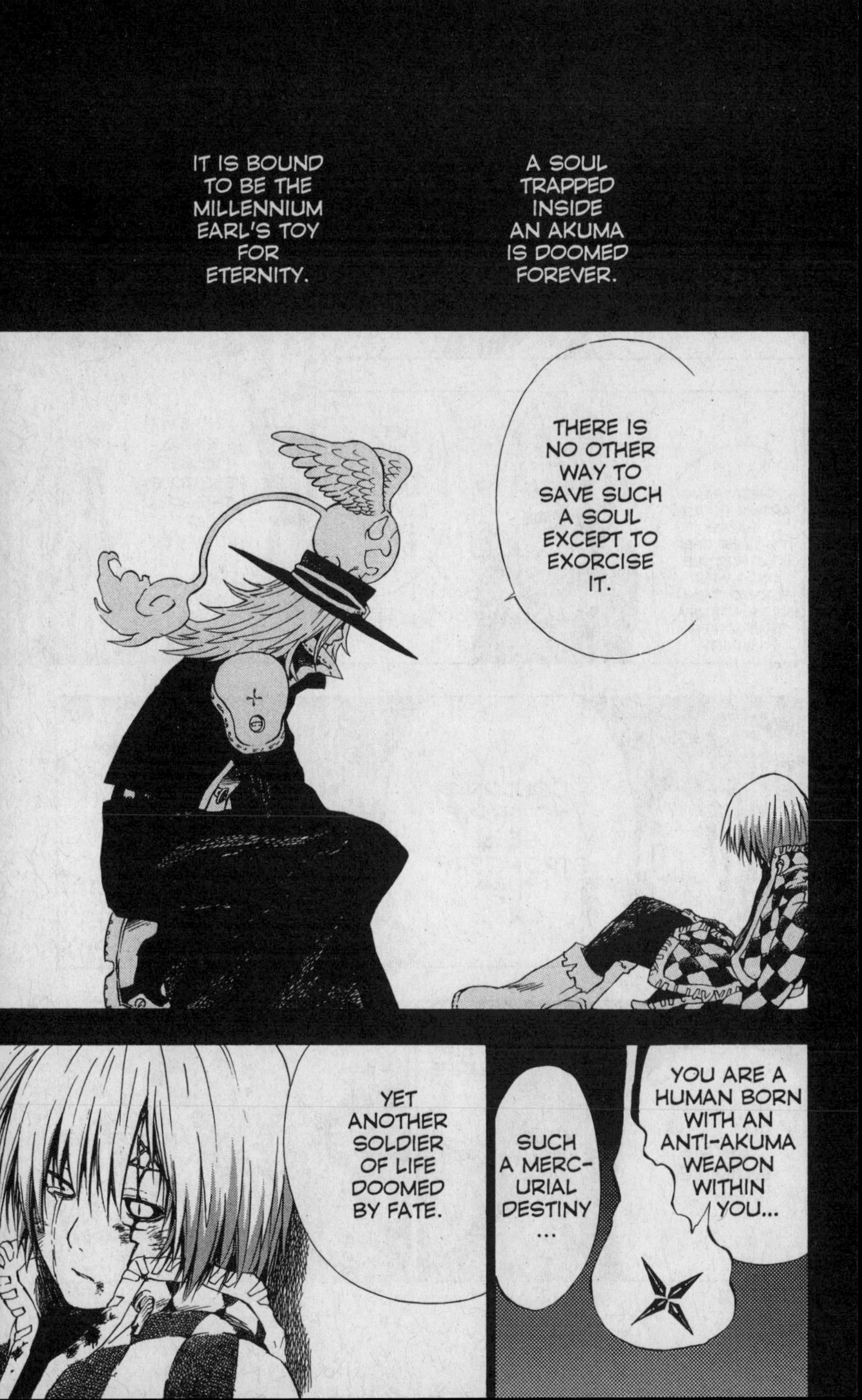
A SOUL TRAPPED INSIDE AN AKUMA IS DOOMED FOREVER.
IT IS BOUND TO BE THE MILLENNIUM EARL'S TOY FOR ETERNITY.
THERE IS NO OTHER WAY TO SAVE SUCH A SOUL EXCEPT TO EXORCISE IT.
YOU ARE A HUMAN BORN WITH AN ANTI-AKUMA WEAPON WITHIN YOU...
SUCH A MERCURIAL DESTINY...
YET ANOTHER SOLDIER OF LIFE DOOMED BY FATE.

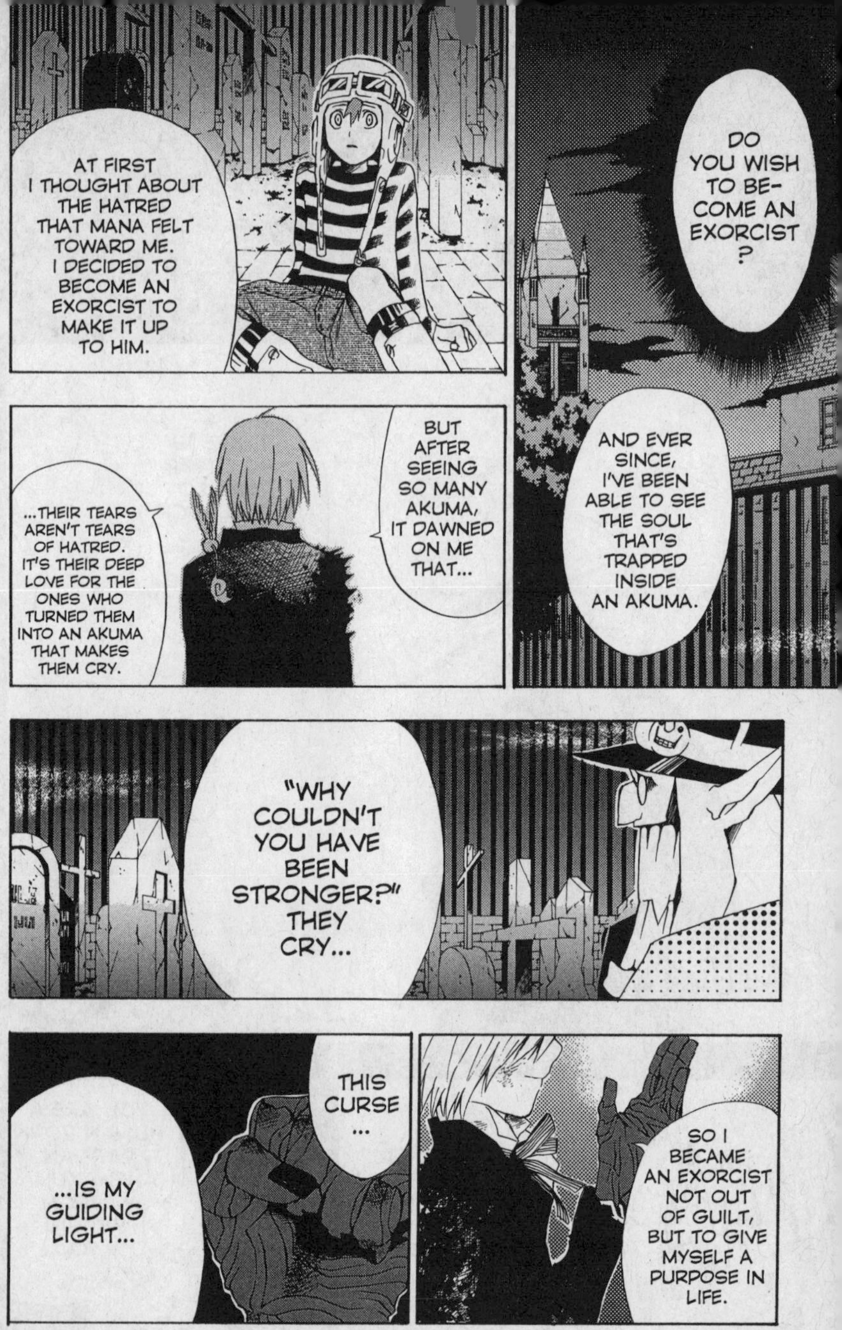
DO YOU WISH TO BE-COME AN EXORCIST?
AND EVER SINCE, I'VE BEEN ABLE TO SEE THE SOUL THAT'S TRAPPED INSIDE AN AKUMA.
AT FIRST I THOUGHT ABOUT THE HATRED THAT MANA FELT TOWARD ME. I DECIDED TO BECOME AN EXORCIST TO MAKE IT UP TO HIM.
BUT AFTER SEEING SO MANY AKUMA, IT DAWNED ON ME THAT...
...THEIR TEARS AREN'T TEARS OF HATRED. IT'S THEIR DEEP LOVE FOR THE ONES WHO TURNED THEM INTO AN AKUMA THAT MAKES THEM CRY.
"WHY COULDN'T YOU HAVE BEEN STRONGER?" THEY CRY...
SO I BECAME AN EXORCIST NOT OUT OF GUILT, BUT TO GIVE MYSELF A PURPOSE IN LIFE.
THIS CURSE...
...IS MY GUIDING LIGHT...

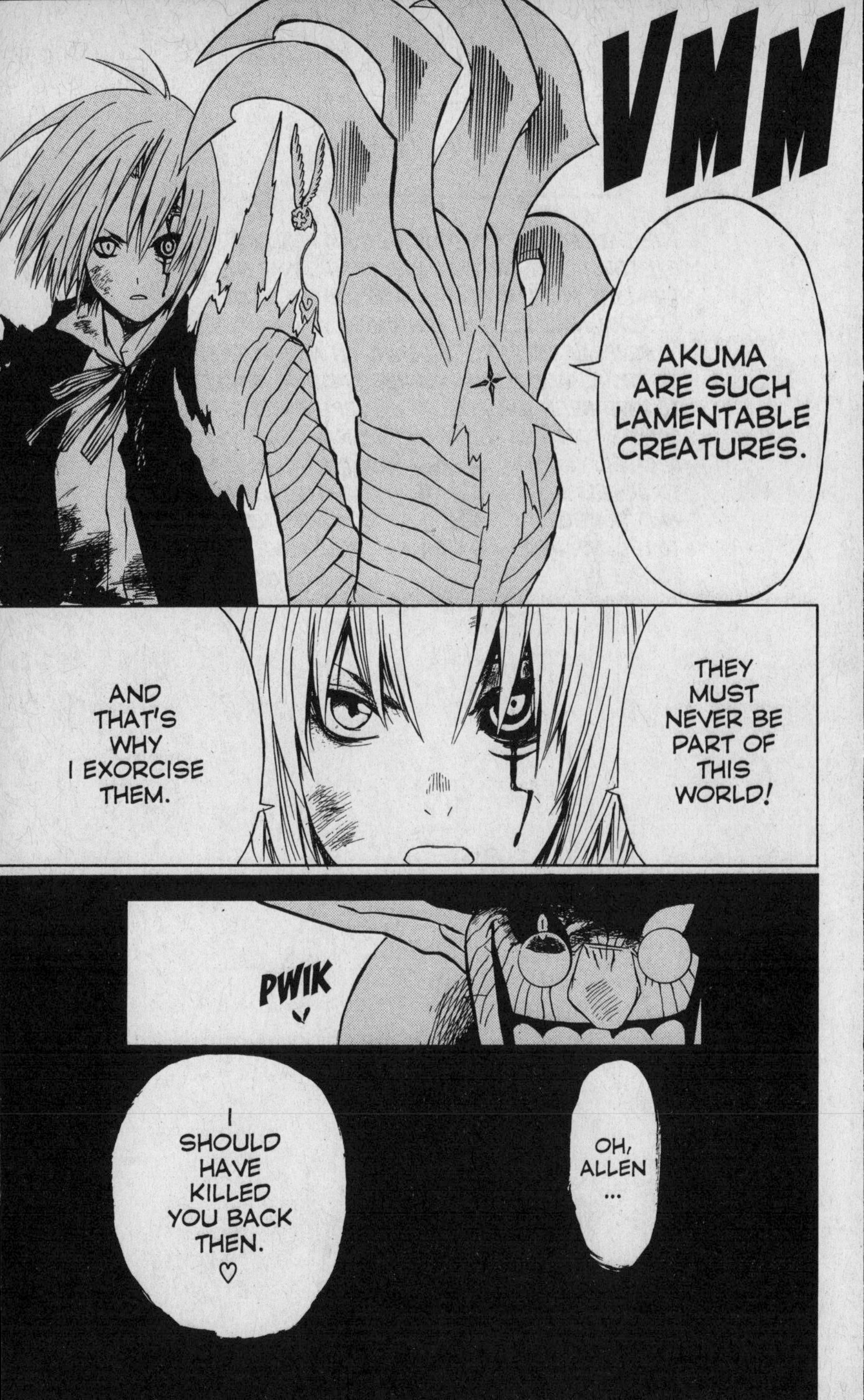
VMM
AKUMA ARE SUCH LAMENTABLE CREATURES.
THEY MUST NEVER BE PART OF THIS WORLD!
AND THAT'S WHY I EXORCISE THEM.
PWIK
OH, ALLEN ...
I SHOULD HAVE KILLED YOU BACK THEN. ♡

THE MILLENNIUM EARL

THE EARL IS BASED ON SOMEONE WHO REALLY EXISTED. I CAN'T SAY HIS NAME, BUT HE WAS ONE OF THE MOST PECULIAR PEOPLE WHO HAD EVER LIVED. HE COMMANDED SEVERAL LANGUAGES, WAS A MASTER OF SEVERAL ACADEMIC FIELDS AND AN ACCOMPLISHED ARTIST. HE WAS ALSO A PROPHET WHO WAS RUMORED TO HAVE BEEN IMMORTAL, AS HIS APPEARANCE DID NOT CHANGE PAST THE AGE OF 50, EVEN AFTER SEVERAL DECADES. THAT'S AMAZING. HE REFERRED TO HIMSELF AS "THE ALCHEMIST WHO TRAVELS TIME". ACCORDING TO LEGEND, HE'S STILL ALIVE SOME- WHERE IN THIS WORLD.

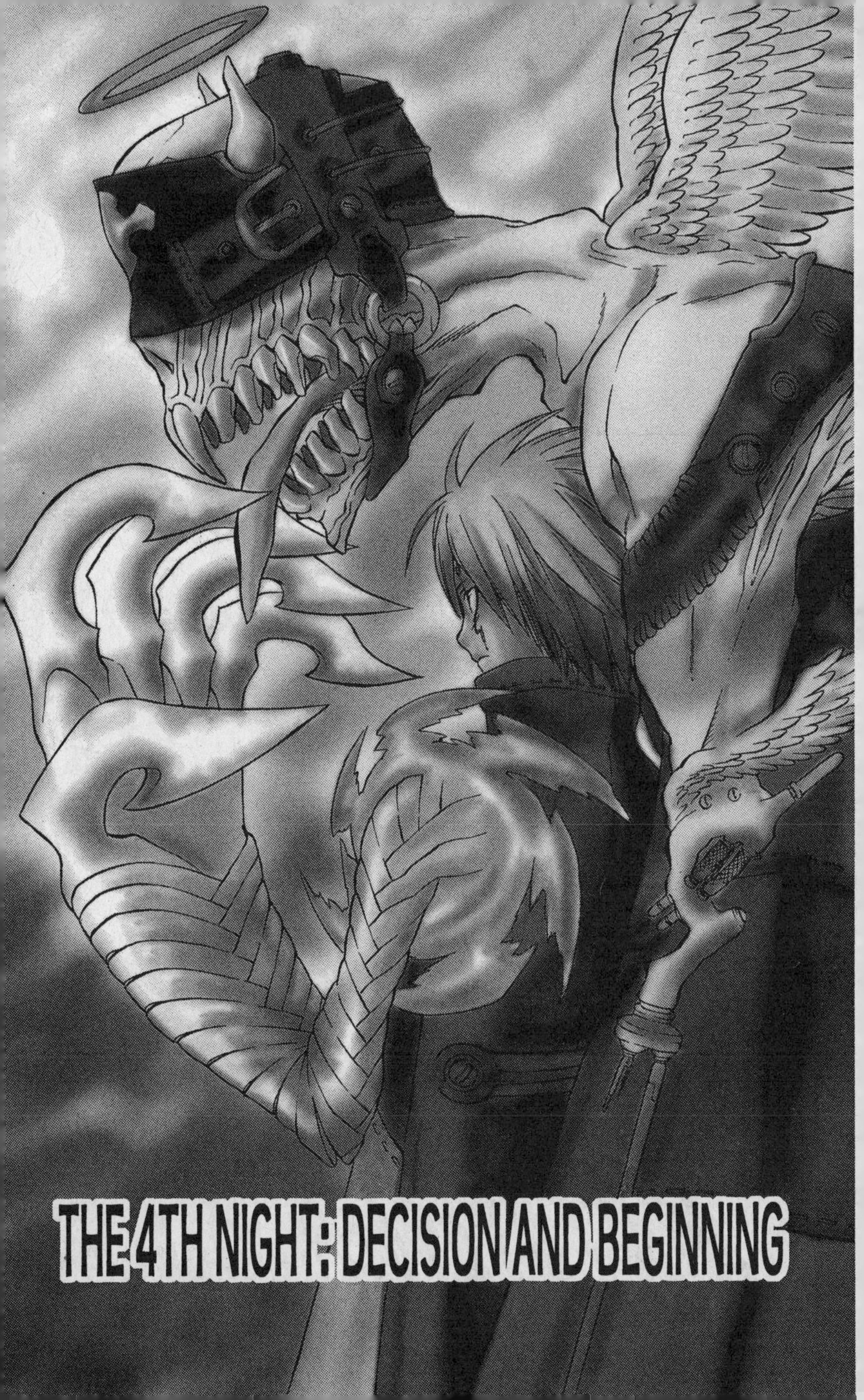
THE 4TH NIGHT: DECISION AND BEGINNING

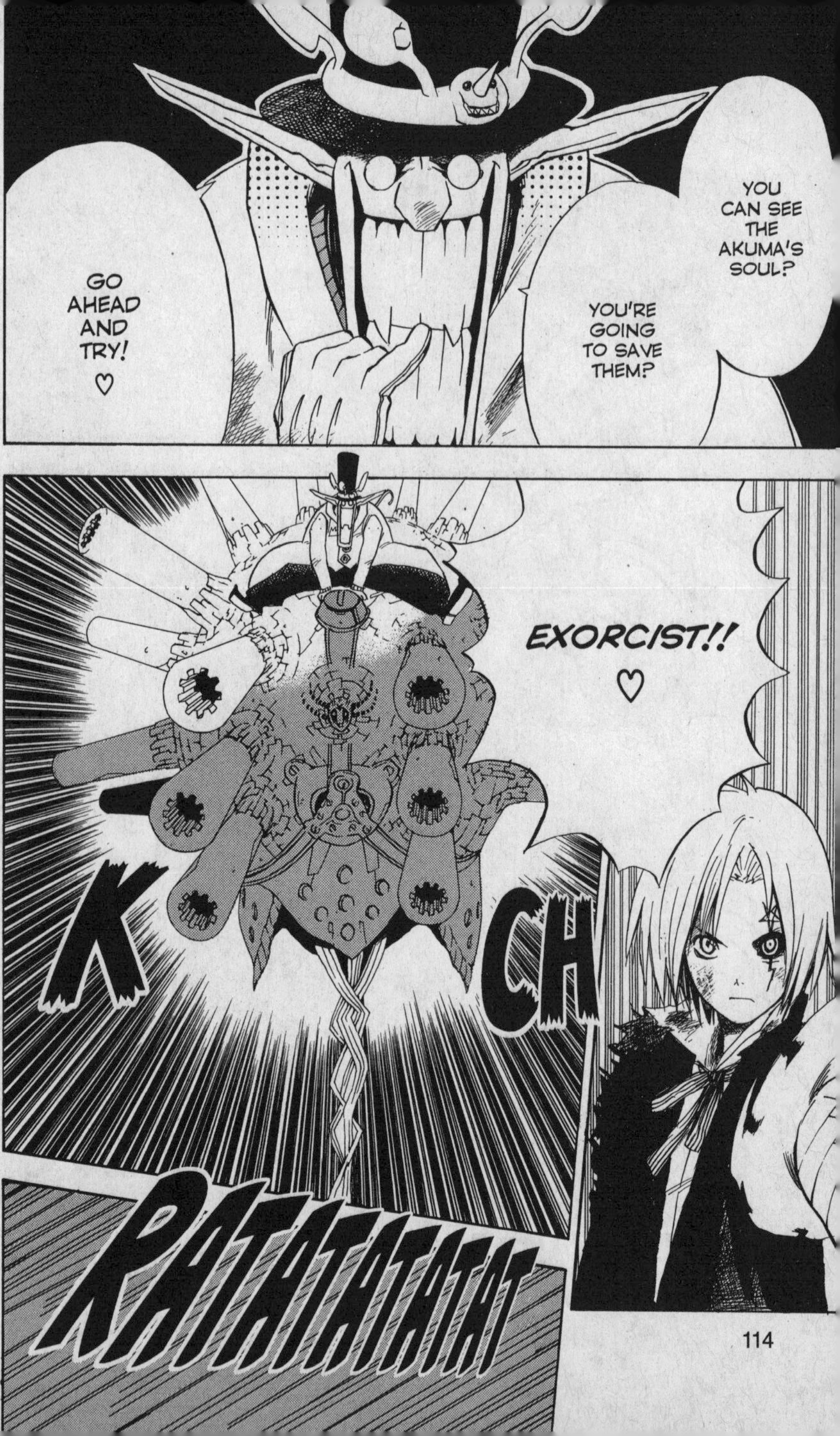

YOU CAN SEE THE AKUMA'S SOUL?
YOU'RE GOING TO SAVE THEM?
GO AHEAD AND TRY! ♡
EXORCIST!! ♡
K
CH
RATATATATAT

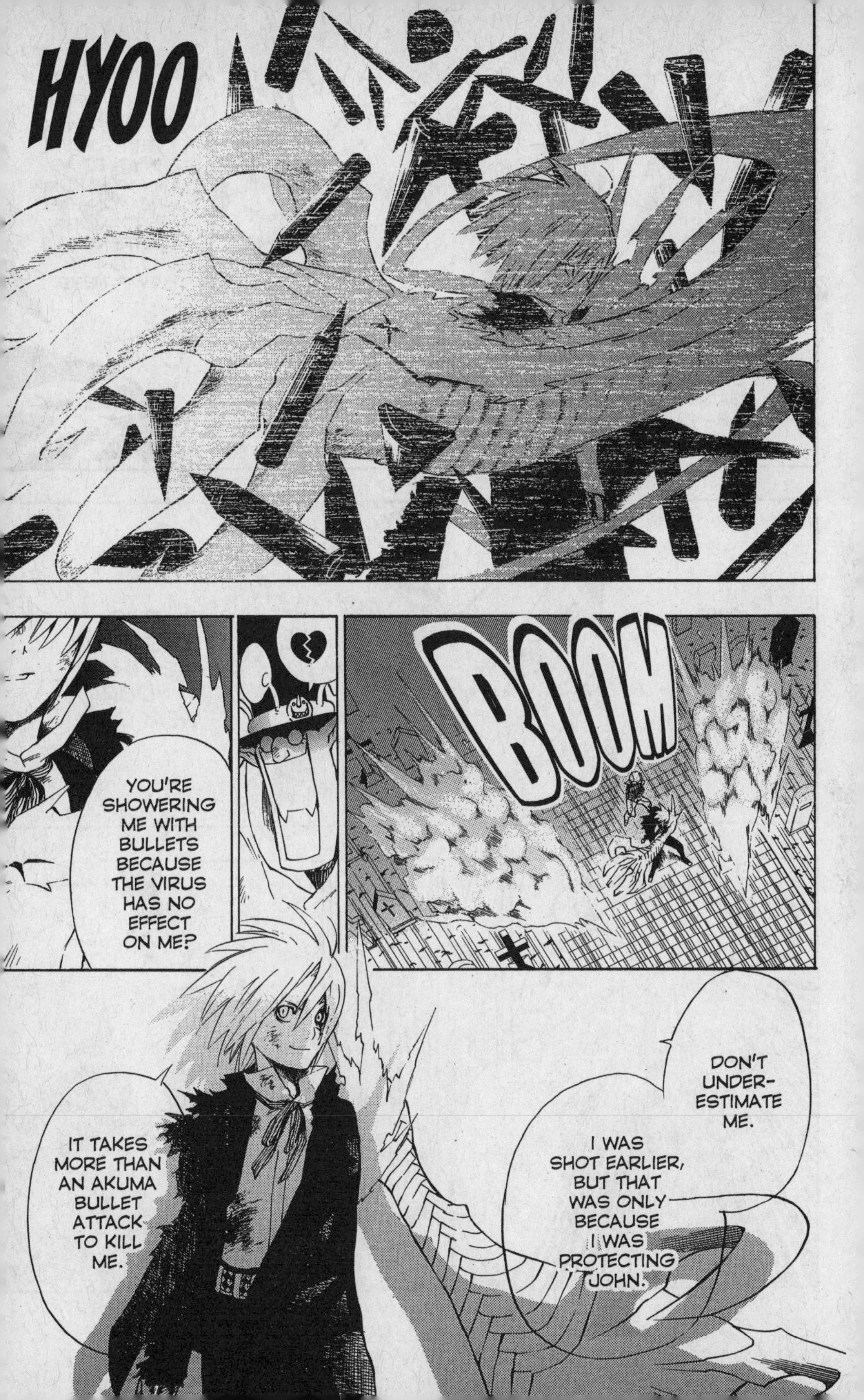
HYOO
BOOM
YOU'RE SHOWERING ME WITH BULLETS BECAUSE THE VIRUS HAS NO EFFECT ON ME?
DON'T UNDER-ESTIMATE ME.
I WAS SHOT EARLIER, BUT THAT WAS ONLY BECAUSE I WAS PROTECTING JOHN.
IT TAKES MORE THAN AN AKUMA BULLET ATTACK TO KILL ME.

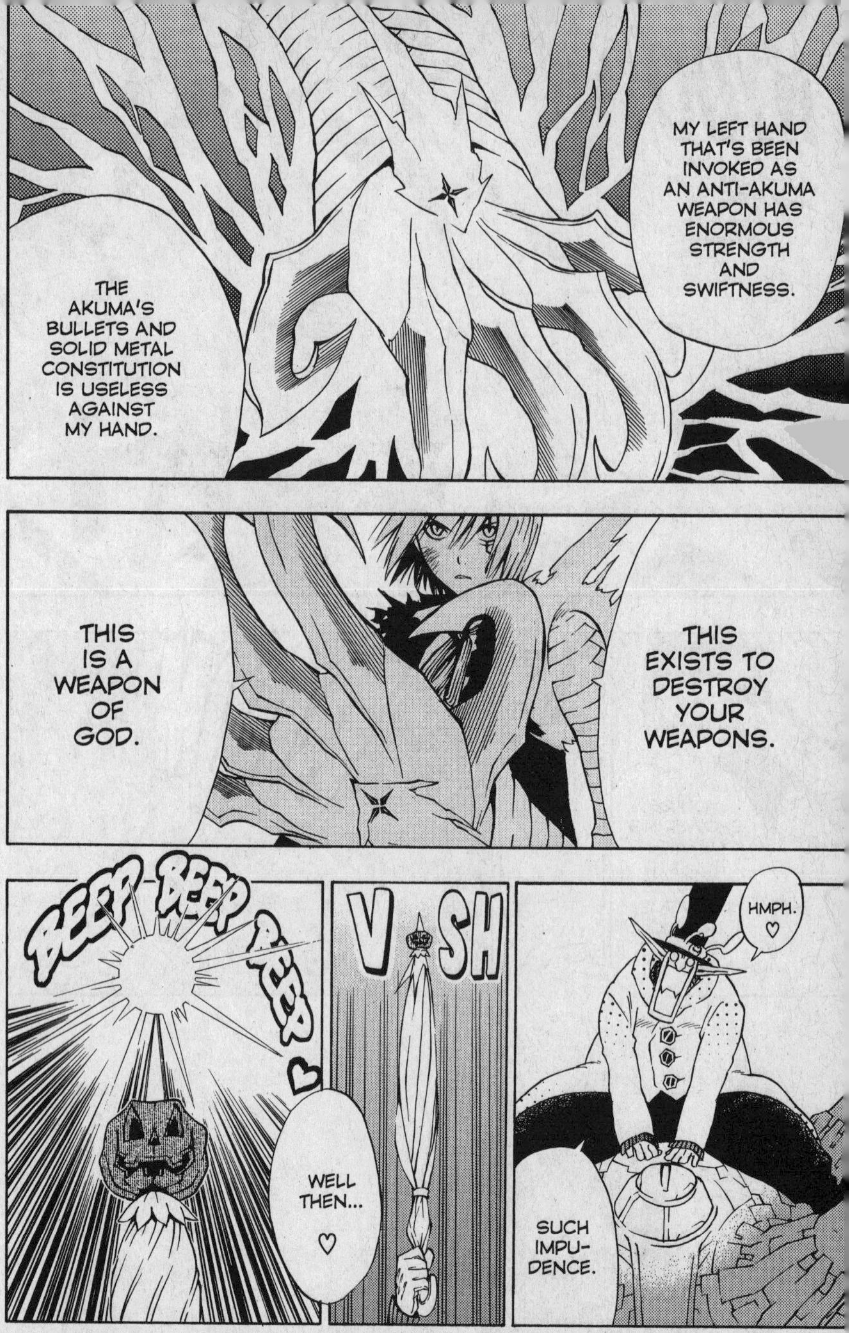
MY LEFT HAND THAT'S BEEN INVOKED AS AN ANTI-AKUMA WEAPON HAS ENORMOUS STRENGTH AND SWIFTNESS.
THE AKUMA'S BULLETS AND SOLID METAL CONSTITUTION IS USELESS AGAINST MY HAND.
THIS EXISTS TO DESTROY YOUR WEAPONS.
THIS IS A WEAPON OF GOD.
HMPH. ♡
SUCH IMPU-DENCE.
VSH
WELL THEN... ♡
BEEP-BEEP BEEP ♡

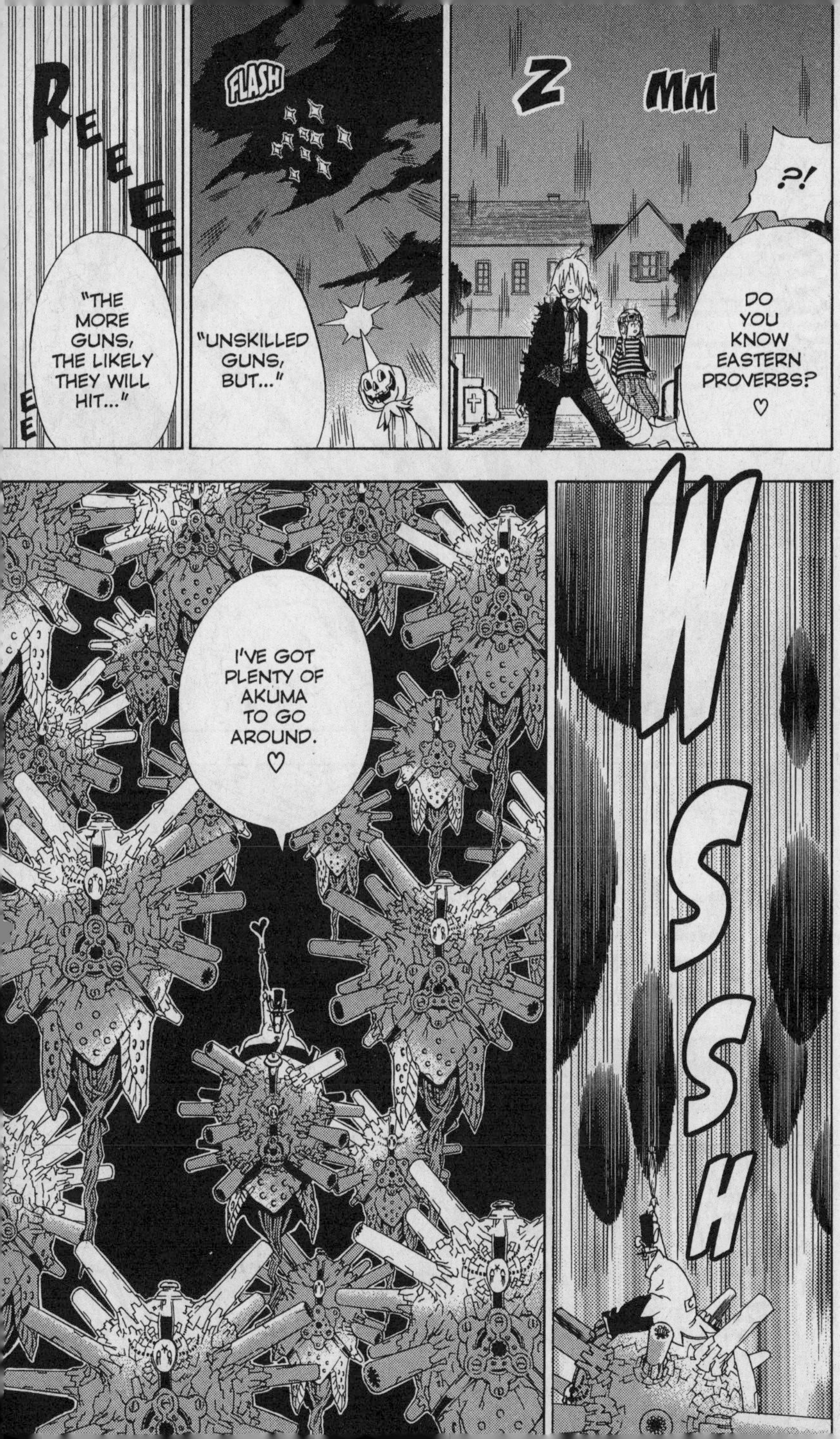
ZMM
?!
DO YOU KNOW EASTERN PROVERBS? ♡
FLASH
"UNSKILLED GUNS, BUT..."
REEEEEEE
"THE MORE GUNS, THE LIKELY THEY WILL HIT..."
WHSSH
I'VE GOT PLENTY OF AKUMA TO GO AROUND. ♡

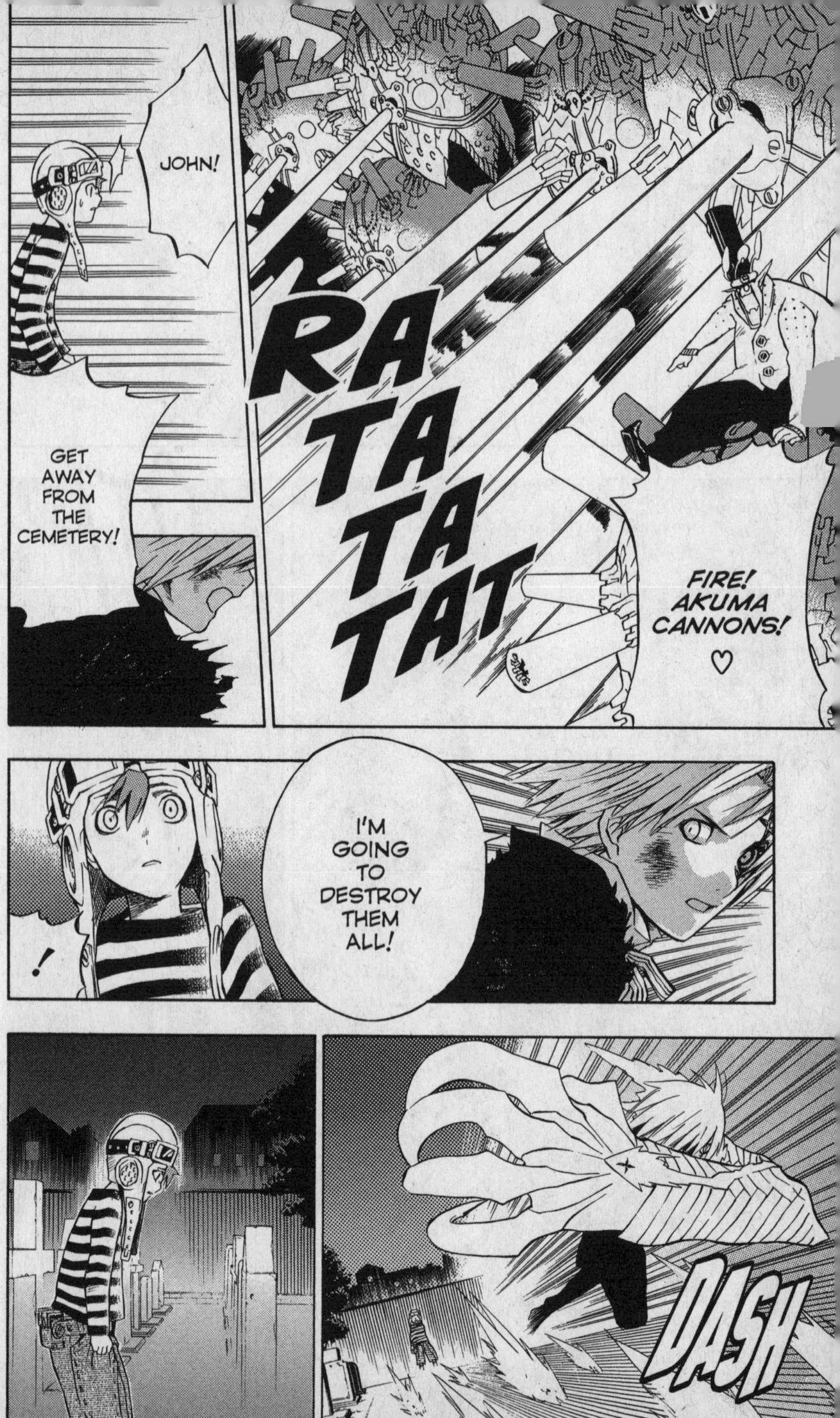
FIRE! AKUMA CANNONS! ♡
RA TA TA TAT
JOHN!
GET AWAY FROM THE CEMETERY!
I'M GOING TO DESTROY THEM ALL!
!
DASH

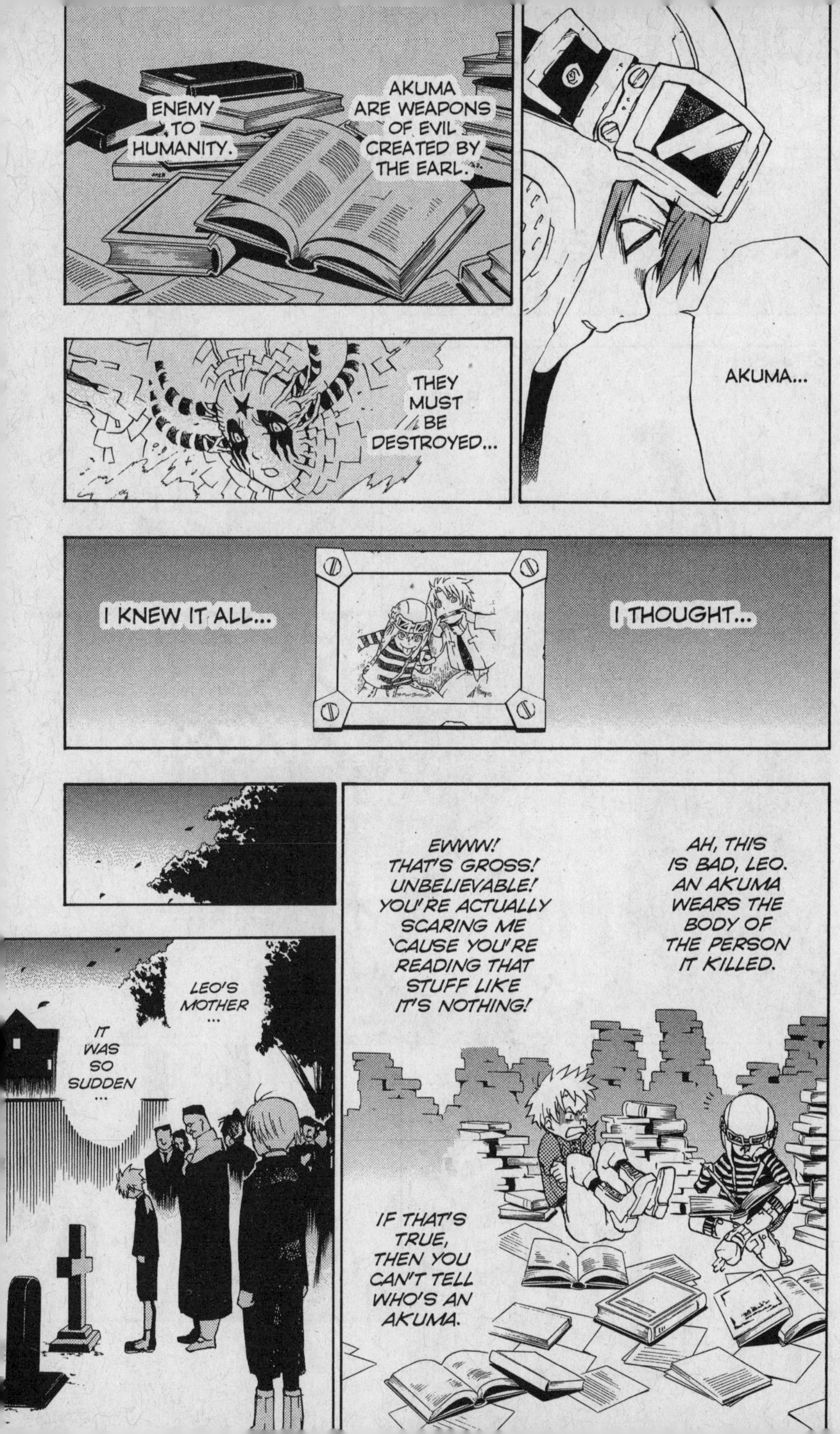
AKUMA...
AKUMA ARE WEAPONS OF EVIL CREATED BY THE EARL.
ENEMY TO HUMANITY.
THEY MUST BE DESTROYED...
I THOUGHT...
I KNEW IT ALL...
AH, THIS IS BAD, LEO. AN AKUMA WEARS THE BODY OF THE PERSON IT KILLED.
EWWW! THAT'S GROSS! UNBELIEVABLE! YOU'RE ACTUALLY SCARING ME 'CAUSE YOU'RE READING THAT STUFF LIKE IT'S NOTHING!
IF THAT'S TRUE, THEN YOU CAN'T TELL WHO'S AN AKUMA.
LEO'S MOTHER...
IT WAS SO SUDDEN...

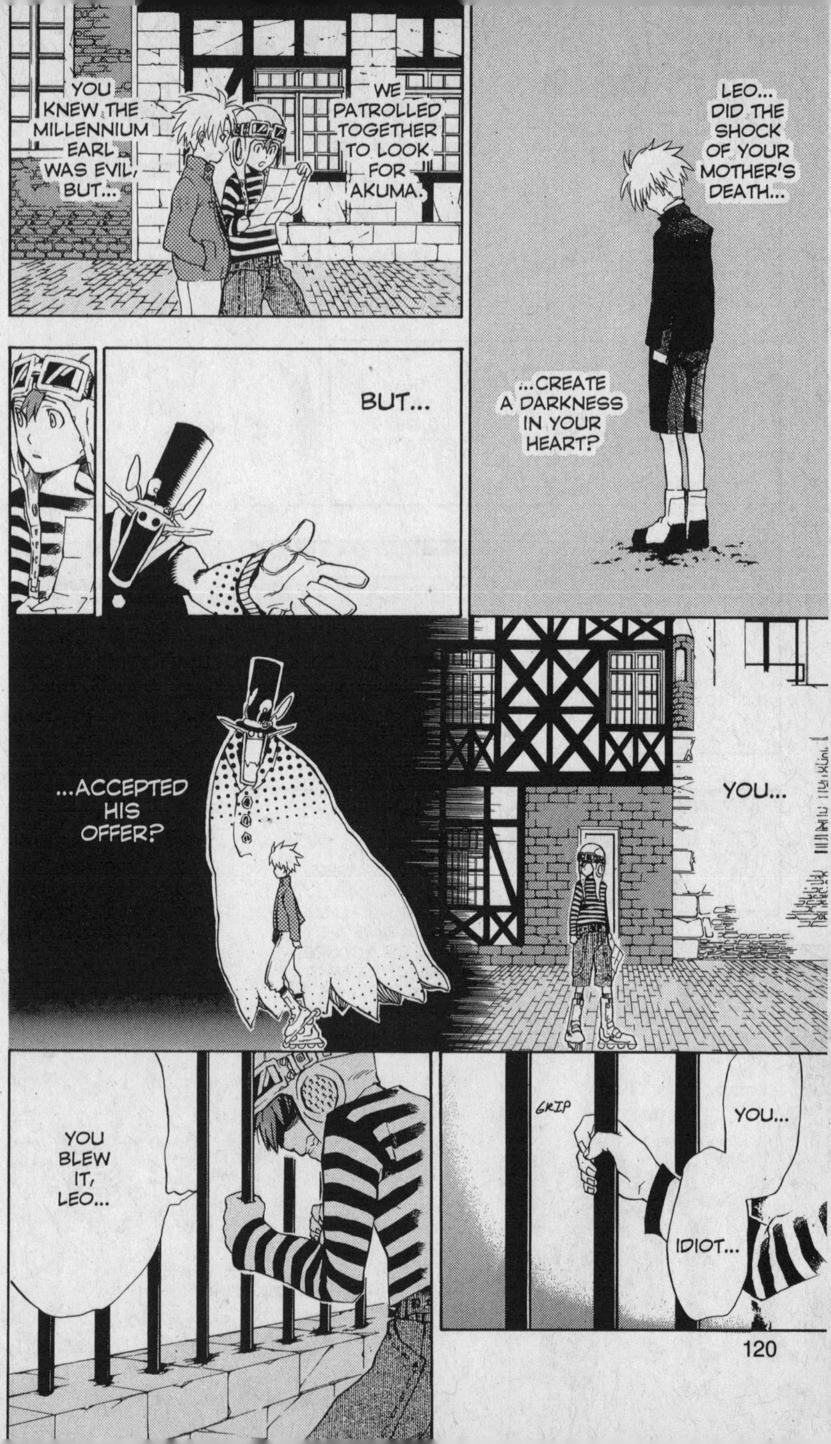

LEO... DID THE SHOCK OF YOUR MOTHER'S DEATH...
...CREATE A DARKNESS IN YOUR HEART?
WE PATROLLED TOGETHER TO LOOK FOR AKUMA.
YOU KNEW THE MILLENNIUM EARL WAS EVIL, BUT...
BUT...
YOU...
...ACCEPTED HIS OFFER?
GRIP
YOU...
IDIOT...
YOU BLEW IT, LEO...

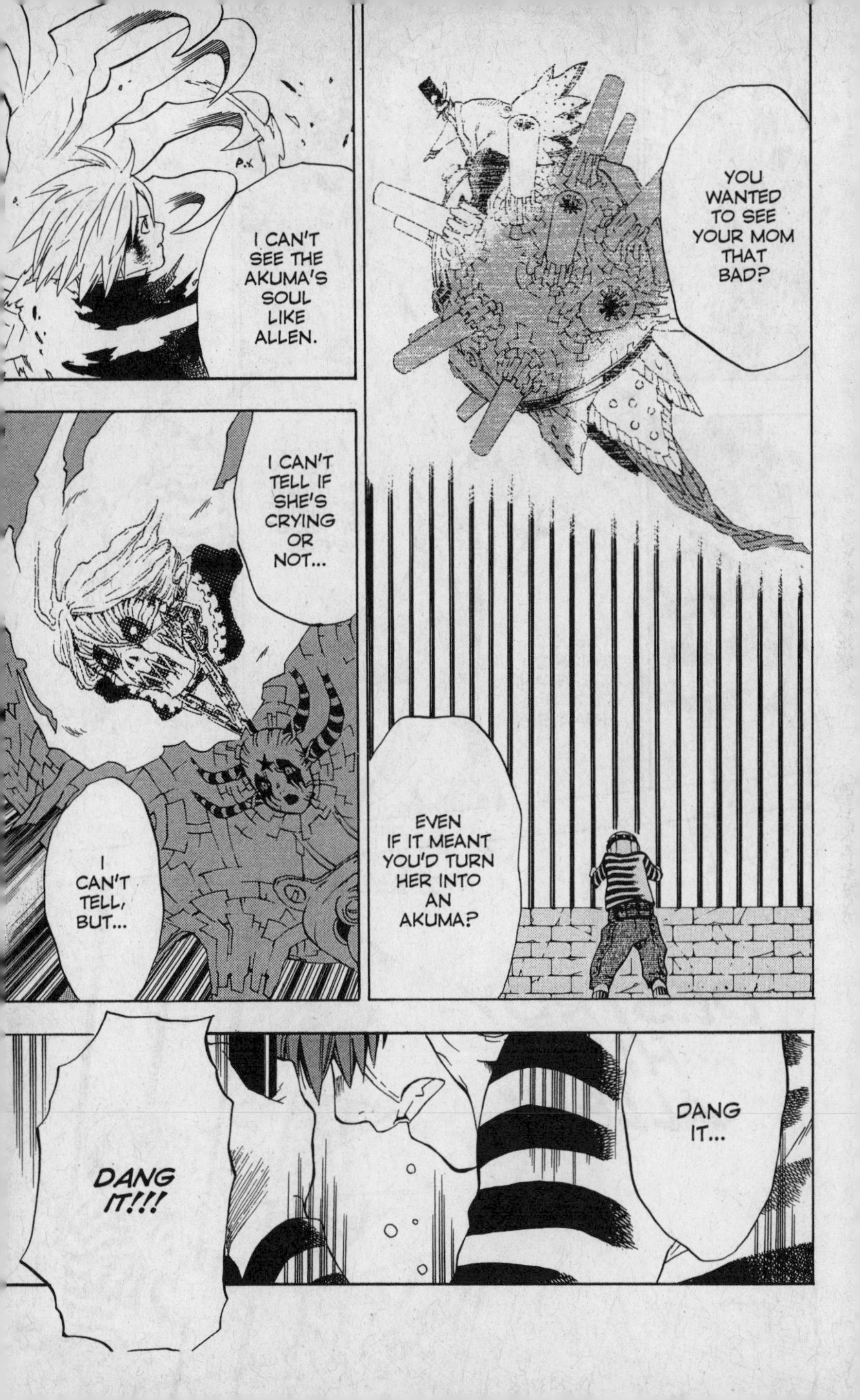
YOU WANTED TO SEE YOUR MOM THAT BAD?
EVEN IF IT MEANT YOU'D TURN HER INTO AN AKUMA?
I CAN'T SEE THE AKUMA'S SOUL LIKE ALLEN.
I CAN'T TELL IF SHE'S CRYING OR NOT...
I CAN'T TELL, BUT...
DANG IT...
DANG IT!!!

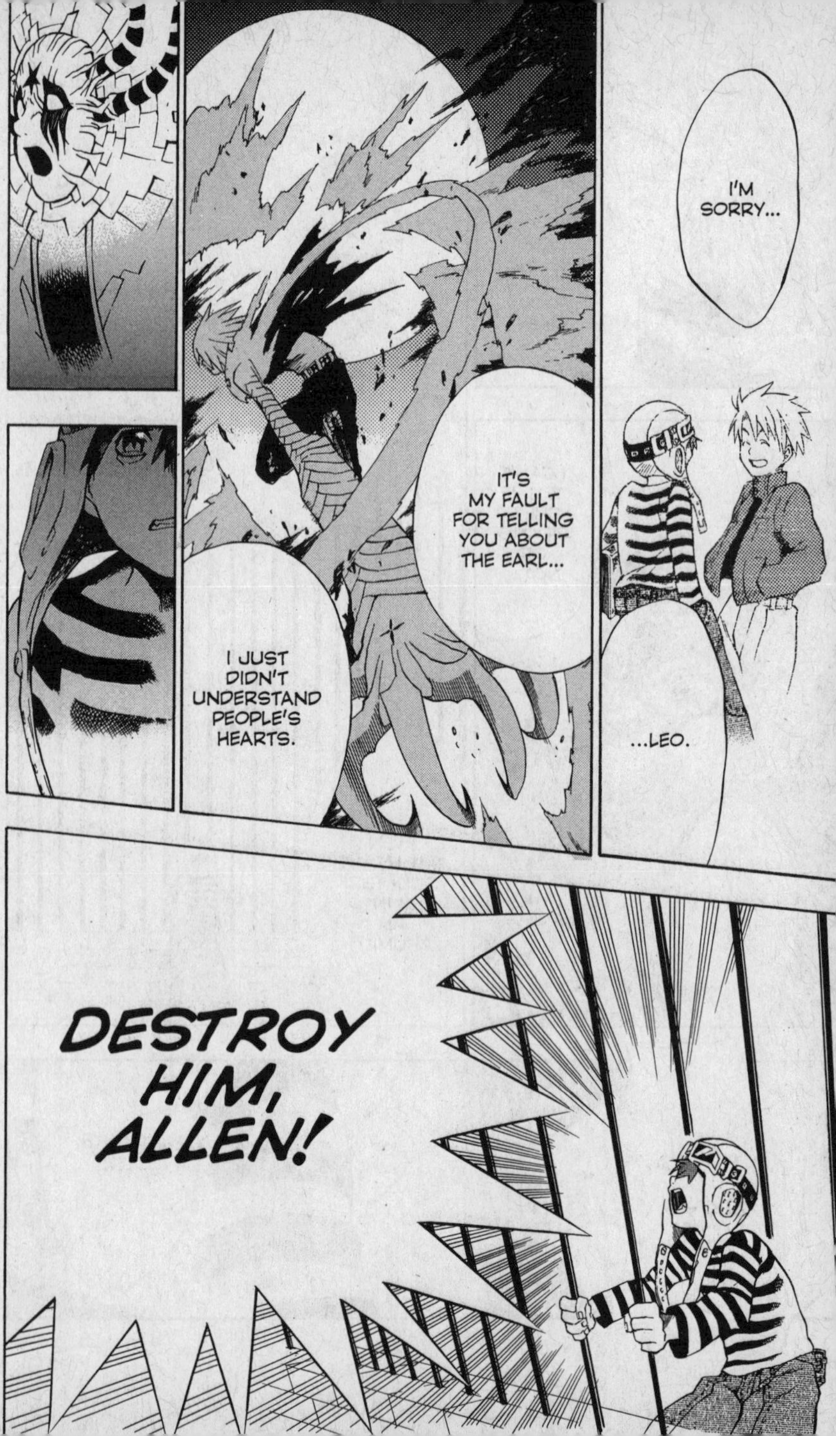
I'M SORRY...
...LEO.
IT'S MY FAULT FOR TELLING YOU ABOUT THE EARL...
I JUST DIDN'T UNDERSTAND PEOPLE'S HEARTS.
DESTROY HIM, ALLEN!

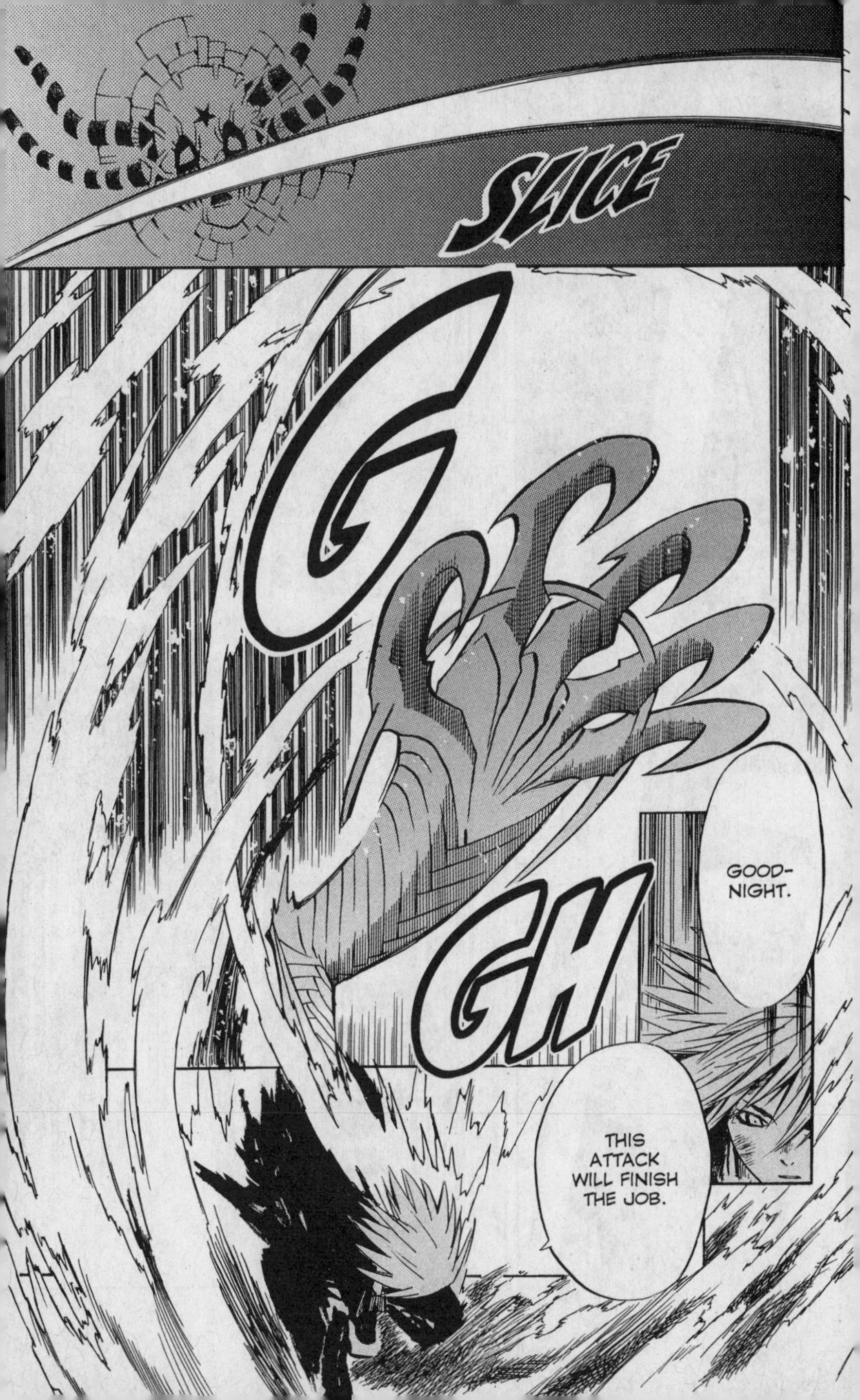
SLICE
GGGGH
GOOD-NIGHT.
THIS ATTACK WILL FINISH THE JOB.

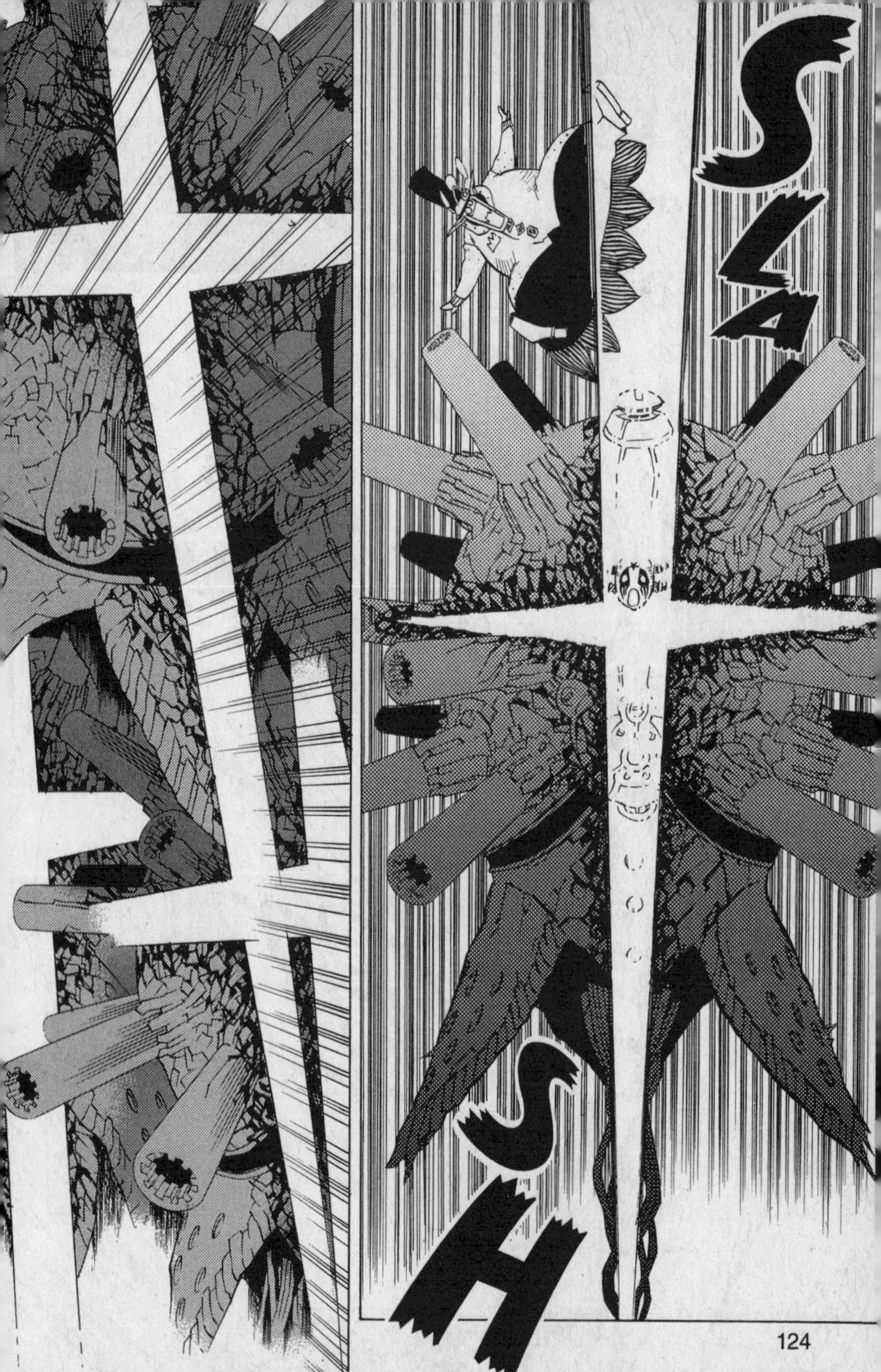
SLASH

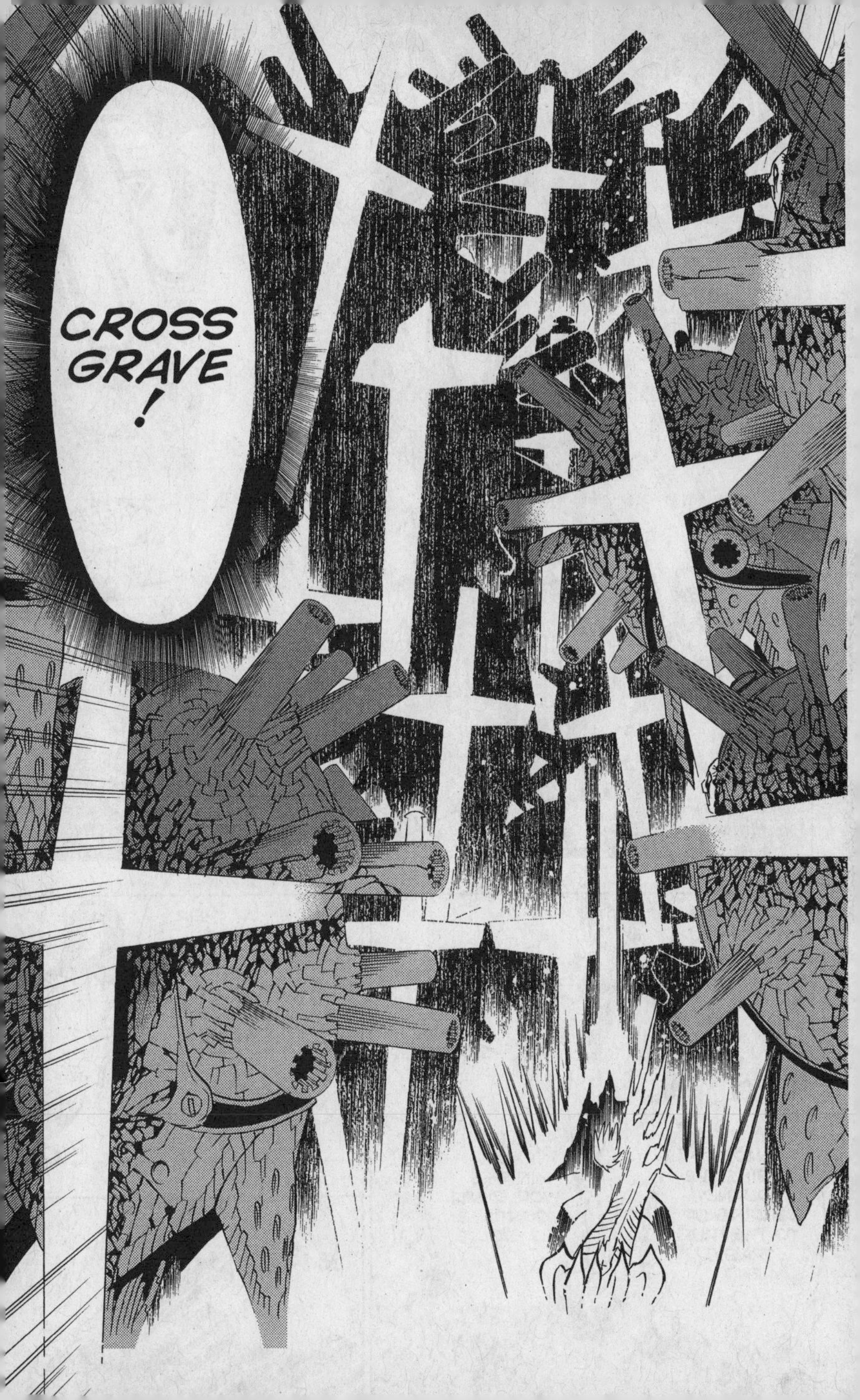
CROSS GRAVE!

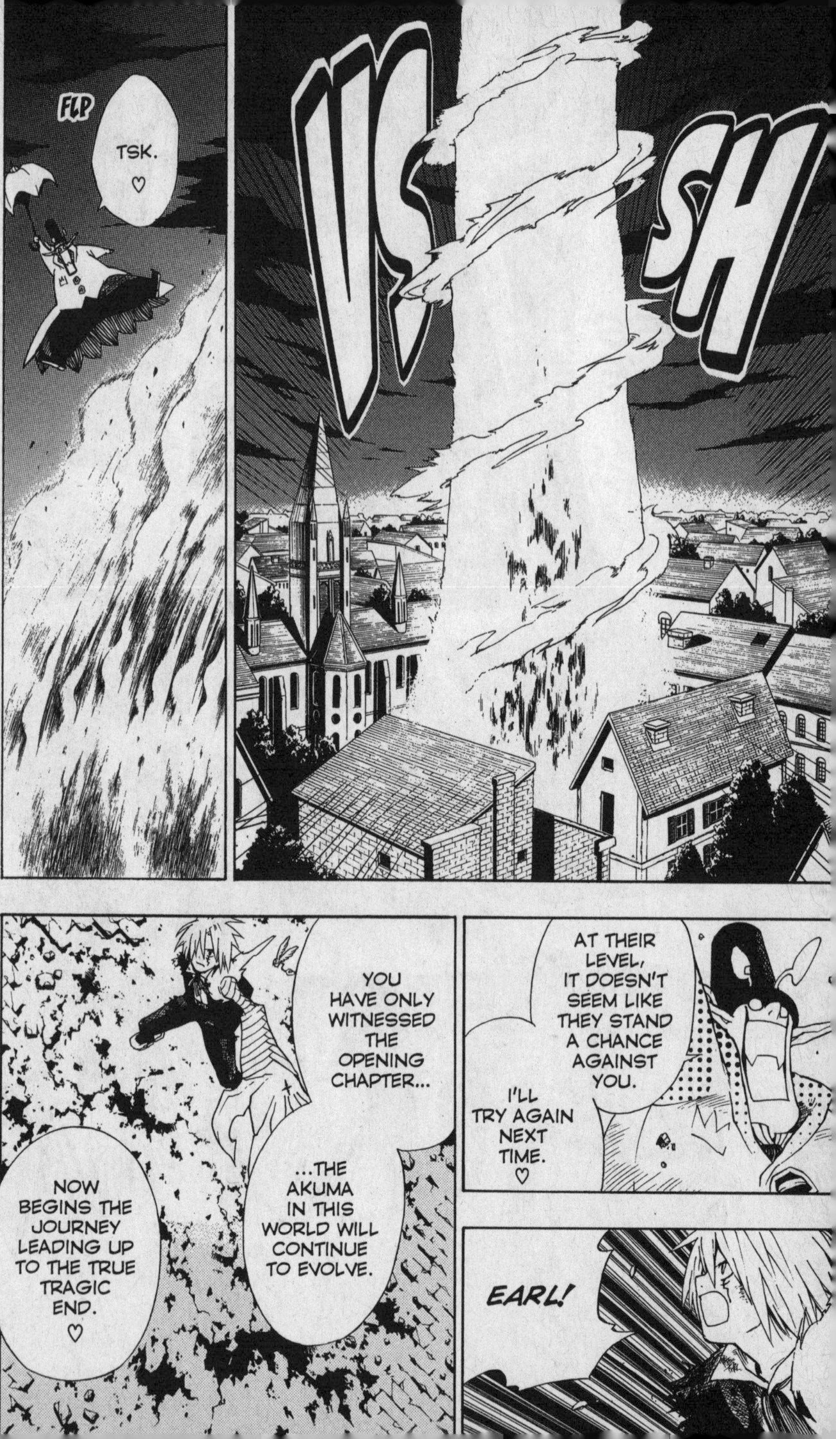
FLP
TSK. ♡
AT THEIR LEVEL, IT DOESN'T SEEM LIKE THEY STAND A CHANCE AGAINST YOU.
I'LL TRY AGAIN NEXT TIME. ♡
EARL!
YOU HAVE ONLY WITNESSED THE OPENING CHAPTER...
...THE AKUMA IN THIS WORLD WILL CONTINUE TO EVOLVE.
NOW BEGINS THE JOURNEY LEADING UP TO THE TRUE TRAGIC END. ♡

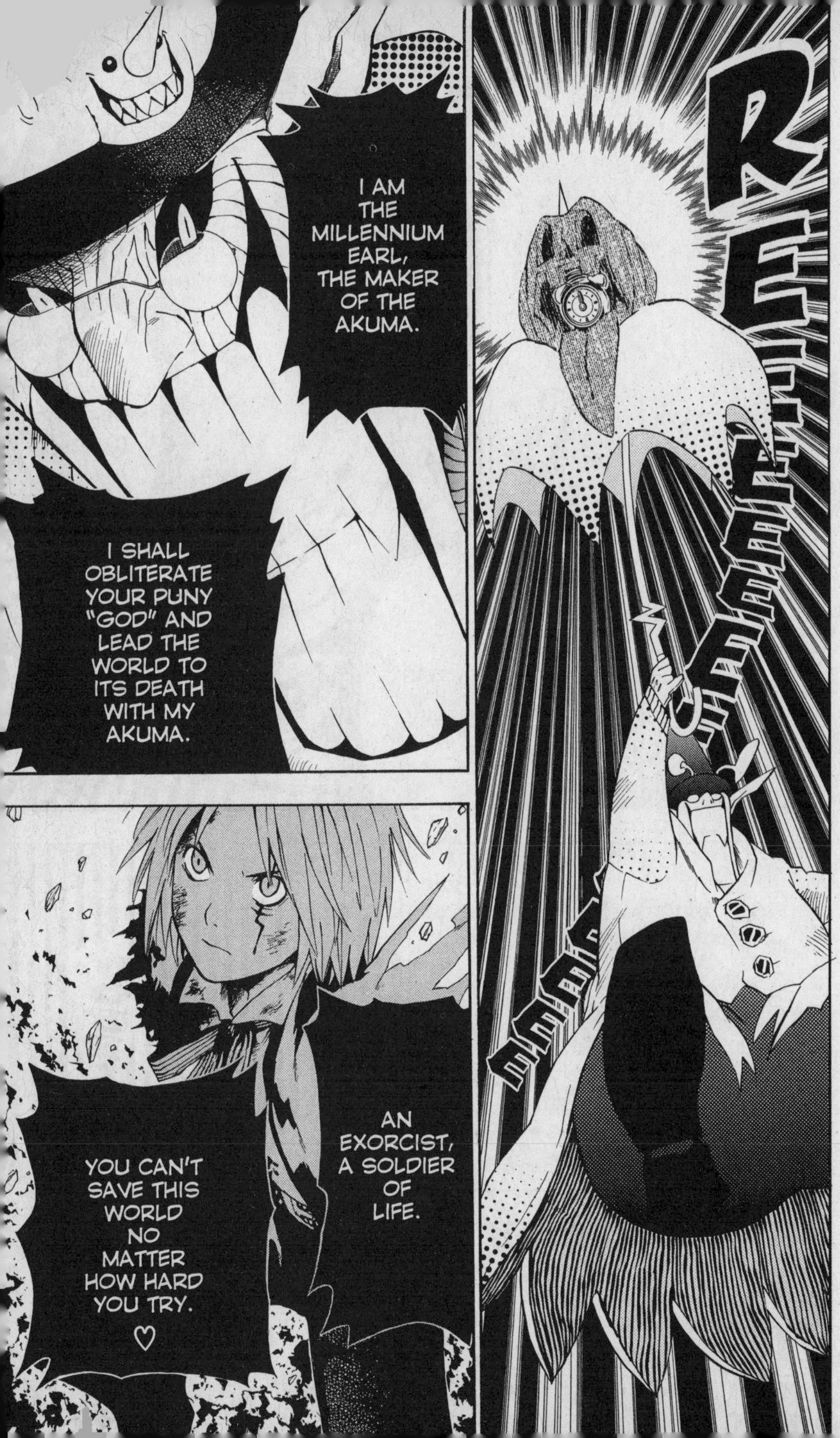
I AM THE MILLENNIUM EARL, THE MAKER OF THE AKUMA.
I SHALL OBLITERATE YOUR PUNY "GOD" AND LEAD THE WORLD TO ITS DEATH WITH MY AKUMA.
AN EXORCIST, A SOLDIER OF LIFE.
YOU CAN'T SAVE THIS WORLD NO MATTER HOW HARD YOU TRY. ♡

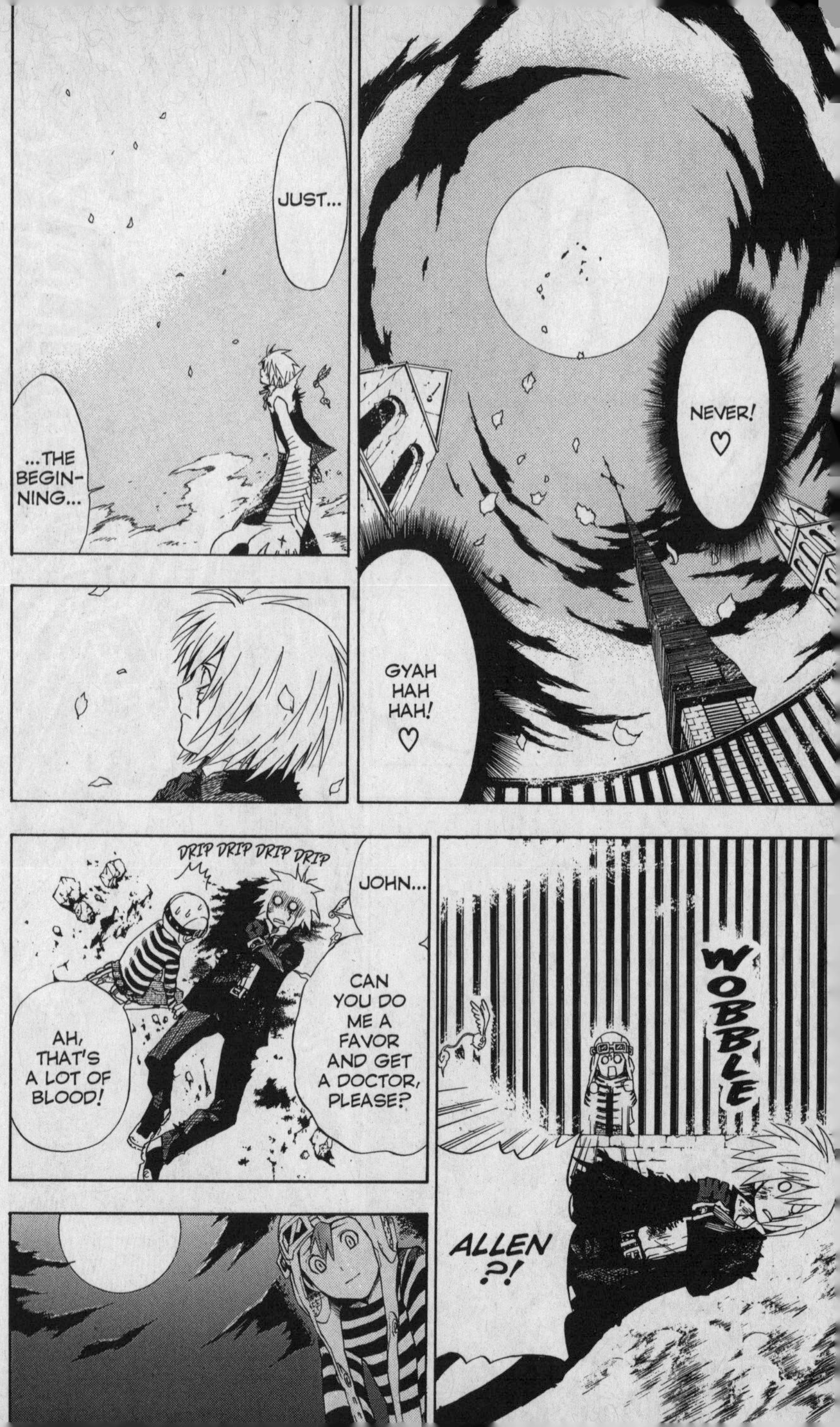
NEVER! ♡
GYAH HAH HAH! ♡
JUST...
...THE BEGIN-NING...
WOBBLE
ALLEN ?!
DRIP DRIP DRIP DRIP
JOHN...
CAN YOU DO ME A FAVOR AND GET A DOCTOR, PLEASE?
AH, THAT'S A LOT OF BLOOD!

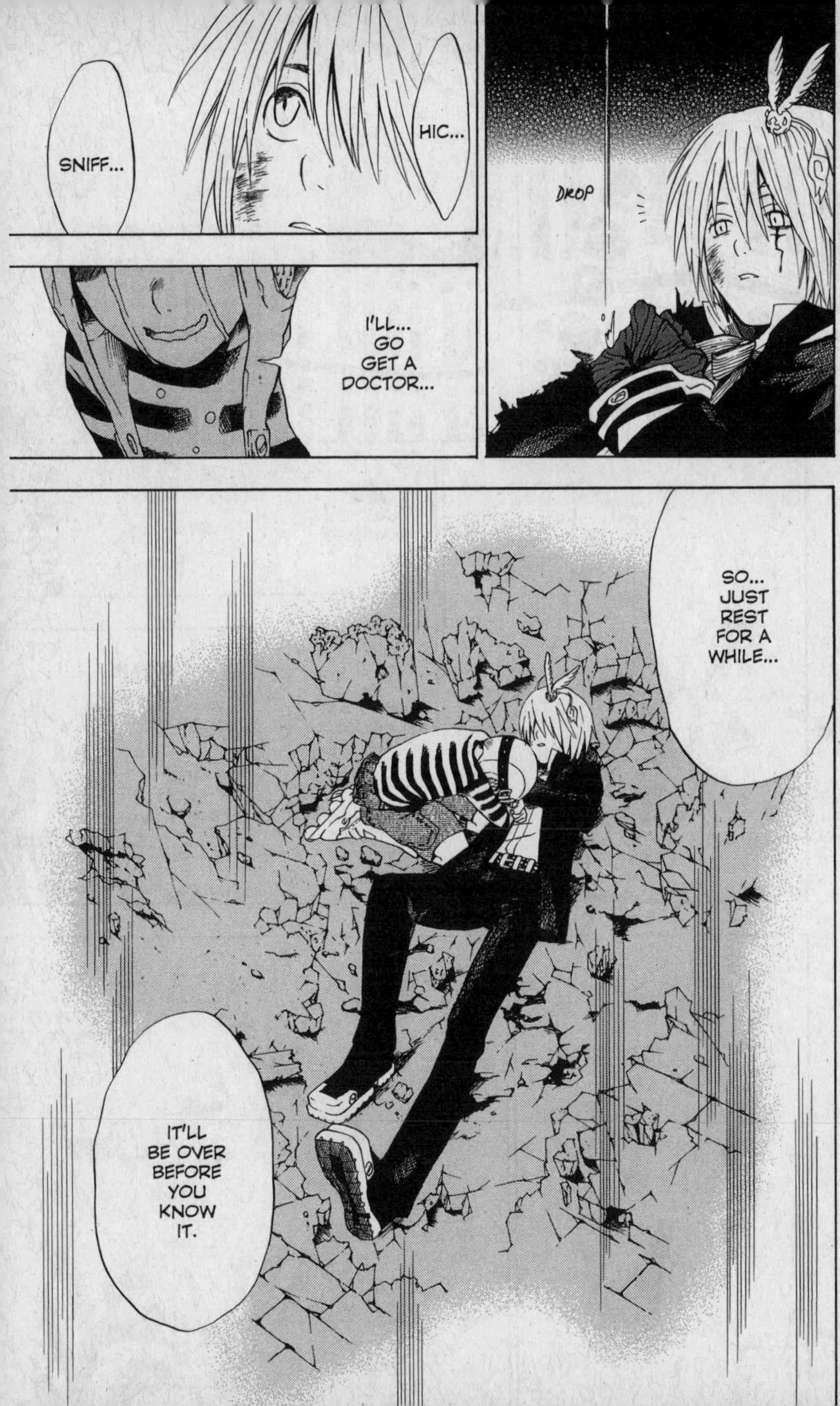
DROP
HIC...
SNIFF...
I'LL... GO GET A DOCTOR...
SO... JUST REST FOR A WHILE...
IT'LL BE OVER BEFORE YOU KNOW IT.

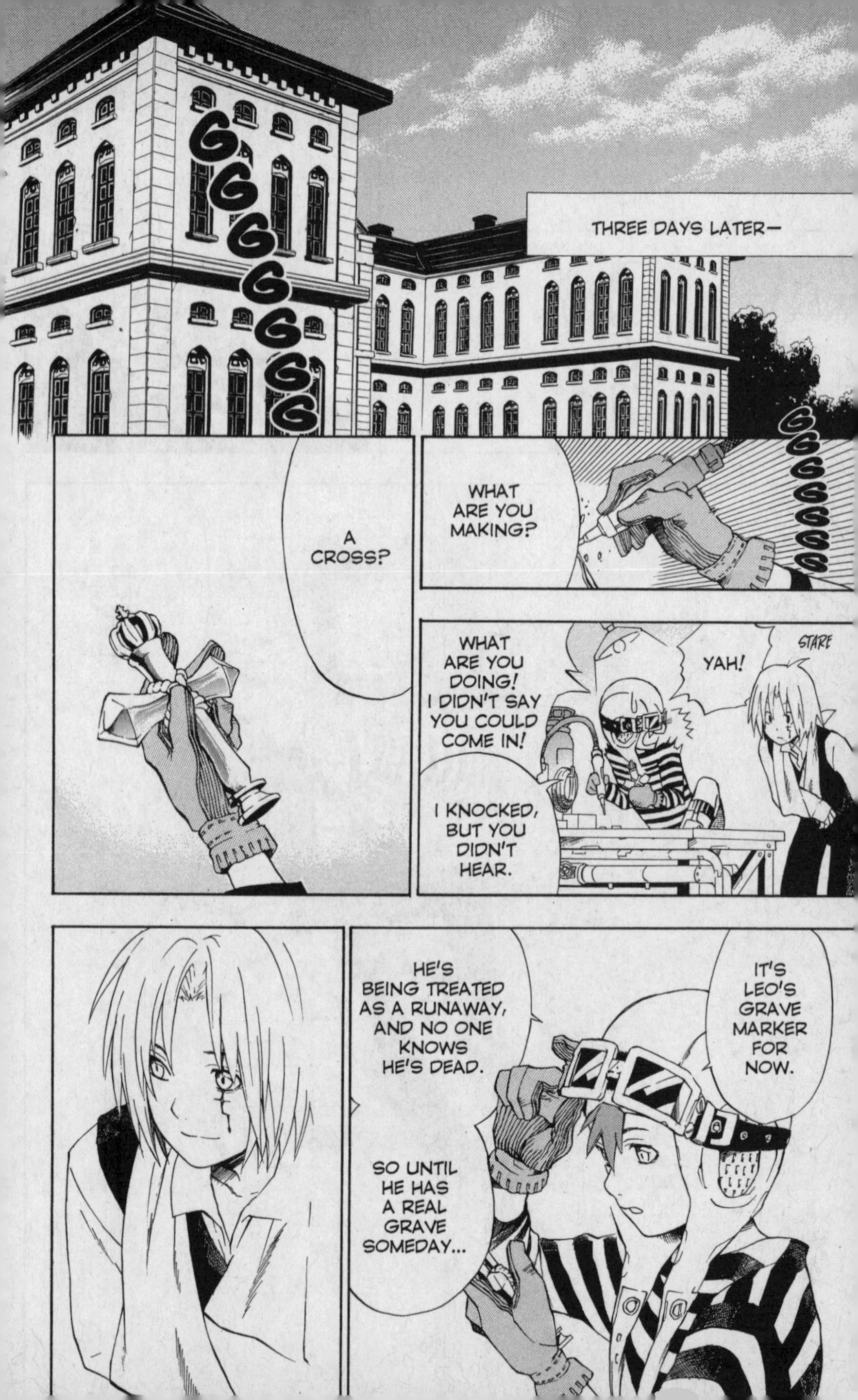
THREE DAYS LATER—
GGGGGG
GGGGGGG
WHAT ARE YOU MAKING?
STARE
YAH!
WHAT ARE YOU DOING! I DIDN'T SAY YOU COULD COME IN!
I KNOCKED, BUT YOU DIDN'T HEAR.
A CROSS?
IT'S LEO'S GRAVE MARKER FOR NOW.
HE'S BEING TREATED AS A RUNAWAY, AND NO ONE KNOWS HE'S DEAD.
SO UNTIL HE HAS A REAL GRAVE SOMEDAY...

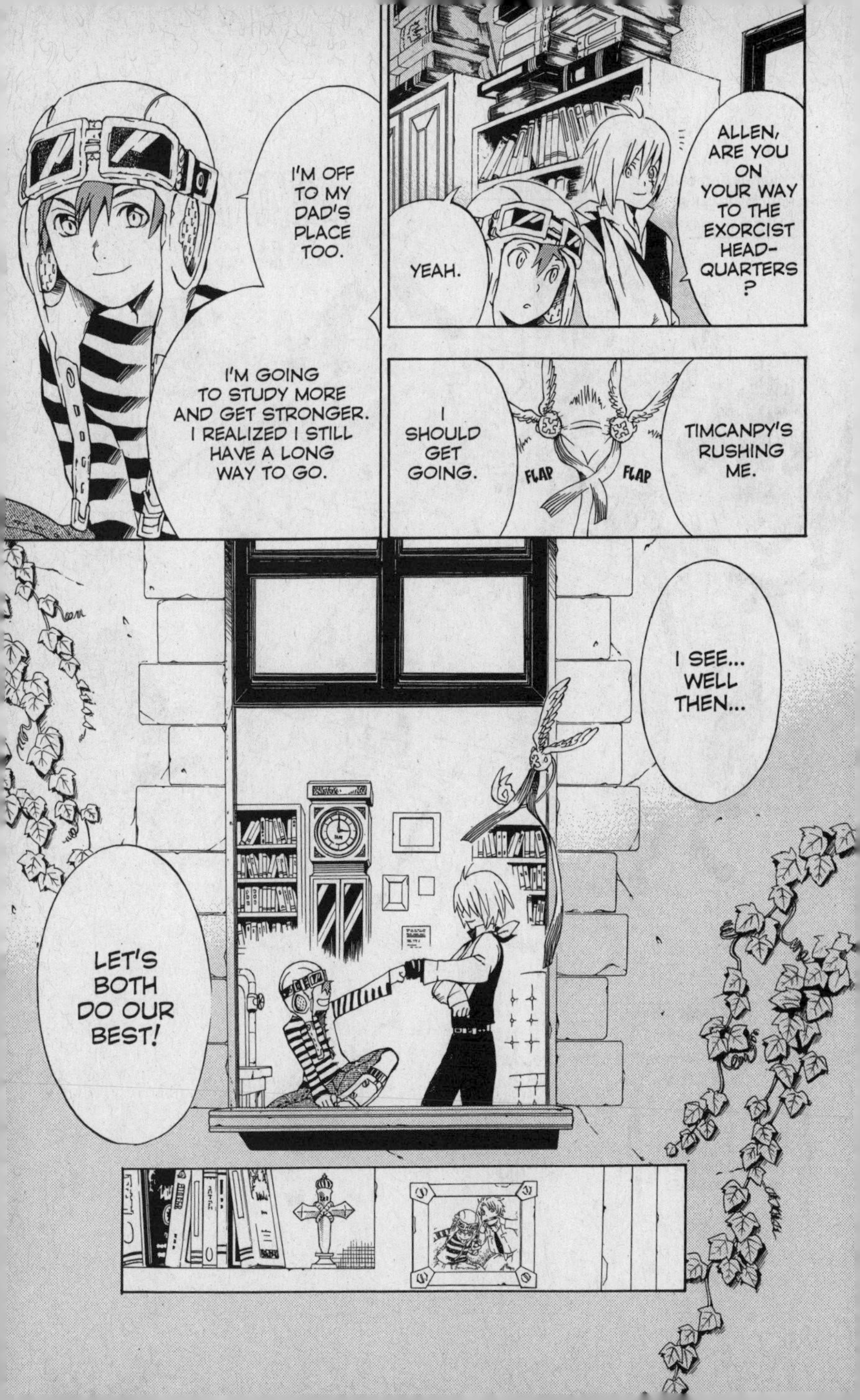
ALLEN, ARE YOU ON YOUR WAY TO THE EXORCIST HEAD-QUARTERS?
YEAH.
TIMCANPY'S RUSHING ME.
FLAP
FLAP
I SHOULD GET GOING.
I'M OFF TO MY DAD'S PLACE TOO.
I'M GOING TO STUDY MORE AND GET STRONGER. I REALIZED I STILL HAVE A LONG WAY TO GO.
I SEE... WELL THEN...
LET'S BOTH DO OUR BEST!

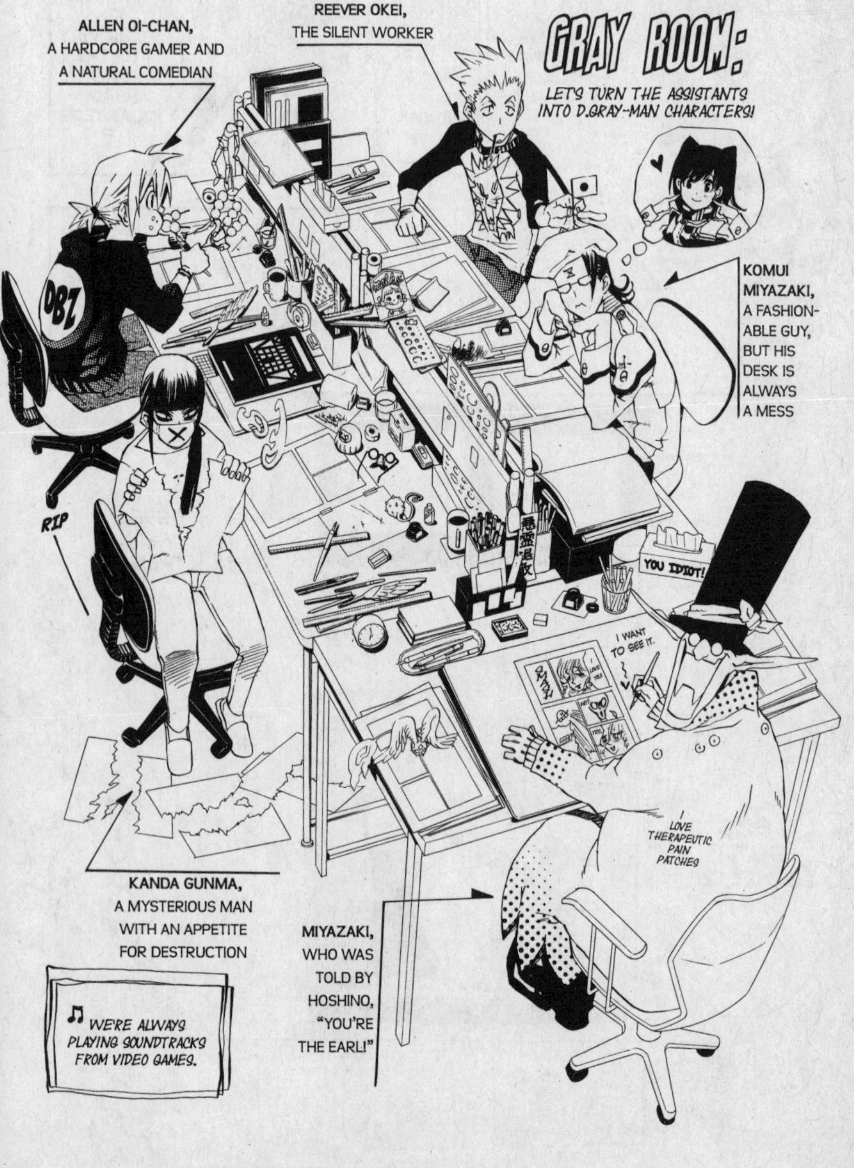
GRAY ROOM:
LET'S TURN THE ASSISTANTS INTO D.GRAY-MAN CHARACTERS!
REEVER OKEI, THE SILENT WORKER
ALLEN OI-CHAN, A HARDCORE GAMER AND A NATURAL COMEDIAN
KOMUI MIYAZAKI, A FASHIONABLE GUY, BUT HIS DESK IS ALWAYS A MESS
RIP
YOU IDIOT!
I WANT TO SEE IT.
I LOVE THERAPEUTIC PAIN PATCHES
KANDA GUNMA, A MYSTERIOUS MAN WITH AN APPETITE FOR DESTRUCTION
MIYAZAKI, WHO WAS TOLD BY HOSHINO, "YOU'RE THE EARL!"
♫ WE'RE ALWAYS PLAYING SOUNDTRACKS FROM VIDEO GAMES.

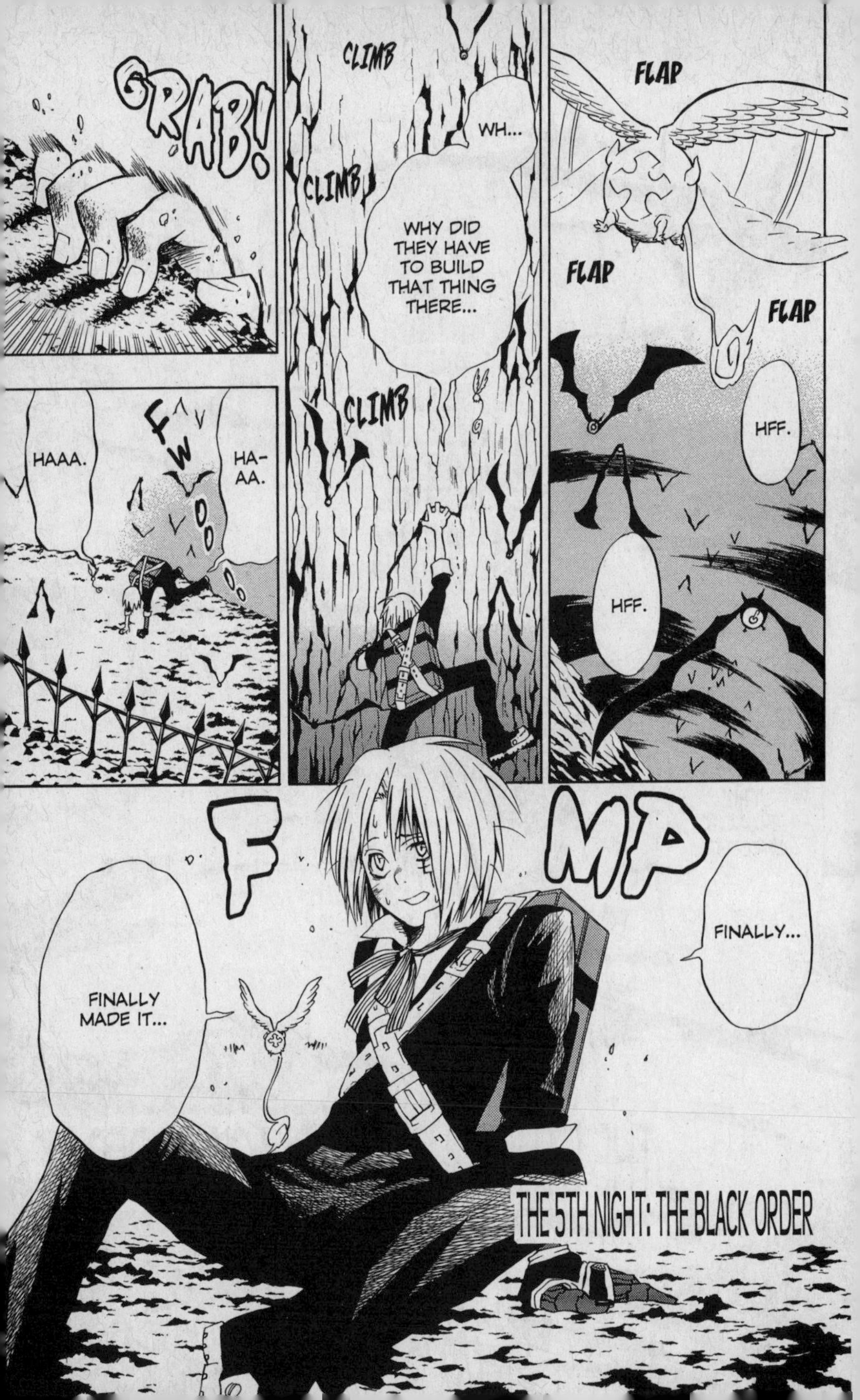

FLAP
FLAP
FLAP
HFF.
HFF.
CLIMB
WH...
WHY DID THEY HAVE TO BUILD THAT THING THERE...
CLIMB
CLIMB
GRAB!
HA-AA.
HAAA.
FMP
FINALLY...
FINALLY MADE IT...
THE 5TH NIGHT: THE BLACK ORDER

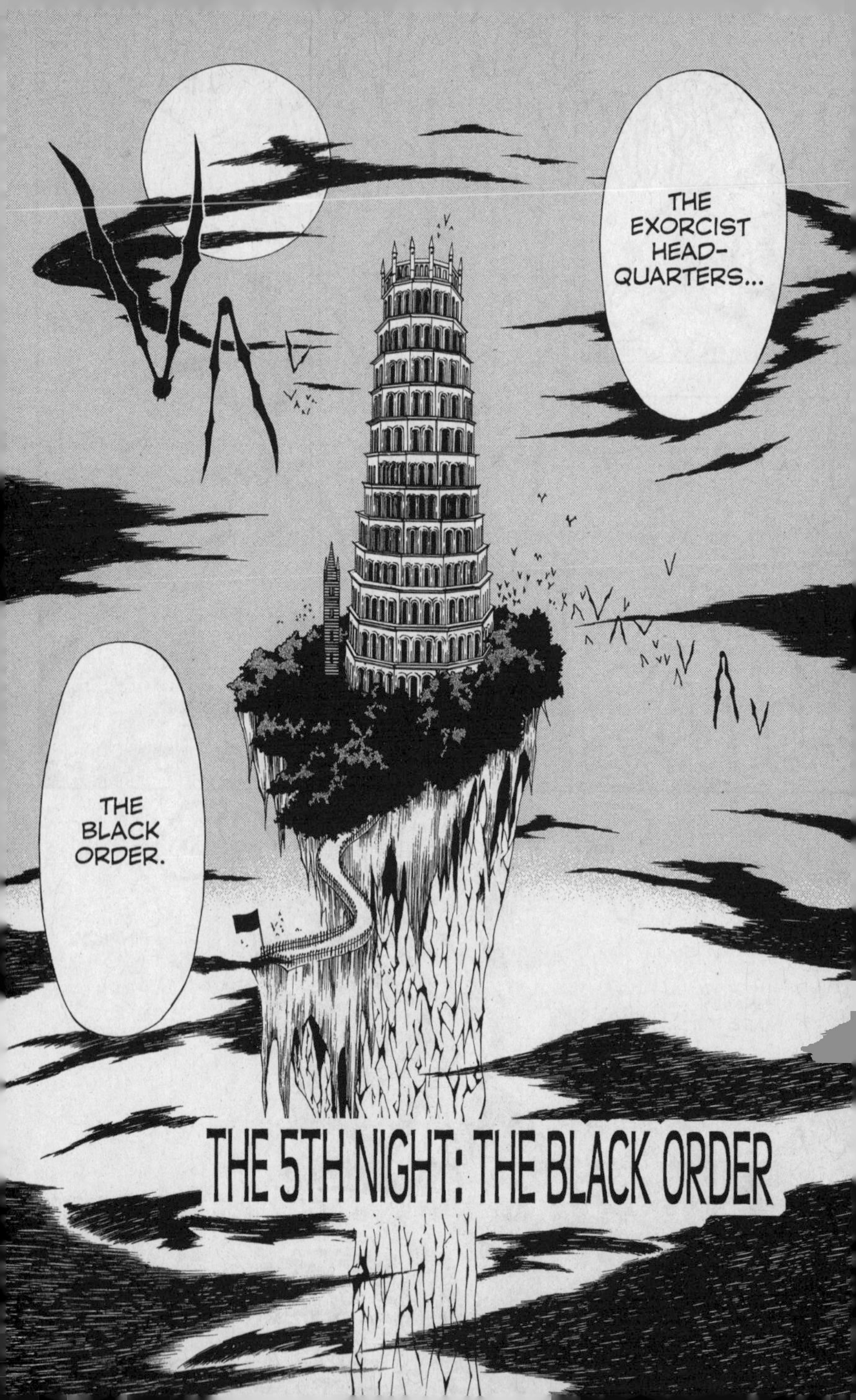
THE EXORCIST HEAD-QUARTERS...
THE BLACK ORDER.
THE 5TH NIGHT: THE BLACK ORDER

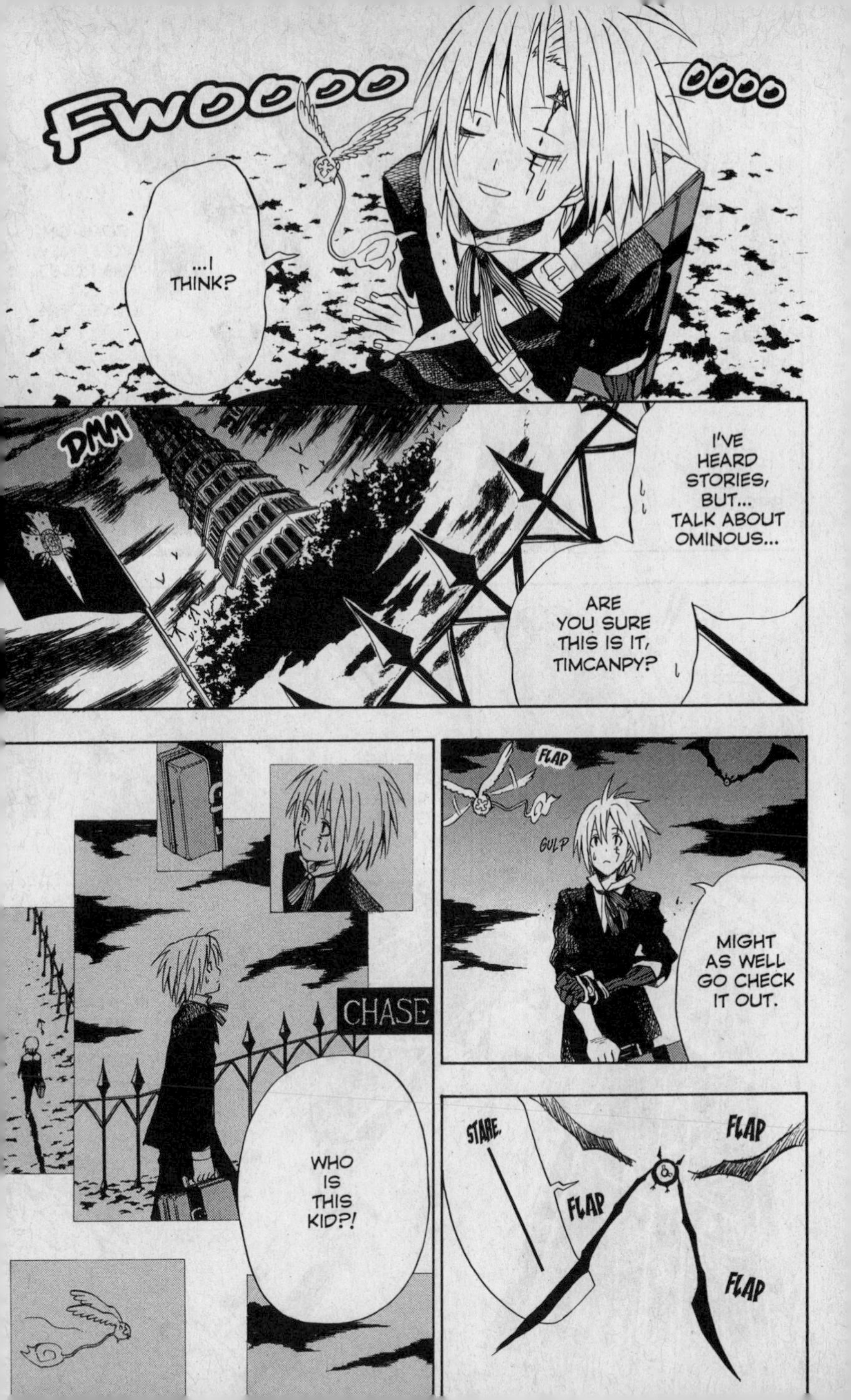
FWOOOOO
OOOO
...I THINK?
DMM
I'VE HEARD STORIES, BUT... TALK ABOUT OMINOUS...
ARE YOU SURE THIS IS IT, TIMCANPY?
FLAP
GULP
MIGHT AS WELL GO CHECK IT OUT.
STARE.
FLAP
FLAP
FLAP
CHASE
WHO IS THIS KID?!

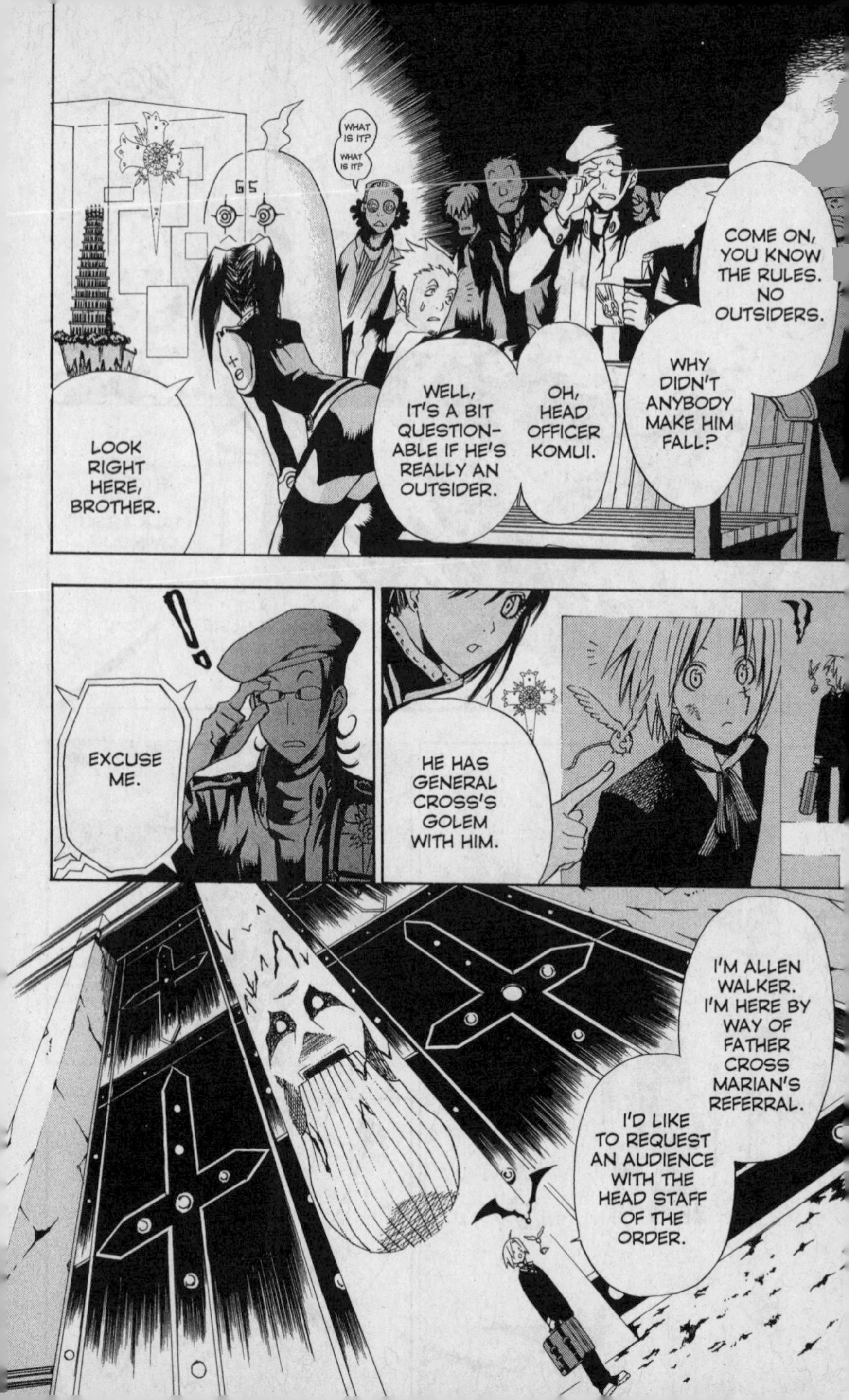
COME ON, YOU KNOW THE RULES. NO OUTSIDERS.
WHY DIDN'T ANYBODY MAKE HIM FALL?
WHAT IS IT? WHAT IS IT?
OH, HEAD OFFICER KOMUI.
WELL, IT'S A BIT QUESTIONABLE IF HE'S REALLY AN OUTSIDER.
LOOK RIGHT HERE, BROTHER.
HE HAS GENERAL CROSS'S GOLEM WITH HIM.
EXCUSE ME.
I'M ALLEN WALKER. I'M HERE BY WAY OF FATHER CROSS MARIAN'S REFERRAL.
I'D LIKE TO REQUEST AN AUDIENCE WITH THE HEAD STAFF OF THE ORDER.

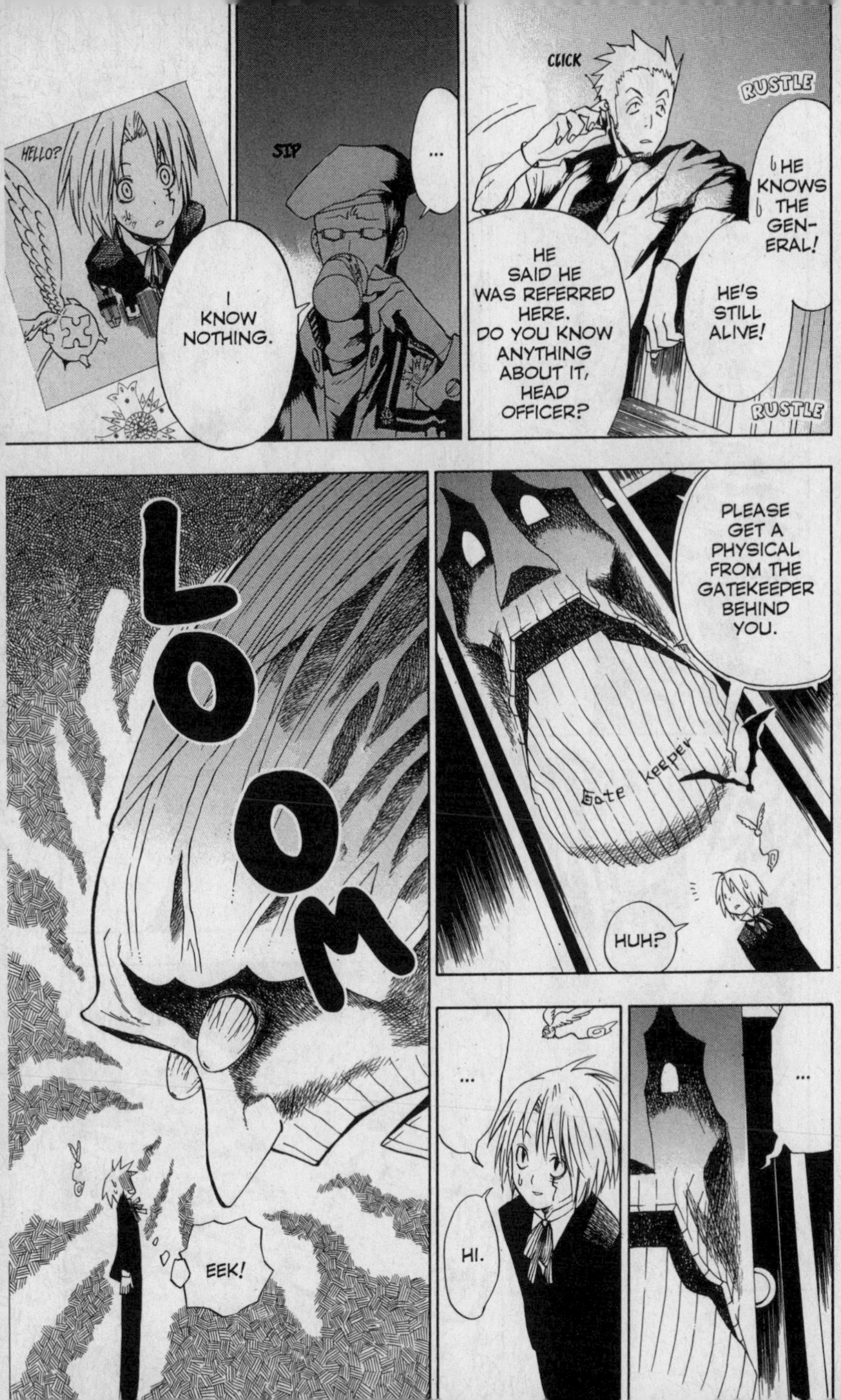
CLICK
RUSTLE
HE KNOWS THE GENERAL!
HE'S STILL ALIVE!
RUSTLE
HE SAID HE WAS REFERRED HERE. DO YOU KNOW ANYTHING ABOUT IT, HEAD OFFICER?
SIP
...
I KNOW NOTHING.
HELLO?
PLEASE GET A PHYSICAL FROM THE GATEKEEPER BEHIND YOU.
Gate keeper
HUH?
...
...
HI.
LOOM
EEK!

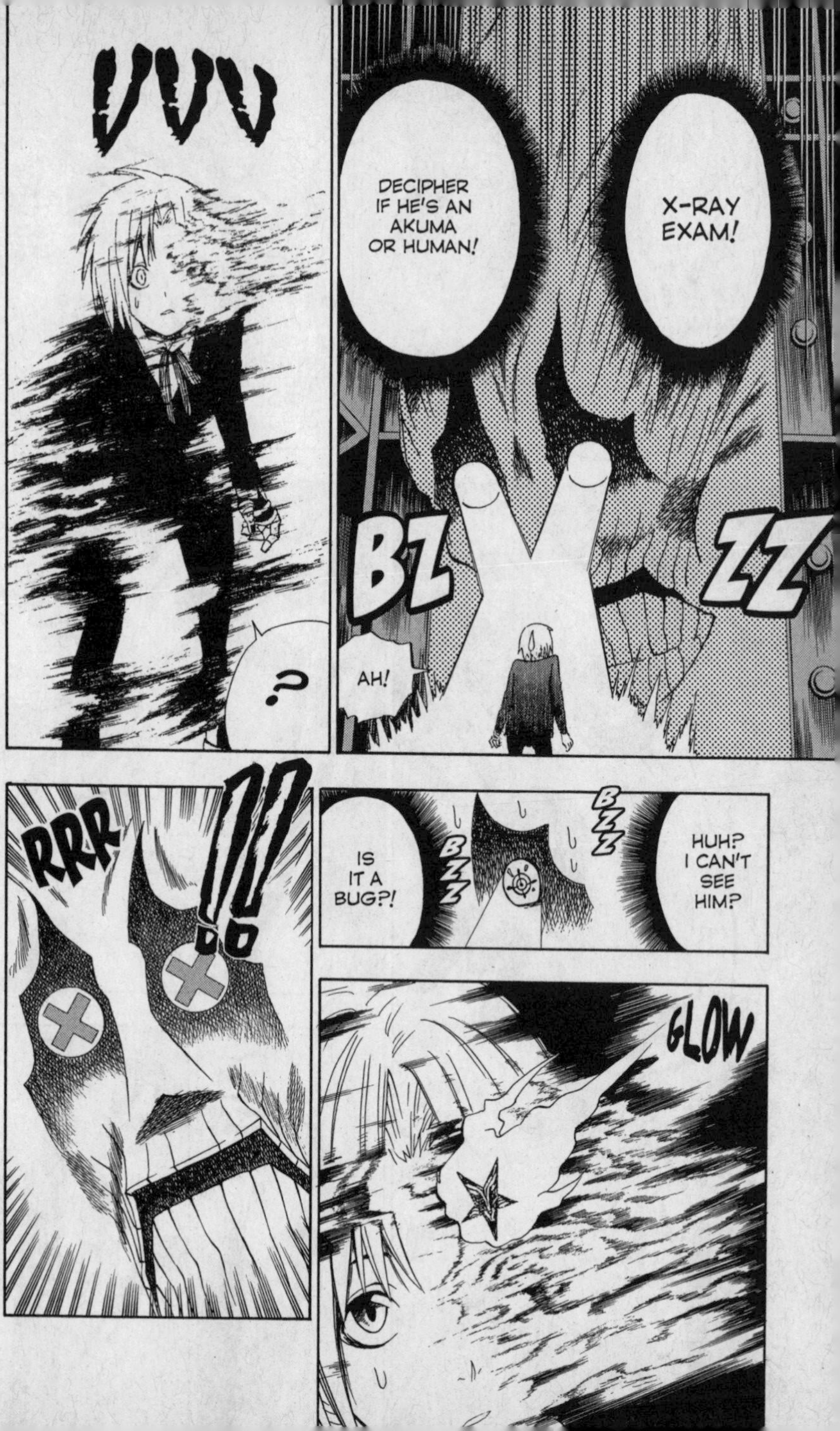
X-RAY EXAM!
DECIPHER IF HE'S AN AKUMA OR HUMAN!
BZ
ZZ
AH!
VVV
?
HUH? I CAN'T SEE HIM?
BZZ
BZZ
IS IT A BUG?!
GLOW
!!
RRR

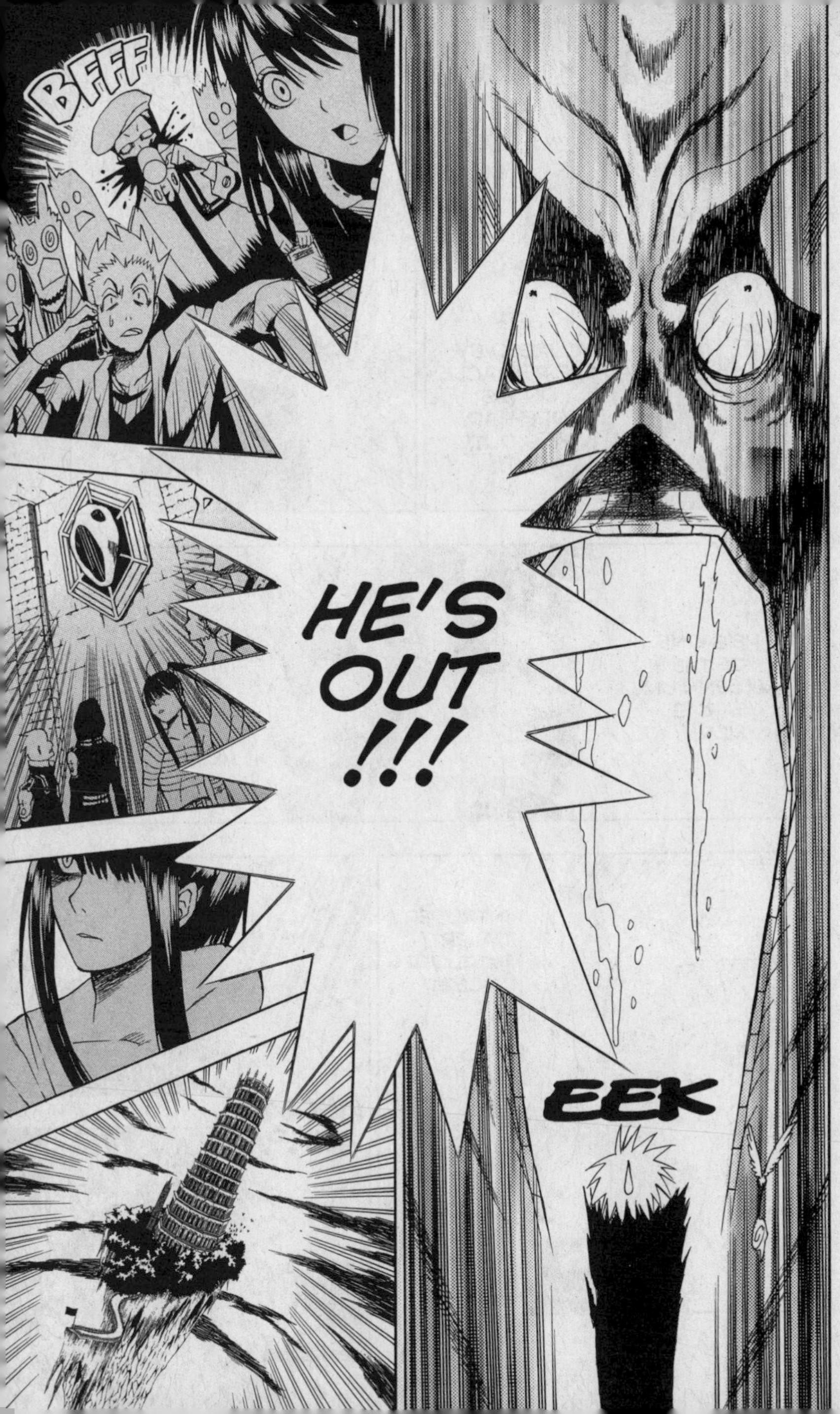
HE'S OUT!!!
EEK
BFFF

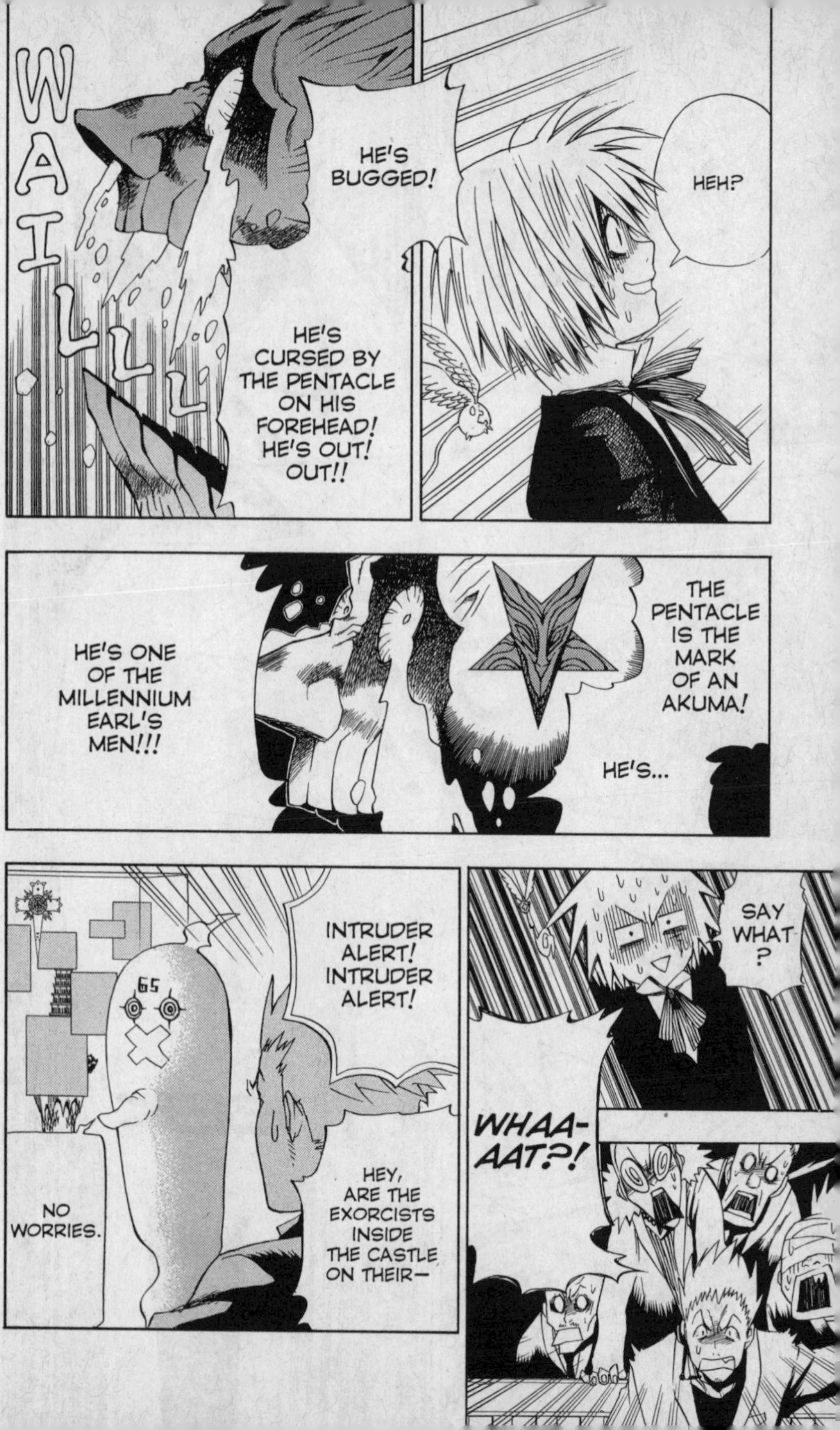
HEH?
HE'S BUGGED!
HE'S CURSED BY THE PENTACLE ON HIS FOREHEAD! HE'S OUT! OUT!!
WAILLLL
THE PENTACLE IS THE MARK OF AN AKUMA!
HE'S...
HE'S ONE OF THE MILLENNIUM EARL'S MEN!!!
SAY WHAT?
WHAAA-AAT?!
INTRUDER ALERT! INTRUDER ALERT!
HEY, ARE THE EXORCISTS INSIDE THE CASTLE ON THEIR—
NO WORRIES.

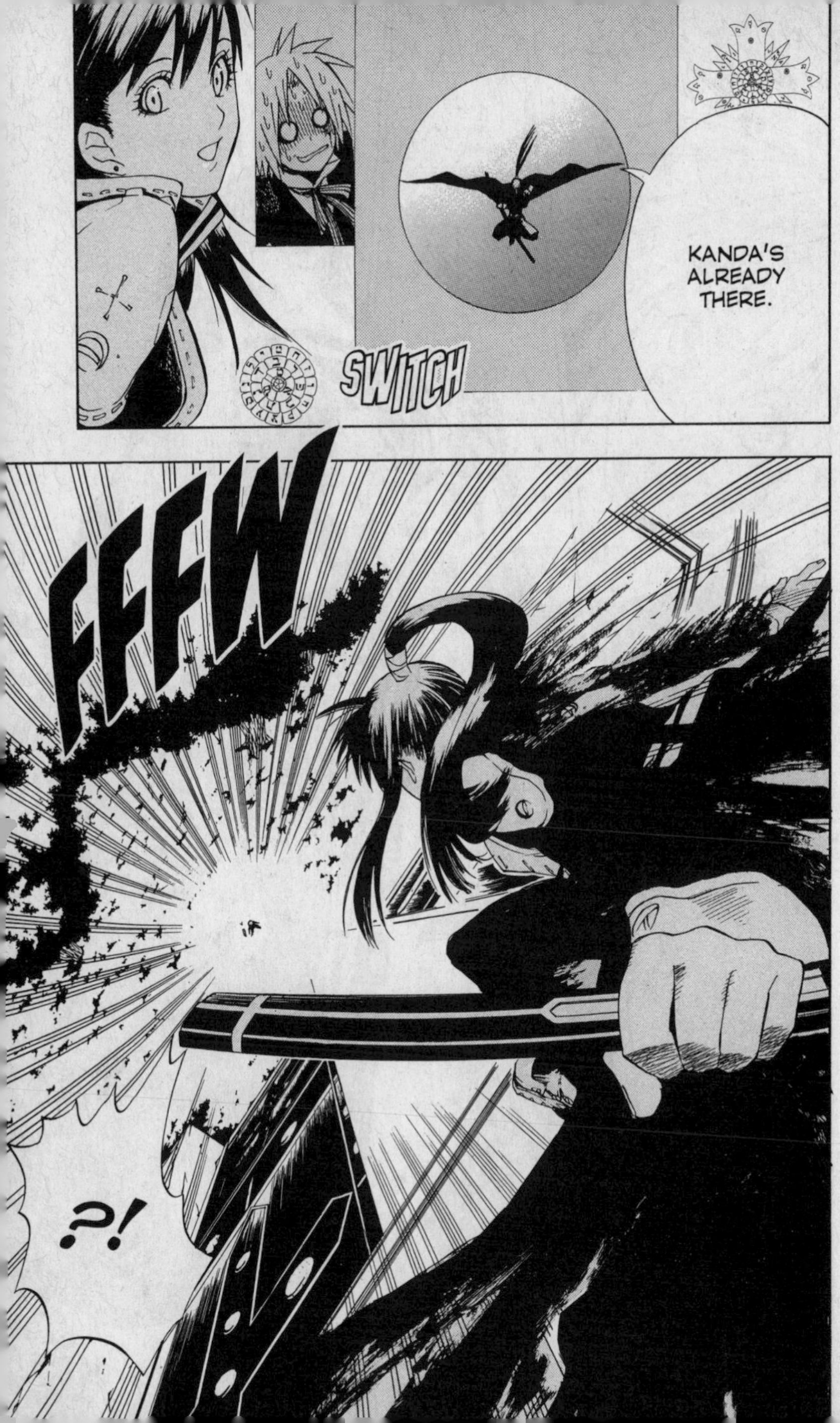
KANDA'S ALREADY THERE.
SWITCH
FFFW
?!

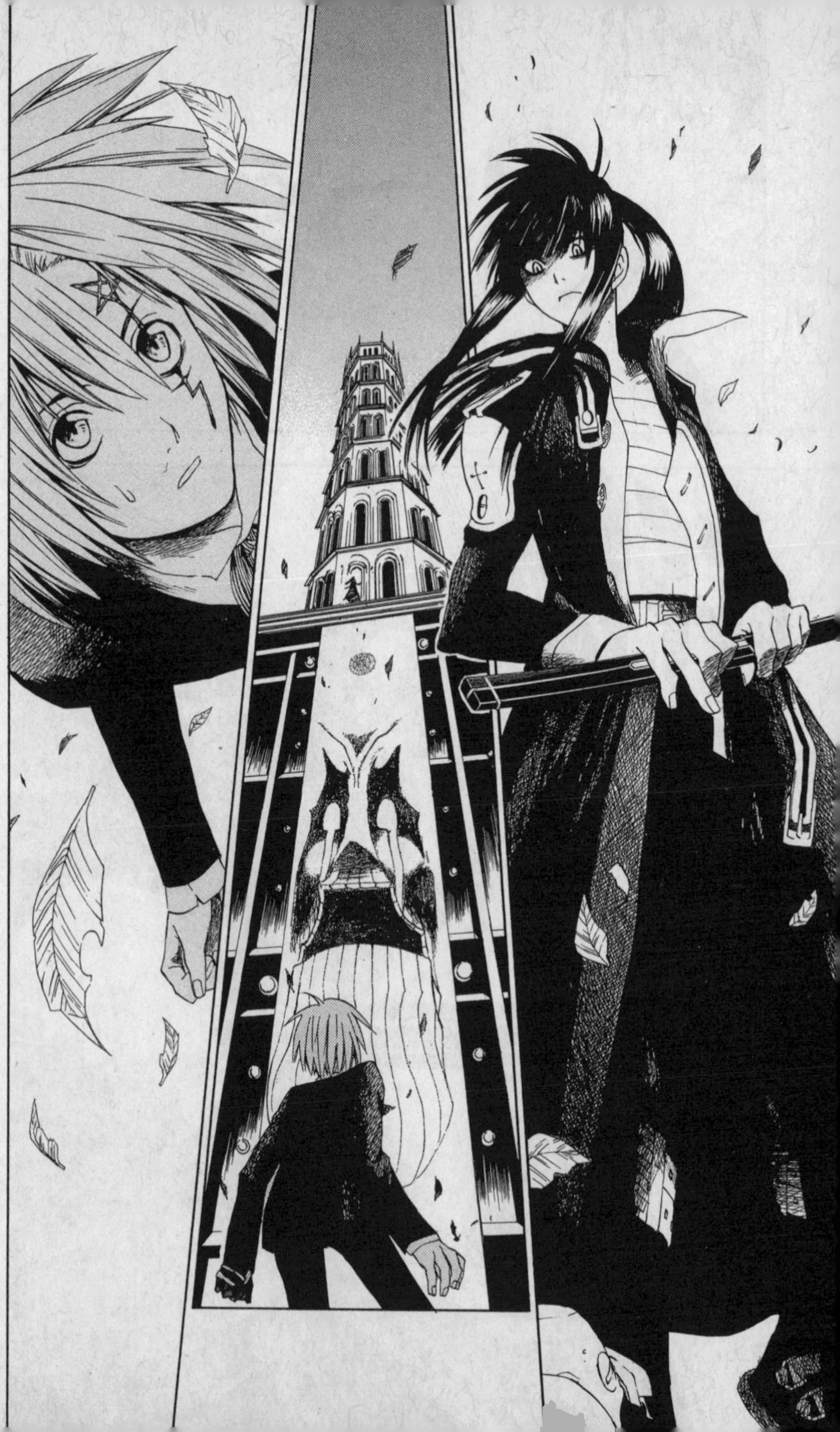

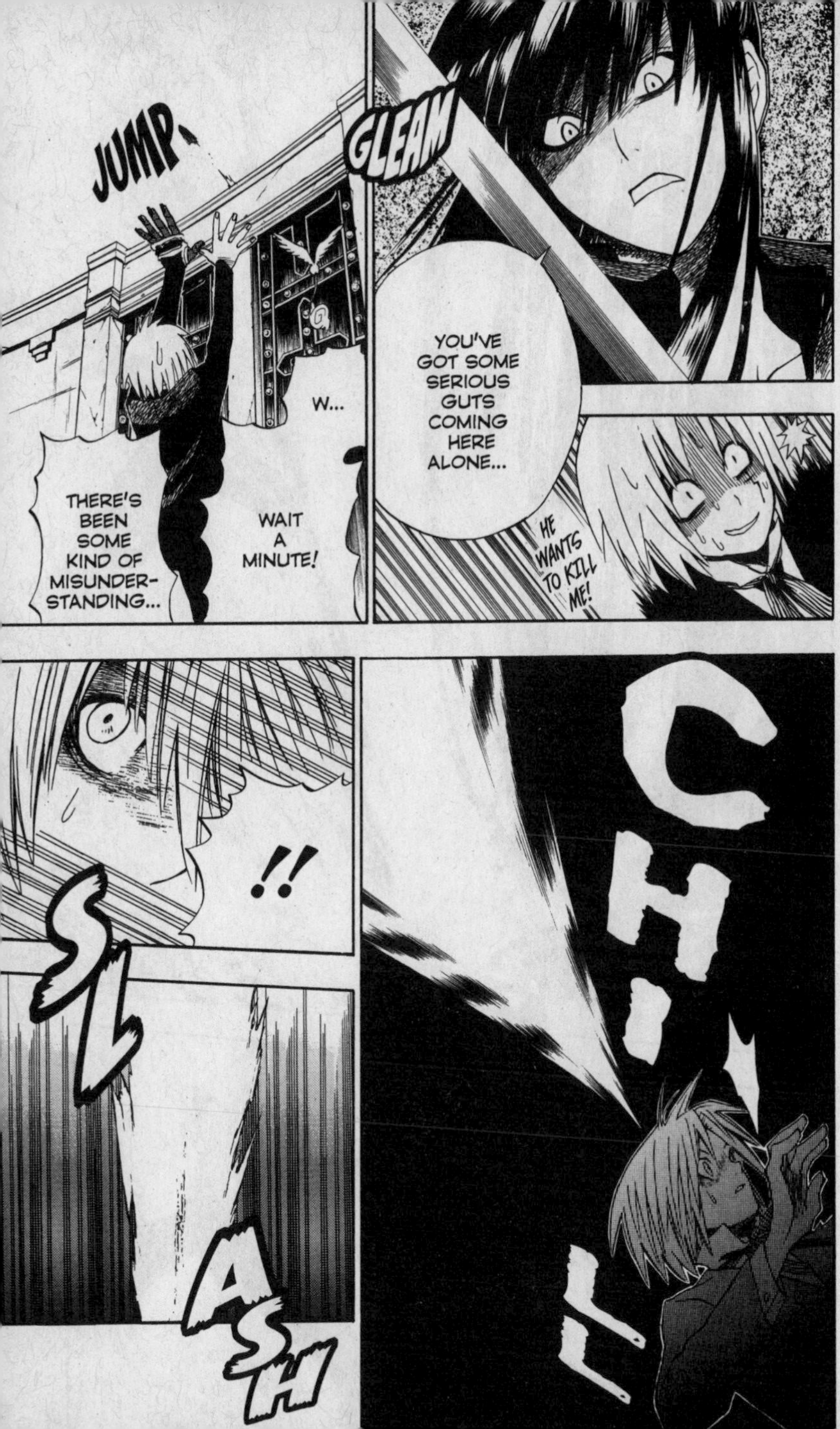
GLEAM
YOU'VE GOT SOME SERIOUS GUTS COMING HERE ALONE...
HE WANTS TO KILL ME!
JUMP
W...
WAIT A MINUTE!
THERE'S BEEN SOME KIND OF MISUNDER-STANDING...
CHILL
!!
SLASH

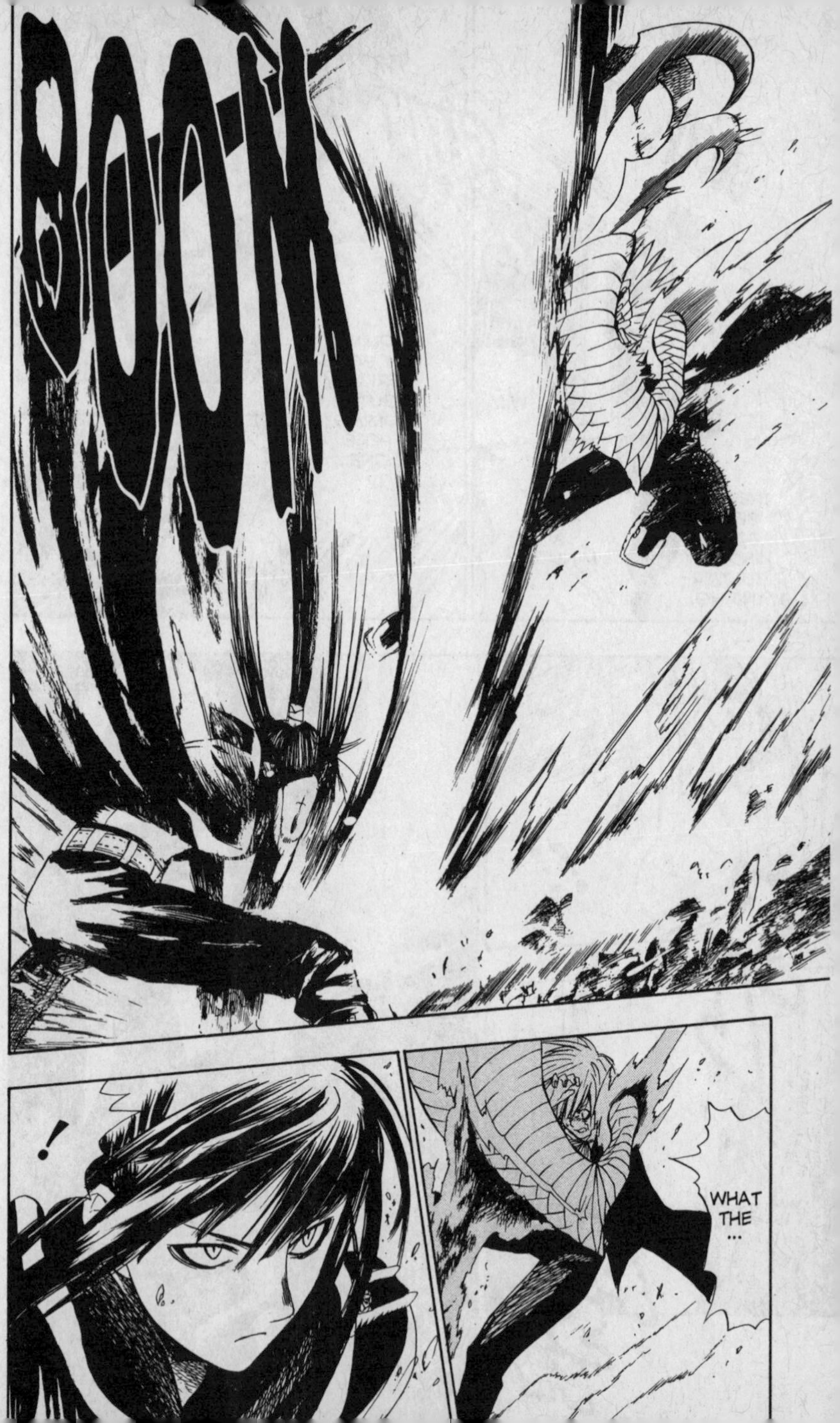
BOOM
WHAT THE ...
!

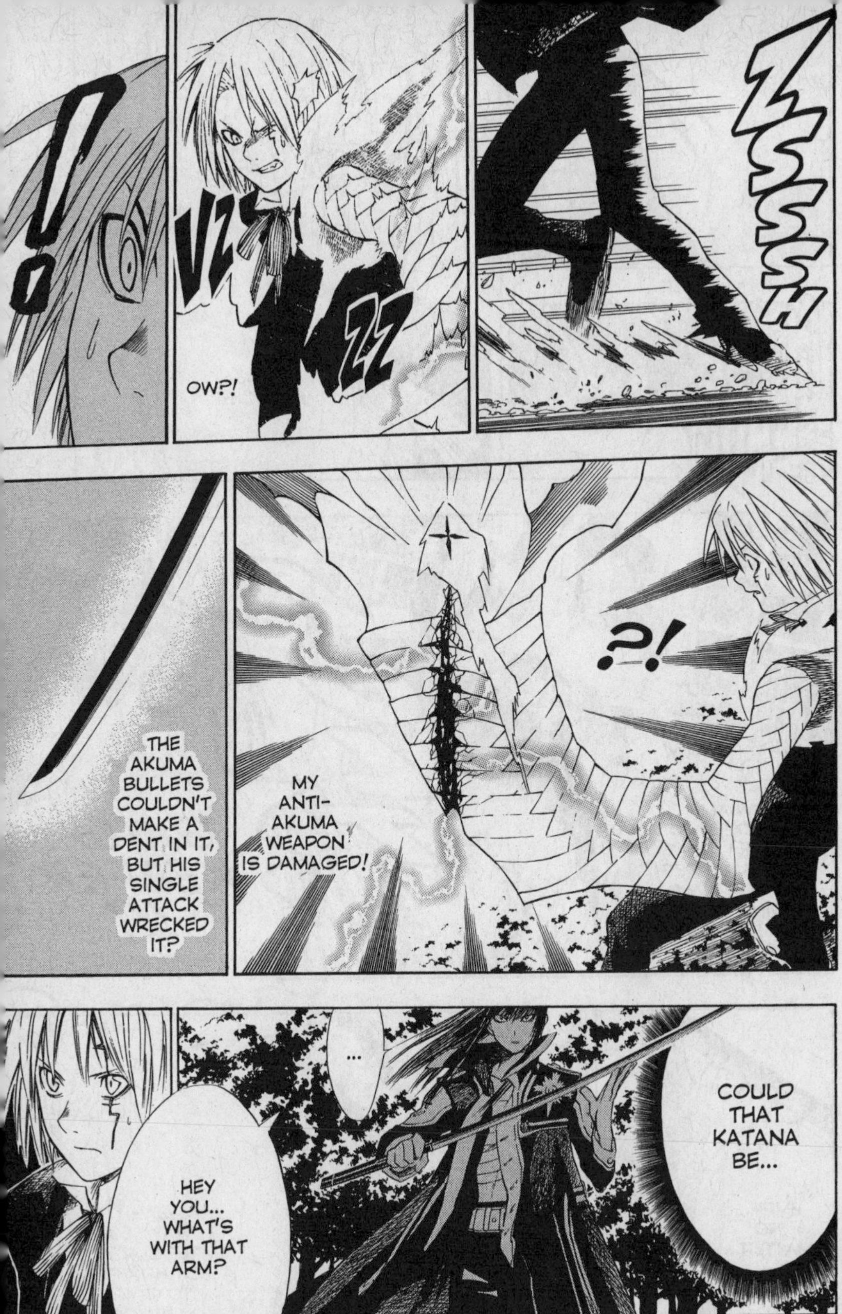
ZSSSSH
OW?!
?!
MY ANTI-AKUMA WEAPON IS DAMAGED!
THE AKUMA BULLETS COULDN'T MAKE A DENT IN IT, BUT HIS SINGLE ATTACK WRECKED IT?
COULD THAT KATANA BE...
...
HEY YOU... WHAT'S WITH THAT ARM?

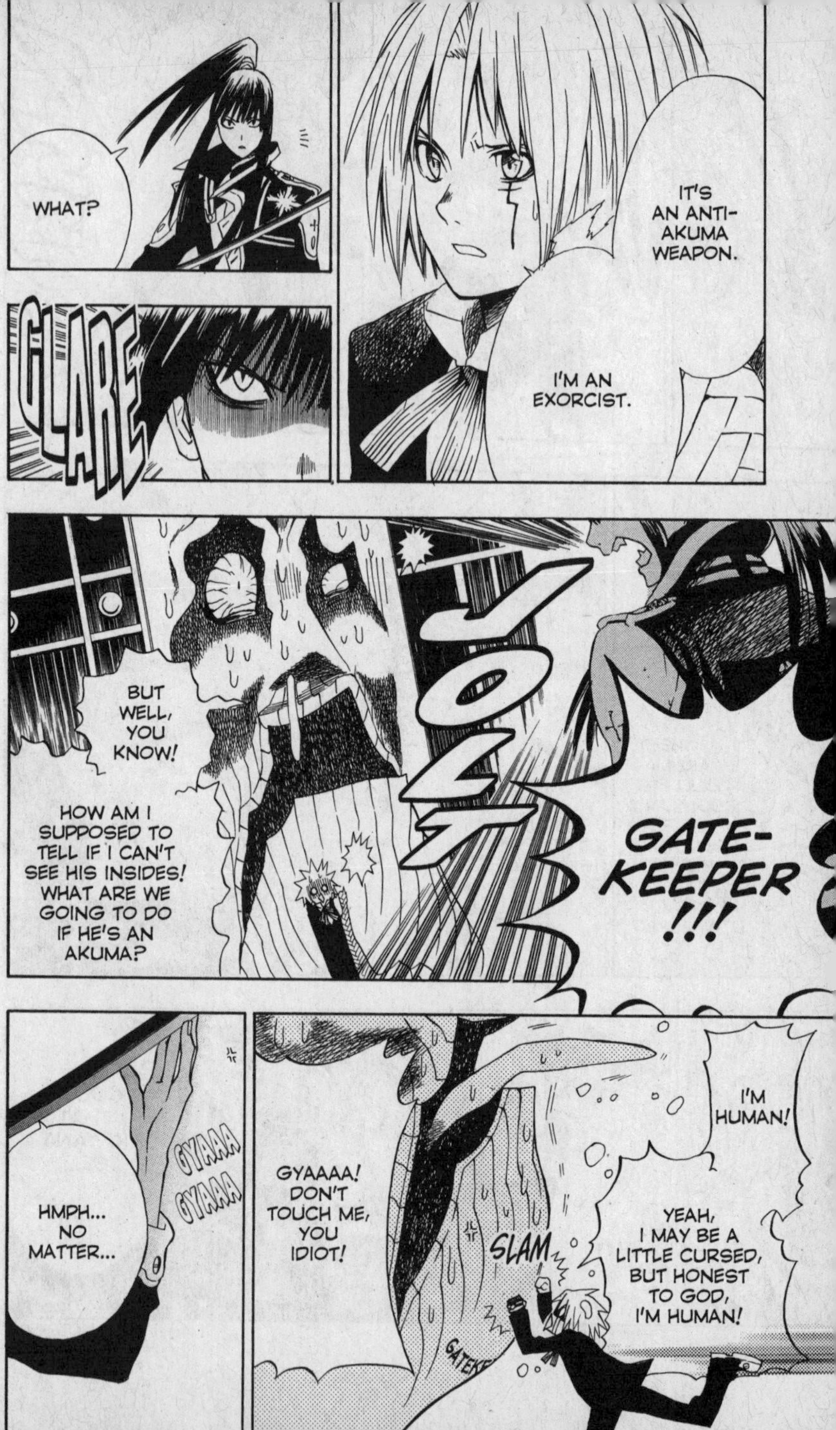
IT'S AN ANTI-AKUMA WEAPON.
I'M AN EXORCIST.
WHAT?
GLARE
GATE-KEEPER!!!
JOLT
BUT WELL, YOU KNOW!
HOW AM I SUPPOSED TO TELL IF I CAN'T SEE HIS INSIDES! WHAT ARE WE GOING TO DO IF HE'S AN AKUMA?
I'M HUMAN!
YEAH, I MAY BE A LITTLE CURSED, BUT HONEST TO GOD, I'M HUMAN!
SLAM
GYAAAA! DON'T TOUCH ME, YOU IDIOT!
GYAAA GYAAA
HMPH... NO MATTER...

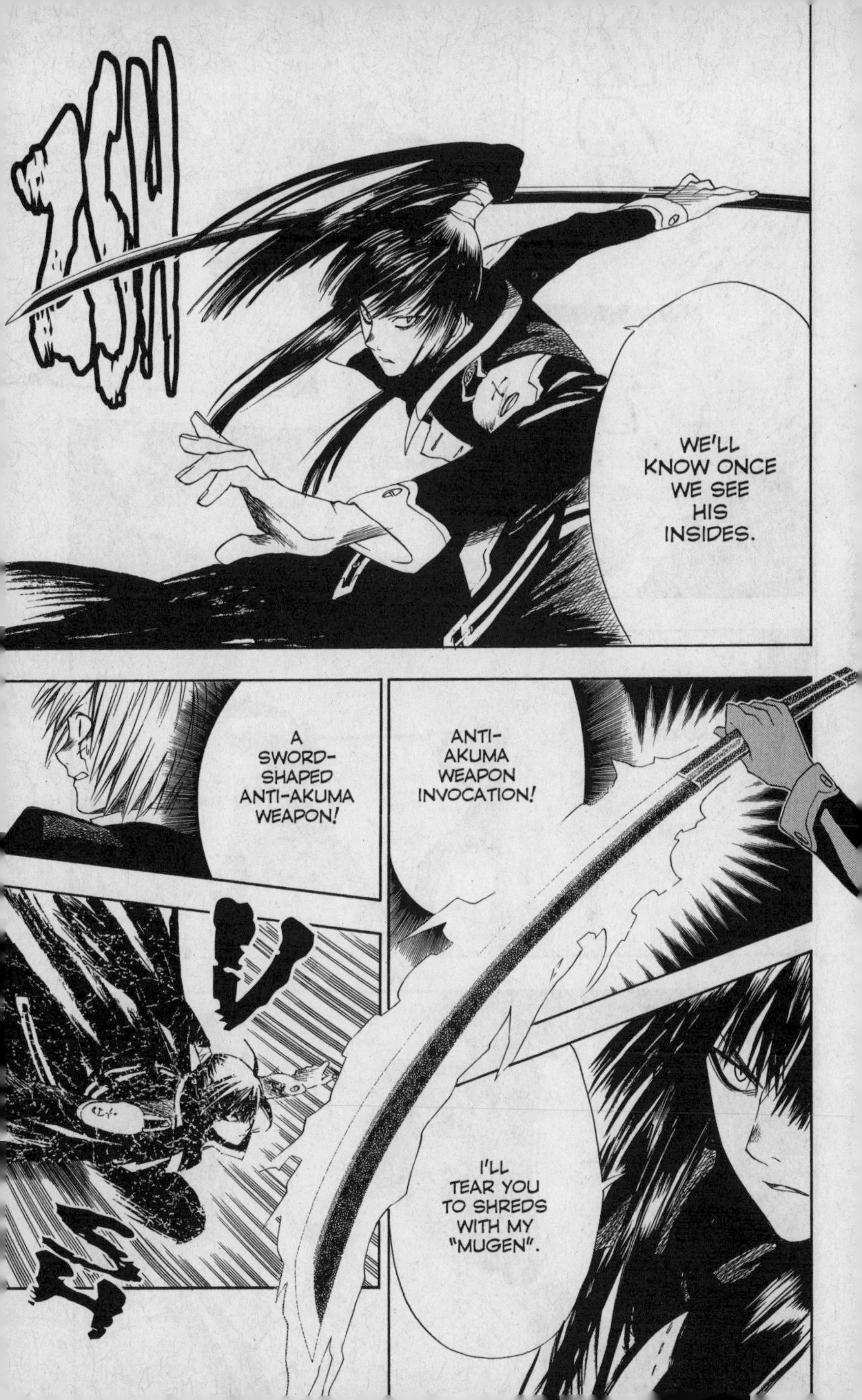
WE'LL KNOW ONCE WE SEE HIS INSIDES.
ANTI-AKUMA WEAPON INVOCATION!
I'LL TEAR YOU TO SHREDS WITH MY "MUGEN".
A SWORD-SHAPED ANTI-AKUMA WEAPON!

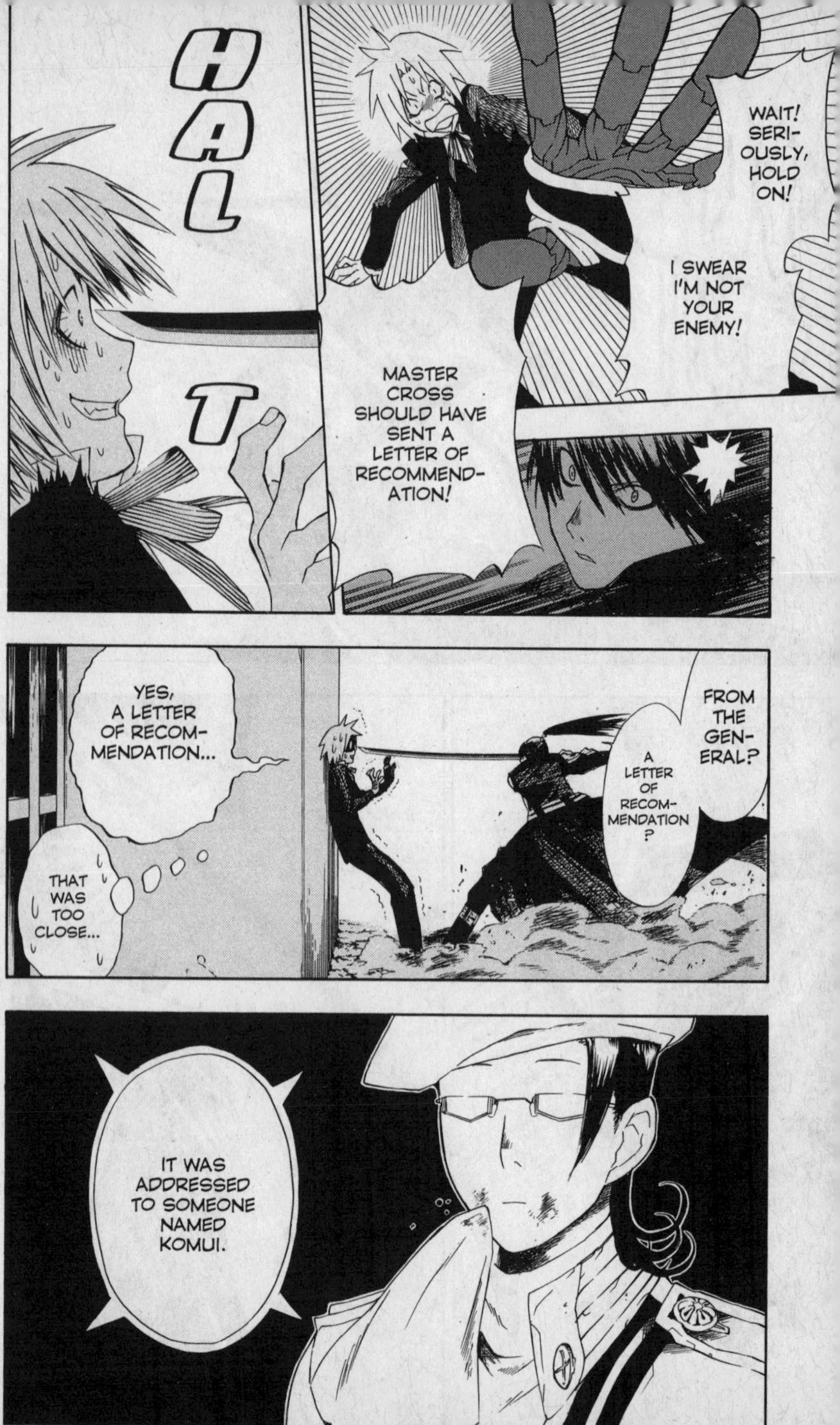
WAIT! SERIOUSLY, HOLD ON!
I SWEAR I'M NOT YOUR ENEMY!
MASTER CROSS SHOULD HAVE SENT A LETTER OF RECOMMENDATION!
HALT
FROM THE GENERAL?
A LETTER OF RECOMMENDATION?
YES, A LETTER OF RECOMMENDATION...
THAT WAS TOO CLOSE...
IT WAS ADDRESSED TO SOMEONE NAMED KOMUI.

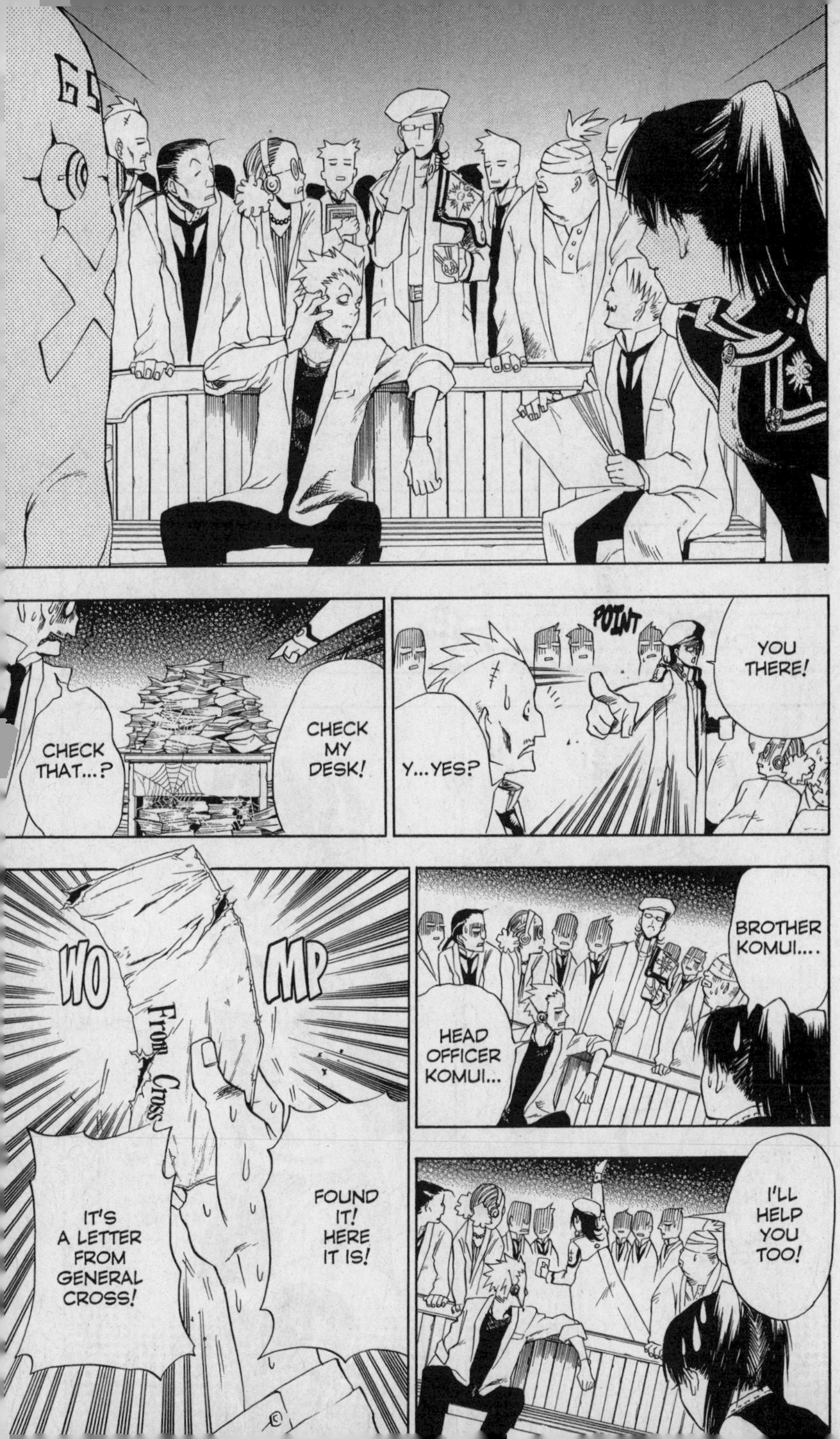
POINT
YOU THERE!
Y...YES?
CHECK MY DESK!
CHECK THAT...?
BROTHER KOMUI....
HEAD OFFICER KOMUI...
I'LL HELP YOU TOO!
WOMP
From Cross
FOUND IT! HERE IT IS!
IT'S A LETTER FROM GENERAL CROSS!

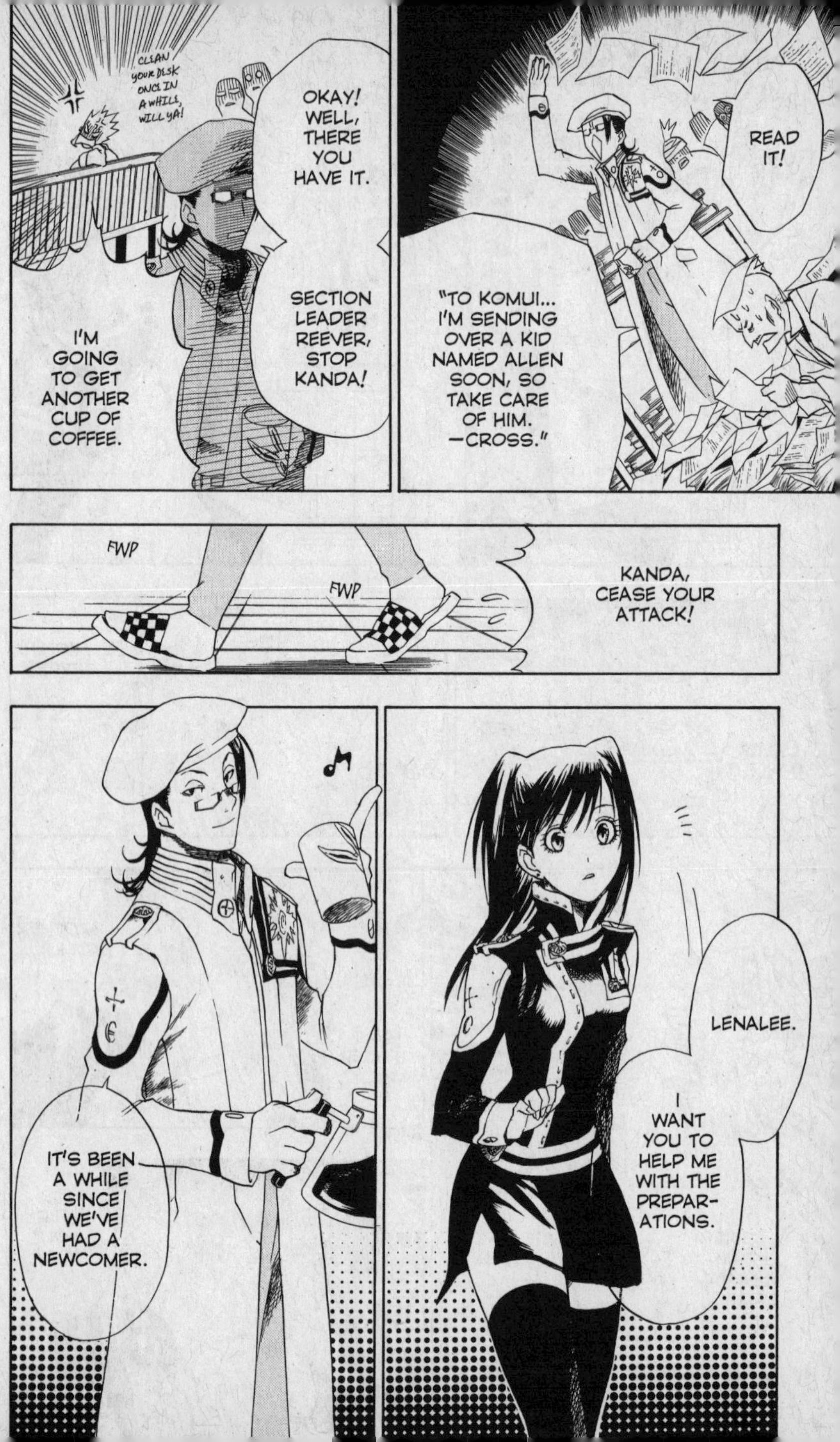
READ IT!
"TO KOMUI... I'M SENDING OVER A KID NAMED ALLEN SOON, SO TAKE CARE OF HIM. —CROSS."
OKAY! WELL, THERE YOU HAVE IT.
SECTION LEADER REEVER, STOP KANDA!
CLEAN YOUR DESK ONCE IN A WHILE, WILL YA!
I'M GOING TO GET ANOTHER CUP OF COFFEE.
KANDA, CEASE YOUR ATTACK!
FWP
FWP
LENALEE.
I WANT YOU TO HELP ME WITH THE PREPAR-ATIONS.
IT'S BEEN A WHILE SINCE WE'VE HAD A NEWCOMER.

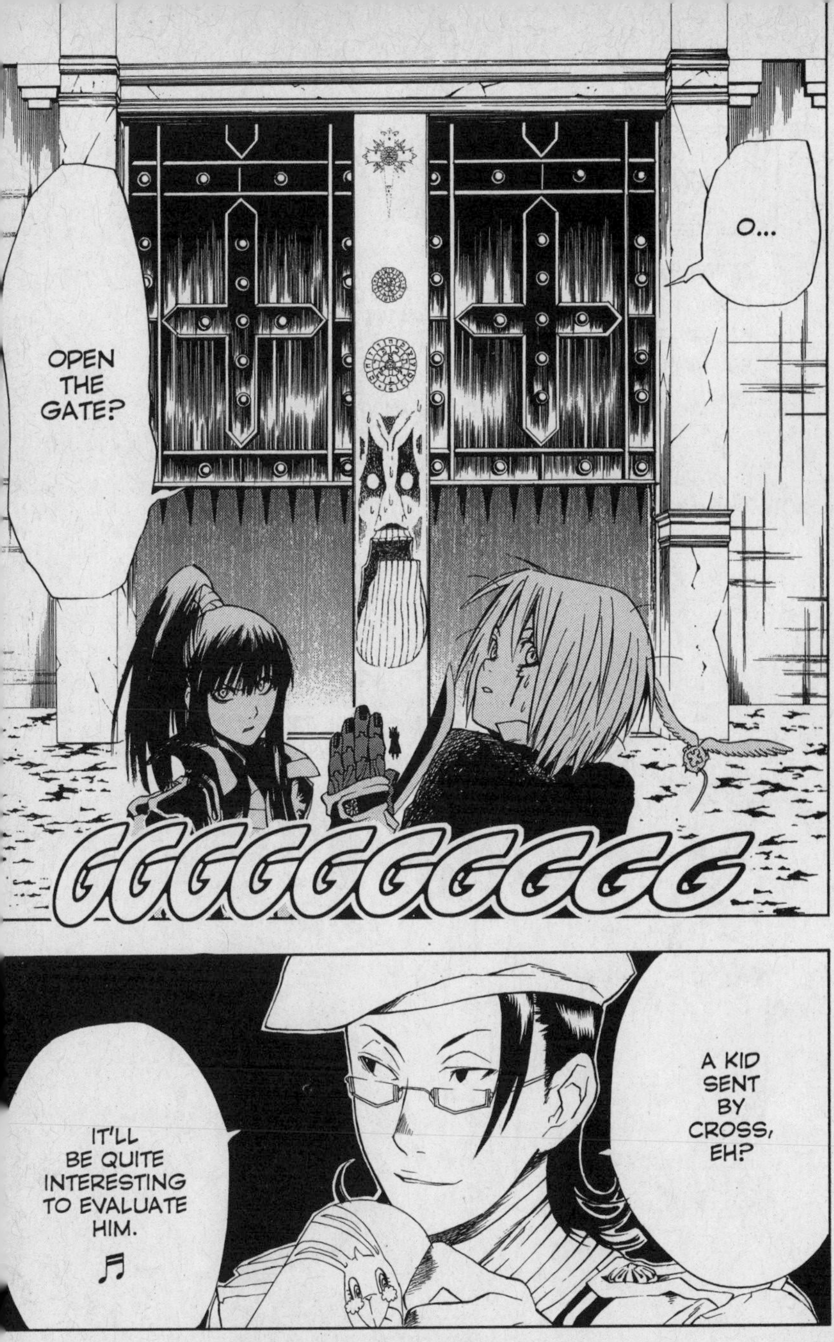
O...
OPEN THE GATE?
GGGGGGGGGGGG
A KID SENT BY CROSS, EH?
IT'LL BE QUITE INTERESTING TO EVALUATE HIM. ♬

KOMUI LEE

CHINESE, 29 YEARS OLD
HEIGHT: 193 CM
WEIGHT: 79 KG
BIRTHDAY: JUNE 13TH
GEMINI, BLOOD TYPE: AB

A YOUNG GENIUS SCIENTIST WITH AN ENDLESS NEED TO FULFILL HIS CURIOSITY...

THE "SCIENTISTS" OF THIS TIME WERE MAINLY MAGICIANS AND ALCHEMISTS. GOLEMS AND OTHER STRANGE THINGS AT THE BLACK ORDER WERE MADE BY THE MAGICIANS FROM THE SCIENCE DEPARTMENT.

WHY DID KOMUI END UP BEING SO STRANGE...? I PATTERNED THIS CHARACTER AFTER YOSHIDA, MY EDITOR. I WONDER IF IT'S OKAY TO SAY THIS...

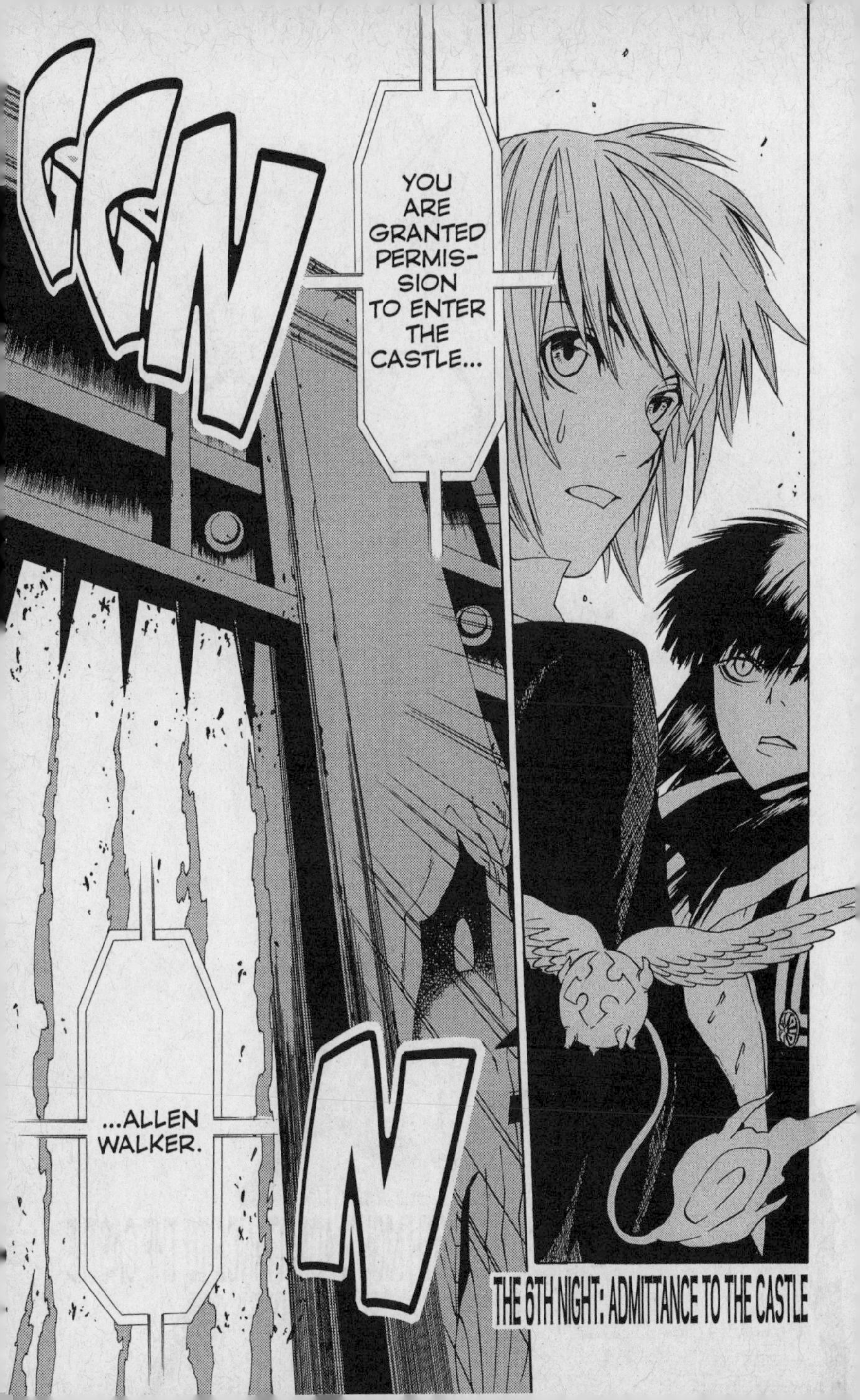
YOU ARE GRANTED PERMISSION TO ENTER THE CASTLE...
THE 6TH NIGHT: ADMITTANCE TO THE CASTLE
GGN
N
...ALLEN WALKER.

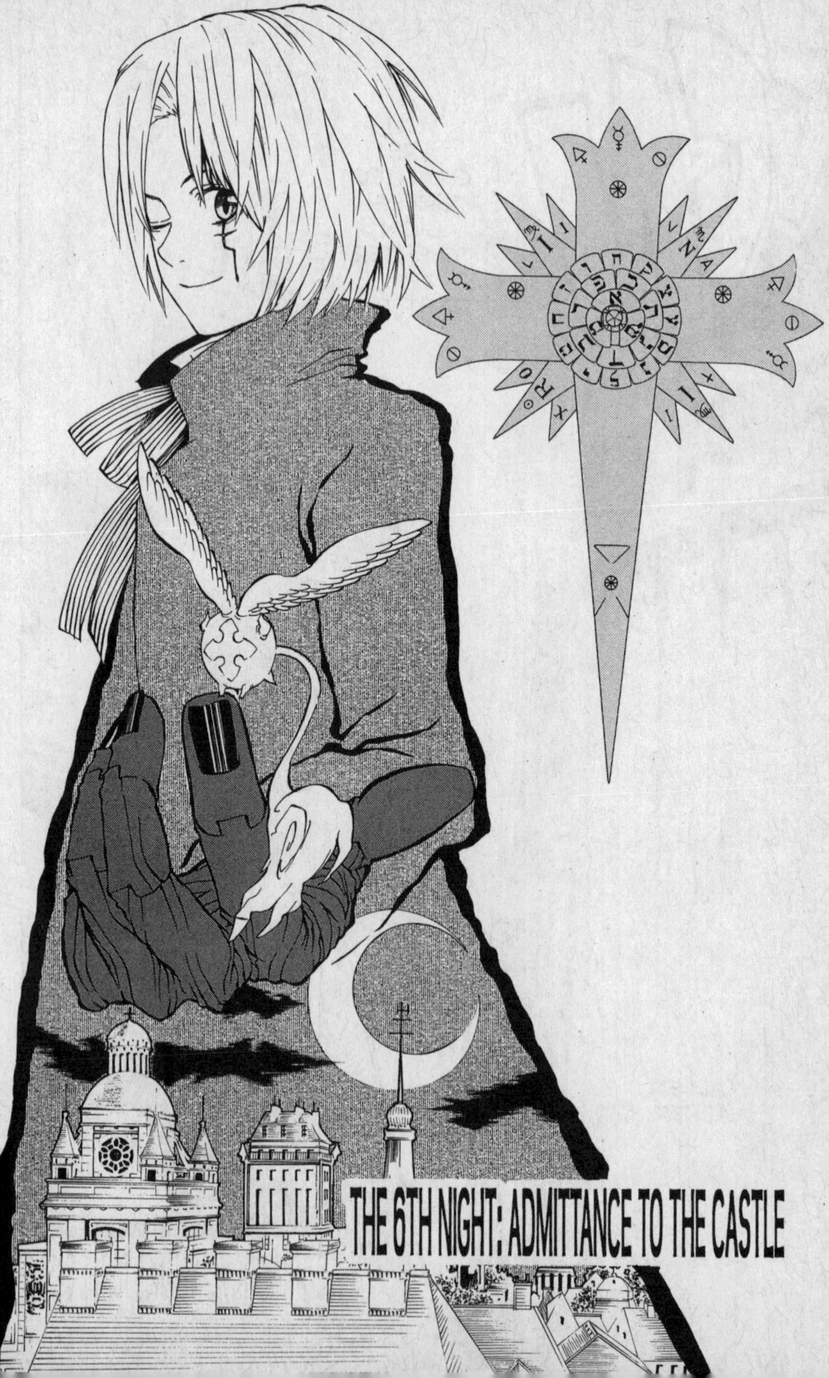

THE 6TH NIGHT: ADMITTANCE TO THE CASTLE

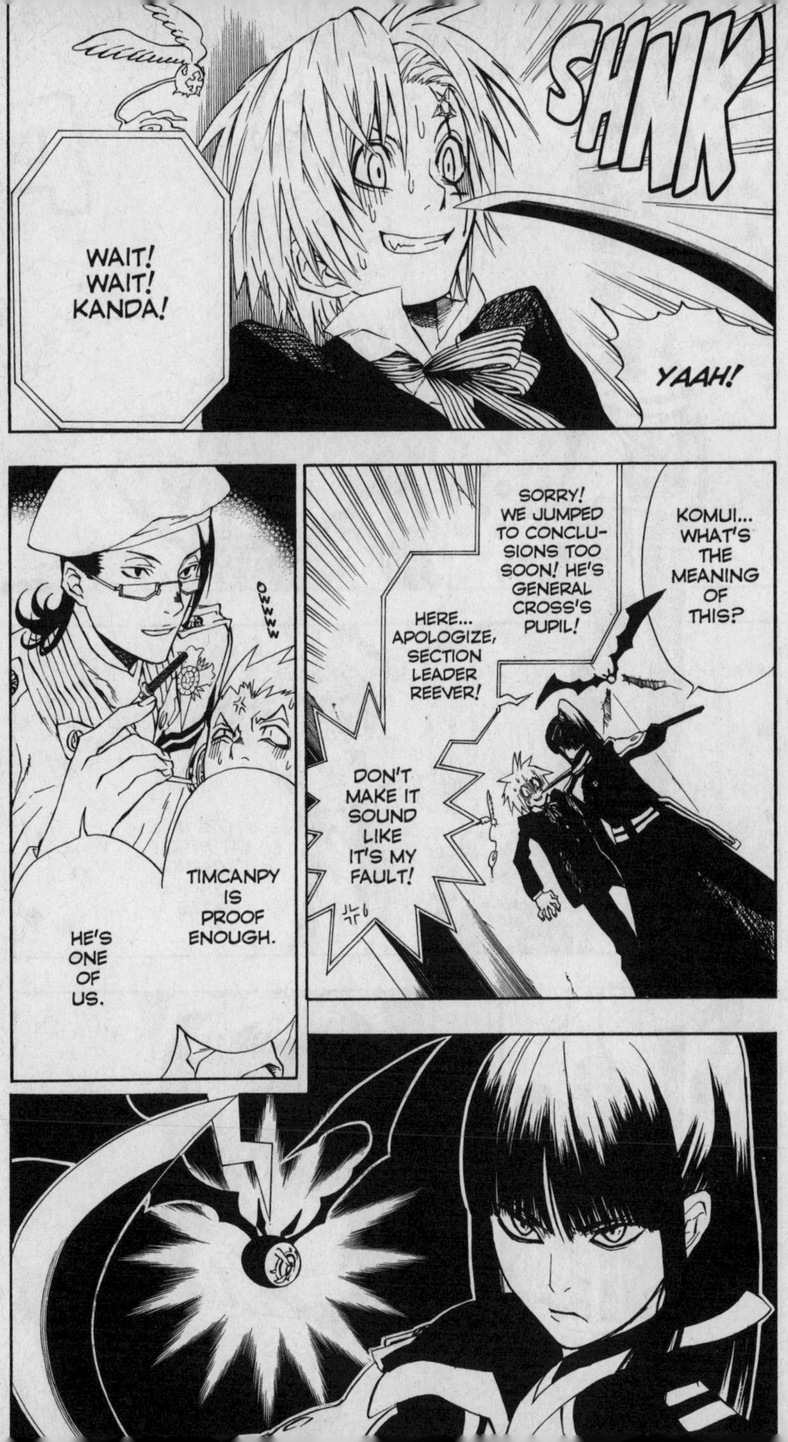
SHNK
YAAH!
WAIT! WAIT! KANDA!
KOMUI... WHAT'S THE MEANING OF THIS?
SORRY! WE JUMPED TO CONCLUSIONS TOO SOON! HE'S GENERAL CROSS'S PUPIL!
HERE... APOLOGIZE, SECTION LEADER REEVER!
DON'T MAKE IT SOUND LIKE IT'S MY FAULT!
OWWWW
TIMCANPY IS PROOF ENOUGH.
HE'S ONE OF US.

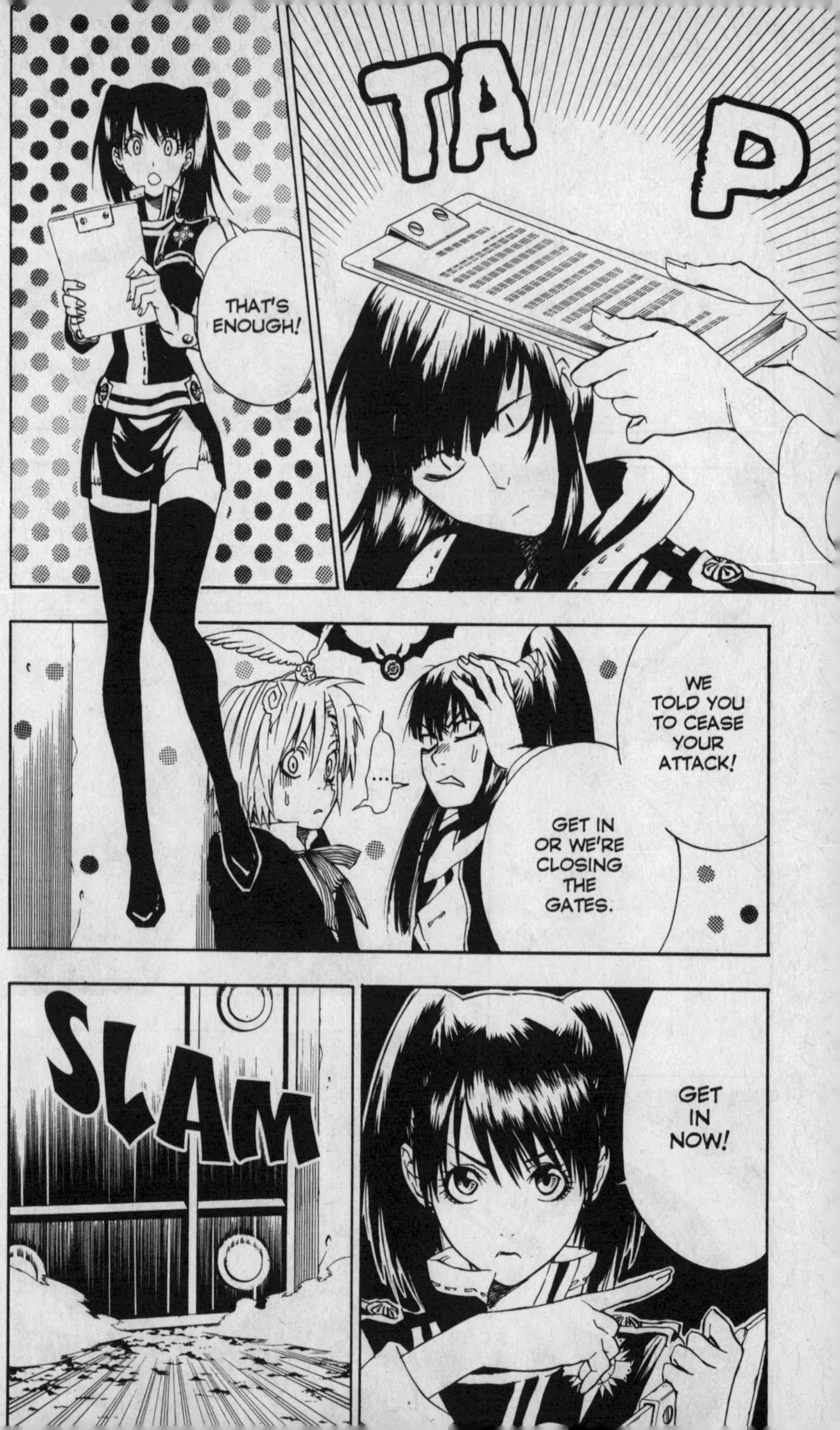
TAP
THAT'S ENOUGH!
WE TOLD YOU TO CEASE YOUR ATTACK!
GET IN OR WE'RE CLOSING THE GATES.
...
GET IN NOW!
SLAM

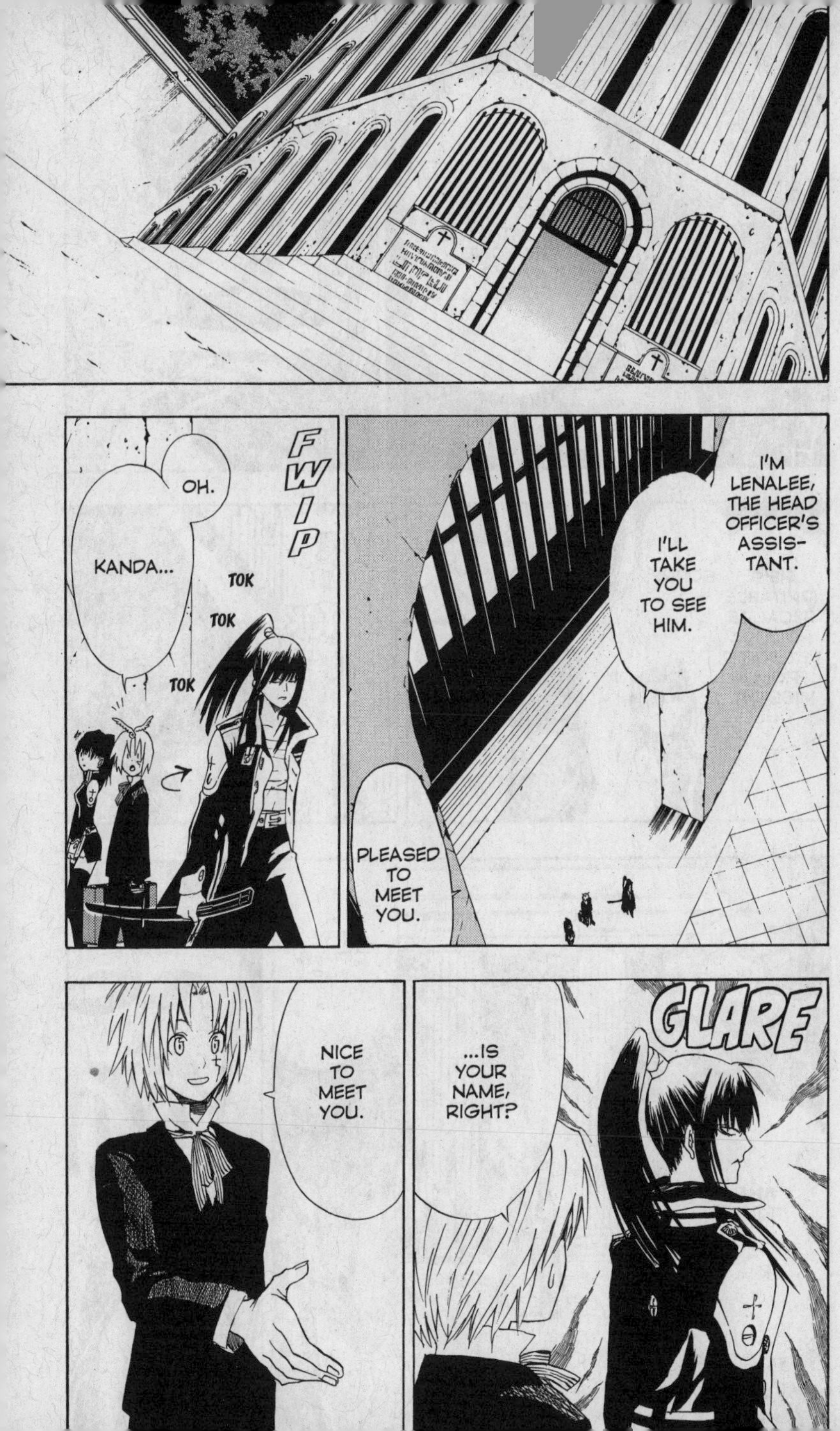
I'M LENALEE, THE HEAD OFFICER'S ASSISTANT.
I'LL TAKE YOU TO SEE HIM.
PLEASED TO MEET YOU.
FWIP
OH.
KANDA...
TOK
TOK
TOK
GLARE
...IS YOUR NAME, RIGHT?
NICE TO MEET YOU.

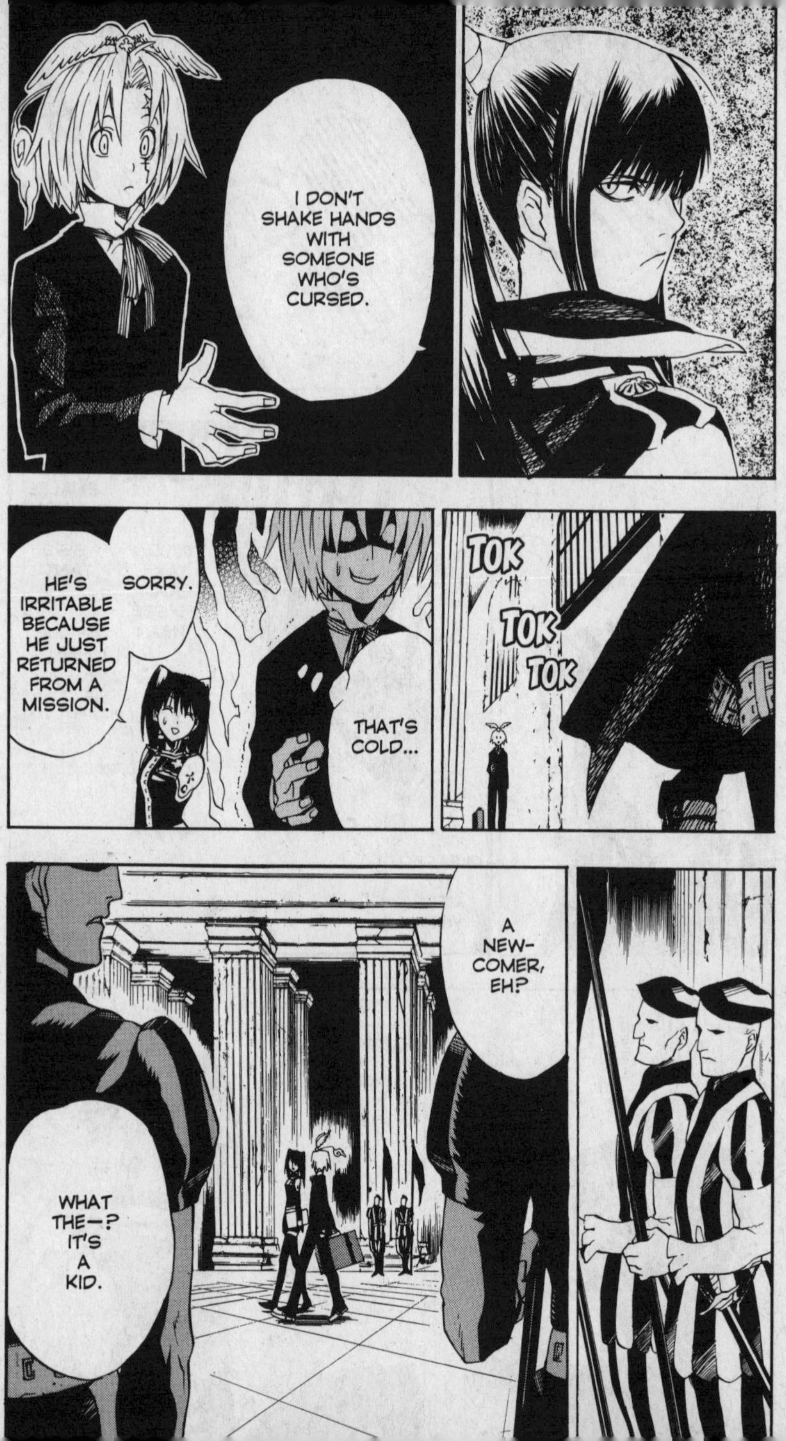
I DON'T SHAKE HANDS WITH SOMEONE WHO'S CURSED.
TOK
TOK
TOK
THAT'S COLD...
SORRY.
HE'S IRRITABLE BECAUSE HE JUST RETURNED FROM A MISSION.
A NEW-COMER, EH?
WHAT THE—? IT'S A KID.

I THOUGHT HE WAS AN OLD MAN AT FIRST... WHAT'S WITH HIS HAIR?

APPARENTLY HE'S CURSED.

ARE THEY SURE ABOUT THAT? WHAT'S A KID LIKE THAT GONNA DO...?

THEY'RE TALKING ABOUT ME...

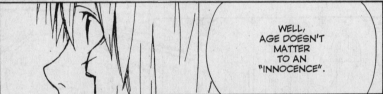

WELL, AGE DOESN'T MATTER TO AN "INNOCENCE".

ALLEN...

... WALKER, EH....

THIS IS THE BLACK ORDER.

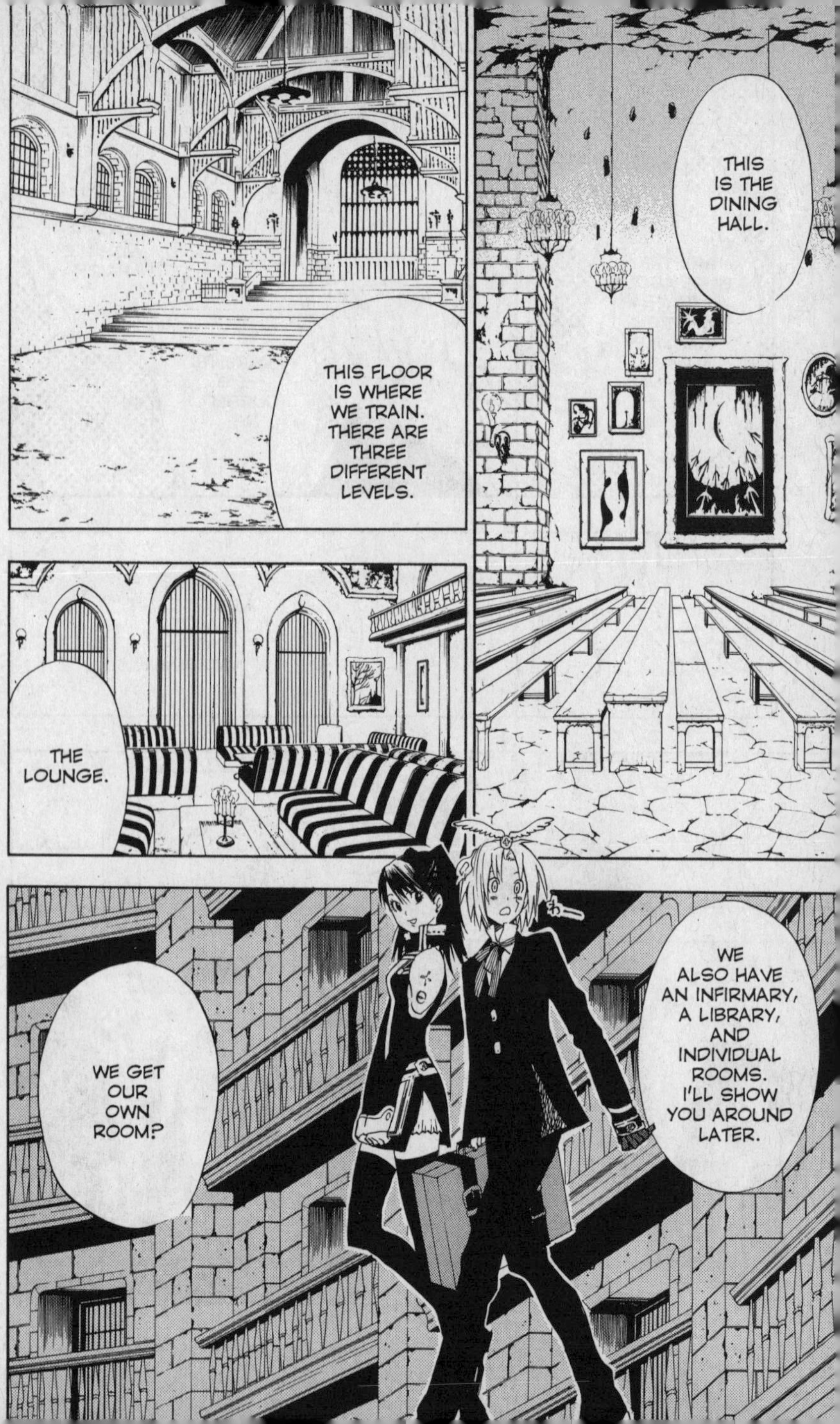
THIS IS THE DINING HALL.
THIS FLOOR IS WHERE WE TRAIN. THERE ARE THREE DIFFERENT LEVELS.
THE LOUNGE.
WE ALSO HAVE AN INFIRMARY, A LIBRARY, AND INDIVIDUAL ROOMS. I'LL SHOW YOU AROUND LATER.
WE GET OUR OWN ROOM?

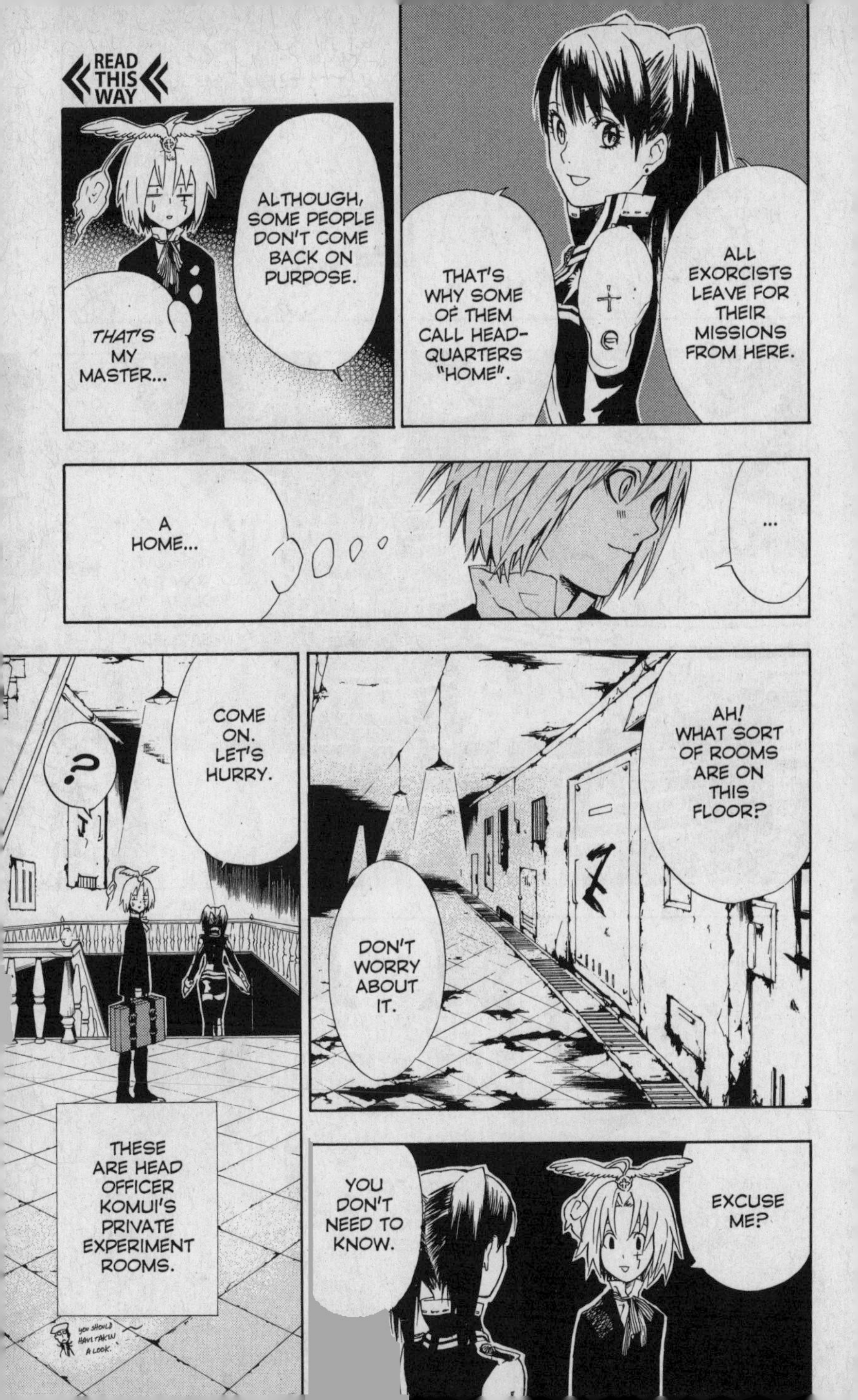
READ THIS WAY
ALL EXORCISTS LEAVE FOR THEIR MISSIONS FROM HERE.
THAT'S WHY SOME OF THEM CALL HEADQUARTERS "HOME".
ALTHOUGH, SOME PEOPLE DON'T COME BACK ON PURPOSE.
THAT'S MY MASTER...
...
A HOME...
AH! WHAT SORT OF ROOMS ARE ON THIS FLOOR?
DON'T WORRY ABOUT IT.
EXCUSE ME?
YOU DON'T NEED TO KNOW.
?
COME ON. LET'S HURRY.
THESE ARE HEAD OFFICER KOMUI'S PRIVATE EXPERIMENT ROOMS.
YOU SHOULD HAVE TAKEN A LOOK.

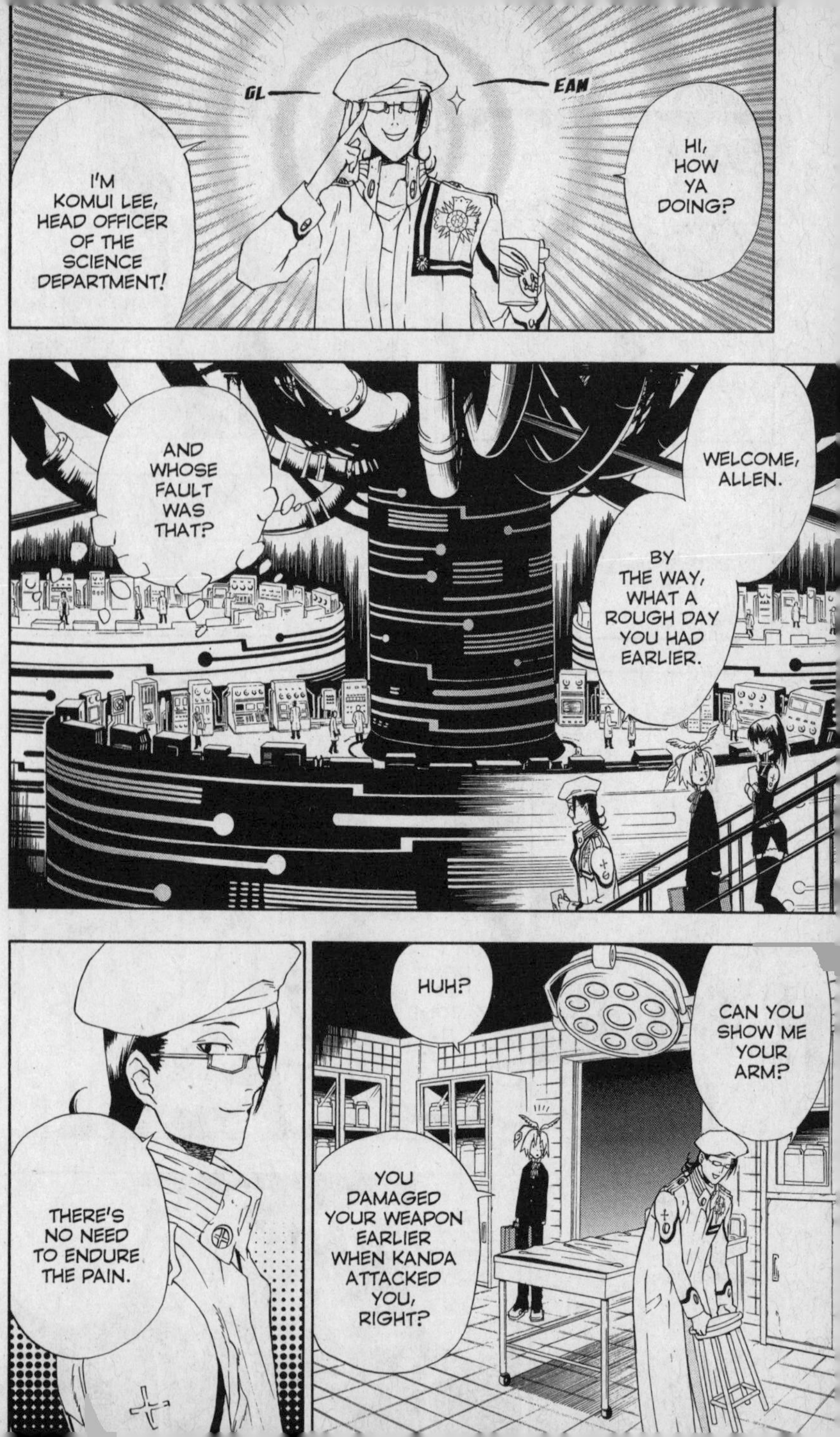
GL——EAM
HI, HOW YA DOING?
I'M KOMUI LEE, HEAD OFFICER OF THE SCIENCE DEPARTMENT!
WELCOME, ALLEN.
BY THE WAY, WHAT A ROUGH DAY YOU HAD EARLIER.
AND WHOSE FAULT WAS THAT?
CAN YOU SHOW ME YOUR ARM?
HUH?
YOU DAMAGED YOUR WEAPON EARLIER WHEN KANDA ATTACKED YOU, RIGHT?
THERE'S NO NEED TO ENDURE THE PAIN.

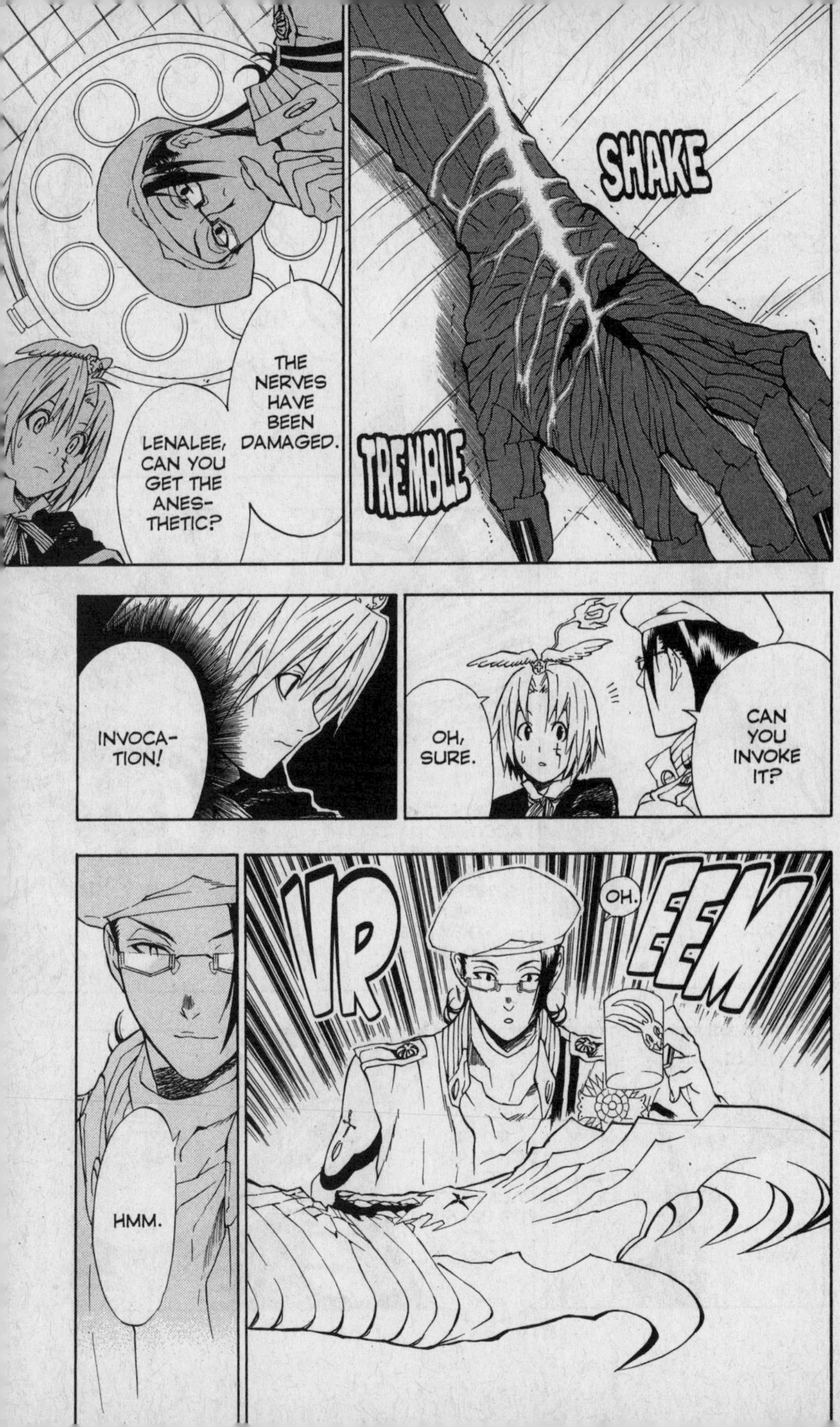
SHAKE
TREMBLE
THE NERVES HAVE BEEN DAMAGED.
LENALEE, CAN YOU GET THE ANES-THETIC?
CAN YOU INVOKE IT?
OH, SURE.
INVOCA-TION!
VR
OH.
EEM
HMM.

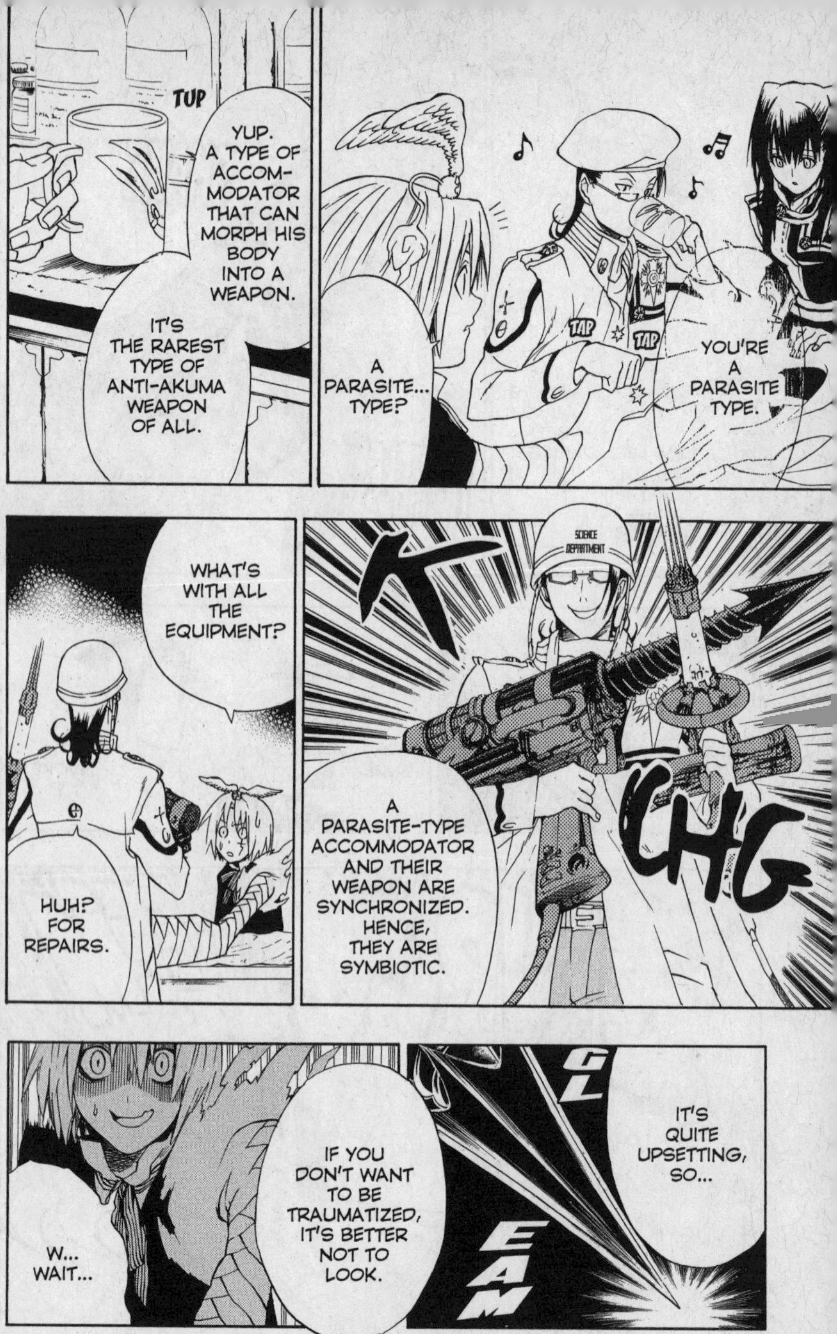
TAP
TAP
YOU'RE A PARASITE TYPE.
A PARASITE... TYPE?
TUP
YUP. A TYPE OF ACCOMMODATOR THAT CAN MORPH HIS BODY INTO A WEAPON.
IT'S THE RAREST TYPE OF ANTI-AKUMA WEAPON OF ALL.
CHG
SCIENCE DEPARTMENT
K
A PARASITE-TYPE ACCOMMODATOR AND THEIR WEAPON ARE SYNCHRONIZED. HENCE, THEY ARE SYMBIOTIC.
WHAT'S WITH ALL THE EQUIPMENT?
HUH? FOR REPAIRS.
GL
IT'S QUITE UPSETTING, SO...
EAM
IF YOU DON'T WANT TO BE TRAUMATIZED, IT'S BETTER NOT TO LOOK.
W... WAIT...

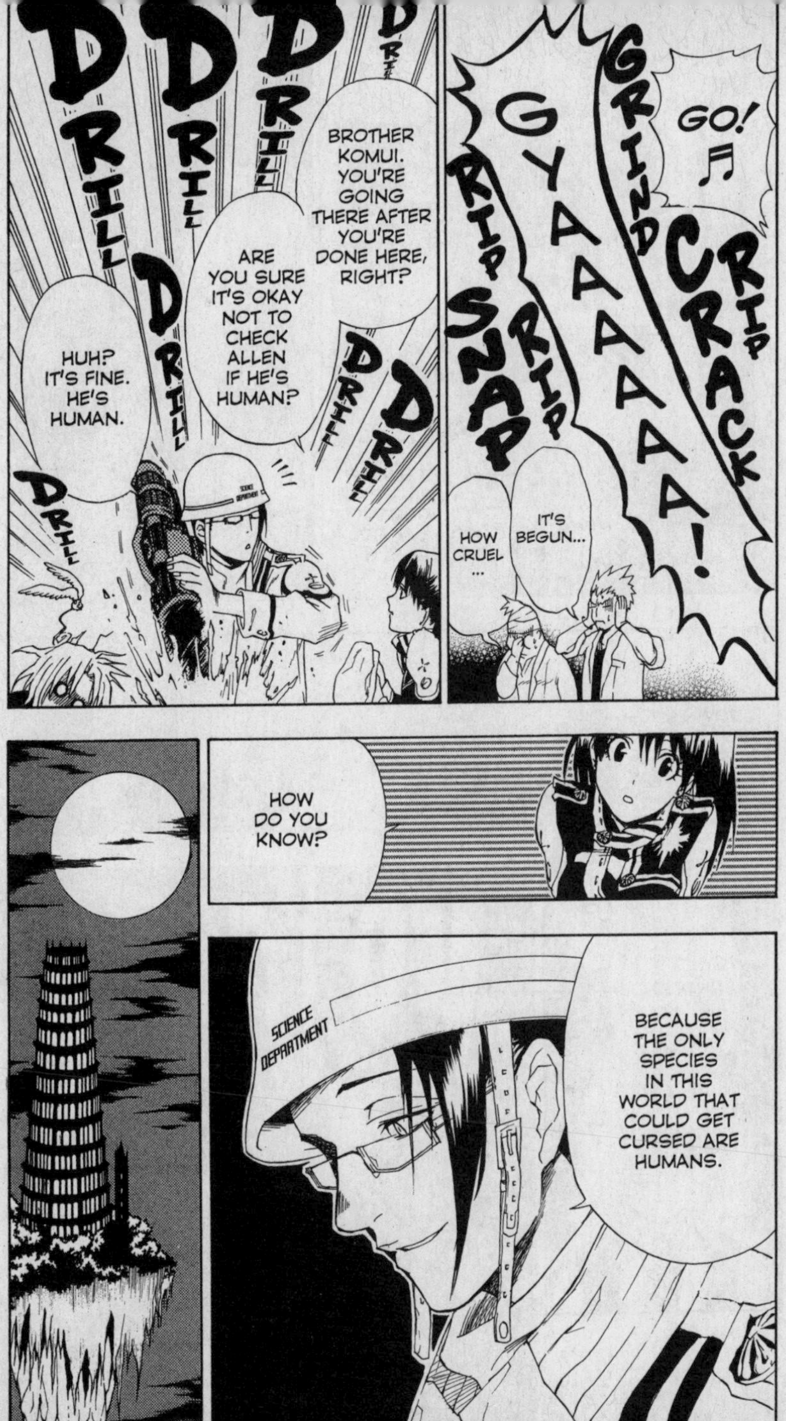
GO! ♫
GRIND
CRACK
RIP RIP
GYAAAAAA!
RIP RIP
SNAP
IT'S BEGUN...
HOW CRUEL...
DRILL
DRILL
DRILL
DRILL
BROTHER KOMUI. YOU'RE GOING THERE AFTER YOU'RE DONE HERE, RIGHT?
ARE YOU SURE IT'S OKAY NOT TO CHECK ALLEN IF HE'S HUMAN?
DRILL
DRILL
DRILL
HUH? IT'S FINE. HE'S HUMAN.
DRILL
HOW DO YOU KNOW?
SCIENCE DEPARTMENT
BECAUSE THE ONLY SPECIES IN THIS WORLD THAT COULD GET CURSED ARE HUMANS.

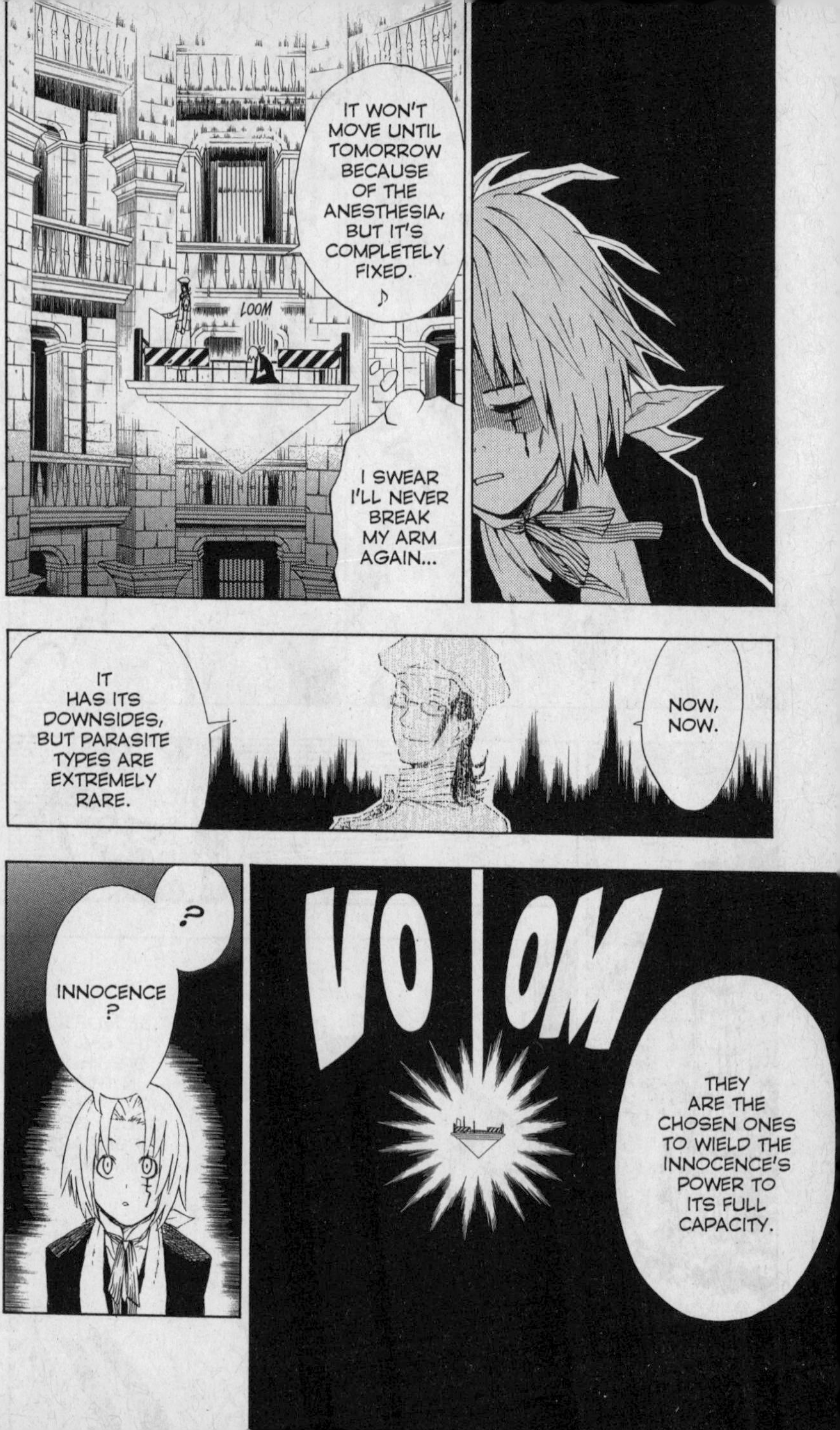
IT WON'T MOVE UNTIL TOMORROW BECAUSE OF THE ANESTHESIA, BUT IT'S COMPLETELY FIXED. ♪
LOOM
I SWEAR I'LL NEVER BREAK MY ARM AGAIN...
NOW, NOW.
IT HAS ITS DOWNSIDES, BUT PARASITE TYPES ARE EXTREMELY RARE.
VOOM
THEY ARE THE CHOSEN ONES TO WIELD THE INNOCENCE'S POWER TO ITS FULL CAPACITY.
? INNOCENCE?

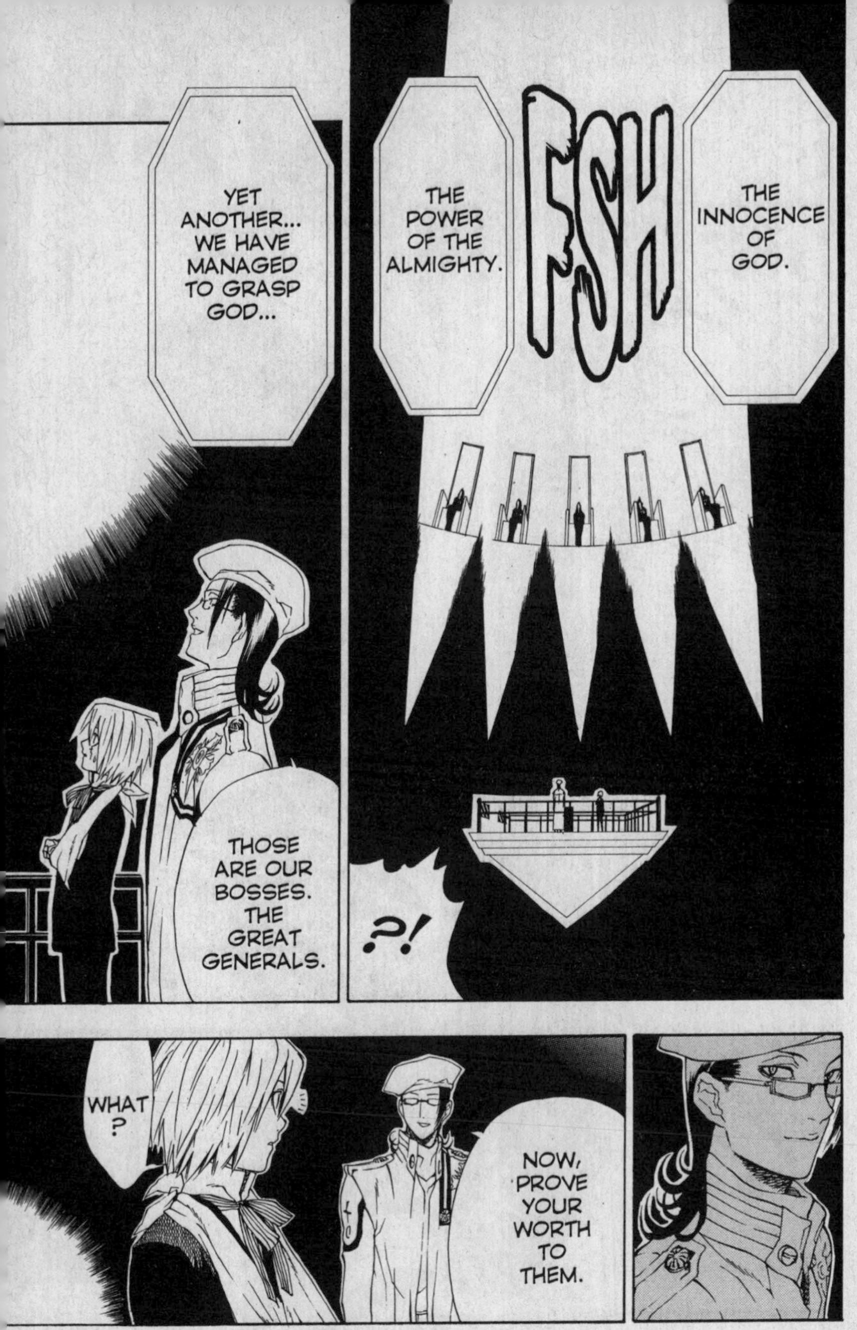
THE INNOCENCE OF GOD.
FSH
THE POWER OF THE ALMIGHTY.
?!
YET ANOTHER... WE HAVE MANAGED TO GRASP GOD...
THOSE ARE OUR BOSSES. THE GREAT GENERALS.
NOW, PROVE YOUR WORTH TO THEM.
WHAT?

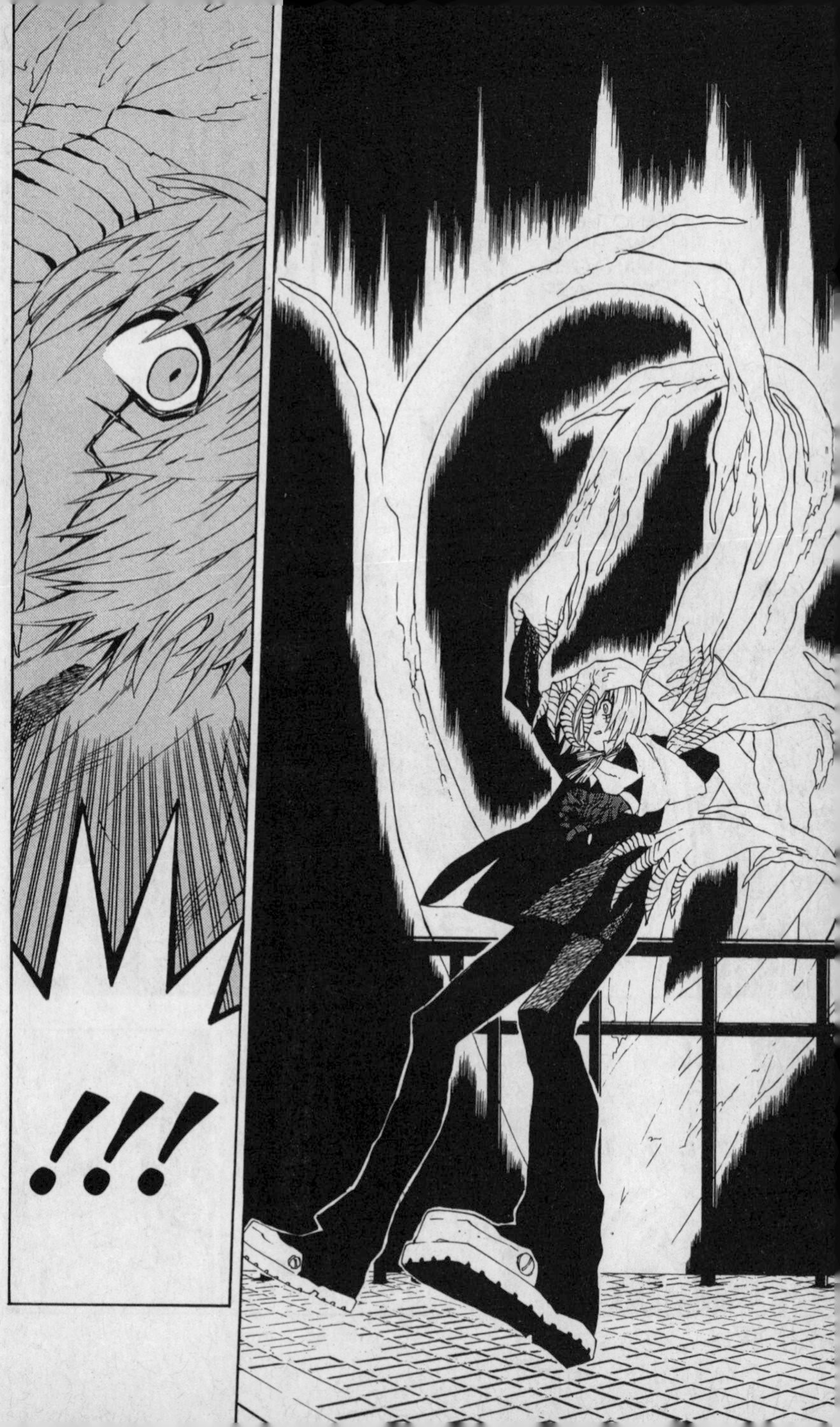
!!!

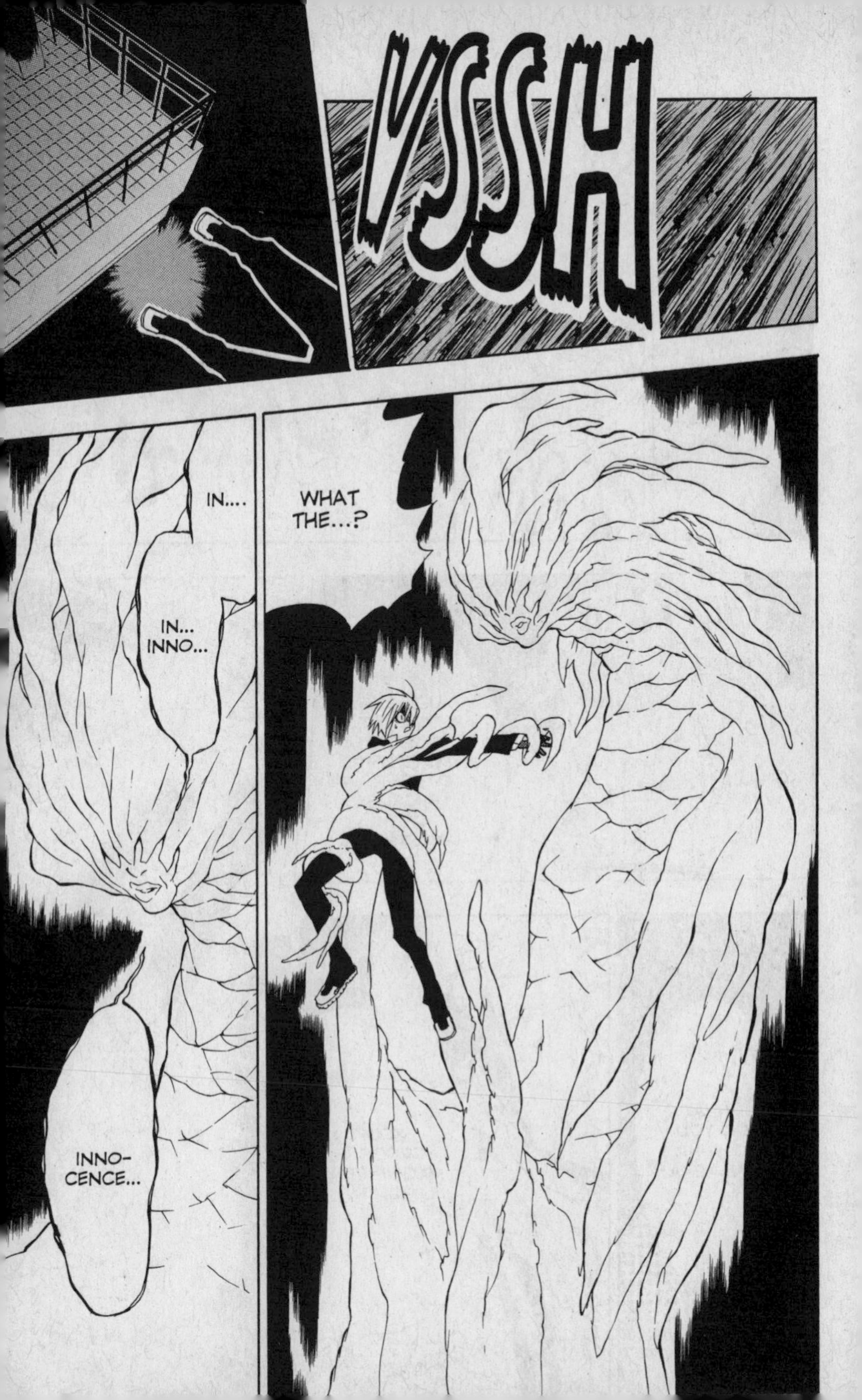
VSSH
WHAT THE...?
IN....
IN... INNO...
INNO-CENCE...

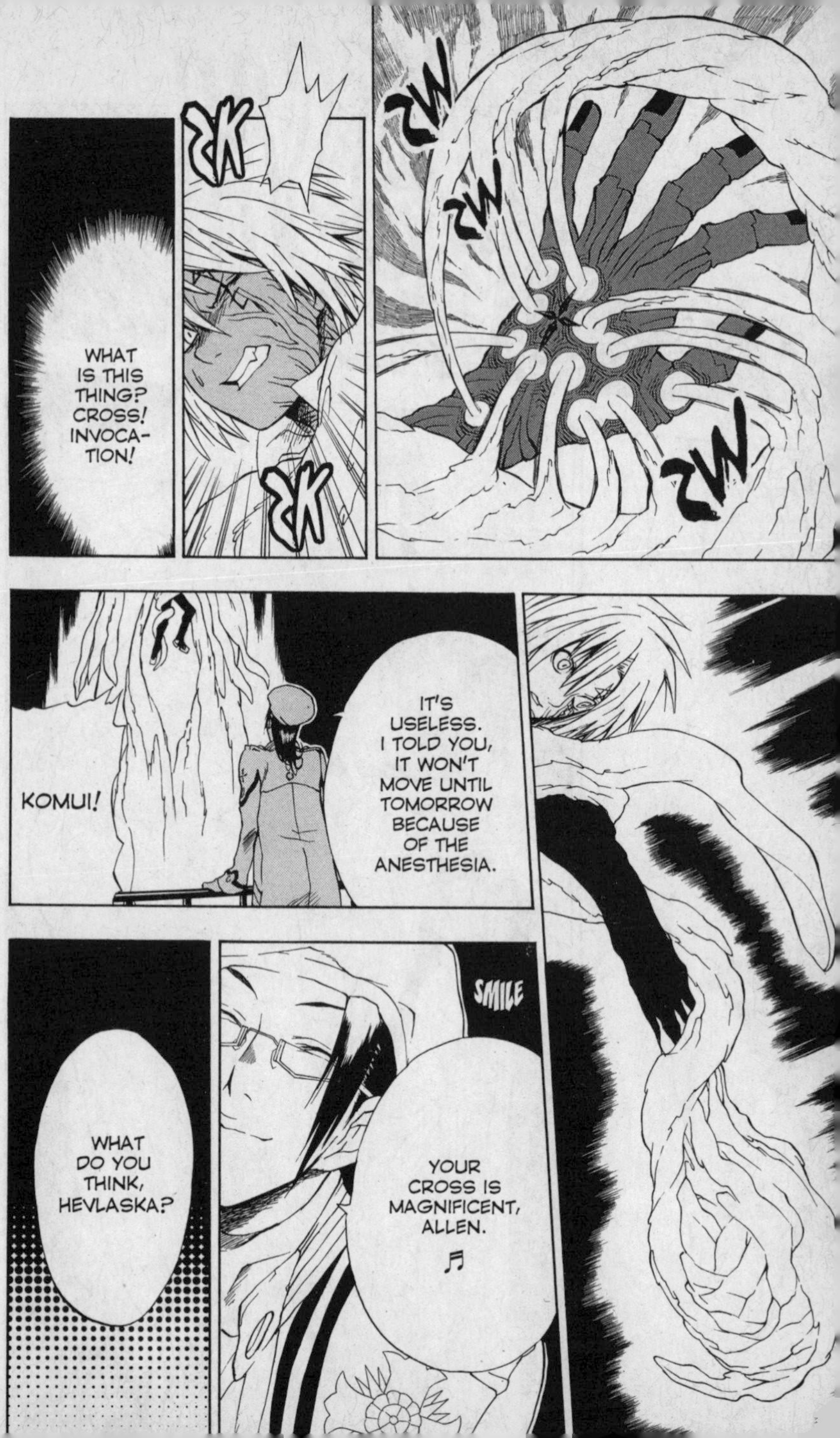
ZW
ZW
ZW
ZK
ZK
WHAT IS THIS THING? CROSS! INVOCATION!
IT'S USELESS. I TOLD YOU, IT WON'T MOVE UNTIL TOMORROW BECAUSE OF THE ANESTHESIA.
KOMUI!
SMILE
YOUR CROSS IS MAGNIFICENT, ALLEN. ♬
WHAT DO YOU THINK, HEVLASKA?

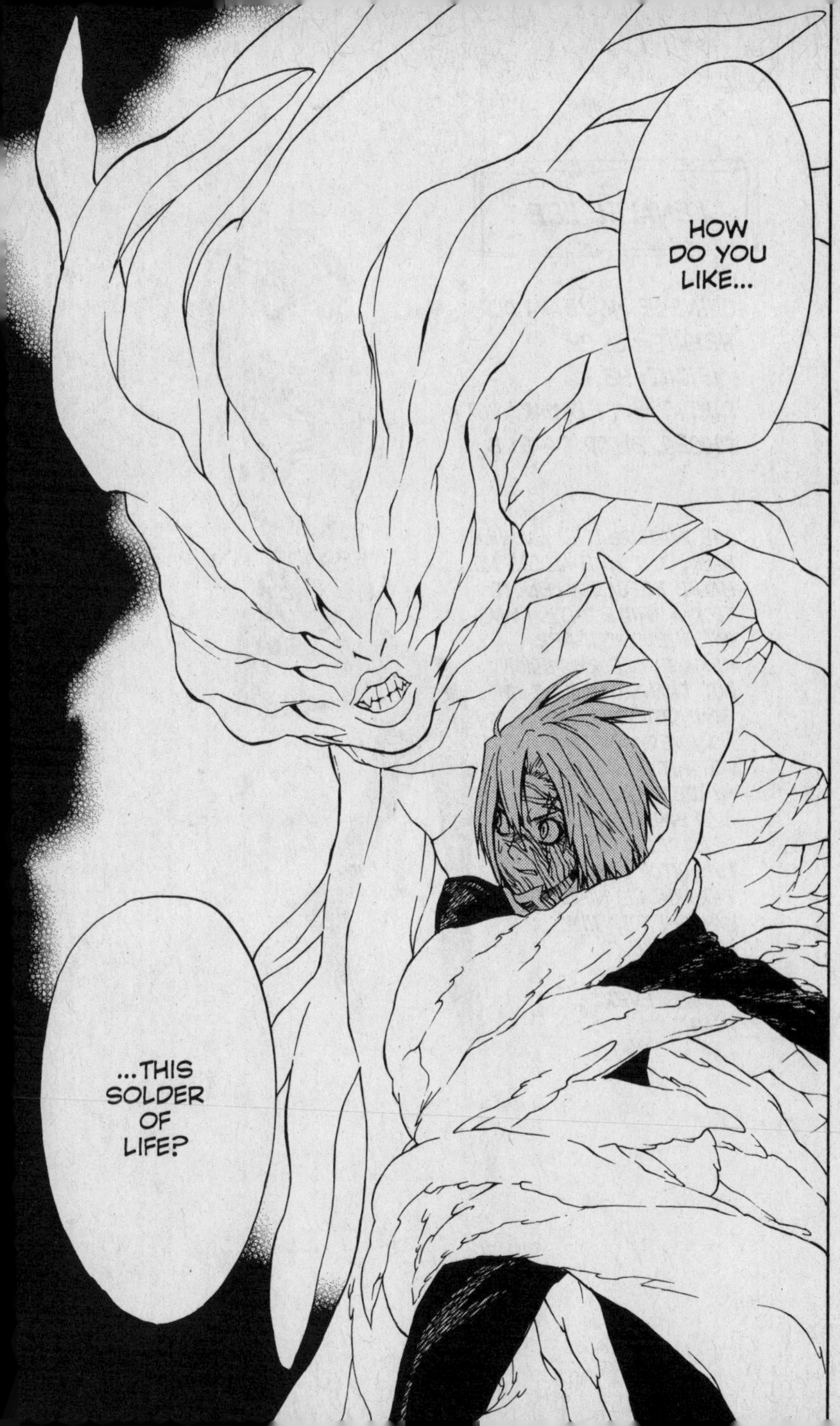
HOW DO YOU LIKE...
...THIS SOLDER OF LIFE?

LENALEE LEE

CHINESE, 16 YEARS OLD
HEIGHT: 166 CM
WEIGHT: 48 KG
BIRTHDAY: FEBRUARY 20TH
PISCES, BLOOD TYPE: B

SHE WAS CREATED A WHILE
BACK, JUST LIKE ALLEN. NO...
MAYBE BEFORE ALLEN. IT
TOOK A WHILE UNTIL I WAS
SATISFIED WITH HER
FEMALE UNIFORM DESIGN,
BUT THANKS TO ALL THAT
BRAINSTORMING, I'M
NOW VERY HAPPY
WITH IT. LENALEE IS
MY IDEAL, AND SHE'S
ALSO BASED ON A
REAL PERSON.
MY EDITOR LAUGHED
THROUGH HIS NOSE
WHEN I TOLD HIM,
SO I SWORE I'D
NEVER TELL
ANYONE EVER
AGAIN.

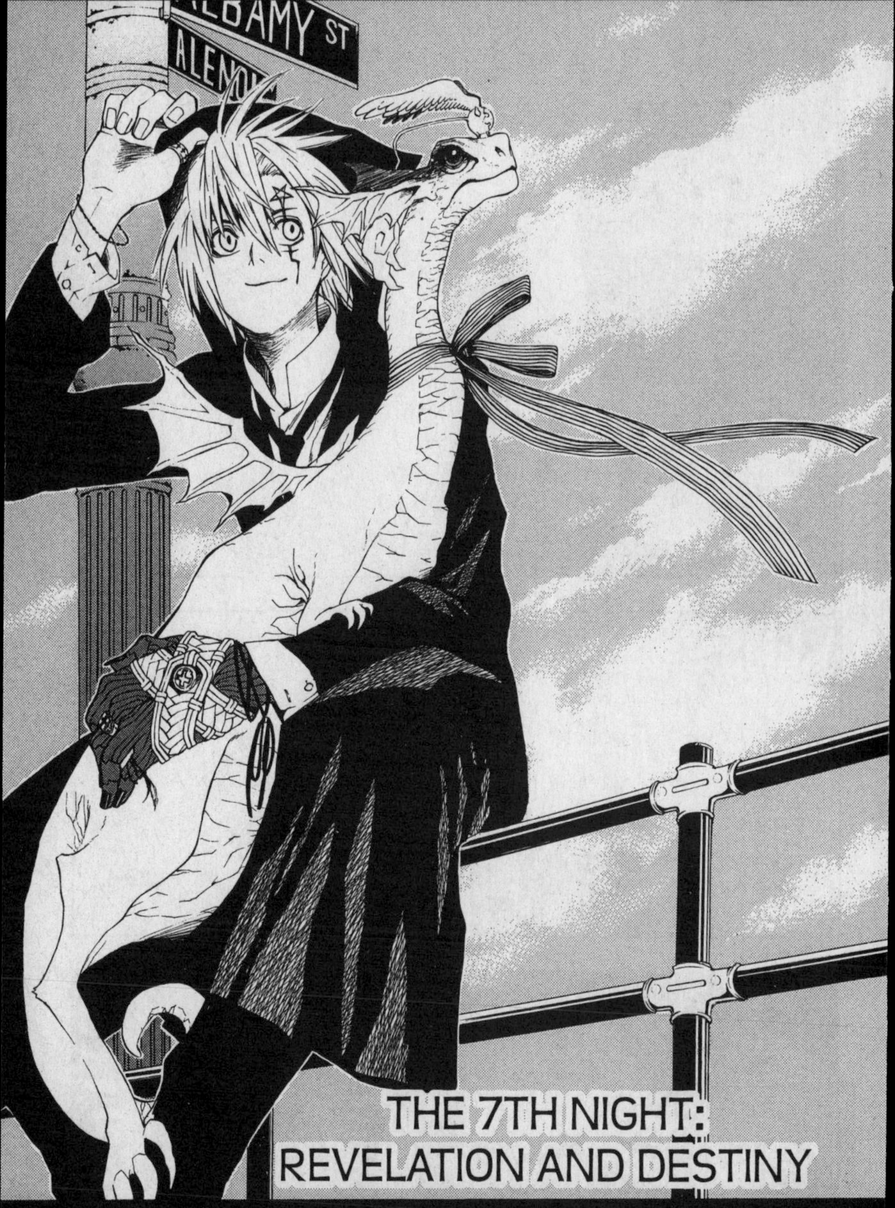
ALBAMY ST
THE 7TH NIGHT:
REVELATION AND DESTINY

GROSS! WHAT IS IT DOING?

IT FEELS LIKE IT'S PROBING THE INSIDE OF MY BODY.

SHK SHK

UGH.

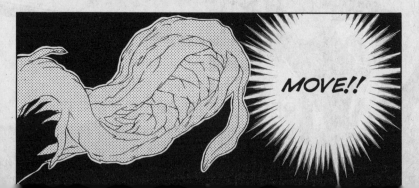

MOVE!!

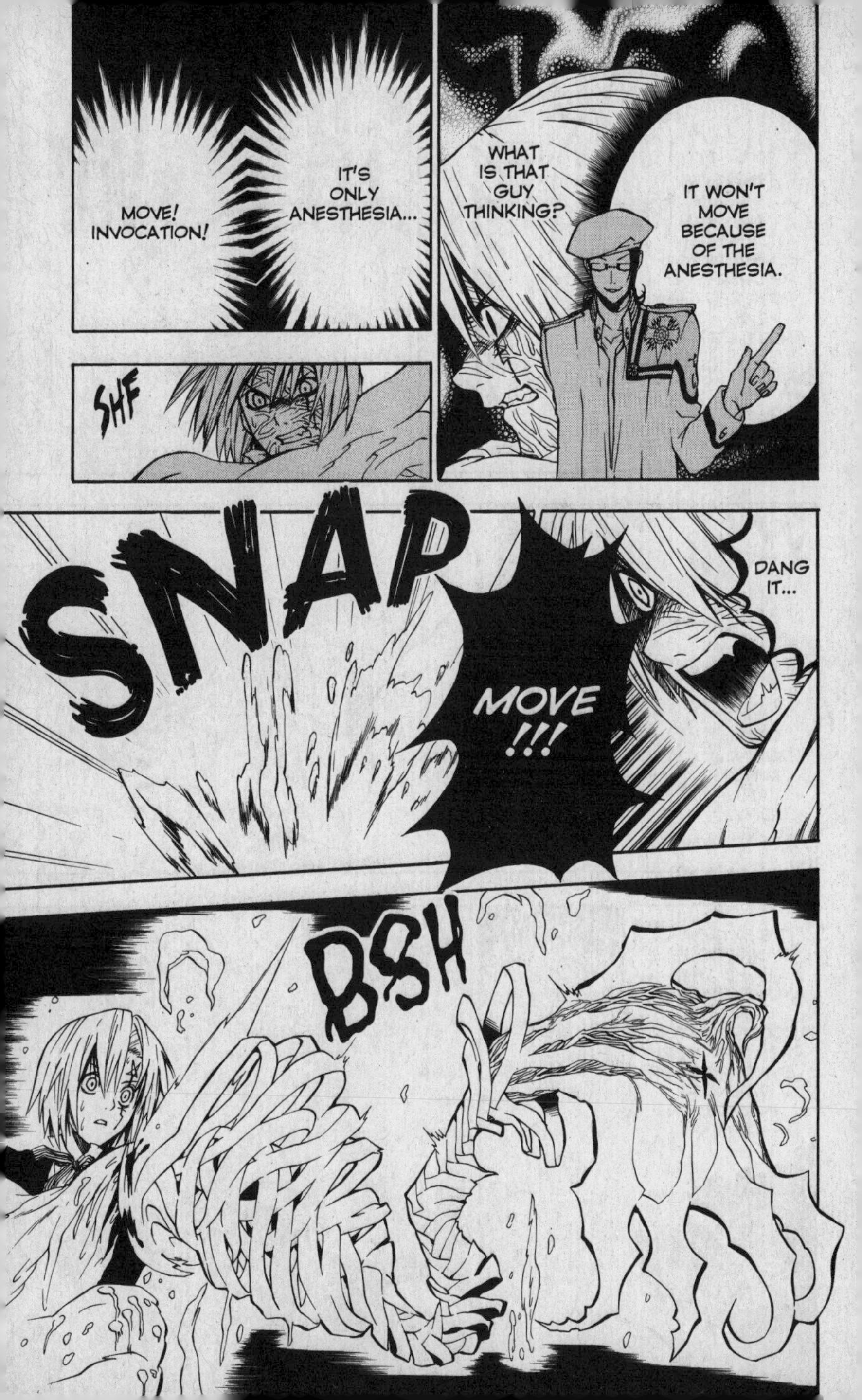
IT WON'T MOVE BECAUSE OF THE ANESTHESIA.
WHAT IS THAT GUY THINKING?
IT'S ONLY ANESTHESIA...
MOVE! INVOCATION!
SHF
DANG IT...
MOVE !!!
SNAP
BSH

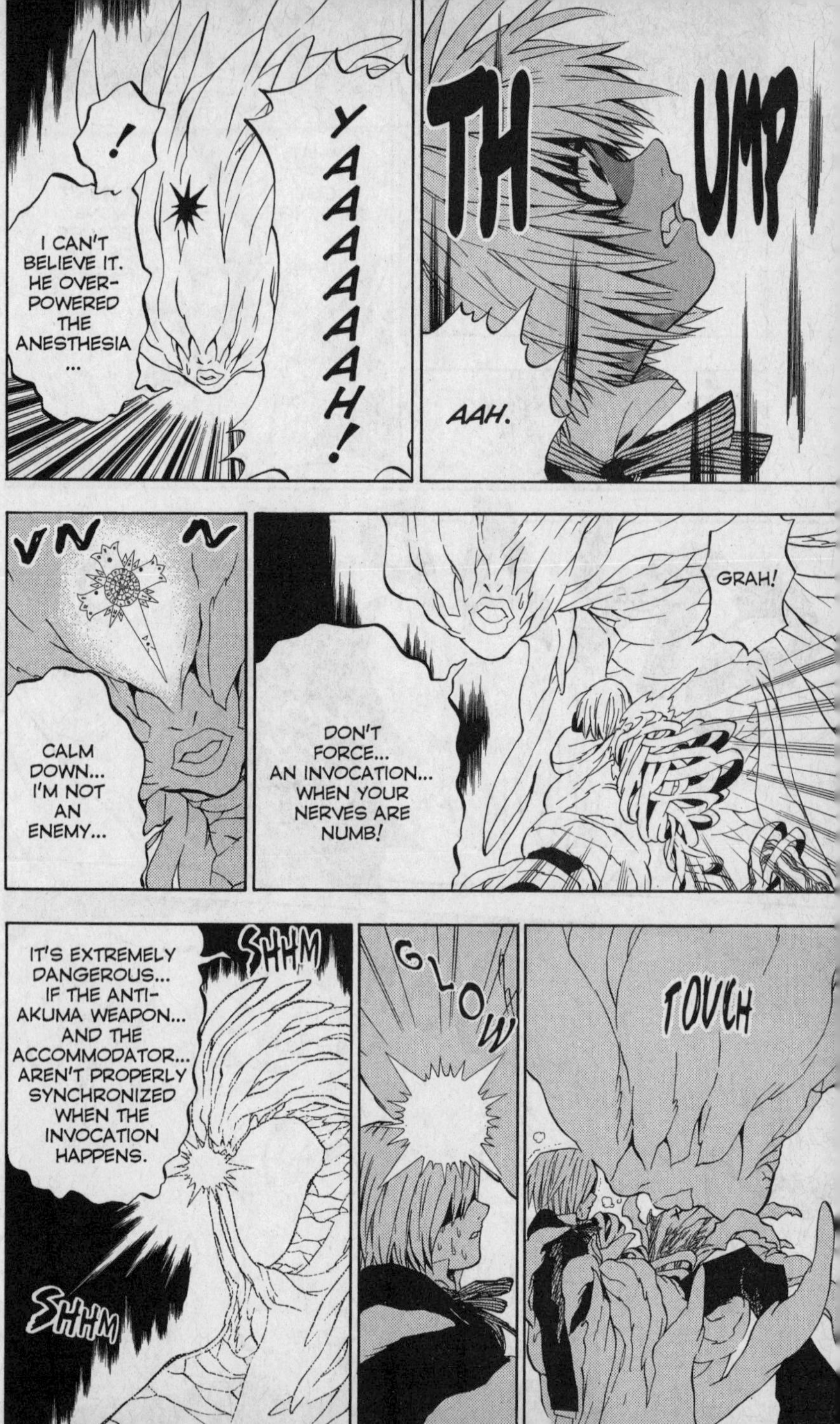
THUMP
AAH.
YAAAAAAAAH!
!
I CAN'T BELIEVE IT. HE OVER-POWERED THE ANESTHESIA ...
GRAH!
DON'T FORCE... AN INVOCATION... WHEN YOUR NERVES ARE NUMB!
VNN
CALM DOWN... I'M NOT AN ENEMY...
TOUCH
GLOW
SHHM
IT'S EXTREMELY DANGEROUS... IF THE ANTI-AKUMA WEAPON... AND THE ACCOMMODATOR... AREN'T PROPERLY SYNCHRONIZED WHEN THE INVOCATION HAPPENS.
SHHM

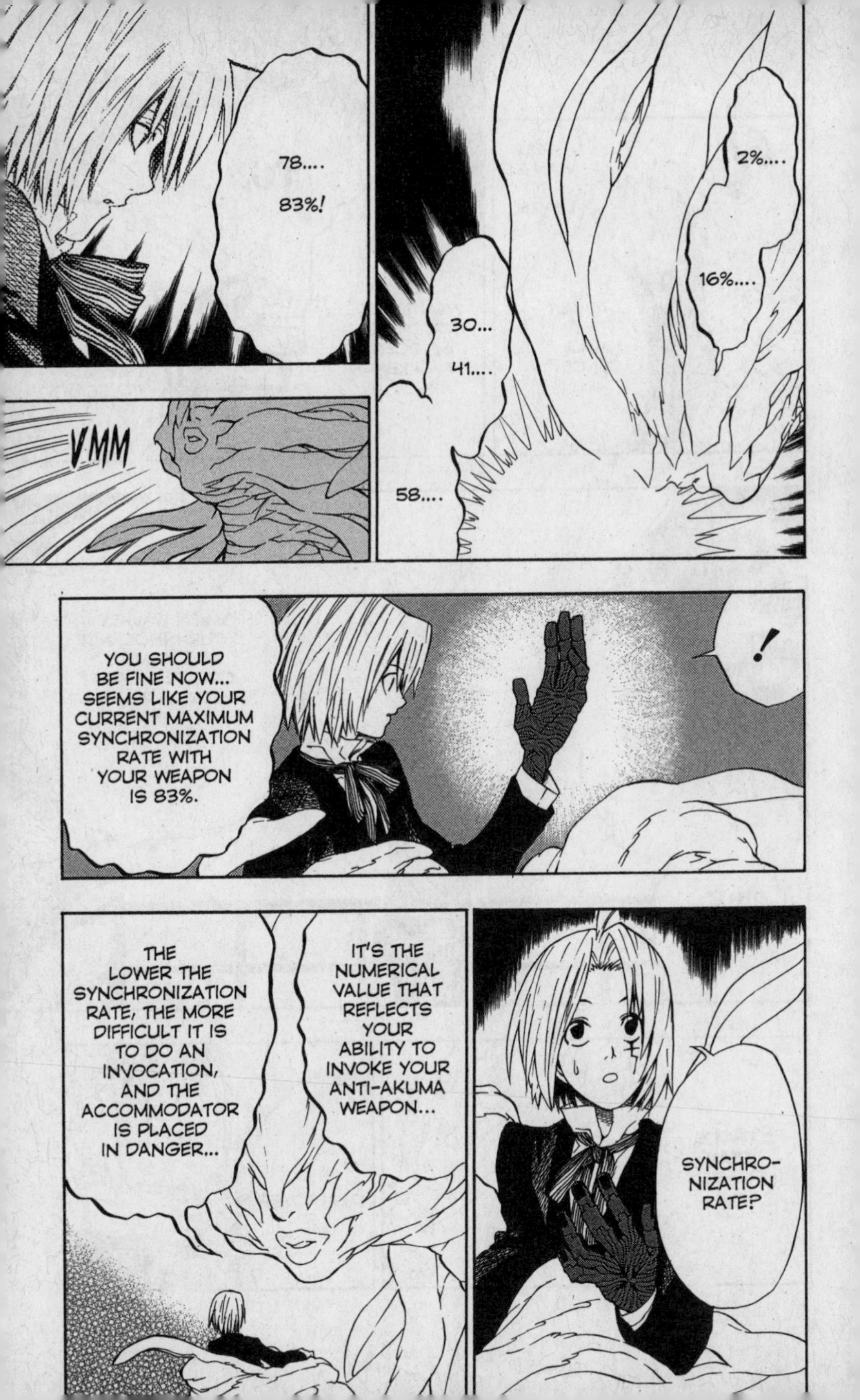
2%....
16%....
30...
41....
58....
78....
83%!
VMM
!
YOU SHOULD BE FINE NOW... SEEMS LIKE YOUR CURRENT MAXIMUM SYNCHRONIZATION RATE WITH YOUR WEAPON IS 83%.
SYNCHRO-NIZATION RATE?
IT'S THE NUMERICAL VALUE THAT REFLECTS YOUR ABILITY TO INVOKE YOUR ANTI-AKUMA WEAPON...
THE LOWER THE SYNCHRONIZATION RATE, THE MORE DIFFICULT IT IS TO DO AN INVOCATION, AND THE ACCOMMODATOR IS PLACED IN DANGER...

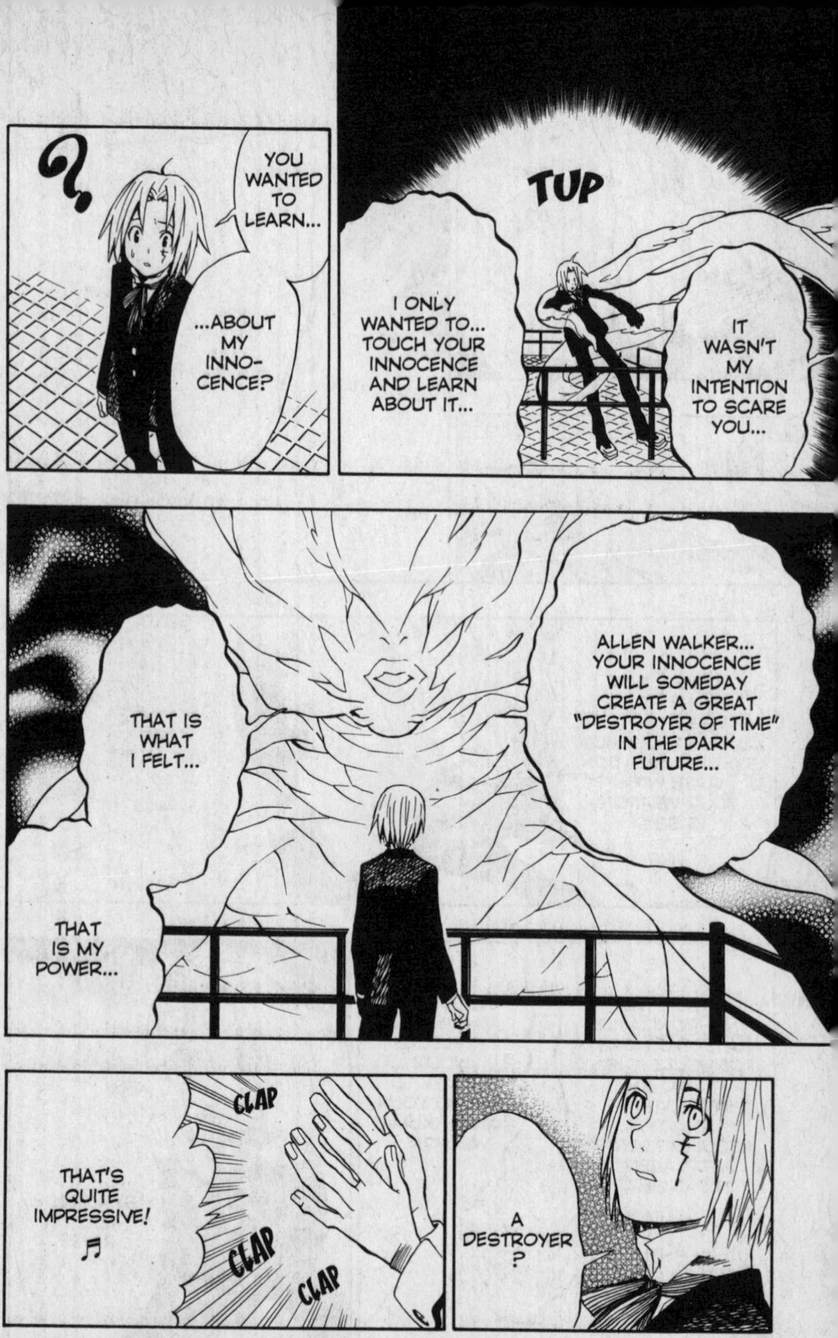
TUP
IT WASN'T MY INTENTION TO SCARE YOU...
I ONLY WANTED TO... TOUCH YOUR INNOCENCE AND LEARN ABOUT IT...
YOU WANTED TO LEARN...
...ABOUT MY INNO-CENCE?
ALLEN WALKER... YOUR INNOCENCE WILL SOMEDAY CREATE A GREAT "DESTROYER OF TIME" IN THE DARK FUTURE...
THAT IS WHAT I FELT...
THAT IS MY POWER...
A DESTROYER?
CLAP
THAT'S QUITE IMPRESSIVE! ♬
CLAP
CLAP

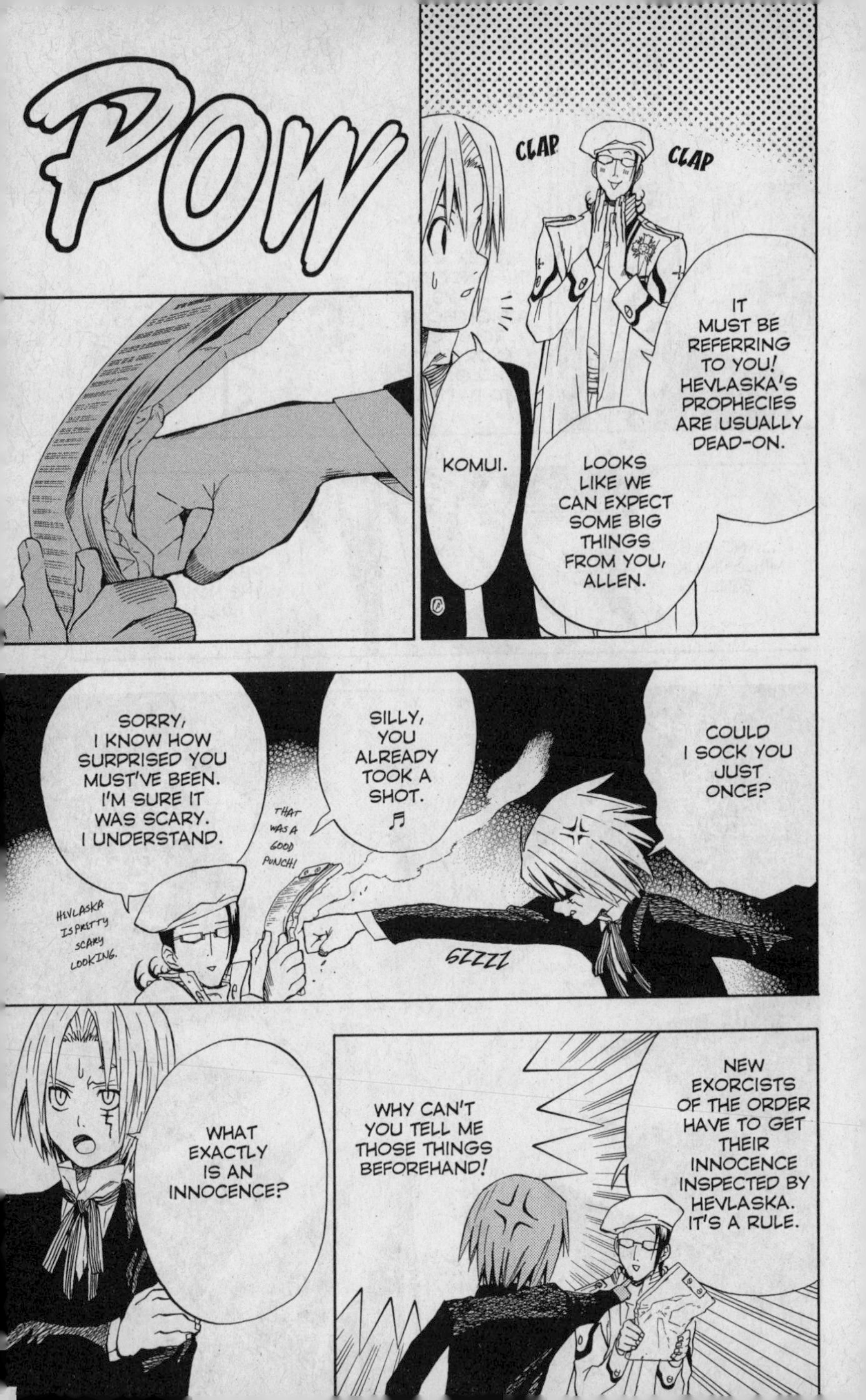
CLAP
CLAP
IT MUST BE REFERRING TO YOU! HEVLASKA'S PROPHECIES ARE USUALLY DEAD-ON.
LOOKS LIKE WE CAN EXPECT SOME BIG THINGS FROM YOU, ALLEN.
KOMUI.
POW
COULD I SOCK YOU JUST ONCE?
SILLY, YOU ALREADY TOOK A SHOT. ♬
THAT WAS A GOOD PUNCH!
SORRY, I KNOW HOW SURPRISED YOU MUST'VE BEEN. I'M SURE IT WAS SCARY. I UNDERSTAND.
HEVLASKA IS PRETTY SCARY LOOKING.
SZZZZ
NEW EXORCISTS OF THE ORDER HAVE TO GET THEIR INNOCENCE INSPECTED BY HEVLASKA. IT'S A RULE.
WHY CAN'T YOU TELL ME THOSE THINGS BEFOREHAND!
WHAT EXACTLY IS AN INNOCENCE?

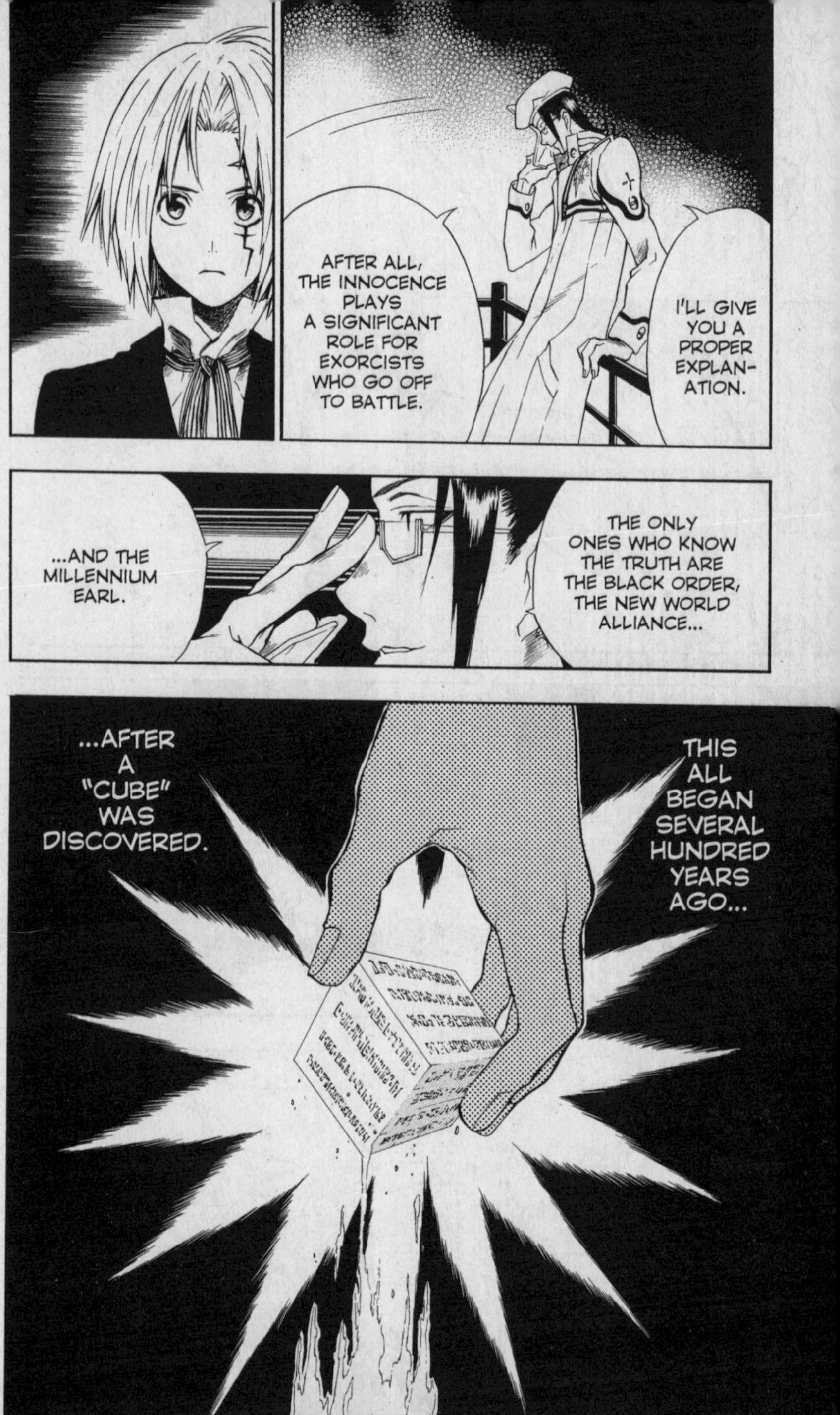
I'LL GIVE YOU A PROPER EXPLANATION.
AFTER ALL, THE INNOCENCE PLAYS A SIGNIFICANT ROLE FOR EXORCISTS WHO GO OFF TO BATTLE.
THE ONLY ONES WHO KNOW THE TRUTH ARE THE BLACK ORDER, THE NEW WORLD ALLIANCE...
...AND THE MILLENNIUM EARL.
THIS ALL BEGAN SEVERAL HUNDRED YEARS AGO...
...AFTER A "CUBE" WAS DISCOVERED.

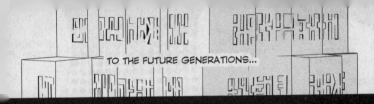

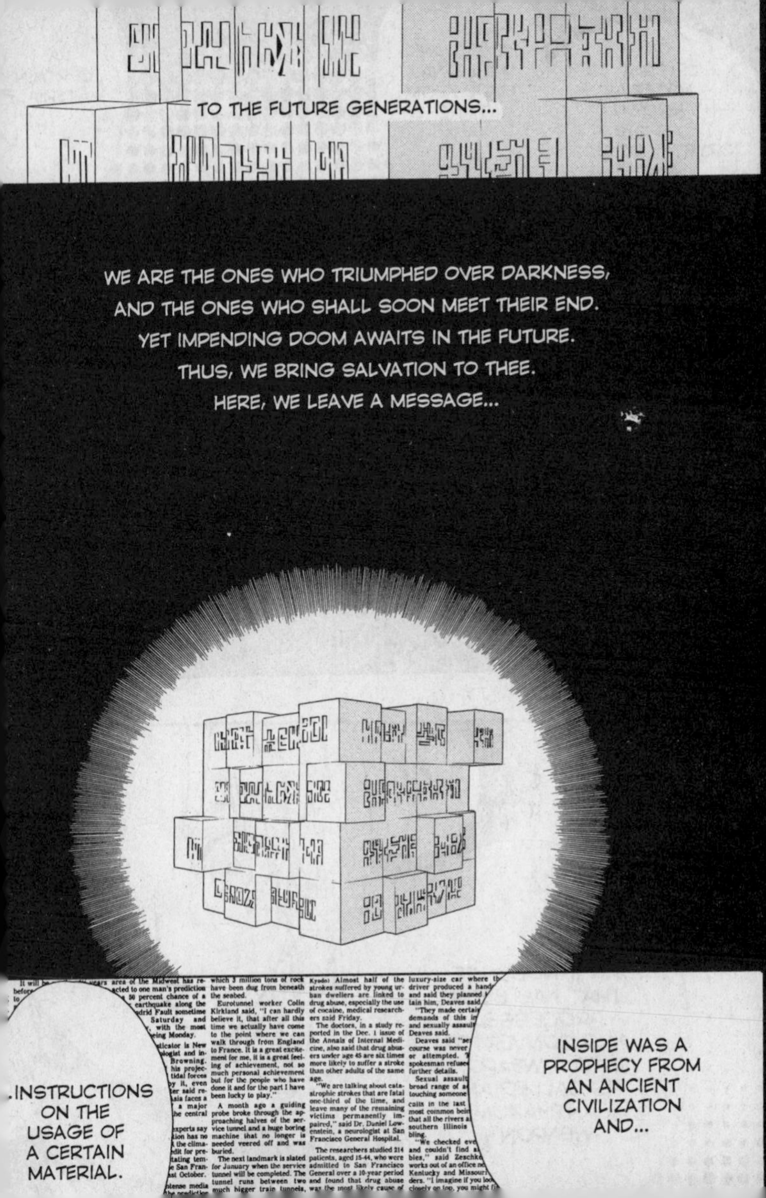

TO THE FUTURE GENERATIONS...
WE ARE THE ONES WHO TRIUMPHED OVER DARKNESS, AND THE ONES WHO SHALL SOON MEET THEIR END. YET IMPENDING DOOM AWAITS IN THE FUTURE. THUS, WE BRING SALVATION TO THEE. HERE, WE LEAVE A MESSAGE...
INSIDE WAS A PROPHECY FROM AN ANCIENT CIVILIZATION AND...
...INSTRUCTIONS ON THE USAGE OF A CERTAIN MATERIAL.

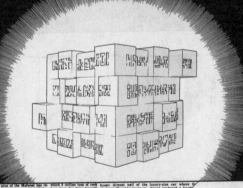

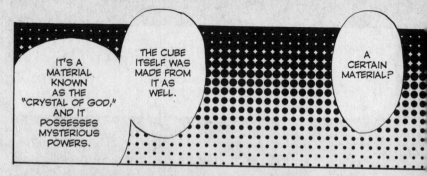

A CERTAIN MATERIAL?
THE CUBE ITSELF WAS MADE FROM IT AS WELL.
IT'S A MATERIAL KNOWN AS THE "CRYSTAL OF GOD," AND IT POSSESSES MYSTERIOUS POWERS.
WE CALL IT "INNOCENCE".
IT'S THE CROSS THAT'S EMBEDDED IN YOUR LEFT HAND.
!!
AN INNOCENCE THAT HAS BEEN PROCESSED AND CONVERTED INTO A WEAPON IS CALLED AN "ANTI-AKUMA WEAPON".

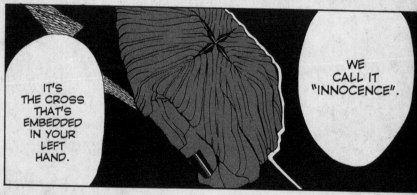

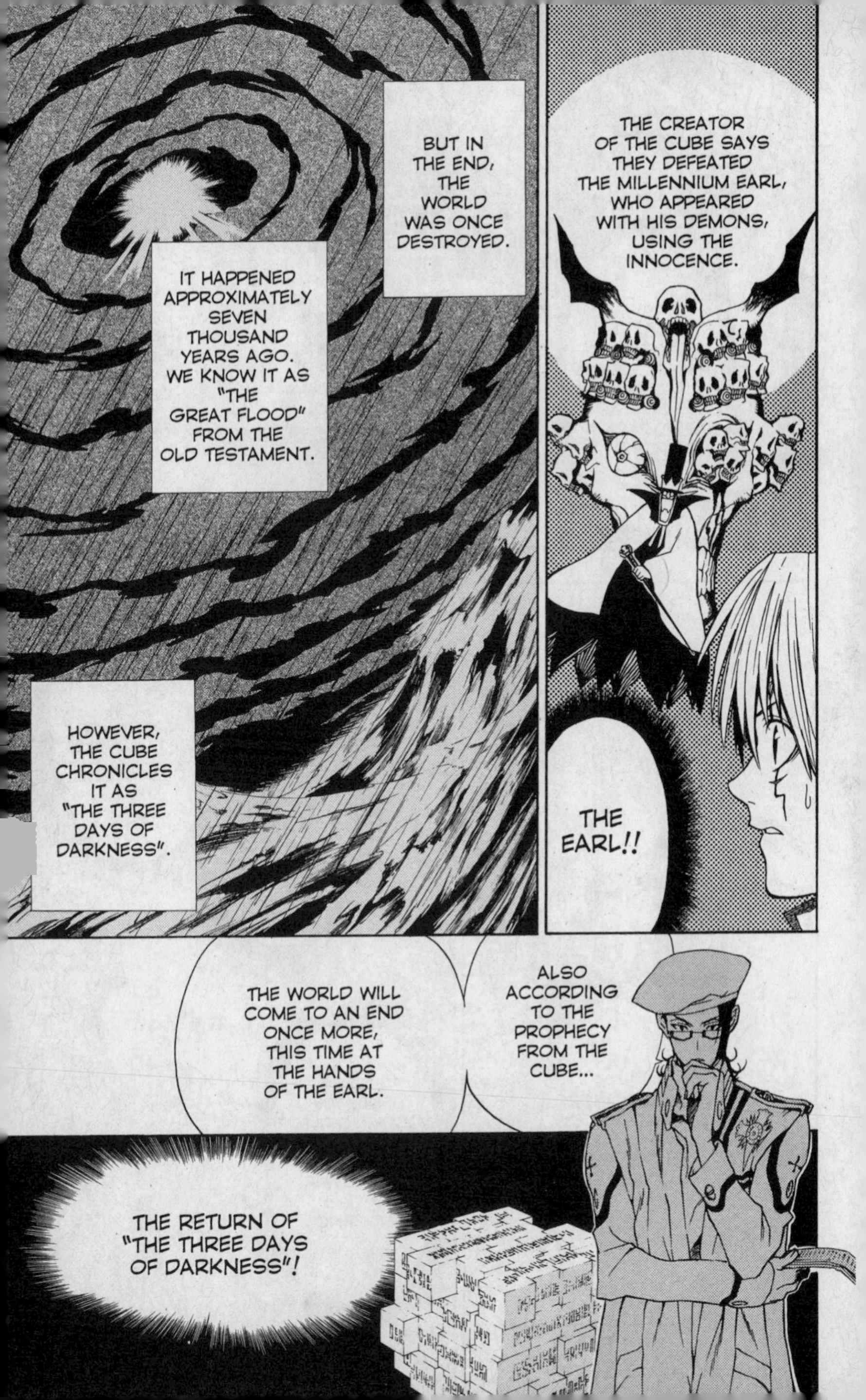
THE CREATOR OF THE CUBE SAYS THEY DEFEATED THE MILLENNIUM EARL, WHO APPEARED WITH HIS DEMONS, USING THE INNOCENCE.
THE EARL!!
BUT IN THE END, THE WORLD WAS ONCE DESTROYED.
IT HAPPENED APPROXIMATELY SEVEN THOUSAND YEARS AGO. WE KNOW IT AS "THE GREAT FLOOD" FROM THE OLD TESTAMENT.
HOWEVER, THE CUBE CHRONICLES IT AS "THE THREE DAYS OF DARKNESS".
ALSO ACCORDING TO THE PROPHECY FROM THE CUBE...
THE WORLD WILL COME TO AN END ONCE MORE, THIS TIME AT THE HANDS OF THE EARL.
THE RETURN OF "THE THREE DAYS OF DARKNESS"!

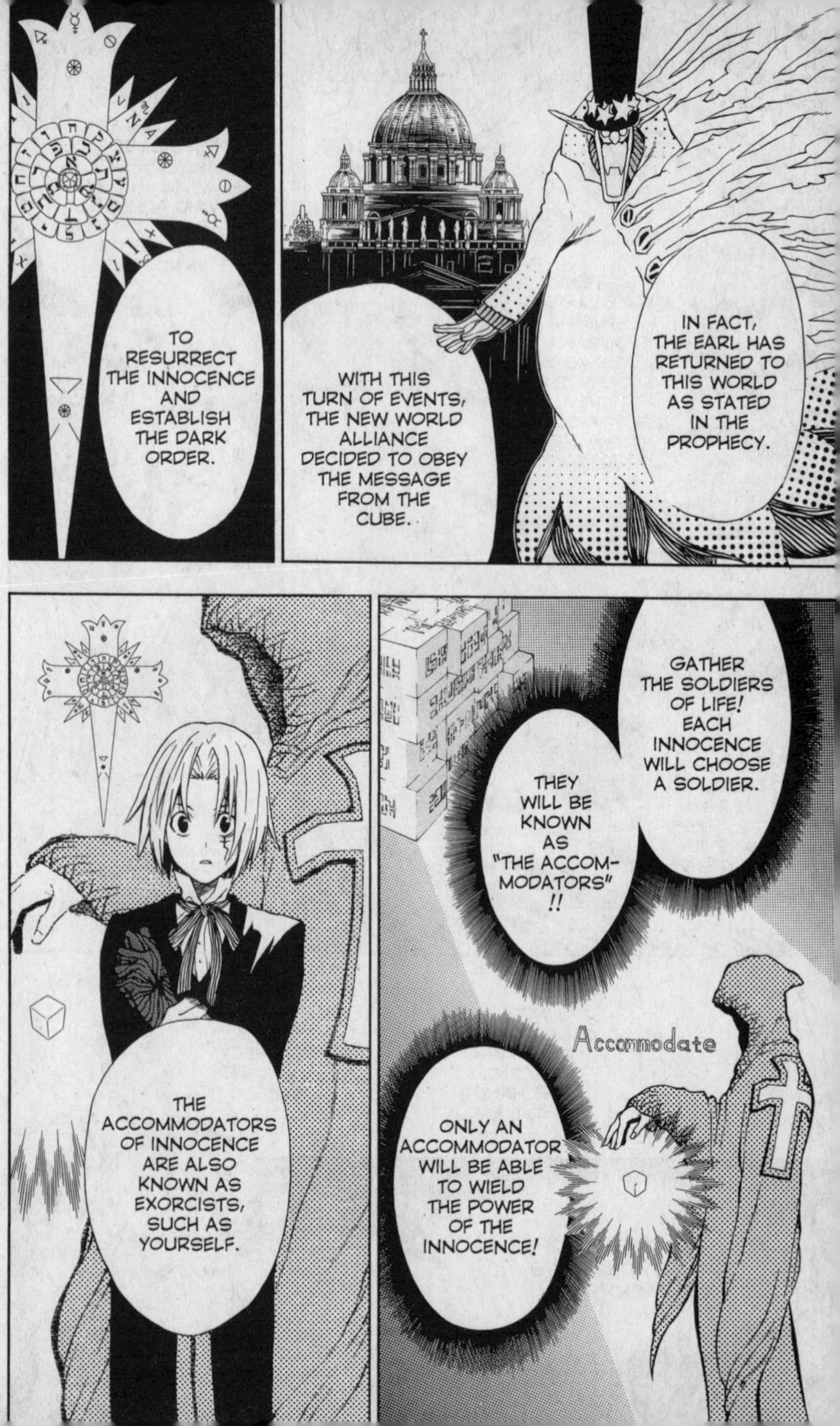
IN FACT, THE EARL HAS RETURNED TO THIS WORLD AS STATED IN THE PROPHECY.
WITH THIS TURN OF EVENTS, THE NEW WORLD ALLIANCE DECIDED TO OBEY THE MESSAGE FROM THE CUBE.
TO RESURRECT THE INNOCENCE AND ESTABLISH THE DARK ORDER.
GATHER THE SOLDIERS OF LIFE! EACH INNOCENCE WILL CHOOSE A SOLDIER.
THEY WILL BE KNOWN AS "THE ACCOM-MODATORS" !!
Accommodate
ONLY AN ACCOMMODATOR WILL BE ABLE TO WIELD THE POWER OF THE INNOCENCE!
THE ACCOMMODATORS OF INNOCENCE ARE ALSO KNOWN AS EXORCISTS, SUCH AS YOURSELF.

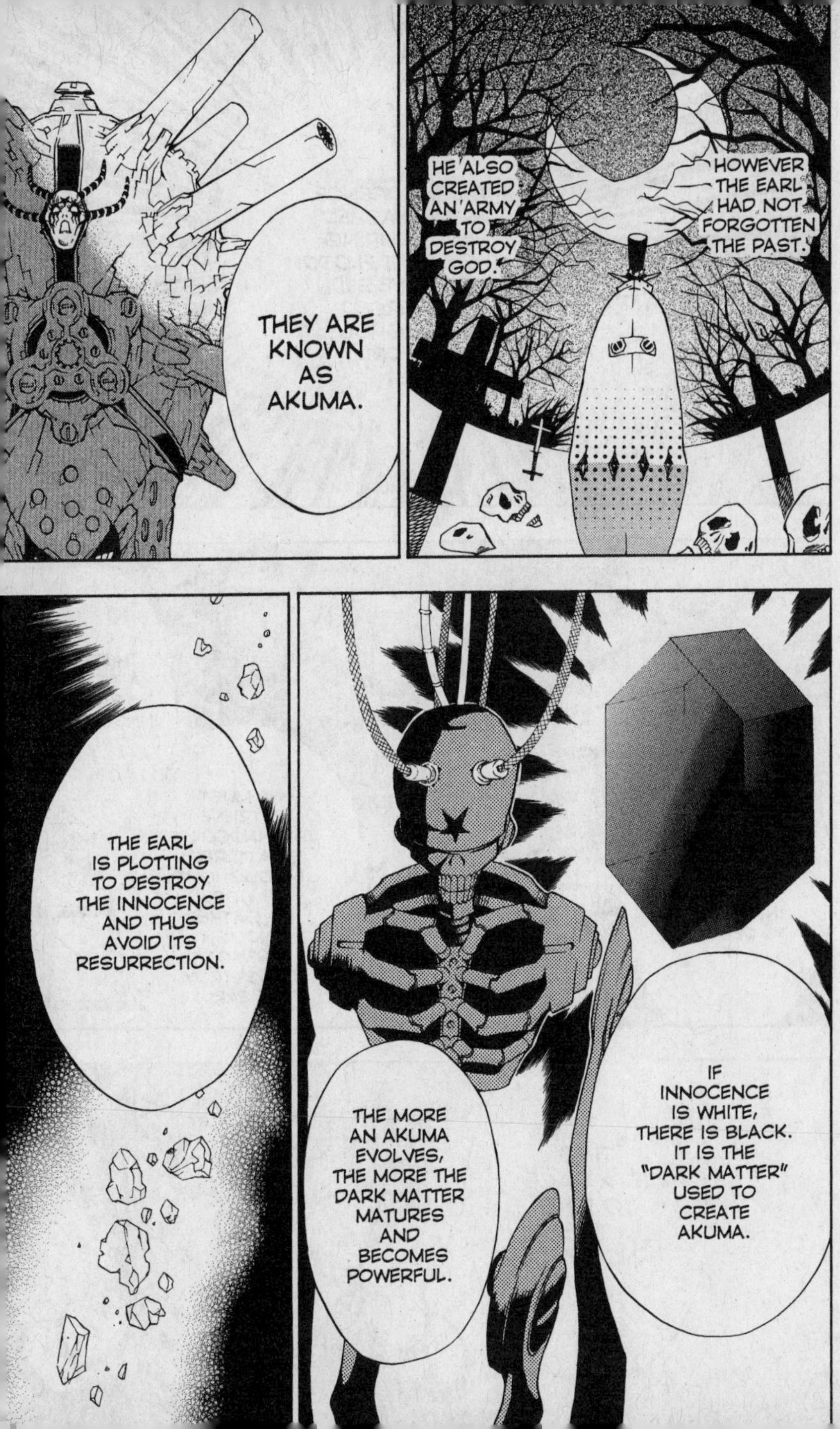
HOWEVER THE EARL HAD NOT FORGOTTEN THE PAST.
HE ALSO CREATED AN ARMY TO DESTROY GOD.
THEY ARE KNOWN AS AKUMA.
IF INNOCENCE IS WHITE, THERE IS BLACK. IT IS THE "DARK MATTER" USED TO CREATE AKUMA.
THE MORE AN AKUMA EVOLVES, THE MORE THE DARK MATTER MATURES AND BECOMES POWERFUL.
THE EARL IS PLOTTING TO DESTROY THE INNOCENCE AND THUS AVOID ITS RESURRECTION.

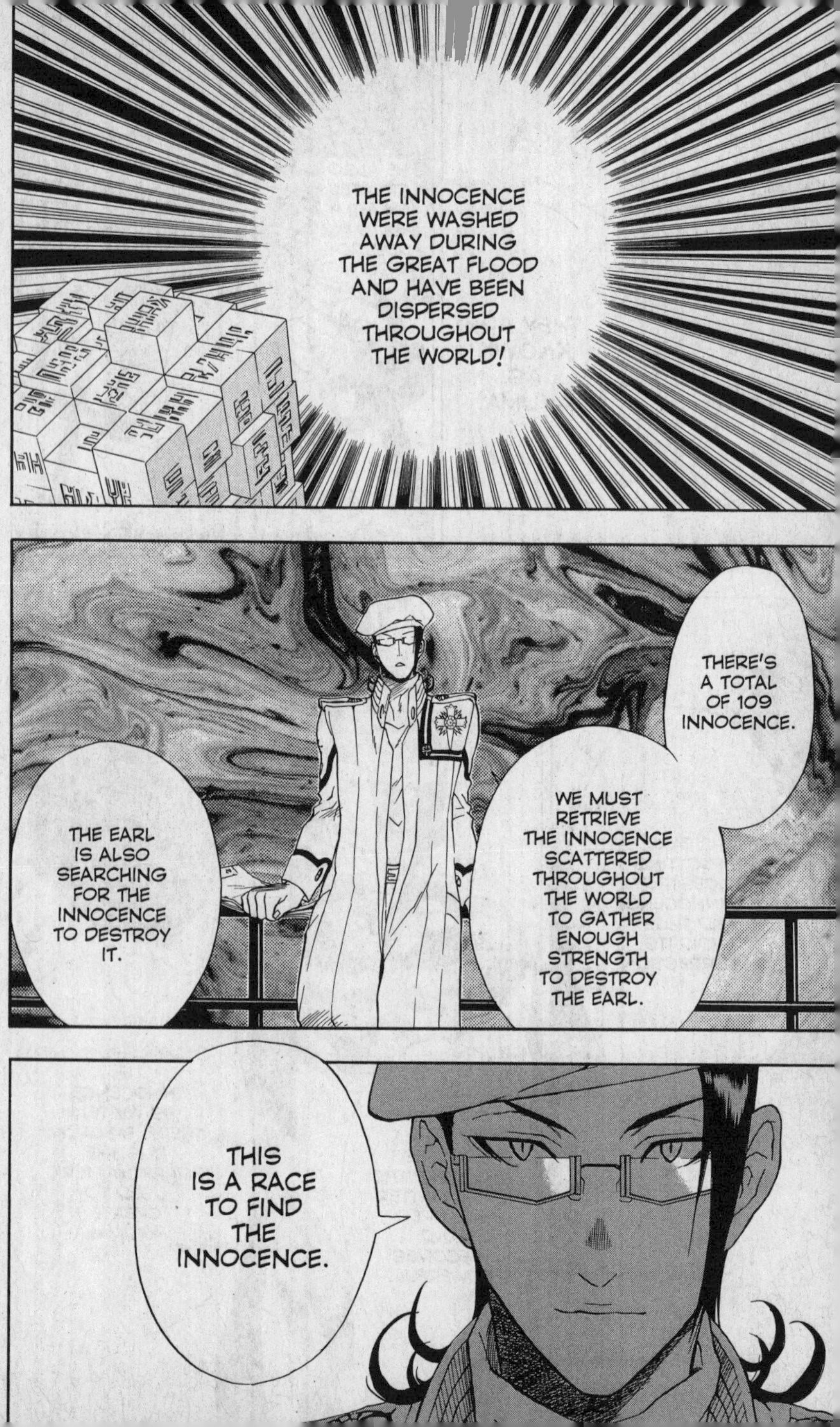
THE INNOCENCE WERE WASHED AWAY DURING THE GREAT FLOOD AND HAVE BEEN DISPERSED THROUGHOUT THE WORLD!
THERE'S A TOTAL OF 109 INNOCENCE.
WE MUST RETRIEVE THE INNOCENCE SCATTERED THROUGHOUT THE WORLD TO GATHER ENOUGH STRENGTH TO DESTROY THE EARL.
THE EARL IS ALSO SEARCHING FOR THE INNOCENCE TO DESTROY IT.
THIS IS A RACE TO FIND THE INNOCENCE.

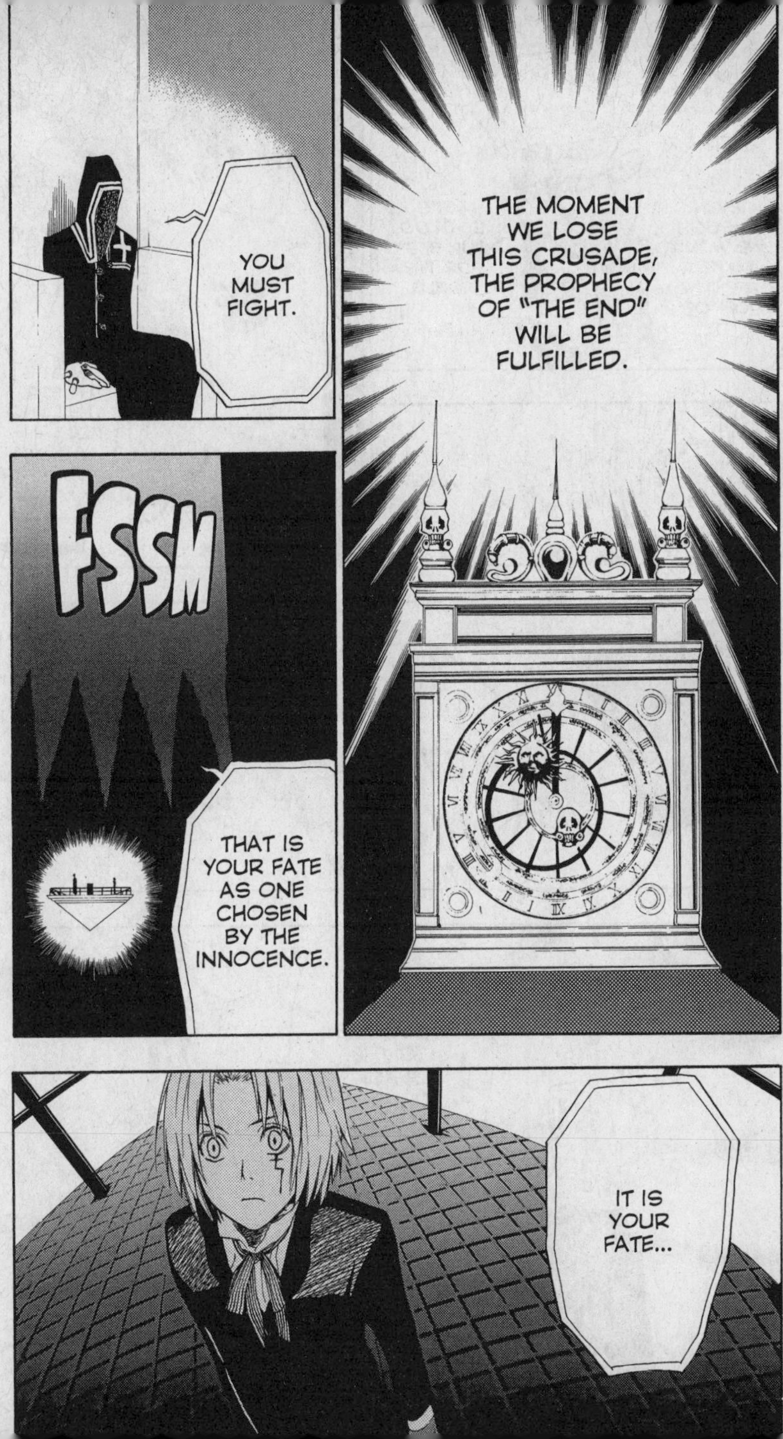
THE MOMENT WE LOSE THIS CRUSADE, THE PROPHECY OF "THE END" WILL BE FULFILLED.
YOU MUST FIGHT.
FSSM
THAT IS YOUR FATE AS ONE CHOSEN BY THE INNOCENCE.
IT IS YOUR FATE...

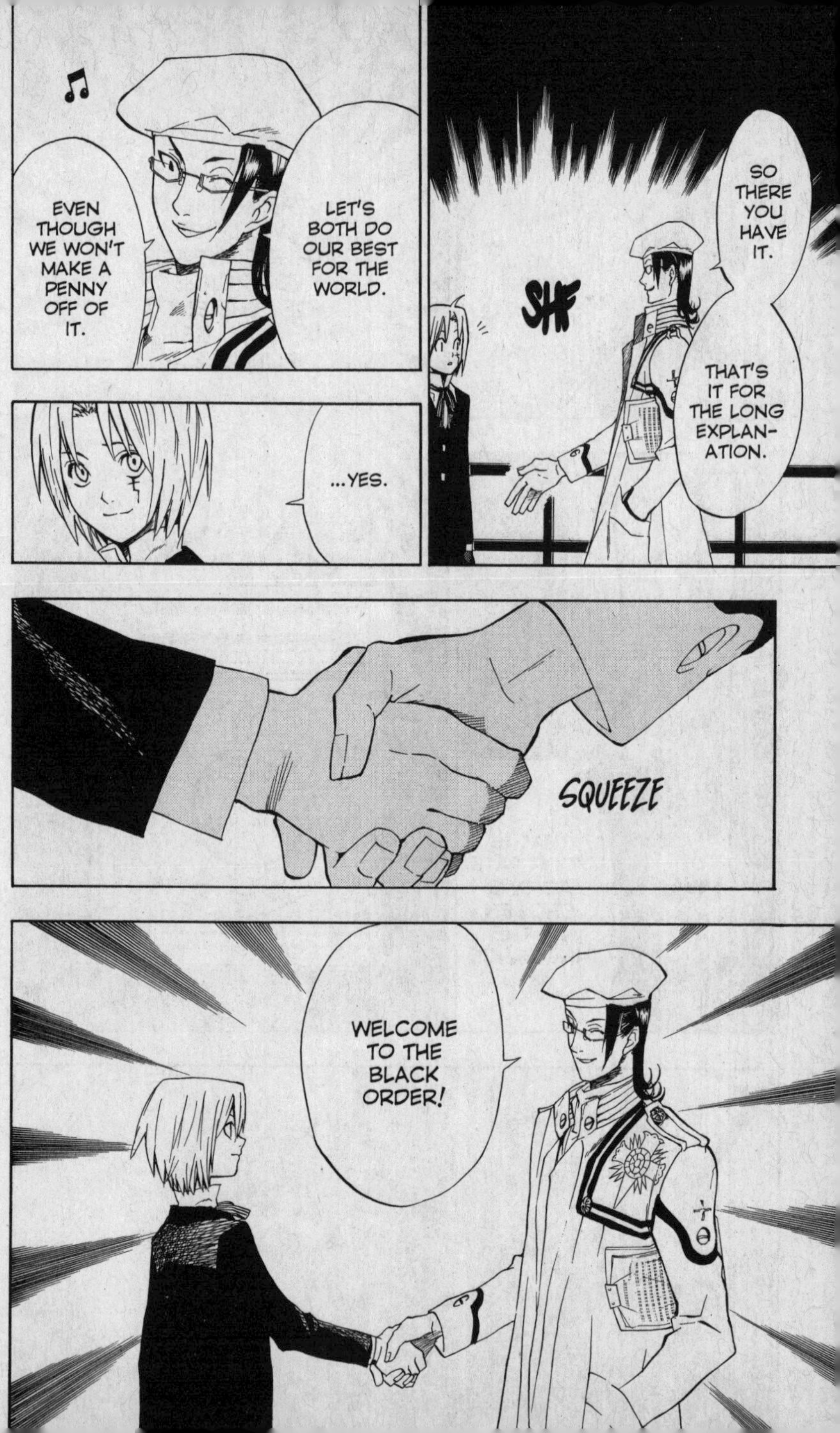
SO THERE YOU HAVE IT.
SHF
THAT'S IT FOR THE LONG EXPLANATION.
LET'S BOTH DO OUR BEST FOR THE WORLD.
EVEN THOUGH WE WON'T MAKE A PENNY OFF OF IT.
...YES.
SQUEEZE
WELCOME TO THE BLACK ORDER!

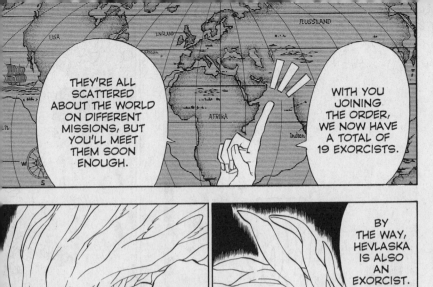

RUSSLAND
ENGLAND
USA
AFRIKA
Indien
WITH YOU JOINING THE ORDER, WE NOW HAVE A TOTAL OF 19 EXORCISTS.
THEY'RE ALL SCATTERED ABOUT THE WORLD ON DIFFERENT MISSIONS, BUT YOU'LL MEET THEM SOON ENOUGH.
BY THE WAY, HEVLASKA IS ALSO AN EXORCIST.
...
WHAT?!
I'M...A DIFFERENT TYPE THAN YOU AND THE OTHERS ...
I'VE BEEN WITH THE ORDER SINCE IT WAS ESTABLISHED... AS THE ACCOMMODATOR OF THE CUBE... I AM THE GUARDIAN OF THE CUBE...
I HAVE MET MANY... EXORCISTS...
ALLEN... MAY THE LORD'S DIVINE PROTECTION ...
...BE WITH YOU...

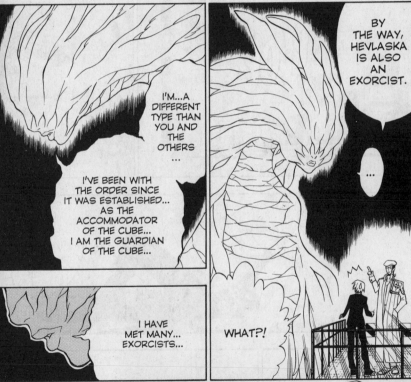

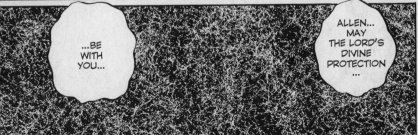

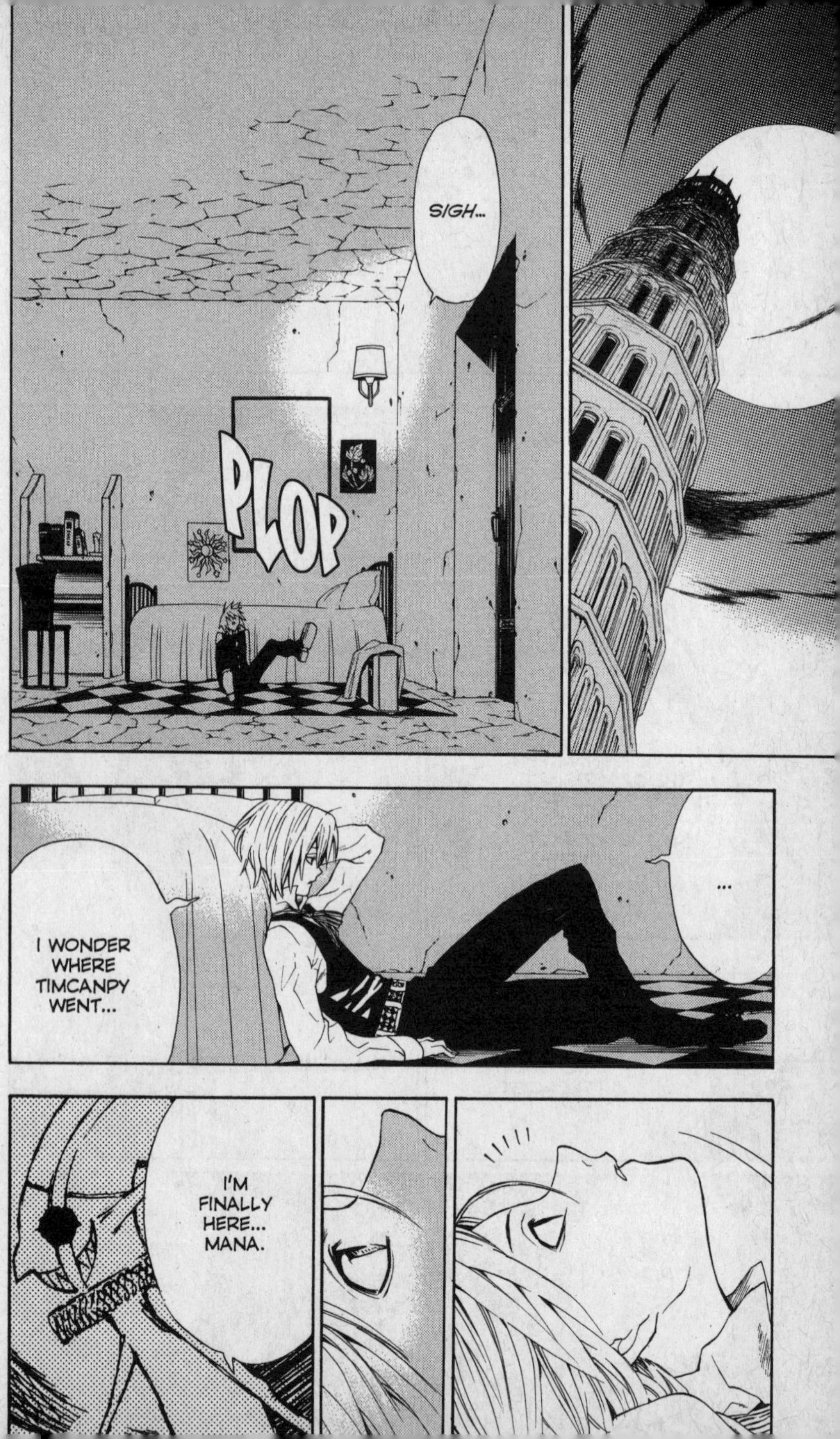
SIGH...
PLOP
...
I WONDER WHERE TIMCANPY WENT...
I'M FINALLY HERE... MANA.

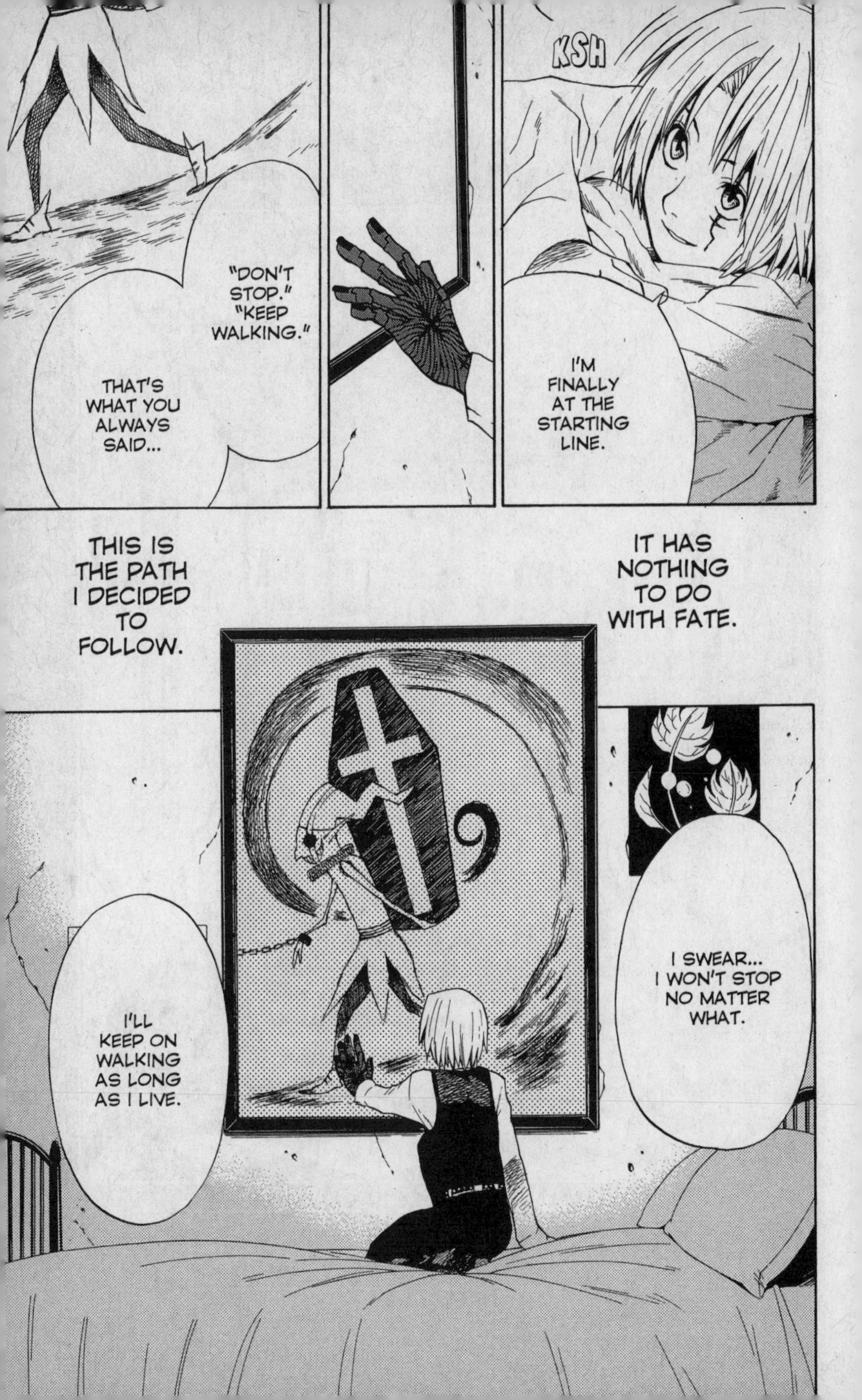
KSH
I'M FINALLY AT THE STARTING LINE.
"DON'T STOP." "KEEP WALKING."
THAT'S WHAT YOU ALWAYS SAID...
IT HAS NOTHING TO DO WITH FATE.
THIS IS THE PATH I DECIDED TO FOLLOW.
I SWEAR... I WON'T STOP NO MATTER WHAT.
I'LL KEEP ON WALKING AS LONG AS I LIVE.

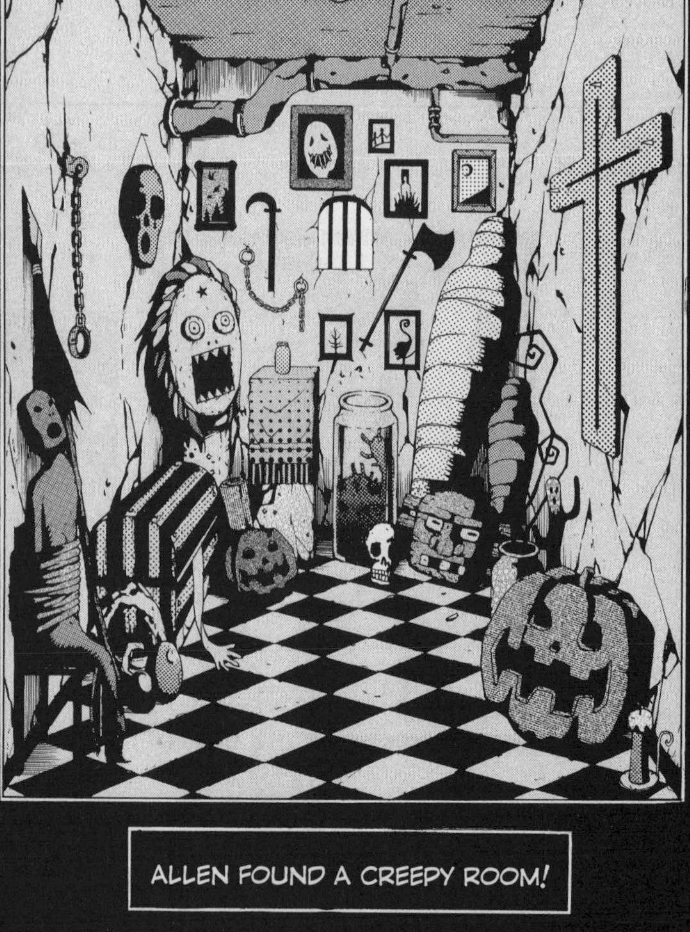

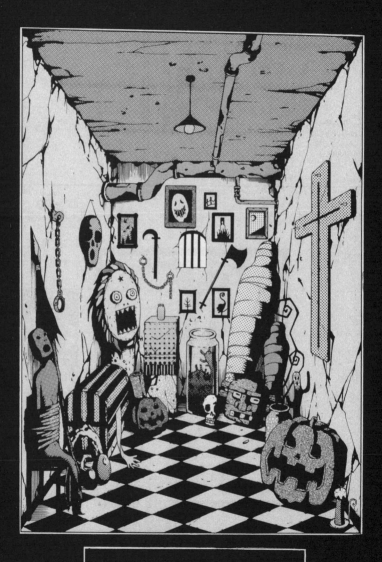

ALLEN FOUND A CREEPY ROOM!

HEAD OFFICER KOMUI'S EXPERIMENT ROOM: UNDERCOVER INVESTIGATION REPORT

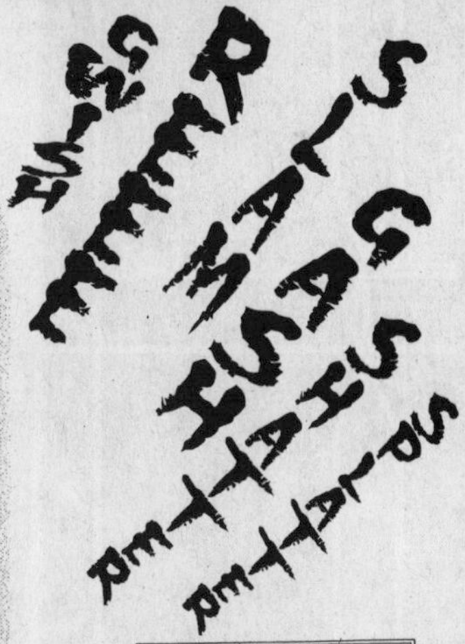

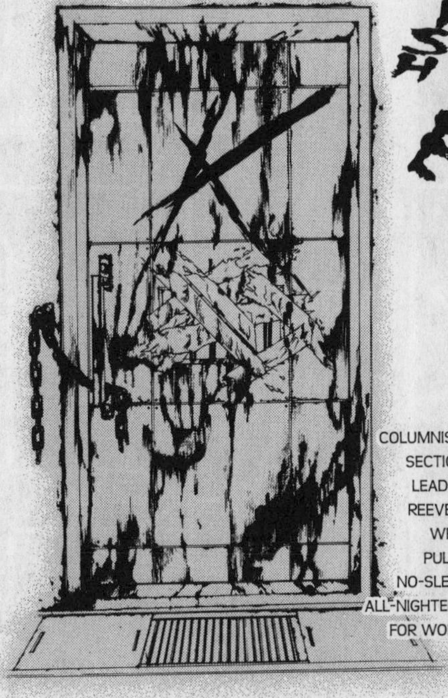

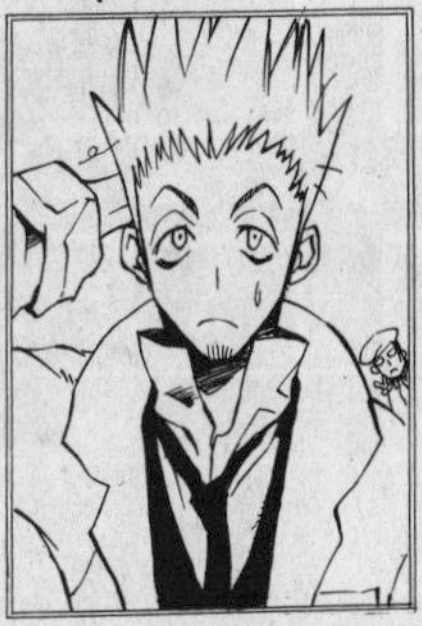

COLUMNIST: SECTION LEADER REEVER,→ WHO PULLS NO-SLEEP, ALL-NIGHTERS FOR WORK.

HI. GOOD EVENING. UMM... I'M REEVER WENHAM, AND I WORK UNDER KOMUI, THE HEAD OFFICER. UMM... I'LL BE GOING UNDERCOVER TO INVESTIGATE THE FORBIDDEN FLOOR, SECTION LEADER KOMUI'S PRIVATE EXPERIMENT ROOMS... ON SECOND THOUGHT, WHY AM I DOING THIS?! THIS IS TOO STRANGE! SHOULDN'T THE MAIN CHARACTER—IN THIS CASE, ALLEN—GO CHECK IT OUT? WILL I BE ABLE TO COME BACK IN ONE PIECE? WILL I BE ABLE TO STAY AS REEVER WENHAM? THERE ARE SOME WEIRD SOUNDS COMING OUT OF THAT DOOR. NO HUMAN SHOULD GO THROUGH THAT DOOR. IT'S WEIRD. IT'S NOT RIGHT. I KNOW HE'S A WEIRDO, BUT I'LL LOSE MY WILL TO WORK IF I FIND OUT HOW MUCH OF A WEIRDO HE REALLY IS. SERIOUSLY... LET ME GO HOME. THE END

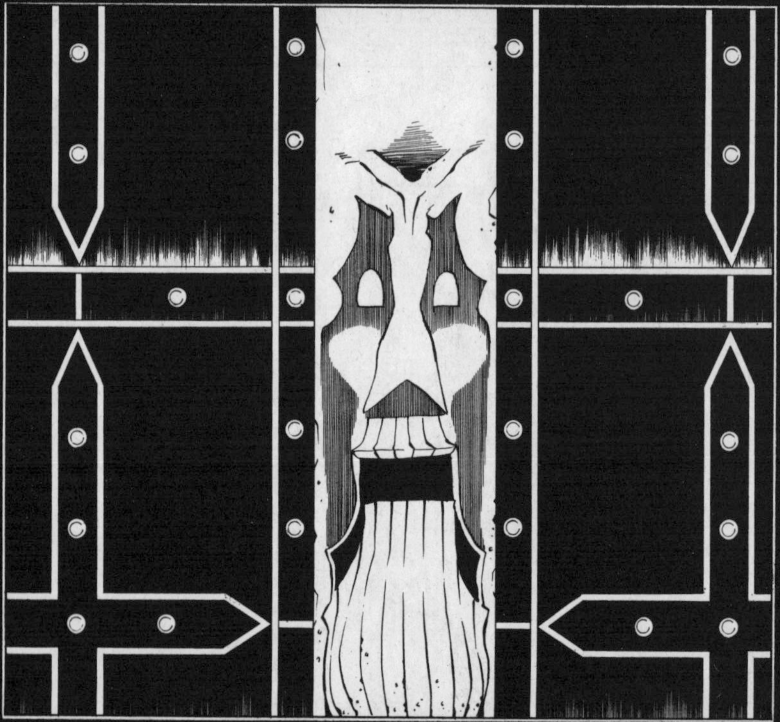

CASTLE ENTRY REPORT

IT COULDN'T HAVE BEEN WORSE.
THANKS TO THAT ALLEN KID,
I WAS IN A TERRIBLE MOOD ALL DAY LONG.
HE'D BETTER WATCH IT. I'LL MAKE SURE I GET MY REVENGE.

DARN IT. MY CHIN BROKE OUT IN HIVES BECAUSE HE TOUCHED ME...

......

GAH! IT'S ITCHY! MY CHIN ITCHES!

IT'S ALL HIS FAULT!!!

GRAAAAAAAA! IT ITCHES! IT ITCHES! IT ITCHES! IT ITCHES!

I KNOW I SHOULDN'T SCRATCH IT, BUT I'M GOING TO DO IT ANYWAY...

WAIT... I DON'T HAVE HANDS!!!

Special Thanks

Abetchi
Otake
Jyusai
Tai

Gunma
Kiyoshi
Makibon
Hiroshi
Tachikawa
Okei
Mamewakame
Mochi

Yoshida
Kobayashi

AKIRA MIYAZAKI

(Adopt-me)

OI-CHAN

MAME ROCK

OKEI

IN THE NEXT VOLUME...

Teen exorcist Allen Walker is dispatched on his first assignment, and his dangerous mission takes him to southern Italy. Along with his fellow exorcist, Kanda, Allen must find the Innocence before an akuma gets to it first!

Available Now!

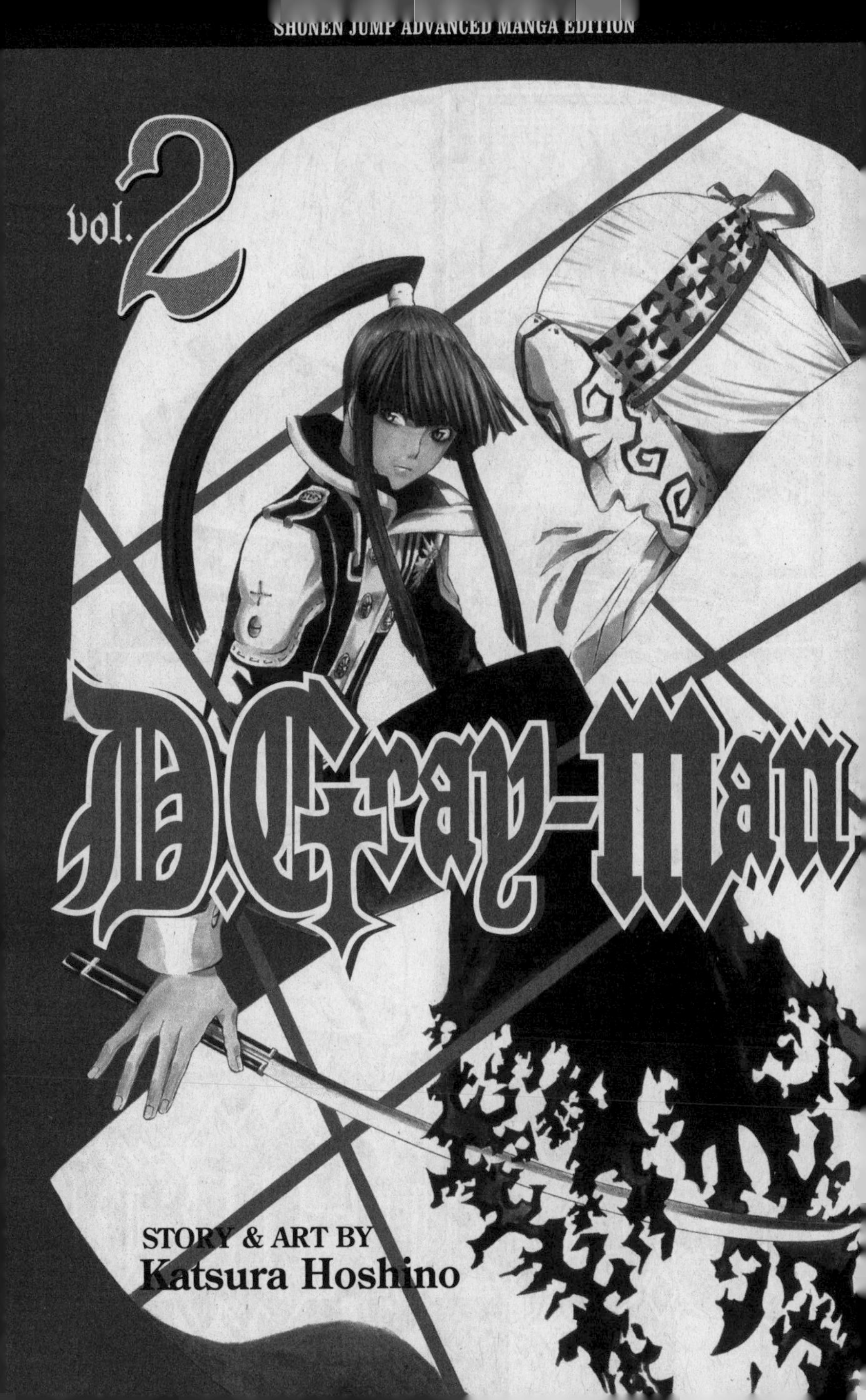
SHONEN JUMP ADVANCED MANGA EDITION
vol. 2
D.Gray-man
STORY & ART BY
Katsura Hoshino

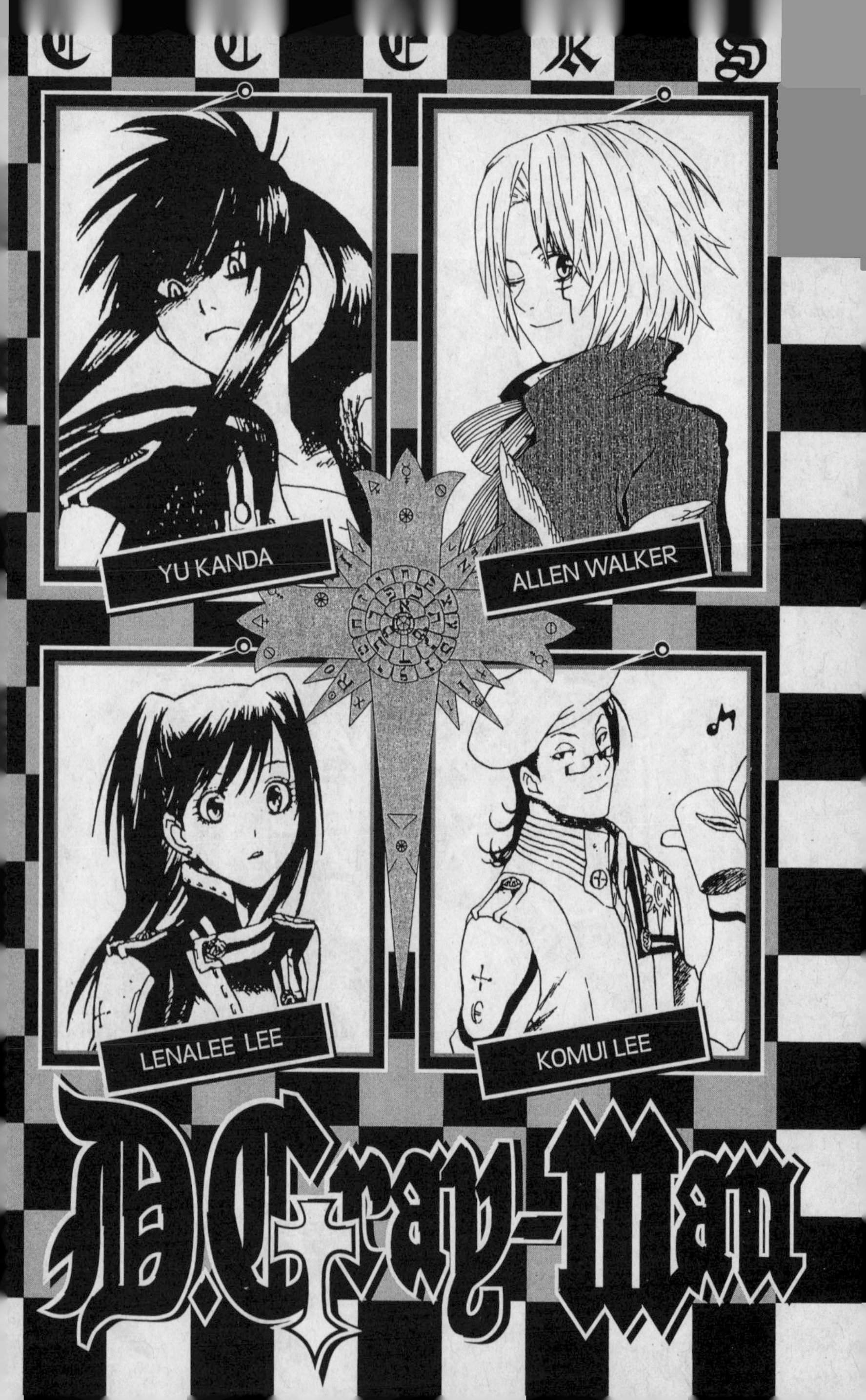
YU KANDA
ALLEN WALKER
LENALEE LEE
KOMUI LEE
D.Gray-man

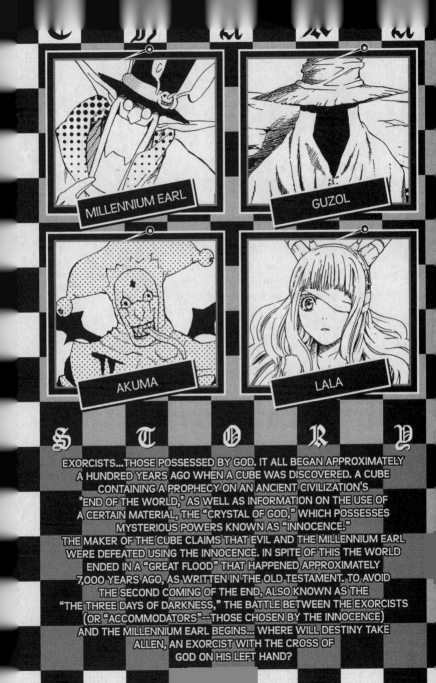

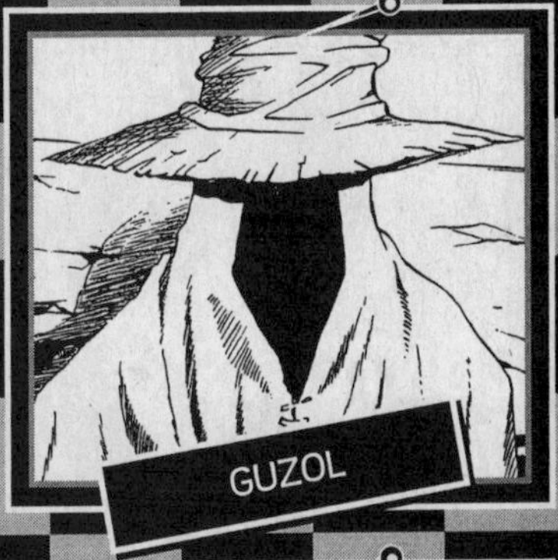
GUZOL

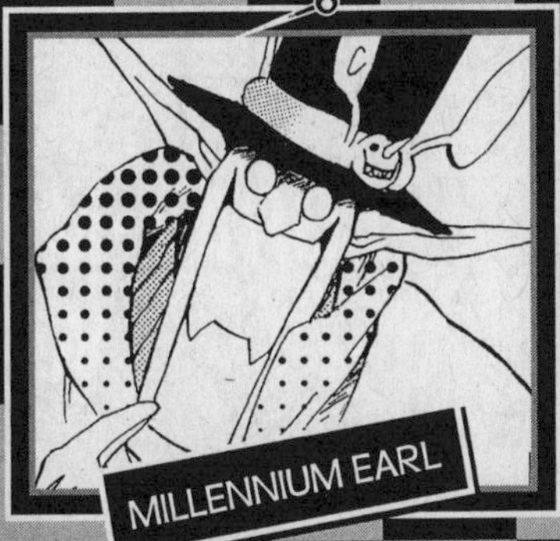
MILLENNIUM EARL

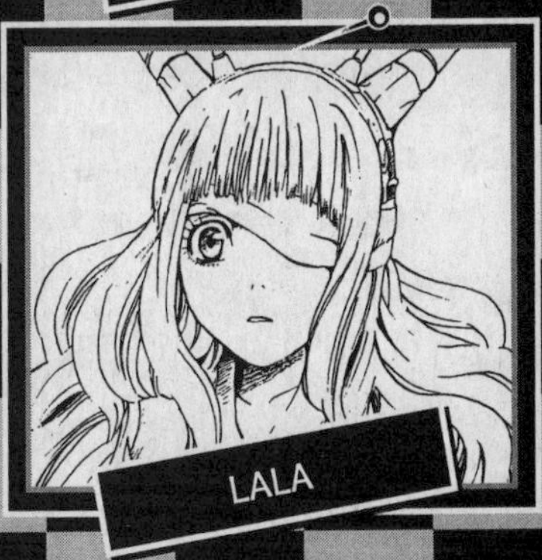
LALA

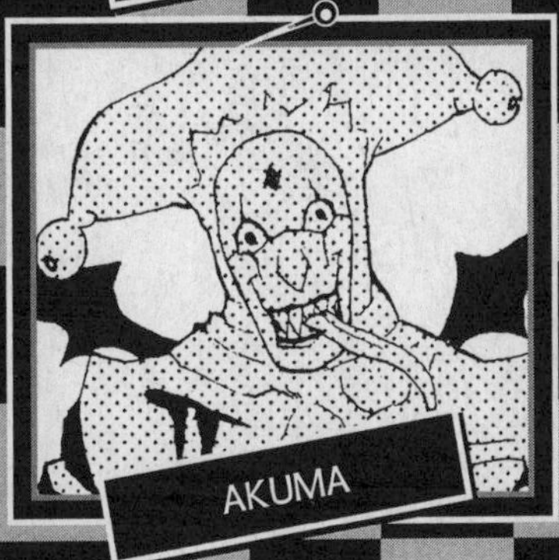
AKUMA

STORY

EXORCISTS...THOSE POSSESSED BY GOD. IT ALL BEGAN APPROXIMATELY A HUNDRED YEARS AGO WHEN A CUBE WAS DISCOVERED. A CUBE CONTAINING A PROPHECY ON AN ANCIENT CIVILIZATION'S "END OF THE WORLD," AS WELL AS INFORMATION ON THE USE OF A CERTAIN MATERIAL, THE "CRYSTAL OF GOD," WHICH POSSESSES MYSTERIOUS POWERS KNOWN AS "INNOCENCE."

THE MAKER OF THE CUBE CLAIMS THAT EVIL AND THE MILLENNIUM EARL WERE DEFEATED USING THE INNOCENCE. IN SPITE OF THIS THE WORLD ENDED IN A "GREAT FLOOD" THAT HAPPENED APPROXIMATELY 7,000 YEARS AGO, AS WRITTEN IN THE OLD TESTAMENT. TO AVOID THE SECOND COMING OF THE END, ALSO KNOWN AS THE "THE THREE DAYS OF DARKNESS," THE BATTLE BETWEEN THE EXORCISTS (OR "ACCOMMODATORS"--THOSE CHOSEN BY THE INNOCENCE) AND THE MILLENNIUM EARL BEGINS... WHERE WILL DESTINY TAKE ALLEN, AN EXORCIST WITH THE CROSS OF GOD ON HIS LEFT HAND?

D.GRAY-MAN
Vol. 2

CONTENTS

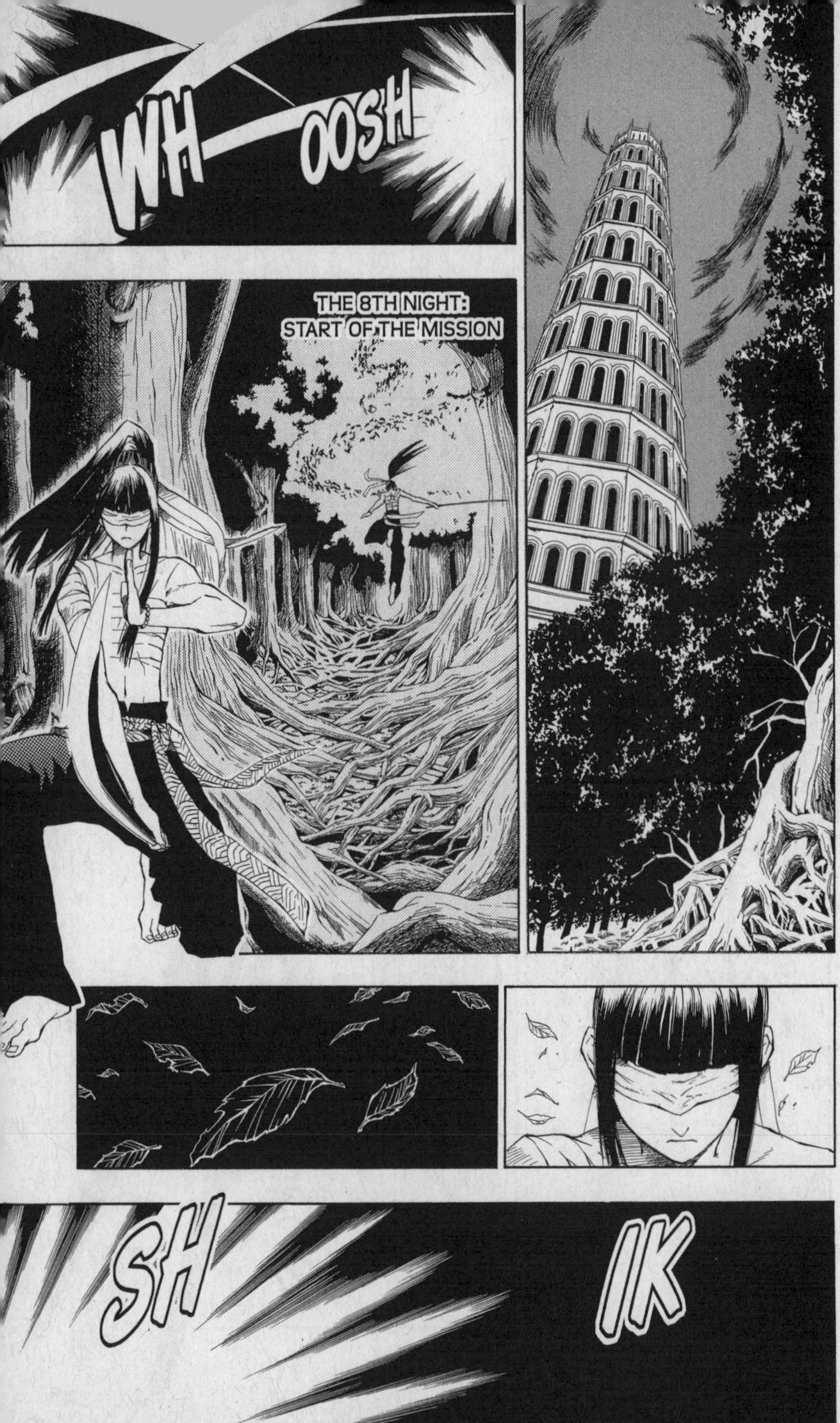
WH OOSH
THE 8TH NIGHT:
START OF THE MISSION
SH IK

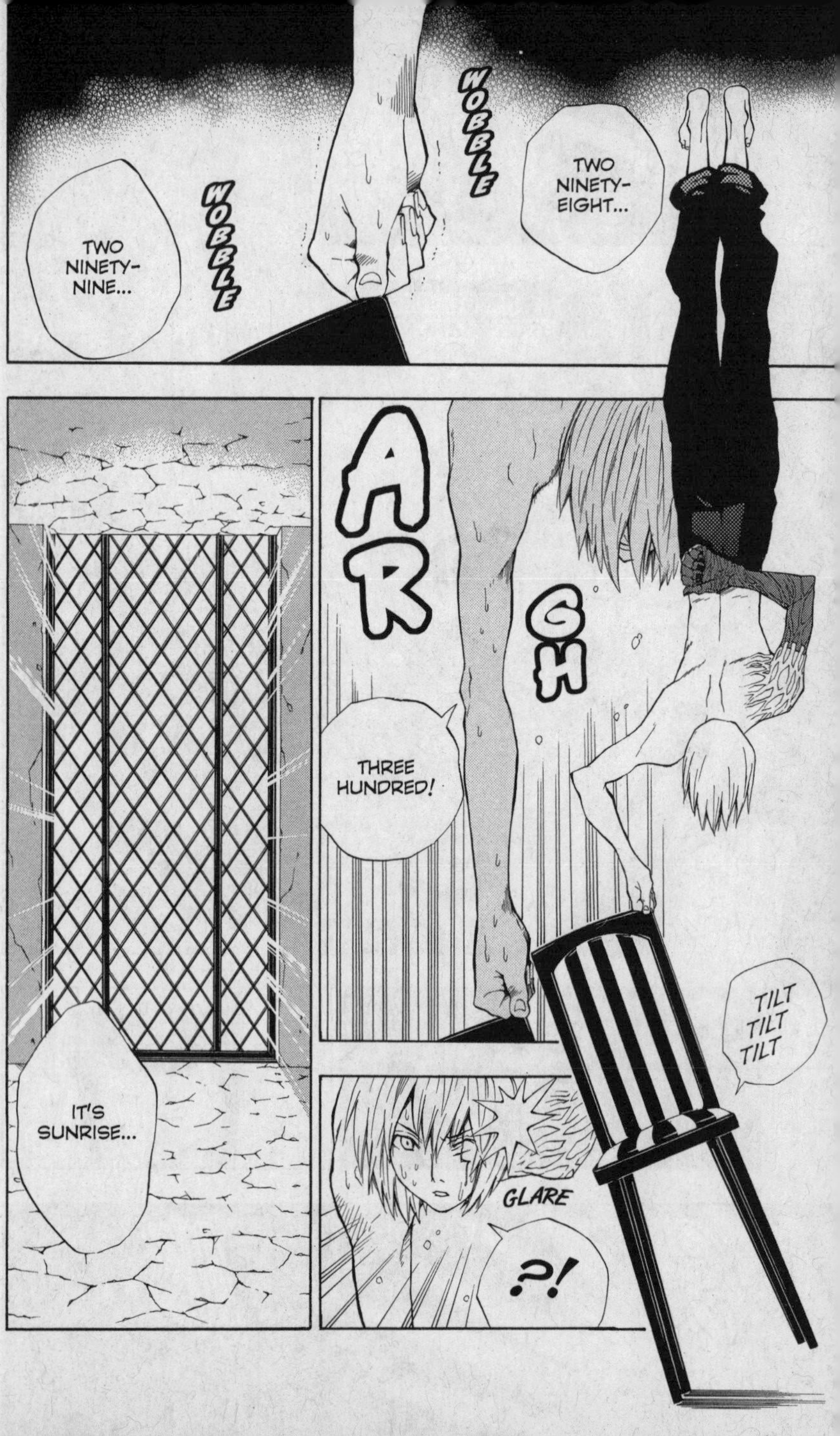
TWO NINETY-EIGHT...
WOBBLE
WOBBLE
TWO NINETY-NINE...
ARGH
THREE HUNDRED!
TILT TILT TILT
GLARE
?!
IT'S SUNRISE...

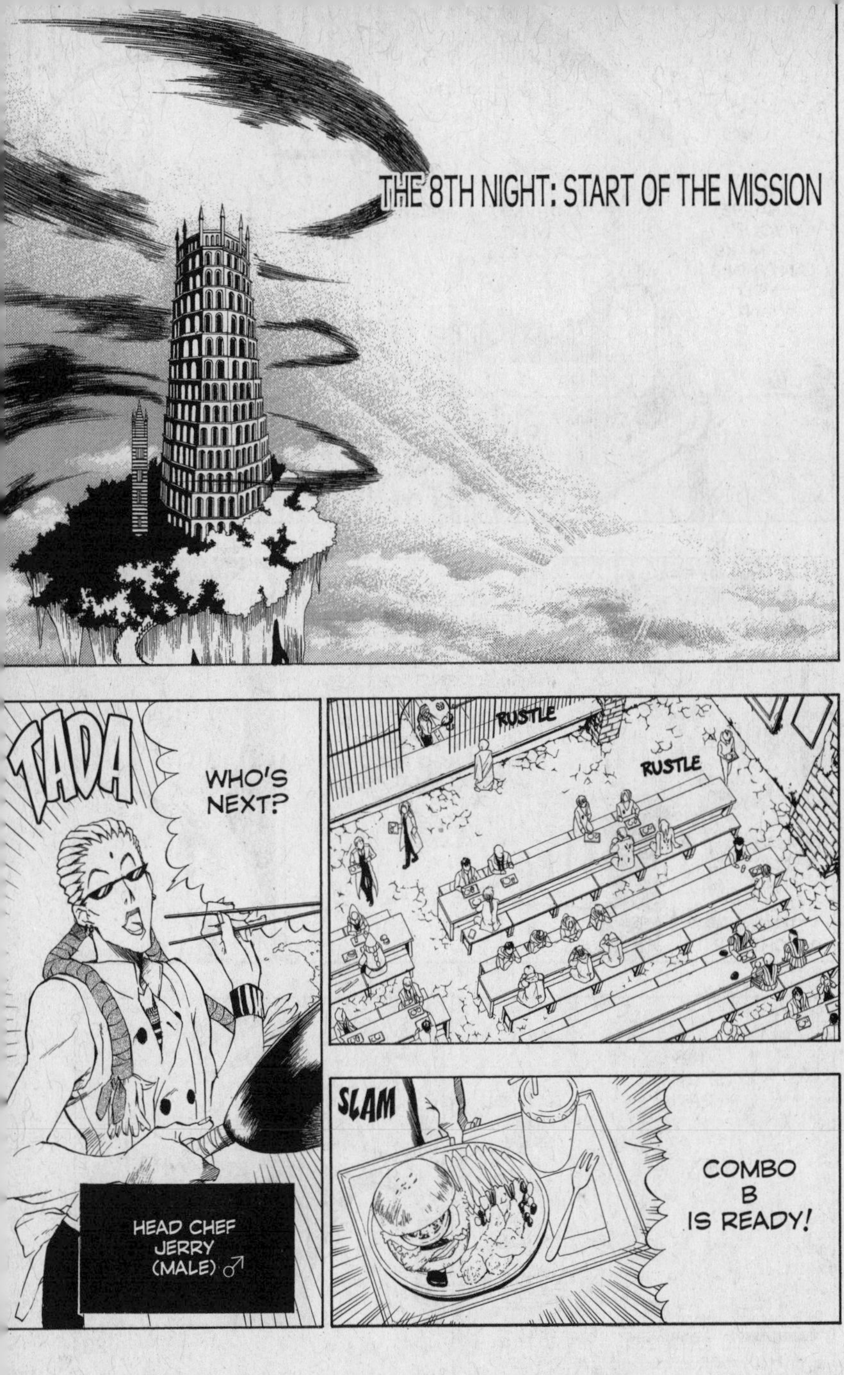
THE 8TH NIGHT: START OF THE MISSION
RUSTLE
RUSTLE
SLAM
COMBO B IS READY!
TADA
WHO'S NEXT?
HEAD CHEF JERRY (MALE) ♂

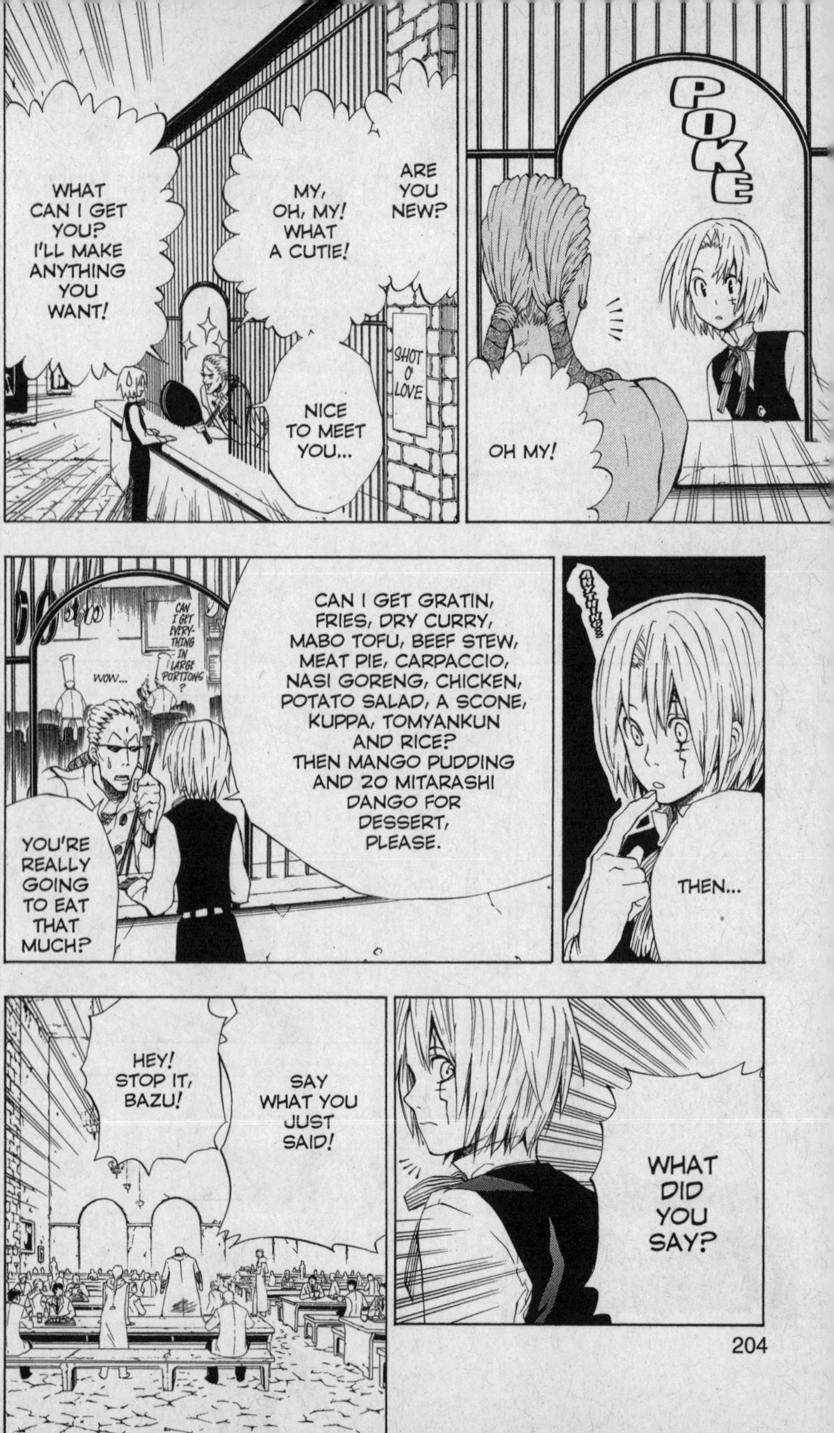
POKE
OH MY!
ARE YOU NEW?
MY, OH, MY! WHAT A CUTIE!
WHAT CAN I GET YOU? I'LL MAKE ANYTHING YOU WANT!
SHOT O' LOVE
NICE TO MEET YOU...
ANYTHING...
THEN...
CAN I GET GRATIN, FRIES, DRY CURRY, MABO TOFU, BEEF STEW, MEAT PIE, CARPACCIO, NASI GORENG, CHICKEN, POTATO SALAD, A SCONE, KUPPA, TOMYANKUN AND RICE? THEN MANGO PUDDING AND 20 MITARASHI DANGO FOR DESSERT, PLEASE.
CAN I GET EVERYTHING IN LARGE PORTIONS?
WOW...
YOU'RE REALLY GOING TO EAT THAT MUCH?
WHAT DID YOU SAY?
SAY WHAT YOU JUST SAID!
HEY! STOP IT, BAZU!

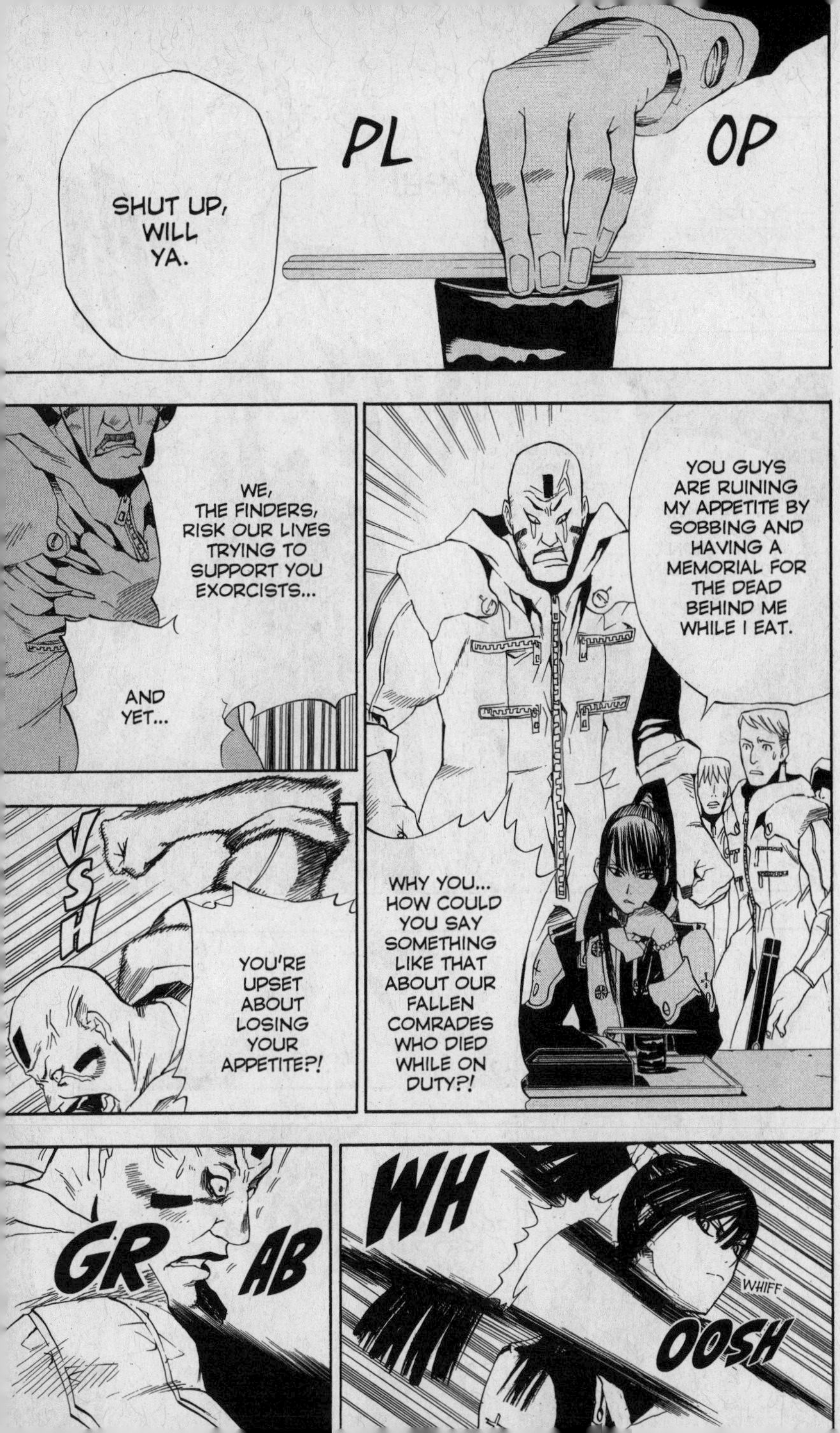
PL OP
SHUT UP, WILL YA.
YOU GUYS ARE RUINING MY APPETITE BY SOBBING AND HAVING A MEMORIAL FOR THE DEAD BEHIND ME WHILE I EAT.
WHY YOU... HOW COULD YOU SAY SOMETHING LIKE THAT ABOUT OUR FALLEN COMRADES WHO DIED WHILE ON DUTY?!
WE, THE FINDERS, RISK OUR LIVES TRYING TO SUPPORT YOU EXORCISTS...
AND YET...
VSH
YOU'RE UPSET ABOUT LOSING YOUR APPETITE?!
WH OOSH
WHIFF
GR AB

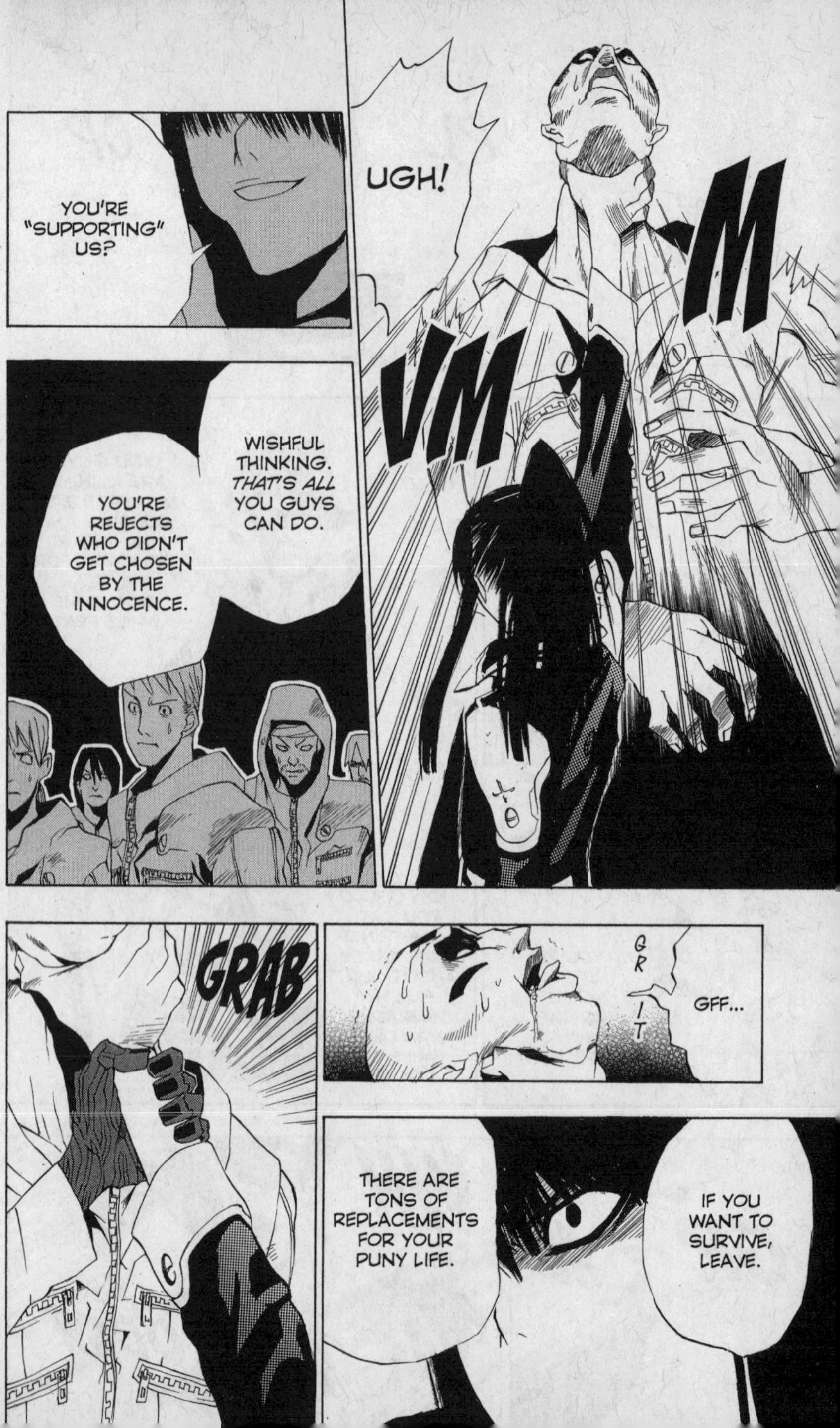
UGH!
VM M
YOU'RE "SUPPORTING" US?
WISHFUL THINKING. *THAT'S ALL* YOU GUYS CAN DO.
YOU'RE REJECTS WHO DIDN'T GET CHOSEN BY THE INNOCENCE.
GRIT
GFF...
IF YOU WANT TO SURVIVE, LEAVE.
THERE ARE TONS OF REPLACEMENTS FOR YOUR PUNY LIFE.
GRAB

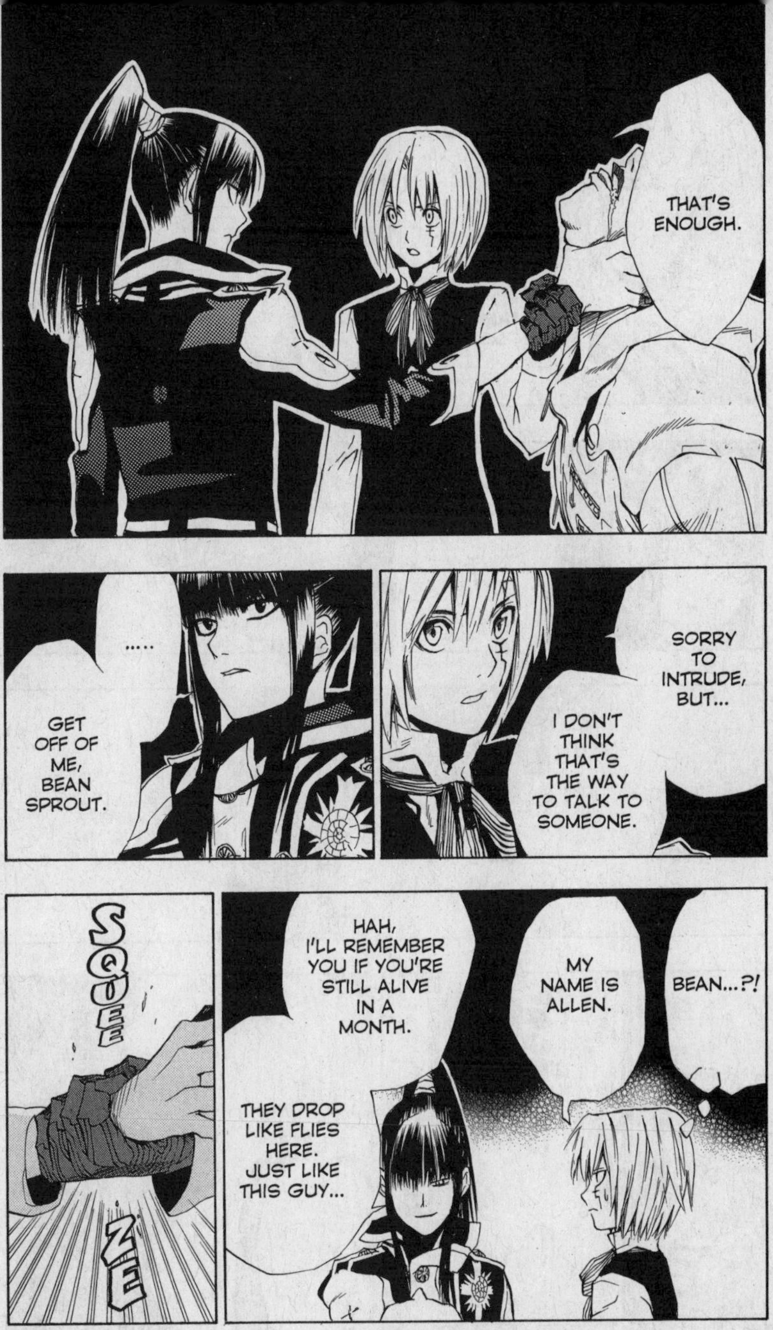
THAT'S ENOUGH.
SORRY TO INTRUDE, BUT...
I DON'T THINK THAT'S THE WAY TO TALK TO SOMEONE.
.....
GET OFF OF ME, BEAN SPROUT.
BEAN...?!
MY NAME IS ALLEN.
HAH, I'LL REMEMBER YOU IF YOU'RE STILL ALIVE IN A MONTH.
THEY DROP LIKE FLIES HERE. JUST LIKE THIS GUY...
SQUEE
ZE

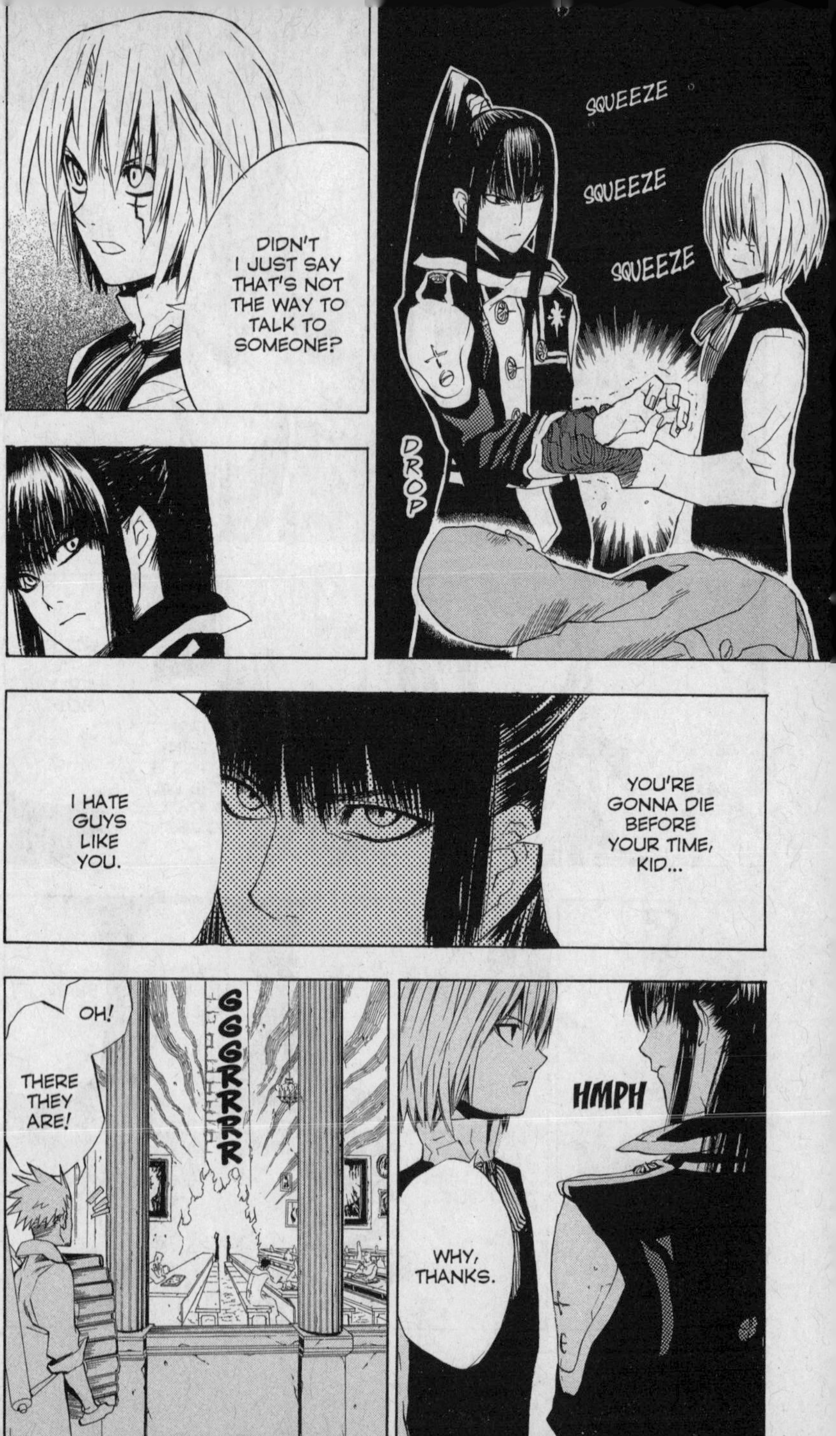
SQUEEZE
SQUEEZE
SQUEEZE
DROP
DIDN'T I JUST SAY THAT'S NOT THE WAY TO TALK TO SOMEONE?
YOU'RE GONNA DIE BEFORE YOUR TIME, KID...
I HATE GUYS LIKE YOU.
HMPH
WHY, THANKS.
OH!
THERE THEY ARE!
GGGRRRR

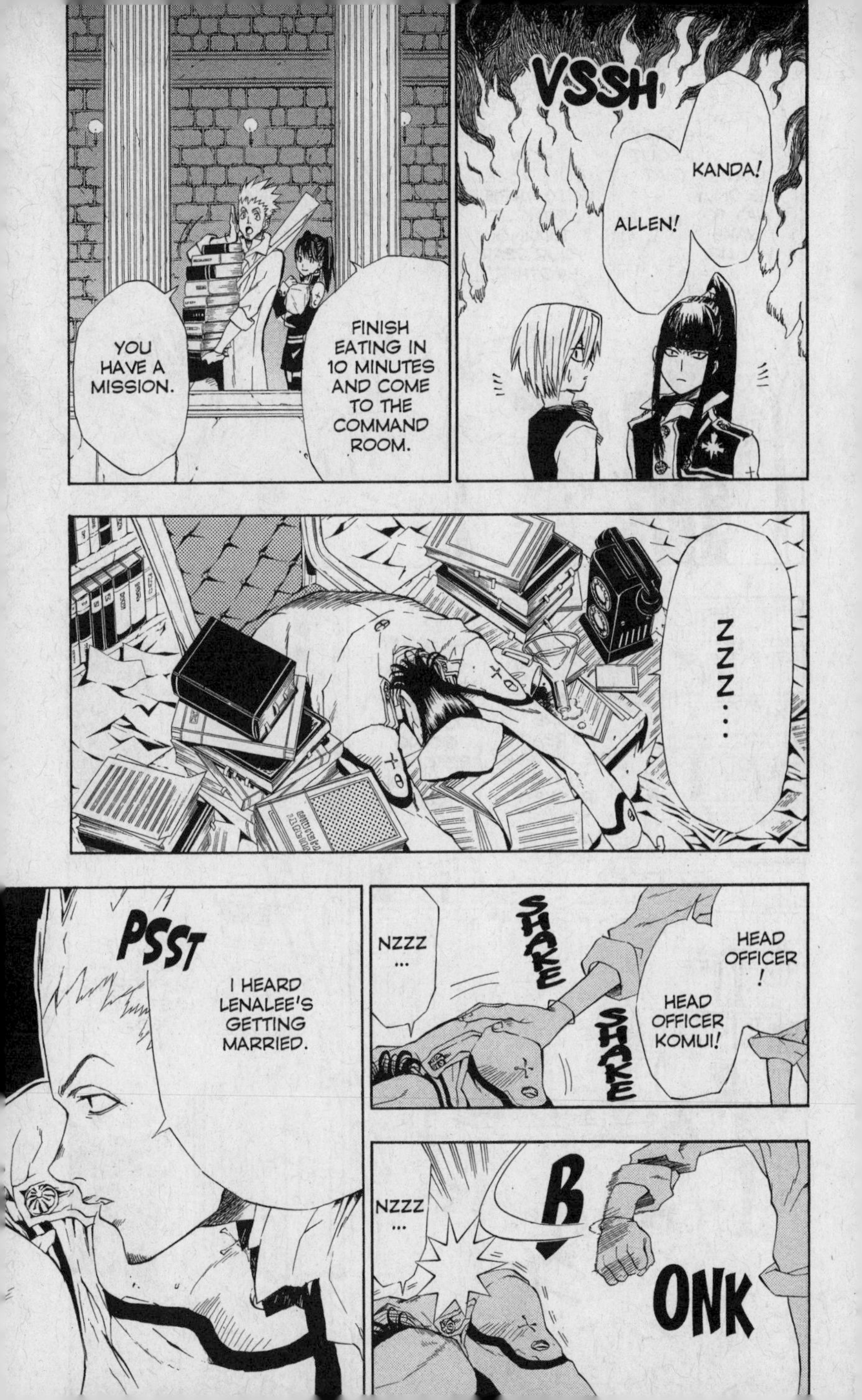
VSSH
KANDA!
ALLEN!
FINISH EATING IN 10 MINUTES AND COME TO THE COMMAND ROOM.
YOU HAVE A MISSION.
ZZZ...
HEAD OFFICER!
HEAD OFFICER KOMUI!
SHAKE
SHAKE
NZZZ...
BONK
NZZZ...
PSST
I HEARD LENALEE'S GETTING MARRIED.

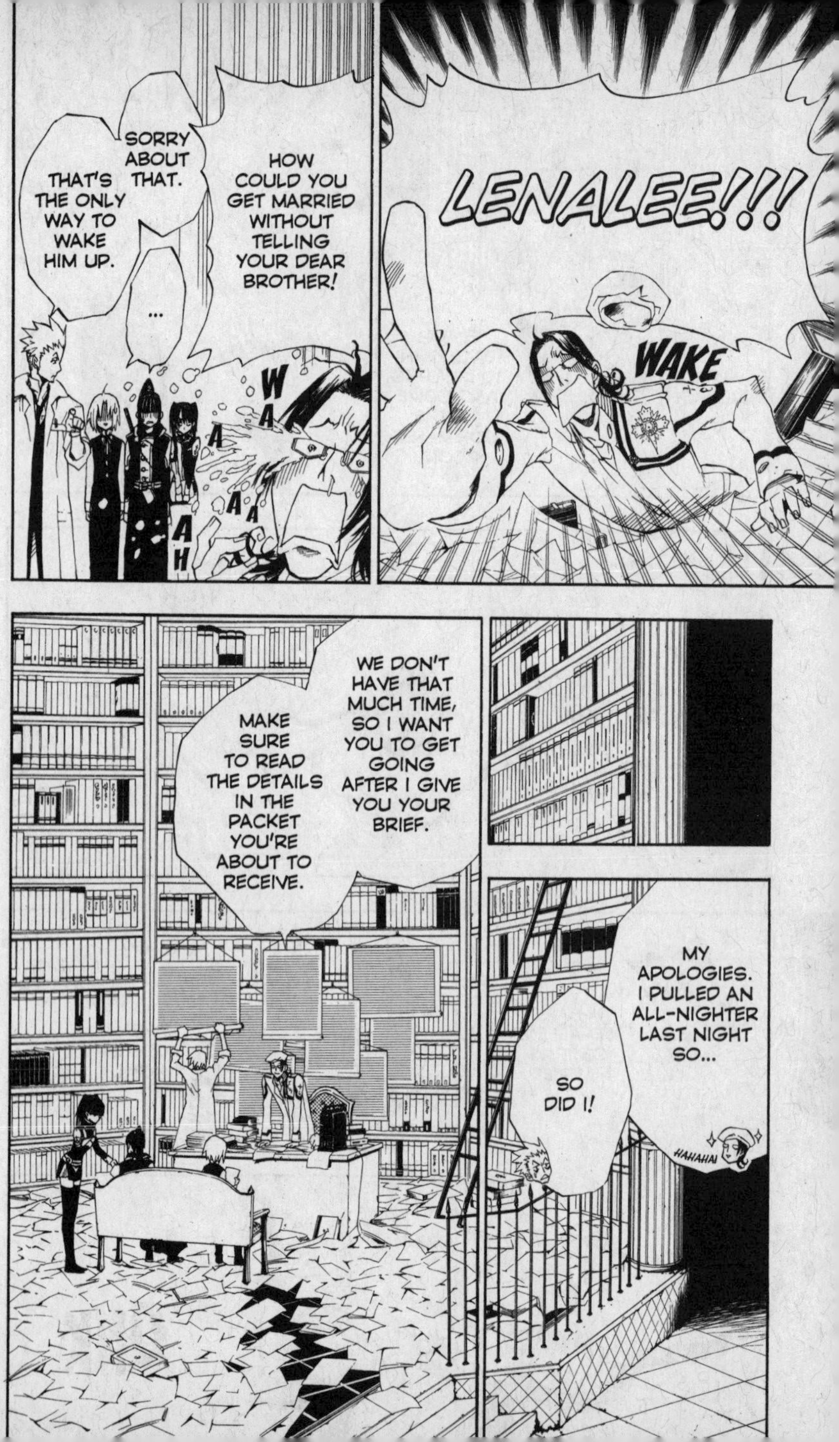
LENALEE!!!
WAKE
HOW COULD YOU GET MARRIED WITHOUT TELLING YOUR DEAR BROTHER!
WAAAAAAH
SORRY ABOUT THAT.
THAT'S THE ONLY WAY TO WAKE HIM UP.
...
MY APOLOGIES. I PULLED AN ALL-NIGHTER LAST NIGHT SO...
SO DID I!
HAHAHA!
WE DON'T HAVE THAT MUCH TIME, SO I WANT YOU TO GET GOING AFTER I GIVE YOU YOUR BRIEF.
MAKE SURE TO READ THE DETAILS IN THE PACKET YOU'RE ABOUT TO RECEIVE.

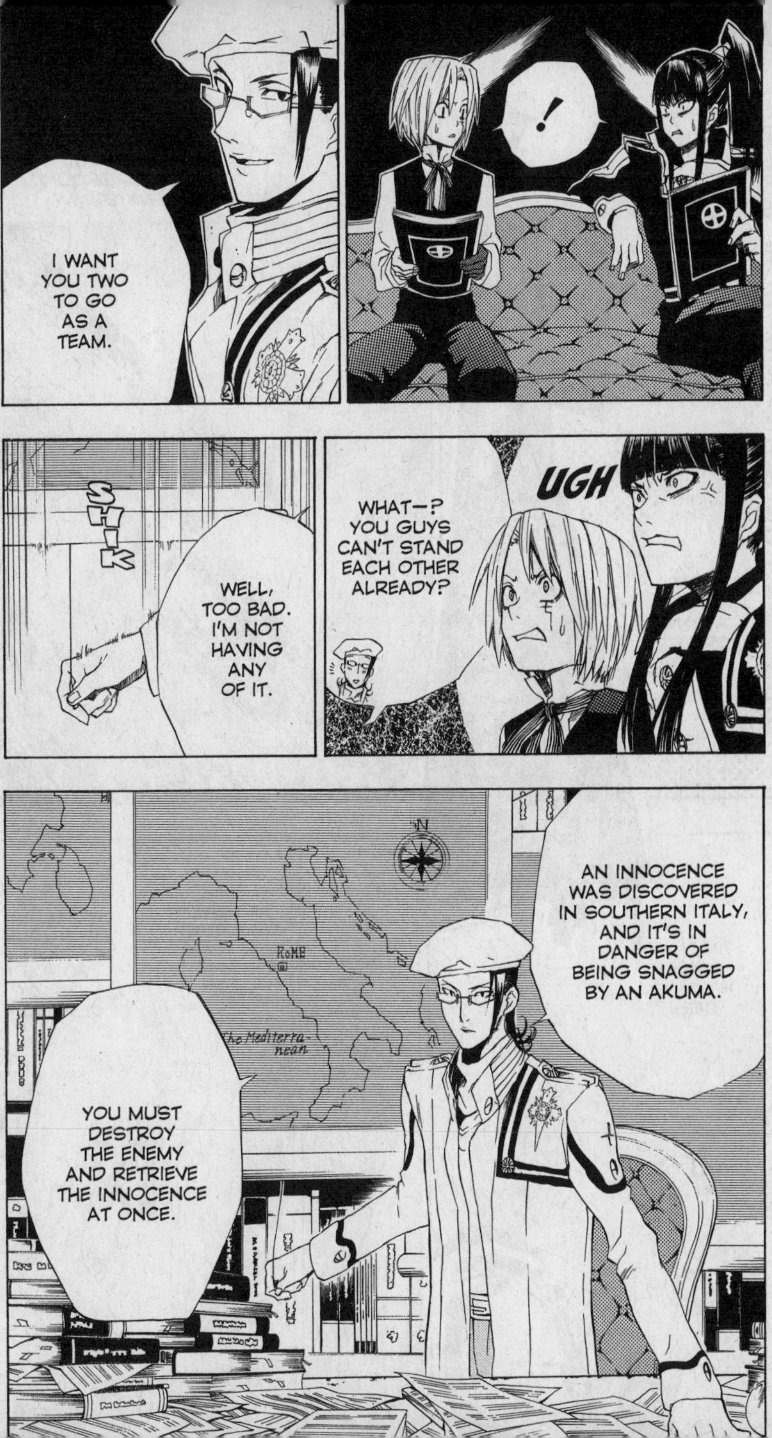
!
I WANT YOU TWO TO GO AS A TEAM.
UGH
WHAT—? YOU GUYS CAN'T STAND EACH OTHER ALREADY?
SHIK
WELL, TOO BAD. I'M NOT HAVING ANY OF IT.
AN INNOCENCE WAS DISCOVERED IN SOUTHERN ITALY, AND IT'S IN DANGER OF BEING SNAGGED BY AN AKUMA.
N
RoME
The Mediterranean
YOU MUST DESTROY THE ENEMY AND RETRIEVE THE INNOCENCE AT ONCE.

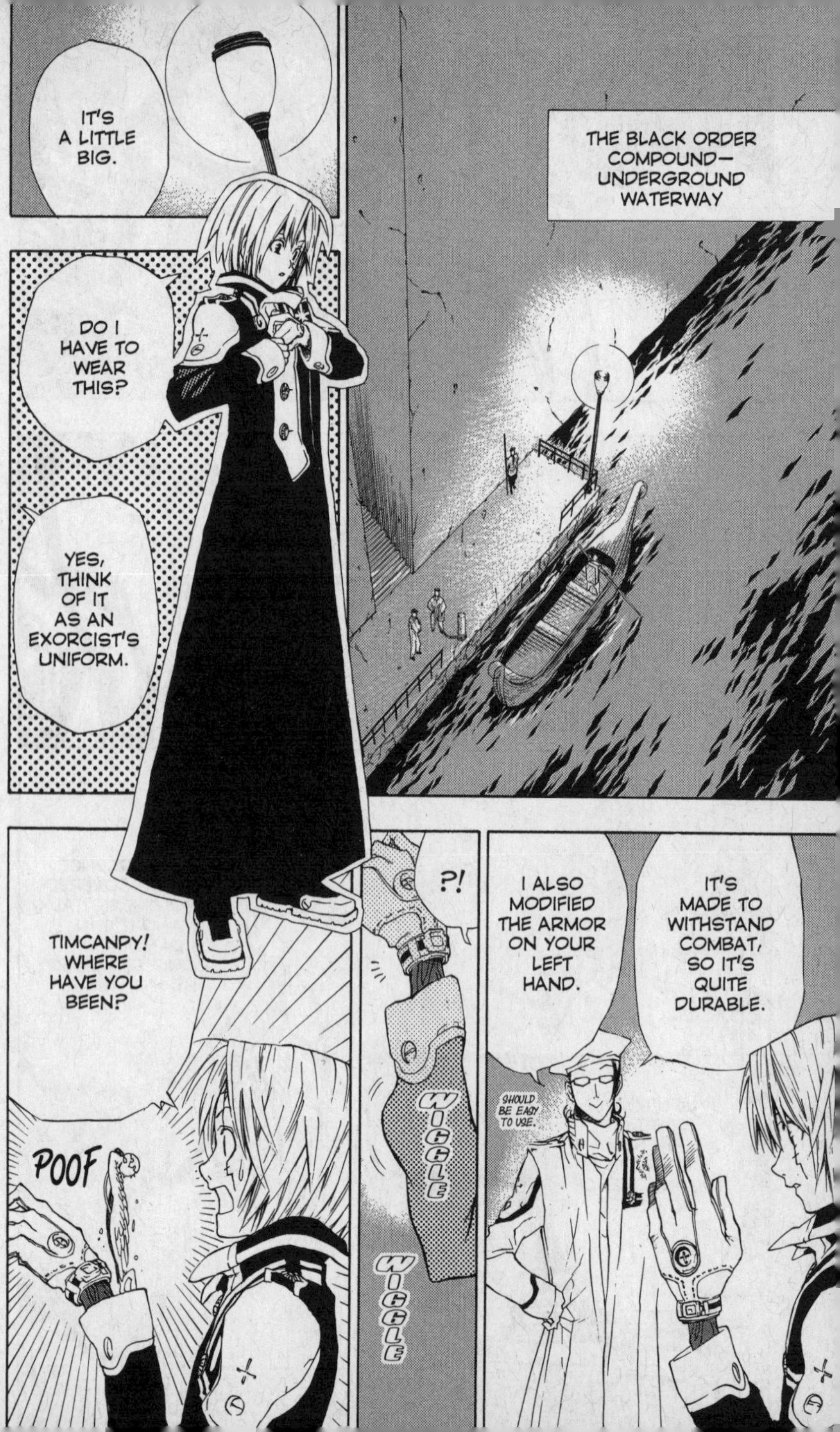
THE BLACK ORDER COMPOUND— UNDERGROUND WATERWAY
IT'S A LITTLE BIG.
DO I HAVE TO WEAR THIS?
YES, THINK OF IT AS AN EXORCIST'S UNIFORM.
IT'S MADE TO WITHSTAND COMBAT, SO IT'S QUITE DURABLE.
I ALSO MODIFIED THE ARMOR ON YOUR LEFT HAND.
SHOULD BE EASY TO USE.
?!
WIGGLE
WIGGLE
TIMCANPY! WHERE HAVE YOU BEEN?
POOF

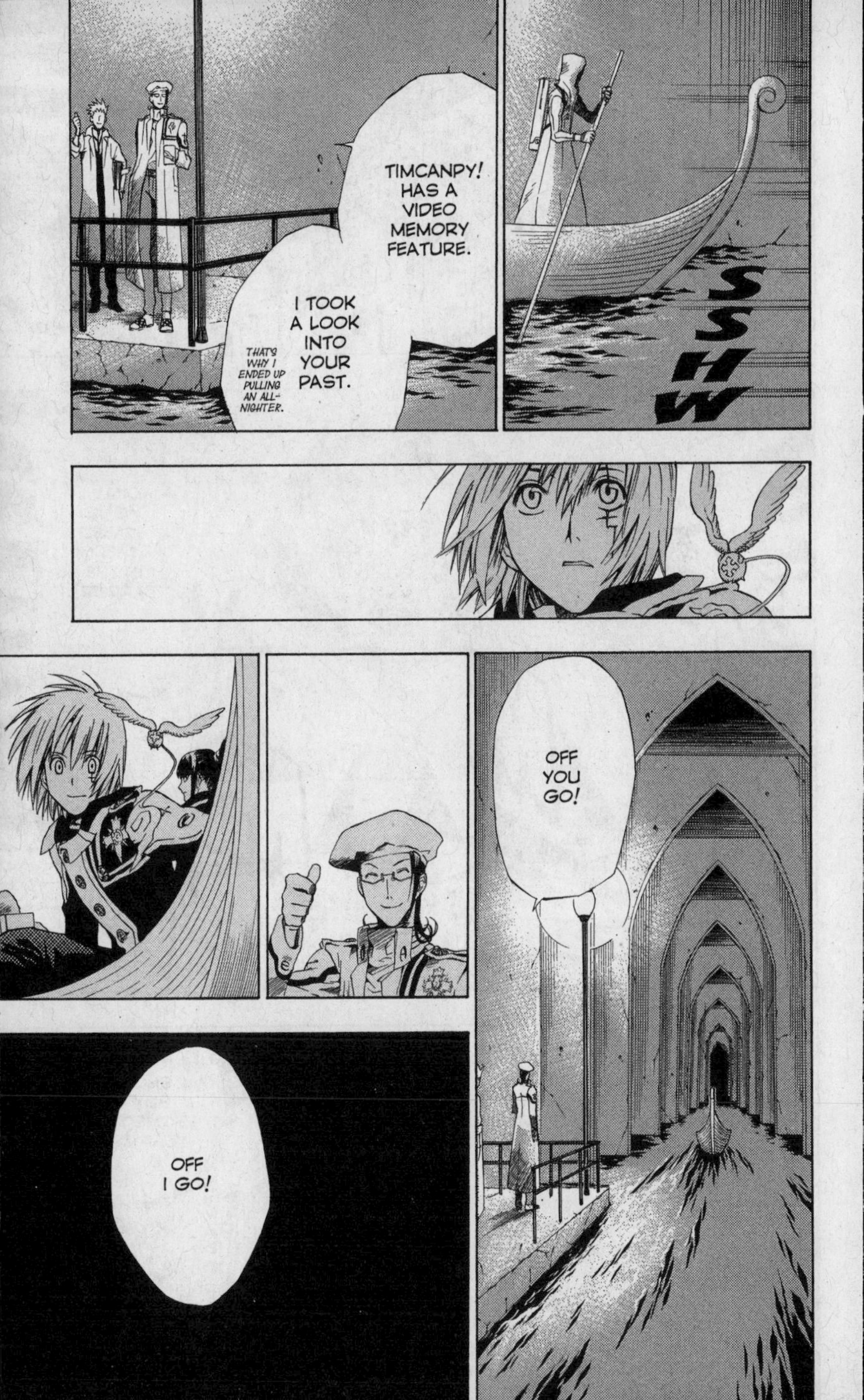
SSHW
TIMCANPY! HAS A VIDEO MEMORY FEATURE.
I TOOK A LOOK INTO YOUR PAST.
THAT'S WHY I ENDED UP PULLING AN ALL-NIGHTER.
OFF YOU GO!
OFF I GO!

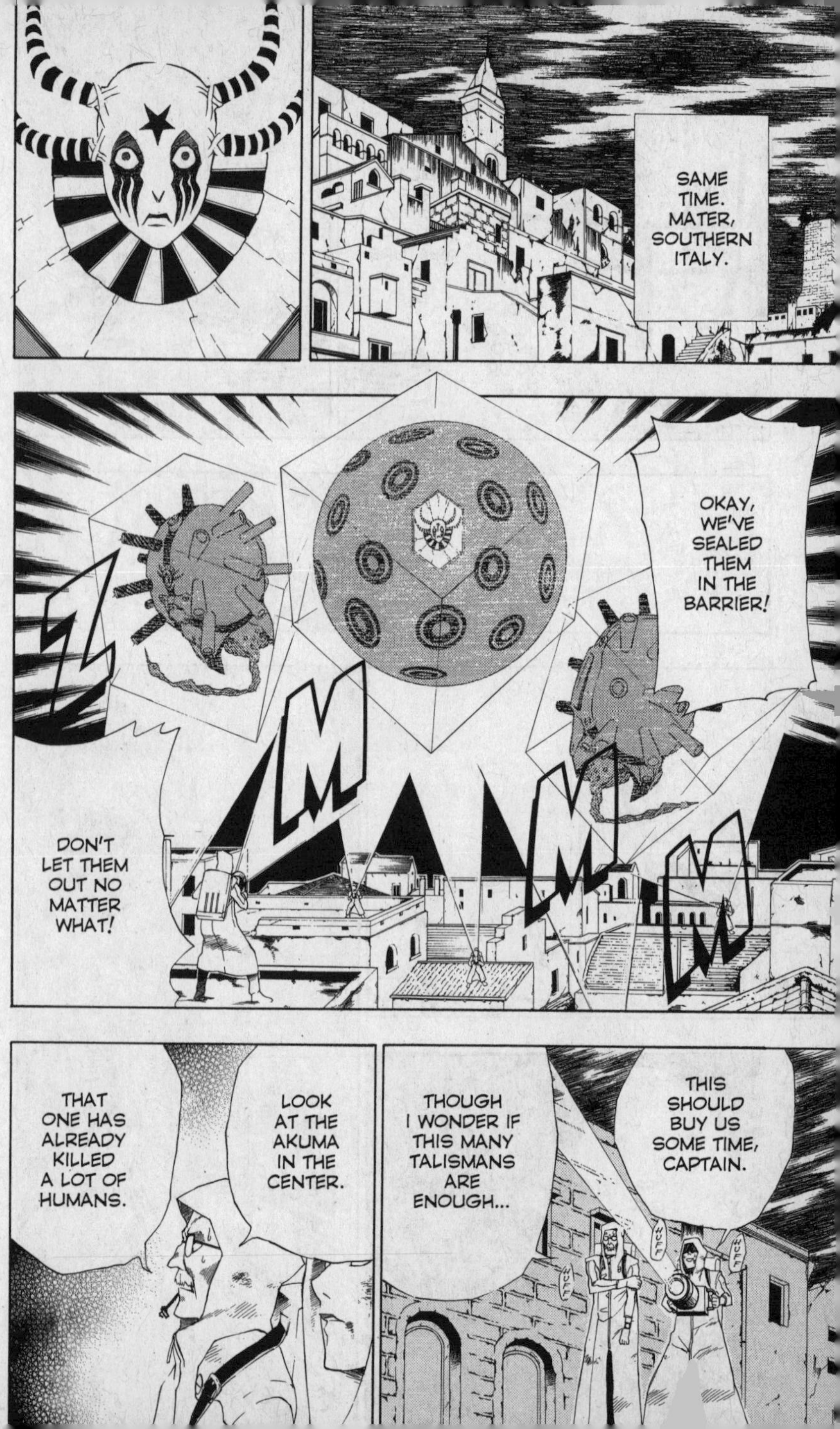
SAME TIME. MATER, SOUTHERN ITALY.
OKAY, WE'VE SEALED THEM IN THE BARRIER!
ZMMM
DON'T LET THEM OUT NO MATTER WHAT!
THIS SHOULD BUY US SOME TIME, CAPTAIN.
HUFF
HUFF
HUFF
THOUGH I WONDER IF THIS MANY TALISMANS ARE ENOUGH...
LOOK AT THE AKUMA IN THE CENTER.
THAT ONE HAS ALREADY KILLED A LOT OF HUMANS.

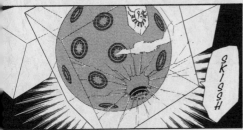

I AM
AN
AKUMA.

HYAH
HYAH
HYAH
HYAH!

HYAH
HYAH!

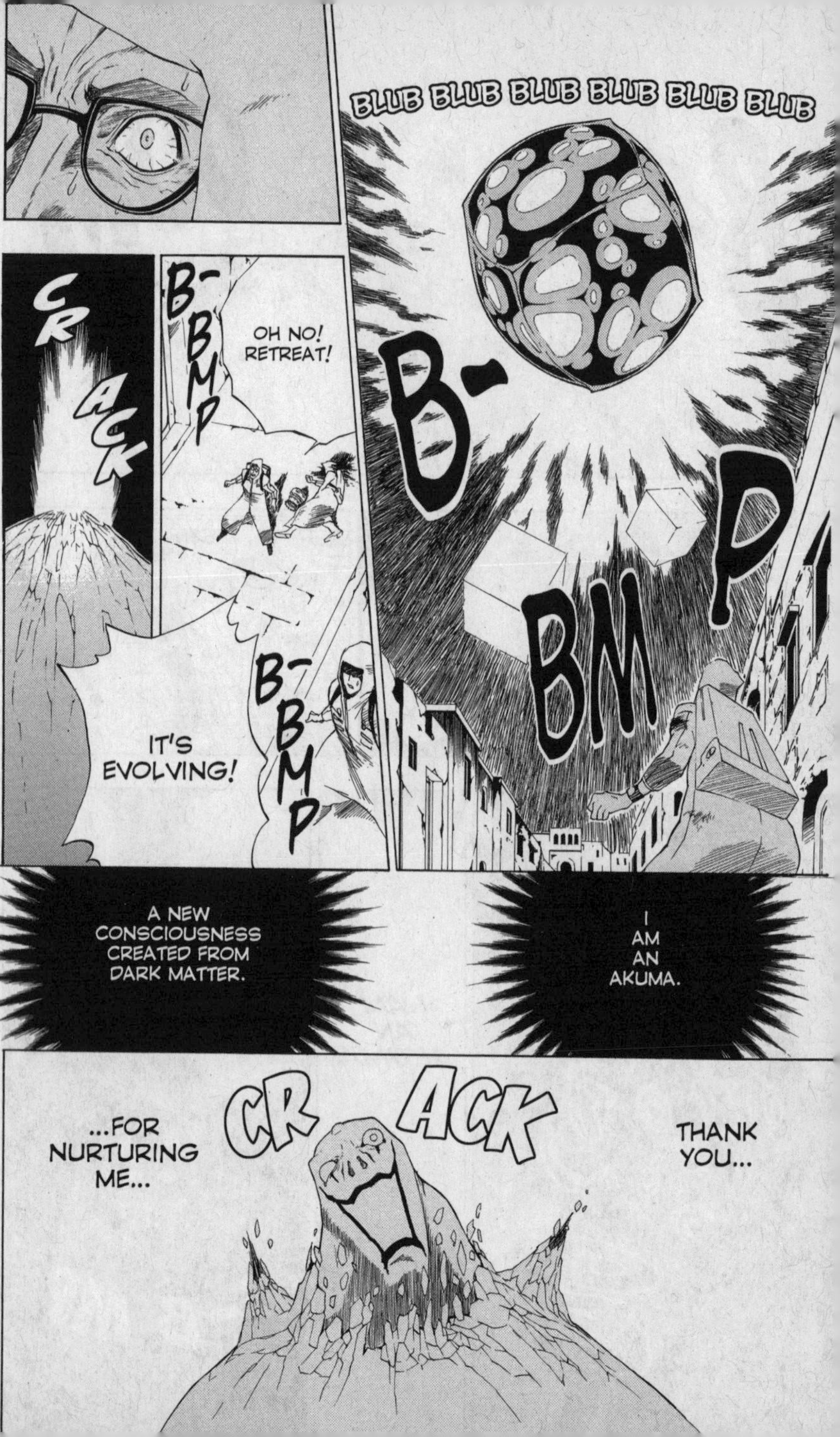

BLUB BLUB BLUB BLUB BLUB BLUB
B-BMP
B-BMP
OH NO! RETREAT!
B-BMP
CRACK
IT'S EVOLVING!
I AM AN AKUMA.
A NEW CONSCIOUSNESS CREATED FROM DARK MATTER.
THANK YOU...
CRACK
...FOR NURTURING ME...

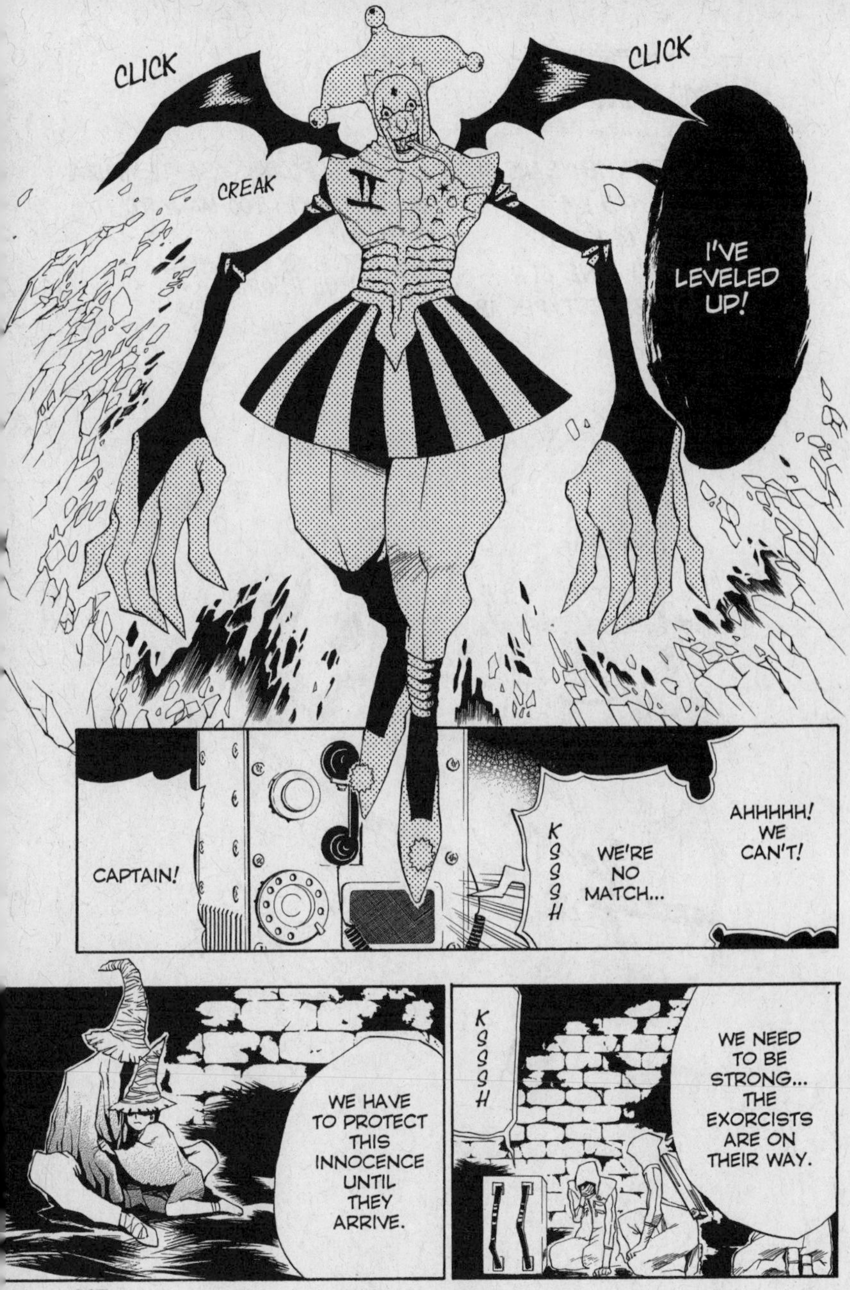
CLICK
CLICK
CREAK
I'VE LEVELED UP!
AHHHHH! WE CAN'T!
WE'RE NO MATCH...
KSSSH
CAPTAIN!
WE NEED TO BE STRONG... THE EXORCISTS ARE ON THEIR WAY.
KSSSH
WE HAVE TO PROTECT THIS INNOCENCE UNTIL THEY ARRIVE.

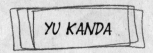

YU KANDA

JAPANESE: 18 YEARS OLD
HEIGHT: 175 CM
WEIGHT: 61 KG
BIRTHDAY: JUNE 6TH
GEMINI: BLOOD TYPE: AB

FAVORITE FOODS: SOBA, TEMPURA
DOESN'T LIKE: TOO MANY TO MENTION

IT'S NOT EASY DRAWING BEAUTIFUL PEOPLE.

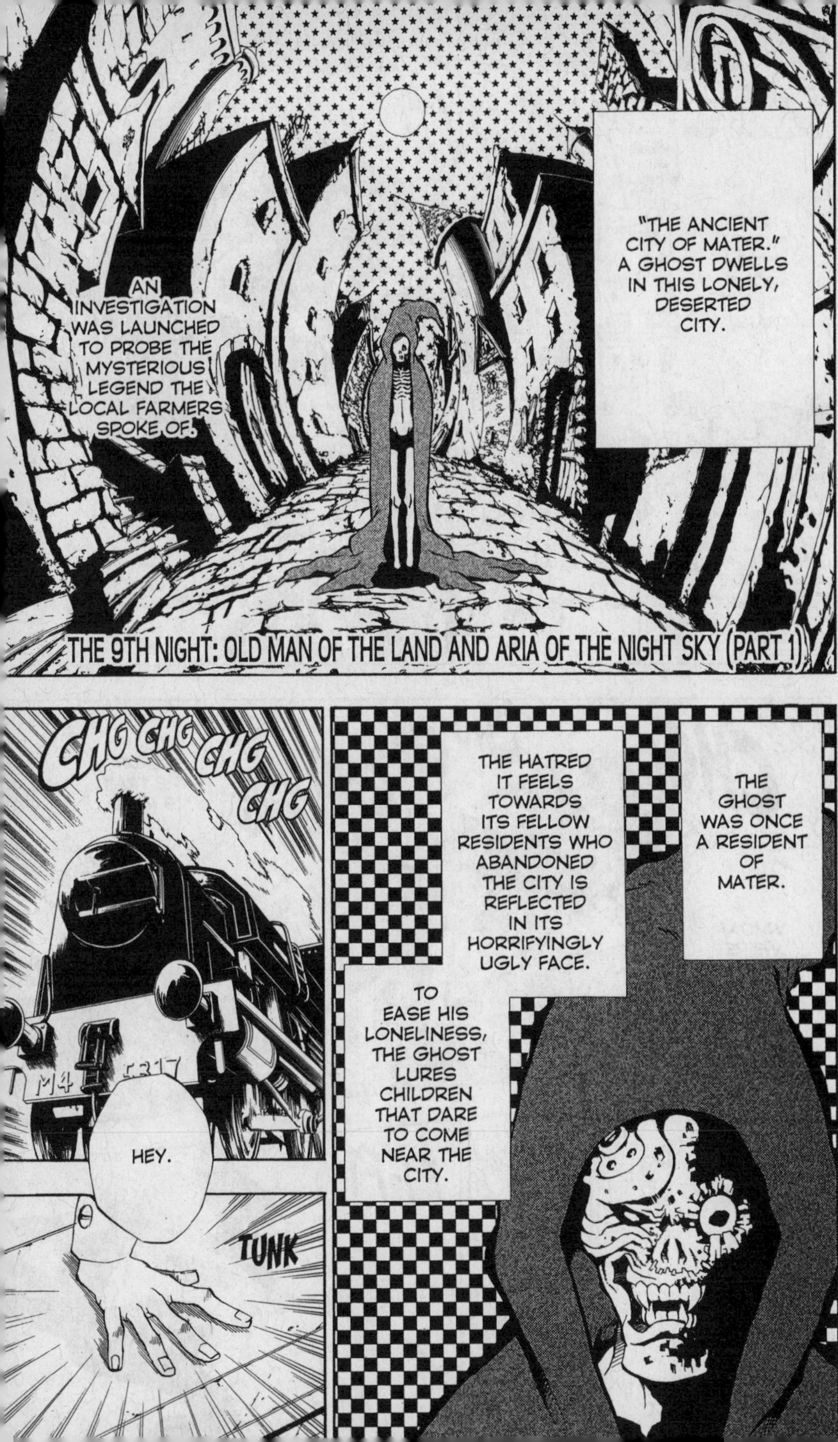
"THE ANCIENT CITY OF MATER." A GHOST DWELLS IN THIS LONELY, DESERTED CITY.
AN INVESTIGATION WAS LAUNCHED TO PROBE THE MYSTERIOUS LEGEND THE LOCAL FARMERS SPOKE OF.
THE 9TH NIGHT: OLD MAN OF THE LAND AND ARIA OF THE NIGHT SKY (PART 1)
THE GHOST WAS ONCE A RESIDENT OF MATER.
THE HATRED IT FEELS TOWARDS ITS FELLOW RESIDENTS WHO ABANDONED THE CITY IS REFLECTED IN ITS HORRIFYINGLY UGLY FACE.
TO EASE HIS LONELINESS, THE GHOST LURES CHILDREN THAT DARE TO COME NEAR THE CITY.
CHG CHG CHG CHG
HEY.
TUNK

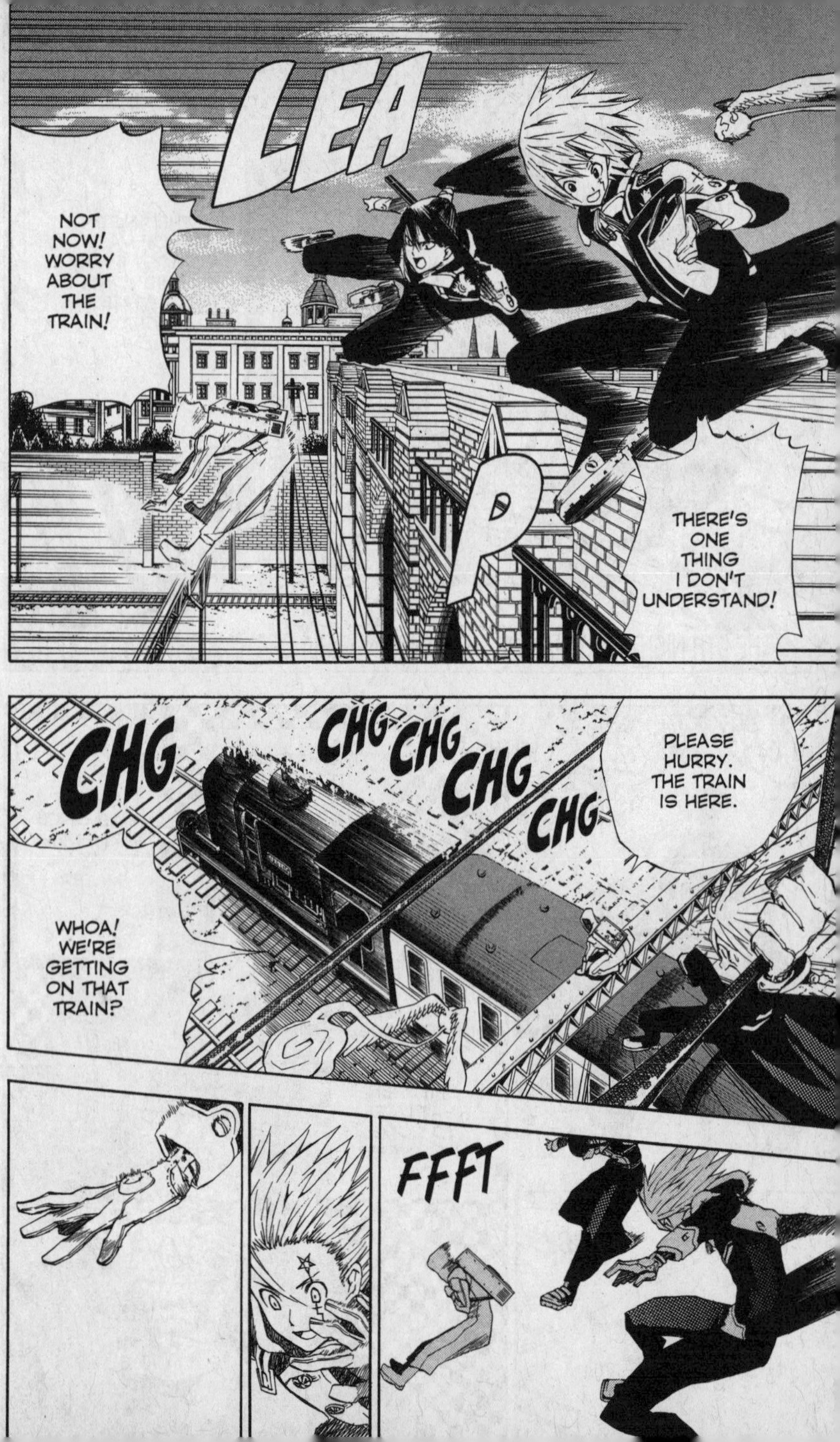
THERE'S ONE THING I DON'T UNDERSTAND!
NOT NOW! WORRY ABOUT THE TRAIN!
LEA
P
PLEASE HURRY. THE TRAIN IS HERE.
CHG
CHG CHG CHG CHG
WHOA! WE'RE GETTING ON THAT TRAIN?
FFFT

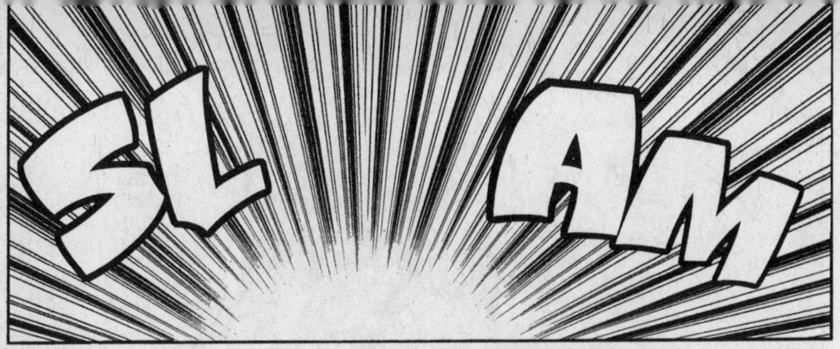
SL AM

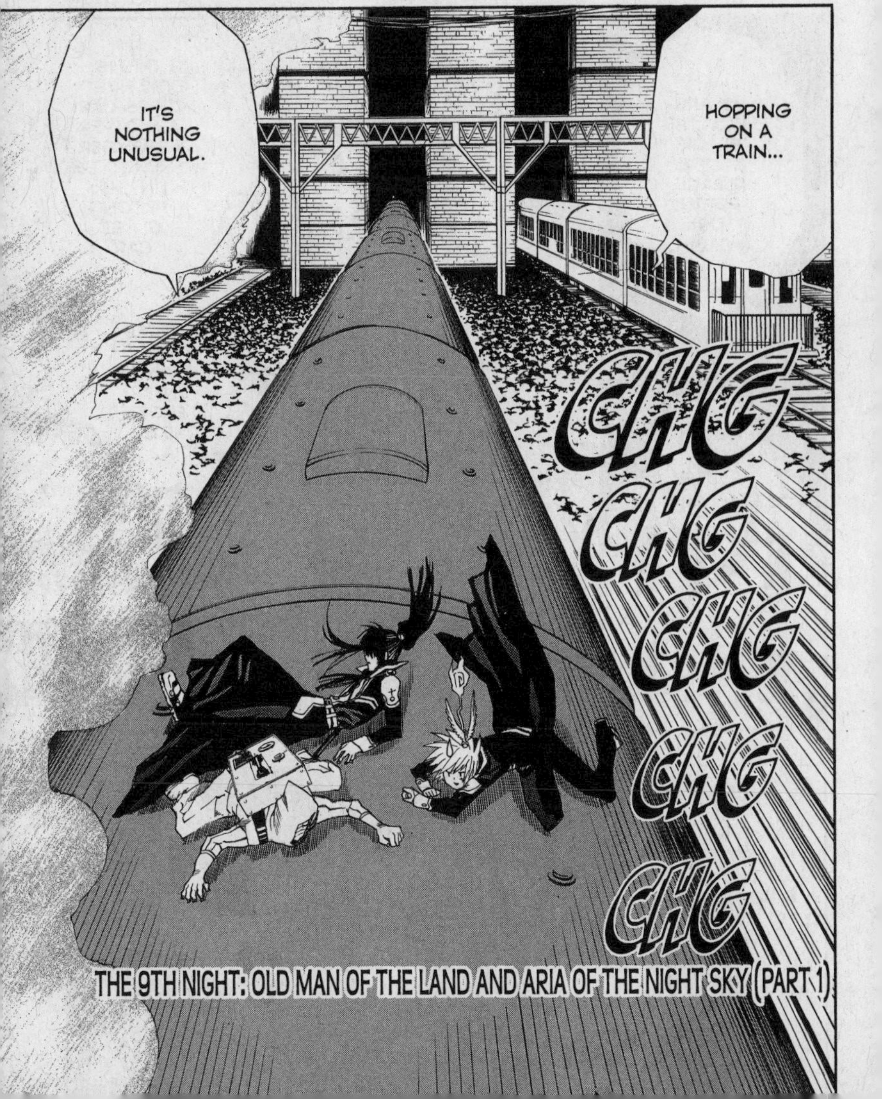
HOPPING ON A TRAIN...
IT'S NOTHING UNUSUAL.
CHG CHG CHG CHG CHG

THE 9TH NIGHT: OLD MAN OF THE LAND AND ARIA OF THE NIGHT SKY (PART 1)

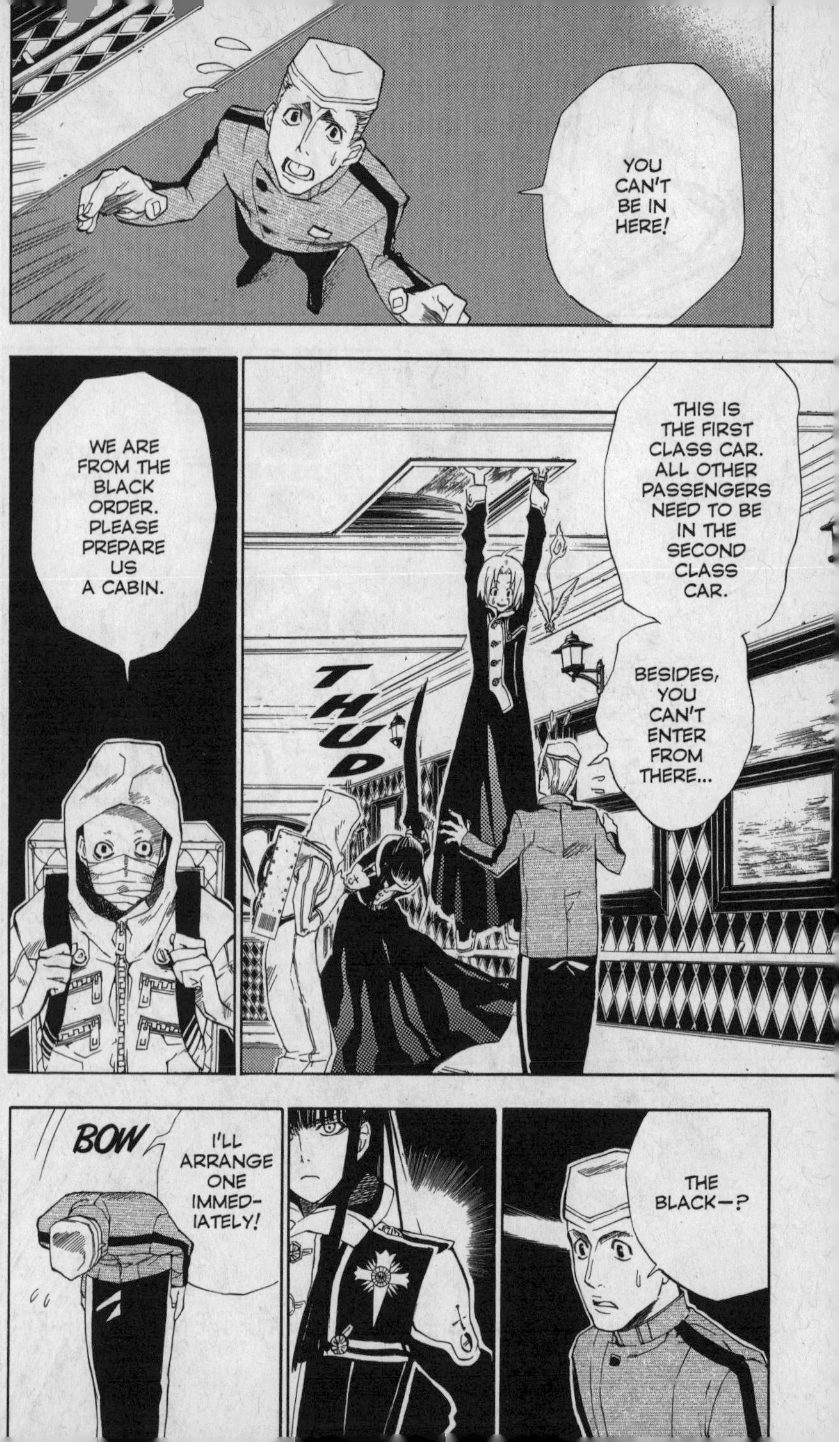
YOU CAN'T BE IN HERE!
THIS IS THE FIRST CLASS CAR. ALL OTHER PASSENGERS NEED TO BE IN THE SECOND CLASS CAR.
BESIDES, YOU CAN'T ENTER FROM THERE...
THUD
WE ARE FROM THE BLACK ORDER. PLEASE PREPARE US A CABIN.
THE BLACK—?
BOW
I'LL ARRANGE ONE IMMEDIATELY!

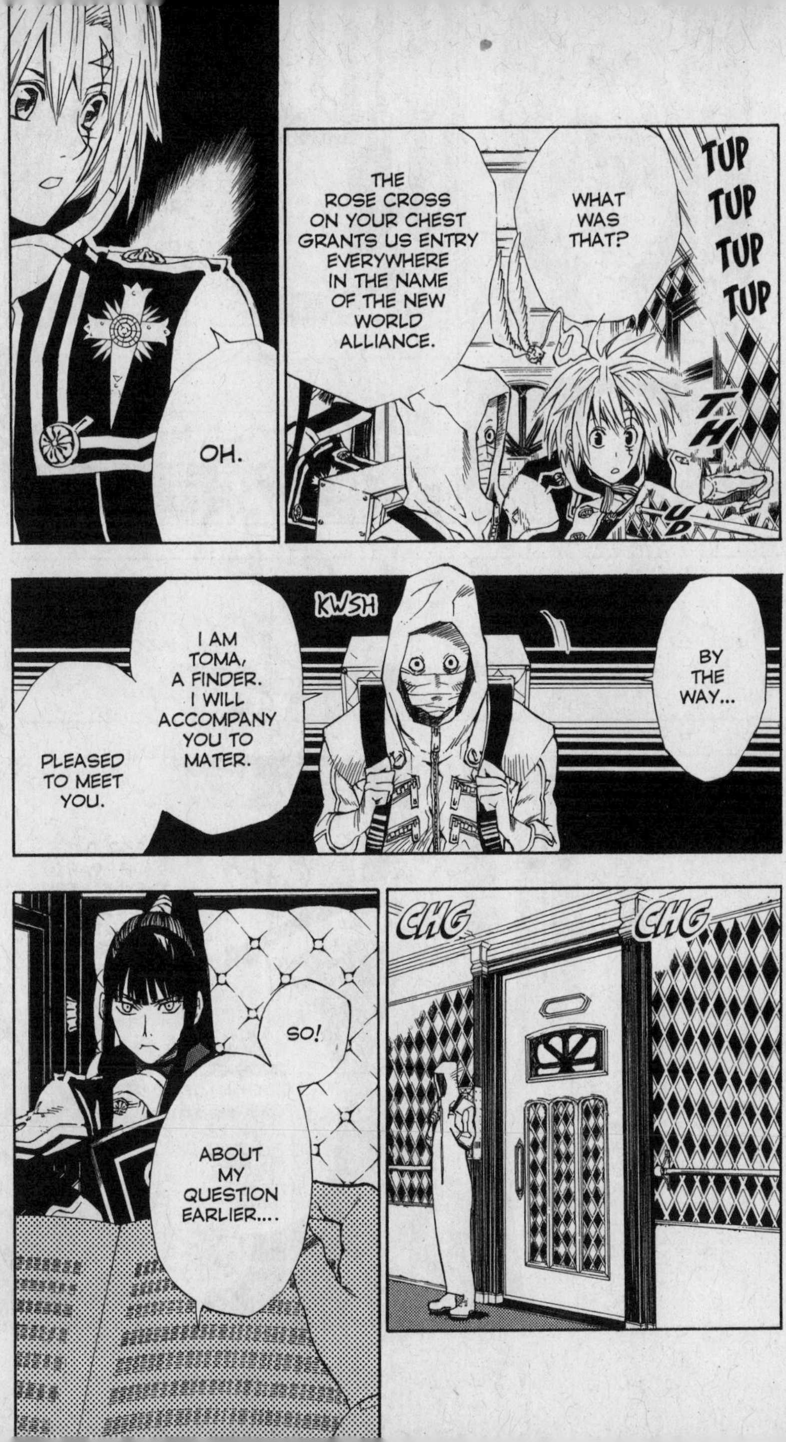
TUP TUP TUP TUP
WHAT WAS THAT?
THE ROSE CROSS ON YOUR CHEST GRANTS US ENTRY EVERYWHERE IN THE NAME OF THE NEW WORLD ALLIANCE.
THUD
OH.
BY THE WAY...
KWSH
I AM TOMA, A FINDER. I WILL ACCOMPANY YOU TO MATER.
PLEASED TO MEET YOU.
CHG CHG
SO!
ABOUT MY QUESTION EARLIER....

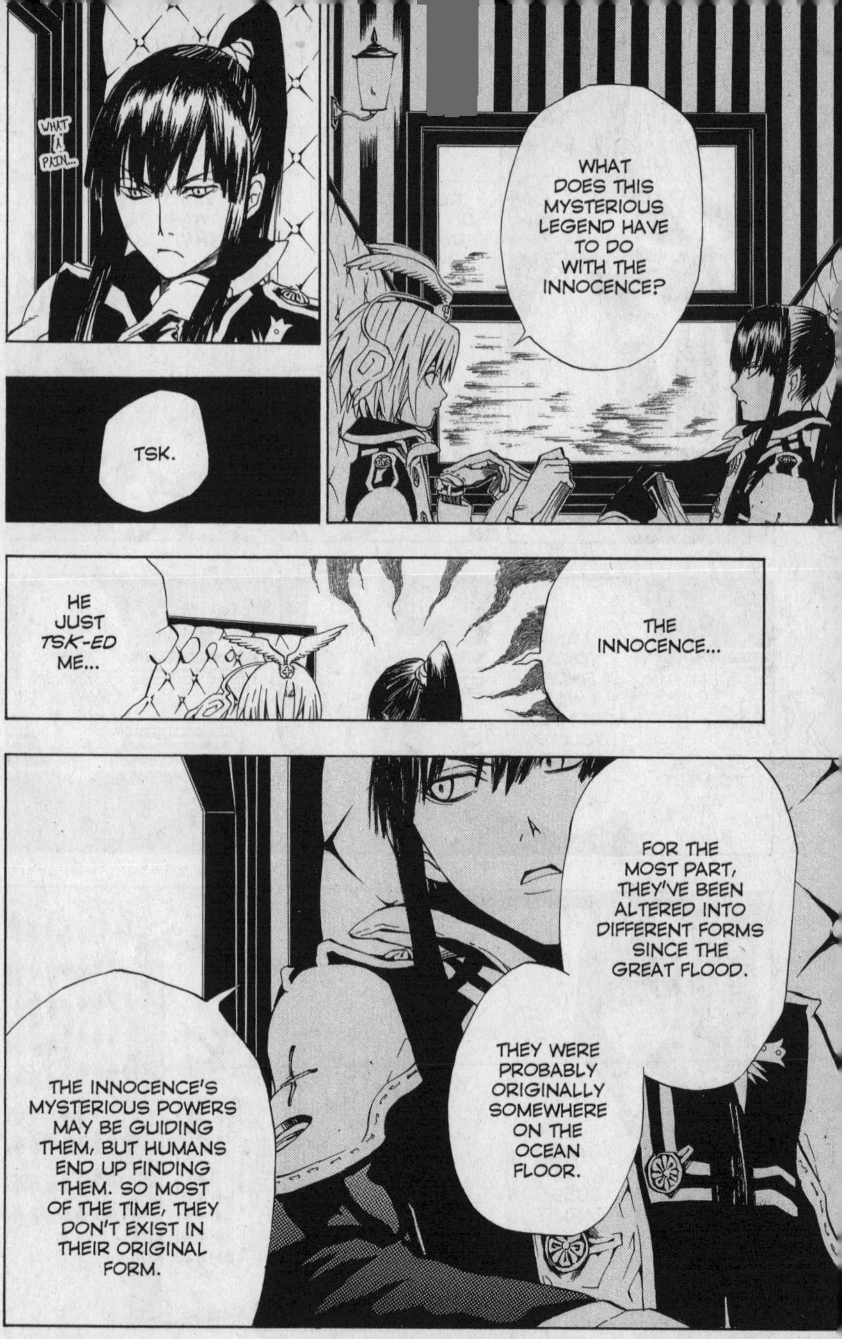
WHAT DOES THIS MYSTERIOUS LEGEND HAVE TO DO WITH THE INNOCENCE?
WHAT A PAIN...
TSK.
THE INNOCENCE...
HE JUST *TSK-ED* ME...
FOR THE MOST PART, THEY'VE BEEN ALTERED INTO DIFFERENT FORMS SINCE THE GREAT FLOOD.
THEY WERE PROBABLY ORIGINALLY SOMEWHERE ON THE OCEAN FLOOR.
THE INNOCENCE'S MYSTERIOUS POWERS MAY BE GUIDING THEM, BUT HUMANS END UP FINDING THEM. SO MOST OF THE TIME, THEY DON'T EXIST IN THEIR ORIGINAL FORM.

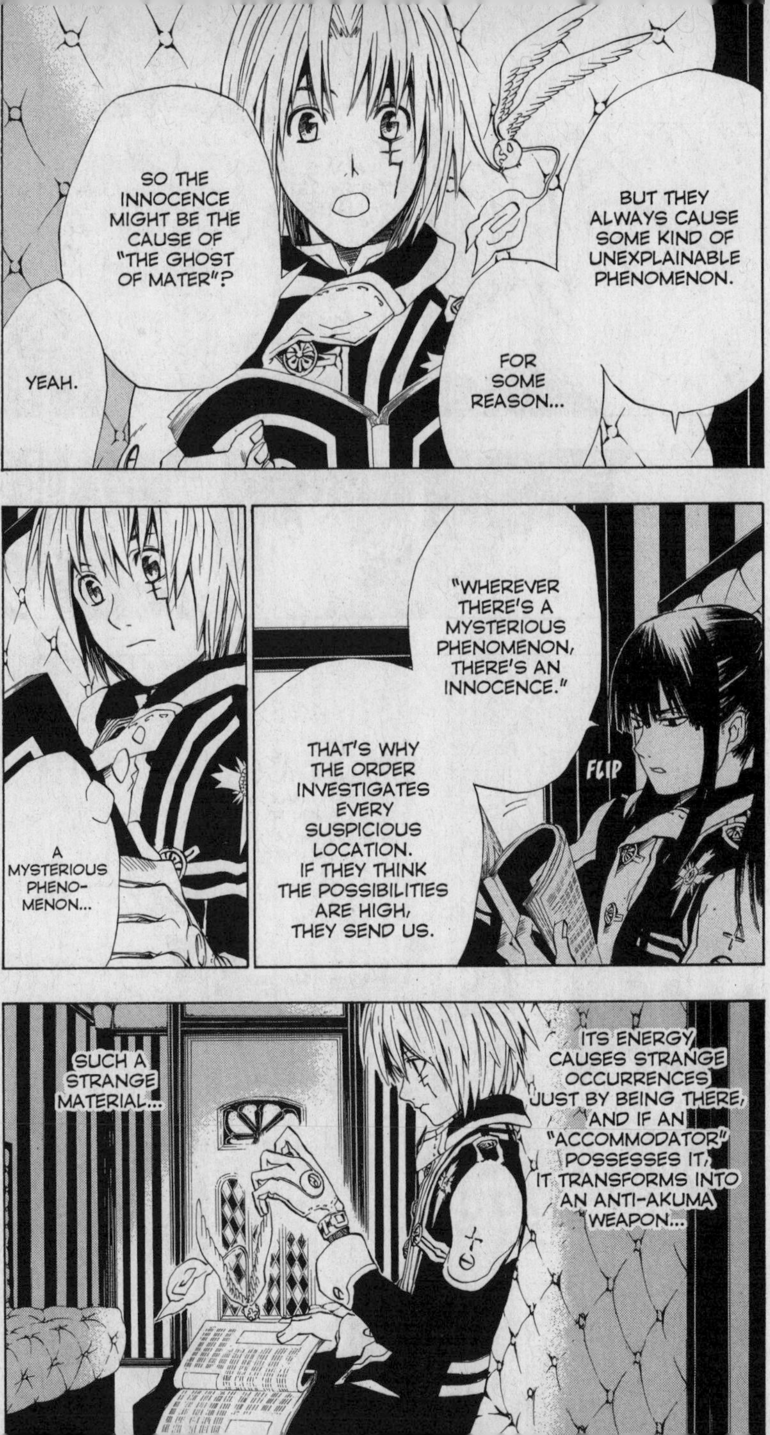

BUT THEY ALWAYS CAUSE SOME KIND OF UNEXPLAINABLE PHENOMENON.
SO THE INNOCENCE MIGHT BE THE CAUSE OF "THE GHOST OF MATER"?
FOR SOME REASON...
YEAH.
"WHEREVER THERE'S A MYSTERIOUS PHENOMENON, THERE'S AN INNOCENCE."
THAT'S WHY THE ORDER INVESTIGATES EVERY SUSPICIOUS LOCATION. IF THEY THINK THE POSSIBILITIES ARE HIGH, THEY SEND US.
FLIP
A MYSTERIOUS PHENO-MENON...
ITS ENERGY CAUSES STRANGE OCCURRENCES JUST BY BEING THERE, AND IF AN "ACCOMMODATOR" POSSESSES IT, IT TRANSFORMS INTO AN ANTI-AKUMA WEAPON...
SUCH A STRANGE MATERIAL...

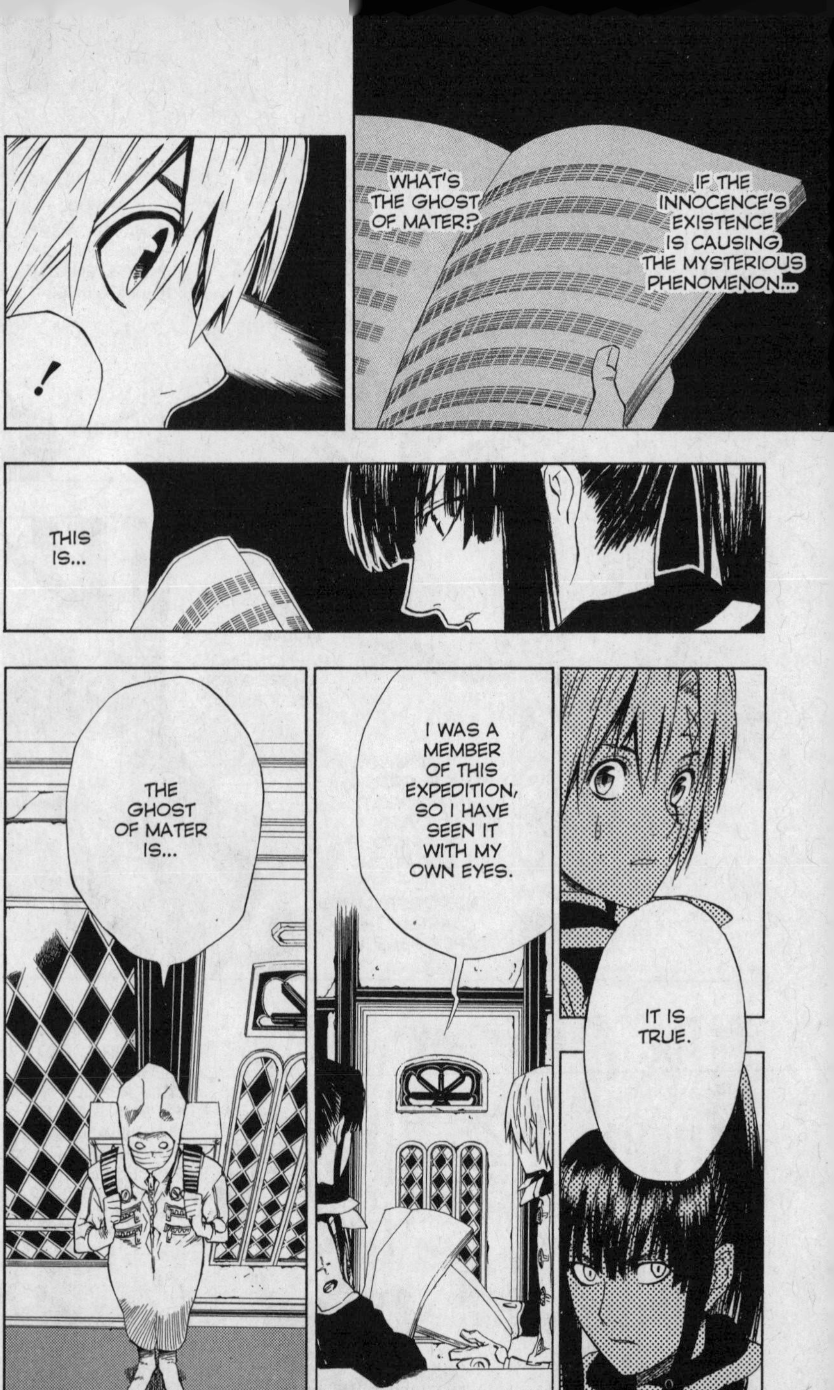
IF THE INNOCENCE'S EXISTENCE IS CAUSING THE MYSTERIOUS PHENOMENON...
WHAT'S THE GHOST OF MATER?
!
THIS IS...
IT IS TRUE.
I WAS A MEMBER OF THIS EXPEDITION, SO I HAVE SEEN IT WITH MY OWN EYES.
THE GHOST OF MATER IS...

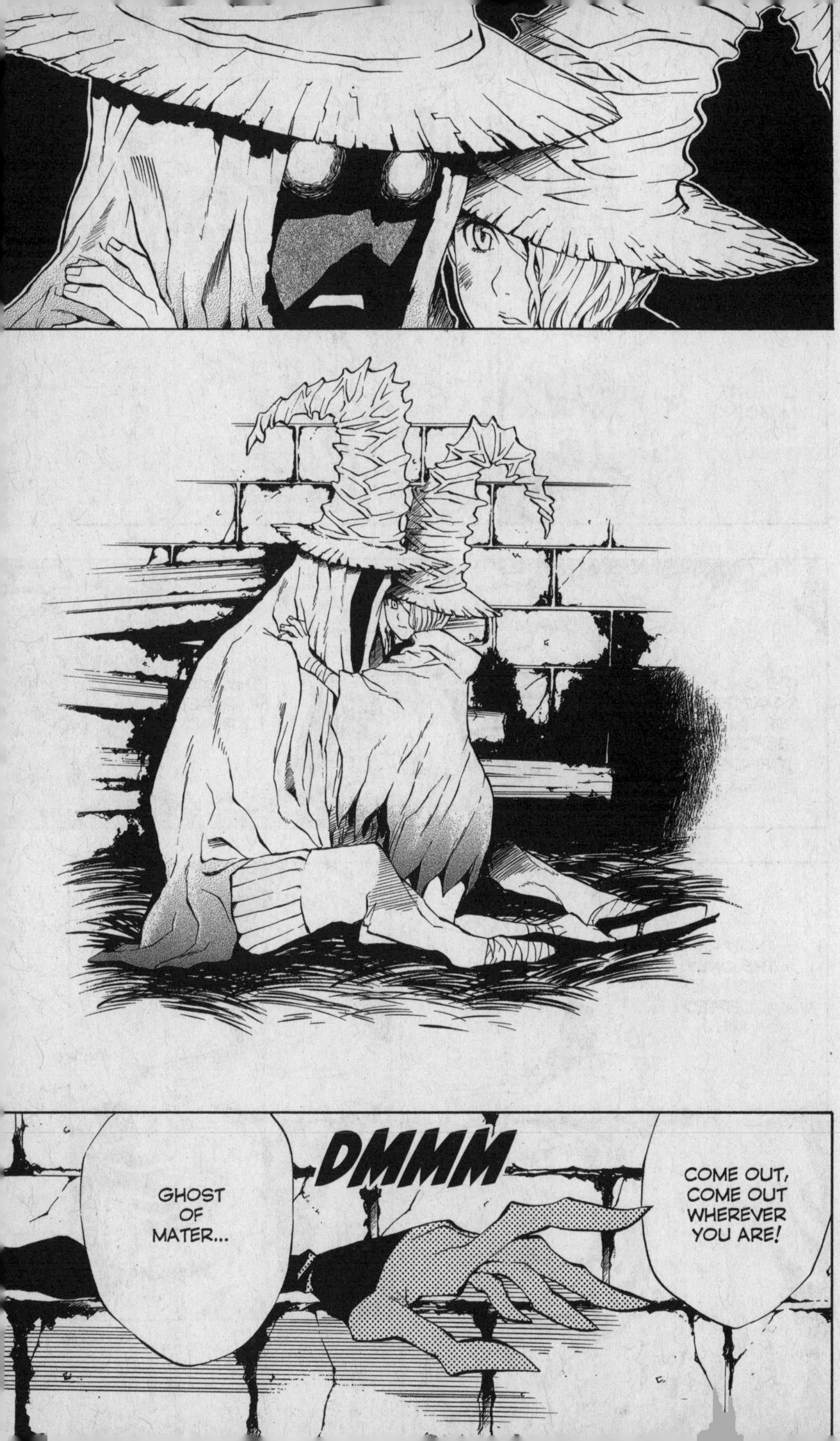
COME OUT, COME OUT WHEREVER YOU ARE!
DMMM
GHOST OF MATER...

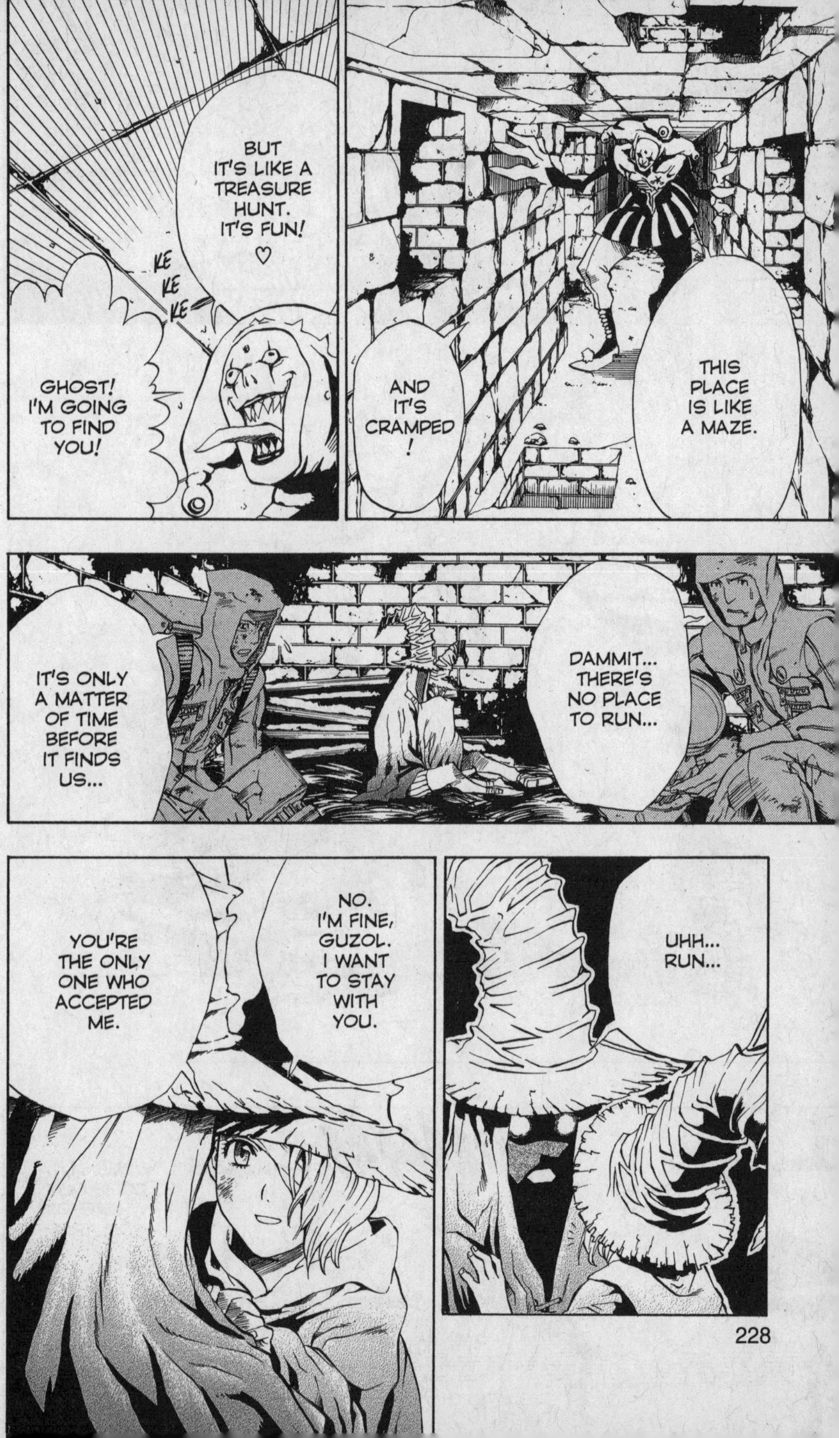
THIS PLACE IS LIKE A MAZE.
AND IT'S CRAMPED!
BUT IT'S LIKE A TREASURE HUNT. IT'S FUN! ♡
KE KE KE
GHOST! I'M GOING TO FIND YOU!
DAMMIT... THERE'S NO PLACE TO RUN...
IT'S ONLY A MATTER OF TIME BEFORE IT FINDS US...
UHH... RUN...
NO. I'M FINE, GUZOL. I WANT TO STAY WITH YOU.
YOU'RE THE ONLY ONE WHO ACCEPTED ME.

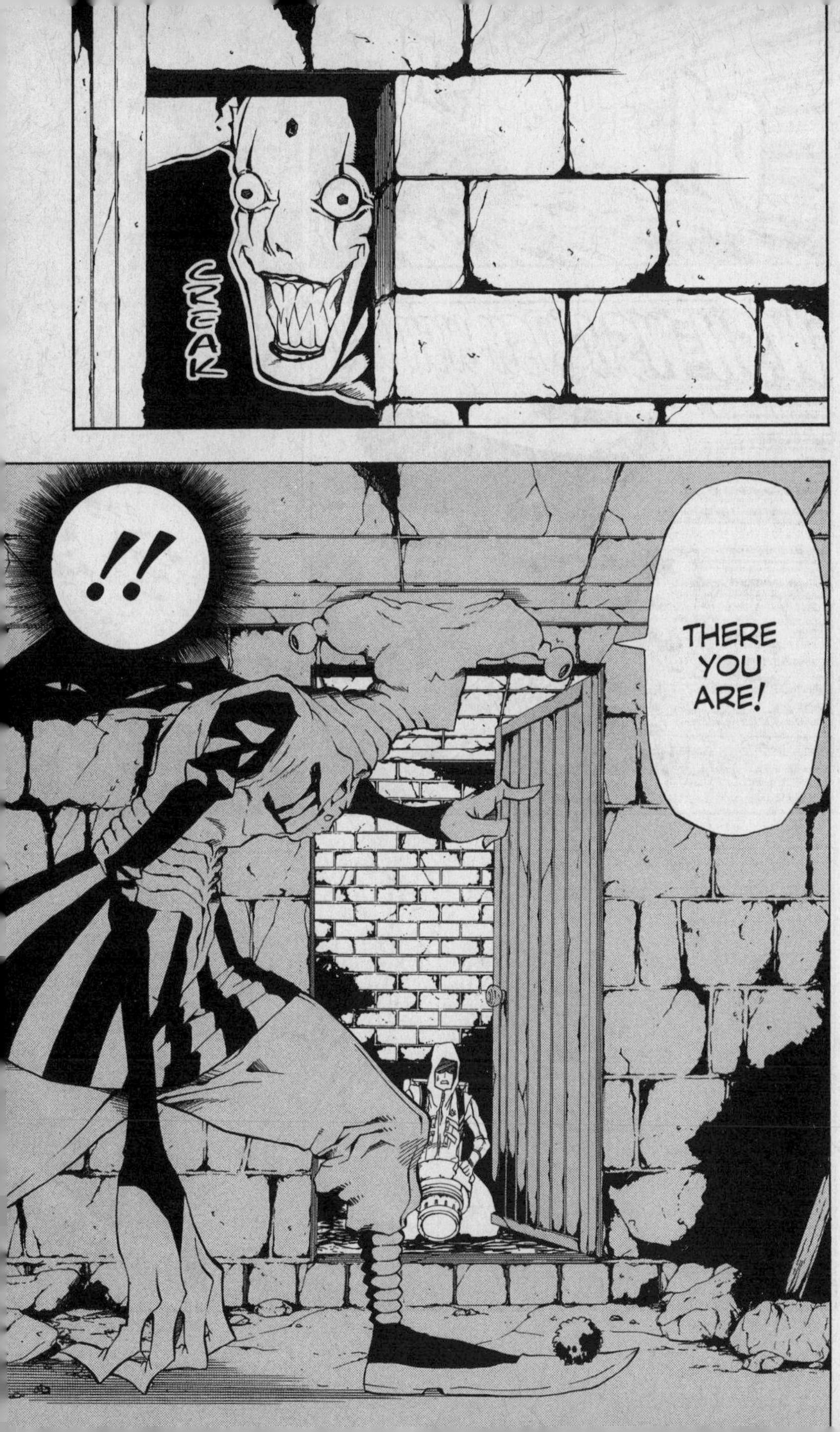
CREAK
THERE YOU ARE!
!!

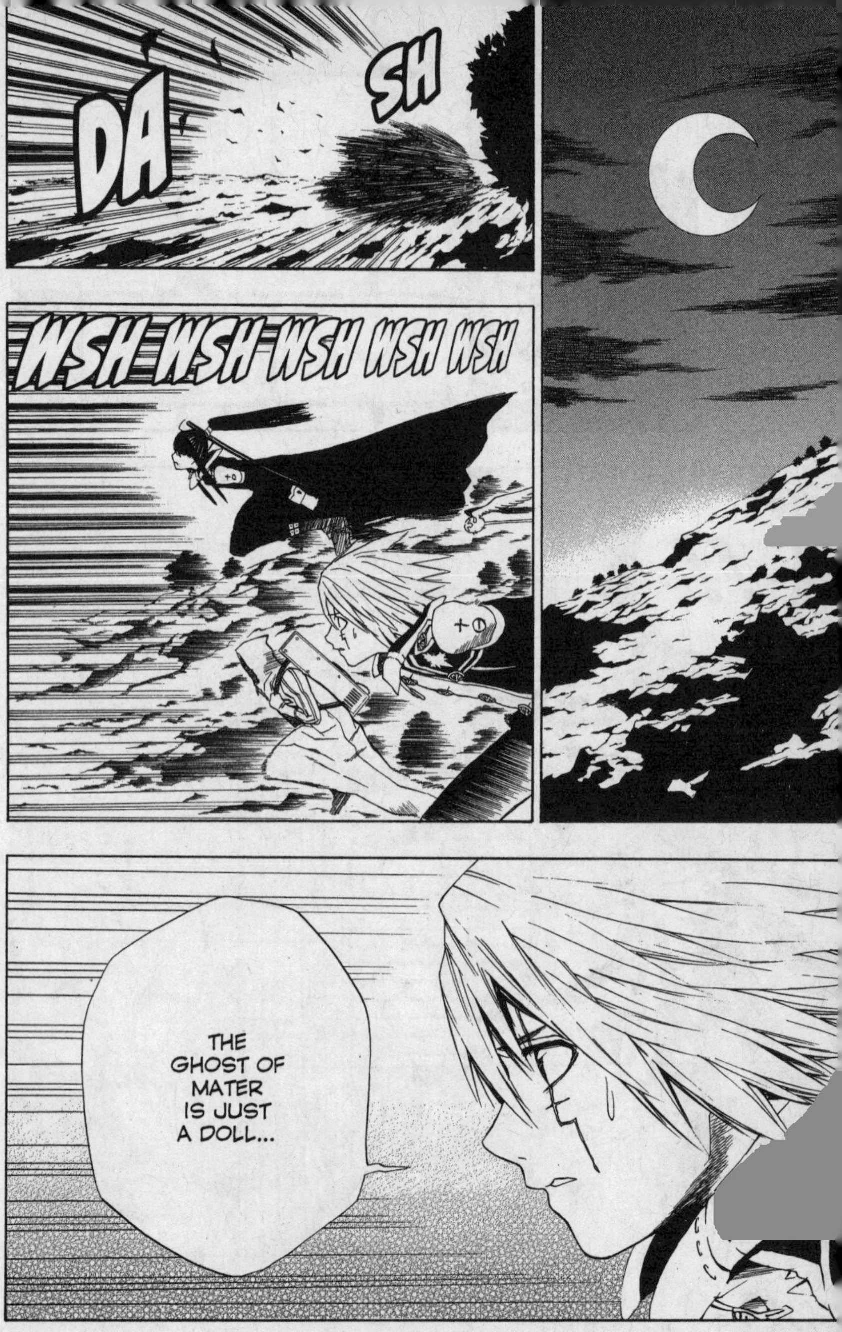
DASH
WSH WSH WSH WSH WSH
THE GHOST OF MATER IS JUST A DOLL...

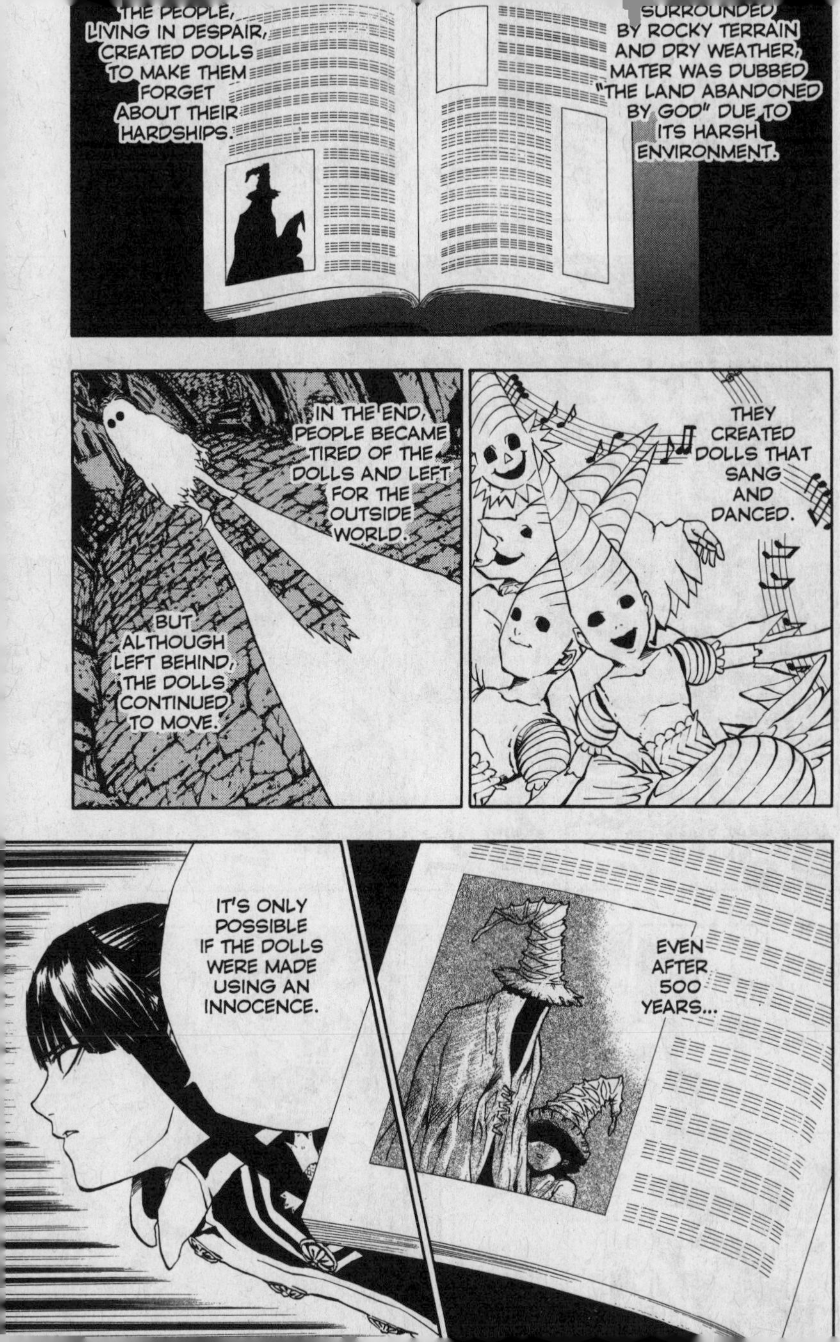
SURROUNDED BY ROCKY TERRAIN AND DRY WEATHER, MATER WAS DUBBED "THE LAND ABANDONED BY GOD" DUE TO ITS HARSH ENVIRONMENT.
THE PEOPLE, LIVING IN DESPAIR, CREATED DOLLS TO MAKE THEM FORGET ABOUT THEIR HARDSHIPS.
THEY CREATED DOLLS THAT SANG AND DANCED.
IN THE END, PEOPLE BECAME TIRED OF THE DOLLS AND LEFT FOR THE OUTSIDE WORLD.
BUT ALTHOUGH LEFT BEHIND, THE DOLLS CONTINUED TO MOVE.
EVEN AFTER 500 YEARS...
IT'S ONLY POSSIBLE IF THE DOLLS WERE MADE USING AN INNOCENCE.

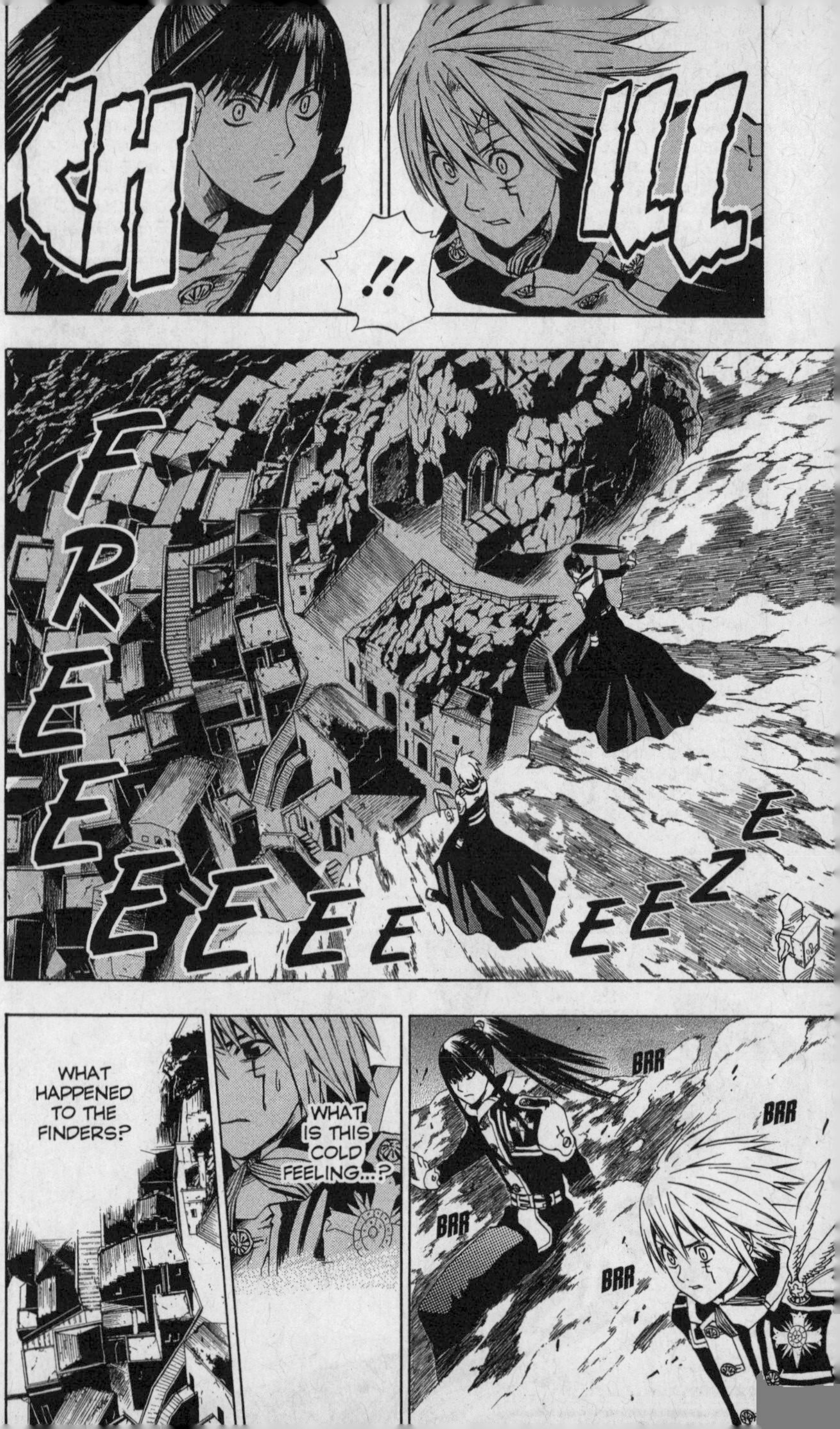
CHILL
!!
FREEEEEEEEZE
BRR
BRR
BRR
BRR
WHAT IS THIS COLD FEELING...?
WHAT HAPPENED TO THE FINDERS?

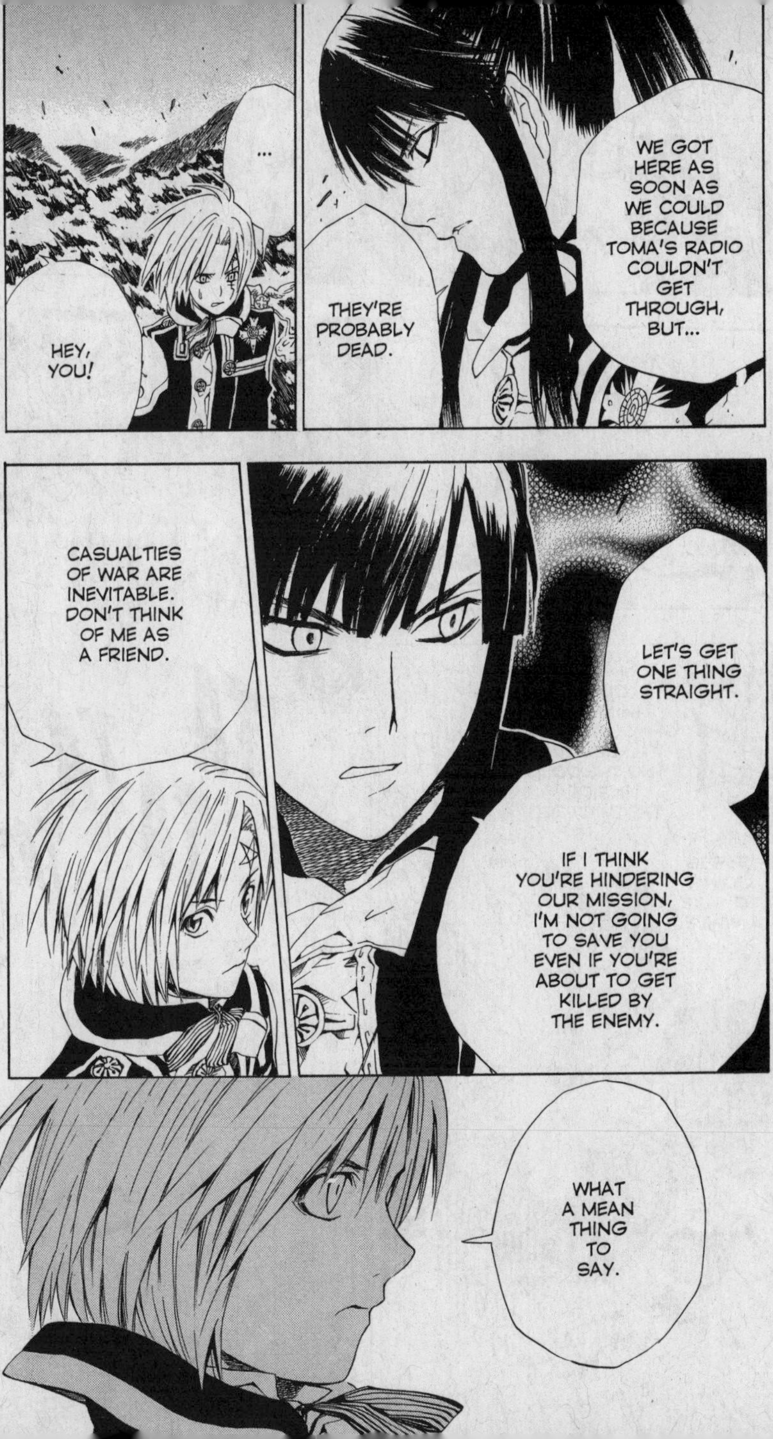
WE GOT HERE AS SOON AS WE COULD BECAUSE TOMA'S RADIO COULDN'T GET THROUGH, BUT...
THEY'RE PROBABLY DEAD.
...
HEY, YOU!
LET'S GET ONE THING STRAIGHT.
IF I THINK YOU'RE HINDERING OUR MISSION, I'M NOT GOING TO SAVE YOU EVEN IF YOU'RE ABOUT TO GET KILLED BY THE ENEMY.
CASUALTIES OF WAR ARE INEVITABLE. DON'T THINK OF ME AS A FRIEND.
WHAT A MEAN THING TO SAY.

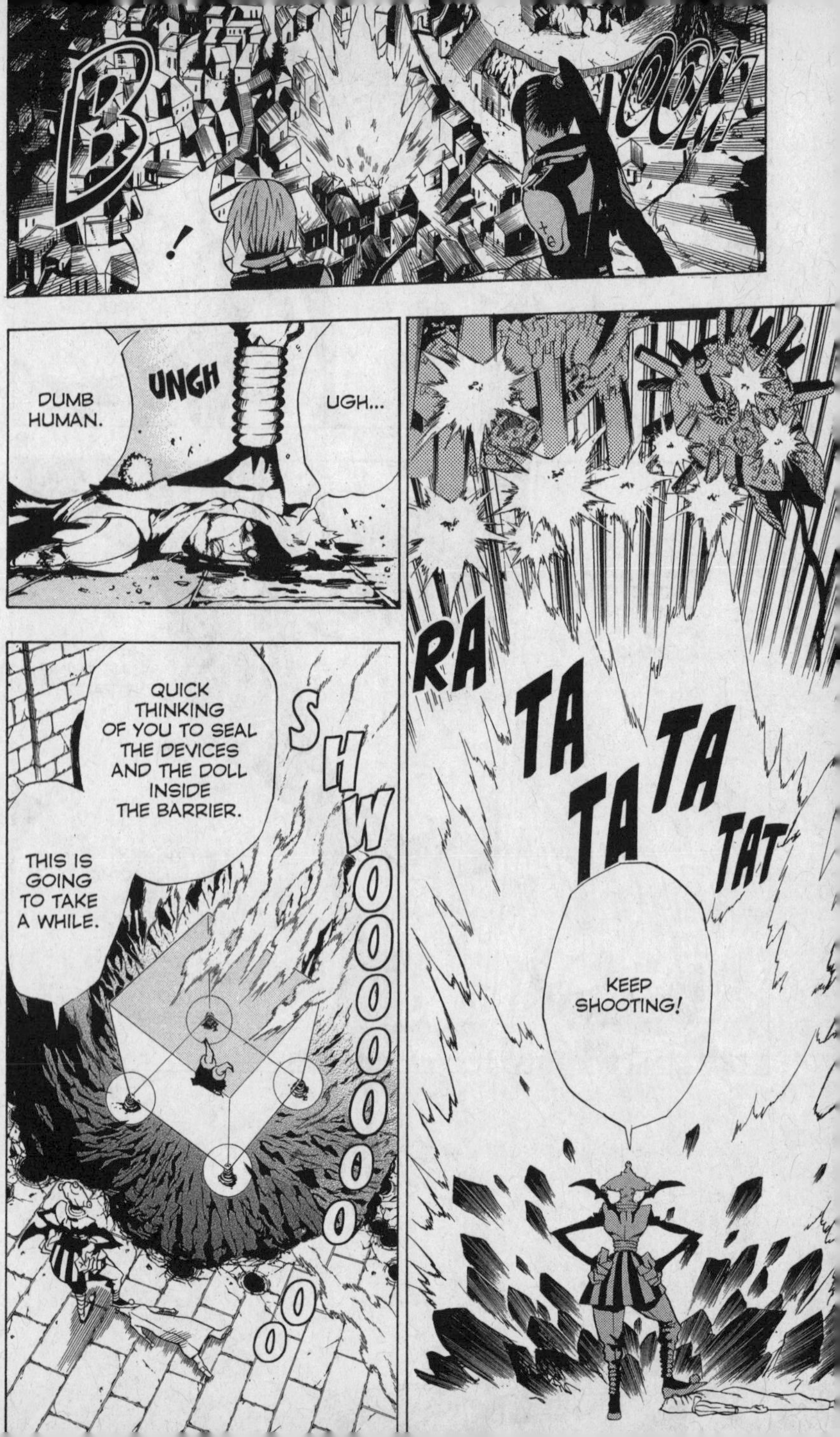
BOOM!
!
RA TA TA TA TA TAT
KEEP SHOOTING!
UGH...
UNGH
DUMB HUMAN.
SHWOOOOOOOOOOOO
QUICK THINKING OF YOU TO SEAL THE DEVICES AND THE DOLL INSIDE THE BARRIER.
THIS IS GOING TO TAKE A WHILE.

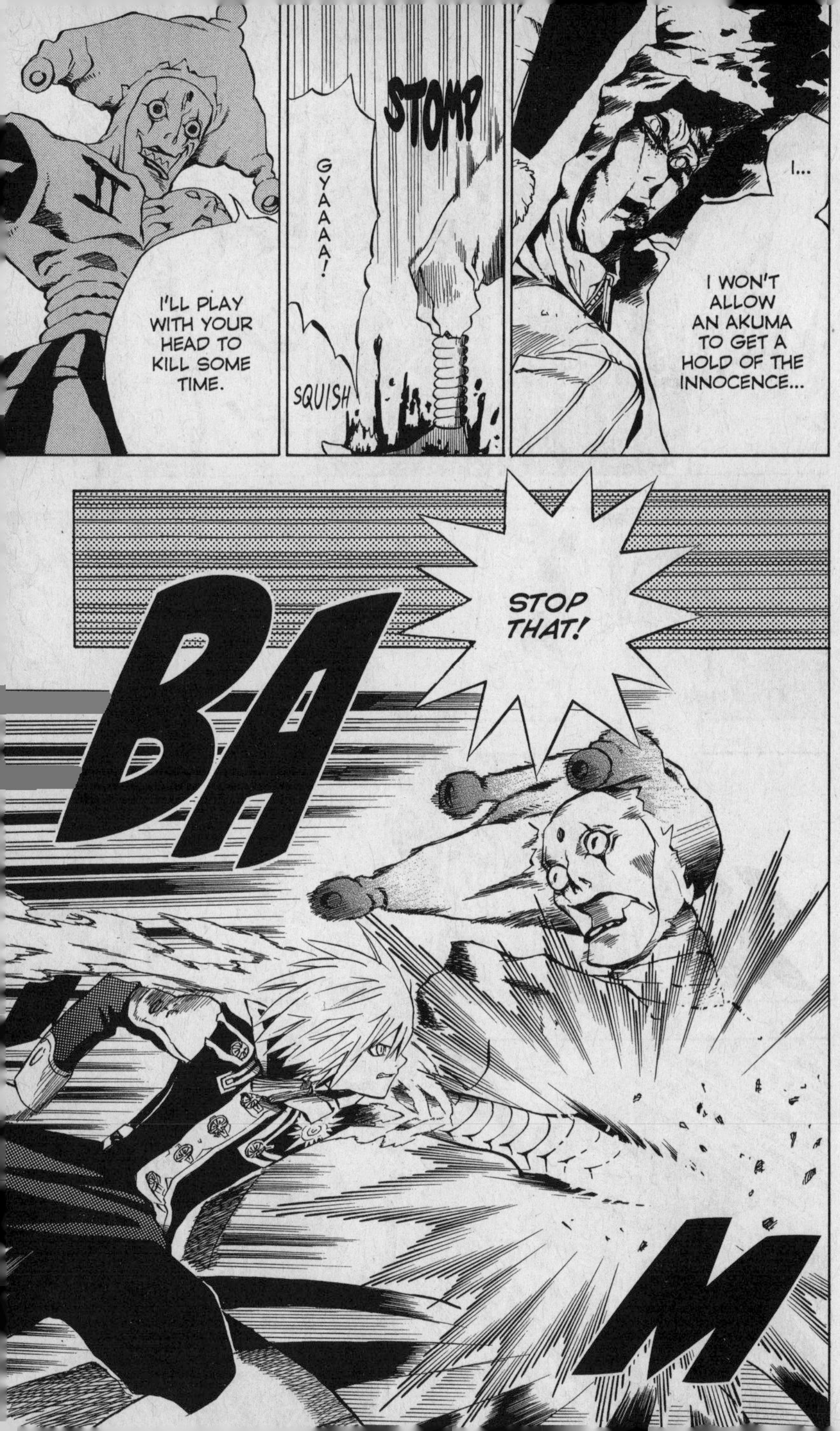

I...
I WON'T ALLOW AN AKUMA TO GET A HOLD OF THE INNOCENCE...
STOMP
GYAAAAA!
SQUISH
I'LL PLAY WITH YOUR HEAD TO KILL SOME TIME.
STOP THAT!
BAM

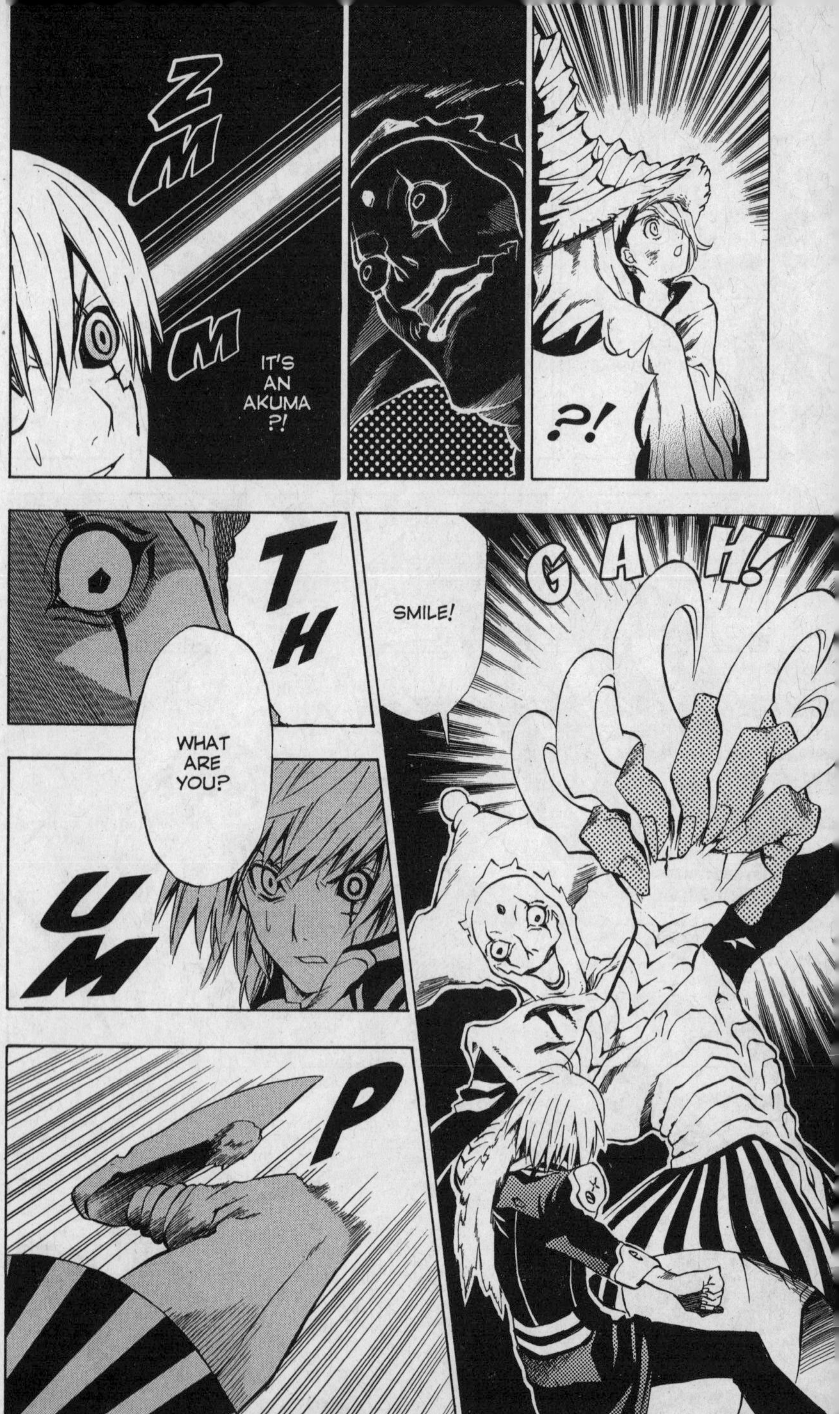
?!
ZMM
IT'S AN AKUMA?!
GAH!
SMILE!
WHAT ARE YOU?
THUMP

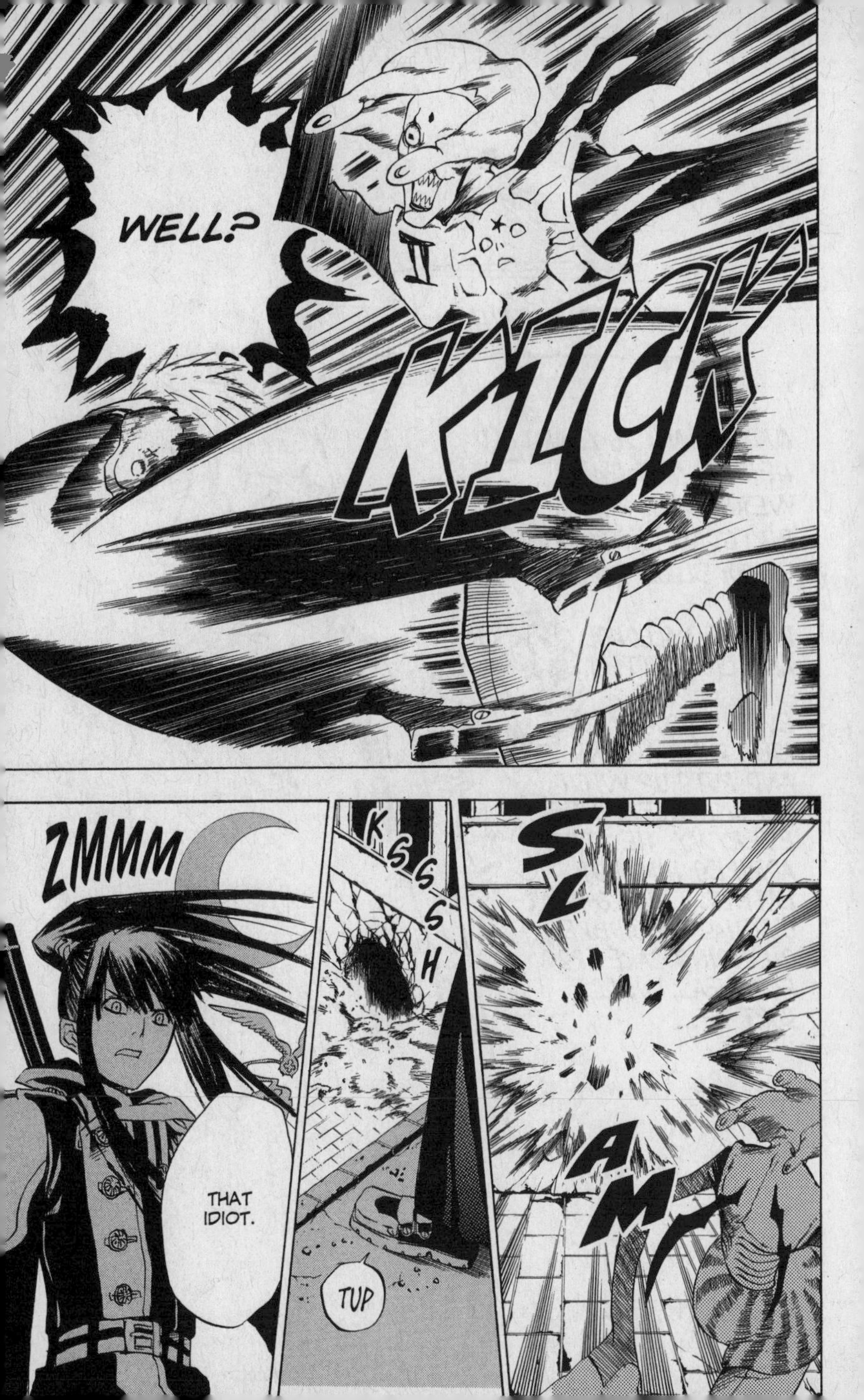
WELL?
KICK
SLAM
KSSSH
TUP
ZMMM
THAT IDIOT.

REEVER WENHAM

AUSTRALIAN: 26 YEARS OLD
HEIGHT: 185 CM
WEIGHT: 75 KG
BIRTHDAY: SEPTEMBER 8TH
VIRGO: BLOOD TYPE: A

DISLIKES ALCOHOL
AND CIGARETTES.

←SODA

BUBBLES

EVEN THOUGH
RIBA RUNS AROUND
AND PUTS UP WITH
KOMUI'S SELFISHNESS
EVERYDAY, HE STILL
ADMIRES HIM. BUT
LATELY, THIS 26-YEAR-
OLD HAS CONSIDERED
CHANGING CAREERS
FOR REAL. WELL,
SORT OF...

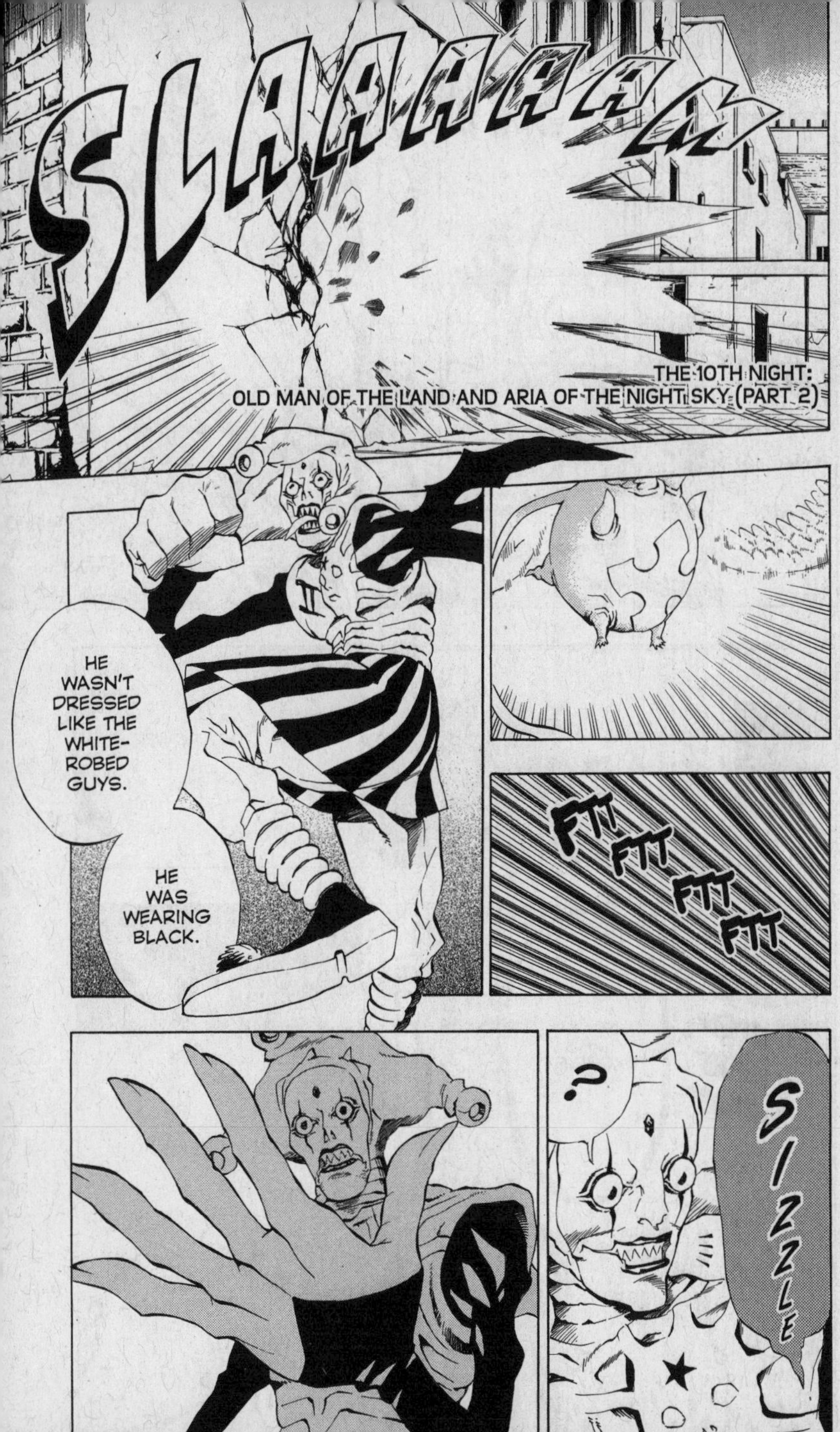
SLAAAAAM
THE 10TH NIGHT:
OLD MAN OF THE LAND AND ARIA OF THE NIGHT SKY (PART 2)
FTT FTT FTT FTT
HE WASN'T DRESSED LIKE THE WHITE-ROBED GUYS.
HE WAS WEARING BLACK.
?
SIZZLE

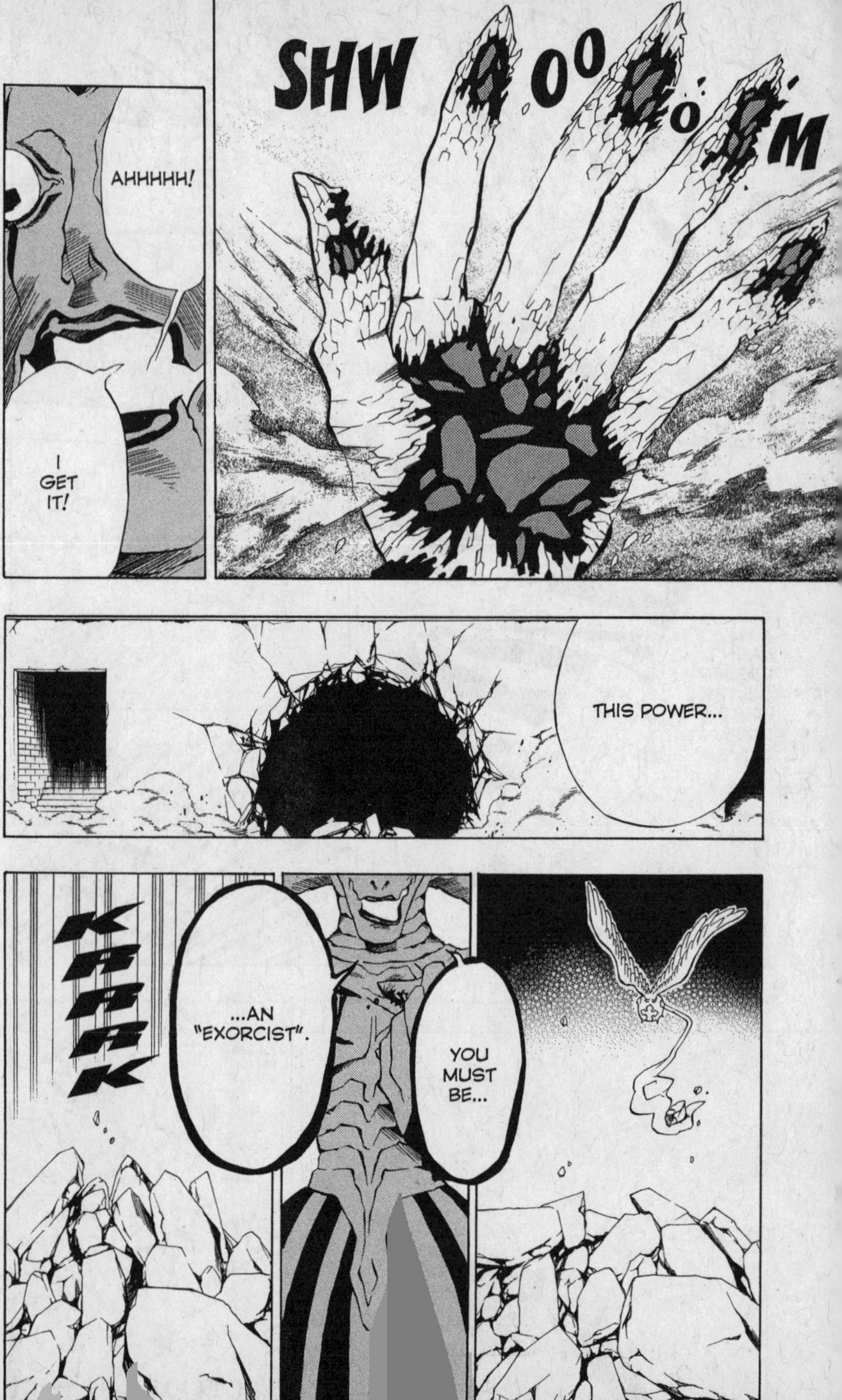
SHWOOOOM
AHHHHH!
I GET IT!
THIS POWER...
YOU MUST BE...
...AN "EXORCIST".
KRAAK

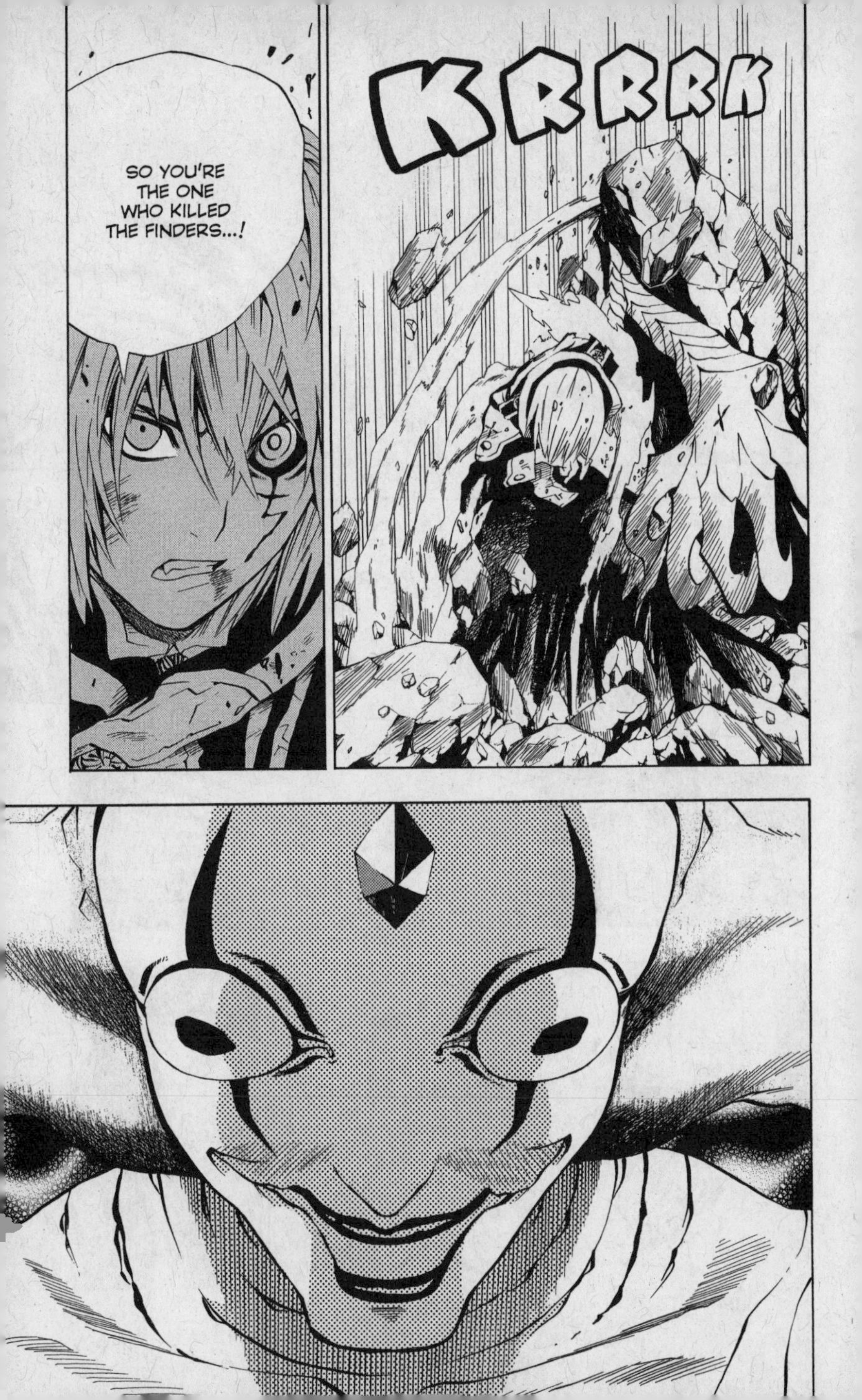
KRRRK
SO YOU'RE THE ONE WHO KILLED THE FINDERS...!

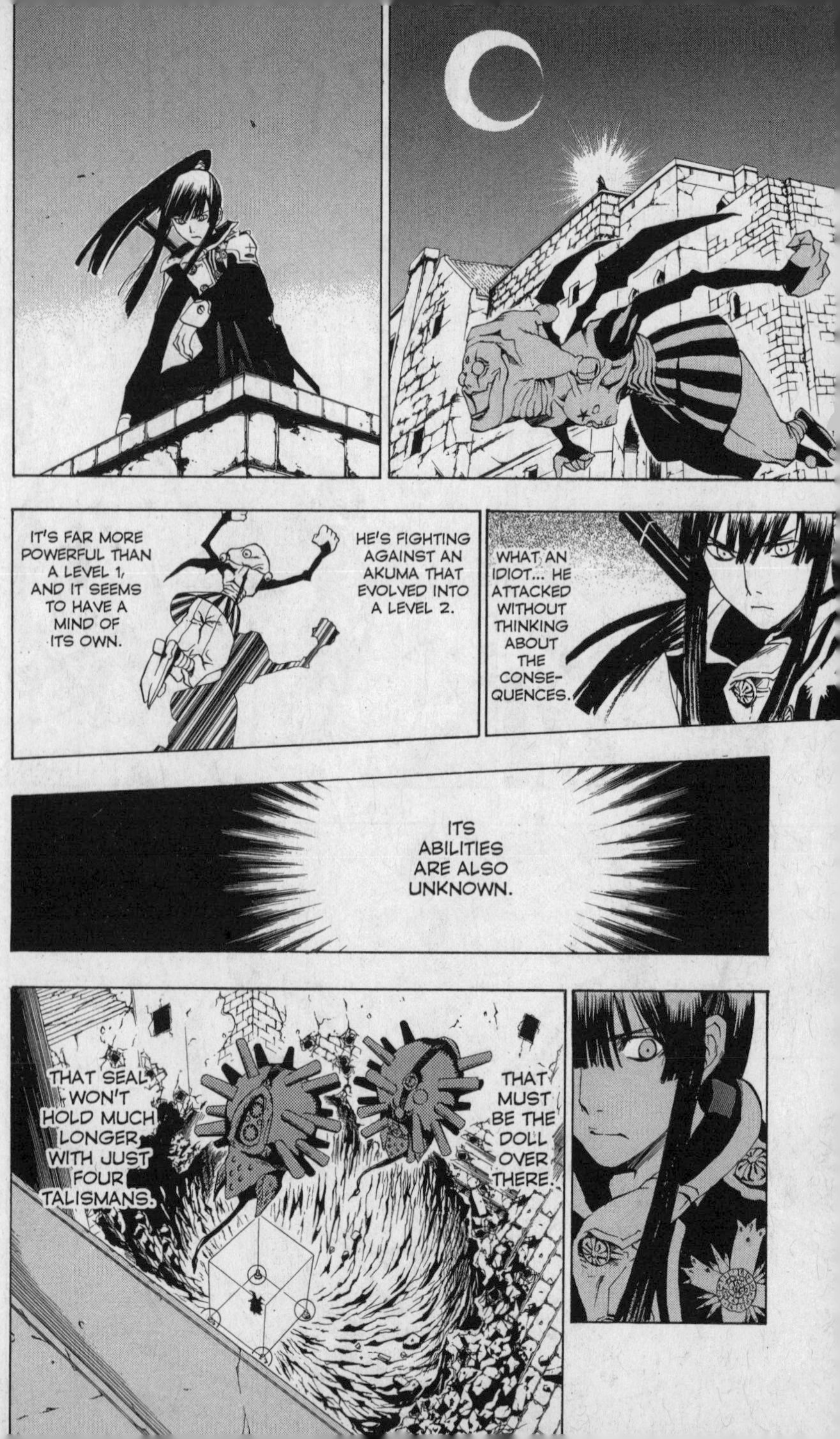
WHAT AN IDIOT... HE ATTACKED WITHOUT THINKING ABOUT THE CONSE-QUENCES.
HE'S FIGHTING AGAINST AN AKUMA THAT EVOLVED INTO A LEVEL 2.
IT'S FAR MORE POWERFUL THAN A LEVEL 1, AND IT SEEMS TO HAVE A MIND OF ITS OWN.
ITS ABILITIES ARE ALSO UNKNOWN.
THAT MUST BE THE DOLL OVER THERE.
THAT SEAL WON'T HOLD MUCH LONGER WITH JUST FOUR TALISMANS.

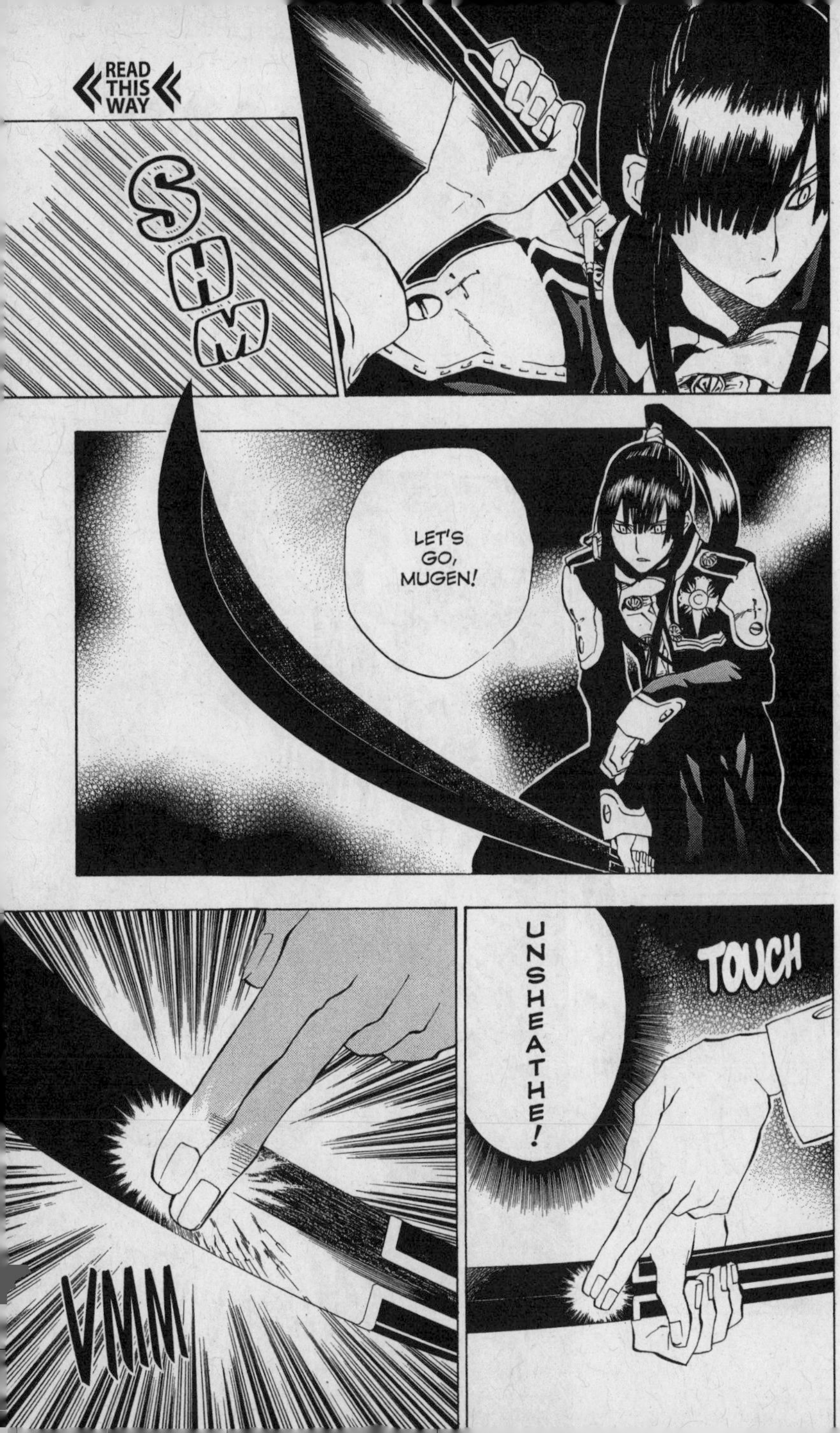
READ THIS WAY
SHM
LET'S GO, MUGEN!
UNSHEATHE!
TOUCH
VMM

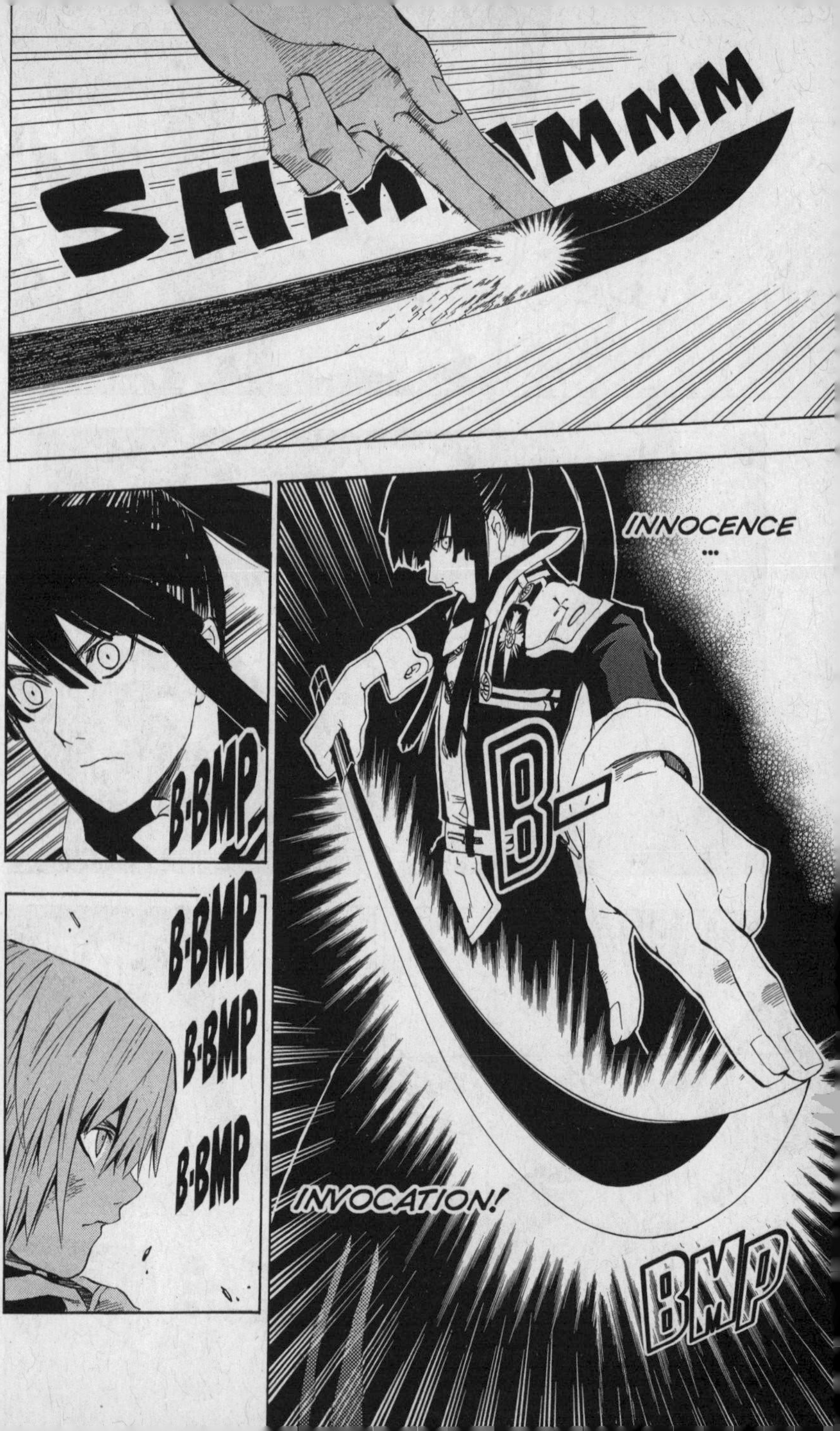
SHIMMMM
INNOCENCE...
B-
INVOCATION!
BMP
B-BMP
B-BMP
B-BMP
B-BMP

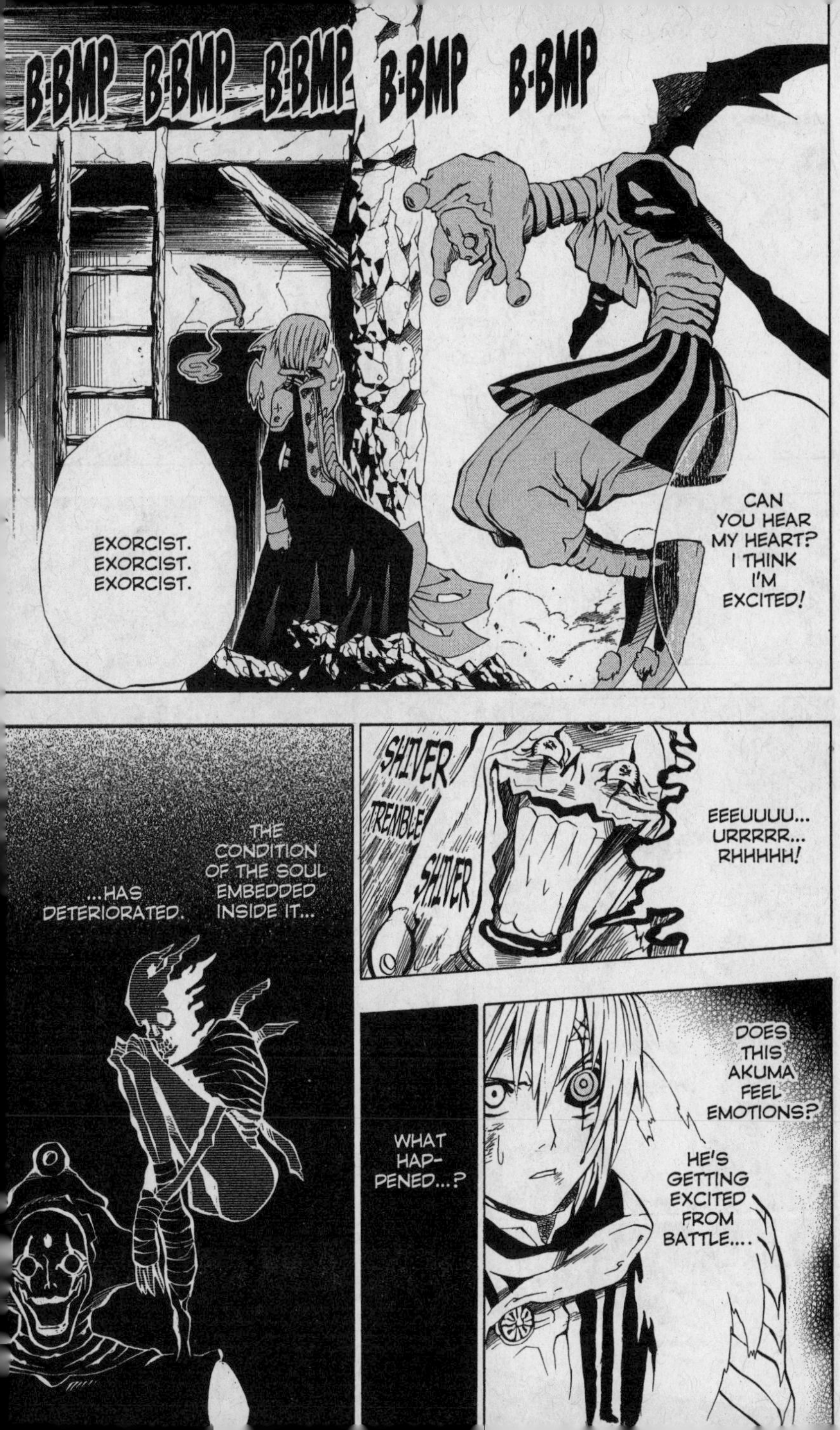
B-BMP B-BMP B-BMP B-BMP B-BMP
CAN YOU HEAR MY HEART? I THINK I'M EXCITED!
EXORCIST. EXORCIST. EXORCIST.
EEEUUUU... URRRRR... RHHHHH!
SHIVER
TREMBLE
SHIVER
DOES THIS AKUMA FEEL EMOTIONS?
HE'S GETTING EXCITED FROM BATTLE....
WHAT HAP-PENED...?
THE CONDITION OF THE SOUL EMBEDDED INSIDE IT...
...HAS DETERIORATED..

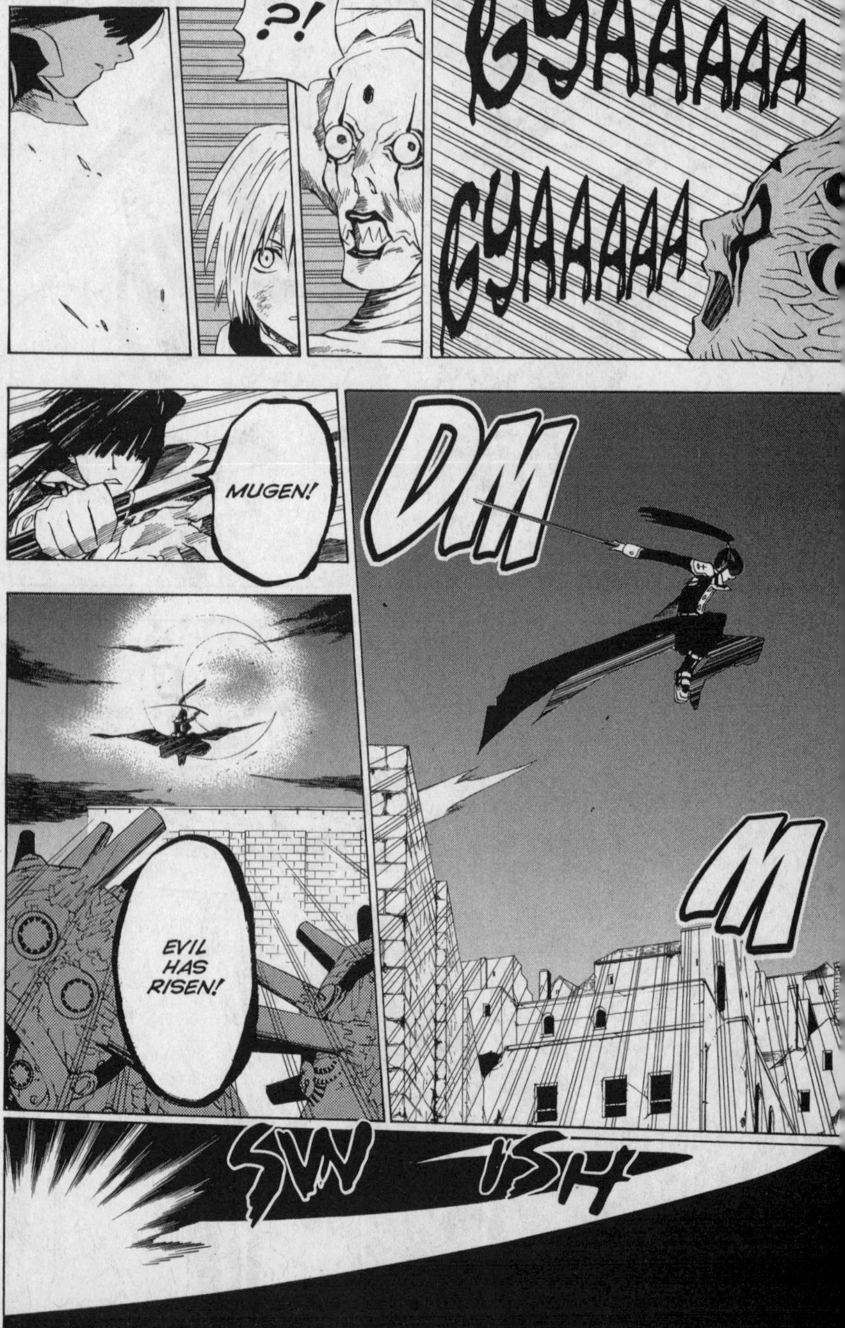
GYAAAAAA
GYAAAAA
?!
DM
M
MUGEN!
EVIL HAS RISEN!
SWISH

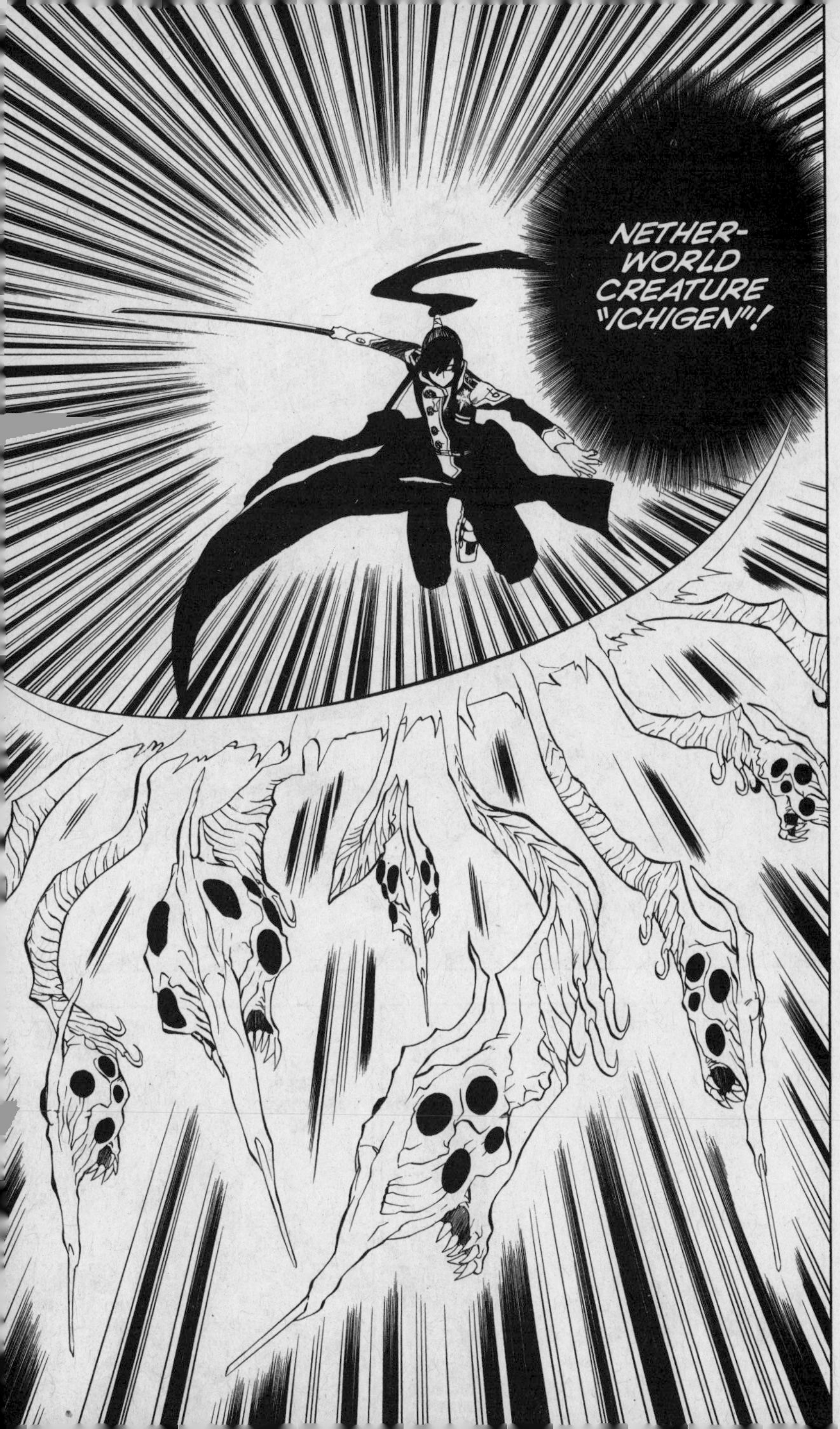
NETHER-WORLD CREATURE "ICHIGEN"!

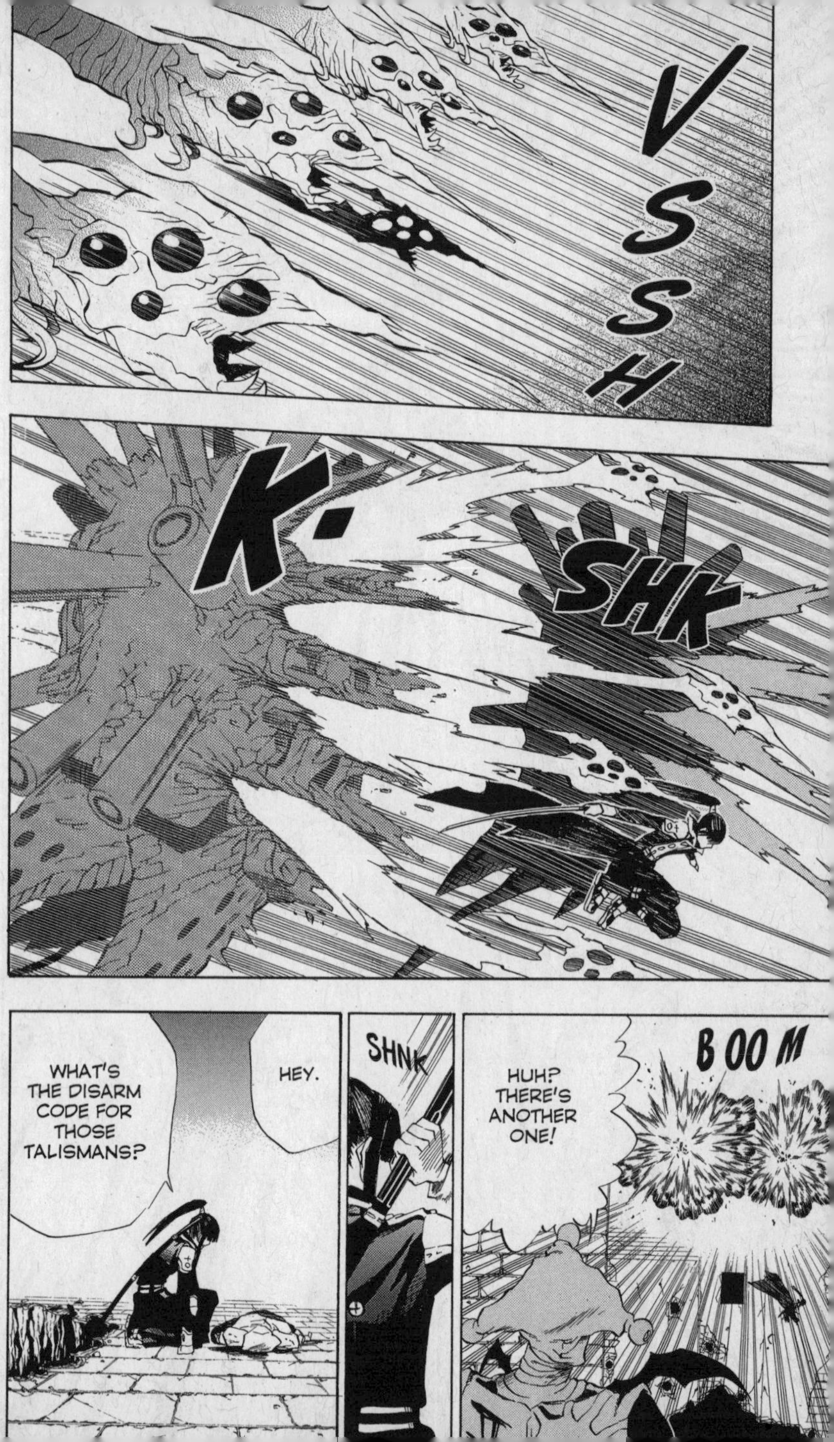
VSSH
K-
SHK
BOOM
HUH? THERE'S ANOTHER ONE!
SHNK
HEY.
WHAT'S THE DISARM CODE FOR THOSE TALISMANS?

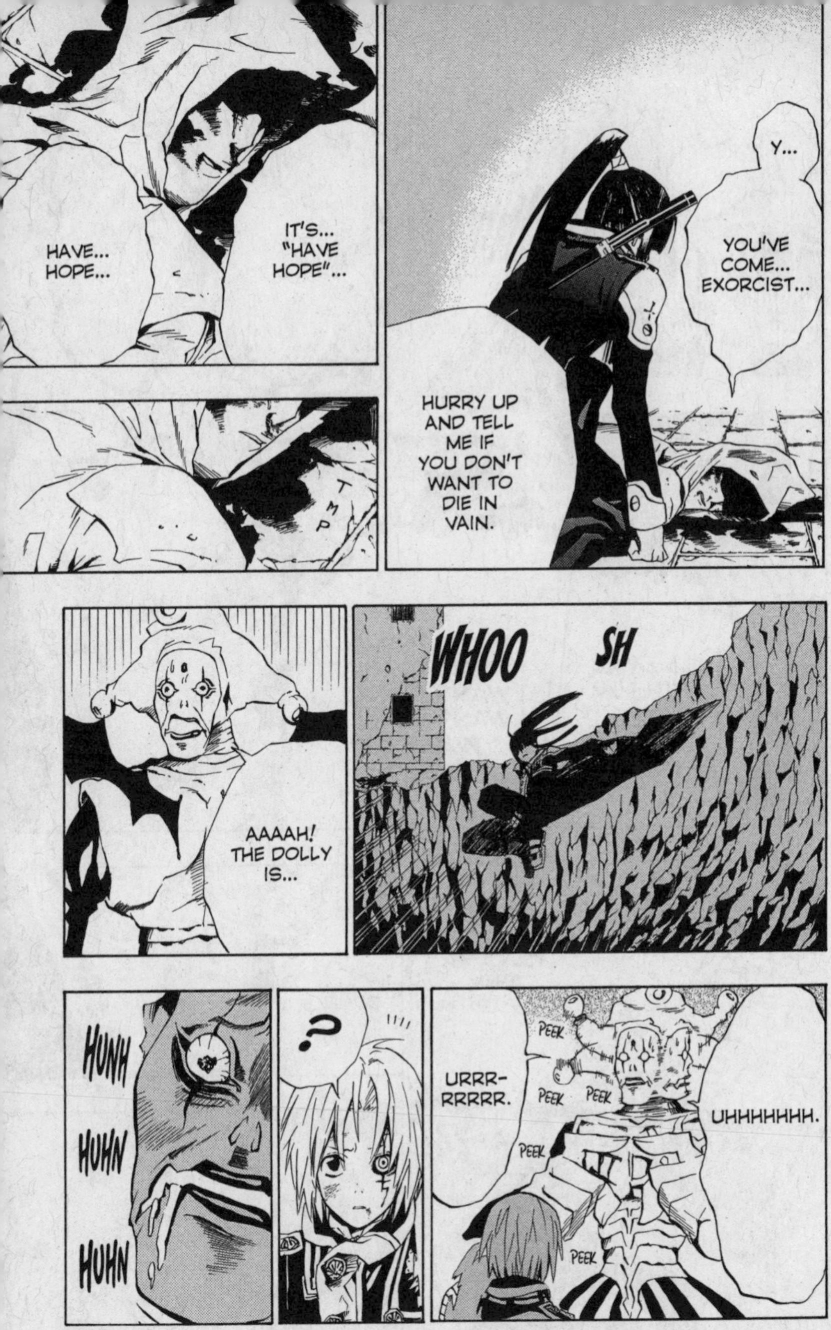
Y...
YOU'VE COME... EXORCIST...
HURRY UP AND TELL ME IF YOU DON'T WANT TO DIE IN VAIN.
IT'S... "HAVE HOPE"...
HAVE... HOPE...
TMP
WHOOSH
AAAAH! THE DOLLY IS...
UHHHHHHH.
PEEK
PEEK
PEEK
URRR-RRRRR.
PEEK
PEEK
?
HUNH
HUHN
HUHN

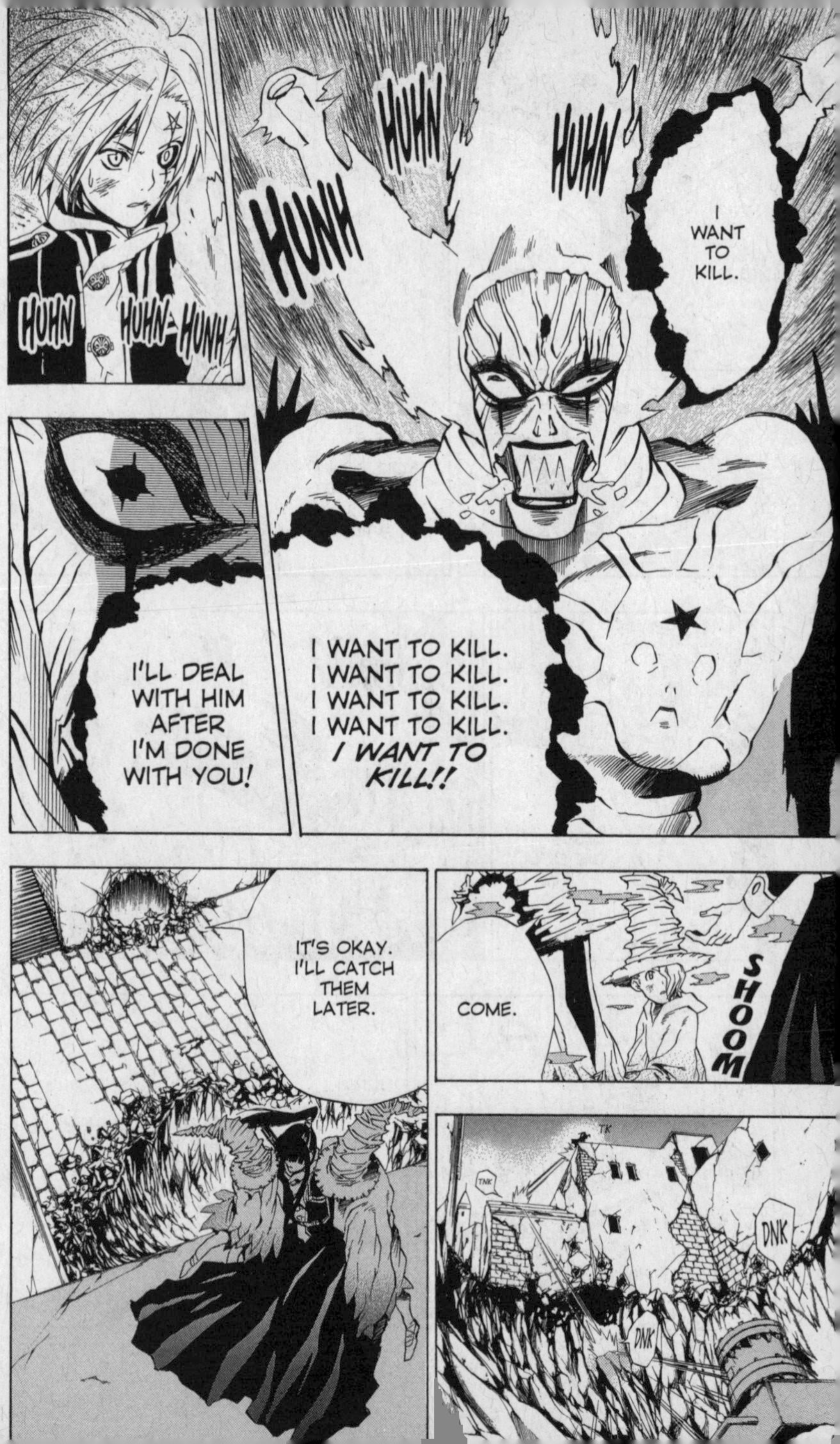
HUHN
HUHN
HUNH
I WANT TO KILL.
I WANT TO KILL.
I WANT TO KILL.
I WANT TO KILL.
I WANT TO KILL.
I WANT TO KILL!!
HUHN
HUHN-HUNH
I'LL DEAL WITH HIM AFTER I'M DONE WITH YOU!
SHOOM
COME.
TK
DNK
TNK
DNK
IT'S OKAY. I'LL CATCH THEM LATER.

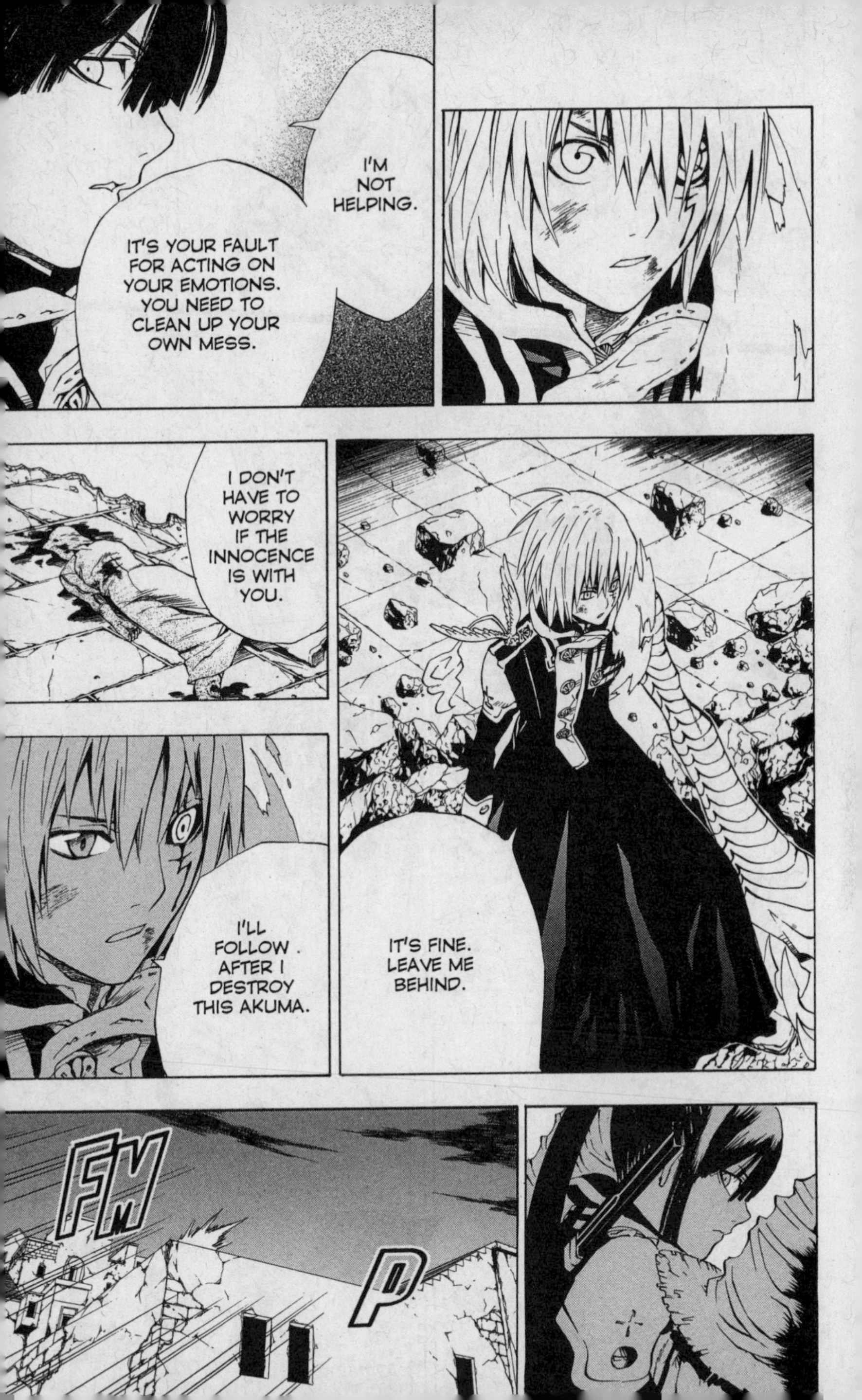
I'M NOT HELPING.
IT'S YOUR FAULT FOR ACTING ON YOUR EMOTIONS. YOU NEED TO CLEAN UP YOUR OWN MESS.
IT'S FINE. LEAVE ME BEHIND.
I DON'T HAVE TO WORRY IF THE INNOCENCE IS WITH YOU.
I'LL FOLLOW AFTER I DESTROY THIS AKUMA.

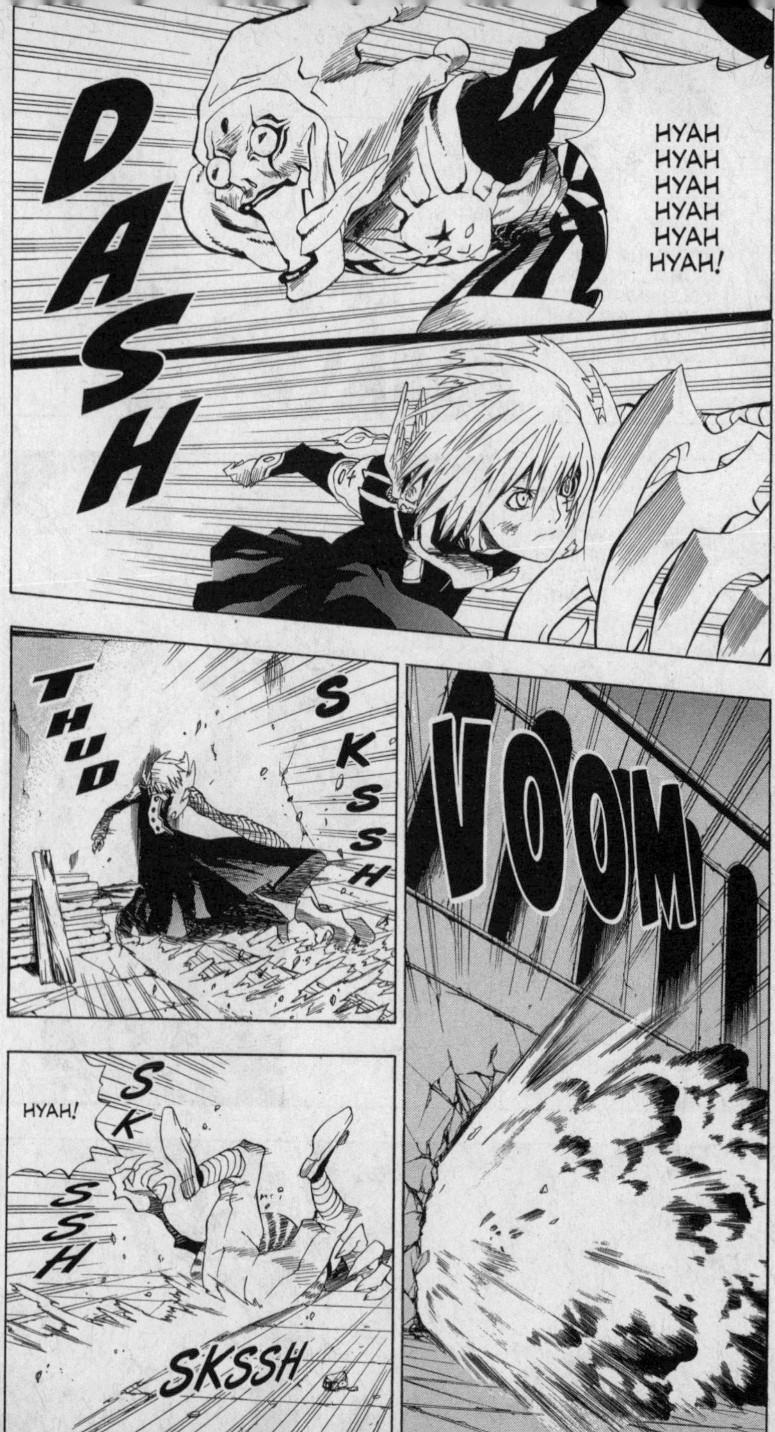
HYAH HYAH HYAH HYAH HYAH HYAH!
DASH
VOOM
SKSSH
THUD
HYAH!
SKSSH
SKSSH

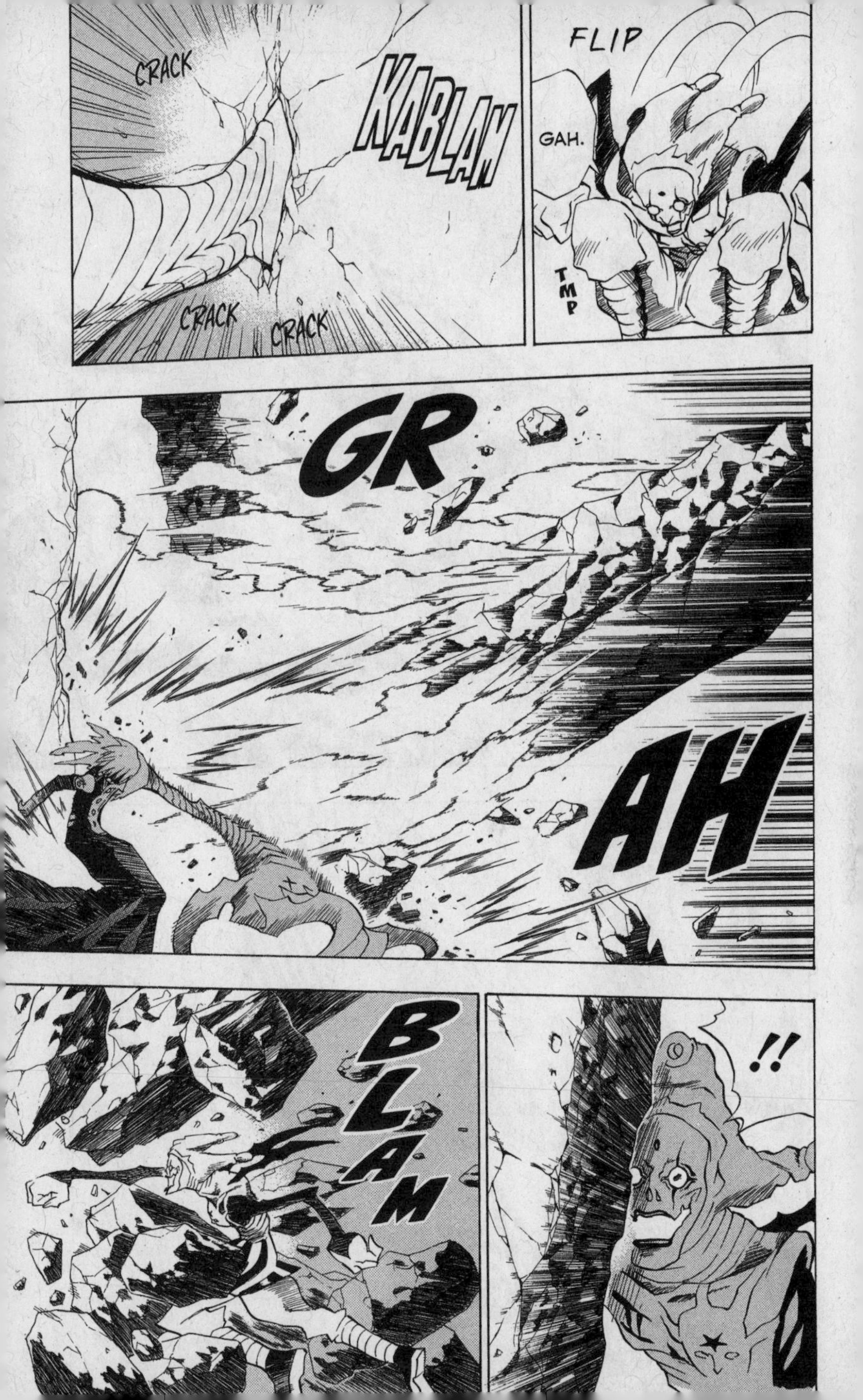
FLIP
GAH.
TMP
KABLAM
CRACK
CRACK
CRACK
GR
AH
!!
BLAM

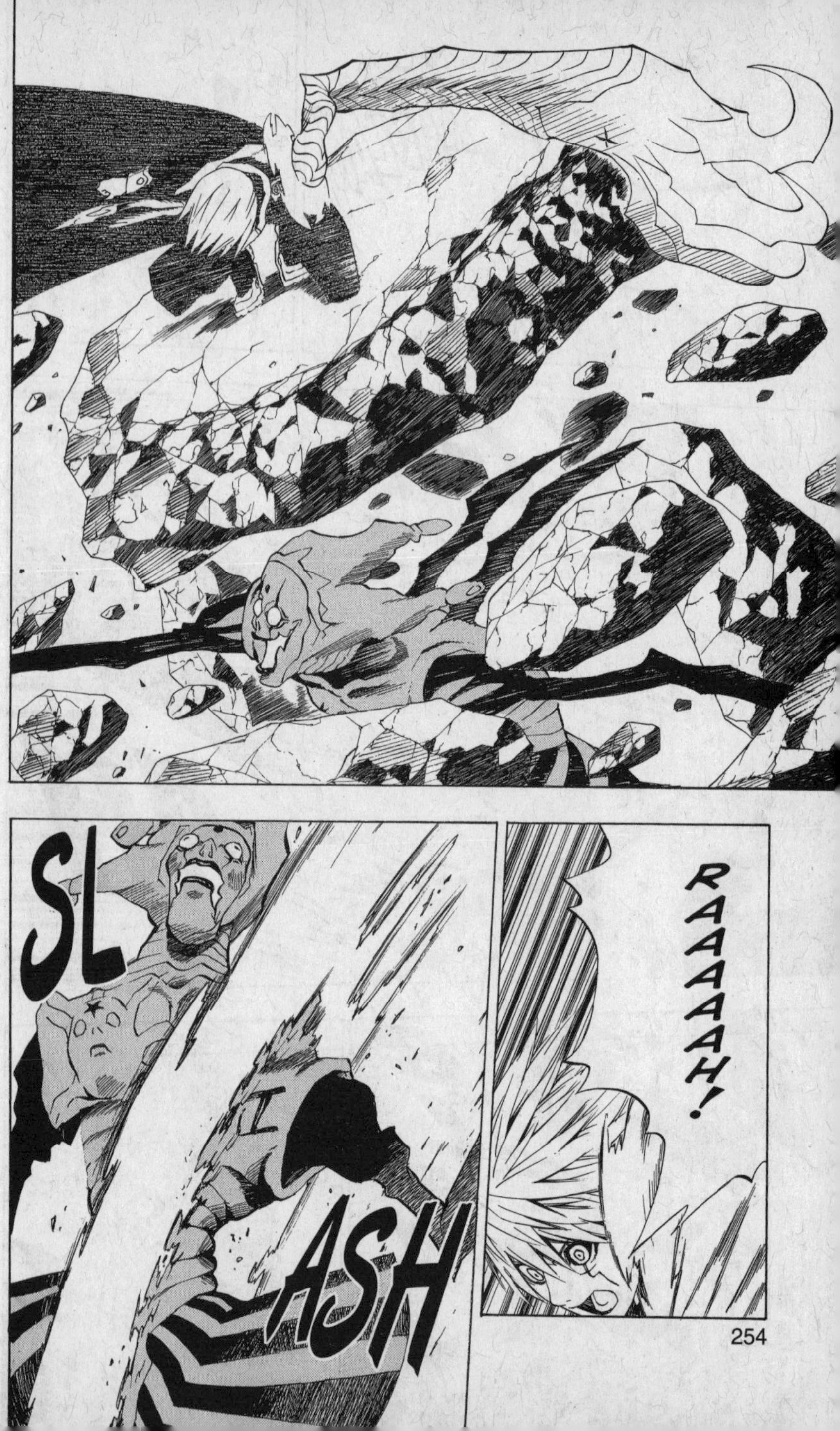
RAAAAAH!
SLASH

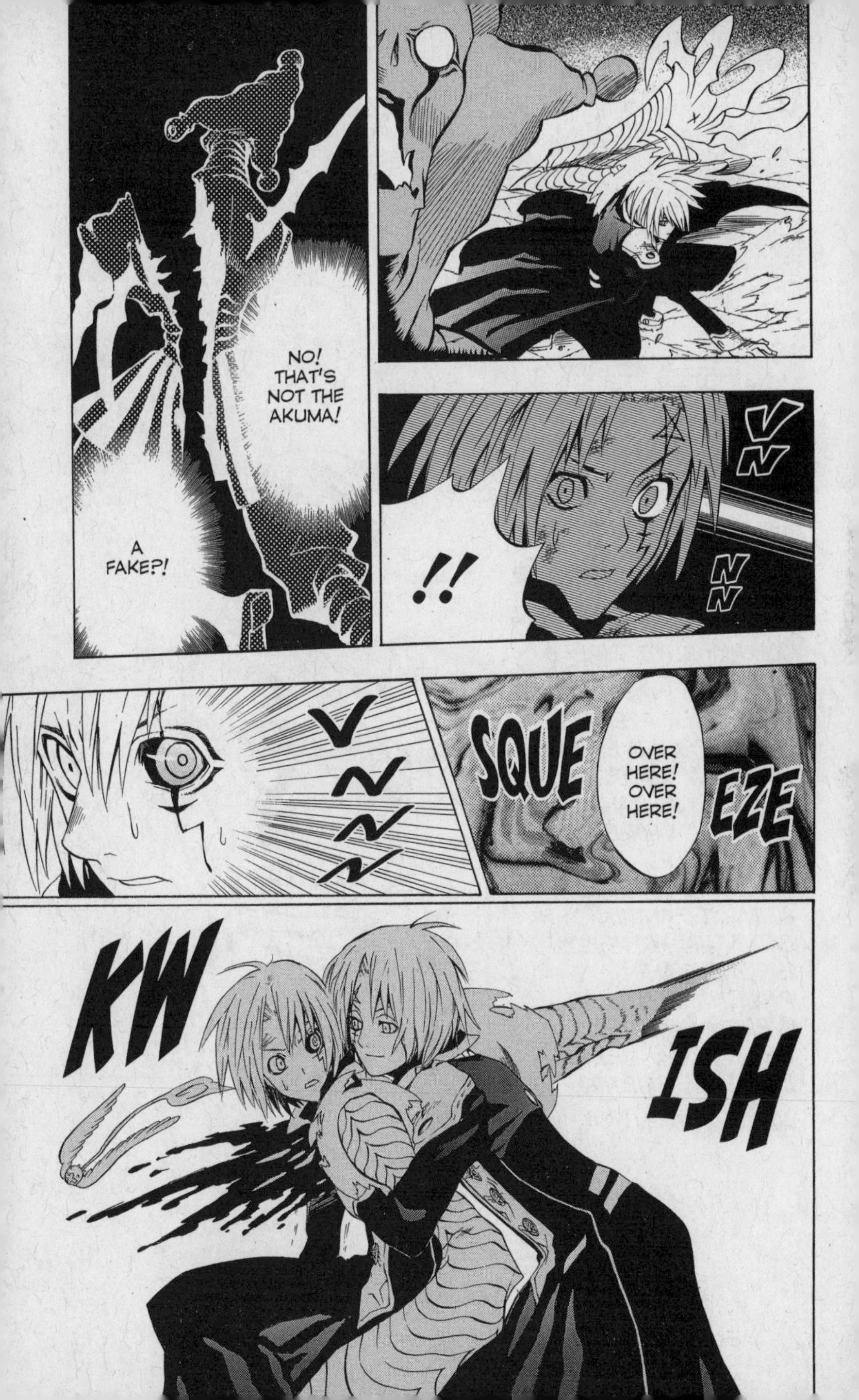
VNNN
!!
NO! THAT'S NOT THE AKUMA!
A FAKE?!
SQUEEZE
OVER HERE! OVER HERE!
VNNN
KWISH

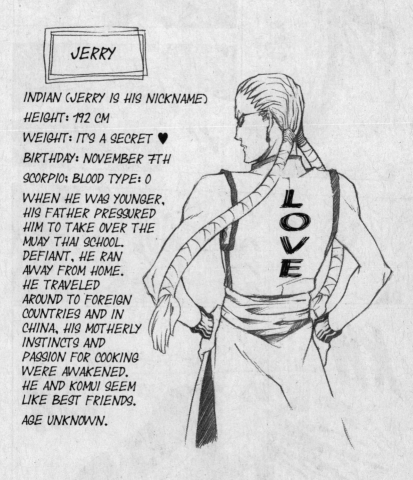

JERRY

INDIAN (JERRY IS HIS NICKNAME)

HEIGHT: 192 CM

WEIGHT: IT'S A SECRET ♥

BIRTHDAY: NOVEMBER 7TH

SCORPIO; BLOOD TYPE: O

WHEN HE WAS YOUNGER, HIS FATHER PRESSURED HIM TO TAKE OVER THE MUAY THAI SCHOOL. DEFIANT, HE RAN AWAY FROM HOME. HE TRAVELED AROUND TO FOREIGN COUNTRIES AND IN CHINA, HIS MOTHERLY INSTINCTS AND PASSION FOR COOKING WERE AWAKENED. HE AND KOMUI SEEM LIKE BEST FRIENDS.

AGE UNKNOWN.

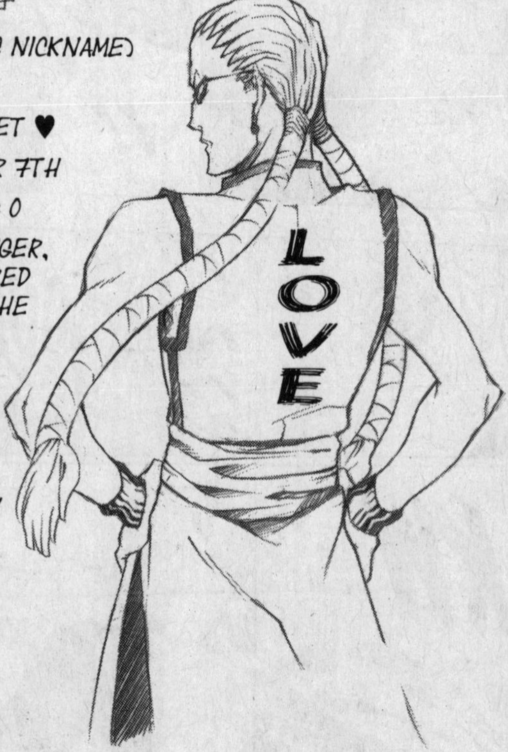
LOVE

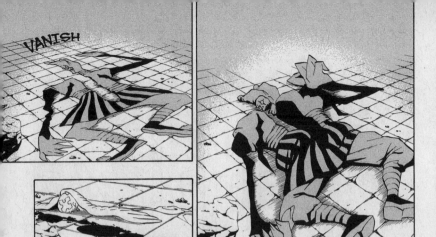

VANISH

ME...?

THE 11TH NIGHT: OLD MAN OF THE LAND AND ARIA OF THE NIGHT SKY (PART 3)

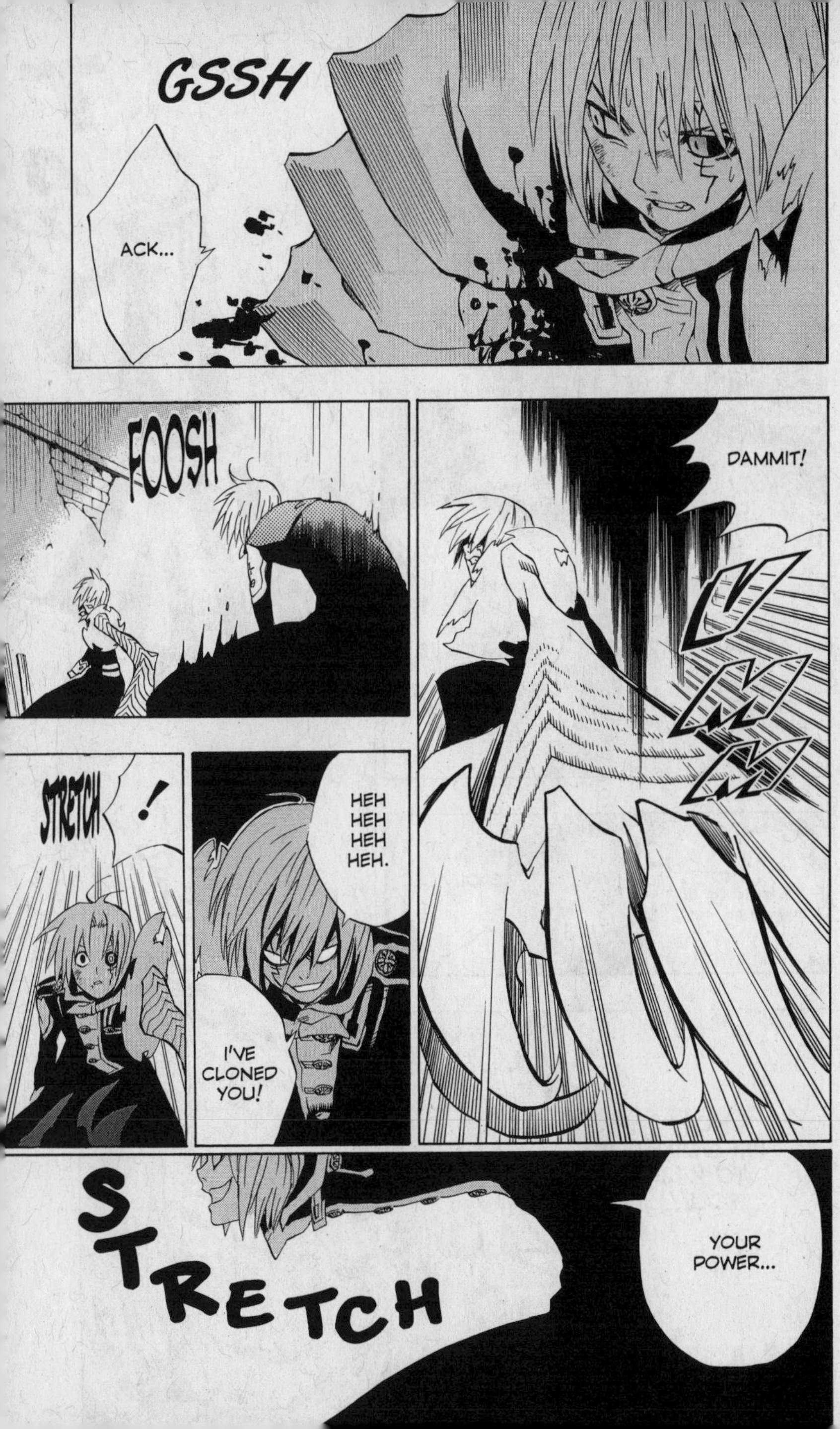
GSSH
ACK...
DAMMIT!
VMMM
FOOSH
HEH HEH HEH HEH.
I'VE CLONED YOU!
STRETCH
!
YOUR POWER...
STRETCH

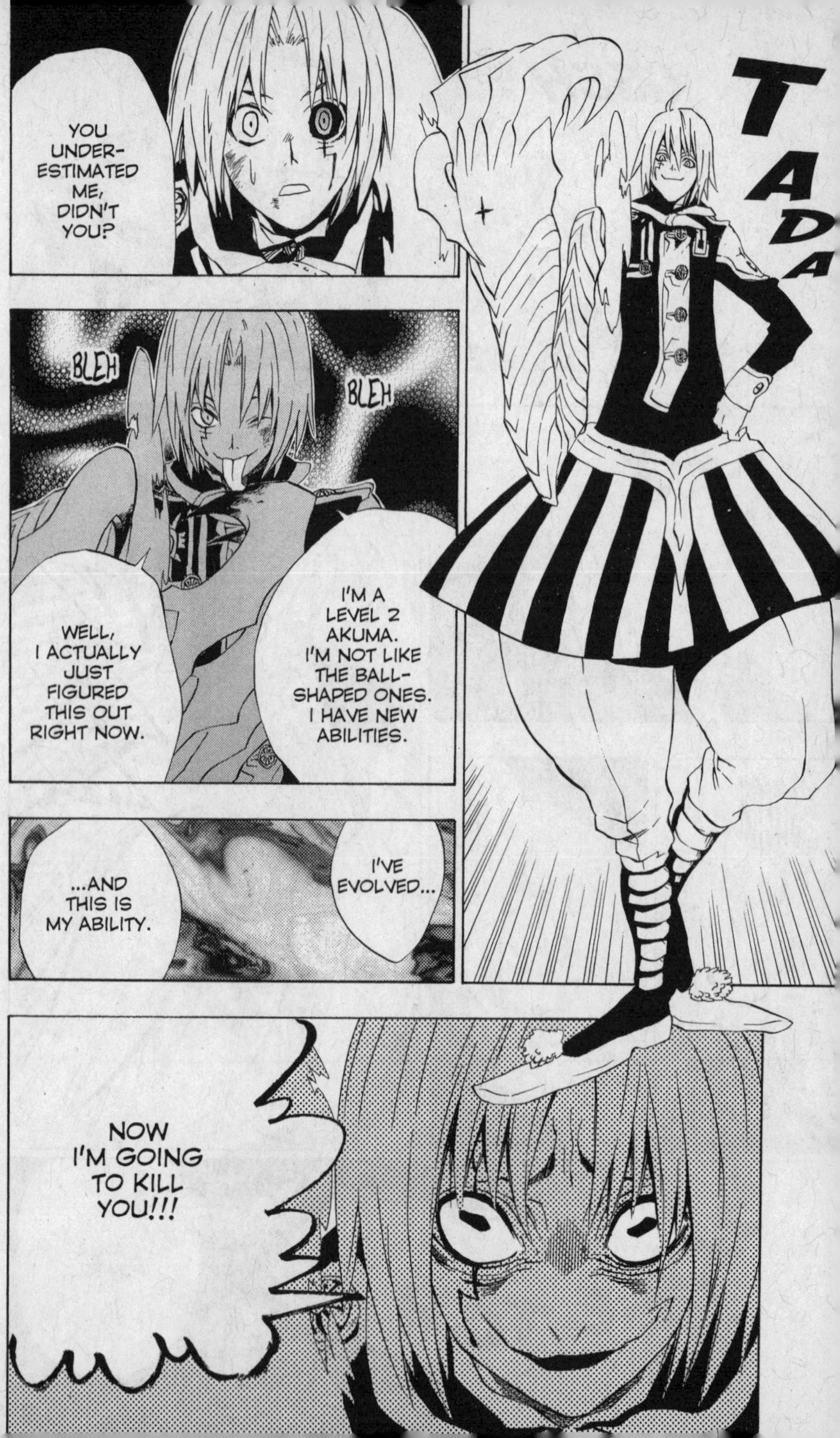
TADA
YOU UNDER-ESTIMATED ME, DIDN'T YOU?
BLEH
BLEH
I'M A LEVEL 2 AKUMA. I'M NOT LIKE THE BALL-SHAPED ONES. I HAVE NEW ABILITIES.
WELL, I ACTUALLY JUST FIGURED THIS OUT RIGHT NOW.
I'VE EVOLVED...
...AND THIS IS MY ABILITY.
NOW I'M GOING TO KILL YOU!!!

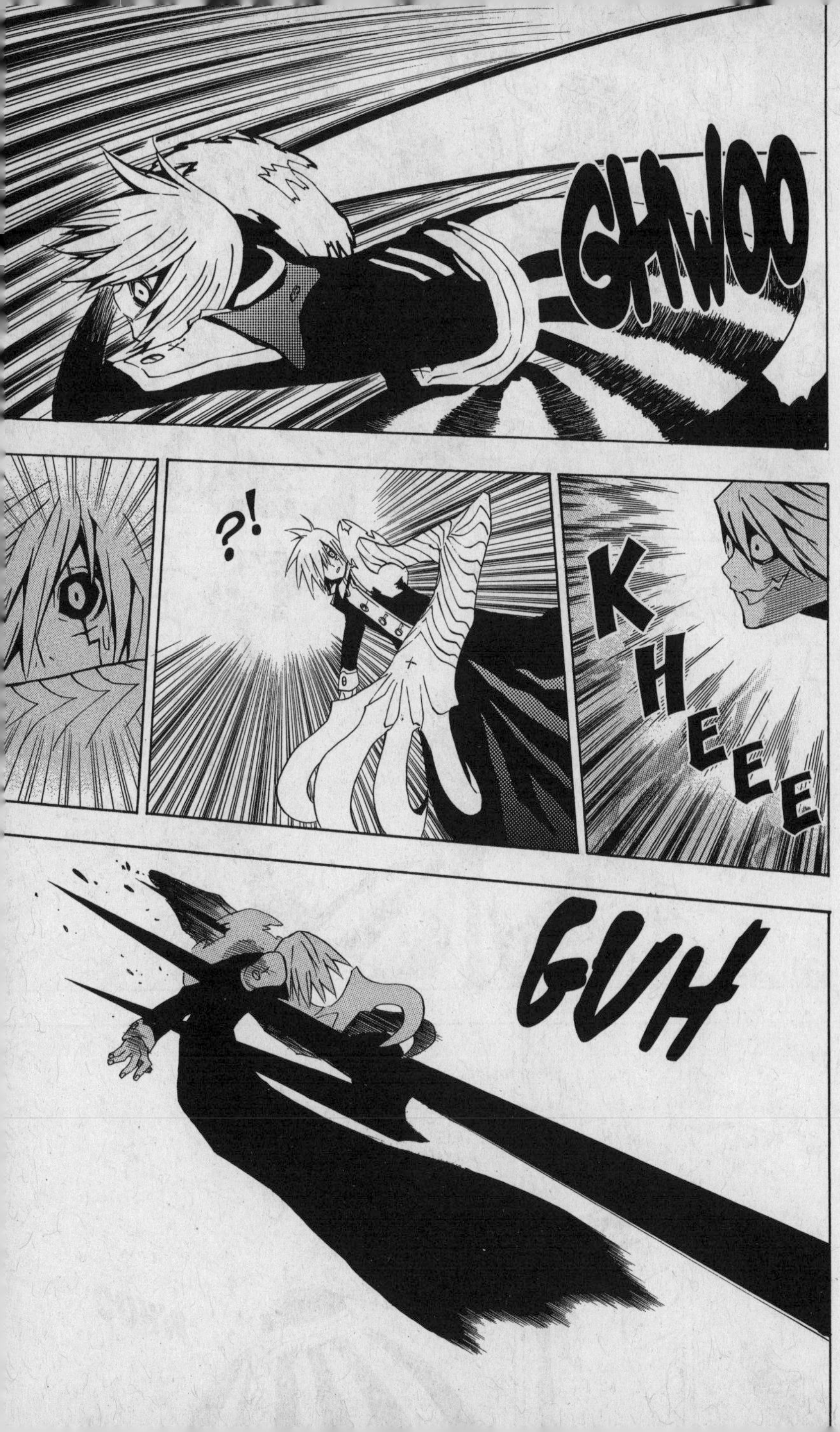
GHWOO
KHEEEE
?!
GUH

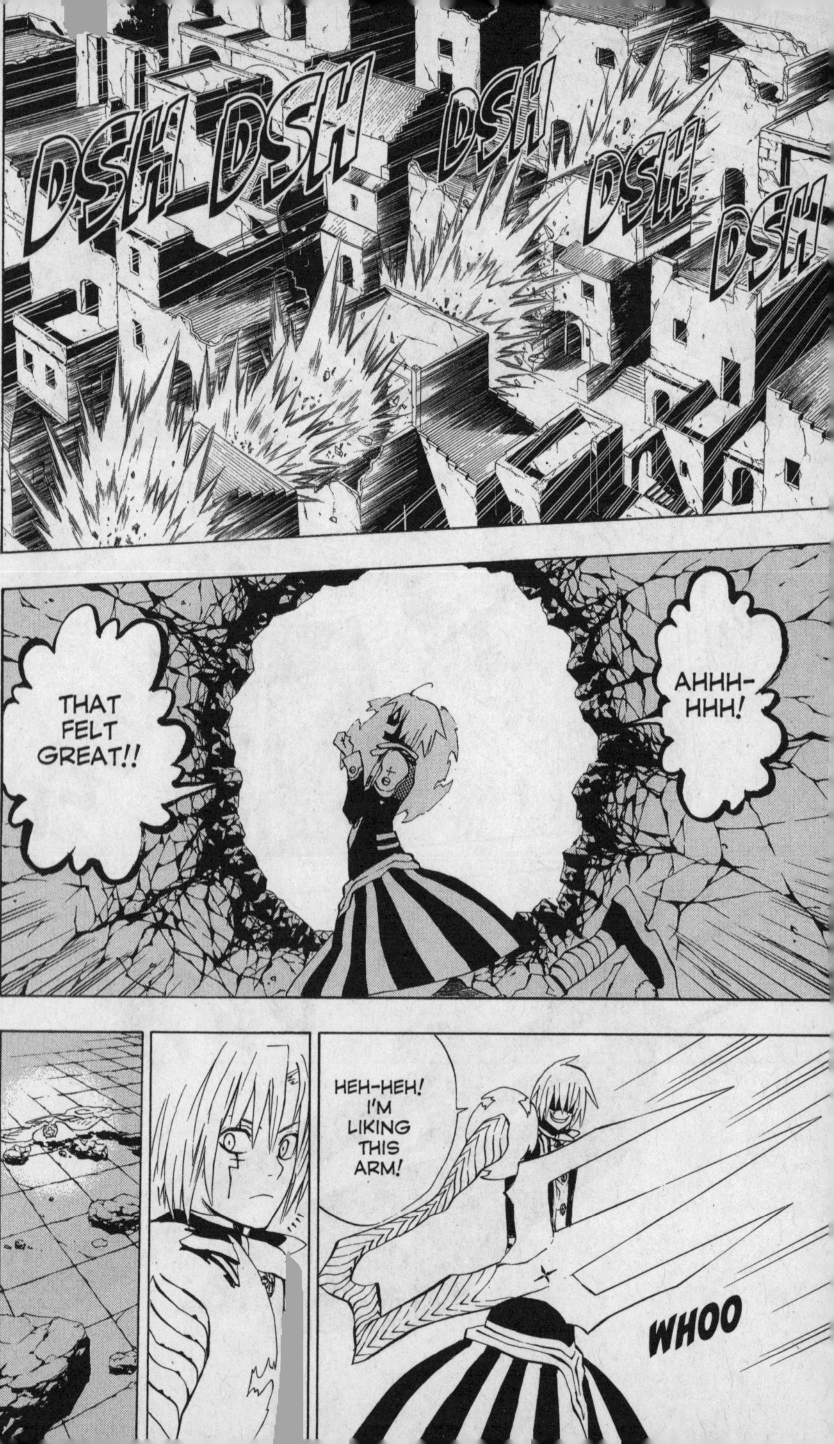
DSH
DSH
DSH
DSH
DSH
AHHH-HHH!
THAT FELT GREAT!!
HEH-HEH! I'M LIKING THIS ARM!
WHOO

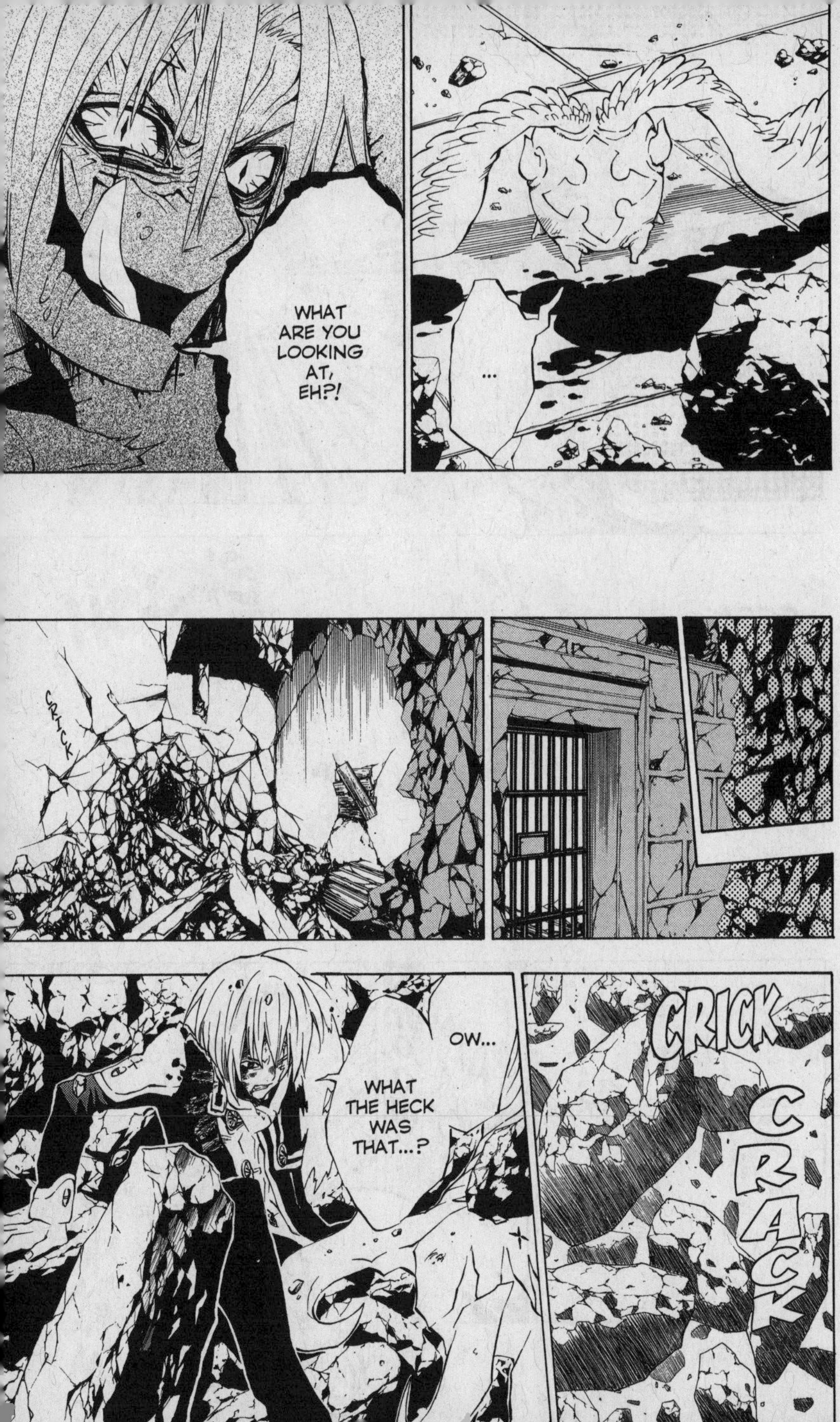
...
WHAT ARE YOU LOOKING AT, EH?!
CRICK
CRICK CRACK
OW...
WHAT THE HECK WAS THAT...?

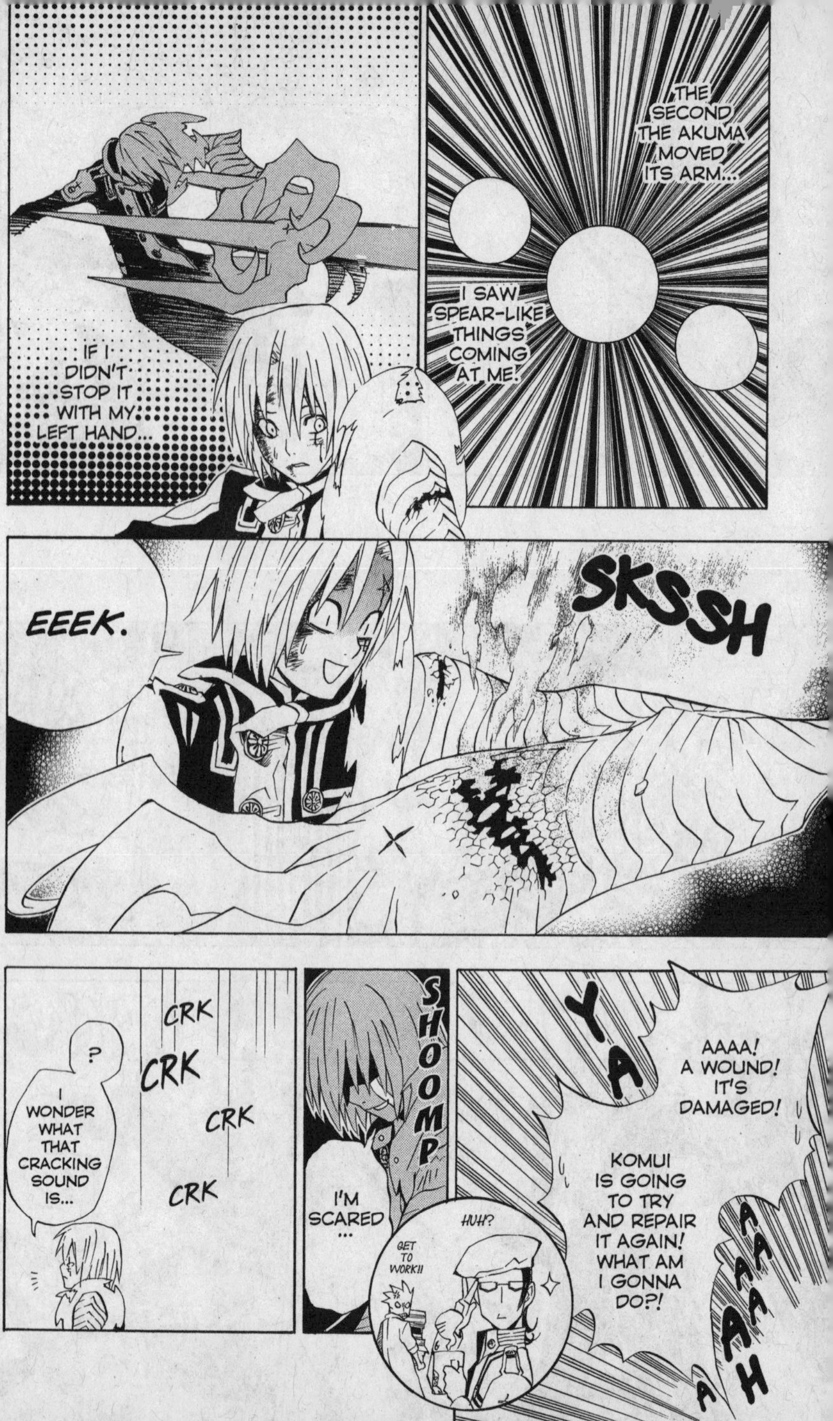
THE SECOND THE AKUMA MOVED ITS ARM...
I SAW SPEAR-LIKE THINGS COMING AT ME.
IF I DIDN'T STOP IT WITH MY LEFT HAND...
EEEK.
SKSSH
YA
AAAA! A WOUND! IT'S DAMAGED!
KOMUI IS GOING TO TRY AND REPAIR IT AGAIN! WHAT AM I GONNA DO?!
AAAAAAH
HUH?
GET TO WORK!!
SHOOMP
I'M SCARED...
CRK
CRK
CRK
CRK
?
I WONDER WHAT THAT CRACKING SOUND IS...

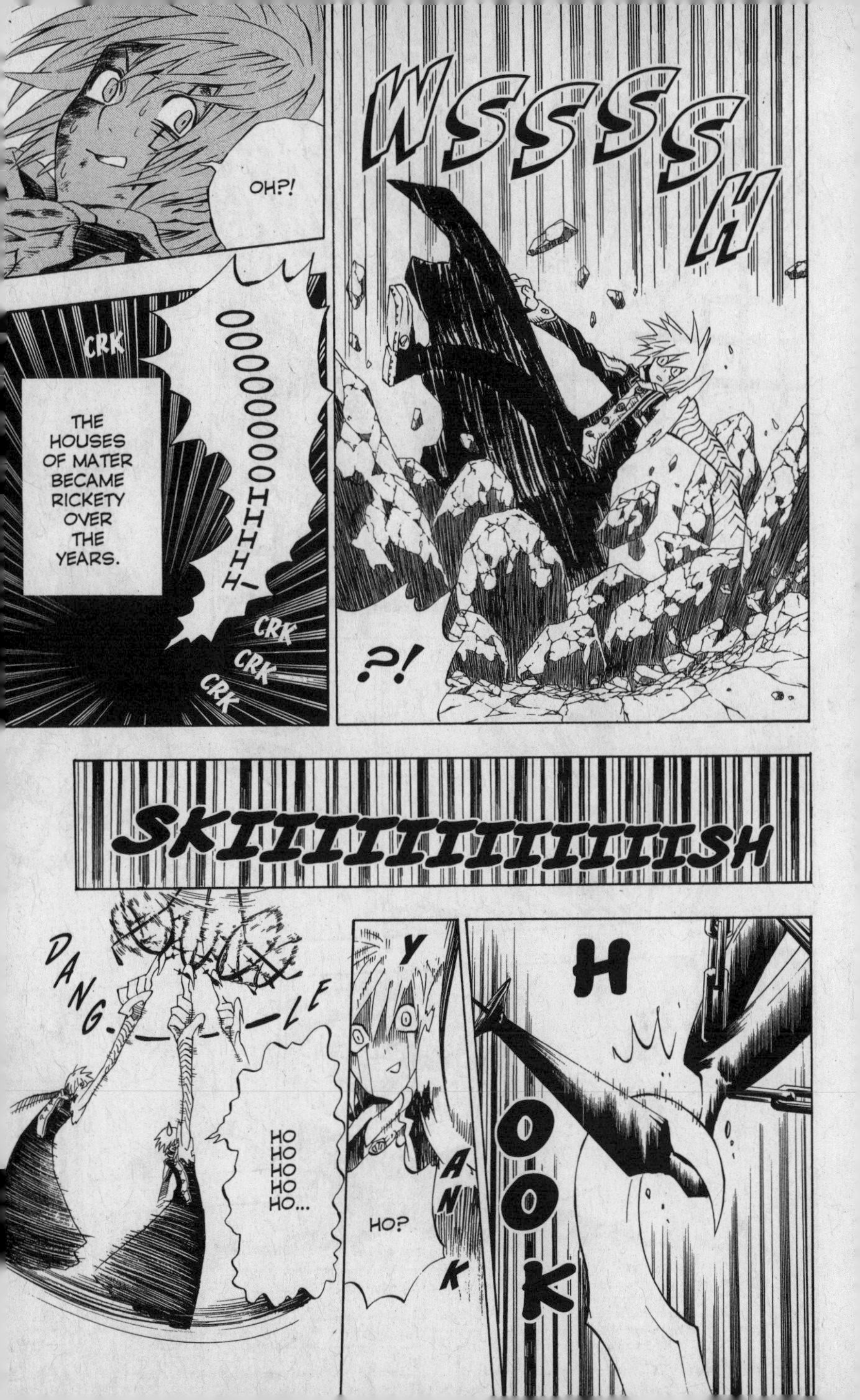
WSSSSH
?!
OH?!
OOOOOOOOOHHHHH-
CRK
THE HOUSES OF MATER BECAME RICKETY OVER THE YEARS.
CRK
CRK
CRK
SKIIIIIIIIIIIIISH
HOOK
YANK
HO?
DANG---LE
HO HO HO HO HO...

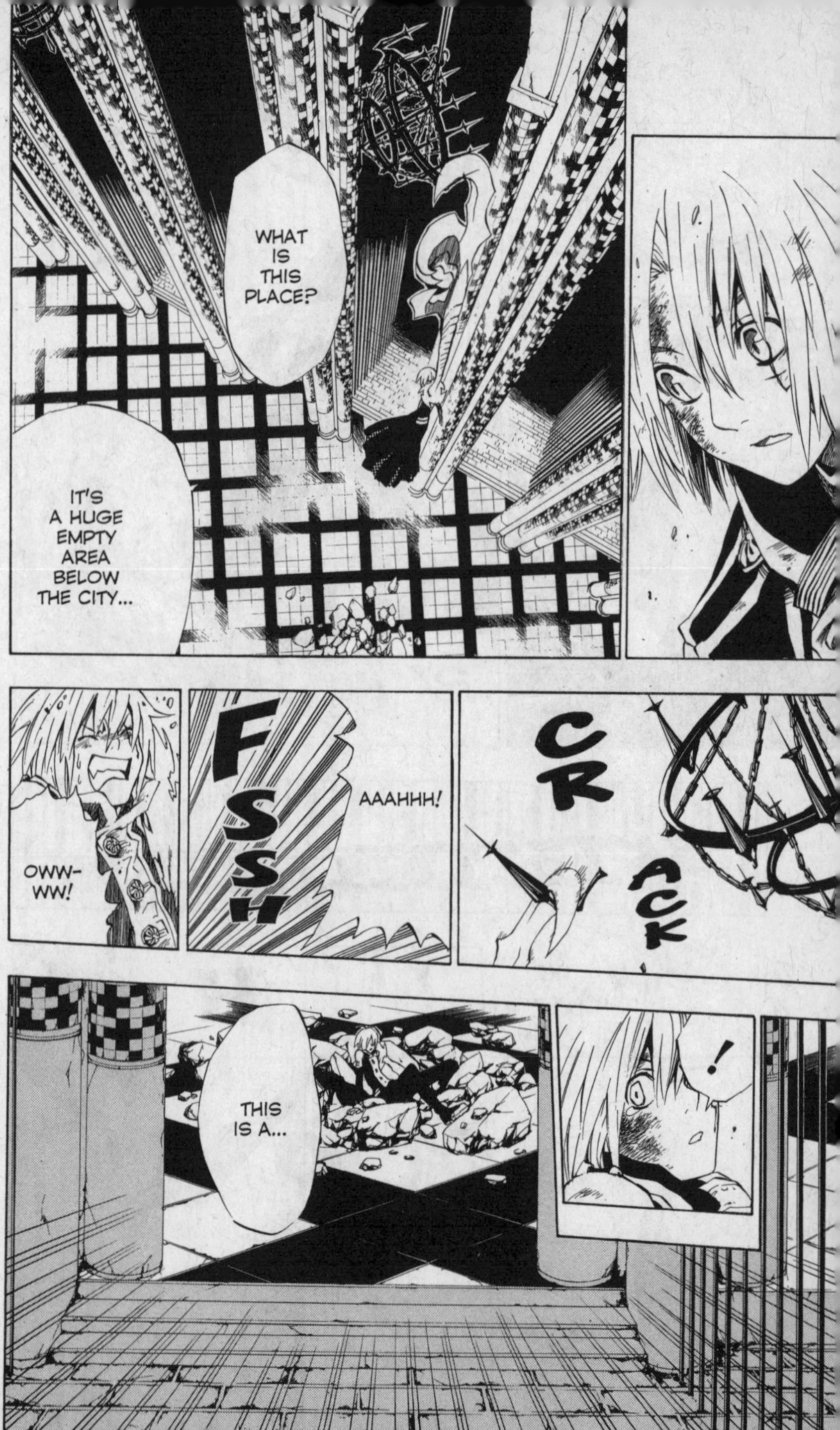
WHAT IS THIS PLACE?
IT'S A HUGE EMPTY AREA BELOW THE CITY...
CRACK
FSSH
AAAHHH!
OWW-WW!
!
THIS IS A...

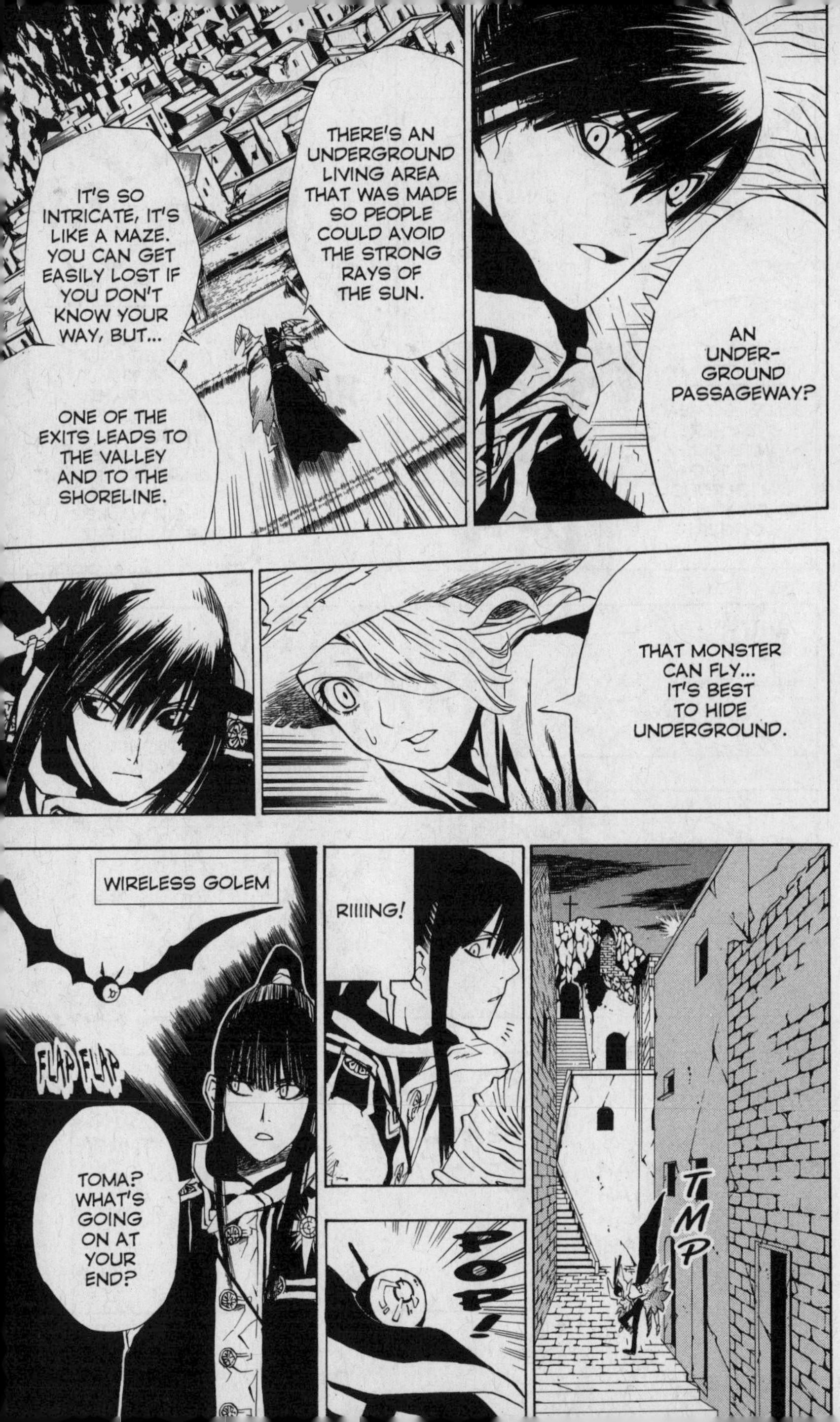
AN UNDER-GROUND PASSAGEWAY?
THERE'S AN UNDERGROUND LIVING AREA THAT WAS MADE SO PEOPLE COULD AVOID THE STRONG RAYS OF THE SUN.
IT'S SO INTRICATE, IT'S LIKE A MAZE. YOU CAN GET EASILY LOST IF YOU DON'T KNOW YOUR WAY, BUT...
ONE OF THE EXITS LEADS TO THE VALLEY AND TO THE SHORELINE.
THAT MONSTER CAN FLY... IT'S BEST TO HIDE UNDERGROUND.
TMP
RIIIING!
POP!
WIRELESS GOLEM
FLAP FLAP
TOMA? WHAT'S GOING ON AT YOUR END?

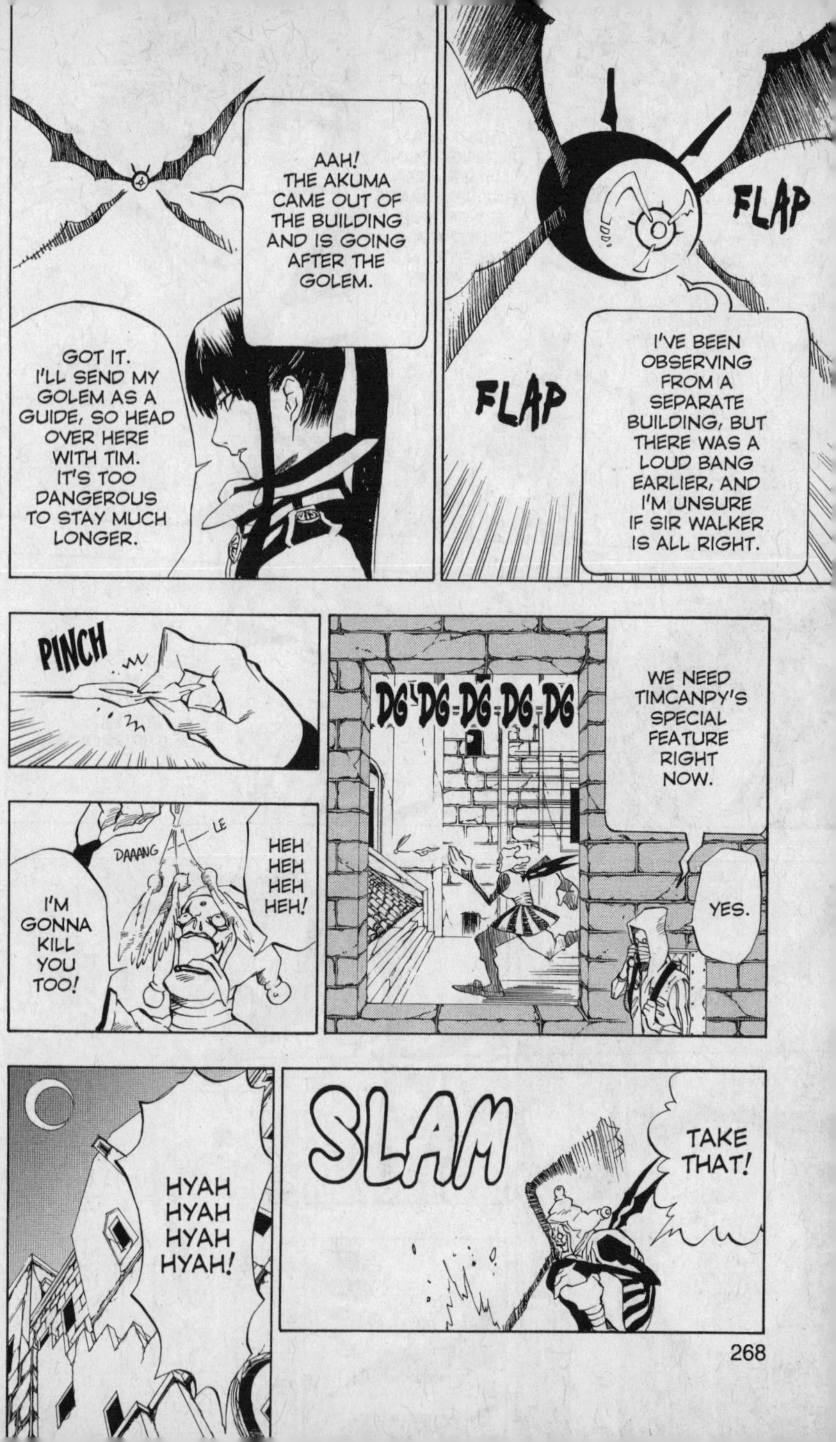
FLAP
I'VE BEEN OBSERVING FROM A SEPARATE BUILDING, BUT THERE WAS A LOUD BANG EARLIER, AND I'M UNSURE IF SIR WALKER IS ALL RIGHT.
FLAP
AAH! THE AKUMA CAME OUT OF THE BUILDING AND IS GOING AFTER THE GOLEM.
GOT IT. I'LL SEND MY GOLEM AS A GUIDE, SO HEAD OVER HERE WITH TIM. IT'S TOO DANGEROUS TO STAY MUCH LONGER.
WE NEED TIMCANPY'S SPECIAL FEATURE RIGHT NOW.
DG DG DG DG DG
YES.
PINCH
HEH HEH HEH HEH!
LE
DAAANG
I'M GONNA KILL YOU TOO!
TAKE THAT!
SLAM
HYAH HYAH HYAH HYAH!

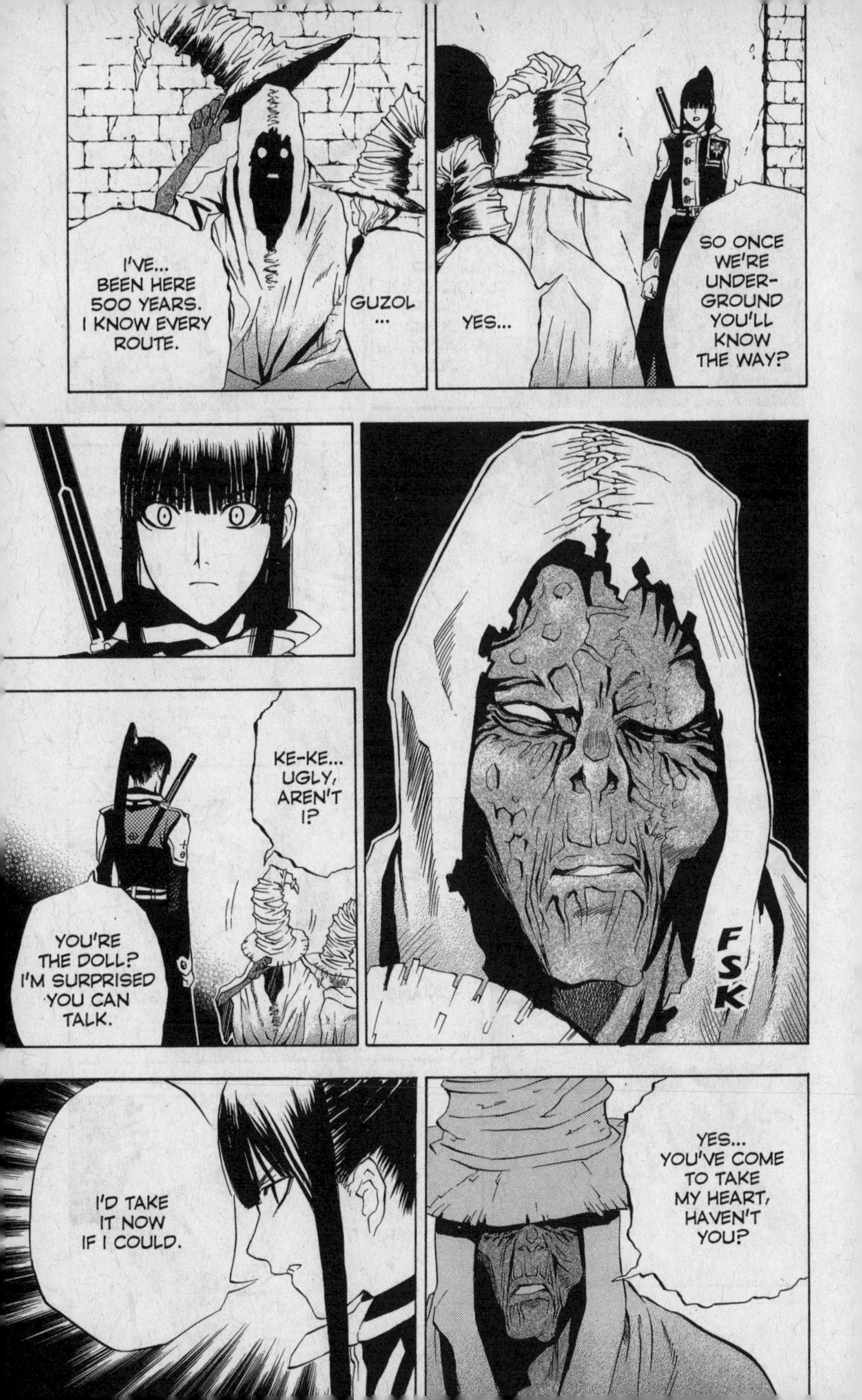
SO ONCE WE'RE UNDER-GROUND YOU'LL KNOW THE WAY?
YES...
GUZOL...
I'VE... BEEN HERE 500 YEARS. I KNOW EVERY ROUTE.
FSK
KE-KE... UGLY, AREN'T I?
YOU'RE THE DOLL? I'M SURPRISED YOU CAN TALK.
YES... YOU'VE COME TO TAKE MY HEART, HAVEN'T YOU?
I'D TAKE IT NOW IF I COULD.

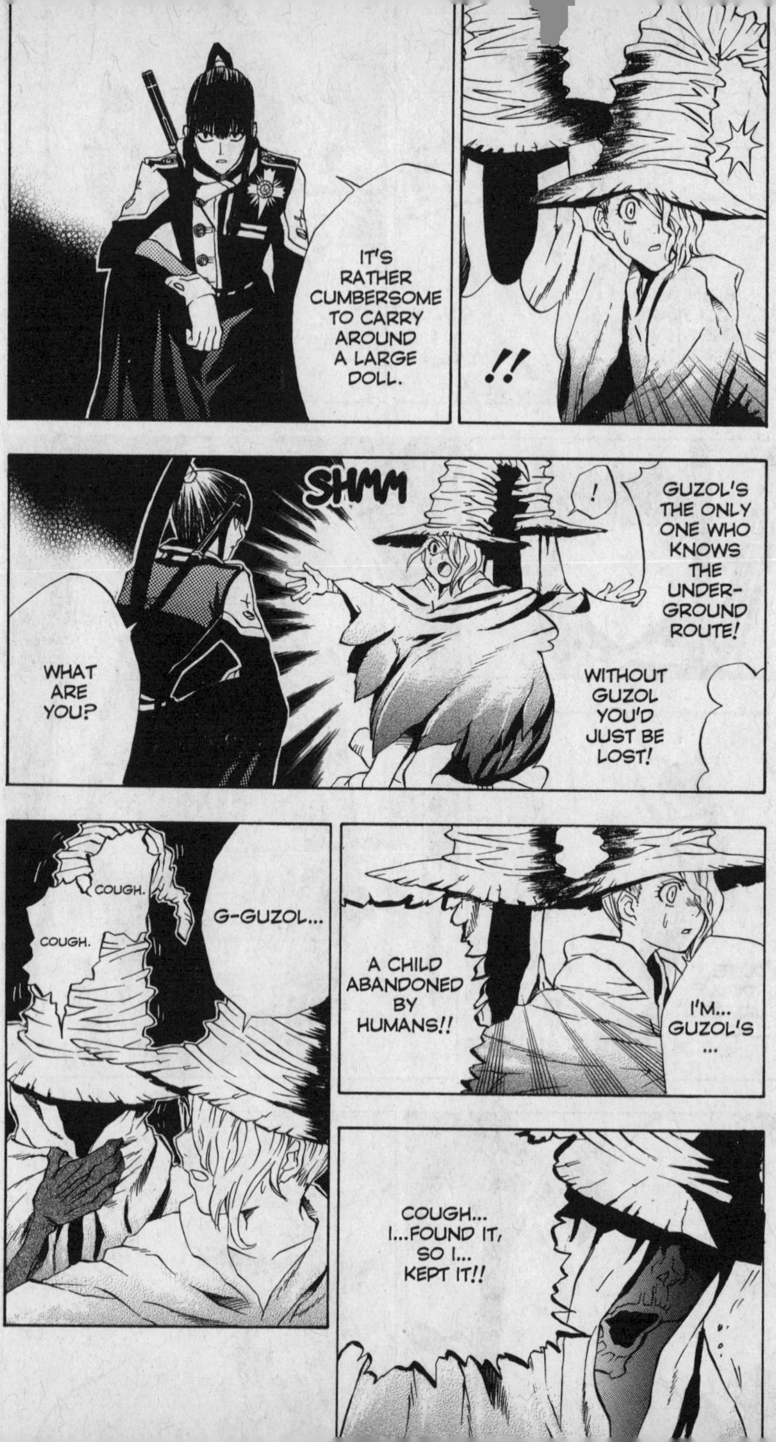
!!
IT'S RATHER CUMBERSOME TO CARRY AROUND A LARGE DOLL.
GUZOL'S THE ONLY ONE WHO KNOWS THE UNDER-GROUND ROUTE!
!
SHMM
WITHOUT GUZOL YOU'D JUST BE LOST!
WHAT ARE YOU?
I'M... GUZOL'S ...
A CHILD ABANDONED BY HUMANS!!
COUGH... I...FOUND IT, SO I... KEPT IT!!
G-GUZOL...
COUGH.
COUGH.

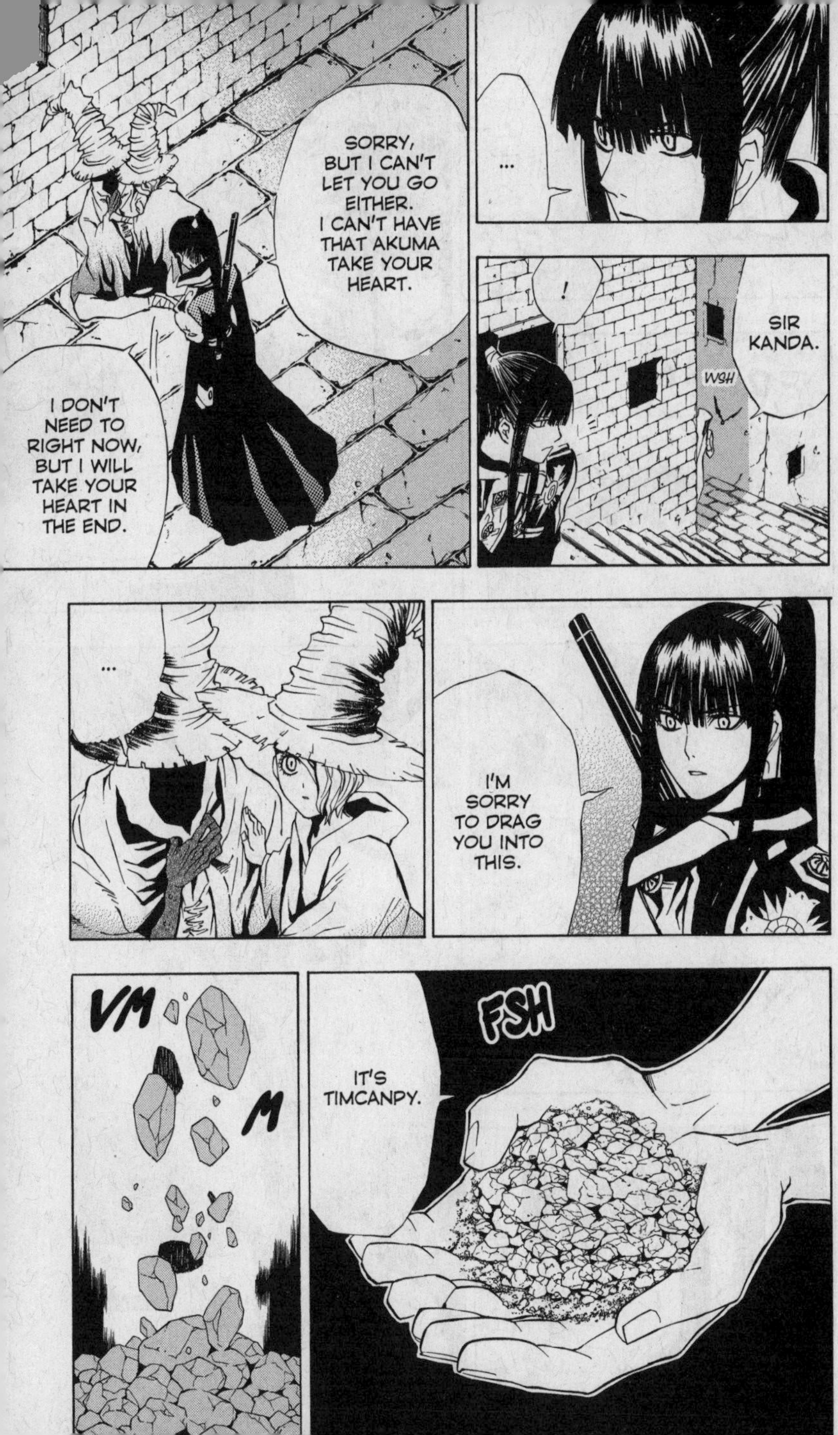
...
SIR KANDA.
WSH
!
SORRY, BUT I CAN'T LET YOU GO EITHER. I CAN'T HAVE THAT AKUMA TAKE YOUR HEART.
I DON'T NEED TO RIGHT NOW, BUT I WILL TAKE YOUR HEART IN THE END.
I'M SORRY TO DRAG YOU INTO THIS.
...
FSH
IT'S TIMCANPY.
VM
M

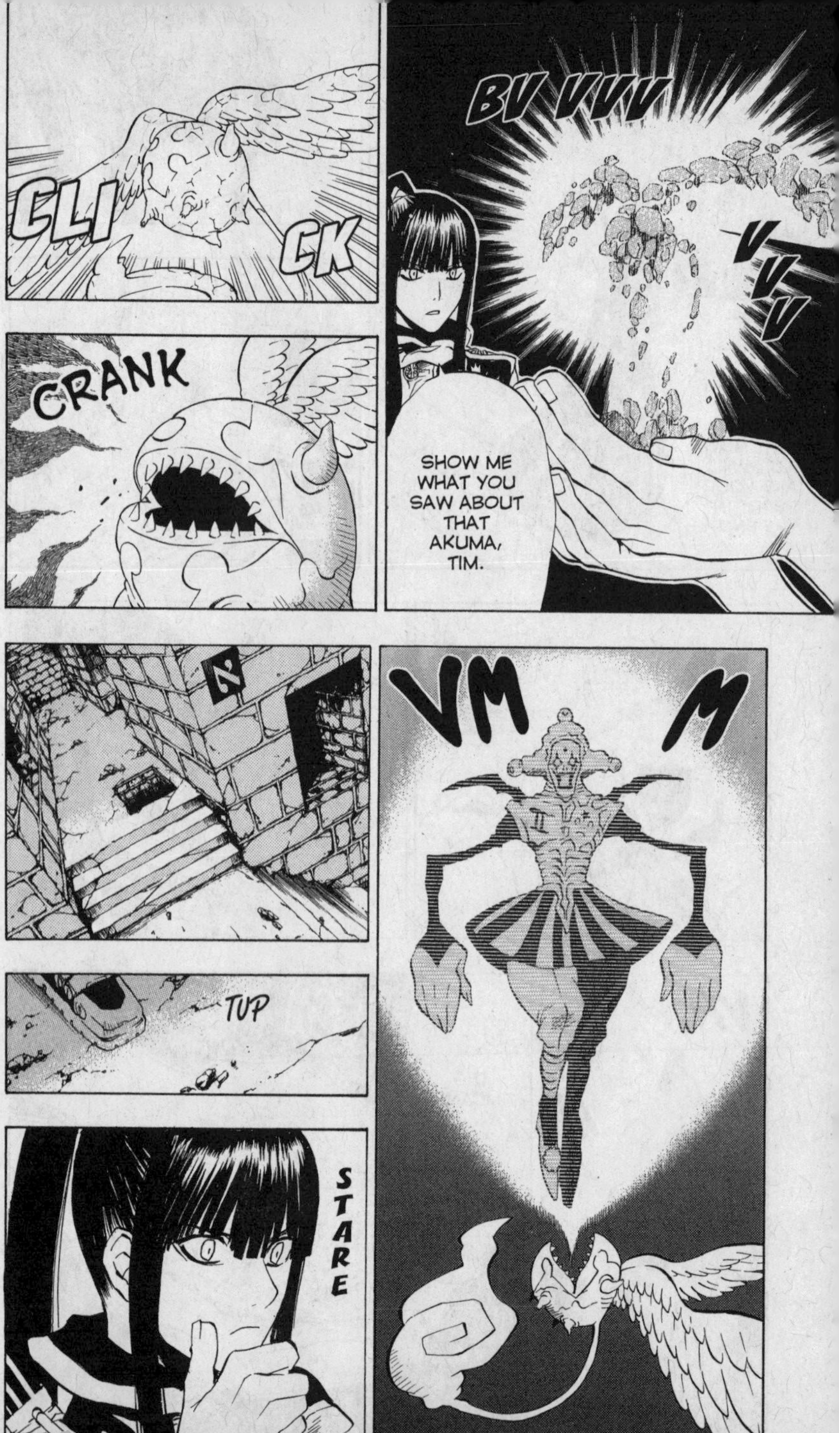
BV VVV
VVVV
SHOW ME WHAT YOU SAW ABOUT THAT AKUMA, TIM.
CLI CK
CRANK
VM M
TUP
STARE

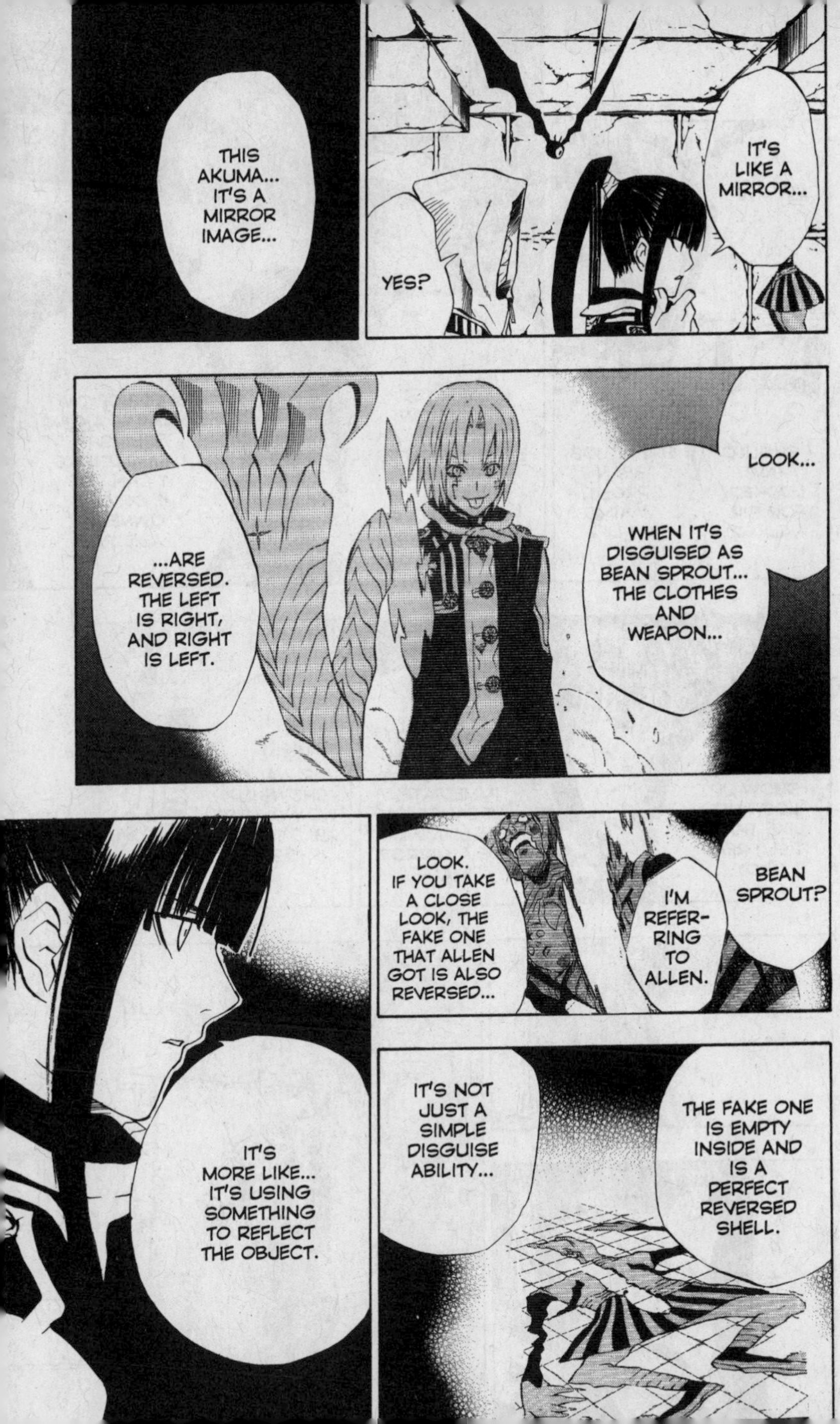
IT'S LIKE A MIRROR...
YES?
THIS AKUMA... IT'S A MIRROR IMAGE...
LOOK...
WHEN IT'S DISGUISED AS BEAN SPROUT... THE CLOTHES AND WEAPON...
...ARE REVERSED. THE LEFT IS RIGHT, AND RIGHT IS LEFT.
BEAN SPROUT?
I'M REFER-RING TO ALLEN.
LOOK. IF YOU TAKE A CLOSE LOOK, THE FAKE ONE THAT ALLEN GOT IS ALSO REVERSED...
THE FAKE ONE IS EMPTY INSIDE AND IS A PERFECT REVERSED SHELL.
IT'S NOT JUST A SIMPLE DISGUISE ABILITY...
IT'S MORE LIKE... IT'S USING SOMETHING TO REFLECT THE OBJECT.

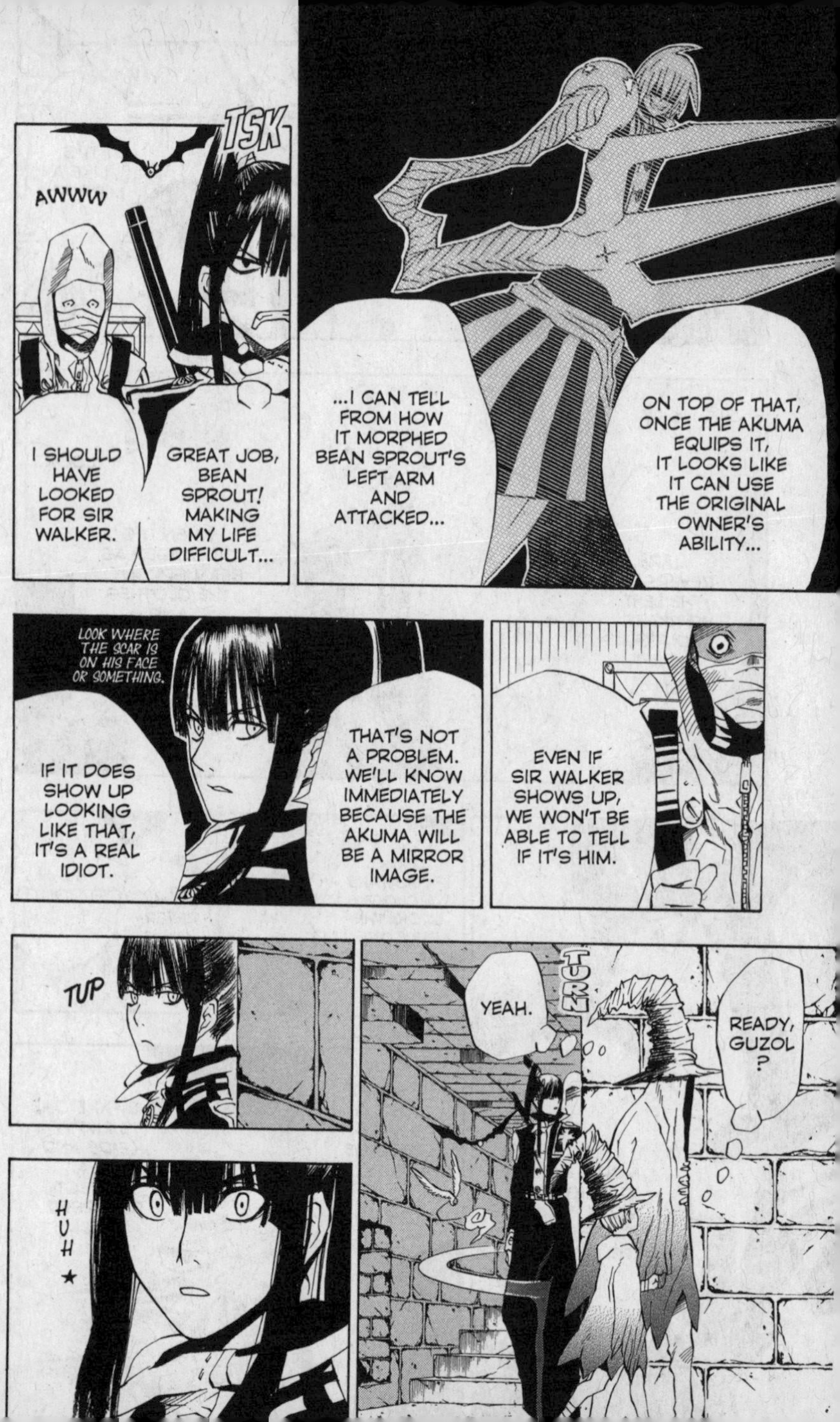
...I CAN TELL FROM HOW IT MORPHED BEAN SPROUT'S LEFT ARM AND ATTACKED...
ON TOP OF THAT, ONCE THE AKUMA EQUIPS IT, IT LOOKS LIKE IT CAN USE THE ORIGINAL OWNER'S ABILITY...
TSK
AWWW
GREAT JOB, BEAN SPROUT! MAKING MY LIFE DIFFICULT...
I SHOULD HAVE LOOKED FOR SIR WALKER.
EVEN IF SIR WALKER SHOWS UP, WE WON'T BE ABLE TO TELL IF IT'S HIM.
THAT'S NOT A PROBLEM. WE'LL KNOW IMMEDIATELY BECAUSE THE AKUMA WILL BE A MIRROR IMAGE.
IF IT DOES SHOW UP LOOKING LIKE THAT, IT'S A REAL IDIOT.
LOOK WHERE THE SCAR IS ON HIS FACE OR SOMETHING.
READY, GUZOL?
TURN
YEAH.
TUP
HUH★

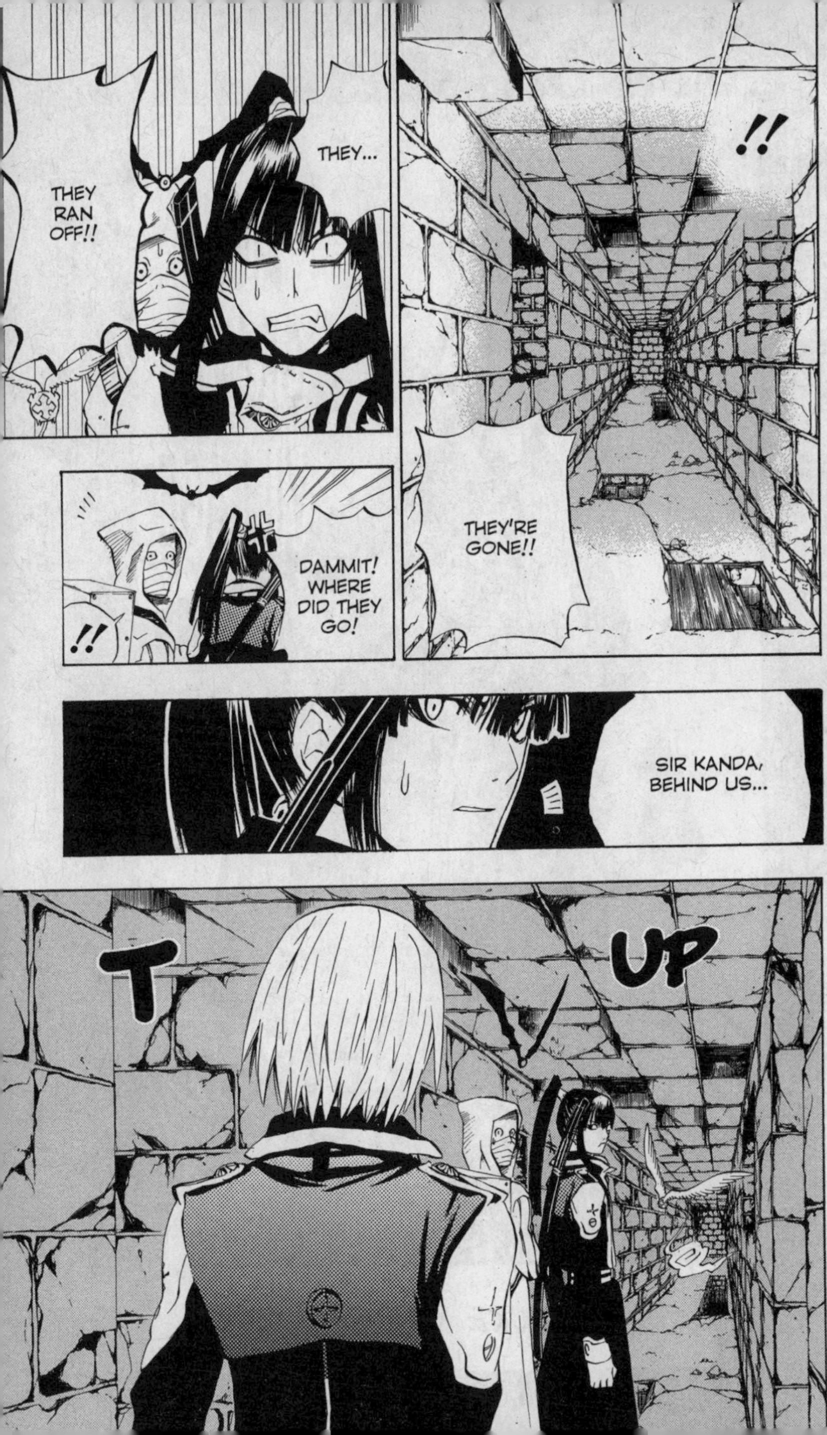
!!
THEY'RE GONE!!
THEY...
THEY RAN OFF!!
DAMMIT! WHERE DID THEY GO!
!!
SIR KANDA, BEHIND US...
UP
T

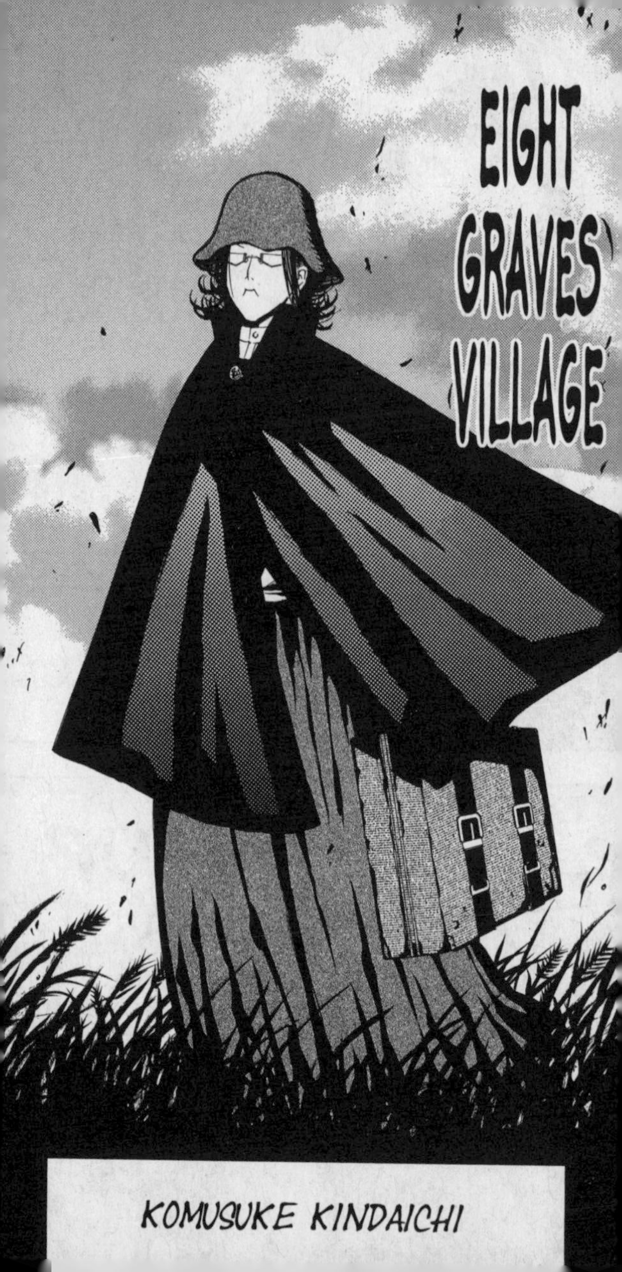
EIGHT GRAVES VILLAGE
KOMUSUKE KINDAICHI

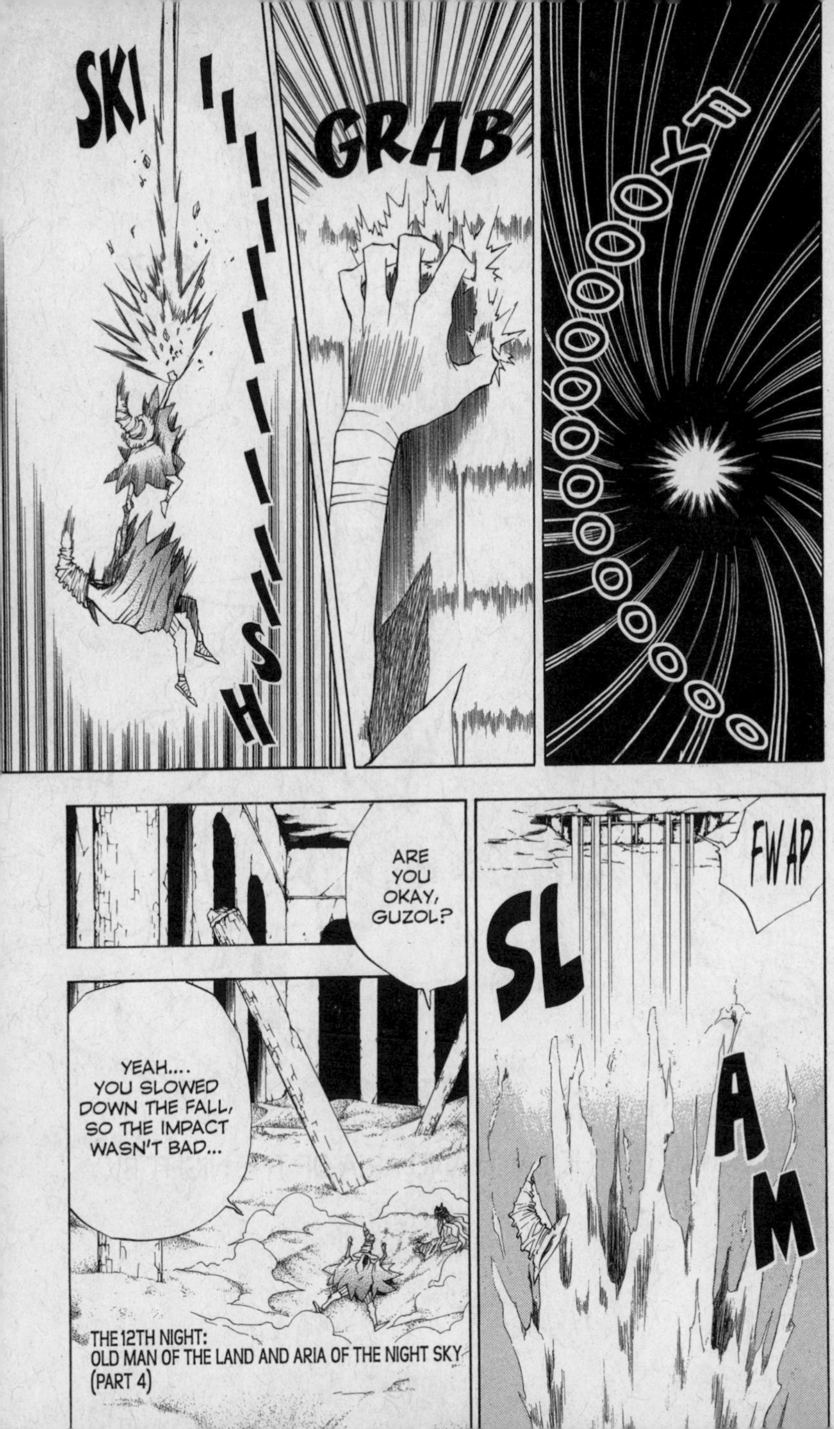
GRAB
SKIIIIIIIIIISH
FWAP
SLAM
ARE YOU OKAY, GUZOL?
YEAH.... YOU SLOWED DOWN THE FALL, SO THE IMPACT WASN'T BAD...
THE 12TH NIGHT: OLD MAN OF THE LAND AND ARIA OF THE NIGHT SKY (PART 4)

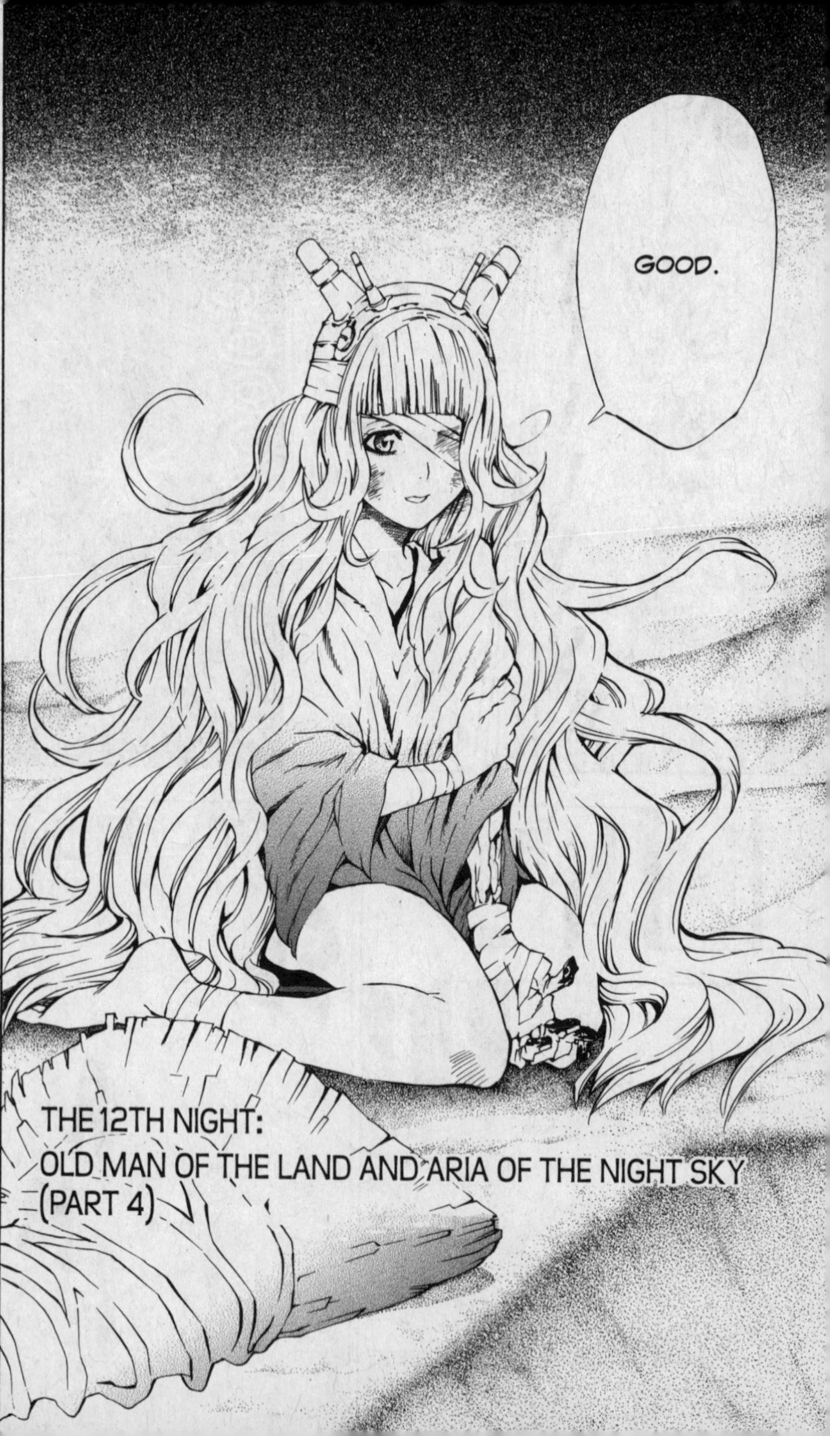
GOOD.

THE 12TH NIGHT:
OLD MAN OF THE LAND AND ARIA OF THE NIGHT SKY (PART 4)

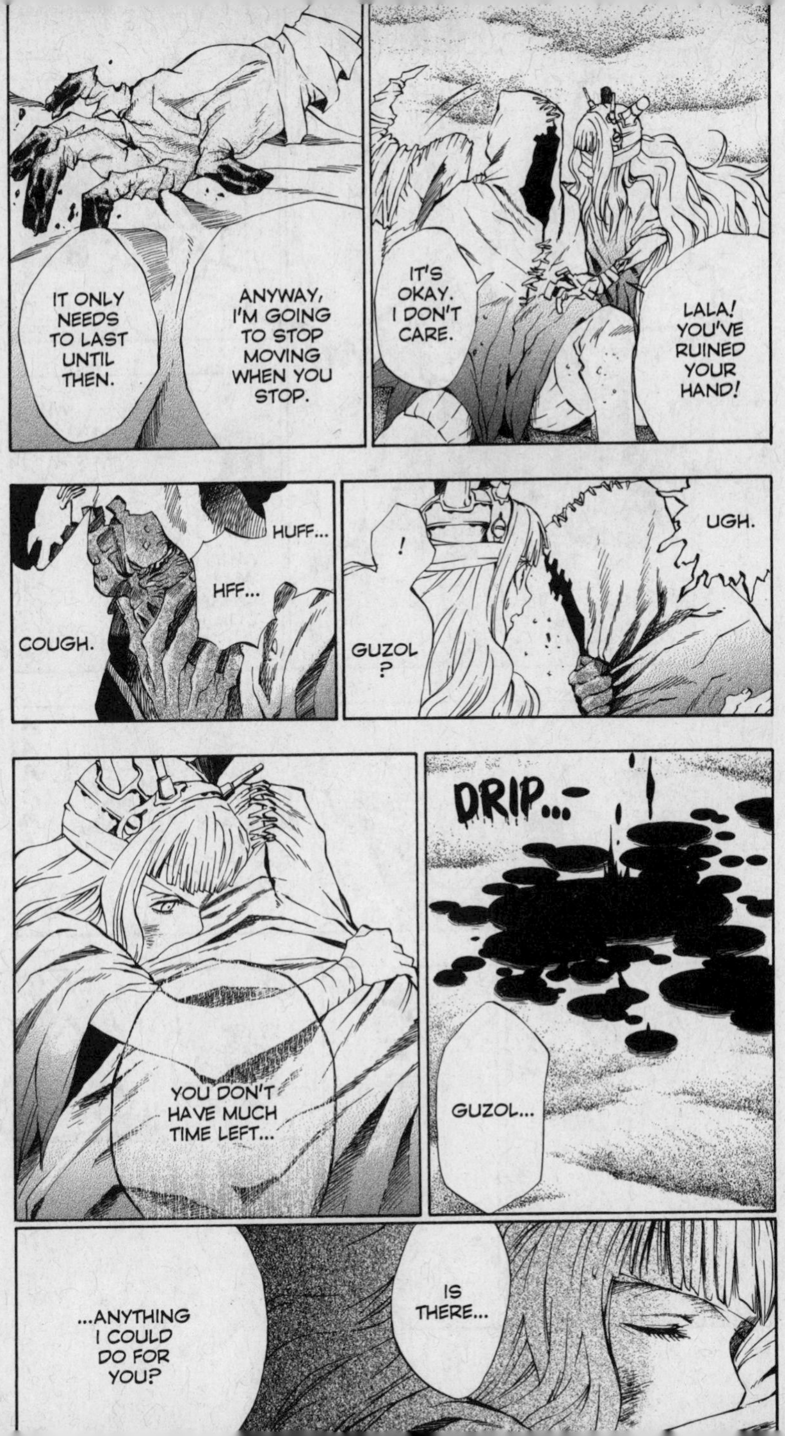
LALA! YOU'VE RUINED YOUR HAND!
IT'S OKAY. I DON'T CARE.
ANYWAY, I'M GOING TO STOP MOVING WHEN YOU STOP.
IT ONLY NEEDS TO LAST UNTIL THEN.
UGH.
!
GUZOL?
HUFF...
HFF...
COUGH.
DRIP...
GUZOL...
YOU DON'T HAVE MUCH TIME LEFT...
IS THERE...
...ANYTHING I COULD DO FOR YOU?

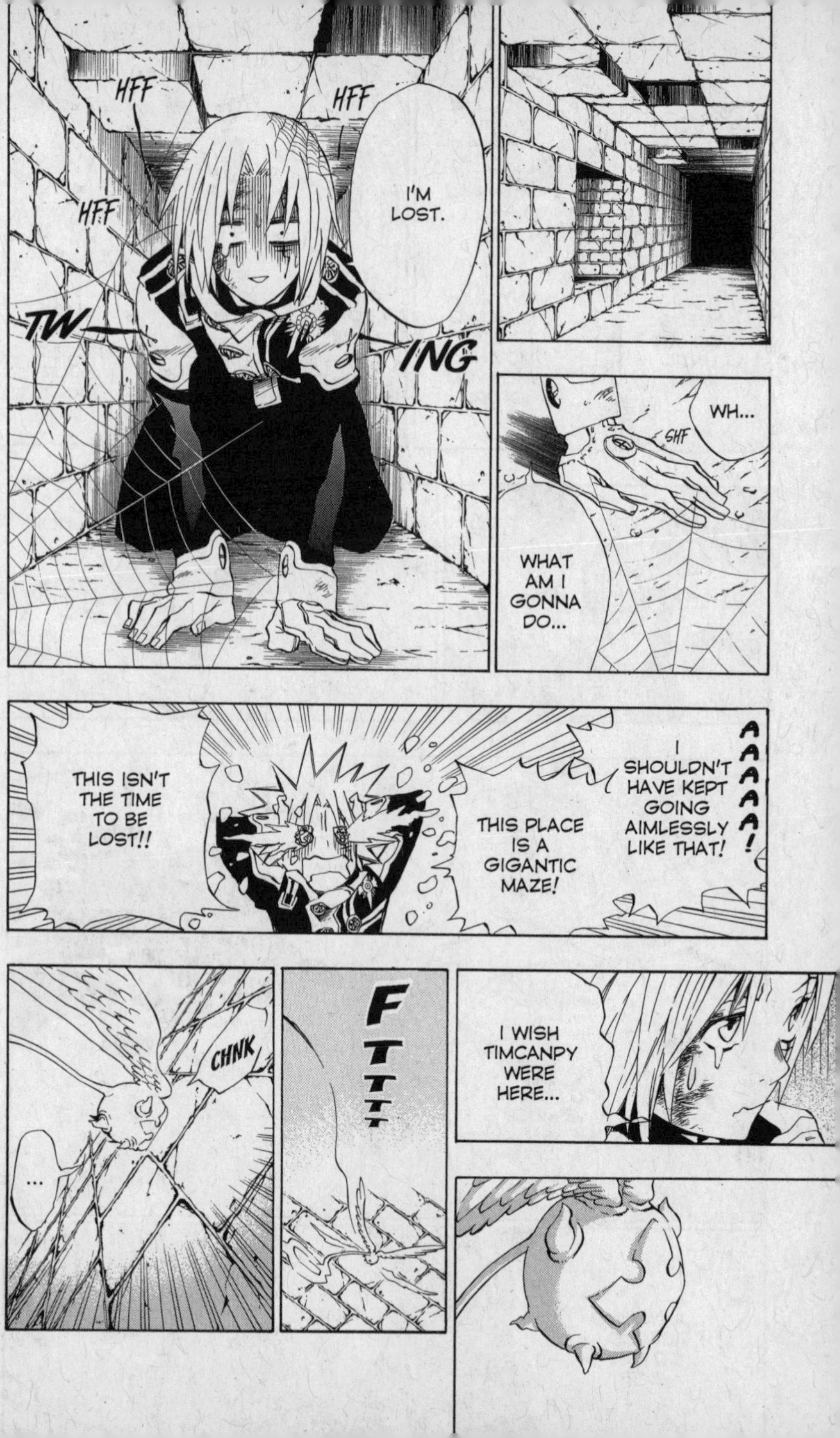
WH...
SHF
WHAT AM I GONNA DO...
HFF
I'M LOST.
HFF
HFF
TW— ING
AAAAAA!
I SHOULDN'T HAVE KEPT GOING AIMLESSLY LIKE THAT!
THIS PLACE IS A GIGANTIC MAZE!
THIS ISN'T THE TIME TO BE LOST!!
I WISH TIMCANPY WERE HERE...
FTTTT
CHNK
...

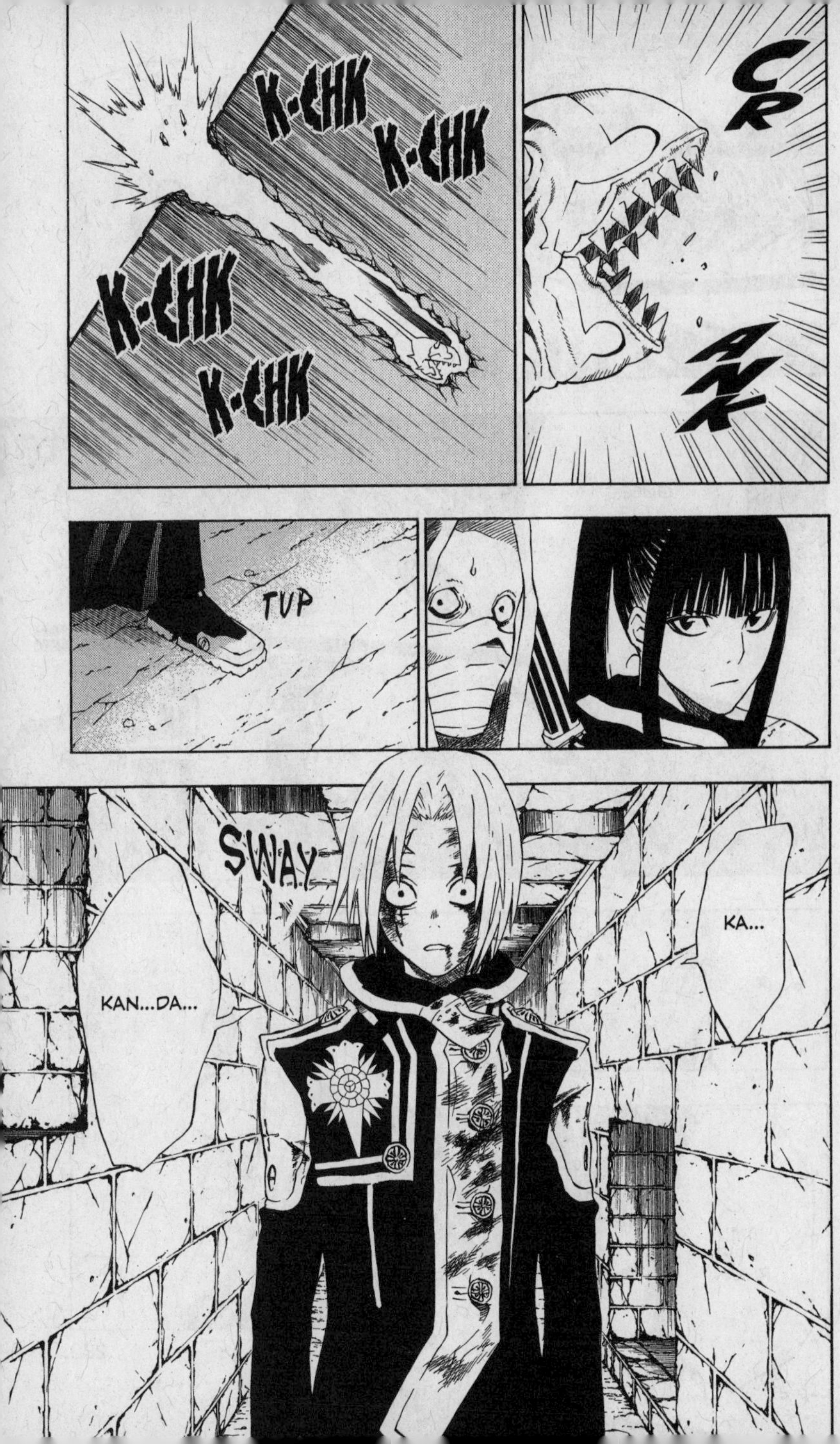
CRANK
K-CHK
K-CHK
K-CHK
K-CHK
TUP
KA...
SWAY
KAN...DA...

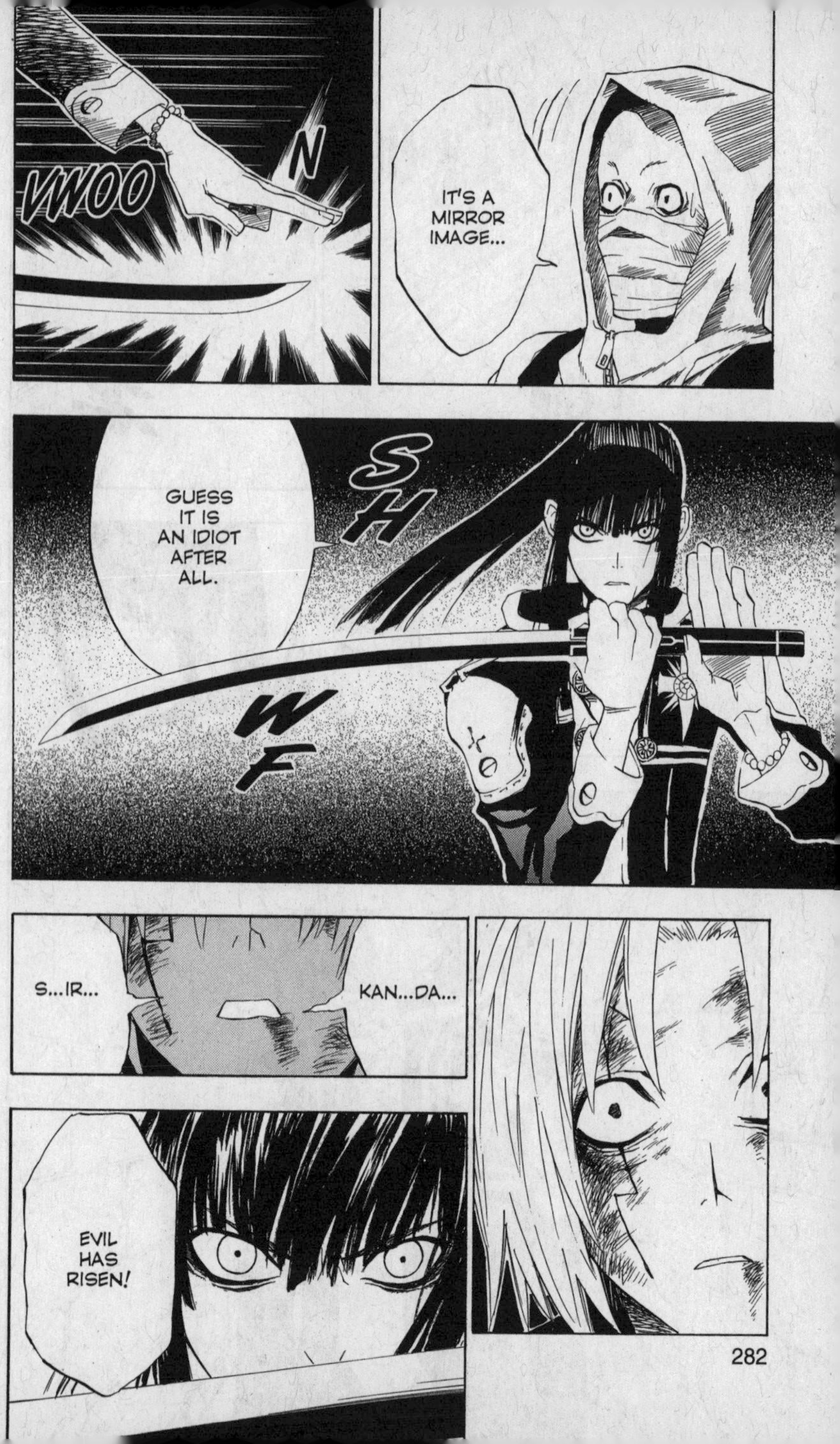
IT'S A MIRROR IMAGE...
VWOO
N
SH
GUESS IT IS AN IDIOT AFTER ALL.
WF
KAN...DA...
S...IR...
EVIL HAS RISEN!

NETHER-WORLD CREATURE "ICHIGEN"!

RETURN TO OBLIVION!

BOOM!

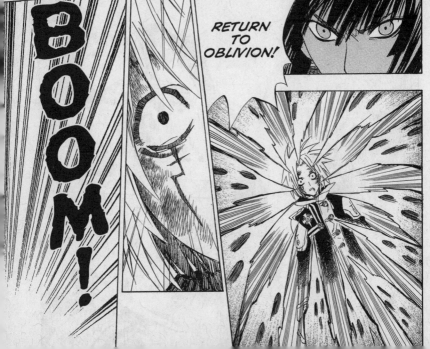

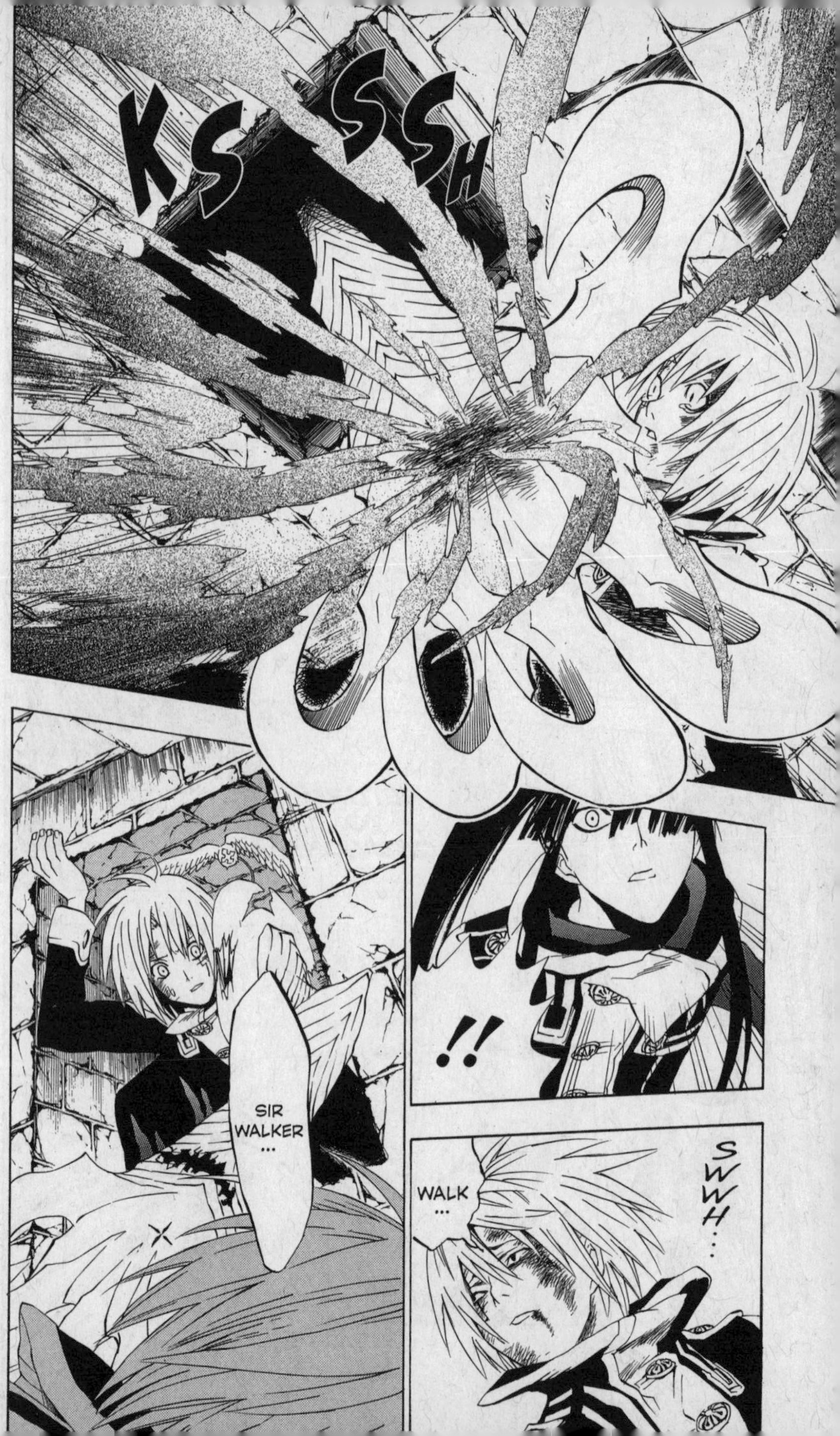
KSSSH
!!
SWWH...
WALK...
SIR WALKER...

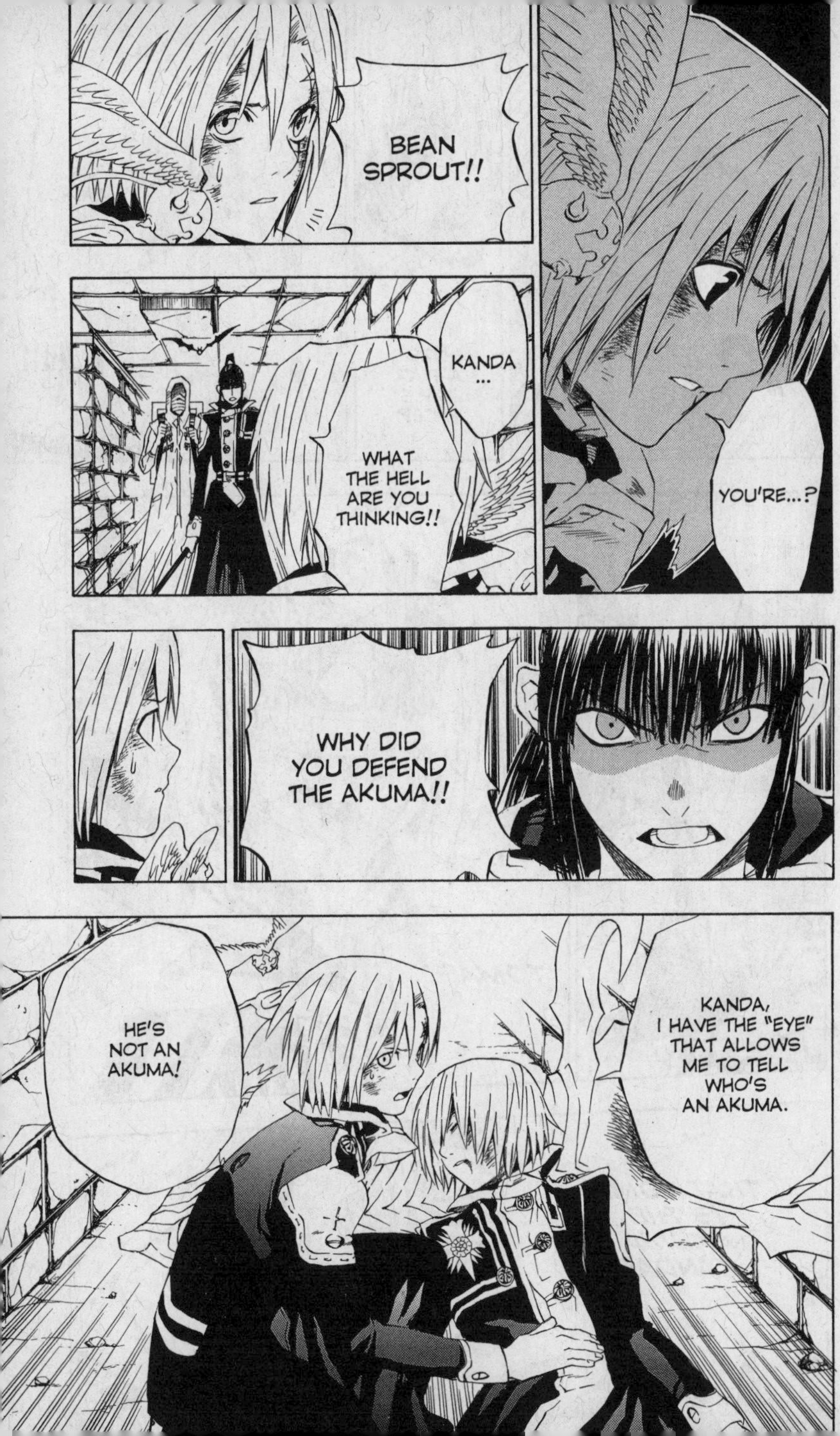
YOU'RE...?
BEAN SPROUT!!
KANDA ...
WHAT THE HELL ARE YOU THINKING!!
WHY DID YOU DEFEND THE AKUMA!!
KANDA, I HAVE THE "EYE" THAT ALLOWS ME TO TELL WHO'S AN AKUMA.
HE'S NOT AN AKUMA!

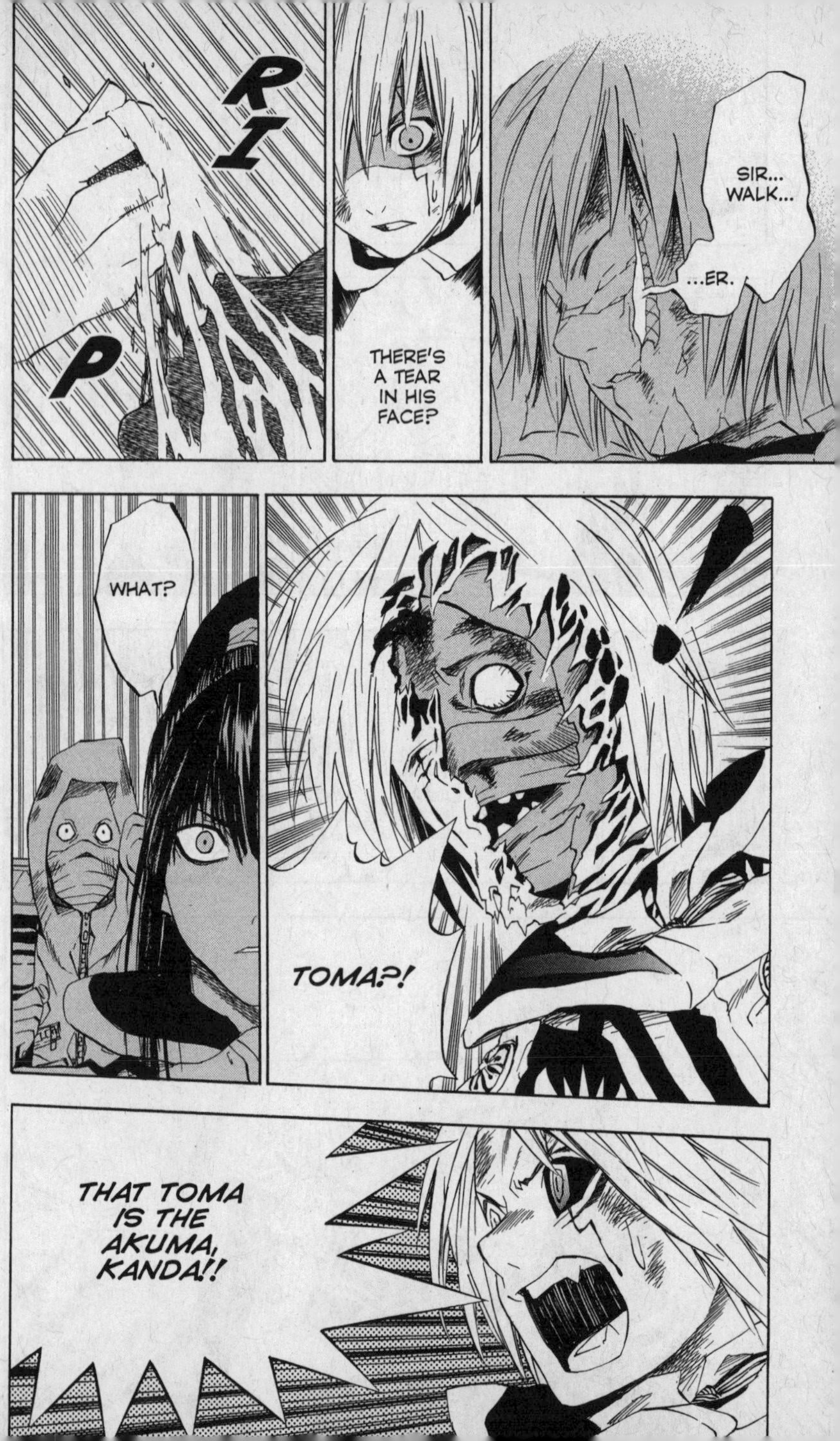
SIR... WALK...
...ER.
THERE'S A TEAR IN HIS FACE?
RIP
TOMA?!
WHAT?
THAT TOMA IS THE AKUMA, KANDA!!

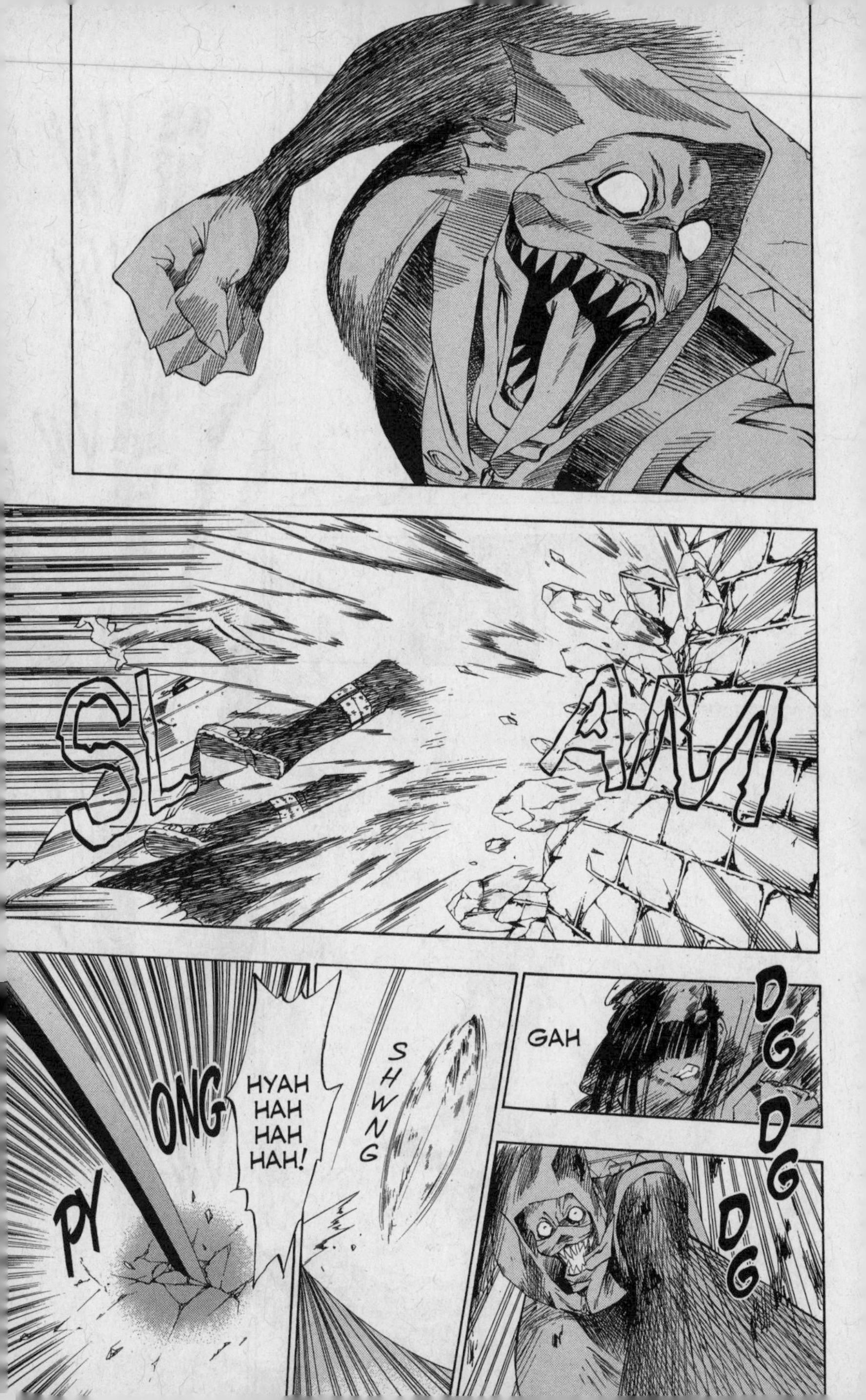

SLAM
GAH
DGDGDG
DGDG
SHWNG
HYAH HAH HAH HAH!
PYONG

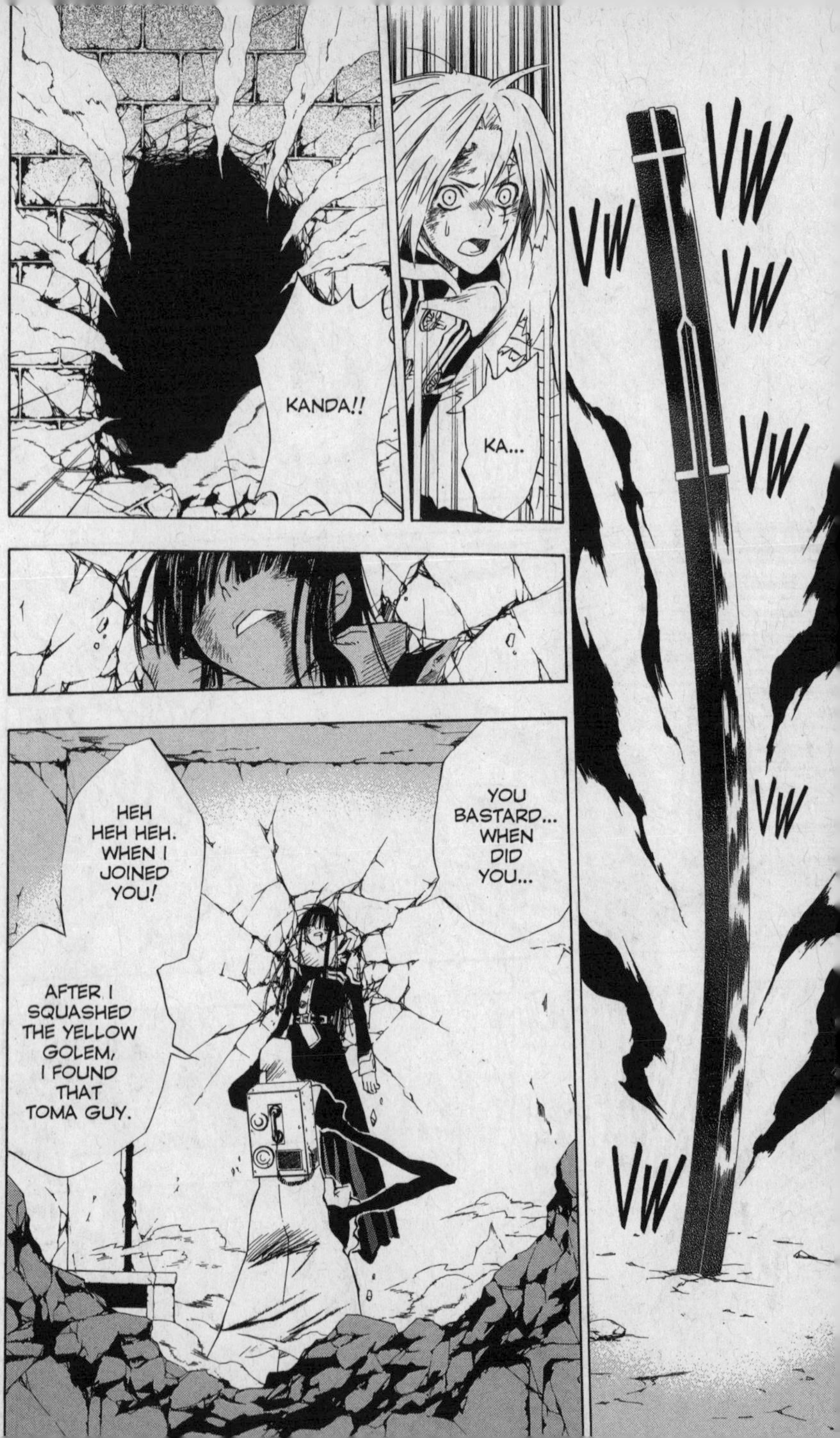
VW
VW
VW
VW
VW
VW
KA...
KANDA!!
YOU BASTARD... WHEN DID YOU...
HEH HEH HEH. WHEN I JOINED YOU!
AFTER I SQUASHED THE YELLOW GOLEM, I FOUND THAT TOMA GUY.

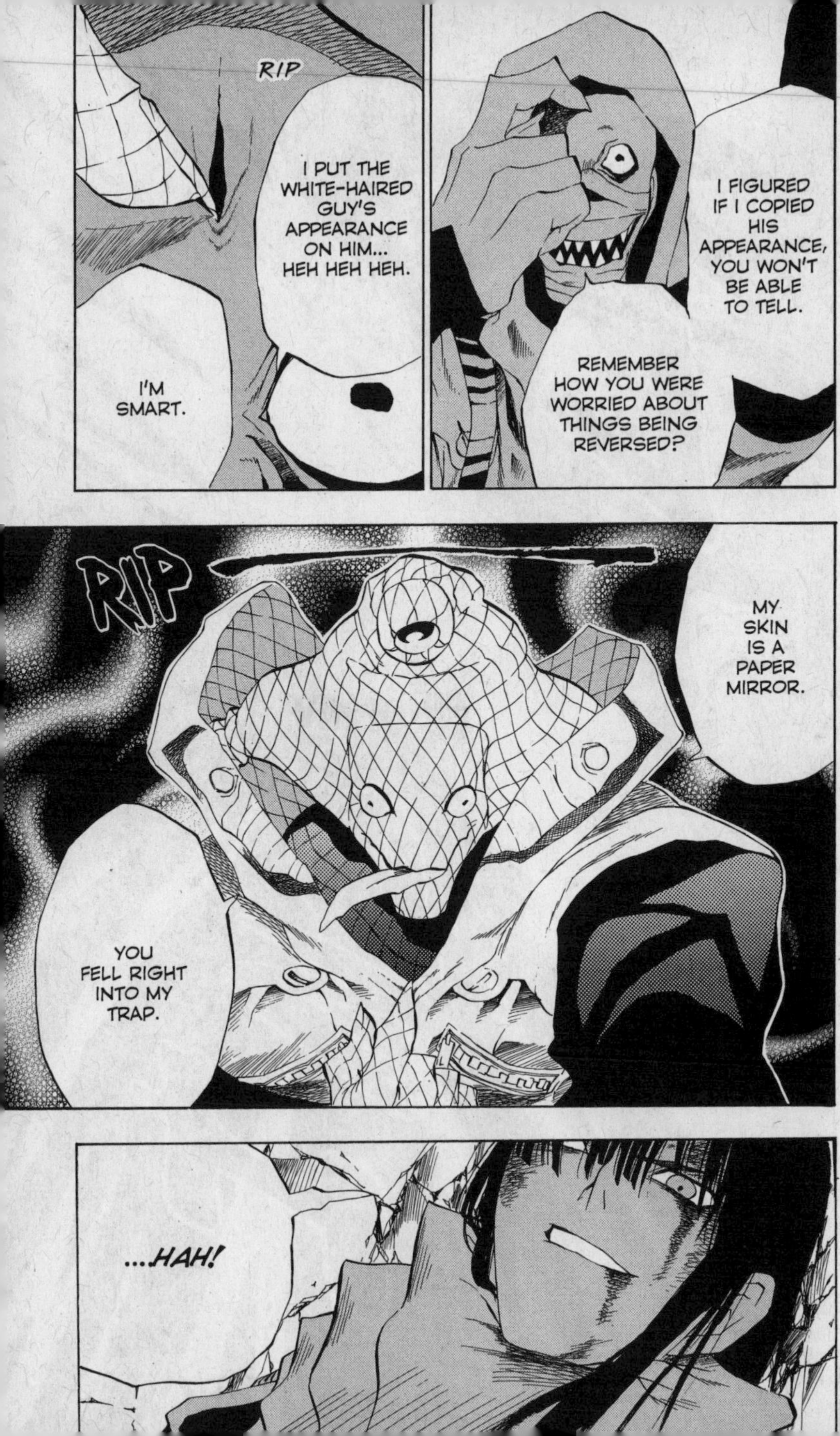
I FIGURED IF I COPIED HIS APPEARANCE, YOU WON'T BE ABLE TO TELL.
REMEMBER HOW YOU WERE WORRIED ABOUT THINGS BEING REVERSED?
RIP
I PUT THE WHITE-HAIRED GUY'S APPEARANCE ON HIM... HEH HEH HEH.
I'M SMART.
MY SKIN IS A PAPER MIRROR.
RIP
YOU FELL RIGHT INTO MY TRAP.
...HAH!

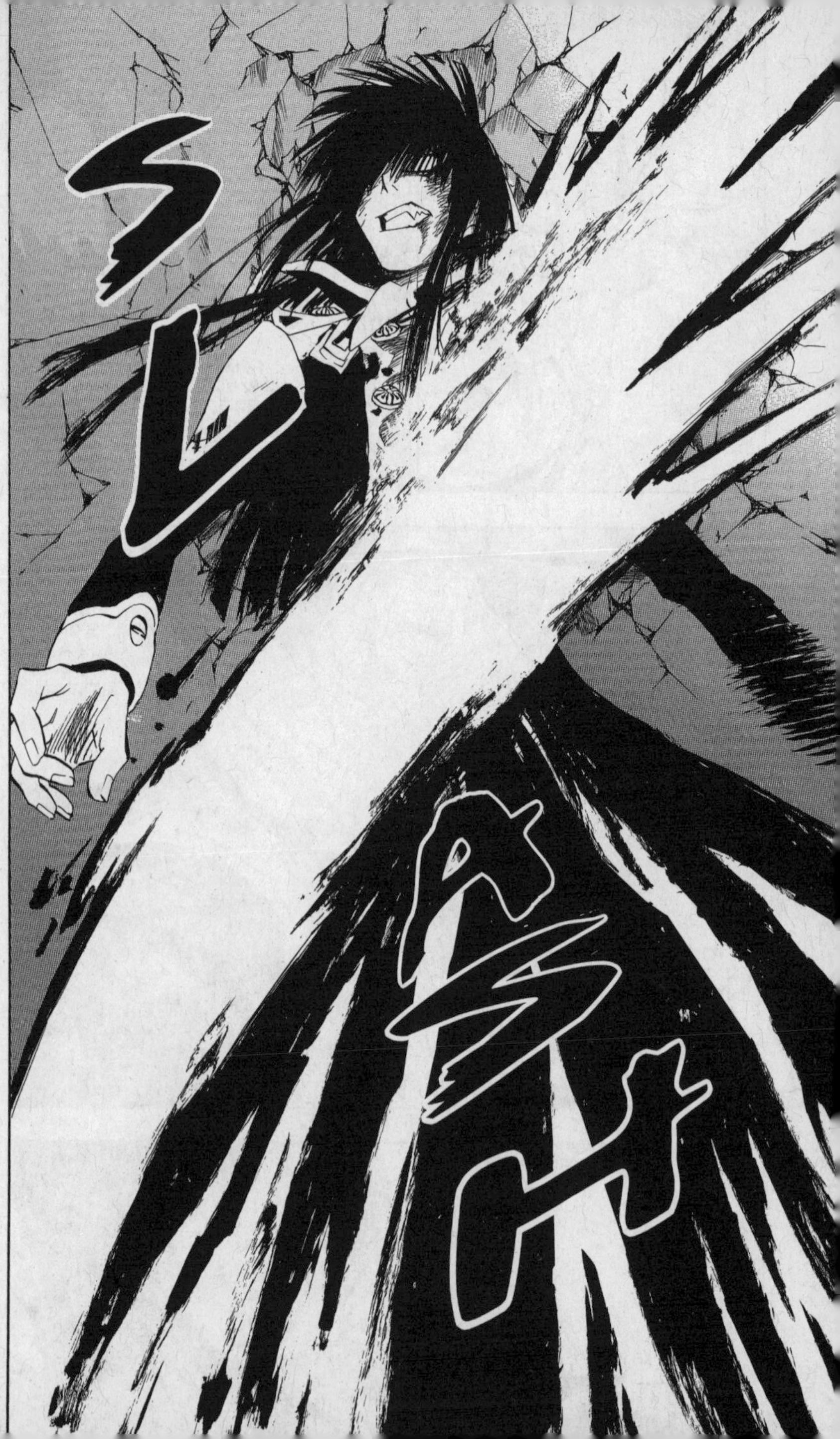

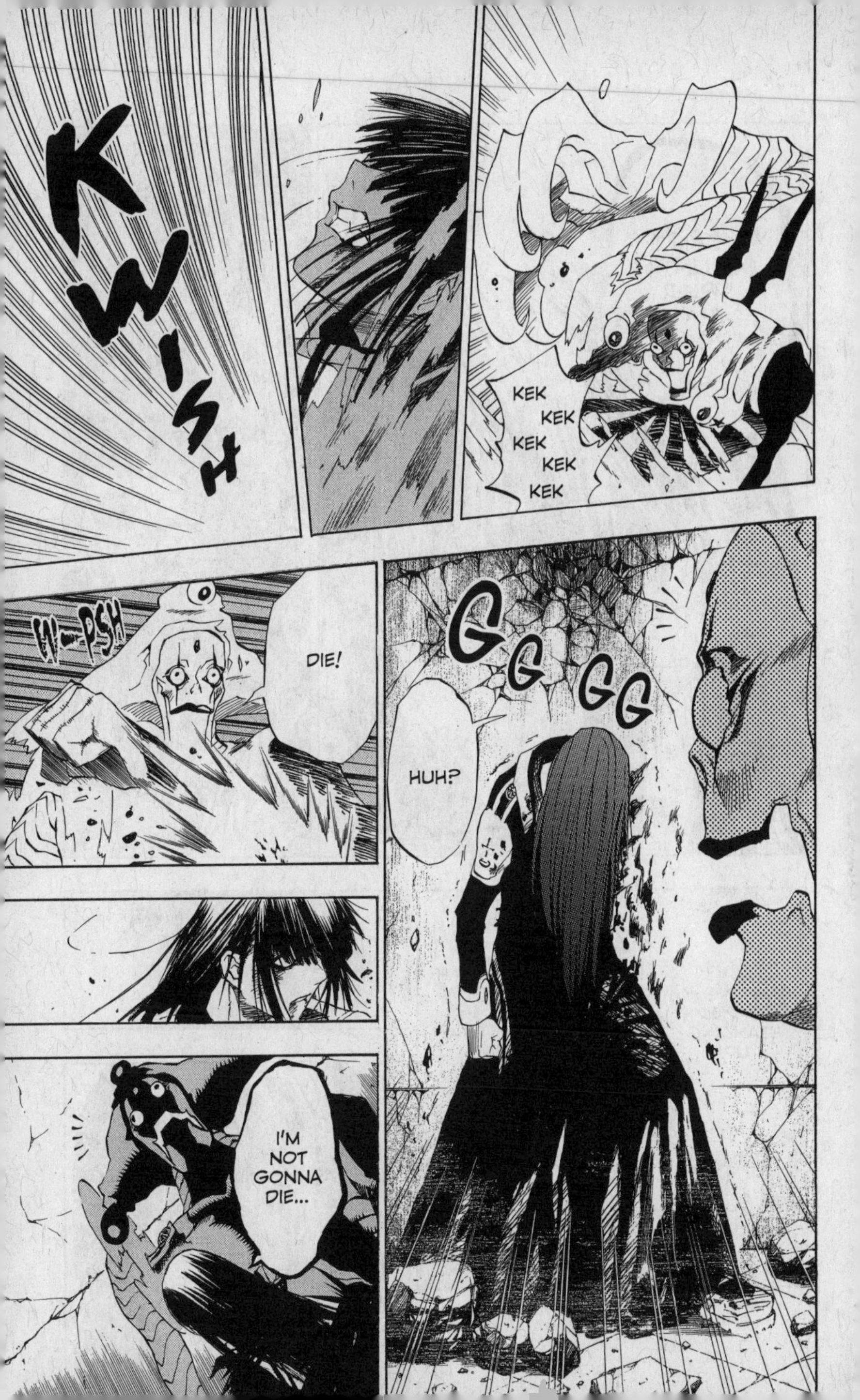
KEK KEK KEK KEK KEK
KWISH
GGGG
HUH?
W—PSH
DIE!
I'M NOT GONNA DIE...

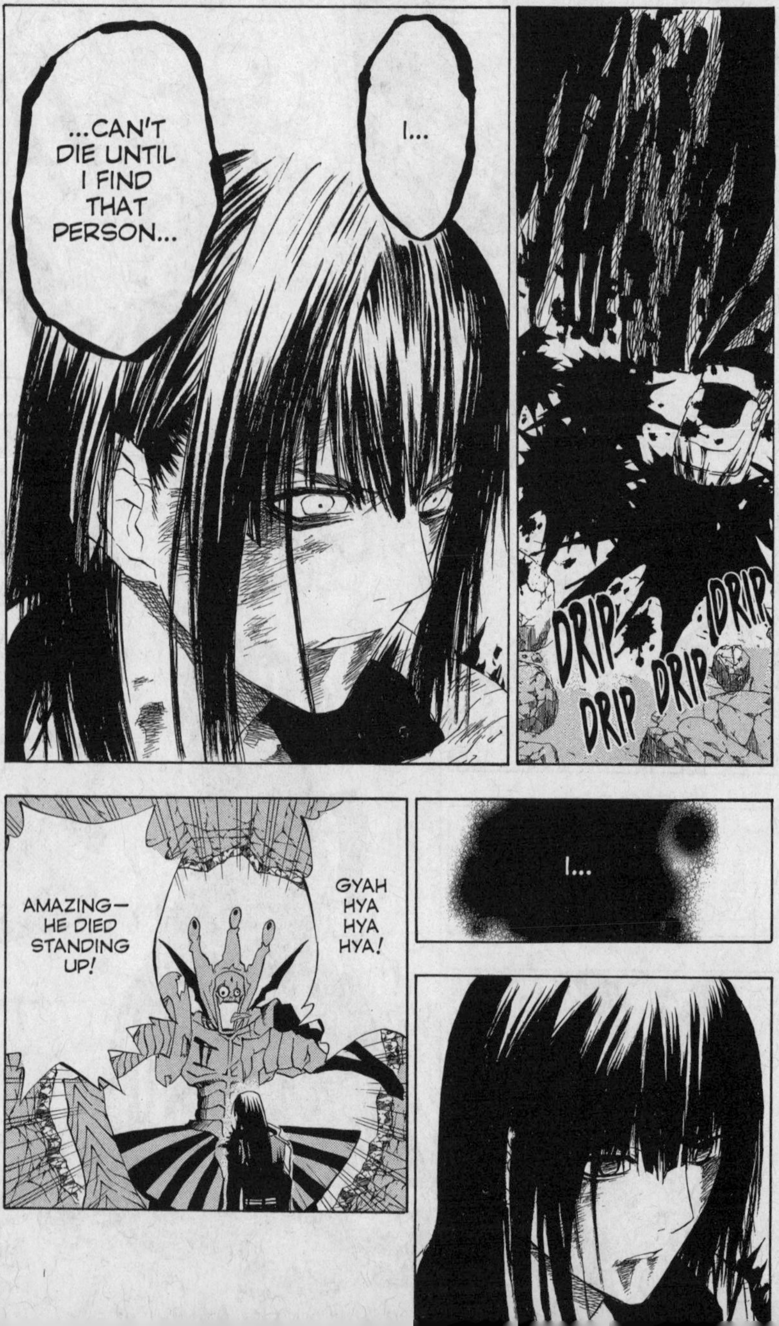
DRIP DRIP DRIP DRIP
I...
...CAN'T DIE UNTIL I FIND THAT PERSON...
I...
GYAH HYA HYA HYA!
AMAZING—HE DIED STANDING UP!

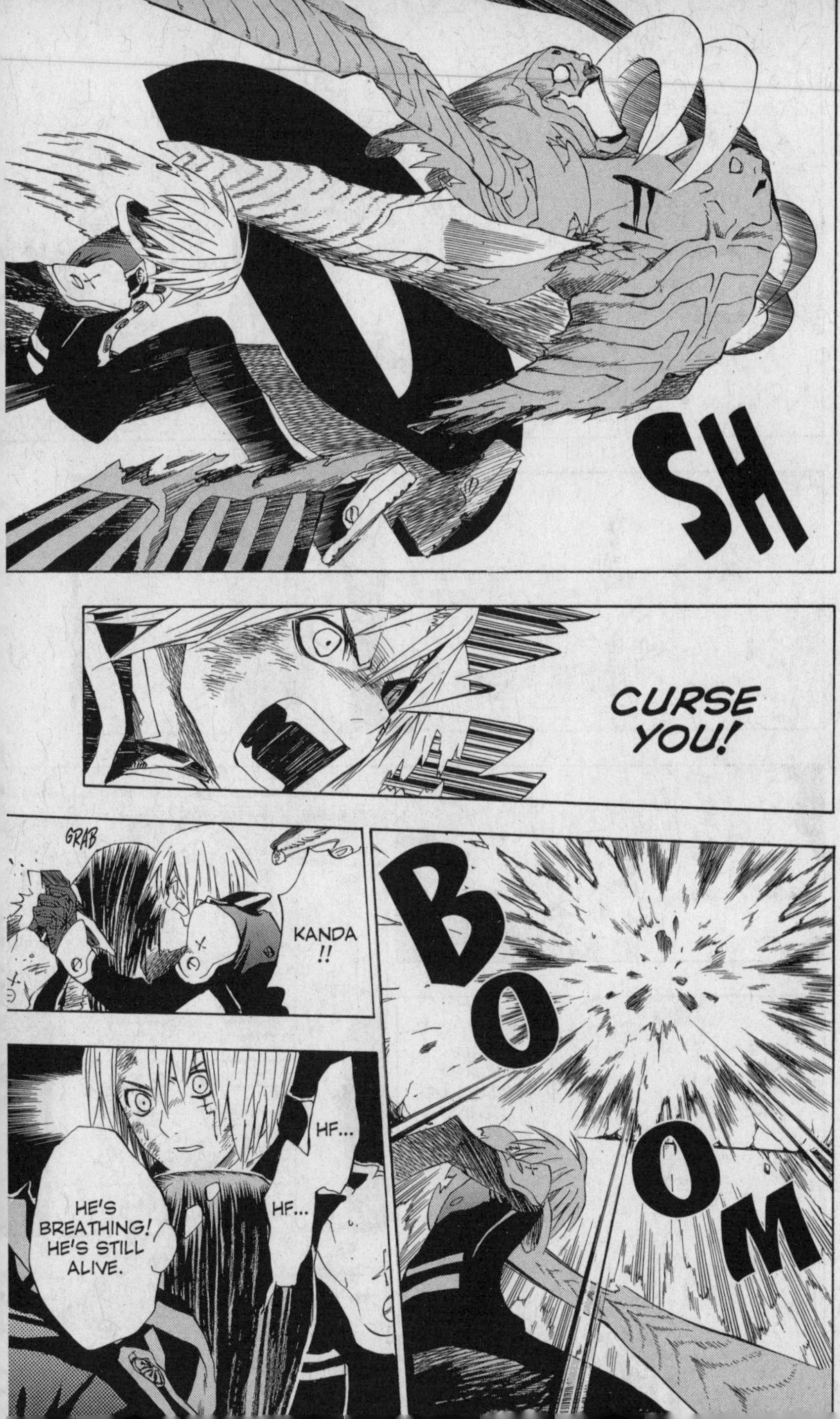
SH
CURSE YOU!
BOOM
GRAB
KANDA !!
HF...
HF...
HE'S BREATHING! HE'S STILL ALIVE.

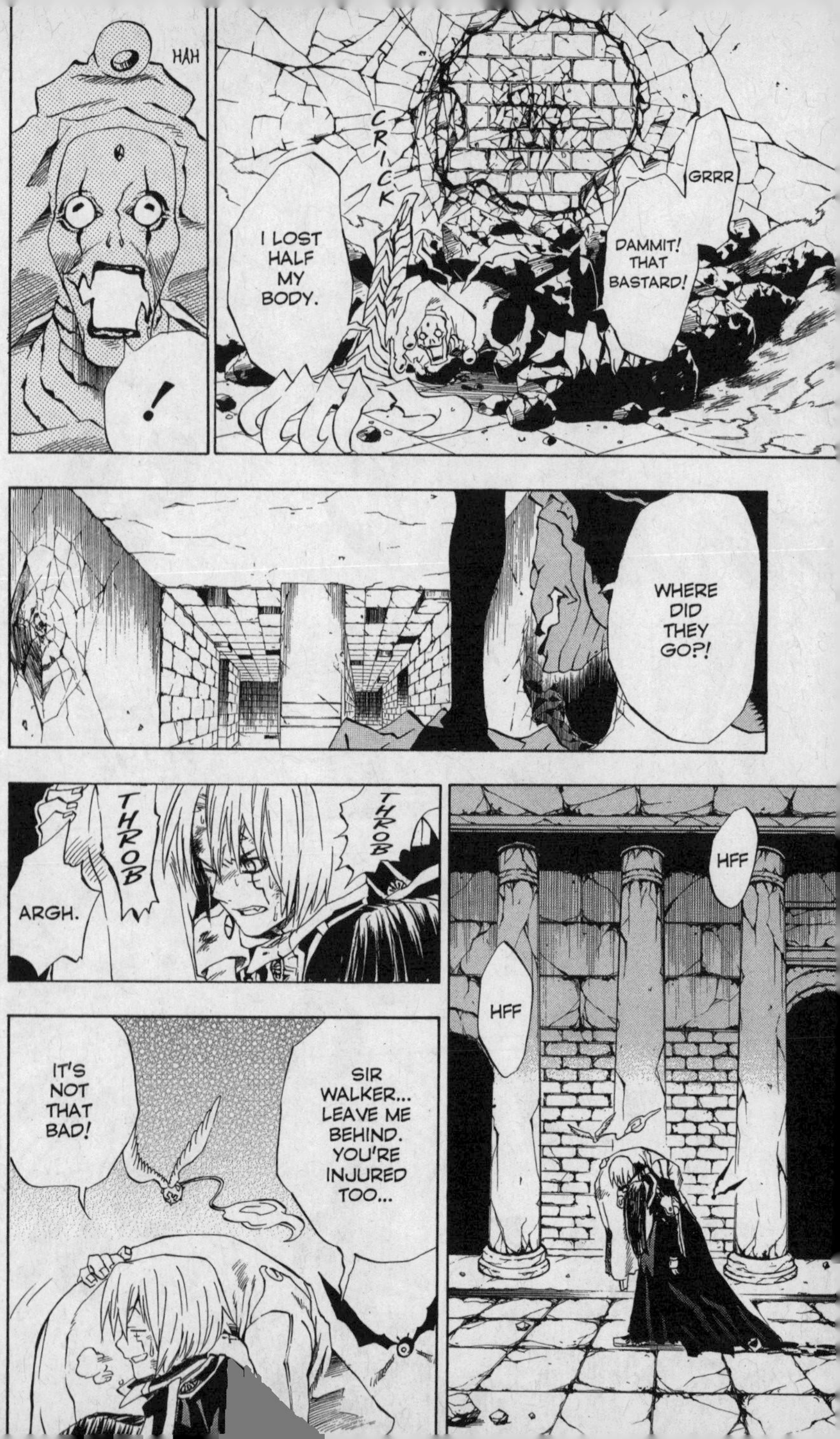
GRRR
DAMMIT! THAT BASTARD!
CRICK
I LOST HALF MY BODY.
HAH
!
WHERE DID THEY GO?!
HFF
HFF
THROB
THROB
ARGH.
SIR WALKER... LEAVE ME BEHIND. YOU'RE INJURED TOO...
IT'S NOT THAT BAD!

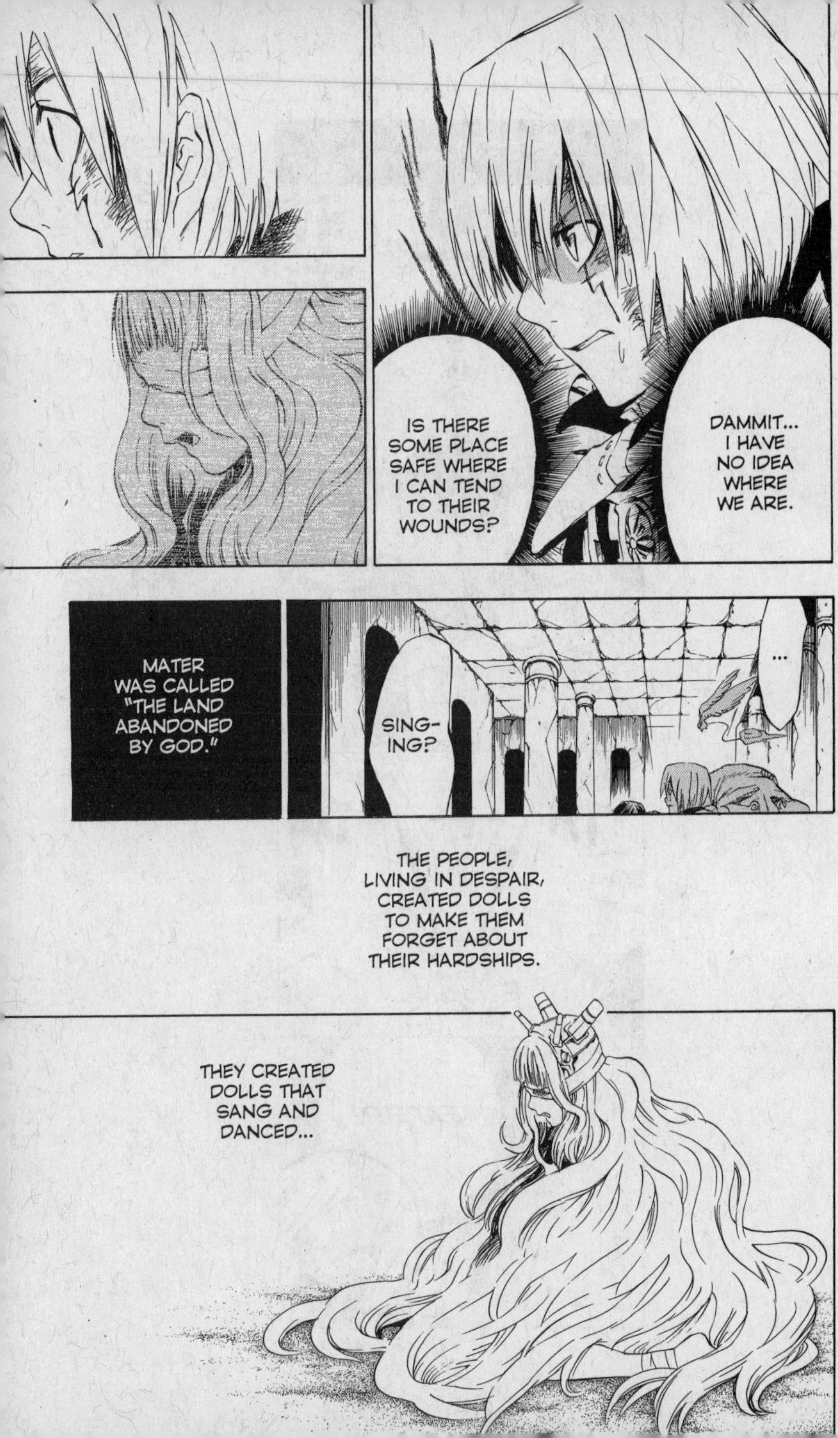
DAMMIT... I HAVE NO IDEA WHERE WE ARE.
IS THERE SOME PLACE SAFE WHERE I CAN TEND TO THEIR WOUNDS?
...
SING-ING?
MATER WAS CALLED "THE LAND ABANDONED BY GOD."
THE PEOPLE, LIVING IN DESPAIR, CREATED DOLLS TO MAKE THEM FORGET ABOUT THEIR HARDSHIPS.
THEY CREATED DOLLS THAT SANG AND DANCED...

SUPER 4 STRIP COMIC ACT

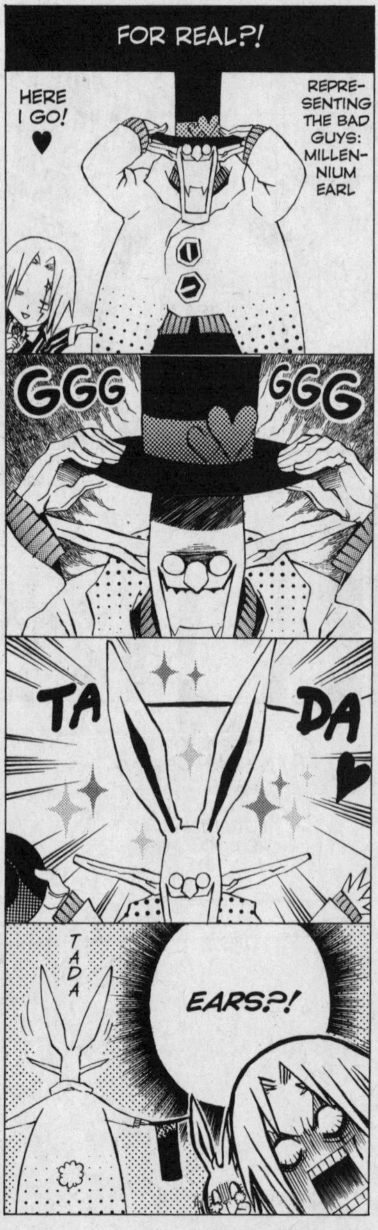

FOR REAL?!
REPRESENTING THE BAD GUYS: MILLENNIUM EARL
HERE I GO! ♥
GGG
GGG
TA DA ♥
EARS?!
TADA

THE 13TH NIGHT: OLD MAN OF THE LAND AND ARIA OF THE NIGHT SKY (PART 5)

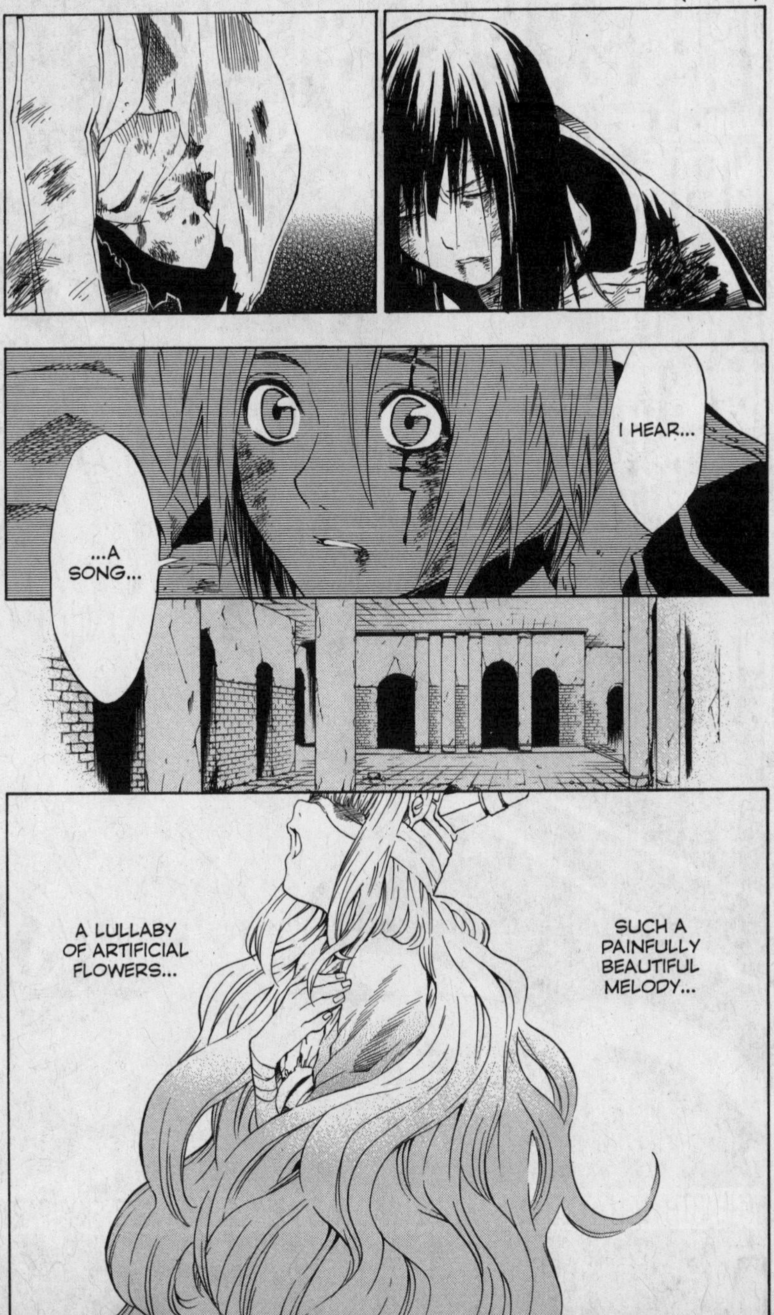
I HEAR...
...A SONG...
SUCH A PAINFULLY BEAUTIFUL MELODY...
A LULLABY OF ARTIFICIAL FLOWERS...

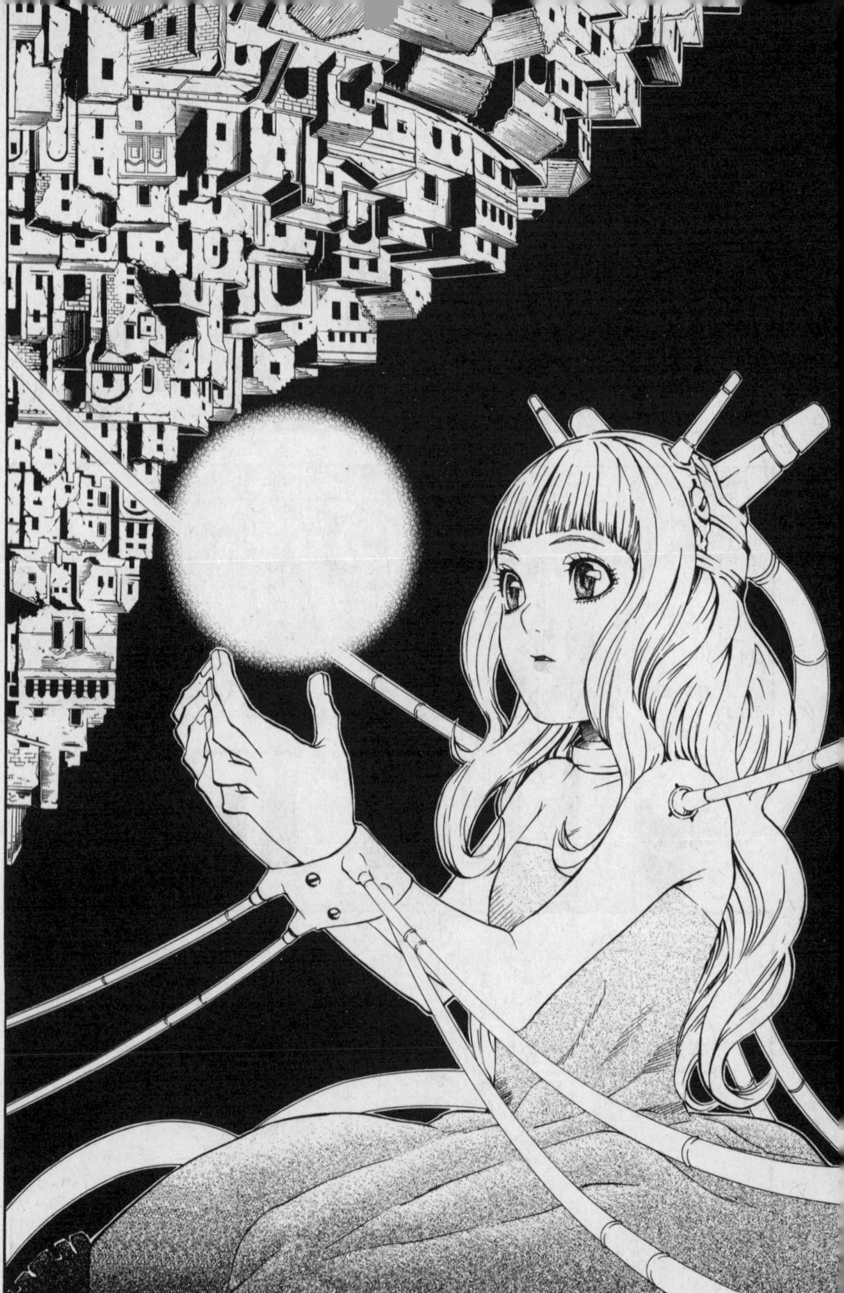

THE 13TH NIGHT: OLD MAN OF THE LAND AND ARIA OF THE NIGHT SKY (PART 5)

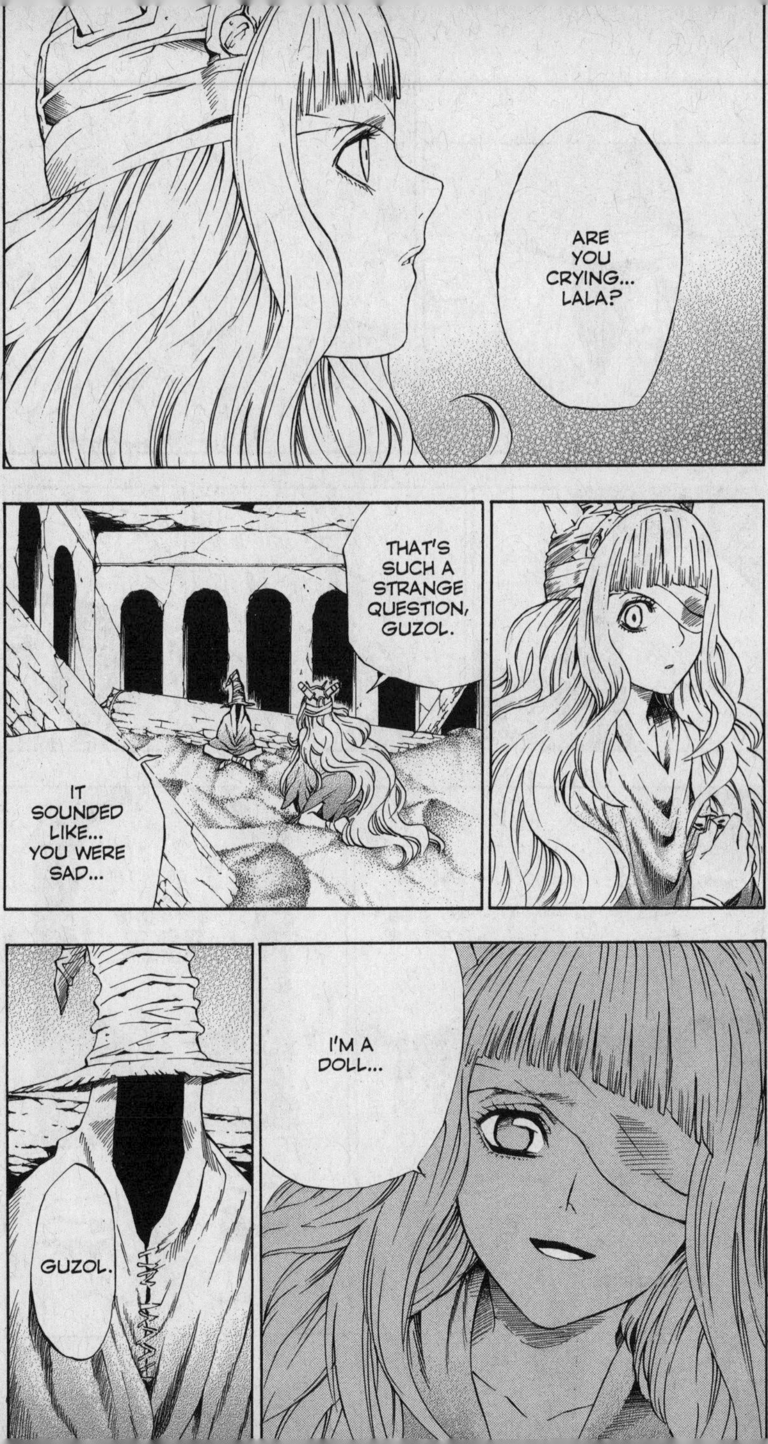
ARE YOU CRYING... LALA?
THAT'S SUCH A STRANGE QUESTION, GUZOL.
IT SOUNDED LIKE... YOU WERE SAD...
I'M A DOLL...
GUZOL.

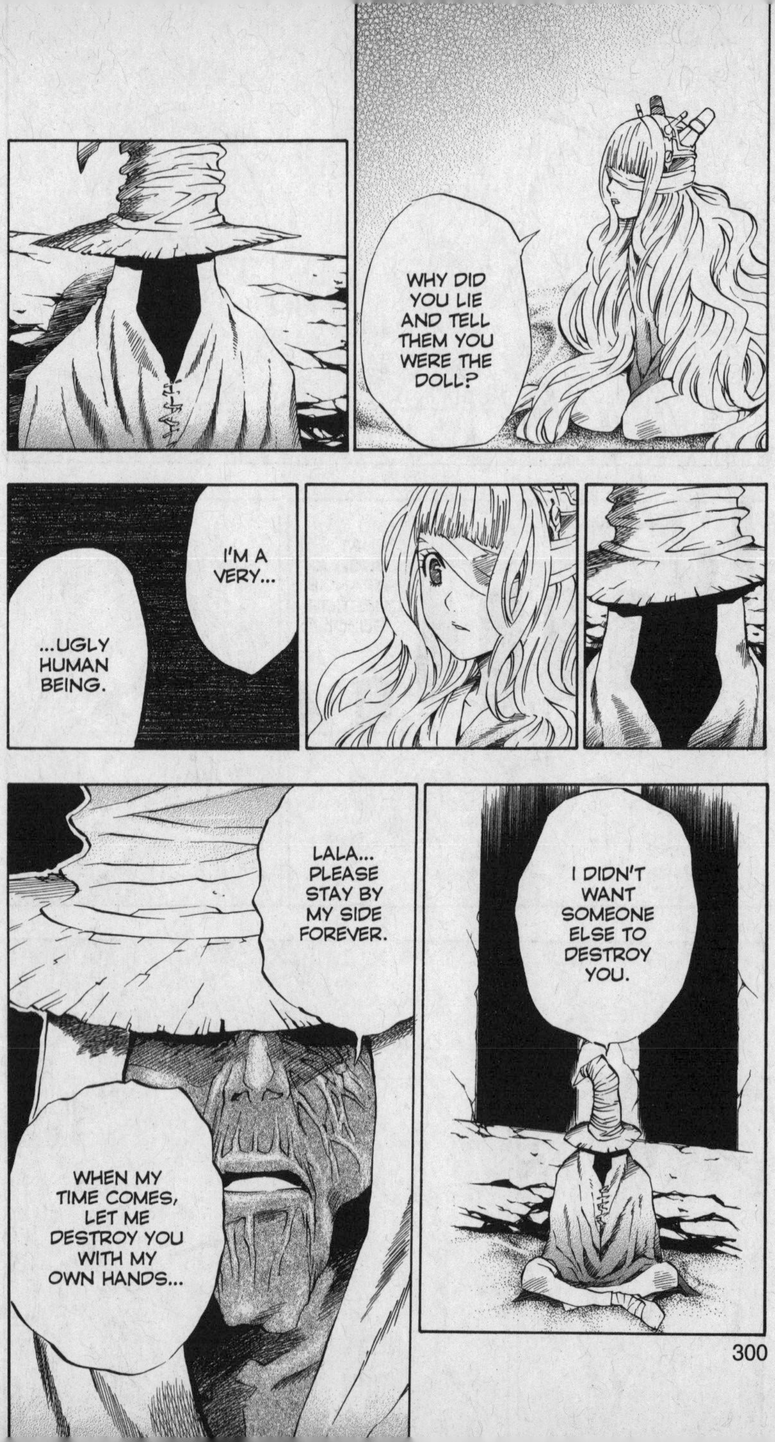
WHY DID YOU LIE AND TELL THEM YOU WERE THE DOLL?
I'M A VERY...
...UGLY HUMAN BEING.
I DIDN'T WANT SOMEONE ELSE TO DESTROY YOU.
LALA... PLEASE STAY BY MY SIDE FOREVER.
WHEN MY TIME COMES, LET ME DESTROY YOU WITH MY OWN HANDS...

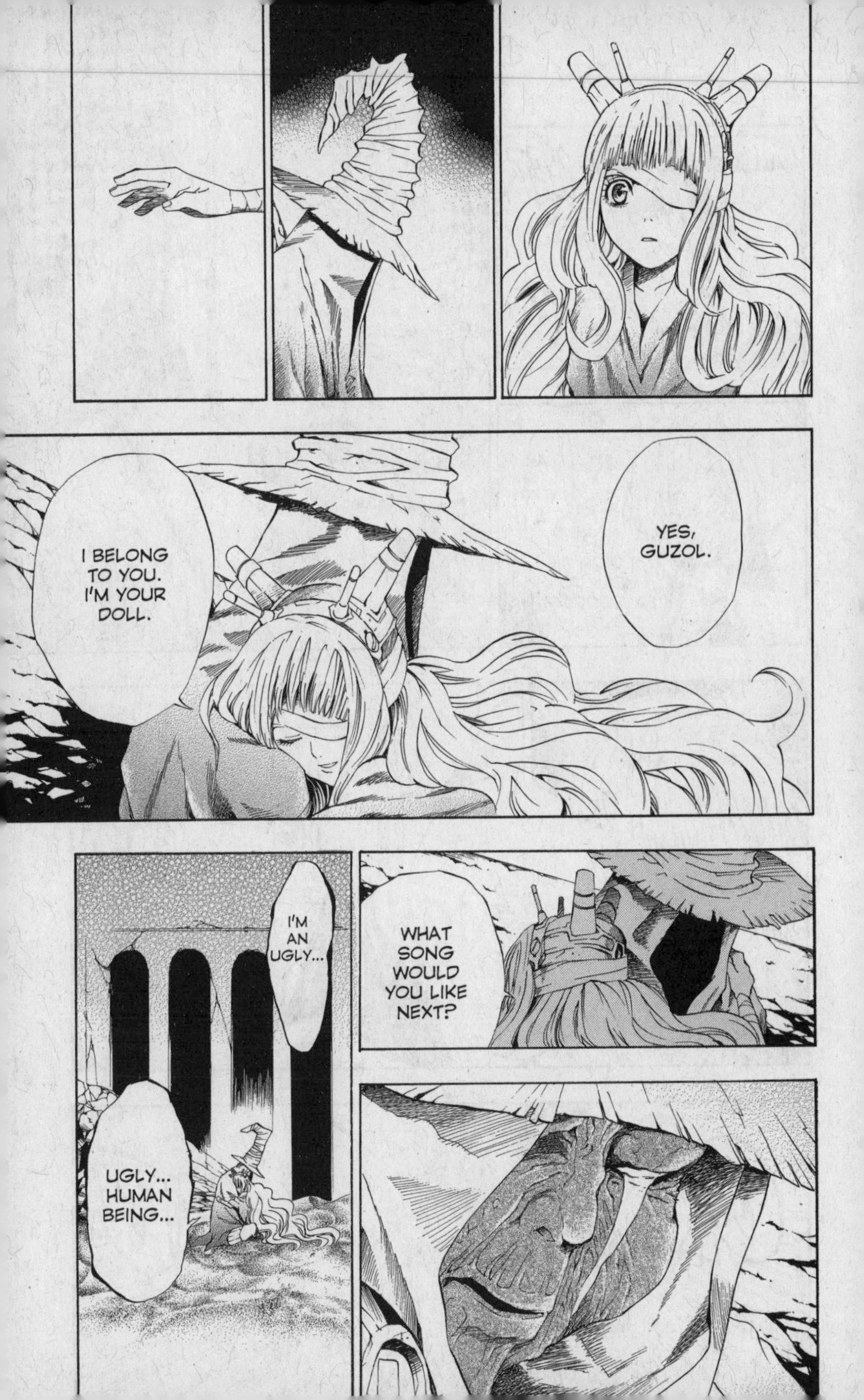
YES, GUZOL.
I BELONG TO YOU. I'M YOUR DOLL.
WHAT SONG WOULD YOU LIKE NEXT?
I'M AN UGLY...
UGLY... HUMAN BEING...

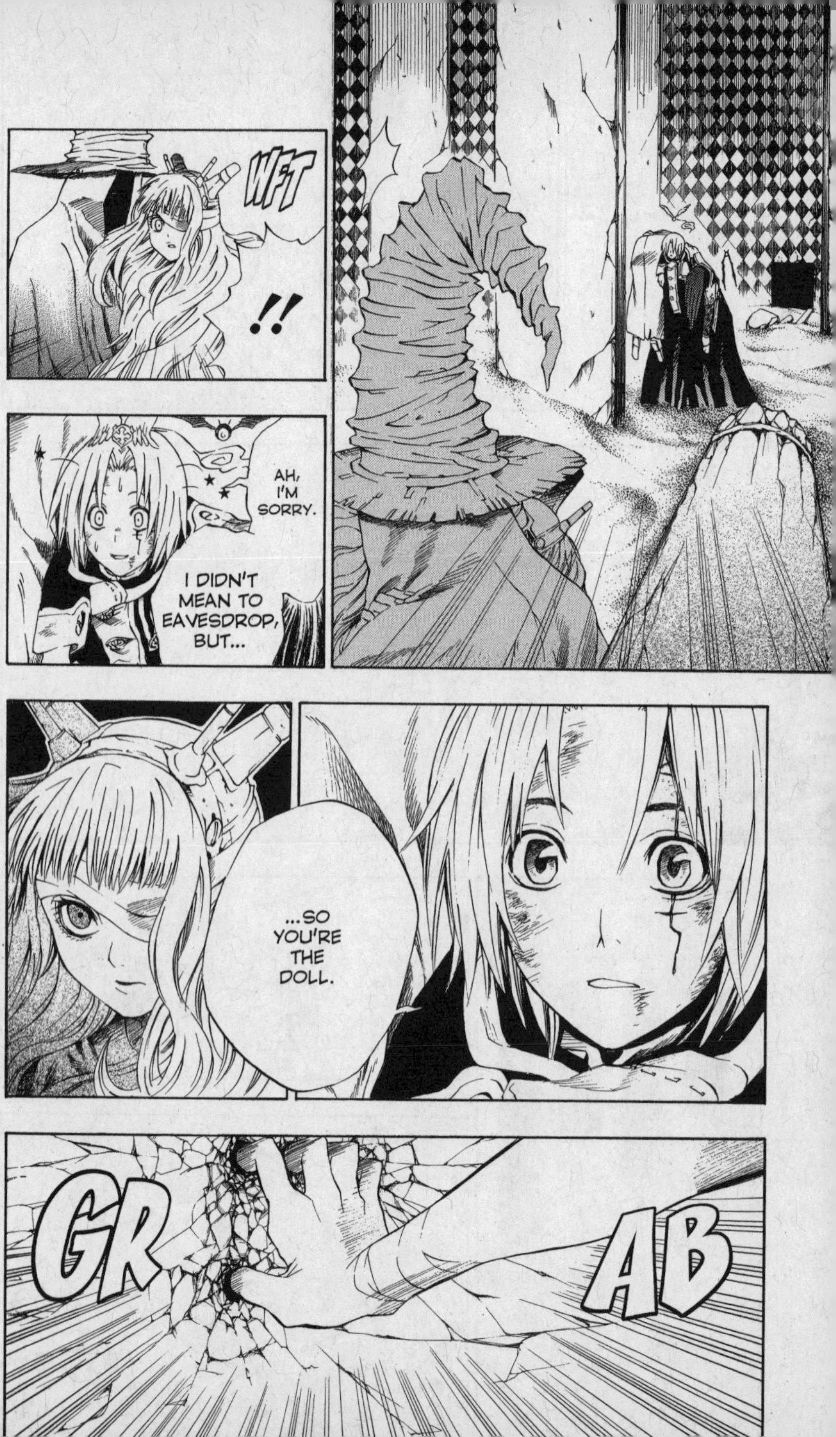
WFT
!!
AH, I'M SORRY.
I DIDN'T MEAN TO EAVESDROP, BUT...
...SO YOU'RE THE DOLL.
GR AB

READ THIS WAY

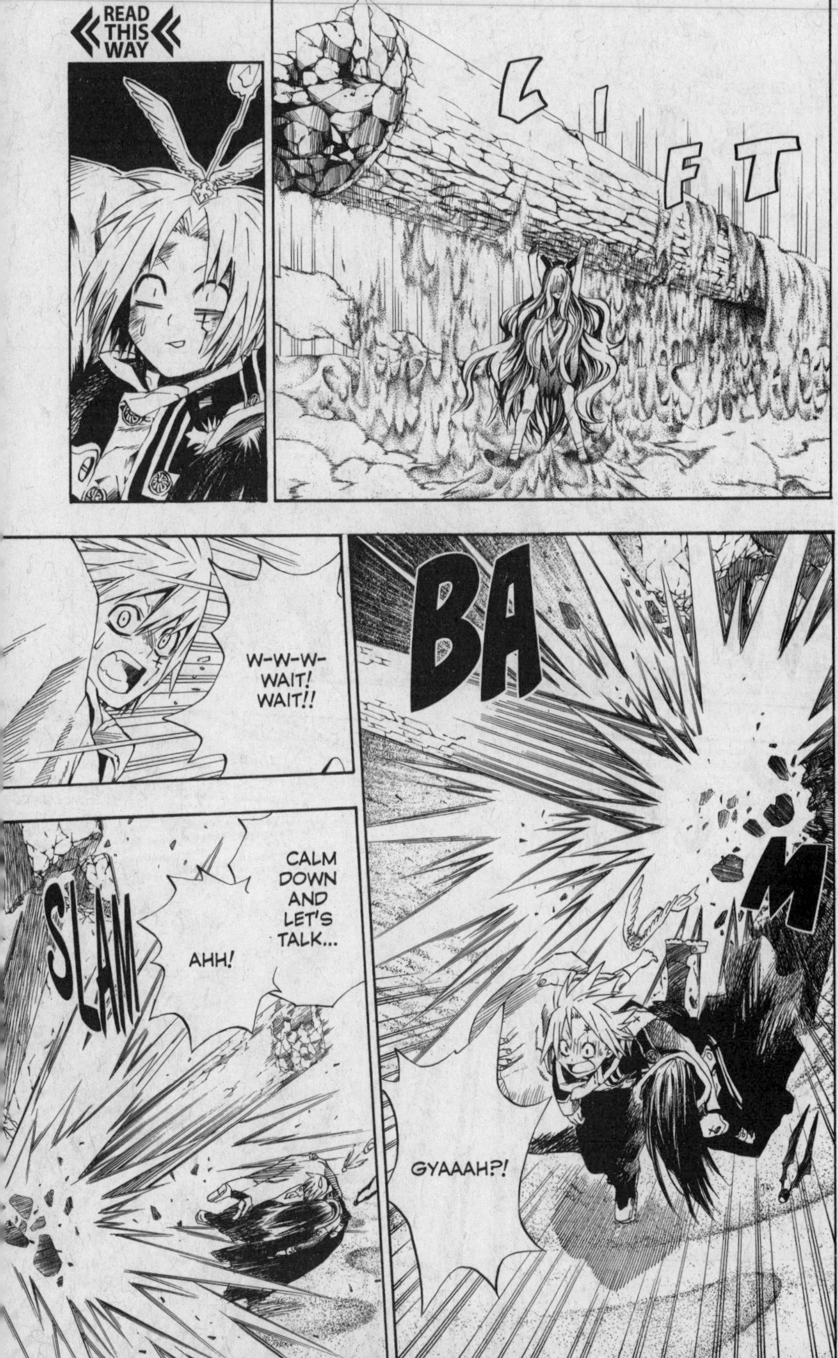
LIFT
BAM
GYAAAH?!
W-W-W-WAIT! WAIT!!
CALM DOWN AND LET'S TALK...
AHH!
SLAM

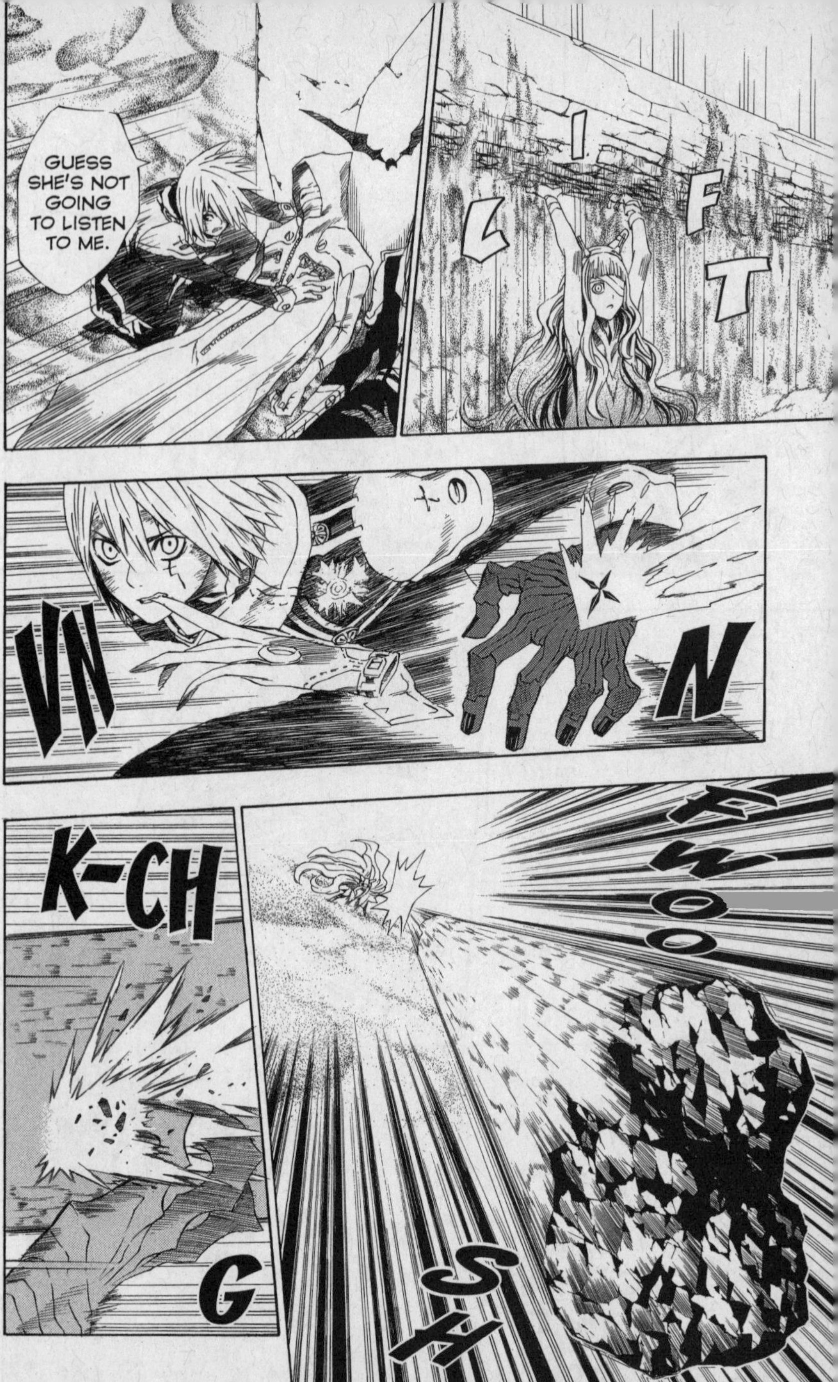

LIFT
GUESS SHE'S NOT GOING TO LISTEN TO ME.
VN
N
FWOOSH
K-CH
G

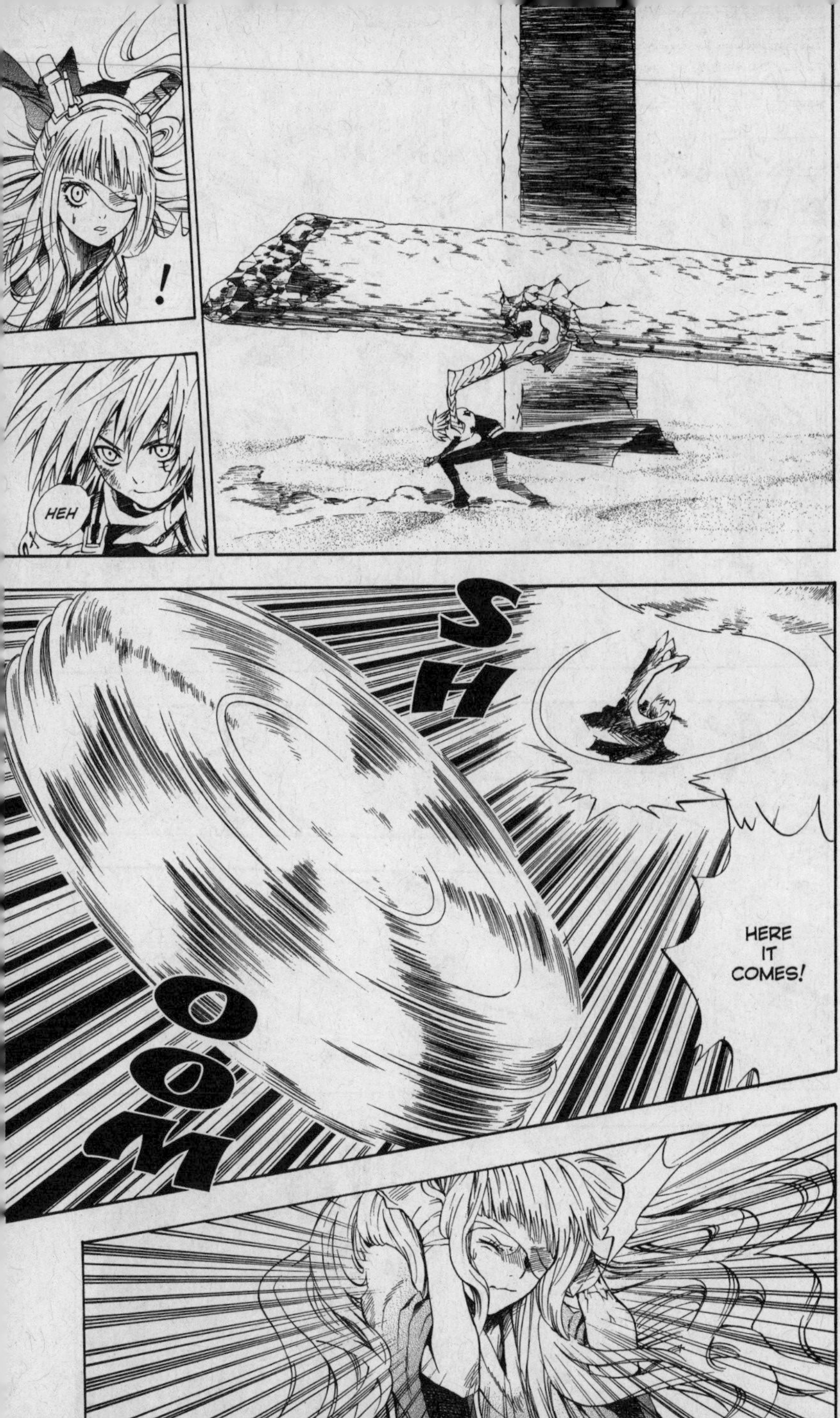
!
HEH
SHOOM
HERE IT COMES!

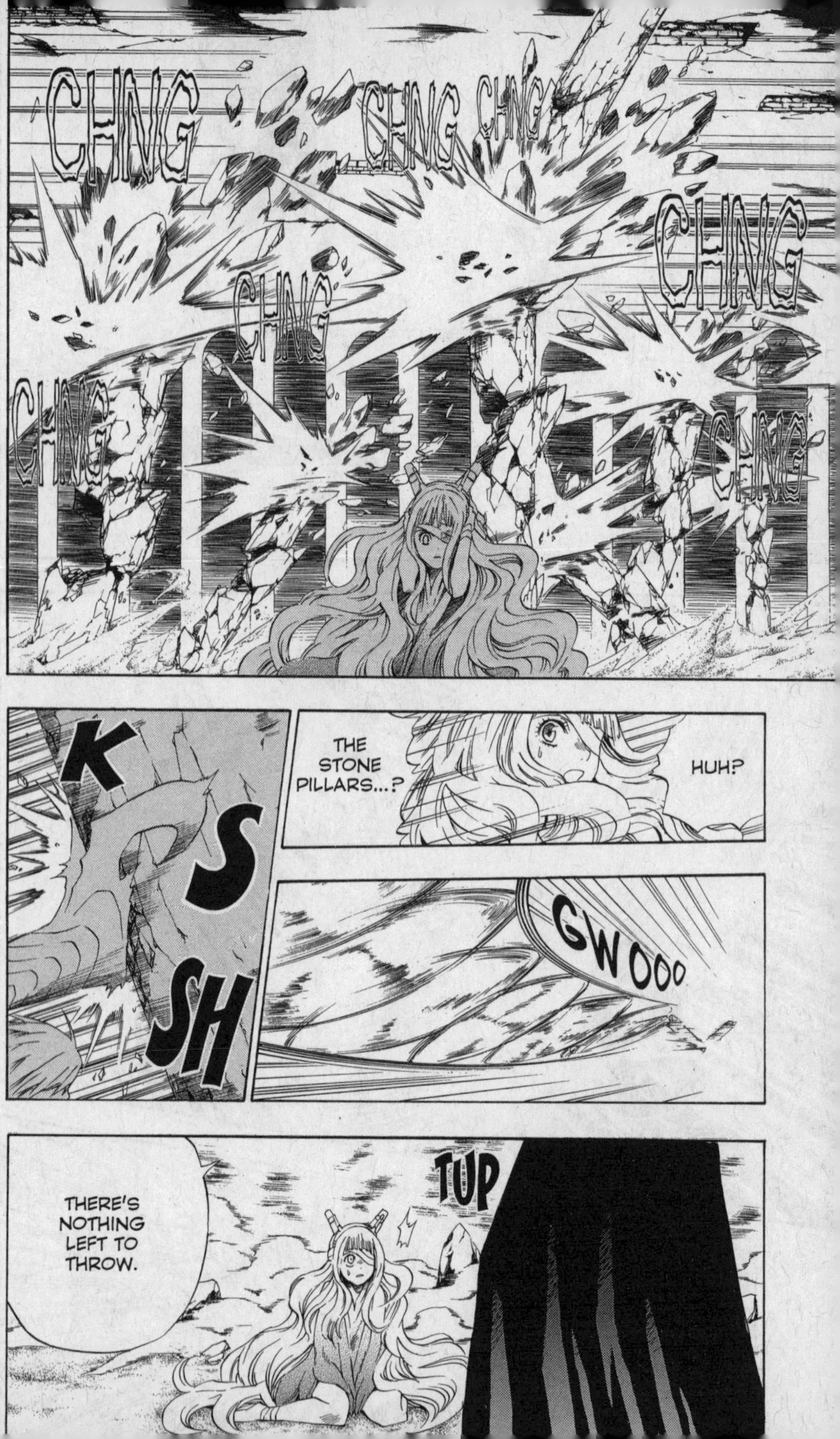
CHING
CHING
CHING
CHING
CHING
CHING
CHING
HUH?
THE STONE PILLARS...?
GWOOO
KSSH
TUP
THERE'S NOTHING LEFT TO THROW.

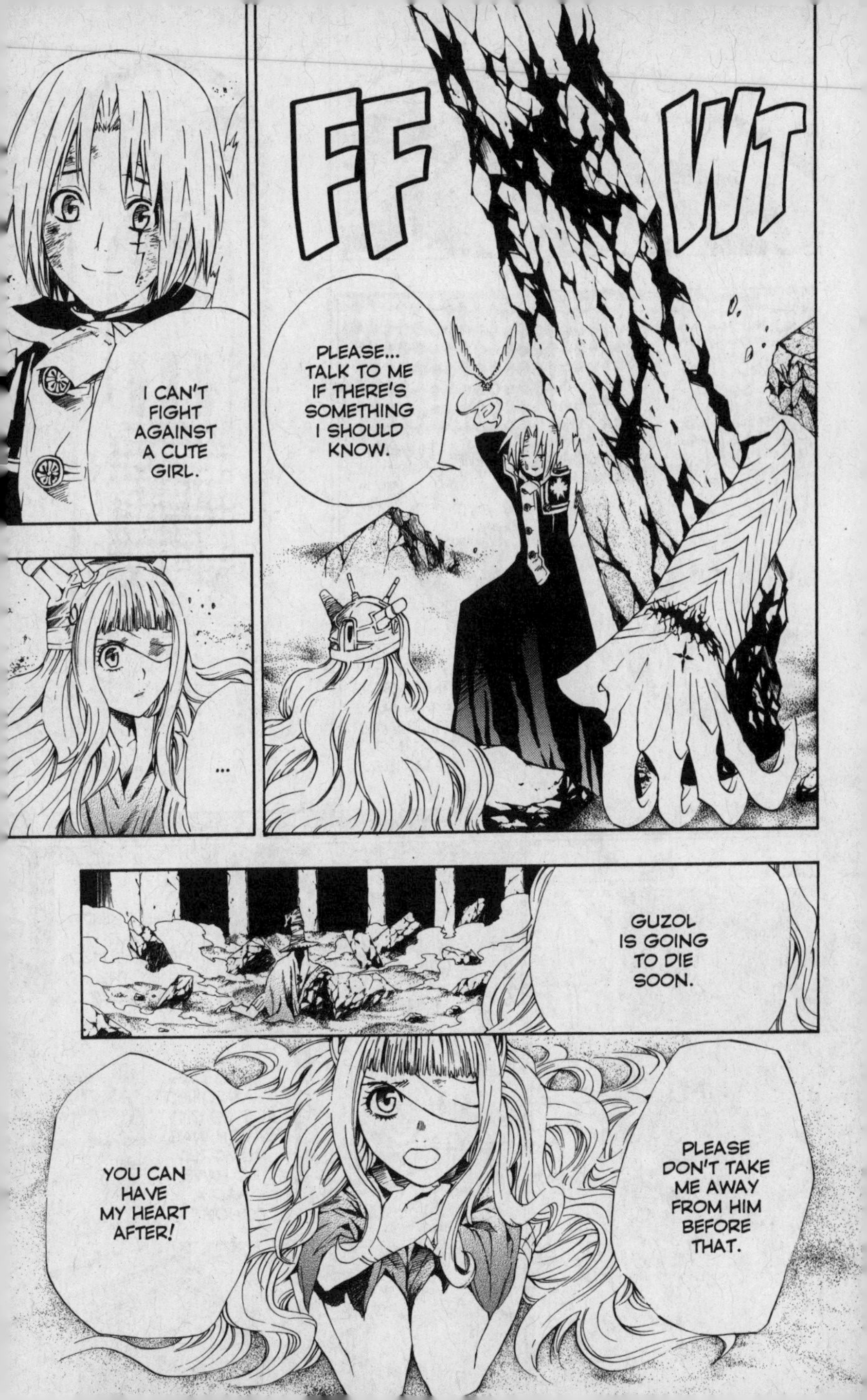

FFWT
PLEASE... TALK TO ME IF THERE'S SOMETHING I SHOULD KNOW.
I CAN'T FIGHT AGAINST A CUTE GIRL.
...
GUZOL IS GOING TO DIE SOON.
PLEASE DON'T TAKE ME AWAY FROM HIM BEFORE THAT.
YOU CAN HAVE MY HEART AFTER!

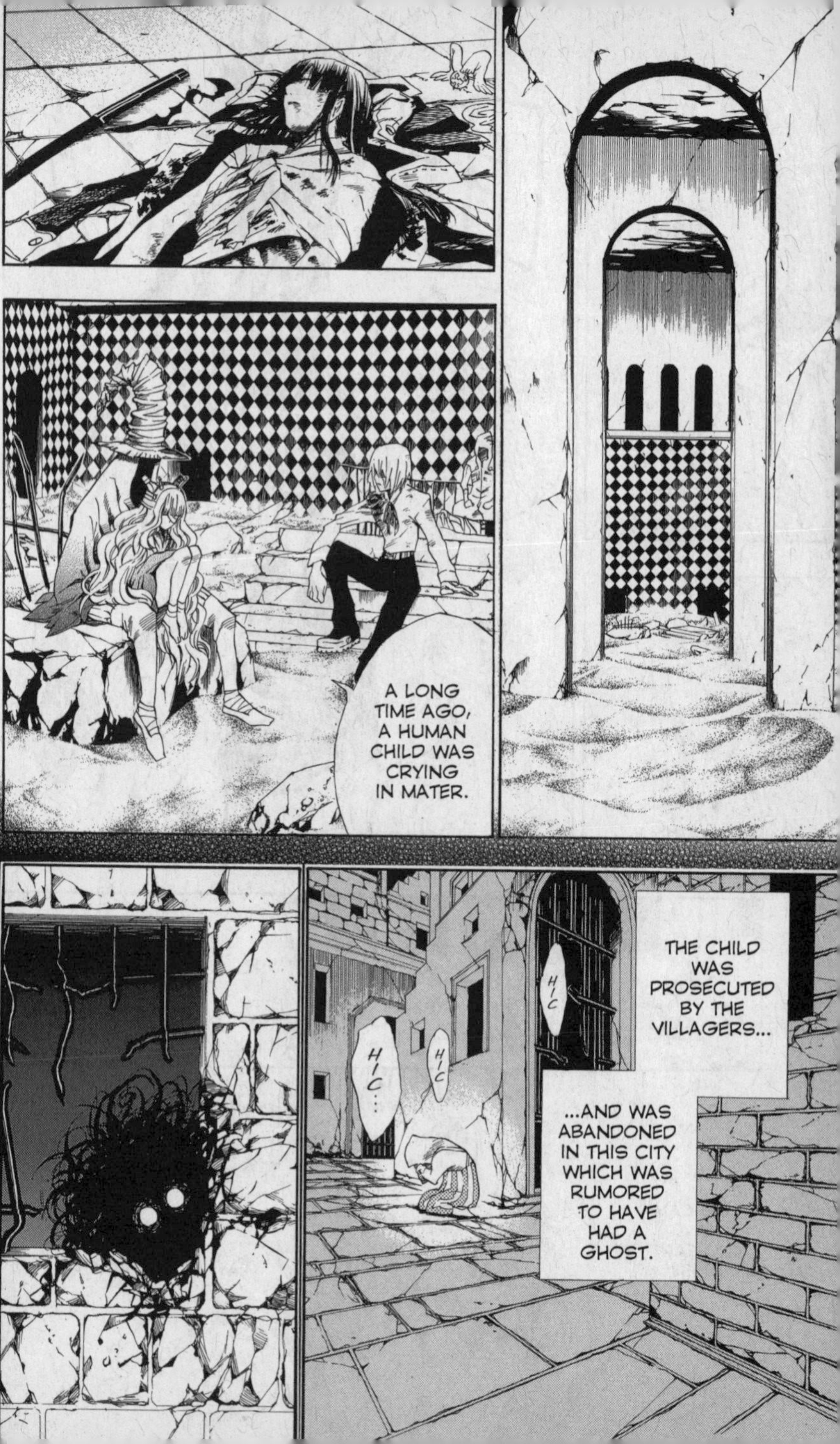
A LONG TIME AGO, A HUMAN CHILD WAS CRYING IN MATER.
THE CHILD WAS PROSECUTED BY THE VILLAGERS...
HIC
HIC
HIC...
...AND WAS ABANDONED IN THIS CITY WHICH WAS RUMORED TO HAVE HAD A GHOST.

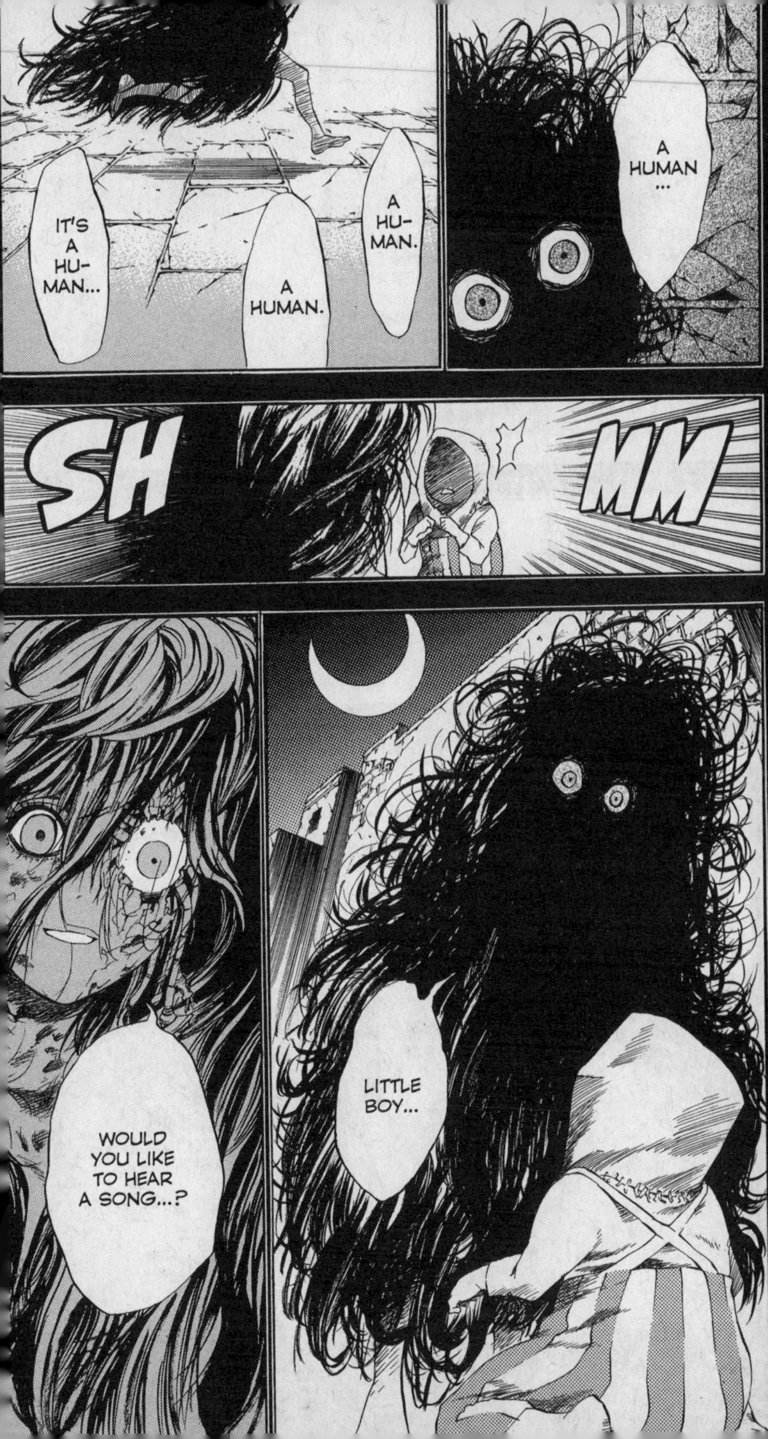
A HUMAN ...
A HU- MAN.
A HUMAN.
IT'S A HU- MAN...
SH MM
LITTLE BOY...
WOULD YOU LIKE TO HEAR A SONG...?

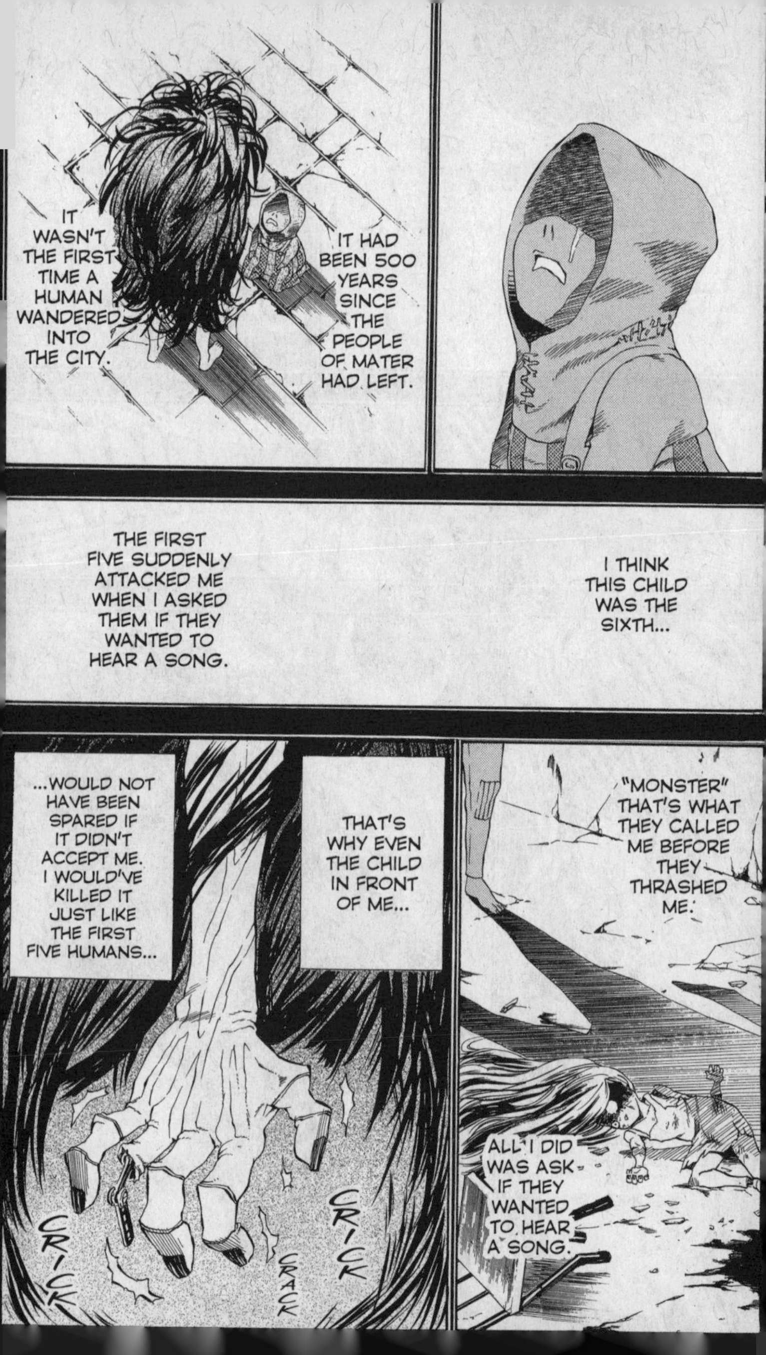
IT HAD BEEN 500 YEARS SINCE THE PEOPLE OF MATER HAD LEFT.
IT WASN'T THE FIRST TIME A HUMAN WANDERED INTO THE CITY.
I THINK THIS CHILD WAS THE SIXTH...
THE FIRST FIVE SUDDENLY ATTACKED ME WHEN I ASKED THEM IF THEY WANTED TO HEAR A SONG.
"MONSTER" THAT'S WHAT THEY CALLED ME BEFORE THEY THRASHED ME.
ALL I DID WAS ASK IF THEY WANTED TO HEAR A SONG.
THAT'S WHY EVEN THE CHILD IN FRONT OF ME...
...WOULD NOT HAVE BEEN SPARED IF IT DIDN'T ACCEPT ME. I WOULD'VE KILLED IT JUST LIKE THE FIRST FIVE HUMANS...
CRICK
CRACK
CRICK

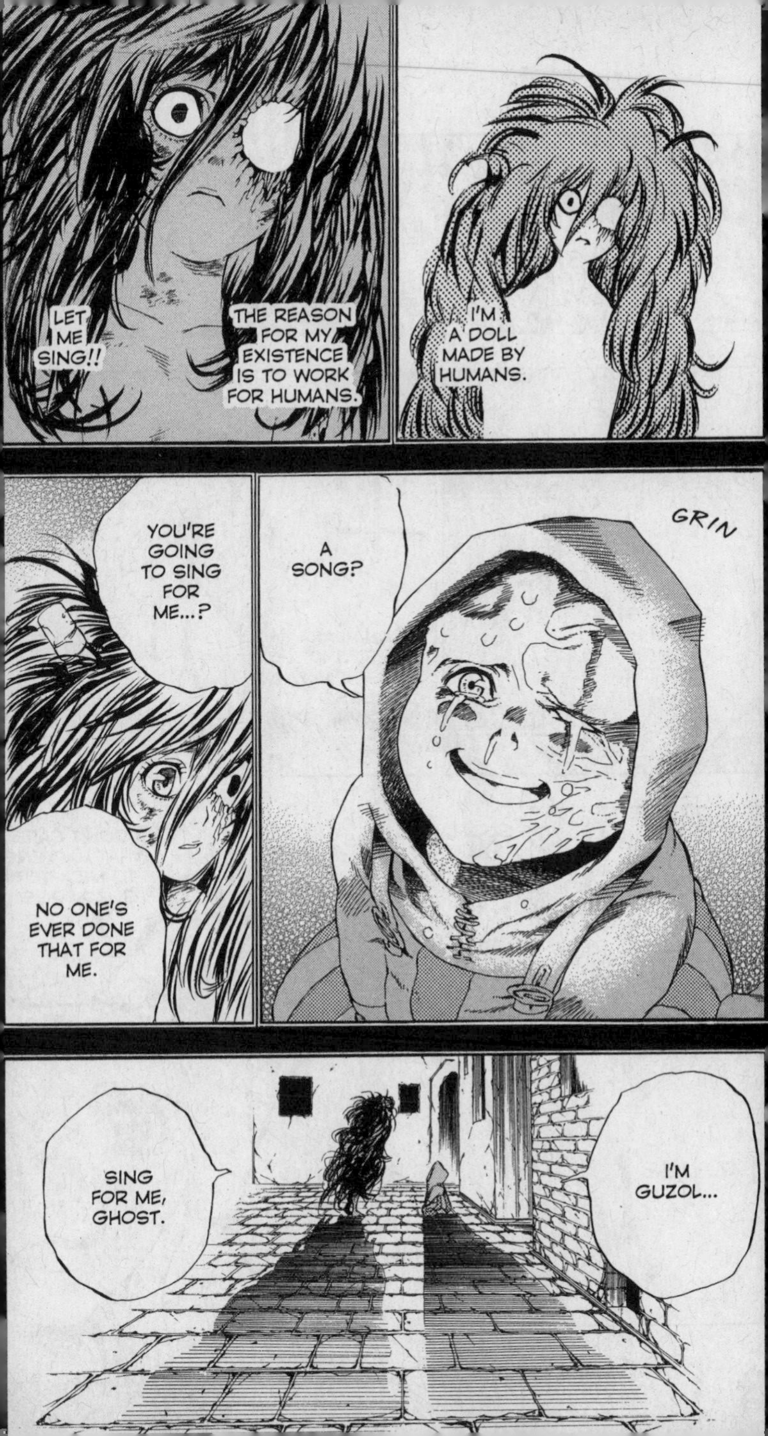

I'M A DOLL MADE BY HUMANS.
THE REASON FOR MY EXISTENCE IS TO WORK FOR HUMANS.
LET ME SING!!
GRIN
A SONG?
YOU'RE GOING TO SING FOR ME...?
NO ONE'S EVER DONE THAT FOR ME.
I'M GUZOL...
SING FOR ME, GHOST.

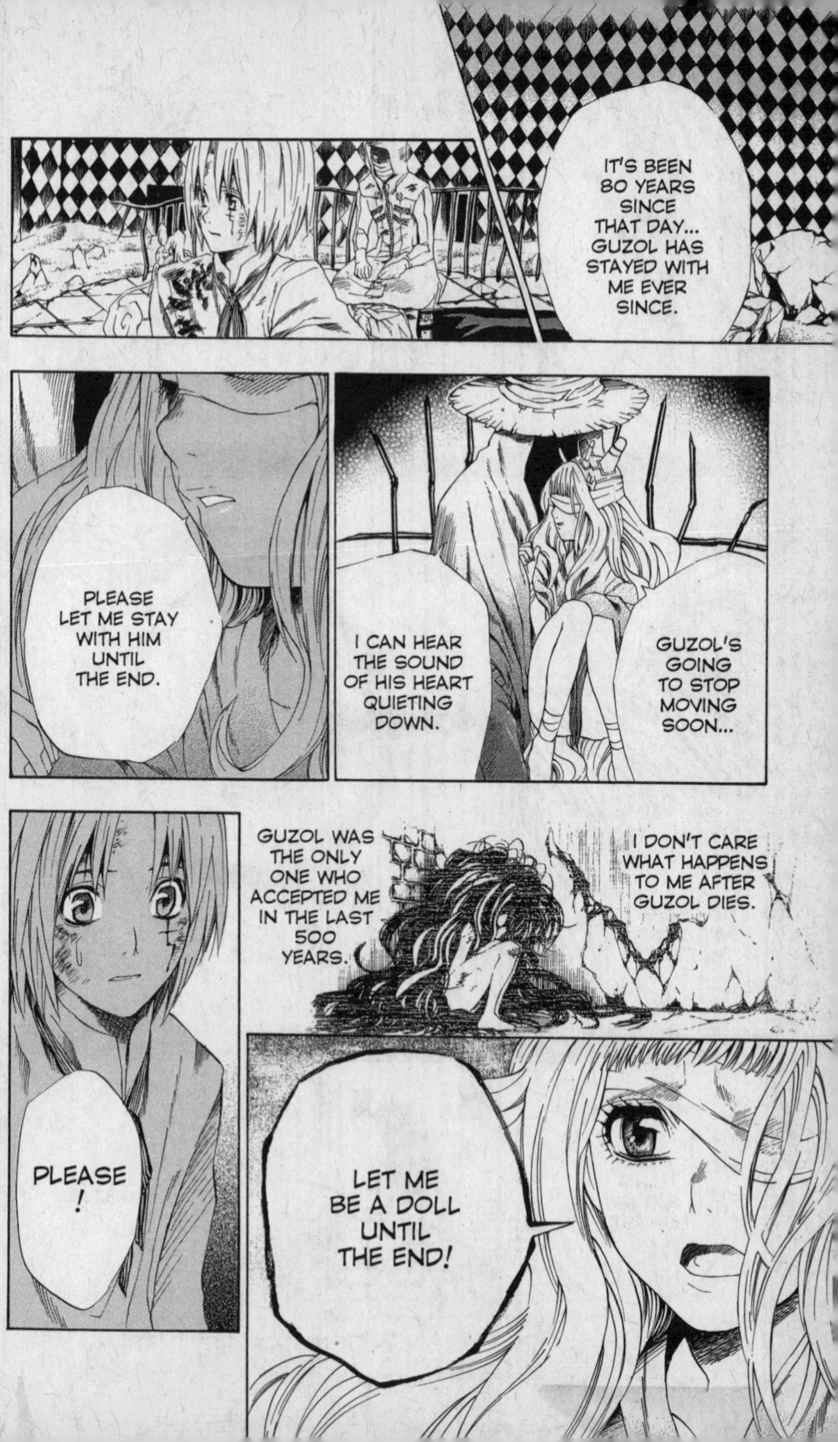
IT'S BEEN 80 YEARS SINCE THAT DAY... GUZOL HAS STAYED WITH ME EVER SINCE.
GUZOL'S GOING TO STOP MOVING SOON...
I CAN HEAR THE SOUND OF HIS HEART QUIETING DOWN.
PLEASE LET ME STAY WITH HIM UNTIL THE END.
I DON'T CARE WHAT HAPPENS TO ME AFTER GUZOL DIES.
GUZOL WAS THE ONLY ONE WHO ACCEPTED ME IN THE LAST 500 YEARS.
LET ME BE A DOLL UNTIL THE END!
PLEASE!

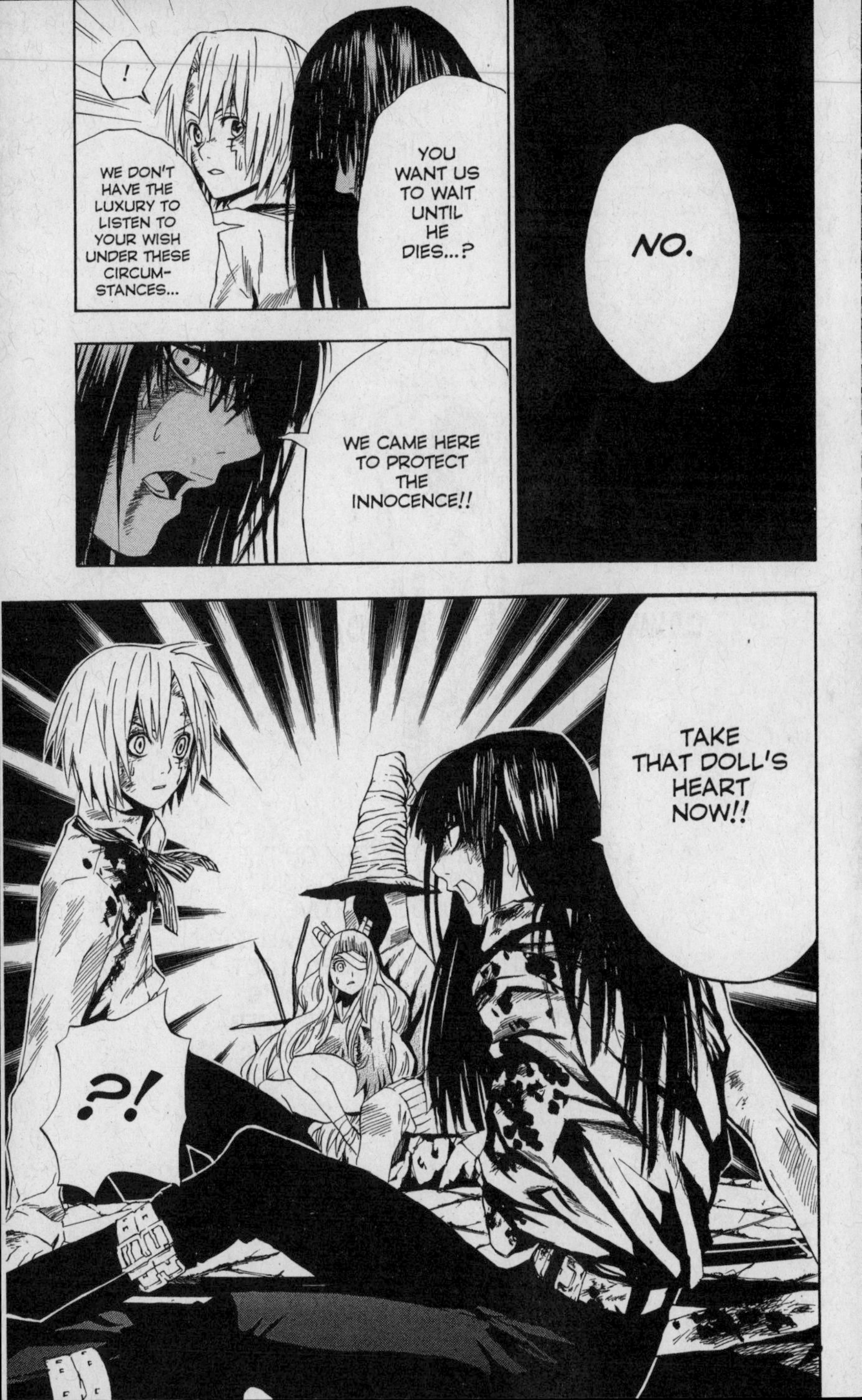
NO.
YOU WANT US TO WAIT UNTIL HE DIES...?
!
WE DON'T HAVE THE LUXURY TO LISTEN TO YOUR WISH UNDER THESE CIRCUM- STANCES...
WE CAME HERE TO PROTECT THE INNOCENCE!!
TAKE THAT DOLL'S HEART NOW!!
?!

OLD MAN OF THE LAND   **AND ARIA OF THE NIGHT SKY**

I LOOSELY BASED THIS STORY ON THE
NOH PLAY CALLED "KOI NO OMONI"
(THE HEAVY BURDEN OF LOVE).
IT'S ABOUT AN OLD MAN WHO FALLS
IN LOVE WITH A YOUNG MAIDEN. I GOT
GUZOL'S NAME FROM "KLINGSOR'S
MAGIC GARDEN" FROM WAGNER'S OPERA
"PARSIFAL." LALA IS A SONGSTRESS;
HENCE, LALA.

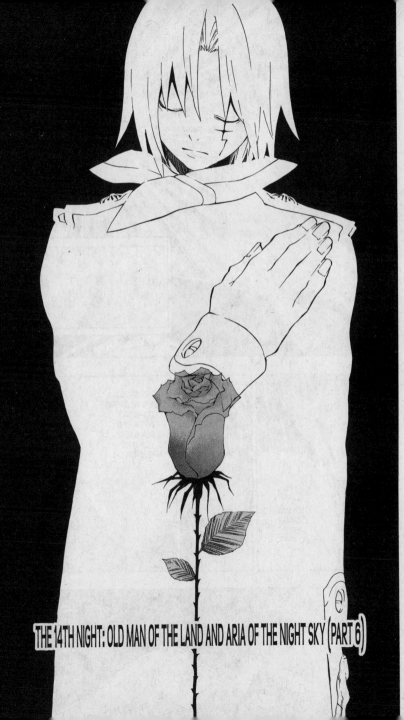

THE 14TH NIGHT: OLD MAN OF THE LAND AND ARIA OF THE NIGHT SKY (PART 6)

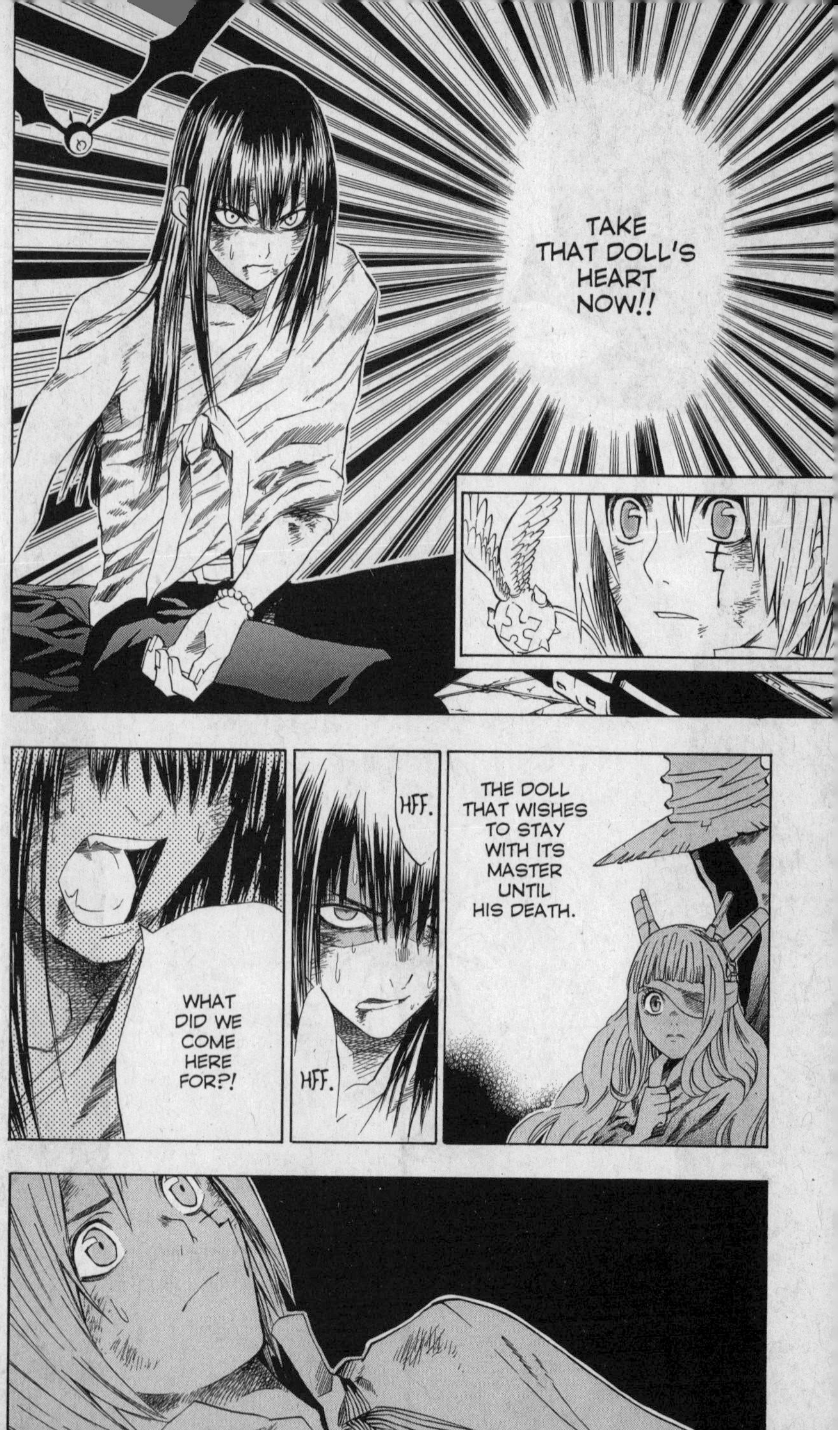
TAKE THAT DOLL'S HEART NOW!!
THE DOLL THAT WISHES TO STAY WITH ITS MASTER UNTIL HIS DEATH.
HFF.
HFF.
WHAT DID WE COME HERE FOR?!

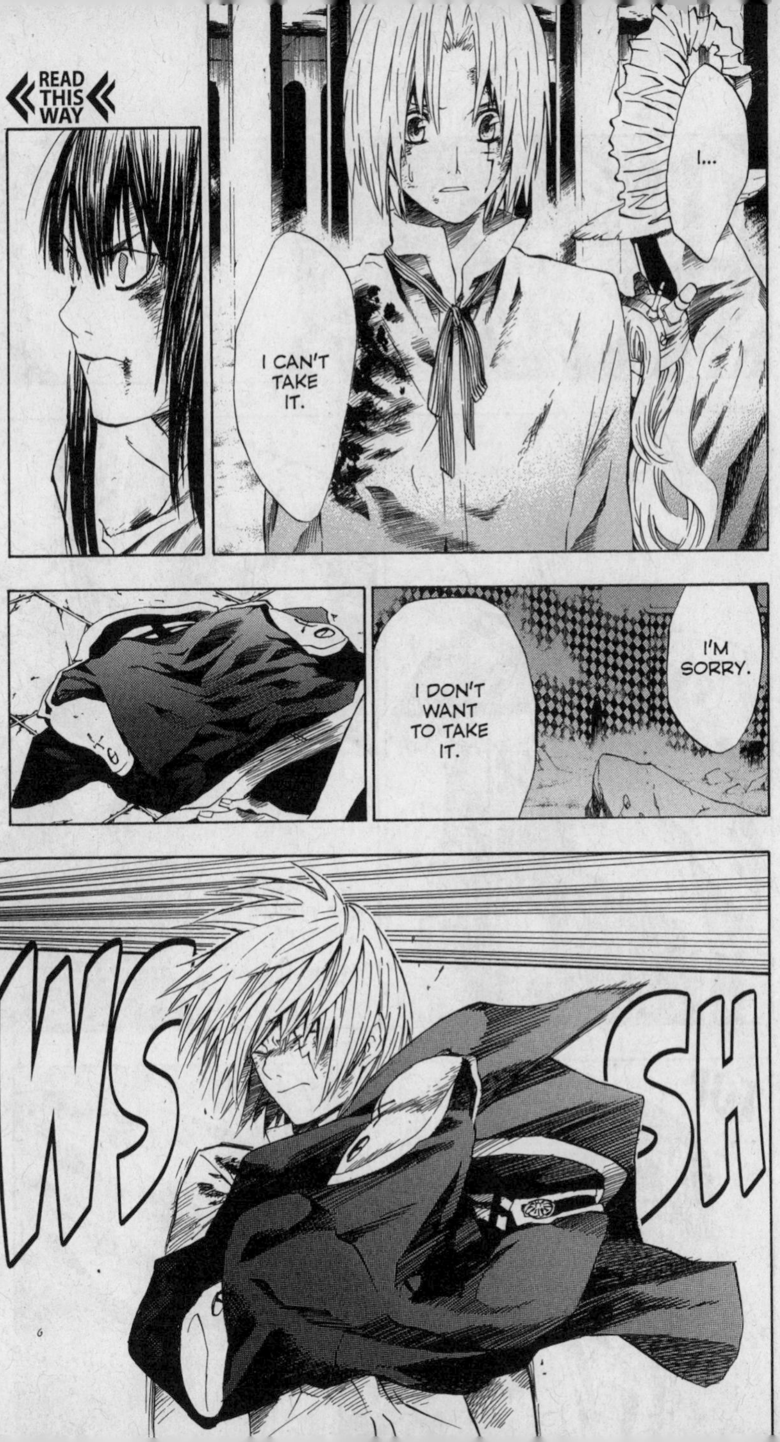
READ THIS WAY
I...
I CAN'T TAKE IT.
I'M SORRY.
I DON'T WANT TO TAKE IT.
WS SH

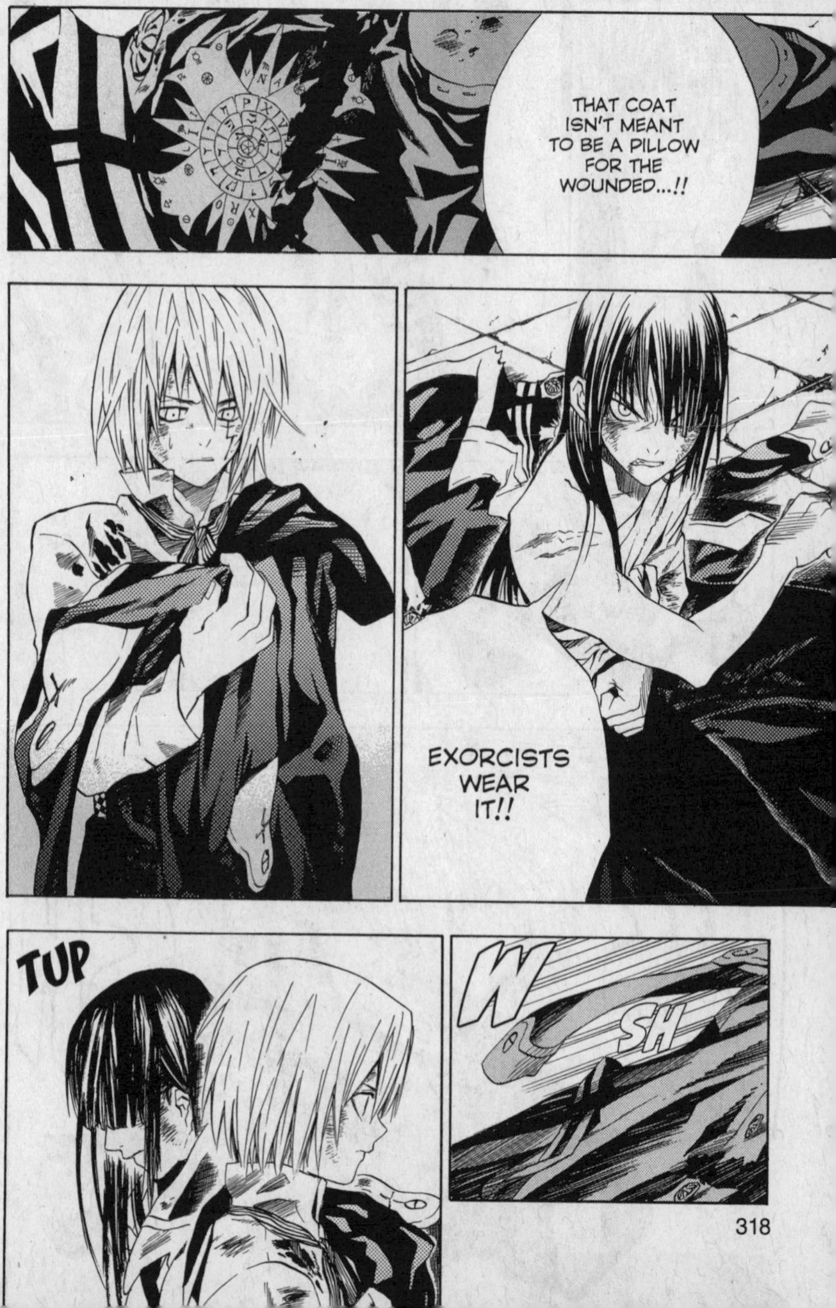
THAT COAT ISN'T MEANT TO BE A PILLOW FOR THE WOUNDED...!!
EXORCISTS WEAR IT!!
WSH
TUP

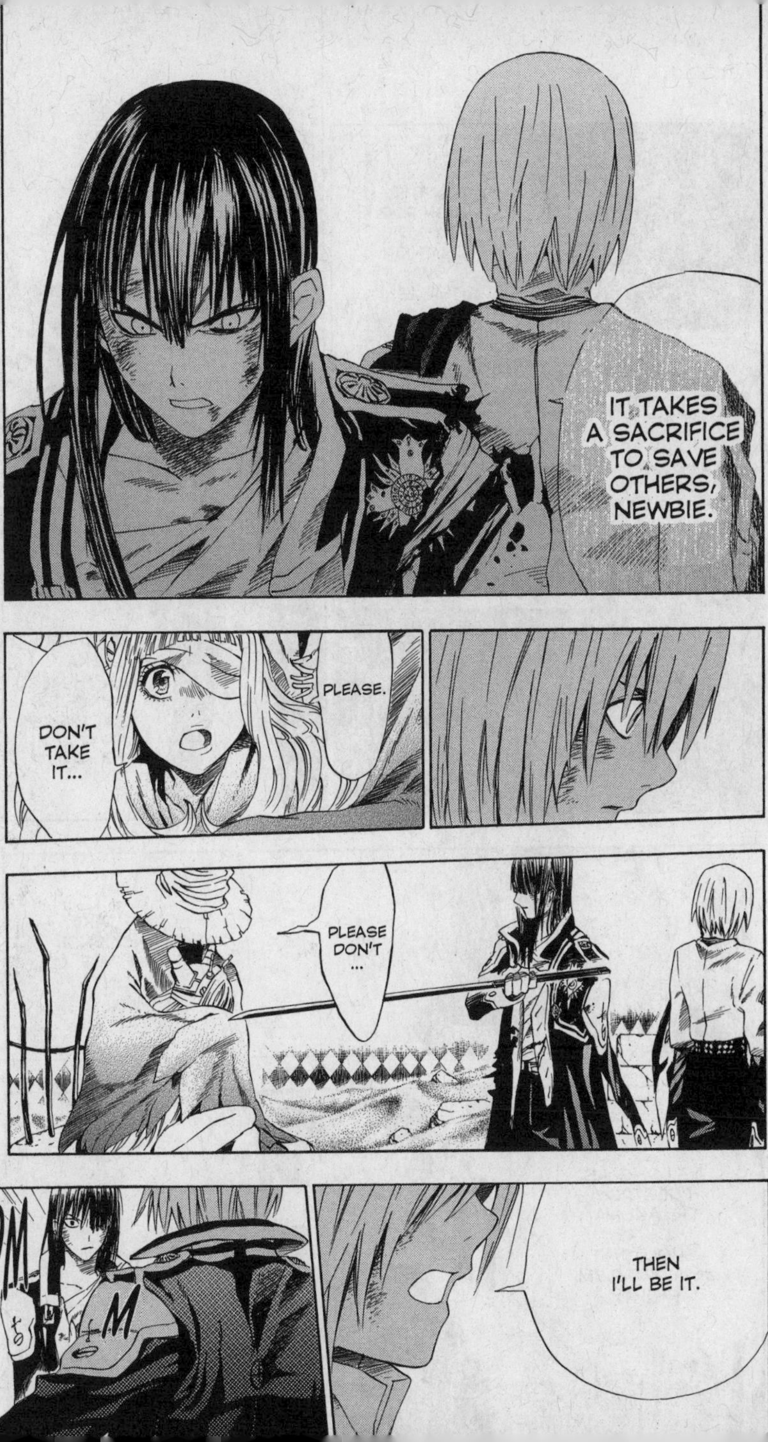
IT TAKES A SACRIFICE TO SAVE OTHERS, NEWBIE.
PLEASE.
DON'T TAKE IT...
PLEASE DON'T ...
THEN I'LL BE IT.
DMM

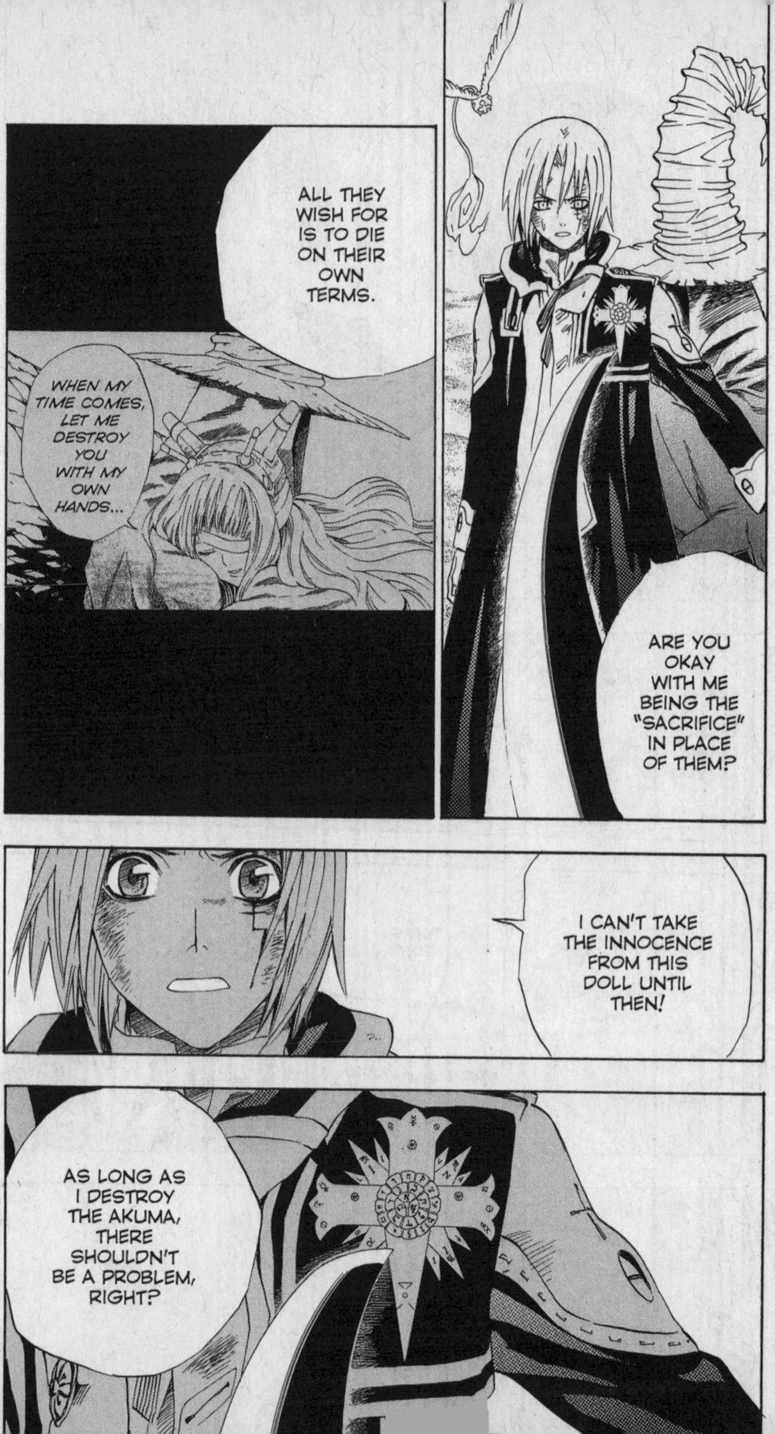
ARE YOU OKAY WITH ME BEING THE "SACRIFICE" IN PLACE OF THEM?
ALL THEY WISH FOR IS TO DIE ON THEIR OWN TERMS.
WHEN MY TIME COMES, LET ME DESTROY YOU WITH MY OWN HANDS...
I CAN'T TAKE THE INNOCENCE FROM THIS DOLL UNTIL THEN!
AS LONG AS I DESTROY THE AKUMA, THERE SHOULDN'T BE A PROBLEM, RIGHT?

READ THIS WAY

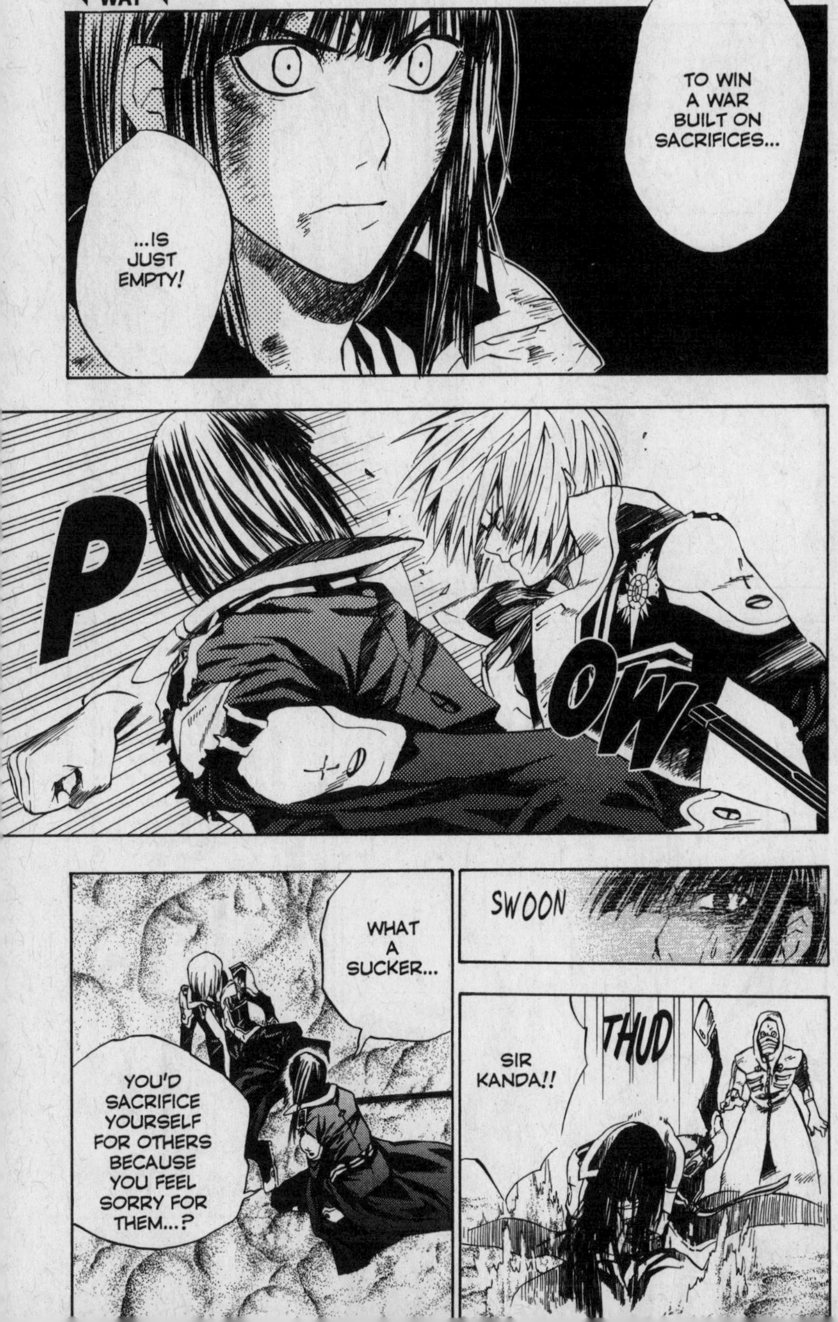
TO WIN A WAR BUILT ON SACRIFICES...
...IS JUST EMPTY!
POW
SWOON
THUD
SIR KANDA!!
WHAT A SUCKER...
YOU'D SACRIFICE YOURSELF FOR OTHERS BECAUSE YOU FEEL SORRY FOR THEM...?

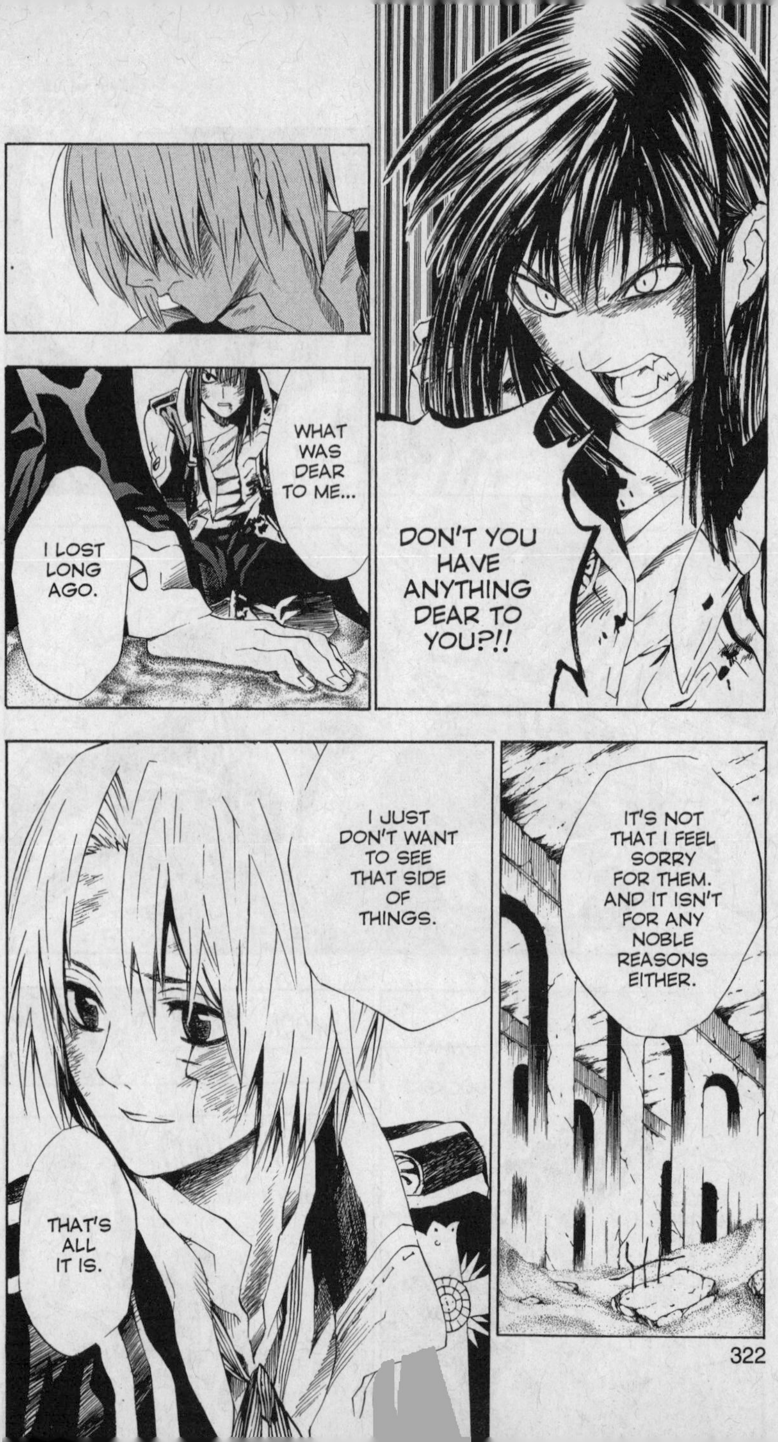
DON'T YOU HAVE ANYTHING DEAR TO YOU?!!
WHAT WAS DEAR TO ME...
I LOST LONG AGO.
IT'S NOT THAT I FEEL SORRY FOR THEM. AND IT ISN'T FOR ANY NOBLE REASONS EITHER.
I JUST DON'T WANT TO SEE THAT SIDE OF THINGS.
THAT'S ALL IT IS.

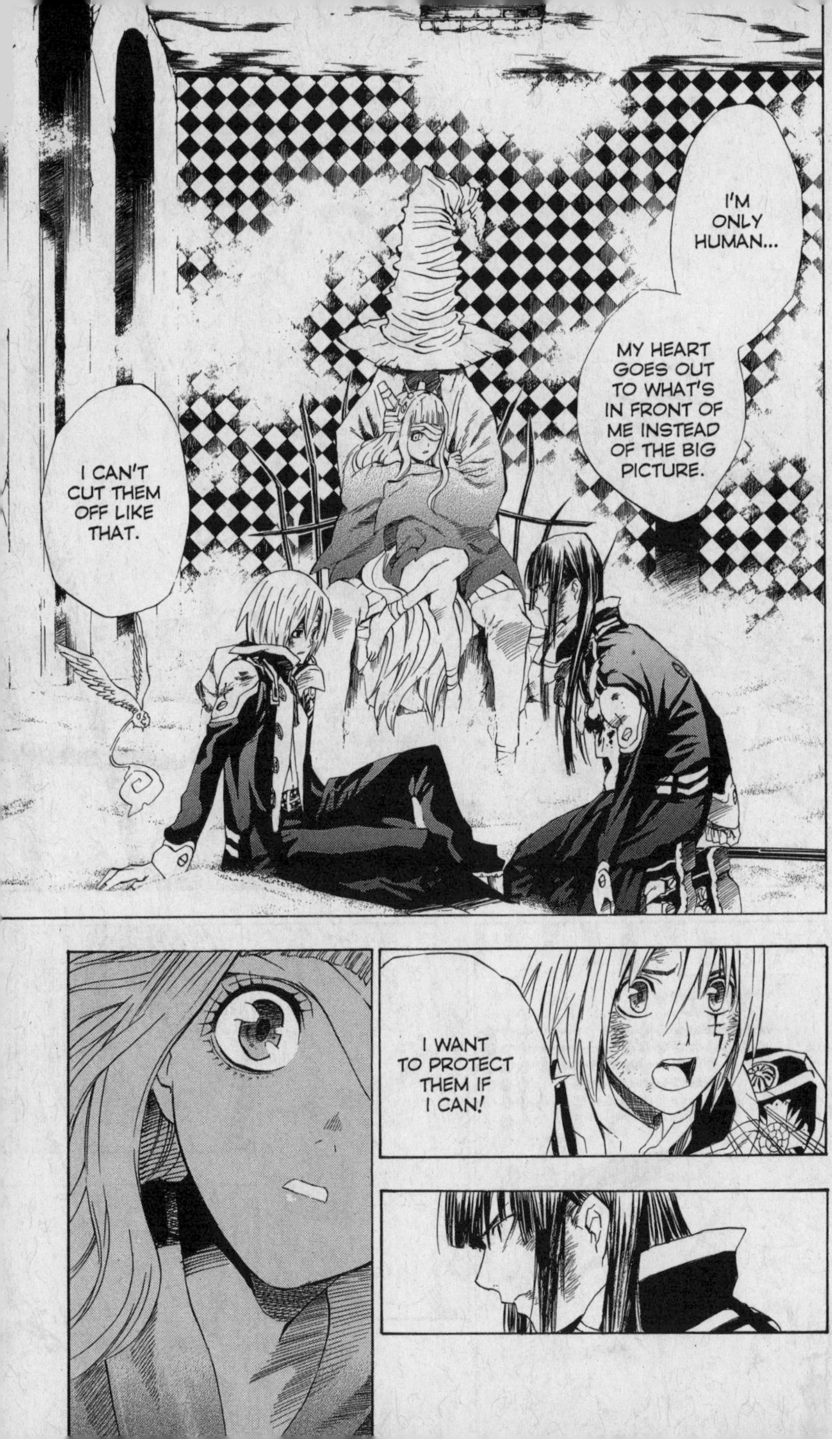
I'M ONLY HUMAN...
MY HEART GOES OUT TO WHAT'S IN FRONT OF ME INSTEAD OF THE BIG PICTURE.
I CAN'T CUT THEM OFF LIKE THAT.
I WANT TO PROTECT THEM IF I CAN!

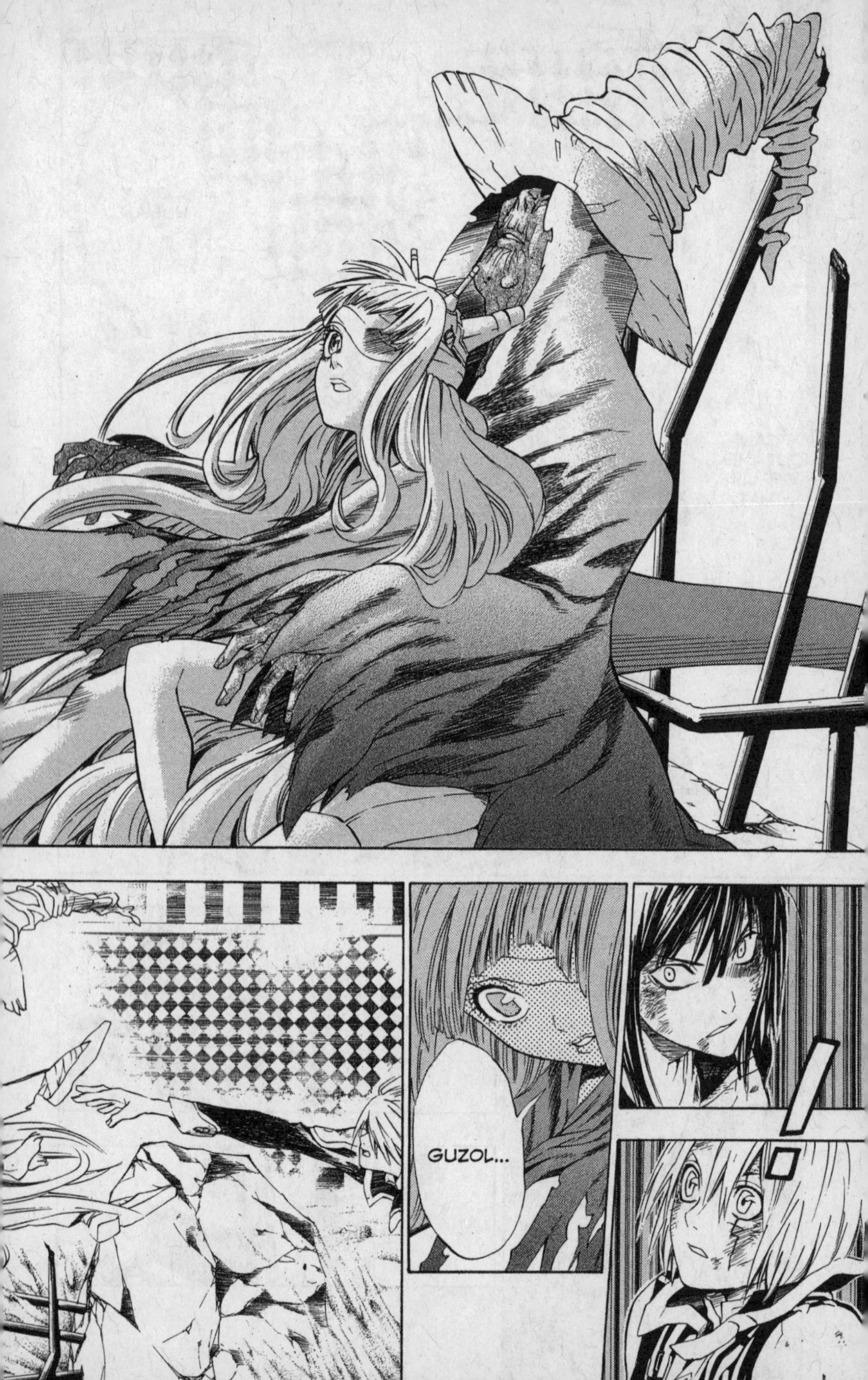
GUZOL...

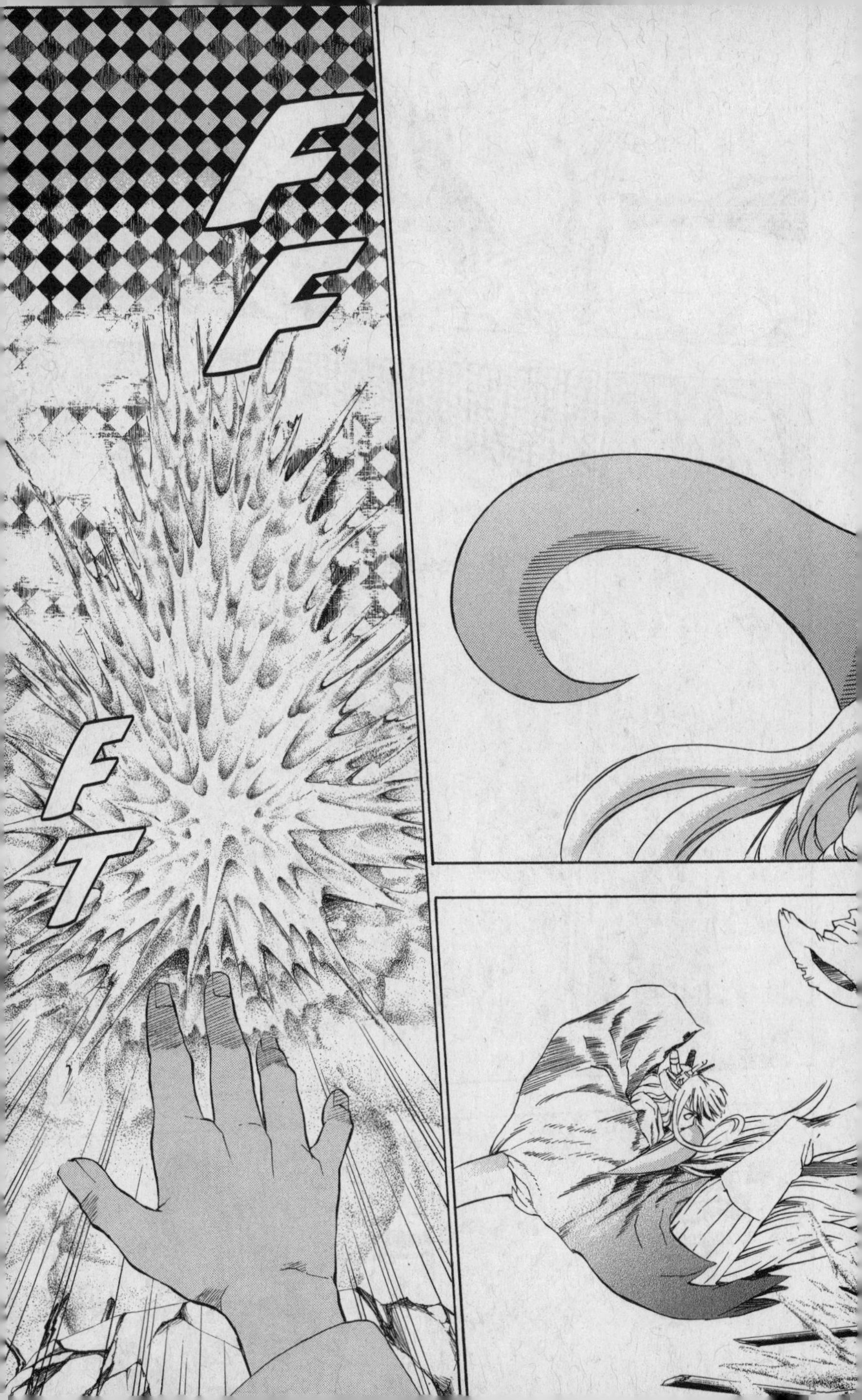
FF
FT

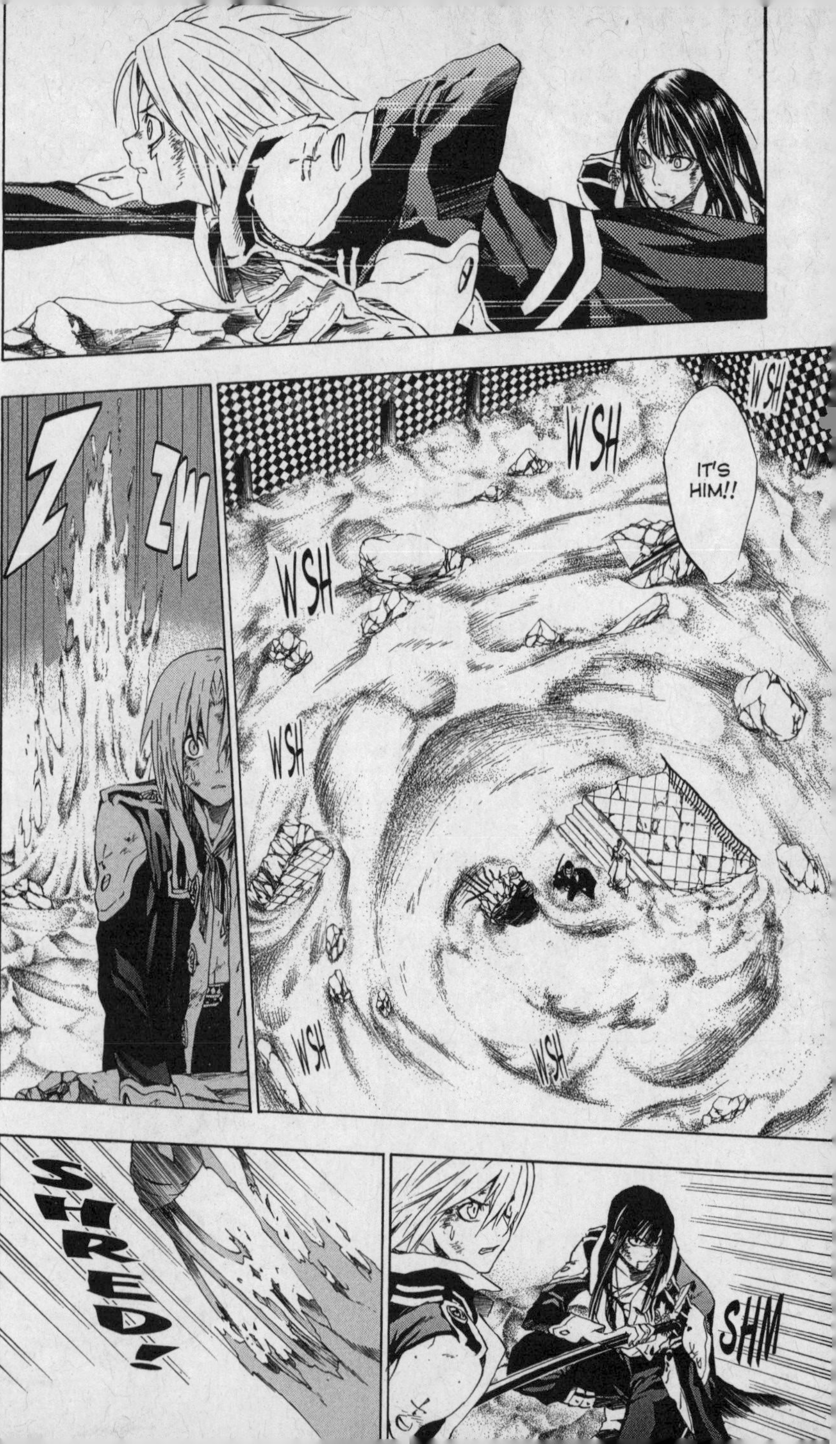

WSH
IT'S HIM!!
WSH
WSH
WSH
WSH
WSH
ZW
Z
SHM
SHRED!

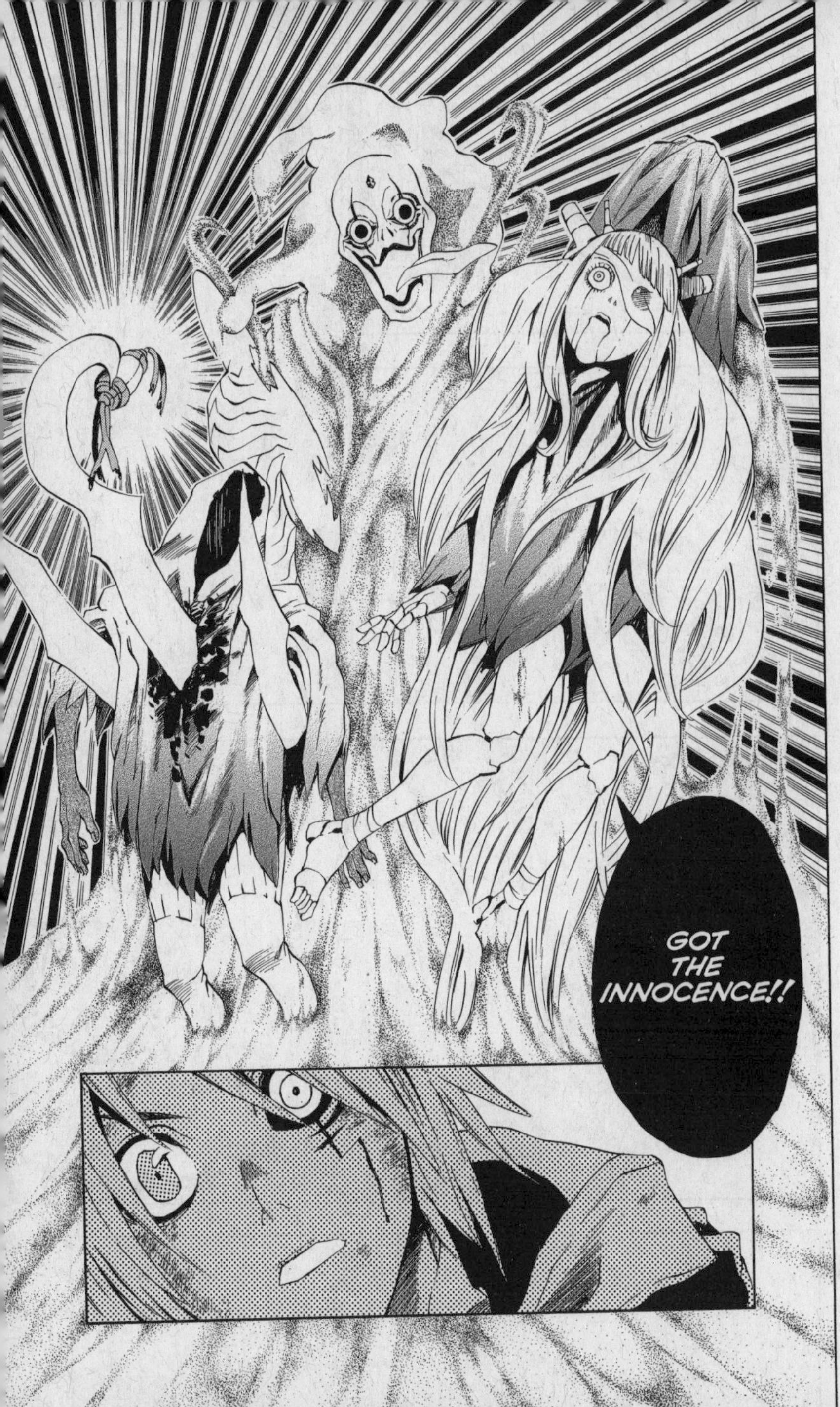
GOT THE INNOCENCE!!

THUD
LA...
LA-LA...
DOZE
LA-LA...
OOOH—
VNN
VNN
VNN
SO THIS IS AN INNOCENCE.
KWSH

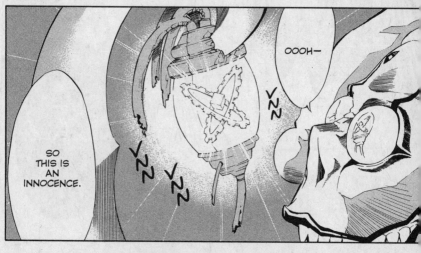

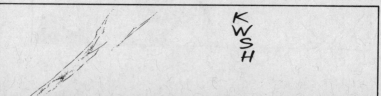

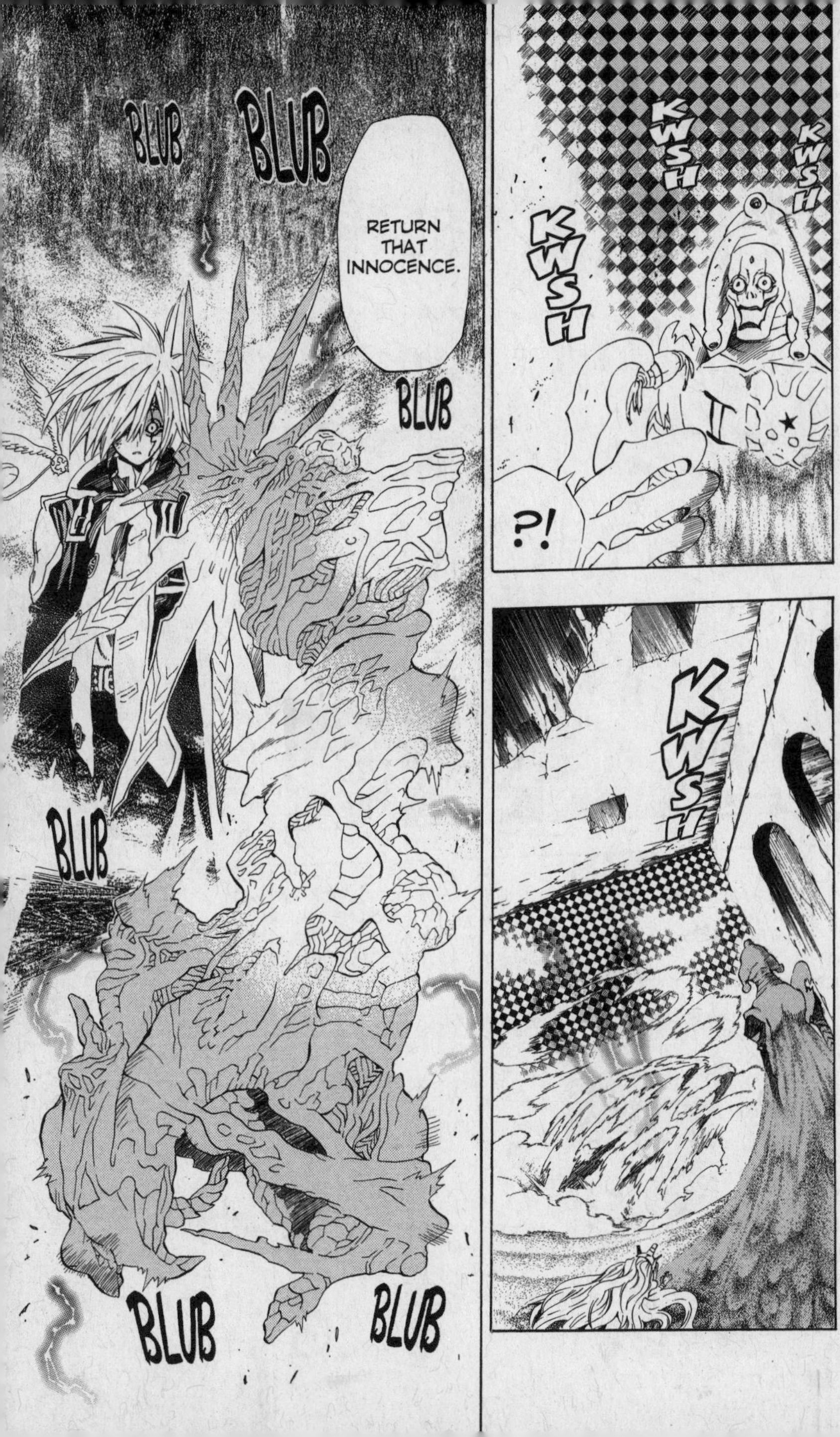
KWSH
KWSH
KWSH
?!
KWSH
RETURN THAT INNOCENCE.
BLUB
BLUB
BLUB
BLUB
BLUB
BLUB

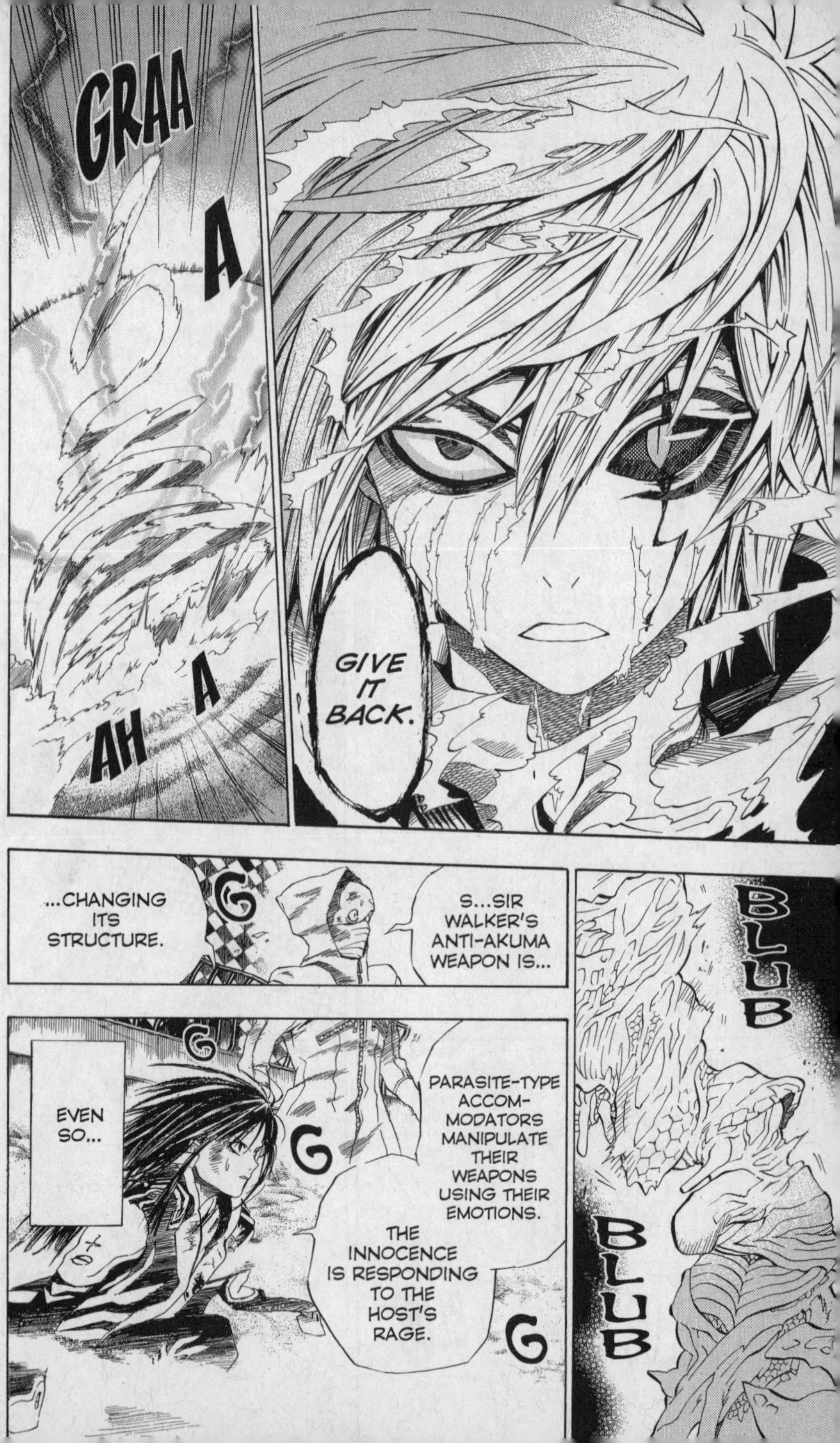
GIVE IT BACK.
GRAA
A
A
AH
BLUB
BLUB
S...SIR WALKER'S ANTI-AKUMA WEAPON IS...
G
...CHANGING ITS STRUCTURE.
G
PARASITE-TYPE ACCOM-MODATORS MANIPULATE THEIR WEAPONS USING THEIR EMOTIONS.
THE INNOCENCE IS RESPONDING TO THE HOST'S RAGE.
G
G
EVEN SO...

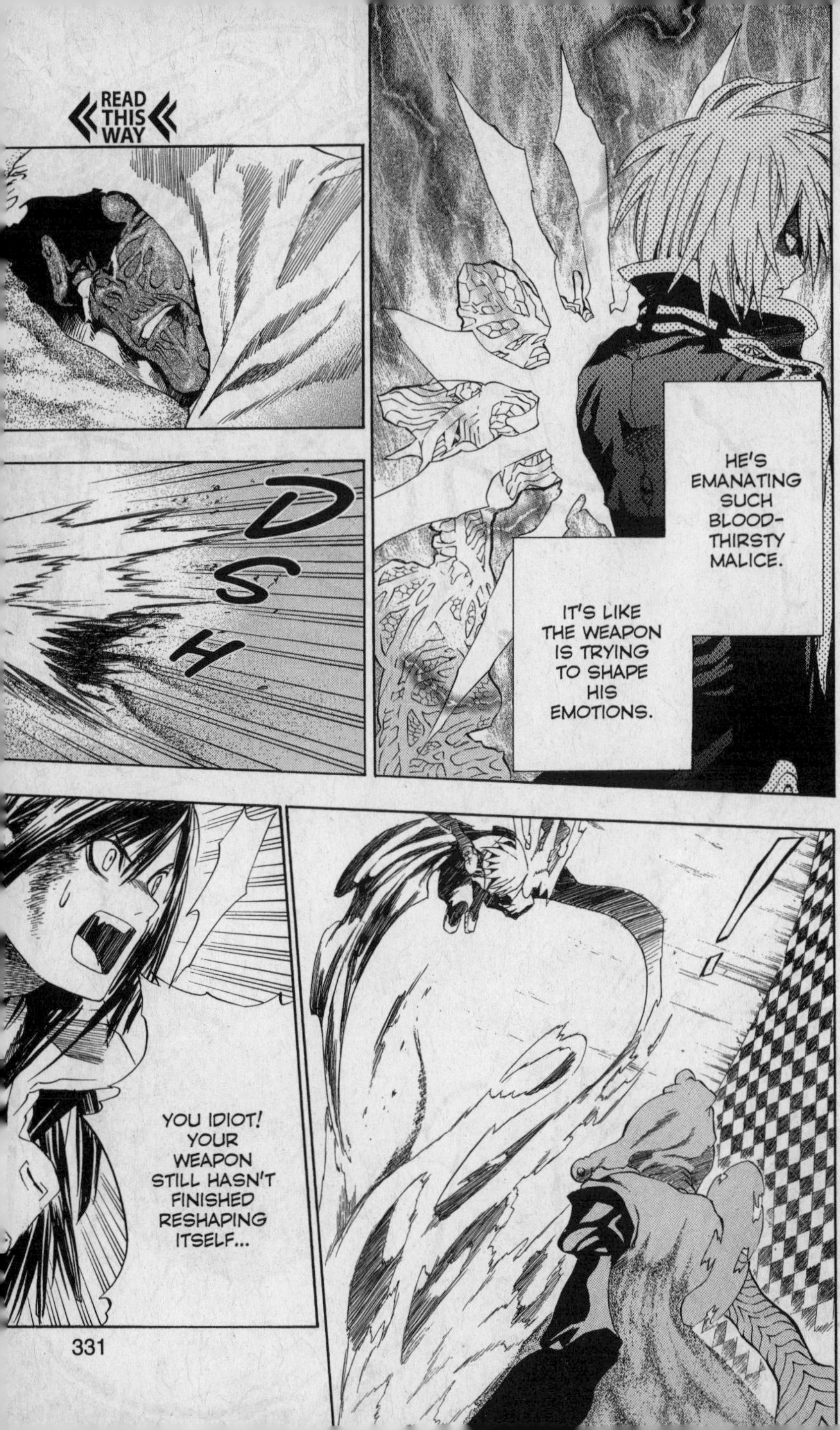
READ THIS WAY
HE'S EMANATING SUCH BLOOD-THIRSTY MALICE.
IT'S LIKE THE WEAPON IS TRYING TO SHAPE HIS EMOTIONS.
DSH
YOU IDIOT! YOUR WEAPON STILL HASN'T FINISHED RESHAPING ITSELF...

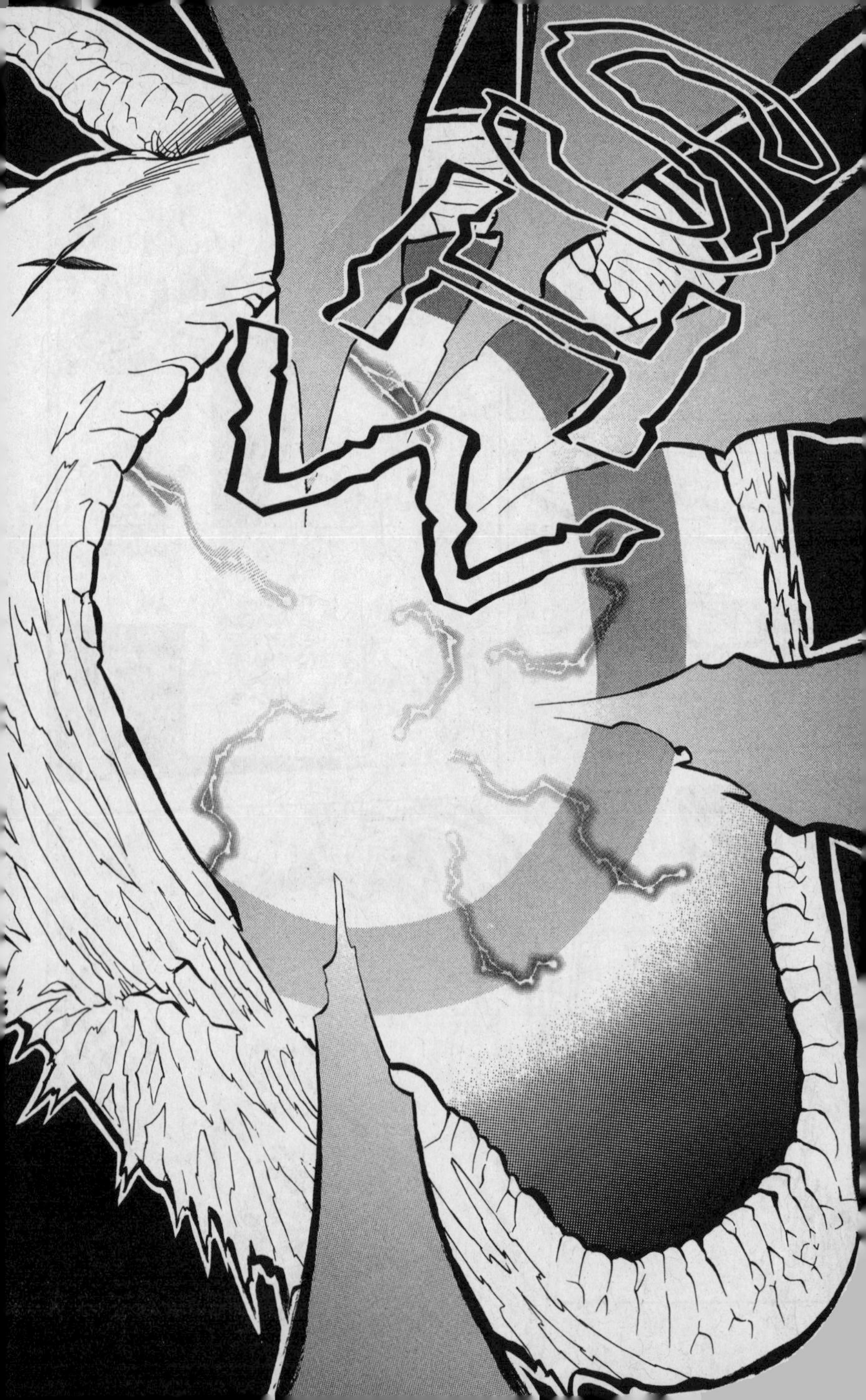

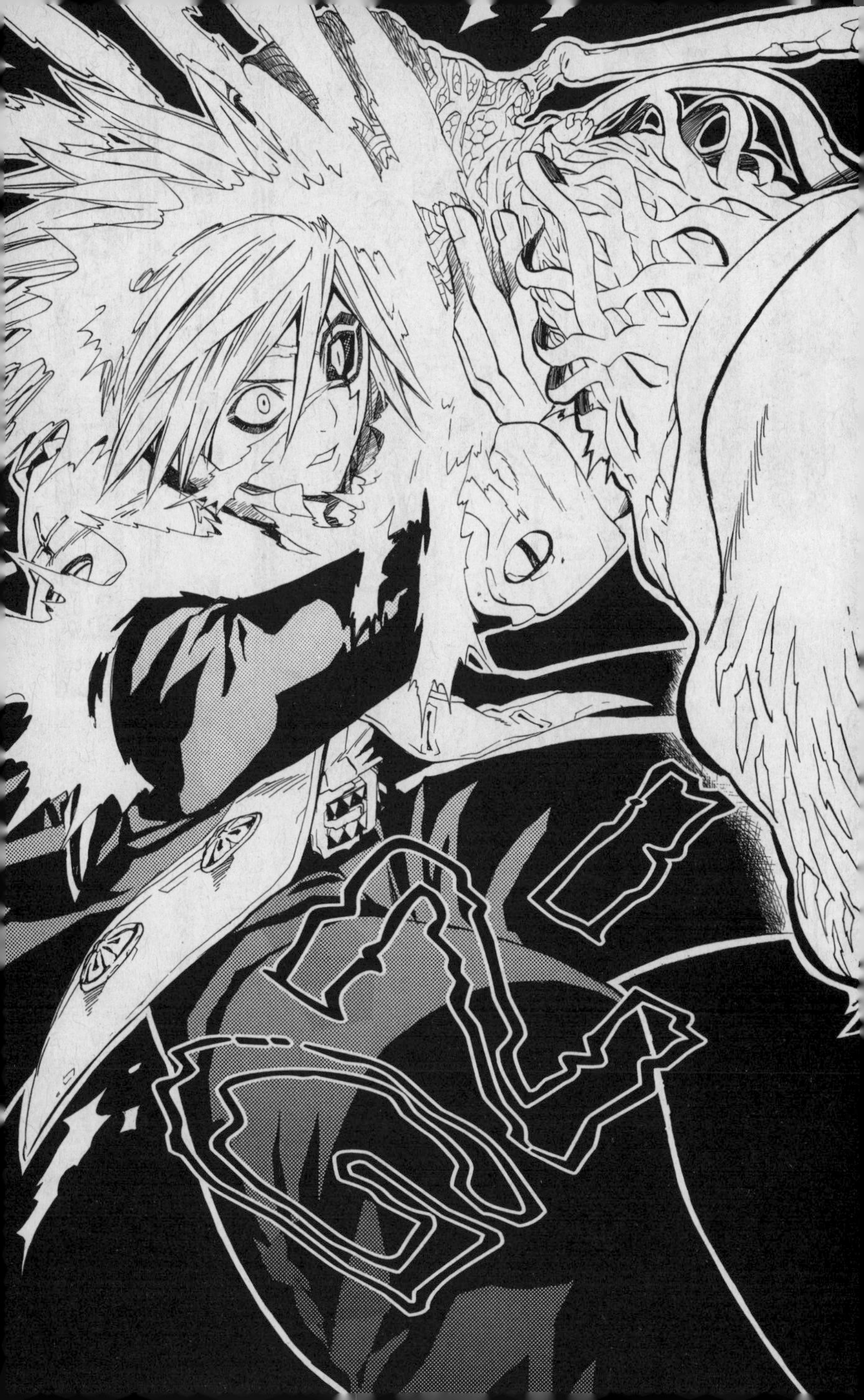

GRAND OPENING!!

READER'S SECTION

KOMUI'S EXPERIMENT ROOM

STARTING NEXT VOLUME—

WE WILL OPEN A READER'S SECTION!

WE'RE GOING TO START OFF WITH THE TWO SECTIONS BELOW!

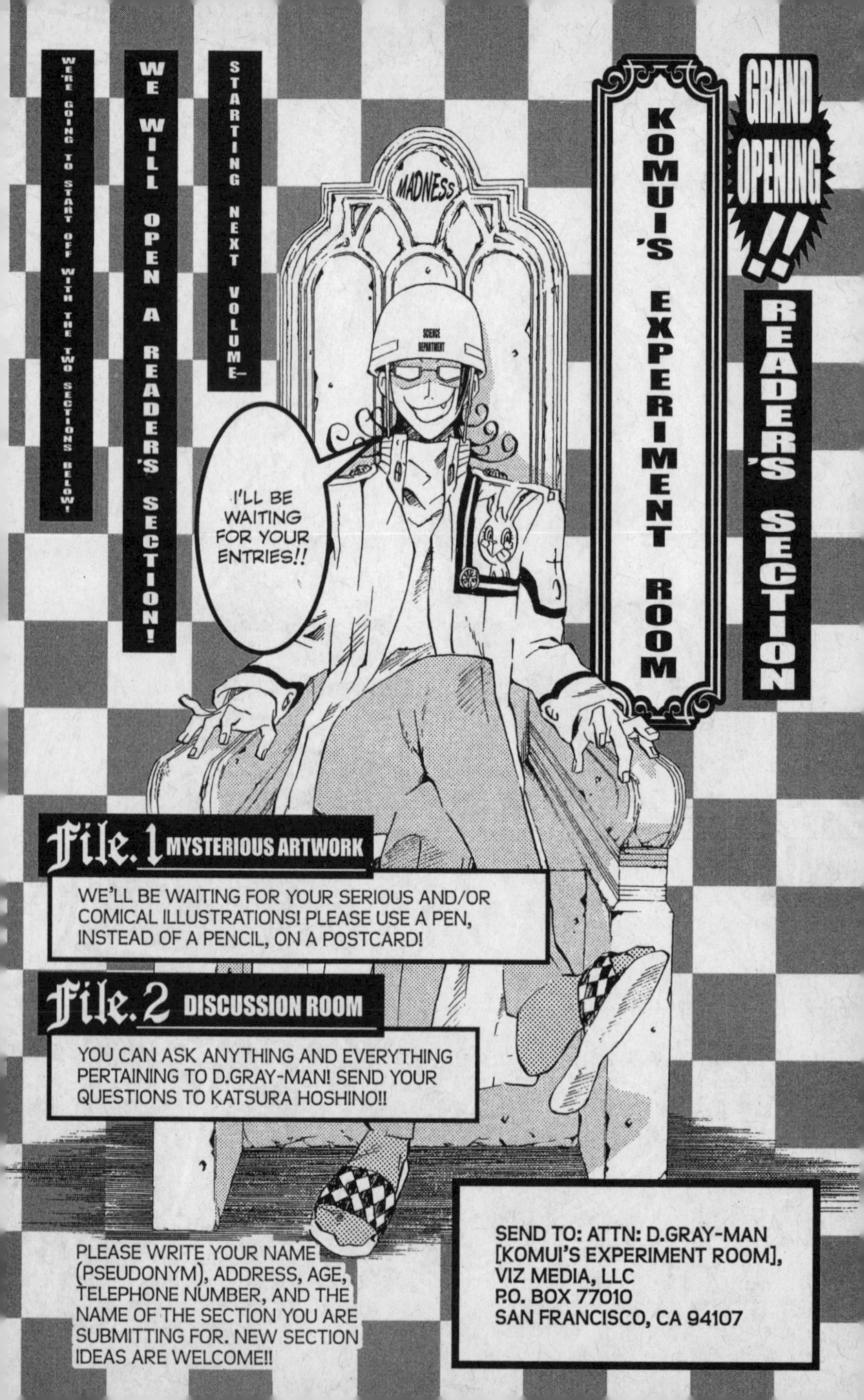
MADNESS
SCIENCE DEPARTMENT
I'LL BE WAITING FOR YOUR ENTRIES!!

File. 1 MYSTERIOUS ARTWORK

WE'LL BE WAITING FOR YOUR SERIOUS AND/OR COMICAL ILLUSTRATIONS! PLEASE USE A PEN, INSTEAD OF A PENCIL, ON A POSTCARD!

File. 2 DISCUSSION ROOM

YOU CAN ASK ANYTHING AND EVERYTHING PERTAINING TO D.GRAY-MAN! SEND YOUR QUESTIONS TO KATSURA HOSHINO!!

PLEASE WRITE YOUR NAME (PSEUDONYM), ADDRESS, AGE, TELEPHONE NUMBER, AND THE NAME OF THE SECTION YOU ARE SUBMITTING FOR. NEW SECTION IDEAS ARE WELCOME!!

SEND TO: ATTN: D.GRAY-MAN
[KOMUI'S EXPERIMENT ROOM],
VIZ MEDIA, LLC
P.O. BOX 77010
SAN FRANCISCO, CA 94107

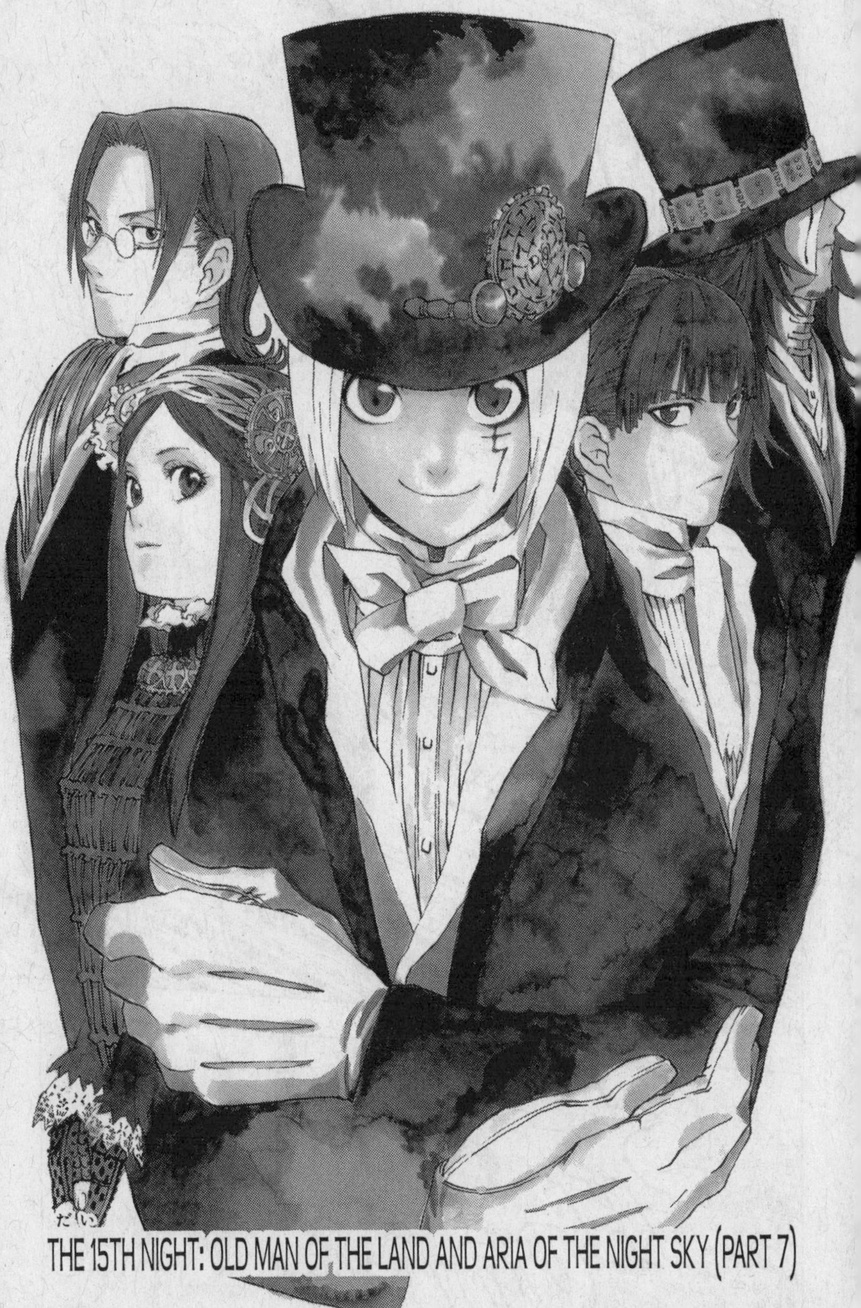

THE 15TH NIGHT: OLD MAN OF THE LAND AND ARIA OF THE NIGHT SKY (PART 7)

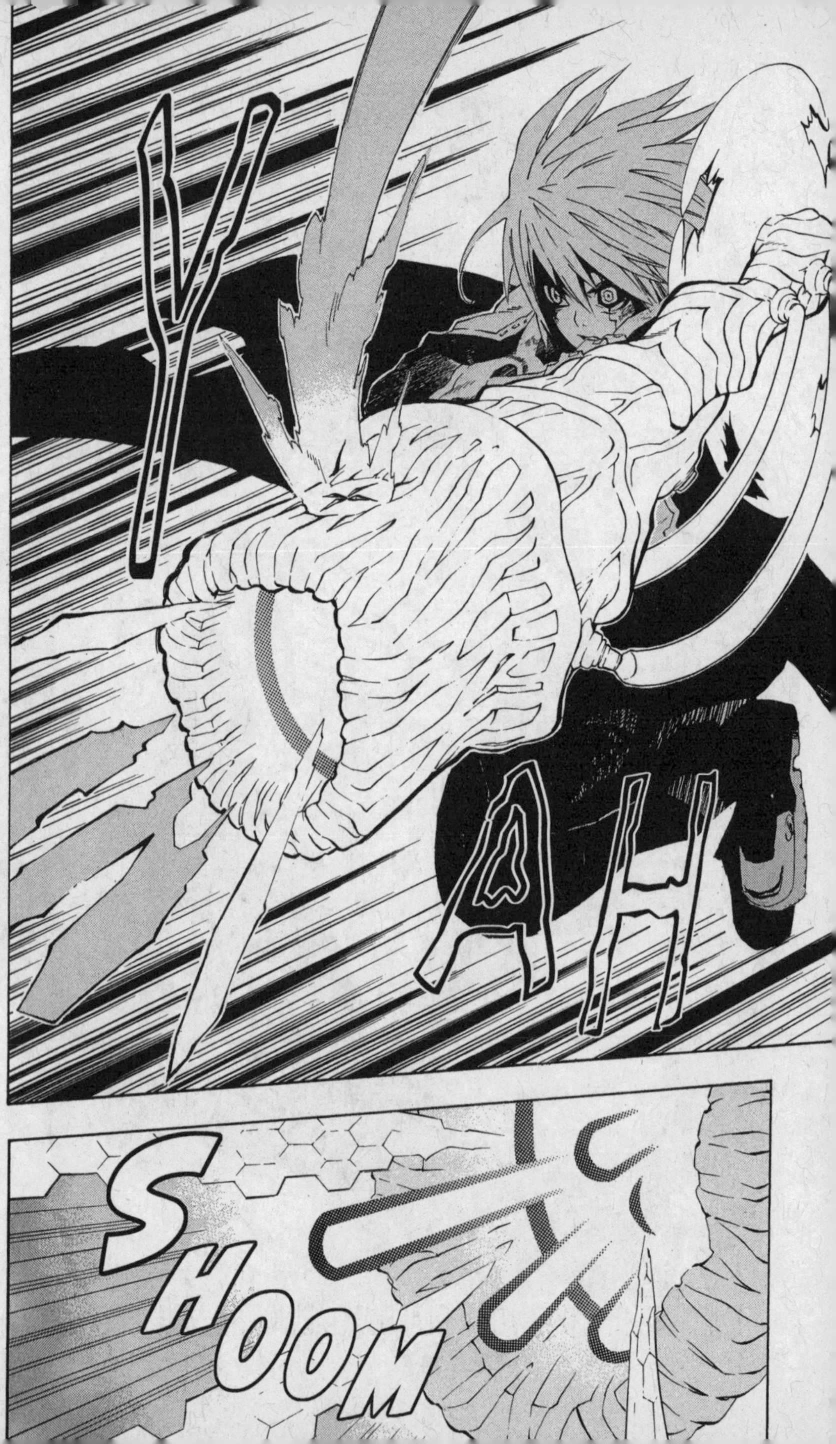
YAH
SHOOM

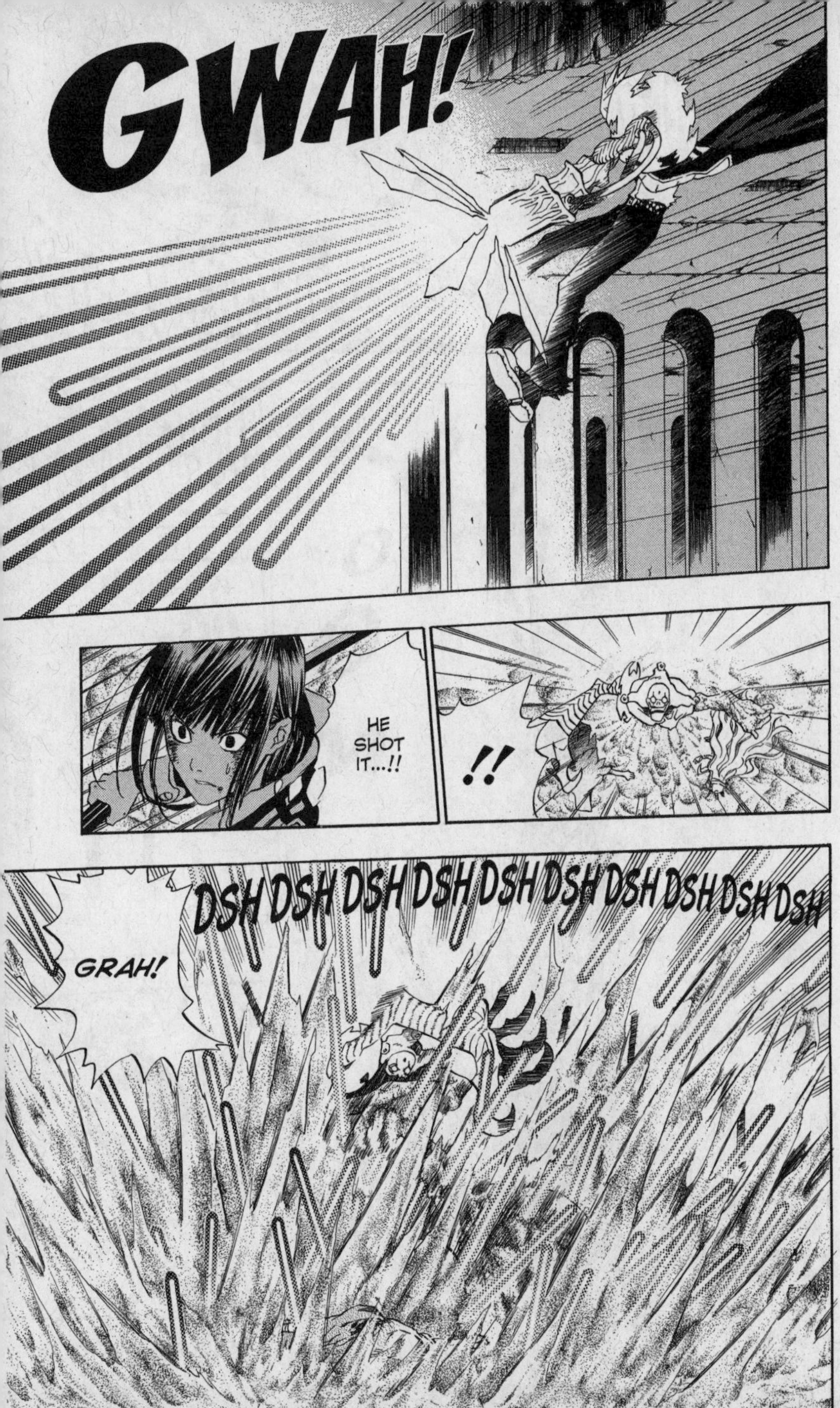

GWAH!
!!
HE SHOT IT...!!
DSH DSH DSH DSH DSH DSH DSH DSH DSH DSH
GRAH!

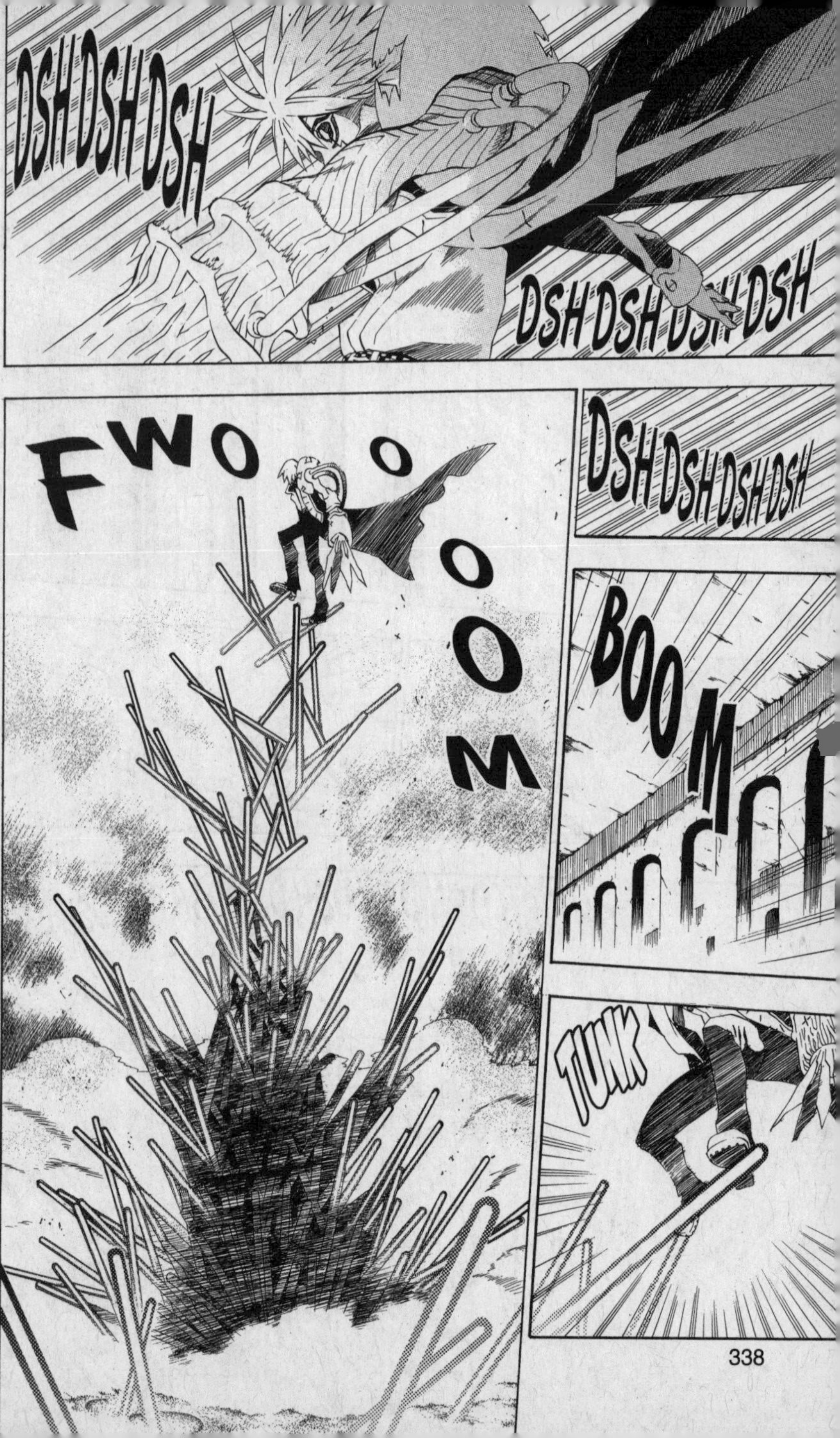
DSH DSH DSH DSH
DSH DSH DSH
DSH DSH DSH DSH
BOOM
TUNK
FWOOOOM

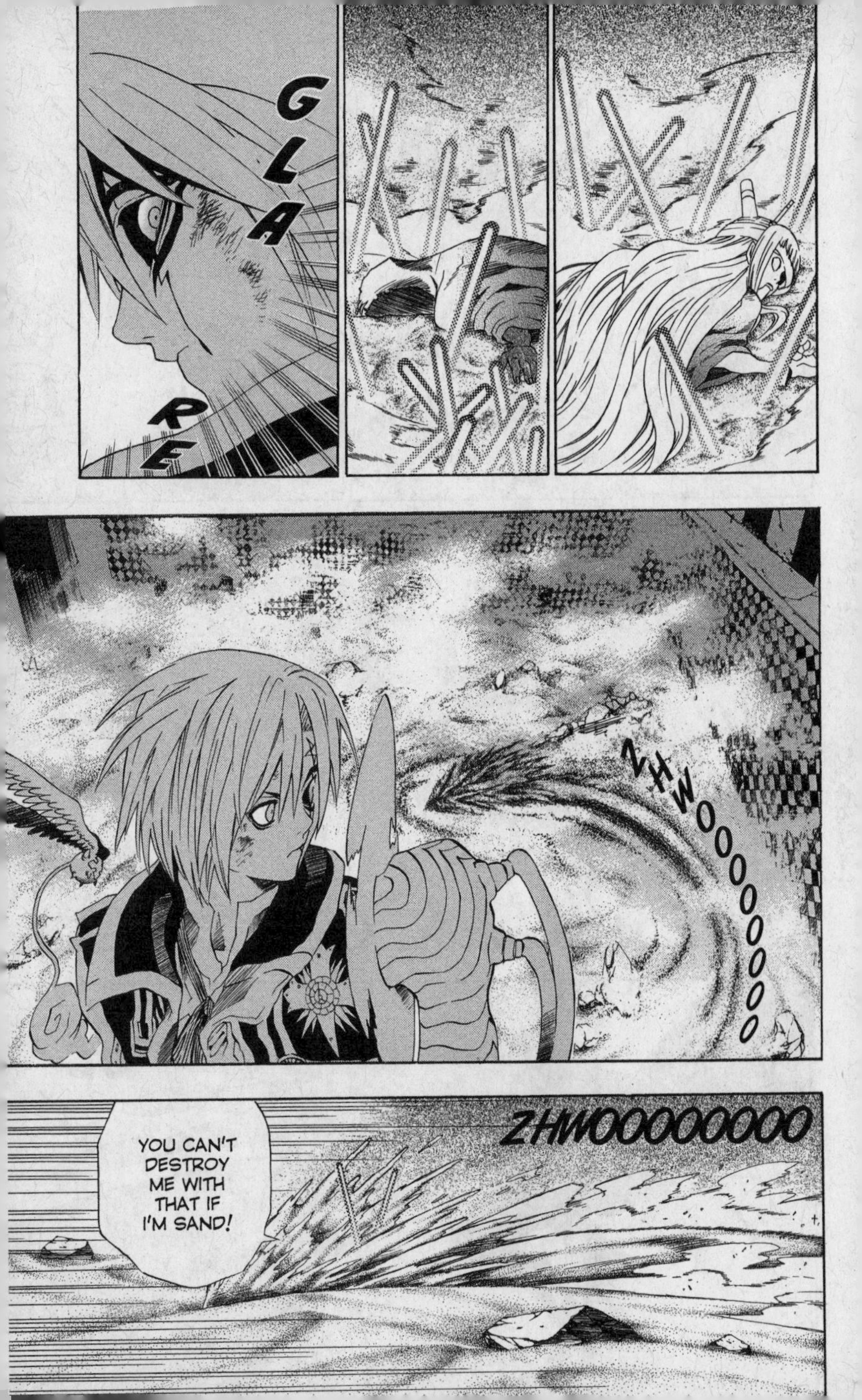
GLARE
ZHWOOOOOOOOO
ZHWOOOOOOOOO
YOU CAN'T DESTROY ME WITH THAT IF I'M SAND!

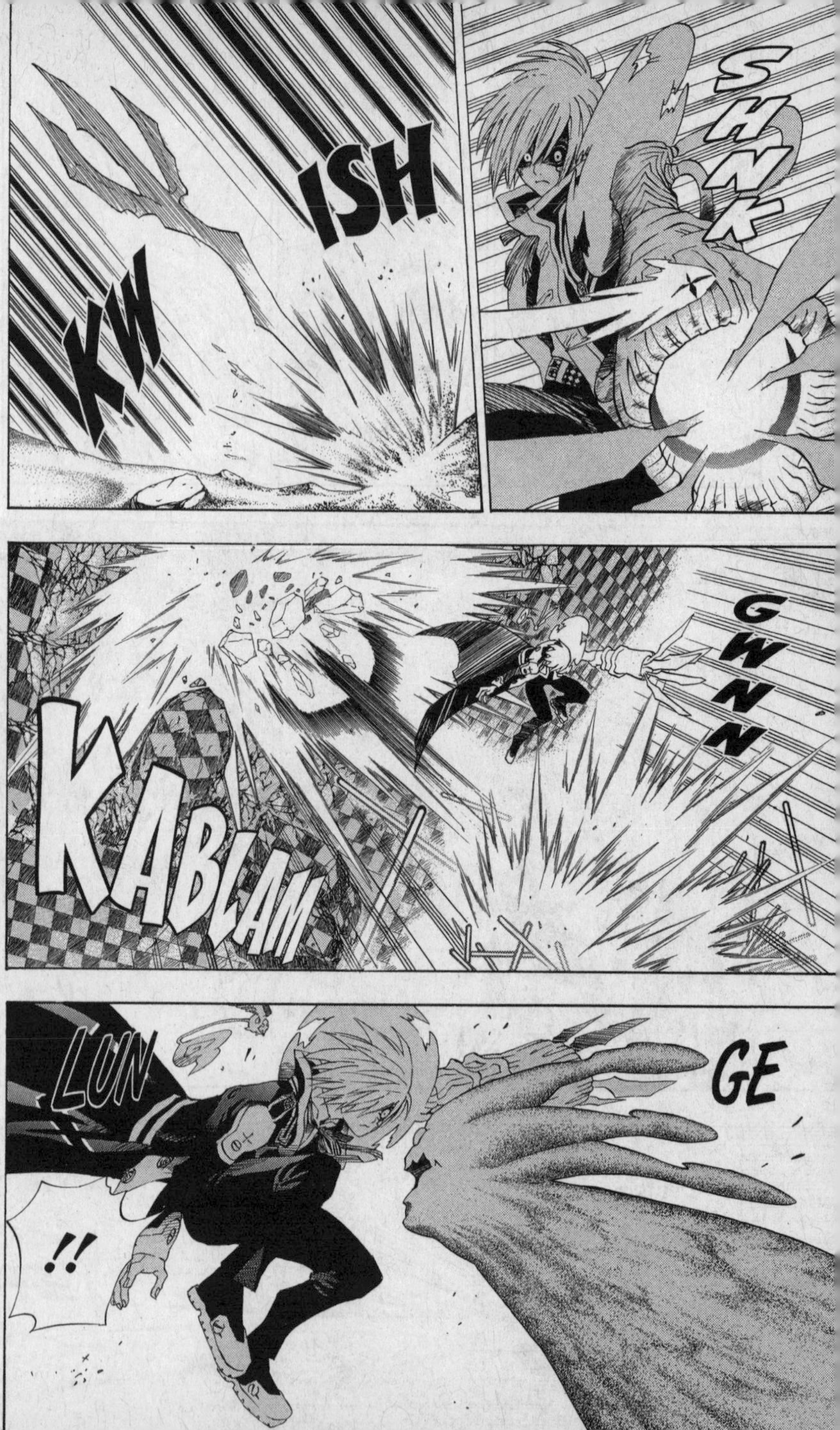
SHNK
KW
ISH
GWNNN
KABLAM
GE
LUN
!!

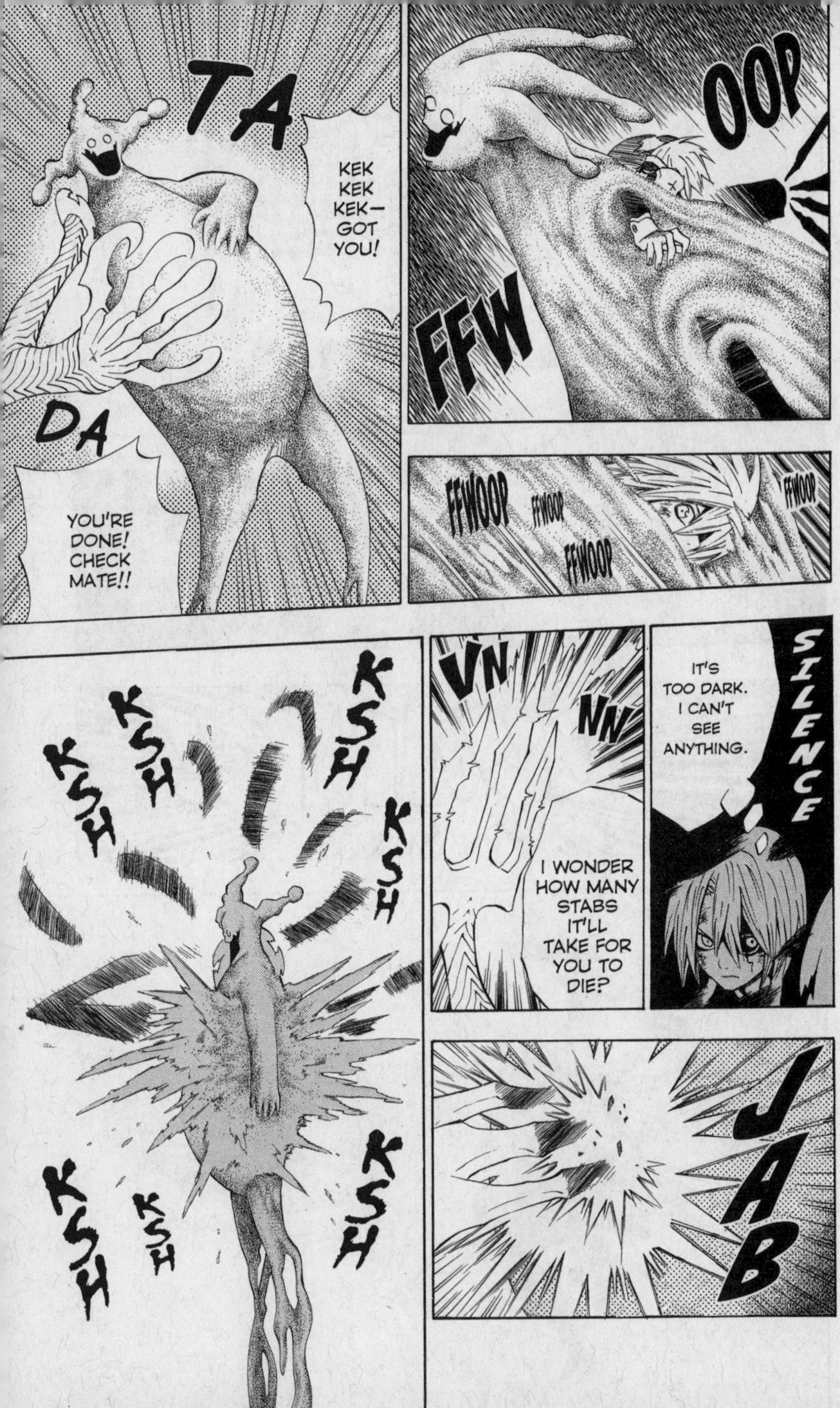
OOP
FFW
FFWOOP
FFWOOP
FFWOOP
FFWOOP
TA
KEK KEK KEK— GOT YOU!
DA
YOU'RE DONE! CHECK MATE!!
SILENCE
IT'S TOO DARK. I CAN'T SEE ANYTHING.
VN
NN
I WONDER HOW MANY STABS IT'LL TAKE FOR YOU TO DIE?
JAB
KSH
KSH
KSH
KSH
KSH
KSH
KSH

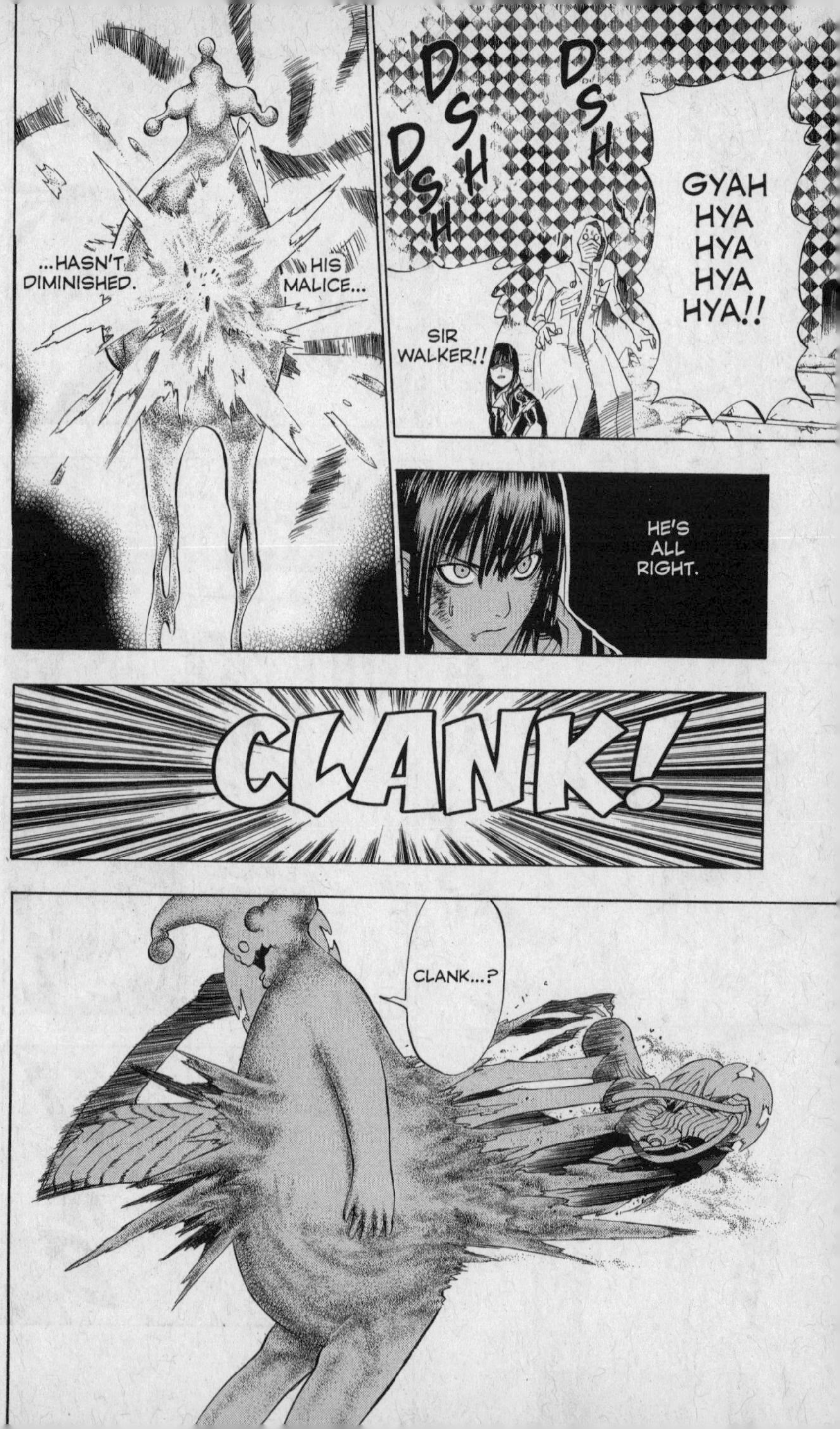
DSH DSH
DSH DSH
GYAH HYA HYA HYA HYA!!
SIR WALKER!!
HE'S ALL RIGHT.
HIS MALICE...
...HASN'T DIMINISHED.
CLANK!
CLANK...?

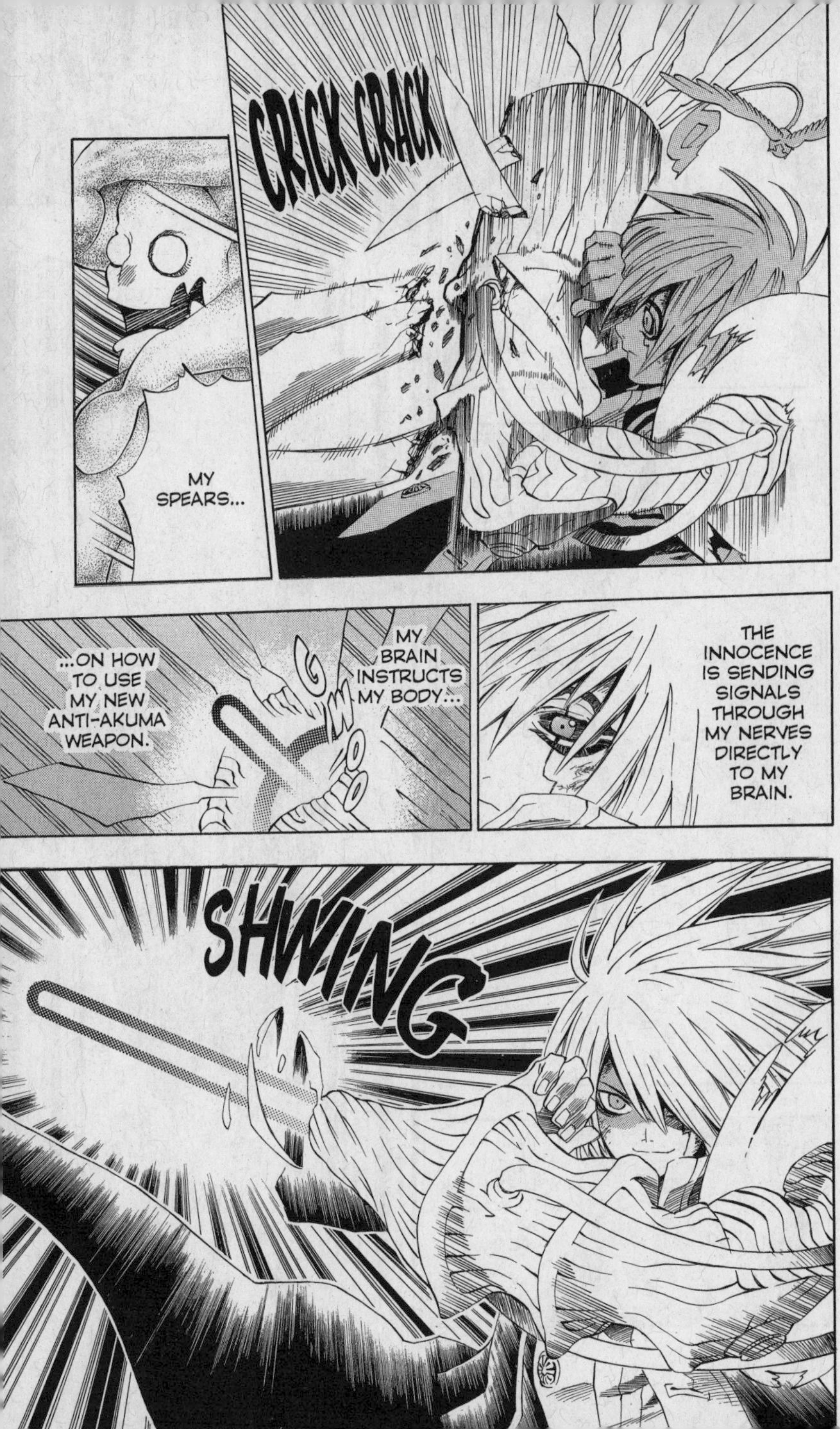
CRICK CRACK
MY SPEARS...
THE INNOCENCE IS SENDING SIGNALS THROUGH MY NERVES DIRECTLY TO MY BRAIN.
MY BRAIN INSTRUCTS MY BODY...
...ON HOW TO USE MY NEW ANTI-AKUMA WEAPON.
SHWING

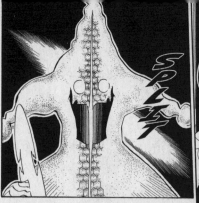

SPLSH

SL ICE

FW AK

FSSH

AAH!
MY
SAND
SKIN!!

NOW
YOU'RE BACK
TO YOUR
ORIGINAL
FORM.

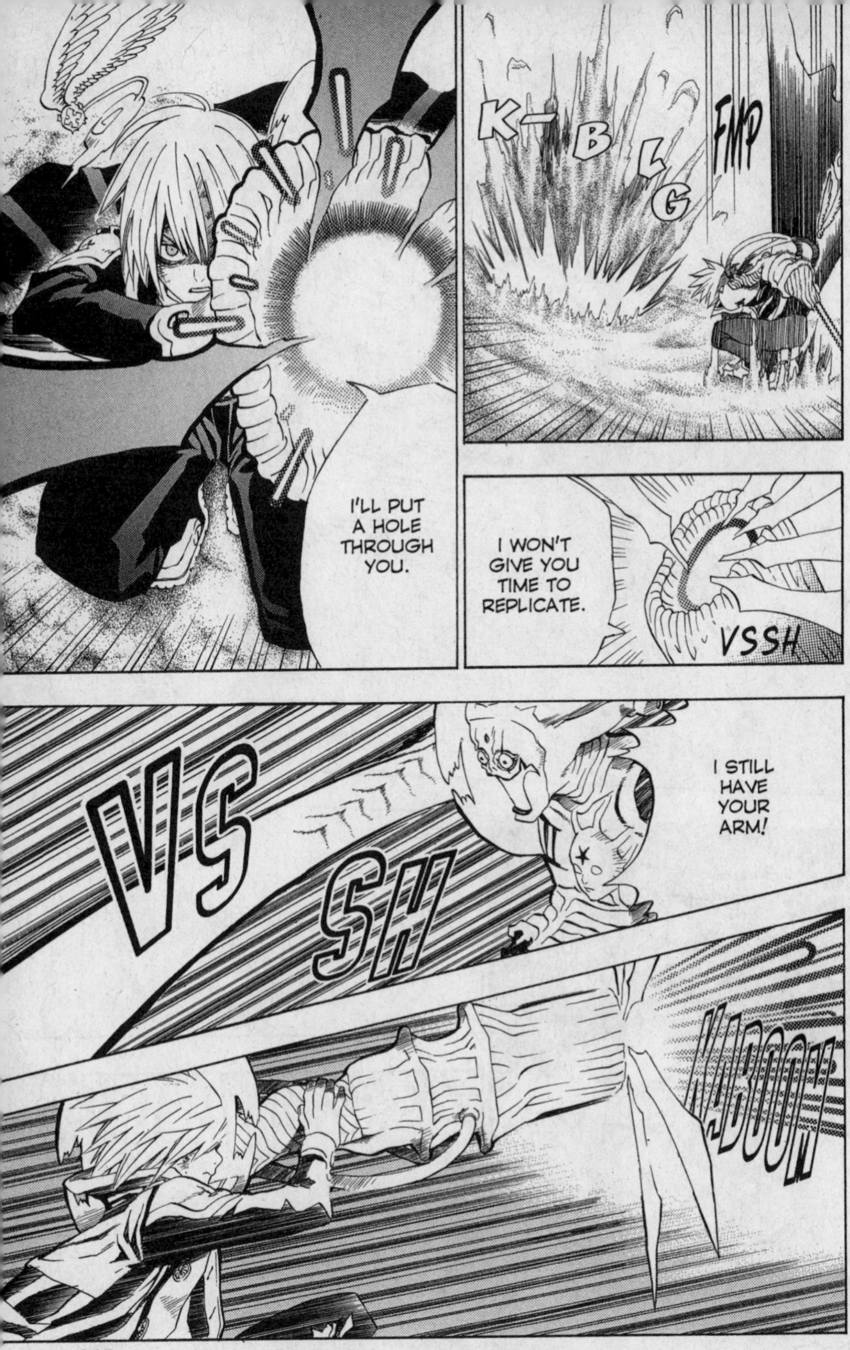
FMP
K-BLG
I WON'T GIVE YOU TIME TO REPLICATE.
VSSH
I'LL PUT A HOLE THROUGH YOU.
I STILL HAVE YOUR ARM!
VSSH
KABOOM

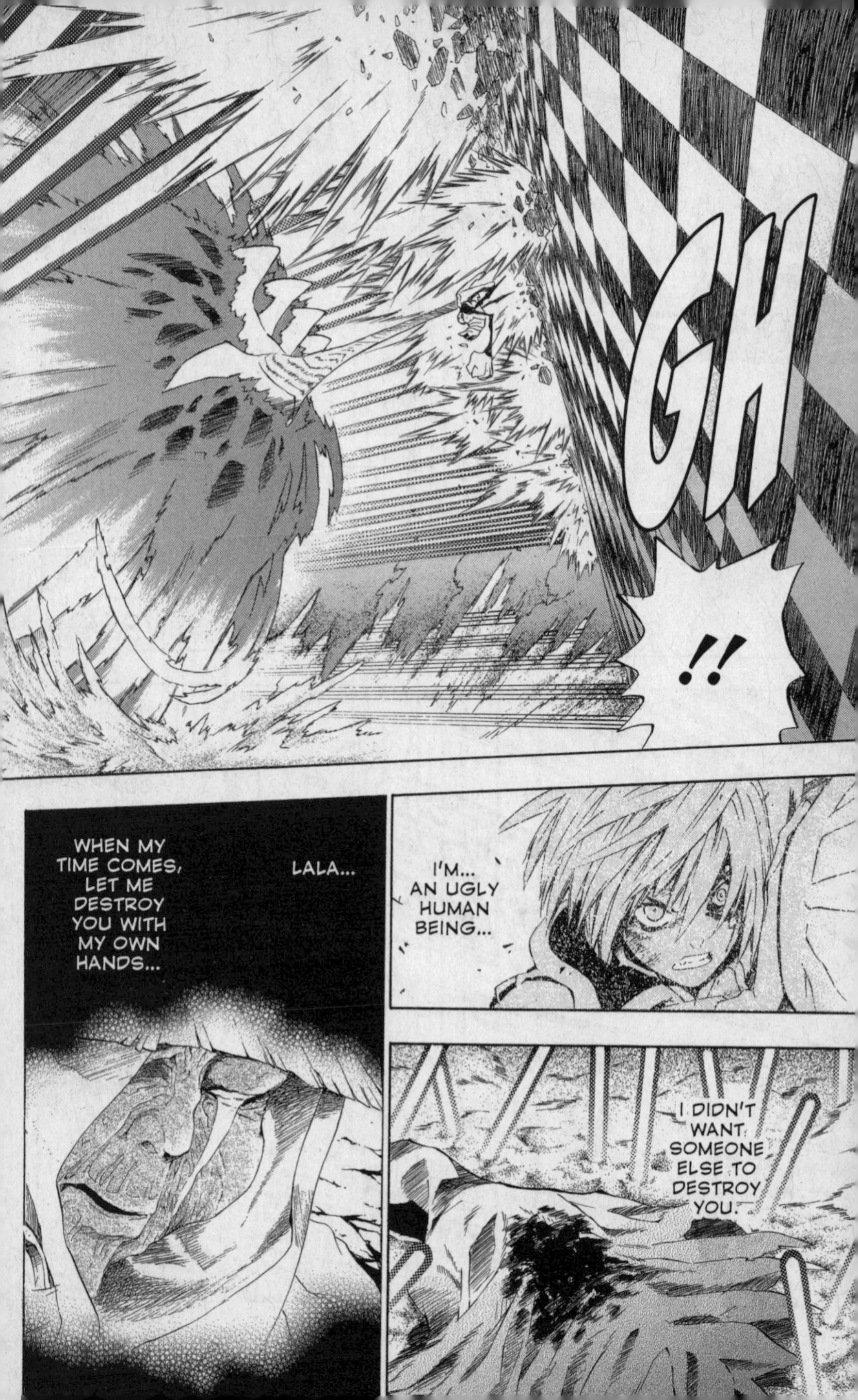
GH
!!
I'M... AN UGLY HUMAN BEING...
I DIDN'T WANT SOMEONE ELSE TO DESTROY YOU.
LALA...
WHEN MY TIME COMES, LET ME DESTROY YOU WITH MY OWN HANDS...

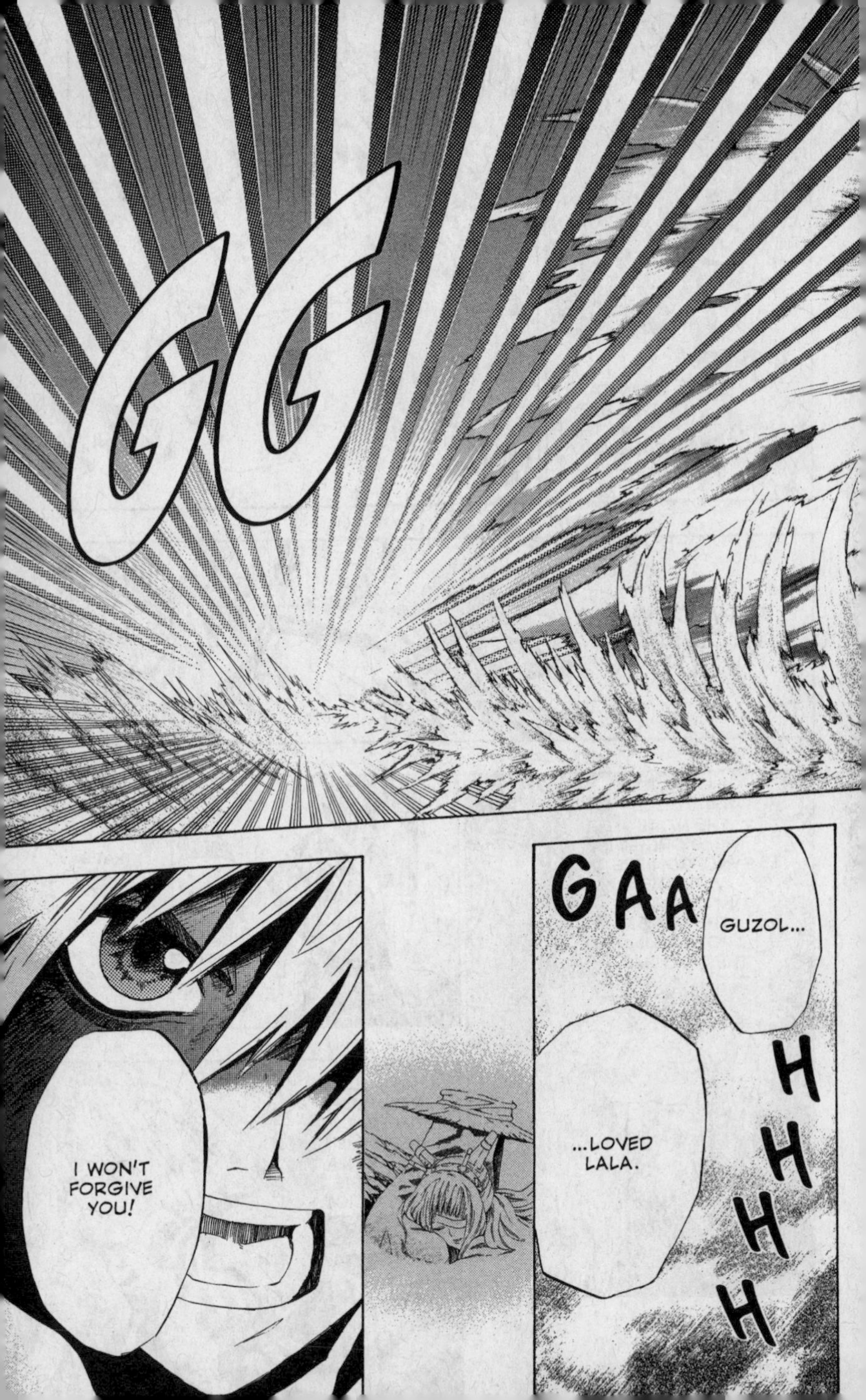
GG
GUZOL...
...LOVED LALA.
GAAHHHH
I WON'T FORGIVE YOU!

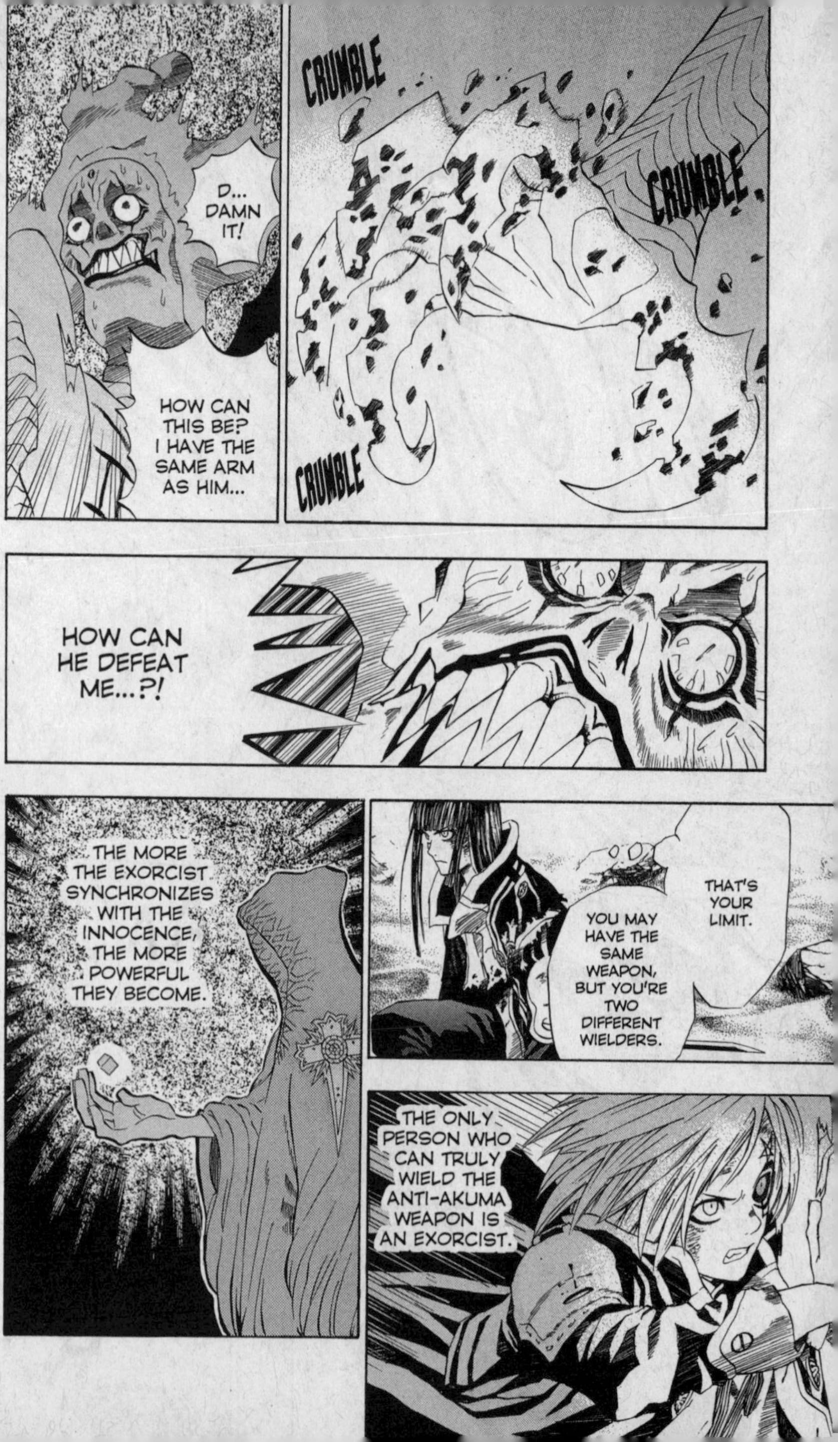
CRUMBLE
CRUMBLE
CRUMBLE
D... DAMN IT!
HOW CAN THIS BE? I HAVE THE SAME ARM AS HIM...
HOW CAN HE DEFEAT ME...?!
THAT'S YOUR LIMIT.
YOU MAY HAVE THE SAME WEAPON, BUT YOU'RE TWO DIFFERENT WIELDERS.
THE ONLY PERSON WHO CAN TRULY WIELD THE ANTI-AKUMA WEAPON IS AN EXORCIST.
THE MORE THE EXORCIST SYNCHRONIZES WITH THE INNOCENCE, THE MORE POWERFUL THEY BECOME.

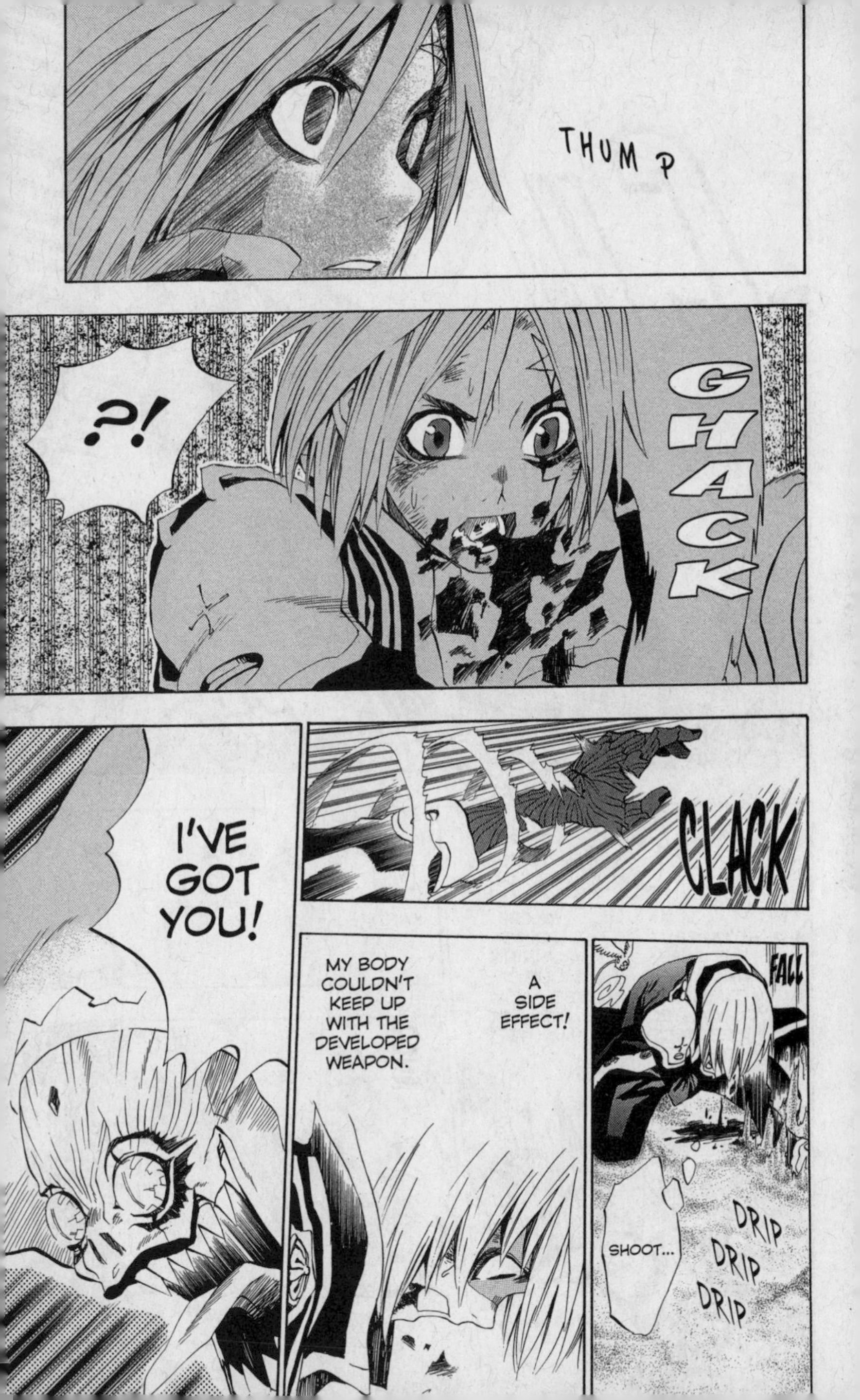

THUMP
GHACK
?!
CLACK
FALL
DRIP DRIP DRIP
SHOOT...
A SIDE EFFECT!
MY BODY COULDN'T KEEP UP WITH THE DEVELOPED WEAPON.
I'VE GOT YOU!

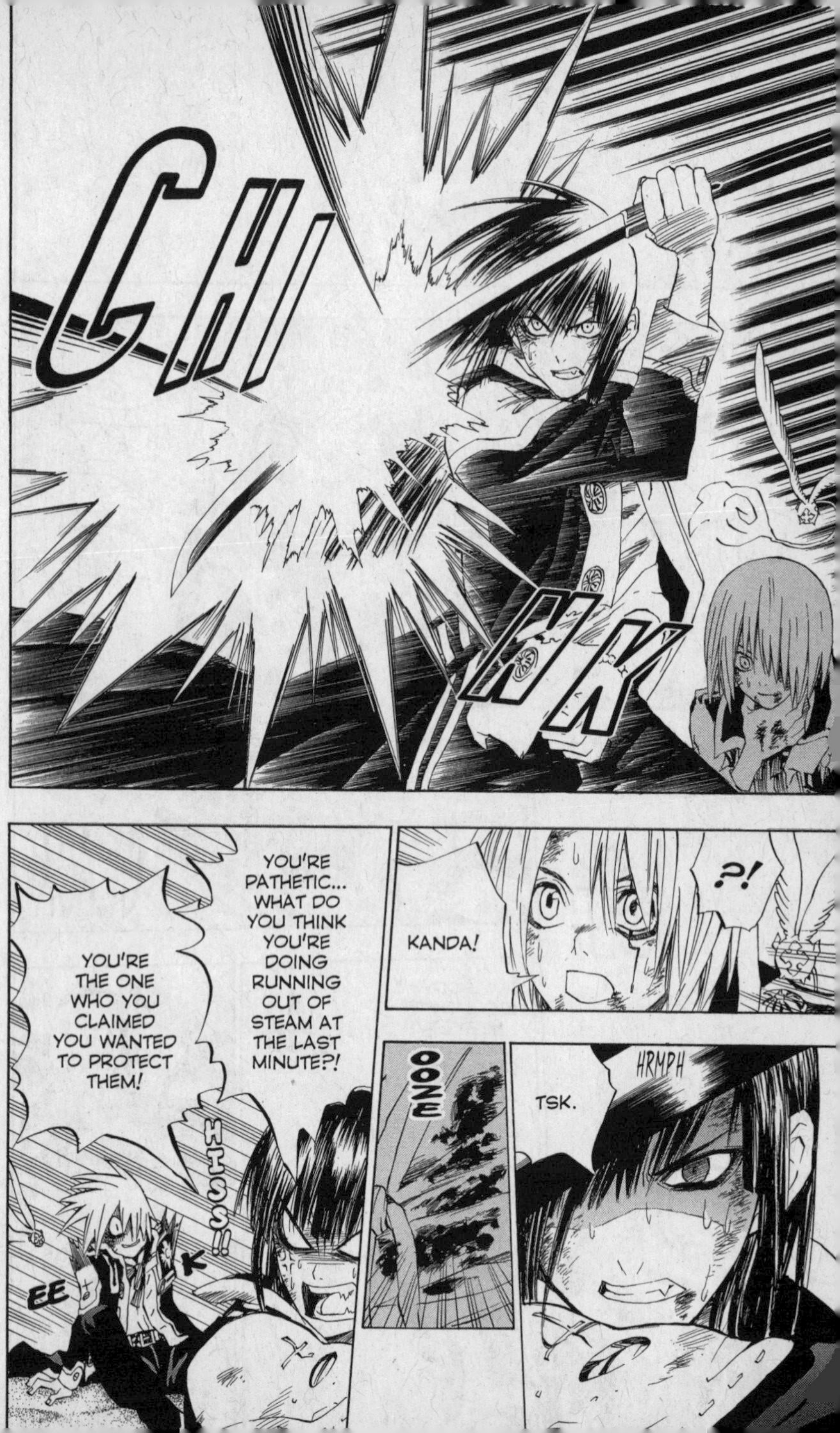
CHI
NK
?!
KANDA!
HRMPH
TSK.
OOZE
YOU'RE PATHETIC... WHAT DO YOU THINK YOU'RE DOING RUNNING OUT OF STEAM AT THE LAST MINUTE?!
YOU'RE THE ONE WHO YOU CLAIMED YOU WANTED TO PROTECT THEM!
HISS!!
K
EE

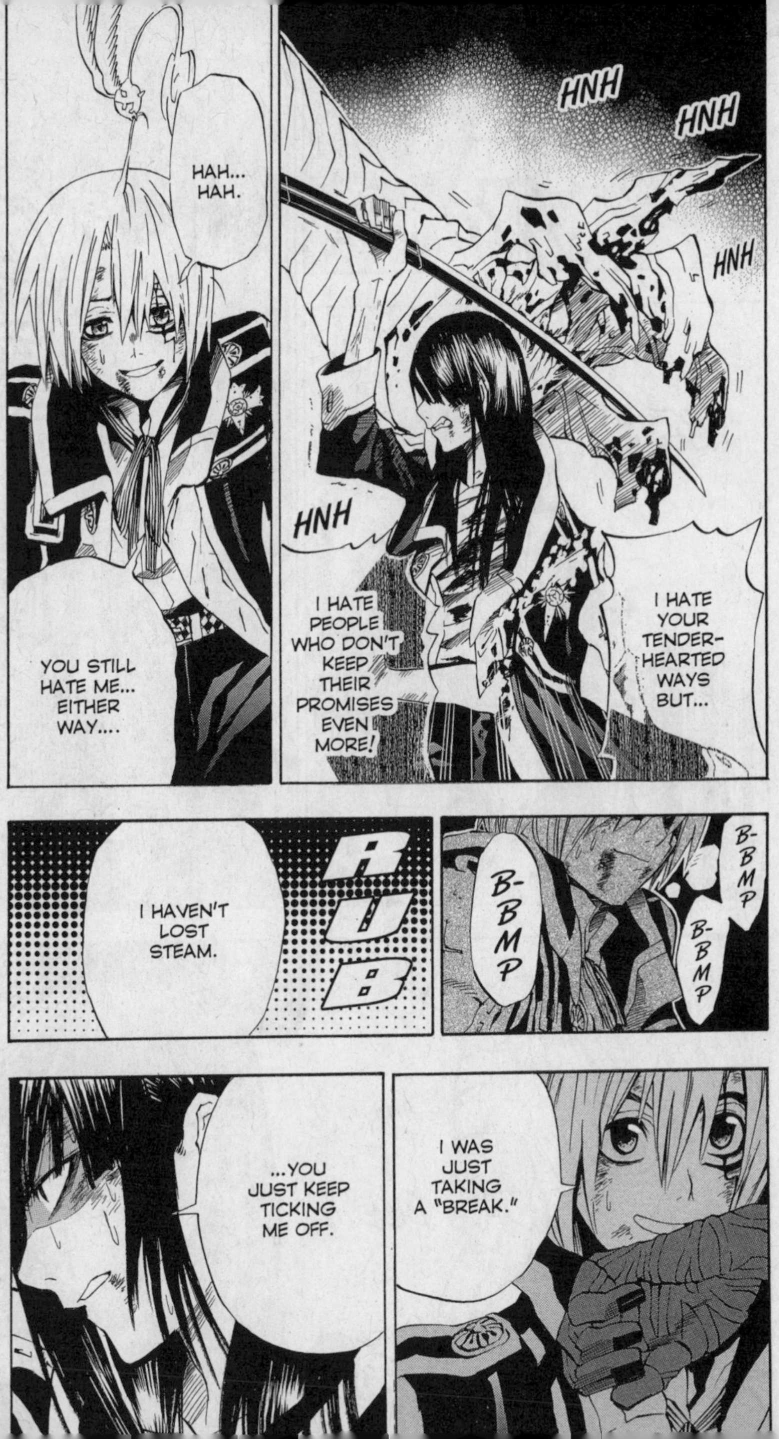
HNH
HNH
HNH
I HATE YOUR TENDER-HEARTED WAYS BUT...
I HATE PEOPLE WHO DON'T KEEP THEIR PROMISES EVEN MORE!
HNH
HAH... HAH.
YOU STILL HATE ME... EITHER WAY....
B-BMP
B-BMP
B-BMP
RUB
I HAVEN'T LOST STEAM.
I WAS JUST TAKING A "BREAK."
...YOU JUST KEEP TICKING ME OFF.

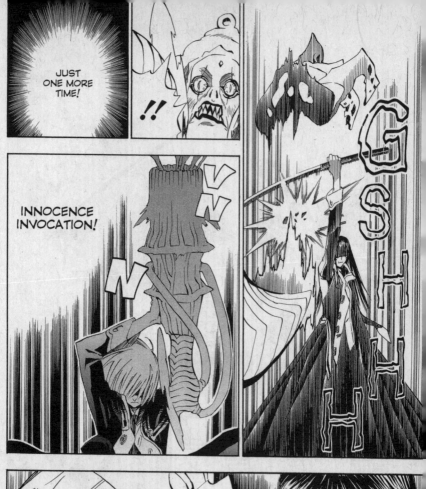

JUST ONE MORE TIME!

!!

INNOCENCE INVOCATION!

TURN TO DUST!

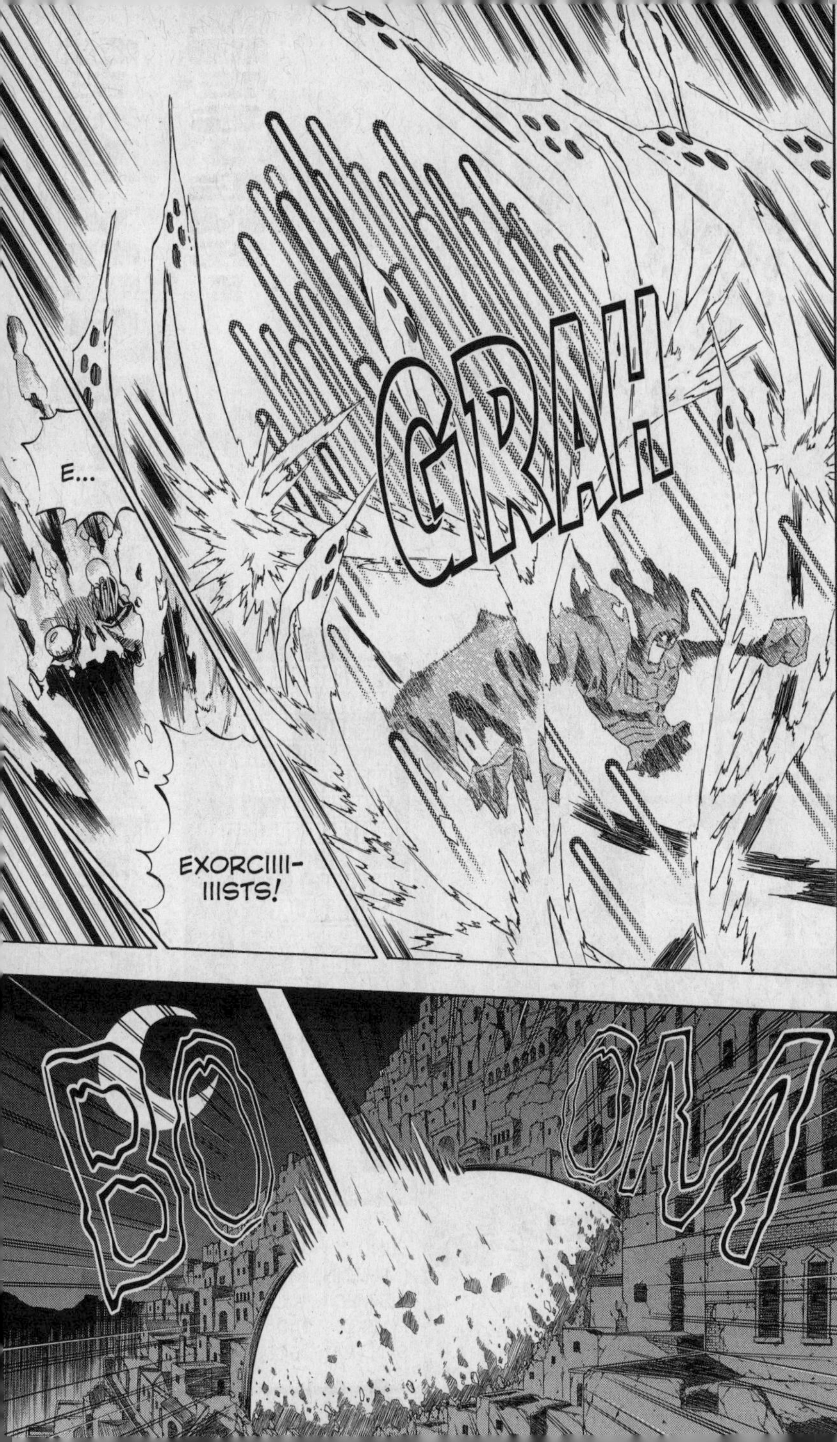
GRAH
E...
EXORCIIII-
IIISTS!
BOOM

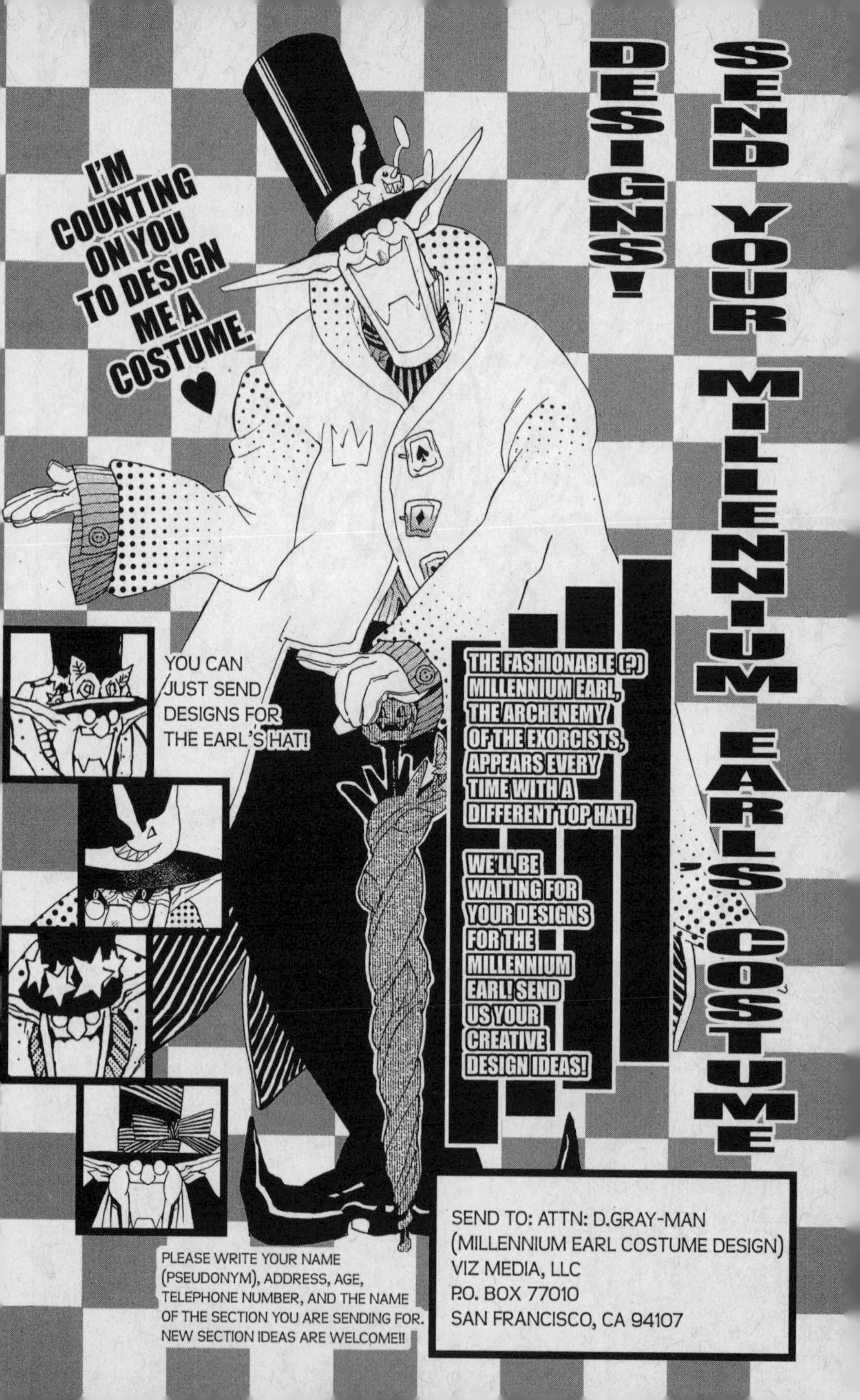
SEND YOUR MILLENNIUM EARL'S COSTUME DESIGNS!
I'M COUNTING ON YOU TO DESIGN ME A COSTUME. ♥
THE FASHIONABLE (?) MILLENNIUM EARL, THE ARCHENEMY OF THE EXORCISTS, APPEARS EVERY TIME WITH A DIFFERENT TOP HAT!
WE'LL BE WAITING FOR YOUR DESIGNS FOR THE MILLENNIUM EARL! SEND US YOUR CREATIVE DESIGN IDEAS!
YOU CAN JUST SEND DESIGNS FOR THE EARL'S HAT!
SEND TO: ATTN: D.GRAY-MAN
(MILLENNIUM EARL COSTUME DESIGN)
VIZ MEDIA, LLC
P.O. BOX 77010
SAN FRANCISCO, CA 94107
PLEASE WRITE YOUR NAME (PSEUDONYM), ADDRESS, AGE, TELEPHONE NUMBER, AND THE NAME OF THE SECTION YOU ARE SENDING FOR. NEW SECTION IDEAS ARE WELCOME!!

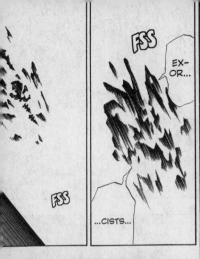

FSS

FSS

EX-
OR...

...CISTS...

BWOO

SH

F
F
W
P

THE 16TH NIGHT: OLD MAN OF THE LAND AND ARIA OF THE NIGHT SKY (PART 8)

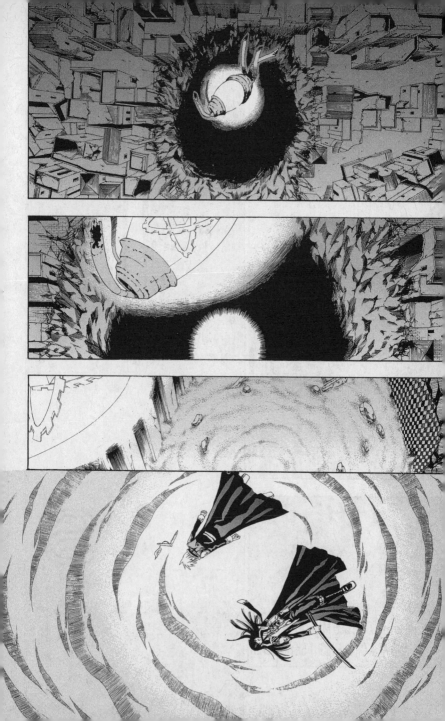

TUNK

PLEASE...
BE
ALIVE...

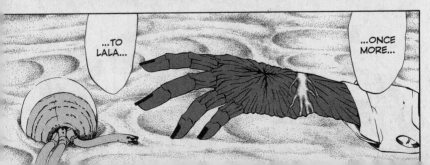

...TO
LALA...

...ONCE
MORE...

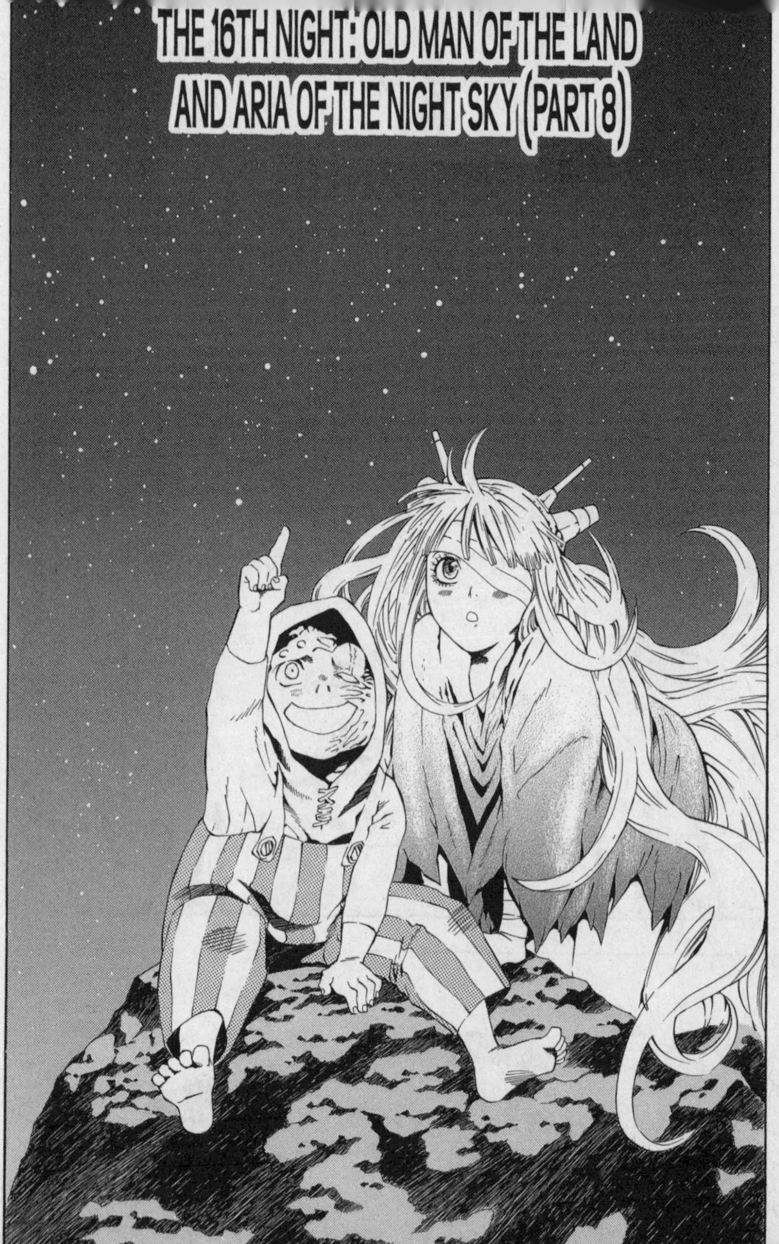
THE 16TH NIGHT: OLD MAN OF THE LAND
AND ARIA OF THE NIGHT SKY (PART 8)

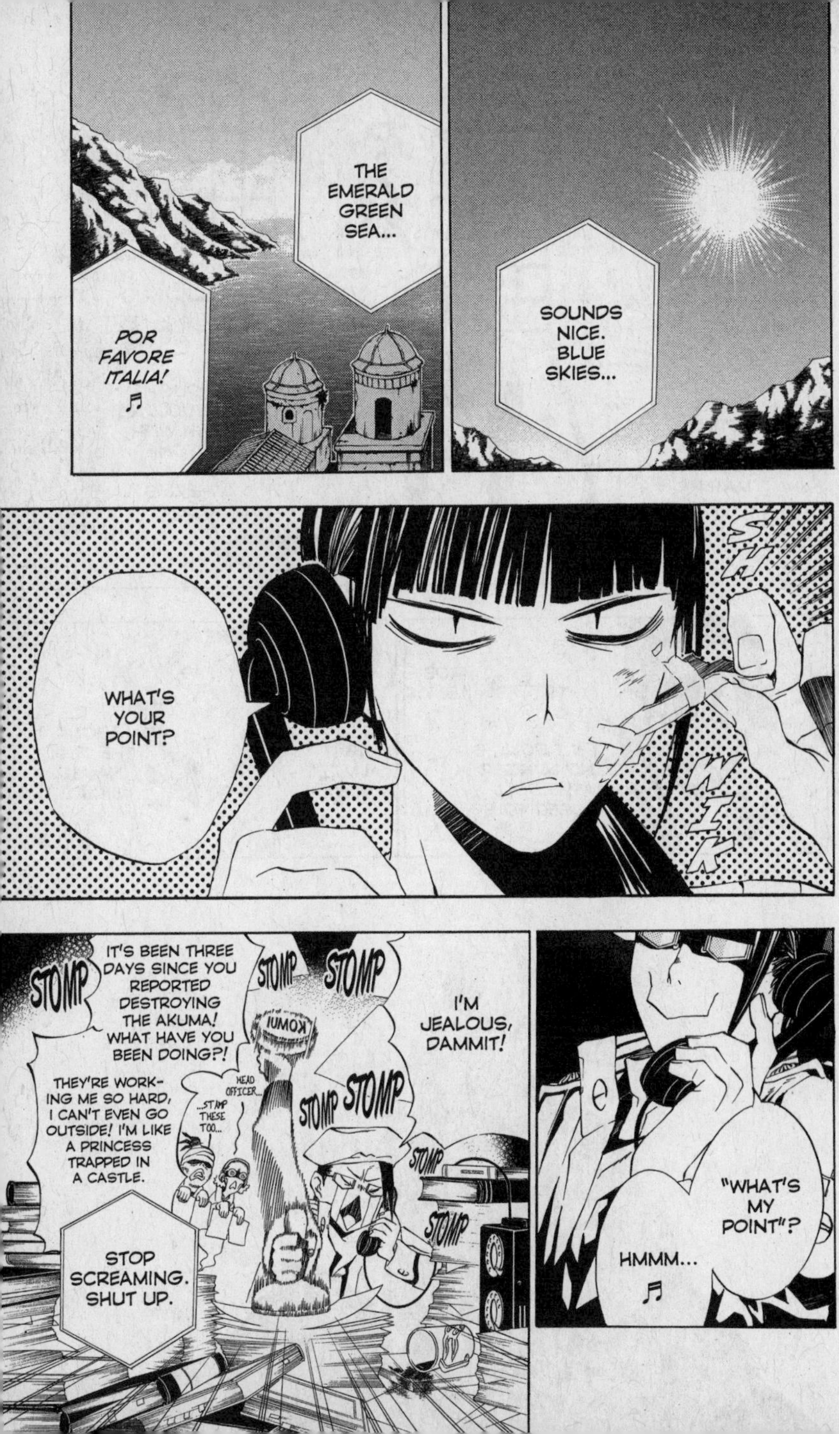
SOUNDS NICE. BLUE SKIES...
THE EMERALD GREEN SEA...
POR FAVORE ITALIA! ♪
SH
WIK
WHAT'S YOUR POINT?
"WHAT'S MY POINT"?
HMMM... ♪
I'M JEALOUS, DAMMIT!
STOMP
STOMP
IT'S BEEN THREE DAYS SINCE YOU REPORTED DESTROYING THE AKUMA! WHAT HAVE YOU BEEN DOING?!
STOMP
KOMUI
STOMP
STOMP
STOMP
STOMP
STOMP
HEAD OFFICER...
...STAMP THESE TOO...
THEY'RE WORKING ME SO HARD, I CAN'T EVEN GO OUTSIDE! I'M LIKE A PRINCESS TRAPPED IN A CASTLE.
STOP SCREAMING. SHUT UP.

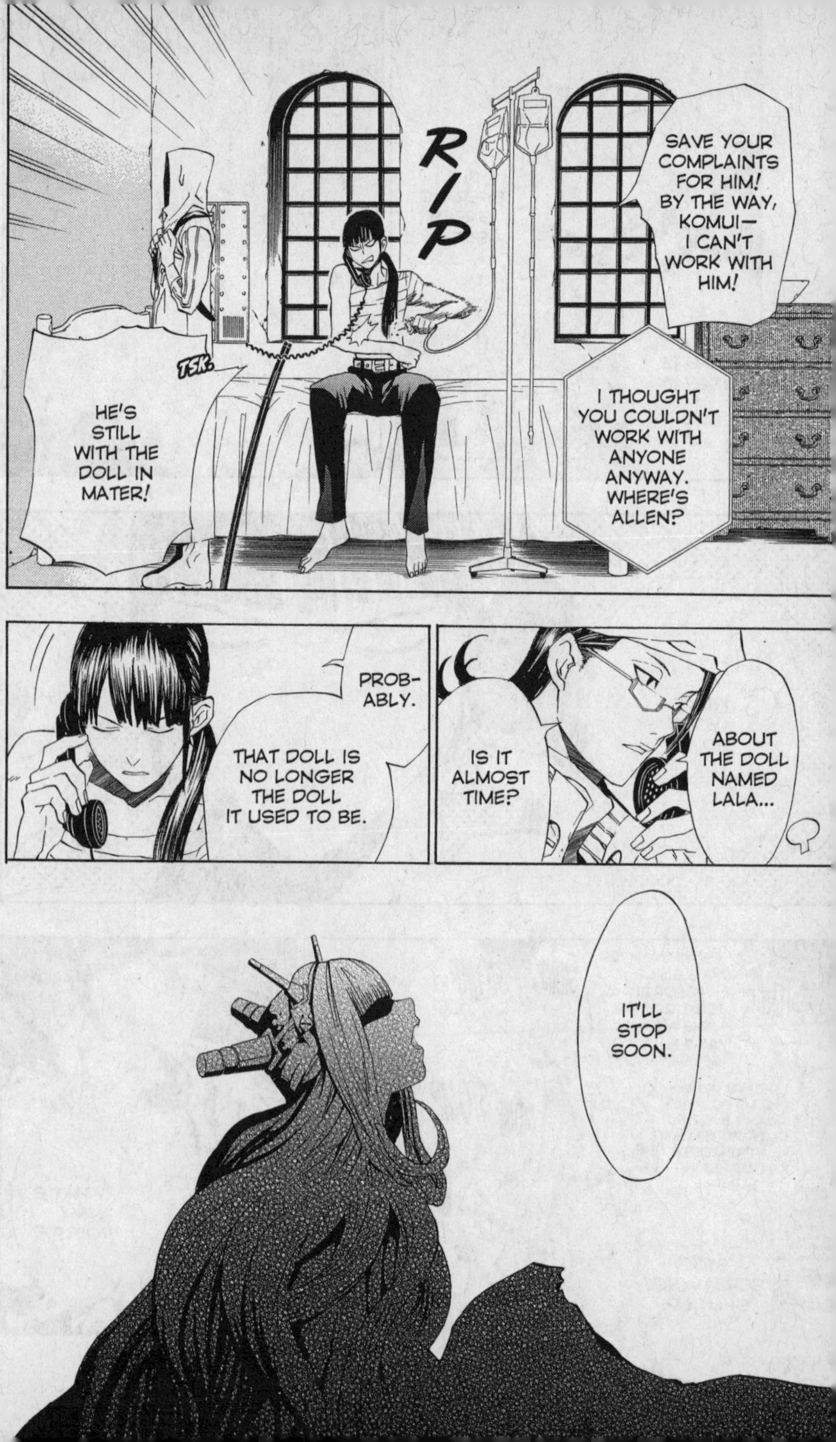
SAVE YOUR COMPLAINTS FOR HIM! BY THE WAY, KOMUI— I CAN'T WORK WITH HIM!
RIP
I THOUGHT YOU COULDN'T WORK WITH ANYONE ANYWAY. WHERE'S ALLEN?
TSK.
HE'S STILL WITH THE DOLL IN MATER!
ABOUT THE DOLL NAMED LALA...
IS IT ALMOST TIME?
PROB-ABLY.
THAT DOLL IS NO LONGER THE DOLL IT USED TO BE.
IT'LL STOP SOON.

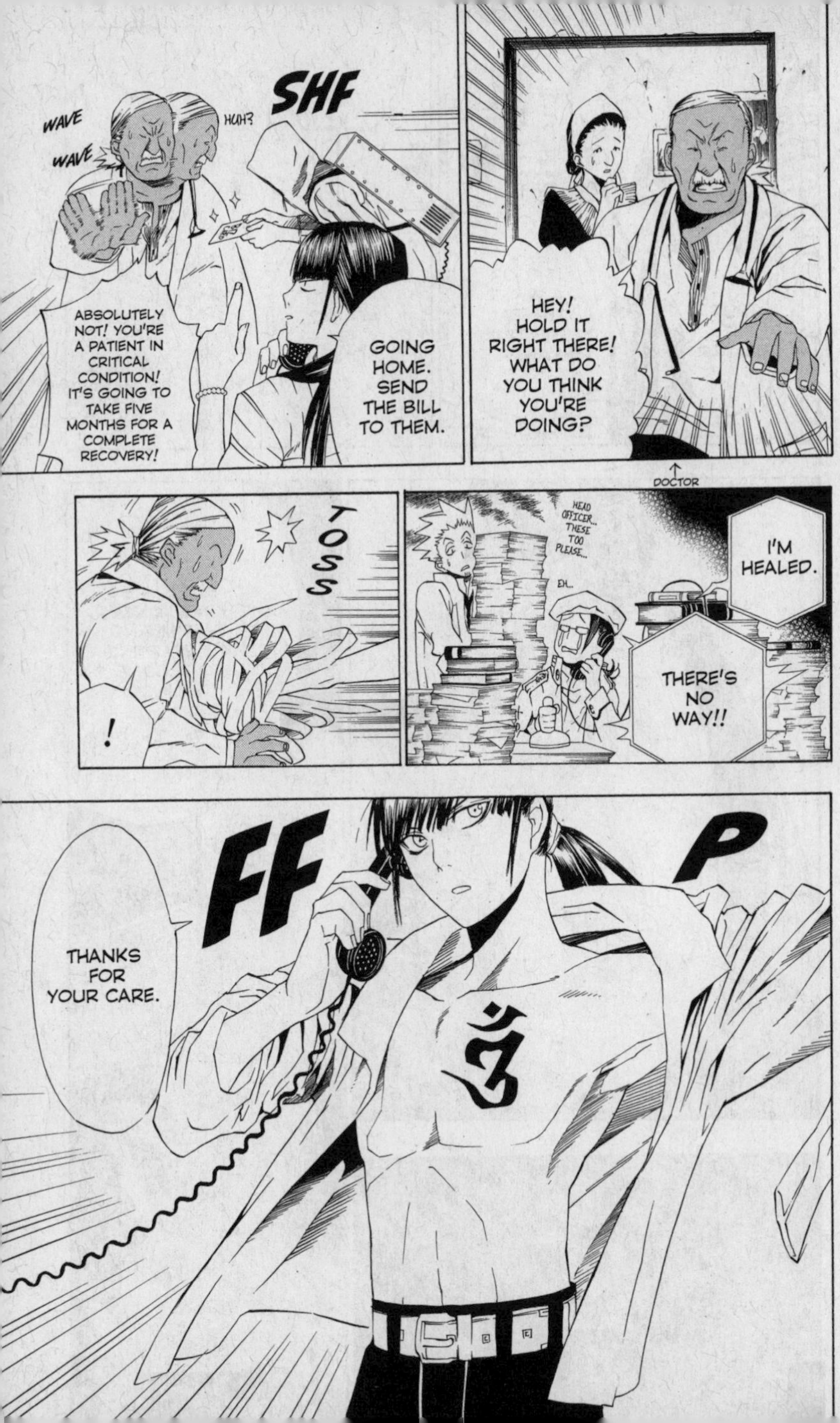
HEY! HOLD IT RIGHT THERE! WHAT DO YOU THINK YOU'RE DOING?
↑ DOCTOR
SHF
GOING HOME. SEND THE BILL TO THEM.
HUH?
WAVE
WAVE
ABSOLUTELY NOT! YOU'RE A PATIENT IN CRITICAL CONDITION! IT'S GOING TO TAKE FIVE MONTHS FOR A COMPLETE RECOVERY!
I'M HEALED.
HEAD OFFICER... THESE TOO PLEASE...
EH..
THERE'S NO WAY!!
TOSS
!
P
FF
THANKS FOR YOUR CARE.

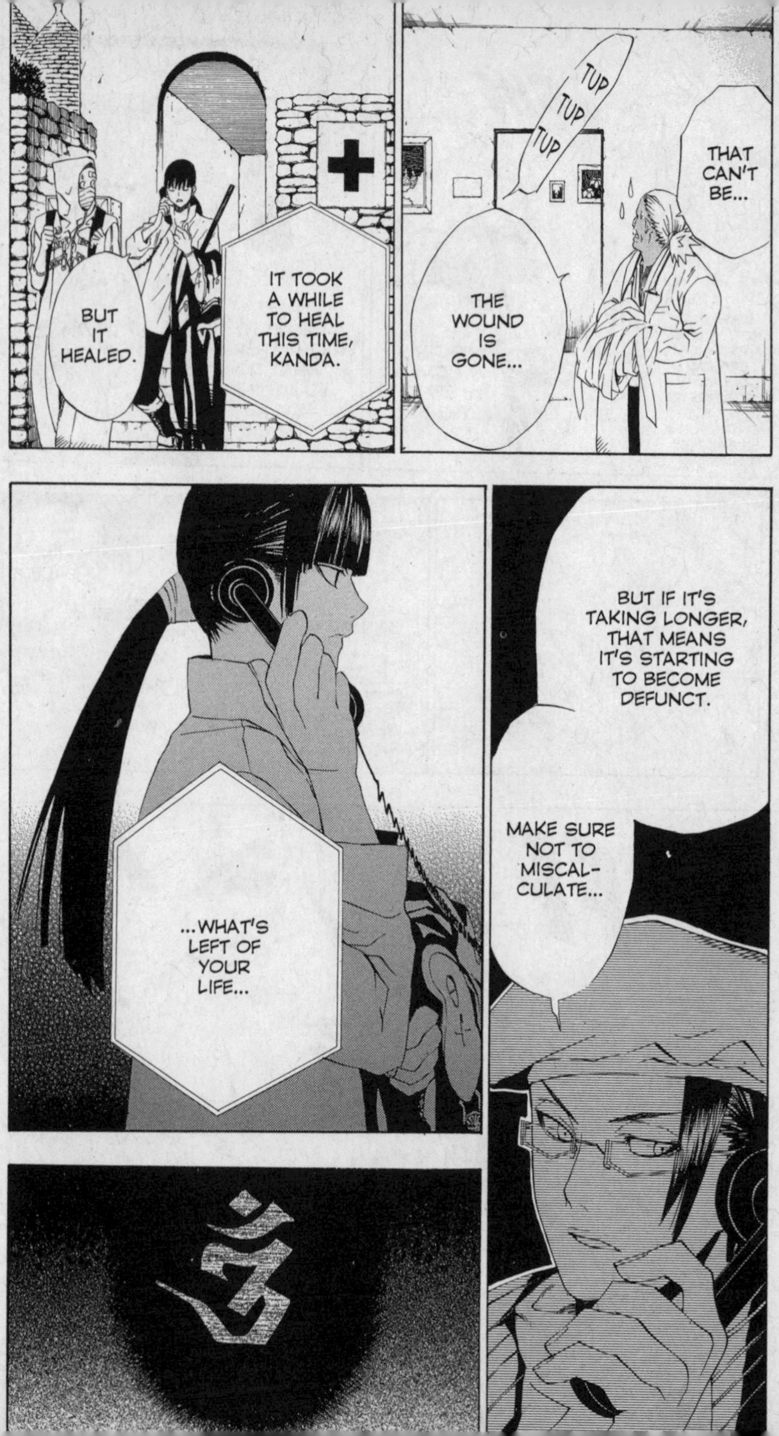
THAT CAN'T BE...
TUP TUP TUP
THE WOUND IS GONE...
IT TOOK A WHILE TO HEAL THIS TIME, KANDA.
BUT IT HEALED.
BUT IF IT'S TAKING LONGER, THAT MEANS IT'S STARTING TO BECOME DEFUNCT.
MAKE SURE NOT TO MISCAL-CULATE...
...WHAT'S LEFT OF YOUR LIFE...

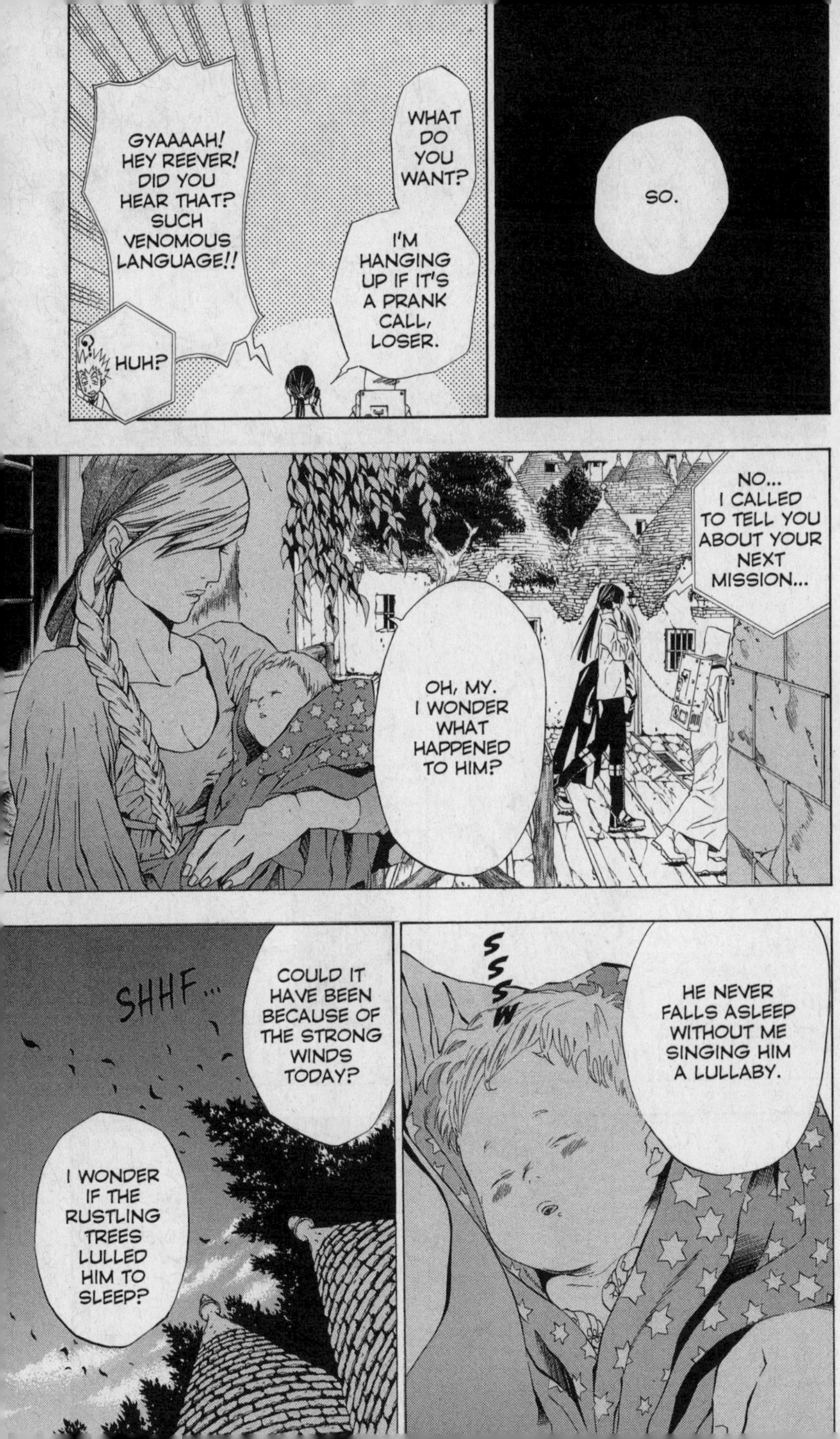
SO.
WHAT DO YOU WANT?
I'M HANGING UP IF IT'S A PRANK CALL, LOSER.
GYAAAAH! HEY REEVER! DID YOU HEAR THAT? SUCH VENOMOUS LANGUAGE!!
HUH?
NO... I CALLED TO TELL YOU ABOUT YOUR NEXT MISSION...
OH, MY. I WONDER WHAT HAPPENED TO HIM?
SSSW
HE NEVER FALLS ASLEEP WITHOUT ME SINGING HIM A LULLABY.
COULD IT HAVE BEEN BECAUSE OF THE STRONG WINDS TODAY?
SHHF...
I WONDER IF THE RUSTLING TREES LULLED HIM TO SLEEP?

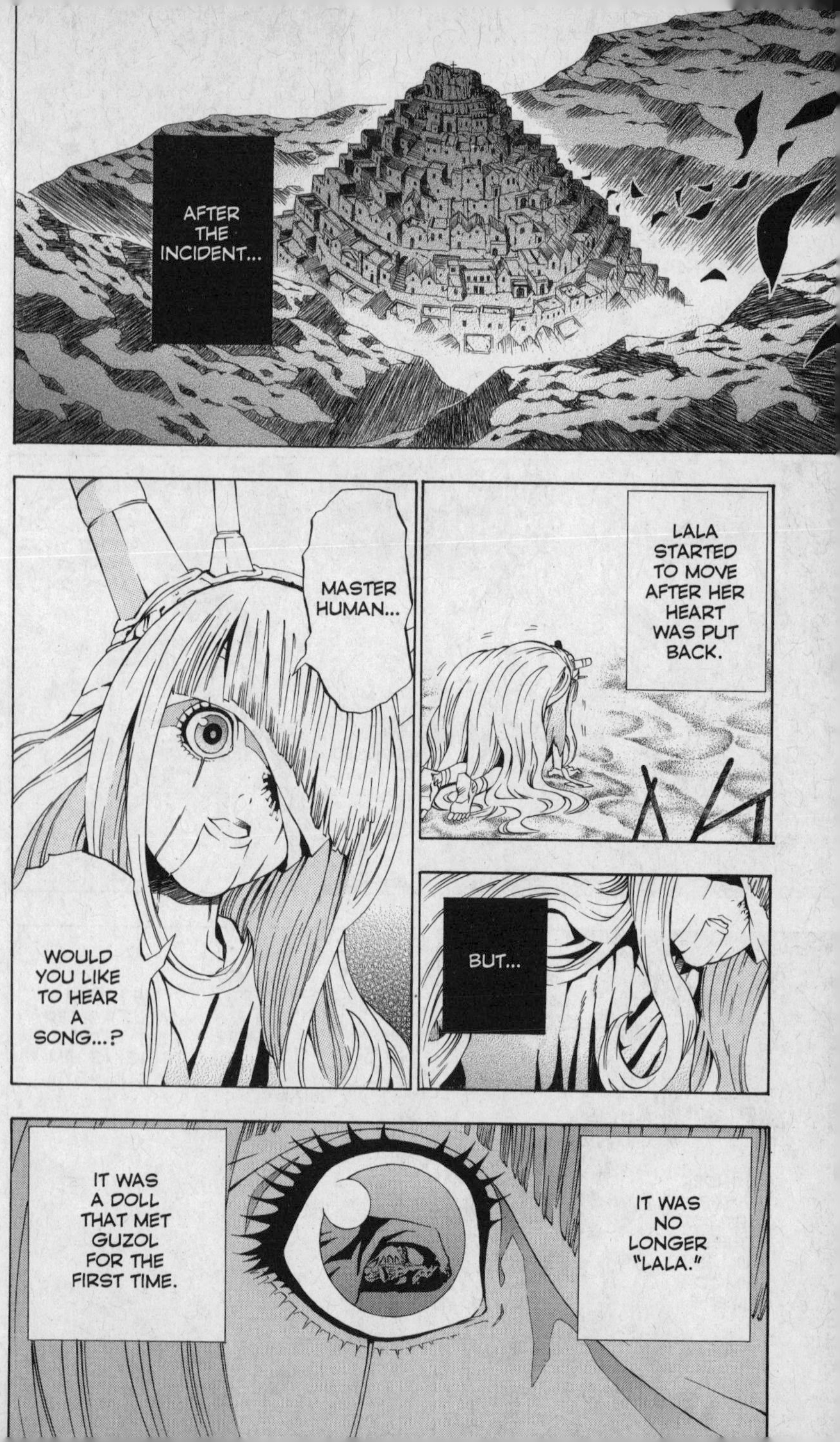
AFTER THE INCIDENT...
LALA STARTED TO MOVE AFTER HER HEART WAS PUT BACK.
BUT...
MASTER HUMAN...
WOULD YOU LIKE TO HEAR A SONG...?
IT WAS NO LONGER "LALA."
IT WAS A DOLL THAT MET GUZOL FOR THE FIRST TIME.

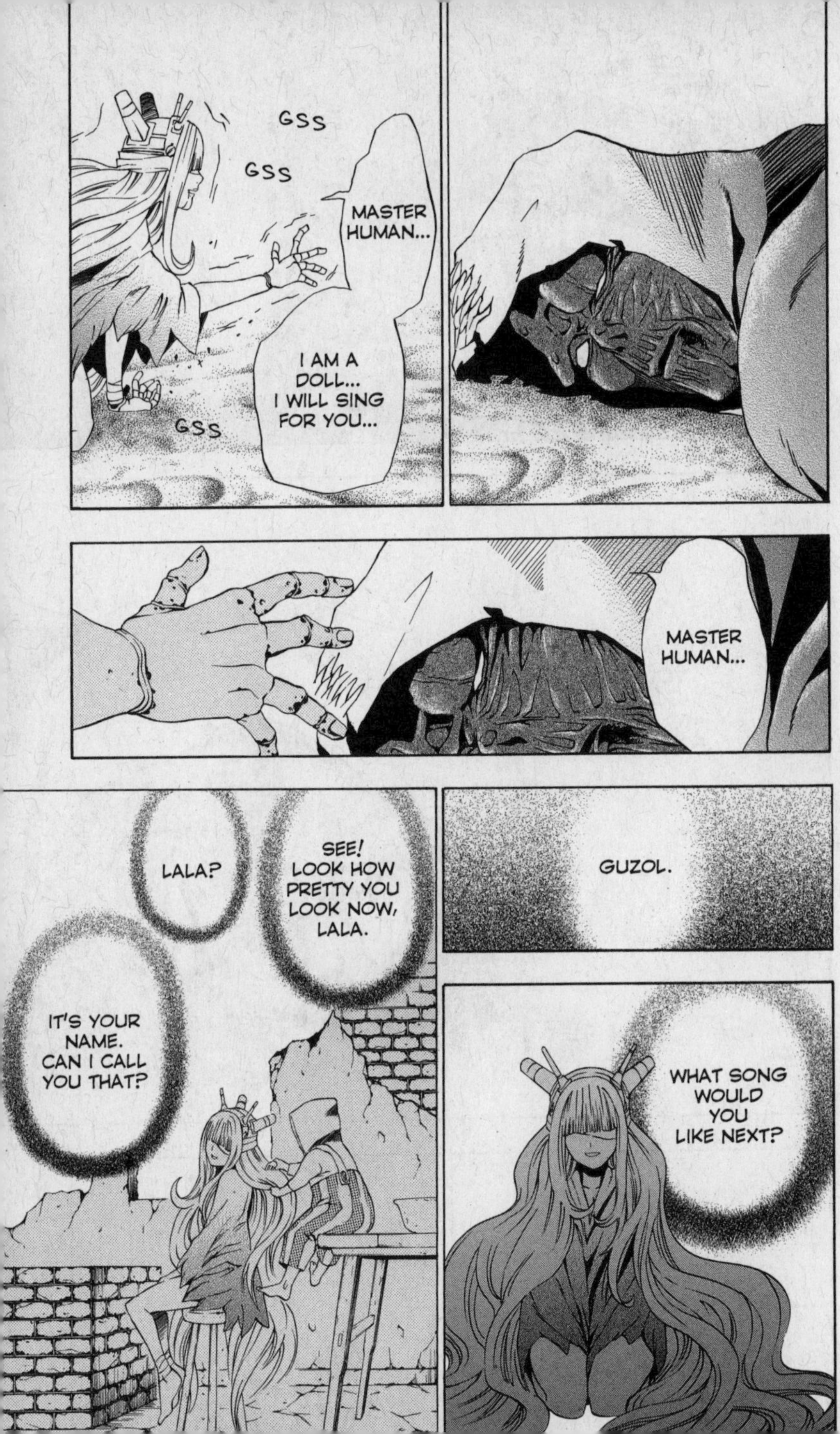
GSS
GSS
MASTER HUMAN...
I AM A DOLL... I WILL SING FOR YOU...
GSS
MASTER HUMAN...
GUZOL.
WHAT SONG WOULD YOU LIKE NEXT?
SEE! LOOK HOW PRETTY YOU LOOK NOW, LALA.
LALA?
IT'S YOUR NAME. CAN I CALL YOU THAT?

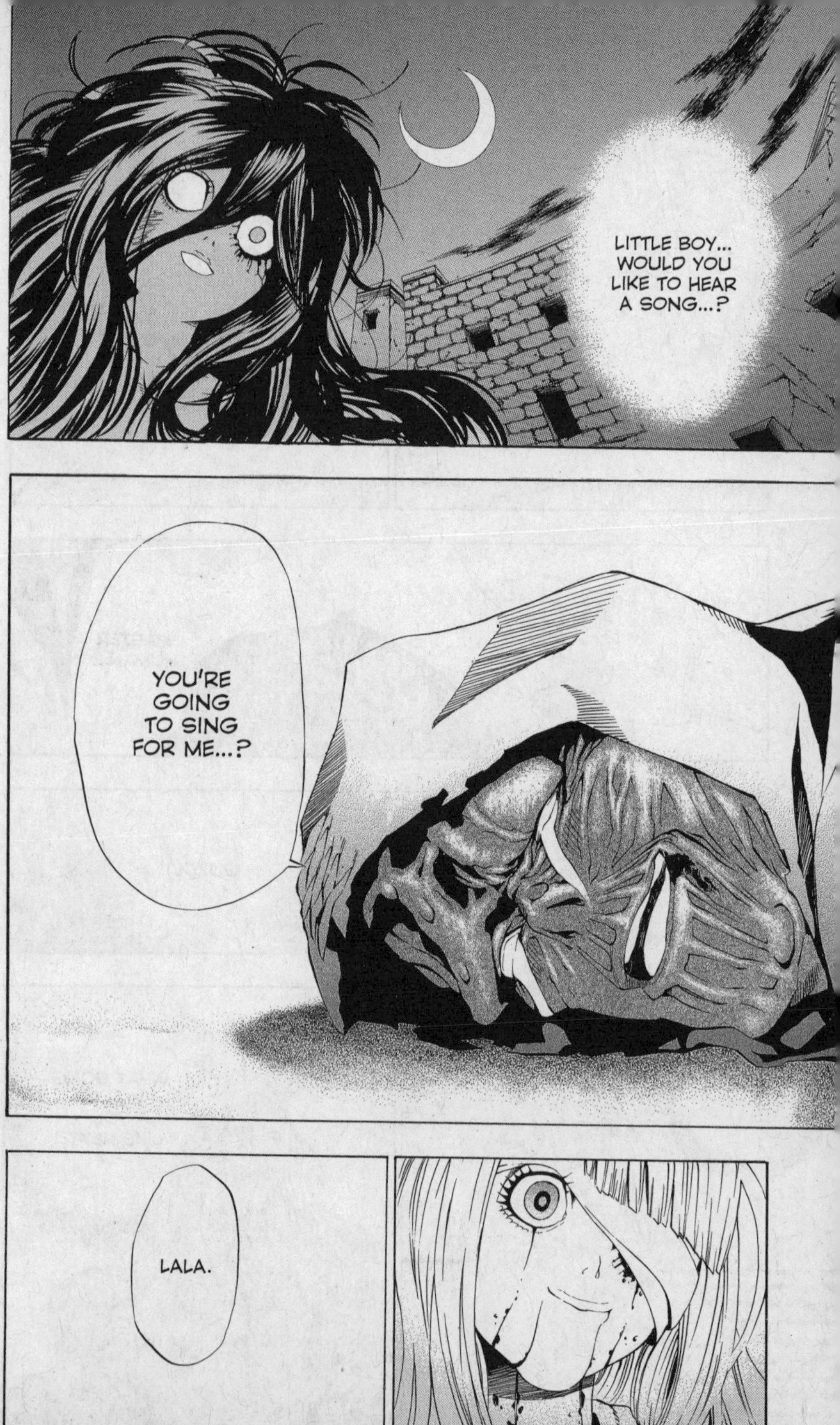
LITTLE BOY... WOULD YOU LIKE TO HEAR A SONG...?
YOU'RE GOING TO SING FOR ME...?
LALA.

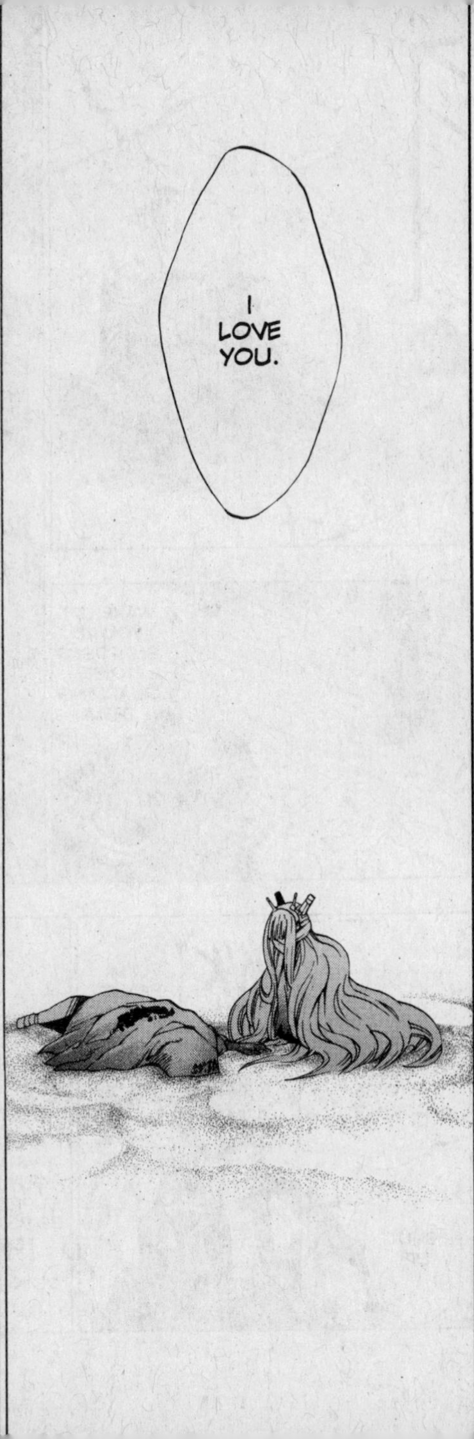
I LOVE YOU.

READ THIS WAY

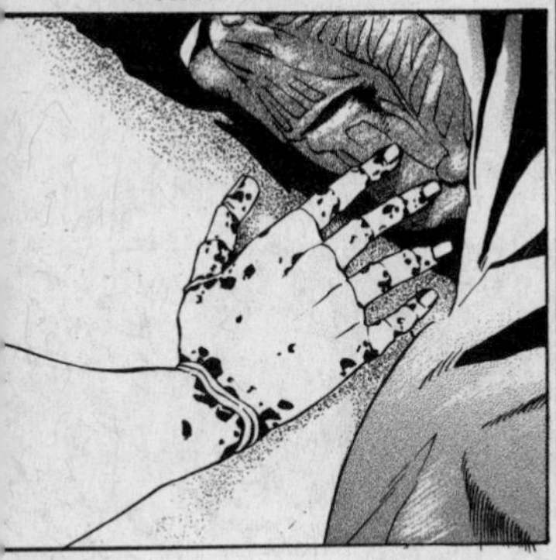

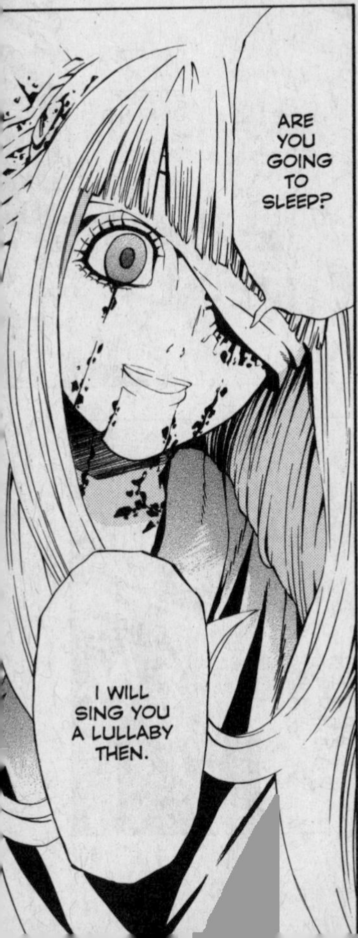
ARE YOU GOING TO SLEEP?
I WILL SING YOU A LULLABY THEN.

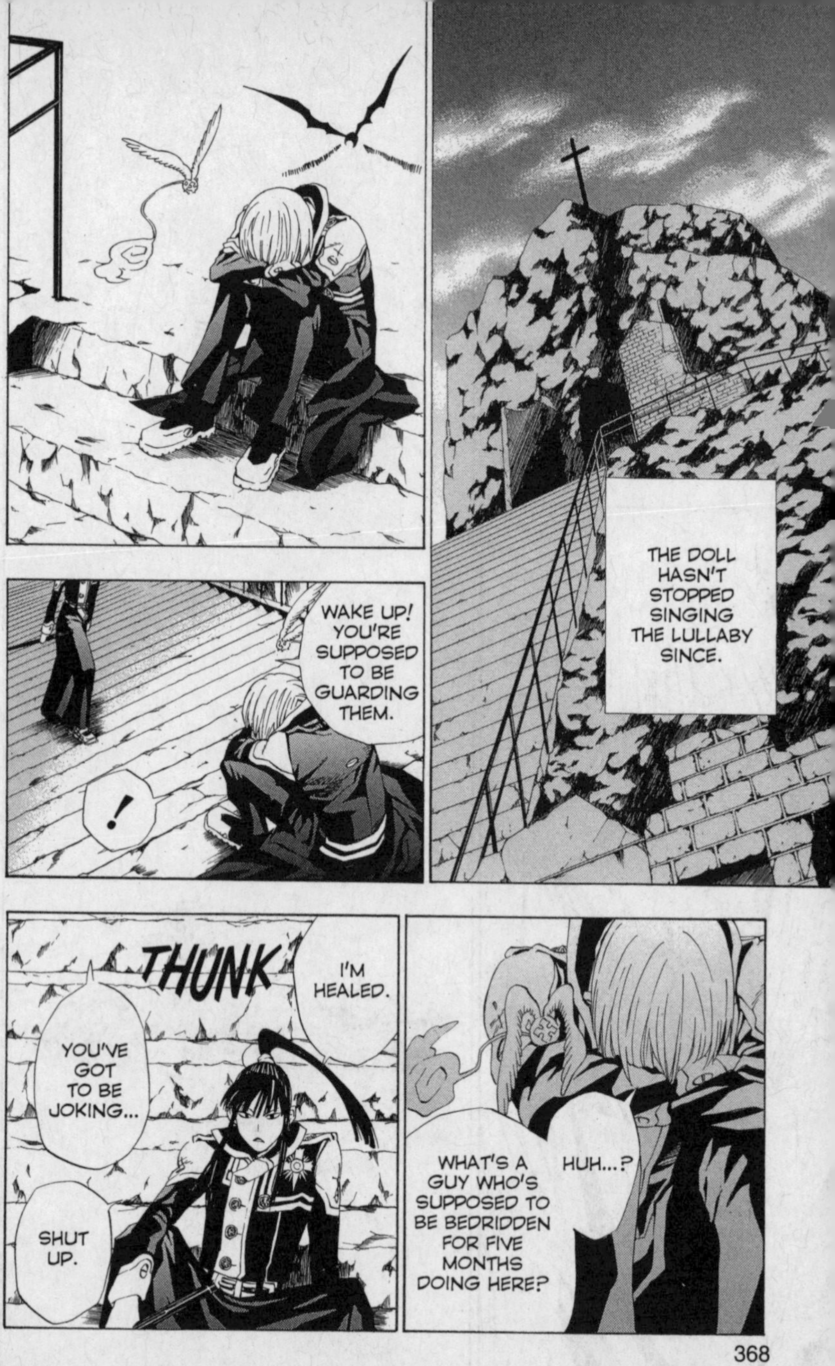
THE DOLL HASN'T STOPPED SINGING THE LULLABY SINCE.
WAKE UP! YOU'RE SUPPOSED TO BE GUARDING THEM.
!
HUH...?
WHAT'S A GUY WHO'S SUPPOSED TO BE BEDRIDDEN FOR FIVE MONTHS DOING HERE?
I'M HEALED.
THUNK
YOU'VE GOT TO BE JOKING...
SHUT UP.

READ THIS WAY

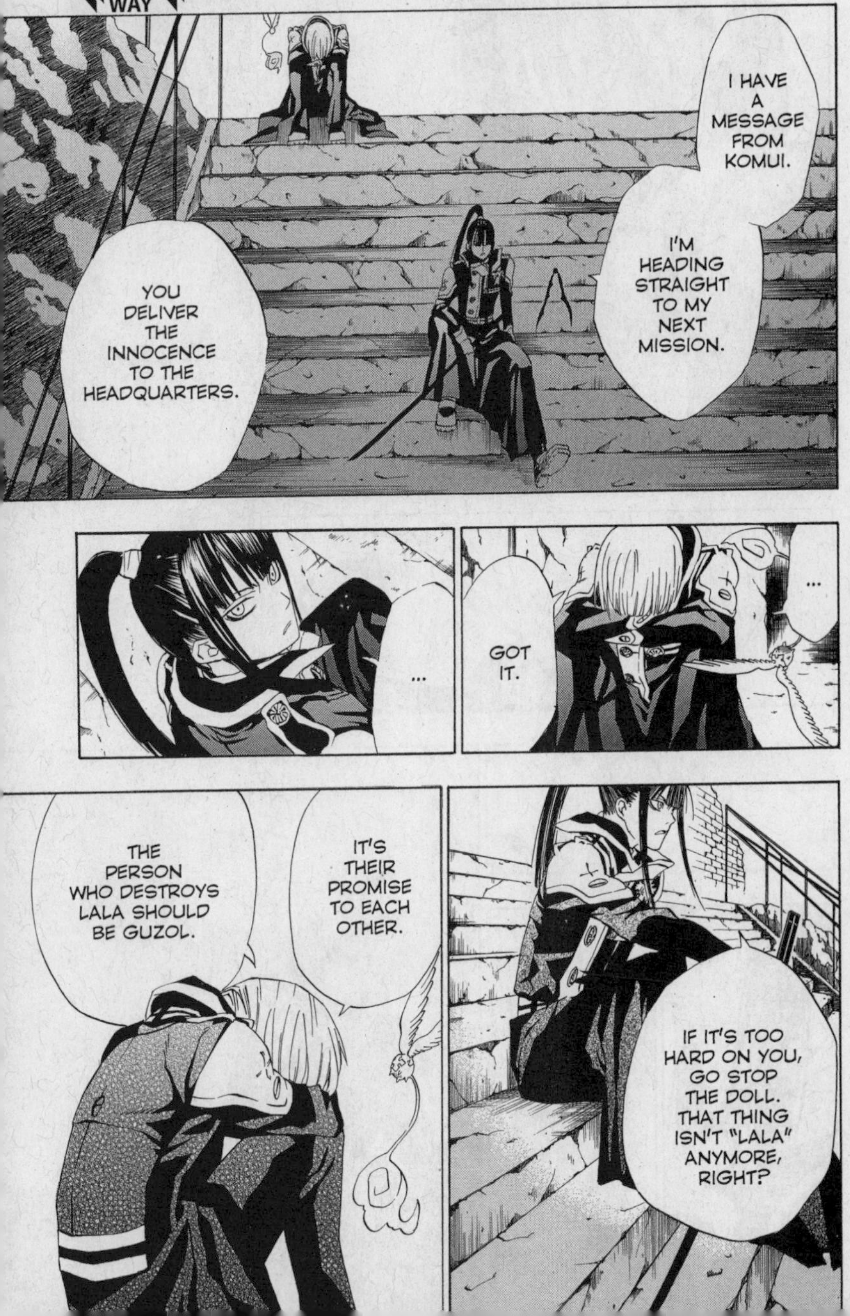
I HAVE A MESSAGE FROM KOMUI.
I'M HEADING STRAIGHT TO MY NEXT MISSION.
YOU DELIVER THE INNOCENCE TO THE HEADQUARTERS.
...
GOT IT.
...
IF IT'S TOO HARD ON YOU, GO STOP THE DOLL. THAT THING ISN'T "LALA" ANYMORE, RIGHT?
IT'S THEIR PROMISE TO EACH OTHER.
THE PERSON WHO DESTROYS LALA SHOULD BE GUZOL.

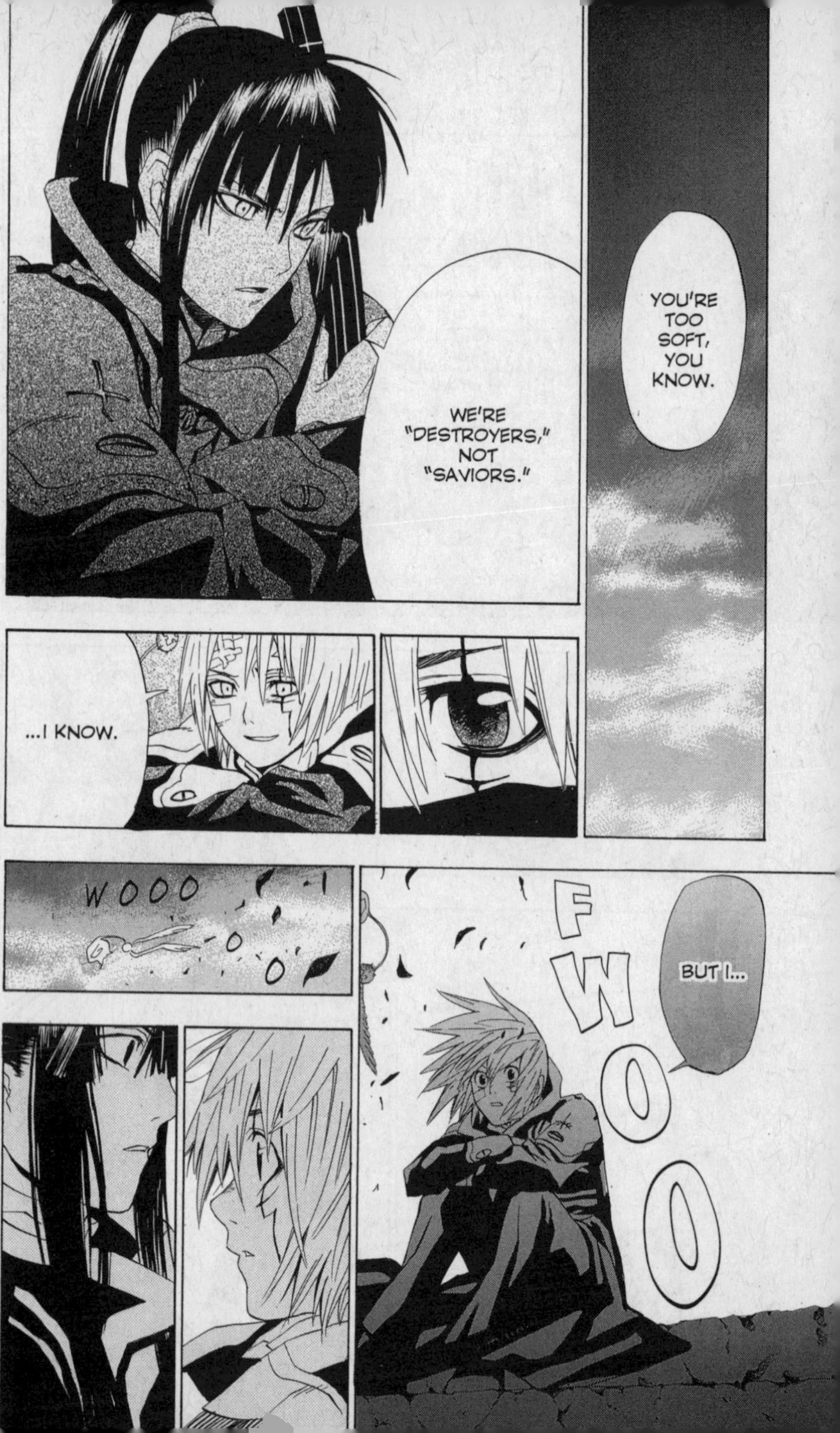

YOU'RE TOO SOFT, YOU KNOW.
WE'RE "DESTROYERS," NOT "SAVIORS."
...I KNOW.
FWOOO
BUT I...
WOOO

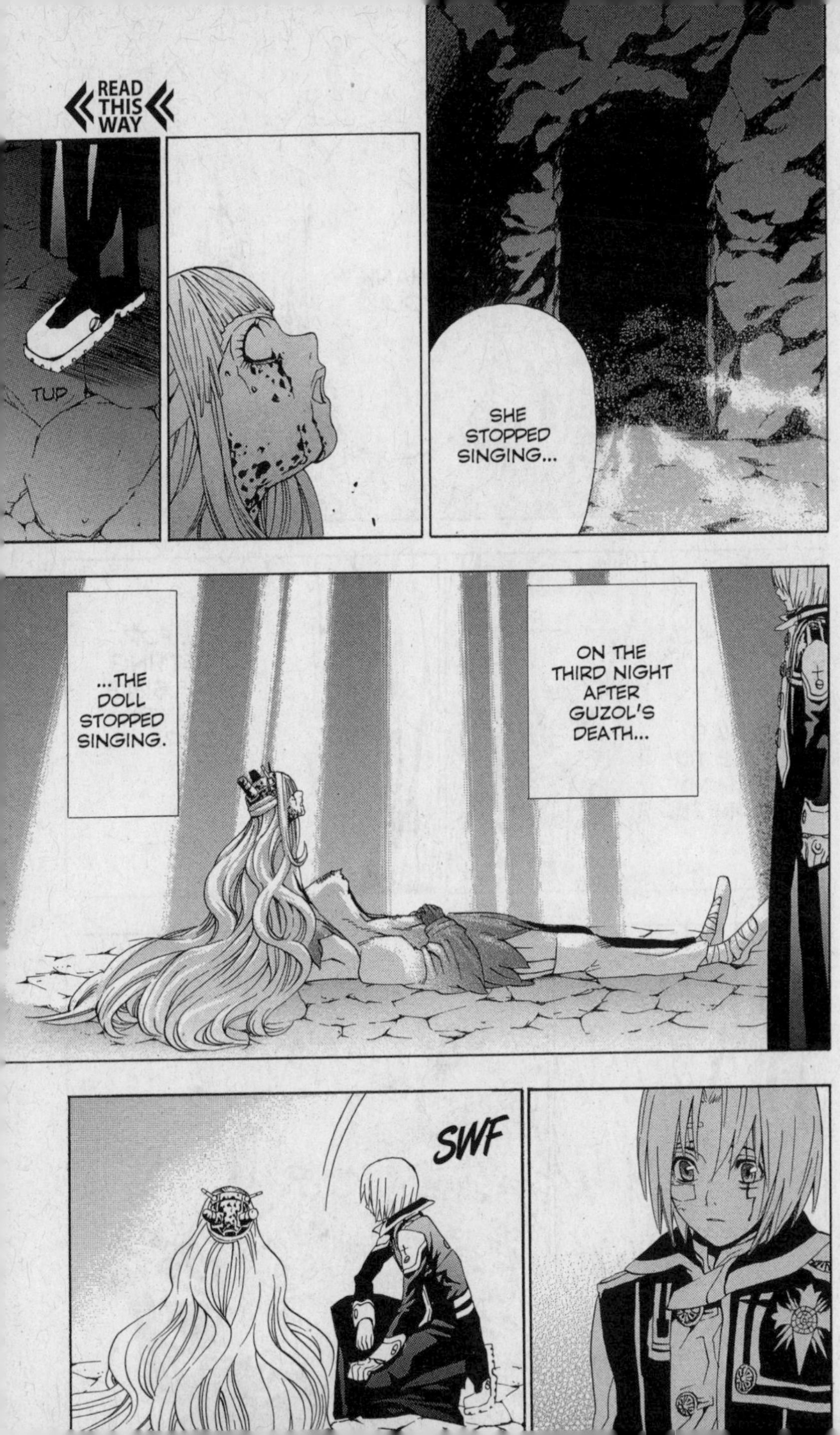
READ THIS WAY
SHE STOPPED SINGING...
TUP
ON THE THIRD NIGHT AFTER GUZOL'S DEATH...
...THE DOLL STOPPED SINGING.
SWF

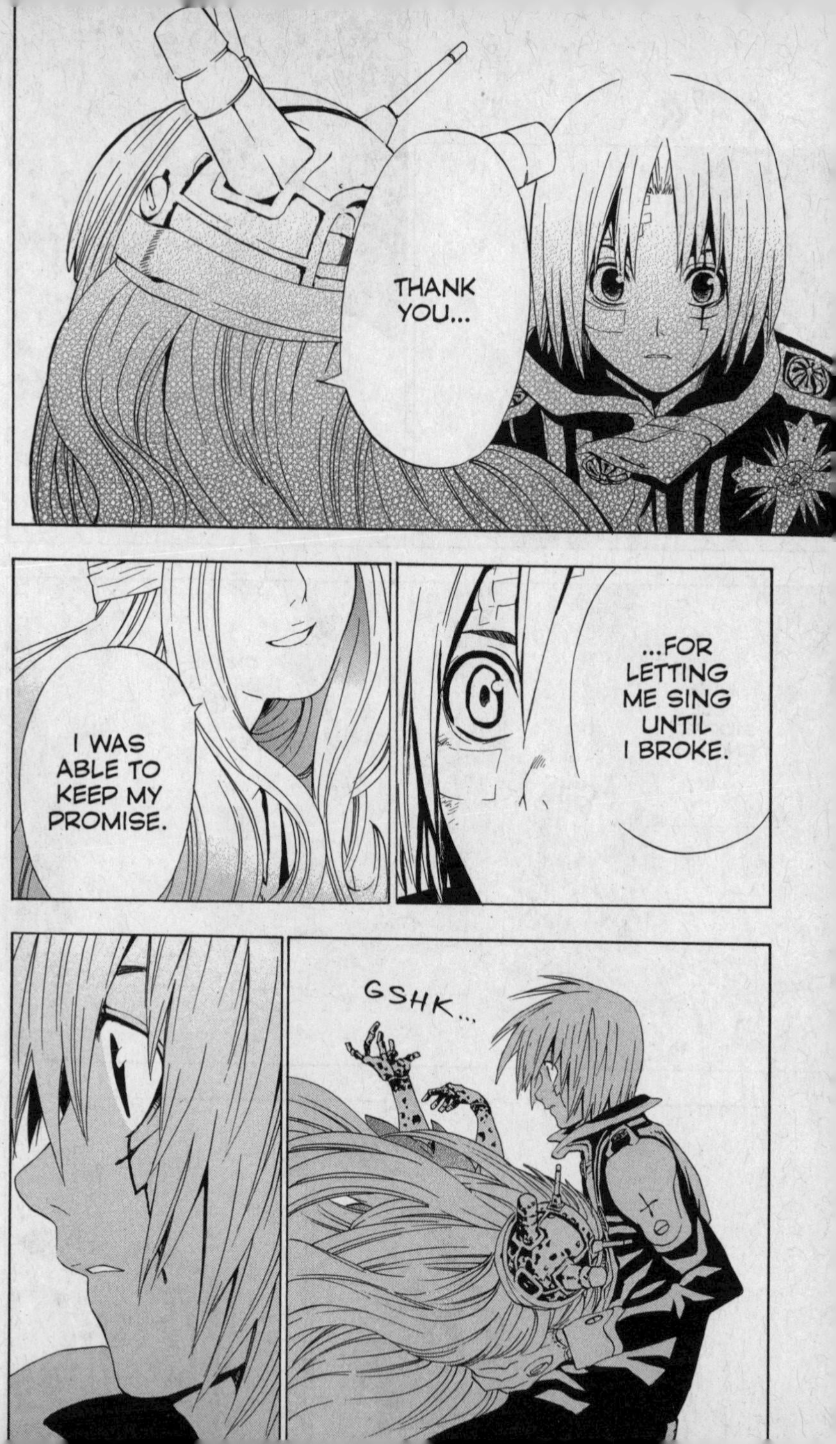
THANK YOU...
...FOR LETTING ME SING UNTIL I BROKE.
I WAS ABLE TO KEEP MY PROMISE.
GSHK...

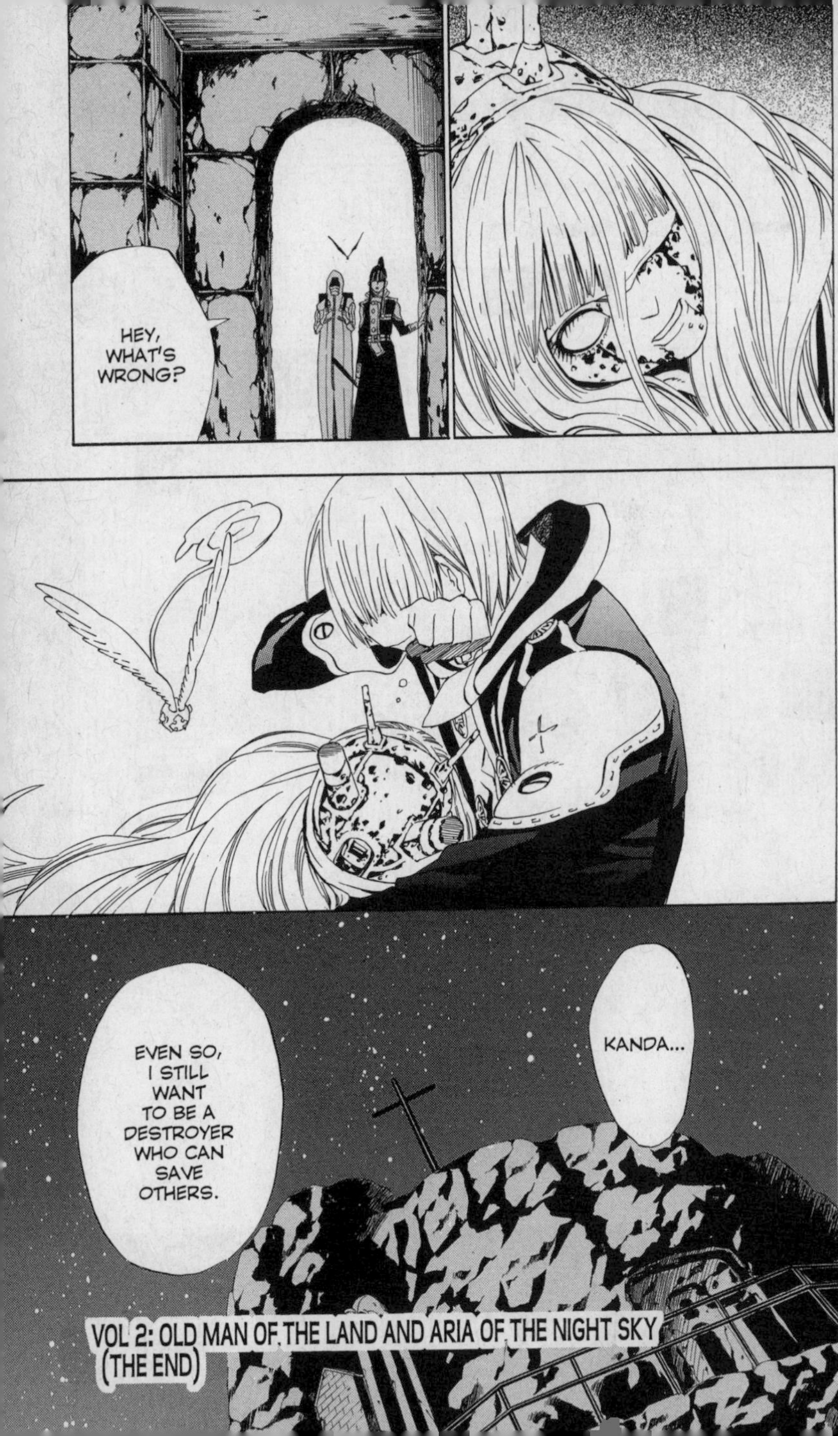
HEY, WHAT'S WRONG?
KANDA...
EVEN SO, I STILL WANT TO BE A DESTROYER WHO CAN SAVE OTHERS.
VOL 2: OLD MAN OF THE LAND AND ARIA OF THE NIGHT SKY (THE END)

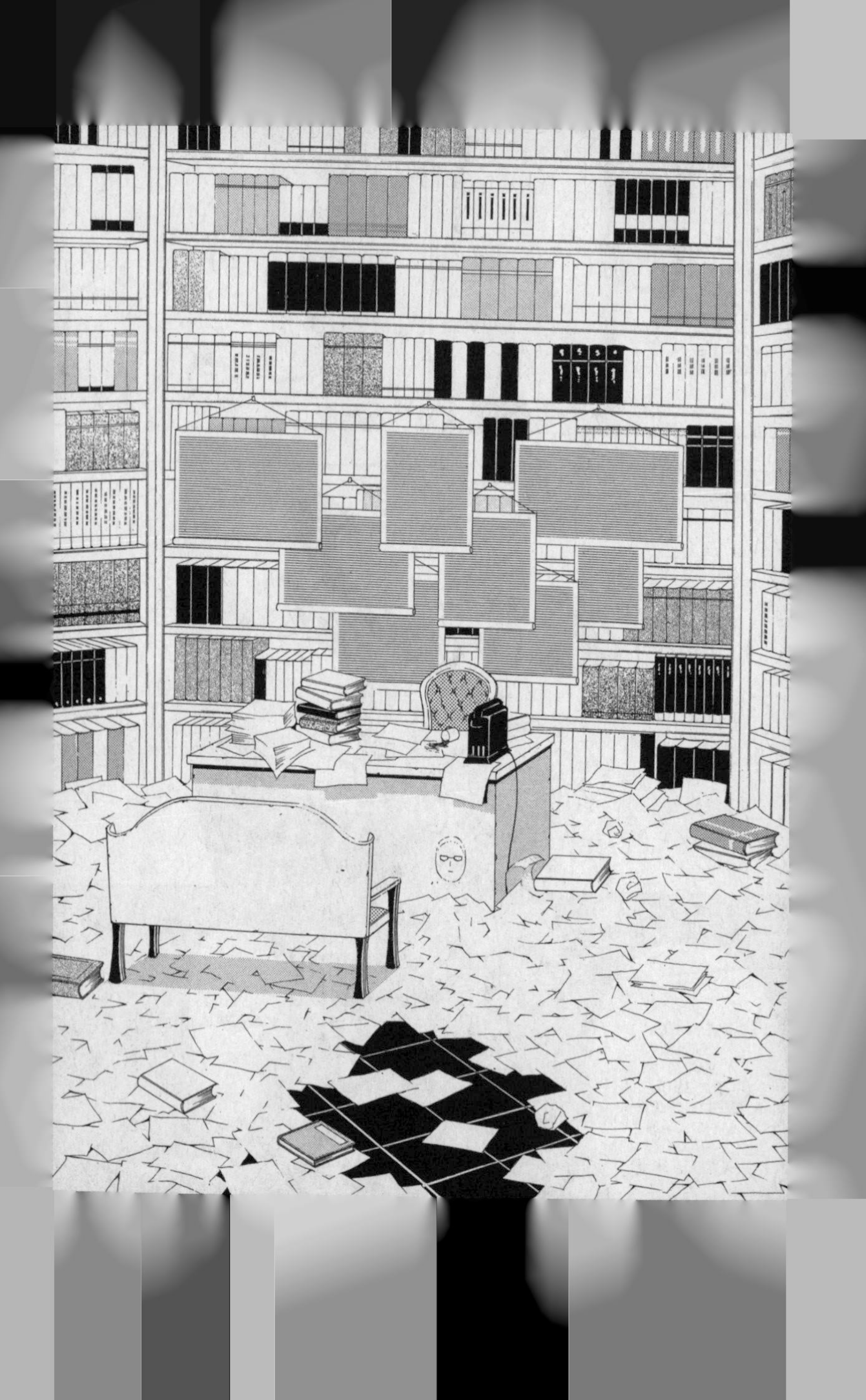

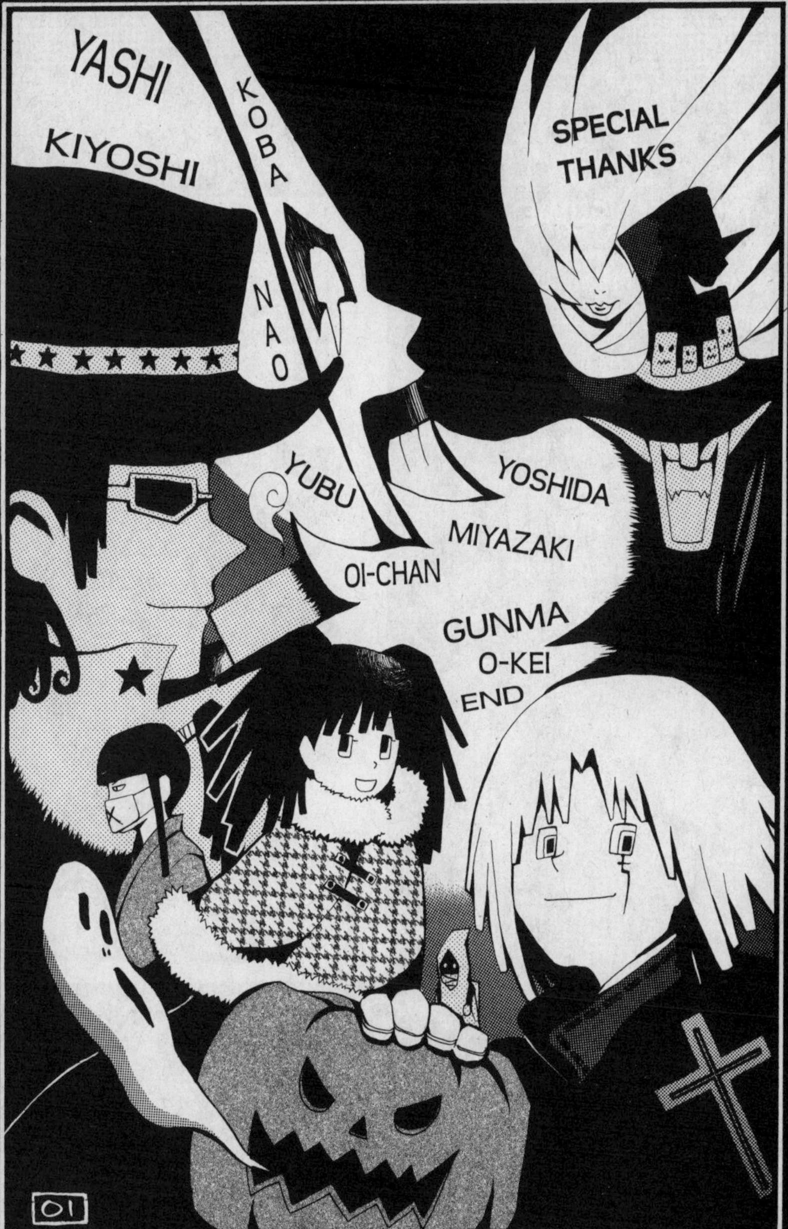
SPECIAL THANKS
YASHI
KIYOSHI
KOBA
NAO
YUBU
YOSHIDA
MIYAZAKI
OI-CHAN
GUNMA
O-KEI
END

IN THE NEXT VOLUME...

Prepare for another bizarre adventure as teenage exorcist Allen Walker and Lenalee of The Black Order are dispatched to a city where time has stood still, a place where the townsfolk forget that every day is the same day repeating itself. Oddly enough, a woman named Miranda is the only one who is unaffected by the time warp. What's her secret?

Available Now!

EDITION

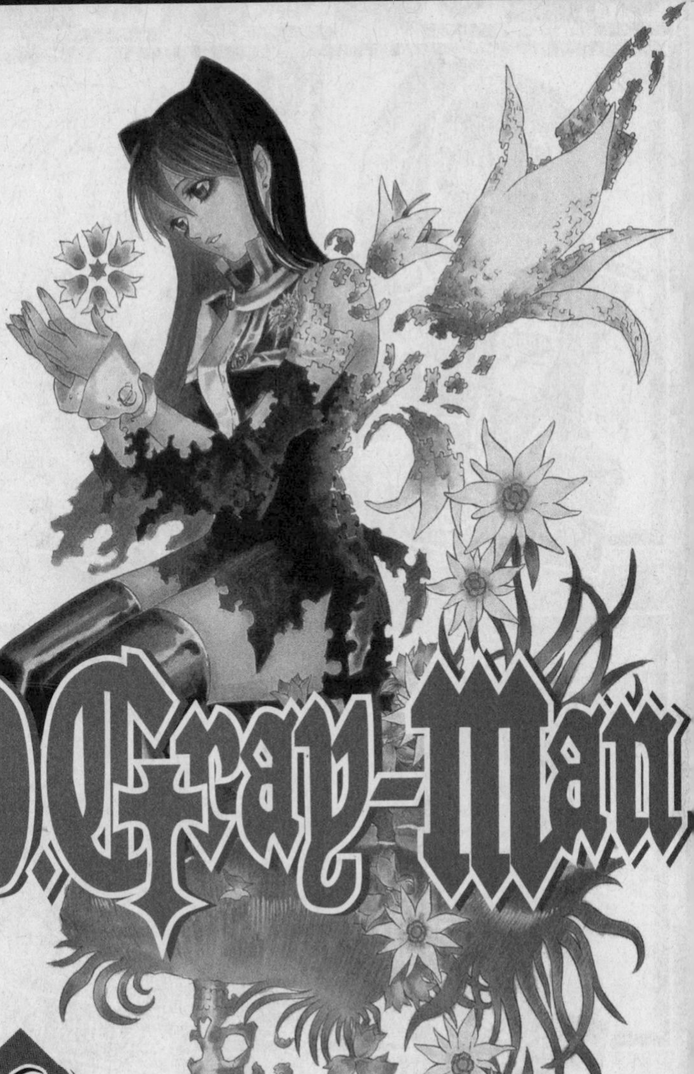

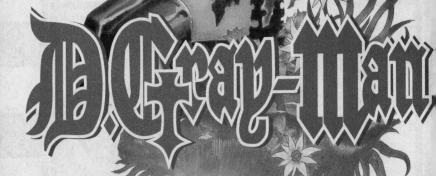

D.Gray-man

vol. 3

STORY & ART BY
Katsura Hoshino

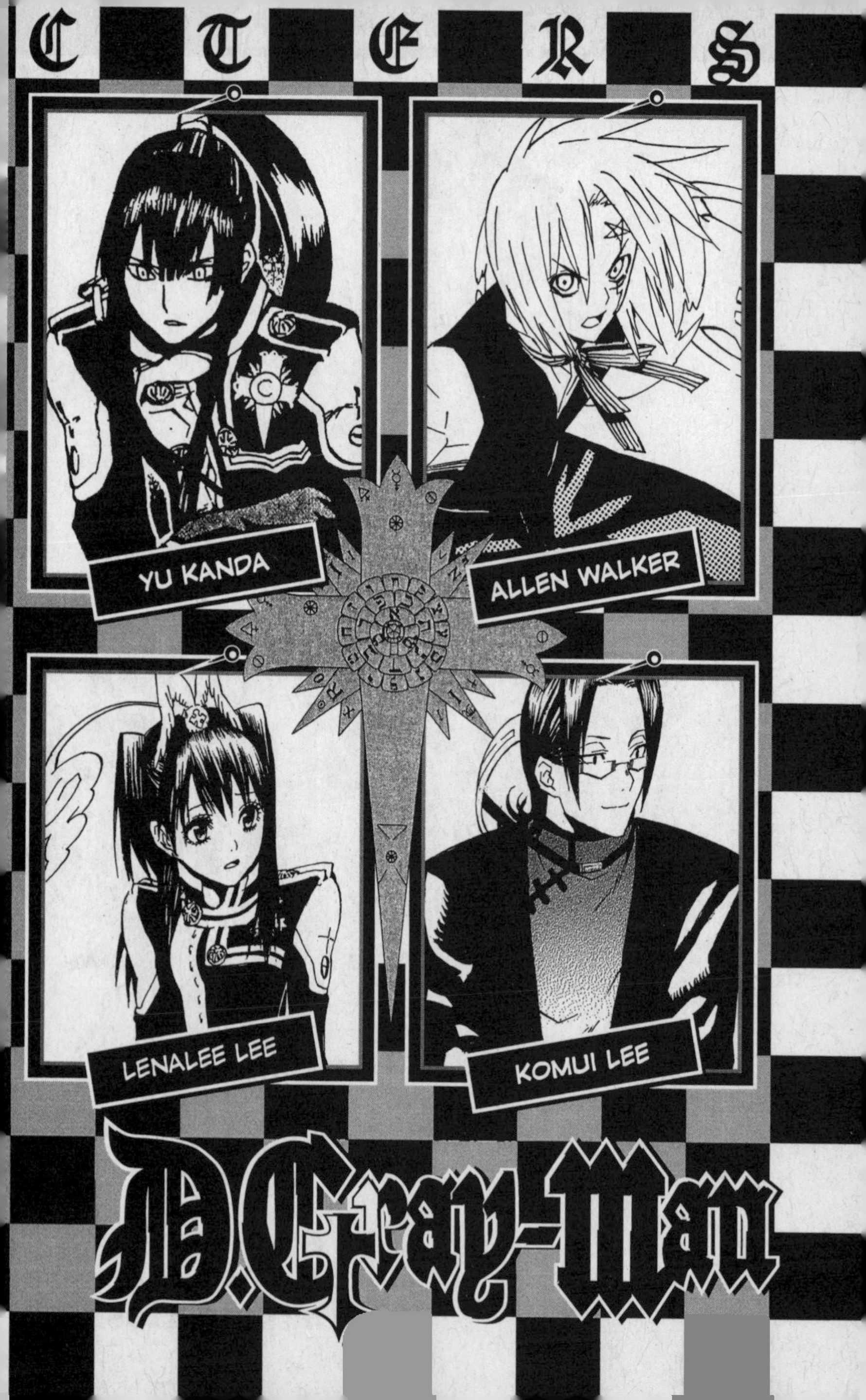
C T E R S
ALLEN WALKER
YU KANDA
KOMUI LEE
LENALEE LEE
D.Gray-man

C H A R A

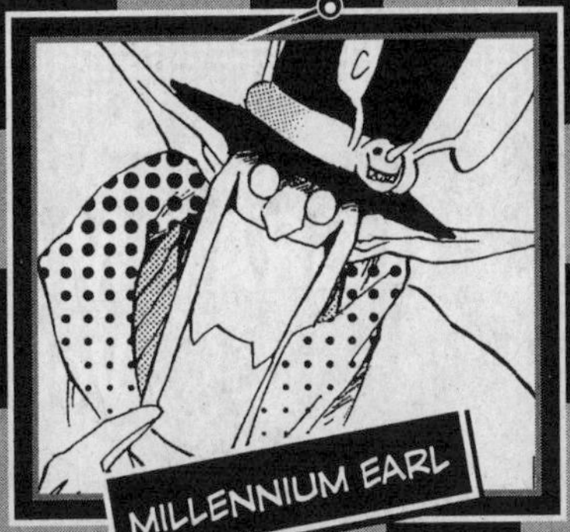

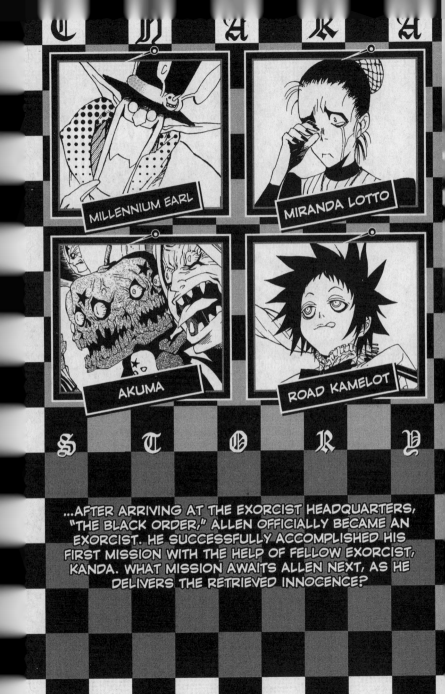

MILLENNIUM EARL

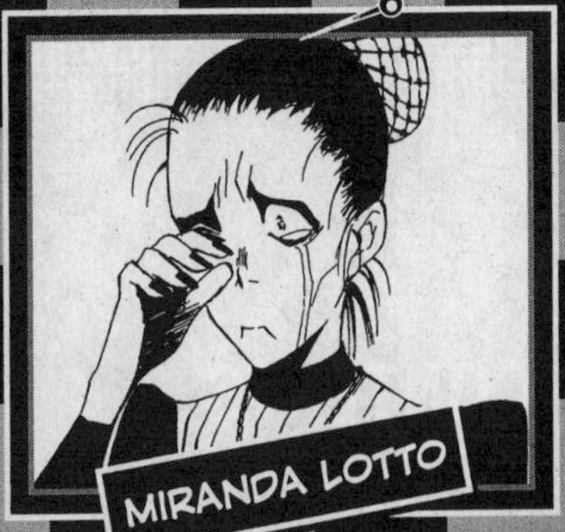

MIRANDA LOTTO

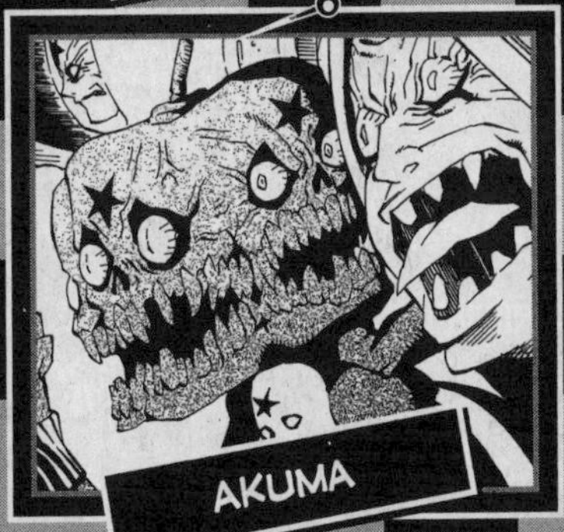

AKUMA

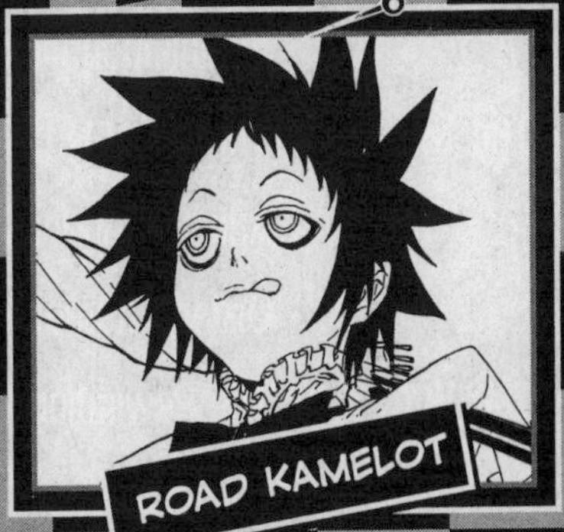

ROAD KAMELOT

S T O R Y

...AFTER ARRIVING AT THE EXORCIST HEADQUARTERS, "THE BLACK ORDER," ALLEN OFFICIALLY BECAME AN EXORCIST. HE SUCCESSFULLY ACCOMPLISHED HIS FIRST MISSION WITH THE HELP OF FELLOW EXORCIST, KANDA. WHAT MISSION AWAITS ALLEN NEXT, AS HE DELIVERS THE RETRIEVED INNOCENCE?

D.GRAY-MAN
Vol. 3

CONTENTS

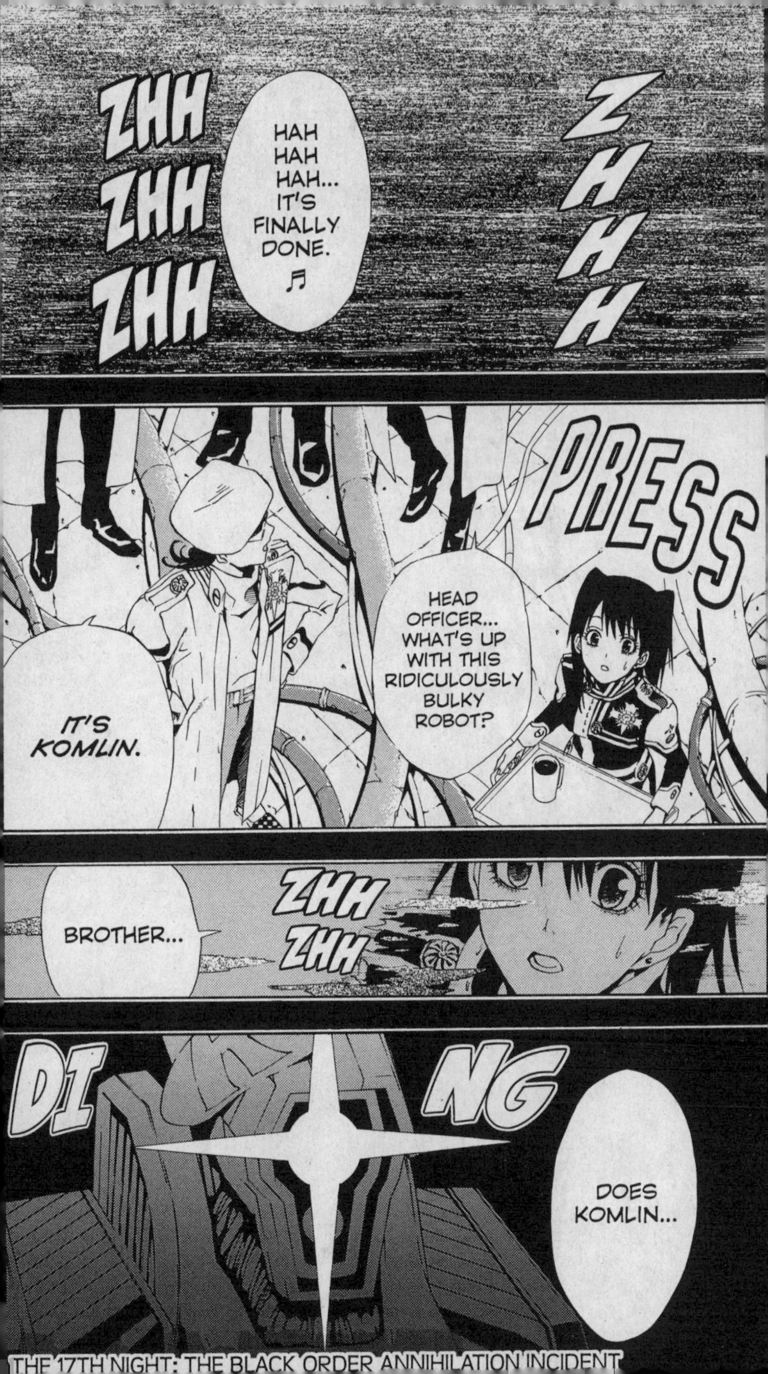
ZHHHH
HAH HAH HAH... IT'S FINALLY DONE. ♬
ZHH ZHH ZHH
PRESS
HEAD OFFICER... WHAT'S UP WITH THIS RIDICULOUSLY BULKY ROBOT?
IT'S KOMLIN.
ZHH ZHH
BROTHER...
DI NG
DOES KOMLIN...

THE 17TH NIGHT: THE BLACK ORDER ANNIHILATION INCIDENT

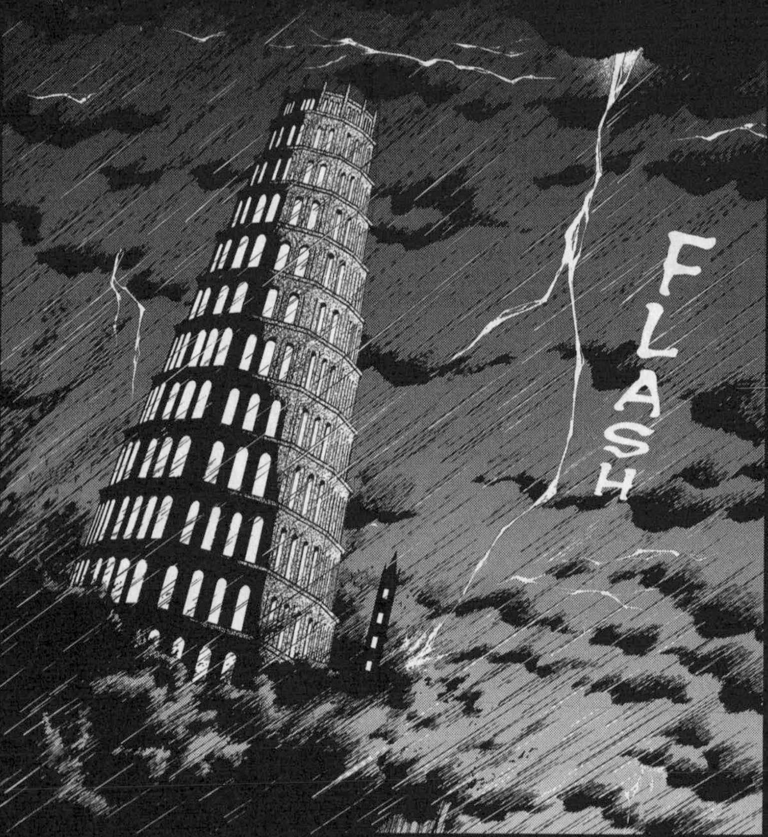
FLASH

THE 17TH NIGHT: THE BLACK ORDER ANNIHILATION INCIDENT

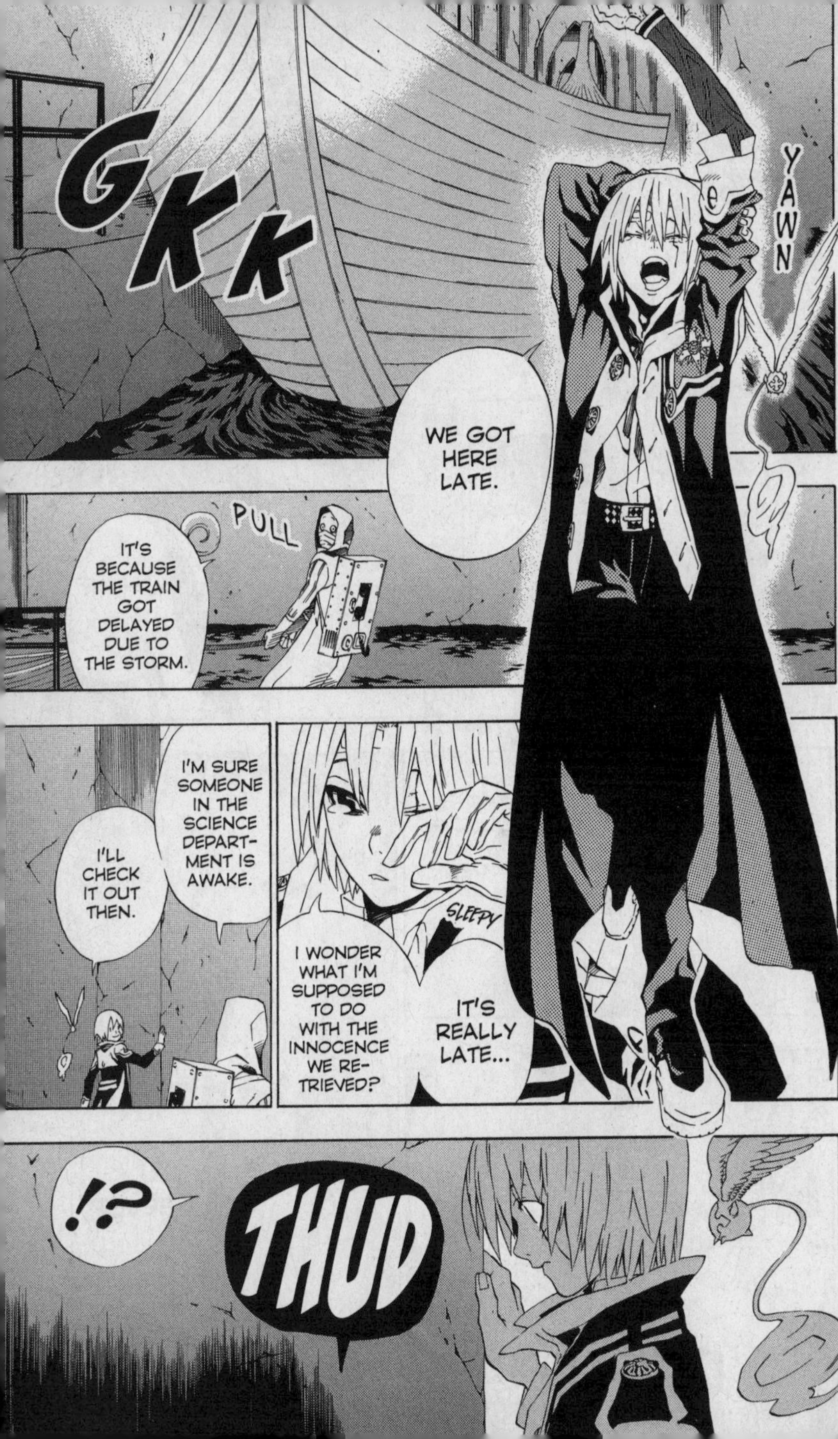
YAWN
WE GOT HERE LATE.
GKK
PULL
IT'S BECAUSE THE TRAIN GOT DELAYED DUE TO THE STORM.
SLEEPY
IT'S REALLY LATE...
I WONDER WHAT I'M SUPPOSED TO DO WITH THE INNOCENCE WE RE-TRIEVED?
I'M SURE SOMEONE IN THE SCIENCE DEPART-MENT IS AWAKE.
I'LL CHECK IT OUT THEN.
THUD
!?

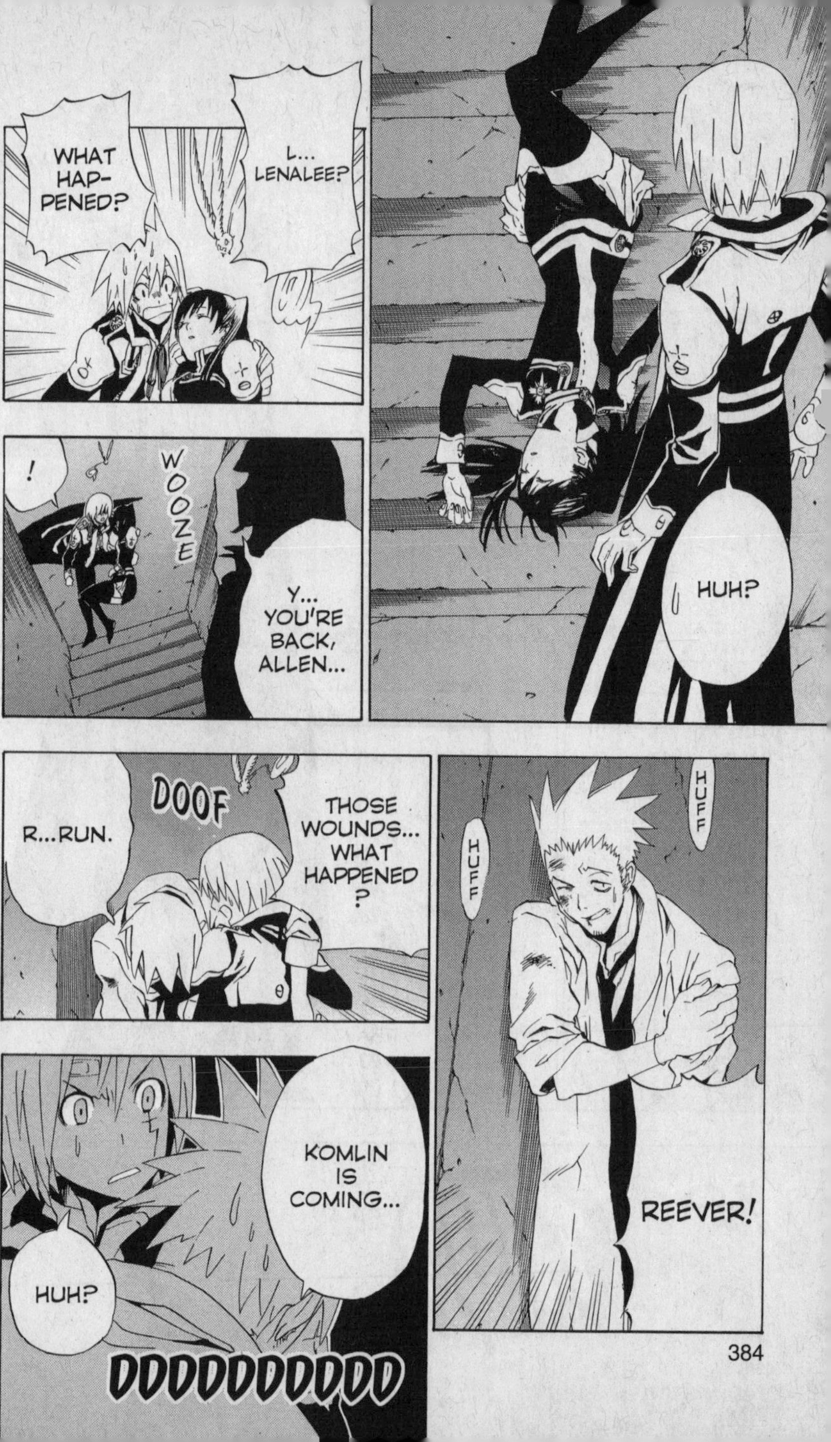
HUH?
L...
LENALEE?
WHAT
HAP-
PENED?
WOOZE
Y...
YOU'RE
BACK,
ALLEN...
!
HUFF
HUFF
REEVER!
THOSE
WOUNDS...
WHAT
HAPPENED
?
DOOF
R...RUN.
KOMLIN
IS
COMING...
HUH?
DDDDDDDDDD

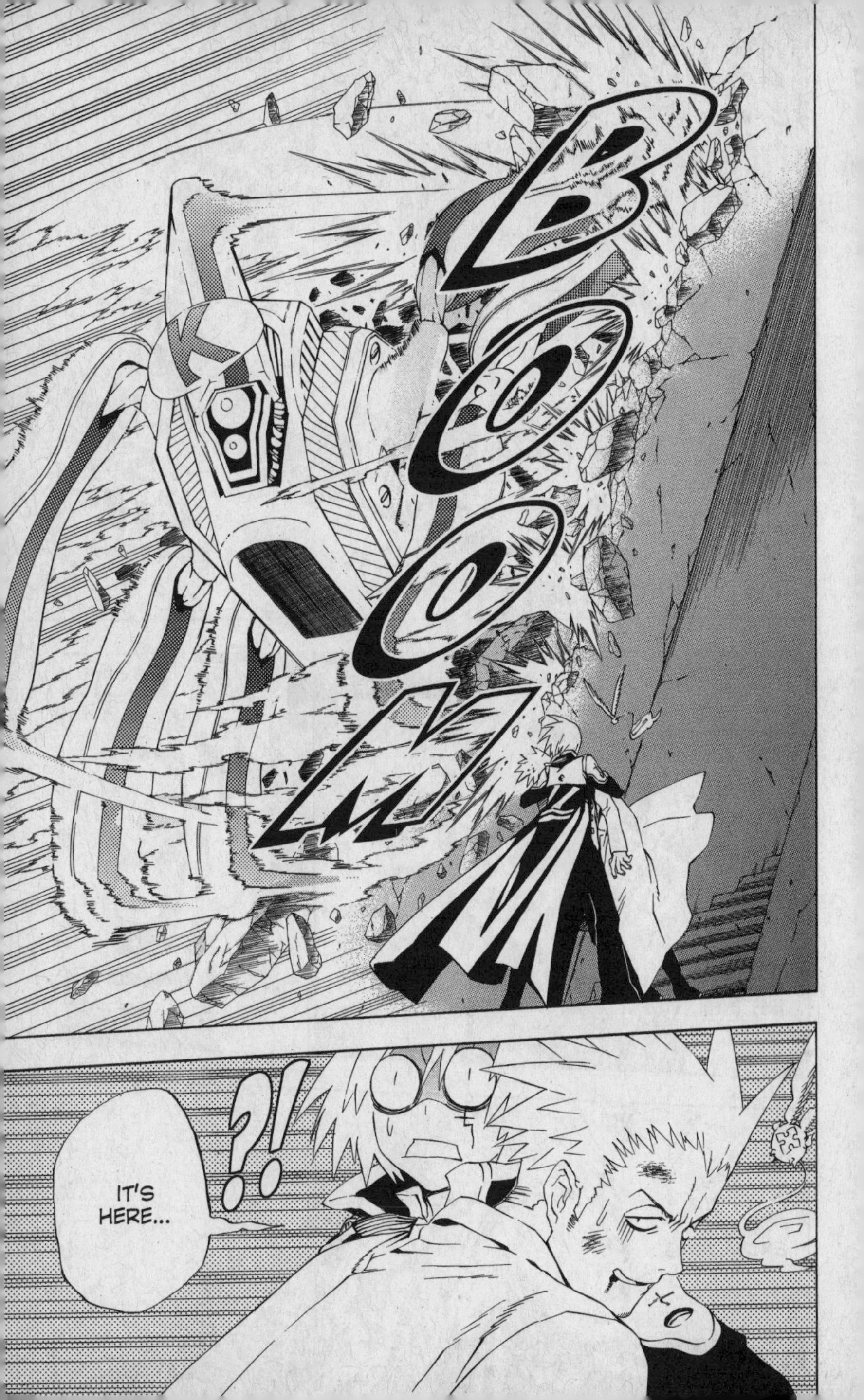
BOOOM
?!!
IT'S HERE...

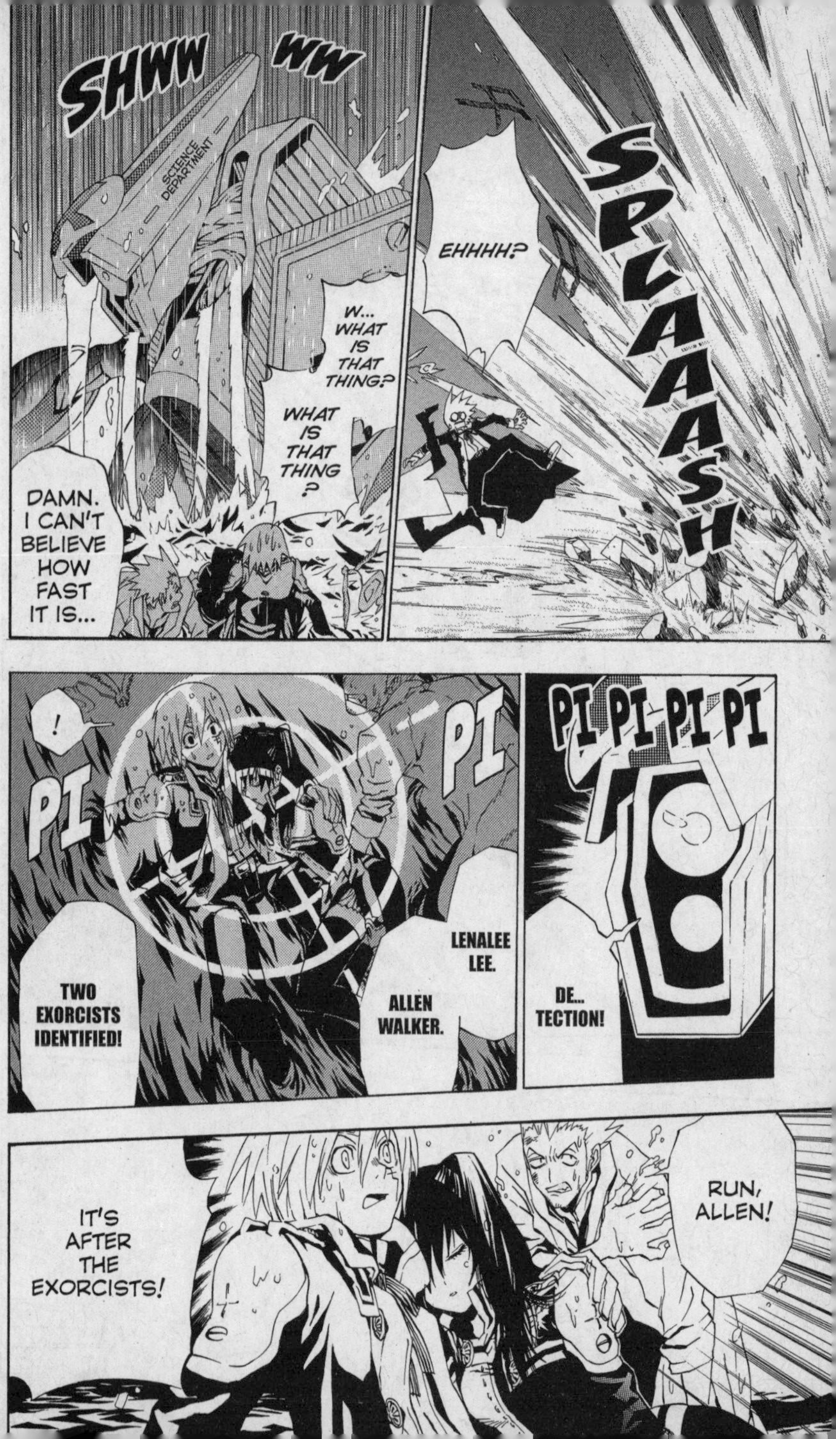
SPLAAASH
EHHHH?
SHWWWW
W... WHAT IS THAT THING?
WHAT IS THAT THING?
DAMN. I CAN'T BELIEVE HOW FAST IT IS...
SCIENCE DEPARTMENT
PI PI PI PI
DE... TECTION!
PI
PI
!
LENALEE LEE.
ALLEN WALKER.
TWO EXORCISTS IDENTIFIED!
RUN, ALLEN!
IT'S AFTER THE EXORCISTS!

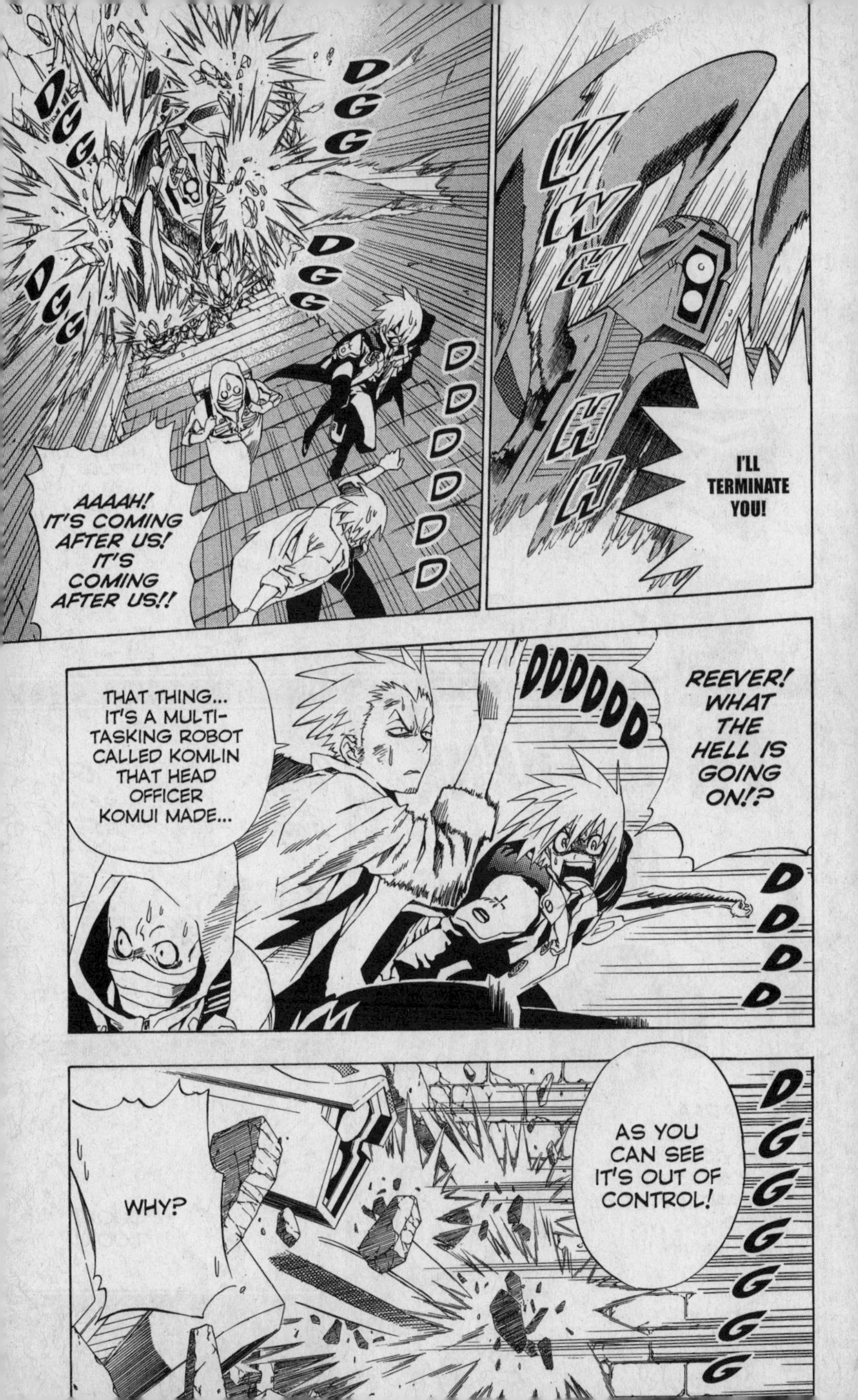
I'LL TERMINATE YOU!
DGG
DGG
DGG
DGG
DDDDDDDD
AAAAH! IT'S COMING AFTER US! IT'S COMING AFTER US!!
REEVER! WHAT THE HELL IS GOING ON!?
DDDDDD
THAT THING... IT'S A MULTI-TASKING ROBOT CALLED KOMLIN THAT HEAD OFFICER KOMUI MADE...
DDDD
DGGGGGGGG
AS YOU CAN SEE IT'S OUT OF CONTROL!
WHY?

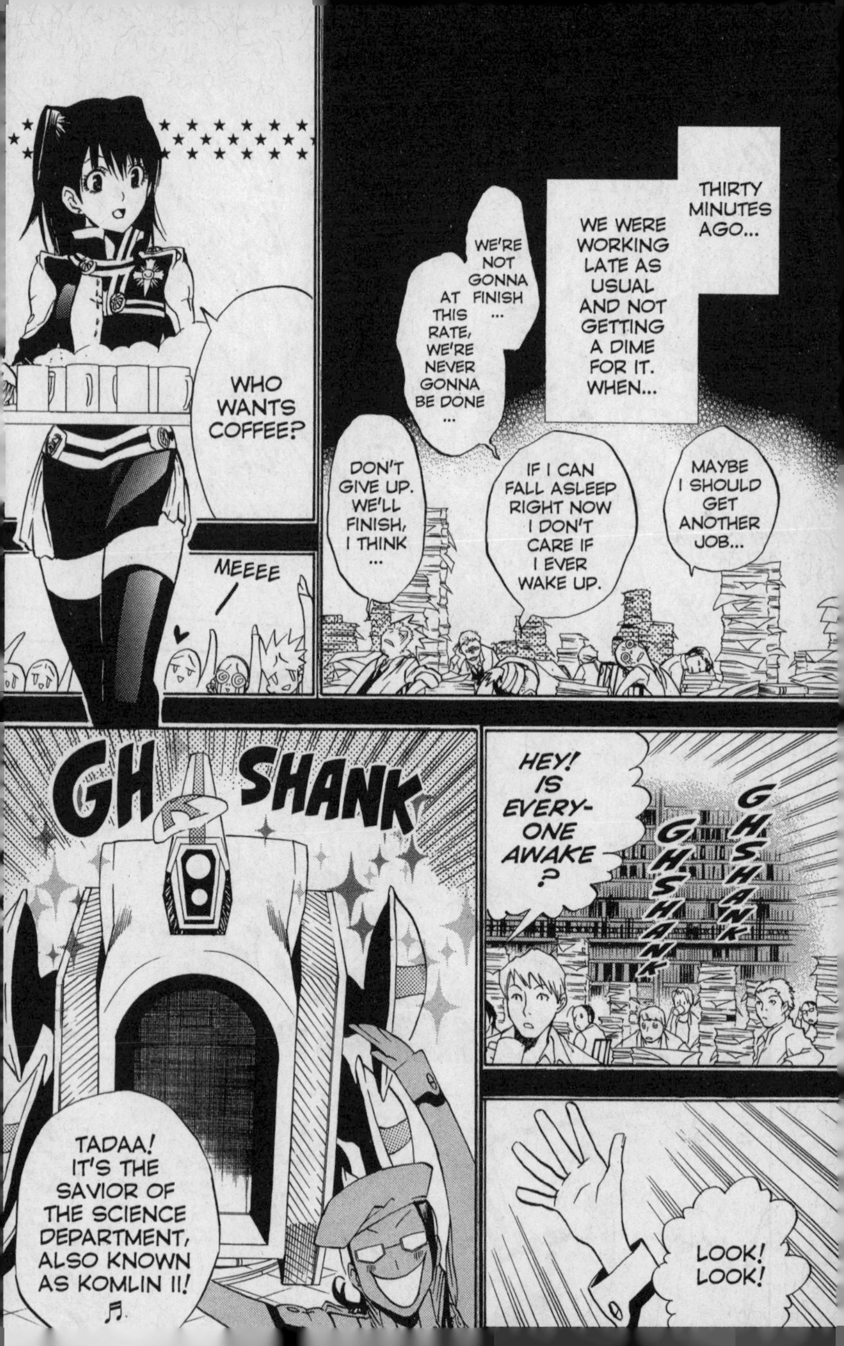
THIRTY MINUTES AGO...
WE WERE WORKING LATE AS USUAL AND NOT GETTING A DIME FOR IT. WHEN...
WE'RE NOT GONNA FINISH ...
AT THIS RATE, WE'RE NEVER GONNA BE DONE ...
MAYBE I SHOULD GET ANOTHER JOB...
IF I CAN FALL ASLEEP RIGHT NOW I DON'T CARE IF I EVER WAKE UP.
DON'T GIVE UP. WE'LL FINISH, I THINK ...
WHO WANTS COFFEE?
MEEEE
HEY! IS EVERY-ONE AWAKE ?
GHSHANK
GHSHANK
LOOK! LOOK!
GH SHANK
TADAA! IT'S THE SAVIOR OF THE SCIENCE DEPARTMENT, ALSO KNOWN AS KOMLIN II! ♬

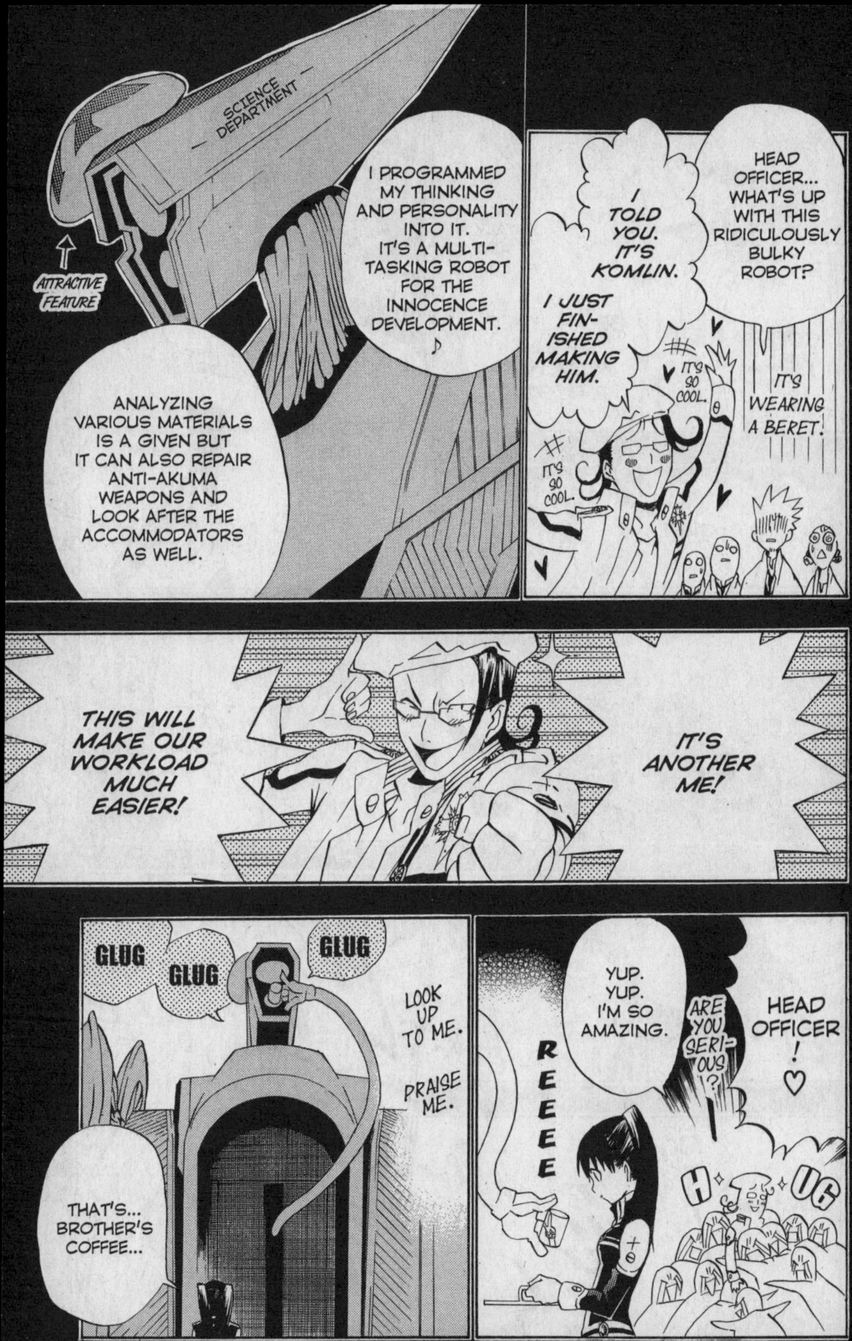
HEAD OFFICER... WHAT'S UP WITH THIS RIDICULOUSLY BULKY ROBOT?
I TOLD YOU. IT'S KOMLIN.
I JUST FIN-ISHED MAKING HIM.
IT'S SO COOL.
IT'S WEARING A BERET.
IT'S SO COOL.
SCIENCE DEPARTMENT
I PROGRAMMED MY THINKING AND PERSONALITY INTO IT. IT'S A MULTI-TASKING ROBOT FOR THE INNOCENCE DEVELOPMENT. ♪
ATTRACTIVE FEATURE
ANALYZING VARIOUS MATERIALS IS A GIVEN BUT IT CAN ALSO REPAIR ANTI-AKUMA WEAPONS AND LOOK AFTER THE ACCOMMODATORS AS WELL.
IT'S ANOTHER ME!
THIS WILL MAKE OUR WORKLOAD MUCH EASIER!
HEAD OFFICER! ♡
ARE YOU SERI-OUS?!
YUP. YUP. I'M SO AMAZING.
REEEE
H UG
GLUG
LOOK UP TO ME.
GLUG
PRAISE ME.
GLUG
THAT'S... BROTHER'S COFFEE...

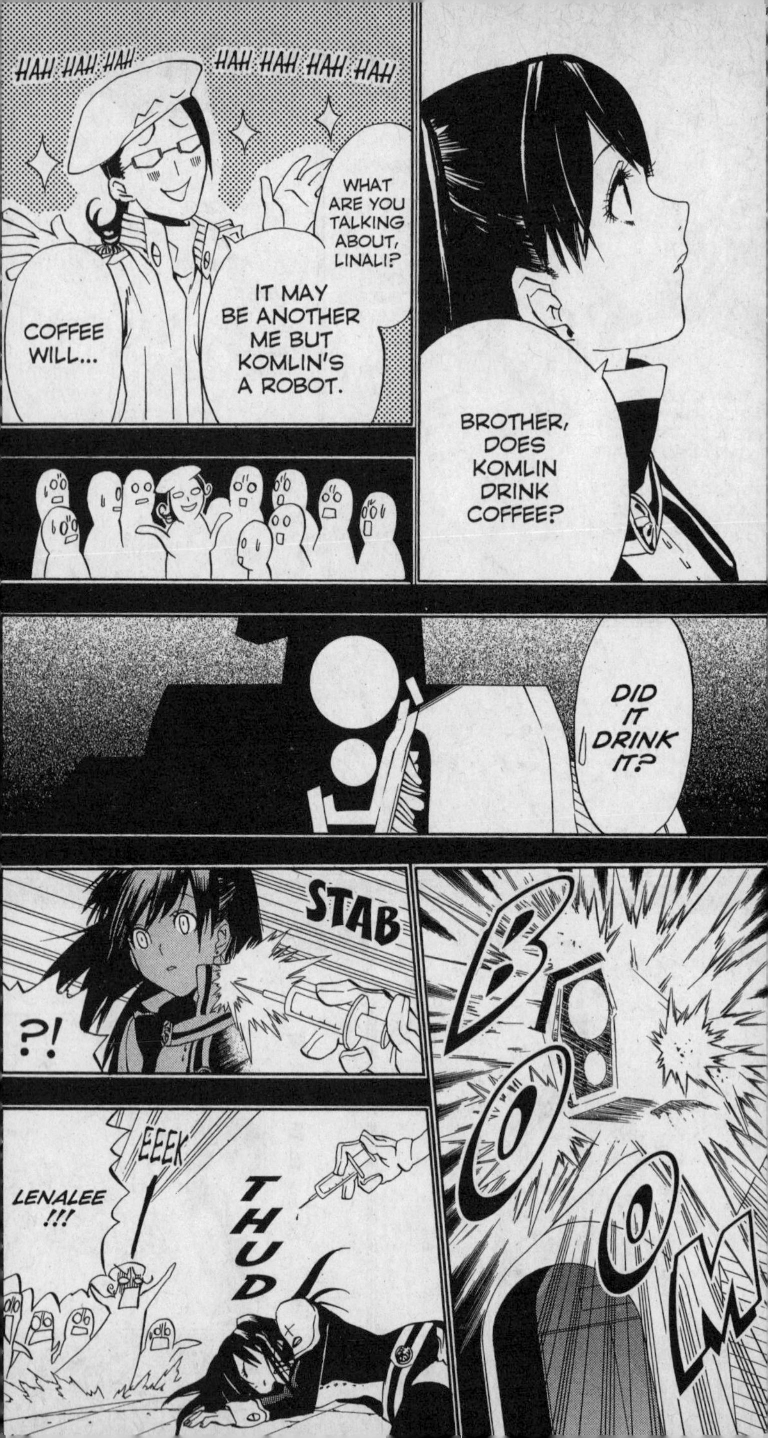
BROTHER, DOES KOMLIN DRINK COFFEE?
HAH HAH HAH HAH
HAH HAH HAH
WHAT ARE YOU TALKING ABOUT, LINALI?
IT MAY BE ANOTHER ME BUT KOMLIN'S A ROBOT.
COFFEE WILL...
DID IT DRINK IT?
BOOM
STAB
?!
EEEK
THUD
LENALEE !!!

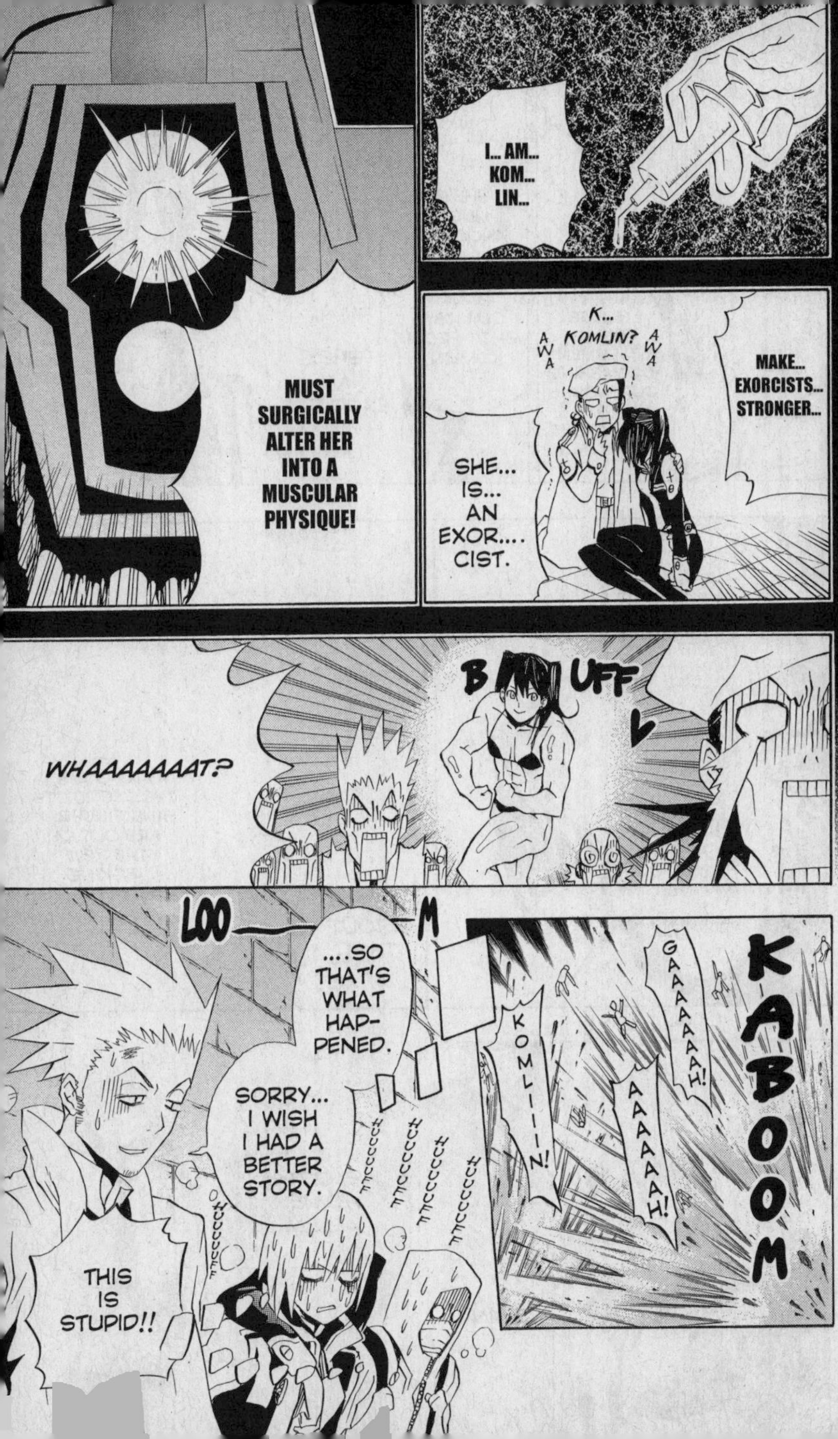
I... AM... KOM... LIN...
MAKE... EXORCISTS... STRONGER...
K... KOMLIN?
AWA
AWA
SHE... IS... AN EXOR.... CIST.
MUST SURGICALLY ALTER HER INTO A MUSCULAR PHYSIQUE!
BUFF
WHAAAAAAAT?
KABOOM
GAAAAAAAAH!
KOMLIIIN!
AAAAAAH!
LOO—M
....SO THAT'S WHAT HAP-PENED.
SORRY... I WISH I HAD A BETTER STORY.
HUUUUUFF
HUUUUUFF
HUUUUUFF
HUUUUUFF
HUUUUUFF
THIS IS STUPID!!

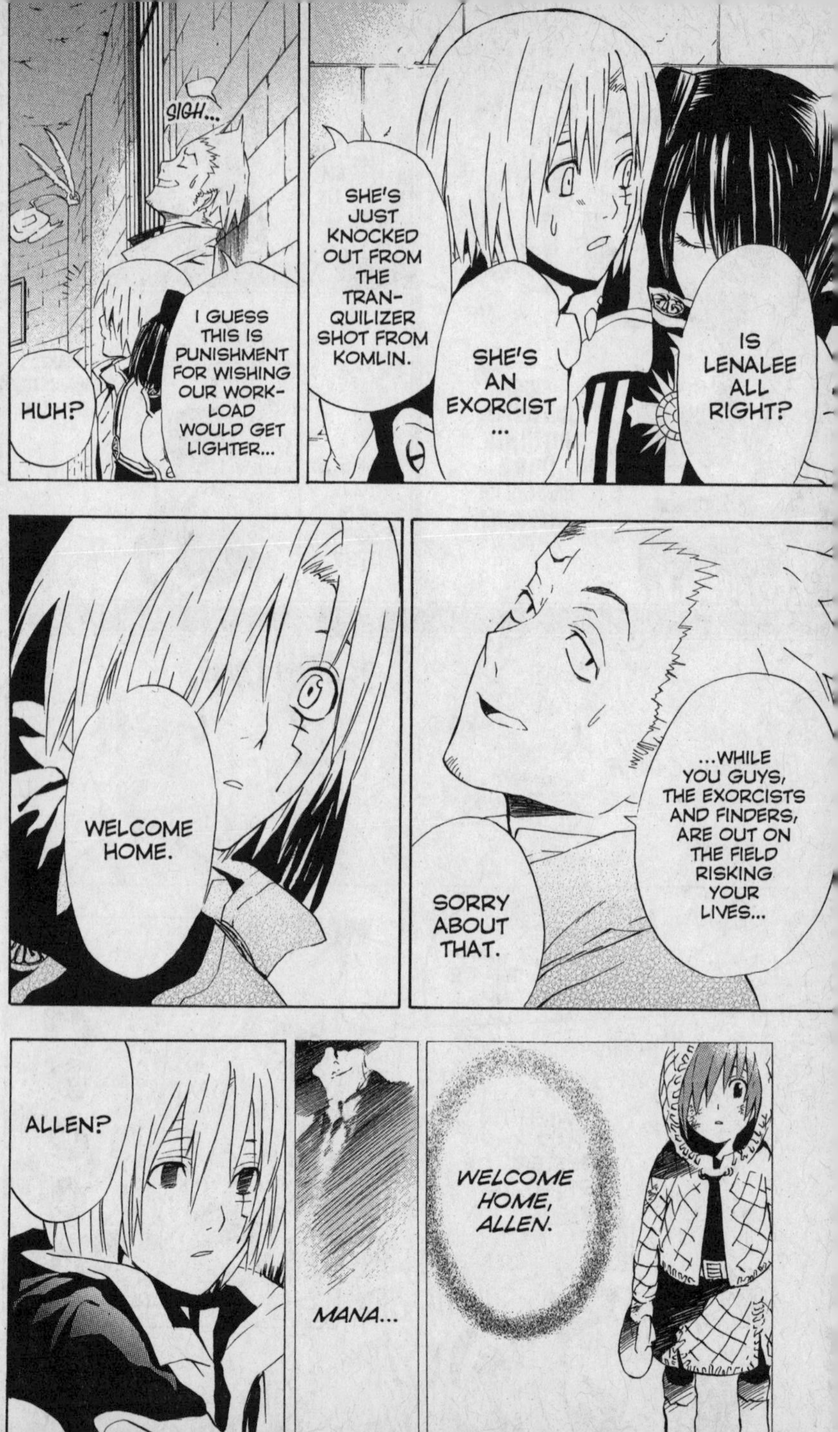
IS LENALEE ALL RIGHT?
SHE'S AN EXORCIST ...
SHE'S JUST KNOCKED OUT FROM THE TRAN-QUILIZER SHOT FROM KOMLIN.
SIGH...
I GUESS THIS IS PUNISHMENT FOR WISHING OUR WORK-LOAD WOULD GET LIGHTER...
HUH?
...WHILE YOU GUYS, THE EXORCISTS AND FINDERS, ARE OUT ON THE FIELD RISKING YOUR LIVES...
SORRY ABOUT THAT.
WELCOME HOME.
WELCOME HOME, ALLEN.
MANA...
ALLEN?

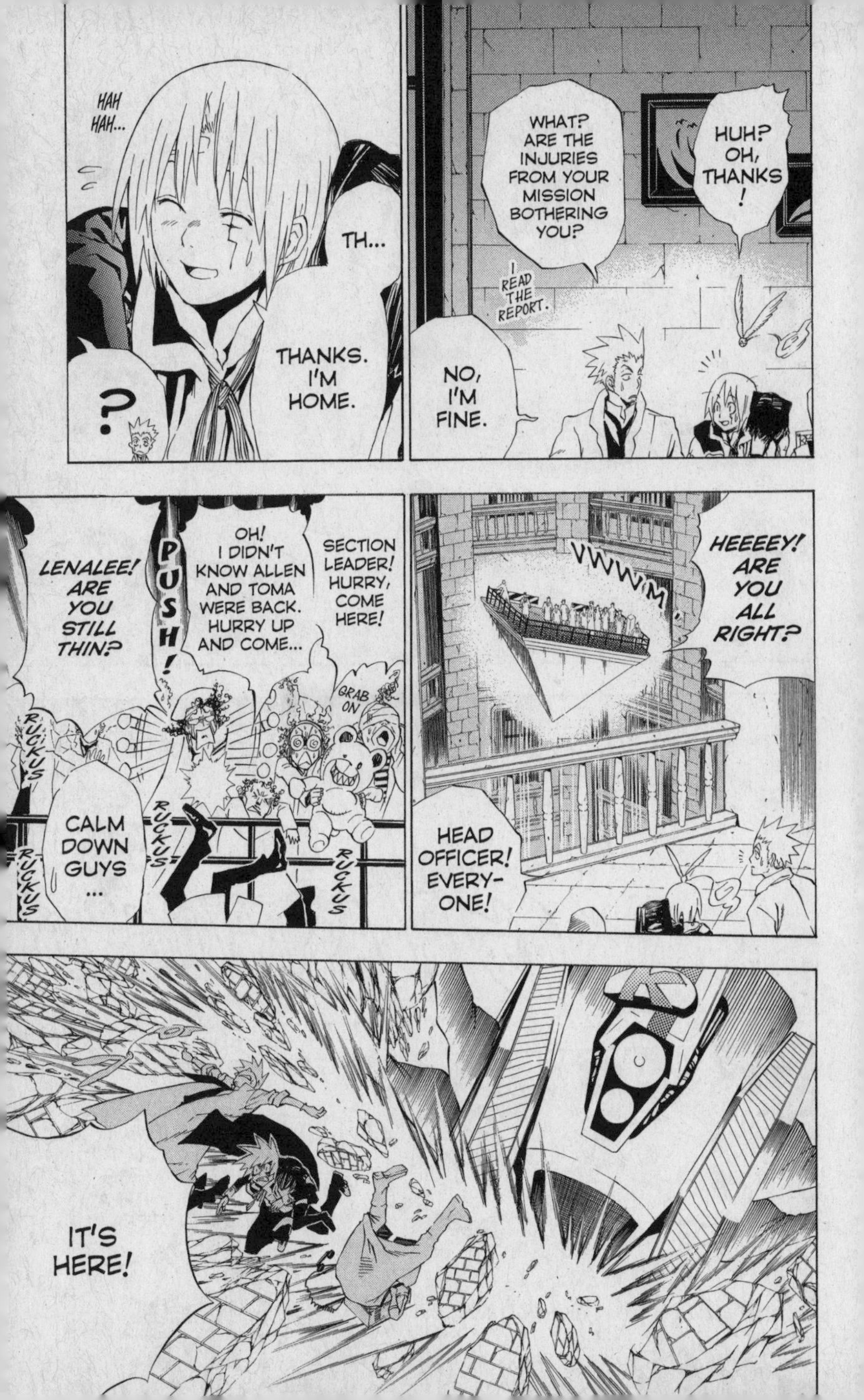

HUH? OH, THANKS!
WHAT? ARE THE INJURIES FROM YOUR MISSION BOTHERING YOU?
I READ THE REPORT.
NO, I'M FINE.
HAH HAH...
TH...
THANKS. I'M HOME.
?
HEEEEY! ARE YOU ALL RIGHT?
VWWWM
HEAD OFFICER! EVERYONE!
SECTION LEADER! HURRY, COME HERE!
OH! I DIDN'T KNOW ALLEN AND TOMA WERE BACK. HURRY UP AND COME...
PUSH!
LENALEE! ARE YOU STILL THIN?
GRAB ON
RUCKUS
RUCKUS
RUCKUS
RUCKUS
CALM DOWN GUYS ...
IT'S HERE!

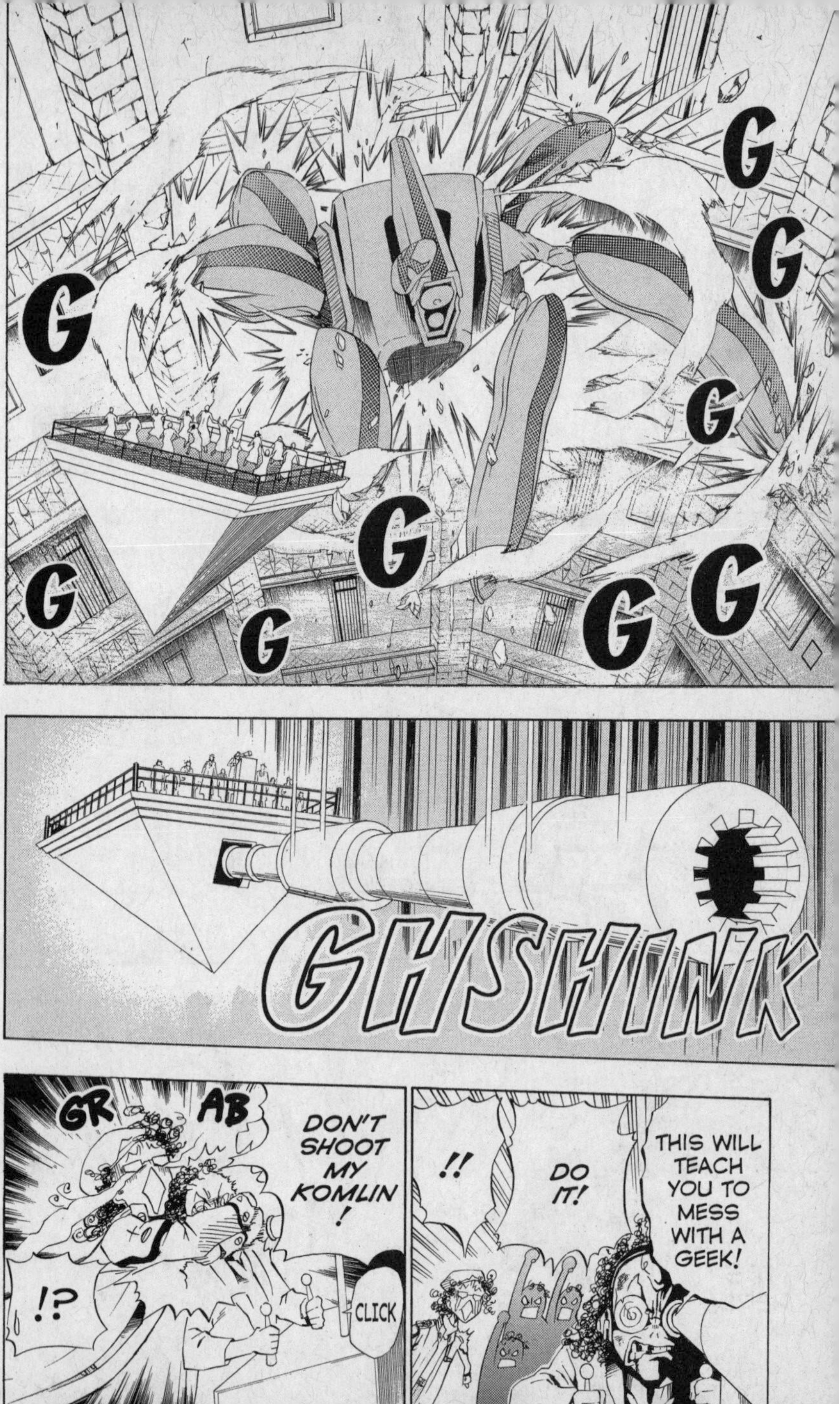
G
G
G
G
G
G
G
G
G
GHSHINK
THIS WILL TEACH YOU TO MESS WITH A GEEK!
DO IT!
!!
DON'T SHOOT MY KOMLIN!
GR AB
CLICK
!?

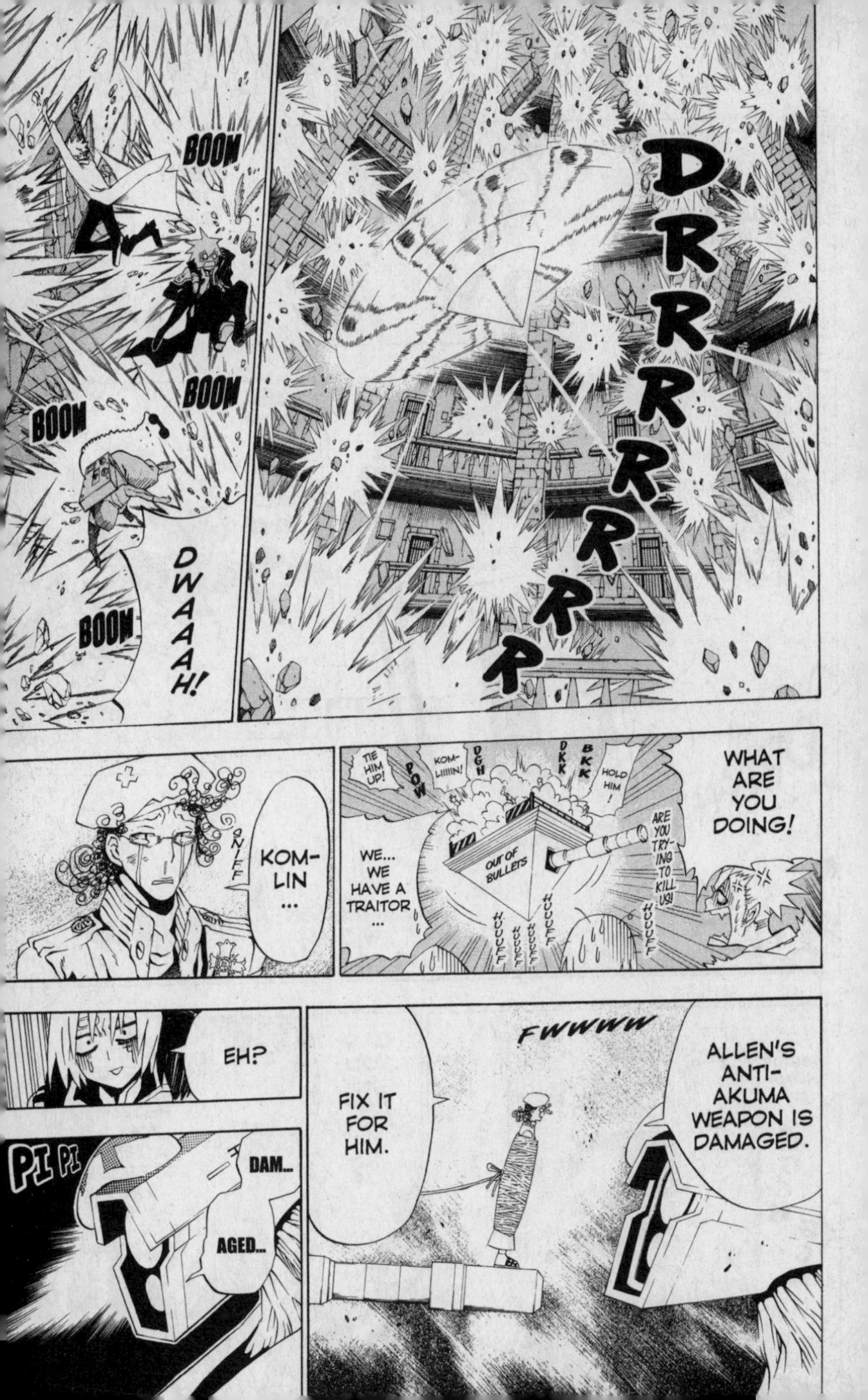
DRRRRRRRR
BOOM
BOOM
BOOM
DWAAAAH!
BOOM
WHAT ARE YOU DOING!
ARE YOU TRYING TO KILL US!
HUUUFF
HOLD HIM!
BKK
DKK
DGH
KOM-LIIIIIN!
TIE HIM UP!
POW
OUT OF BULLETS
HUUUFF
HUUUFF
HUUUFF
H..UUUFF
WE... WE HAVE A TRAITOR...
KOM-LIN...
SNIFF
ALLEN'S ANTI-AKUMA WEAPON IS DAMAGED.
FWWWW
FIX IT FOR HIM.
EH?
PI PI
DAM...
AGED...

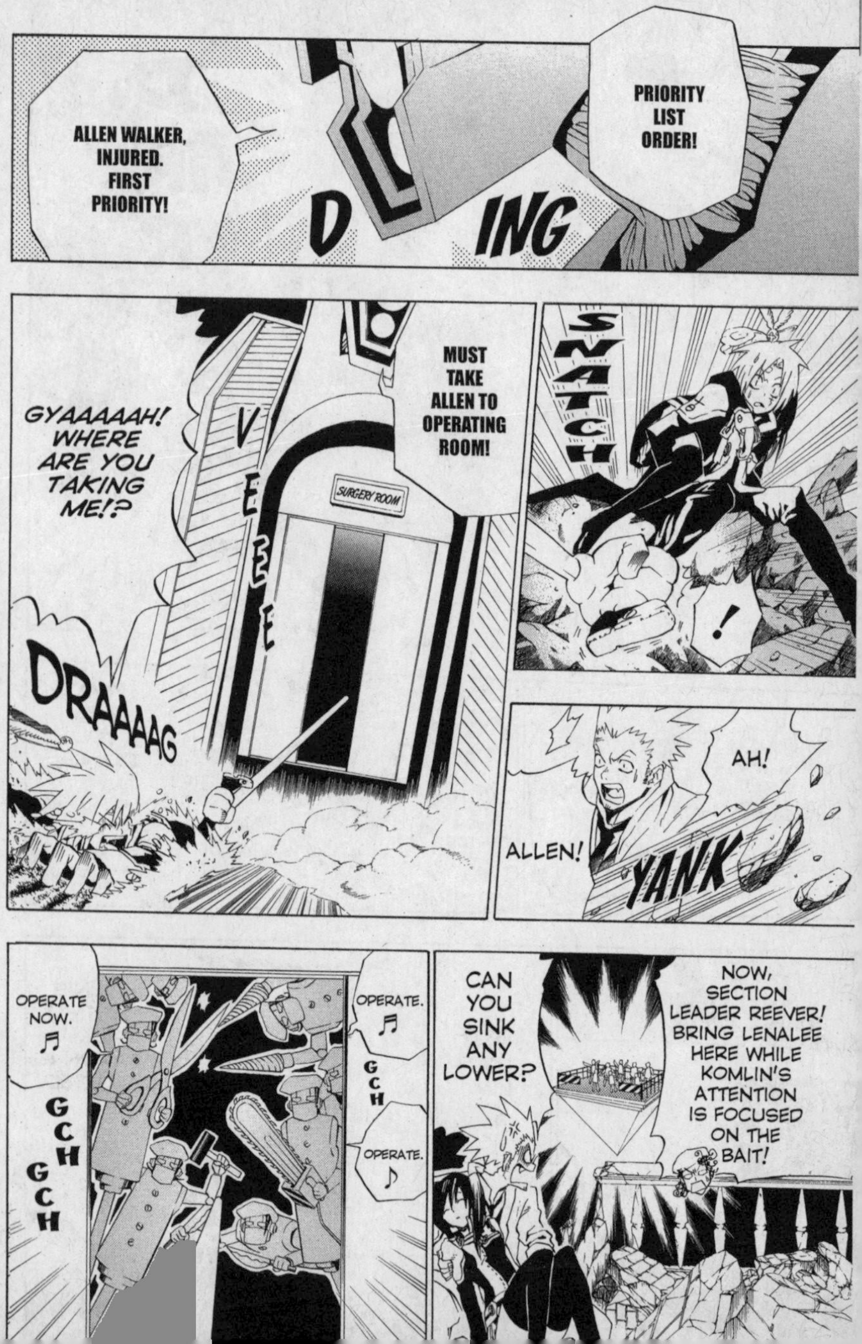
PRIORITY LIST ORDER!
ALLEN WALKER, INJURED. FIRST PRIORITY!
D ING
SNATCH
!
AH!
ALLEN!
YANK
MUST TAKE ALLEN TO OPERATING ROOM!
VEEE
SURGERY ROOM
GYAAAAAH! WHERE ARE YOU TAKING ME!?
DRAAAAG
NOW, SECTION LEADER REEVER! BRING LENALEE HERE WHILE KOMLIN'S ATTENTION IS FOCUSED ON THE BAIT!
CAN YOU SINK ANY LOWER?
OPERATE. ♬
GCH
OPERATE. ♪
OPERATE NOW. ♬
GCH
GCH
GCH

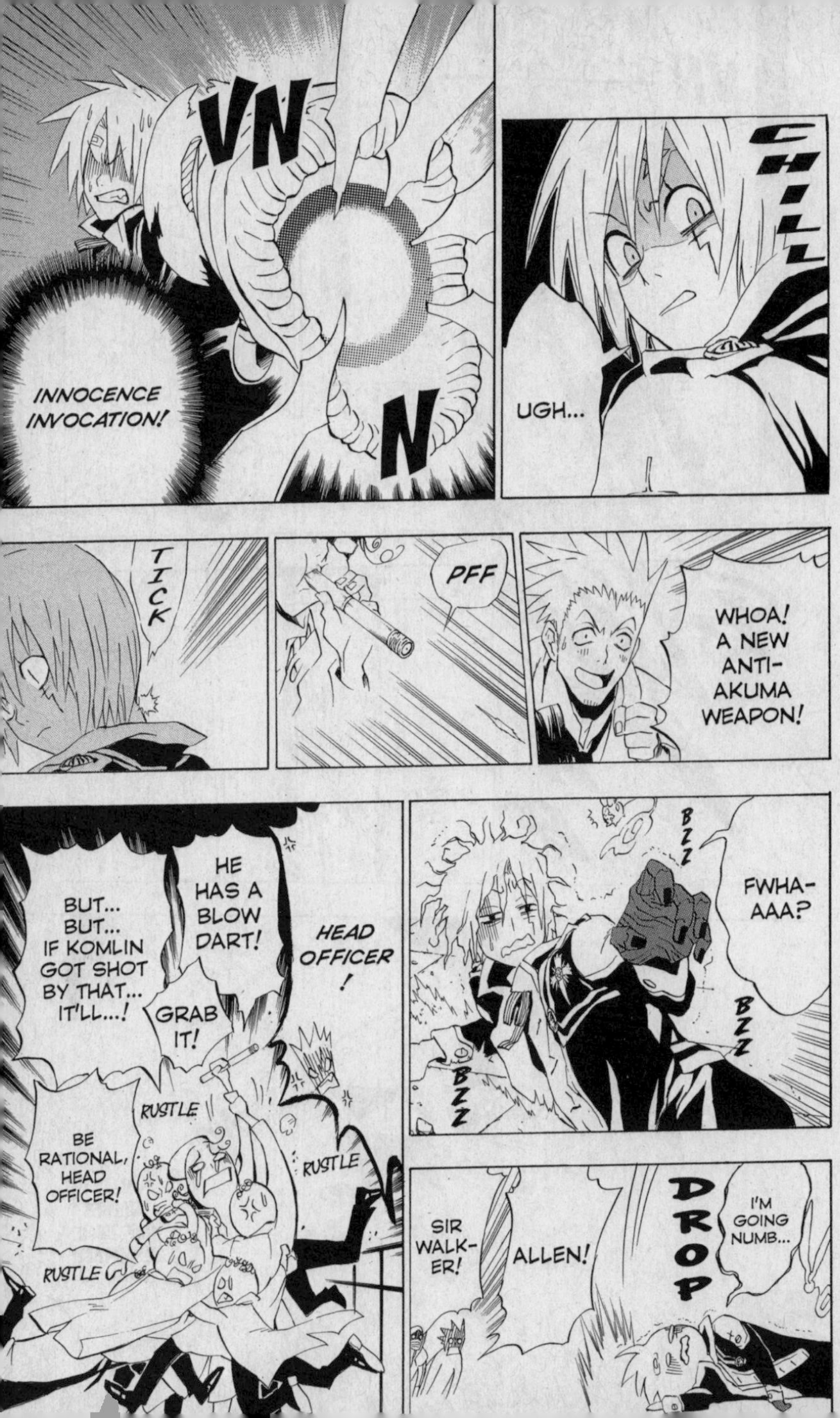
CHILL
UGH...
VN
INNOCENCE INVOCATION!
N
WHOA! A NEW ANTI-AKUMA WEAPON!
PFF
TICK
FWHA-AAA?
BZZ
BZZ
BZZ
I'M GOING NUMB...
DROP
ALLEN!
SIR WALK-ER!
HEAD OFFICER!
HE HAS A BLOW DART!
BUT... BUT... IF KOMLIN GOT SHOT BY THAT... IT'LL...!
GRAB IT!
RUSTLE
RUSTLE
BE RATIONAL, HEAD OFFICER!
RUSTLE

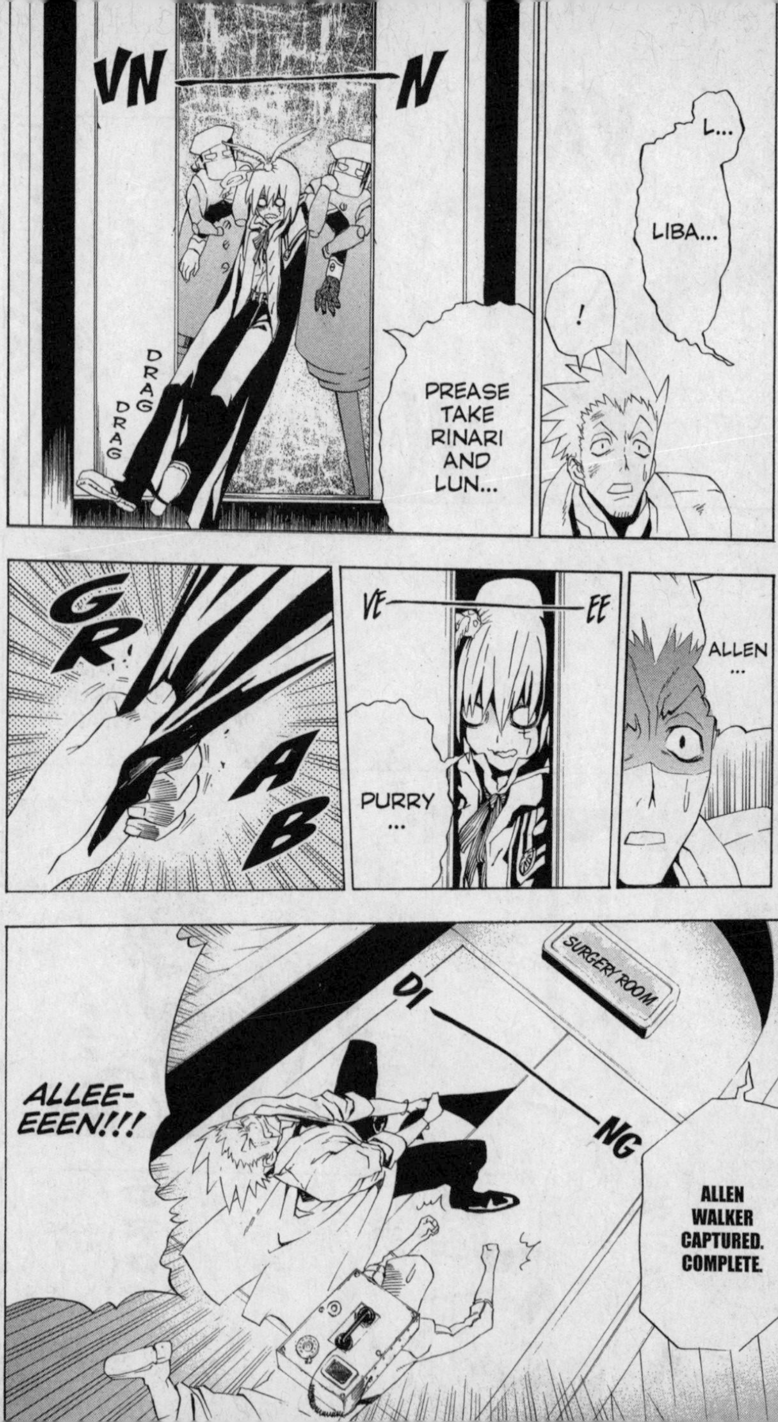
L...
LIBA...
!
PREASE TAKE RINARI AND LUN...
VN—N
DRAG DRAG
DRAG DRAG
ALLEN ...
VE—EE
PURRY ...
GRAB
SURGERY ROOM
DI—NG
ALLEN WALKER CAPTURED. COMPLETE.
ALLEE-EEEN!!!

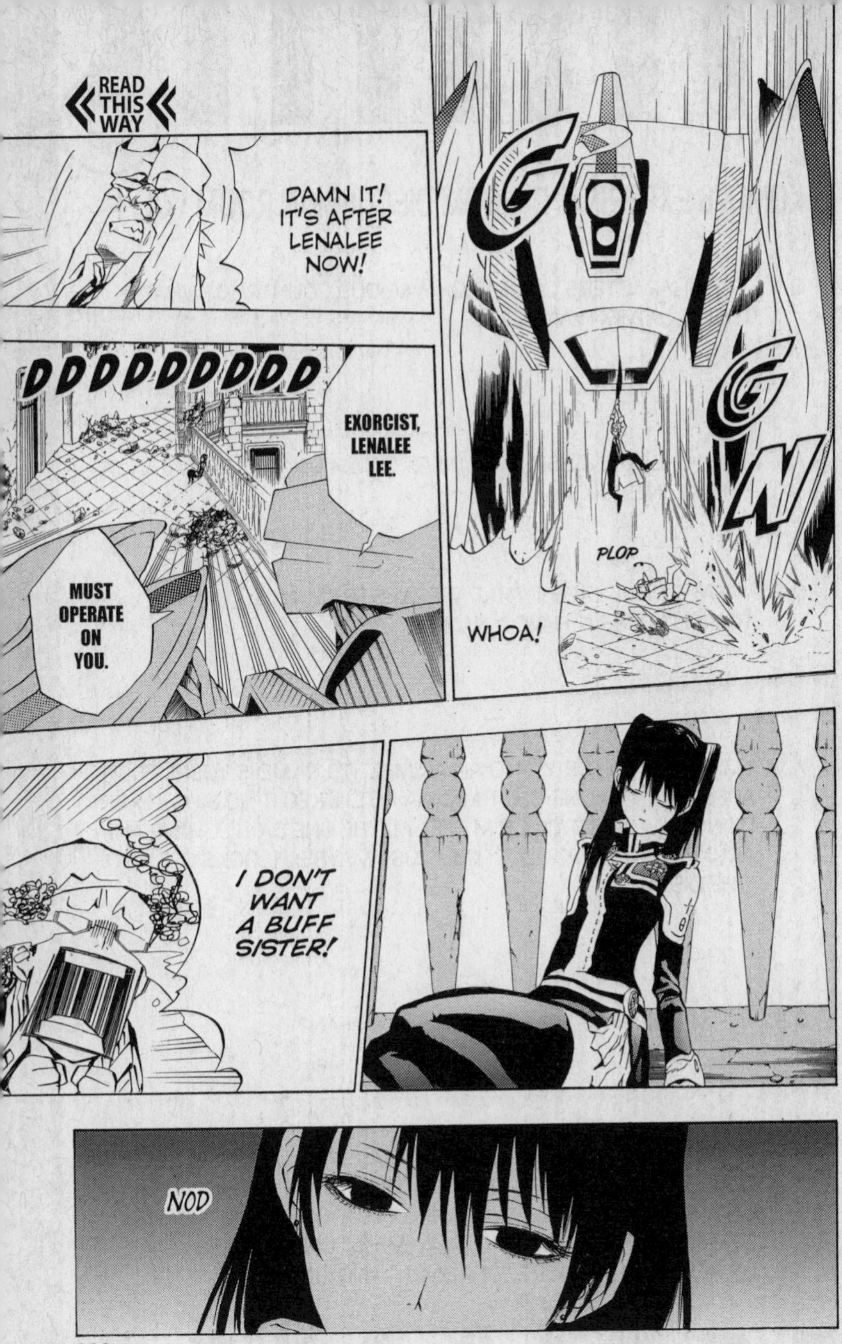
READ THIS WAY
GOGON
PLOP
WHOA!
DAMN IT! IT'S AFTER LENALEE NOW!
DDDDDDDDD
EXORCIST, LENALEE LEE.
MUST OPERATE ON YOU.
I DON'T WANT A BUFF SISTER!
NOD

KOMUI'S EXPERIMENT ROOM DISCUSSION ROOM VOL. 1

Q 1. THE CHARACTERS COME FROM VARIOUS COUNTRIES. WHAT'S THEIR COMMON LANGUAGE?

A. THEY SPEAK ENGLISH, THE UNIVERSAL LANGUAGE. EVEN KANDA SPEAKS IN ENGLISH.

Q 2. WHAT'S THAT RABBIT THAT APPEARS FROM TIME TO TIME? DOES IT HAVE A NAME?

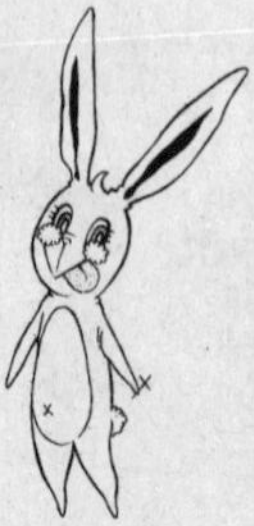

A. I MADE MY EDITOR Y INTO AN ANIMAL. ITS NAME IS YOSHI. YOSHI APPEARED IN A ONE-SHOT MANGA BUT I LIKED IT SO MUCH I KEPT USING IT (JUST TO TICK HIM OFF). MAYBE ONE DAY I'LL HAVE AN AKUMA THAT LOOKS LIKE HIM... JUST MAYBE... (LOOKS OFF INTO THE DISTANCE).

Q 3. WHAT DOES THE TITLE, D.GRAY-MAN MEAN?

A. IT'S A WORD THAT I MADE UP AND HAS VARIOUS MEANINGS. IT COULD APPLY TO ALLEN AND THE OTHER CHARACTERS AS WELL... ON A SEPARATE NOTE, I WAS THINKING "DOLLS" FOR THE TITLE BEFORE I CAME UP WITH "D.GRAY-MAN." OTHER TITLES I CAME UP BEFORE THAT WERE "CHRONOA" AND "ZONE."

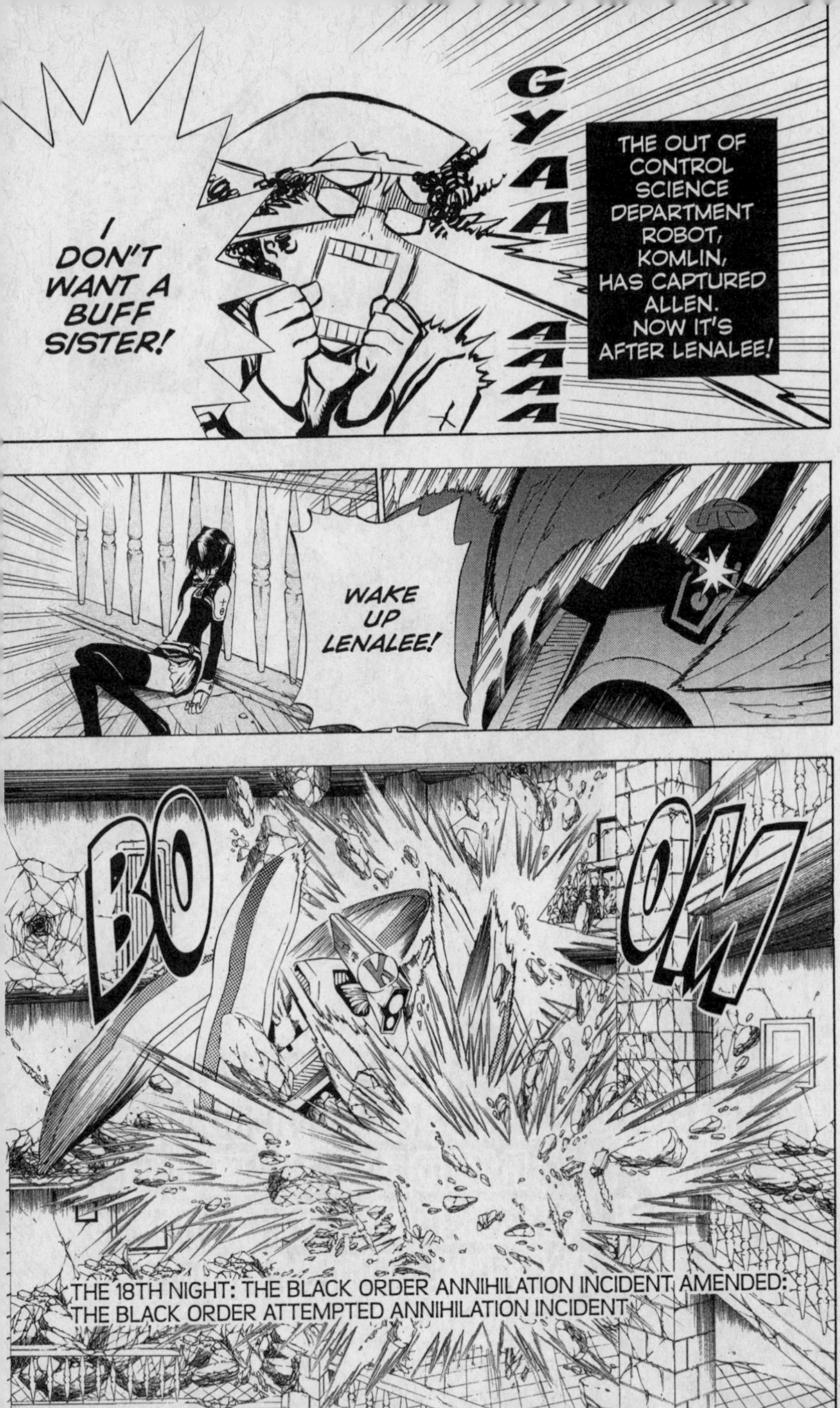
THE OUT OF CONTROL SCIENCE DEPARTMENT ROBOT, KOMLIN, HAS CAPTURED ALLEN. NOW IT'S AFTER LENALEE!
GYAAAAAA
I DON'T WANT A BUFF SISTER!
WAKE UP LENALEE!
BOOM
THE 18TH NIGHT: THE BLACK ORDER ANNIHILATION INCIDENT AMENDED: THE BLACK ORDER ATTEMPTED ANNIHILATION INCIDENT

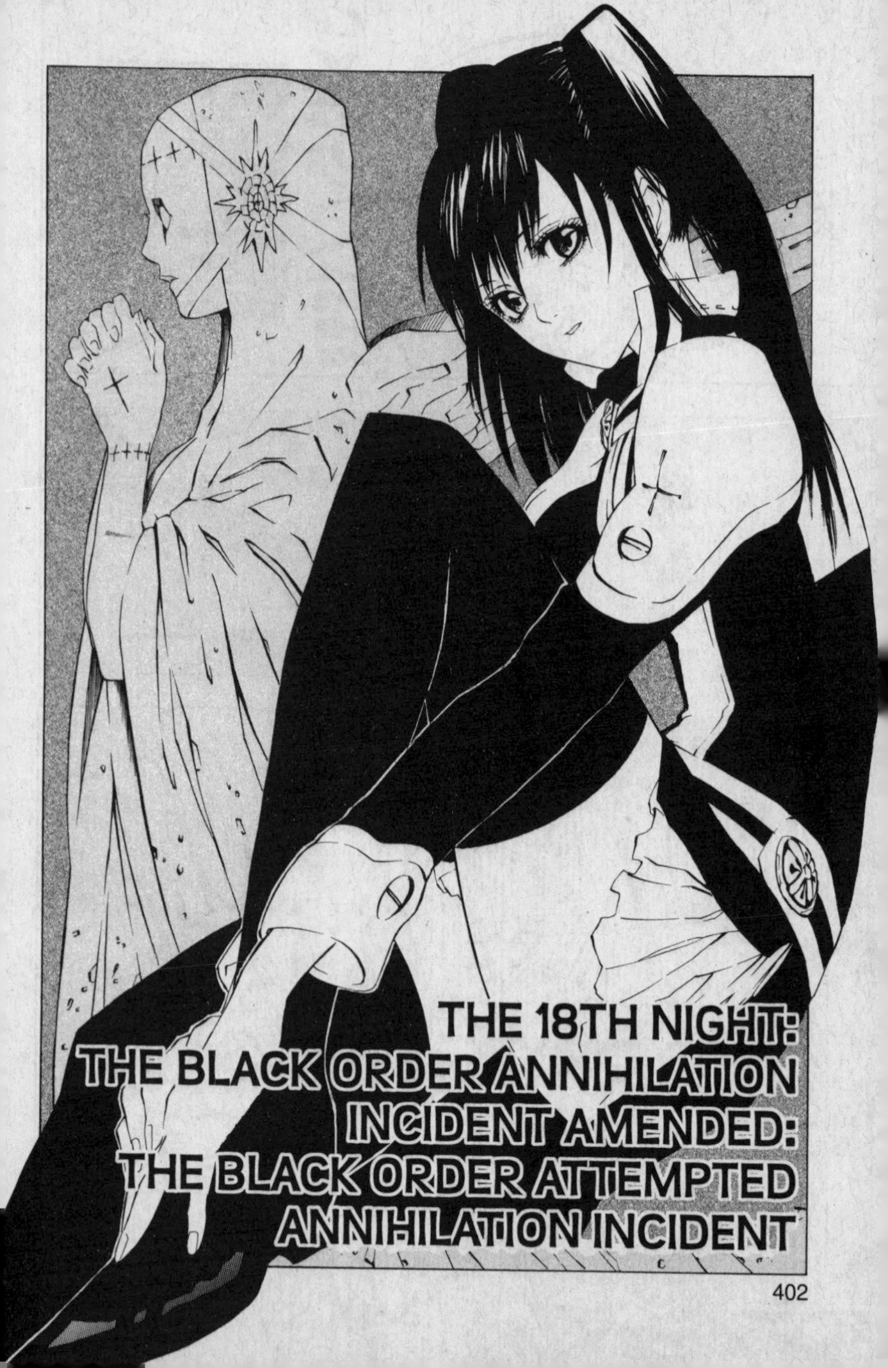
THE 18TH NIGHT:
THE BLACK ORDER ANNIHILATION INCIDENT AMENDED:
THE BLACK ORDER ATTEMPTED ANNIHILATION INCIDENT

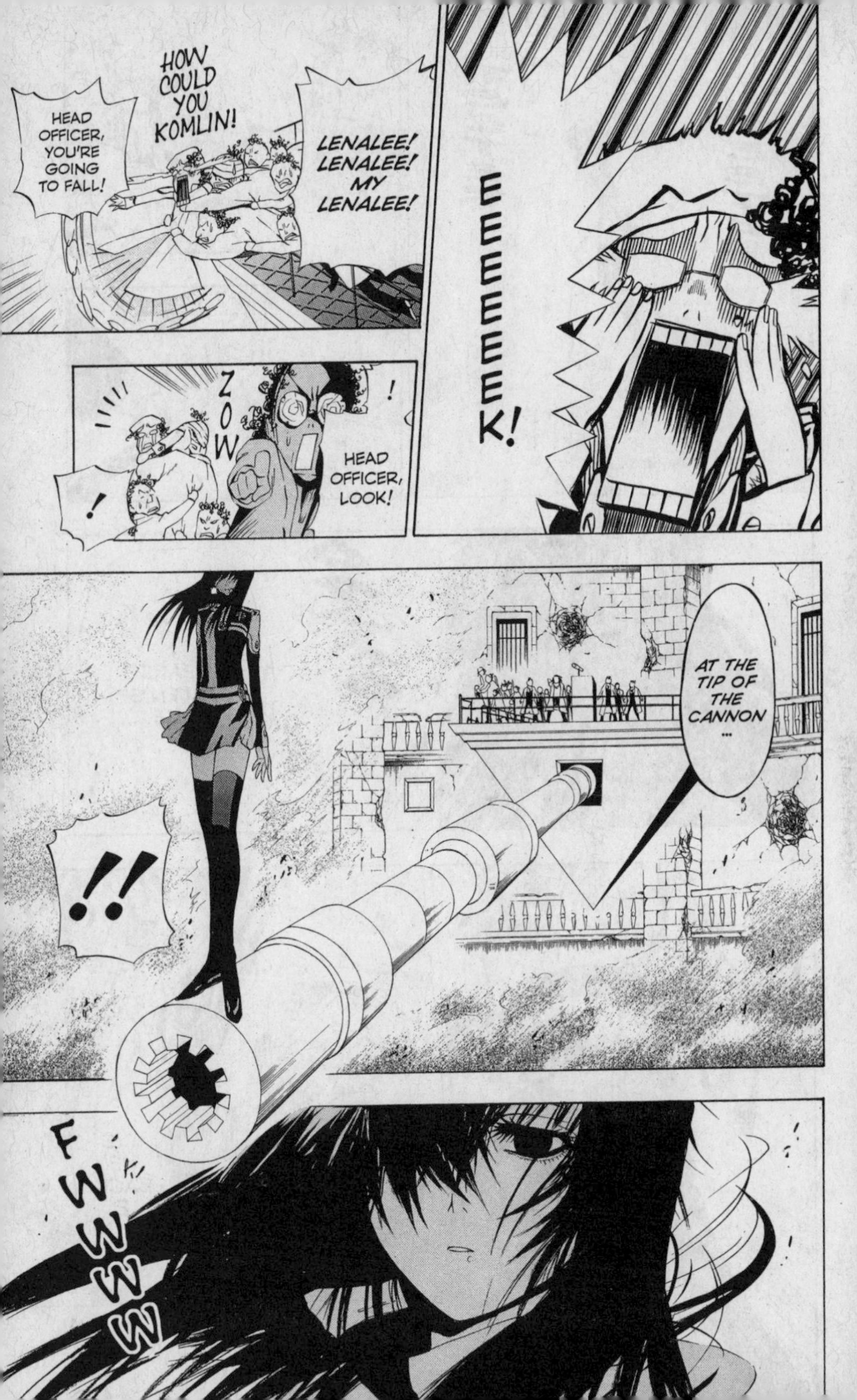
EEEEEEEK!
LENALEE! LENALEE! MY LENALEE!
HOW COULD YOU KOMLIN!
HEAD OFFICER, YOU'RE GOING TO FALL!
HEAD OFFICER, LOOK!
ZOW
AT THE TIP OF THE CANNON...
!!
FWWWW

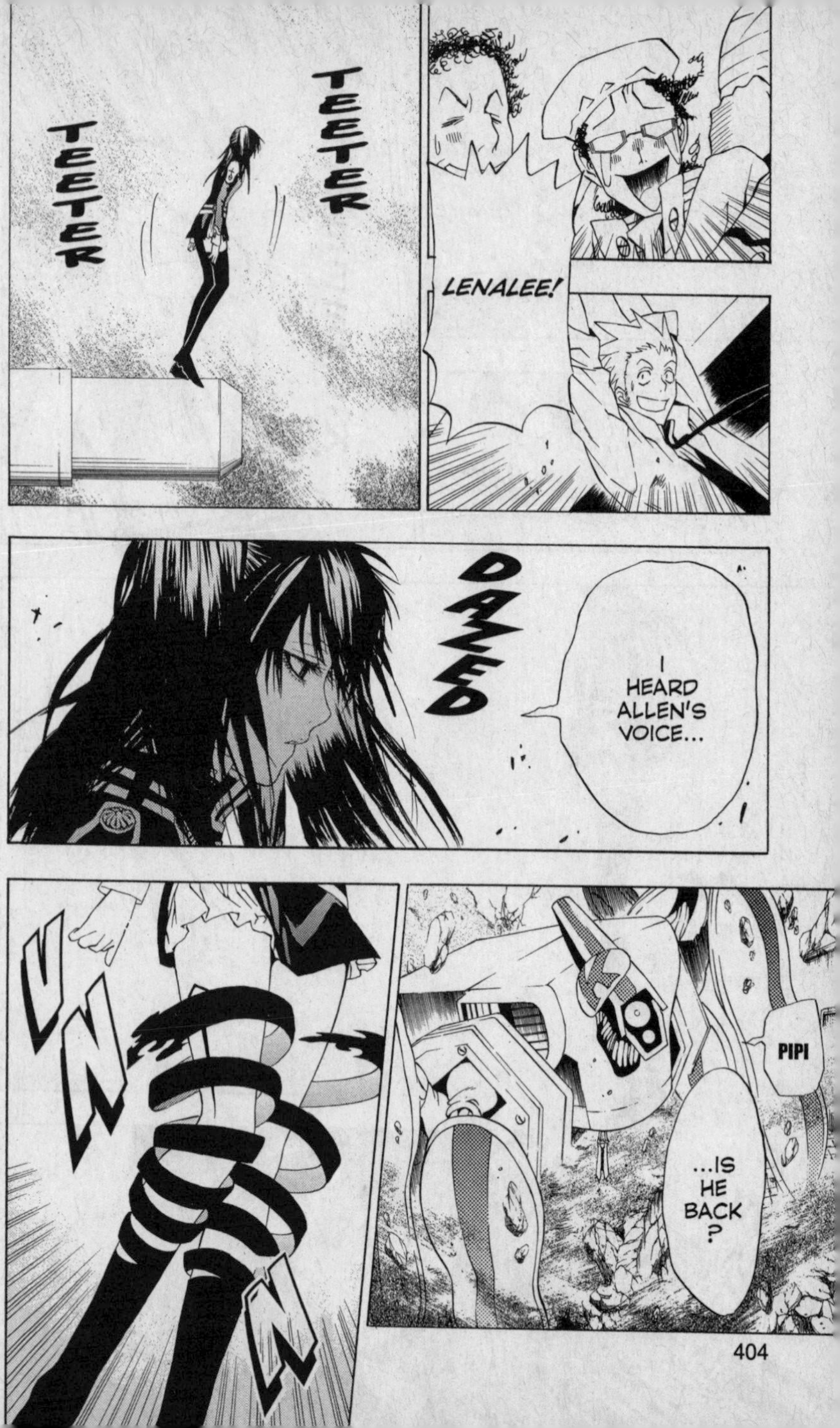
LENALEE!
TEETER
TEETER
DAZED
I HEARD ALLEN'S VOICE...
PIPI
...IS HE BACK?
VNN

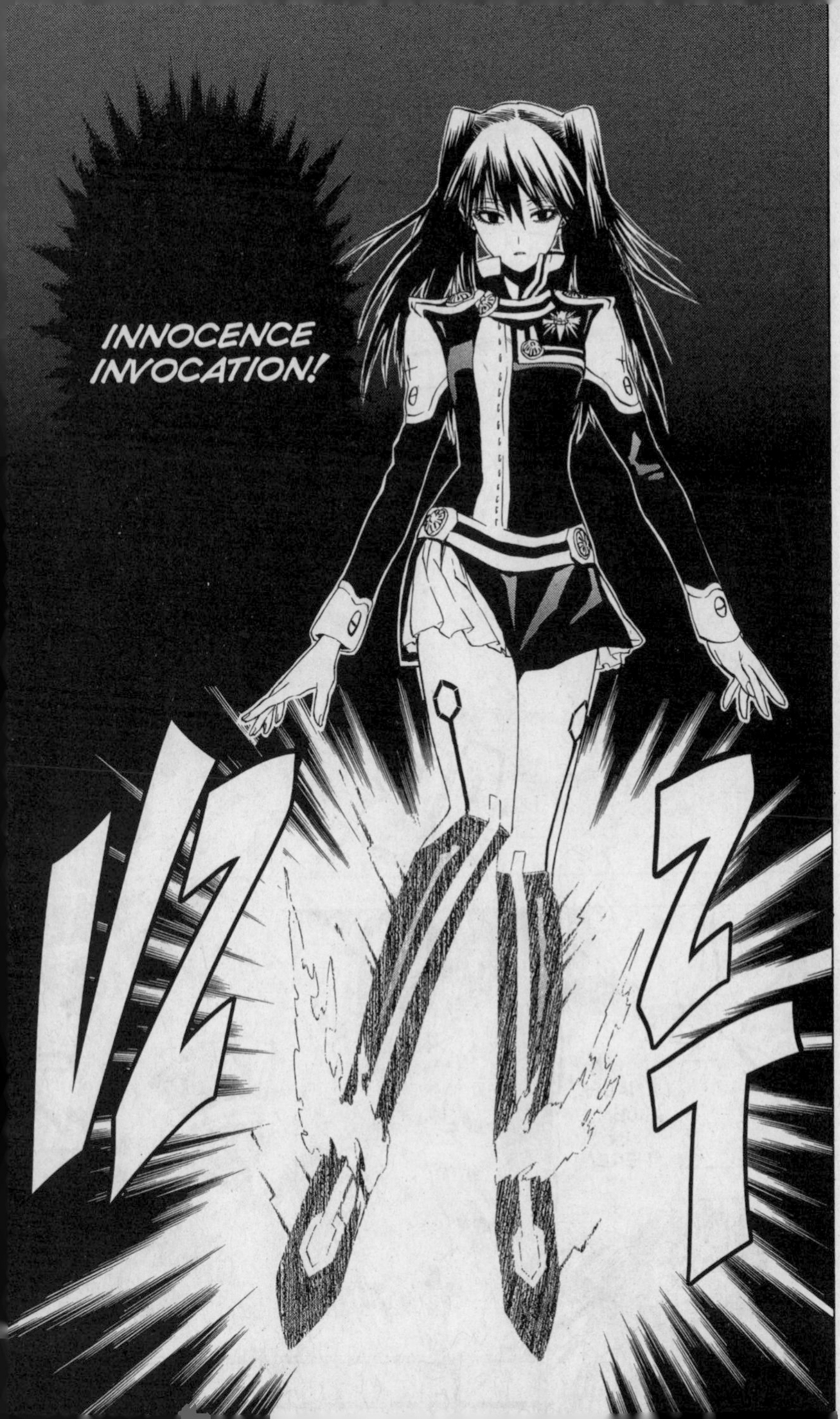
INNOCENCE INVOCATION!

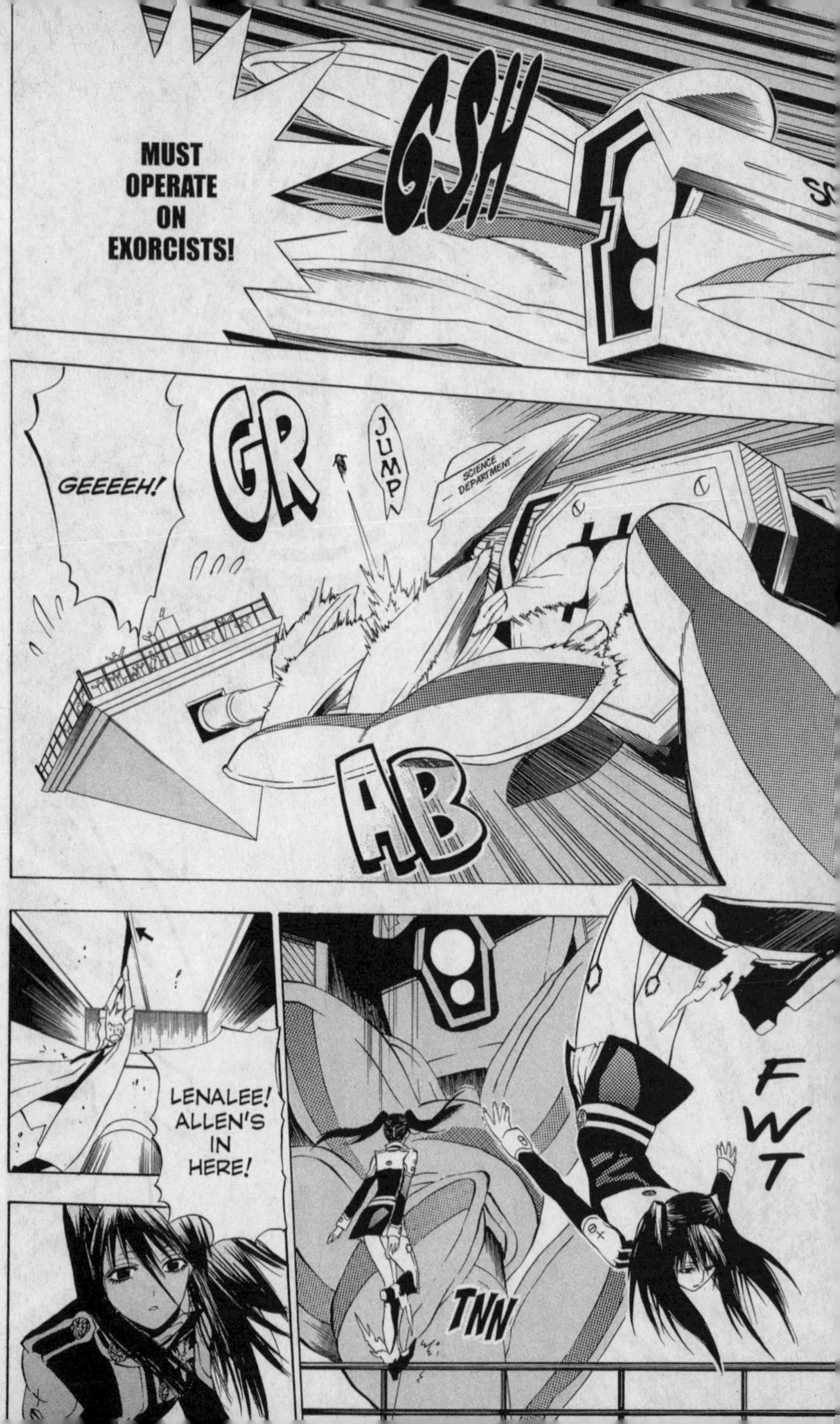
MUST OPERATE ON EXORCISTS!
GSH
SCIENCE DEPARTMENT
JUMP
GR
GEEEEH!
AB
FWT
TNN
LENALEE! ALLEN'S IN HERE!

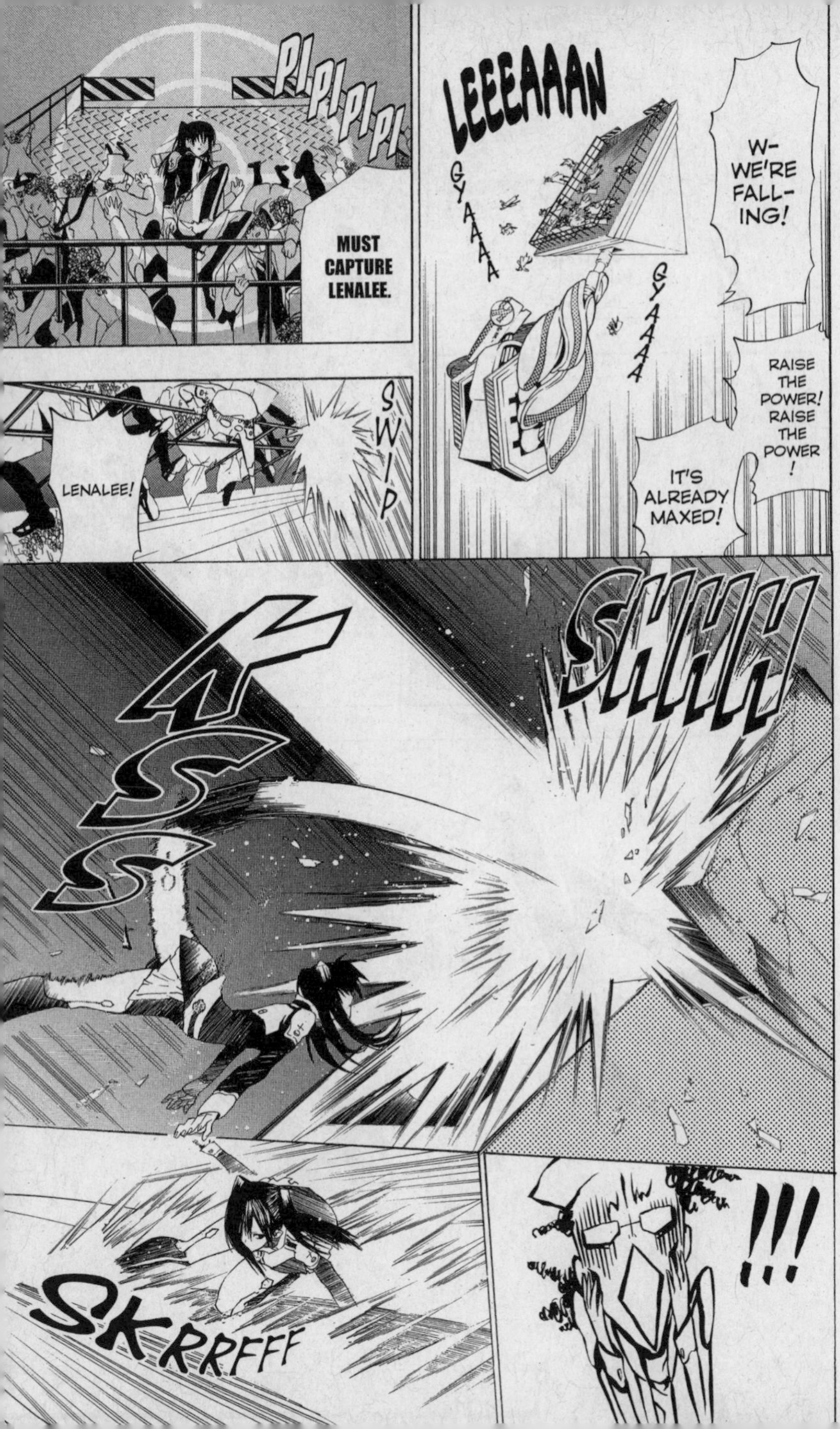
W- WE'RE FALL- ING!
LEEEAAAN
GYAAAA
GYAAAA
RAISE THE POWER! RAISE THE POWER!
IT'S ALREADY MAXED!
PI PI PI PI
MUST CAPTURE LENALEE.
SWIP
LENALEE!
SHHH
KSSS
!!!
SKRRFFF

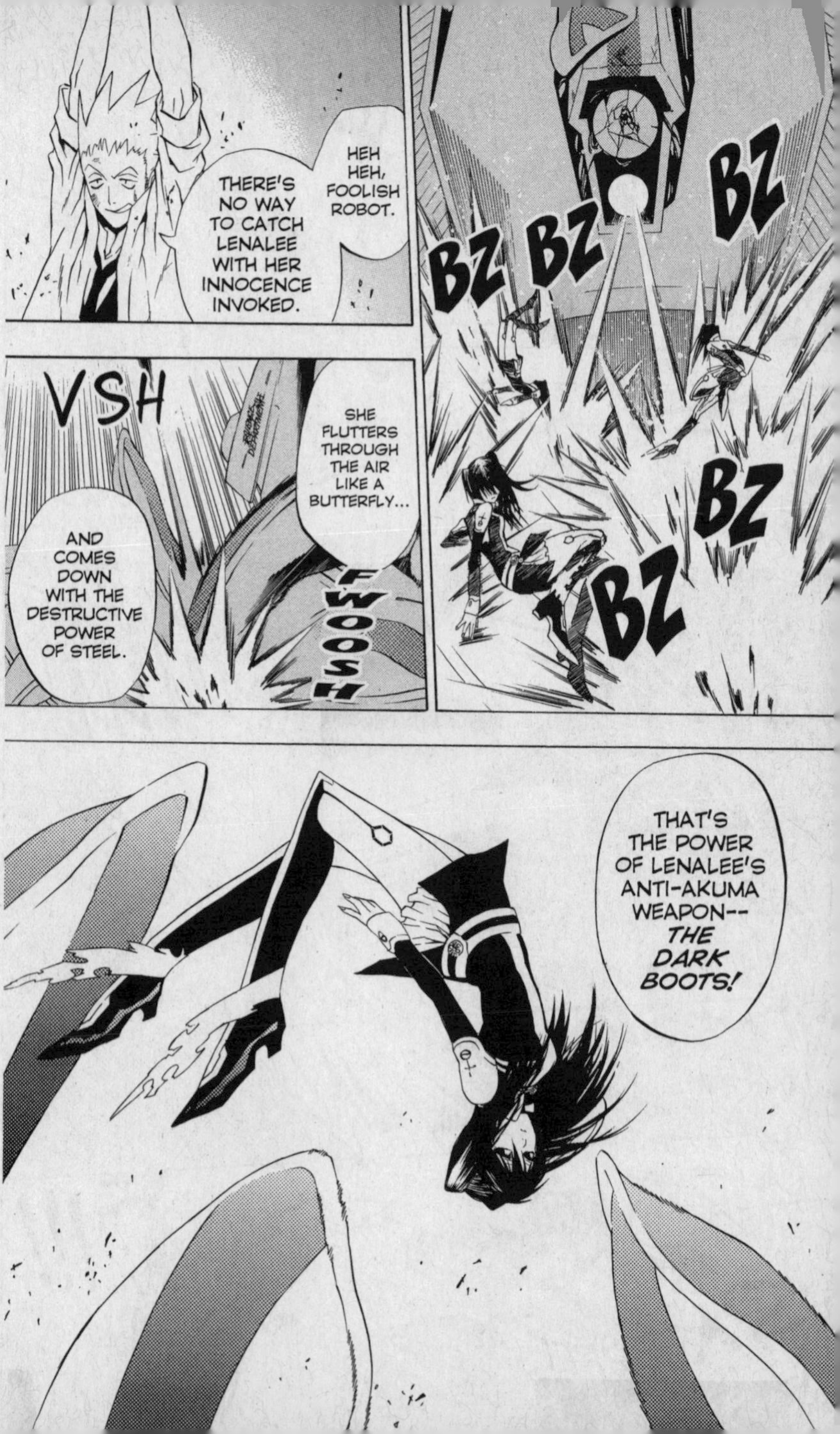
BZ
BZ
BZ
BZ
BZ
BZ
HEH HEH, FOOLISH ROBOT.
THERE'S NO WAY TO CATCH LENALEE WITH HER INNOCENCE INVOKED.
VSH
SHE FLUTTERS THROUGH THE AIR LIKE A BUTTERFLY...
AND COMES DOWN WITH THE DESTRUCTIVE POWER OF STEEL.
FWOOSH
THAT'S THE POWER OF LENALEE'S ANTI-AKUMA WEAPON-- *THE DARK BOOTS!*

READ THIS WAY

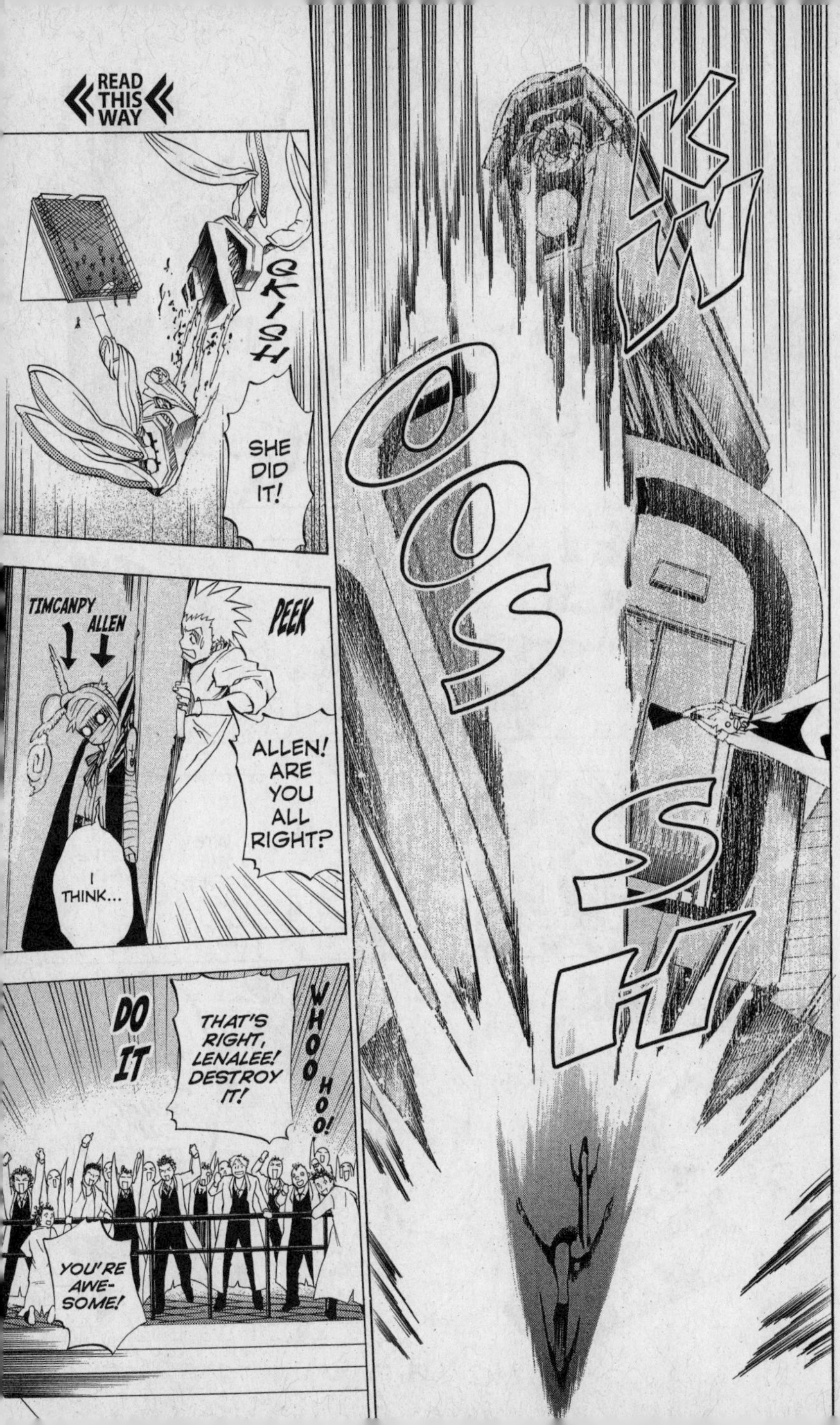
KWWOOSSH
GKISH
SHE DID IT!
PEEK
ALLEN! ARE YOU ALL RIGHT?
TIMCANPY
ALLEN
I THINK...
WHOO HOO!
DO IT
THAT'S RIGHT, LENALEE! DESTROY IT!
YOU'RE AWE-SOME!

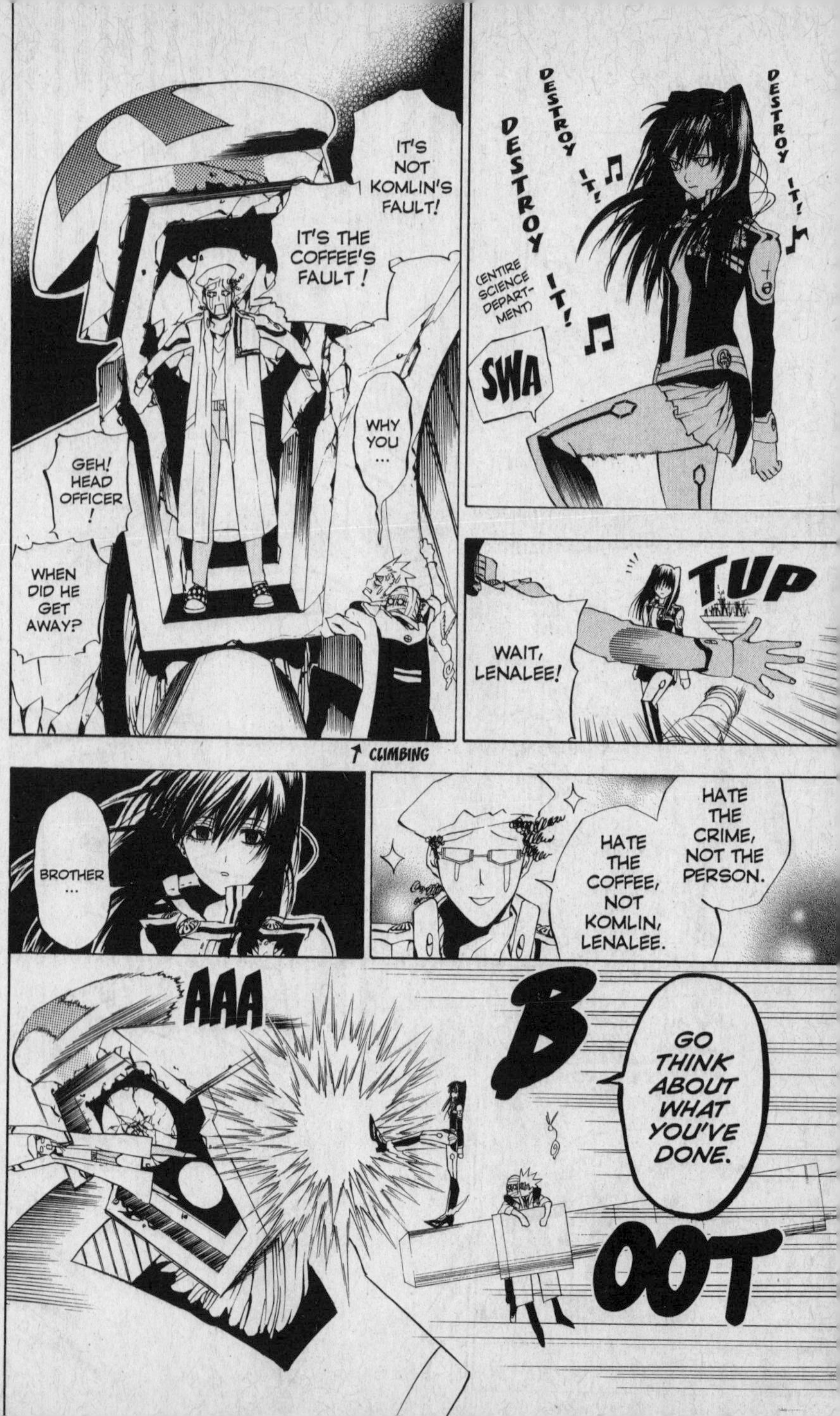

DESTROY IT!
DESTROY IT!
DESTROY IT!
(ENTIRE SCIENCE DEPARTMENT)
SWA
TUP
WAIT, LENALEE!
IT'S NOT KOMLIN'S FAULT!
IT'S THE COFFEE'S FAULT!
WHY YOU...
GEH! HEAD OFFICER!
WHEN DID HE GET AWAY?
↑ CLIMBING
HATE THE CRIME, NOT THE PERSON.
HATE THE COFFEE, NOT KOMLIN, LENALEE.
BROTHER...
GO THINK ABOUT WHAT YOU'VE DONE.
B
OOT
AAA

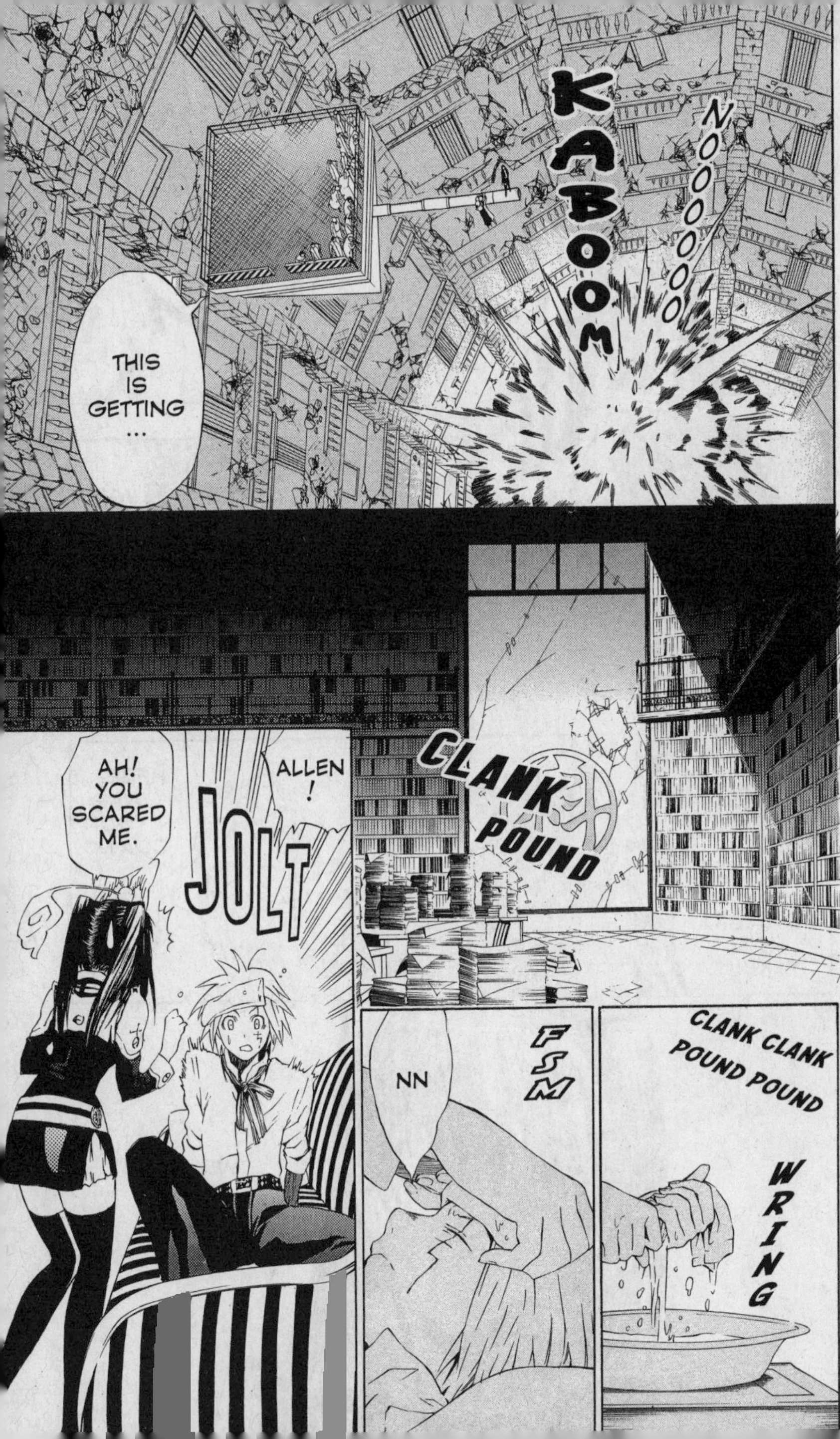
NOOOOOO
KABOOM
THIS IS GETTING ...
CLANK
POUND
CLANK CLANK POUND POUND
WRING
FSM
NN
ALLEN!
JOLT
AH! YOU SCARED ME.

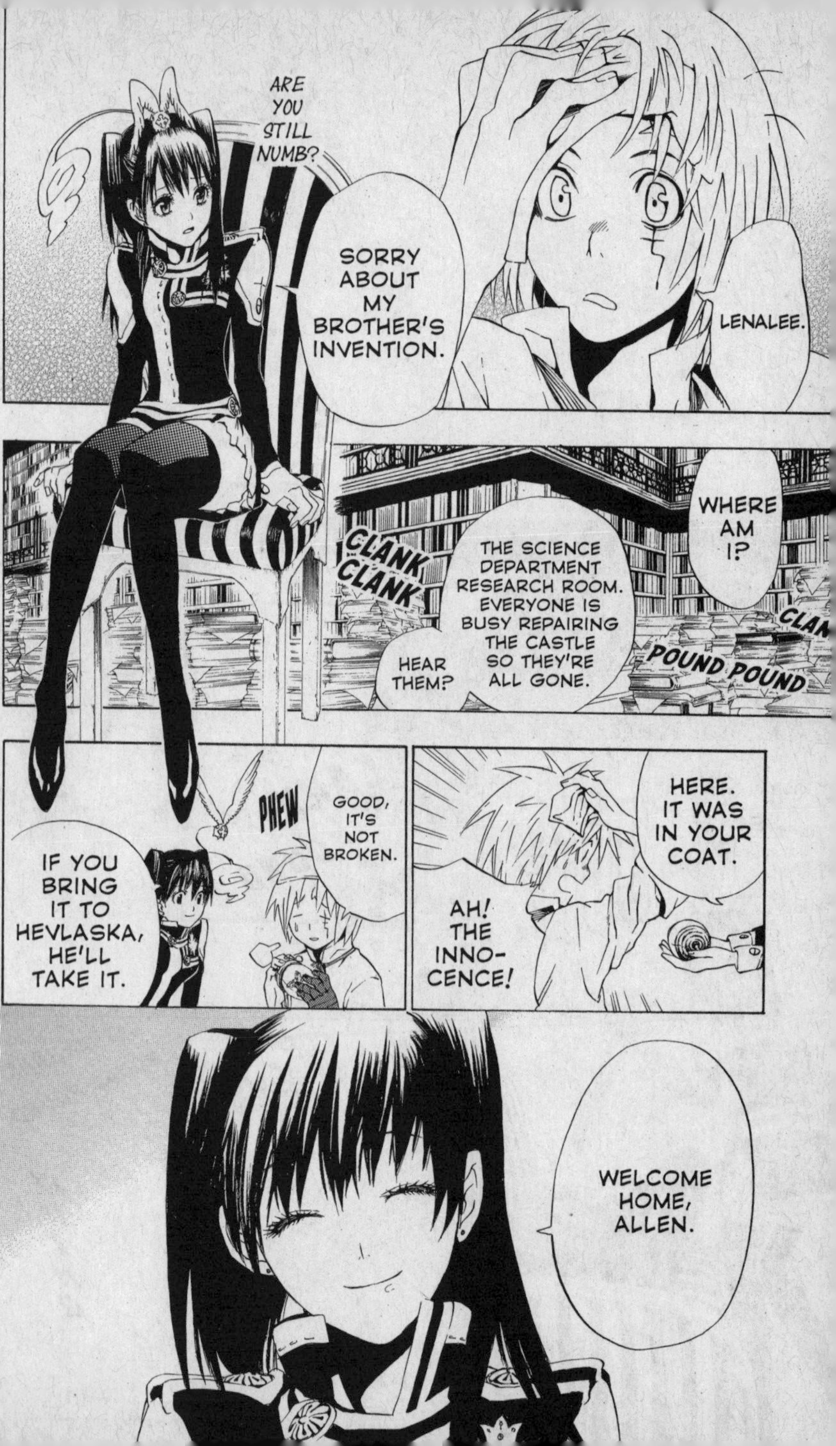
LENALEE.
SORRY ABOUT MY BROTHER'S INVENTION.
WHERE AM I?
CLAN
POUND POUND
THE SCIENCE DEPARTMENT RESEARCH ROOM. EVERYONE IS BUSY REPAIRING THE CASTLE SO THEY'RE ALL GONE.
HEAR THEM?
CLANK CLANK
ARE YOU STILL NUMB?
HERE. IT WAS IN YOUR COAT.
AH! THE INNO-CENCE!
GOOD, IT'S NOT BROKEN.
PHEW
IF YOU BRING IT TO HEVLASKA, HE'LL TAKE IT.
WELCOME HOME, ALLEN.

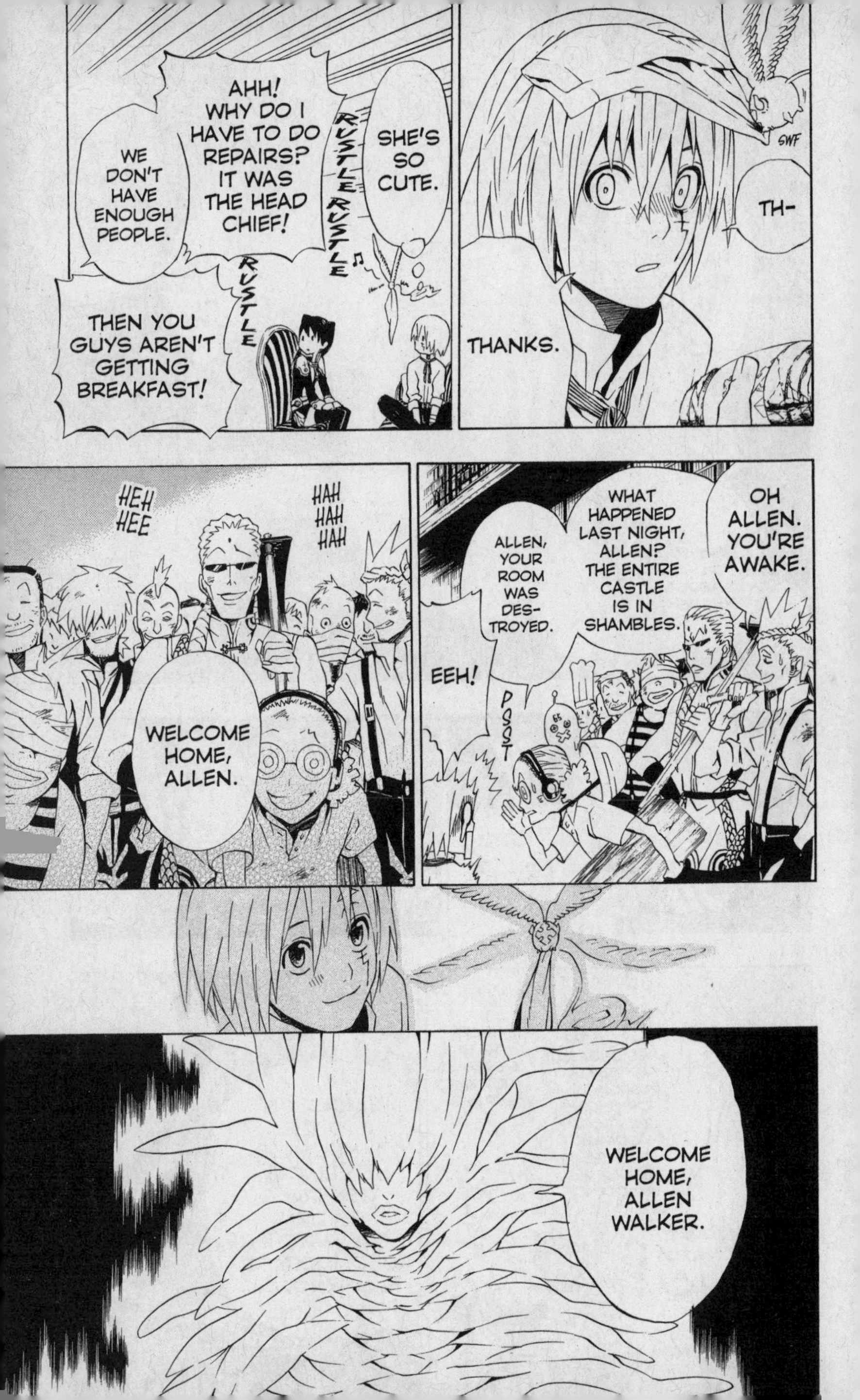
SWF
TH-
THANKS.
SHE'S SO CUTE.
RUSTLE RUSTLE
AHH! WHY DO I HAVE TO DO REPAIRS? IT WAS THE HEAD CHIEF!
RUSTLE
WE DON'T HAVE ENOUGH PEOPLE.
THEN YOU GUYS AREN'T GETTING BREAKFAST!
OH ALLEN. YOU'RE AWAKE.
WHAT HAPPENED LAST NIGHT, ALLEN? THE ENTIRE CASTLE IS IN SHAMBLES.
ALLEN, YOUR ROOM WAS DES-TROYED.
PSST
EEH!
HAH HAH HAH
HEH HEE
WELCOME HOME, ALLEN.
WELCOME HOME, ALLEN WALKER.

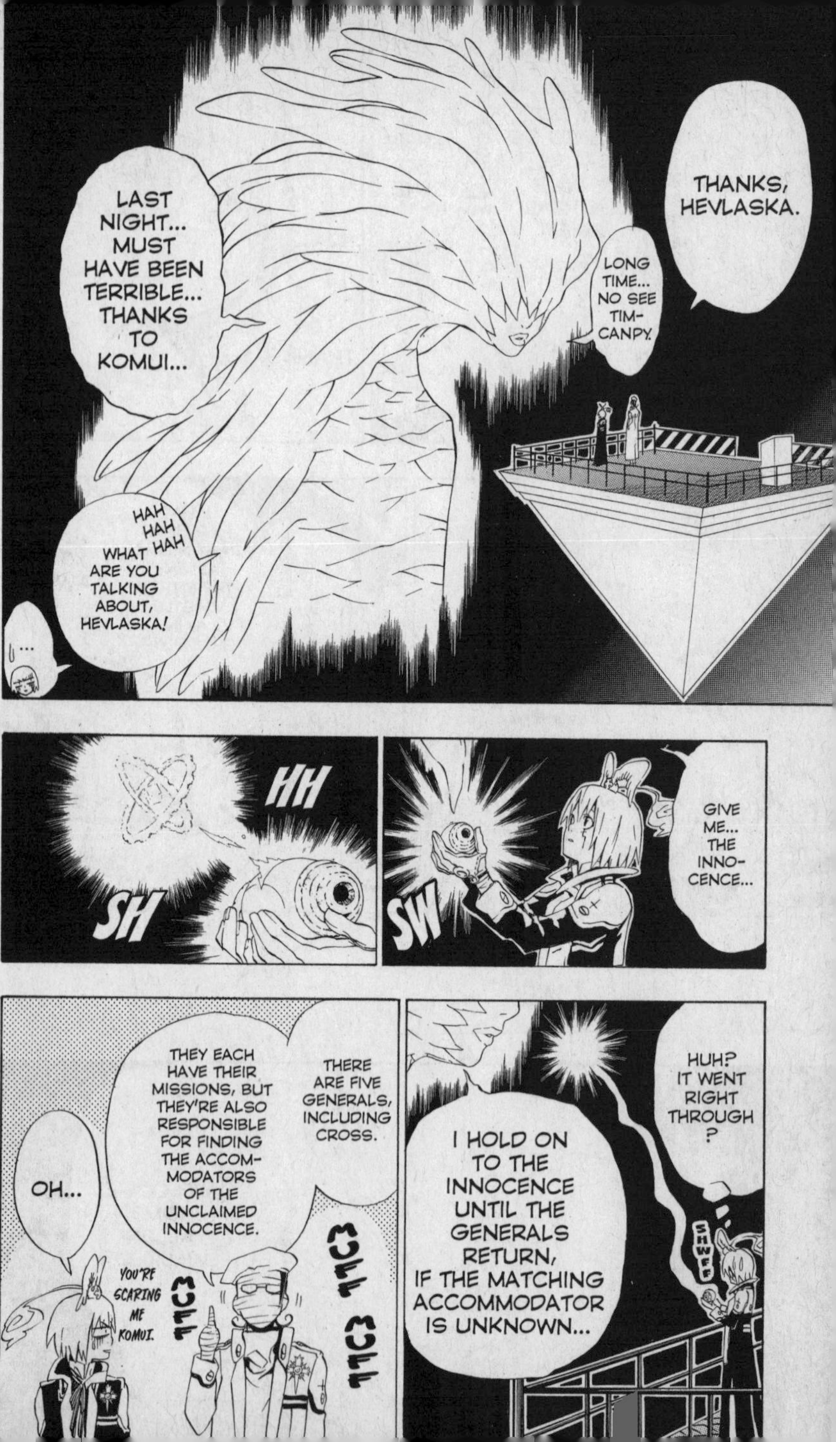
THANKS, HEVLASKA.
LONG TIME... NO SEE TIM-CANPY.
LAST NIGHT... MUST HAVE BEEN TERRIBLE... THANKS TO KOMUI...
HAH HAH HAH WHAT ARE YOU TALKING ABOUT, HEVLASKA!
...
GIVE ME... THE INNO-CENCE...
SW
HH
SH
HUH? IT WENT RIGHT THROUGH?
SHWFF
I HOLD ON TO THE INNOCENCE UNTIL THE GENERALS RETURN, IF THE MATCHING ACCOMMODATOR IS UNKNOWN...
THERE ARE FIVE GENERALS, INCLUDING CROSS.
THEY EACH HAVE THEIR MISSIONS, BUT THEY'RE ALSO RESPONSIBLE FOR FINDING THE ACCOM-MODATORS OF THE UNCLAIMED INNOCENCE.
MUFF MUFF
MUFF
OH...
YOU'RE SCARING ME KOMUI.
MUFF

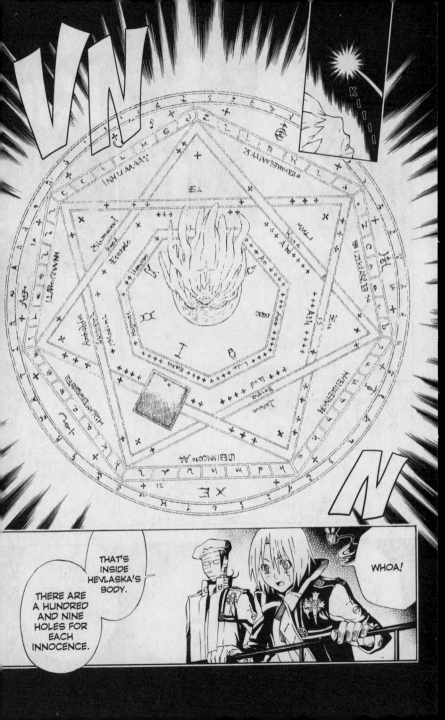

THAT'S INSIDE HEVLASKA'S BODY.

THERE ARE A HUNDRED AND NINE HOLES FOR EACH INNOCENCE.

WHOA!

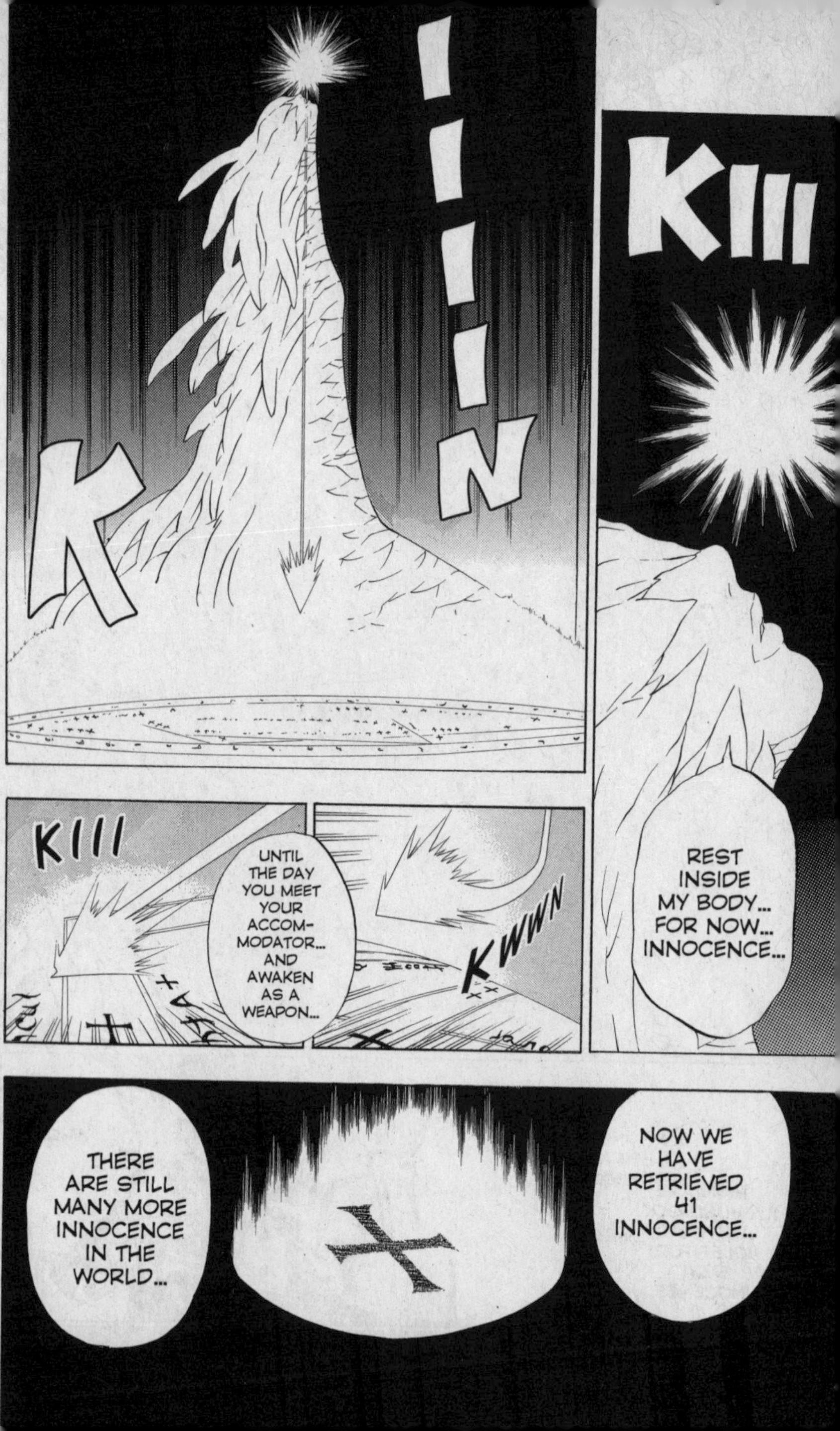
KIII
REST INSIDE MY BODY... FOR NOW... INNOCENCE...
KIIIIIN
KWWN
UNTIL THE DAY YOU MEET YOUR ACCOM-MODATOR... AND AWAKEN AS A WEAPON...
KIII
NOW WE HAVE RETRIEVED 41 INNOCENCE...
THERE ARE STILL MANY MORE INNOCENCE IN THE WORLD...

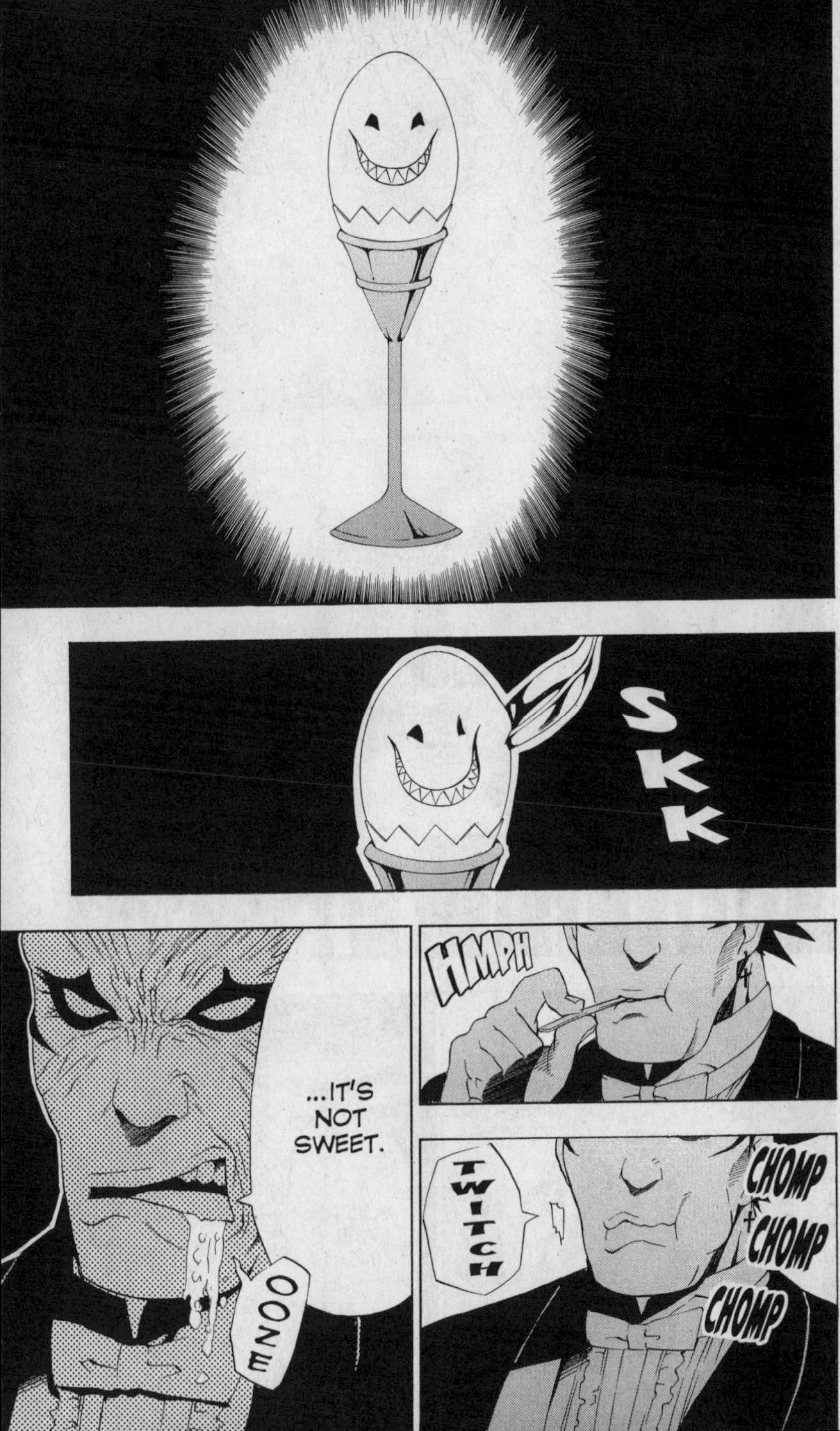
SKK
HMPH
CHOMP
CHOMP
CHOMP
TWITCH
...IT'S NOT SWEET.
OONE

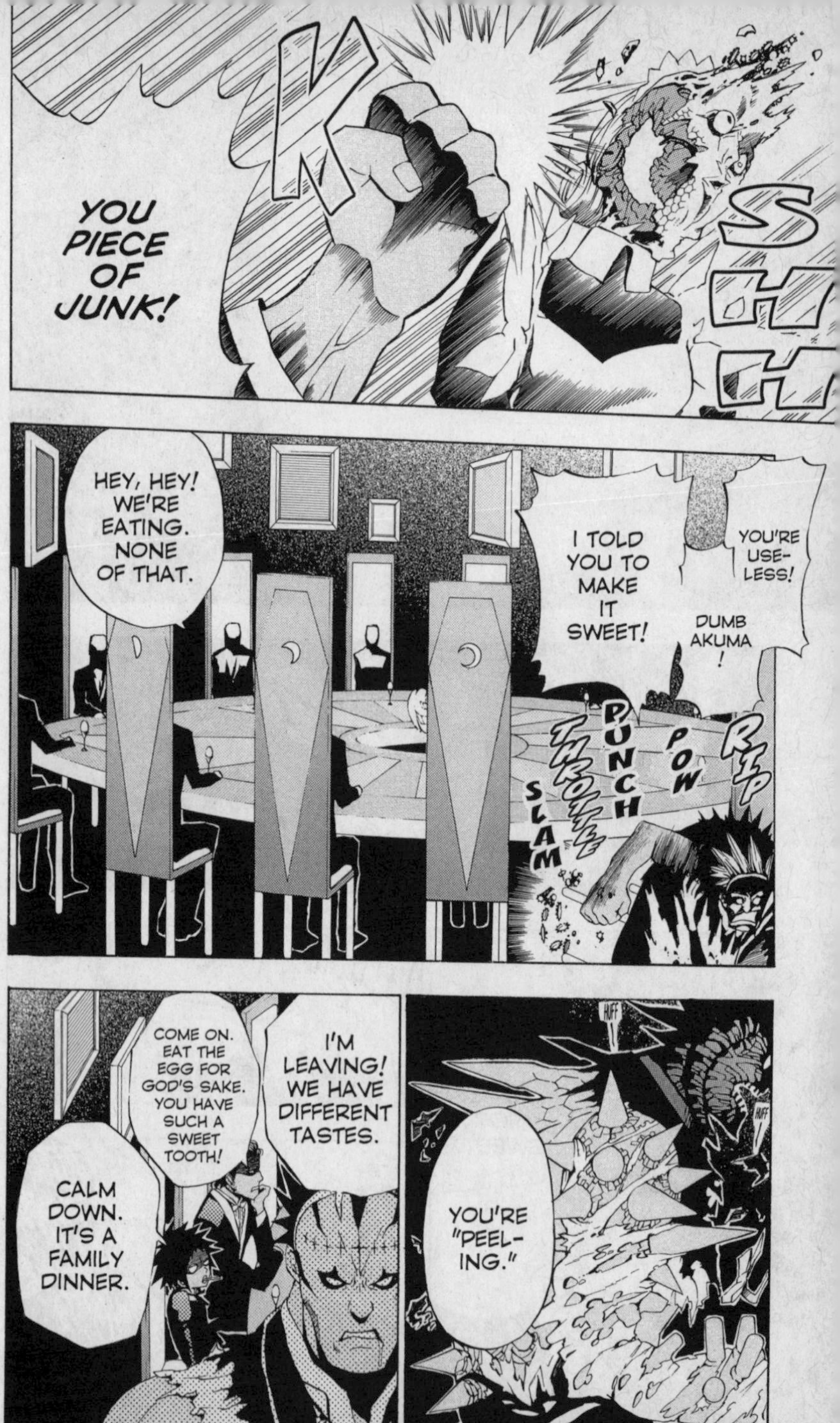
YOU PIECE OF JUNK!
YOU'RE USE-LESS!
DUMB AKUMA!
I TOLD YOU TO MAKE IT SWEET!
RIP
POW
PUNCH
THROWW
SLAM
HEY, HEY! WE'RE EATING. NONE OF THAT.
HUFF
HUFF
YOU'RE "PEEL-ING."
I'M LEAVING! WE HAVE DIFFERENT TASTES.
COME ON. EAT THE EGG FOR GOD'S SAKE. YOU HAVE SUCH A SWEET TOOTH!
CALM DOWN. IT'S A FAMILY DINNER.

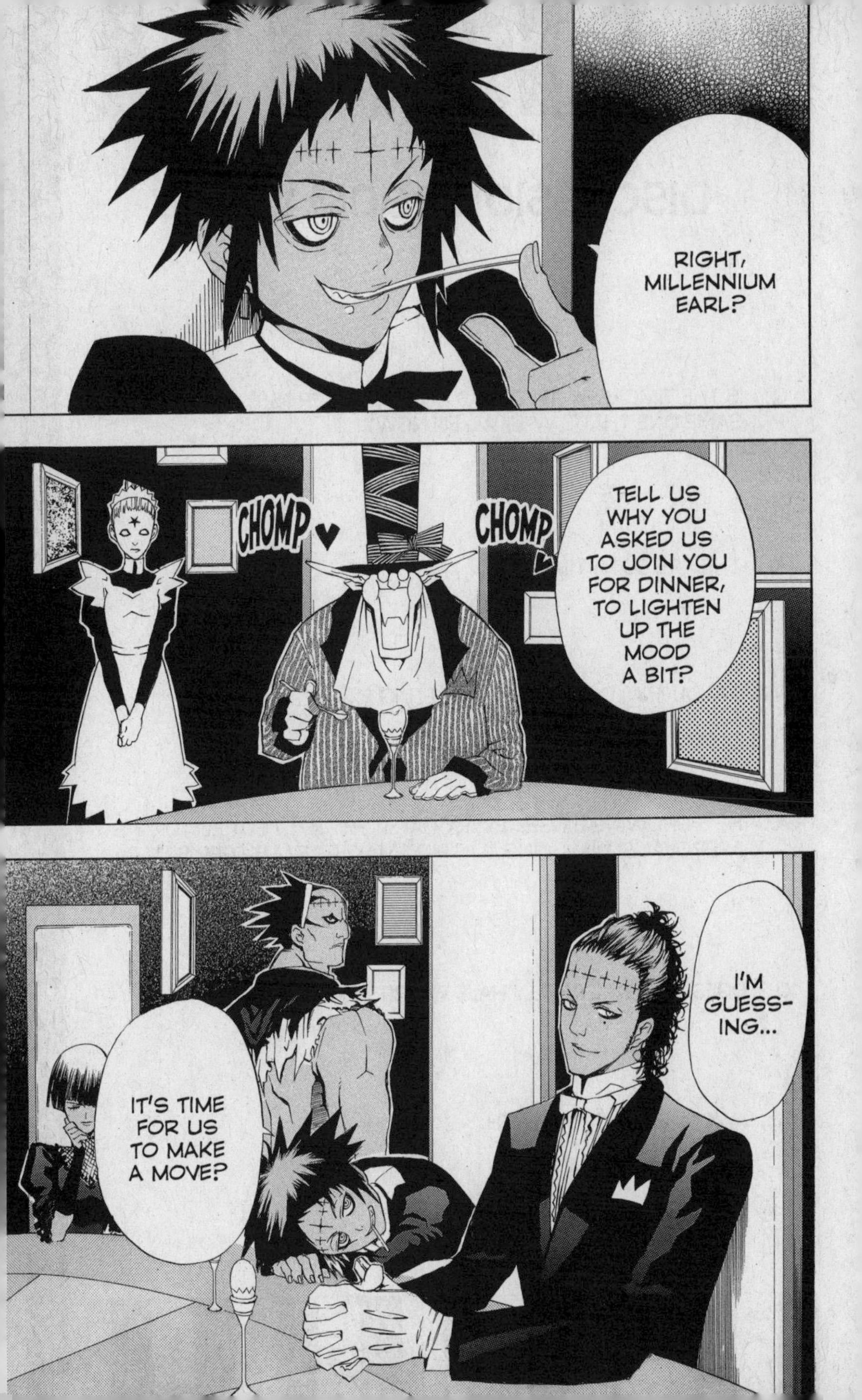
RIGHT, MILLENNIUM EARL?
TELL US WHY YOU ASKED US TO JOIN YOU FOR DINNER, TO LIGHTEN UP THE MOOD A BIT?
CHOMP
CHOMP
I'M GUESS- ING...
IT'S TIME FOR US TO MAKE A MOVE?

DISCUSSION ROOM VOL. 2

Q 1. IS THE TIMCANPY THAT WAS ON MASTER CROSS'S HEAD THE SAME ONE THAT'S WITH ALLEN NOW?

A.   THEY'RE BOTH TIMCANPY.

Q 2. TIMCANPY LOOKS LIKE IT'S GETTING BIGGER.

A.   HE'S GROWING BIGGER EVERY DAY (I THINK?). I GOT EDITOR Y'S APPROVAL SO I'M GOING TO START MAKING HIM BIGGER STILL!!

Q 3. DOES THE EARL REALLY HAVE RABBIT EARS?

A... I WONDER... HEH HEH HEH.

THE 19TH NIGHT: THE REWINDING CITY

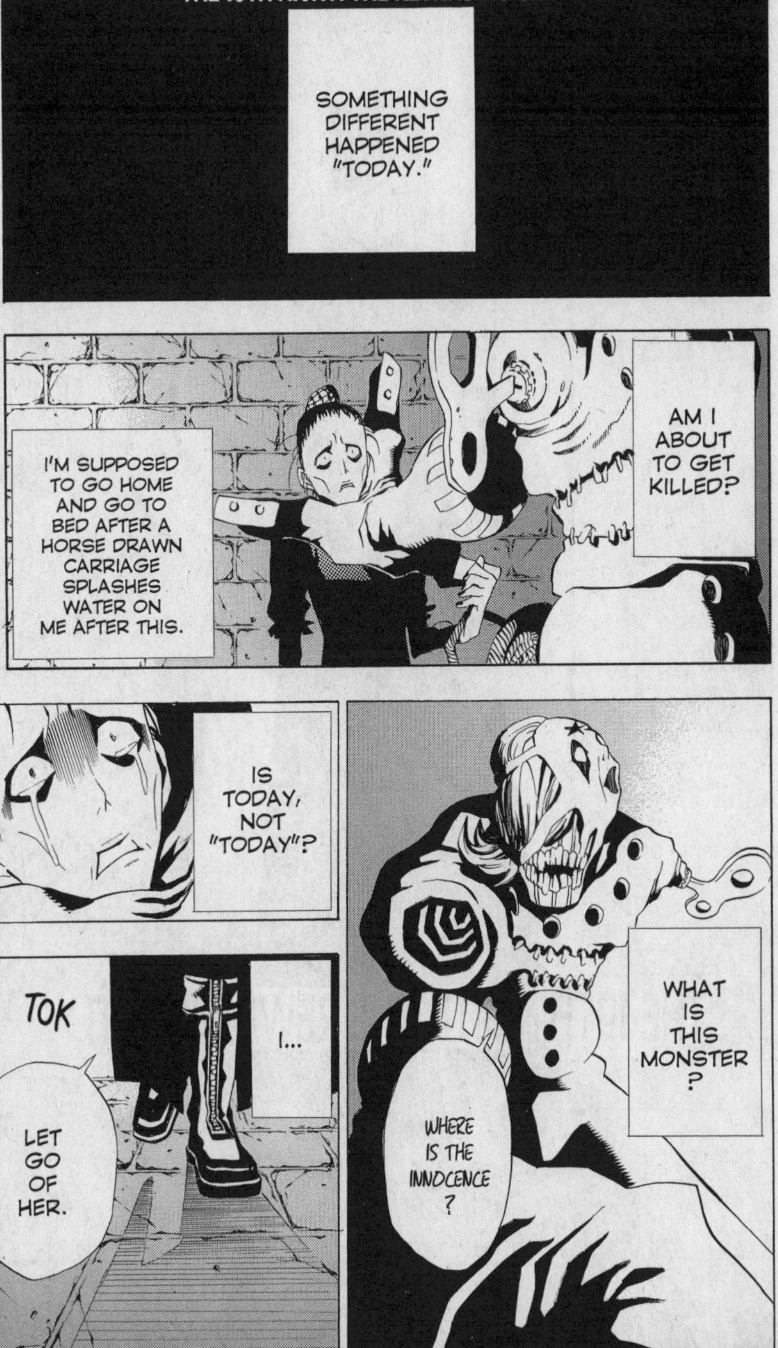
SOMETHING DIFFERENT HAPPENED "TODAY."
AM I ABOUT TO GET KILLED?
I'M SUPPOSED TO GO HOME AND GO TO BED AFTER A HORSE DRAWN CARRIAGE SPLASHES WATER ON ME AFTER THIS.
WHAT IS THIS MONSTER ?
WHERE IS THE INNOCENCE ?
IS TODAY, NOT "TODAY"?
I...
TOK
LET GO OF HER.

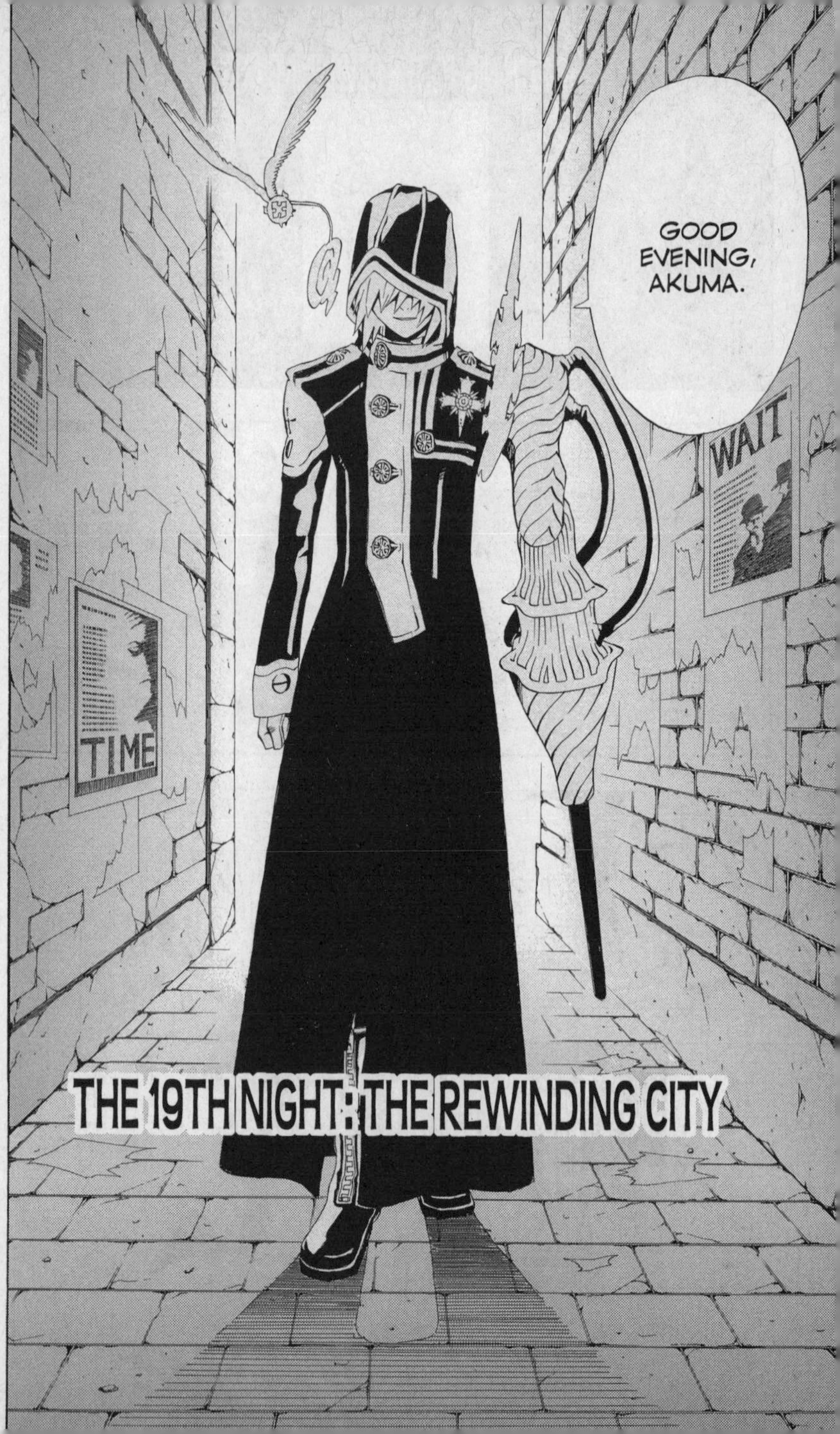
GOOD EVENING, AKUMA.
WAIT
TIME
THE 19TH NIGHT: THE REWINDING CITY

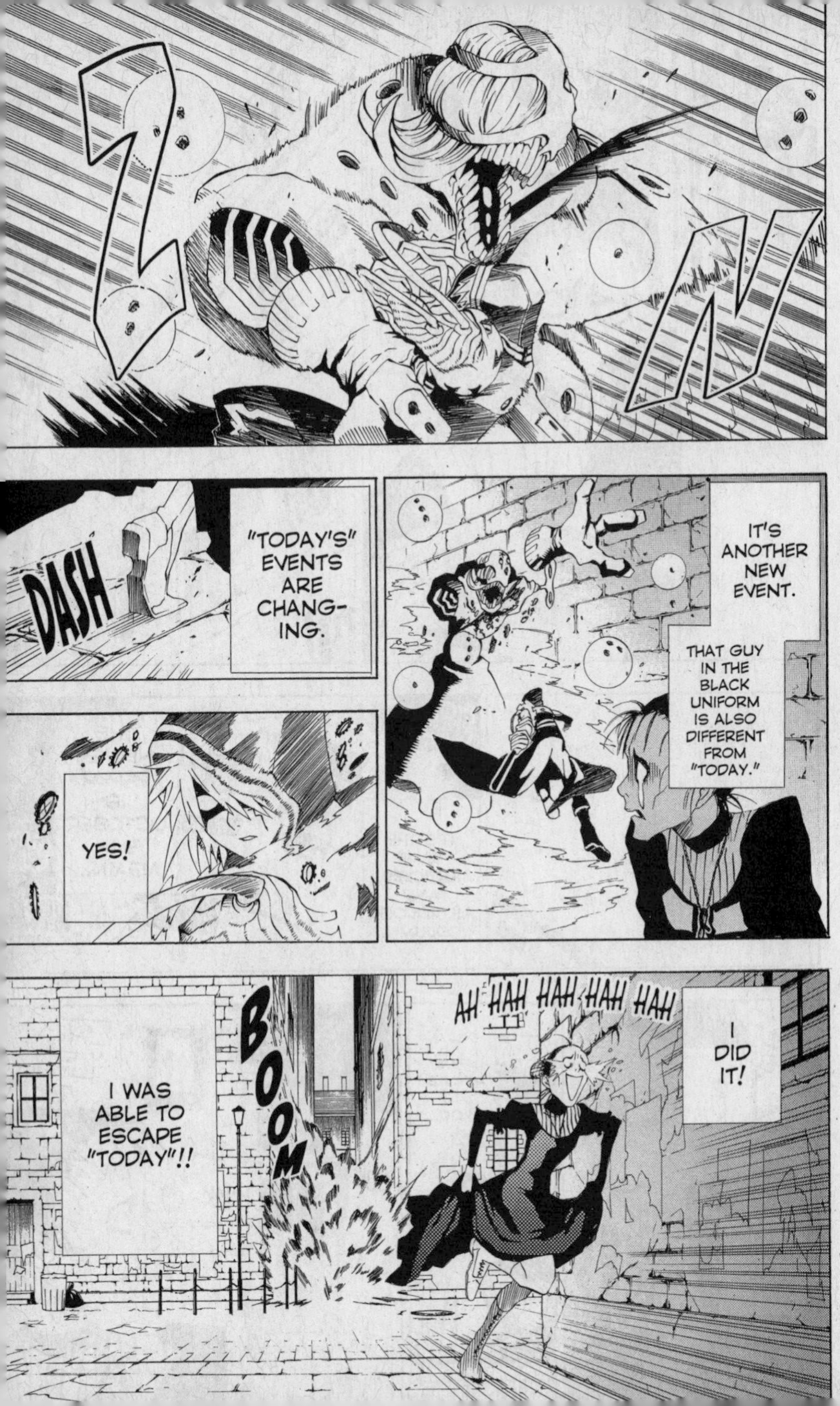
IT'S ANOTHER NEW EVENT.
THAT GUY IN THE BLACK UNIFORM IS ALSO DIFFERENT FROM "TODAY."
"TODAY'S" EVENTS ARE CHANG-ING.
DASH
YES!
I DID IT!
AH HAH HAH HAH HAH
BOOM
I WAS ABLE TO ESCAPE "TODAY"!!

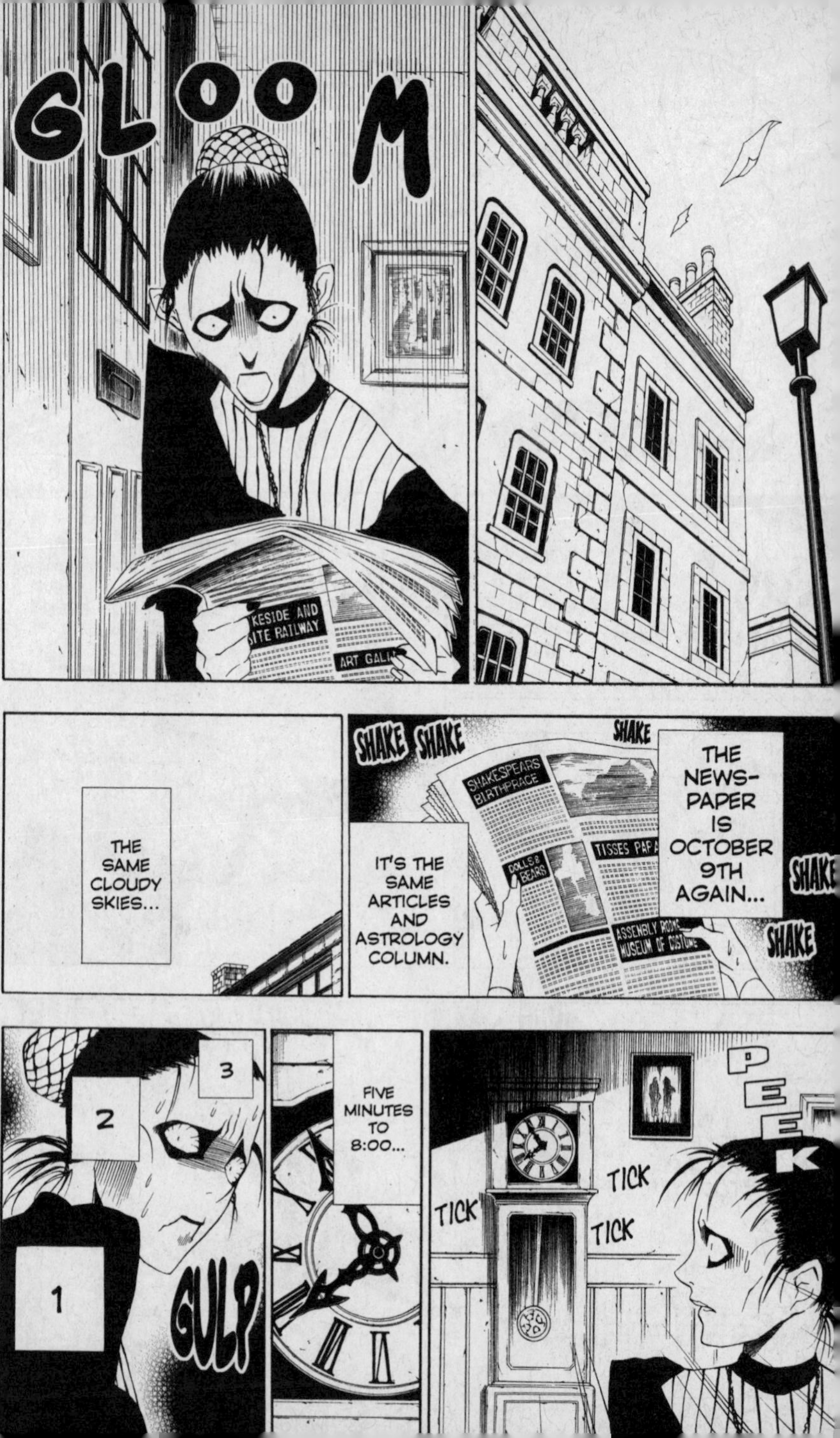
GLOOM
KESIDE AND
SITE RAILWAY
ART GALL
SHAKE
THE NEWS-PAPER IS OCTOBER 9TH AGAIN...
SHAKE
SHAKE
SHAKESPEARS BIRTHPRACE
TISSES PAPA
DOLLS & BEARS
ASSENBLY ROOMS MUSEUM OF COSTUME
SHAKE SHAKE
IT'S THE SAME ARTICLES AND ASTROLOGY COLUMN.
THE SAME CLOUDY SKIES...
PEEK
TICK
TICK
TICK
FIVE MINUTES TO 8:00...
3
2
GULP
1

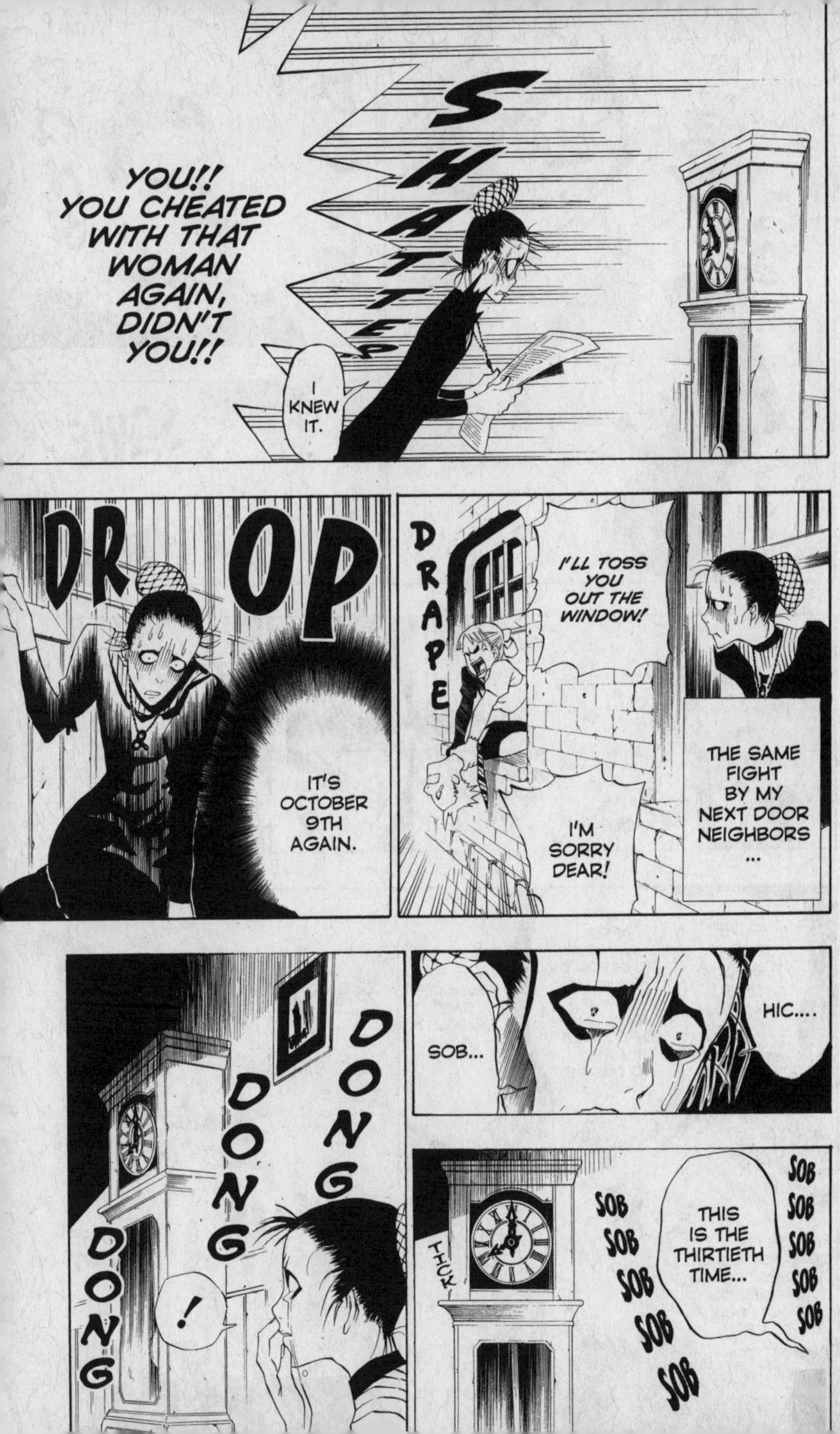
SHATTER
YOU!! YOU CHEATED WITH THAT WOMAN AGAIN, DIDN'T YOU!!
I KNEW IT.
I'LL TOSS YOU OUT THE WINDOW!
DRAPE
THE SAME FIGHT BY MY NEXT DOOR NEIGHBORS...
I'M SORRY DEAR!
DROP
IT'S OCTOBER 9TH AGAIN.
HIC....
SOB...
SOB SOB SOB SOB SOB
THIS IS THE THIRTIETH TIME...
SOB SOB SOB SOB SOB SOB
TICK
DONG
DONG
DONG
DONG
!

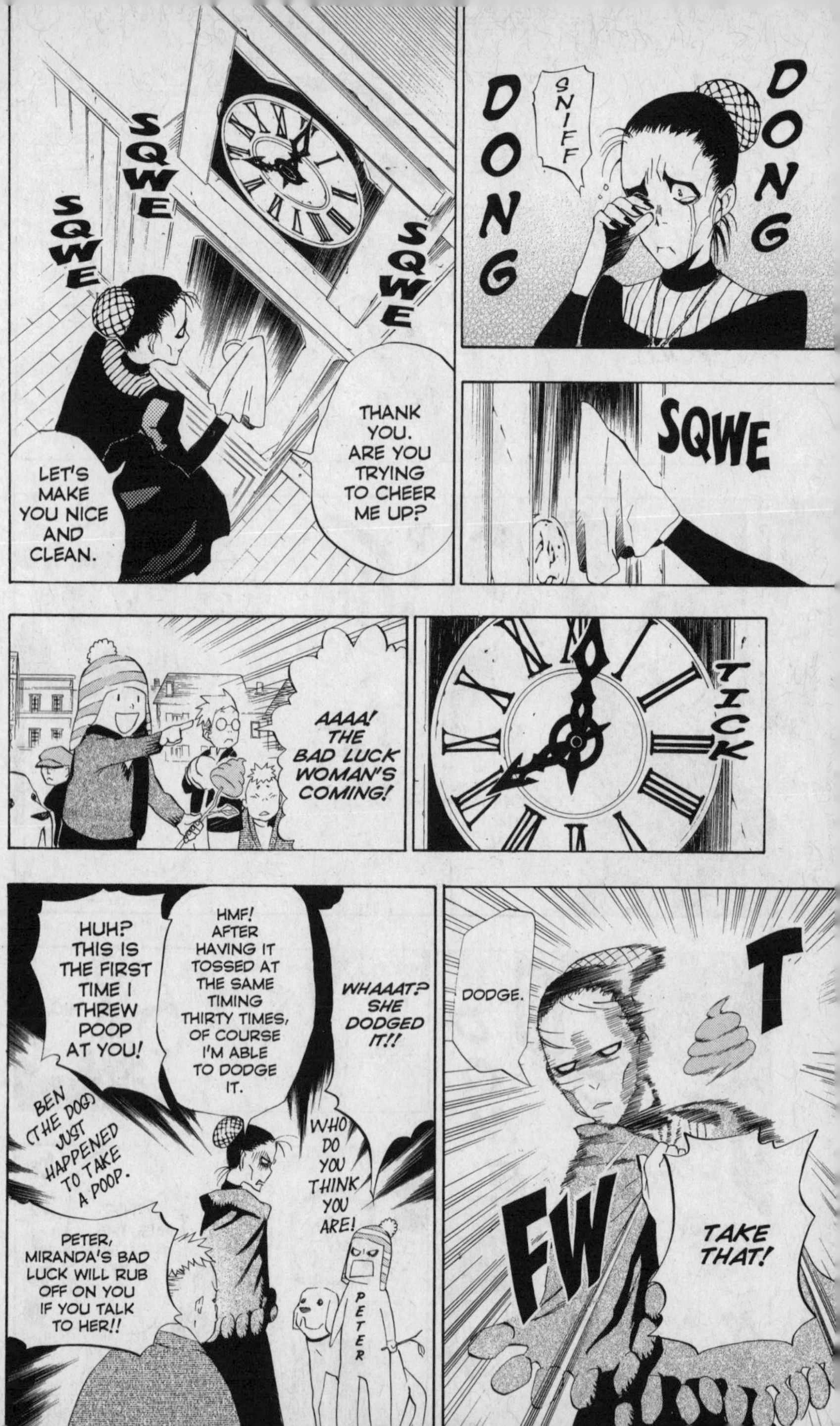
DONG
SNIFF
DONG
SQWE
SQWE
SQWE
SQWE
THANK YOU. ARE YOU TRYING TO CHEER ME UP?
LET'S MAKE YOU NICE AND CLEAN.
TICK
AAAA! THE BAD LUCK WOMAN'S COMING!
T
DODGE.
FW
TAKE THAT!
WHAAAT? SHE DODGED IT!!
HMF! AFTER HAVING IT TOSSED AT THE SAME TIMING THIRTY TIMES, OF COURSE I'M ABLE TO DODGE IT.
HUH? THIS IS THE FIRST TIME I THREW POOP AT YOU!
WHO DO YOU THINK YOU ARE!
BEN (THE DOG) JUST HAPPENED TO TAKE A POOP.
PETER, MIRANDA'S BAD LUCK WILL RUB OFF ON YOU IF YOU TALK TO HER!!
PETER

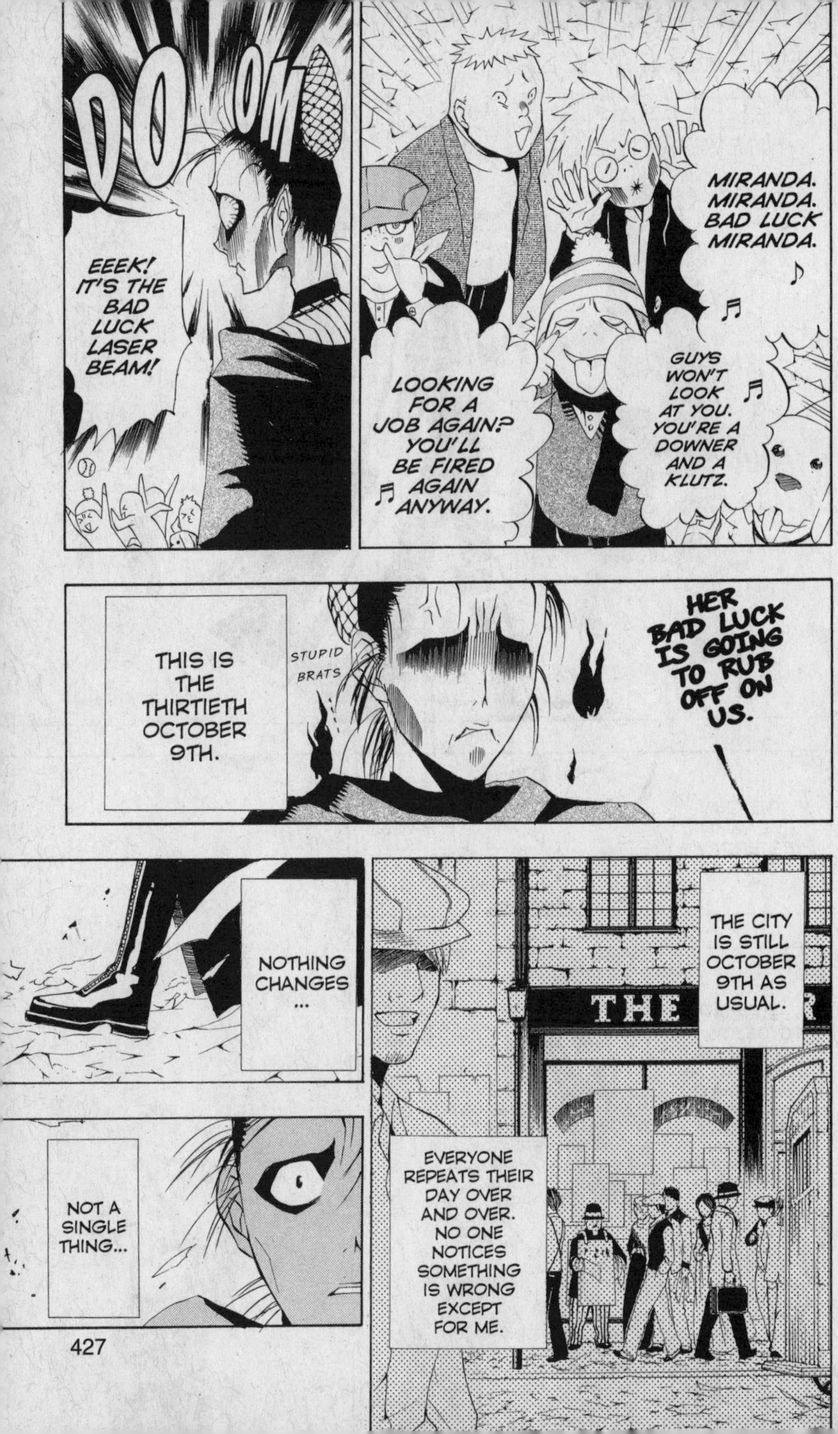
MIRANDA. MIRANDA. BAD LUCK MIRANDA. ♪
GUYS WON'T LOOK AT YOU. YOU'RE A DOWNER AND A KLUTZ. ♬
LOOKING FOR A JOB AGAIN? YOU'LL BE FIRED AGAIN ANYWAY. ♬
DOOM
EEEK! IT'S THE BAD LUCK LASER BEAM!
HER BAD LUCK IS GOING TO RUB OFF ON US.
STUPID BRATS
THIS IS THE THIRTIETH OCTOBER 9TH.
THE CITY IS STILL OCTOBER 9TH AS USUAL.
THE
EVERYONE REPEATS THEIR DAY OVER AND OVER. NO ONE NOTICES SOMETHING IS WRONG EXCEPT FOR ME.
NOTHING CHANGES ...
NOT A SINGLE THING...

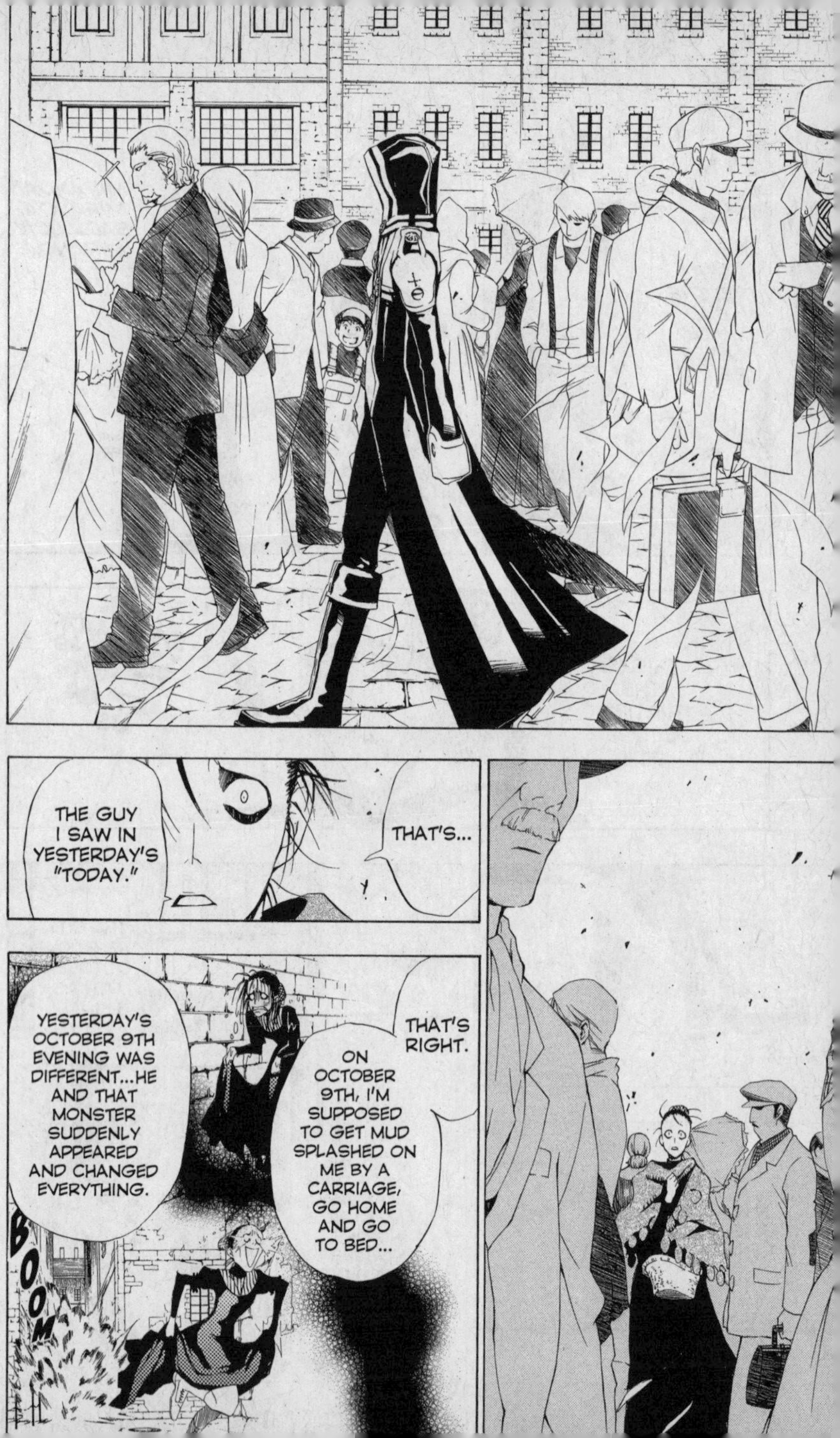
THAT'S...
THE GUY I SAW IN YESTERDAY'S "TODAY."
THAT'S RIGHT.
ON OCTOBER 9TH, I'M SUPPOSED TO GET MUD SPLASHED ON ME BY A CARRIAGE, GO HOME AND GO TO BED...
YESTERDAY'S OCTOBER 9TH EVENING WAS DIFFERENT...HE AND THAT MONSTER SUDDENLY APPEARED AND CHANGED EVERYTHING.
BOOM

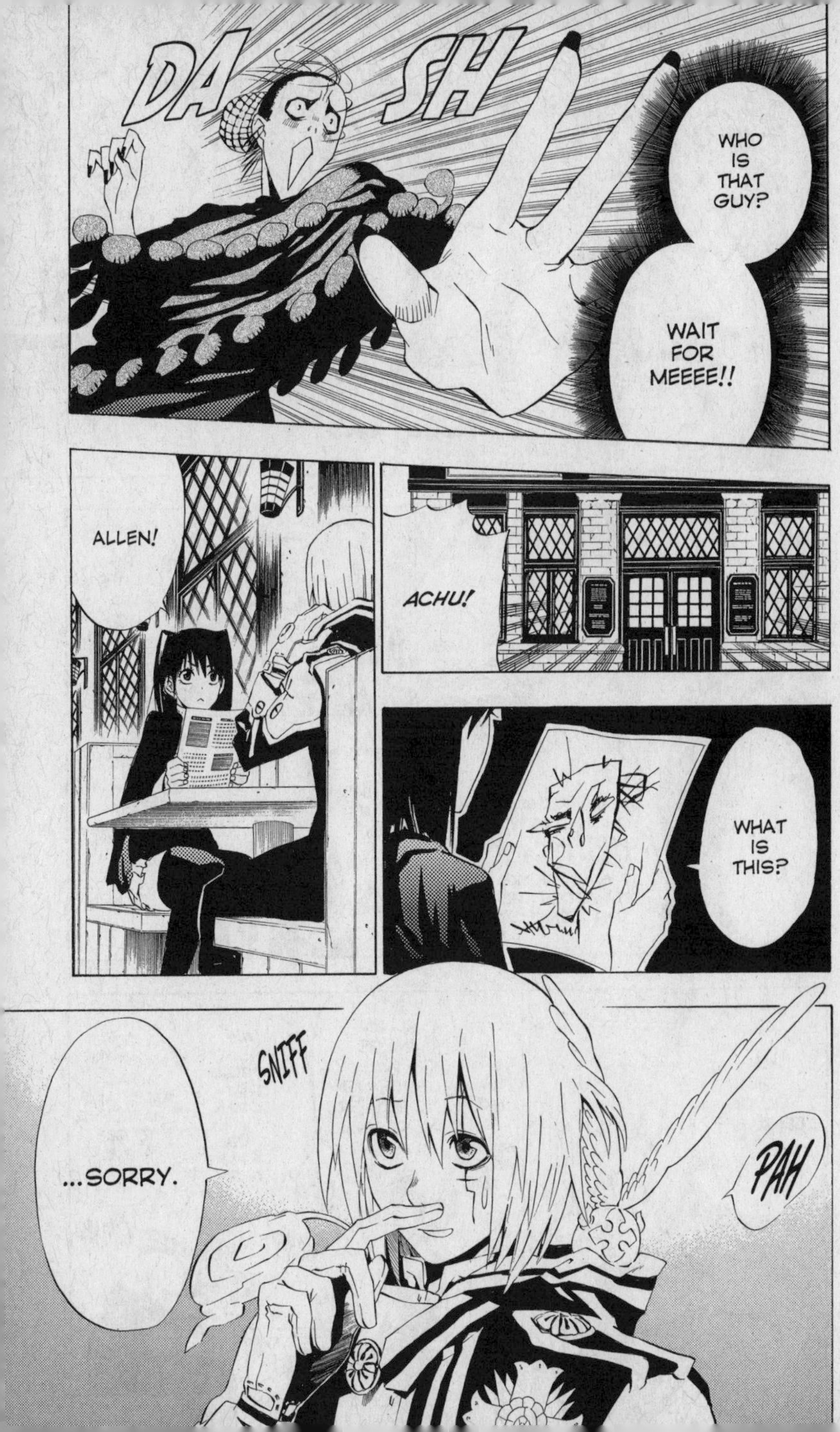
WHO IS THAT GUY?
WAIT FOR MEEEE!!
DASH
ACHU!
WHAT IS THIS?
ALLEN!
PAH
SNIFF
...SORRY.

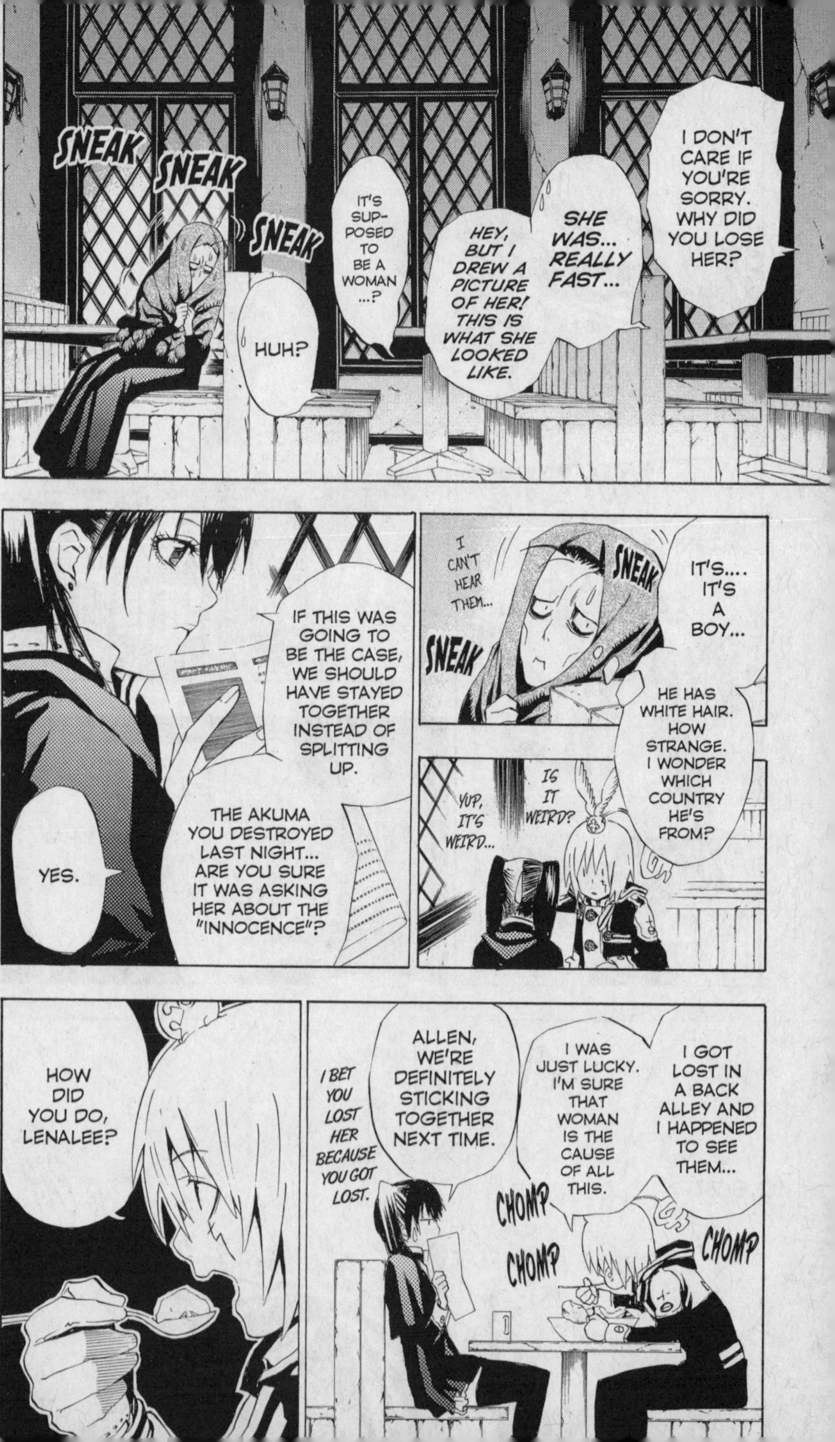
I DON'T CARE IF YOU'RE SORRY. WHY DID YOU LOSE HER?
SHE WAS... REALLY FAST...
HEY, BUT I DREW A PICTURE OF HER! THIS IS WHAT SHE LOOKED LIKE.
IT'S SUP-POSED TO BE A WOMAN ...?
HUH?
SNEAK
SNEAK
SNEAK
IT'S.... IT'S A BOY...
SNEAK
I CAN'T HEAR THEM...
SNEAK
HE HAS WHITE HAIR. HOW STRANGE. I WONDER WHICH COUNTRY HE'S FROM?
IS IT WEIRD?
YUP, IT'S WEIRD...
IF THIS WAS GOING TO BE THE CASE, WE SHOULD HAVE STAYED TOGETHER INSTEAD OF SPLITTING UP.
THE AKUMA YOU DESTROYED LAST NIGHT... ARE YOU SURE IT WAS ASKING HER ABOUT THE "INNOCENCE"?
YES.
I GOT LOST IN A BACK ALLEY AND I HAPPENED TO SEE THEM...
I WAS JUST LUCKY. I'M SURE THAT WOMAN IS THE CAUSE OF ALL THIS.
ALLEN, WE'RE DEFINITELY STICKING TOGETHER NEXT TIME.
I BET YOU LOST HER BECAUSE YOU GOT LOST.
CHOMP
CHOMP
CHOMP
HOW DID YOU DO, LENALEE?

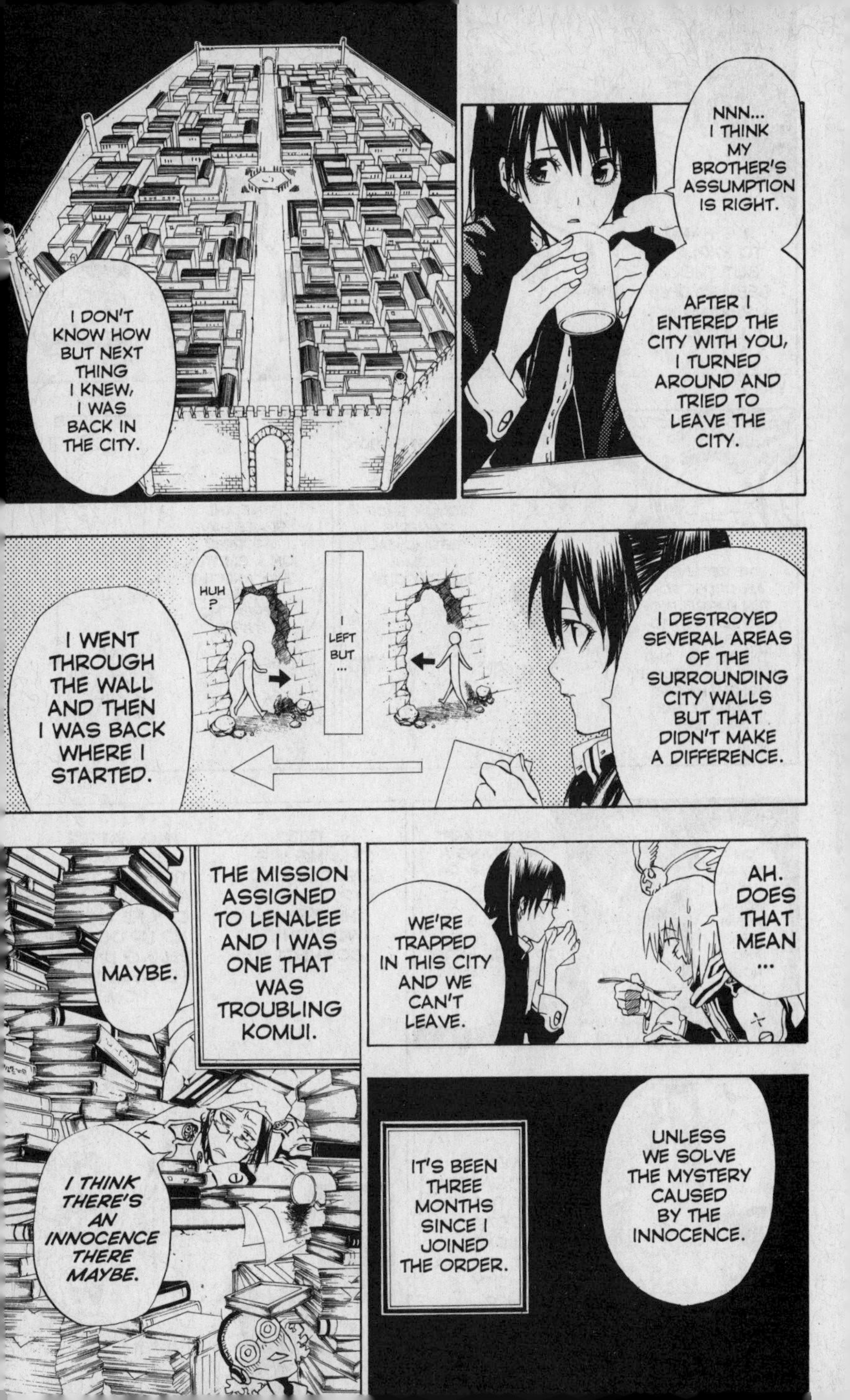
NNN... I THINK MY BROTHER'S ASSUMPTION IS RIGHT.
AFTER I ENTERED THE CITY WITH YOU, I TURNED AROUND AND TRIED TO LEAVE THE CITY.
I DON'T KNOW HOW BUT NEXT THING I KNEW, I WAS BACK IN THE CITY.
I DESTROYED SEVERAL AREAS OF THE SURROUNDING CITY WALLS BUT THAT DIDN'T MAKE A DIFFERENCE.
I LEFT BUT ...
HUH ?
I WENT THROUGH THE WALL AND THEN I WAS BACK WHERE I STARTED.
AH. DOES THAT MEAN ...
WE'RE TRAPPED IN THIS CITY AND WE CAN'T LEAVE.
UNLESS WE SOLVE THE MYSTERY CAUSED BY THE INNOCENCE.
IT'S BEEN THREE MONTHS SINCE I JOINED THE ORDER.
THE MISSION ASSIGNED TO LENALEE AND I WAS ONE THAT WAS TROUBLING KOMUI.
MAYBE.
I THINK THERE'S AN INNOCENCE THERE MAYBE.

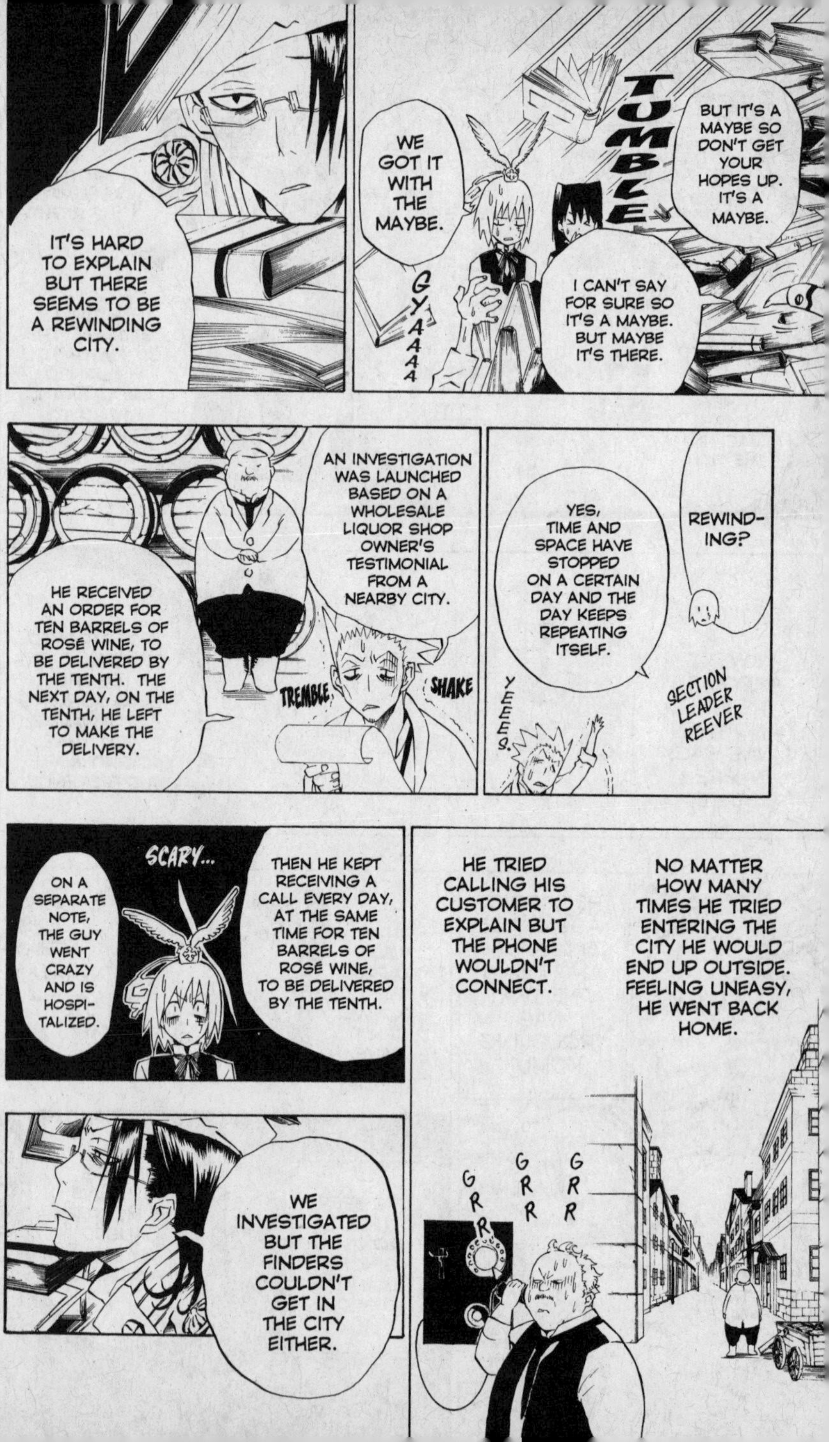
BUT IT'S A MAYBE SO DON'T GET YOUR HOPES UP. IT'S A MAYBE.
TUMBLE
I CAN'T SAY FOR SURE SO IT'S A MAYBE. BUT MAYBE IT'S THERE.
WE GOT IT WITH THE MAYBE.
GYAAAA
IT'S HARD TO EXPLAIN BUT THERE SEEMS TO BE A REWINDING CITY.
REWINDING?
YES, TIME AND SPACE HAVE STOPPED ON A CERTAIN DAY AND THE DAY KEEPS REPEATING ITSELF.
YEEES.
SECTION LEADER REEVER
AN INVESTIGATION WAS LAUNCHED BASED ON A WHOLESALE LIQUOR SHOP OWNER'S TESTIMONIAL FROM A NEARBY CITY.
SHAKE
TREMBLE
HE RECEIVED AN ORDER FOR TEN BARRELS OF ROSÉ WINE, TO BE DELIVERED BY THE TENTH. THE NEXT DAY, ON THE TENTH, HE LEFT TO MAKE THE DELIVERY.
NO MATTER HOW MANY TIMES HE TRIED ENTERING THE CITY HE WOULD END UP OUTSIDE. FEELING UNEASY, HE WENT BACK HOME.
HE TRIED CALLING HIS CUSTOMER TO EXPLAIN BUT THE PHONE WOULDN'T CONNECT.
GRR
GRR
GRR
THEN HE KEPT RECEIVING A CALL EVERY DAY, AT THE SAME TIME FOR TEN BARRELS OF ROSÉ WINE, TO BE DELIVERED BY THE TENTH.
SCARY...
ON A SEPARATE NOTE, THE GUY WENT CRAZY AND IS HOSPITALIZED.
WE INVESTIGATED BUT THE FINDERS COULDN'T GET IN THE CITY EITHER.

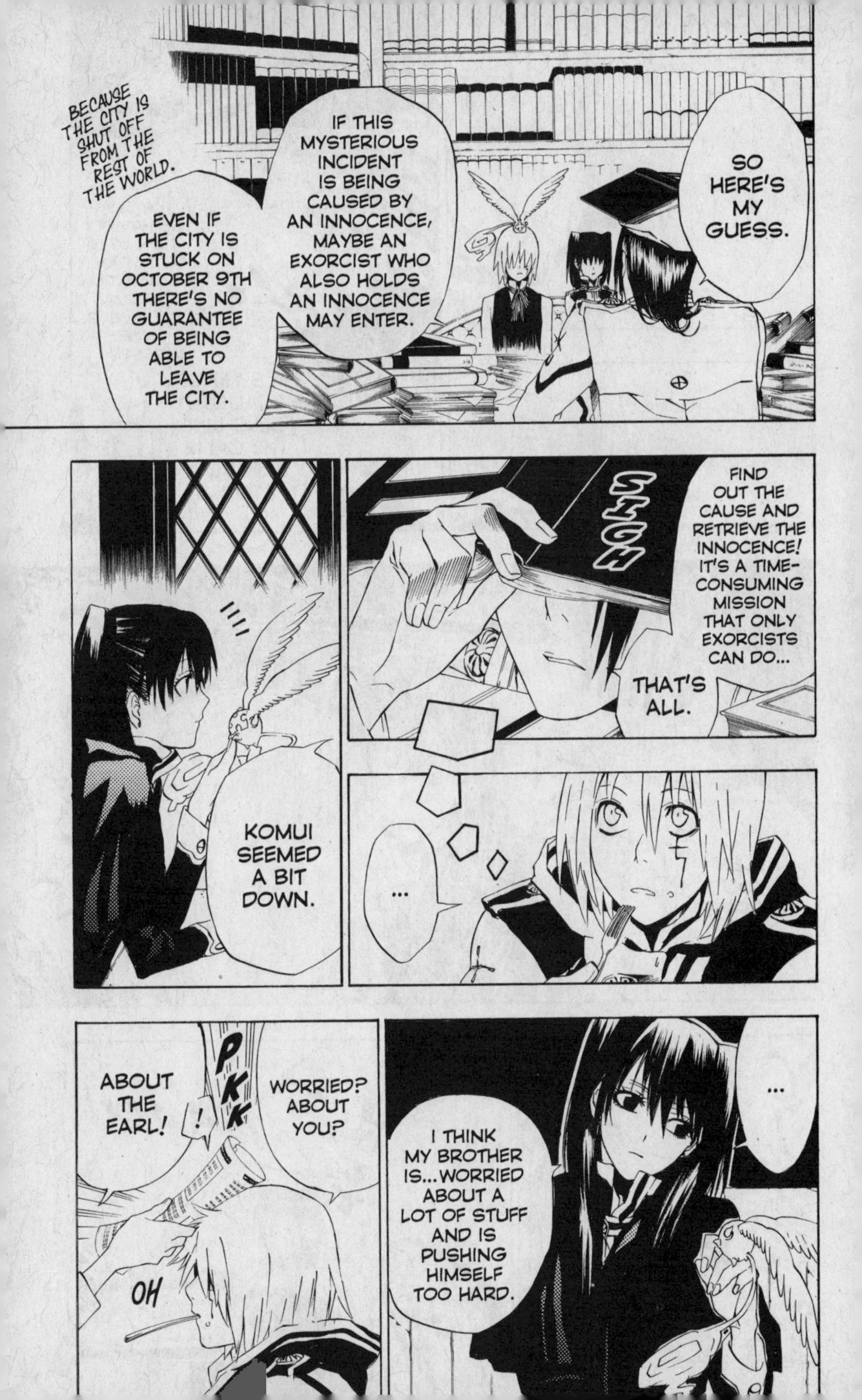
SO HERE'S MY GUESS.
IF THIS MYSTERIOUS INCIDENT IS BEING CAUSED BY AN INNOCENCE, MAYBE AN EXORCIST WHO ALSO HOLDS AN INNOCENCE MAY ENTER.
BECAUSE THE CITY IS SHUT OFF FROM THE REST OF THE WORLD.
EVEN IF THE CITY IS STUCK ON OCTOBER 9TH THERE'S NO GUARANTEE OF BEING ABLE TO LEAVE THE CITY.
SIGH
FIND OUT THE CAUSE AND RETRIEVE THE INNOCENCE! IT'S A TIME-CONSUMING MISSION THAT ONLY EXORCISTS CAN DO...
THAT'S ALL.
...
KOMUI SEEMED A BIT DOWN.
...
I THINK MY BROTHER IS...WORRIED ABOUT A LOT OF STUFF AND IS PUSHING HIMSELF TOO HARD.
WORRIED? ABOUT YOU?
PKK
ABOUT THE EARL!
!
OH

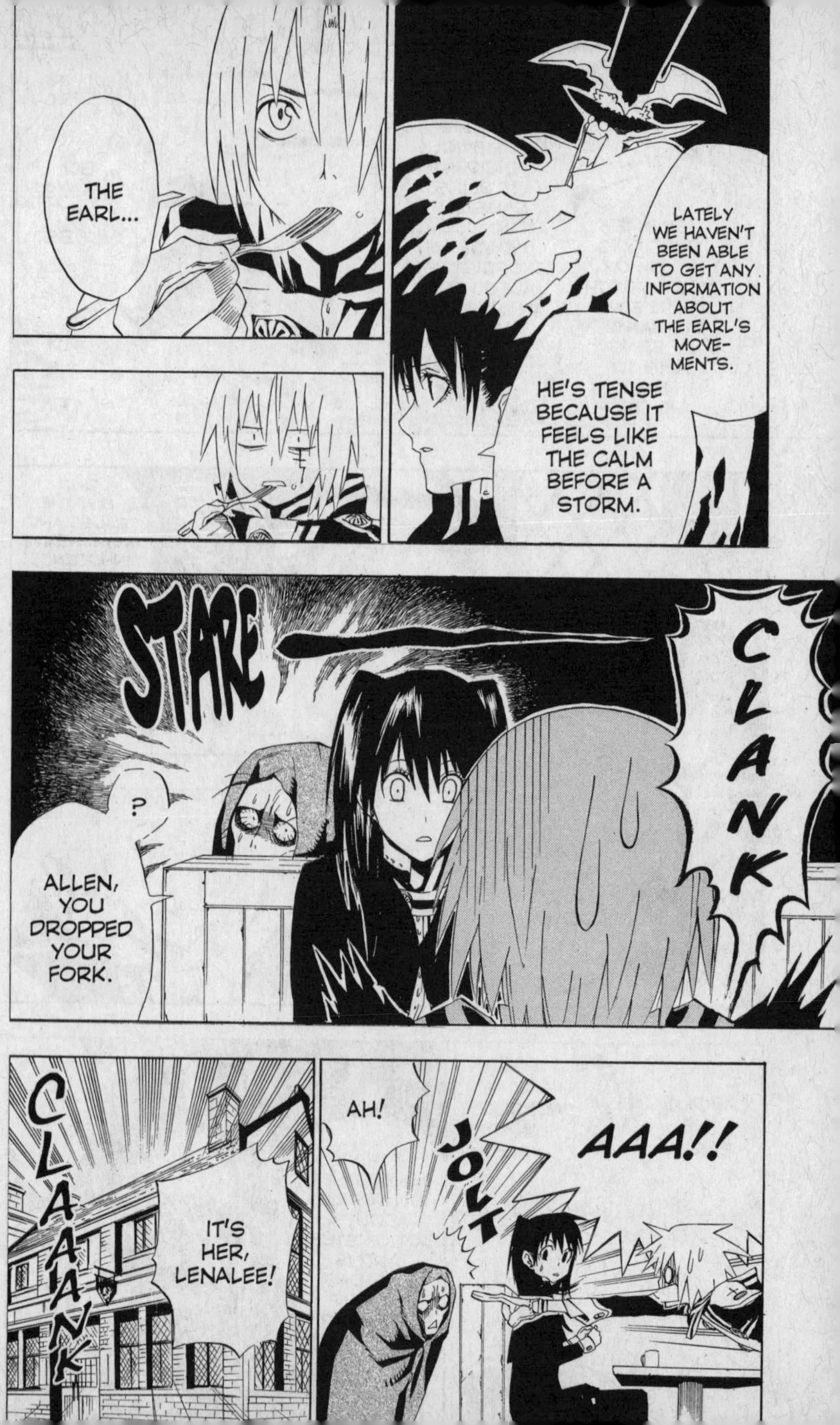
LATELY WE HAVEN'T BEEN ABLE TO GET ANY INFORMATION ABOUT THE EARL'S MOVEMENTS.
HE'S TENSE BECAUSE IT FEELS LIKE THE CALM BEFORE A STORM.
THE EARL...
CLANK
STARE
?
ALLEN, YOU DROPPED YOUR FORK.
AAA!!
JOLT
AH!
CLAAANK
IT'S HER, LENALEE!

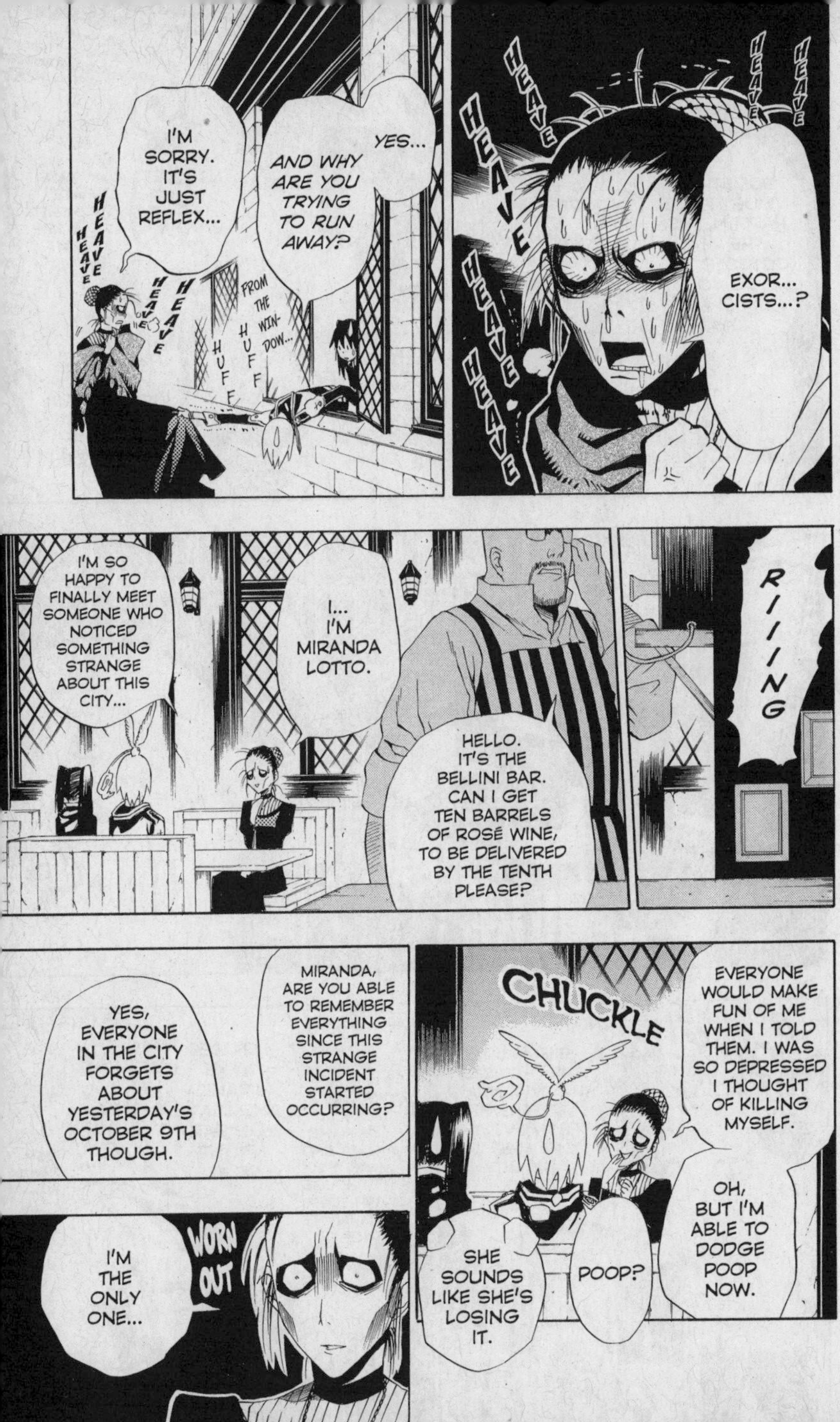
HEAVE HEAVE HEAVE HEAVE HEAVE HEAVE HEAVE
EXOR... CISTS...?
YES...
AND WHY ARE YOU TRYING TO RUN AWAY?
I'M SORRY. IT'S JUST REFLEX...
HEAVE HEAVE HEAVE HEAVE
HUFF HUFF
FROM THE WINDOW...
RIIIING
HELLO. IT'S THE BELLINI BAR. CAN I GET TEN BARRELS OF ROSÉ WINE, TO BE DELIVERED BY THE TENTH PLEASE?
I... I'M MIRANDA LOTTO.
I'M SO HAPPY TO FINALLY MEET SOMEONE WHO NOTICED SOMETHING STRANGE ABOUT THIS CITY...
CHUCKLE
EVERYONE WOULD MAKE FUN OF ME WHEN I TOLD THEM. I WAS SO DEPRESSED I THOUGHT OF KILLING MYSELF.
OH, BUT I'M ABLE TO DODGE POOP NOW.
POOP?
SHE SOUNDS LIKE SHE'S LOSING IT.
MIRANDA, ARE YOU ABLE TO REMEMBER EVERYTHING SINCE THIS STRANGE INCIDENT STARTED OCCURRING?
YES, EVERYONE IN THE CITY FORGETS ABOUT YESTERDAY'S OCTOBER 9TH THOUGH.
WORN OUT
I'M THE ONLY ONE...

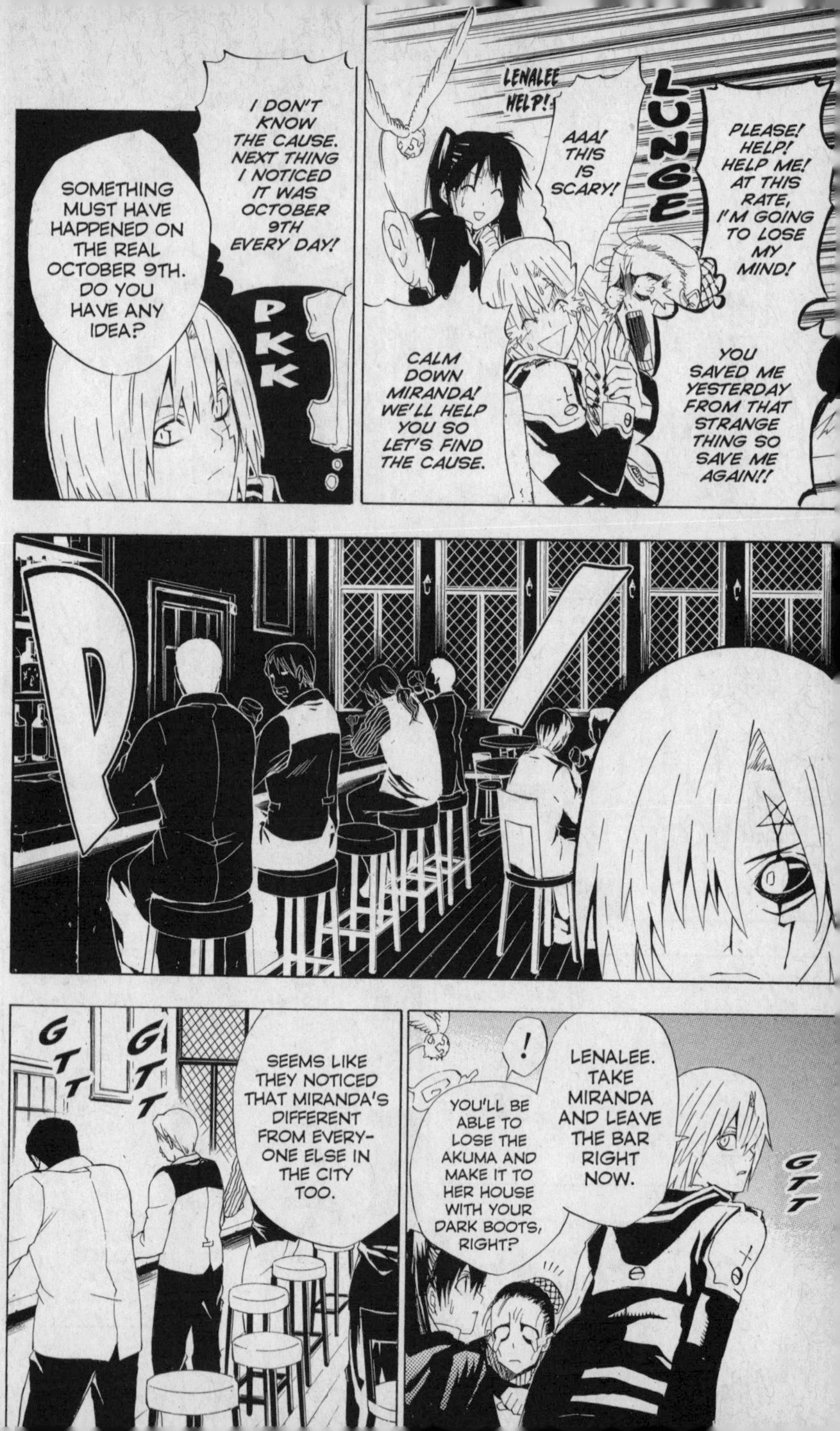
PLEASE! HELP! HELP ME! AT THIS RATE, I'M GOING TO LOSE MY MIND!
LUNGE
AAA! THIS IS SCARY!
LENALEE HELP?!
YOU SAVED ME YESTERDAY FROM THAT STRANGE THING SO SAVE ME AGAIN!!
CALM DOWN MIRANDA! WE'LL HELP YOU SO LET'S FIND THE CAUSE.
I DON'T KNOW THE CAUSE. NEXT THING I NOTICED IT WAS OCTOBER 9TH EVERY DAY!
PKK
SOMETHING MUST HAVE HAPPENED ON THE REAL OCTOBER 9TH. DO YOU HAVE ANY IDEA?
!
LENALEE. TAKE MIRANDA AND LEAVE THE BAR RIGHT NOW.
YOU'LL BE ABLE TO LOSE THE AKUMA AND MAKE IT TO HER HOUSE WITH YOUR DARK BOOTS, RIGHT?
GTT
SEEMS LIKE THEY NOTICED THAT MIRANDA'S DIFFERENT FROM EVERY-ONE ELSE IN THE CITY TOO.
GTT
GTT

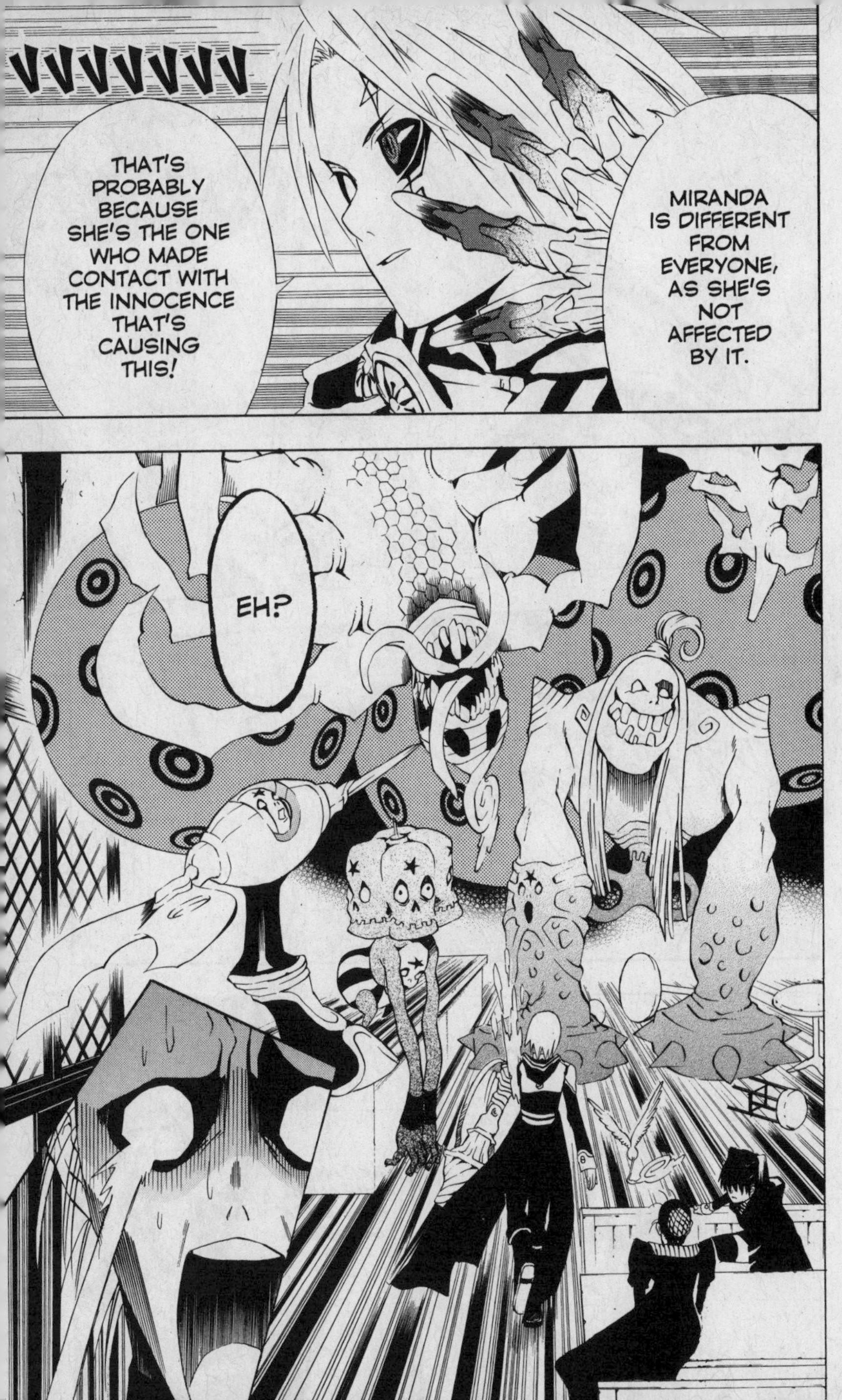
MIRANDA IS DIFFERENT FROM EVERYONE, AS SHE'S NOT AFFECTED BY IT.
VVVVVVVV
THAT'S PROBABLY BECAUSE SHE'S THE ONE WHO MADE CONTACT WITH THE INNOCENCE THAT'S CAUSING THIS!
EH?

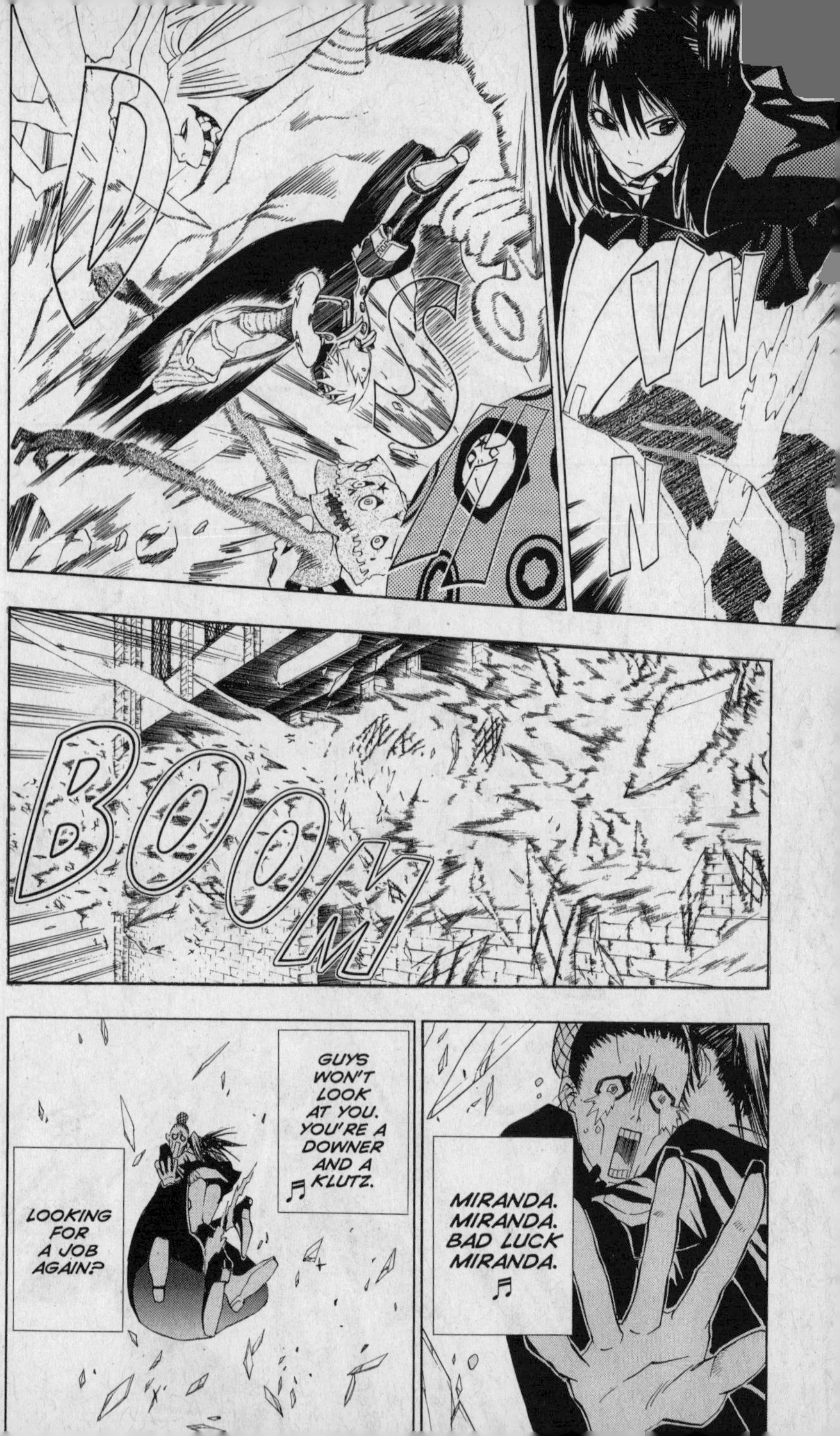
BOOM
MIRANDA. MIRANDA. BAD LUCK MIRANDA. ♪
GUYS WON'T LOOK AT YOU. YOU'RE A DOWNER AND A KLUTZ. ♪
LOOKING FOR A JOB AGAIN?

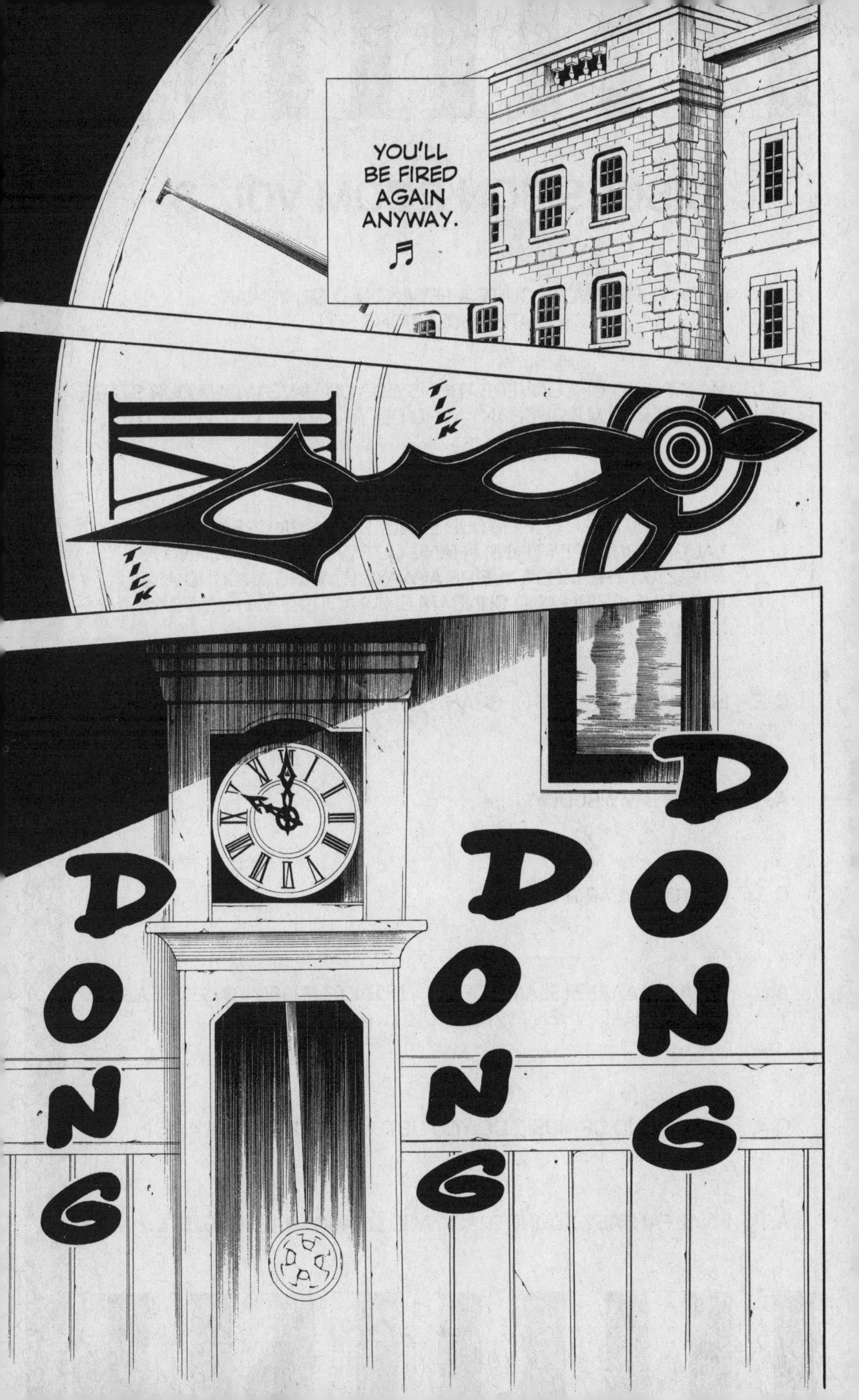
YOU'LL BE FIRED AGAIN ANYWAY. ♬
TICK
TICK
DONG
DONG
DONG

DISCUSSION ROOM VOL. 3

★THERE WERE QUITE A FEW NON-D.GRAY-MAN-
RELATED QUESTIONS SO...

Q 1.　WHAT KIND OF CONVERSATIONS DO YOU HAVE WITH YOUR STAFF
MEMBERS, LIKE OI-CHAN? WHO DO YOU HANG OUT WITH THE
MOST?

A.　WE SHOW EACH OTHER OUR EARLIER MANGA CREATIONS AND
LAUGH ABOUT IT. I THINK I HANG OUT WITH OI-CHAN AND
MIYAZAKI THE MOST. WE'RE ALWAYS PLAYING AROUND AND
IMITATING GHIBLI AND GUNDAM CHARACTERS WHEN WE'RE
WORKING.

Q 2.　IS YOUR ASSISTANT OI-CHAN YOUR NEPHEW?

A.　NO, HE'S MY BUDDY.

Q 3.　DO YOU WEAR A TOUPEE?

A.　WHAAAAAAA!!? (SLAMS DESK!) I DO NOT! I USED TO GET TEASED
ABOUT THAT WHEN I WAS YOUNG...

Q 4.　WHAT KIND OF MUSIC DO YOU LISTEN TO WHILE WORKING?

A.　FINAL FANTASY SOUNDTRACK AND DRAGONBALL CDS, ETC.

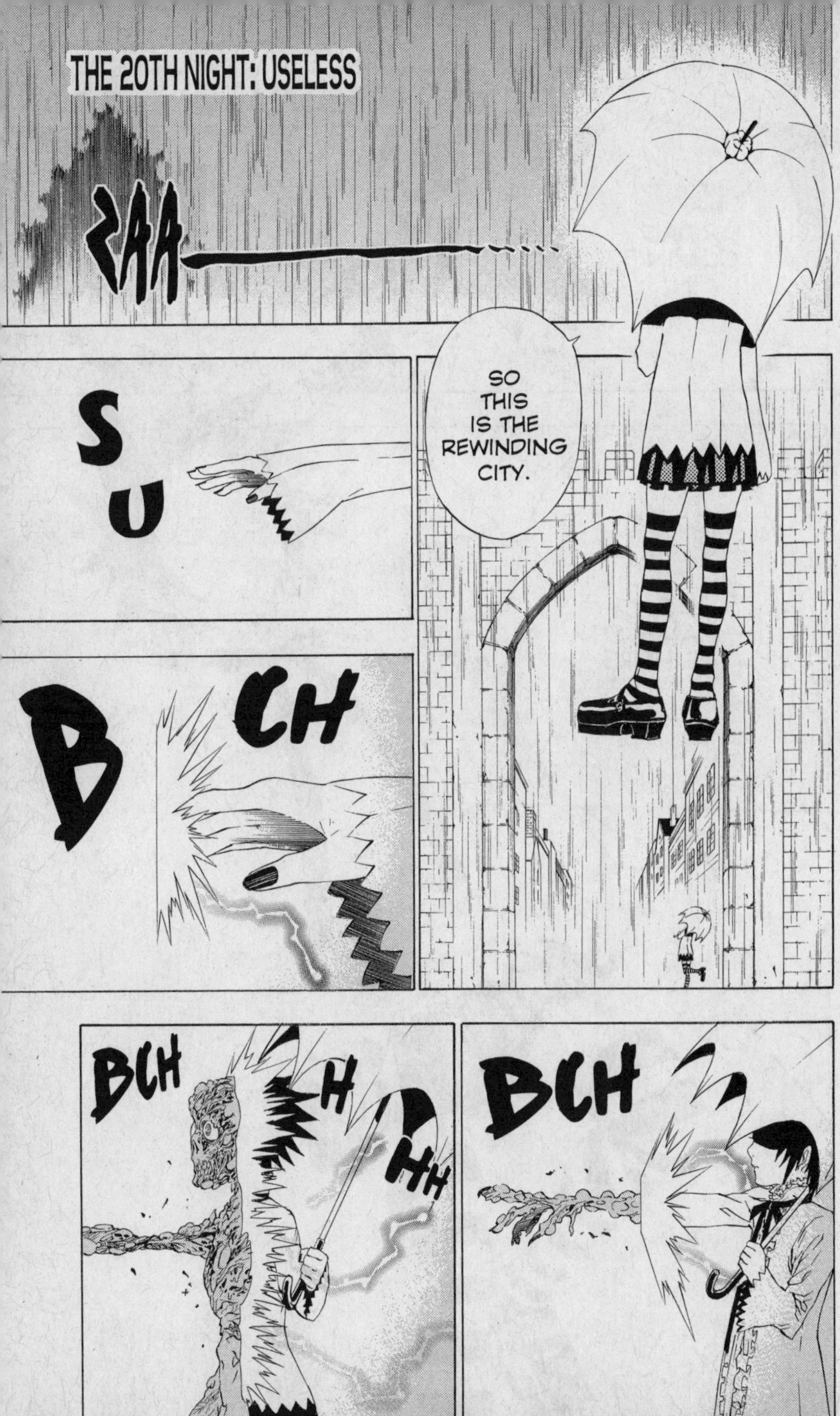
THE 20TH NIGHT: USELESS
ZAA
SO THIS IS THE REWINDING CITY.
SU
BCH
BCH
BCH

THE 20TH NIGHT: USELESS

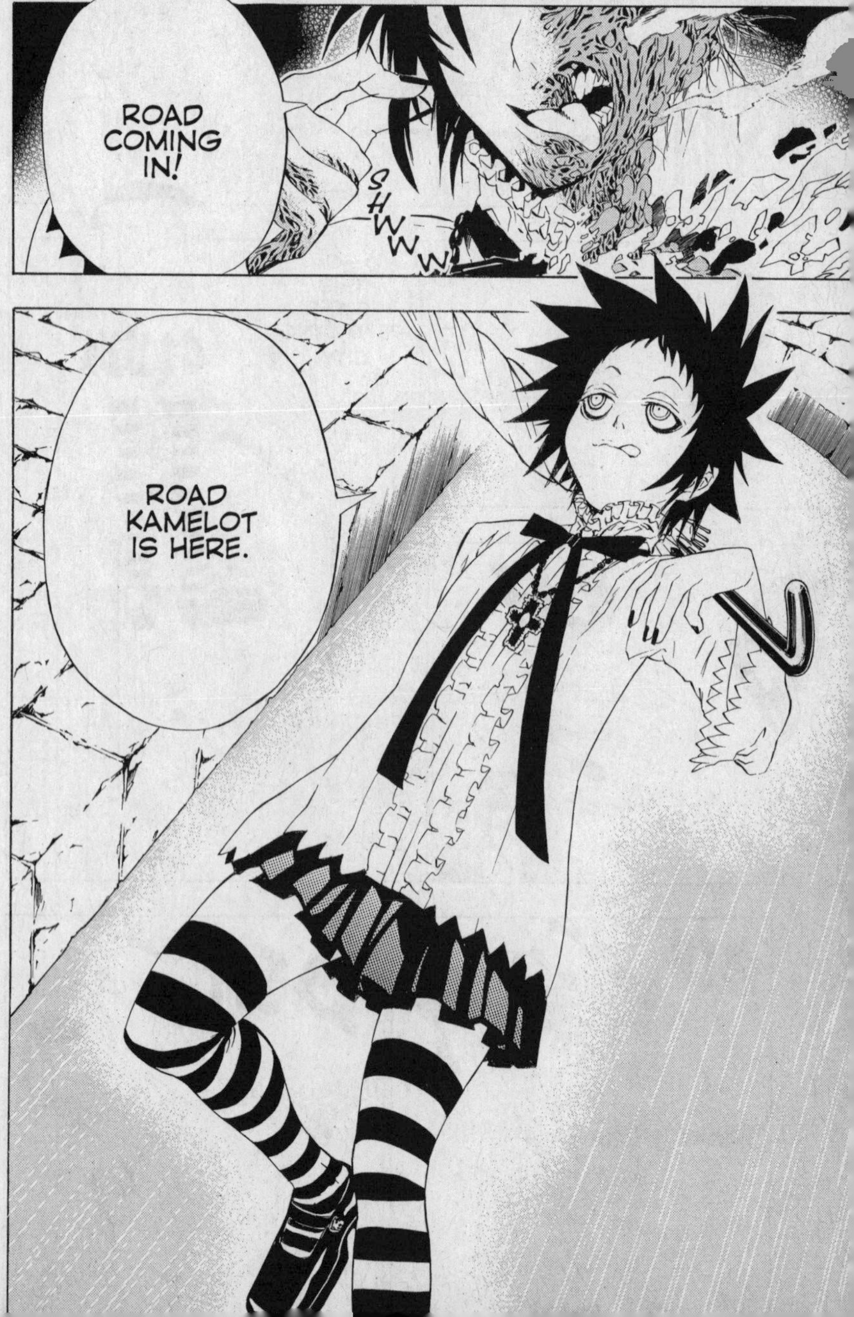
ROAD COMING IN!
SHWWW
ROAD KAMELOT IS HERE.

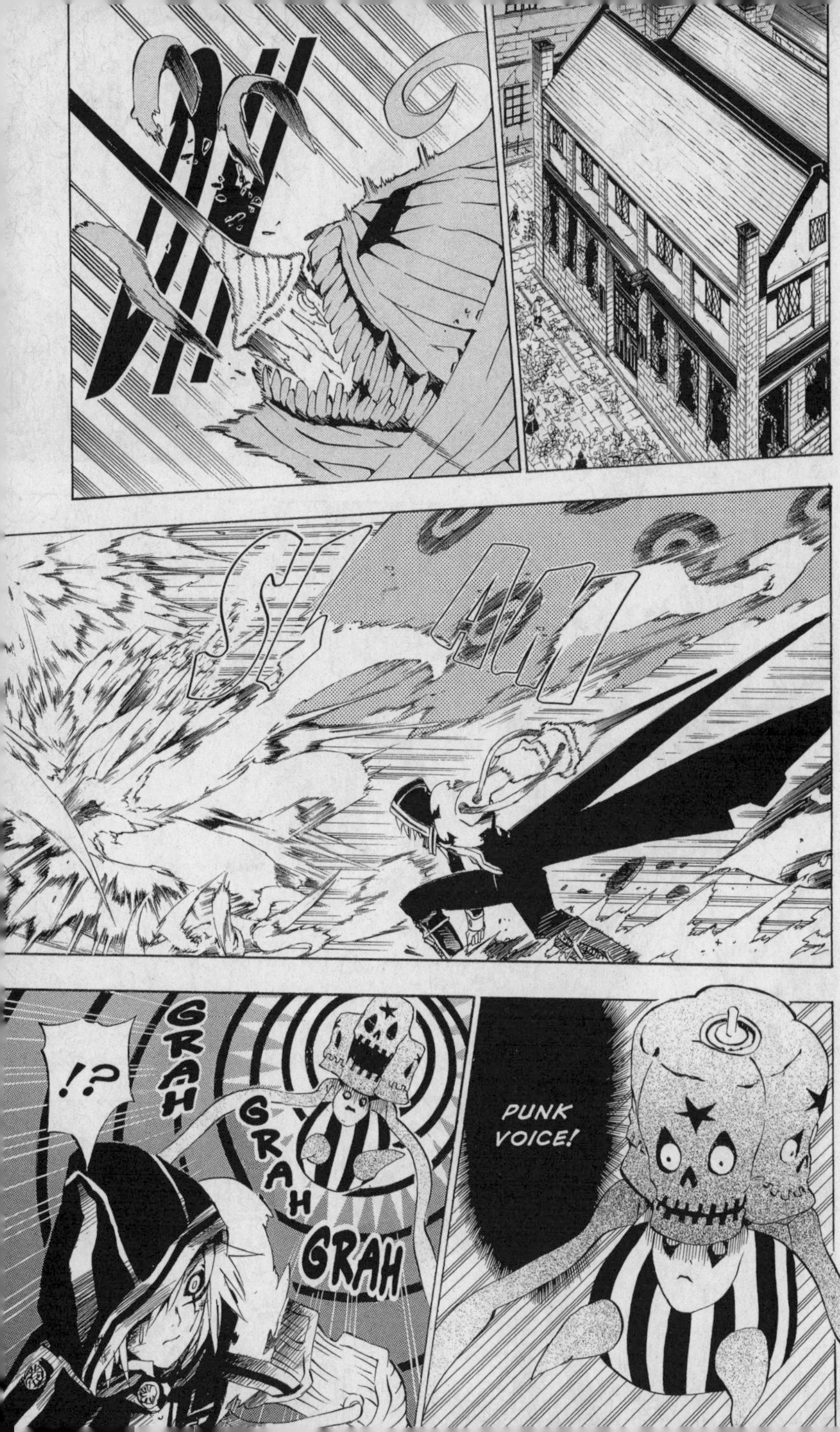
SLAM
PUNK VOICE!
GRAH
GRAH
GRAH
GRAH
!?

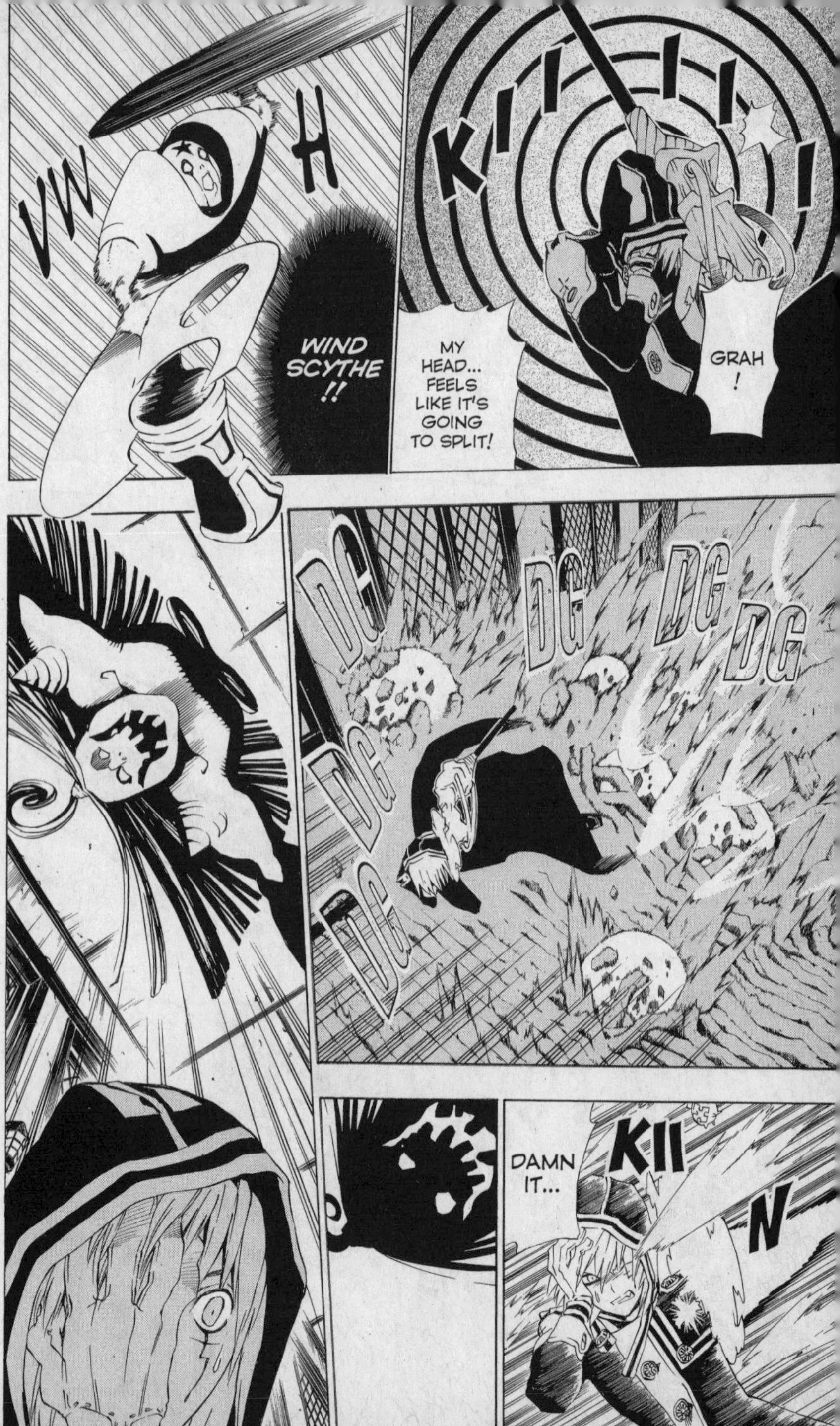
KIIIIII
GRAH!
MY HEAD... FEELS LIKE IT'S GOING TO SPLIT!
VWH
WIND SCYTHE!!
DG DG DG DG DG DG DG DG
KIIN
DAMN IT...

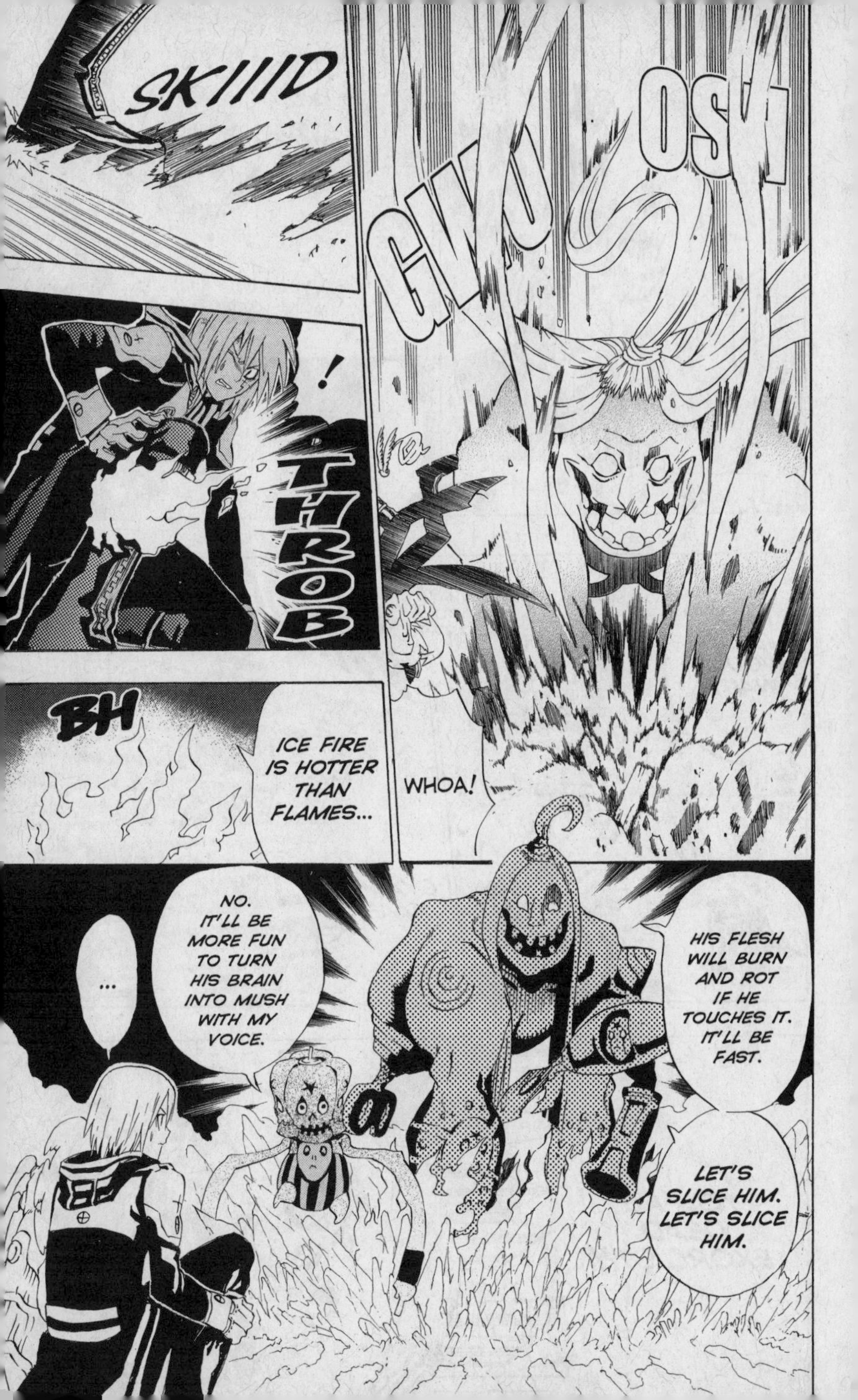
GWOOSH
WHOA!
SKIIID
!
THROB
BH
ICE FIRE IS HOTTER THAN FLAMES...
HIS FLESH WILL BURN AND ROT IF HE TOUCHES IT. IT'LL BE FAST.
LET'S SLICE HIM. LET'S SLICE HIM.
NO. IT'LL BE MORE FUN TO TURN HIS BRAIN INTO MUSH WITH MY VOICE.
...

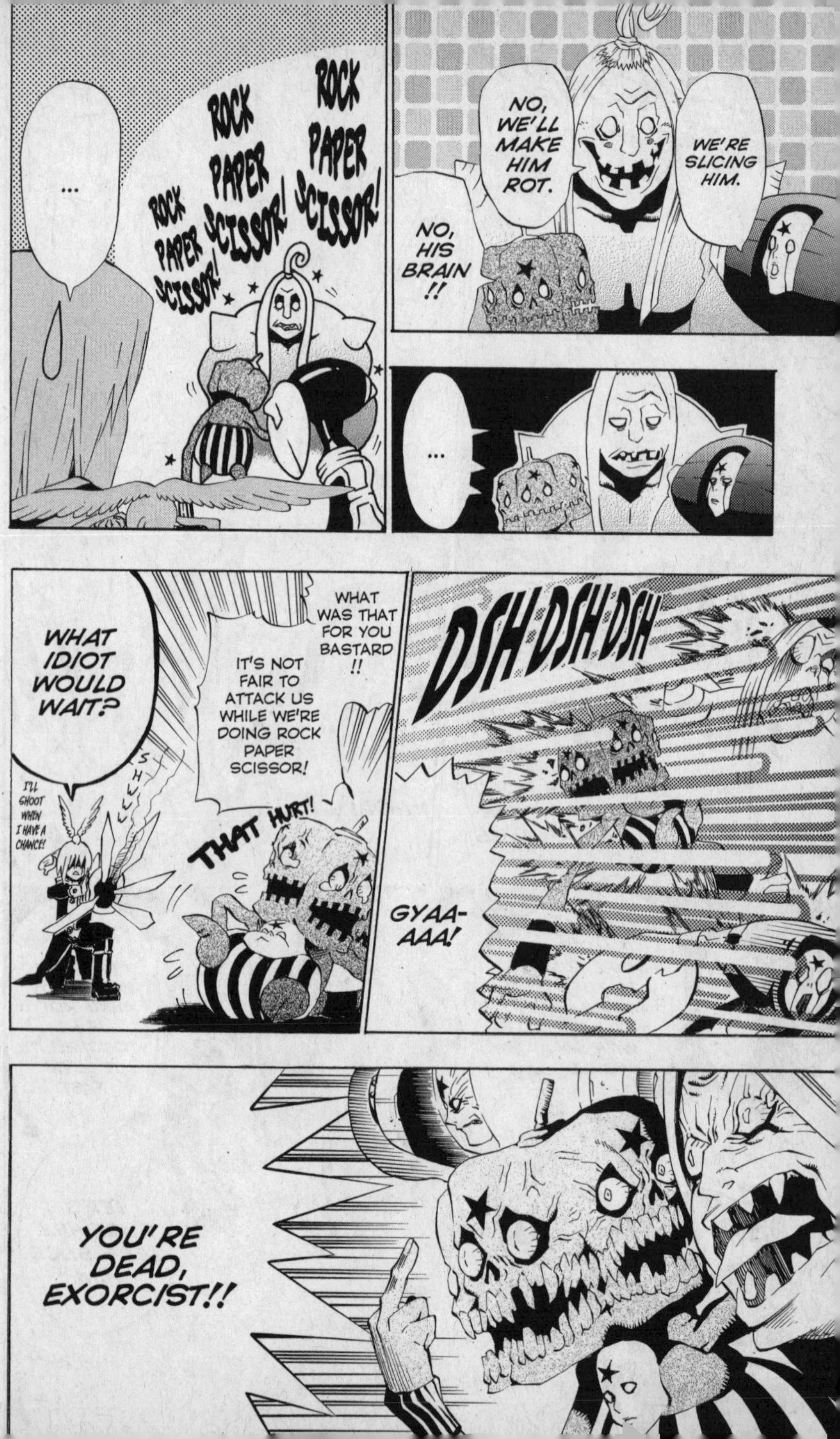
WE'RE SLICING HIM.
NO, WE'LL MAKE HIM ROT.
NO, HIS BRAIN!!
...
ROCK PAPER SCISSOR!
ROCK PAPER SCISSOR!
ROCK PAPER SCISSOR!
...
DSH DSH DSH
GYAA-AAA!
WHAT WAS THAT FOR YOU BASTARD!!
IT'S NOT FAIR TO ATTACK US WHILE WE'RE DOING ROCK PAPER SCISSOR!
THAT HURT!
WHAT IDIOT WOULD WAIT?
I'LL SHOOT WHEN I HAVE A CHANCE!
YOU'RE DEAD, EXORCIST!!

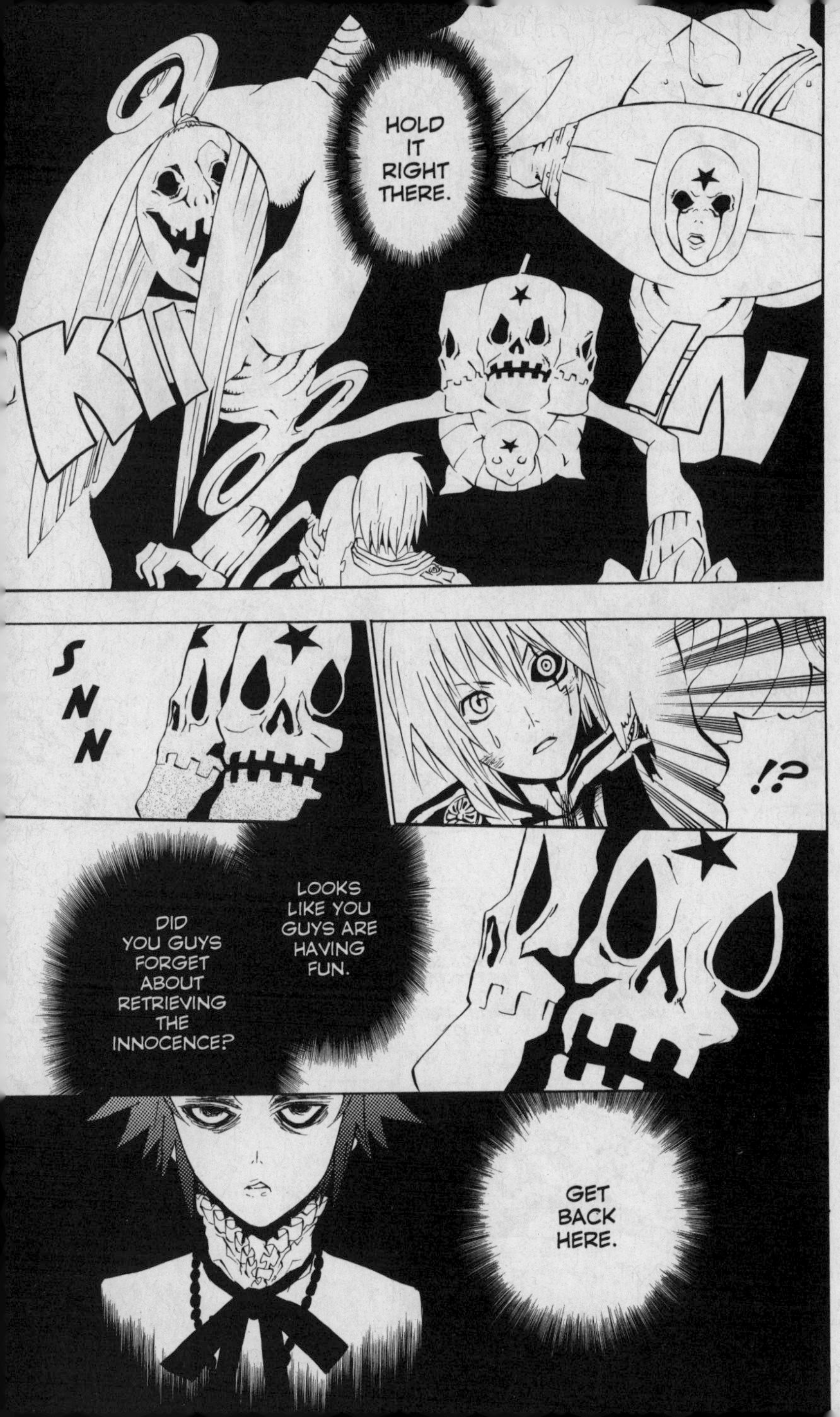
KII IN
HOLD IT RIGHT THERE.
!?
SNN
LOOKS LIKE YOU GUYS ARE HAVING FUN.
DID YOU GUYS FORGET ABOUT RETRIEVING THE INNOCENCE?
GET BACK HERE.

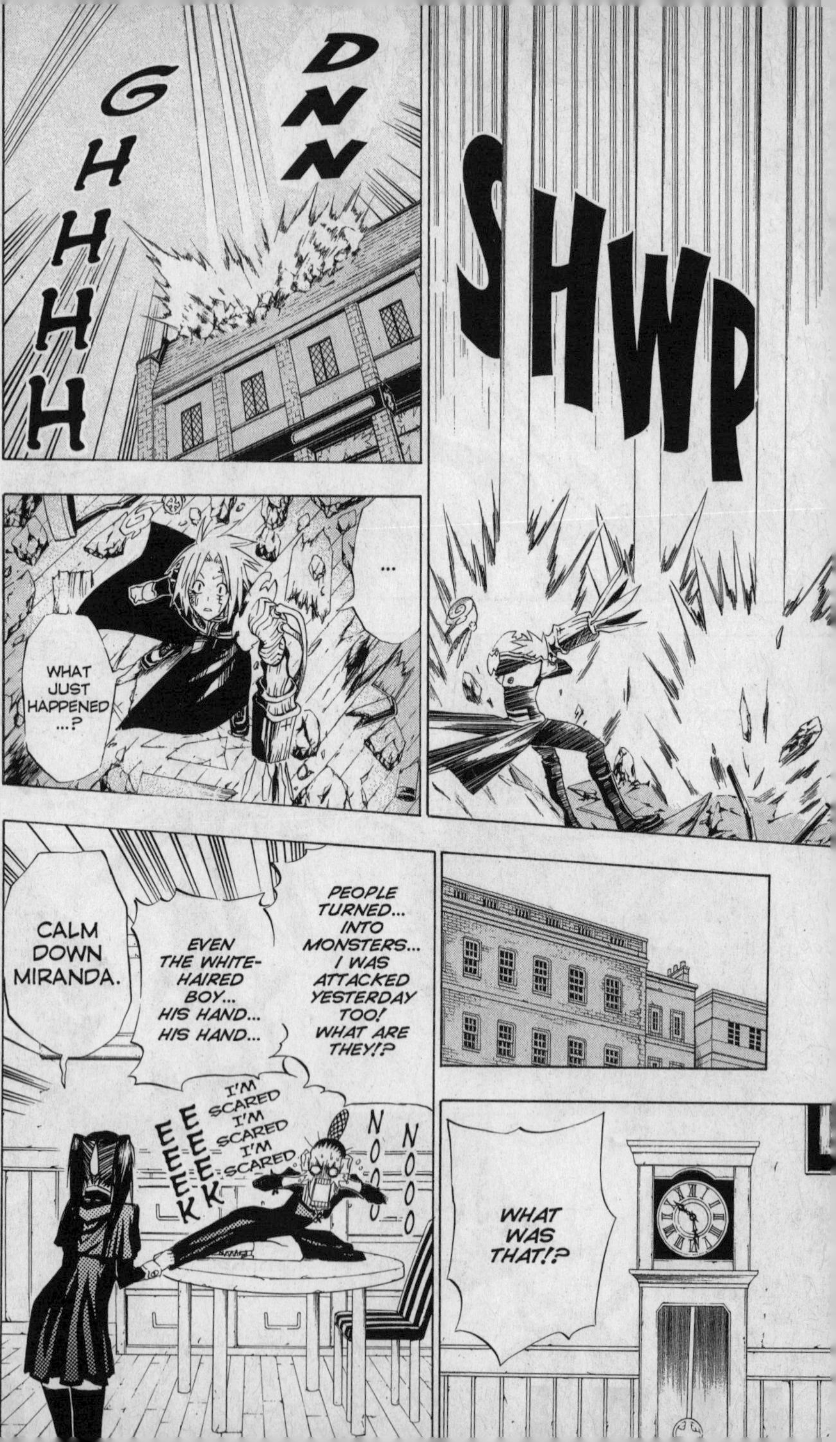
SHWP
DNN
GHHHHH
...
WHAT JUST HAPPENED ...?
WHAT WAS THAT!?
PEOPLE TURNED... INTO MONSTERS... I WAS ATTACKED YESTERDAY TOO! WHAT ARE THEY!?
EVEN THE WHITE-HAIRED BOY... HIS HAND... HIS HAND...
CALM DOWN MIRANDA.
NOOOO
NOOOO
I'M SCARED I'M SCARED I'M SCARED
EEEEK
EEEK

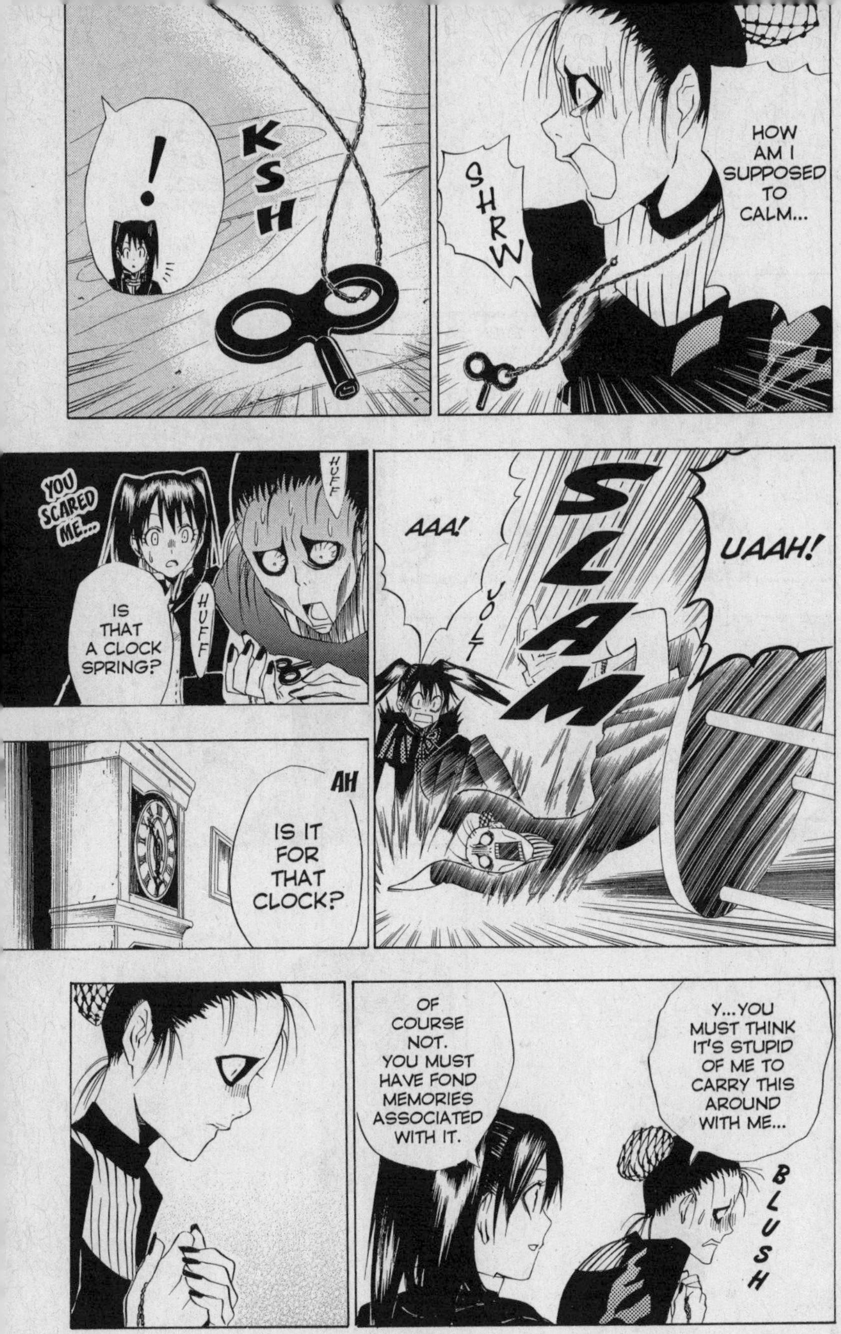
HOW AM I SUPPOSED TO CALM...
SHRW
KSH
!
UAAH!
SLAM
AAA!
JOLT
HUFF
YOU SCARED ME...
HUFF
IS THAT A CLOCK SPRING?
AH
IS IT FOR THAT CLOCK?
Y...YOU MUST THINK IT'S STUPID OF ME TO CARRY THIS AROUND WITH ME...
BLUSH
OF COURSE NOT. YOU MUST HAVE FOND MEMORIES ASSOCIATED WITH IT.

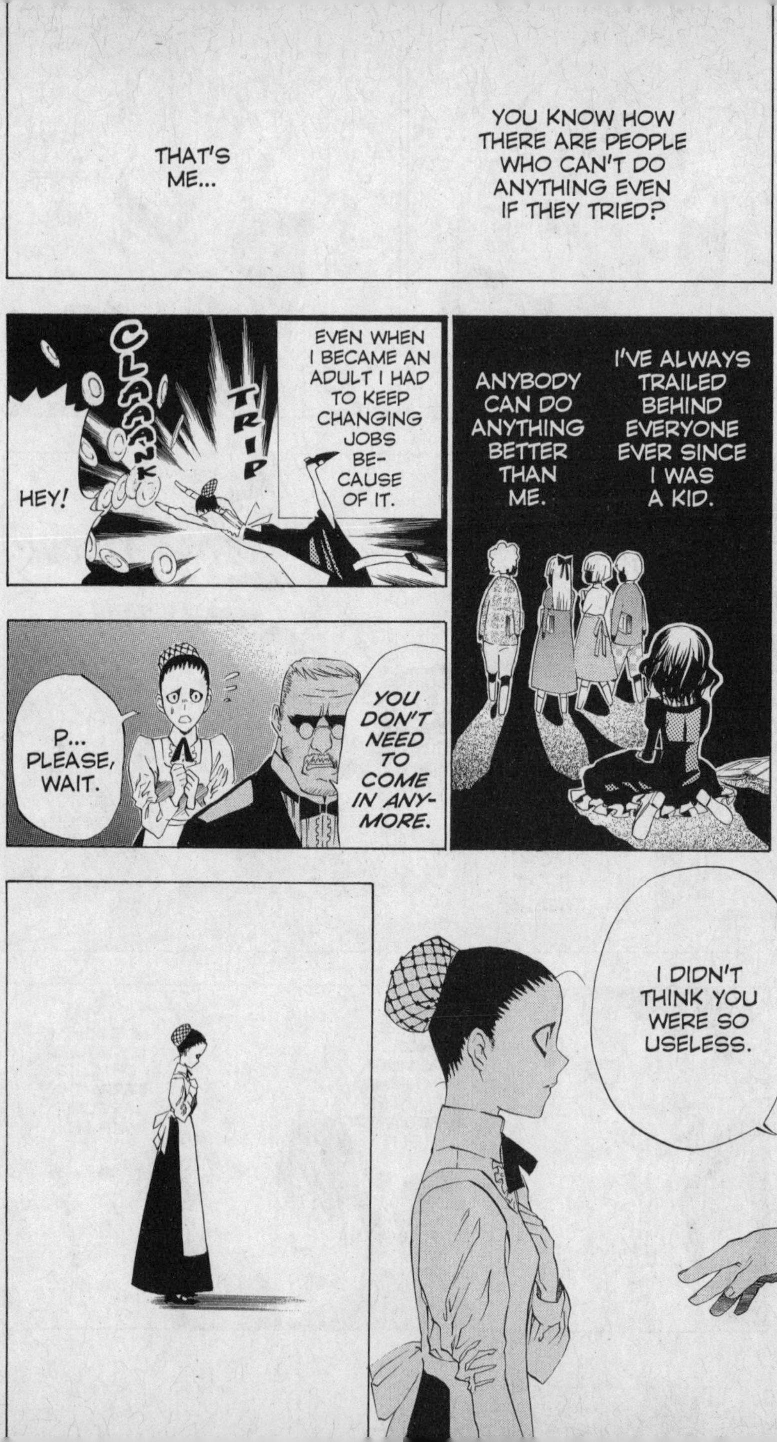
YOU KNOW HOW THERE ARE PEOPLE WHO CAN'T DO ANYTHING EVEN IF THEY TRIED?
THAT'S ME...
I'VE ALWAYS TRAILED BEHIND EVERYONE EVER SINCE I WAS A KID.
ANYBODY CAN DO ANYTHING BETTER THAN ME.
EVEN WHEN I BECAME AN ADULT I HAD TO KEEP CHANGING JOBS BE-CAUSE OF IT.
TRIP
CLAAANK
HEY!
YOU DON'T NEED TO COME IN ANY-MORE.
P... PLEASE, WAIT.
I DIDN'T THINK YOU WERE SO USELESS.

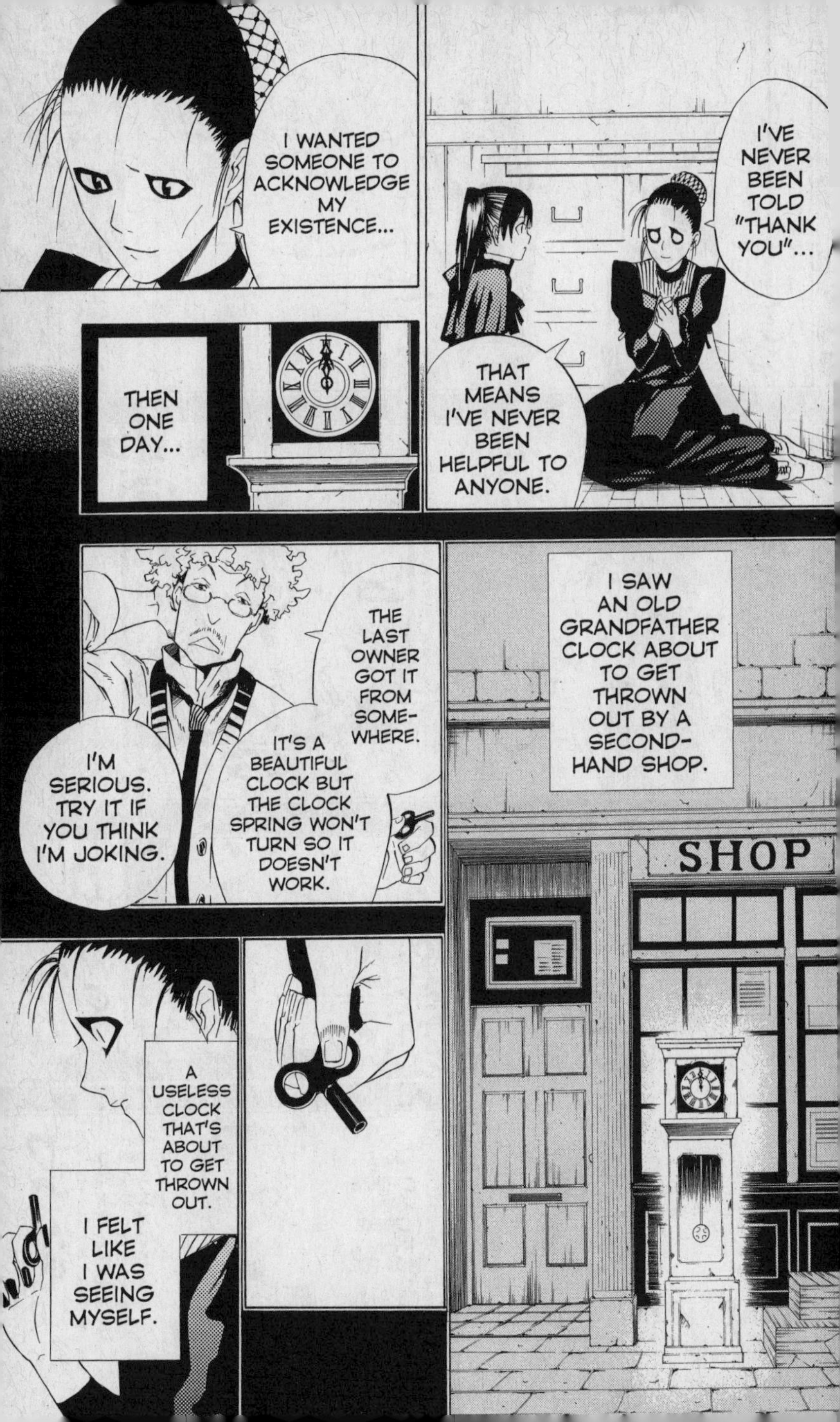
I'VE NEVER BEEN TOLD "THANK YOU"...
THAT MEANS I'VE NEVER BEEN HELPFUL TO ANYONE.
I WANTED SOMEONE TO ACKNOWLEDGE MY EXISTENCE...
THEN ONE DAY...
I SAW AN OLD GRANDFATHER CLOCK ABOUT TO GET THROWN OUT BY A SECOND-HAND SHOP.
SHOP
THE LAST OWNER GOT IT FROM SOMEWHERE.
IT'S A BEAUTIFUL CLOCK BUT THE CLOCK SPRING WON'T TURN SO IT DOESN'T WORK.
I'M SERIOUS. TRY IT IF YOU THINK I'M JOKING.
A USELESS CLOCK THAT'S ABOUT TO GET THROWN OUT.
I FELT LIKE I WAS SEEING MYSELF.

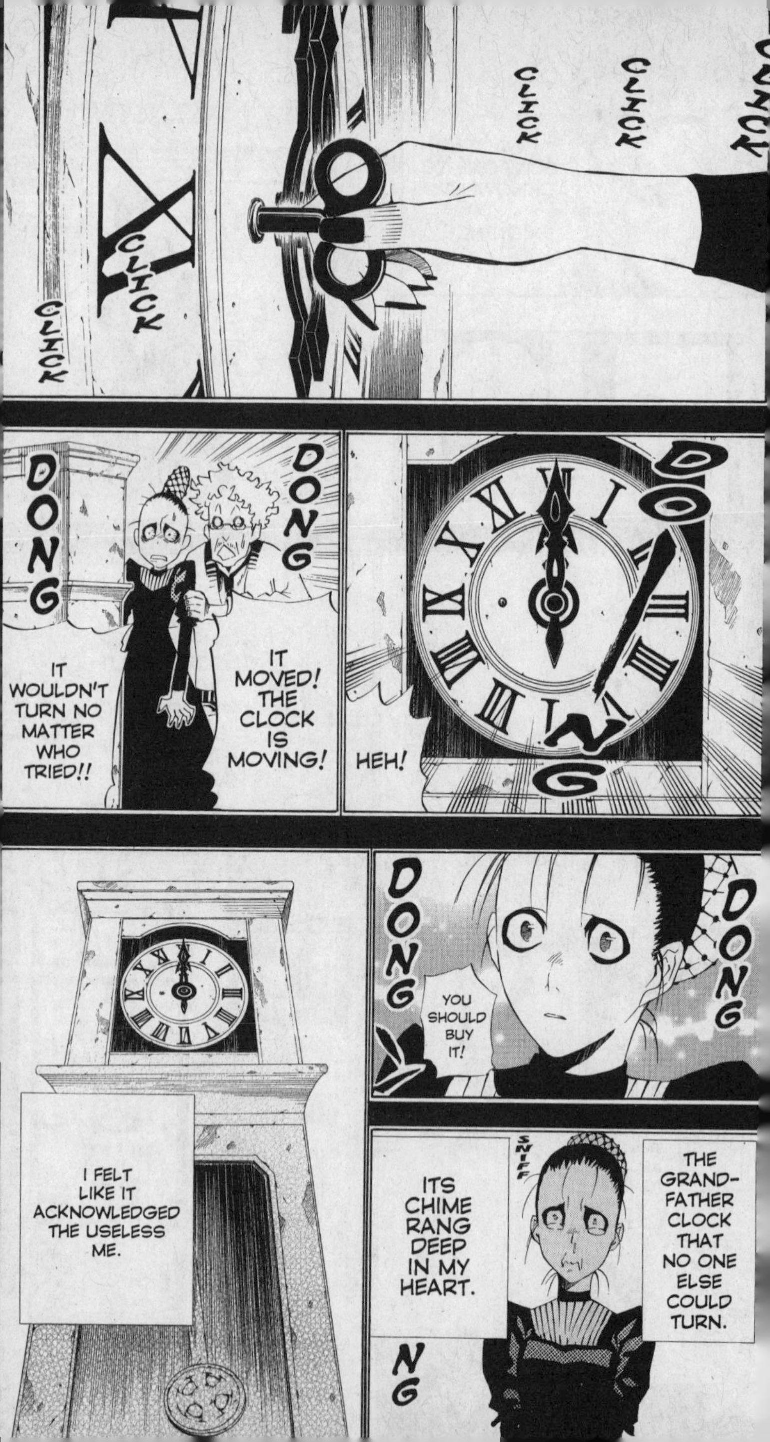
CLICK
CLICK
CLICK
CLICK
CLICK
DONG
HEH!
DONG
IT MOVED! THE CLOCK IS MOVING!
DONG
IT WOULDN'T TURN NO MATTER WHO TRIED!!
DONG
YOU SHOULD BUY IT!
DONG
THE GRAND-FATHER CLOCK THAT NO ONE ELSE COULD TURN.
SNIFF
ITS CHIME RANG DEEP IN MY HEART.
NG
I FELT LIKE IT ACKNOWLEDGED THE USELESS ME.

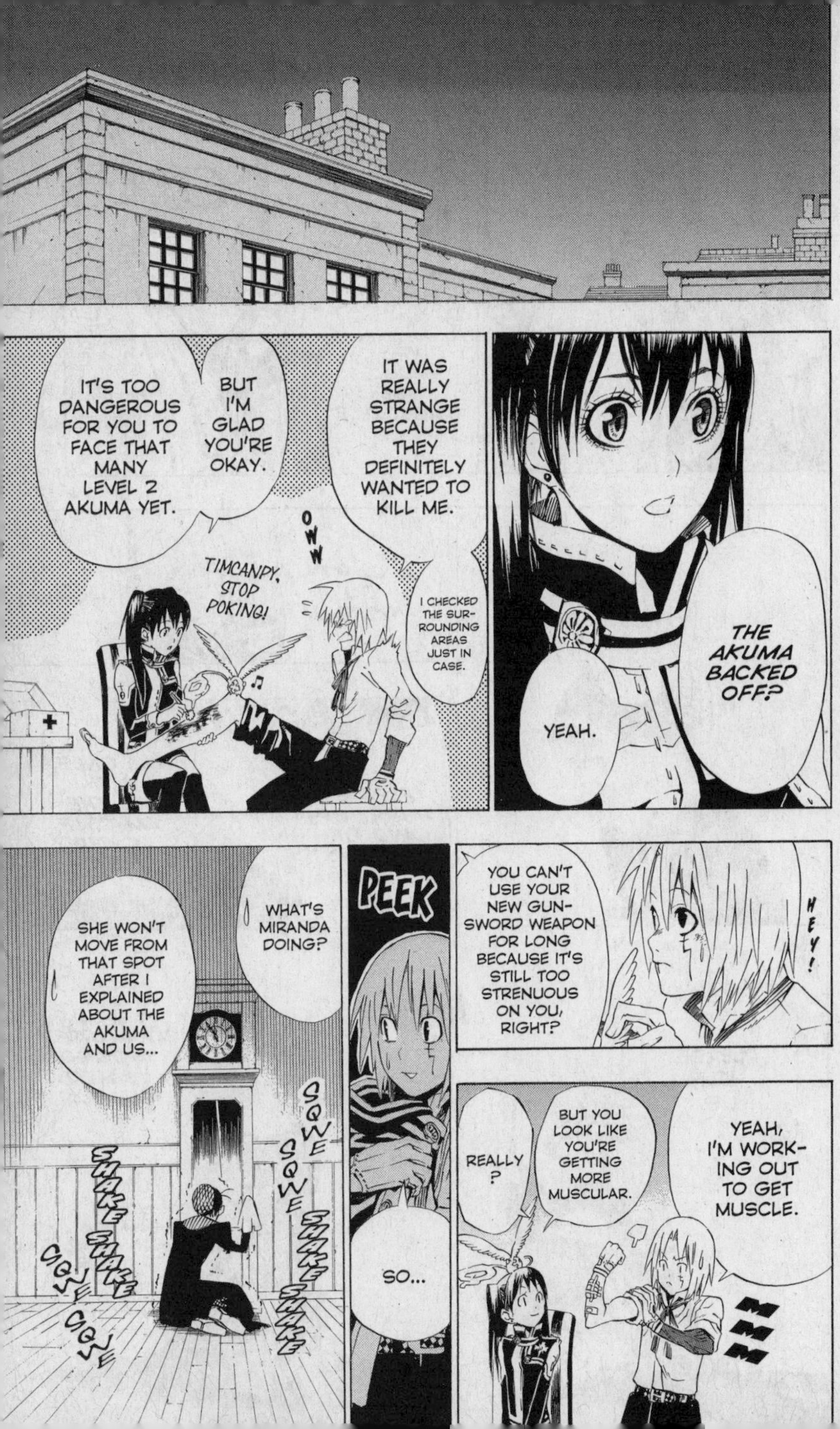
THE AKUMA BACKED OFF?
YEAH.
IT WAS REALLY STRANGE BECAUSE THEY DEFINITELY WANTED TO KILL ME.
BUT I'M GLAD YOU'RE OKAY.
IT'S TOO DANGEROUS FOR YOU TO FACE THAT MANY LEVEL 2 AKUMA YET.
OWW
I CHECKED THE SUR-ROUNDING AREAS JUST IN CASE.
TIMCANPY, STOP POKING!
HEY!
YOU CAN'T USE YOUR NEW GUN-SWORD WEAPON FOR LONG BECAUSE IT'S STILL TOO STRENUOUS ON YOU, RIGHT?
YEAH, I'M WORK-ING OUT TO GET MUSCLE.
BUT YOU LOOK LIKE YOU'RE GETTING MORE MUSCULAR.
REALLY?
MMM
PEEK
SO...
WHAT'S MIRANDA DOING?
SHE WON'T MOVE FROM THAT SPOT AFTER I EXPLAINED ABOUT THE AKUMA AND US...
SQWE SQWE
SHAKE SHAKE
SHAKE SHAKE
SQWE SQWE

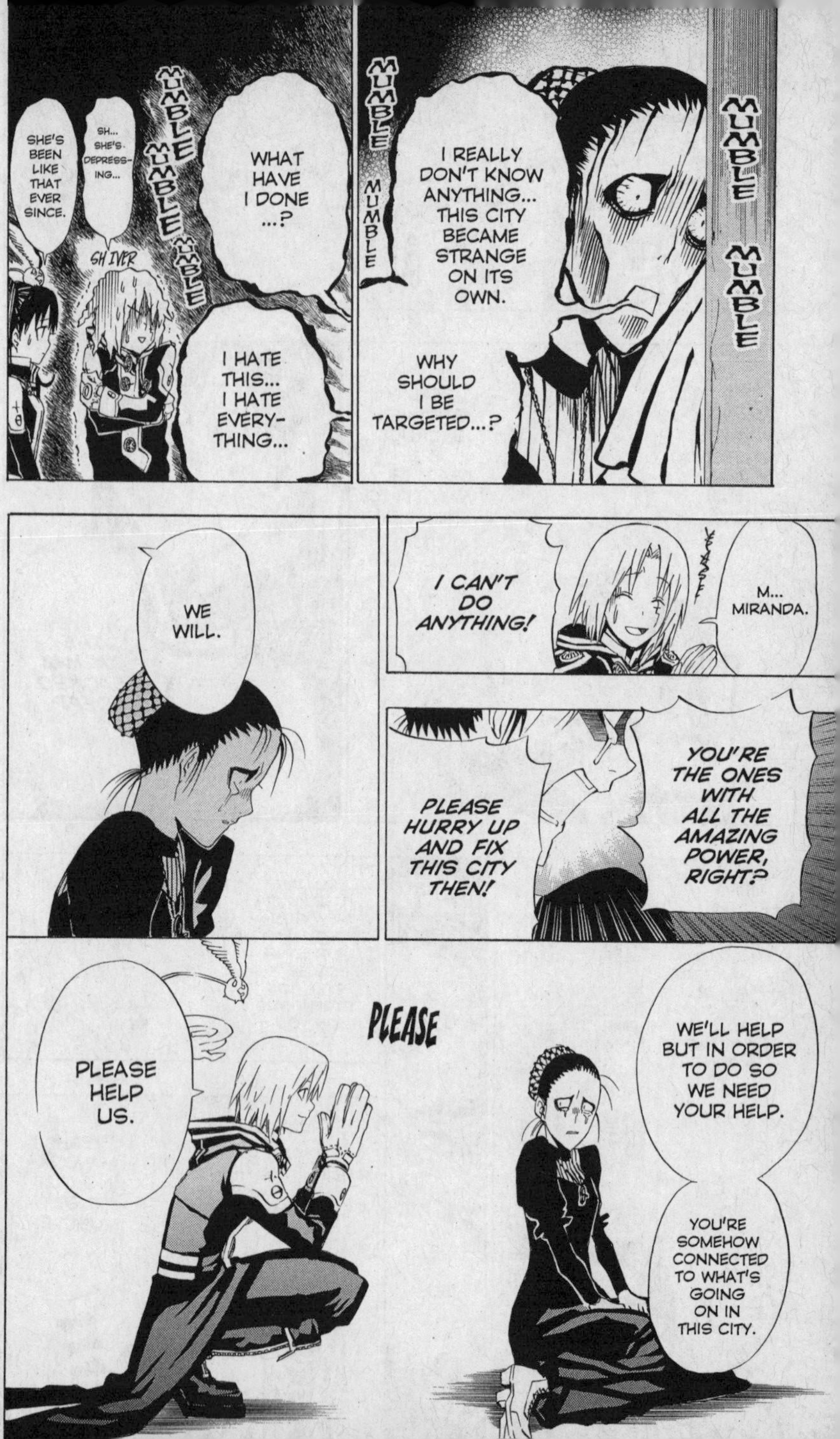
MUMBLE MUMBLE
I REALLY DON'T KNOW ANYTHING... THIS CITY BECAME STRANGE ON ITS OWN.
WHY SHOULD I BE TARGETED...?
MUMBLE MUMBLE
WHAT HAVE I DONE ...?
I HATE THIS... I HATE EVERY-THING...
MUMBLE MUMBLE MUMBLE
SH... SHE'S DEPRESS-ING...
SHIVER
SHE'S BEEN LIKE THAT EVER SINCE.
M... MIRANDA.
I CAN'T DO ANYTHING!
YOU'RE THE ONES WITH ALL THE AMAZING POWER, RIGHT?
PLEASE HURRY UP AND FIX THIS CITY THEN!
WE WILL.
WE'LL HELP BUT IN ORDER TO DO SO WE NEED YOUR HELP.
YOU'RE SOMEHOW CONNECTED TO WHAT'S GOING ON IN THIS CITY.
PLEASE
PLEASE HELP US.

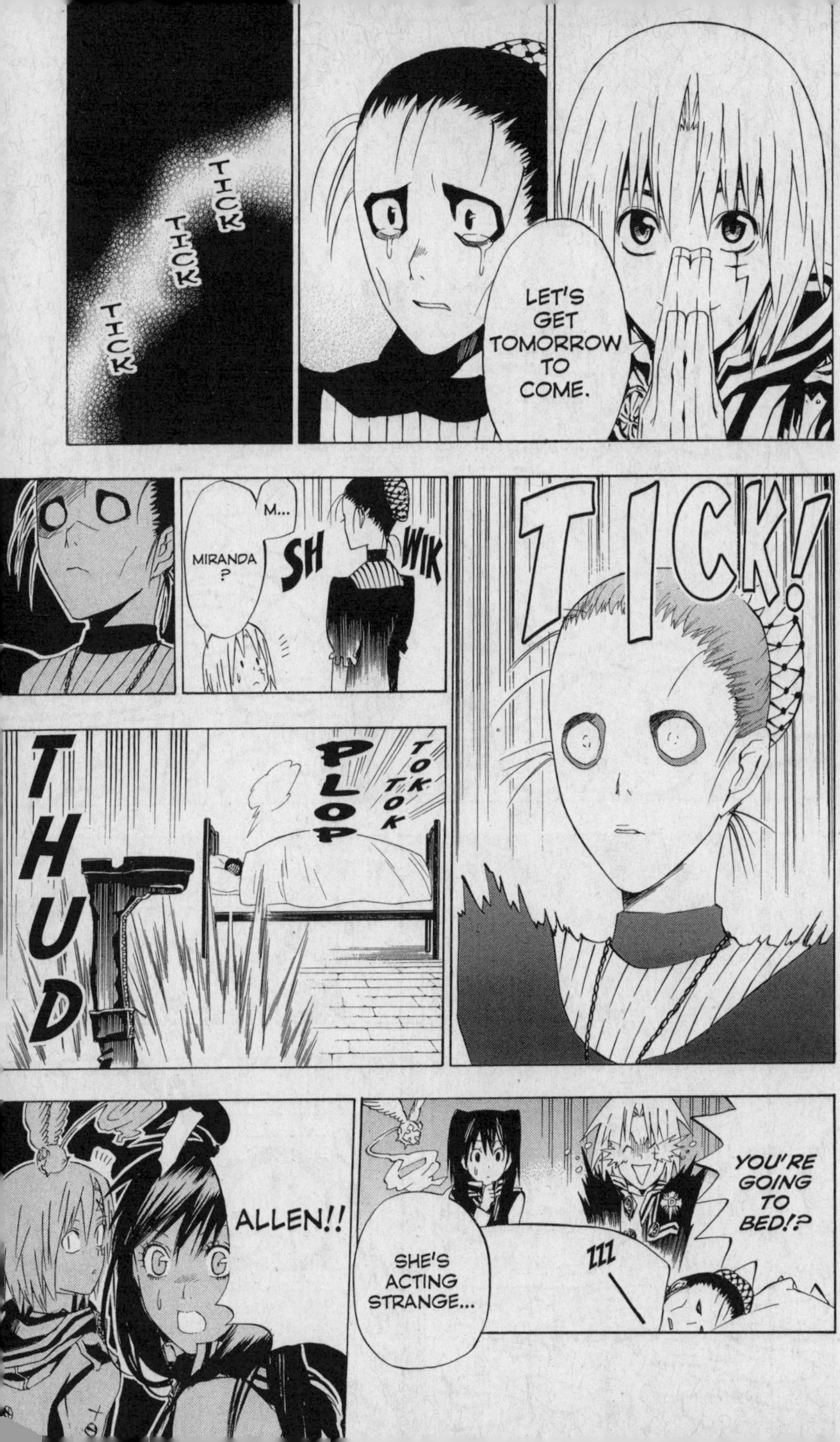
LET'S GET TOMORROW TO COME.
TICK
TICK
TICK
TICK!
M... MIRANDA?
SHWIK
PLOP
TOK TOK
THUD
YOU'RE GOING TO BED!?
ZZZ
SHE'S ACTING STRANGE...
ALLEN!!

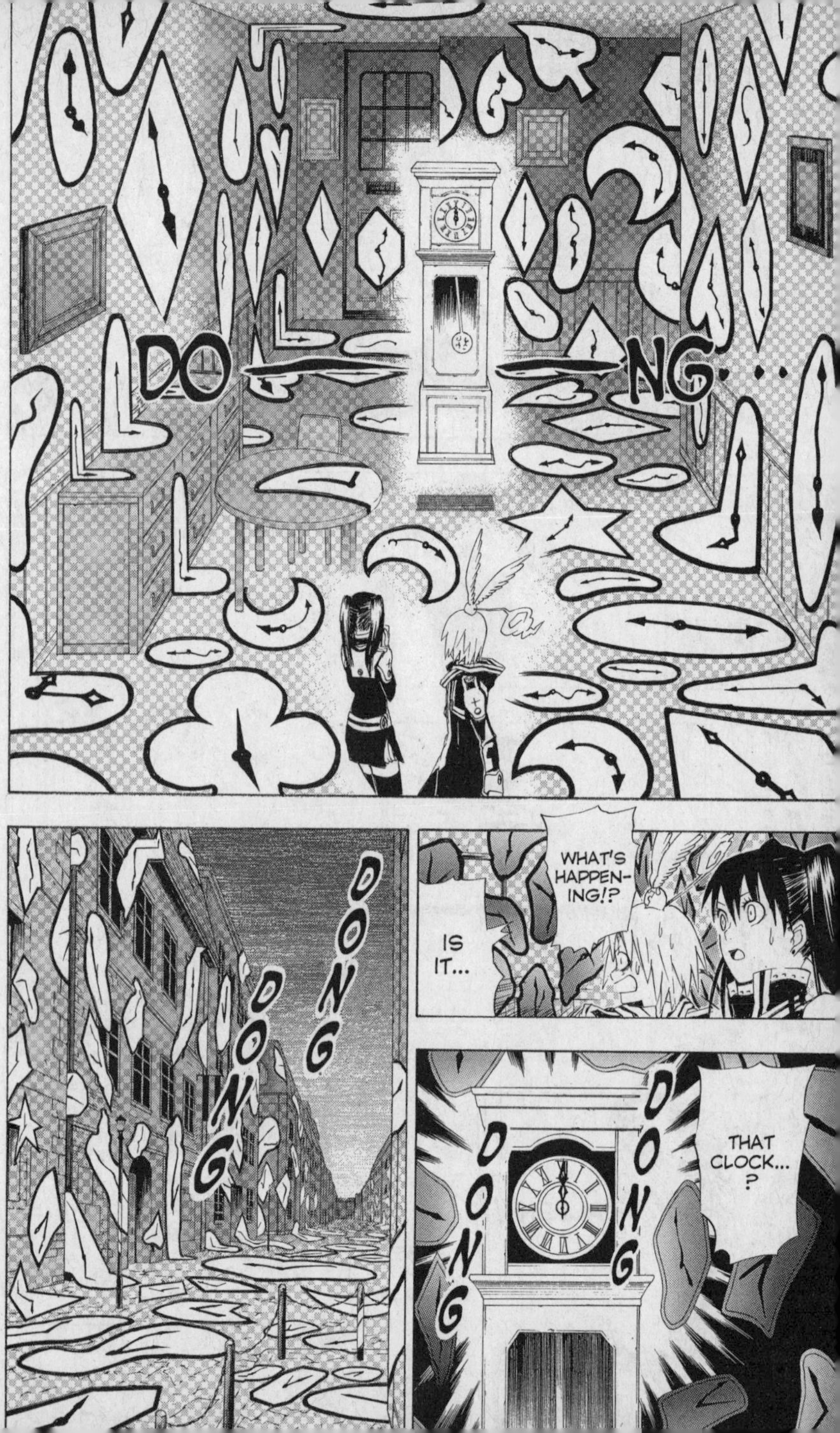
DO—NG...
WHAT'S HAPPEN-ING!?
IS IT...
THAT CLOCK...?
DOONG
DOONG
DOONG
DOONG

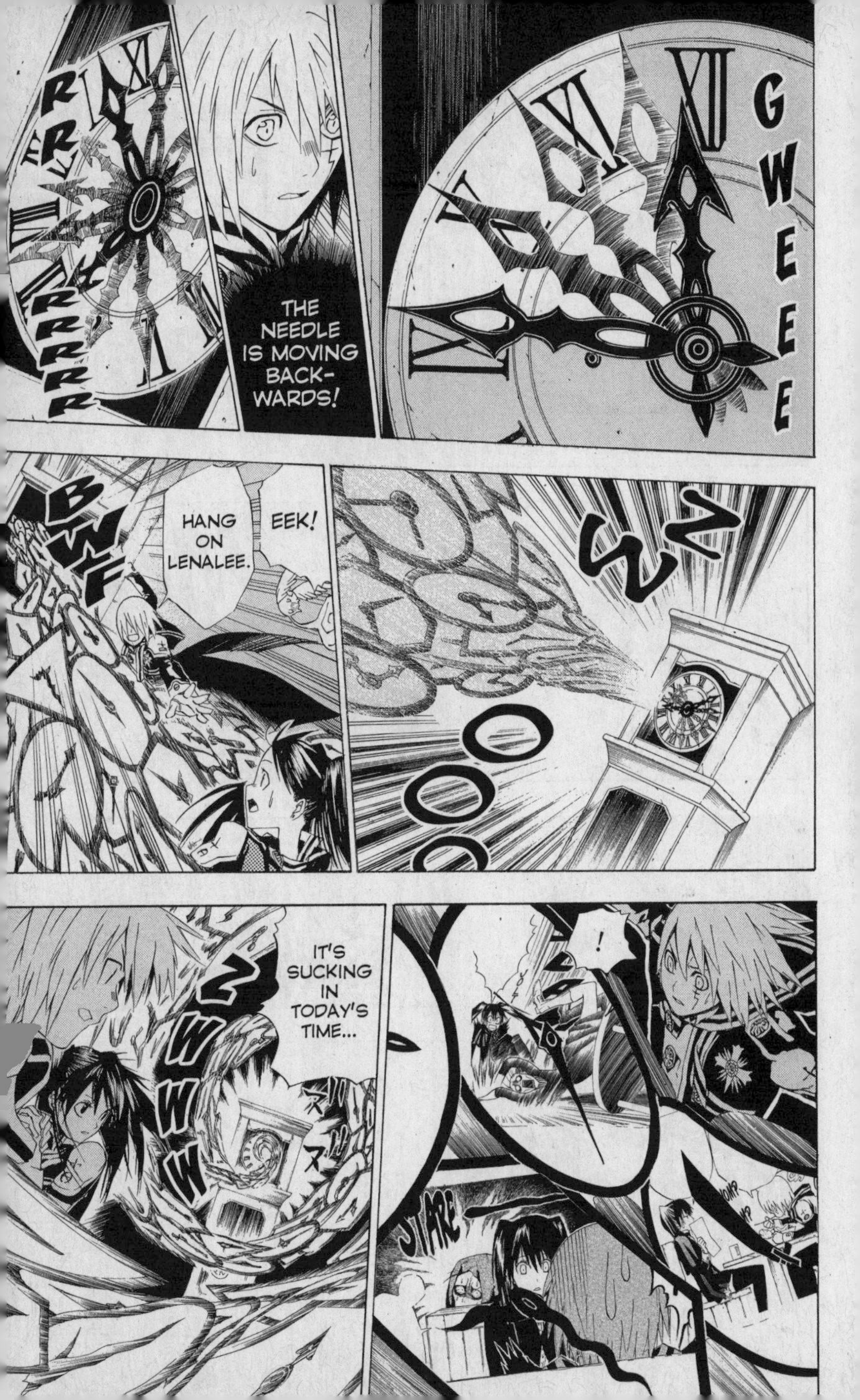
GWEEE
THE NEEDLE IS MOVING BACKWARDS!
EEK!
HANG ON LENALEE.
!
STARE
IT'S SUCKING IN TODAY'S TIME...

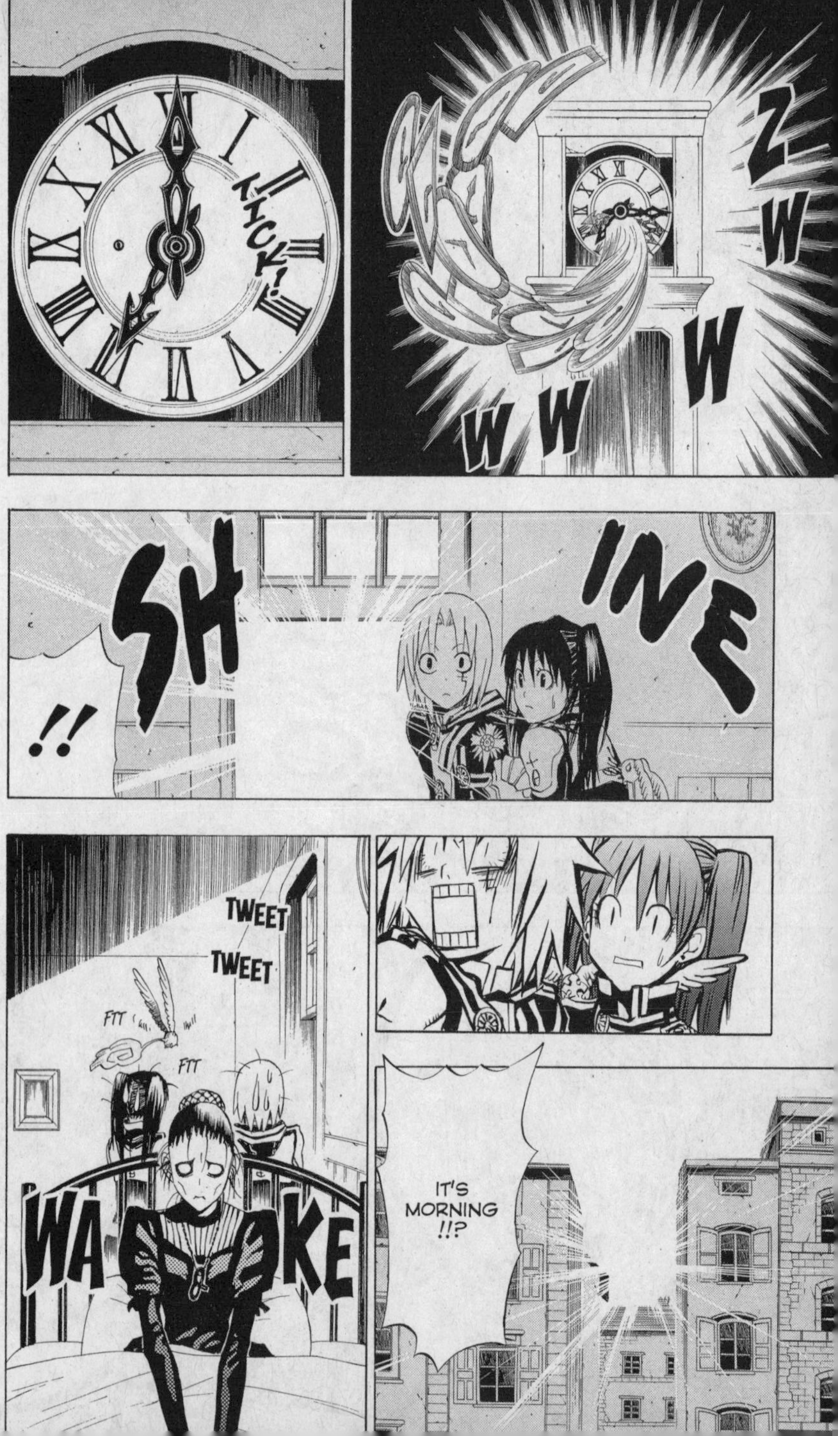
WWWWZ
TICK!
SHINE
!!
IT'S MORNING !!?
TWEET
TWEET
FTT
FTT
WAKE

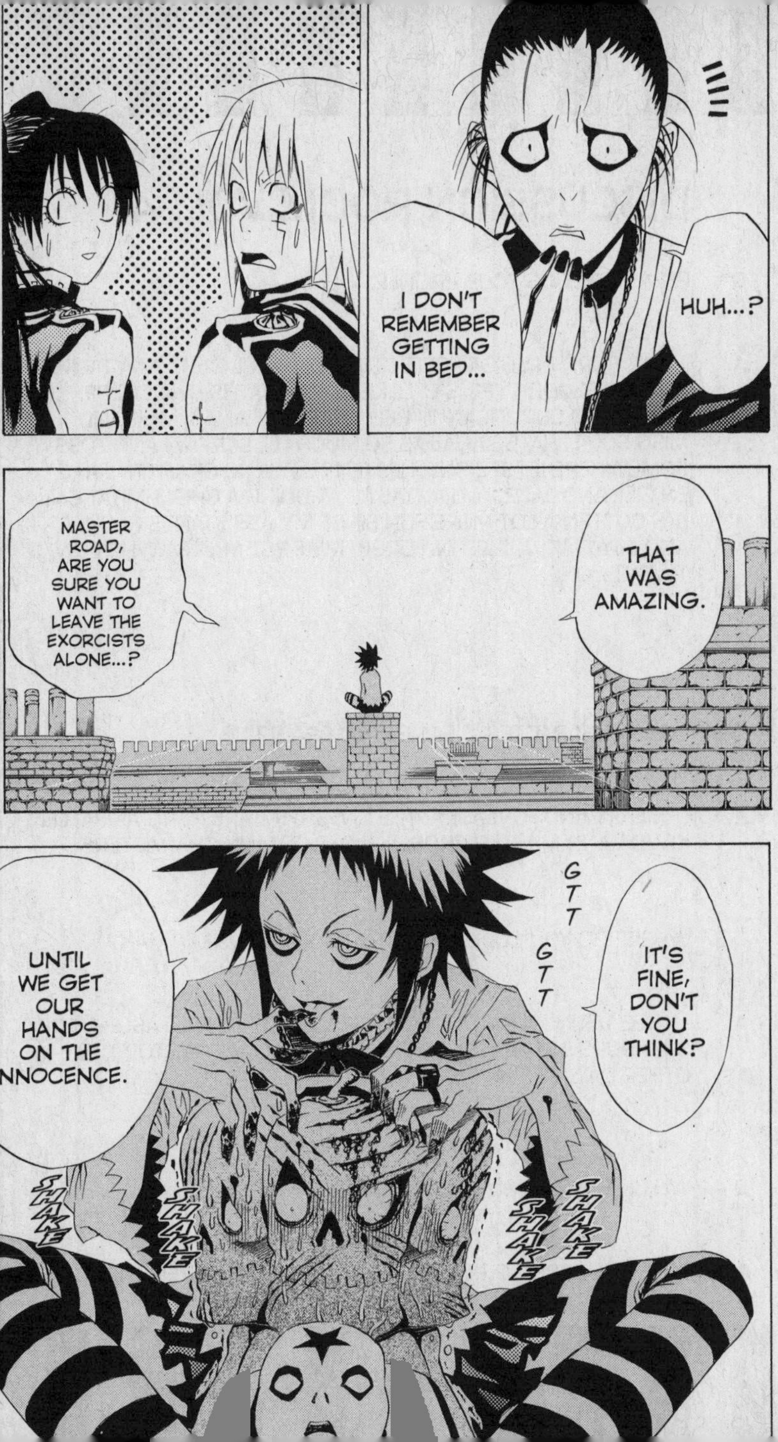
HUH...?
I DON'T REMEMBER GETTING IN BED...
THAT WAS AMAZING.
MASTER ROAD, ARE YOU SURE YOU WANT TO LEAVE THE EXORCISTS ALONE...?
GTT GTT
IT'S FINE, DON'T YOU THINK?
UNTIL WE GET OUR HANDS ON THE INNOCENCE.
SHAKE SHAKE
SHAKE SHAKE

DISCUSSION ROOM VOL. 4

Q 1.   PLEASE TELL US YOUR PROFILE.

A.   I WAS BORN IN SHIGA PREFECTURE ON APRIL 21ST. I'M A TAURUS
      AND MY BLOOD TYPE IS O. I LIKE CURRY, BATHS, THE COLOR
      BLACK AND CURLING UP IN BED. I HATE BANANAS, MILK AND
      MISO SOUP. I HATE BANANAS SO MUCH I'LL SCREAM AND TOSS IT
      SOMEWHERE IF I SEE ONE. I LISTEN TO PORNO GRAFITTI, L'ARC
      EN CIEL AND JAZZ. I'M FANTASTIC AT DOING A GHIBLI IMITATION.
      IT'S GOTTEN A LOT MORE FUN SINCE MY ASSISTANTS OI-CHAN
      AND MIYAZAKI JOINED IN. I DREW MY FIRST MANGA WHEN I WAS
      TWENTY ONE.

Q 2.   WHICH CHARACTER IS EASIEST TO DRAW?

A.   THE EARL AND HEVLASKA. THE ONES THAT ARE HARD ARE ALLEN,
      KANDA AND MASTER CROSS... (LOTS OF MAIN CHARACTERS)

Q 3.   WHERE DO YOU COME UP WITH IDEAS FOR D.GRAY-MAN?

A.   WHILE TAKING A BATH. I HAVE A TENDENCY TO FALL ASLEEP FOR
      SIX HOURS IN THE TUB. MY EDITOR Y TOLD ME TO STOP THE
      OTHER DAY.

Q 4.   WHICH PEN DO YOU USE TO DRAW?

A.   I USE THE ZEBRA G-PEN AND CIRCLE PEN. I USE THEIR STANDARD
      MODELS.

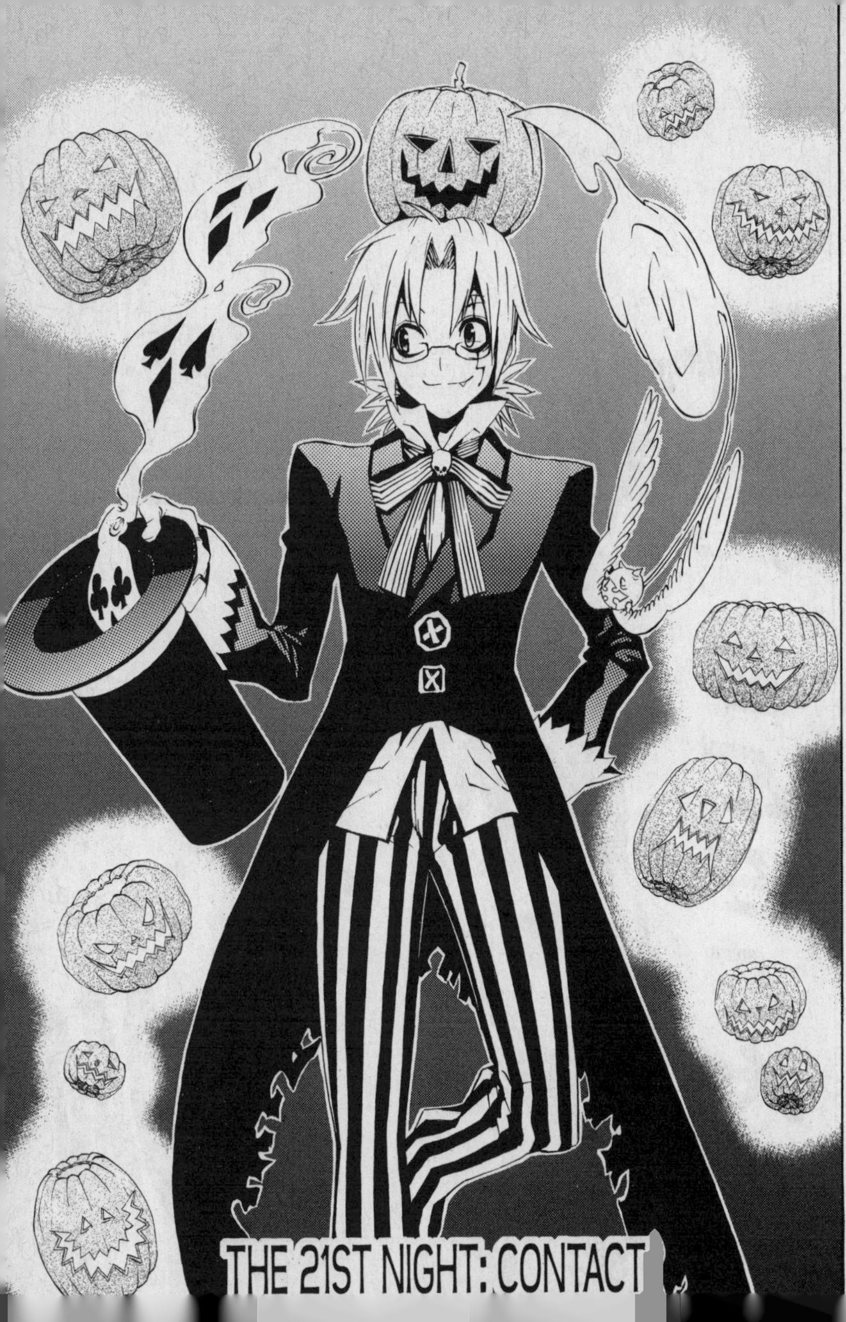
THE 21ST NIGHT: CONTACT

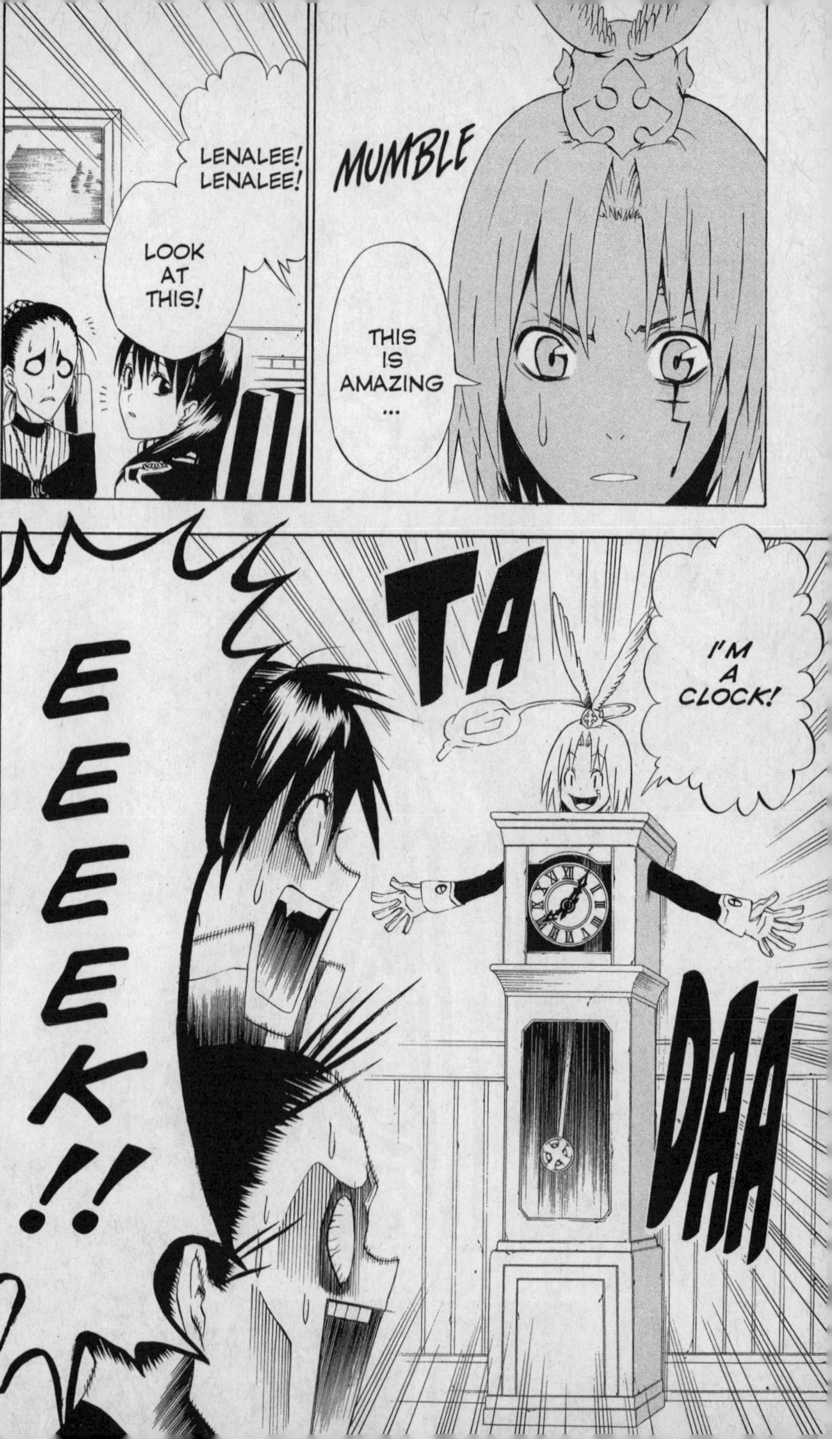
MUMBLE
THIS IS AMAZING ...
LENALEE! LENALEE!
LOOK AT THIS!
I'M A CLOCK!
TA
DAA
EEEEEK!!

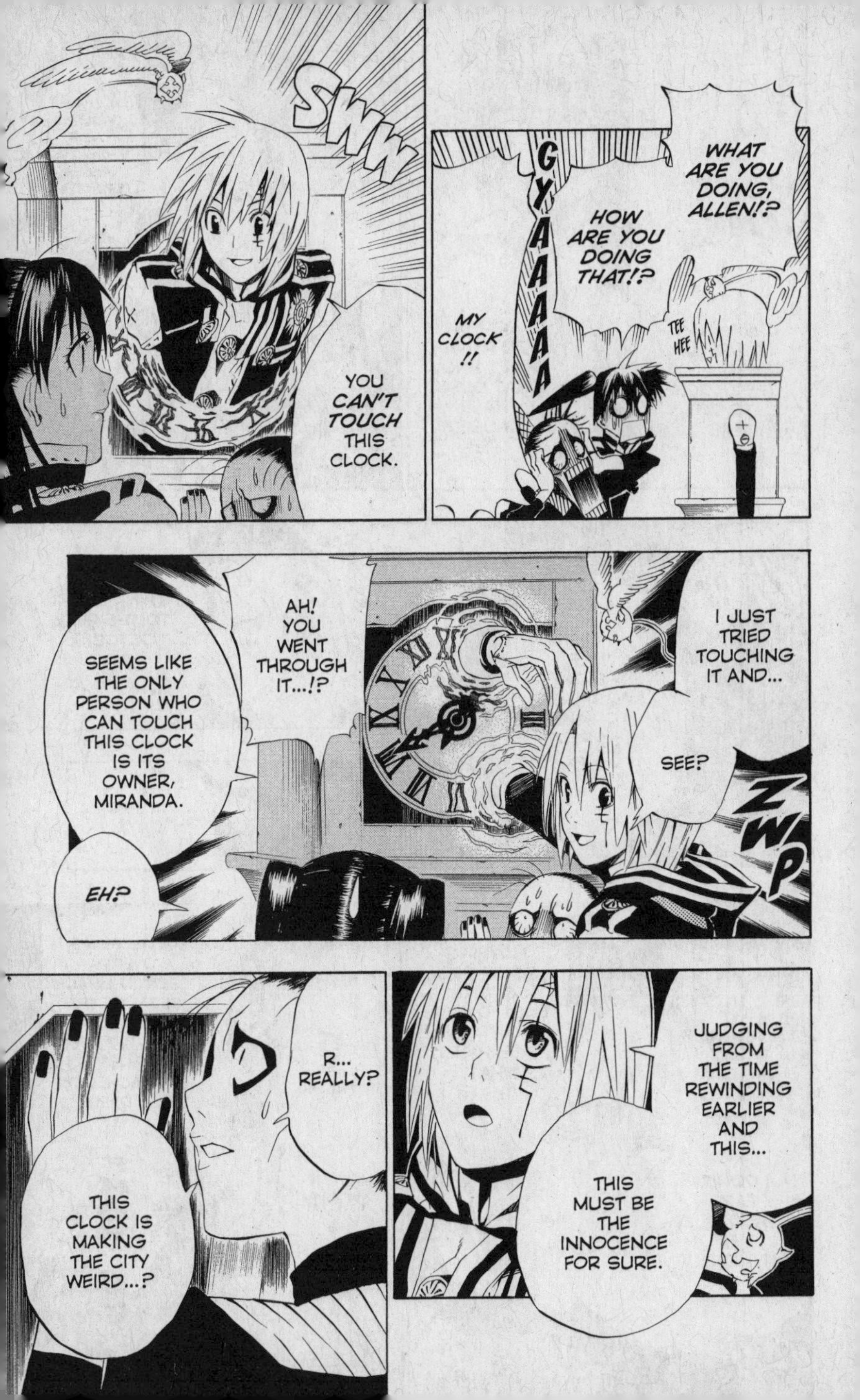
WHAT ARE YOU DOING, ALLEN!?
HOW ARE YOU DOING THAT!?
GYAAAAA
MY CLOCK !!
TEE HEE
SWW
YOU CAN'T TOUCH THIS CLOCK.
I JUST TRIED TOUCHING IT AND...
SEE?
ZWP
AH! YOU WENT THROUGH IT...!?
SEEMS LIKE THE ONLY PERSON WHO CAN TOUCH THIS CLOCK IS ITS OWNER, MIRANDA.
EH?
JUDGING FROM THE TIME REWINDING EARLIER AND THIS...
THIS MUST BE THE INNOCENCE FOR SURE.
R... REALLY?
THIS CLOCK IS MAKING THE CITY WEIRD...?

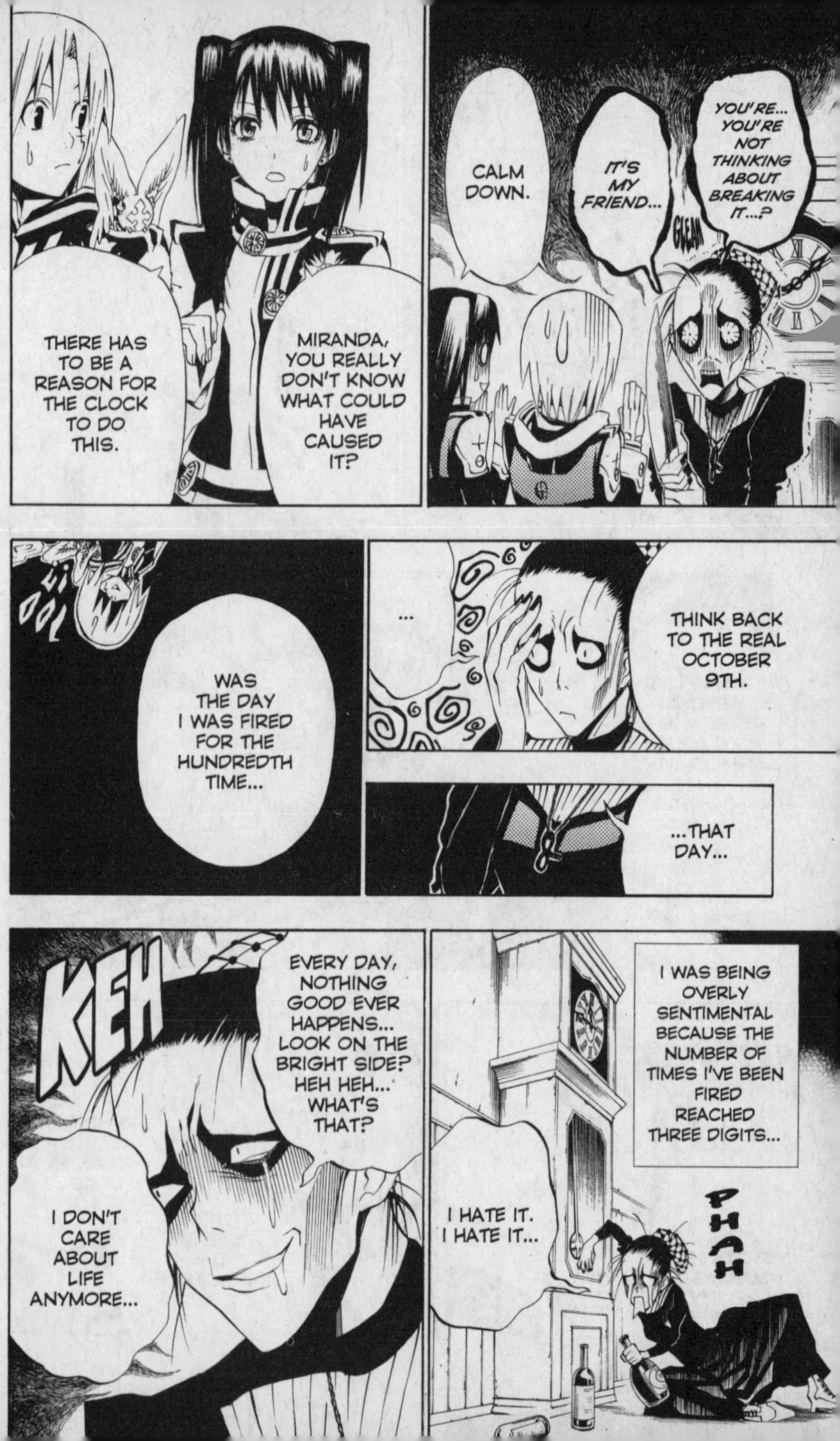
YOU'RE... YOU'RE NOT THINKING ABOUT BREAKING IT...?
GLEAM
IT'S MY FRIEND...
CALM DOWN.
MIRANDA, YOU REALLY DON'T KNOW WHAT COULD HAVE CAUSED IT?
THERE HAS TO BE A REASON FOR THE CLOCK TO DO THIS.
THINK BACK TO THE REAL OCTOBER 9TH.
...
...THAT DAY...
WAS THE DAY I WAS FIRED FOR THE HUNDREDTH TIME...
I WAS BEING OVERLY SENTIMENTAL BECAUSE THE NUMBER OF TIMES I'VE BEEN FIRED REACHED THREE DIGITS...
PHAH
I HATE IT. I HATE IT...
EVERY DAY, NOTHING GOOD EVER HAPPENS... LOOK ON THE BRIGHT SIDE? HEH HEH... WHAT'S THAT?
KEH
I DON'T CARE ABOUT LIFE ANYMORE...

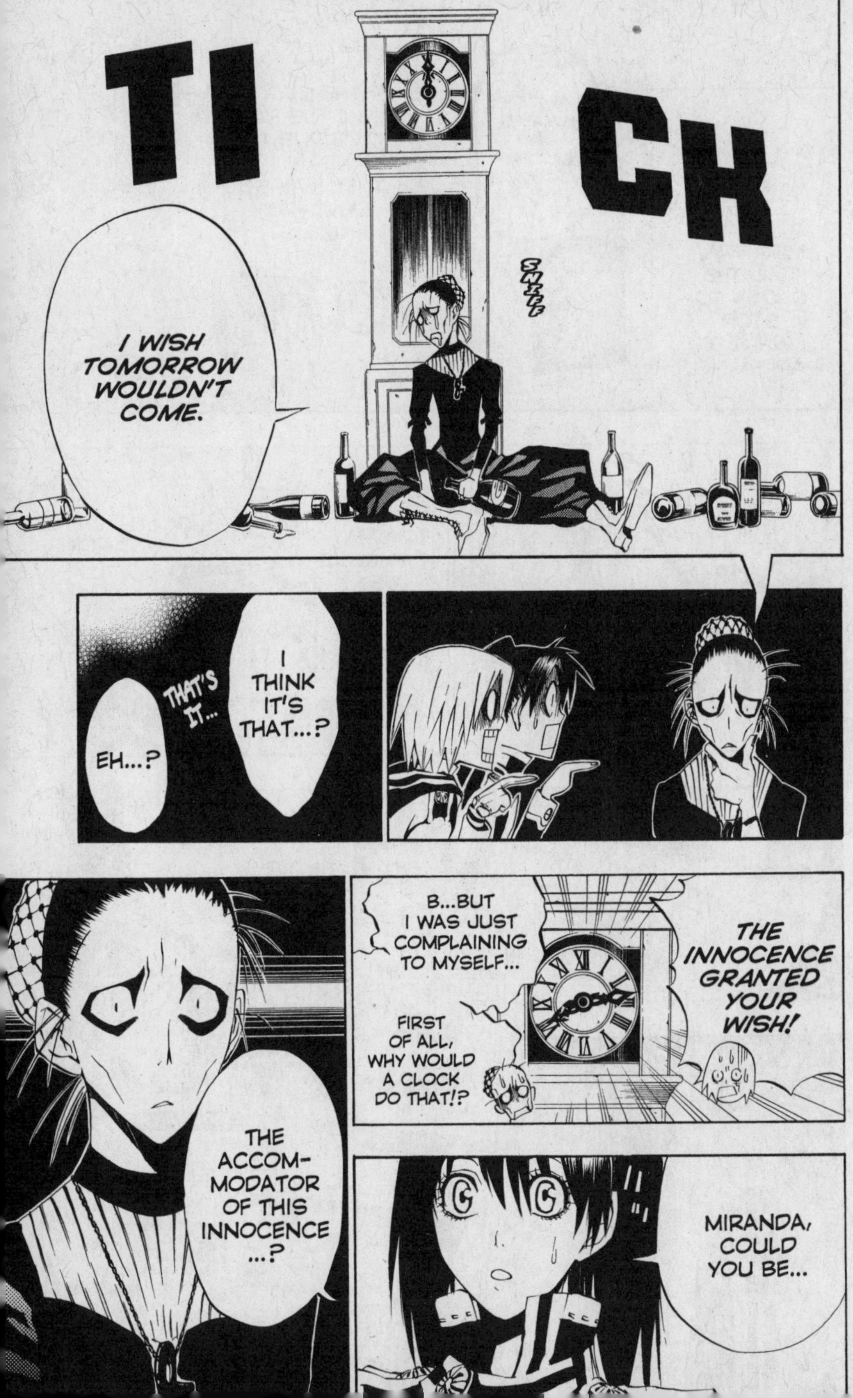
TI
CK
SNIFF
I WISH TOMORROW WOULDN'T COME.
I THINK IT'S THAT...?
THAT'S IT...
EH...?
THE INNOCENCE GRANTED YOUR WISH!
B...BUT I WAS JUST COMPLAINING TO MYSELF...
FIRST OF ALL, WHY WOULD A CLOCK DO THAT!?
MIRANDA, COULD YOU BE...
THE ACCOM-MODATOR OF THIS INNOCENCE ...?

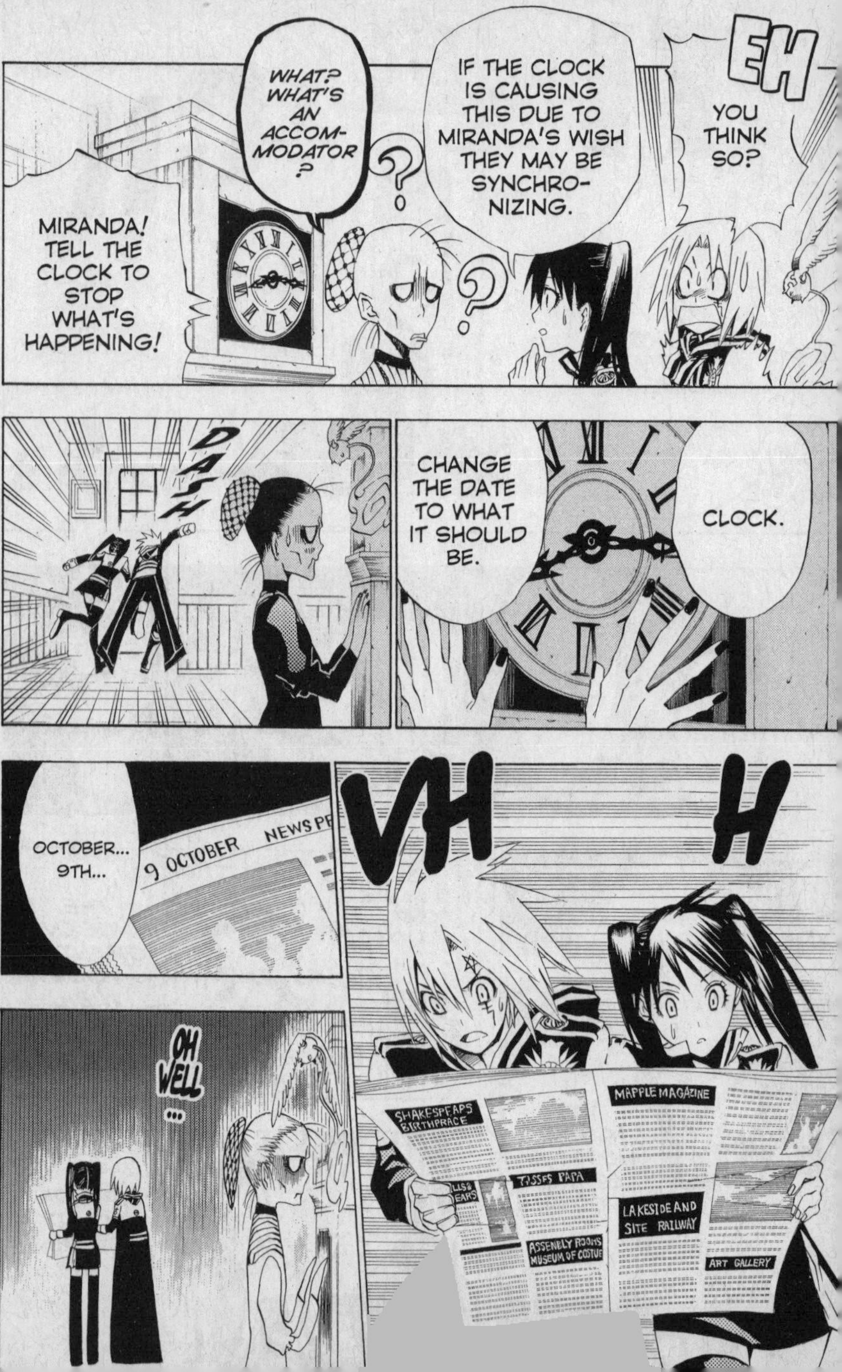
EH
YOU THINK SO?
IF THE CLOCK IS CAUSING THIS DUE TO MIRANDA'S WISH THEY MAY BE SYNCHRO-NIZING.
WHAT? WHAT'S AN ACCOM-MODATOR?
MIRANDA! TELL THE CLOCK TO STOP WHAT'S HAPPENING!
CLOCK.
CHANGE THE DATE TO WHAT IT SHOULD BE.
DASH
VH H
MAPPLE MAGAZINE
SHAKESPEAPS BIRTHPRACE
TISSES PAPA
LAKESIDE AND SITE RAILWAY
ASSENBLY ROOMS MUSEUM OF COSTUE
ART GALLERY
OCTOBER... 9TH...
9 OCTOBER
NEWS
OH WELL...

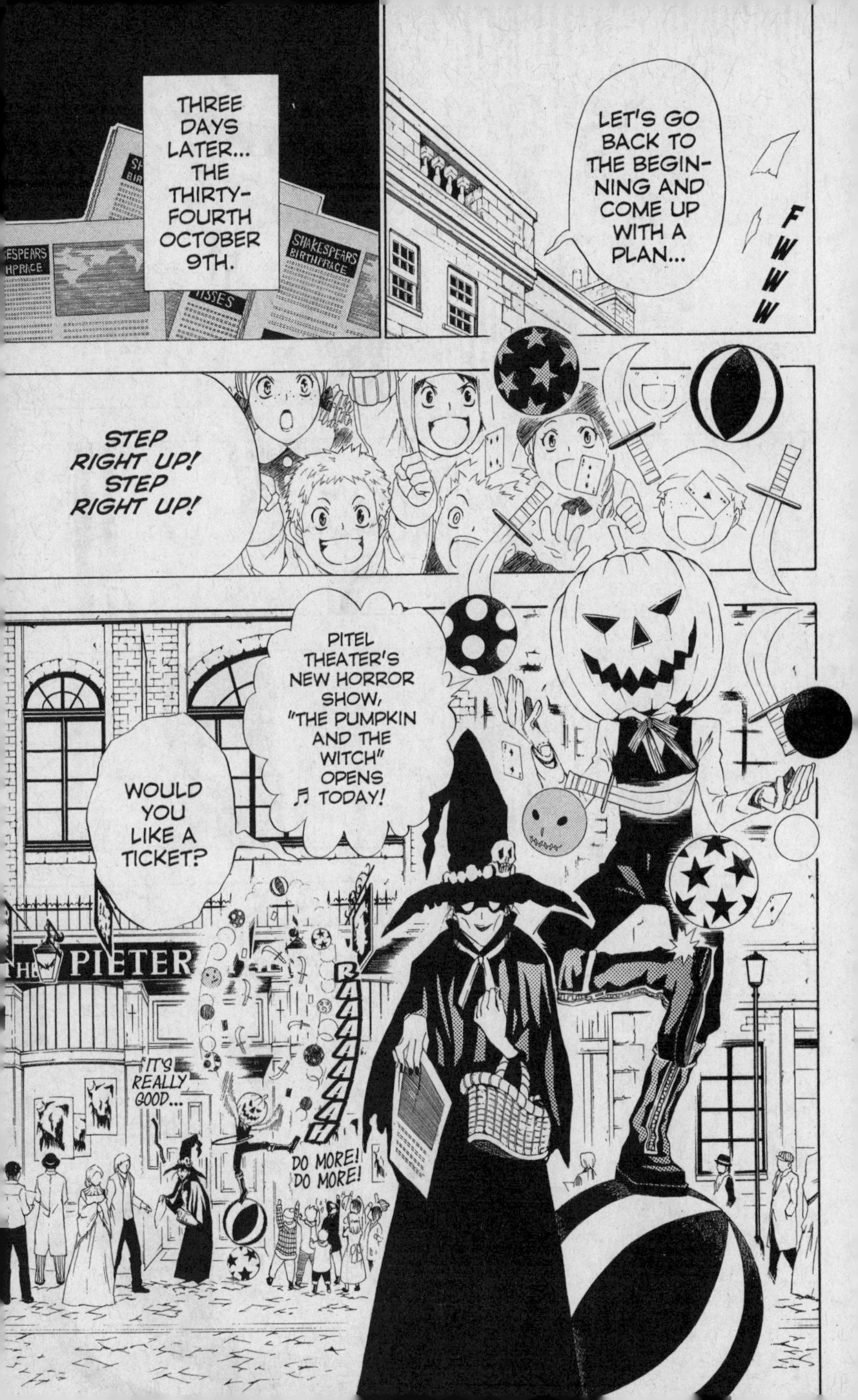
LET'S GO BACK TO THE BEGINNING AND COME UP WITH A PLAN...
FWWW
THREE DAYS LATER... THE THIRTY-FOURTH OCTOBER 9TH.
SHAKESPEARS BIRTHPRACE
ESPEARS HPRACE
ISSES
STEP RIGHT UP! STEP RIGHT UP!
PITEL THEATER'S NEW HORROR SHOW, "THE PUMPKIN AND THE WITCH" OPENS ♫ TODAY!
WOULD YOU LIKE A TICKET?
PIETER
RAAAAAAAAH
DO MORE! DO MORE!
IT'S REALLY GOOD...

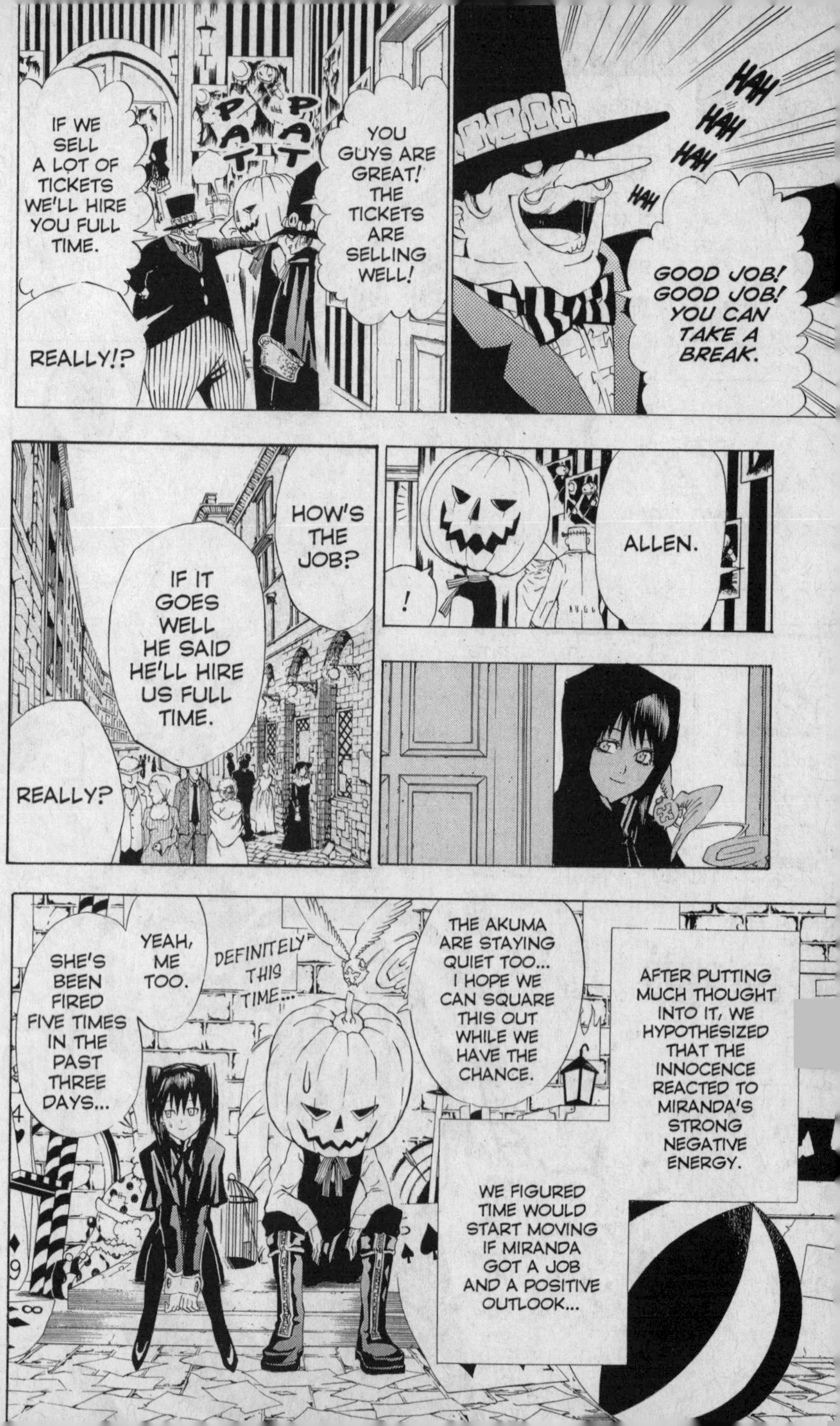
HAH HAH HAH HAH
GOOD JOB! GOOD JOB! YOU CAN TAKE A BREAK.
YOU GUYS ARE GREAT! THE TICKETS ARE SELLING WELL!
PAT PAT
IF WE SELL A LOT OF TICKETS WE'LL HIRE YOU FULL TIME.
REALLY!?
ALLEN.
!
HOW'S THE JOB?
IF IT GOES WELL HE SAID HE'LL HIRE US FULL TIME.
REALLY?
AFTER PUTTING MUCH THOUGHT INTO IT, WE HYPOTHESIZED THAT THE INNOCENCE REACTED TO MIRANDA'S STRONG NEGATIVE ENERGY.
WE FIGURED TIME WOULD START MOVING IF MIRANDA GOT A JOB AND A POSITIVE OUTLOOK...
THE AKUMA ARE STAYING QUIET TOO... I HOPE WE CAN SQUARE THIS OUT WHILE WE HAVE THE CHANCE.
DEFINITELY THIS TIME...
YEAH, ME TOO.
SHE'S BEEN FIRED FIVE TIMES IN THE PAST THREE DAYS...

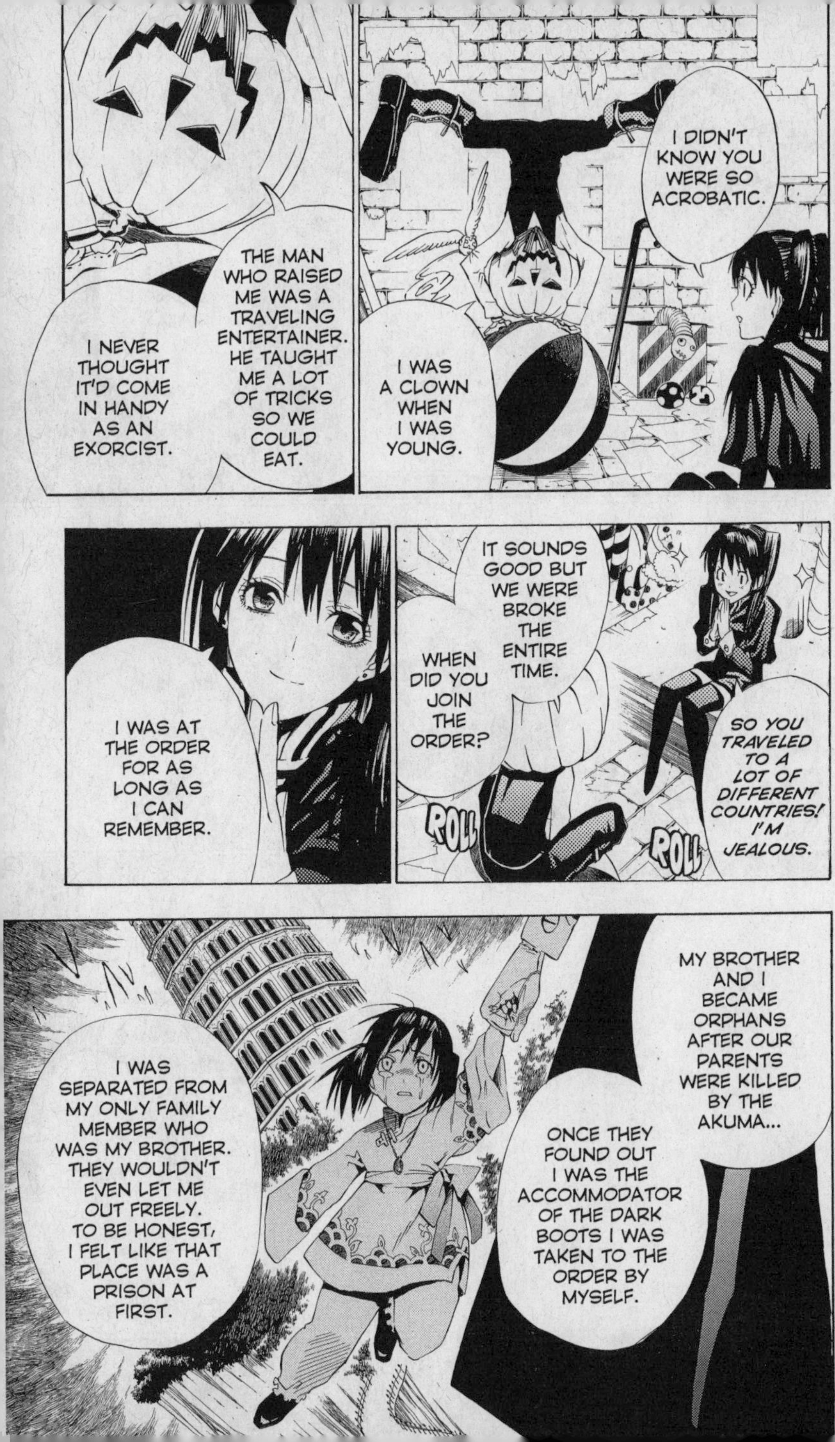
I DIDN'T KNOW YOU WERE SO ACROBATIC.
I WAS A CLOWN WHEN I WAS YOUNG.
THE MAN WHO RAISED ME WAS A TRAVELING ENTERTAINER. HE TAUGHT ME A LOT OF TRICKS SO WE COULD EAT.
I NEVER THOUGHT IT'D COME IN HANDY AS AN EXORCIST.
SO YOU TRAVELED TO A LOT OF DIFFERENT COUNTRIES! I'M JEALOUS.
ROLL
ROLL
IT SOUNDS GOOD BUT WE WERE BROKE THE ENTIRE TIME.
WHEN DID YOU JOIN THE ORDER?
I WAS AT THE ORDER FOR AS LONG AS I CAN REMEMBER.
MY BROTHER AND I BECAME ORPHANS AFTER OUR PARENTS WERE KILLED BY THE AKUMA...
ONCE THEY FOUND OUT I WAS THE ACCOMMODATOR OF THE DARK BOOTS I WAS TAKEN TO THE ORDER BY MYSELF.
I WAS SEPARATED FROM MY ONLY FAMILY MEMBER WHO WAS MY BROTHER. THEY WOULDN'T EVEN LET ME OUT FREELY. TO BE HONEST, I FELT LIKE THAT PLACE WAS A PRISON AT FIRST.

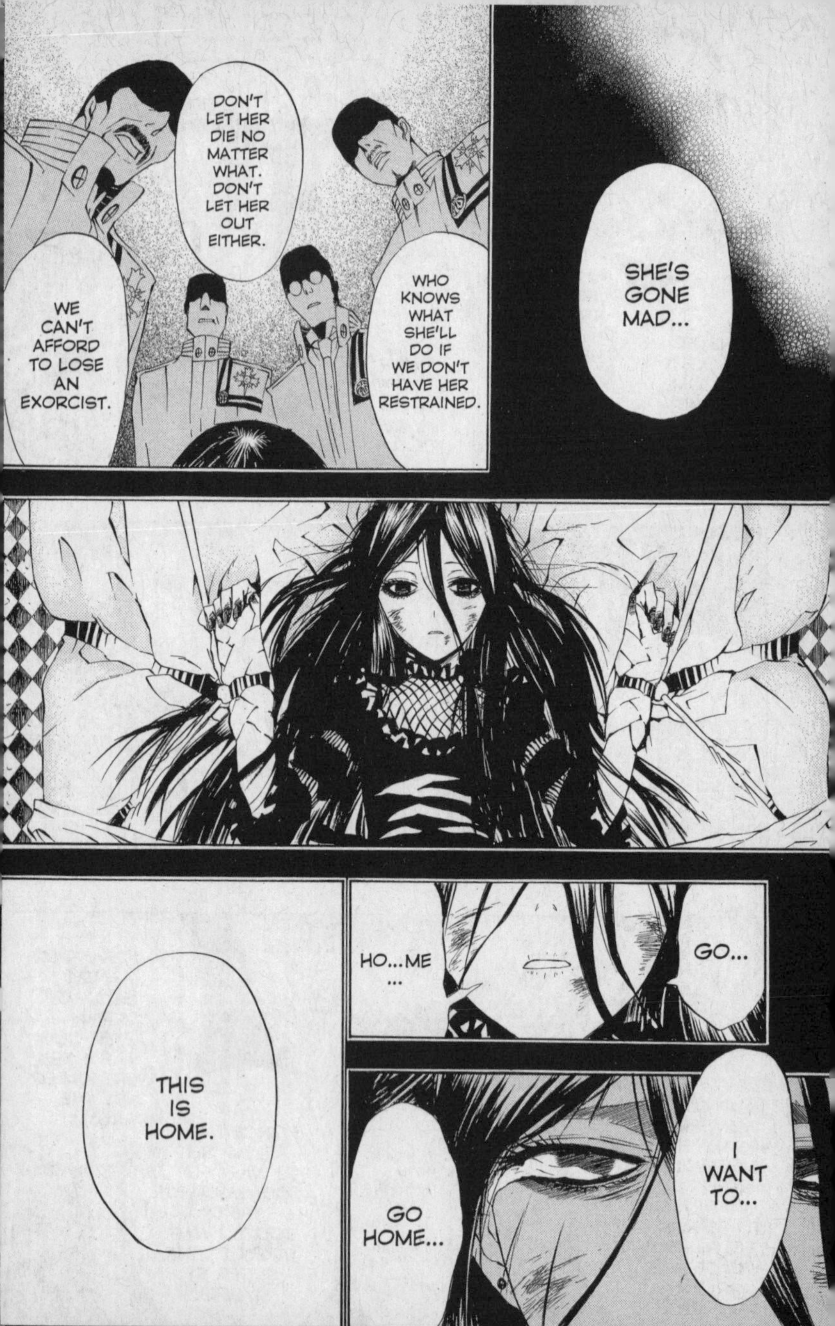
SHE'S GONE MAD...
DON'T LET HER DIE NO MATTER WHAT. DON'T LET HER OUT EITHER.
WHO KNOWS WHAT SHE'LL DO IF WE DON'T HAVE HER RESTRAINED.
WE CAN'T AFFORD TO LOSE AN EXORCIST.
GO...
HO...ME ...
I WANT TO...
GO HOME...
THIS IS HOME.

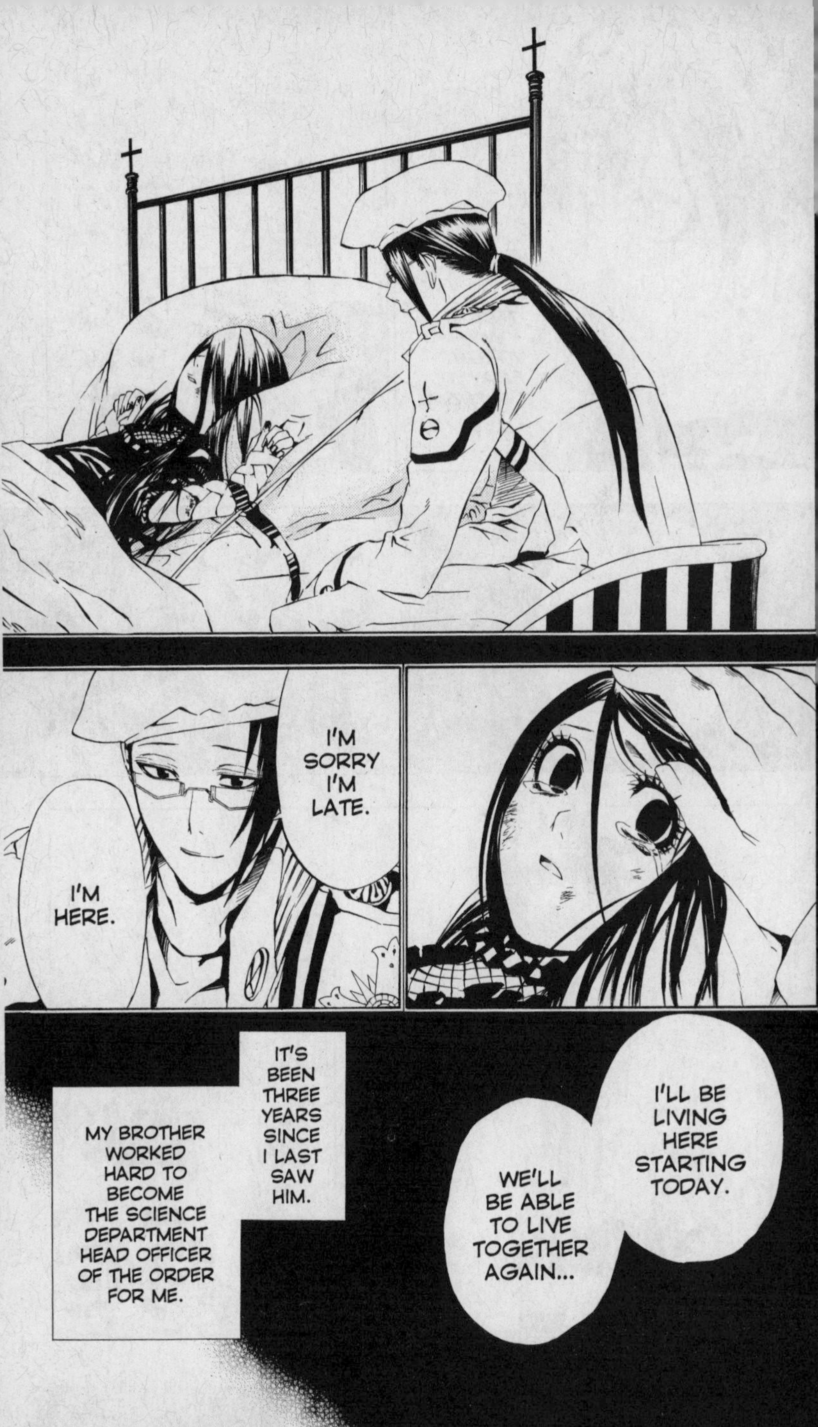
I'M SORRY I'M LATE.
I'M HERE.
I'LL BE LIVING HERE STARTING TODAY.
WE'LL BE ABLE TO LIVE TOGETHER AGAIN...
IT'S BEEN THREE YEARS SINCE I LAST SAW HIM.
MY BROTHER WORKED HARD TO BECOME THE SCIENCE DEPARTMENT HEAD OFFICER OF THE ORDER FOR ME.

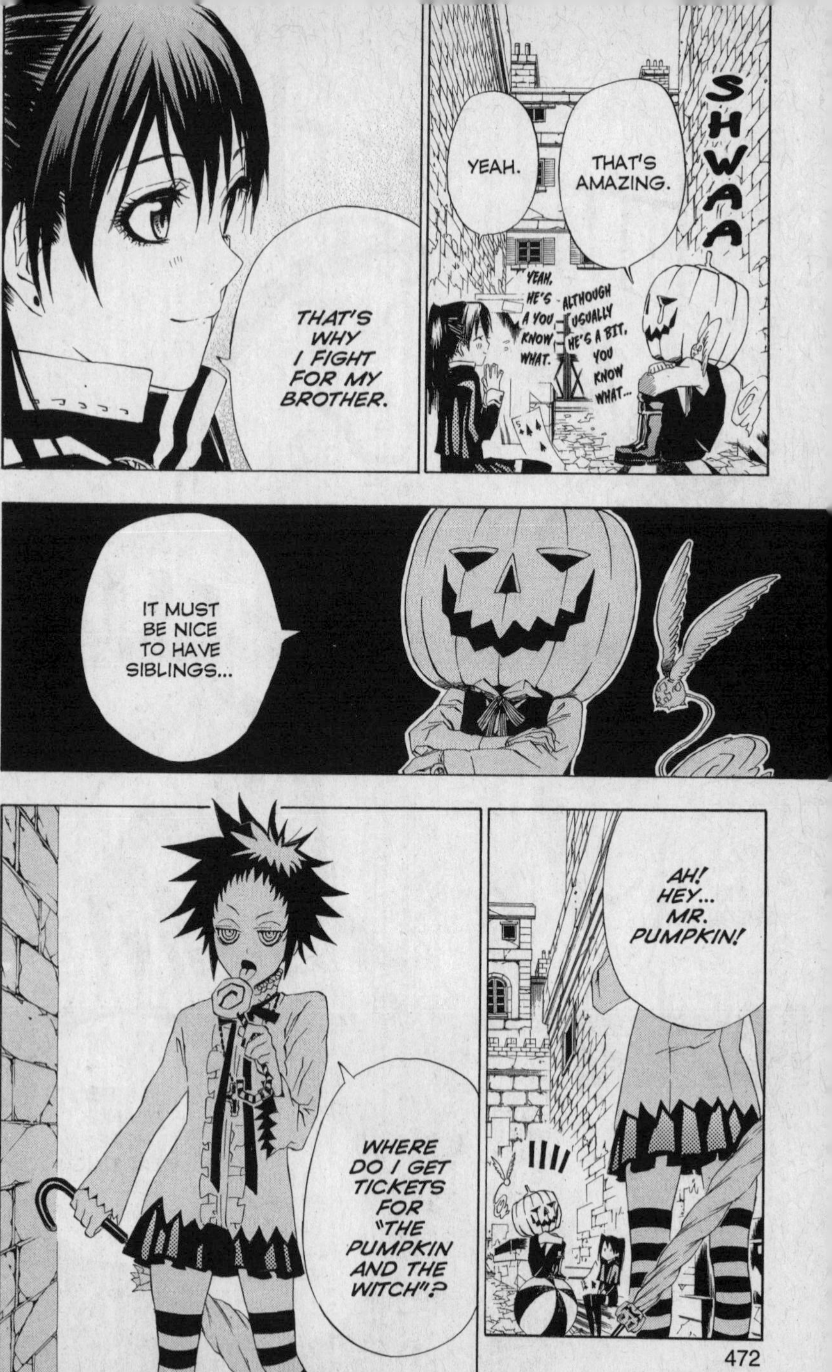
SHWAA
THAT'S AMAZING.
YEAH.
ALTHOUGH USUALLY HE'S A BIT, YOU KNOW WHAT...
YEAH, HE'S A YOU KNOW WHAT.
THAT'S WHY I FIGHT FOR MY BROTHER.
IT MUST BE NICE TO HAVE SIBLINGS...
AH! HEY... MR. PUMPKIN!
WHERE DO I GET TICKETS FOR "THE PUMPKIN AND THE WITCH"?

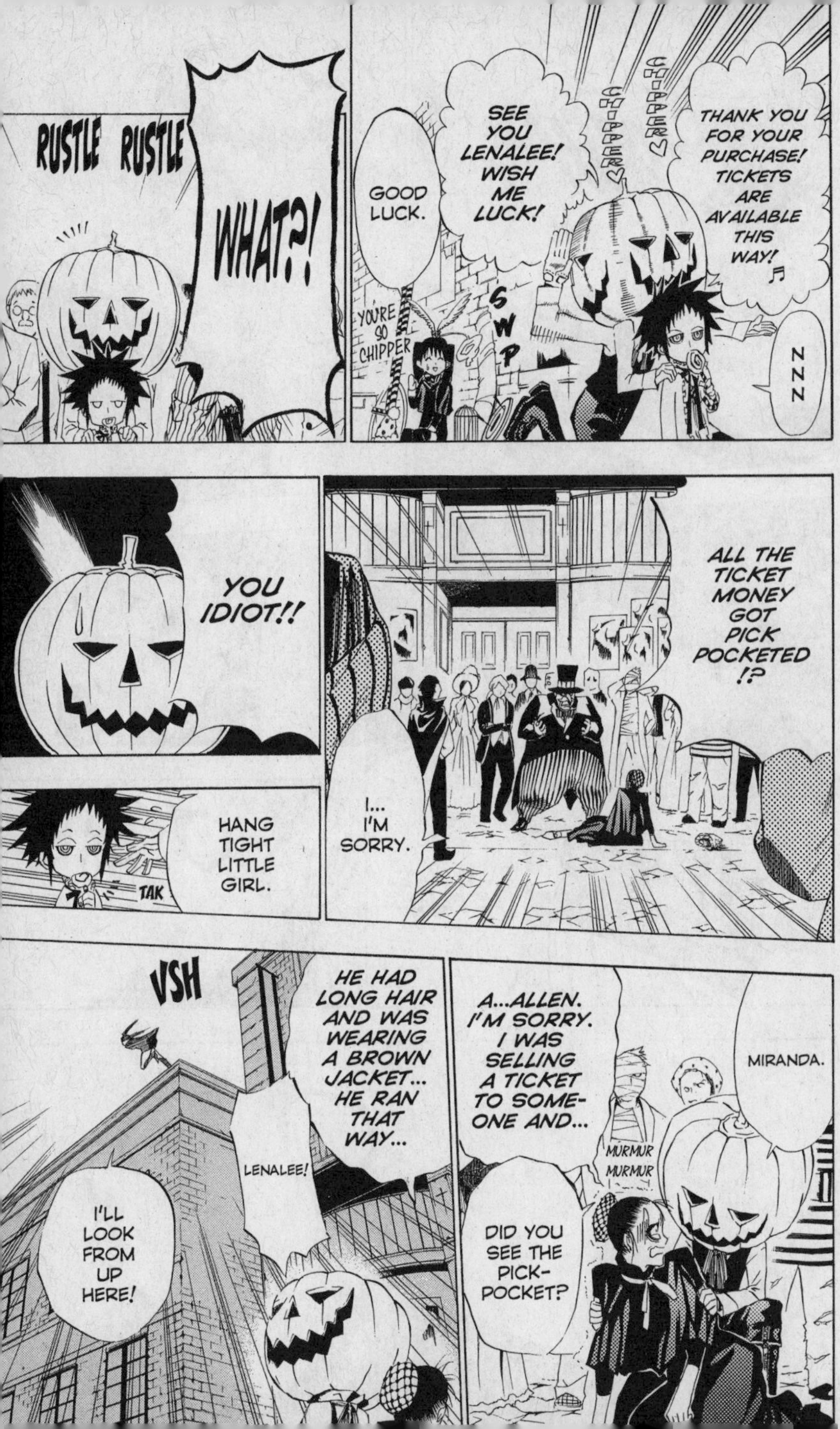
THANK YOU FOR YOUR PURCHASE! TICKETS ARE AVAILABLE THIS WAY! ♪
NNN
CHIPPER♡ CHIPPER♡
SEE YOU LENALEE! WISH ME LUCK!
SWP
GOOD LUCK.
YOU'RE SO CHIPPER
WHAT?!
RUSTLE RUSTLE
ALL THE TICKET MONEY GOT PICK POCKETED !?
I... I'M SORRY.
YOU IDIOT!!
HANG TIGHT LITTLE GIRL.
TAK
MIRANDA.
A...ALLEN. I'M SORRY. I WAS SELLING A TICKET TO SOME-ONE AND...
MURMUR MURMUR
DID YOU SEE THE PICK-POCKET?
HE HAD LONG HAIR AND WAS WEARING A BROWN JACKET... HE RAN THAT WAY...
LENALEE!
VSH
I'LL LOOK FROM UP HERE!

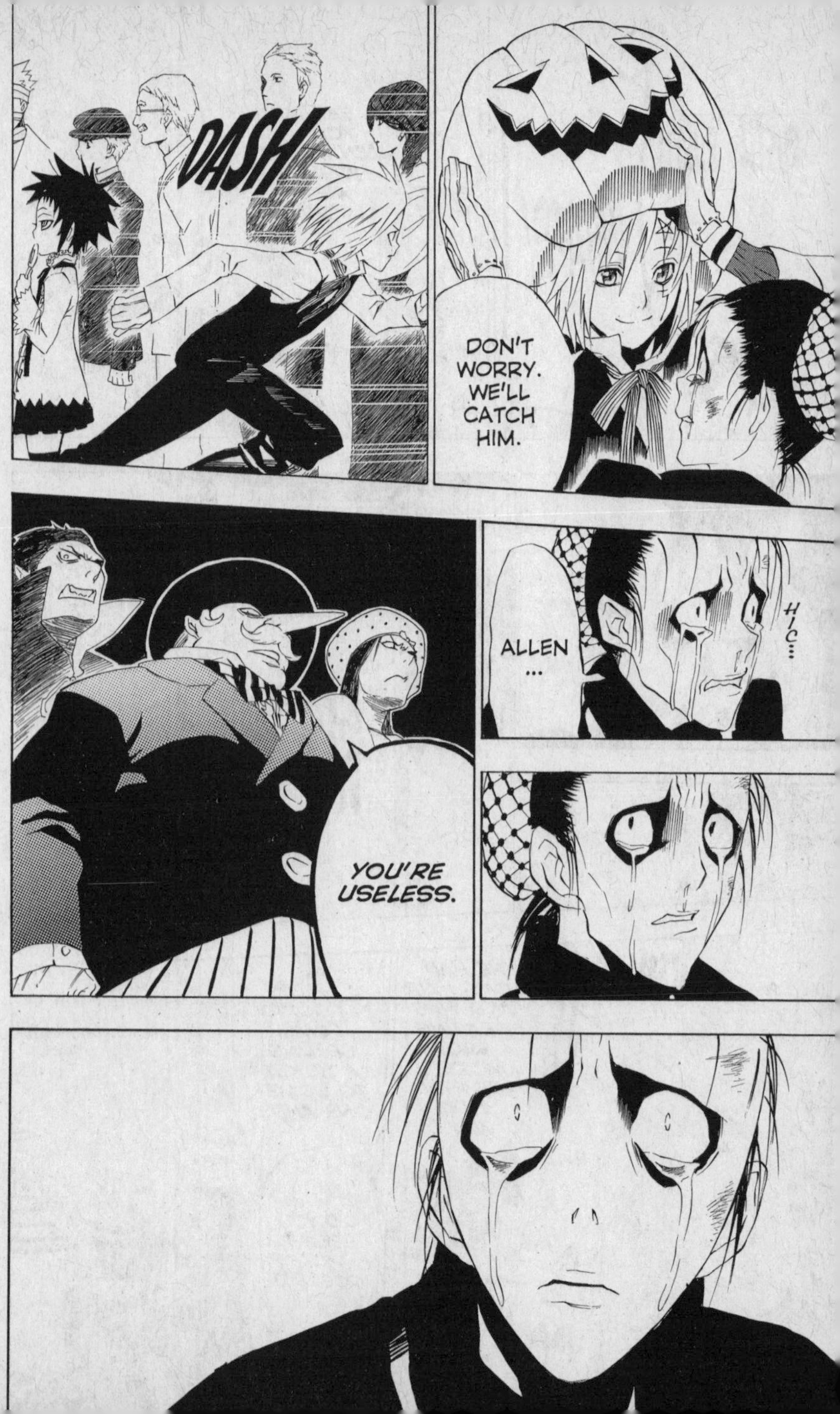
DON'T WORRY. WE'LL CATCH HIM.
DASH
ALLEN ...
HIC...
YOU'RE USELESS.

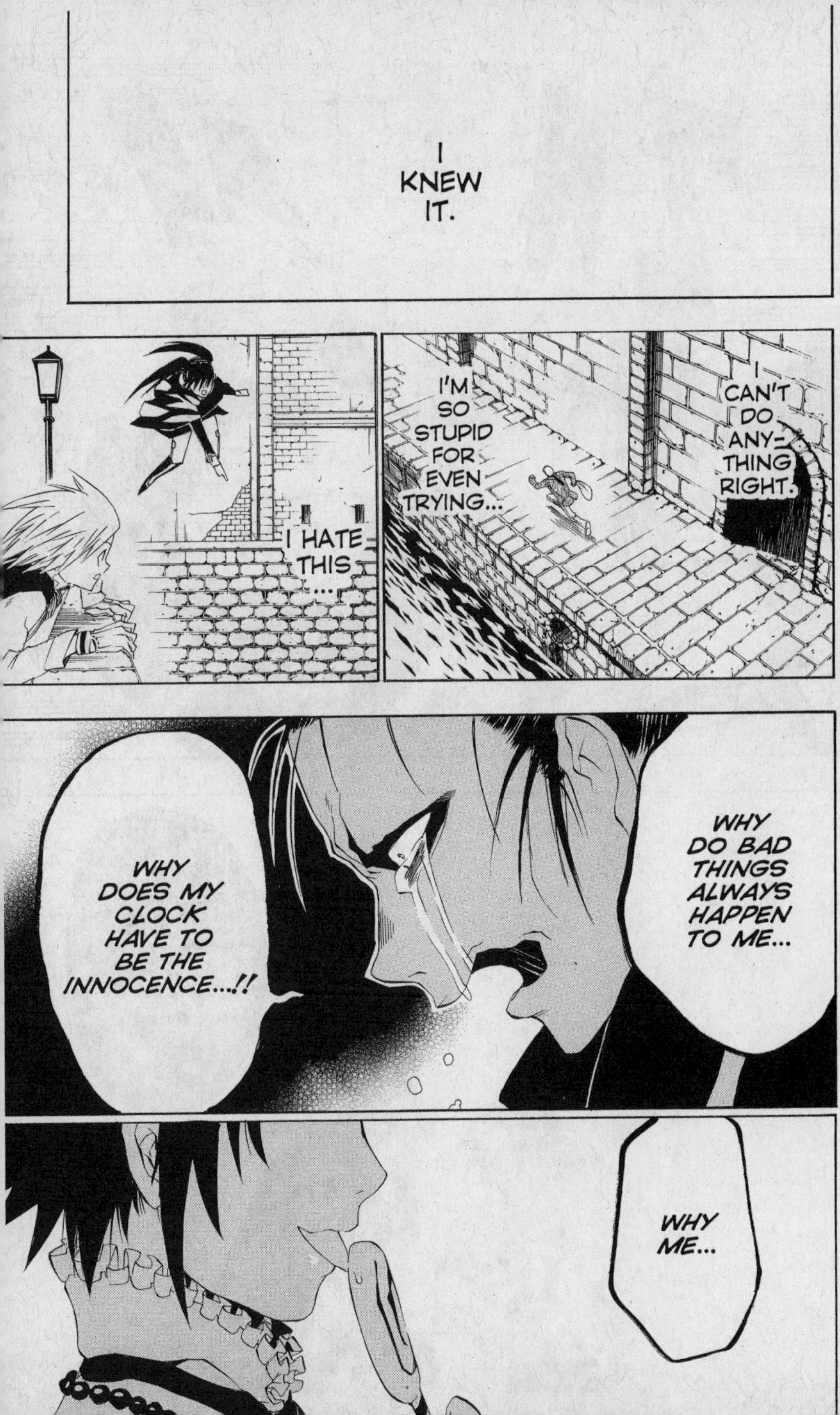
I KNEW IT.
I CAN'T DO ANYTHING RIGHT.
I'M SO STUPID FOR EVEN TRYING...
I HATE THIS...
WHY DO BAD THINGS ALWAYS HAPPEN TO ME...
WHY DOES MY CLOCK HAVE TO BE THE INNOCENCE...!!
WHY ME...

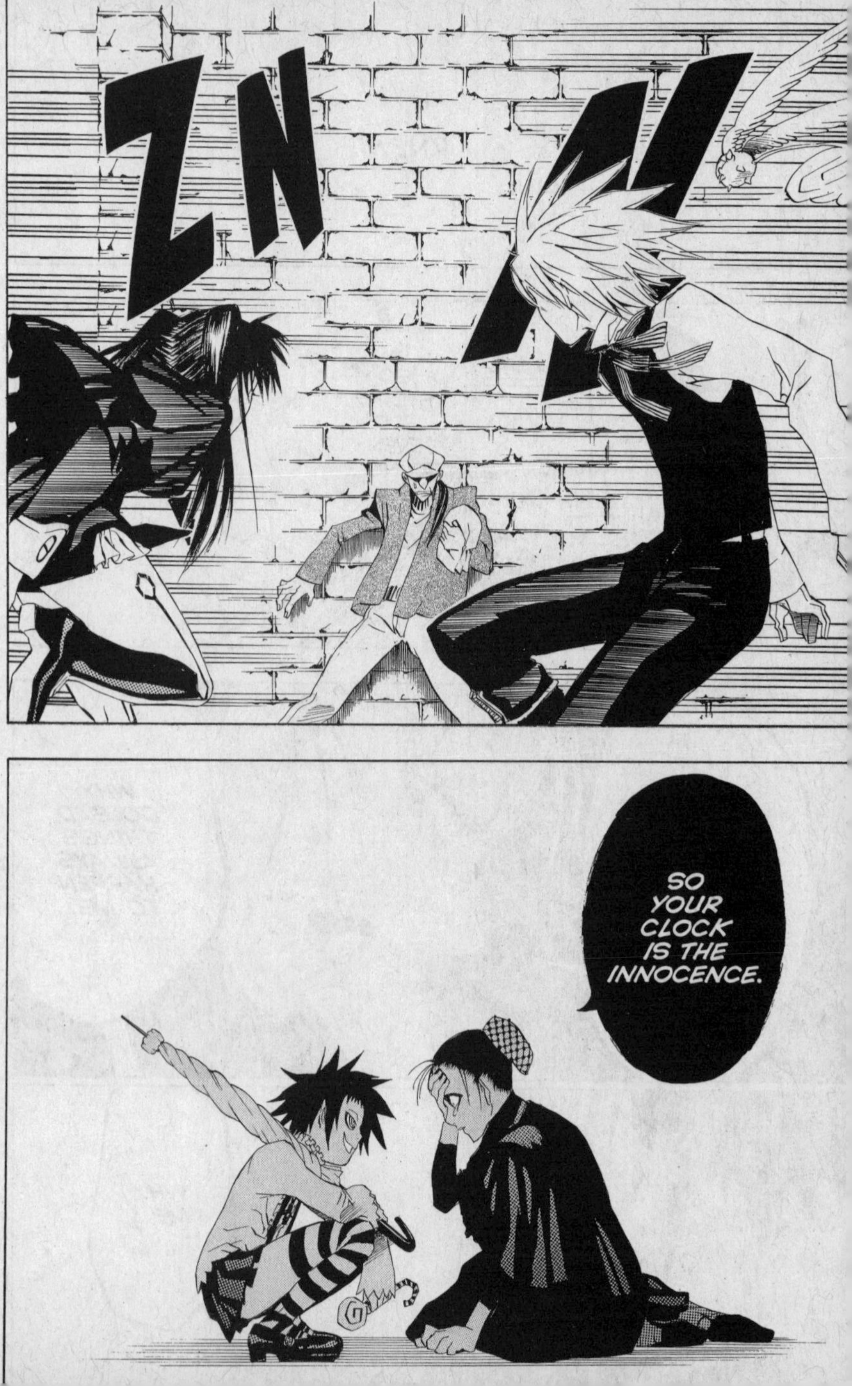
ZNN
SO YOUR CLOCK IS THE INNOCENCE.

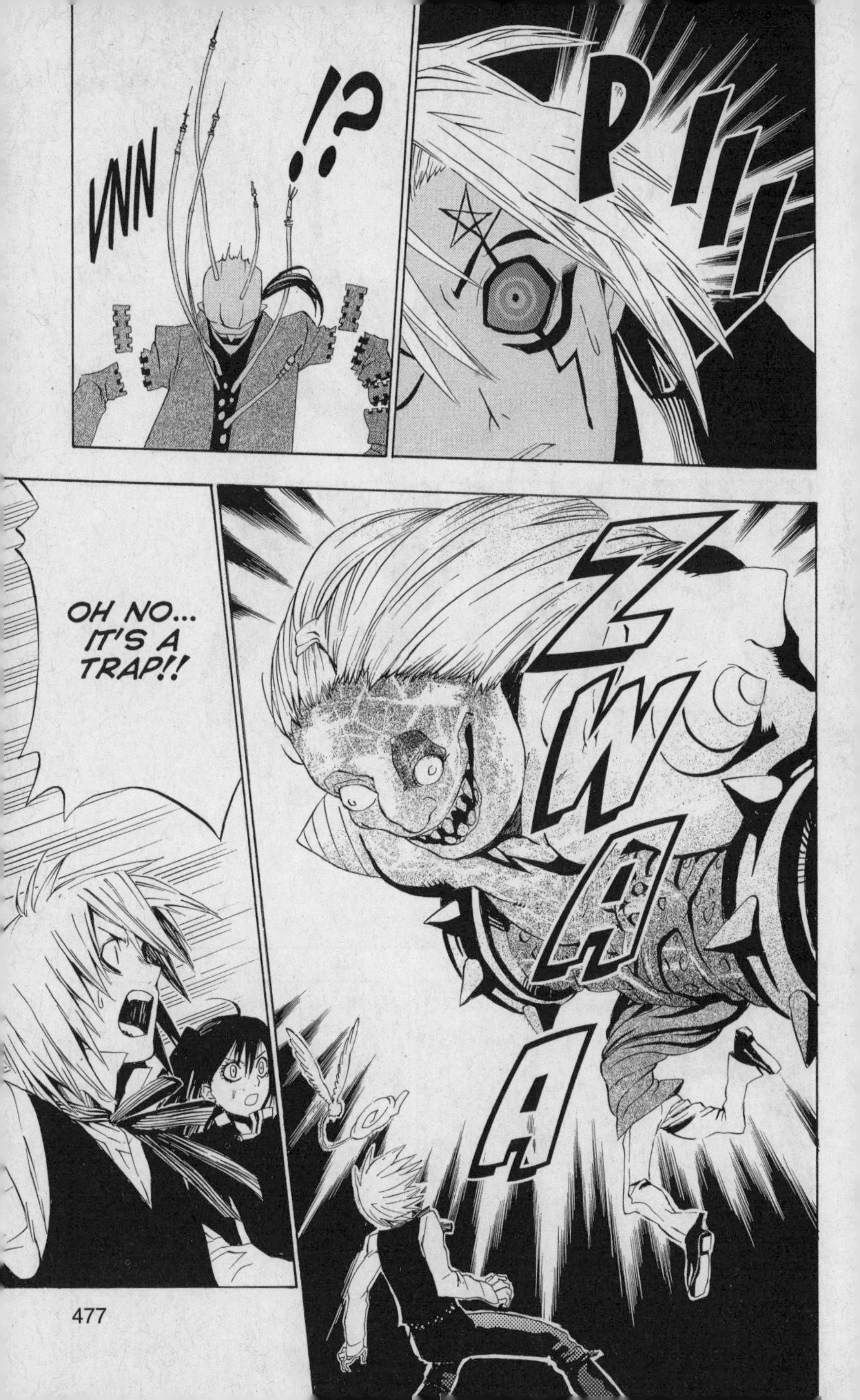
PIIII
!?
VNN
ZWAAA
OH NO... IT'S A TRAP!!

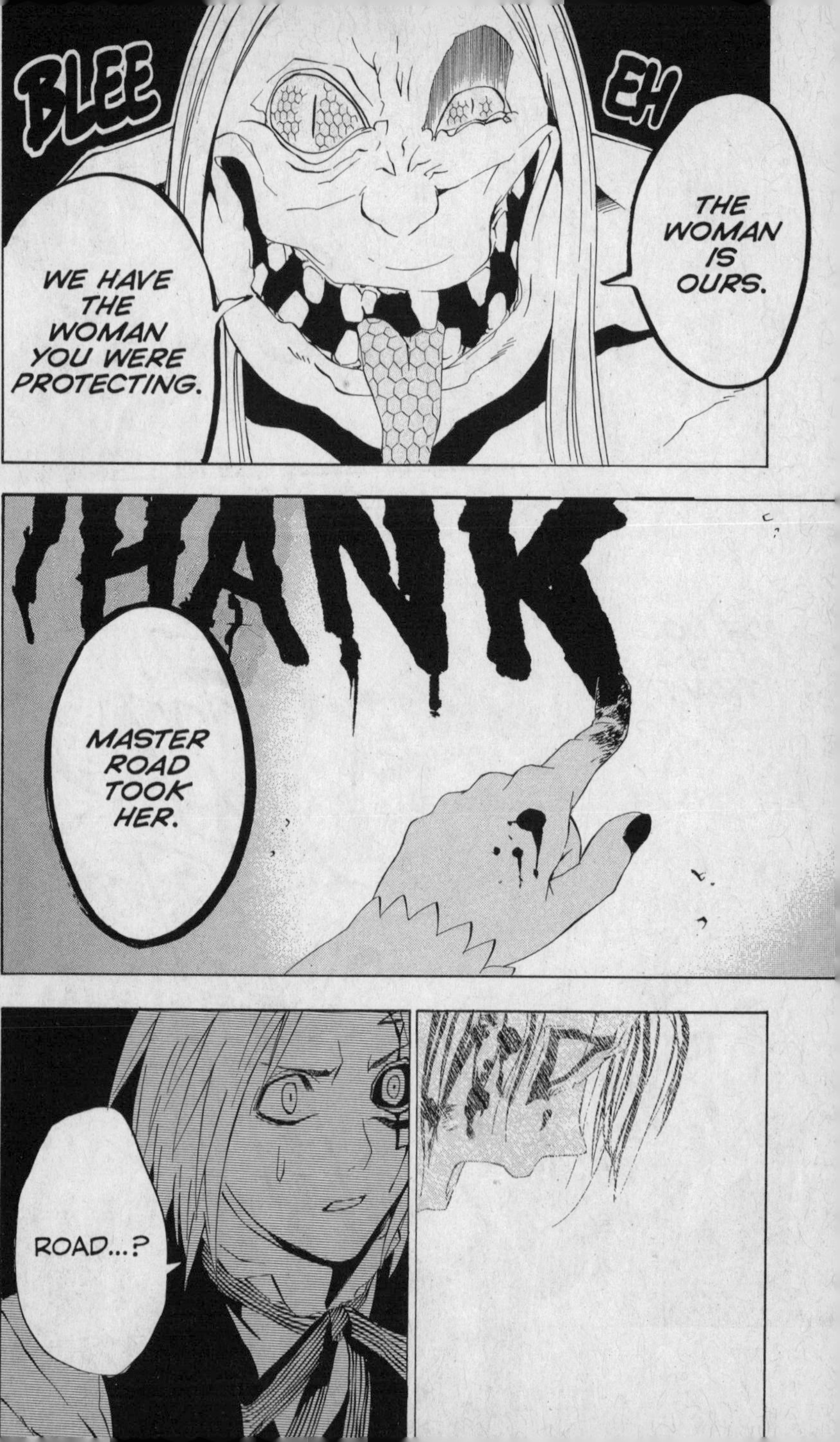

BLEE EH
THE WOMAN IS OURS.
WE HAVE THE WOMAN YOU WERE PROTECTING.
MASTER ROAD TOOK HER.
ROAD...?

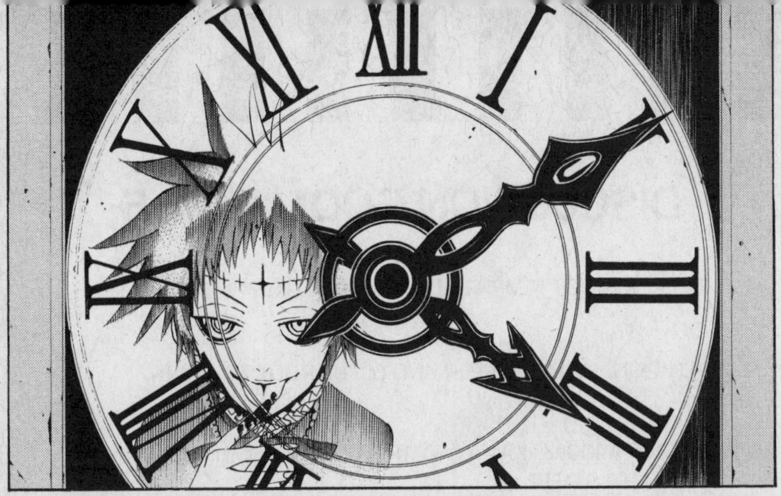

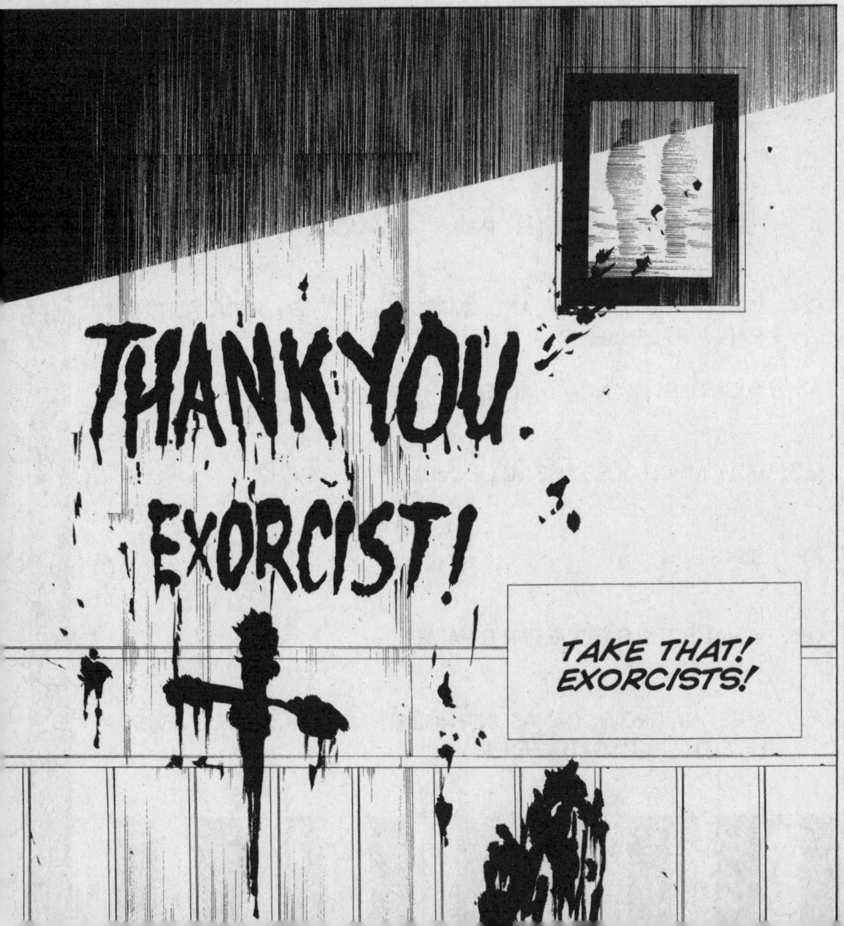
THANK YOU. EXORCIST!
TAKE THAT! EXORCISTS!

DISCUSSION ROOM VOL. 5

Q 1. WHAT KIND OF TEMPURA DOES KANDA LIKE?

A. PUMPKIN, SWEET PEPPER AND LOTUS ROOT TEMPURA.

Q 2. OUT OF A 100%, HOW MUST TRUST DOES KOMUI COMMAND FROM HIS STAFF?

A. 99% TRUST AND 1% MURDEROUS HATE.

Q 3. IS KOMUI A COFFEE SNOB OR DOES HE DRINK INSTANT COFFEE? PLEASE TELL US WHAT KIND HE DRINKS.

A. HE'S A COFFEE SNOB. HE DRINKS BLUE MOUNTAIN COFFEE.

Q 4. WHO'S THE DUMBEST AND SMARTEST OUT OF KANDA, ALLEN, RABI AND LENALEE?

A. (DUMBEST) KANDA -> ALLEN -> RABI -> LENALEE (SMARTEST)

Q 5. HOW MUCH DOES THE MILLENNIUM EARL WEIGH?

A. 85KG.

Q 6. WHAT'S THE GATEKEEPER'S NAME?

A. ALESTINA DROW JOANASON P. ROBATHAN GIA AMADEUS NO. 5. HE'S THE FIFTH GATEKEEPER.

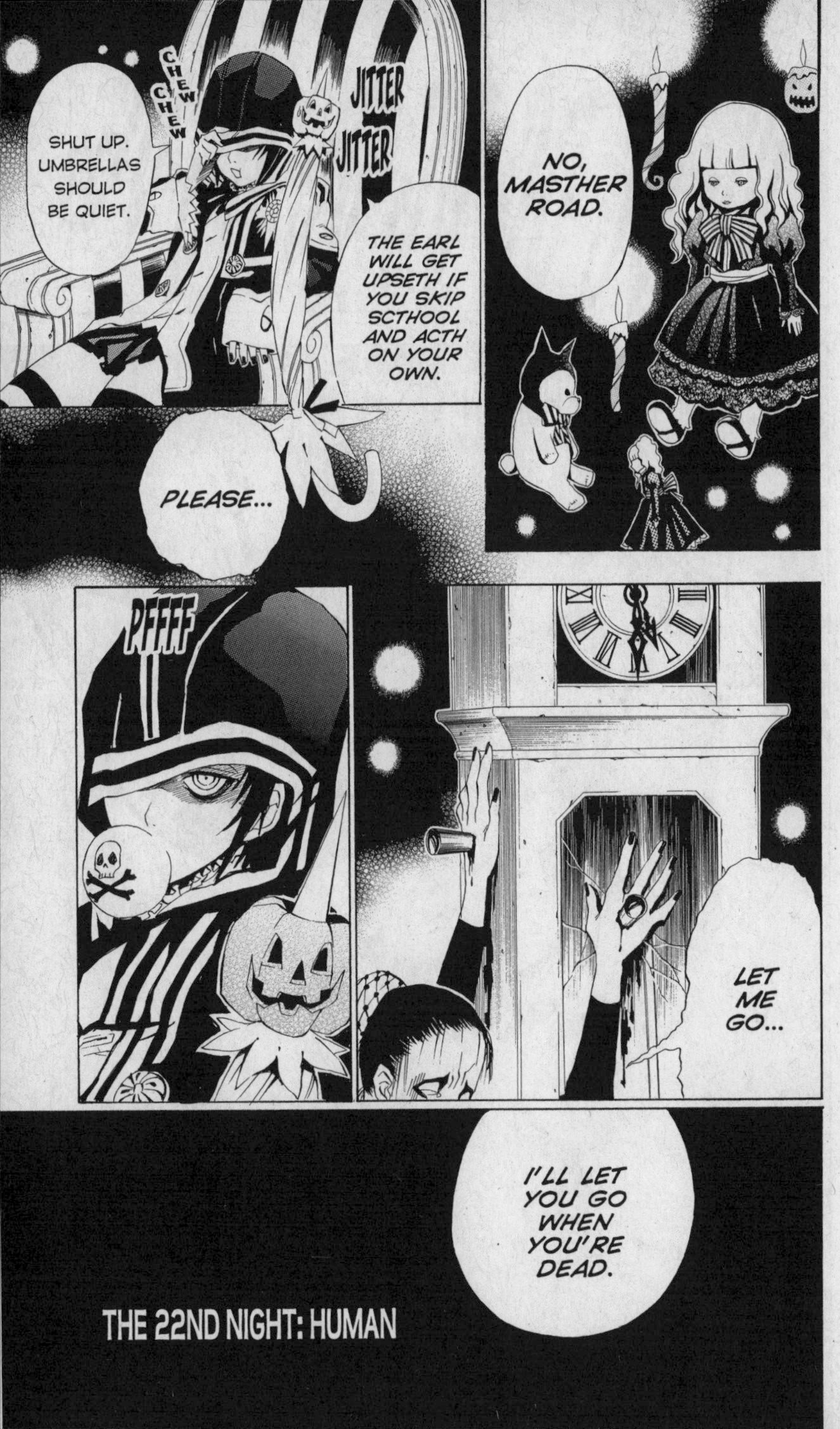
NO, MASTHER ROAD.
JITTER JITTER
THE EARL WILL GET UPSETH IF YOU SKIP SCTHOOL AND ACTH ON YOUR OWN.
CHEW CHEW
SHUT UP. UMBRELLAS SHOULD BE QUIET.
PLEASE...
LET ME GO...
PFFFF
I'LL LET YOU GO WHEN YOU'RE DEAD.
THE 22ND NIGHT: HUMAN

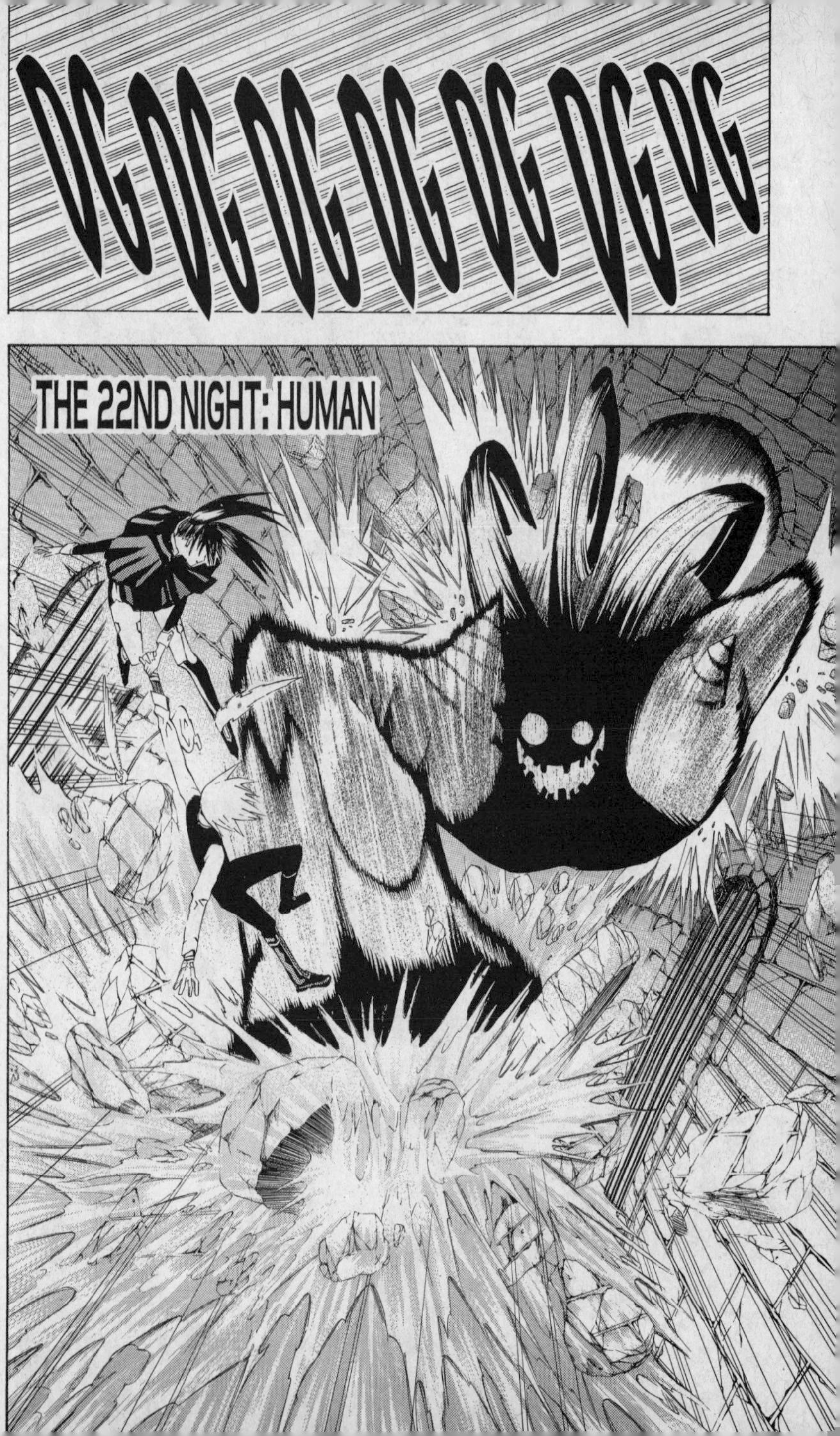
DG DG DG DG DG DG DG DG
THE 22ND NIGHT: HUMAN

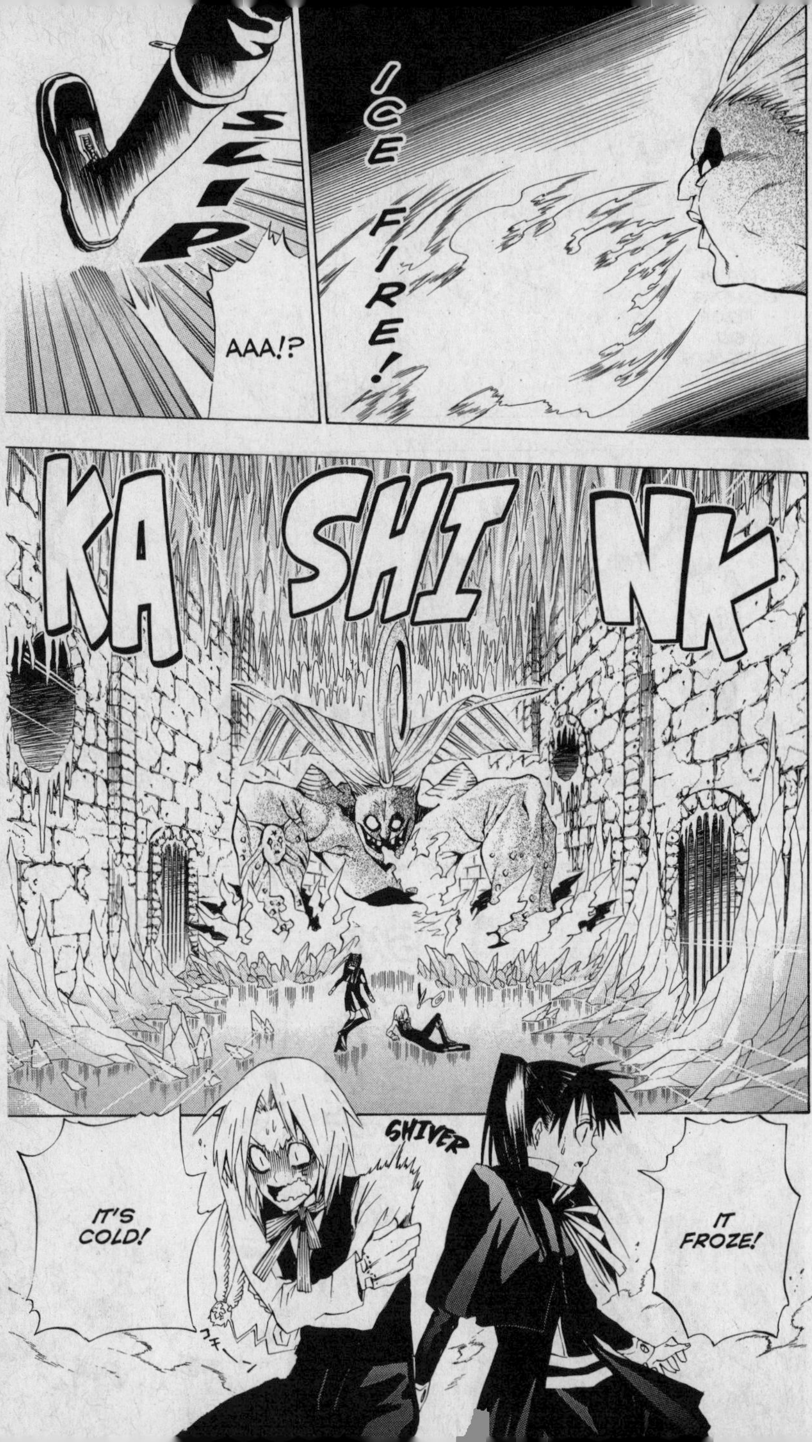
ICE FIRE!
SLIP
AAA!?
KA SHI NK
IT FROZE!
SHIVER
IT'S COLD!

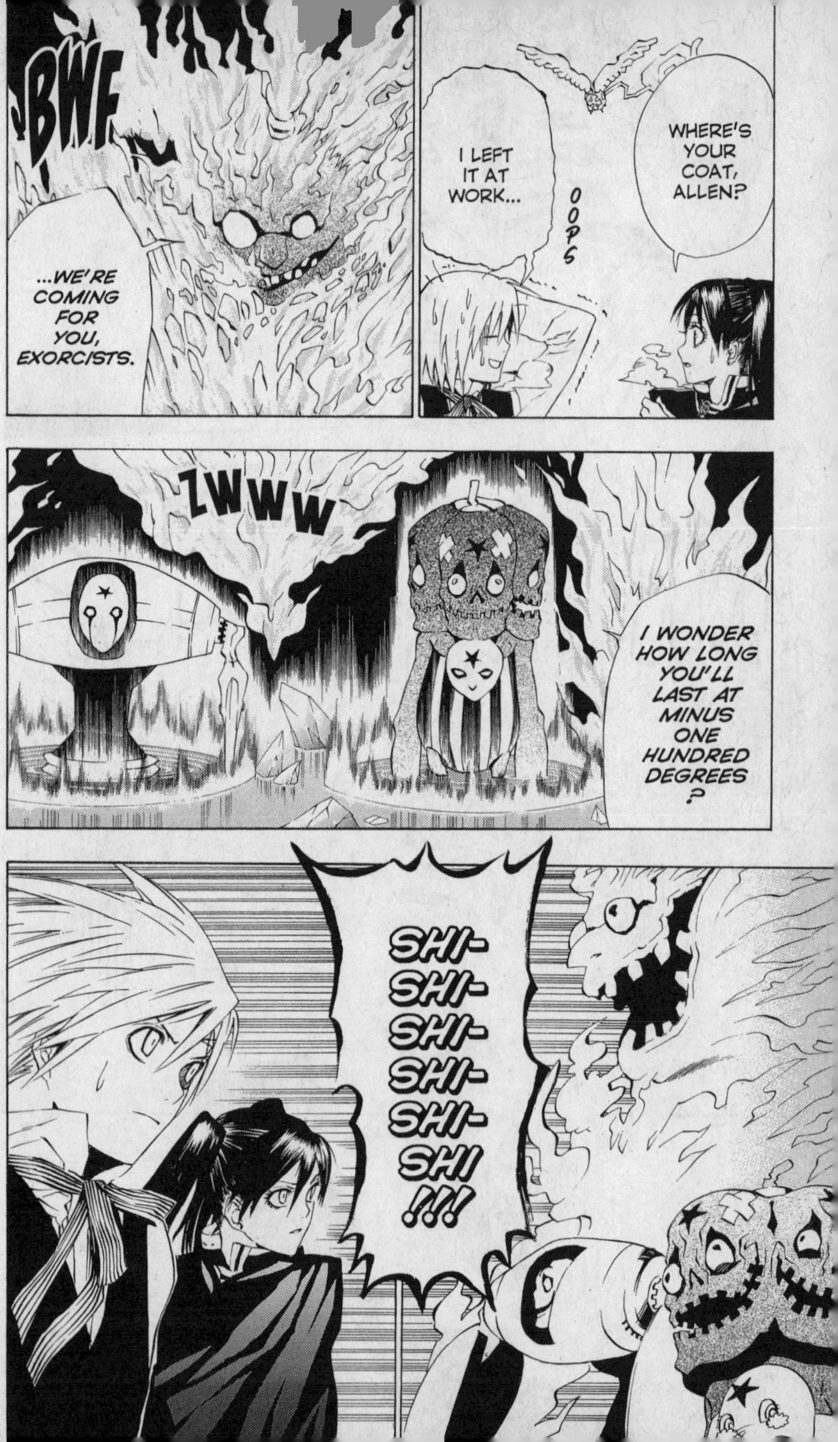
WHERE'S YOUR COAT, ALLEN?
I LEFT IT AT WORK...
OOPS
BWF
...WE'RE COMING FOR YOU, EXORCISTS.
ZWWW
I WONDER HOW LONG YOU'LL LAST AT MINUS ONE HUNDRED DEGREES?
SHI-SHI-SHI-SHI-SHI-SHI!!!

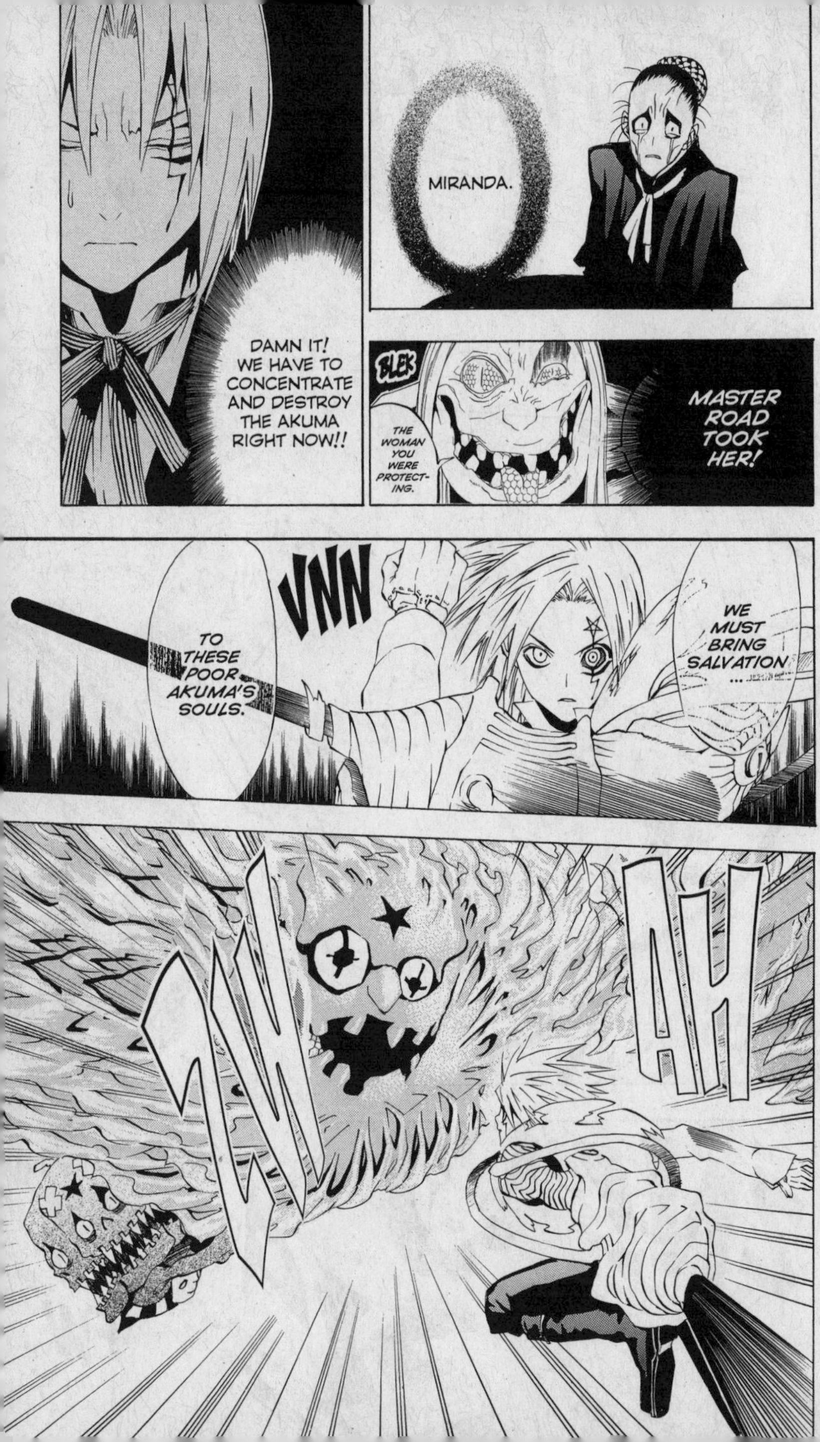
MIRANDA.
BLEK
MASTER ROAD TOOK HER!
THE WOMAN YOU WERE PROTECTING.
DAMN IT! WE HAVE TO CONCENTRATE AND DESTROY THE AKUMA RIGHT NOW!!
WE MUST BRING SALVATION ...
VNN
TO THESE POOR AKUMA'S SOULS.
AH

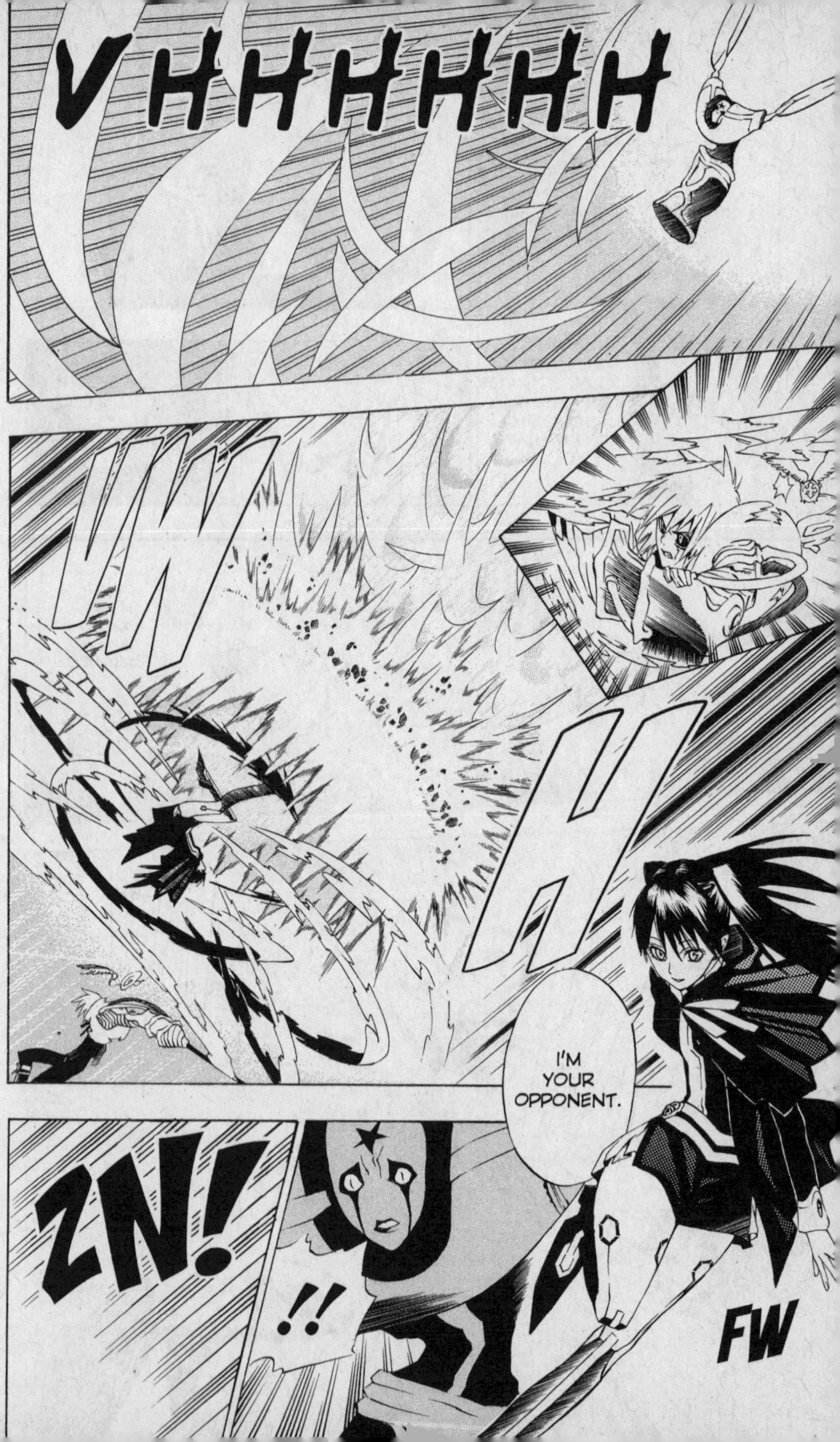
VHHHHHH
VN
H
I'M YOUR OPPONENT.
ZN!
!!
FW

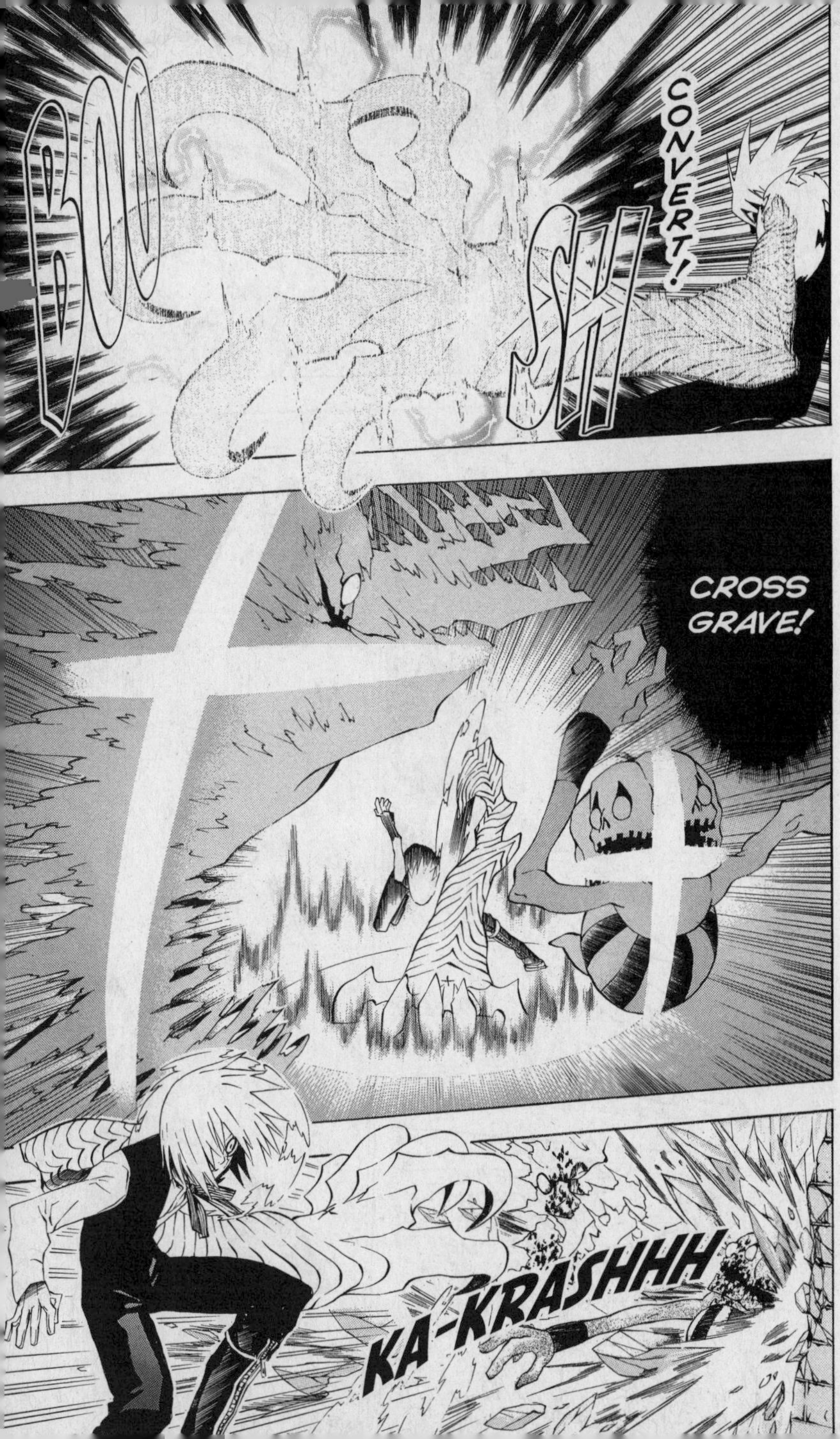
CONVERT!
SH
BOO
CROSS GRAVE!
KA-KRASHHH

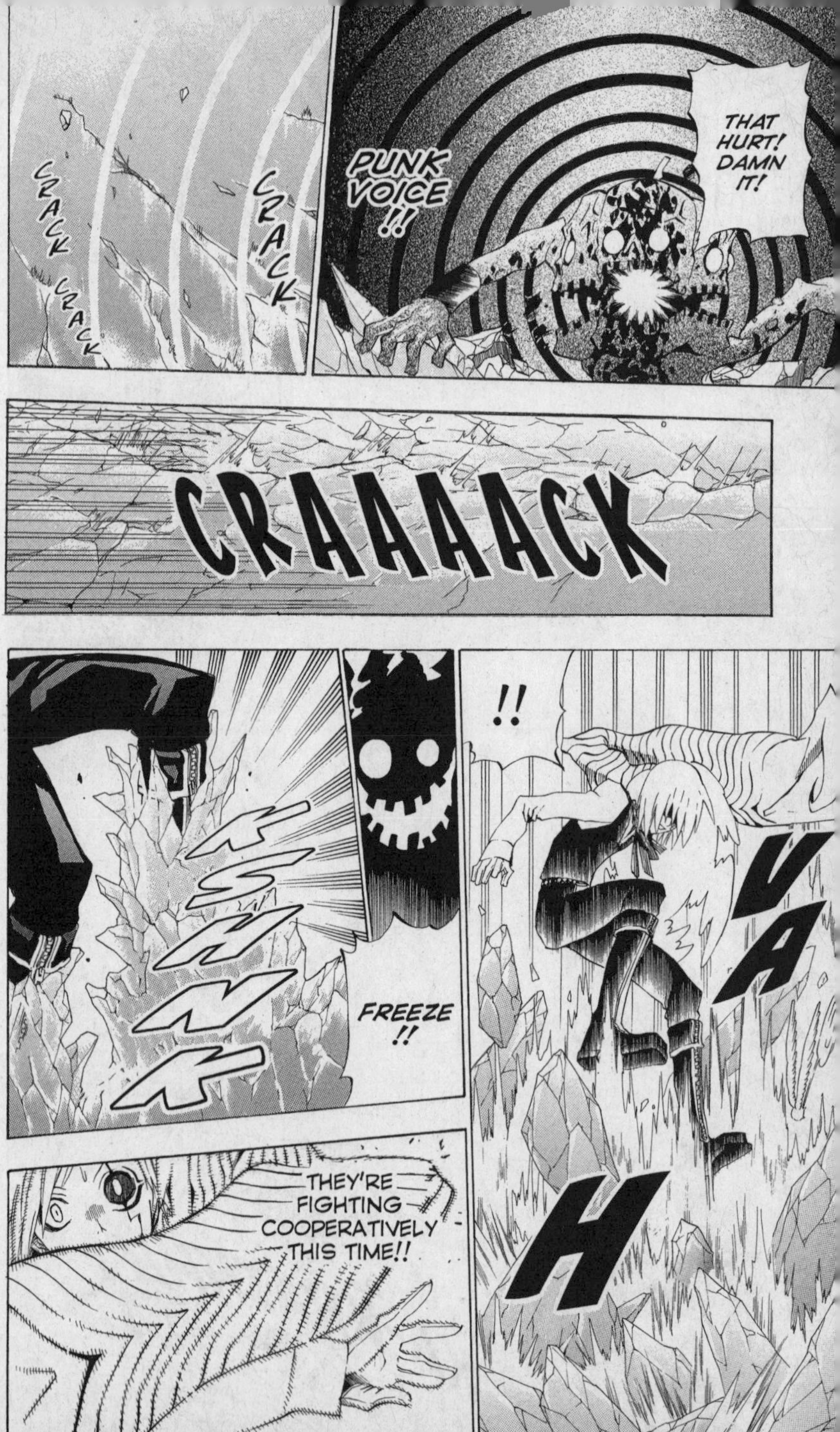
THAT HURT! DAMN IT!
PUNK VOICE!!
CRACK
CRACK CRACK
CRAAAACK
!!
VAH
KSHNNK
FREEZE!!
THEY'RE FIGHTING COOPERATIVELY THIS TIME!!

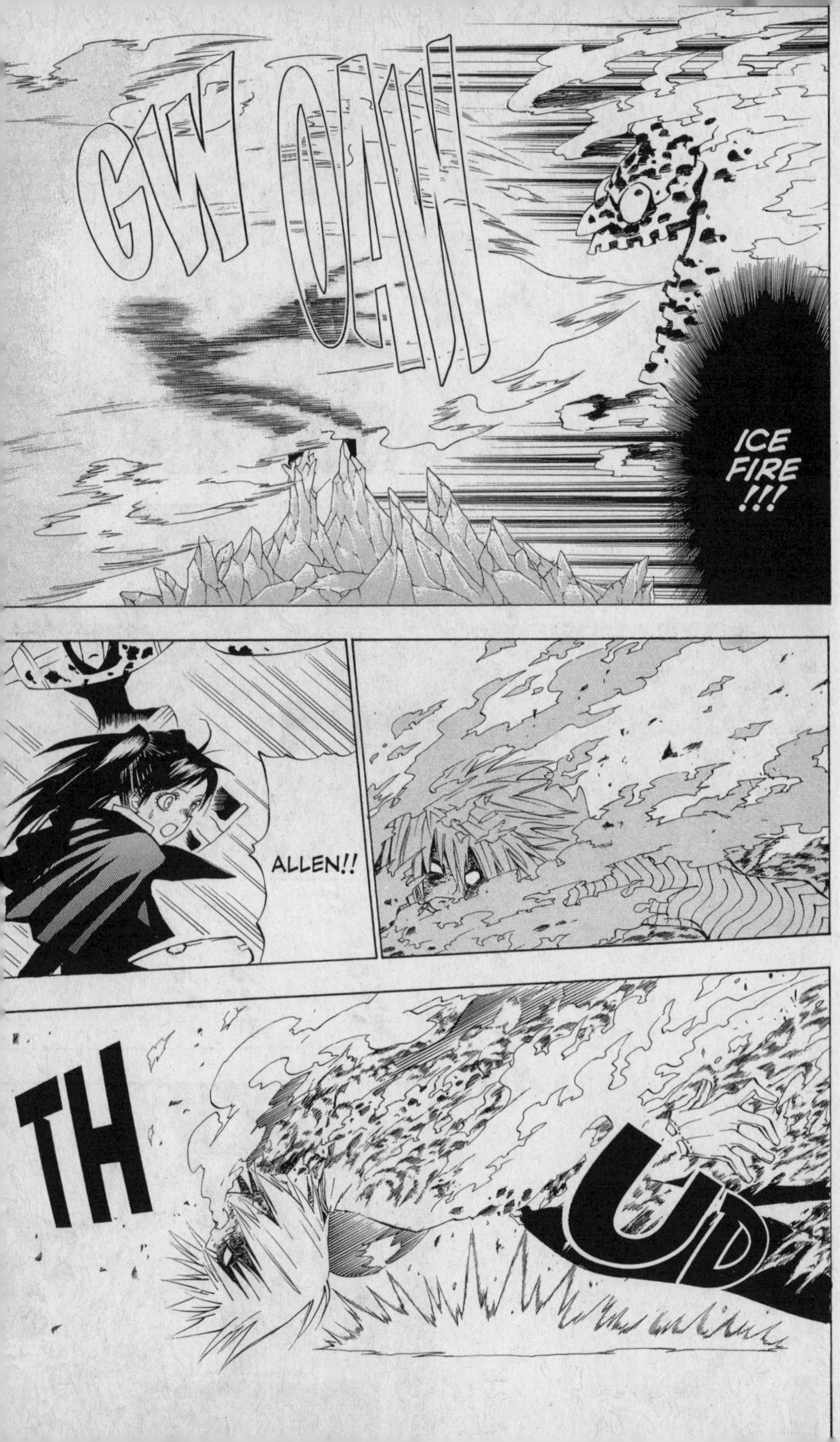
ICE FIRE!!!
GWOAAM
ALLEN!!
THUD

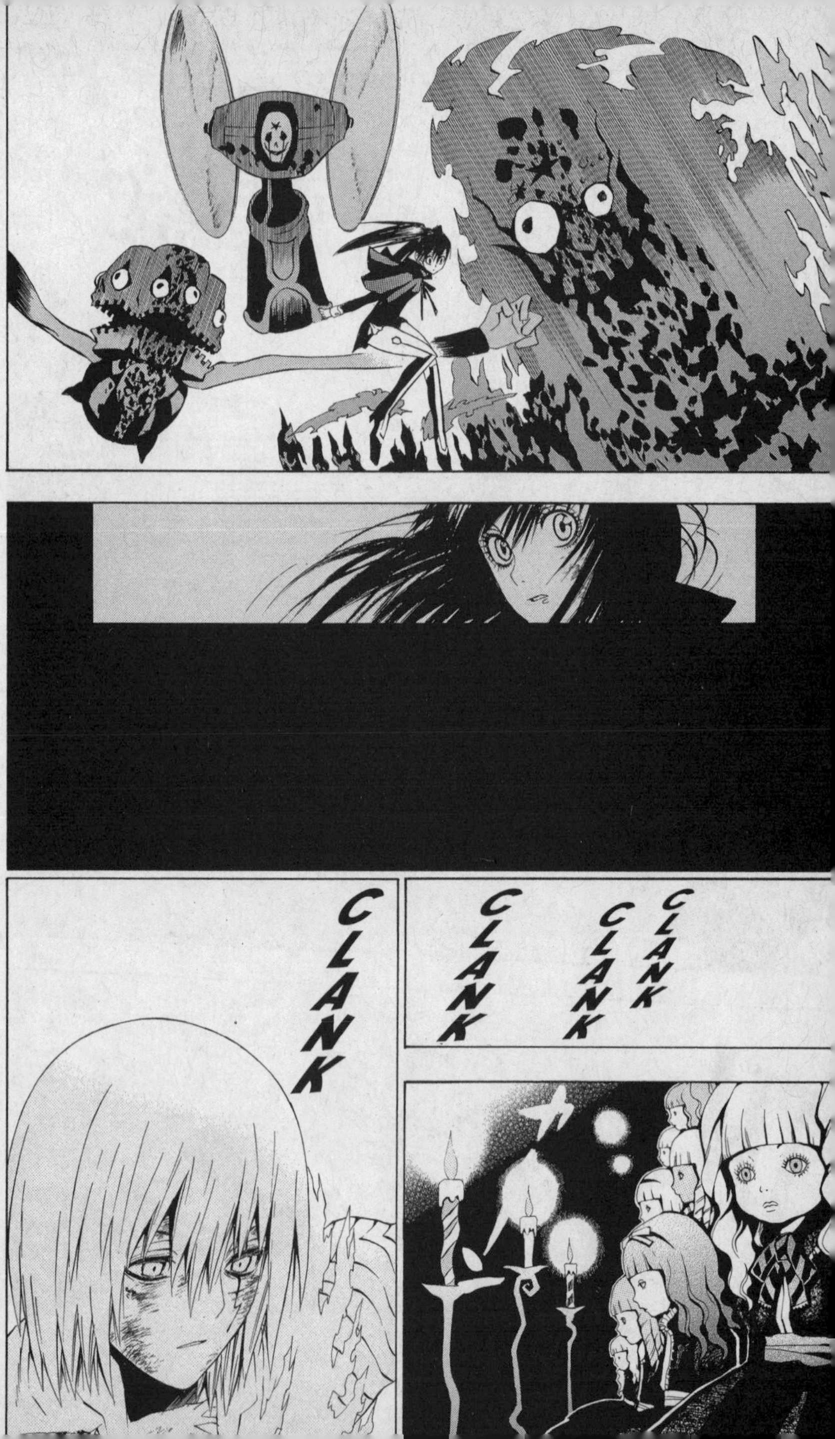
CLANK
CLANK
CLANK
CLANK

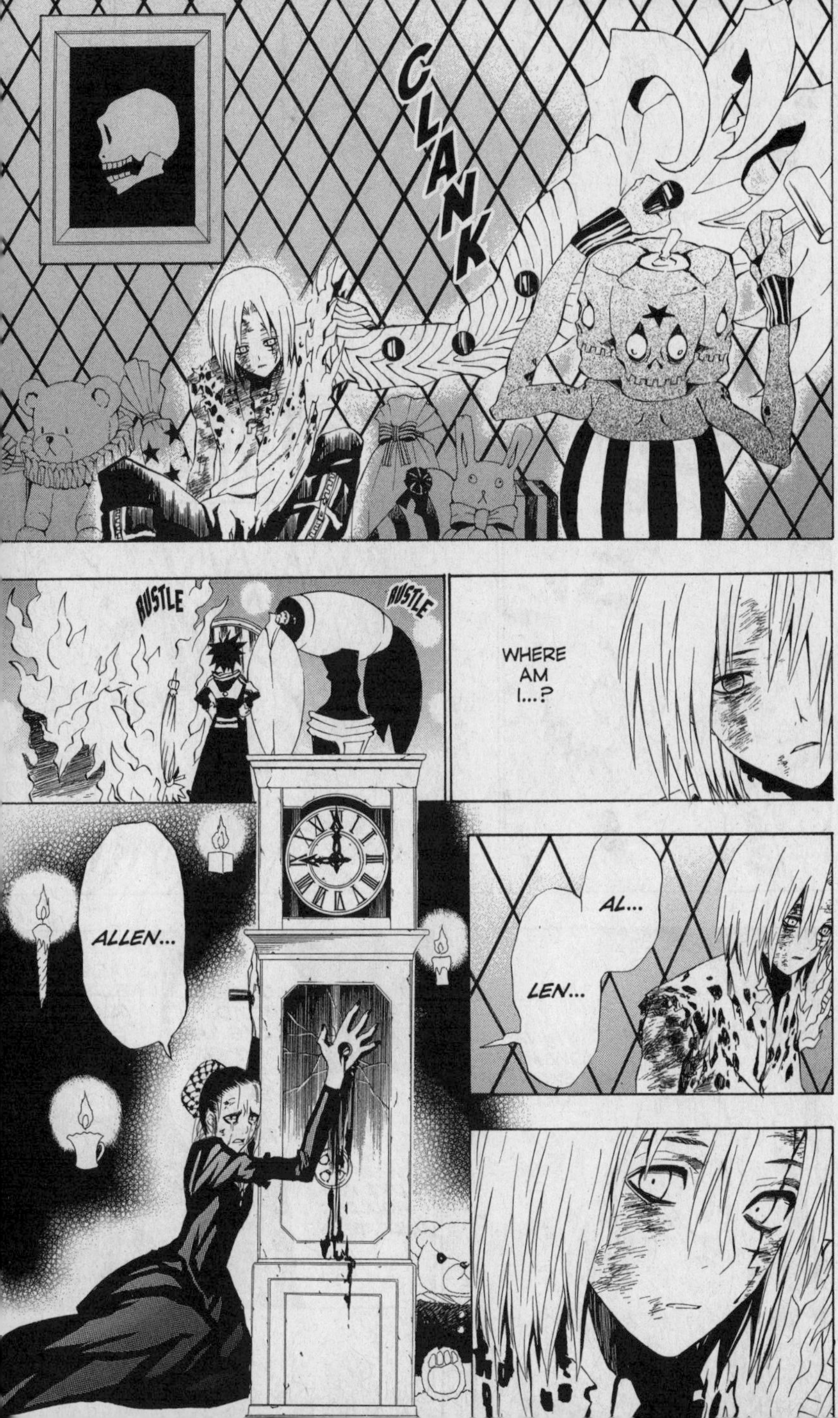
CLANK
WHERE AM I...?
RUSTLE
RUSTLE
AL...
LEN...
ALLEN...

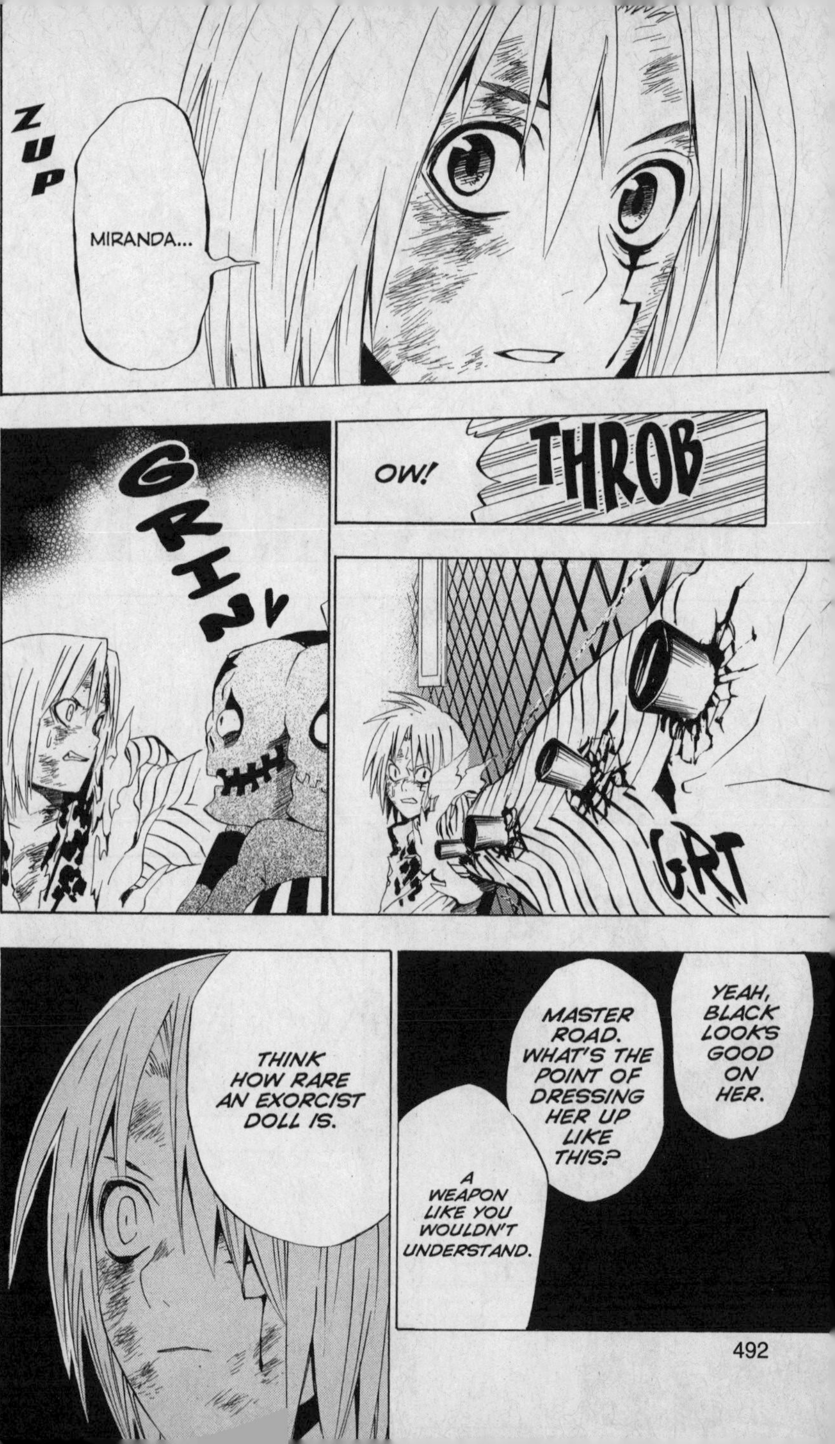
ZUP
MIRANDA...
OW!
THROB
GRT
GRIZ
YEAH, BLACK LOOKS GOOD ON HER.
MASTER ROAD. WHAT'S THE POINT OF DRESSING HER UP LIKE THIS?
A WEAPON LIKE YOU WOULDN'T UNDERSTAND.
THINK HOW RARE AN EXORCIST DOLL IS.

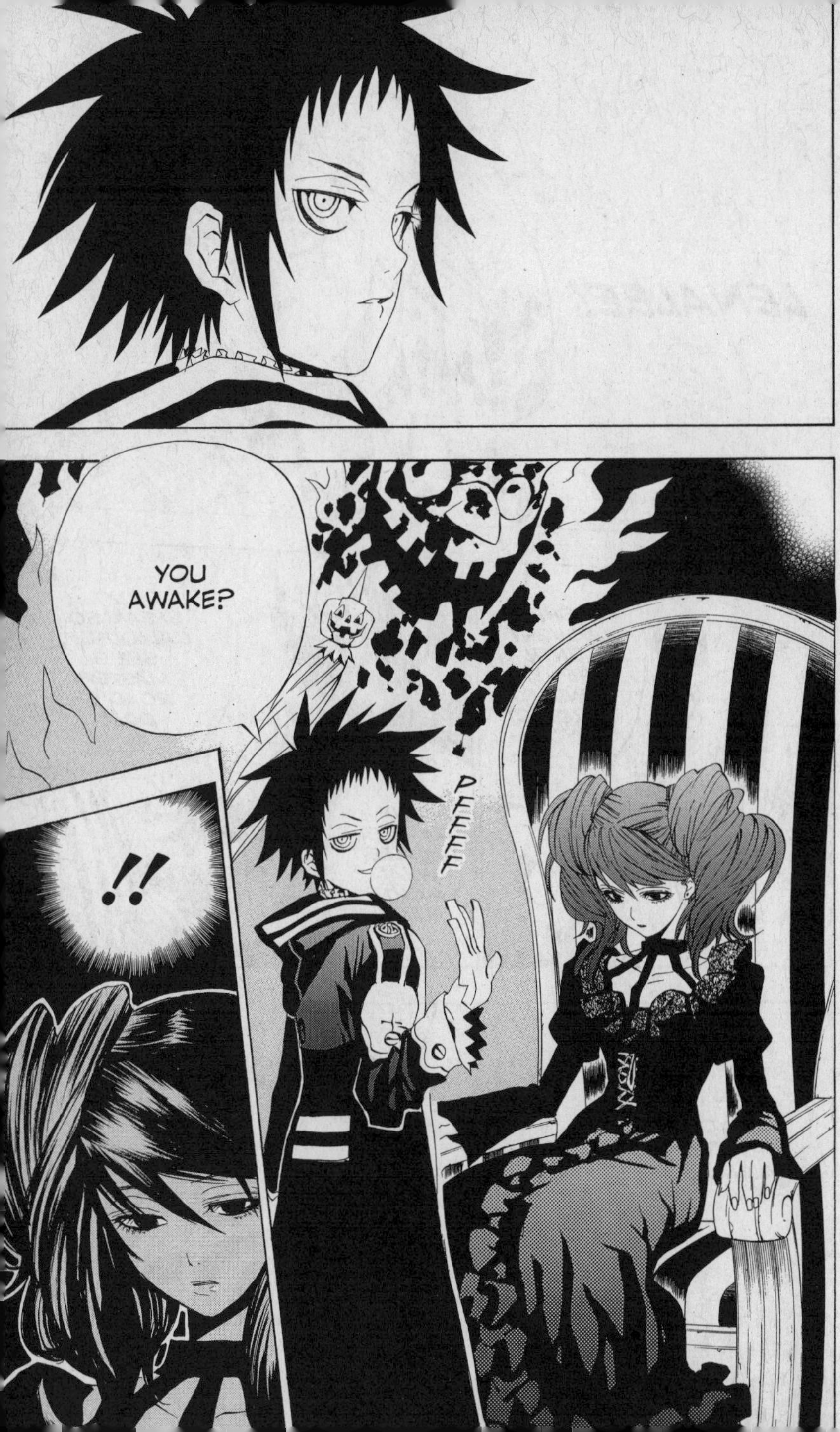
YOU AWAKE?
PFFFFF
!!

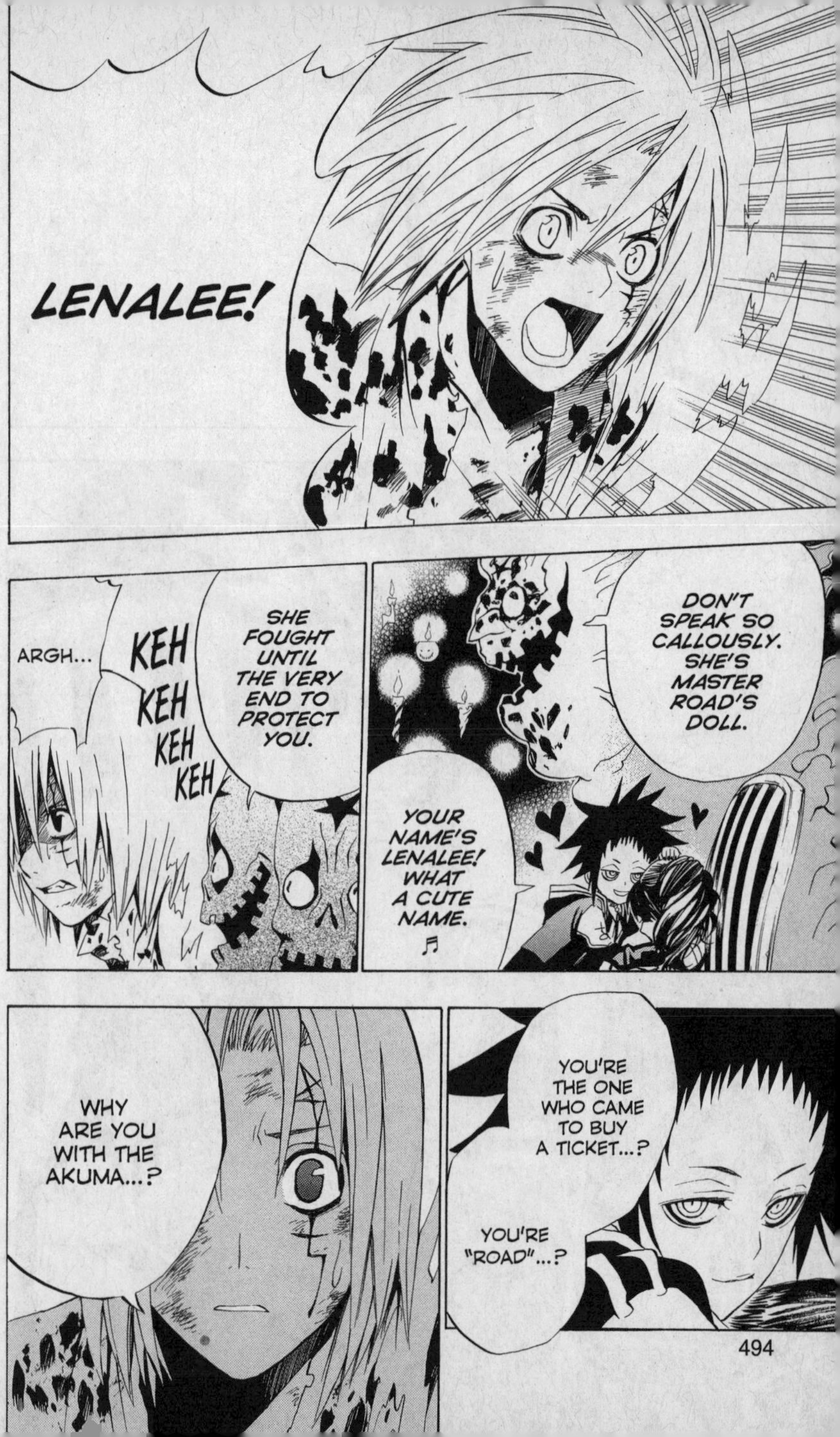
LENALEE!
DON'T SPEAK SO CALLOUSLY. SHE'S MASTER ROAD'S DOLL.
YOUR NAME'S LENALEE! WHAT A CUTE NAME. ♬
SHE FOUGHT UNTIL THE VERY END TO PROTECT YOU.
KEH KEH KEH KEH
ARGH...
YOU'RE THE ONE WHO CAME TO BUY A TICKET...?
YOU'RE "ROAD"...?
WHY ARE YOU WITH THE AKUMA...?

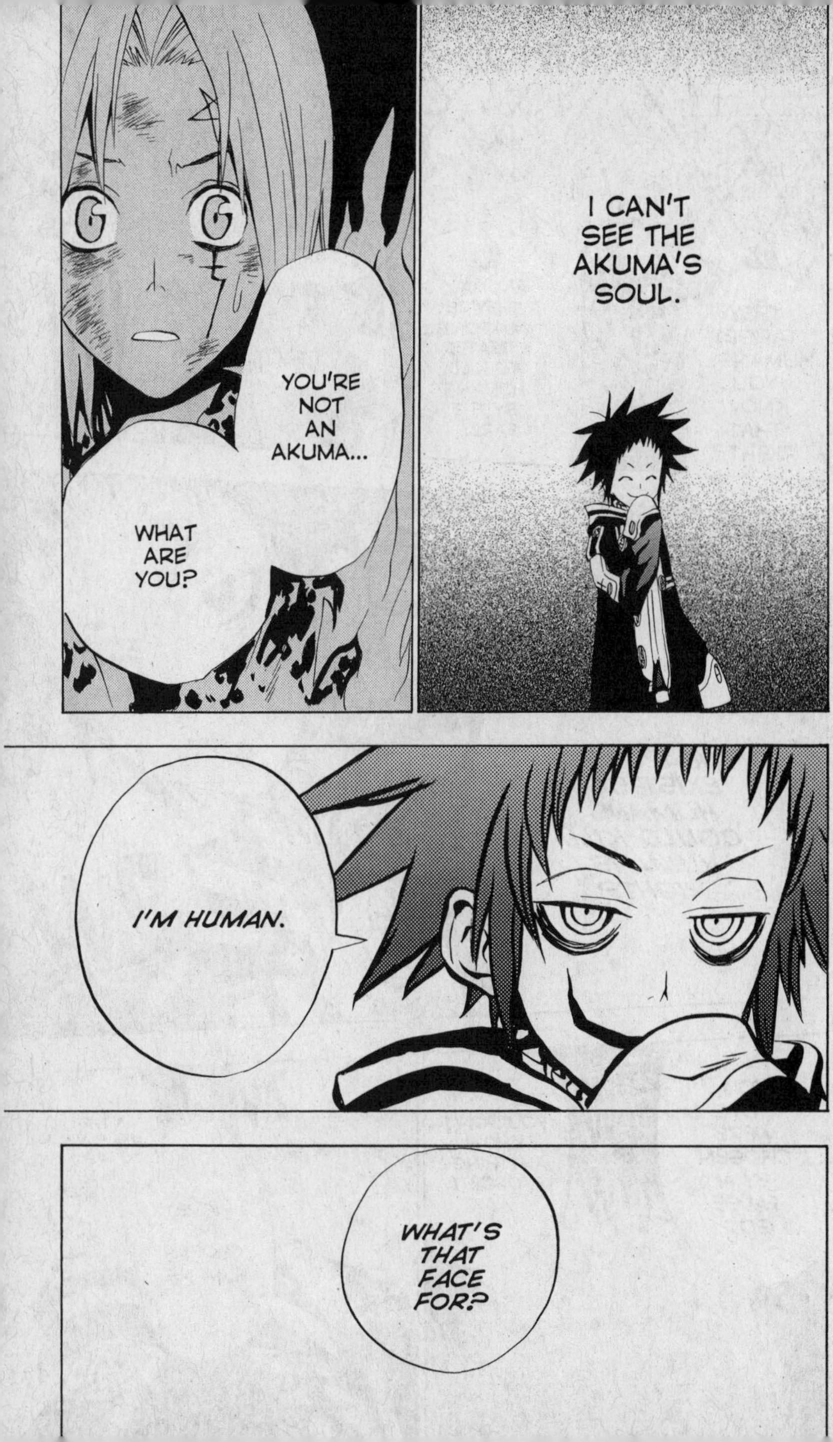
I CAN'T SEE THE AKUMA'S SOUL.
YOU'RE NOT AN AKUMA...
WHAT ARE YOU?
I'M HUMAN.
WHAT'S THAT FACE FOR?

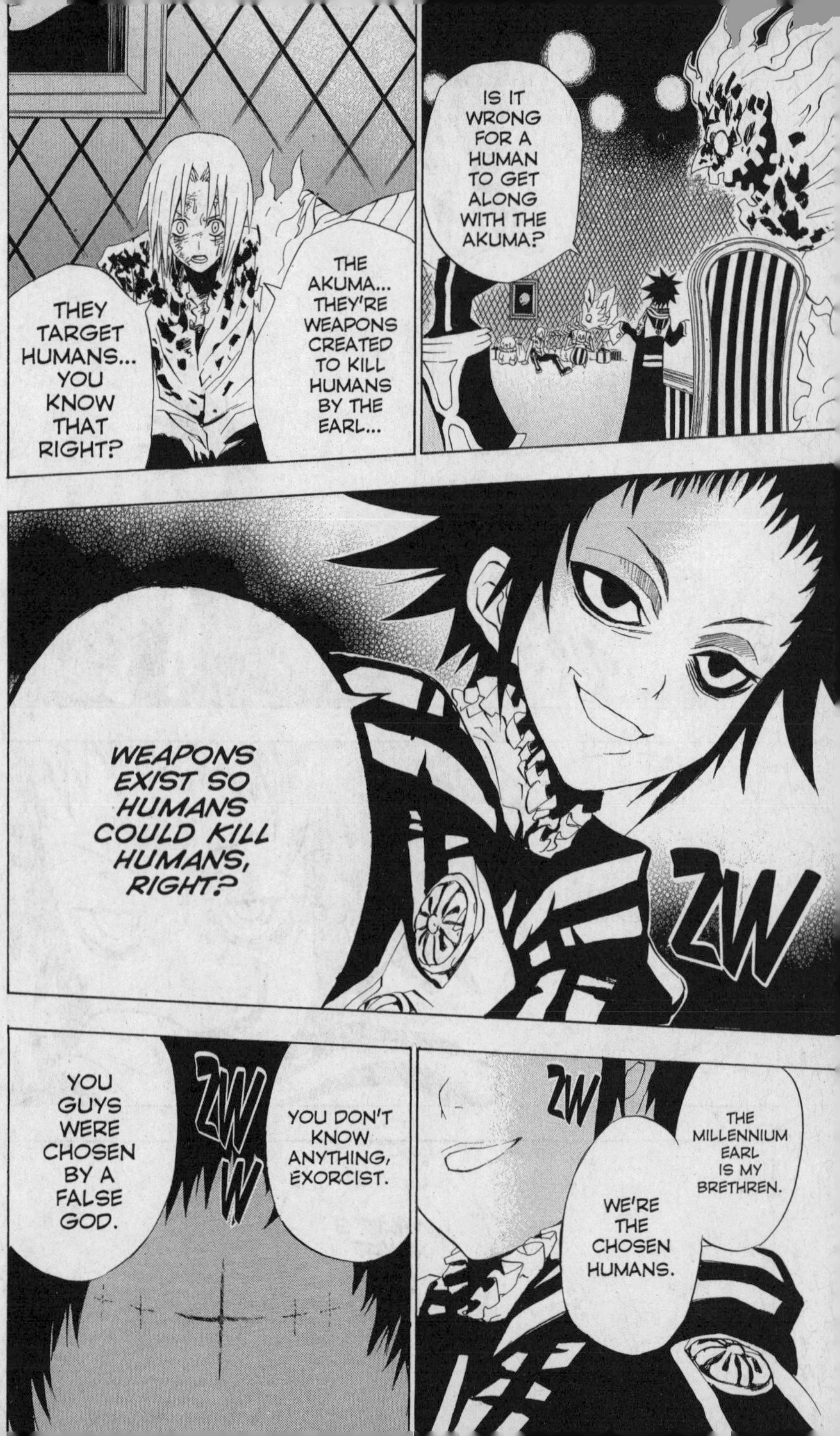
IS IT WRONG FOR A HUMAN TO GET ALONG WITH THE AKUMA?
THE AKUMA... THEY'RE WEAPONS CREATED TO KILL HUMANS BY THE EARL...
THEY TARGET HUMANS... YOU KNOW THAT RIGHT?
WEAPONS EXIST SO HUMANS COULD KILL HUMANS, RIGHT?
ZW
ZW
THE MILLENNIUM EARL IS MY BRETHREN.
WE'RE THE CHOSEN HUMANS.
ZW
W
YOU DON'T KNOW ANYTHING, EXORCIST.
YOU GUYS WERE CHOSEN BY A FALSE GOD.

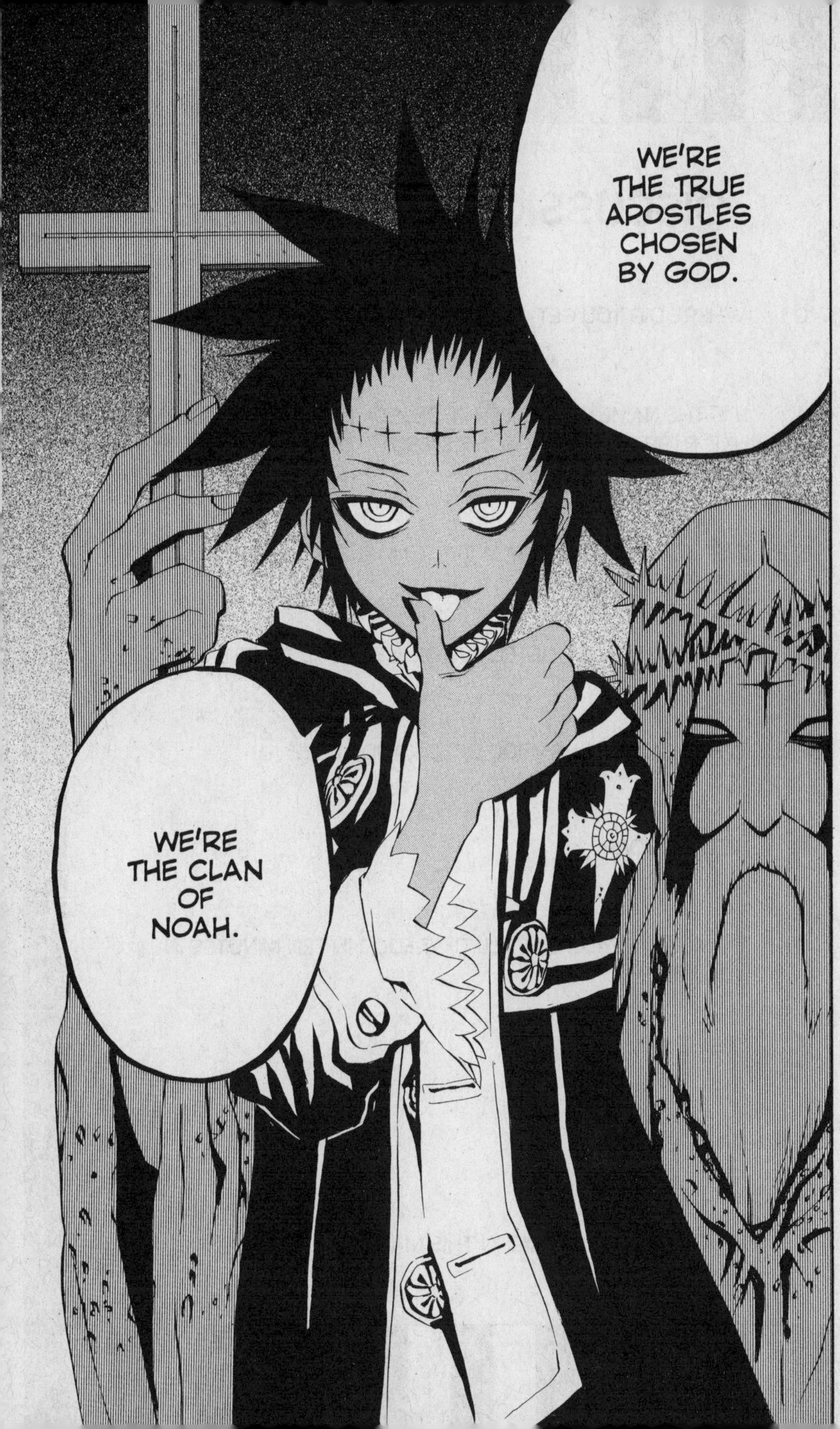
WE'RE THE TRUE APOSTLES CHOSEN BY GOD.
WE'RE THE CLAN OF NOAH.

DISCUSSION ROOM VOL. 6

Q 1. WHERE DID YOU GET TIMCANPY'S NAME FROM?

A. IT'S THE NAME OF A SILVER ACCESSORY BRAND NAME. I REALLY LIKE THEIR STUFF SO I'VE TAKEN SOME OTHER CHARACTER NAMES FROM THEM TOO.

Q 2. IF SECTION LEADER RIBA WERE TO MAKE A CAREER CHANGE WHAT WOULD HE DO?

A. HE'D BE A PRIVATE DETECTIVE OR A SCHOOL TEACHER.

Q 3. WHAT KIND OF SHAMPOO DOES KANDA USE?

A. HE USES SOAP.

Q 4. DID ALLEN REALLY EAT ALL THAT FOOD IN TEN MINUTES IN VOLUME TWO?

A. YES HE DID.

Q 5. WHAT IS LOVE?

A. ...I HOPE TO DRAW THAT IN THIS MANGA.

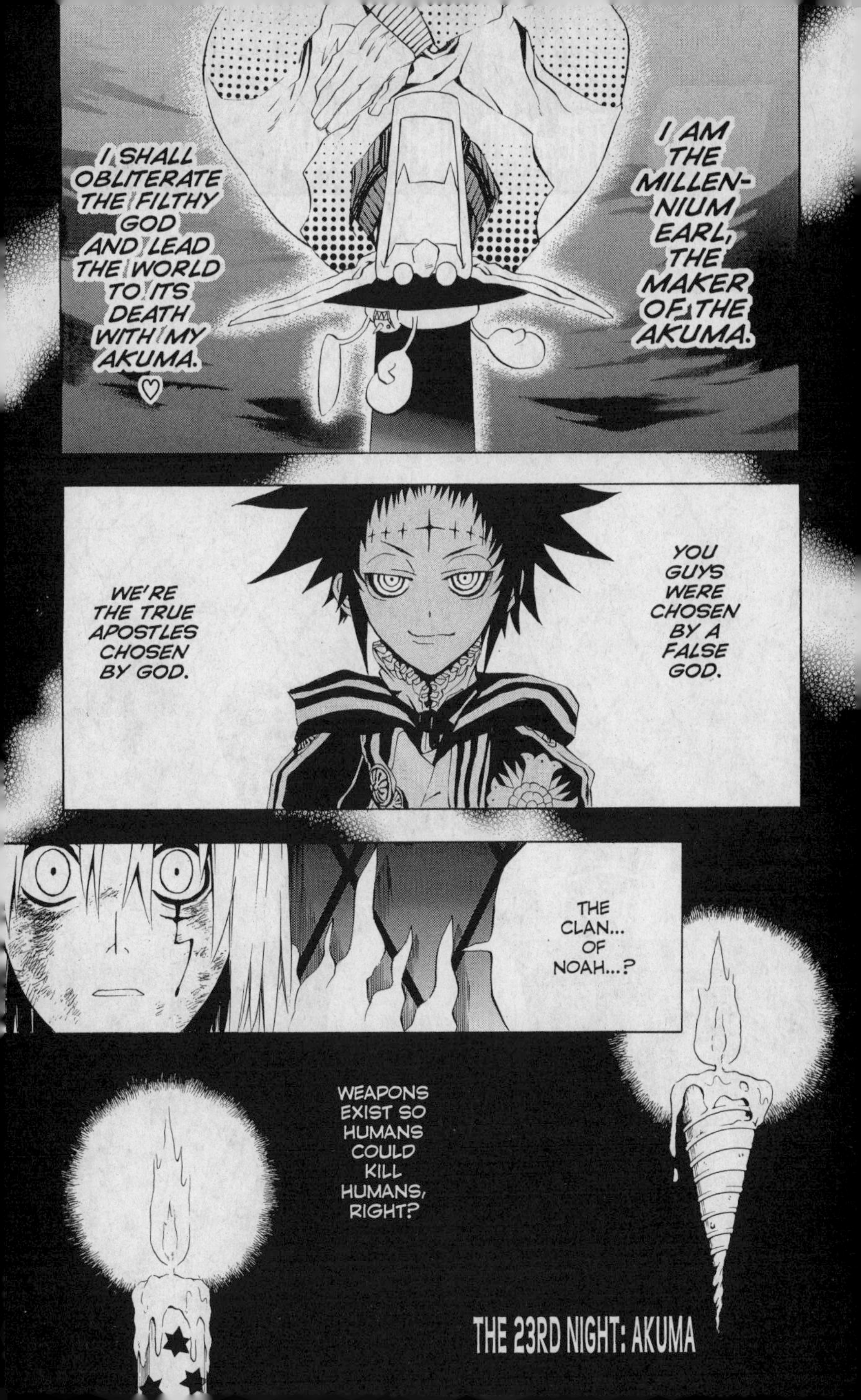
I AM THE MILLENNIUM EARL, THE MAKER OF THE AKUMA.
I SHALL OBLITERATE THE FILTHY GOD AND LEAD THE WORLD TO ITS DEATH WITH MY AKUMA. ♡
YOU GUYS WERE CHOSEN BY A FALSE GOD.
WE'RE THE TRUE APOSTLES CHOSEN BY GOD.
THE CLAN... OF NOAH...?
WEAPONS EXIST SO HUMANS COULD KILL HUMANS, RIGHT?
THE 23RD NIGHT: AKUMA

THE 23RD NIGHT: AKUMA

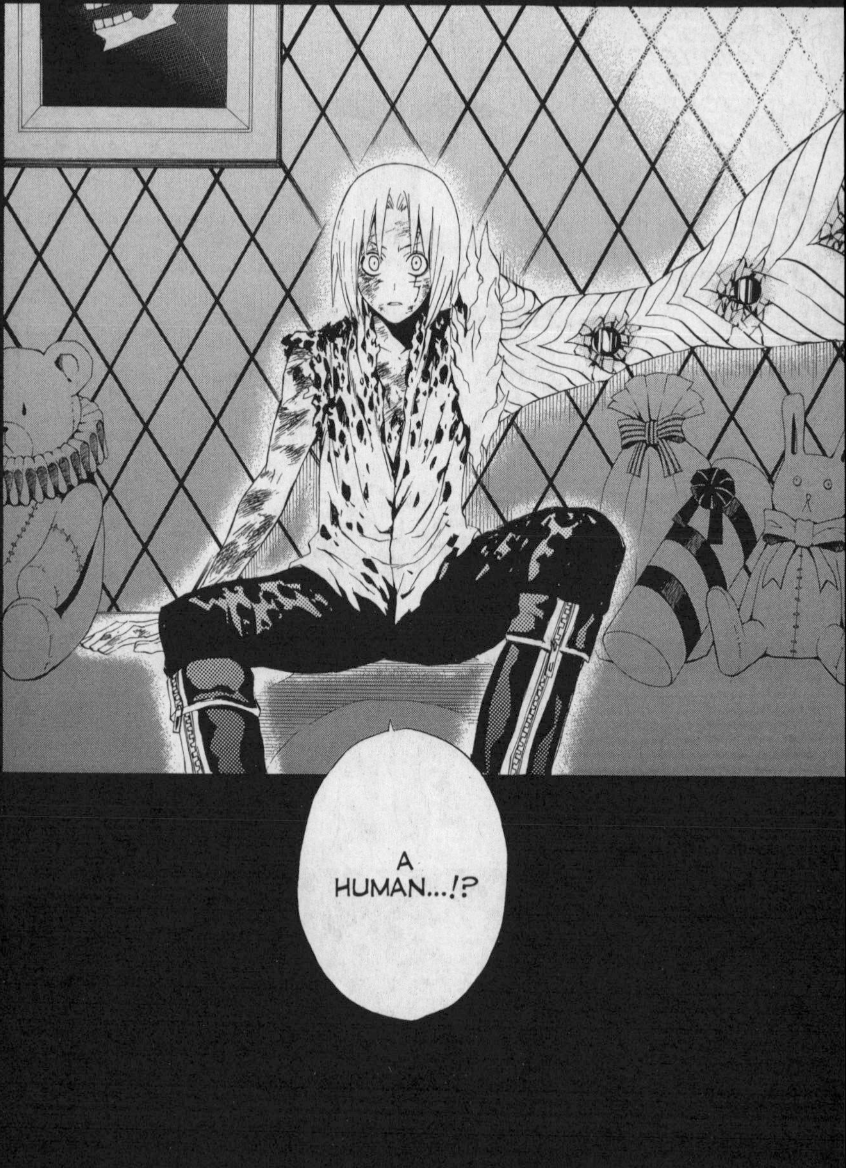
A HUMAN...!?

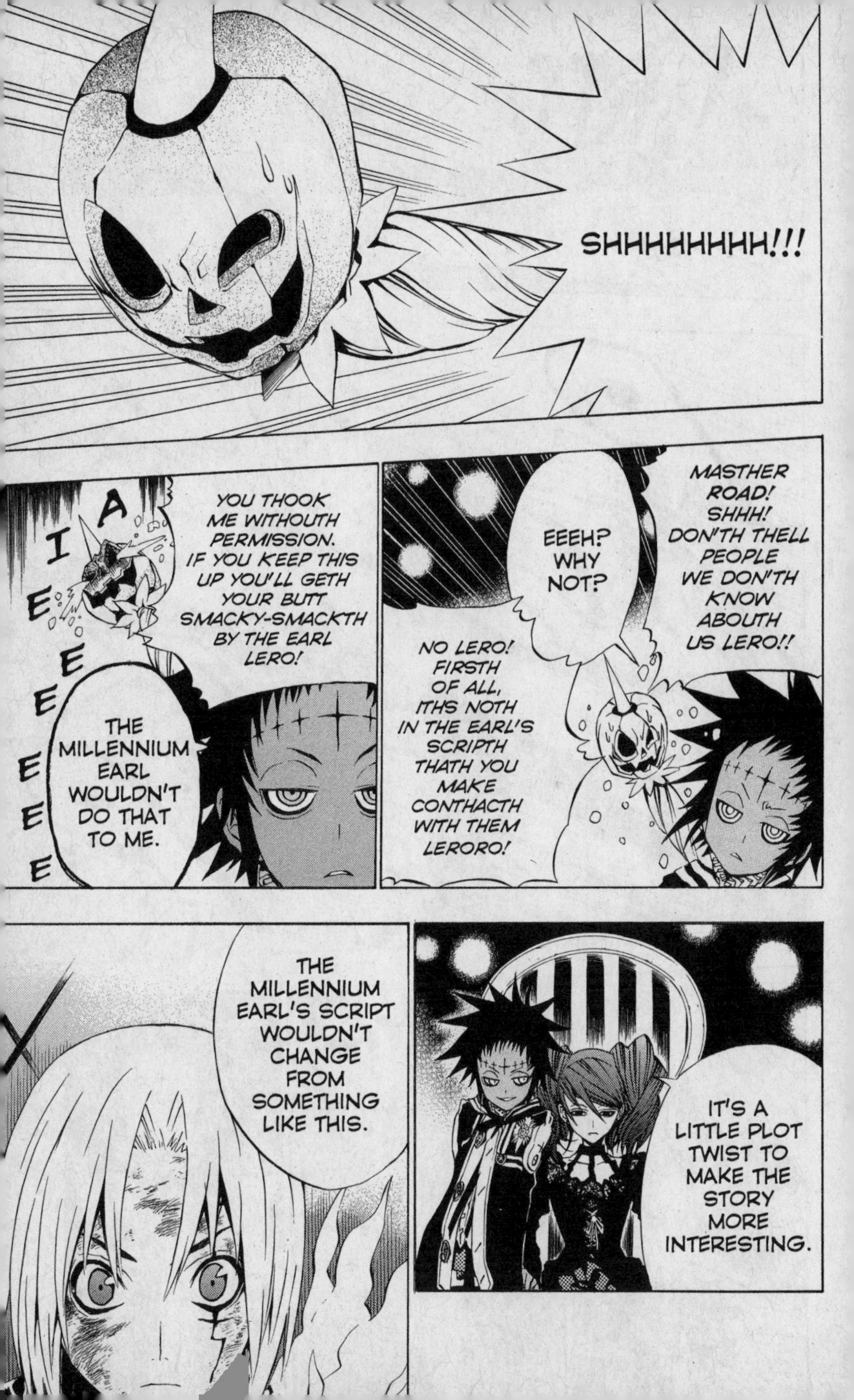
SHHHHHHHH!!!
MASTHER ROAD! SHHH! DON'TH THELL PEOPLE WE DON'TH KNOW ABOUTH US LERO!!
EEEH? WHY NOT?
NO LERO! FIRSTH OF ALL, ITHS NOTH IN THE EARL'S SCRIPTH THATH YOU MAKE CONTHACTH WITH THEM LERORO!
YOU THOOK ME WITHOUTH PERMISSION. IF YOU KEEP THIS UP YOU'LL GETH YOUR BUTT SMACKY-SMACKTH BY THE EARL LERO!
AIEEEEEE
THE MILLENNIUM EARL WOULDN'T DO THAT TO ME.
IT'S A LITTLE PLOT TWIST TO MAKE THE STORY MORE INTERESTING.
THE MILLENNIUM EARL'S SCRIPT WOULDN'T CHANGE FROM SOMETHING LIKE THIS.

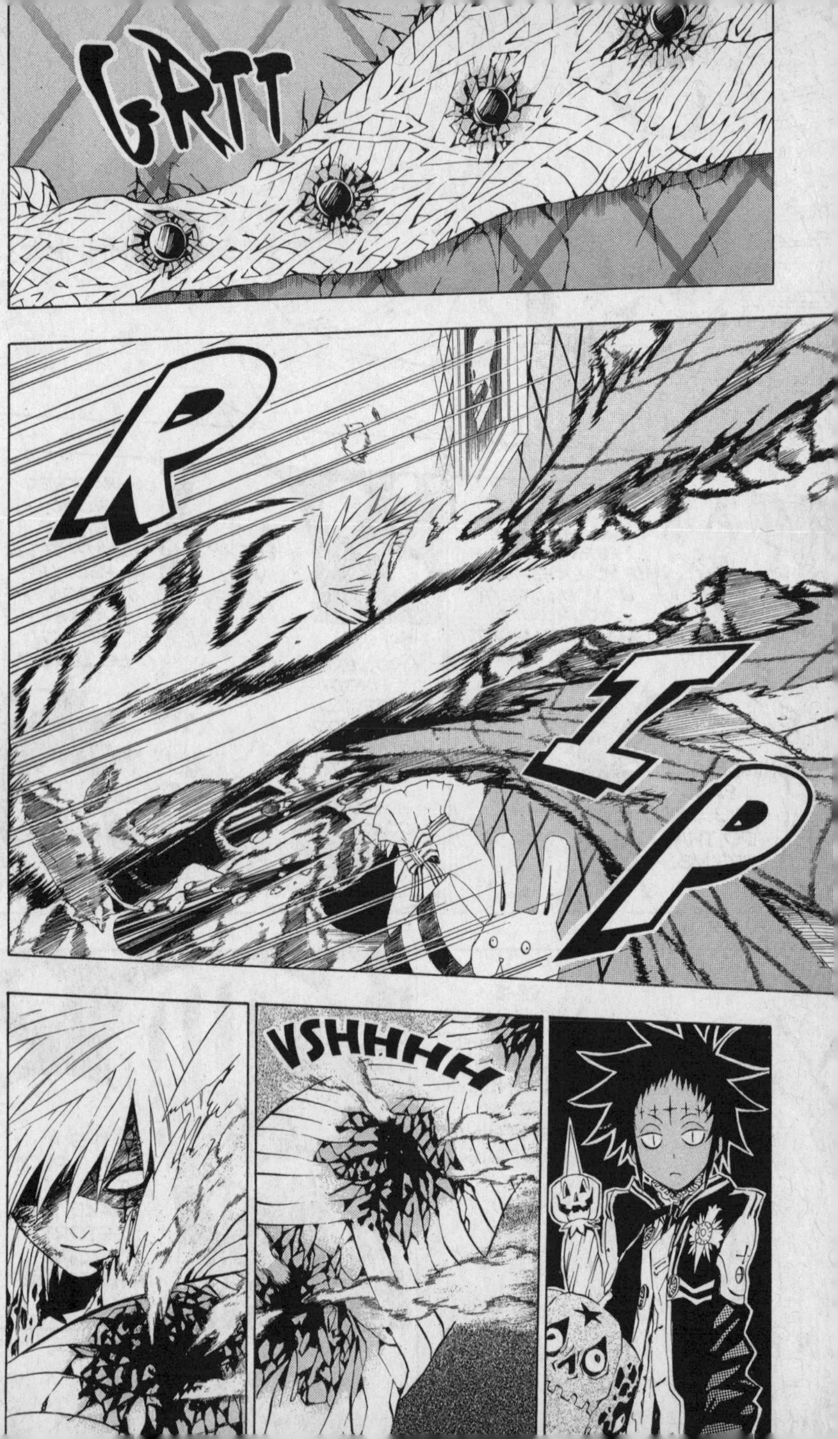
GRTT
RIP
VSHHHH

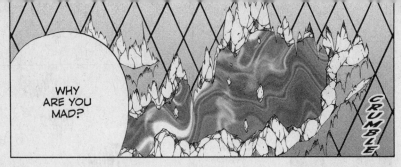

WHY ARE YOU MAD?

CRUMBLE

YOU CAN'T BELIEVE I'M HUMAN?

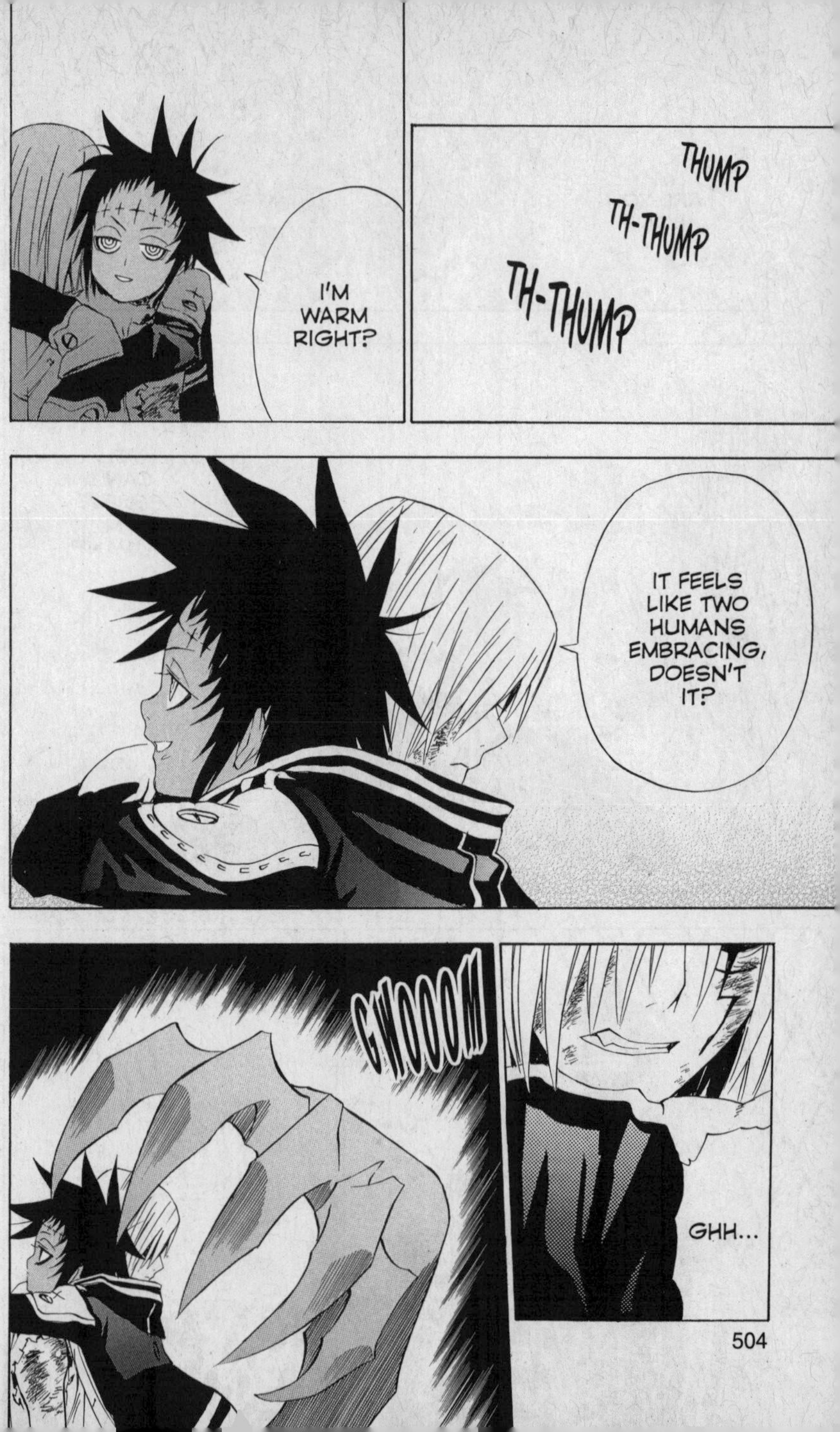
THUMP
TH-THUMP
TH-THUMP
I'M WARM RIGHT?
IT FEELS LIKE TWO HUMANS EMBRACING, DOESN'T IT?
GHH...
GWOOOM

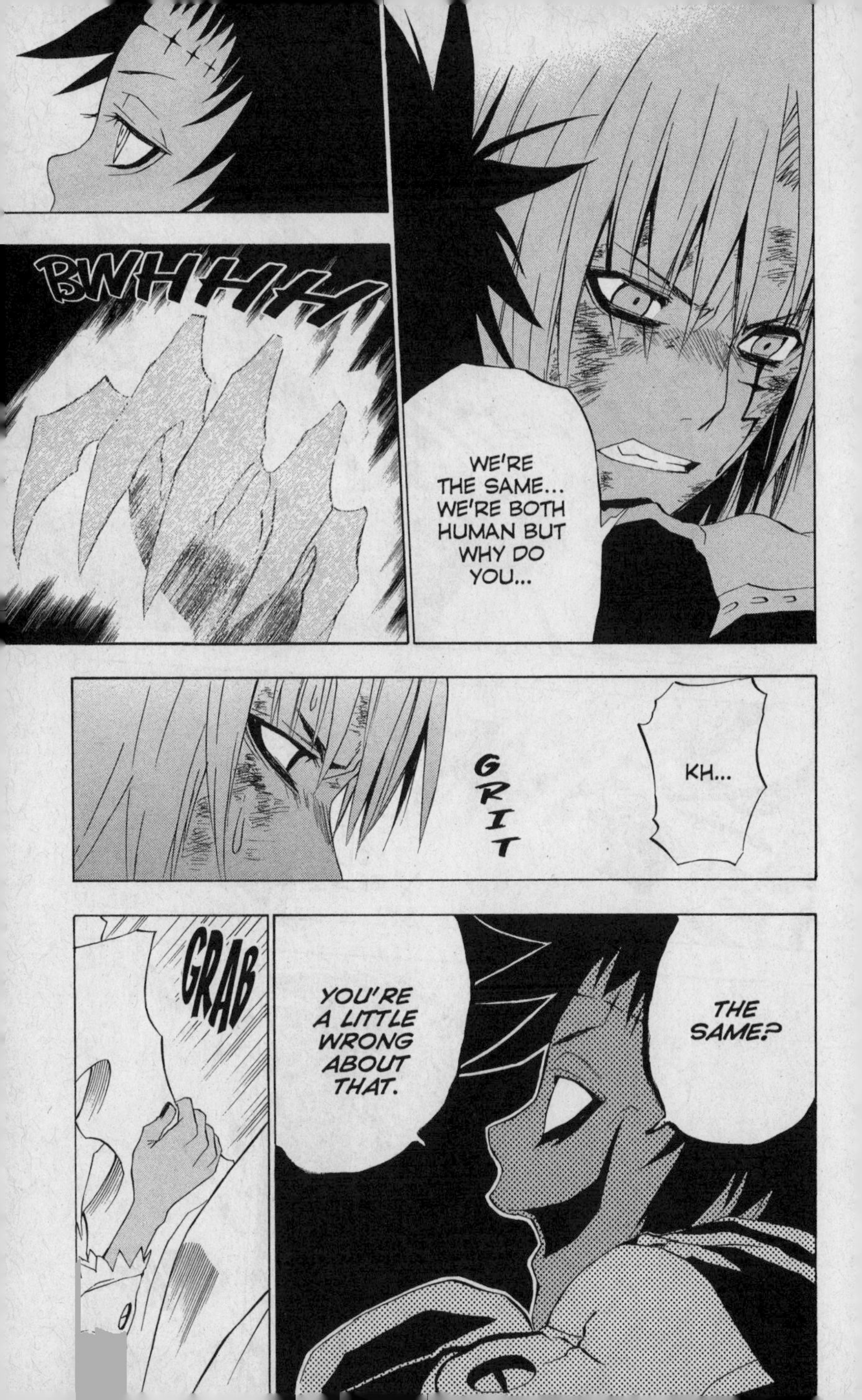
WE'RE THE SAME... WE'RE BOTH HUMAN BUT WHY DO YOU...
BWHHHH
KH...
GRIT
THE SAME?
YOU'RE A LITTLE WRONG ABOUT THAT.
GRAB

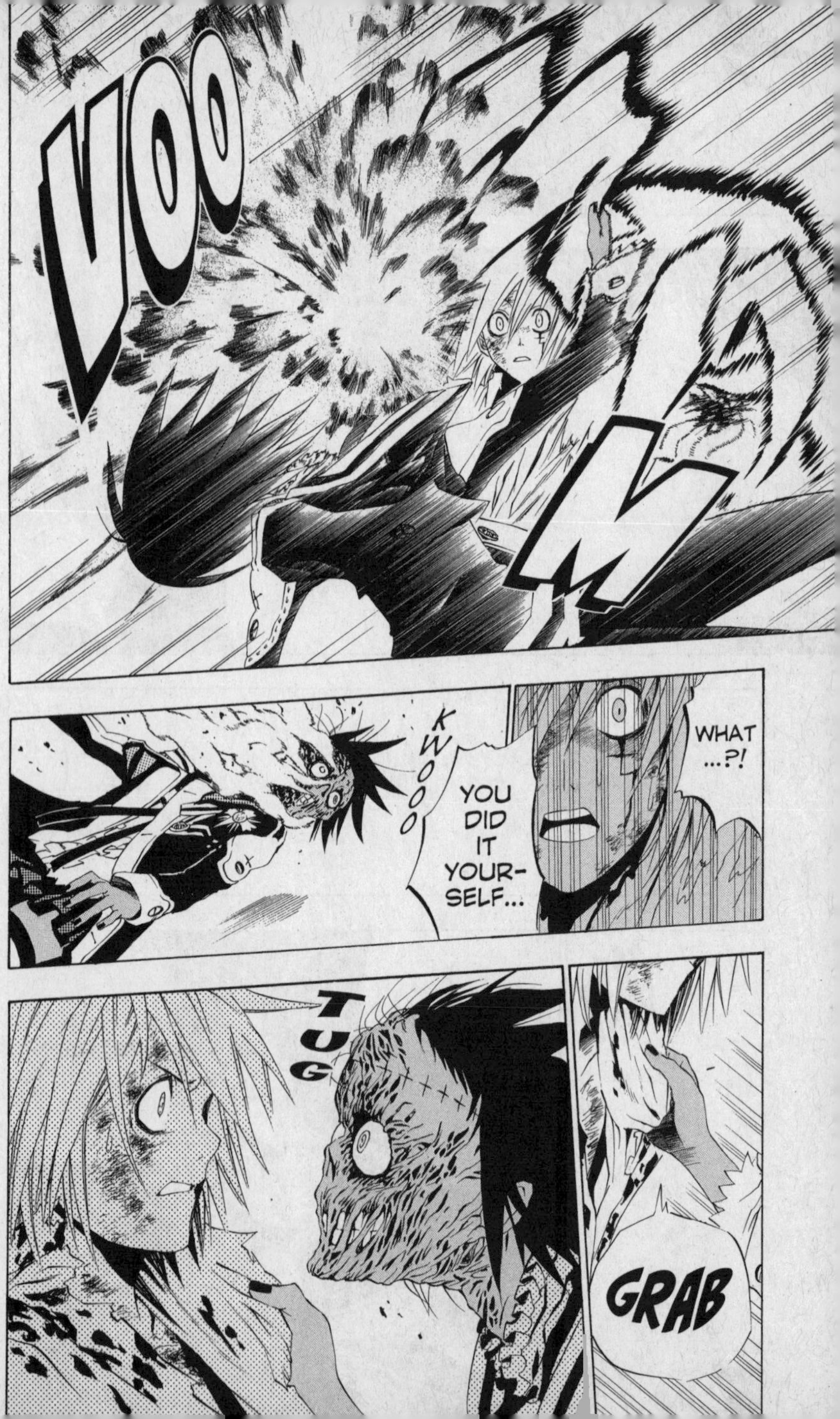
VOOM
WHAT ...?!
KWOOOO
YOU DID IT YOUR-SELF...
TUG
GRAB

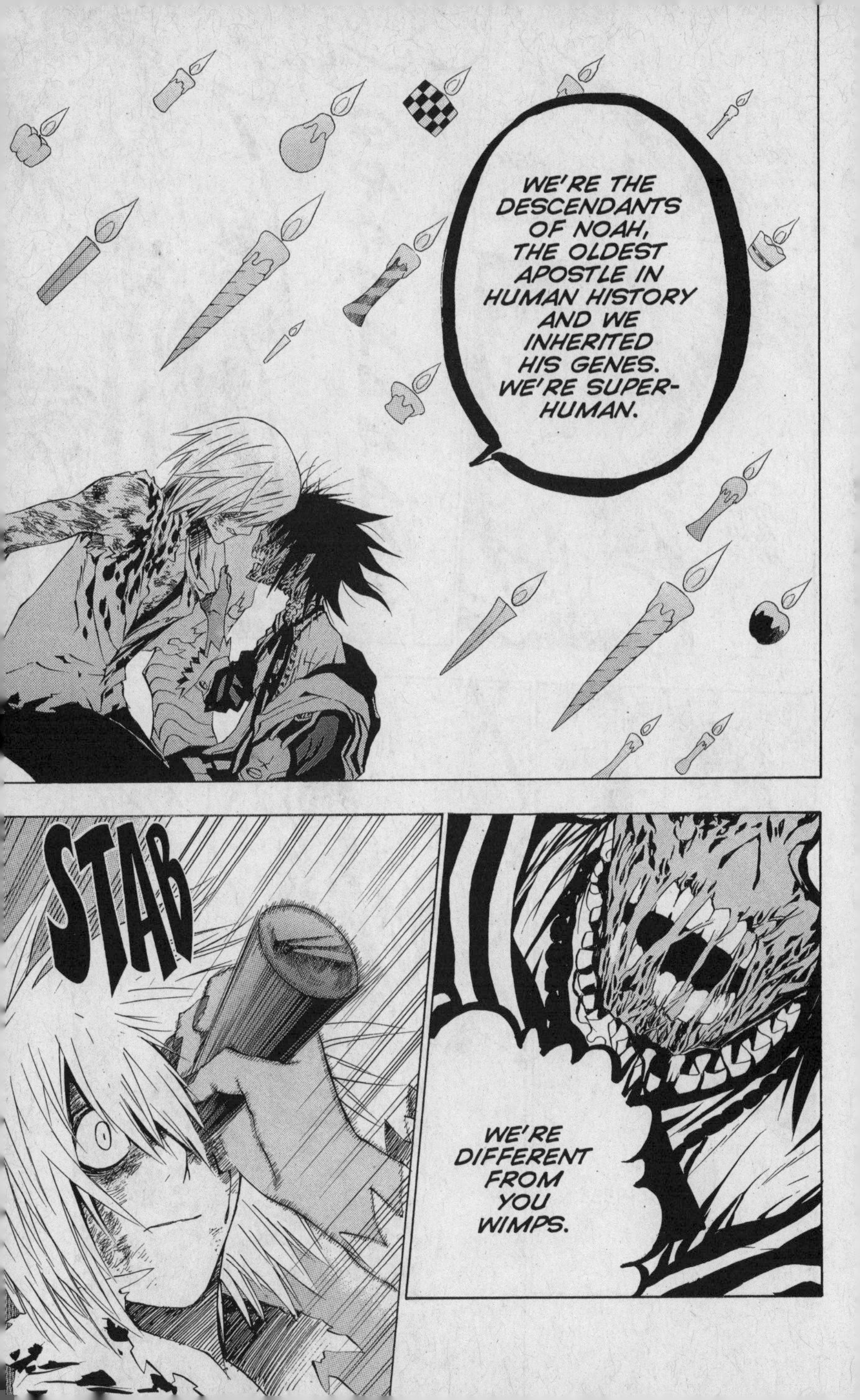
WE'RE THE DESCENDANTS OF NOAH, THE OLDEST APOSTLE IN HUMAN HISTORY AND WE INHERITED HIS GENES. WE'RE SUPER-HUMAN.
WE'RE DIFFERENT FROM YOU WIMPS.
STAB

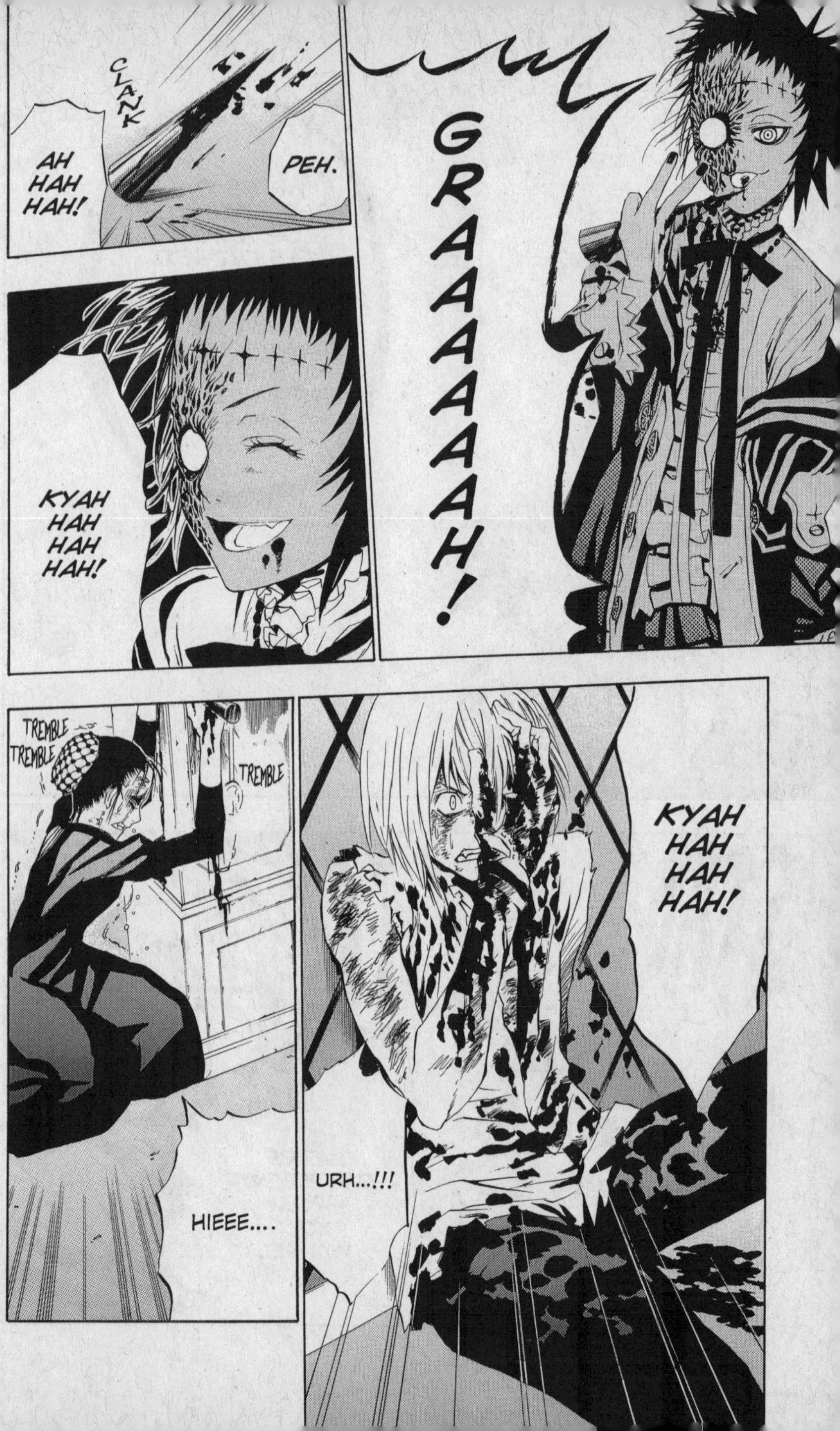
GRAAAAAAAH!
CLANK
PEH.
AH HAH HAH!
KYAH HAH HAH HAH!
KYAH HAH HAH HAH!
URH...!!!
TREMBLE TREMBLE
TREMBLE
HIEEE....

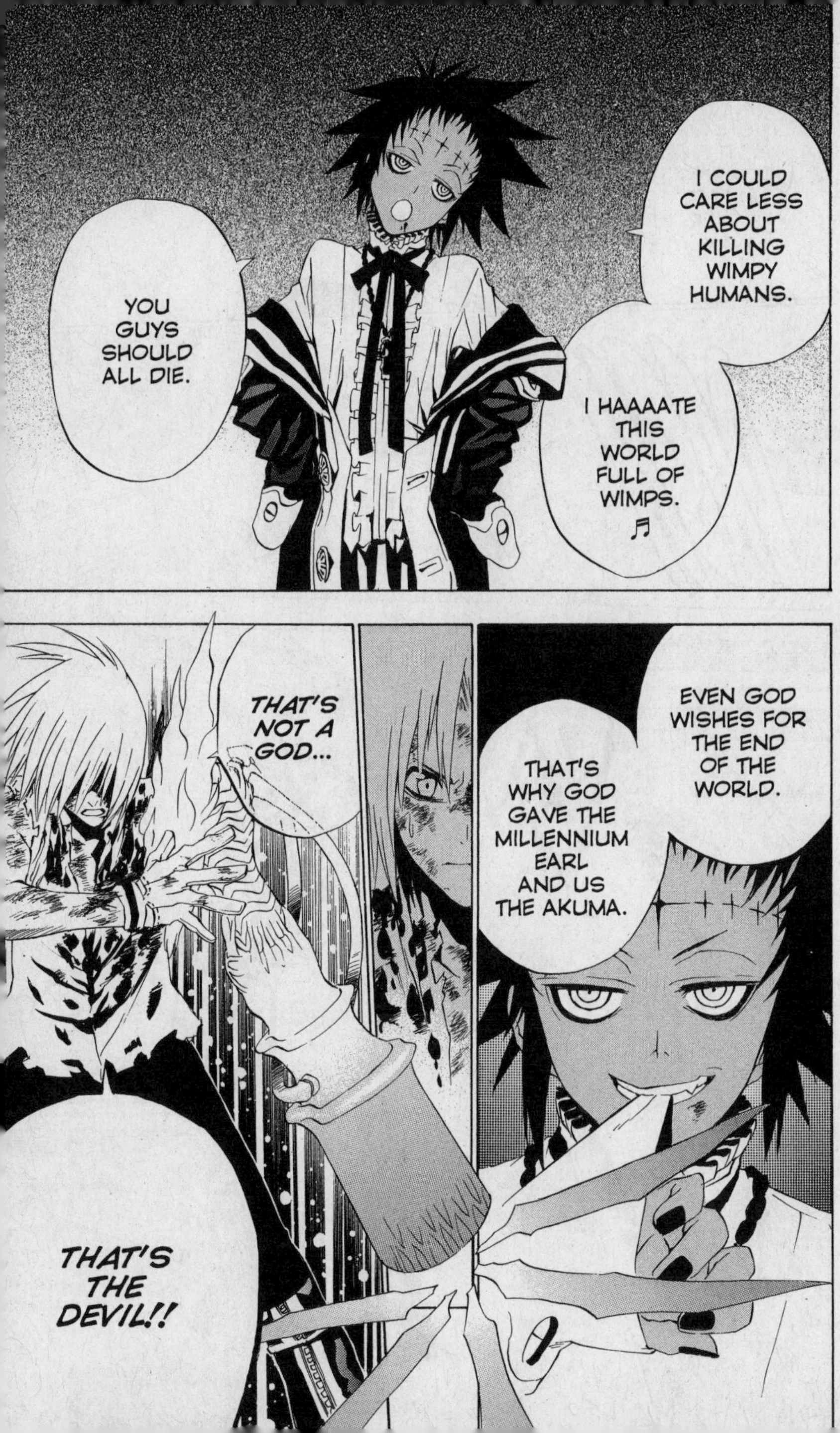
I COULD CARE LESS ABOUT KILLING WIMPY HUMANS.
I HAAAATE THIS WORLD FULL OF WIMPS. ♬
YOU GUYS SHOULD ALL DIE.
EVEN GOD WISHES FOR THE END OF THE WORLD.
THAT'S WHY GOD GAVE THE MILLENNIUM EARL AND US THE AKUMA.
THAT'S NOT A GOD...
THAT'S THE DEVIL!!

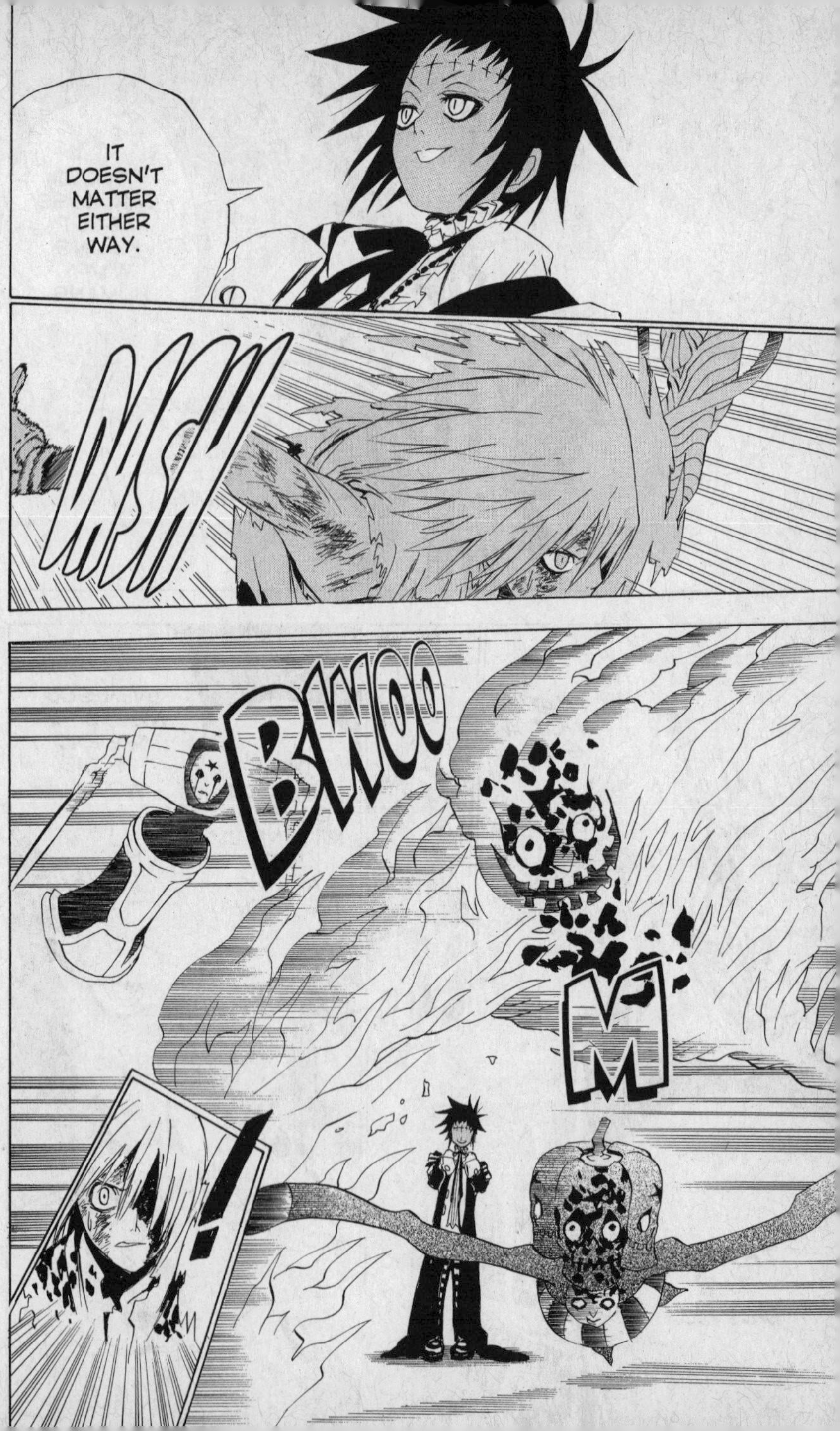
IT DOESN'T MATTER EITHER WAY.
DASH
BWOOM

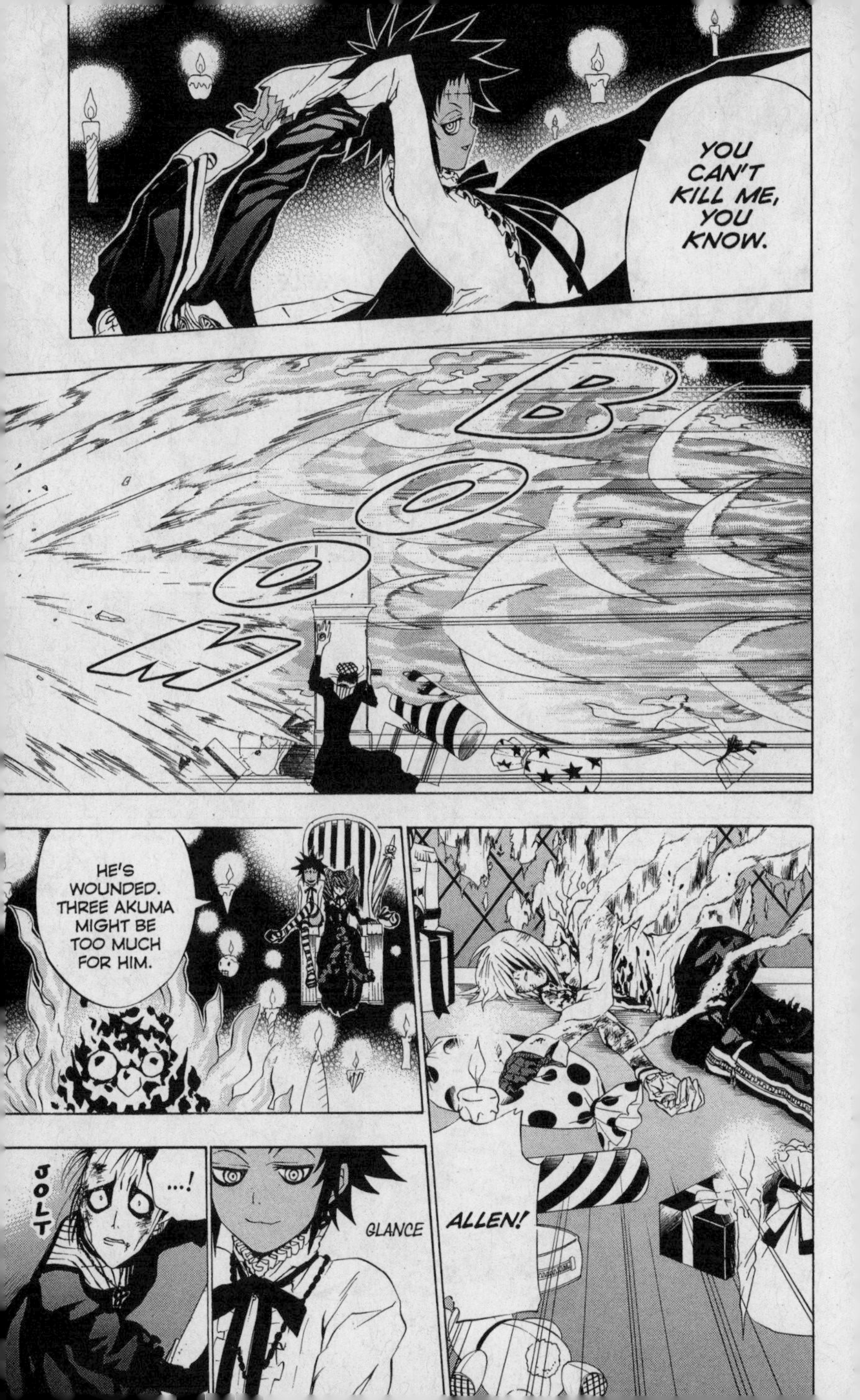
YOU CAN'T KILL ME, YOU KNOW.
BOOOM
ALLEN!
HE'S WOUNDED. THREE AKUMA MIGHT BE TOO MUCH FOR HIM.
GLANCE
JOLT
...!

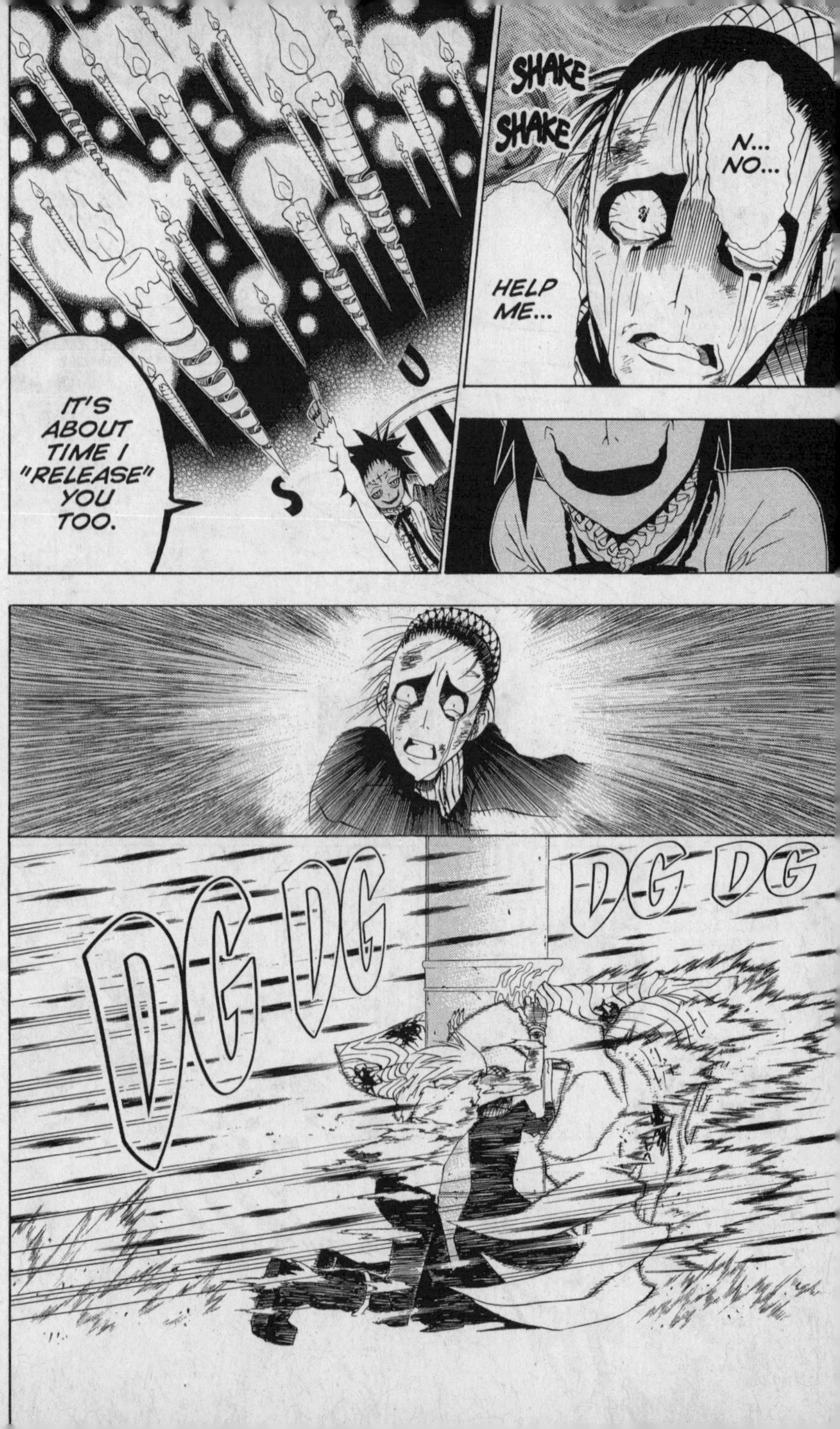
SHAKE
SHAKE
N... NO...
HELP ME...
IT'S ABOUT TIME I "RELEASE" YOU TOO.
DG DG
DG DG

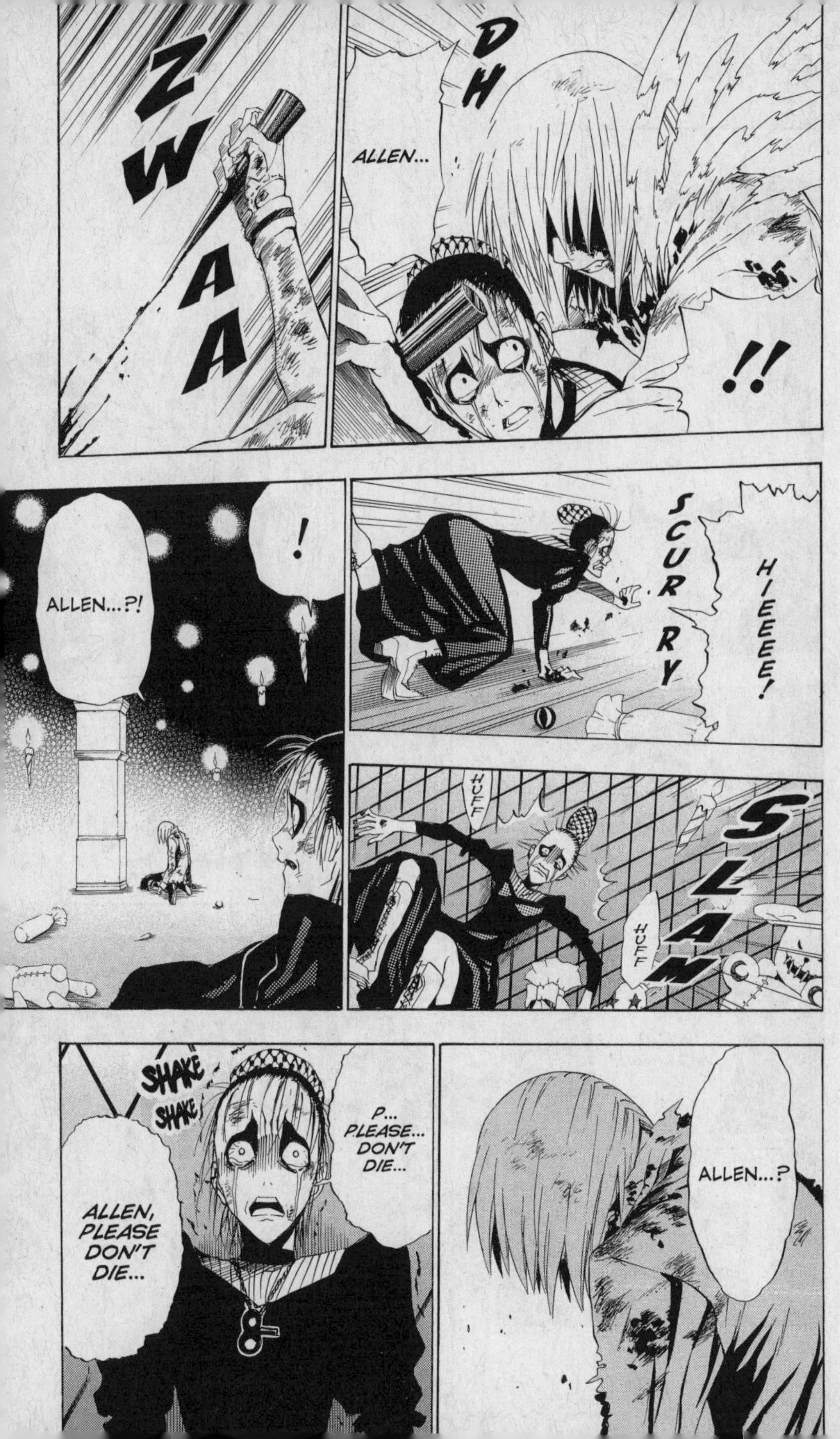
DH
ALLEN...
!!
ZWAA
HIEEEE!
SCURRY
SLAM
HUFF
HUFF
!
ALLEN...?!
ALLEN...?
P... PLEASE... DON'T DIE...
SHAKE SHAKE
ALLEN, PLEASE DON'T DIE...

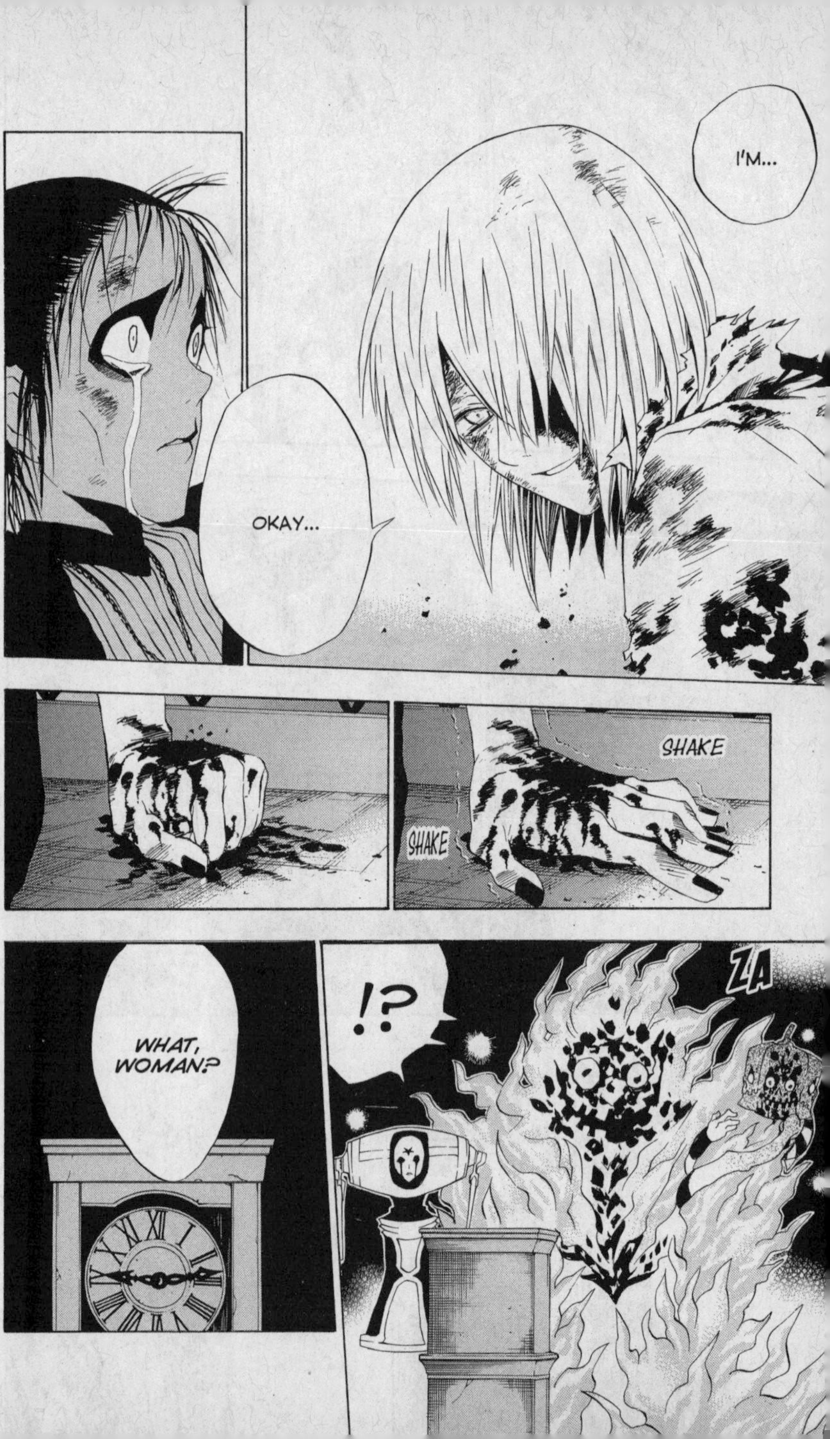
I'M...
OKAY...
SHAKE
SHAKE
ZA
!?
WHAT, WOMAN?

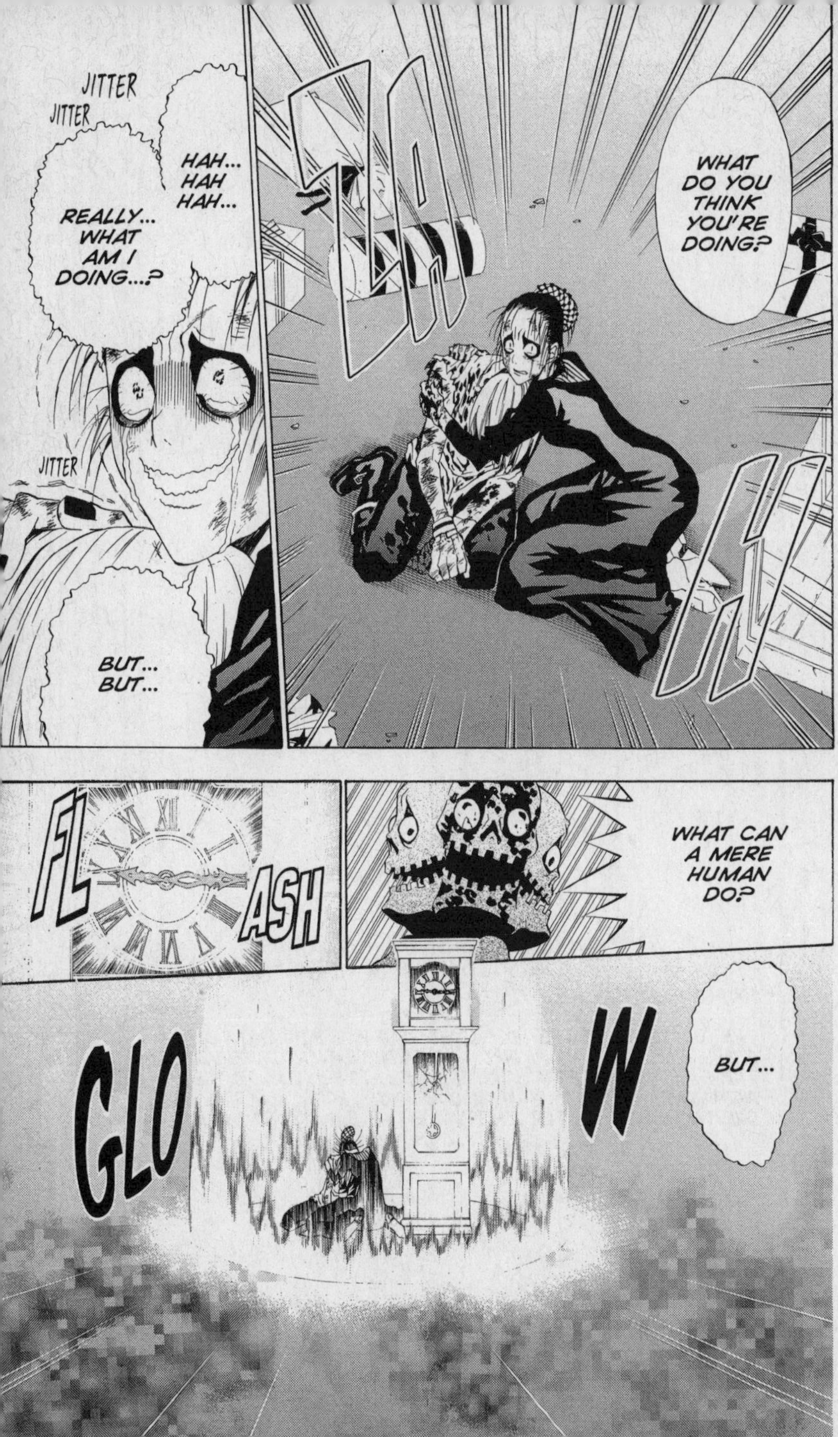
WHAT DO YOU THINK YOU'RE DOING?
JITTER JITTER
HAH... HAH HAH...
REALLY... WHAT AM I DOING...?
JITTER
BUT... BUT...
WHAT CAN A MERE HUMAN DO?
FLASH
GLOW
BUT...

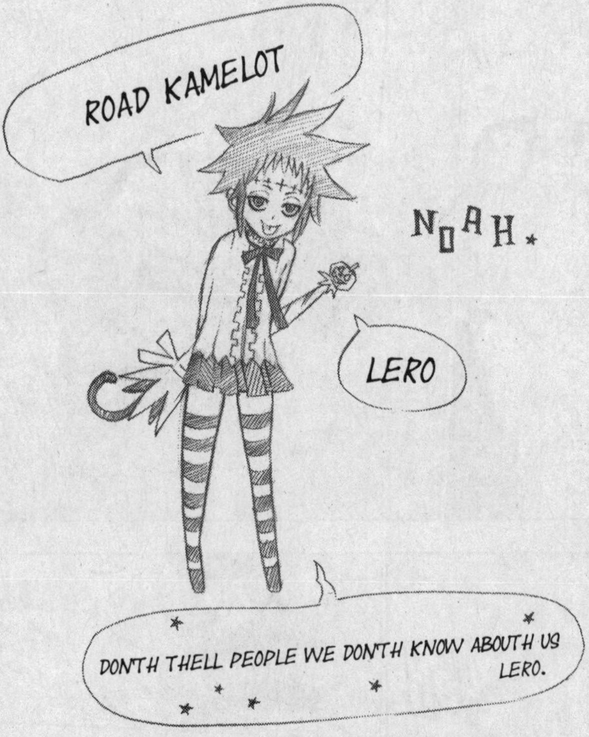
ROAD KAMELOT
NOAH.
LERO
DONTH THELL PEOPLE WE DONTH KNOW ABOUTH US LERO.

MY PROFILE DETAILS ARE STILL A SECRET.

THE QUESTION I GOT THE MOST ABOUT ROAD WAS IF SHE IS A BOY OR A GIRL. SHE'S A FEMALE, A GIRL. HER FAVORITE THINGS ARE CANDY AND THE EARL. SHE HATES HUMANS. SHE LIKES TO BE MEAN TO THE AKUMA AND LIKES TO PLAY JOKES ON PEOPLE, ESPECIALLY THE EARL. SHE TAKES LERO ALL THE TIME WHILE THE EARL TAKES A NAP.

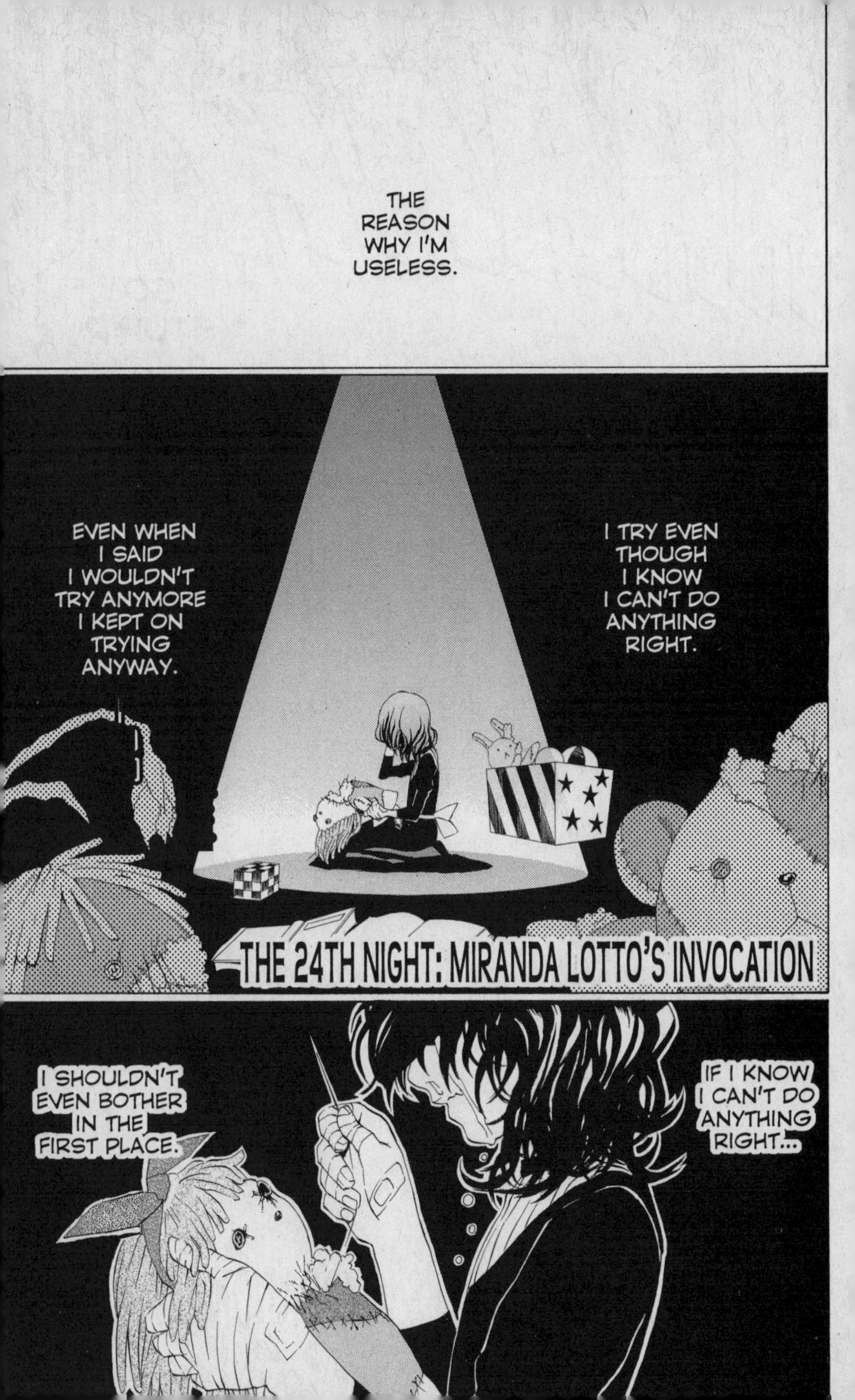
THE REASON WHY I'M USELESS.
I TRY EVEN THOUGH I KNOW I CAN'T DO ANYTHING RIGHT.
EVEN WHEN I SAID I WOULDN'T TRY ANYMORE I KEPT ON TRYING ANYWAY.
THE 24TH NIGHT: MIRANDA LOTTO'S INVOCATION
IF I KNOW I CAN'T DO ANYTHING RIGHT...
I SHOULDN'T EVEN BOTHER IN THE FIRST PLACE.

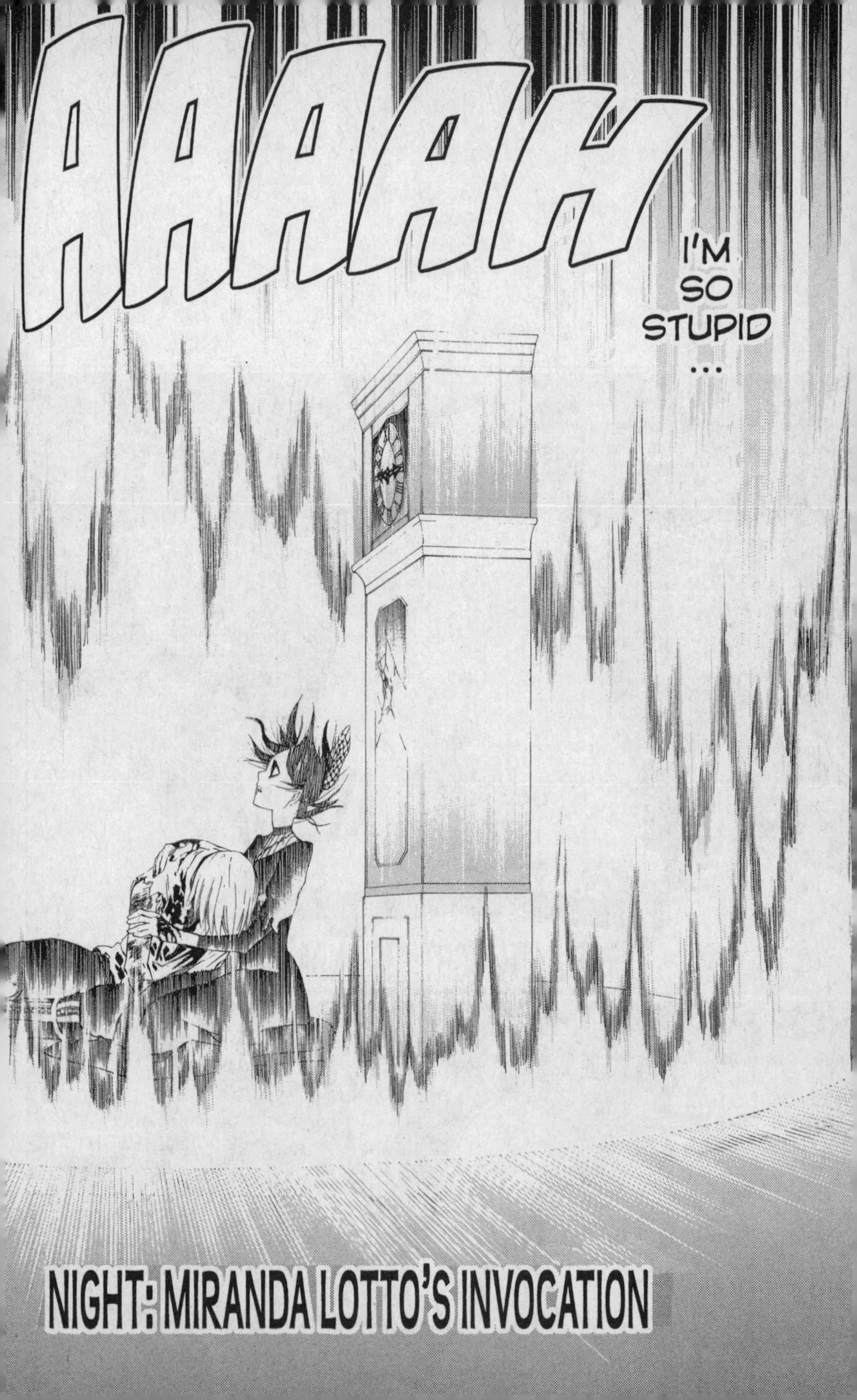
AAAAH
I'M SO STUPID ...

NIGHT: MIRANDA LOTTO'S INVOCATION

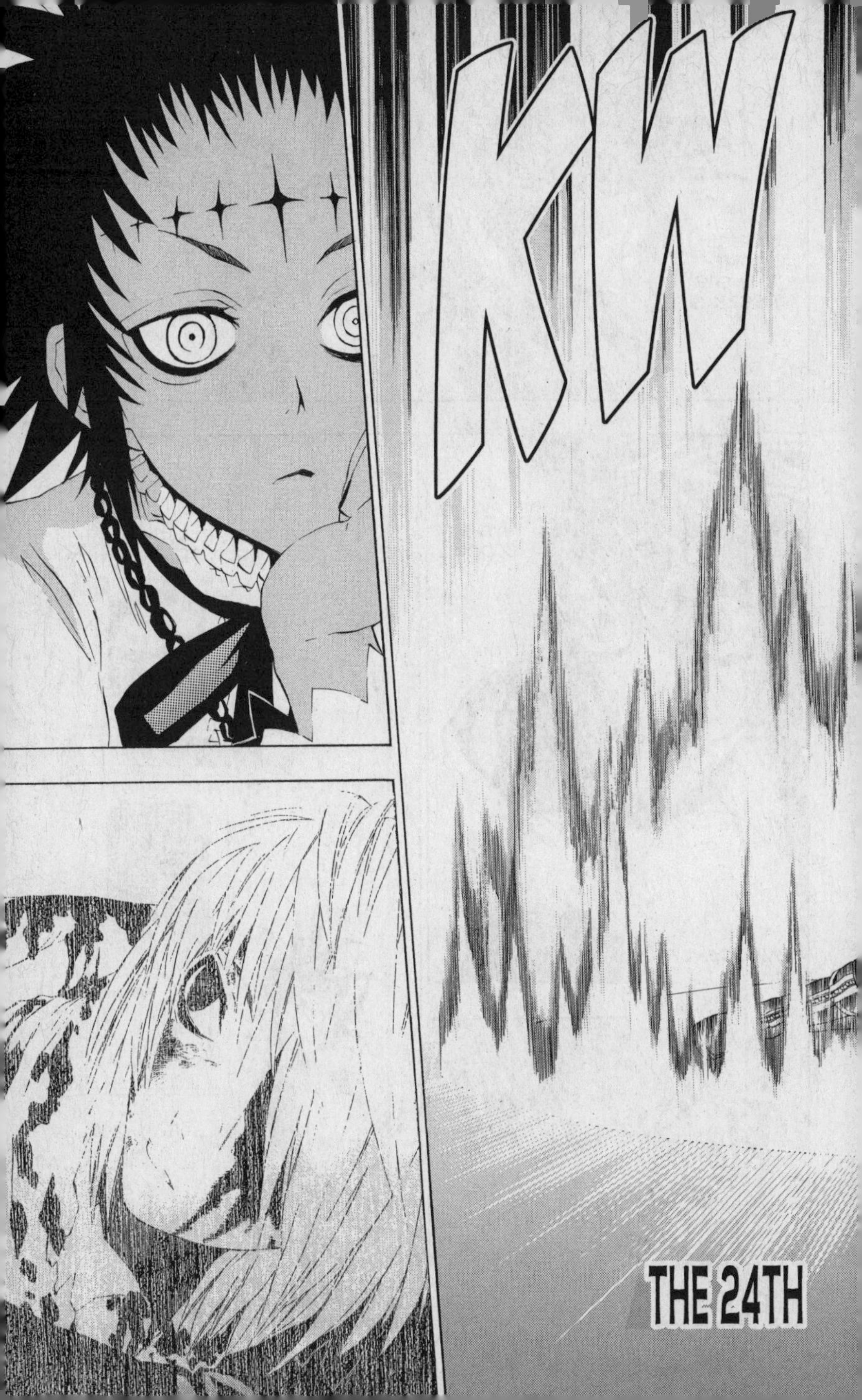
KIN
THE 24TH

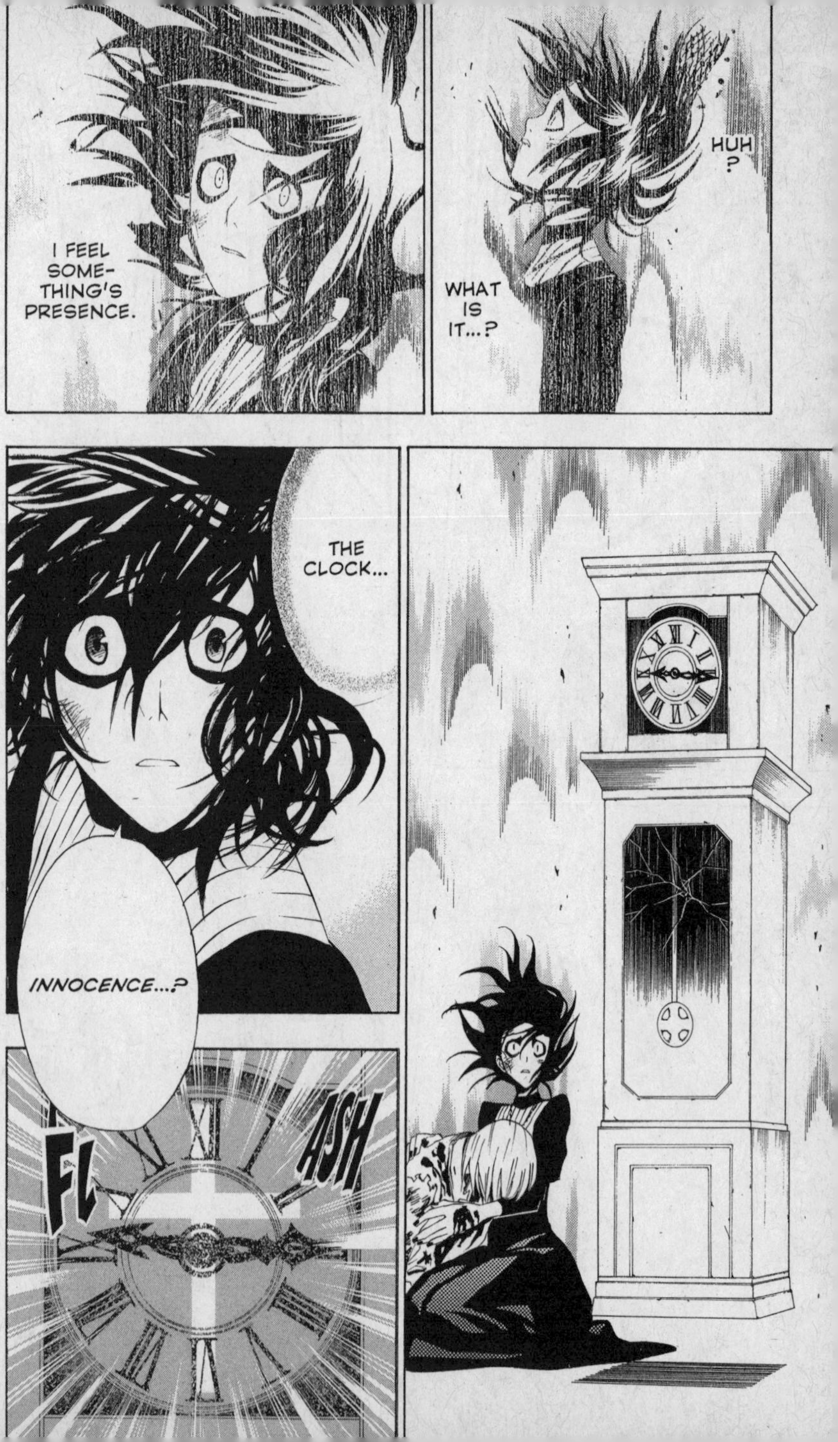
HUH?
WHAT IS IT...?
I FEEL SOMETHING'S PRESENCE.
THE CLOCK...
INNOCENCE...?
FLASH

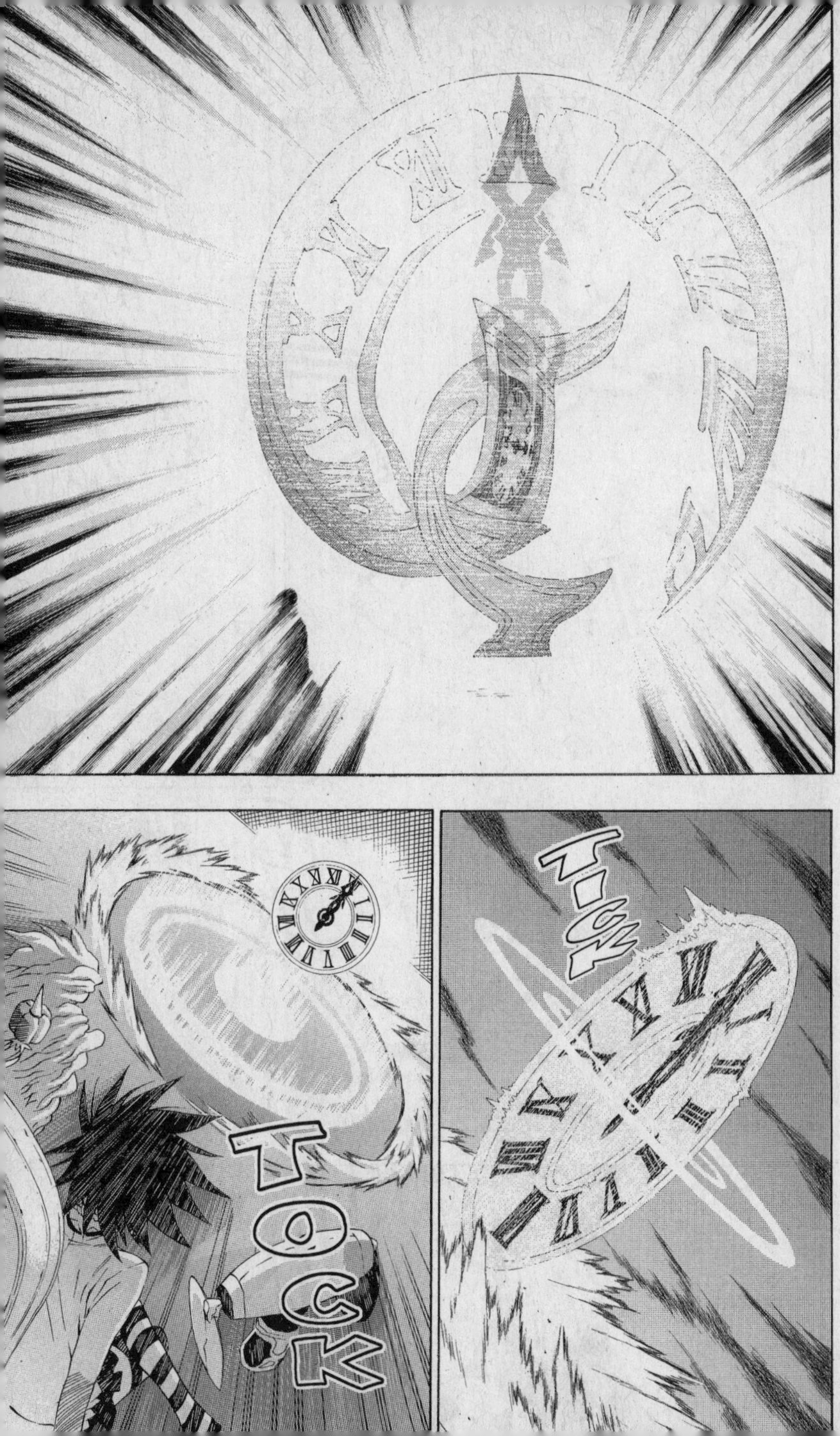
TICK
TOCK

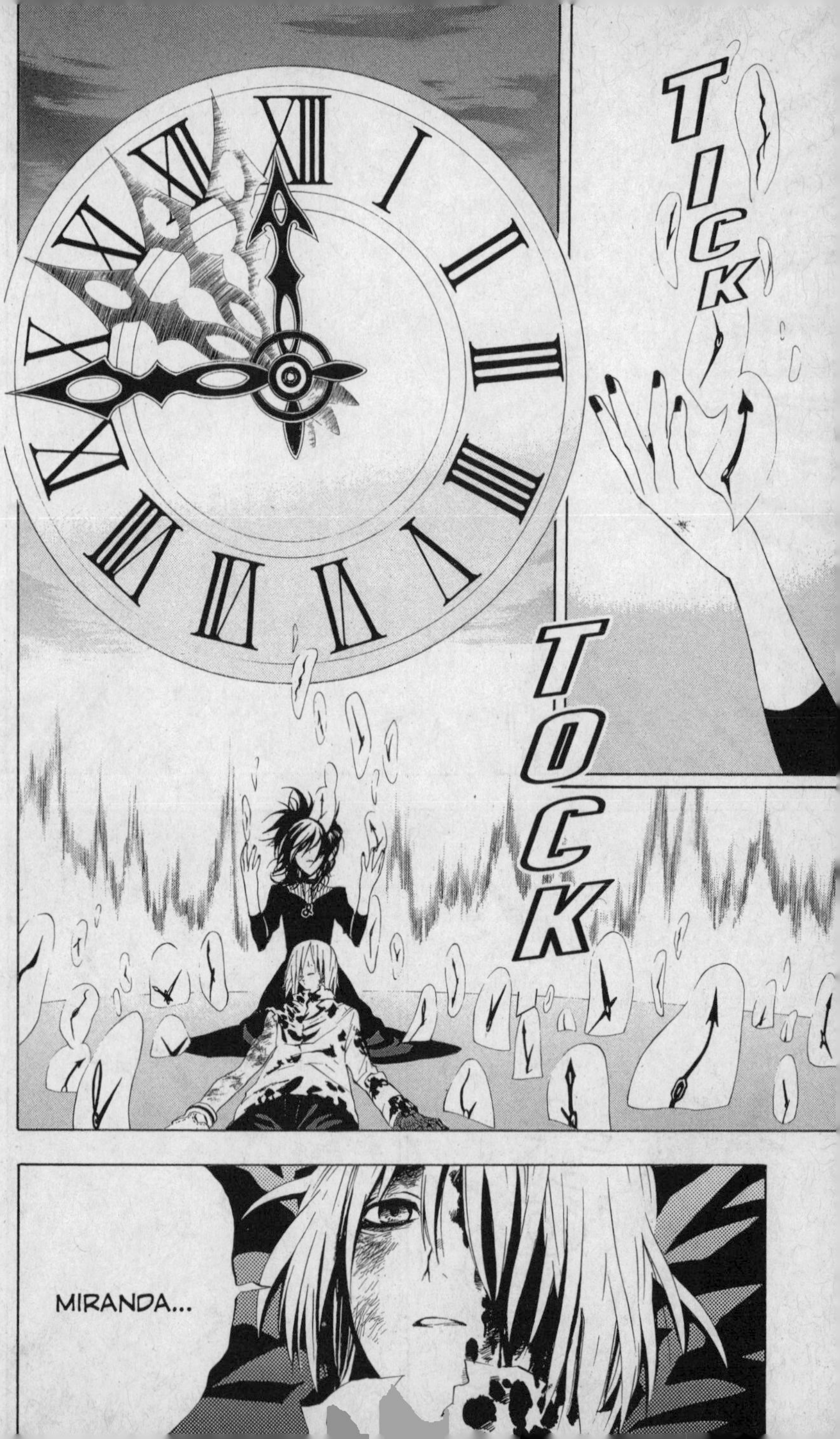
TICK
TOCK
MIRANDA...

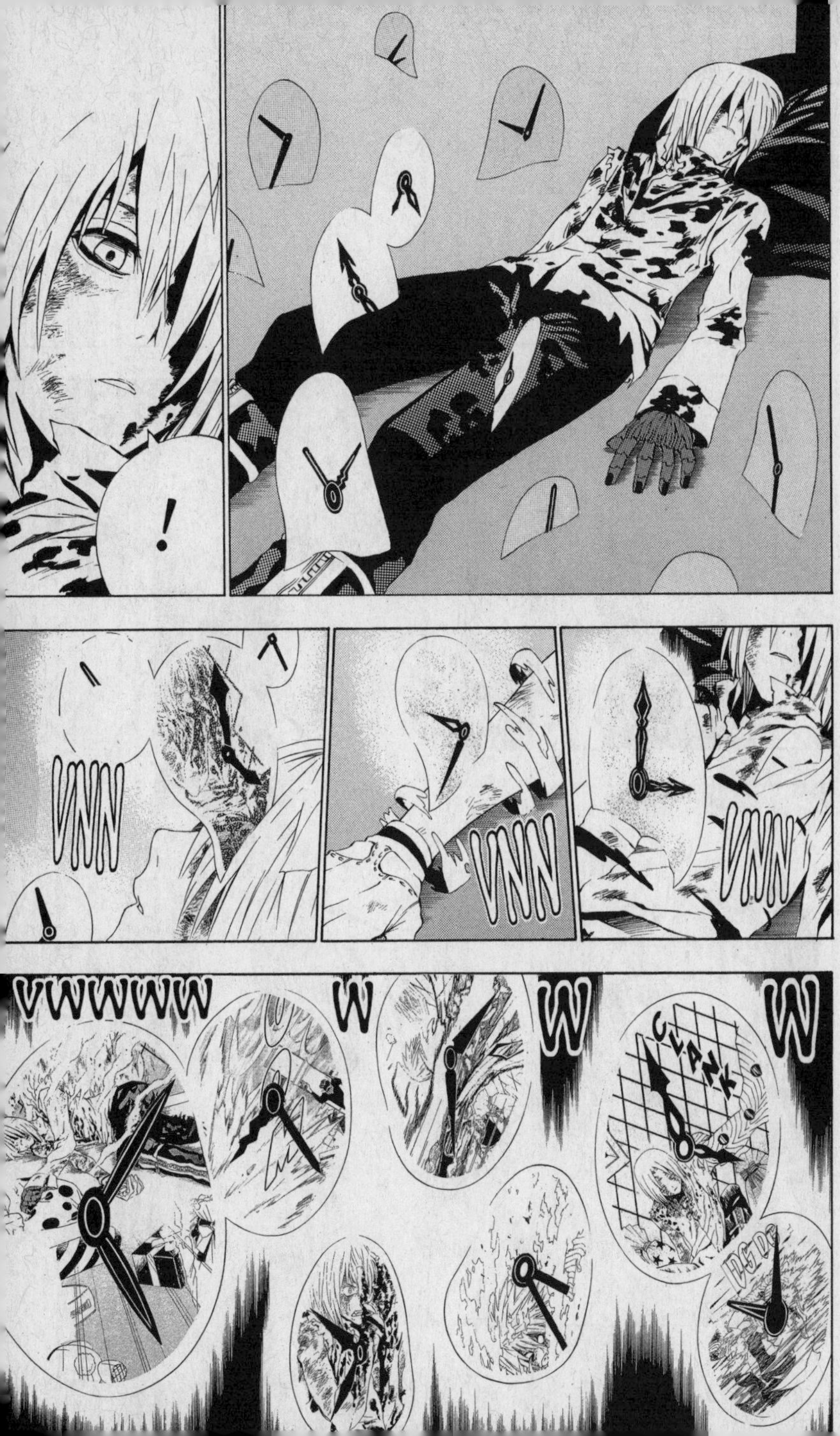
!
VNN
VNN
VNN
VWWWWW
W
W
W
CLANK
DGDG

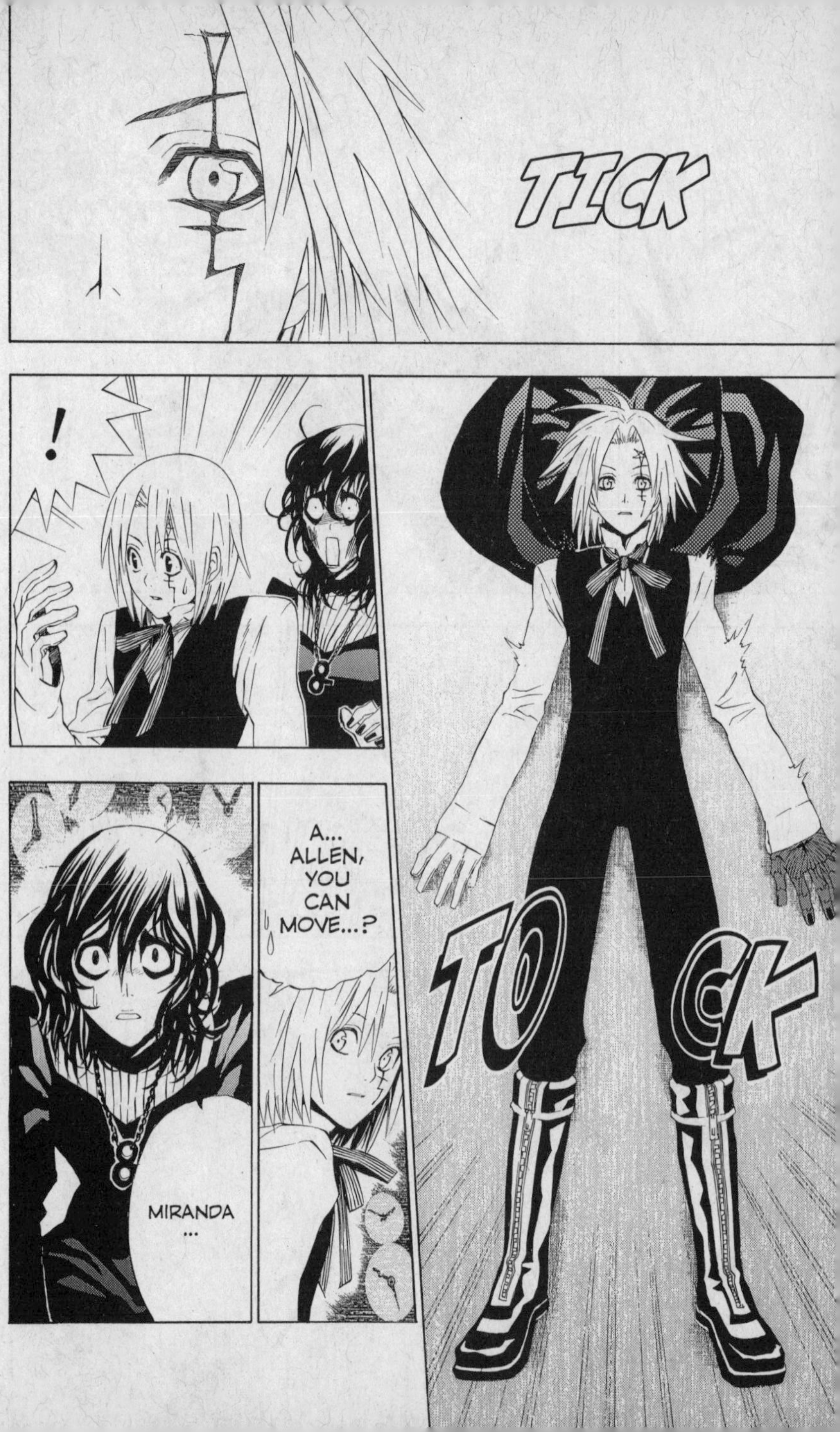

TICK
TOCK
!
A... ALLEN, YOU CAN MOVE...?
MIRANDA ...

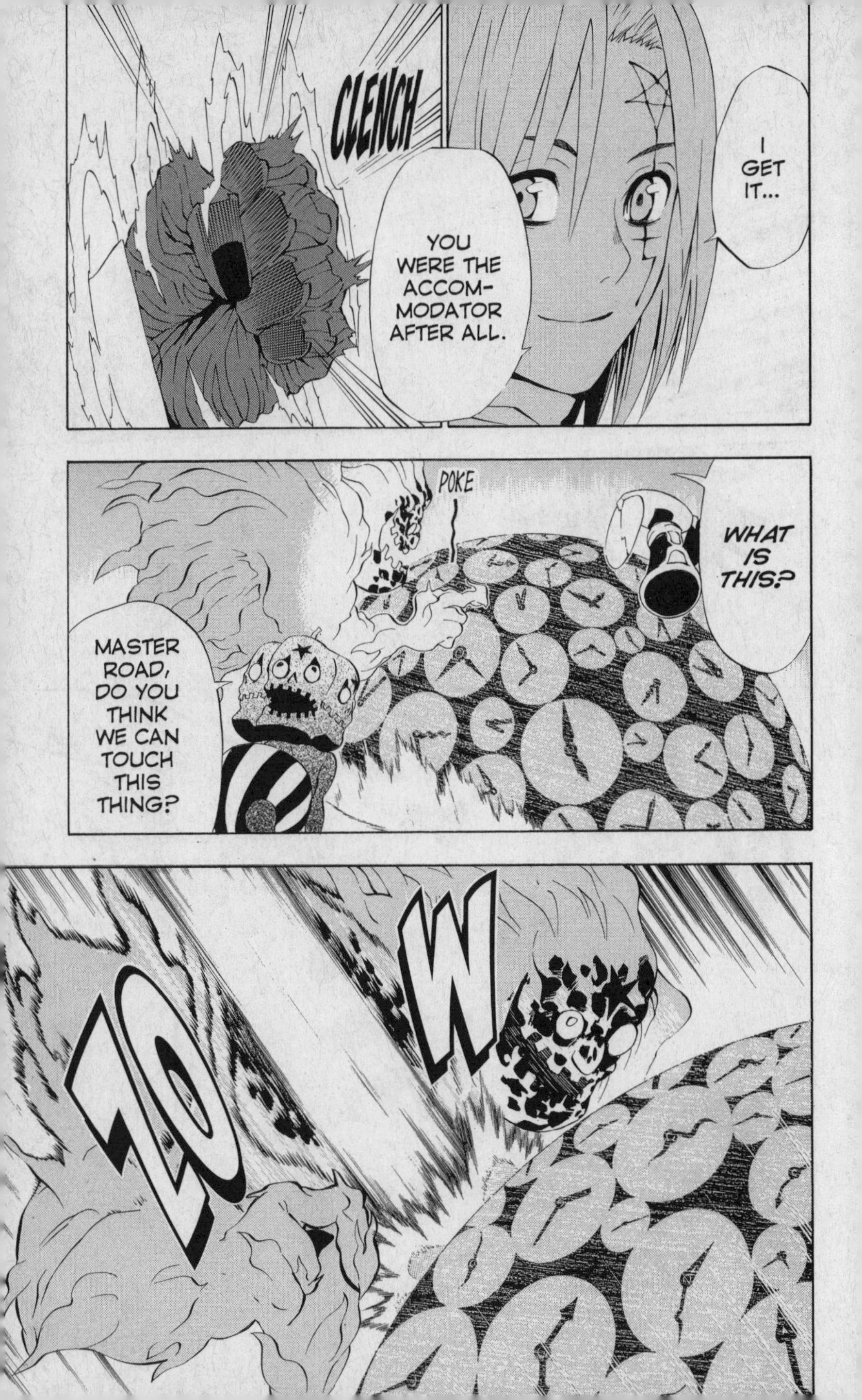
I GET IT...
CLENCH
YOU WERE THE ACCOM-MODATOR AFTER ALL.
WHAT IS THIS?
POKE
MASTER ROAD, DO YOU THINK WE CAN TOUCH THIS THING?
ZOW

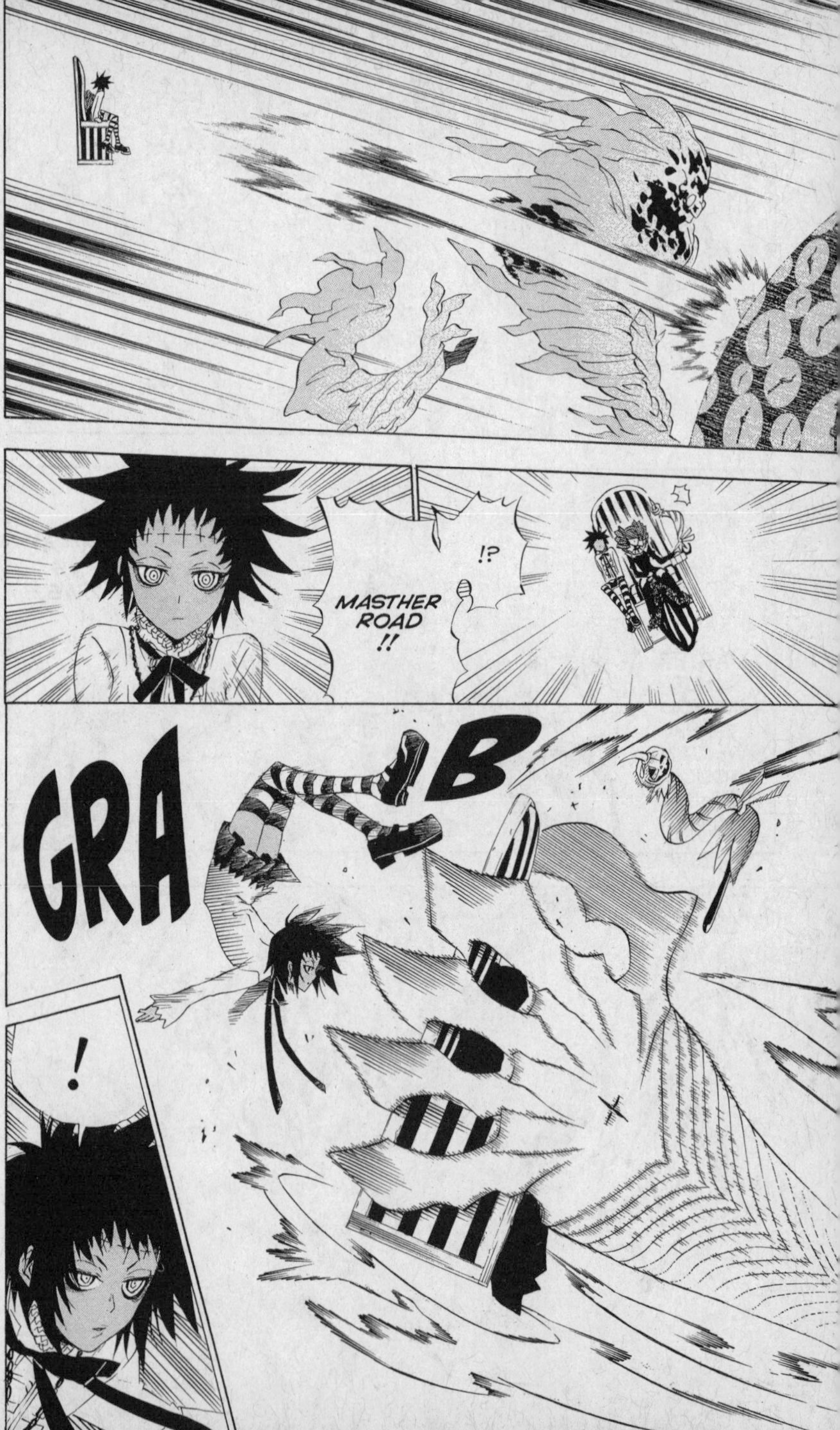
!?
MASTHER ROAD !!
GRAB
!

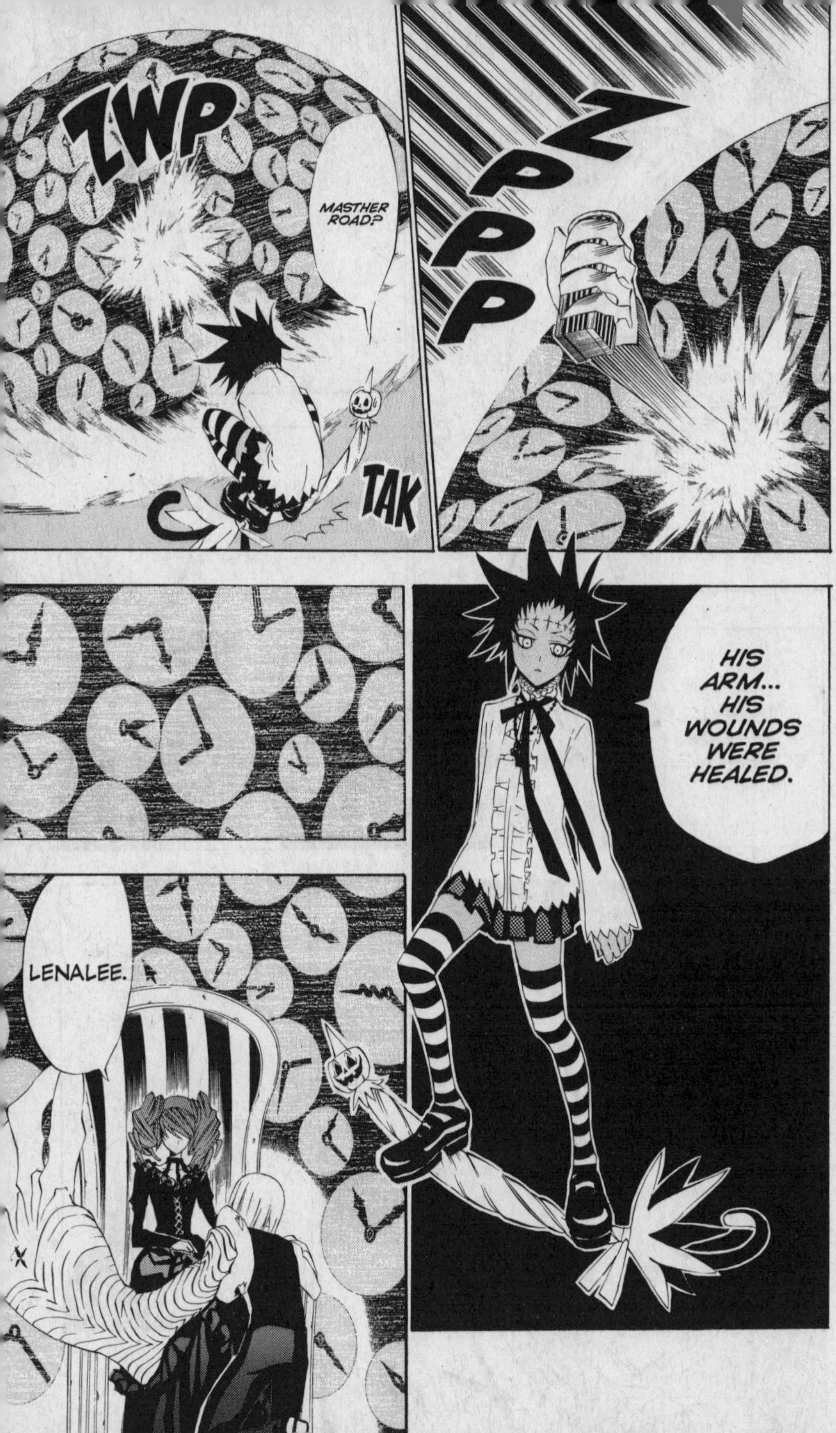
ZPPP
ZWP
MASTHER ROAD?
TAK
HIS ARM... HIS WOUNDS WERE HEALED.
LENALEE.

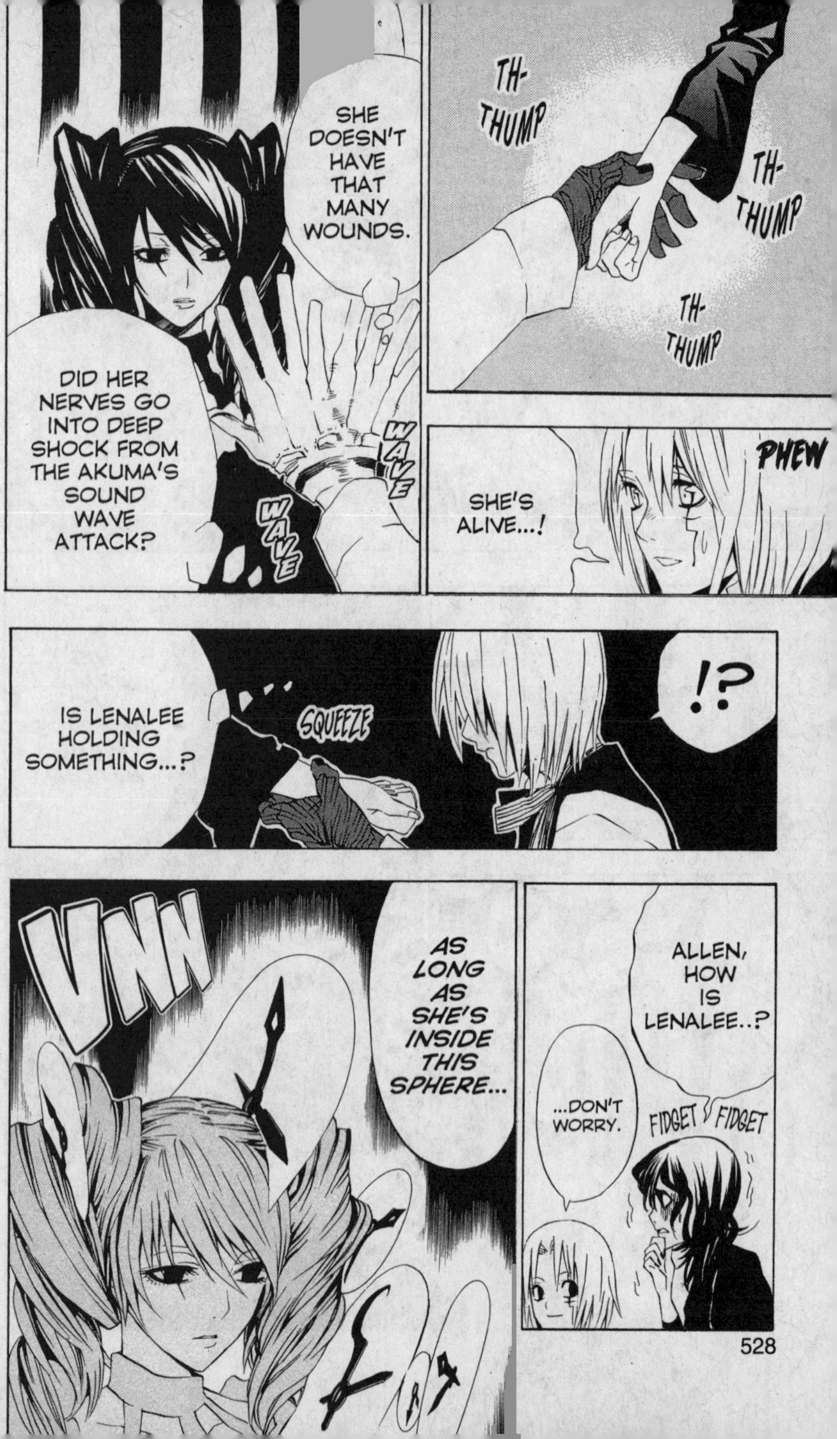
TH-THUMP
TH-THUMP
TH-THUMP
PHEW
SHE'S ALIVE...!
SHE DOESN'T HAVE THAT MANY WOUNDS.
DID HER NERVES GO INTO DEEP SHOCK FROM THE AKUMA'S SOUND WAVE ATTACK?
WAVE
WAVE
!?
IS LENALEE HOLDING SOMETHING...?
SQUEEZE
ALLEN, HOW IS LENALEE..?
FIDGET FIDGET
...DON'T WORRY.
AS LONG AS SHE'S INSIDE THIS SPHERE...
VNN

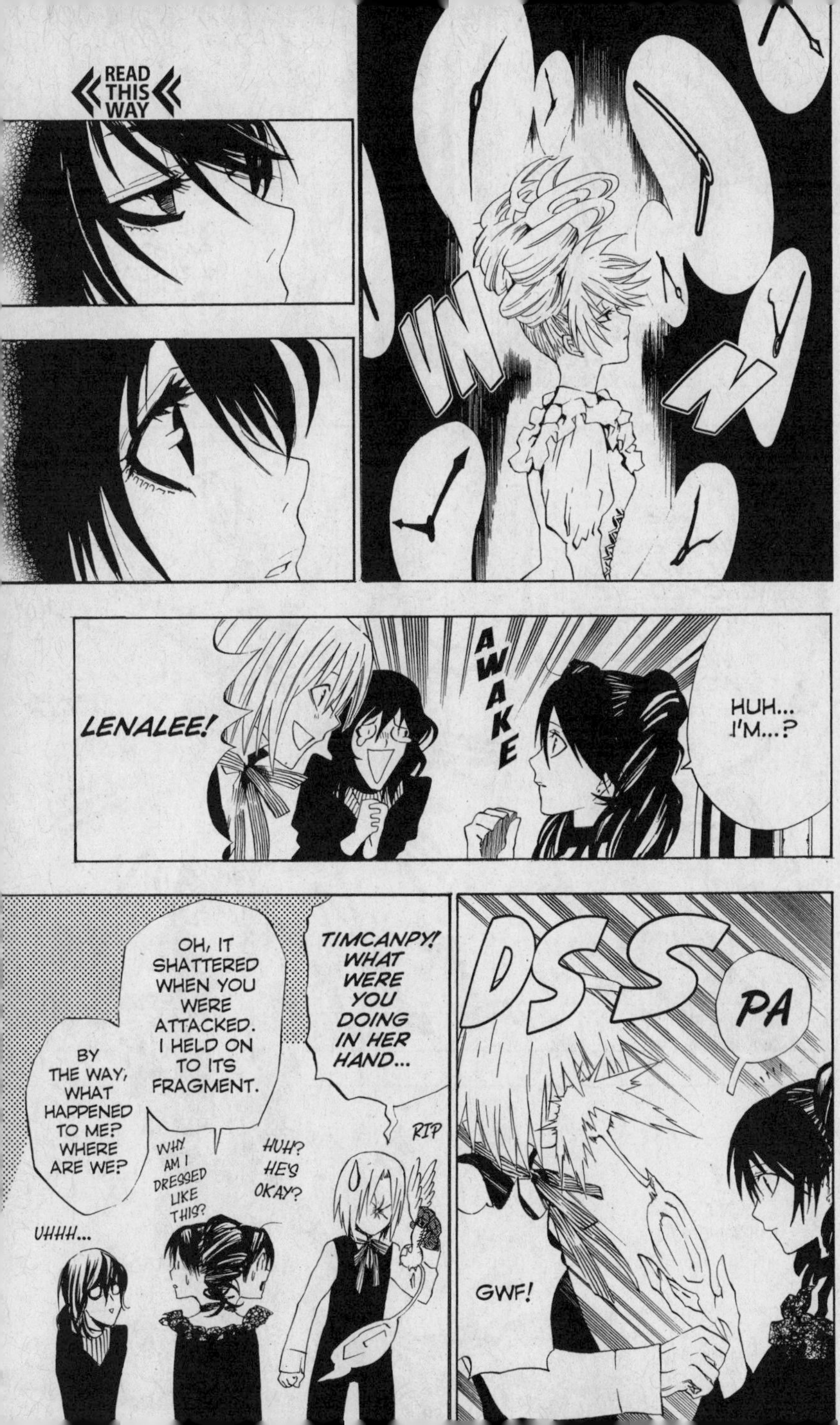
READ THIS WAY
VNNN
HUH... I'M...?
AWAKE
LENALEE!
DSS
PA
GWF!
TIMCANPY! WHAT WERE YOU DOING IN HER HAND...
RIP
HUH? HE'S OKAY?
OH, IT SHATTERED WHEN YOU WERE ATTACKED. I HELD ON TO ITS FRAGMENT.
WHY AM I DRESSED LIKE THIS?
BY THE WAY, WHAT HAPPENED TO ME? WHERE ARE WE?
UHHH...

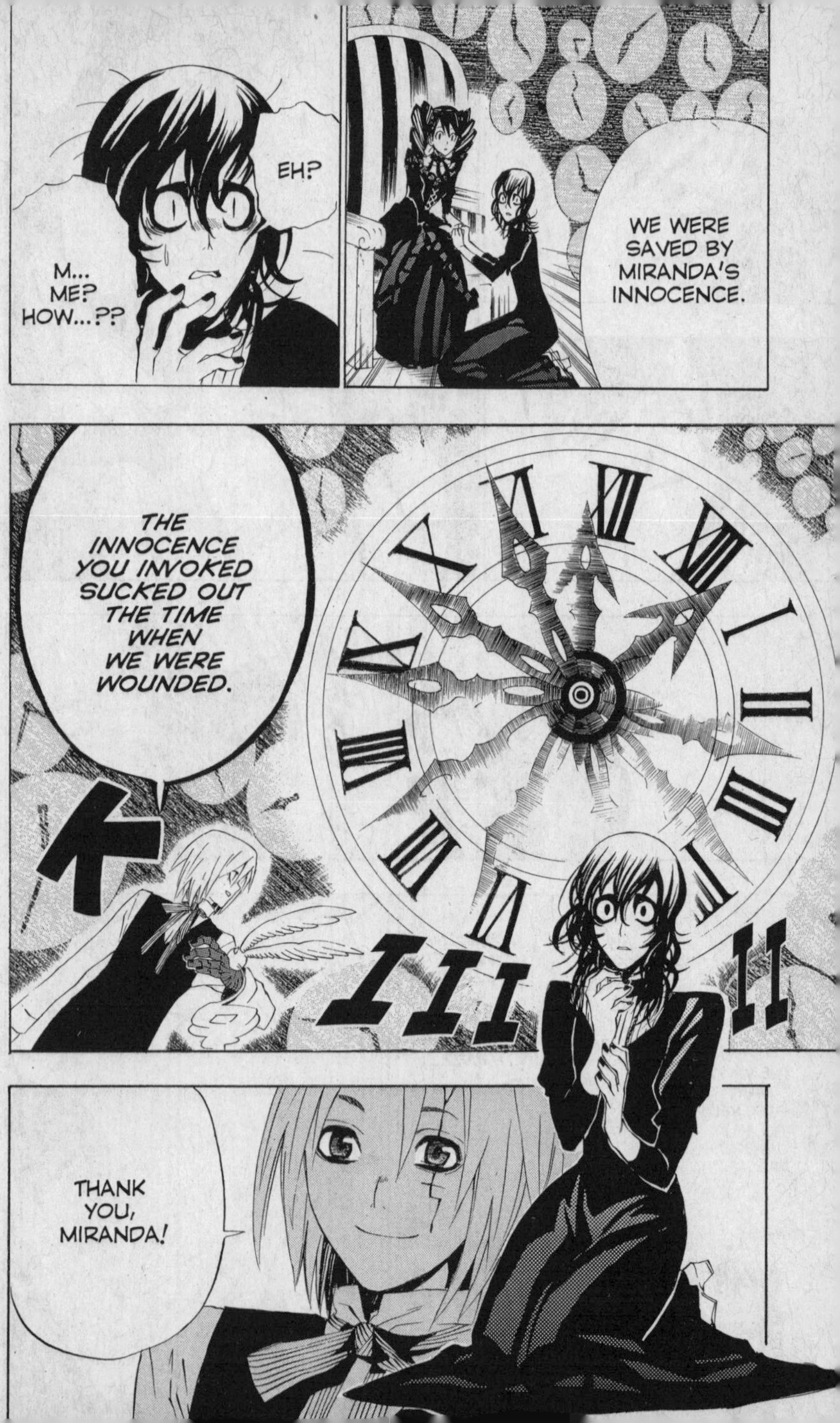
WE WERE SAVED BY MIRANDA'S INNOCENCE.
EH?
M... ME? HOW...??
THE INNOCENCE YOU INVOKED SUCKED OUT THE TIME WHEN WE WERE WOUNDED.
THANK YOU, MIRANDA!

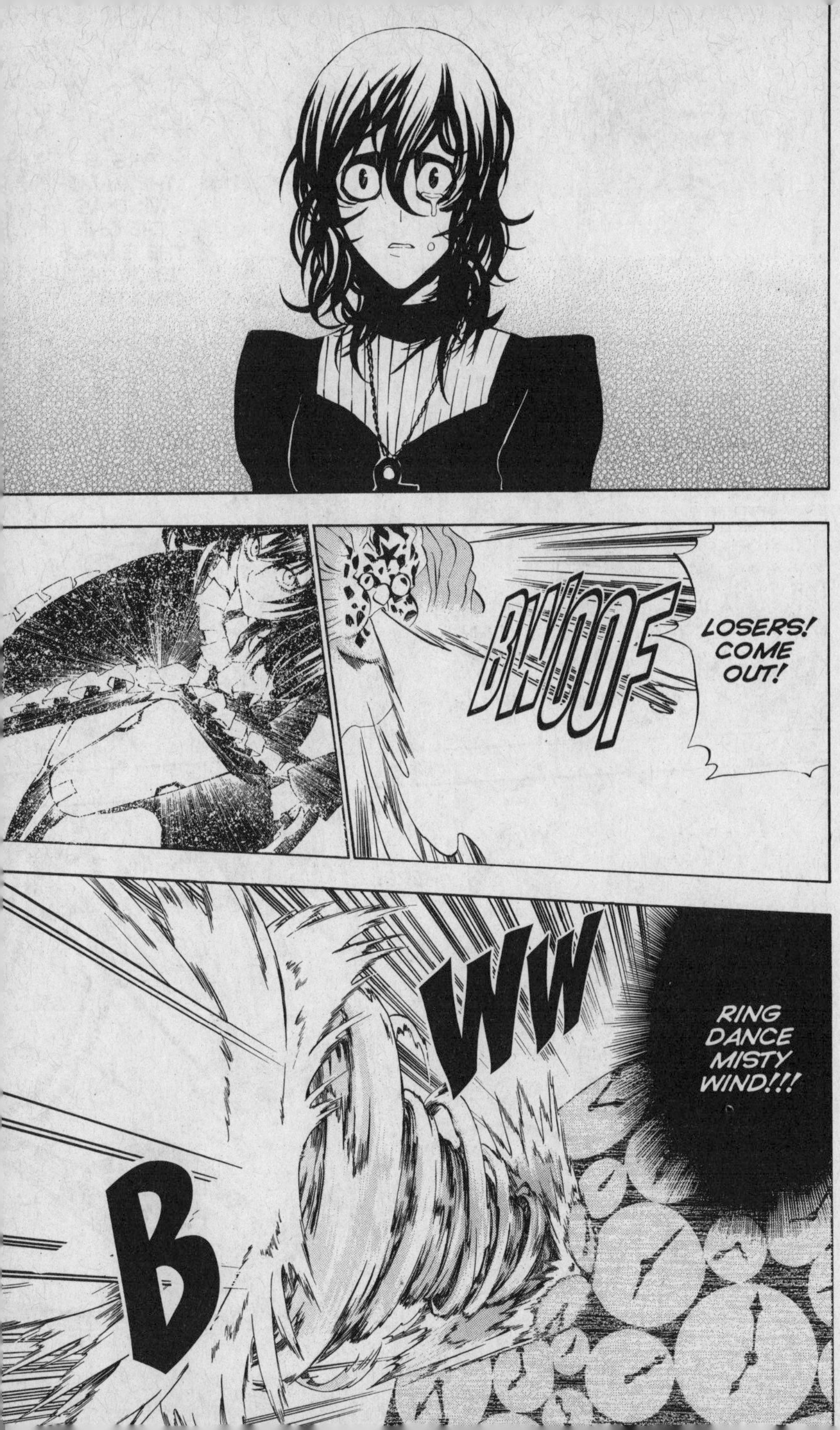
LOSERS! COME OUT!
BWOOF
RING DANCE MISTY WIND!!!
WW
B

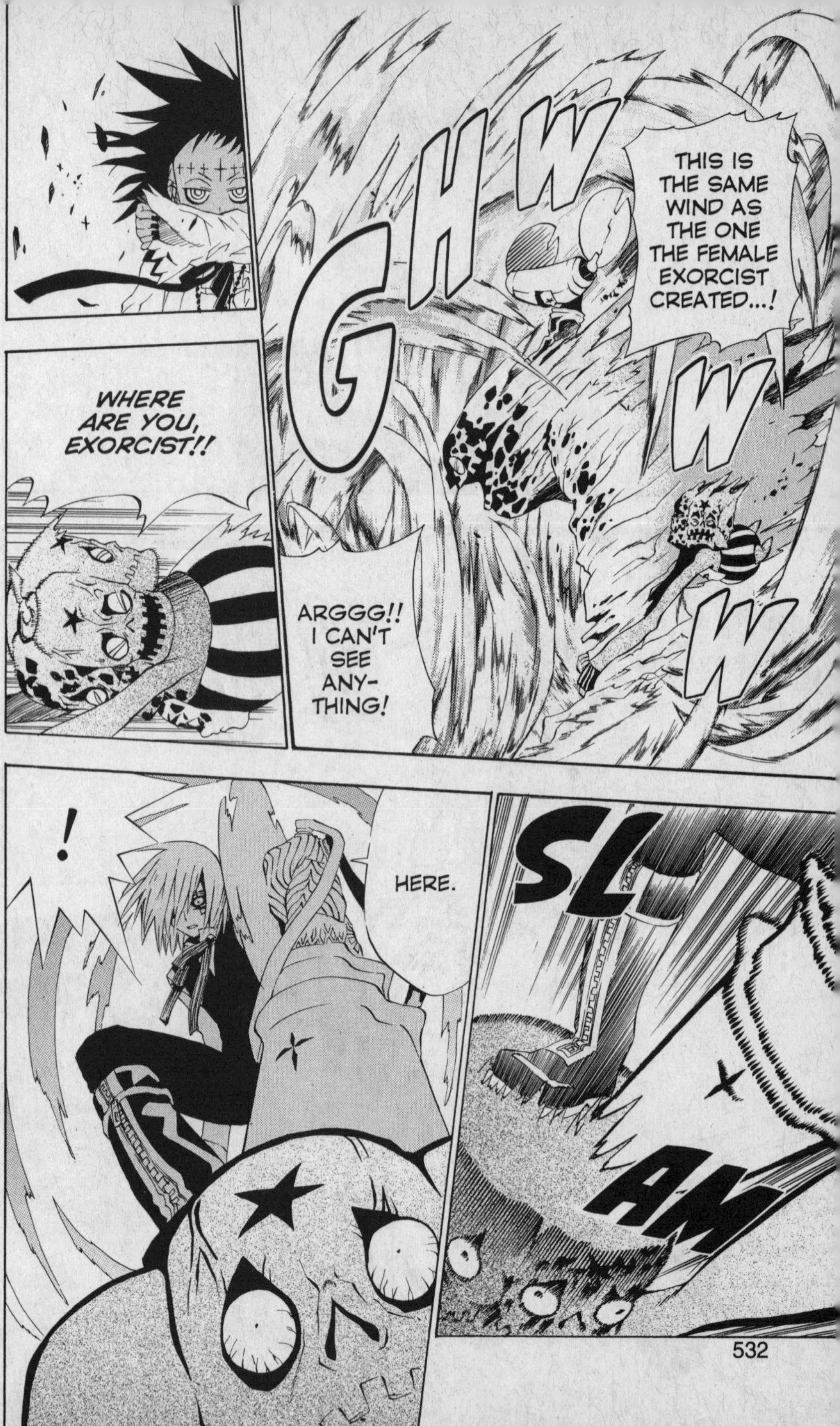
GHWWWW
THIS IS THE SAME WIND AS THE ONE THE FEMALE EXORCIST CREATED...!
ARGGG!! I CAN'T SEE ANY-THING!
WHERE ARE YOU, EXORCIST!!
SLAM
!
HERE.

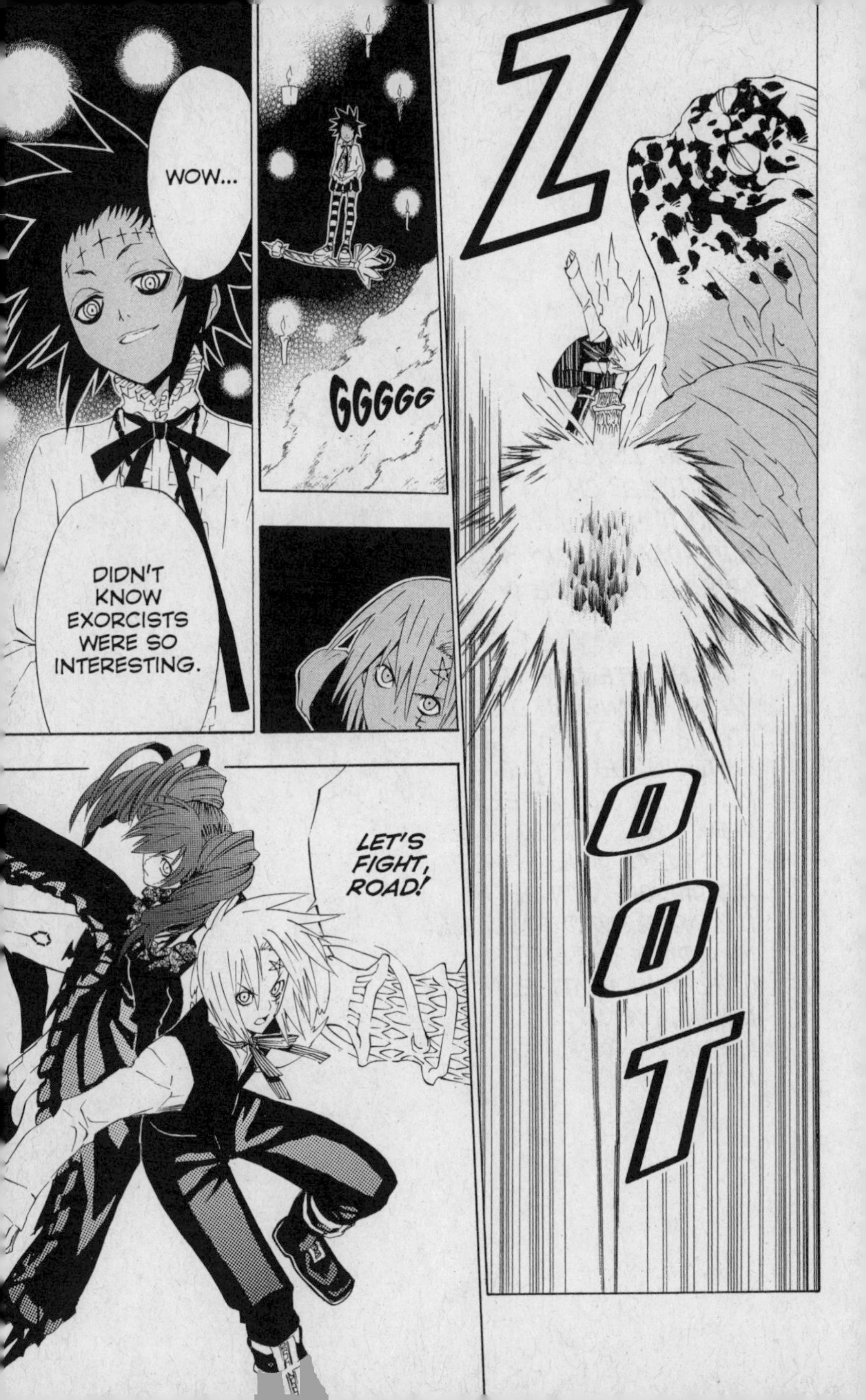
ZOOT
GGGGG
WOW...
DIDN'T KNOW EXORCISTS WERE SO INTERESTING.
LET'S FIGHT, ROAD!

MIRANDA LOTTO

GERMAN 25 YEARS OLD
HEIGHT 168 CM
WEIGHT 45KG
BIRTHDAY JANUARY 1ST
ARIES BLOOD TYPE O

I HAD NO INTENTION OF
MAKING MIRANDA AN EXORCIST
AT THE TIME I DREW THE
FIRST CHAPTER OF THE
REWINDING CITY. AFTER I
DREW HER I STARTED TO SEE
THAT WE'RE SIMILAR INSIDE
AND SHE GREW ON ME. I'M
LOOKING FORWARD TO DRAWING
MIRANDA IN THE ORDER'S
UNIFORM IN A BATTLE. I'M
LOOKING FORWARD TO
SEEING YOU SOON,
MIRANDA.

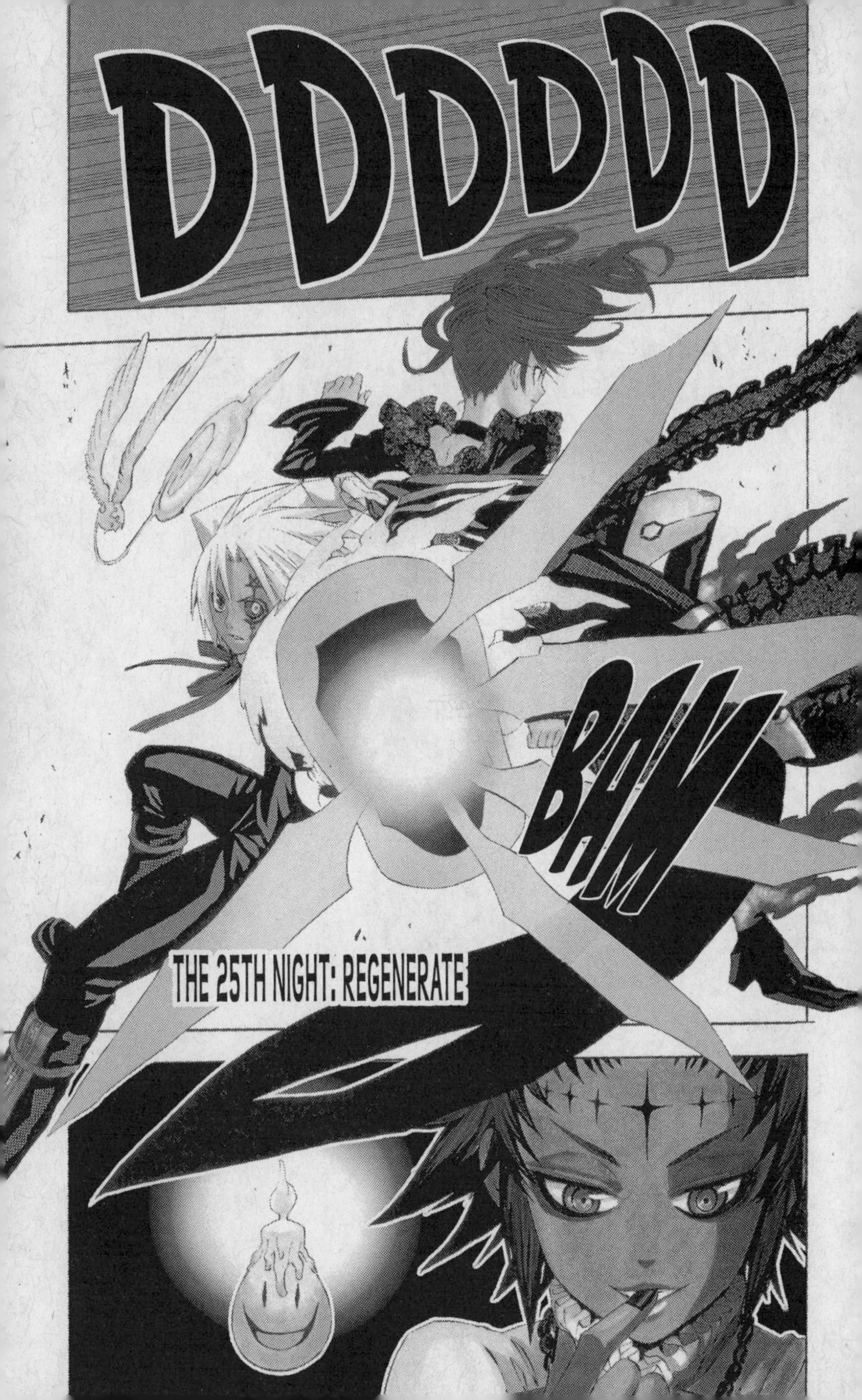
DDDDDD
BAM
THE 25TH NIGHT: REGENERATE

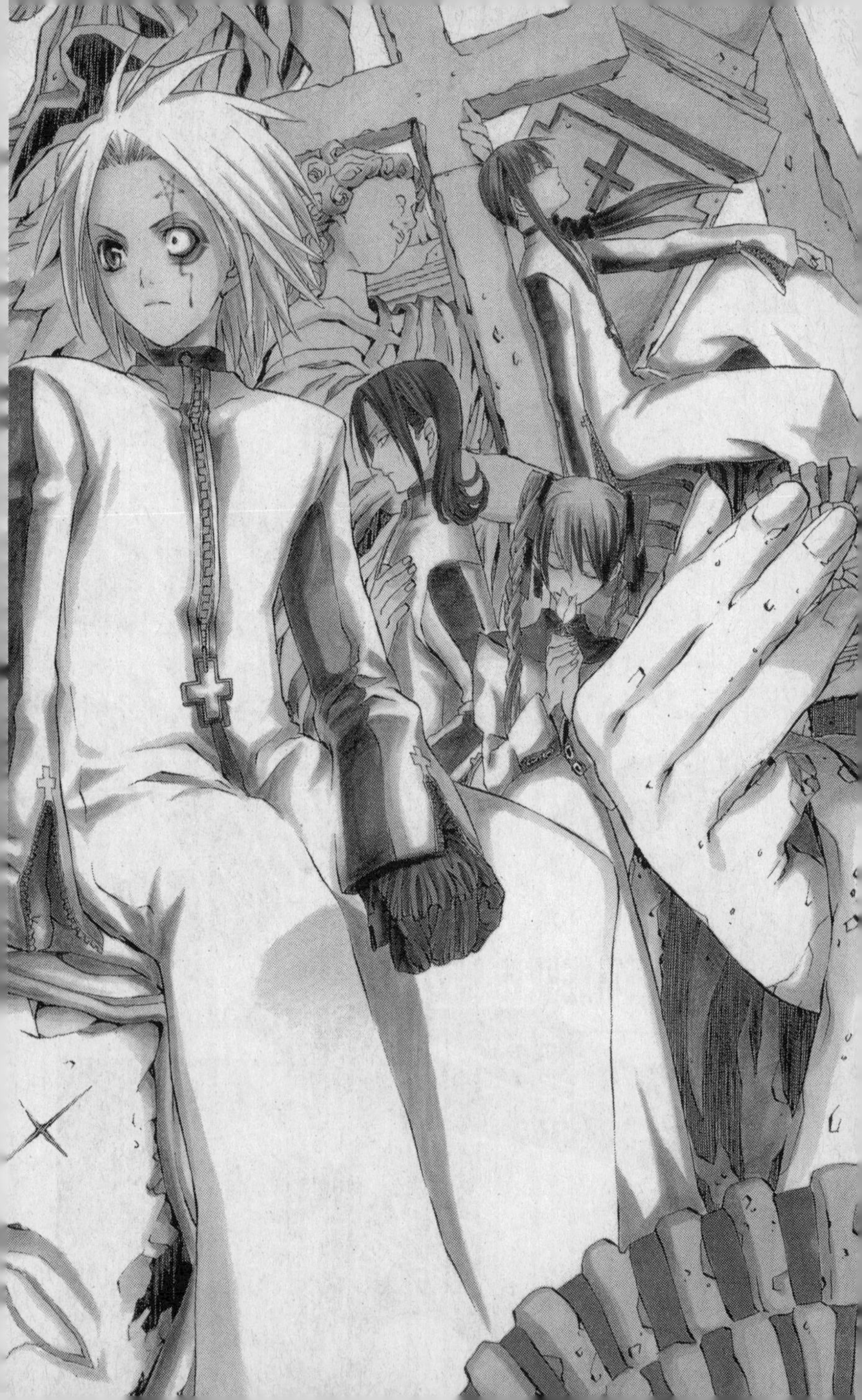

THE 25TH NIGHT: REGENERATE

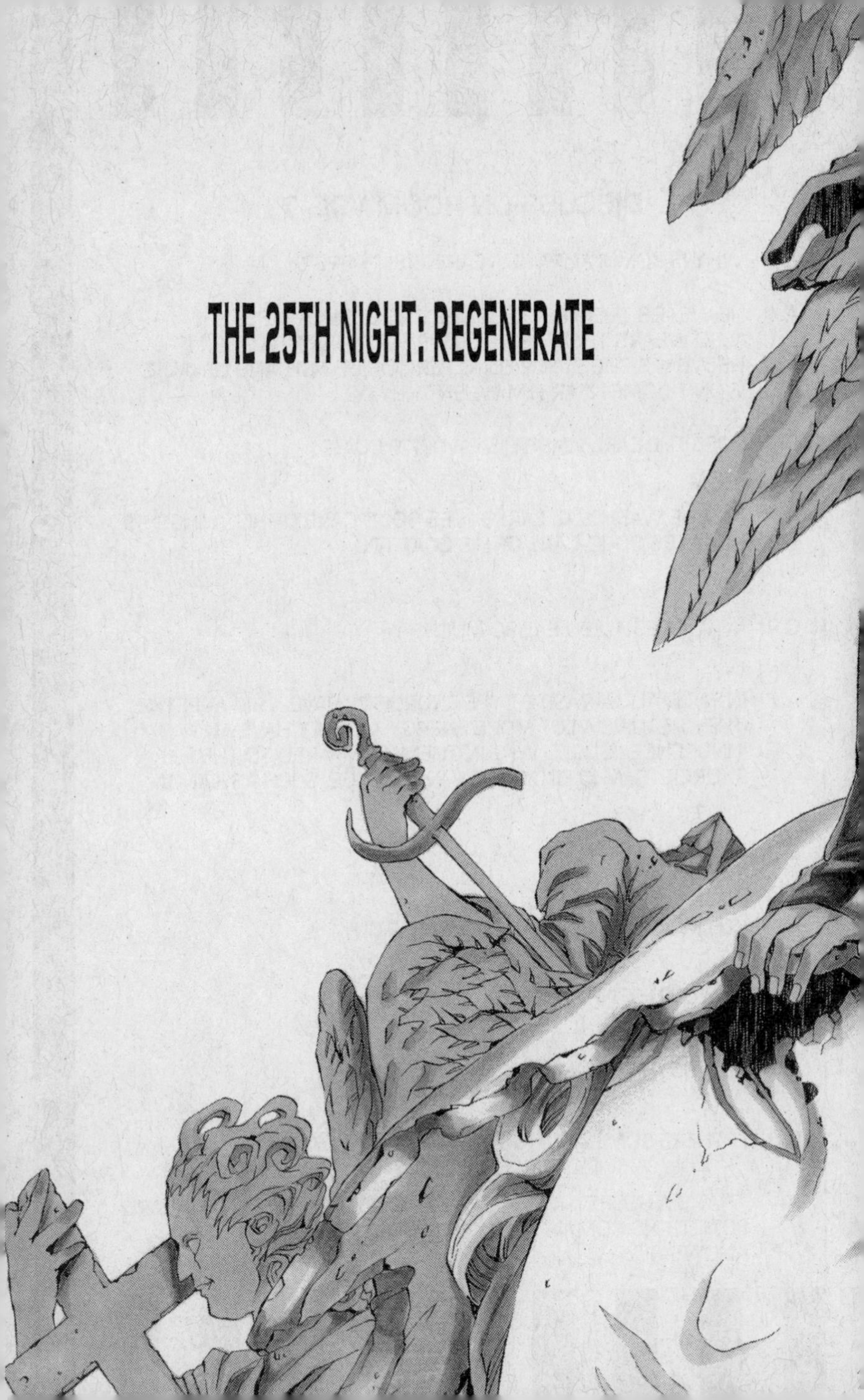

DISCUSSION ROOM VOL. 7

Q 1. WHY IS KOMUI ALWAYS WEARING SLIPPERS?

A. HE WEARS THEM BECAUSE THEY'RE COMFORTABLE. HE
ALSO WEARS THEM BECAUSE HIS FEET START TO STINK IF
HE WEARS SHOES FOR LONG PERIODS OF TIME AND LENALEE
WON'T COME NEAR HIM WHEN THEY DO.

Q 2. DOES THE EARL WASH HIS FAVORITE COAT?

A. YES, HE WASHES IT. EARL TAKES GOOD CARE OF HIS THINGS SO
HE TAKES GOOD CARE OF HIS COAT TOO.

Q 3. WHY DOES ALLEN EAT SO MUCH?

A. IN FACT, ALL PARASITE-TYPE EXORCISTS HAVE A BIG APPETITE.
THEY REQUIRE A LOT MORE ENERGY AS THEY HAVE AN
INNOCENCE LODGED WITHIN THEM, COMPARED TO THE
EXORCISTS WHO EQUIP THEIR INNOCENCE, SUCH AS KANDA.

Q 4. IS KANDA A GUY OR A GIRL?

A. NO DOUBT ABOUT THAT ONE. HE'S A GUY.

Q 5. IS ALLEN LEFT-HANDED?

A. HE'S BOTH-HANDED.

Q 6. IS THERE SOME CONTRAPTION IN KOMUI'S BERET?

A. THAT'S A SECRET. APPARENTLY ONE OF HIS ASSISTANTS HEARD
SOMETHING COMING FROM AROUND THAT AREA BUT WHO
KNOWS...

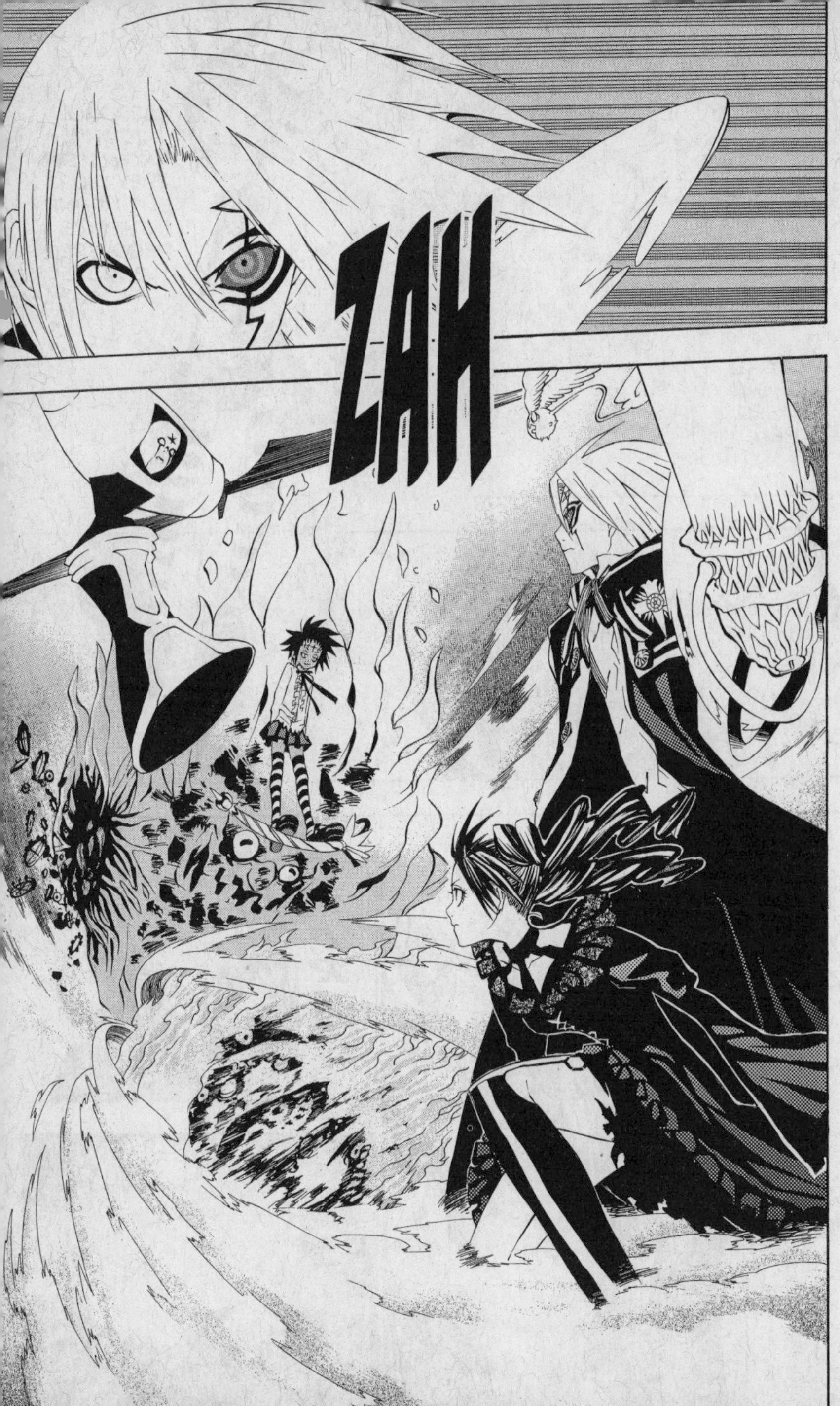
ZAH

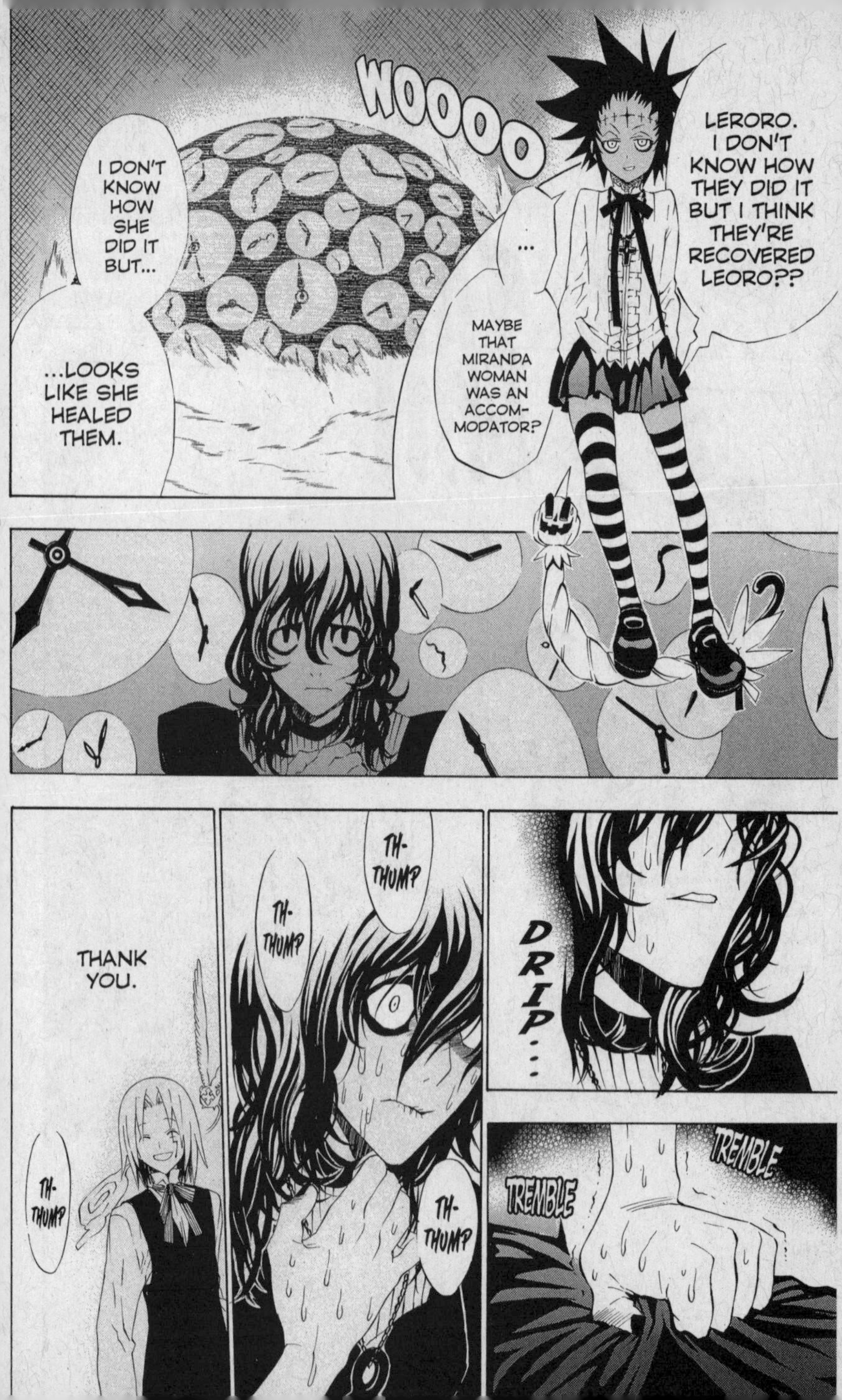
WOOOO
LERORO. I DON'T KNOW HOW THEY DID IT BUT I THINK THEY'RE RECOVERED LEORO??
...
MAYBE THAT MIRANDA WOMAN WAS AN ACCOM-MODATOR?
I DON'T KNOW HOW SHE DID IT BUT...
...LOOKS LIKE SHE HEALED THEM.
DRIP...
TREMBLE
TREMBLE
TH-THUMP
TH-THUMP
TH-THUMP
THANK YOU.
TH-THUMP

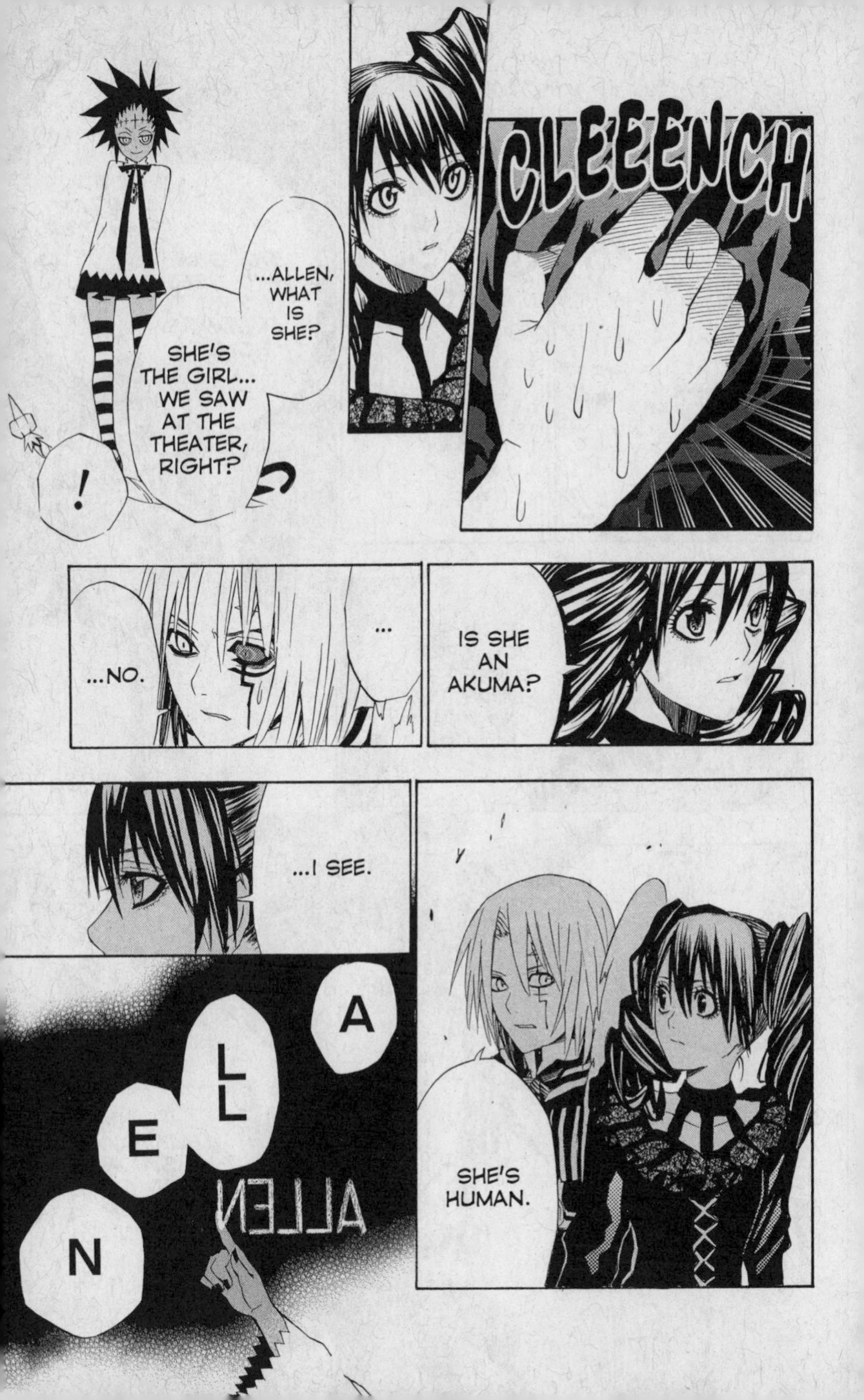
CLEEENCH
...ALLEN, WHAT IS SHE?
SHE'S THE GIRL... WE SAW AT THE THEATER, RIGHT?
!
IS SHE AN AKUMA?
...
...NO.
SHE'S HUMAN.
...I SEE.
A
L
L
E
N

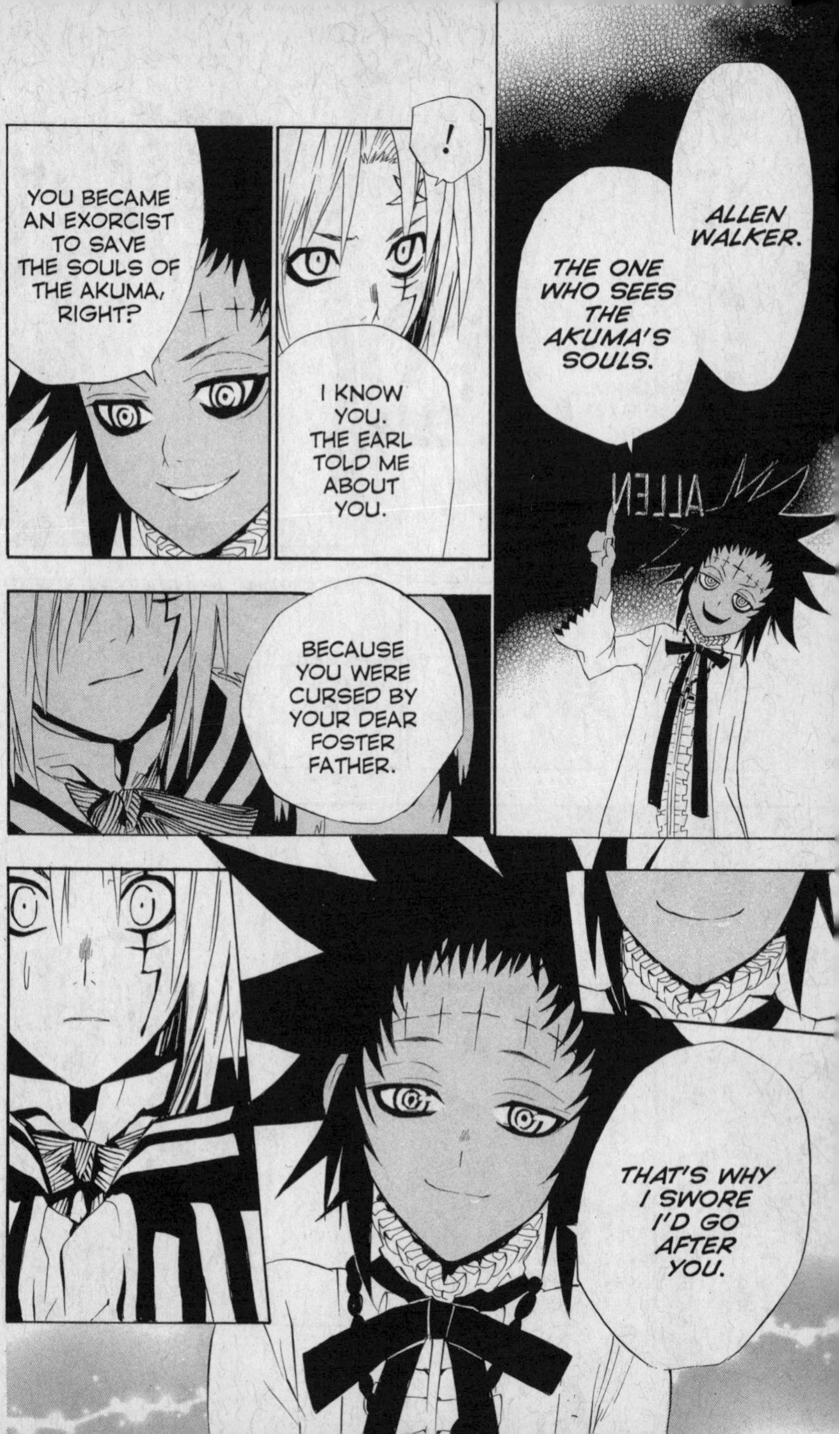
ALLEN WALKER.
THE ONE WHO SEES THE AKUMA'S SOULS.
ALLEN
!
I KNOW YOU. THE EARL TOLD ME ABOUT YOU.
YOU BECAME AN EXORCIST TO SAVE THE SOULS OF THE AKUMA, RIGHT?
BECAUSE YOU WERE CURSED BY YOUR DEAR FOSTER FATHER.
THAT'S WHY I SWORE I'D GO AFTER YOU.

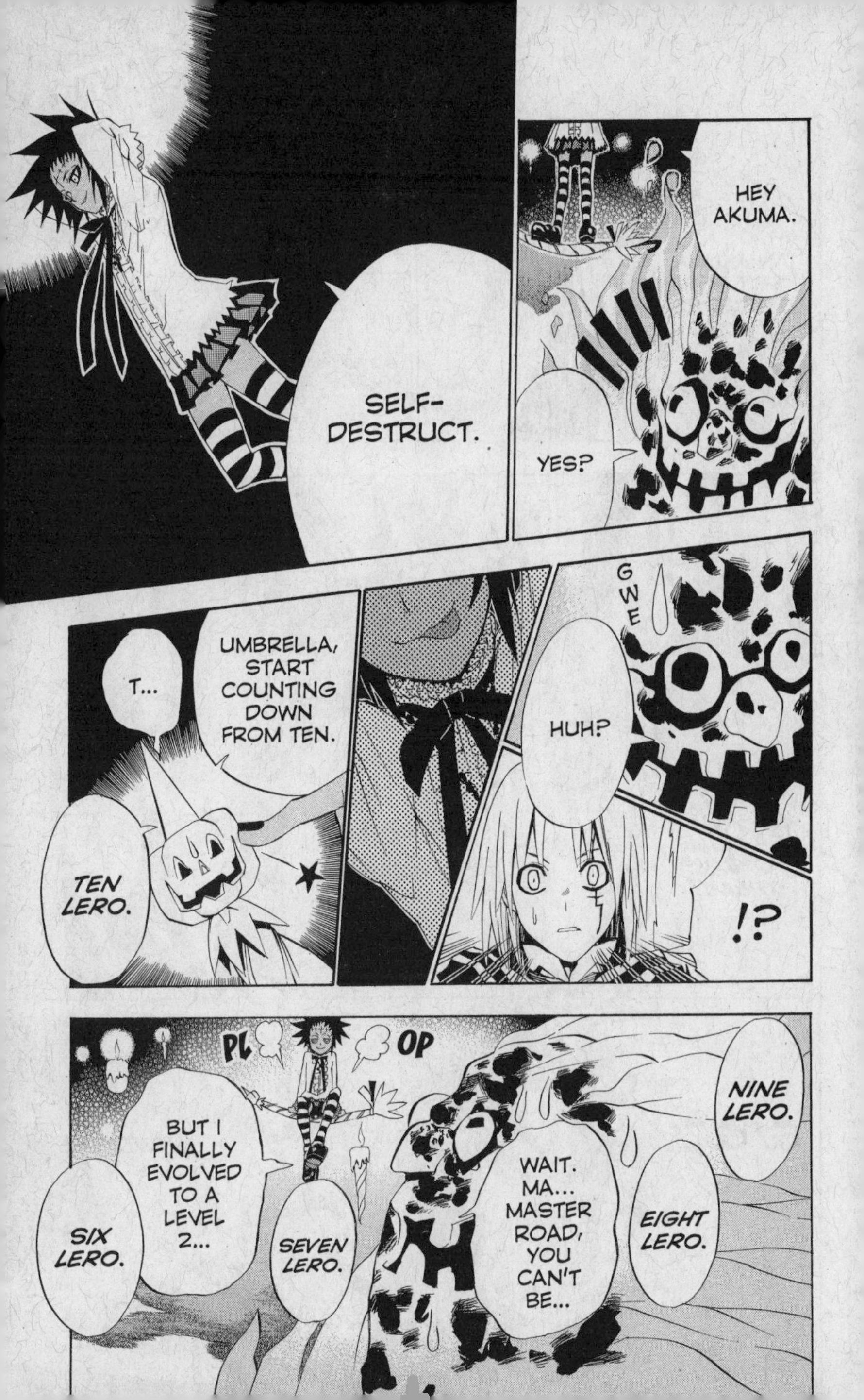
HEY AKUMA.
YES?
SELF-DESTRUCT.
GWE
HUH?
!?
UMBRELLA, START COUNTING DOWN FROM TEN.
T...
TEN LERO.
NINE LERO.
PL OP
EIGHT LERO.
WAIT. MA... MASTER ROAD, YOU CAN'T BE...
SEVEN LERO.
BUT I FINALLY EVOLVED TO A LEVEL 2...
SIX LERO.

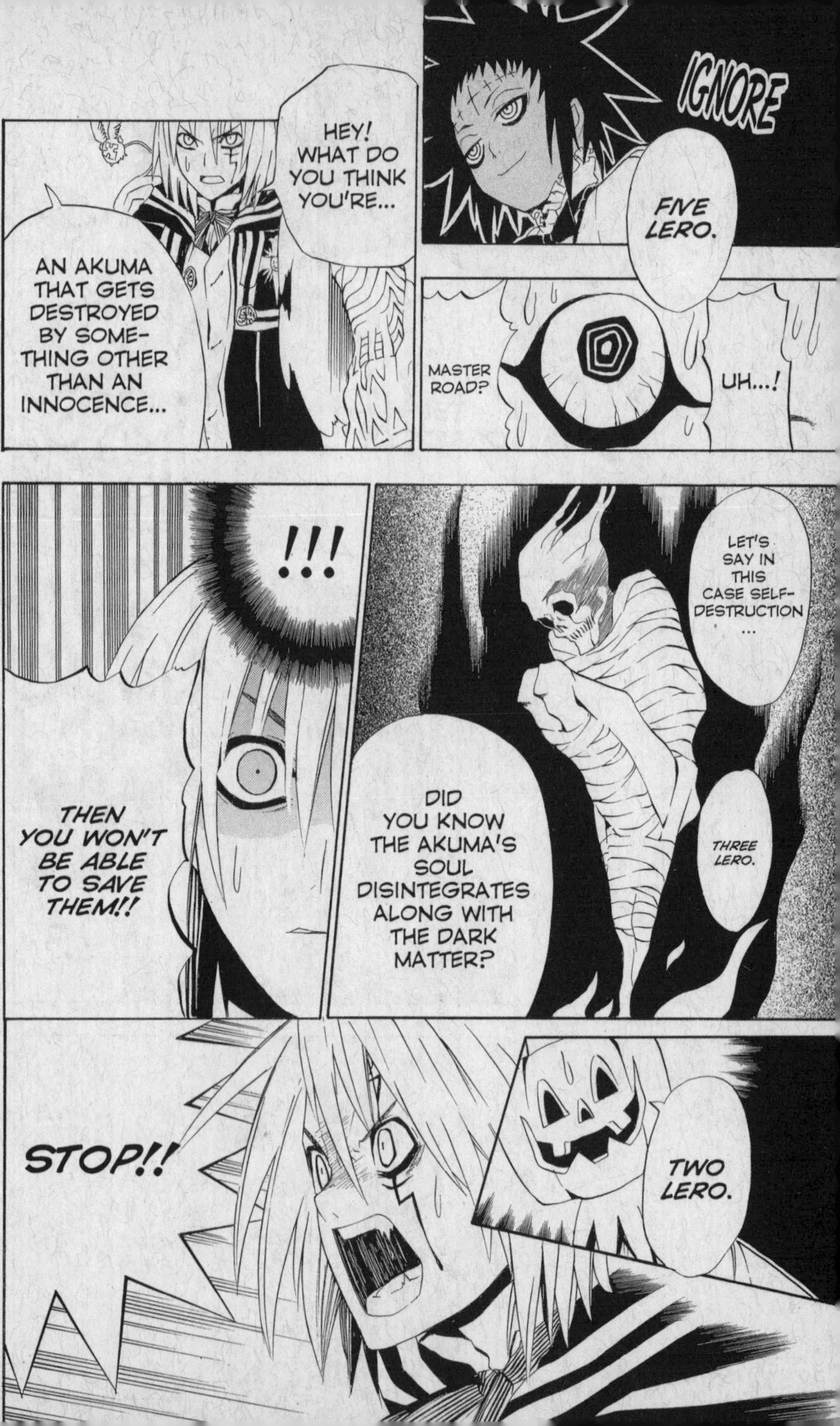
IGNORE
FIVE LERO.
UH...!
MASTER ROAD?
HEY! WHAT DO YOU THINK YOU'RE...
AN AKUMA THAT GETS DESTROYED BY SOME-THING OTHER THAN AN INNOCENCE...
LET'S SAY IN THIS CASE SELF-DESTRUCTION ...
THREE LERO.
DID YOU KNOW THE AKUMA'S SOUL DISINTEGRATES ALONG WITH THE DARK MATTER?
!!!
THEN YOU WON'T BE ABLE TO SAVE THEM!!
TWO LERO.
STOP!!

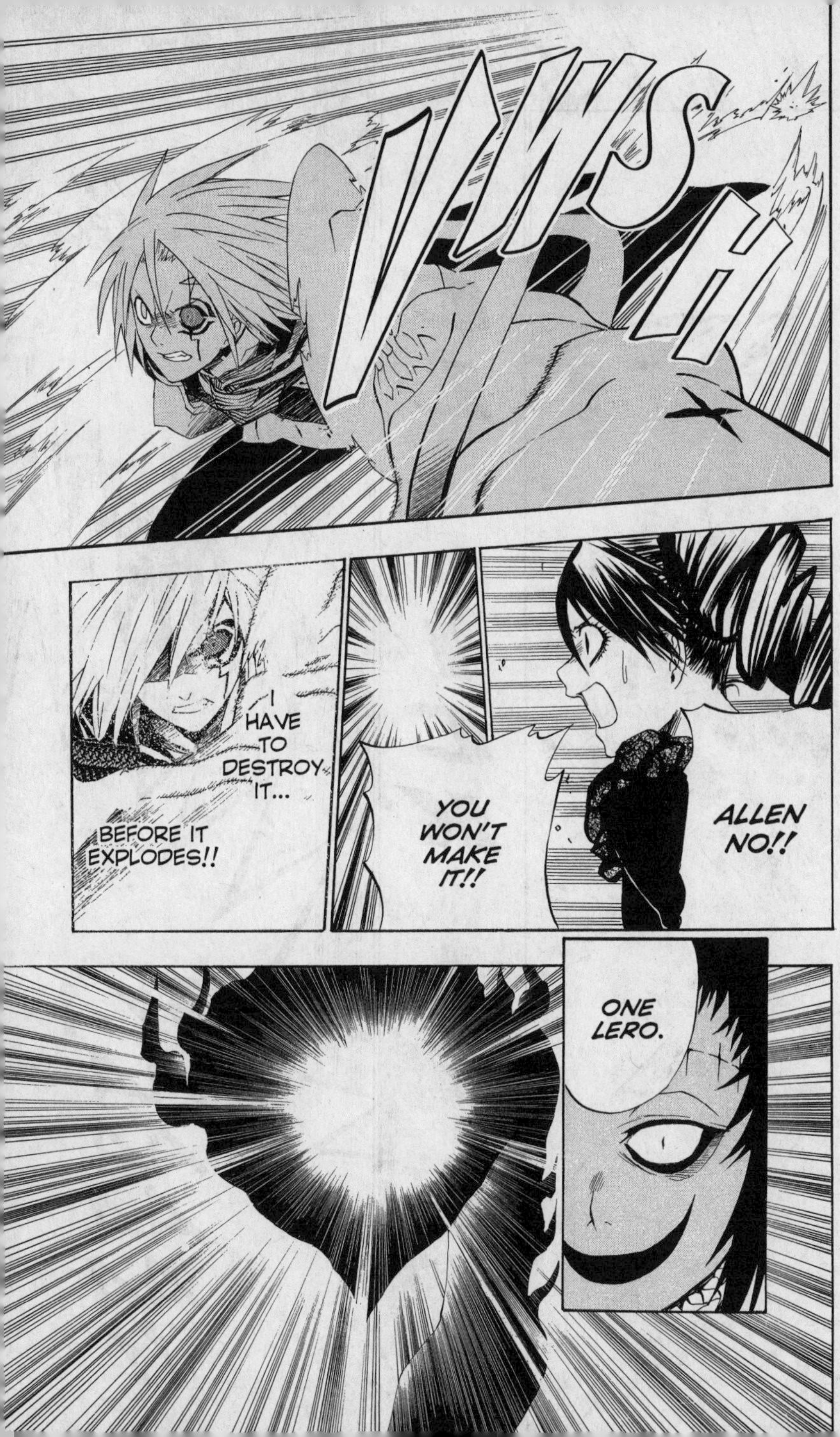
VWSH
ALLEN NO!!
YOU WON'T MAKE IT!!
I HAVE TO DESTROY IT...
BEFORE IT EXPLODES!!
ONE LERO.

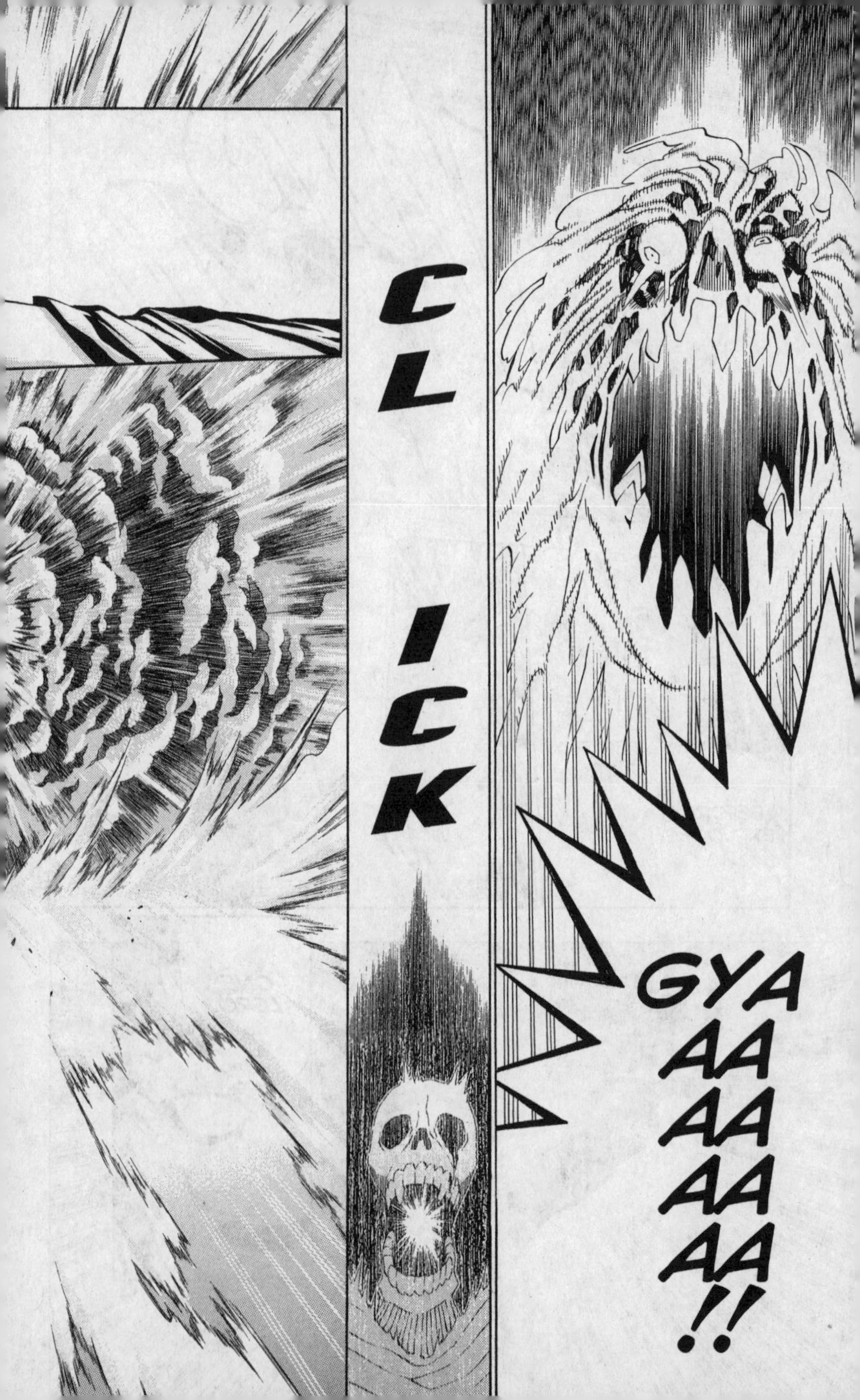
GYAAAAAAAAA!!
CLICK

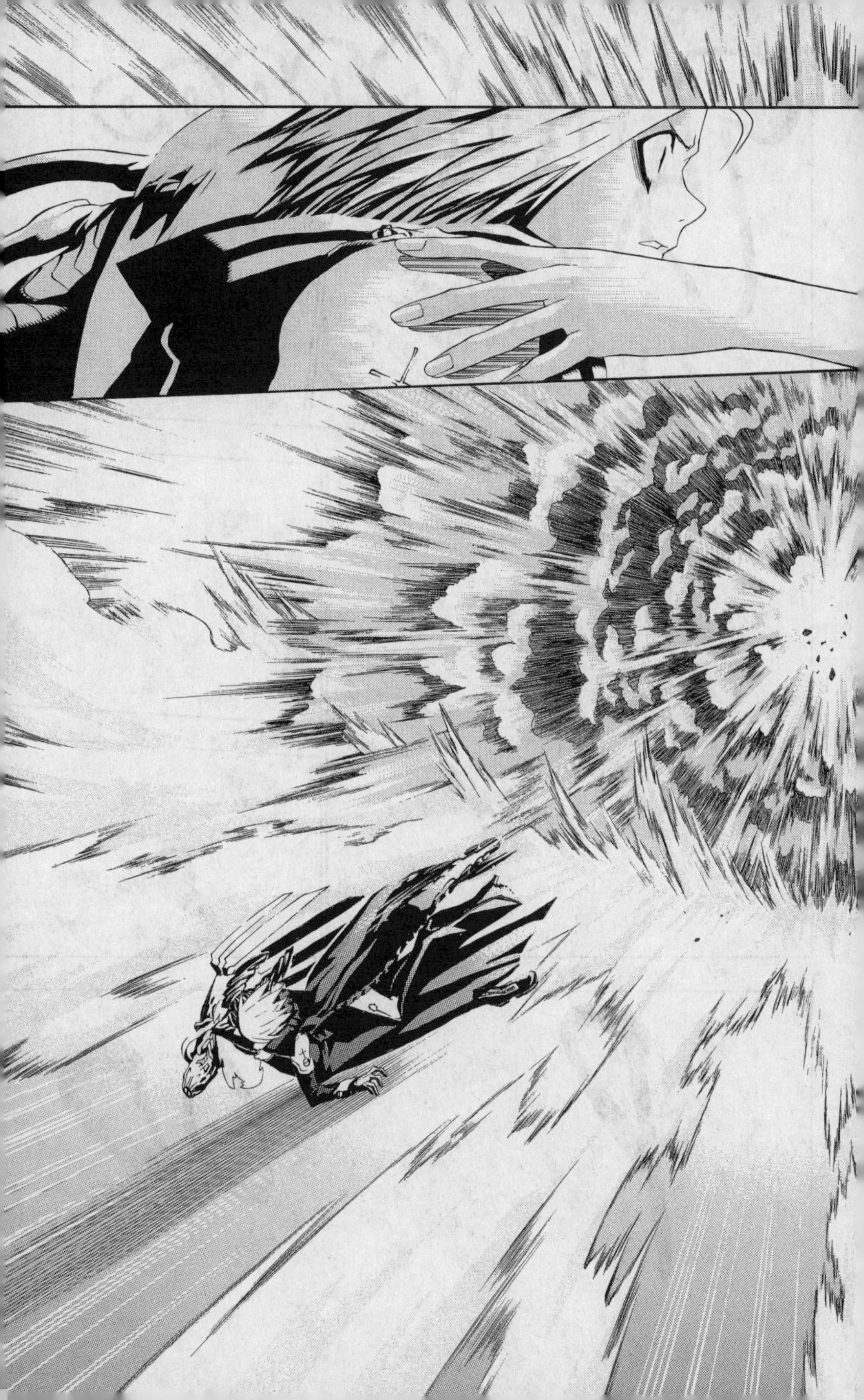

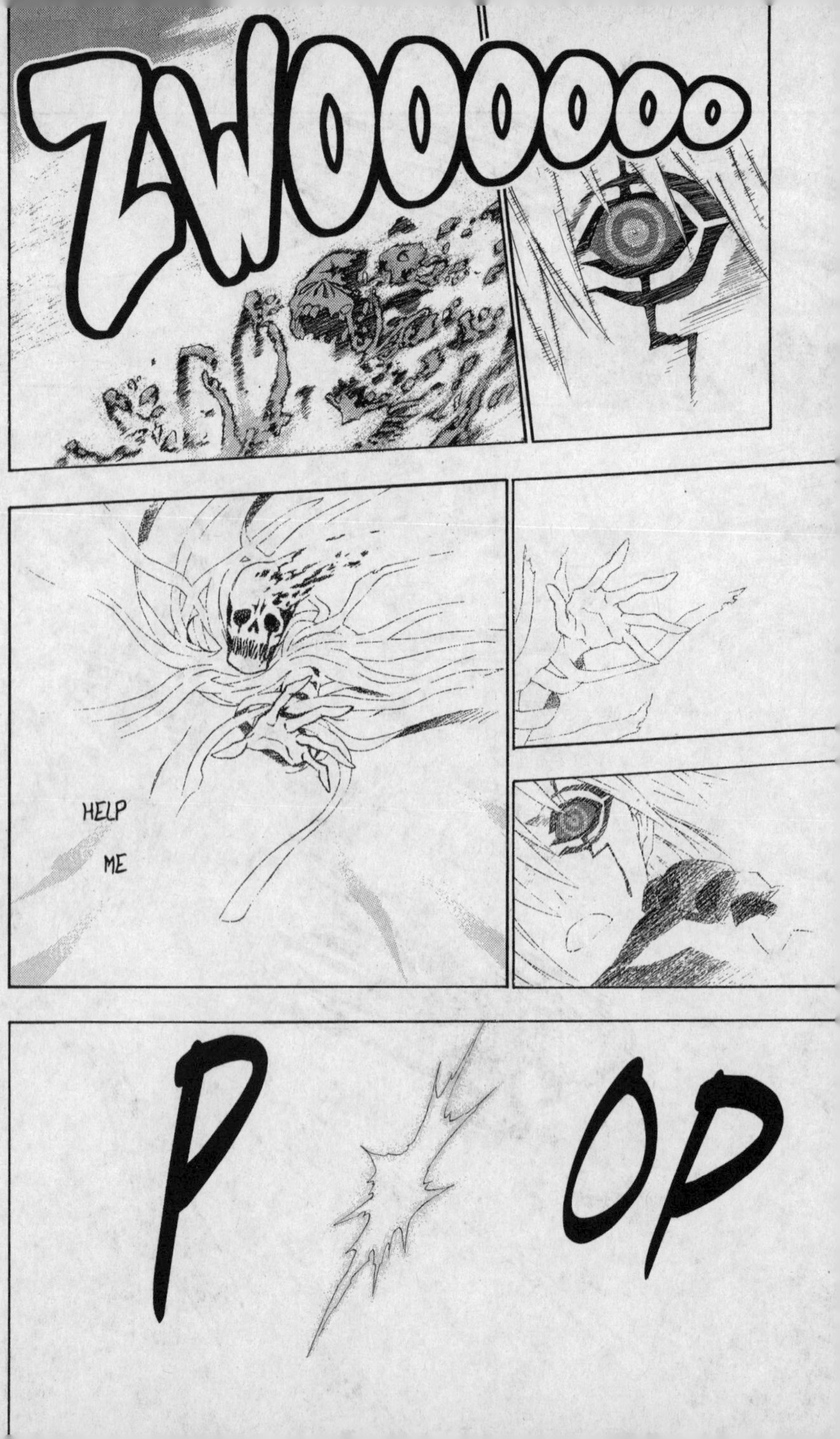
ZWOOOOOO
HELP ME
P OP

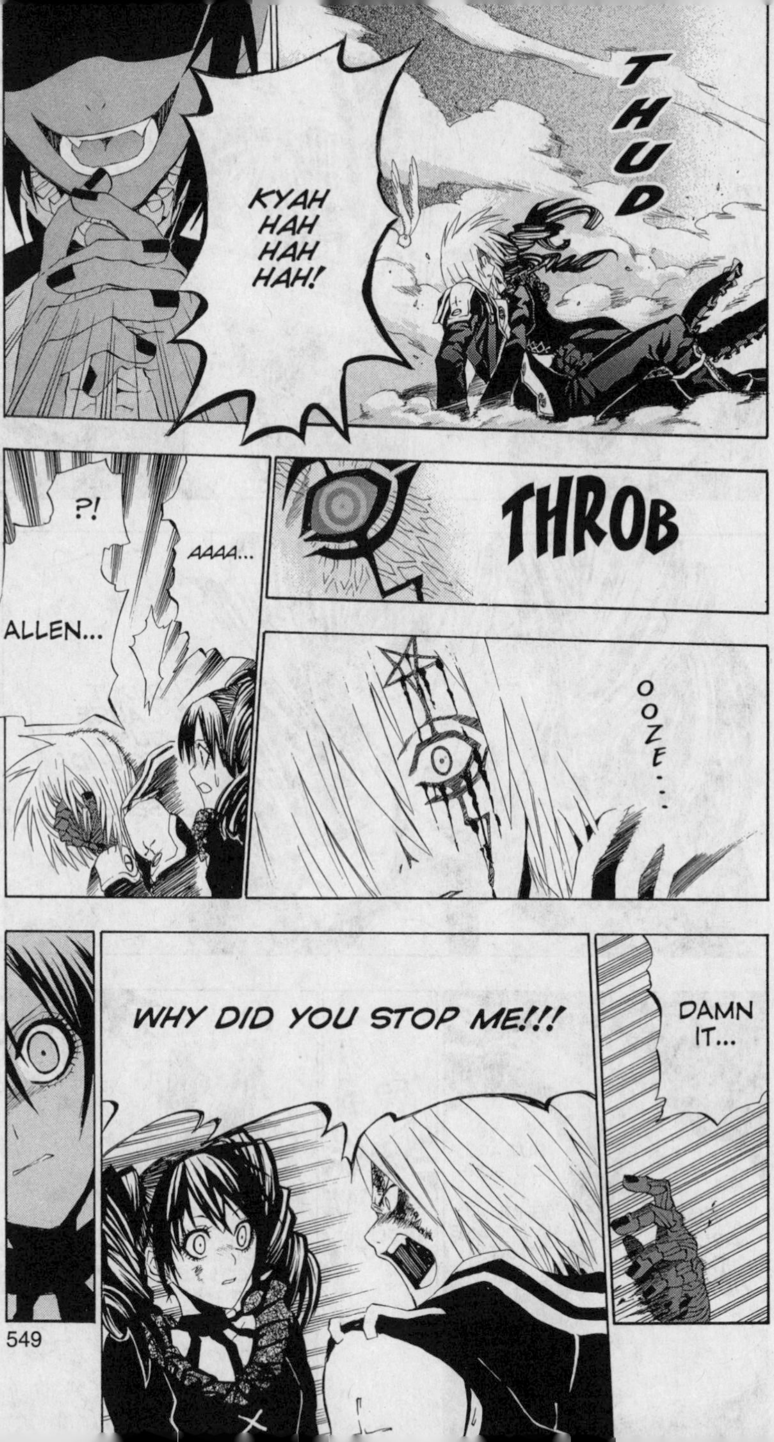
THUD
KYAH HAH HAH HAH!
THROB
OOZE...
?!
AAAA...
ALLEN...
DAMN IT...
WHY DID YOU STOP ME!!!

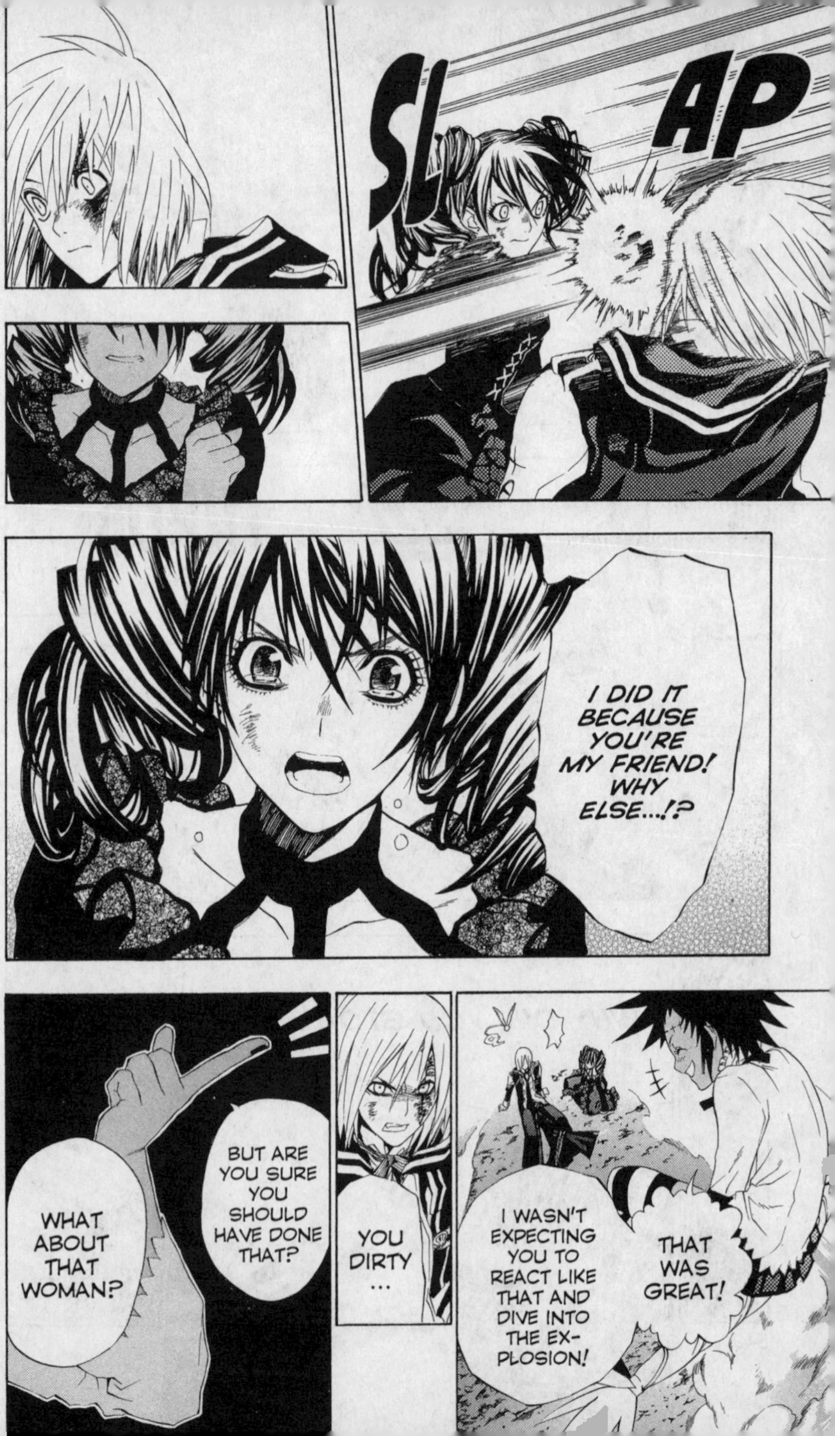
SLAP
I DID IT BECAUSE YOU'RE MY FRIEND! WHY ELSE...!?
THAT WAS GREAT!
I WASN'T EXPECTING YOU TO REACT LIKE THAT AND DIVE INTO THE EX-PLOSION!
YOU DIRTY ...
BUT ARE YOU SURE YOU SHOULD HAVE DONE THAT?
WHAT ABOUT THAT WOMAN?

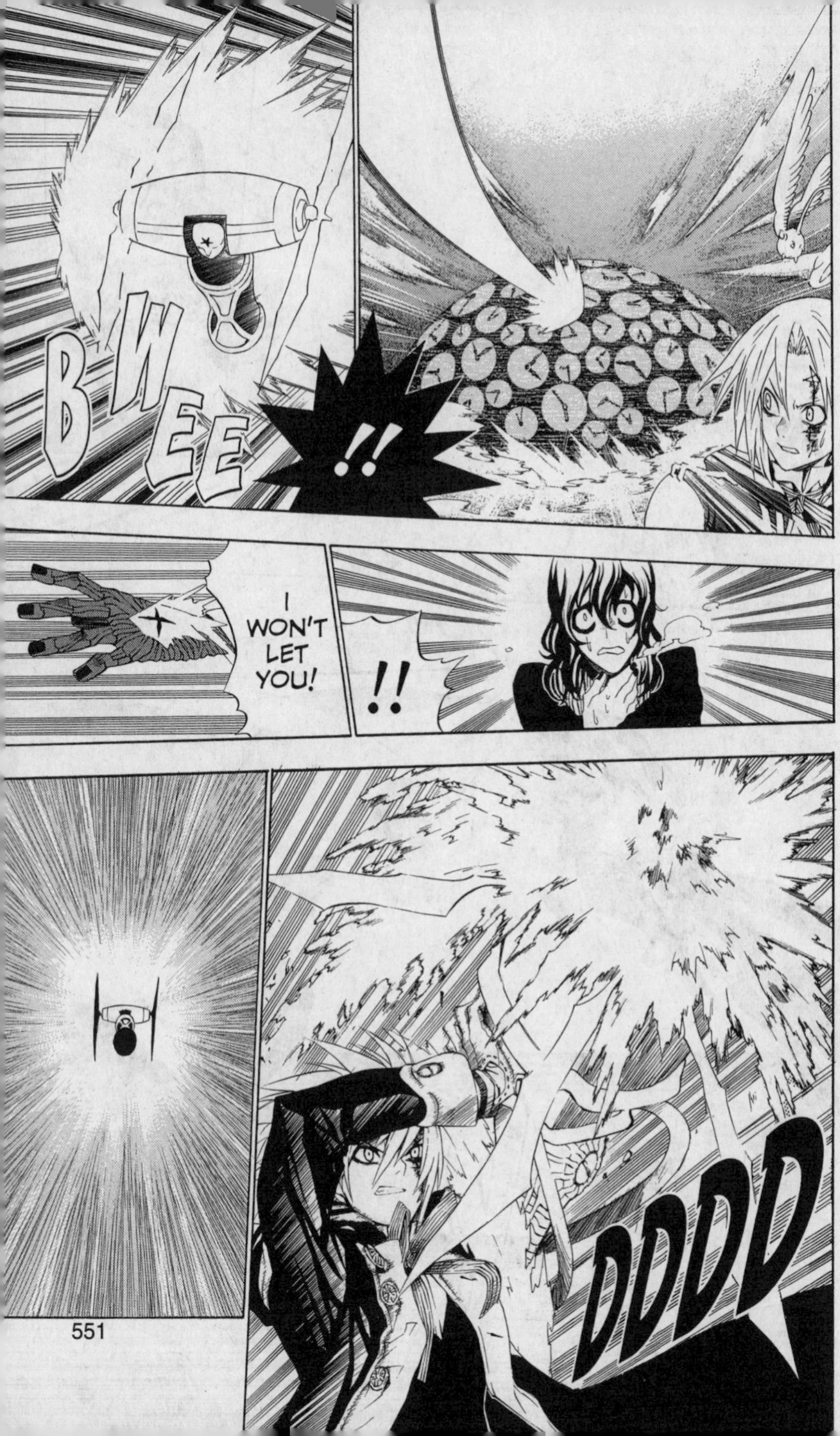
!!
BWEE
!!
I WON'T LET YOU!
DDDD

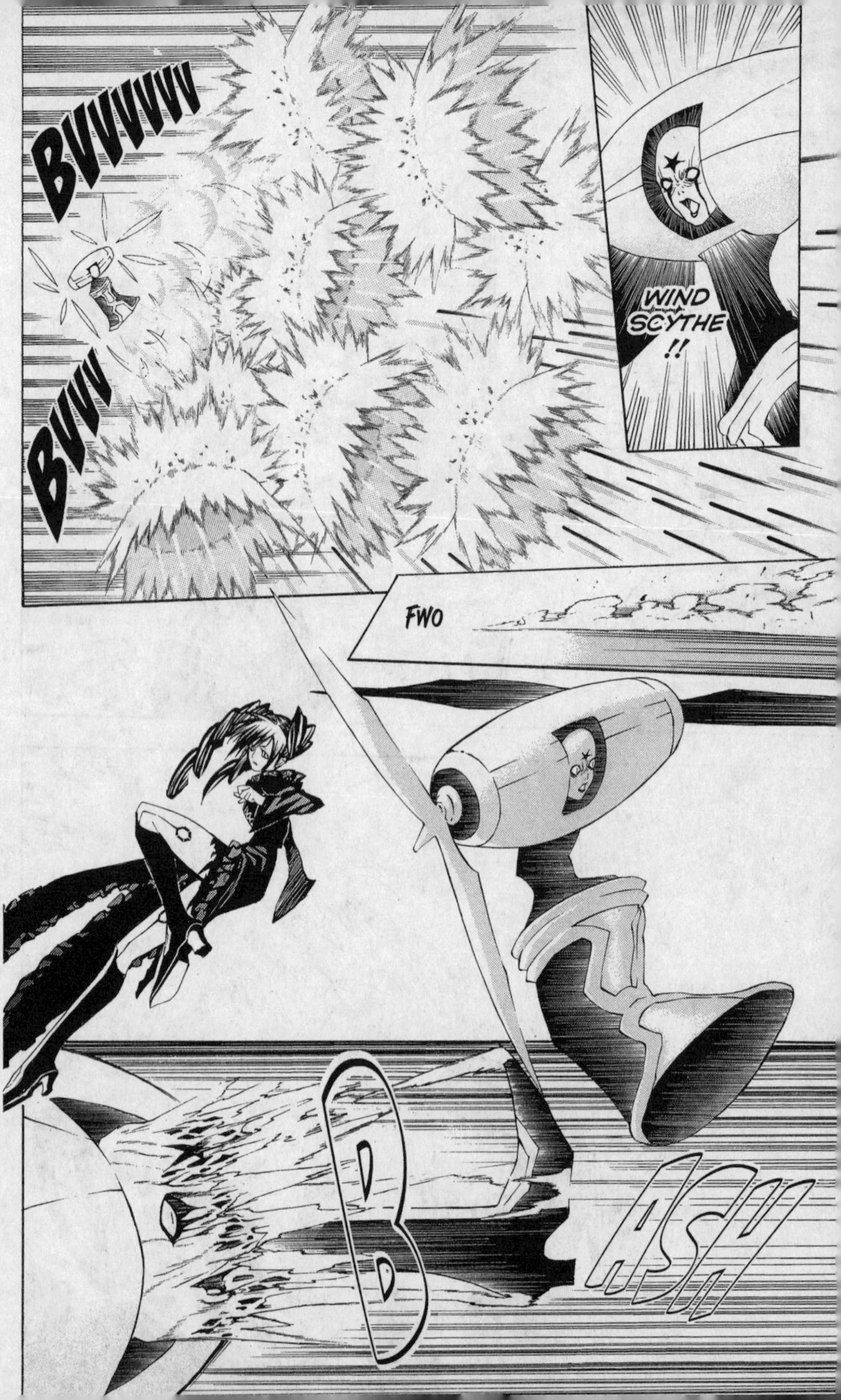
WIND SCYTHE !!
BVVVVVV
BVVV
FWO
BASH

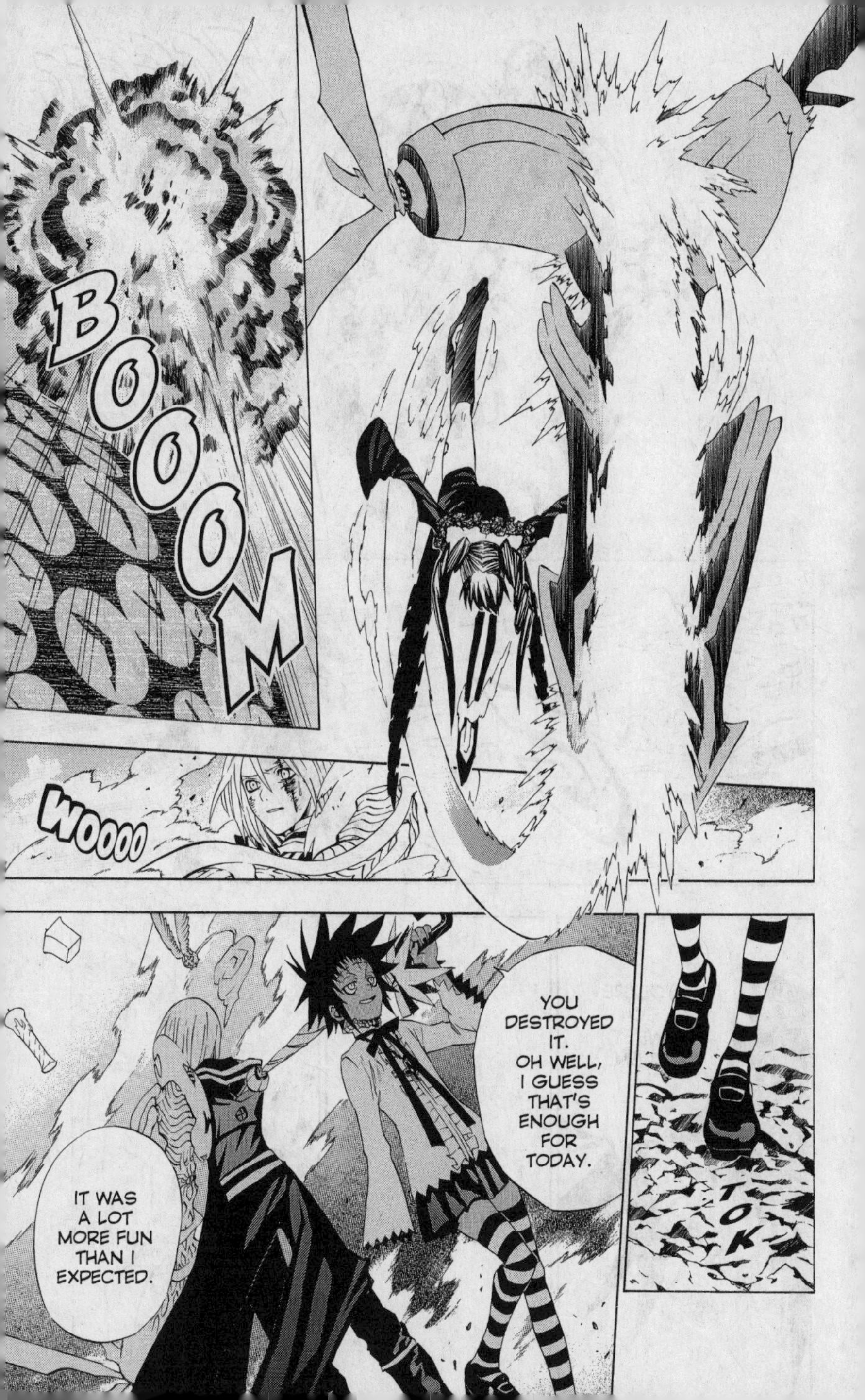
BOOOOM
WOOOO
TOK
YOU DESTROYED IT. OH WELL, I GUESS THAT'S ENOUGH FOR TODAY.
IT WAS A LOT MORE FUN THAN I EXPECTED.

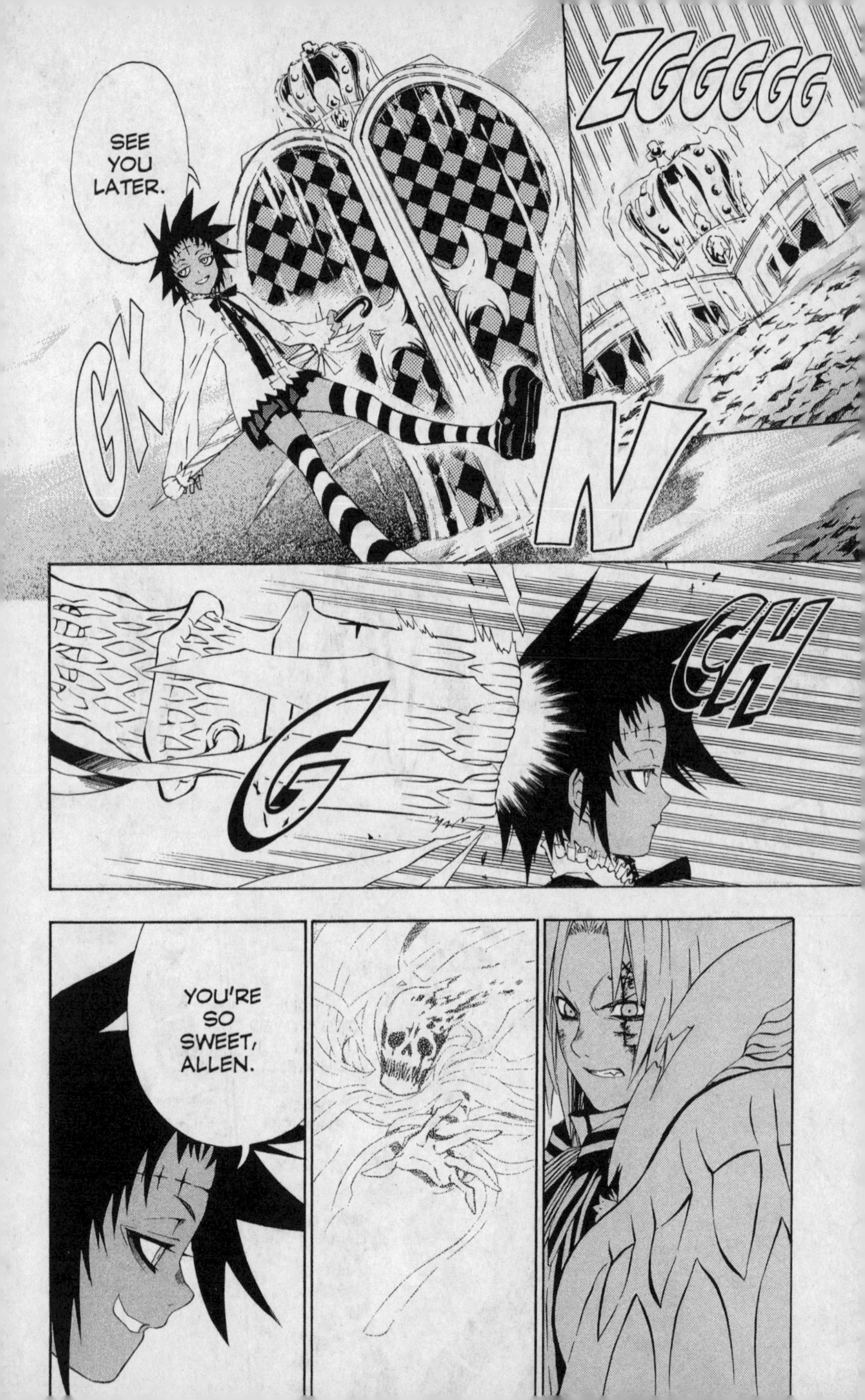
ZGGGGG
SEE YOU LATER.
N
GK
CH
G
YOU'RE SO SWEET, ALLEN.

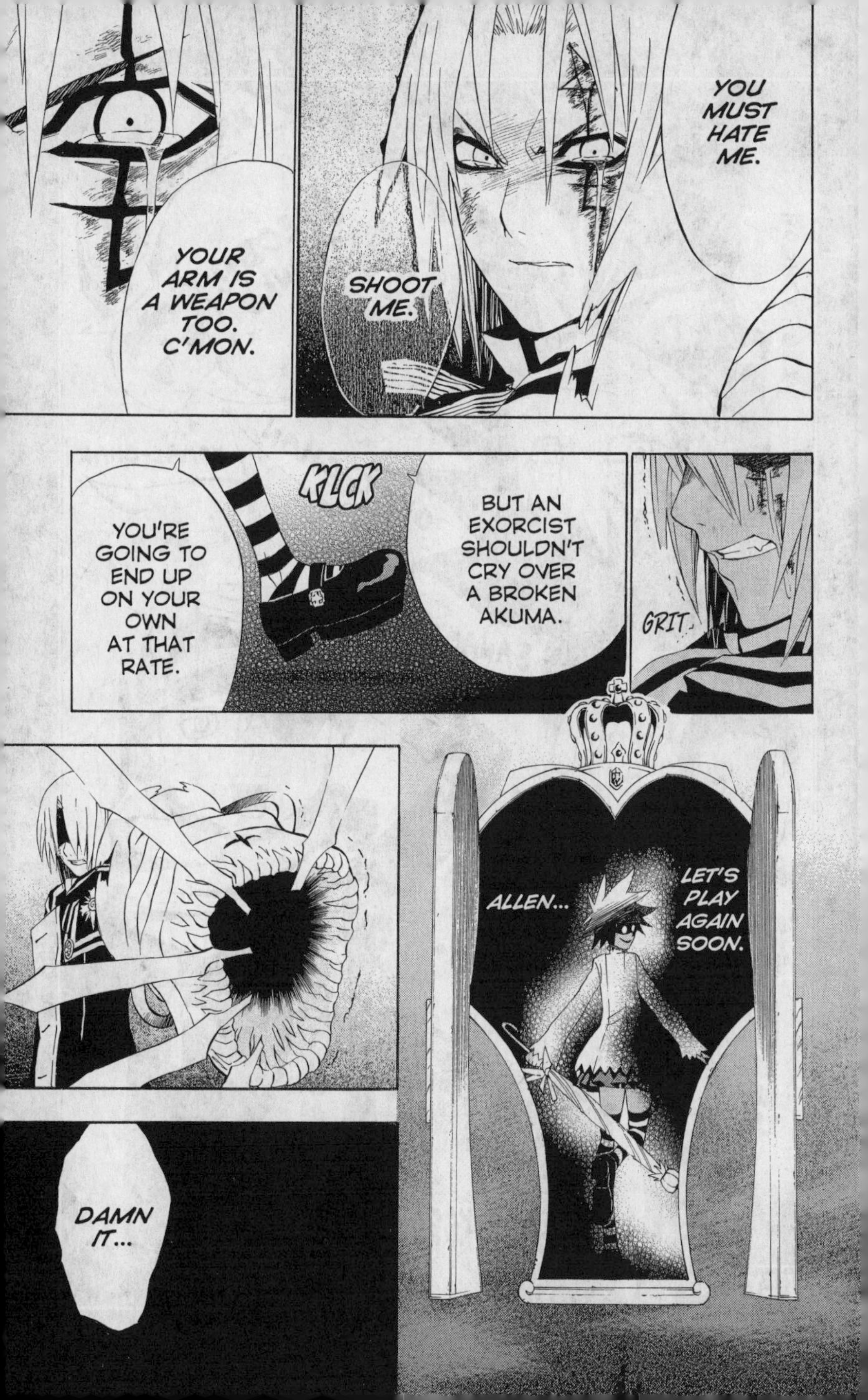
YOU MUST HATE ME.
SHOOT ME.
YOUR ARM IS A WEAPON TOO. C'MON.
GRIT
KLCK
BUT AN EXORCIST SHOULDN'T CRY OVER A BROKEN AKUMA.
YOU'RE GOING TO END UP ON YOUR OWN AT THAT RATE.
LET'S PLAY AGAIN SOON.
ALLEN...
DAMN IT...

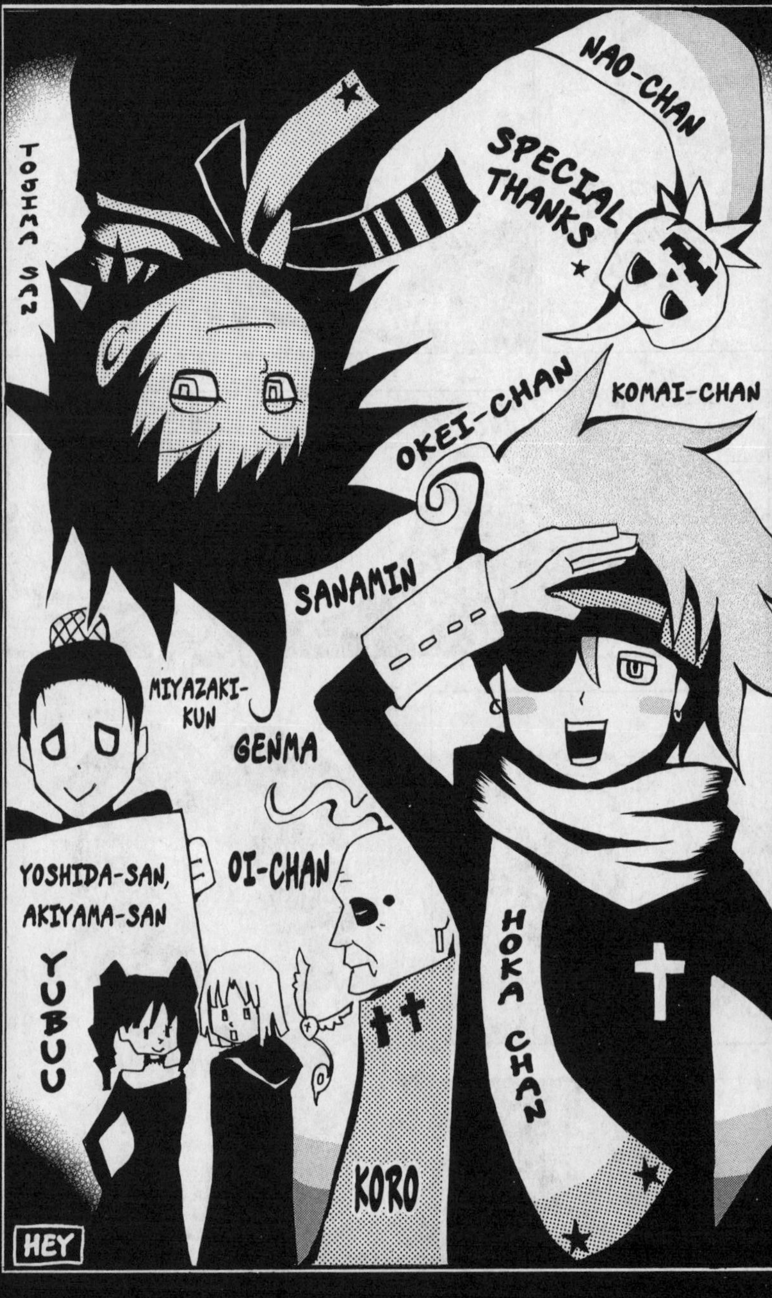
NAO-CHAN
SPECIAL THANKS ★
TOJIMA SAN
KOMAI-CHAN
OKEI-CHAN
SANAMIN
MIYAZAKI-KUN
GENMA
HOKA CHAN
OI-CHAN
YOSHIDA-SAN, AKIYAMA-SAN
YUBUU
KORO
HEY

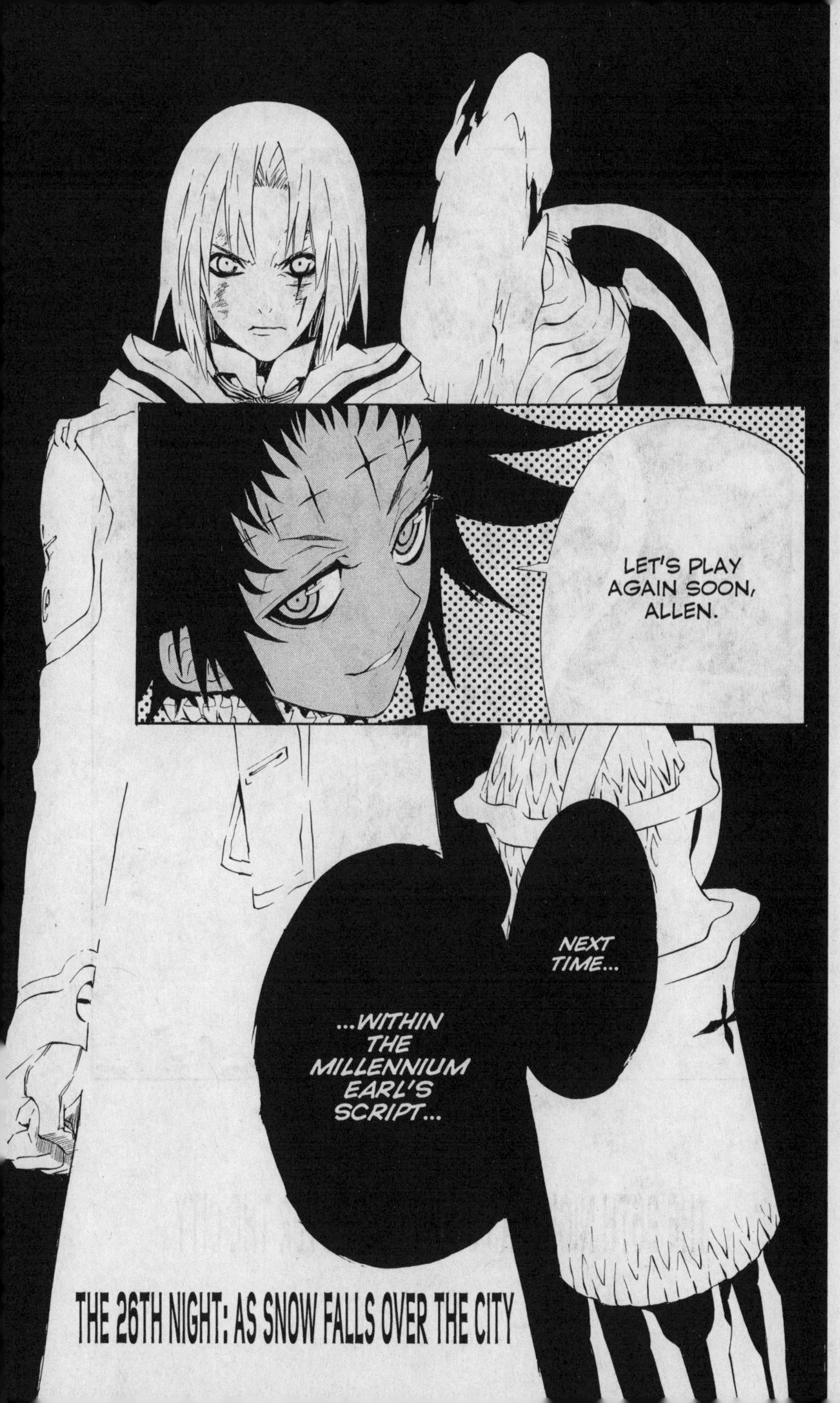
LET'S PLAY AGAIN SOON, ALLEN.
NEXT TIME...
...WITHIN THE MILLENNIUM EARL'S SCRIPT...

THE 26TH NIGHT: AS SNOW FALLS OVER THE CITY

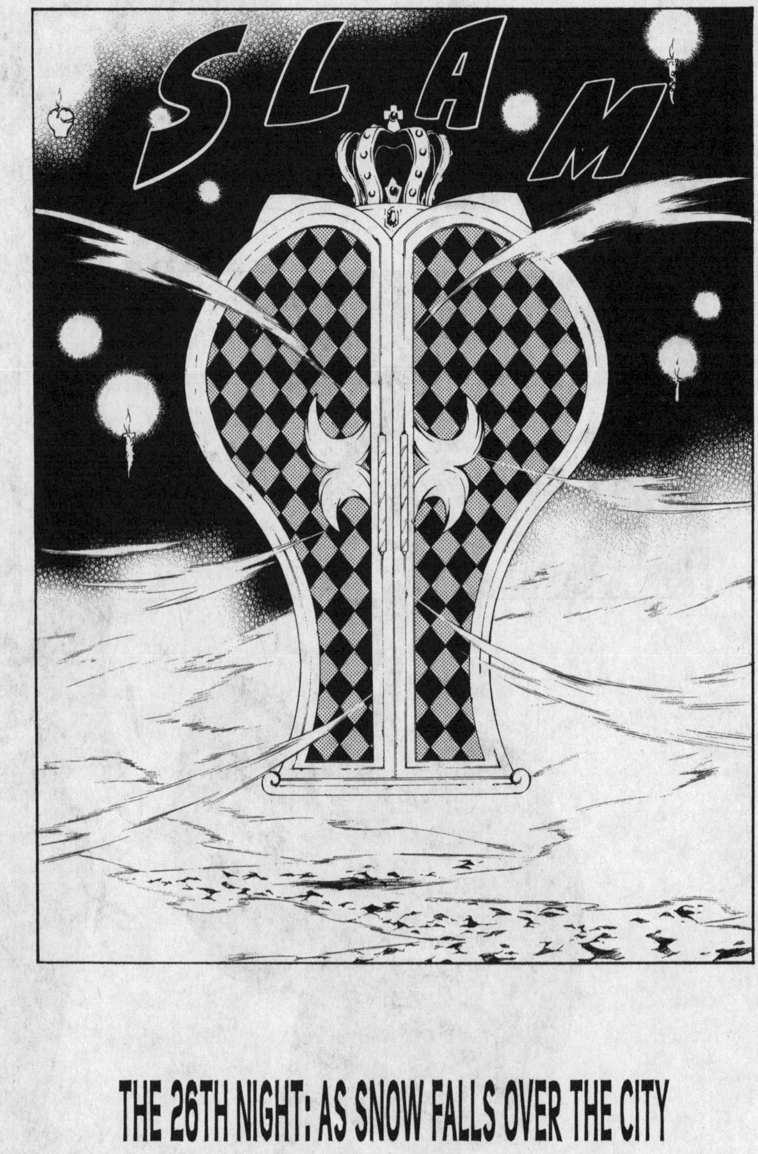
SLAM

THE 26TH NIGHT: AS SNOW FALLS OVER THE CITY

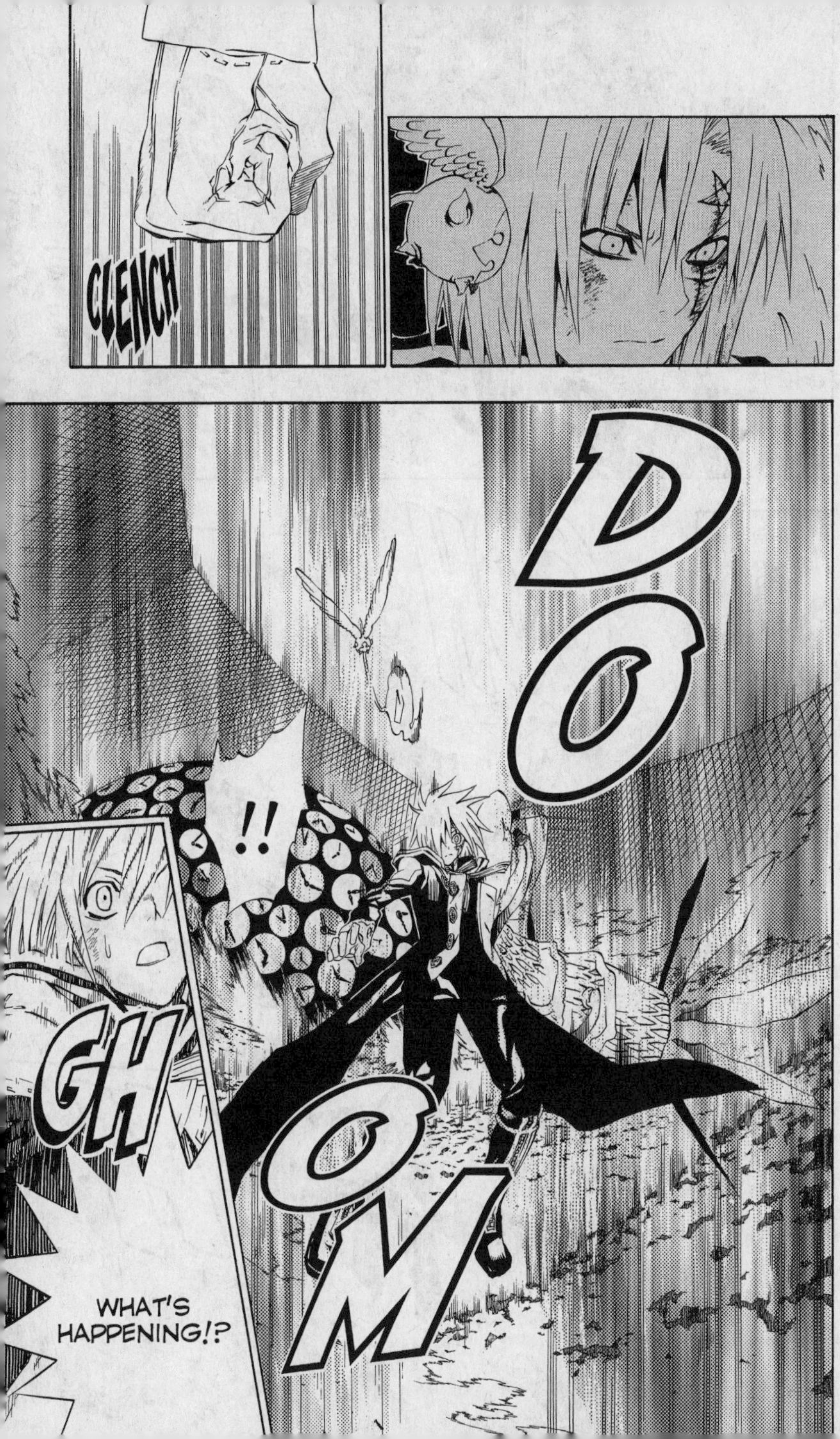
CLENCH
DOOM
!!
GH
WHAT'S HAPPENING!?

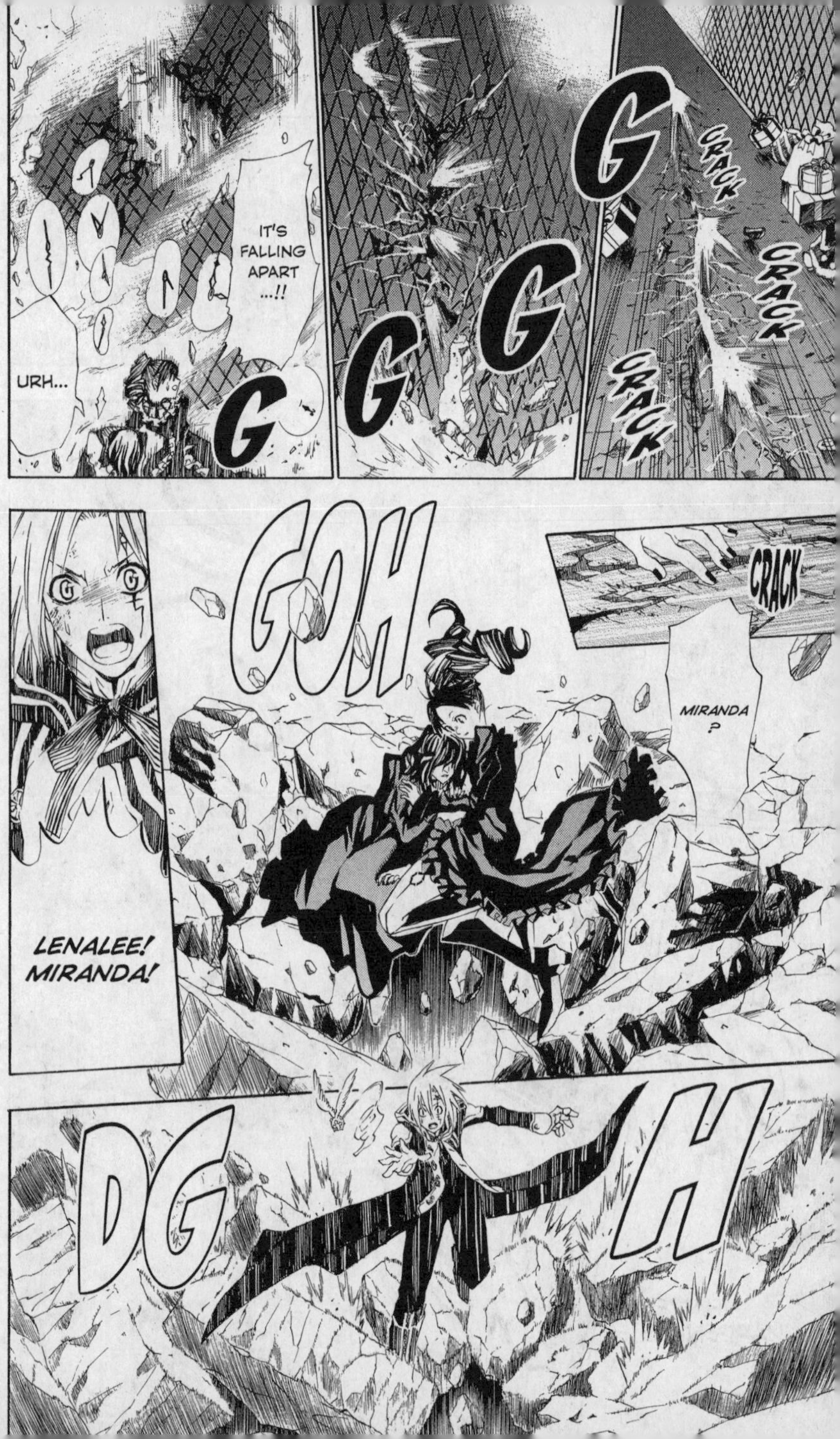
CRACK
CRACK
CRACK
CRACK
CRACK
G
G
G
G
G
IT'S FALLING APART ...!!
URH...
CRACK
MIRANDA ?
GOH
LENALEE! MIRANDA!
DGH

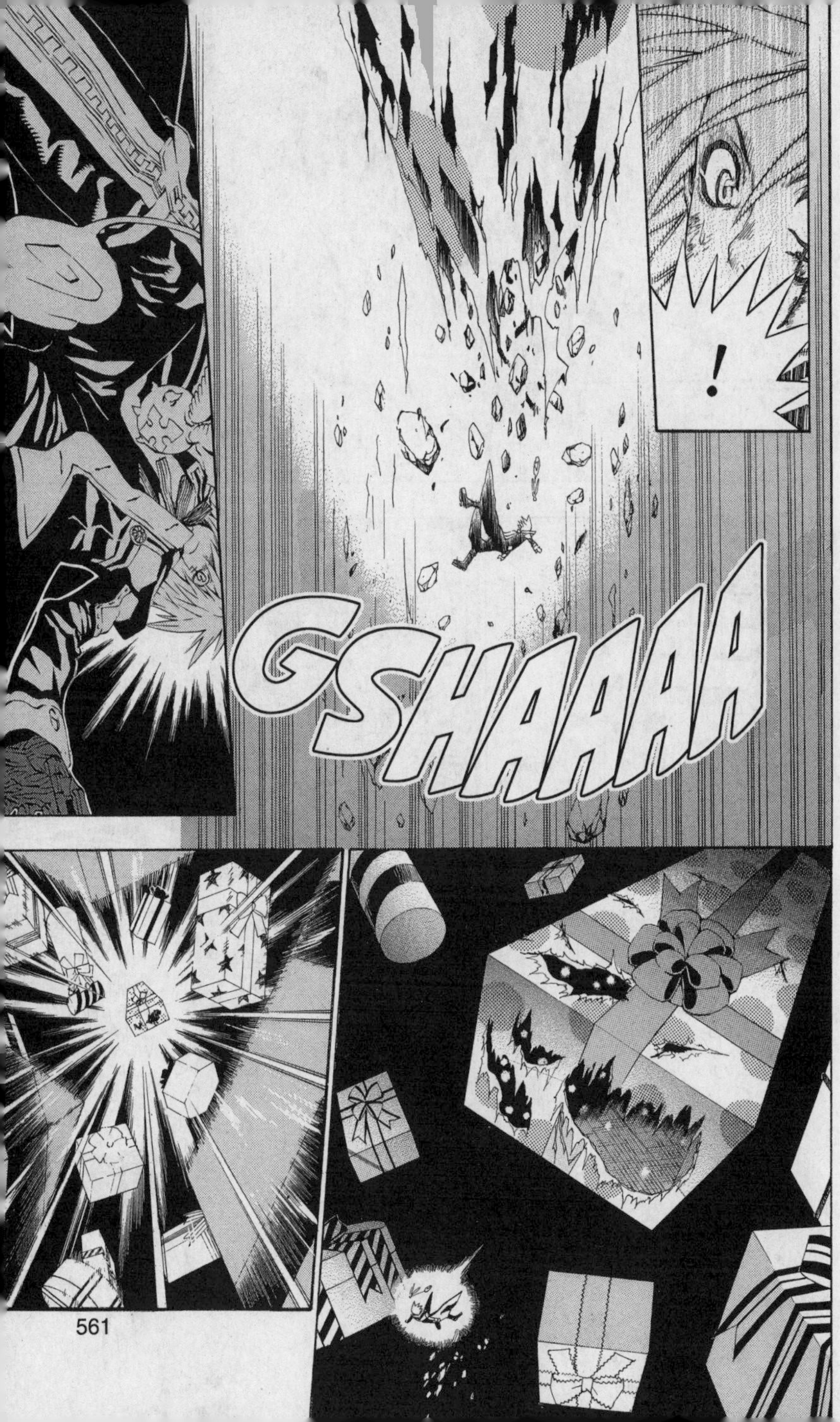
!
GSHAAAA

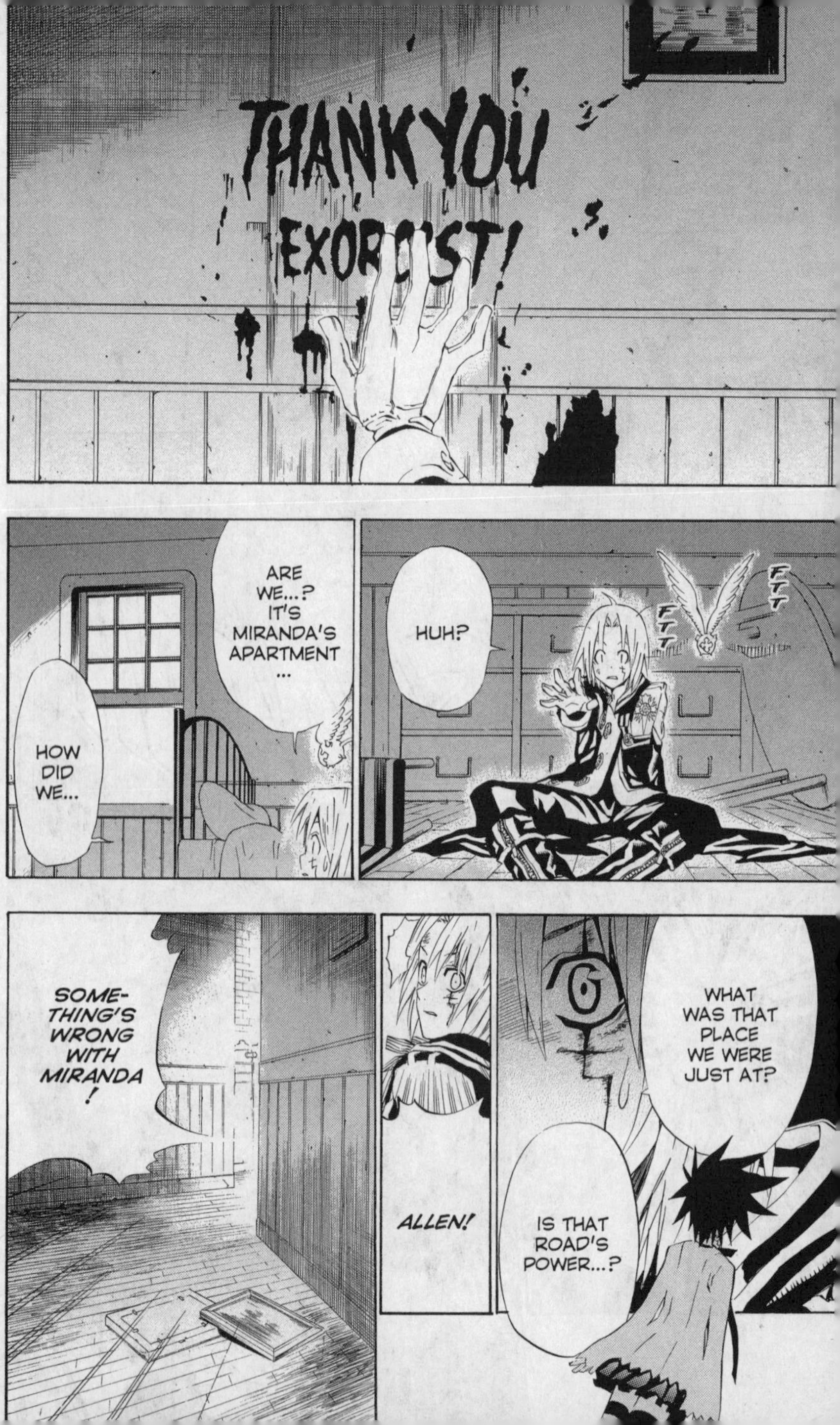
THANK YOU EXORCIST!
FTT
HUH?
FTT
ARE WE...? IT'S MIRANDA'S APARTMENT...
HOW DID WE...
WHAT WAS THAT PLACE WE WERE JUST AT?
IS THAT ROAD'S POWER...?
ALLEN!
SOME-THING'S WRONG WITH MIRANDA!

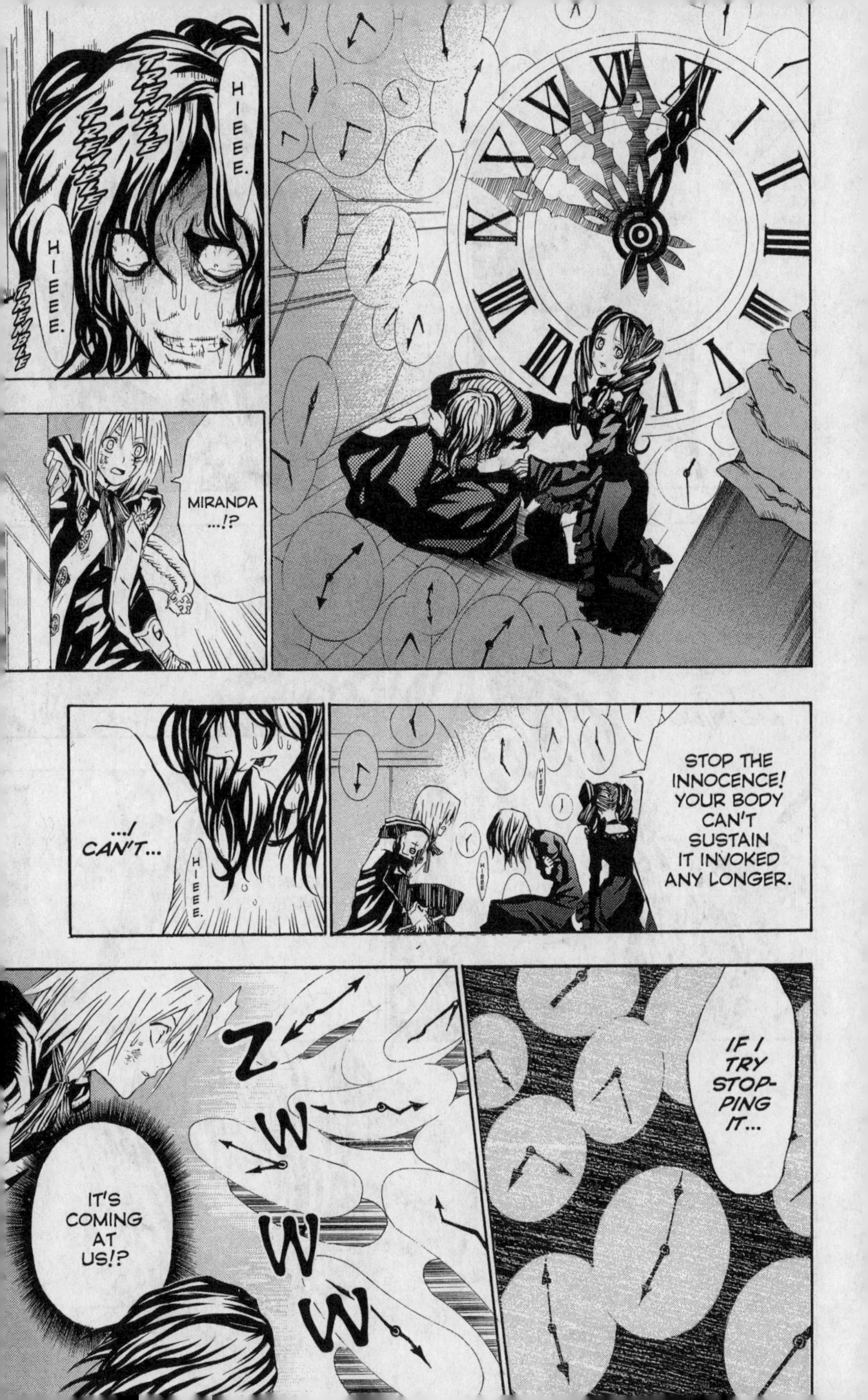

HIEEE.
TREMBLE TREMBLE
HIEEE.
TREMBLE
MIRANDA ...!?
STOP THE INNOCENCE! YOUR BODY CAN'T SUSTAIN IT INVOKED ANY LONGER.
...I CAN'T...
HIEEE.
IF I TRY STOPPING IT...
ZWWWW
IT'S COMING AT US!?

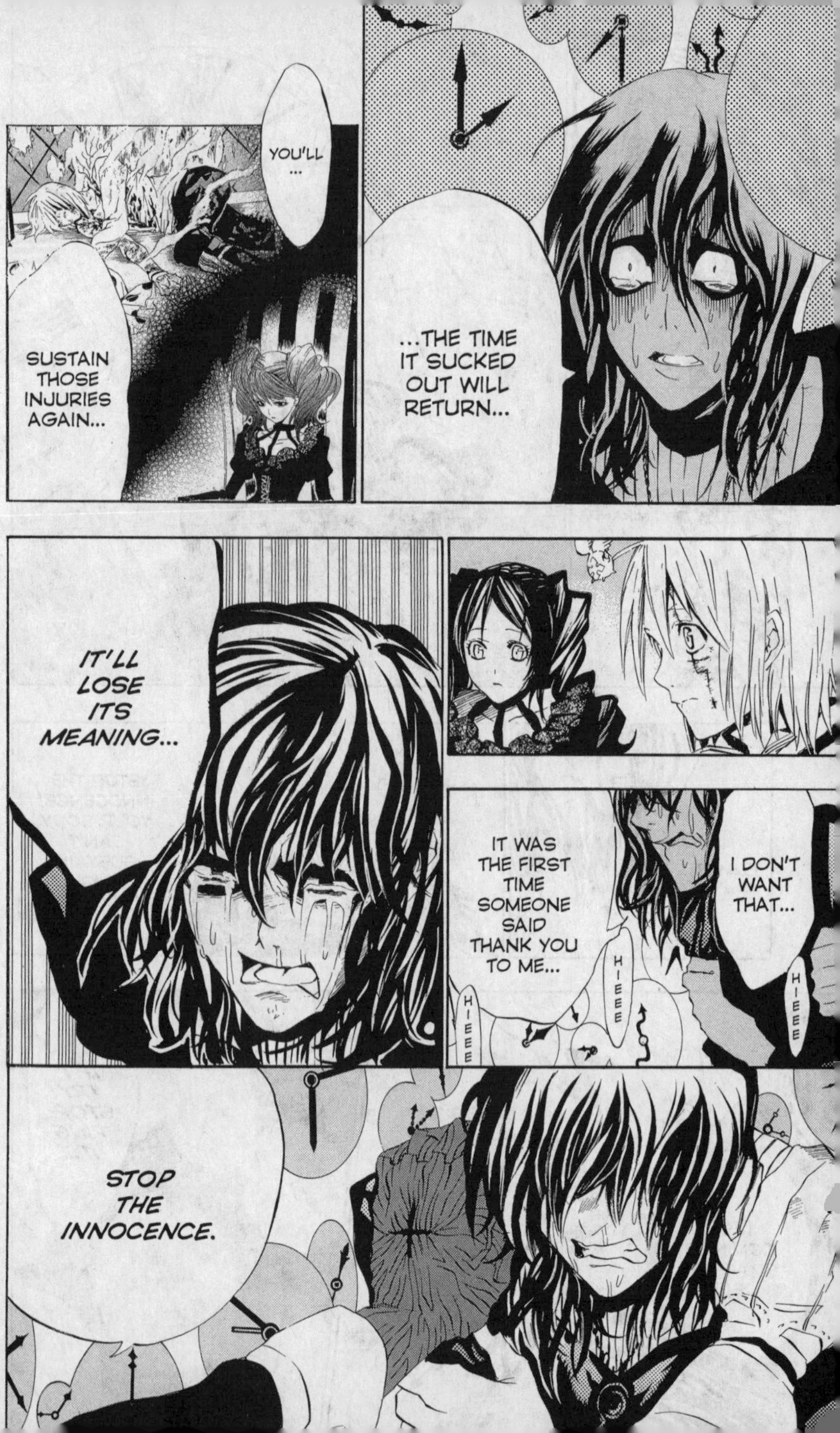
...THE TIME IT SUCKED OUT WILL RETURN...
YOU'LL ...
SUSTAIN THOSE INJURIES AGAIN...
I DON'T WANT THAT...
HIEEE
IT WAS THE FIRST TIME SOMEONE SAID THANK YOU TO ME...
HIEEE
HIEEE
IT'LL LOSE ITS MEANING...
STOP THE INNOCENCE.

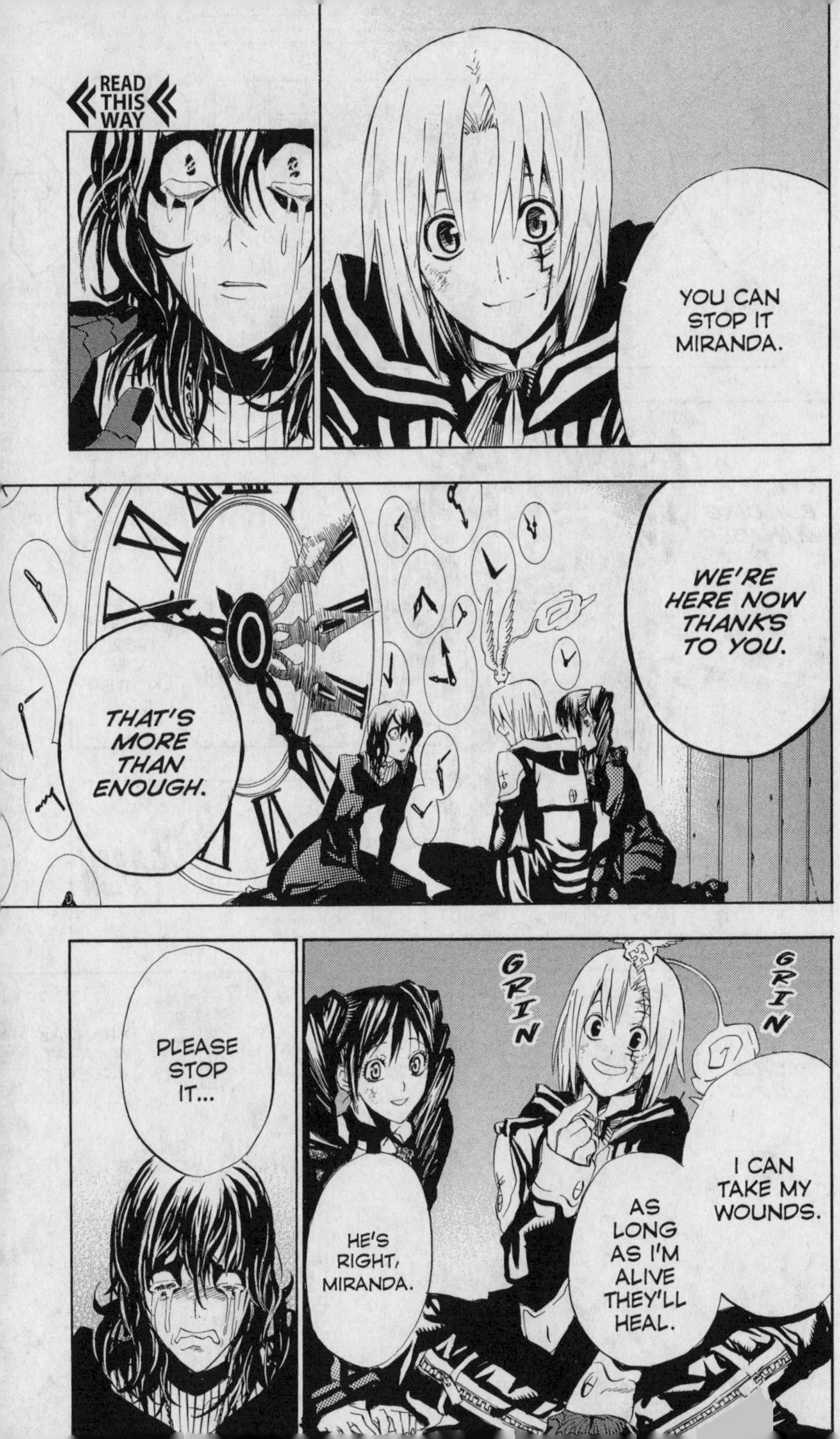
READ THIS WAY
YOU CAN STOP IT MIRANDA.
WE'RE HERE NOW THANKS TO YOU.
THAT'S MORE THAN ENOUGH.
GRIN
GRIN
I CAN TAKE MY WOUNDS.
AS LONG AS I'M ALIVE THEY'LL HEAL.
HE'S RIGHT, MIRANDA.
PLEASE STOP IT...

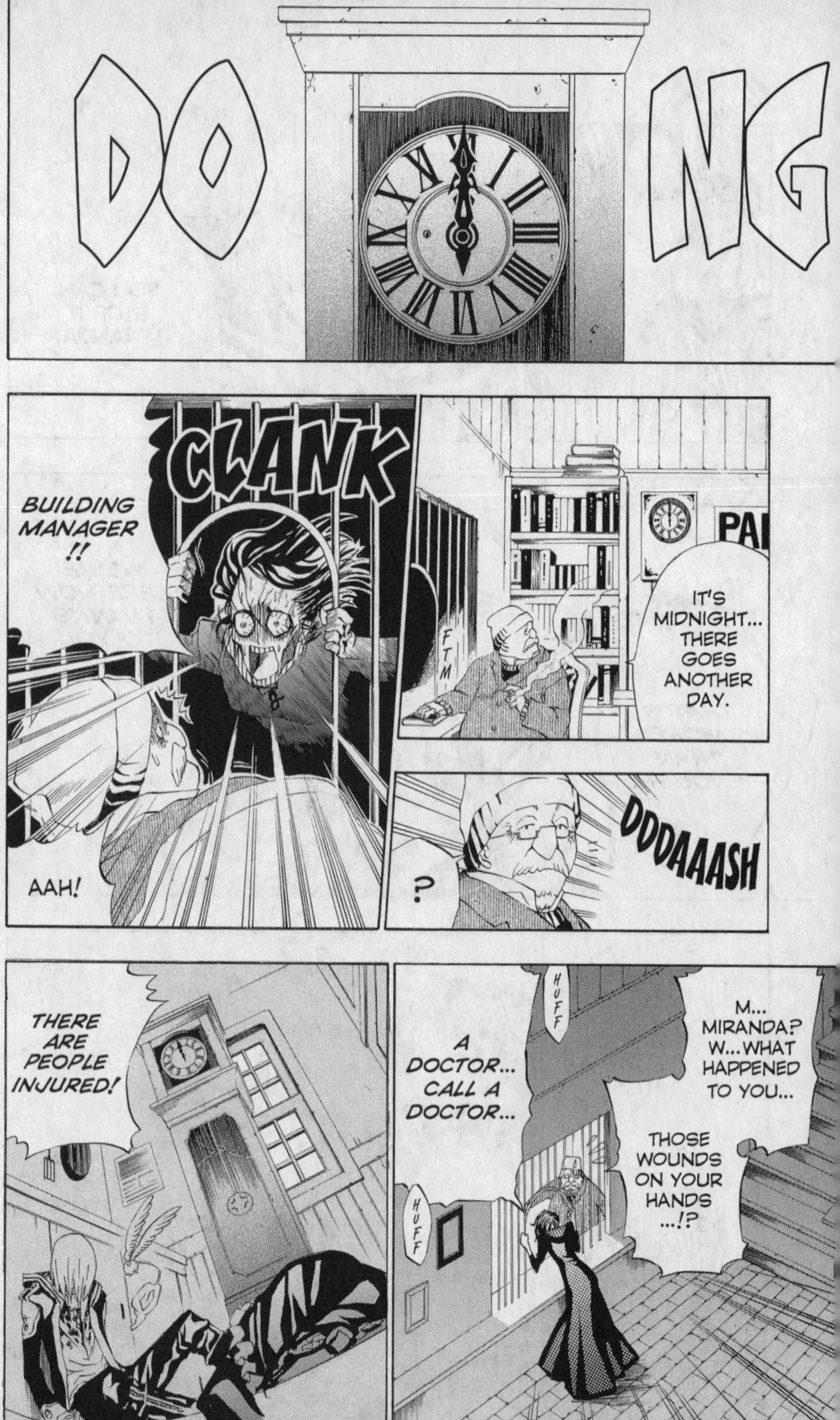
DONG
PA
IT'S MIDNIGHT... THERE GOES ANOTHER DAY.
FTM
DDDAAASH
?
CLANK
BUILDING MANAGER !!
AAH!
M... MIRANDA? W...WHAT HAPPENED TO YOU...
HUFF
A DOCTOR... CALL A DOCTOR...
THOSE WOUNDS ON YOUR HANDS ...!?
HUFF
THERE ARE PEOPLE INJURED!

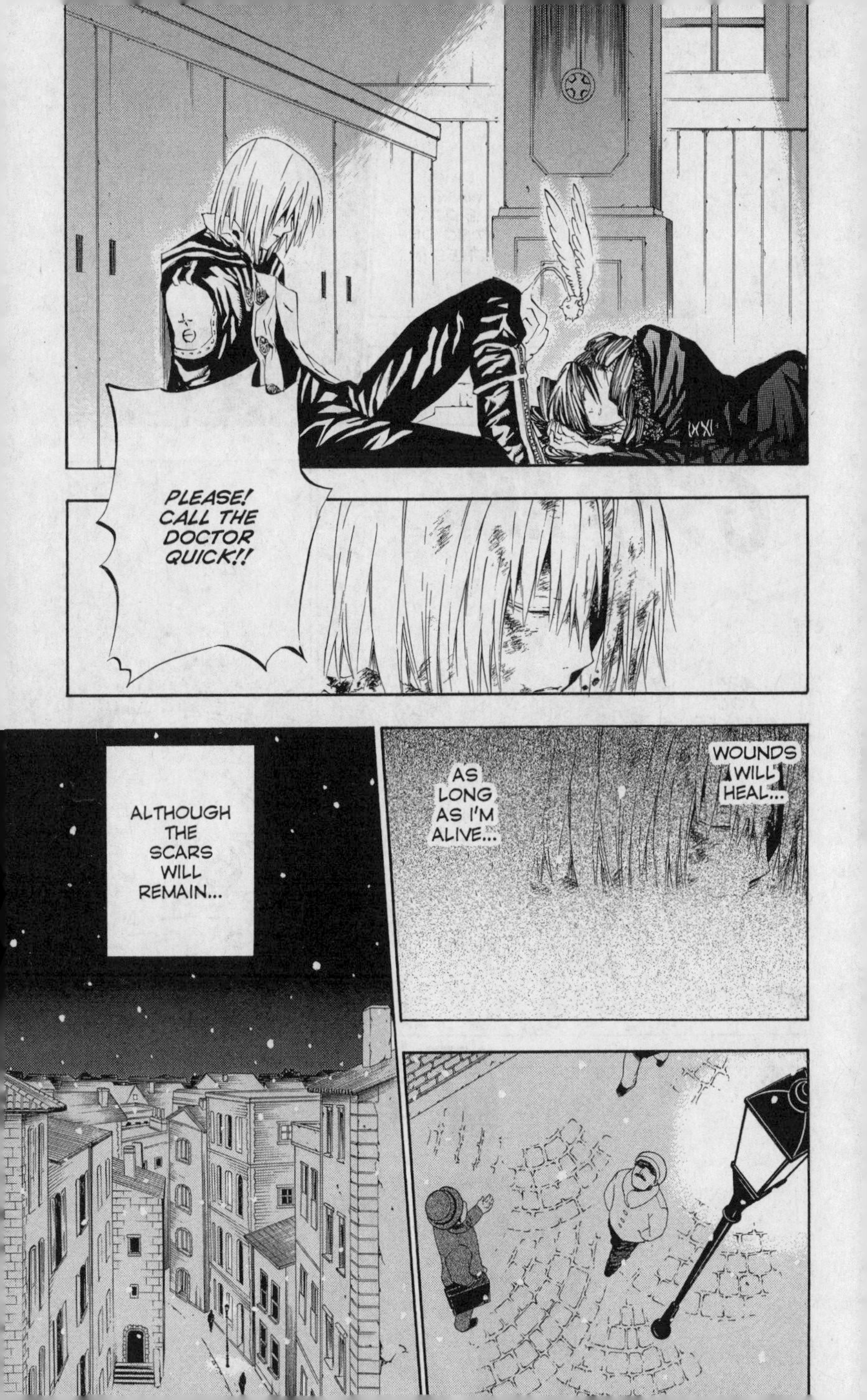
PLEASE! CALL THE DOCTOR QUICK!!
WOUNDS WILL HEAL...
AS LONG AS I'M ALIVE...
ALTHOUGH THE SCARS WILL REMAIN...

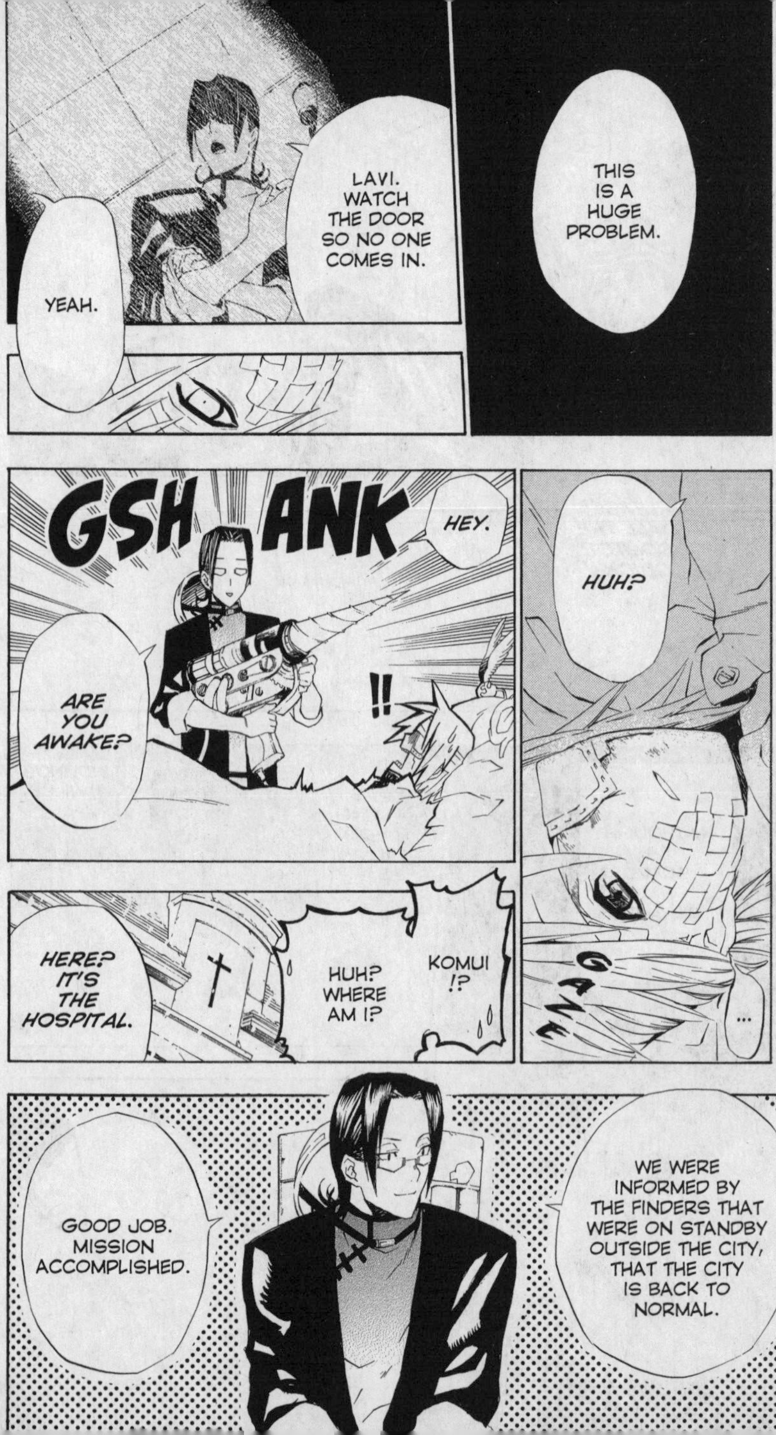
THIS IS A HUGE PROBLEM.
LAVI. WATCH THE DOOR SO NO ONE COMES IN.
YEAH.
HUH?
GAZE
...
HEY.
GSH ANK
!!
ARE YOU AWAKE?
KOMUI !?
HUH? WHERE AM I?
HERE? IT'S THE HOSPITAL.
WE WERE INFORMED BY THE FINDERS THAT WERE ON STANDBY OUTSIDE THE CITY, THAT THE CITY IS BACK TO NORMAL.
GOOD JOB. MISSION ACCOMPLISHED.

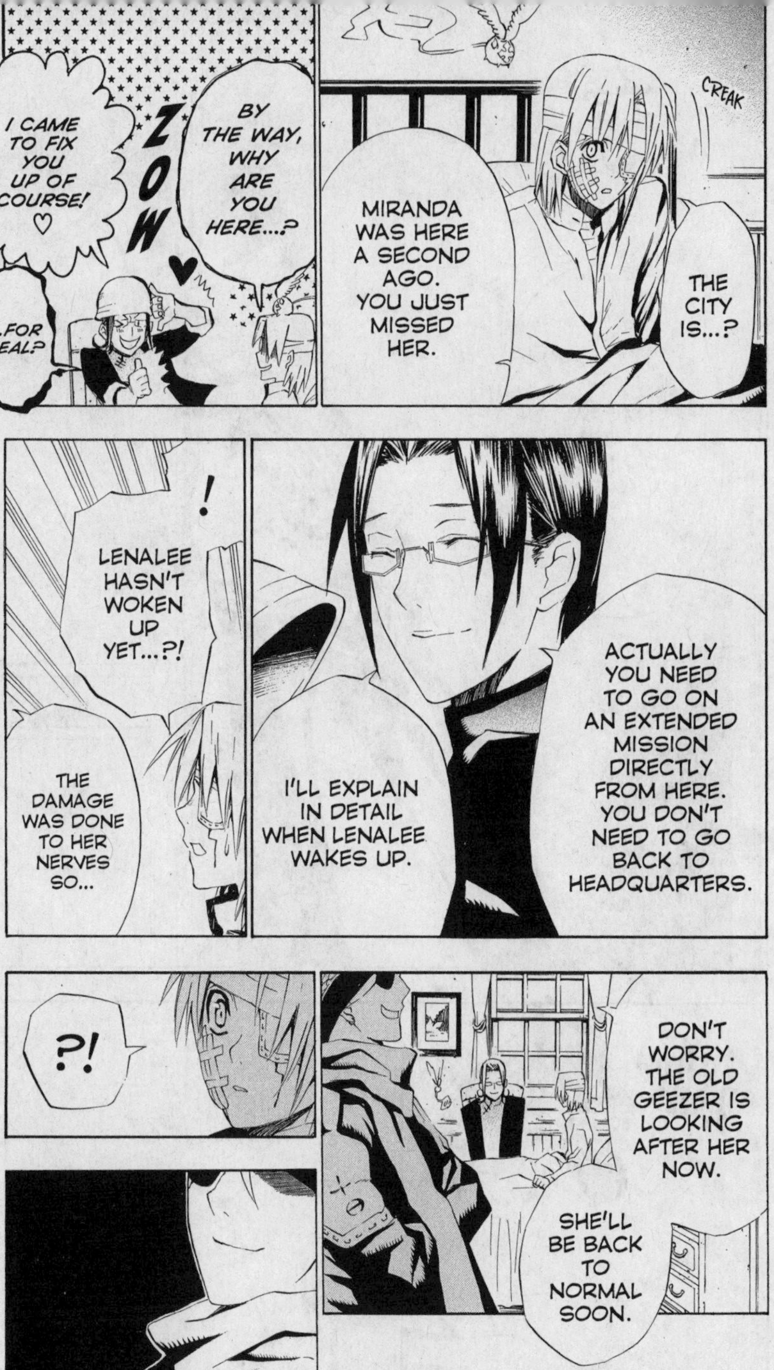
CREAK
THE CITY IS...?
MIRANDA WAS HERE A SECOND AGO. YOU JUST MISSED HER.
BY THE WAY, WHY ARE YOU HERE...?
ZOW
I CAME TO FIX YOU UP OF COURSE! ♡
...FOR REAL?
ACTUALLY YOU NEED TO GO ON AN EXTENDED MISSION DIRECTLY FROM HERE. YOU DON'T NEED TO GO BACK TO HEADQUARTERS.
I'LL EXPLAIN IN DETAIL WHEN LENALEE WAKES UP.
!
LENALEE HASN'T WOKEN UP YET...?!
THE DAMAGE WAS DONE TO HER NERVES SO...
DON'T WORRY. THE OLD GEEZER IS LOOKING AFTER HER NOW.
SHE'LL BE BACK TO NORMAL SOON.
?!

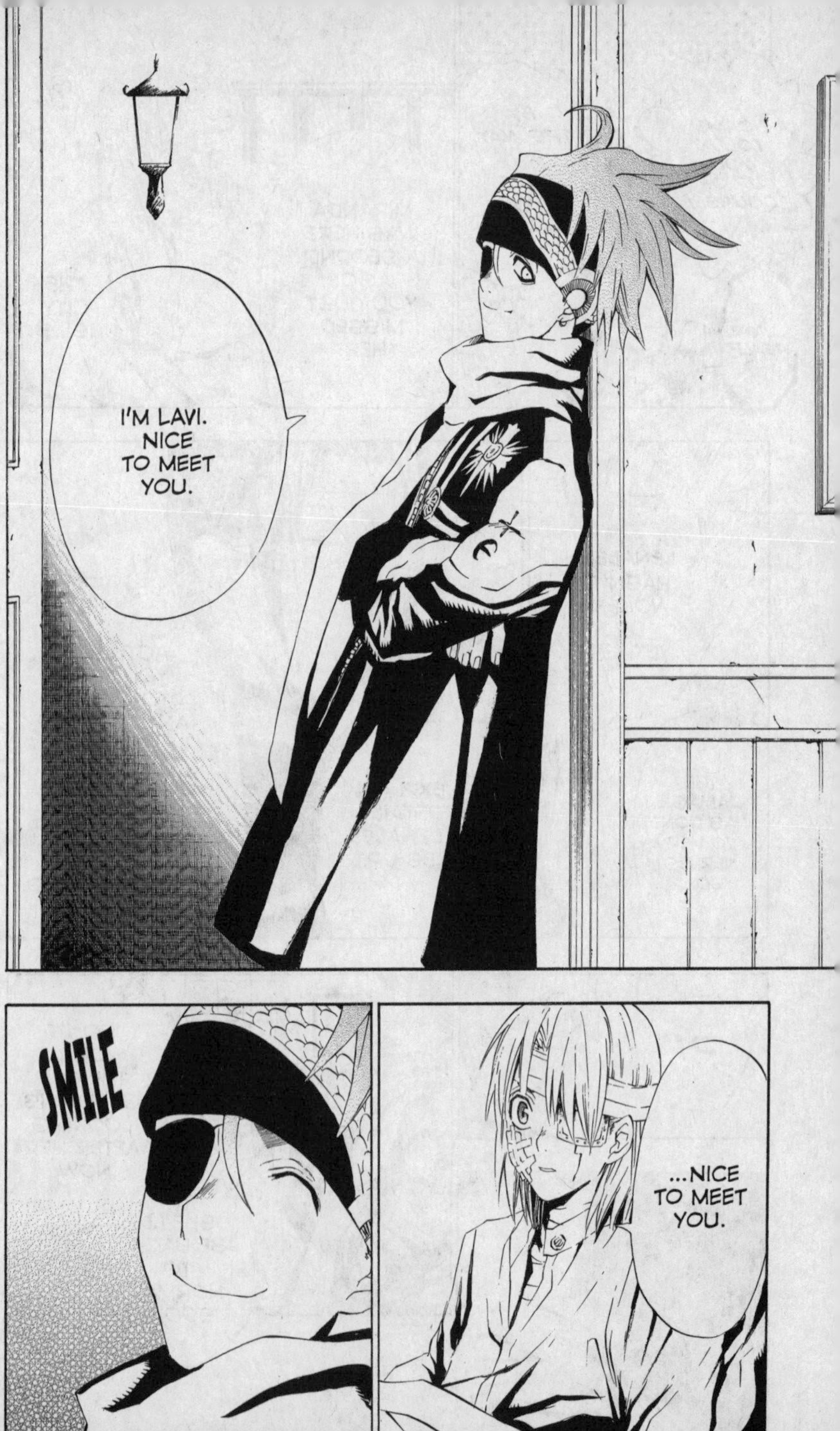
I'M LAVI. NICE TO MEET YOU.
...NICE TO MEET YOU.
SMILE

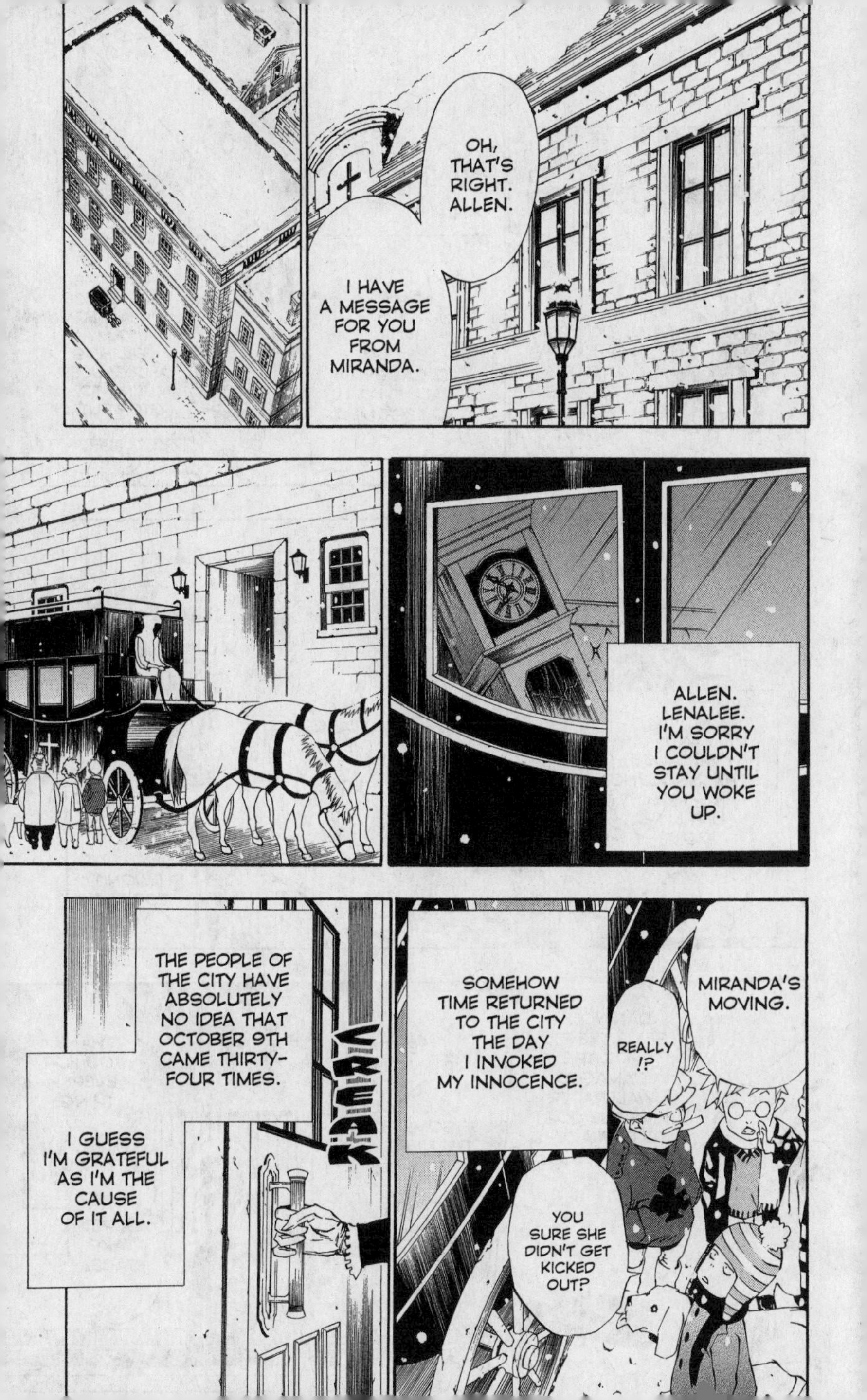
OH, THAT'S RIGHT. ALLEN.
I HAVE A MESSAGE FOR YOU FROM MIRANDA.
ALLEN. LENALEE. I'M SORRY I COULDN'T STAY UNTIL YOU WOKE UP.
MIRANDA'S MOVING.
SOMEHOW TIME RETURNED TO THE CITY THE DAY I INVOKED MY INNOCENCE.
REALLY!?
YOU SURE SHE DIDN'T GET KICKED OUT?
THE PEOPLE OF THE CITY HAVE ABSOLUTELY NO IDEA THAT OCTOBER 9TH CAME THIRTY-FOUR TIMES.
CREAK
I GUESS I'M GRATEFUL AS I'M THE CAUSE OF IT ALL.

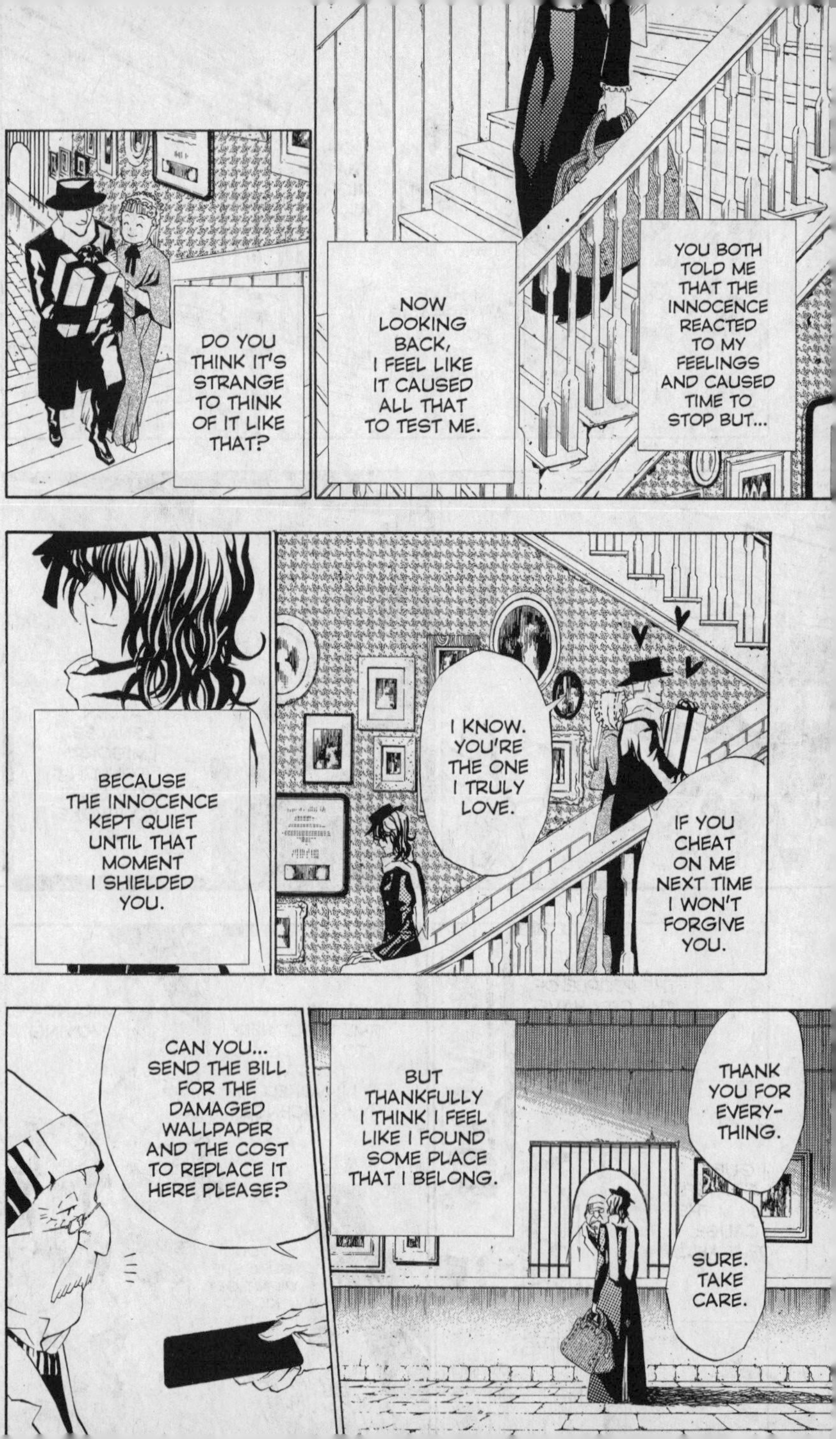
YOU BOTH TOLD ME THAT THE INNOCENCE REACTED TO MY FEELINGS AND CAUSED TIME TO STOP BUT...
NOW LOOKING BACK, I FEEL LIKE IT CAUSED ALL THAT TO TEST ME.
DO YOU THINK IT'S STRANGE TO THINK OF IT LIKE THAT?
IF YOU CHEAT ON ME NEXT TIME I WON'T FORGIVE YOU.
I KNOW. YOU'RE THE ONE I TRULY LOVE.
BECAUSE THE INNOCENCE KEPT QUIET UNTIL THAT MOMENT I SHIELDED YOU.
THANK YOU FOR EVERY-THING.
SURE. TAKE CARE.
BUT THANKFULLY I THINK I FEEL LIKE I FOUND SOME PLACE THAT I BELONG.
CAN YOU... SEND THE BILL FOR THE DAMAGED WALLPAPER AND THE COST TO REPLACE IT HERE PLEASE?